Preface

The publication of the tenth edition of INTER-MEDIATE ACCOUNTING represents a milestone. No other intermediate accounting text has been in use for as long as this text, which has benefited from the suggestions of thousands of students and teachers. The tenth edition builds on and maintains the strengths of past editions. At the same time, this edition represents a totally updated and current revision of this widely accepted textbook. All relevant FASB pronouncements issued through July 1, 1989, are incorporated in the tenth edition, including the FASB's important recent statements No. 95 (Statement of Cash Flows) and No. 96 (Accounting for Income Taxes), and its exposure draft on Employers' Accounting for Postretirement Benefits Other Than Pensions. In addition, recent changes in tax laws, such as uniform cost capitalization rules and MACRS, have been incorporated.

The underlying objective of this edition is to continue to provide the most teachable and student-oriented text on the market. Topics are introduced and developed in a logical sequence and explained in a manner that is clear and understandable to students. Many real-world examples have been added to enhance student understanding and interest. The student-oriented approach of INTERMEDIATE ACCOUNTING is one of the main reasons why it has been a leading intermediate text for so many years. The emphasis on student understanding and teachability has been retained and strengthened in the tenth edition.

Important Features of the Tenth Edition

The overall structure of the tenth edition is similar to that of the ninth edition. The following new features have been added to aid students in their reading and studying of the text material:

Chapter Topics Each chapter begins with an outline of the main topics to be covered in that chapter. This will help instructors and students see the organizational flow of the chapter. These chapter topics also will help students evaluate their understanding of the main points of each chapter.

Key Terms Important terms and concepts are highlighted in color throughout the text. At the end of each chapter, there is a list of key terms for that chapter with appropriate page references. This will help students to identify the key terms they should know and to locate the page in the text where a particular term is defined and discussed.

Glossary A glossary is provided at the end of the book. This glossary lists all key terms in alphabetical order and provides a succinct definition of each term.

Several chapters have been significantly revised, and the chapters on deferred income taxes and the statement of cash flows have been totally rewritten. The revisions reflect extensive feedback from users of the ninth edition and from several accounting educators who reviewed the new and revised material for the tenth edition. Following is a summary of the most significant features of the tenth edition of INTERMEDIATE ACCOUNTING.

Comprehensive Coverage of Topics

The tenth edition has been expanded to provide more comprehensive coverage of important topics and issues in financial accounting and reporting. Many new illustrations, examples, and applications have been added throughout the text to clarify and reinforce discussions and explanations. Just as important, the coverage of some topics has been reduced or eliminated, where appropriate, to allow time for concentration on the major topics.

Real-World Perspective

Real-world examples and events are used extensively to illustrate important points and to enhance student interest. This feature enables students to view financial accounting and reporting from a broader, business-oriented perspective. These illustrations provide a frame of reference that is helpful for students in making the transition from text knowledge to application of principles.

Current Accounting Standards

The text has been updated to include all current pronouncements of the FASB that are relevant to intermediate accounting. These include the standards relating to accounting for income taxes, the statement of cash flows, and the Board's proposed standard on postretirement benefits other than pensions.

End-of-Chapter Materials

Many new and revised questions, cases, exercises, and problems are included at the end of each chapter. The questions and cases provide a vehicle for promoting class discussion of important issues. The number of exercises and problems have been increased to allow instructors more flexibility in making assignments.

Readability

The authors have focused their efforts on making this text the most readable intermediate text on the market. The discussion of topics within each chapter progresses logically and concentrates effectively on the points being discussed. The discussion is streamlined to emphasize major points, allowing much of the technical detail to be obtained, if needed, on specific job assignments. The result is a balanced mix of theory and practice that is needed by students preparing for careers in accounting.

Highlights of Specific Changes

The tenth edition of INTERMEDIATE AC-COUNTING consists of twenty-six chapters organized into five logically related parts. Every chapter in the text has been revised, and many have been extensively rewritten. Following is a summary of the most significant content changes.

Review of the Accounting Process Chapter 3 reviews the accounting cycle, including the basic relationships of accounts. Three appendixes also are included. The appendix on special journals and subsidiary ledgers has been revised extensively to make it more consistent with practice; an appendix has been added illustrating the closing method for inventory in a periodic system; and an appendix providing a comprehensive illustration of accrual versus cash accounting is retained.

Balance Sheet and Statement of Cash Flows A new comprehensive balance sheet illustration for a hypothetical company has been added in Chapter 5. In addition, the discussion and illustration of the statement of cash flows has been completely revised and updated.

Accounting for Long-Term Debt Securities New current material has been included in Chapter 15. Definitions and examples of such topics as junk bonds, leveraged buyouts, and off-balance-sheet financing make this chapter particularly relevant in today's business world.

Stockholders' Equity Chapters 16 and 17 have been revised to include more examples and illustrations of stockholders' equity. Where applicable, entries for the investor have been added to those shown for the issuer for further clarification.

Accounting for Income Taxes Chapter 20 has been completely rewritten to incorporate the asset and liability approach required by FASB Statement No. 96. The chapter includes a discussion of the conceptual justification for interperiod income tax allocation, and a clear description of temporary differences between taxable income and financial income. The asset and liability approach is presented in a series of examples that clearly illustrate the scheduling of temporary difference reversals required under FASB Statement No. 96. A discussion of the strengths and weaknesses of this controversial statement concludes the chapter. Expanded discussion and illustration of

Intermediate Accounting

Comprehensive Volume

Tenth Edition

Jay M. Smith, PhD, CPA
Brigham Young University

K. Fred Skousen, PhD, CPA
Brigham Young University

AC92JA
PUBLISHED BY
SOUTH-WESTERN PUBLISHING CO.
CINCINNATI, OH   WEST CHICAGO, IL   DALLAS, TX   LIVERMORE, CA

1 2 3 4 5 Ki 3 2 1 0 9

Printed in the United States of America

Smith, Jay M.
    Intermediate accounting : comprehensive volume / Jay M.
Smith, Jr., K. Fred Skousen, -- 10th ed.
        p.   cm.
    Bibliography: p.
    Includes index.
    ISBN 0-538-80500-5
    1. Accounting.   I. Skousen, K. Fred.   II. Title.
HF5635.S5946   1990   89-11556
657'.044--dc20   CIP

intraperiod income tax allocation and accounting for the investment tax credit are included in appendixes to the chapter for those instructors who wish to cover these topics.

Accounting for Pensions Chapter 22 has been expanded to include a comprehensive illustration of accounting for pensions from one period to another according to the requirements of FASB Statement No. 87. The interplay between recorded information and memorandum information for purposes of pension note disclosure is clarified with added exhibits to aid students in understanding these important relationships. The new exposure draft dealing with accounting for other postemployment benefits is presented in an appendix to Chapter 22. Because the recording of these additional employee benefits could have a significant impact on employer's financial statements, emphasis is placed on the conceptual basis for the exposure draft and on the factors that make accounting for these benefits particularly difficult.

Statement of Cash Flows Chapter 24 has been completely rewritten to incorporate FASB Statement Nos. 95 and 102. The statement of cash flows replaces the statement of changes in financial position (funds statement) as one of the three primary financial statements that must be presented to external users. The requirements of Statement No. 95 are explained clearly, including a discussion of both the direct and indirect methods of computing net cash flow from operations. Illustrations are provided that highlight the required format for classifying cash flows according to operating, investing, and financing activities. To provide an historical perspective, the chapter also includes a brief explanation of the development of the cash flow statement.

Supplementary Materials

A comprehensive package of supplementary materials is provided with the tenth edition to assist both instructors and students.

Available to Instructors

Solutions Manual. This manual contains the answers to all end-of-chapter questions, cases, exercises, and problems.

Instructor's Manual, prepared by Andrew H. Barnett, San Diego State University. This new manual contains objectives, chapter outlines, teaching suggestions and strategies, topical overviews of end-of-chapter materials, assignment classifications with level of difficulty and estimated completion time, suggested readings on chapter topics, and teaching transparency masters. The text of the Instructor's Manual is available on diskette.

Transparencies. Transparencies of solutions for all end-of-chapter exercises and problems are available with the tenth edition of the text.

Examinations. A test bank is available in both printed and microcomputer (MicroSWAT II) versions. The test bank, which has been significantly revised and expanded, includes true-false, matching, and multiple-choice questions and examination problems for each chapter, accompanied by solutions.

Template Diskette. The template diskette is used with Lotus® 1-2-3®[1] for solving selected end-of-chapter exercises and problems that are identified with the symbol at the right. The diskette for the tenth edition includes a greater number of exercises and problems and may be ordered free of charge from South-Western Publishing Co.

Key for Practice Case. The key provides a complete solution for *SporTime Inc. II.*

Available to Students

Study Guide, prepared by Frank J. Imke, The University of Texas of the Permian Basin. The study guide provides review and reinforcement materials for each chapter, including learning objectives, a glossary of key terms in the chapter, chapter review outlines, objective questions, and short problems. Answers for all questions and problems are provided in a separate section at the end of the study guide.

Practice Case, prepared by Donald C. Dwyer, Berkshire Community College. The practice case, *SporTime Inc. II*, provides a comprehensive review of accounting principles.

Electronic Spreadsheet Applications for Intermediate Accounting, prepared by Gaylord N.

Smith, Albion College. This supplemental text-workbook with template diskette includes intermediate accounting applications and a Lotus 1-2-3 tutorial. It requires approximately 25-30 hours for completion.

Working Papers. Printed forms for solving end-of-chapter problems are contained in a single bound volume and are perforated for easy removal.

Check Figures. Instructors may order check figures for students to use in verifying their solutions to end-of-chapter problems.

Acknowledgements

Relevant pronouncements of the Financial Accounting Standards Board and other authoritative publications are paraphrased, quoted, discussed, and referenced throughout the textbook. We are indebted to the American Accounting Association, the American Institute of Certified Public Accountants, the Financial Accounting Standards Board, and the Securities and Exchange Commission for material from their publications.

We thank the following faculty who reviewed the previous edition or manuscript for this edition and provided many helpful suggestions:

Ted Bainbridge
Concordia College

Andrew H. Barnett
San Diego State University

Linda C. Bowen
University of North Carolina—Chapel Hill

H. Lawrence Dennis
North Georgia College

Napoleon Lucchini
South Puget Sound Community College

Donald C. Dwyer
Berkshire Community College

Delbert B. Hurst
Lambuth College

Eileen M. Kapinos
Holyoke Community College

Richard T. King
Dickinson State University

Robert Leshin
Miami-Dade Community College

Penny Marquette
University of Akron

John A. Marts
University of North Carolina—Wilmington

John D. O'Connell
College of the Holy Cross

Craig Pence
Highland Community College

Donald R. Suttles
Catawba College

Thomas F. Schaefer
Florida State University

Arthur R. Wyatt
Arthur Andersen and Company

We also wish to thank the faculty and students who have used INTERMEDIATE ACCOUNTING and volunteered their comments and suggestions.

Jay M. Smith, Jr.
K. Fred Skousen

About the Authors

Jay M. Smith, PhD, CPA is Professor of Accounting at the School of Accountancy, Brigham Young University. He holds a bachelor's and master's degree from BYU and a PhD from Stanford University. He has over thirty years teaching experience at BYU, Stanford University, the University of Minnesota where he served as department chairman, and at the University of Hawaii. In 1984 he spent a year as a faculty resident at Arthur Andersen & Co.'s St. Charles, Illinois professional educational center. He has received several awards and recognitions in accounting, including fellowships from the Danforth and Sloan Foundations and teaching excellence awards from Brigham Young University and the Utah Association of Certified Public Accountants. Professor Smith has served on several national accounting education committees, and has served on the Practice Subcommittee of the AICPA Board of Examiners with responsibility for writing the practice section of the CPA examination (1986-89). He is currently a member of the Faculty Advisory Group working with Coopers & Lybrand in their Excellence in Auditing educational project. He is a member of the American Institute of CPAs, the Utah Association of CPAs, and the American Accounting Association and has served on numerous committees of these organizations.

K. Fred Skousen, PhD, CPA, is Peat Marwick Professor and the past Director of the School of Accountancy, Brigham Young University. He holds a bachelor's degree from BYU and the master's and PhD degrees from the University of Illinois. Professor Skousen has taught at the University of Illinois, the University of Minnesota, the University of California at Berkeley, and the University of Missouri. He received Distinguished Faculty Awards at the University of Minnesota and at BYU and was recognized as the National Beta Alpha Psi Academic Accountant of the Year in 1979. Professor Skousen is the author or co-author of over 40 articles, research reports, and books. He served as Director of Research and a member of the Executive Committee of the American Accounting Association and is a member of the American Institute of CPAs, and the Utah Association of CPAs. He has served as president of the UACPA and on Council for the AICPA. Dr. Skousen also has served as a consultant to the Controller General of the United States, the Federal Trade Commission, the California Society of CPAs, and several large companies. He was a Faculty Resident on the staff of the Securities and Exchange Commission and a Faculty Fellow with Price Waterhouse and Co.

Contents in Brief

Contents

Part Three   Liabilities and Equity

PART ONE

Overview of Accounting and its Theoretical Foundation

Chapter 1

Financial Reporting and the Accounting Profession

Chapter Topics **Financial Reporting to Users of Accounting Information**

Elements of the Accounting Profession

Role of the FASB and Various Governmental and Professional Organizations in the Development of Accounting Standards

Impact of Accounting Standards and the Importance of Professional Judgment in Applying the Standards

Financial Reporting in a Complex Business Environment

Conflict Between Public and Private Sectors in Establishing Accounting Standards

The time has arrived for United Exploration Inc.'s annual meeting. The purpose of the meeting is to elect members to the Board of Directors, to take care of miscellaneous corporate matters, and to answer stockholders' questions concerning the recently issued financial statements. The attendance at this year's meeting is unusually large because of a significant decline in net income reported for the current year.

Three groups are represented at the meeting: (1) management (2) external auditors, and (3) stockholders. Much of the technical discussion involves the impact of changing the method of depreciation used for the financial statements. Management explains to the stockholders that the new method makes United's statements more comparable to those of competitors. The stockholders are especially concerned because the decline in net income has had a negative effect in the stock market. There is some expressed concern that management is purposefully manipulating income. The stockholders are interested in the impact of the accounting change because they must decide whether to buy additional shares in the company, sell the shares they have, or maintain their present position.

The above scenario describing a stockholders' meeting is repeated hundreds of times each year as various interested parties meet to discuss the financial affairs of their companies. The audited financial statements contained in annual reports are the primary source of financial information available to stockholders about the profitability and financial soundness of a corporation. The accountants who are responsible for preparing these financial statements play a vital role in the functioning of our nation's economy. This chapter will discuss that role along with other aspects of the accounting profession.

Accounting and Financial Reporting

As implied in the introductory scenario and as indicated in the following quotation, the overall objective of accounting* is to provide information that can be used in making economic decisions.

Accounting is a service activity. Its function is to provide quantitative information, primarily financial in nature, about economic entities that is intended

*A glossary of key terms appears in Appendix B at the end of the text. The terms included in the glossary are printed in color and are listed at the end of each chapter.

to be useful in making economic decisions—in making reasoned choices among alternative courses of action.[1]

Several key features of this definition should be noted. First, accounting provides a vital **service** in today's business environment. Economists and environmentalists remind us constantly that we live in a world with limited resources. We must use our natural resources, our labor, and our financial wealth wisely so as to maximize their benefit to society. The better the accounting system that measures and reports the cost of using these resources, the better the decisions that are made for allocating them. Second, accounting is concerned primarily with **quantitative financial information** that is used in conjunction with qualitative evaluations in making judgments. Finally, although accountants place much emphasis on reporting what has already occurred, this past information is intended to be useful in making **economic decisions** about the future.

Users of Accounting Information

If accounting is to meet its objective of providing useful information for economic decision making, the following questions must be answered: (1) Who are the users of accounting information, and (2) what information do they require to meet their decision making needs?

User groups are normally divided into two major classifications: (1) **internal users** who make decisions directly affecting the internal operations of the enterprise, and (2) **external users** who make decisions concerning their relationship to the enterprise. Major internal and external user groups are listed in Exhibit 1-1.

Internal users need information to assist in planning and controlling enterprise operations and managing (allocating) enterprise resources. The accounting system must provide timely information needed to control day-to-day operations and to make major planning decisions, such as "Do we make this product or another one? Do we build a new production plant or expand existing facilities? Must we increase prices or can we cut costs?"

Exhibit 1-1   Internal and External User Groups

Internal users

Company management
Company employees
Board of directors

External users

Creditors
Investors
Potential investors
Governmental agencies
General public

---

[1]*Statement of the Accounting Principles Board No. 4*, "Basic Concepts and Accounting Principles Underlying Financial Statements of Business Enterprises" (New York: American Institute of Certified Public Accountants, 1970), par. 40.

The types of decisions made by external users vary widely, thus their information needs are highly diverse. Considerable time and effort have been devoted to studying the information needs of external users. As a result, two groups, creditors and investors, have been identified as the principal external users of financial information. Two reasons cited for the importance of these groups are:[2]

1. Their decisions significantly affect the allocation of resources in the economy.
2. Information provided to meet investors' and creditors' needs is likely to be generally useful to members of other groups who are interested in essentially the same financial aspects of business enterprises as investors and creditors.

Creditors need information about the profitability and stability of the enterprise to answer such questions as: "Do we lend the money, and with what provisions?" Investors (both existing stockholders and potential investors) need information concerning the safety and profitability of their investment. As noted in the introduction to this chapter, stockholders must decide whether to increase, decrease, terminate, or maintain their interest in an enterprise.

Financial Reporting The two major classifications of users, internal and external, have led to a distinction between two major areas of accounting. Management accounting (sometimes referred to as managerial or cost accounting) is concerned primarily with financial reporting for internal users. Internal users, especially management, have control over the accounting system and can specify precisely what information is needed and how the information is to be reported. Financial accounting focuses on the development and communication of financial information for external users primarily in the form of general purpose financial statements. The statements include a balance sheet, income statement, statement of cash flows, and usually a statement of changes in retained earnings or in owners' equity.

Most accounting systems are designed to generate information for both internal and external reporting. Generally, the external information is much more highly summarized than the information reported internally. The internal decisions made by management require information regarding, for example, specific product lines, specific financing alternatives, individual sales territories, detailed expense classifications, and differences between actual and budgeted revenues and costs. The decisions made by external users require broader indications of overall profitability and financial stability.

While internal financial reporting is governed by the needs of manage-

---

[2]*Statement of Financial Accounting Concepts No. 1,* "Objectives of Financial Reporting by Business Enterprises" (Stamford: Financial Accounting Standards Board, 1978), par. 30.

ment, external financial reporting is governed by an established body of standards or principles[3] that are designed to reflect the external users' needs. The development of these standards is discussed in some detail later in this chapter.

This textbook focuses on financial accounting and external reporting. The remaining chapters present the concepts, standards, and procedures applied in the development of the basic financial statements.

The Accounting Profession

Professional accountants perform their work in many different roles and environments. To meet its various reporting needs, a business enterprise may employ **financial accountants**, who are primarily concerned with external financial reporting; **management accountants**, who are primarily concerned with internal financial reporting; and **tax accountants**, who prepare the necessary federal, state, and local tax returns and advise management in matters relating to taxation. In smaller organizations, there is less specialization and more combining of responsibility for the various accounting functions.

Larger business enterprises typically employ **internal auditors** who review the work performed by accountants and others within the enterprise and report their findings to management. In addition to auditing financial reports generated by the accounting system, they review the operational policies of the company and make recommendations for improving efficiency and effectiveness. Although internal auditors are employees of the enterprise, they must be independent with respect to the employees whose work they review. Thus, internal auditors generally report to top management or a special audit committee of the board of directors.

Some accountants, known as Certified Public Accountants (CPAs), do not work for a single business enterprise. Rather, they provide a variety of services for many different individual and business clients. With respect to external financial reporting, the most important service provided by CPAs is the independent audit of financial statements.

The External Audit Function

As independent or external auditors, CPAs play a critical role in the reporting of financial information to external users. In performing an **external audit**, their responsibility is to independently examine the financial statements to be furnished to external users and to express an opinion as to the fairness of the statements in adhering to generally accepted accounting principles. The auditor's opinion is communicated in a report that accompanies the financial statements. The opinion is based on evidence gathered by the auditor from the detailed records and documents maintained by the company and from a review of the controls over the accounting system. A revised, three-paragraph auditor's report

[3]The terms "standards" and "principles" are used interchangeably by the accounting profession and in this text.

was adopted by the accounting profession effective July 15, 1988. The new report form replaced a standard two-paragraph report that had been used for forty years. The revision emphasizes the separate responsibilities that management and the auditors have for the accounting system and for the information in the financial statements. An example of the new report form is included in the 1988 annual report of The Procter & Gamble Company and is reproduced on page 8.[4] Modifications to the standard report are required in some cases, for example when the auditor determines that the financial statements contain a departure from generally accepted accounting principles.

The need for independent audits resulted from the emergence of the corporate form of business and the resulting separation of ownership and management. A significant proportion of the productive activity in the United States is conducted by publicly held corporations; that is, by corporations whose securities are sold to the general public. The stockholders who own the corporations are primarily investors and are generally not involved in enterprise operations. These investor-owners rely on management to operate the business and report periodically on the performance and financial status of the enterprise. Those companies registered nationally with the Securities and Exchange Commission are *required* to have an annual independent audit as an assurance to the stockholders.

Management has control over the information reported to stockholders and other external users and is responsible for the content of the financial statements. A statement emphasizing this responsibility is included in the annual report to stockholders, as illustrated for The Procter & Gamble Company on page 8. Management is also accountable for the profitability and financial condition of the enterprise as reflected in the statements. Obviously, there is a motivation on the part of management to present the financial information in the most favorable manner possible. It is the responsibility of the auditors to review management's reports and to independently decide if the reports are indeed representative of the actual conditions existing within the enterprise. The auditor's opinion adds credibility to the financial statements of enterprises, whether large or small, or privately or publicly held.

Other Services Provided by CPAs

In addition to performing independent audits, CPAs assist clients in **tax planning** and reporting to various government entities. CPAs also function as management consultants, offering advice to clients in such areas as systems design, organization, personnel, finance, internal control, and employee benefits. These services are frequently referred to as **management advisory services**. Various accounting services are also provided for smaller, privately owned businesses.

---

[4]See also the auditor's report that accompanies the financial statements of General Mills, Inc., reproduced in Appendix A at the end of the book.

Exhibit 1–2   The Procter & Gamble Company

Report Of Independent Accountants

Deloitte
Haskins+Sells

250 East Fifth Street
Cincinnati, Ohio 45202

To the Board of Directors and Shareholders of The Procter & Gamble Company:

We have audited the accompanying consolidated balance sheets of The Procter & Gamble Company and subsidiaries as of June 30, 1988 and 1987, and the related consolidated statements of earnings, retained earnings, and changes in financial position for each of the three years in the period ended June 30, 1988. These financial statements are the responsibility of the companies' management. Our responsibility is to express an opinion on these financial statements based on our audit.

We conducted our audit in accordance with generally accepted auditing standards. Those standards require that we plan and perform the audit to obtain reasonable assurance about whether the financial statements are free of material misstatement. An audit includes examining, on a test basis, evidence supporting the amounts and disclosures in the financial statements. An audit also includes assessing the accounting principles used and significant estimates made by management, as well as evaluating the overall financial statement presentation. We believe that our audit provides a reasonable basis for our opinion.

In our opinion, the financial statements referred to above present fairly, in all material respects, the financial position of the companies at June 30, 1988 and 1987, and the results of their operations and the changes in their financial position for each of the three years in the period ended June 30, 1988, in conformity with generally accepted accounting principles.

Deloitte Haskins + Sells

August 10, 1988

Responsibility For The Financial Statements

The financial statements of The Procter & Gamble Company and its subsidiaries are the responsibility of, and have been prepared by, the Company, in accordance with generally accepted accounting principles. To help insure the accuracy and integrity of its financial data, the Company has developed and maintains internal accounting controls which are designed to provide reasonable assurances that transactions are executed as authorized and accurately recorded, and that assets are properly safeguarded. These controls are monitored by an extensive program of internal audits.

The financial statements have been examined by the Company's independent public accountants, Deloitte Haskins & Sells. Their report is shown on page 31.

The Board of Directors has an Audit Committee composed entirely of outside Directors. The Committee meets periodically with representatives of Deloitte Haskins & Sells and financial management to review accounting, control, auditing, and financial reporting matters. To help assure the independence of the public accountants, Deloitte Haskins & Sells regularly meets privately with the Audit Committee.

The Practice of Public Accounting

CPAs practice either individually or in firms. Because of the importance of personal liability for professional conduct, public accounting firms are generally organized as either proprietorships or partnerships. Most state laws now permit CPAs to be organized as professional corporations. These corporations provide many of the benefits of the corporate structure, but still retain personal liability for the professionals involved.

Almost all big, publicly held corporations are audited by a few large CPA firms. Listed in alphabetical order, the eight largest firms are Arthur

Andersen & Co.; Arthur Young & Company; Coopers & Lybrand; Deloitte Haskins & Sells; Ernst & Whinney; Peat, Marwick, Main & Co.; Price Waterhouse & Co.; and Touche Ross & Co. Each of these firms is an international organization with many offices in the United States and abroad.

Many small businesses and nonprofit entities are serviced by regional and local CPA firms, including a large number of sole practitioners. In these firms, the role of auditing is often less important than the areas of tax reporting and planning and systems consulting. A CPA in a smaller firm is expected to be something of an accounting generalist, as opposed to the more specialized positions of CPAs in large regional and national firms. A vital role is played by the smaller public accounting firms in serving the thousands of small entities in the United States that are crucial to the nation's economy.[5]

The Development of Accounting Standards

Accounting principles and procedures have evolved over hundreds of years. The formal standard-setting process that exists today, however, has developed in the past fifty years. Because accounting grew so rapidly with the advent of the Industrial Revolution, accounting procedures were often developed without extended debate or discussion. Accountants developed methods that seemed to meet the needs of their respective companies, resulting in diverse procedures among companies in accounting for similar activities. The comparability of the resulting financial reports, therefore, was often questionable.

During the 1920's, these differences led to financial statements that were often inflated in value. Market values of stocks rose higher than the underlying real values warranted until the entire structure collapsed in the stock market crash of 1929. The government of the United States, under the leadership of President Franklin D. Roosevelt, vigorously attacked the ensuing depression and, among other things, created the Securities and Exchange Commission (SEC). This new agency was given the responsibility to protect the interests of investors by ensuring full and fair disclosure in the regulation of the capital markets. The broad power granted to the SEC by Congress will be more fully discussed in a separate section. The emergence of the SEC forced the accounting profession to unite and to become more diligent in developing accounting principles and ethics to govern the profession. This led over time to the formation of several different private sector organizations, each having the responsibility of issuing accounting standards. These organizations, their publications, and the time they were in existence are identified in Exhibit 1-2 and discussed in subsequent sections of the chapter.

---

[5]According to a newsnote in *Forbes*, 98% of all the businesses in the United States are private proprietorships or partnerships. They account for one-third of the U.S. output, and 65 of them have revenues over $1 billion. "Who Needs Stockholders?" *Forbes* (November 18, 1985), p. 6.

Exhibit 1–3   Accounting Standard-Setting Bodies

Standard-Setting Body	Date	Authoritative Publications
AICPA Committee on Accounting Procedures	1939-1959	Accounting Research Bulletins
Accounting Principles Board	1959-1973	APB Opinions
Financial Accounting Standards Board	1973-present	Statements of Financial Accounting Standards Interpretations

In the previous pages, three important groups that are involved with general purpose financial statements were identified; users, managers of business enterprises, and external auditors. As has been demonstrated, each of these groups has its own specific function to perform in the complex business environment that constitutes our economy. In many instances, these functions may be in conflict with each other. This condition provides another reason for the establishment of accounting standards—to resolve those different points of view that lead to different accounting methods being applied in similar circumstances.

Standards are designed to help accountants apply consistent principles for different businesses. They are recognized by the profession as representing the generally accepted position of the profession, and must be followed in the preparation of financial statements unless circumstances warrant an exception to a standard. These standards are commonly referred to as **generally accepted accounting principles (GAAP)**. If the management of an enterprise feels the circumstances do not warrant compliance with the standard, an exception can be taken. Under these circumstances, the auditor's report must clearly disclose the nature of and the reason for the exception in the financial statements.[6]

Financial Accounting Standards Board

The **Financial Accounting Standards Board (FASB)** is an independent organization consisting of seven full-time members drawn from professional accounting, business, government, and academia.[7] The members are required to sever all connections with their firms or institutions prior to assuming membership on the Board. Members are appointed for five-year terms and are eligible for reappointment to one additional term. Headquartered in Norwalk, Connecticut, the Board has its own research staff and an annual budget in excess of 10 million dollars.

[6]American Institute of Certified Public Accountants, *Code of Professional Conduct*, Rule 203.

[7]Maintaining this independence is sometimes difficult when complex issues affect so many groups in material ways. For example, in 1985, executives of business enterprises openly expressed their desire for more business representation on the FASB to assure that their interests were being considered. In a newspaper article, "The F.A.S.B. Comes Under Fire," Eric Berg, writing for *The New York Times*, stated that "It (business) has deluged foundation members with telephone calls and letters and has formed a committee with some of the most powerful financial executives in America to make sure more business executives get on the board." *The New York Times,* August 18, 1985, Section 3, page 4.

Funding for the FASB is obtained through the **Financial Accounting Foundation (FAF),** an organization that is also responsible for selecting members of the FASB and its Advisory Council. (See Exhibit 1–4 for Financial Accounting Foundation organization chart.) The **Financial Accounting Standards Advisory Council** consults with the Board on major policy questions, selects major project task forces to work on specific projects, and conducts such other activities as may be requested by the FASB. The Foundation is administered by a Board of Trustees whose 16 members are made up of representatives from eight sponsoring institutions as follows:

  · American Accounting Association (AAA)
  · American Institute of Certified Public Accountants (AICPA)
  · Financial Analysts Federation (FAF)
  · Financial Executives Institute (FEI)
  · National Association of Accountants (NAA)
  · Securities Industry Associates (SIA)
  · National Association of State Auditors, Comptrollers, and Treasurers (NASACT)
  · Government Finance Officers Association (GFOA)

The latter two organizations were added in 1984 when the Foundation assumed responsibility for selecting members for a newly established organization, the **Governmental Accounting Standards Board (GASB).** This Board was organized to establish standards in the governmental area.

Exhibit 1–4   Financial Accounting Foundation Organizational Chart

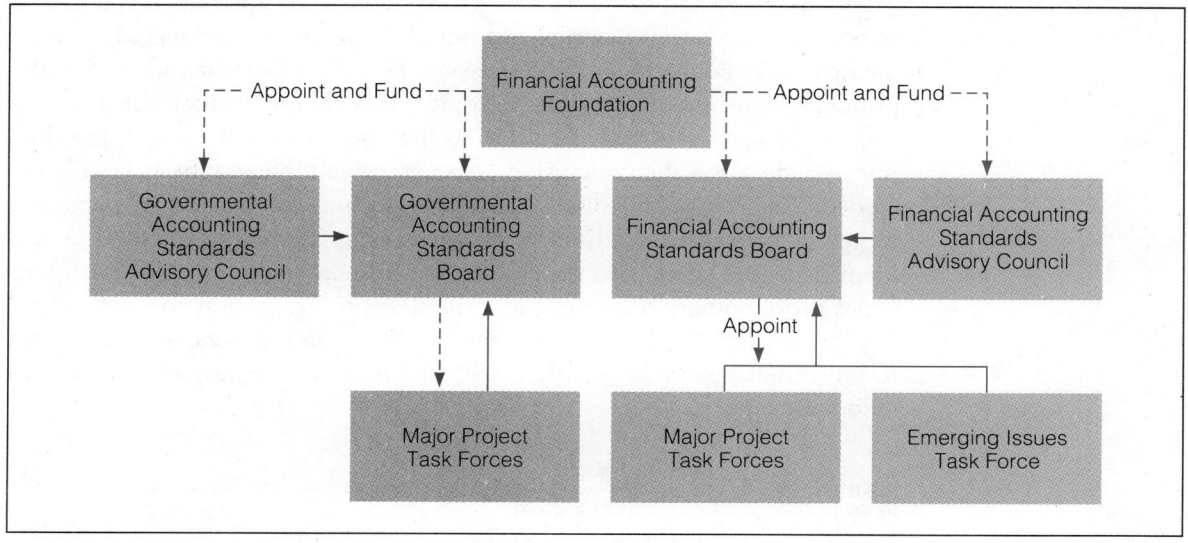

The major function of the FASB is to study accounting issues and
establish accounting standards. These standards are published as
Statements of Financial Accounting Standards. The FASB also issues
Statements of Financial Accounting Concepts. The concepts identified in
the statements are intended as guides for establishing standards. That is,
they provide a framework within which specific accounting standards
can be developed.[9]

Because the actions of the FASB have an impact on many individuals
and groups within the economy, the Board follows a standard-setting process that is open to public observation and participation. The Board sepa-
rates the topics it deals with into two areas: (1) Major Projects and (2)
Implementation and Practice Problems. The process for the first area is
very extensive and often requires from two to four years or more to complete. For example, significant events in the development of FASB Statement No. 87, issued in late 1985, are listed in Exhibit 1–5. While the
eleven years required to complete this project exceed the normal period,
this example illustrates how difficult it is to resolve some of the more complex accounting issues. The process for the second area, Implementation
and Practice Problems, though still subject to public input, is designed for
completion within a six-to-twelve-month period.

The long-term nature of the standard-setting process has been one of
the principal points of criticism of the Board. There seems to be no alternative to the lengthy process, however, given the philosophy that arriving
at a consensus among the members of the accounting profession and other
interested parties is important to the Board's credibility.

Major Projects

For each major project undertaken by the Board, a task force of outside
experts is appointed to study the existing literature. When available literature is deemed insufficient, additional research is conducted. Subsequently, the Board issues a Discussion Memorandum that identifies the
principal issues involved with the topic. This document includes a discussion of the various points of view as to the resolution of the issues, but does
not include a specific conclusion. An extensive bibliography is usually included. Readers of the discussion memorandum are invited to comment
either in writing or orally at a public hearing. Sometimes a topic is not
identified well enough to issue a discussion memorandum, and the FASB
issues a preliminary document identified as an "Invitation to Comment."
The topic is briefly discussed in the document, and readers are encouraged
to send their comments to the FASB for more definite formulation of specific issues.

---

[8]For a more detailed description of the FASB and its operations see "Facts about FASB," published annually
by the Financial Accounting Standards Board.

[9]The conceptual framework of the FASB is discussed fully in Chapter 2.

Exhibit 1–5   Significant Events in the Development of FASB Statement No. 87, "Employers' Accounting for Pensions"

1974	Pensions added to FASB agenda
1975	Task force appointed
1975	Discussion Memorandum #1 issued
1976	Public hearing #1 held
1977	Exposure Draft #1 issued
1979	Exposure Draft #1 revised
1980	FASB background paper issued
1981	Discussion Memorandum #2 issued
1981	Public hearing #2 held
1982	Preliminary Views document issued
1983	Supplement to Discussion Memorandum #2 issued
1984	Public hearing #3 held
1985	Exposure Draft #2 issued
1985	Public hearing #4 held
1985	Statement No. 87 issued in December

After a Discussion Memorandum has been issued and comments from interested parties have been evaluated, the Board meets as many times as necessary to resolve the issues. These meetings are open to the public, and the agenda is published in advance. From these meetings, the Board develops an Exposure Draft of a Statement that includes specific recommendations for financial accounting and reporting. A majority of the seven-member Board is required to approve the Exposure Draft for issuance. Again, reaction to this document is requested from the accounting and business community. At the end of the exposure period, usually 60 days or more, all comment papers are reviewed by the Staff and the Board. Further deliberation by the Board leads to either the issuance of a Statement of Financial Accounting Standards, to a revised Exposure Draft, or in some cases to abandonment of the project.

The final statement not only sets forth the actual standards, but also establishes the effective date and method of transition, and gives pertinent background information and the basis for the Board's conclusions, including reasons for rejecting significant alternative solutions. If any members dissent from the majority view, they may include the reasons for their dissent as part of the document.

Implementation and Practice Problems

The second category of issues dealt with by the Board involves implementation and practice problems that relate to previously issued standards. Depending on the nature of a problem, the Board may issue a Statement of Financial Accounting Standards or an Interpretation of a Statement of Financial Accounting Standards. The interpretation may be issued without appointing a task force, issuing a Discussion Memorandum, or holding public hearings. Exposure of these publications, however, to either the public or the Advisory Council is required as part of the due process followed by the Board.

Problems that arise in practice are also addressed in Technical Bulletins prepared and issued by the staff of the FASB. The Bulletins, which are reviewed by the Board prior to being issued, provide guidance for particular situations that arise in practice. In contrast with Standards and Interpretations, the staff Technical Bulletins do not have the authority of GAAP.

The procedures of the Board are intended to help accomplish its mission, which is to establish and improve standards of financial accounting and reporting. The credibility of the Board has fluctuated through the years as different issues have been resolved.[10] The FASB has no legislative power, but must depend on the general acceptance of its pronouncements by the accounting profession and other interested groups. This acceptability is directly influenced by two other organizations: the AICPA and the SEC.

American Institute of Certified Public Accountants

The American Institute of Certified Public Accountants is the professional organization of practicing CPAs in the United States. The organization was founded in 1887, and publishes a monthly journal, the *Journal of Accountancy*. Membership in the AICPA is voluntary, and over 275,000 CPAs are members. The AICPA has several important responsibilities that include standard-setting, quality control, and certification and continuing education for CPAs.

Standard-Setting Responsibilities

Prior to the formation of the FASB, accounting principles were established under the direction of the AICPA. From 1939-1959, principles were formed by the Committee on Accounting Procedures (CAP). Their pronouncements were known as Accounting Research Bulletins (ARBs). From 1959 to 1973, accounting principles were formed by the Accounting Principles Board (APB) and issued as Opinions. Dissatisfaction with the part-time nature of these boards, their failure to react quickly to some issues, and the lack of broad representation on the boards because of their direct relationship to the AICPA led to the formation in 1973 of the FASB.

Although the FASB replaced the APB as the official standard-setting body for the profession, the AICPA continues to influence the establishment of accounting standards through its issuance of Accounting and Audit Guides and Statements of Position (SOPs). The Guides are issued by specially appointed committees of the AICPA and relate to specific industries, such as construction, insurance, banking, and real estate. These Guides not only contain information concerning the auditing of these entities, but also discuss alternative accounting methods that may be employed by the industry. The Guides often recommend a preferred accounting method. The SOPs were issued by the Accounting Standards Executive Committee

---

[10]An evaluation of the FASB's success was undertaken in 1984 by the Harris Research Group. Over 600 individuals were queried on a variety of topics. In response to the query as to the overall view of the FASB, 87% ranked its success as good or excellent. Louis Harris, "A Study of Attitudes Towards an Assessment of the FASB," Executive Summary, *FASB Viewpoints*, p. 4.

(AcSEC), an AICPA committee established when the FASB assumed the standard-setting role. SOPs often dealt with emerging issues that had not yet been placed on the FASB agenda, but which needed to be addressed by the profession for improved comparability in financial reporting. In 1984, the Financial Accounting Standards Board created a new organization, the **Emerging Issues Task Force (EITF)**. This task force was created to deal with the criticism that had been levied against the Board for its intermittent failure to provide timely guidance on new accounting issues, and to reclaim an area of standard-setting that was being assumed by the Accounting Standards Executive Committee of the AICPA. Members of the task force are drawn from the accounting profession and industry, and are selected for their expertise in dealing with emerging issues. The primary responsibilities of the task force are to: (1) identify new accounting issues for which no authoritative statements exist and (2) to discuss alternative approaches to the issues and, where possible, arrive at a consensus statement that provides standards for the issues until such time as they may be addressed formally by the FASB. Although the Guides, SOPs, and EITF consensus statements are not part of GAAP, they are considered Preferable Accounting Principles and may be looked upon as another important source of standards guidance.

The FASB became concerned about this growing volume of "other" standards, and in 1979 adopted the Guides and SOPs as officially preferred accounting principles subject to their review and possible subsequent issuance of FASB Statements.[11] Beginning in the early 1980s, many specialized industry guides were adopted as FASB Standards. (See list of FASB standards in Appendix C of the text). Although no longer issuing SOPs, AcSEC still helps the FASB identify emerging issues and communicates the concerns of CPAs on accounting issues to the FASB. Thus, the AICPA continues to influence greatly the establishment of accounting standards.

In addition to influencing the establishment of accounting standards, the AICPA assumes direct responsibility for the establishment of auditing standards. The Auditing Standards Board is a part-time board of 21 members from the public accounting practice with the responsibility of establishing guidelines for the proper conduct of audits. Similar committees of the AICPA are responsible for establishing standards for tax professionals and systems consultants.

Quality Control

The AICPA is also concerned with maintaining the integrity of the profession through its Code of Professional Conduct and through a quality control program that includes a process of peer review of CPA firms con-

---

[11]*Statement of Financial Accounting Standards No. 32*, "Specialized Accounting and Reporting Principles and Practices in AICPA Statements of Position and Guides on Accounting and Auditing Matters" (Stamford: Financial Accounting Standards Board, 1979).

ducted by other CPAs. Although membership in the AICPA traditionally has been individual, the influence of the firm has become increasingly important. In the late 1970s the AICPA instituted a firm membership in one of two sections: (1) the **SEC Practice Section (SECPS)** for firms that have clients subject to government regulation through the Securities and Exchange Commission (SEC), and (2) the **Private Companies Practice Section (PCPS)** for firms that do not have clients regulated by the SEC. The SEC practice firms are subject to more stringent regulation than the private companies practice firms, although a high quality of performance is expected of all firms. At the present time, membership in these sections is voluntary. A firm may belong to both sections, and most of the larger firms do. One of the requirements for membership in a section is for firms to have a periodic peer review of its operations by other CPAs. Because all firms have not elected to belong to a practice section, some firms have not had peer reviews. The membership of the AICPA voted in 1988 to make a quality review program a condition of AICPA membership. Of course, those firms in the practice sections already meet this requirement.

The quality review requirement was only one of several requirements approved by the AICPA membership to address an issue that arose primarily in the 1980s referred to as the expectation or perception gap. This gap is identified as the difference between how users of financial statements interpreted the auditor's responsibilities and how auditors themselves viewed their responsibilities. Users felt auditors should alert them earlier to a firm's financial difficulties, and thus protect their investments from loss. The auditing profession addressed this gap, and issued a group of ten new auditing standards in mid-1988 to identify more clearly the auditor's responsibility for detection of fraud, evaluation of a company's internal control, and responsibility for identification of companies unlikely to be able to continue operations. The impact of these new regulations and standards will not be fully discernible for several years. It is likely, however, that they will have a favorable impact on reporting to decision makers.

Certification and Continuing Education

Another important function of the AICPA is preparation and grading of the Uniform CPA examination. This examination, covering two and one half days, is given twice each year simultaneously in all fifty states. In addition to passing all four parts of the examination, an individual must meet the state education and experience requirements in order to obtain state certification as a CPA. Most states now require CPAs to meet continuing education requirements in order to retain their certificate to practice. The AICPA assists its members in meeting these requirements through an extensive Continuing Professional Education (CPE) program that includes course offerings throughout the United States.

Securities and Exchange Commission

The **Securities and Exchange Commission** was created by an act of Congress in 1934. Its primary role is to regulate the issuance and trading of securities by corporations to the general public. Prior to offering securities for sale to the public, a company must file a registration statement with the Commission that contains financial and organizational disclosures. In addition, all publicly held companies are required to furnish annual and other periodical information to the Commission and to have their external financial statements examined by independent accountants.

The Commission's intent is not to prevent the trading of speculative securities, but to insist that investors have adequate information. As a result, the SEC is vitally interested in financial reporting and the development of accounting standards. The Commission carefully monitors the standard-setting process and responds to Discussion Memorandums and Exposure Drafts issued by the FASB. The Commission also brings to the Board's attention emerging problems that need to be addressed.

When the Commission was formed, Congress gave it power to establish accounting principles as follows:

> The Commission may prescribe, in regard to reports made pursuant to this title, the form or forms in which the required information shall be set forth, the items or details to be shown in the balance sheet and the earning statement, and the methods to be followed in the preparation of reports, in the appraisal or valuation of assets and liabilities . . .[12]

The Commission has generally refrained from fully using these powers, preferring to work through the private sector in the development of standards. Throughout its existence, however, the Commission has issued statements pertaining to accounting and auditing issues. Most of them are quite specific in nature and deal with a particular company or a specific situation. At present, SEC statements are referred to as either **Financial Reporting Releases (FRRs)** or **Accounting and Auditing Enforcement Releases (AAERs)**. Prior to 1982, they were referred to as **Accounting Series Releases (ASRs)**. Although the SEC is generally supportive of the FASB, from time to time the Commission intervenes in the standard-setting process. The SEC has been credited, for example, with requiring experimentation with current value disclosure when it appeared that the FASB was going to recommend an alternative approach to reporting inflation information.

American Accounting Association

The **American Accounting Association** is primarily an organization for accounting academicians, although practicing professional accountants also belong in large numbers. A quarterly journal, *The Accounting Review* is published by the AAA. Several specialized sections have been organized within the AAA, and many of these also publish journals. Accounting academicians are very interested in the development of accounting

---

[12]Securities Exchange Act of 1934, Section 13(b).

standards. They have the unique position of being professionals not directly involved with the preparation or audit of financial statements. Thus, they are able to consider objectively the needs of users as well as business enterprises and auditors. The AAA was instrumental in encouraging development by the FASB of a conceptual framework for accounting that would assist in the development of standards to govern financial reporting. AAA committee members review FASB Discussion Memorandums and Exposure Drafts and respond to the proposals of the FASB. Individual members of the association participate actively in research projects that are used by the FASB as the basis for many of its recommendations.[13]

The members of the American Accounting Association hold many different opinions and points of view. One of the major roles of the AAA is to serve as a forum within which educators can express their views, either individually or in specially appointed committees. The AAA, however, does not claim to serve as a majority voice for accounting academicians and, until recently, had a firm policy against taking positions on accounting issues as an association. A new policy was adopted in 1988 that permits the Executive Committee of the AAA to take positions representing its membership as needed. The impact of the academic arm of accounting on the establishment of accounting standards has increased through the years, as evidenced by inclusion of an educator as a member of the FASB and the large number of educators included on FASB task forces and the FASB staff.

Other Organizations   Although the preceding groups have traditionally exercised the most direct influence upon the regulation of accountants and the development of accounting principles, the influence of other groups has also been felt. Professional accountants from business enterprises are represented on the Board of Trustees of the Financial Accounting Foundation by two organizations, the **Financial Executives Institute** and the **National Association of Accountants**.

The FEI is a national organization composed of financial executives employed by large corporations. The FEI membership includes treasurers, controllers, and financial vice-presidents. The FEI has sponsored several research projects through the years related to financial reporting problems.

The NAA is more concerned with the information needs of internal users than with external reporting. Its monthly publication, *Management Accounting*, has traditionally dealt mainly with problems involving information systems and the development and use of accounting data within the

---

[13]Indicative of this type of research are the following reports commissioned and issued by the FASB as background for its issued Concepts Statement No. 5. Yuji Ijiri, *Recognition of Contractual Rights and Obligations* (Stamford: Financial Accounting Standards Board, 1980); Henry Jaenicke, *Survey of Present Practices in Recognizing Revenues, Expenses, Gains, and Losses* (Stamford: Financial Accounting Standards Board, 1981); L. Todd Johnson and Reed K. Storey, *Recognition in Financial Statements: Underlying Concepts and Practical Conventions* (Stamford: Financial Accounting Standards Board, 1982).

business organization. It awards the **Certificate of Management Accounting (CMA)** to those management accountants who pass a 2½-day qualifying examination and meet specified experience requirements. Because a firm's information system usually provides data for both internal and external reporting, the NAA is often concerned about the activities of the FASB and responds to its invitations to comment on issues that are related to internal reporting.

The users of external financial reports are also represented on the Financial Accounting Foundation's Board of Trustees by two organizations. The **Financial Analysts Federation** represents the large number of analysts who advise the investing public on the meaning of the financial reports issued by America's businesses. Members of this group have often been critical of corporate financial reporting practices and have continually requested increased disclosure of pertinent financial data. The **Securities Industry Associates** is the organization that represents the investment bankers who manage the portfolios of the large institutional investors that have affected the stock market so dramatically in the past decade. The large amount of investment capital controlled by insurance companies and banks has significantly diminished the influence of the small investor in the market. The strong "bull market" of the mid 1980's was characterized by large daily swings in the stock market prices caused by heavy trading by institutional investors. In October 1987, a steep decline in stock prices was triggered partly by investors who relied on computer programs to determine when securities should be bought and sold. As the market fell, computers initiated sell orders that further depressed the market prices. This trading was referred to as "program trading" and became too automatic to buffer the decline. Institutional investors represent a major group of external users of financial information and have become increasingly vocal with regard to financial reporting and the establishment of accounting standards.

Although the preceding discussion of accounting standards has focused on reporting by business enterprises, the accounting profession is also concerned with the reporting by the numerous government institutions in our economy. This includes not only the Federal Government and its agencies, but also the large number of states, counties, and municipal governments. It is estimated that the total expenditures by these government organizations exceed 1.5 trillion dollars per year. Two government organizations were added to the list of sponsors of the FAF in 1984—the **National Association of State Auditors, Treasurers, and Controllers** and the **Government Finance Officers Association**. These organizations are especially interested in the standards issued by the **Governmental Accounting Standards Board**, a companion board to the FASB organized in 1984 to focus on reporting by the public sector of our economy. Although the statements issued by governmental organizations do not have a direct impact on investors, the magnitude of their impact on such vital economic factors as the interest rate, tax policies, and employment rates cannot be ignored in any financial planning. Creditors are especially affected by the financial activities of governmental units that require funding through various forms of bonds and long-term notes.

Impact of Accounting Standards

As discussed earlier in this chapter, accounting information plays a critical role in the economic decision-making process. Thus, the standards applied in financial reporting have a significant impact on the allocation of resources in our economy.

Professional Judgment

Many accounting standards provide general guidelines rather than precise rules. The accountant, therefore, must exercise professional judgment in interpreting and applying standards. For example, FASB Statement No. 5, "Accounting for Contingencies," states that a contingent loss and the related liability should be recognized in the financial statements only if it is "probable" that an actual future loss will be sustained. It is up to the accountant and the auditor to decide whether it is "probable" that an event, such as a lawsuit, will result in a definite liability. The accountant's decision has a direct impact on the information reported on the financial statements.

Texaco Inc. provides an interesting example of the difficulty in applying the contingent liability standards. On December 10, 1985, a Texas district court entered judgment for Pennzoil Company against Texaco Inc. for $11 billion. This was only $3 billion less than Texaco's total stockholders' equity at the time of the judgment. Texaco appealed the ruling, which arose from a conflict over attempts to acquire Getty Oil Company, claiming it was excessive and would destroy the company. In its 1985 and 1986 financial statements, Texaco included a lengthy note describing the litigation and the appeal process. The note stated that because Texaco Inc. "believes that there is no legal basis for the judgment, which it believes is contrary to the evidence and applicable law",[13] no provision for the judgment was included in the balance sheet or the income statement at December 31, 1985 or 1986. On April 12, 1987, Texaco filed a petition for relief under Chapter 11 bankruptcy laws, and agreed to a restructuring of its assets and liabilities. On December 19, 1987, after failing to obtain a reversal of the judgment, Texaco Inc. reached an agreement with Pennzoil. The agreed settlement included a $3 billion cash payment to Pennzoil from Texaco as full settlement of the earlier judgment.

The 1987 financial statements included the agreed settlement of $3 billion as an expense. The 1987 statements also included a lengthy note on "Chapter 11—Plan of Reorganization." The auditor's report that accompa-

---

[13]Texaco Inc. and Subsidiary Companies 1986 Consolidated Financial Statements, Note 17.

nied the 1987 financial statements included the following explanatory paragraph and conclusion:

Exhibit 1–6	**Texaco Inc.**

As more fully described in Notes 1 and 16 to the consolidated financial statements, a judgment, which may be subject to further appeal, has been rendered against Texaco Inc. in the Pennzoil litigation. On April 12, 1987, Texaco Inc. and two of its subsidiaries (the Debtor Companies) each filed a Voluntary Petition for Relief under Chapter 11, Title 11 of the United States Code. The Debtor Companies are operating their businesses as debtors-in-possession subject to the jurisdiction of the U.S. Federal Court. The accompanying financial statements have been prepared on a going-concern basis which contemplates the realization of assets and payment of liabilities in the ordinary course of business. The financial statements do not give effect to all reclassifications and may not give effect to all adjustments that could result from any plans, arrangements or actions which might arise out of the reorganization proceedings, as the eventual outcome of these proceedings is not presently determinable.

In our opinion, subject to the effect, if any, that might have been required had the outcome of the uncertainties referred to in the preceding paragraph been known, the financial statements referred to above present fairly the financial position of Texaco Inc. and subsidiary companies as of December 31, 1987 and 1986, and the results of their operations and the changes in their financial position for each of the three years in the period ended December 31, 1987, in conformity with generally accepted accounting principles applied on a consistent basis.

Alternative Accounting Principles

In many areas, there is more than one generally accepted principle or standard for reporting events or transactions. Examples include depreciation of plant assets, inventory valuation, and costs of long-term construction contracts. The choice of one standard rather than another can have a material effect on financial statements.

For example, Revere Copper and Brass Inc. changed its method of valuing some of its inventory from FIFO to LIFO. The income statement for that year reported net income of $15,042,000 and income tax expense of $1,801,000. Had Revere continued to value its inventories under the FIFO method, net income would have been approximately $20,986,000 and the company would have incurred a much larger tax liability. The balance sheet reported inventories of $90,491,000, whereas using FIFO, inventories would have been reported at approximately $98,000,000.

Reported financial information, particularly net income, can have far-reaching effects. Thus, a decrease in net income could cause a decline in stock prices or a reduction of dividends paid to stockholders. Also, some companies have employee compensation and benefit plans that are directly related to net income. Thus, when employee bonuses or contributions to employee profit-sharing plans are calculated as a percentage of net income, the employees would suffer a direct economic loss as a result of lower reported earnings.

These are just a few examples of the impact of accounting standards and their application. They are intended to underscore the importance of accounting information and the standards applied in developing that information.

Financial Reporting in a Complex Business Environment

The environment within which business and accounting function has become increasingly complex. One of its characteristic features is the many social, political, legal, and economic influences that create continual change in that environment. Technology has developed new products that have led to a dramatic shift from a capital-intensive industrial economy in the United States to a labor-intensive information technology economy. Government continues to influence the economy through its tremendous federal deficits, tax regulations, international trade policy, and actions to control inflation. World markets have become closer as businesses have increased their international involvement and funds have become increasingly fluid in movement around the world. If accounting is to continue to be the "language of business," it must adapt to these complex, changing relationships.

This dynamic environment means that financial reporting must reflect these environmental factors. For example, the technological revolution of the past few years has included a significant increase in the use of computers, both in business and in the home. The programs that make the computer so adaptable to varied uses are known as "computer software." Thousands of companies, many quite small, have been formed to produce wide varieties of software for public consumption. The financial reporting issue involved concerns the treatment of costs to develop the software. There is always uncertainty as to whether the cost to develop the software will be recovered in the market place. Should these costs be reported as assets before the judgment of the market place is known, or should they be charged to expense and written off against revenue?[14]

Another example of how our complex environment affects financial reporting is the financial market place. It is continuing to develop new instruments that also adapt to the rapid changes in the economy. Variable interest debt, zero-interest-rate discounted bonds, and leveraged leases describe financial instruments that have emerged in the past few years. In establishing reporting standards for these instruments, both the lender and the investor must be considered to assure comparable treatment by business enterprises.

The changing business environment creates the need to continually review existing standards to see if they require revision. The FASB has adopted a policy of reviewing its pronouncements to see if modification is needed. As a result of such review, the standards dealing with recording fluctuations in foreign exchange rates were modified after a seven year period.[15]

The magnitude of the growth in the standards is demonstrated by the fact that in the first 15 years of the FASB's existence, it issued 98 stan-

---

[14]The FASB responded to this question by issuing *Statement of Financial Accounting Standards No. 86,* "Accounting for Computer Software Costs" (Stamford: Financial Accounting Standards Board, 1985). See Chapter 11 for detailed discussion of this topic.

[15]*Statement of Financial Accounting Standards No. 52,* issued in 1981, replaced *Statement of Financial Accounting Standards No. 8,* issued in 1975.

dards. This compares with 31 opinions issued in a similar period by the Accounting Principles Board, predecessor to the FASB. While it is true that some of the FASB standards are quite narrow in their coverage, there is still significantly more output from the FASB than was true of earlier standard-setting bodies.

Conflict between Public and Private Sector

As indicated previously, the SEC has historically left the standard-setting process to the private sector. The Commission's influence, however, has often been felt on specific issues. From time to time, Congress has urged the SEC to exercise a more critical role in setting financial accounting standards and in evaluating the independence and quality control of CPA firms. Over the past two decades, there have been many legal actions brought against CPA firms for failure to fairly disclose the financial condition of a company. These legal actions have become more common, and as they arise, Congress, through its committee structure, again raises difficult questions about whether the system in the private sector is working for the benefit of the public.

In 1978 there were two significant Congressional committees that conducted hearings concerning the accounting profession: the Metcalf Committee, chaired by Senator Lee Metcalf (Montana), and the Moss Committee, chaired by Representative John E. Moss (California). A Senate staff report entitled "The Accounting Establishment" was used extensively by the committees as they probed such issues as the possible monopoly position of the eight largest U.S. accounting firms (the "Big 8"); the independence of auditors whose firms employ tax consultants and management advisory counselors who work directly with audit clients; and the poor quality of audit work being performed in some instances. Although no definite legislative action was taken, these committees attracted a great deal of attention from the profession, and several changes were made by the AICPA as a result of these hearings, including its establishment of the firm membership divisions. Also, as a result of these hearings, annual reports from the SEC on the auditing profession are now required by Congress. These reports have generally been positive; however, another increase in business failures in the mid and late 1980s, including many bank failures, led to another round of hearings under the direction of Representative John Dingell of Michigan. The SEC commissioned a blue-ribbon committee to study the issue of fraudulent financial reporting. Their report, known as the Treadway Report after its chairman Robert Treadway, made several specific recommendations to management, auditors, and educators to help detect and deter management fraud.[16] The congressional Dingell Committee urged

---

[16]Several large fraud cases emerged in the late 1980s. Among the more prominent were EMS Securities, a case where the auditor accepted money to issue fraudulent reports, and ZZZZ Best, a case where millions of dollars of phony business was not detected by the auditors before fraudulent reports were issued.

the various sectors to study the Treadway Report carefully, and generally agreed with the recommendations to improve audit quality.

Although much attention is paid to the audit function by these congressional committees, there also has been concern over the establishment of accounting standards. Critics of standard-setting in the private sector ask if it is realistic to assume that the profession can establish and administer standards and still retain an independent posture. Congress continues to prod the SEC to exercise a more active role in assuring that financial reporting is adequately measuring and disclosing the true status of companies and their activities. The FASB has responded to this pressure by its open discussion policy and its attempt to arrive at standards that balance theory and varying user needs.

Regardless of who sets accounting standards, the task is difficult. As will be discussed in the next chapter, there are very few absolutes in accounting principles. As evidenced by the voluminous tax legislation and the extreme difficulty in achieving tax simplification, passing the responsibility for accounting standard setting to the SEC or a similar governmental agency would probably lead to an even greater complexity in financial reporting. If accountants are to retain their role as professionals, they must be able to exercise judgment in applying general guidelines to specific problems. Users, managers of business enterprises, and professional auditors must balance their needs and views and continue to work toward more meaningful accounting and financial reporting. If these users cannot obtain meaningful reports through the private sector organizations such as the FASB, there will be increased demand from the public through Congress to do it by legislation.

Overview of Intermediate Accounting

This first chapter is designed to emphasize the importance of accounting and financial reporting in today's complex business environment and the challenges that face those who are members of the accounting profession. The remaining chapters of the text cover in depth the elements contained in the basic financial statements presented to external users. To help students realize that the issues discussed are not just textbook issues, extensive examples of actual businesses are included throughout the book.

Although there has been a growing body of standards that constitute GAAP, there are many unresolved areas. In some cases, the existing standards have been questioned, and recommendations for revision of the standards have been made. It is important that those who plan to enter the profession of accounting have a foundation as to not only what GAAP currently is, but also have a theoretical understanding of why it developed to its present state.

Key Terms   Accounting 3
Accounting and Audit Guides 14
Accounting and Auditing
  Enforcement Releases (AAER) 17
Accounting Principles Board (APB)
  14
Accounting Research Bulletins
  (ARB) 14
Accounting Series Releases (ASRs)
  17
American Accounting Association
  (AAA) 17
American Institute of Certified Public
  Accountants (AICPA) 14
Committee on Accounting
  Procedures (CAP) 14
Discussion Memorandum 12
Emerging Issues Task Force (EITF)
  15
Exposure Draft 13
External audit 6
Financial accounting 5
Financial Accounting Foundation
  (FAF) 11
Financial Accounting Standards
  Advisory Council 11
Financial Accounting Standards
  Board (FASB) 10
Financial Analysts Federation 19

Financial Executives Institute (FEI)
  18
Financial Reporting Releases (FRR)
  17
Generally accepted accounting
  principles (GAAP) 10
General purpose financial statements
  5
Governmental Accounting Standards
  Board (GASB) 11
Interpretation of a Statement of
  Financial Accounting Standards 13
Management accounting 5
National Association of Accountants
  (NAA) 18
Opinions 14
Private Companies Practice Section
  (PCPS) 16
Securities and Exchange Commission
  (SEC) 17
SEC Practice Section (SECPS) 16
Securities Industry Associates 19
Statements of Financial Accounting
  Concepts 12
Statements of Financial Accounting
  Standards (SFAS) 13
Statements of Position (SOPs) 14
Technical Bulletins 14

Questions   1. Accounting has been defined as a service activity. Who is served by accounting and how are they benefitted?
2. Accounting is sometimes characterized as dealing only with the past. Give three examples of how accounting information can be of value in dealing with the future.
3. How does the fact that there are limited resources in the world relate to accounting information?
4. Distinguish between management accounting and financial accounting.
5. Contrast the roles of an accountant and an auditor.
6. Why are independent audits necessary?
7. What conditions led to the establishment of accounting standard-setting bodies?
8. What are the differences in purpose and scope of the FASB's Statements of Financial Accounting Standards, Statements of Financial Accounting Concepts, Interpretations of Financial Accounting Standards, and Technical Bulletins?
9. What characteristics of the standard-setting process are designed to increase the acceptability of standards established by the FASB?
10. What is the relationship of the AICPA and the AAA to the FASB?

11. How does the SEC influence the accounting profession?
12. Why is standard setting such a difficult and complex task?
13. Why is Congress conducting hearings on the accounting profession? What type of legislation has been proposed to increase control over accounting?

Discussion Cases   **Case 1–1   (How should I invest?)**

Changing economic conditions have made equity securities (stock) a desirable investment alternative. Assume you have funds to invest in common stock, but you are not sure which companies you should invest in. You send for and receive the annual reports of several companies in three growth industries, but your background in accounting is limited to an introductory course. With your limited experience, what information would you expect to find to assist you in making an investment decision in (a) the balance sheet, (b) the income statement, and (c) the statement of cash flows?

Case 1–2   (How large is too large?)

The existence of a relatively few large CPA firms that service virtually all of the major industrial and financial firms and thus dominate the accounting profession has led to criticism through the years. In a staff study for Senator Metcalf and his Subcommittee on Reporting, Accounting, and Management, the following assertion was made:

> The AICPA has developed prestige because of its size, resources, management, and the professional reputation of CPAs for objectivity, which has been accepted by the public and governmental authorities until recent years. Analysis of AICPA activities reveals that the organization primarily promotes the perceived interest of the large national accounting firms. Those interests are generally sympathetic to the management interests of large corporate clients which are primary sources of revenue for large accounting firms. (p. 129, 1976 report)

What dangers do you see from this concentration of power? What advantages are present because of the emergence of a relatively few large firms?

Case 1–3   (Here comes Congress again!)

Congressional hearings continue to be held on the question of control of the accounting profession. There are many critics of accounting who would like to see more government control of accounting standards and of the auditors who examine financial statements of business enterprises.

(a) What points would you expect to hear from the president of the AICPA defending retention of private-sector control?

(b) What points would you expect to hear from a senator advocating installation of government controls over the accounting profession?

Case 1–4   (What do users need?)

The definition of accounting quoted in this chapter stresses that information generated by an accounting system should be useful for making decisions. There are two basic types of users: those external to the company and those who are within the company, or internal users. Distinguish between the types of information these two user groups would need in order to make their decisions.

Case 1–5   (SEC: A necessary evil?)

Annette Wilson and Henry Wall were selected to present a case in competition with students from other universities dealing with the need for a government agency with oversight responsibility to monitor the quality of accounting in the private sector. Draft an outline showing the points you think Annette and Henry should make.

Case 1–6   (We aren't getting what we expect.)

Quality Enterprises Inc. issued its 1990 financial statements on February 22, 1991. The auditors expressed a "clean" opinion in the audit report. On July 14, 1991, the company filed for bankruptcy as a result of an inability to meet currently maturing long-term debt obligations. Reasons cited for the action include (1) large losses on inventory due to overproduction of product lines that did not sell, (2) failure to collect on a large account receivable due to the customer's bankruptcy, and (3) a deteriorating economic environment caused by a severe recession in the spring of 1991. John Stevens, a large stockholder of Quality, is concerned that a company with a clean audit opinion could have financial difficulty leading to bankruptcy just four months after the audit report was issued. "Where were the auditors?" he inquired. In reply, the auditors contend that at December 31, 1990, the date of the financial statements, the statements were presented in accordance with GAAP. What is the auditor's responsibility for protecting users from losses? How does this case illustrate the "expectation gap" issue?

Chapter 2

A Conceptual Framework of Accounting

The general public often views accounting as a scientific discipline based on a fixed set of rules and procedures. This is a natural perception since the public's exposure to accounting generally relates to financial statements, tax returns, and other reports showing dollar amounts that give an impression of exactness. Those within the profession, however, recognize that accounting is more an art than a science and that the operating results and other accounting measurements are based on estimates and judgments relative to the measurement and communication of business activity.

Even though accounting professionals must rely on their judgment, accounting and financial reporting are governed by a well-established body of "generally accepted accounting principles," referred to as GAAP. As explained in Chapter 1, GAAP includes standards and interpretations issued by the FASB and those pronouncements issued by previous standard-setting bodies that have not been suspended or superseded. Underlying these principles or standards are several fundamental concepts and assumptions that, collectively, provide a theoretical or conceptual framework of accounting. This chapter focuses on the need for such a framework and examines the major components of the FASB's conceptual framework.

Need For A Conceptual Framework

Much has been written about the theoretical foundation or conceptual framework that underlies accounting practice. There are several reasons why such a framework is important. One major purpose is to provide broad definitions of the objectives, terms, and concepts involved in the practice of accounting. This definitional aspect of the framework prescribes the boundaries of accounting and financial reporting.

A strong theoretical foundation is essential if accounting practice is to keep pace with a changing business environment. Accountants are continually faced with new situations, technological advances, and business innovations that present new accounting and reporting problems. These problems must be dealt with in an organized and consistent manner. If their impact is sufficiently broad, specific issues may be resolved through the FASB's standard-setting process. The conceptual framework plays a vital role in the development of new standards and in the revision of previously issued standards. Recognizing the importance of this role, the FASB stated that fundamental concepts "guide the Board in developing accounting and reporting standards by providing . . . a common foundation and basic reasoning on which to consider merits of alternatives."[1] In a very real sense, then, the FASB itself is a primary beneficiary of a conceptual framework.

A conceptual framework also brings together the objectives and fundamentals of existing accounting practice and financial reporting. This helps users to better understand the purposes, content, and characteristics of information provided by accounting.

A conceptual framework not only helps in understanding existing practice, but it also provides a guide for future practice. When accountants are confronted with new developments that are not covered by GAAP, a conceptual framework provides a reference for analyzing and resolving emerging issues.

A conceptual framework is also useful in selecting the most appropriate methods for reporting enterprise activity. Often, there is more than one justifiable or generally accepted reporting alternative for a particular transaction or event, and accountants must use their judgment in selecting among available alternatives. Fundamental concepts provide guidance in choosing the alternative that most accurately reflects the financial position and results of operations for the entity given the specific circumstances involved. If businesses and their activities were identical, reporting alternatives could be eliminated. However, that is not the case. Even within a particular industry, companies are not organized in exactly the same way. They do not produce identical products or provide identical services, and their accounting systems and the reports generated therefrom are not uniform. Thus, accountants must exercise professional judgment in fulfilling their roles as suppliers of useful information for decision makers. A conceptual framework helps make the results of the reporting process more comparable than they would be otherwise.

In summary, a conceptual framework of accounting should:

1. define the boundaries of accounting by providing definitions of basic objectives, key terms, and fundamental concepts,

2. assist the FASB in the standard-setting process by providing a basis for developing new and revised accounting and reporting standards,

3. provide a description of current practice and a frame of reference for resolving new issues not covered by GAAP, and

4. assist accountants and others in selecting from among reporting alterna-

[1]*Statement of Financial Accounting Concepts No. 6,* "Elements of Financial Statements" (Stamford: Financial Accounting Standards Board, December, 1985), p. i.

tives the method that best represents the economic reality of the situation.

If these purposes are accomplished, the overall result should be a reporting of the most useful information for decision-making purposes, which is the ultimate goal of accounting.

Nature and Components of the FASB's Conceptual Framework

Serious attempts to develop a theoretical foundation of accounting can be traced to the 1930s. Among the leaders in such attempts were accounting educators, both individually and collectively as a part of the American Accounting Association (AAA). In 1936, the Executive Committee of the AAA began issuing a series of publications devoted to accounting theory, the last of which was published in 1965 and entitled "A Statement of Basic Accounting Theory." During the period from 1936 to 1973, there were several additional publications issued by the AAA and also by the American Institute of Certified Public Accountants (AICPA), each attempting to develop a conceptual foundation for the practice of accounting.[2]

While these publications made significant contributions to the development of accounting thought, no unified structure of accounting theory emerged from these efforts. When the Financial Accounting Standards Board was established in 1973, it responded to the need for a general theoretical framework by undertaking a comprehensive project to develop a "conceptual framework for financial accounting and reporting." This project has been described as an attempt to establish a constitution for accounting. The goal of the FASB was to provide "a coherent system of interrelated objectives and fundamentals that is expected to lead to consistent standards and that prescribes the nature, function, and limits of financial accounting and reporting."[3]

The conceptual framework project was one of the original FASB agenda items. It was viewed as a long-term, continuing project to be developed in stages. Because of its significant potential impact on many aspects of financial reporting, and therefore its controversial nature, progress was deliberate. The project had high priority and received a large share of FASB resources. In December, 1985, the FASB issued the last of six State-

---

[2]Among the most prominent of these publications were: Maurice Moonitz, *Accounting Research Study No. 1*, "The Basic Postulates of Accounting" (New York: American Institute of Certified Public Accountants, 1961); William A. Paton and A. C. Littleton, *An Introduction to Corporate Accounting Standards*, Monograph 3 (Evanston, Ill.: American Accounting Association, 1940); Thomas H. Sanders, Henry R. Hatfield, and W. Moore, *A Statement of Accounting Principles* (New York: American Institute of Accountants, Inc., 1938); Robert T. Sprouse, and Maurice Moonitz, *Accounting Research Study No. 3*, "A Tentative Set of Broad Accounting Principles for Business Enterprises" (New York: American Institute of Certified Public Accountants, 1962); *Statement of the Accounting Principles Board No. 4*, "Basic Concepts and Accounting Principles Underlying Financial Statements of Business Enterprises" (New York: American Institute of Certified Public Accountants, October 1970), *Report of the Study Group on the Objectives of Financial Statements*, "Objectives of Financial Statements" (New York: American Institute of Certified Public Accountants, October 1973).

[3]*Statement of Financial Accounting Concepts No. 6*, p. i.

ments of Financial Accounting Concepts (frequently referred to as Concepts Statements), which provide the basis for the conceptual framework.[4]

The FASB's framework incorporates many widely accepted concepts and principles developed in earlier works. In addition, several traditional assumptions underlying accounting practice are explicitly or implicitly recognized in the framework. The assumptions are discussed later in the chapter and include economic entity, going concern, arm's-length transactions, stable monetary unit, accounting periods, and accrual accounting. The main components of the FASB's conceptual framework, including the underlying assumptions, are presented in Exhibit 2-1.

The first area addressed by the FASB was the basic purposes or **objectives** of financial reporting. The Board sought answers to the questions: Who are the users of accounting information? What kinds of information do they require for decision making? Based on the objectives, the FASB proceeded to develop fundamental concepts that define the important **qualitative characteristics** of useful information and the specific **elements** to be included in financial statements.

Building on the objectives and fundamental concepts, the FASB addressed the issues of **recognition, measurement,** and **reporting.** In this final phase of the framework project, the Board established broad implementation guidelines relating to the questions: When should revenues and expenses be recognized? How should revenues and expenses and other financial statement elements be measured (valued)? How should financial information be reported or displayed?

Each of the framework components is discussed in the following sections. In considering the individual components, the interrelationships become apparent. Decisions concerning one part of the framework influence other parts.

Objectives of Financial Reporting

The starting point for the FASB's conceptual framework was to establish the objectives of financial reporting, since they determine the purposes and overall direction of accounting. Without identifying the goals for financial reporting, e.g., who needs what kind of information and for what reasons, accountants cannot determine the recognition criteria needed, which measurements are useful, or how best to report accounting information.

The financial reporting objectives discussed in this chapter and listed in Exhibit 2–2 are summaried and adapted from FASB Concepts Statement No. 1. Some general observations regarding these objectives should be made. First, because the FASB is currently the primary standard-setting

---

[4]The six Concepts Statements issued by the FASB are:
1. Objectives of Financial Reporting by Business Enterprises
2. Qualitative Characteristics of Accounting Information
3. Elements of Financial Statements of Business Enterprises
4. Objectives of Financial Reporting by Nonbusiness Organizations
5. Recognition and Measurement in Financial Statements of Business Enterprises
6. Elements of Financial Statements (a replacement of No. 3, broadened to include not-for-profit as well as business enterprises).

Exhibit 2–1   A Conceptual Framework for Accounting

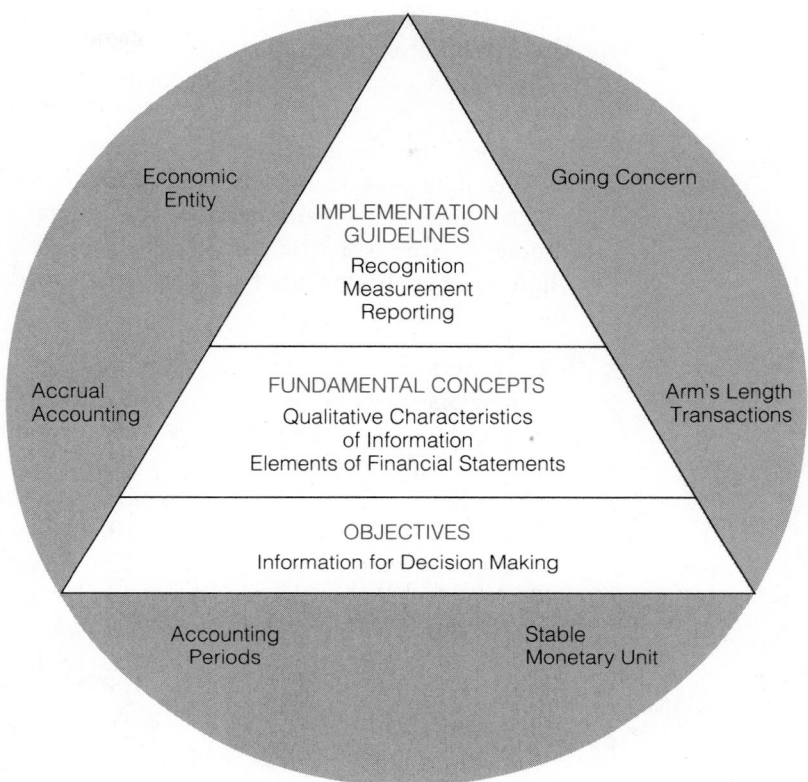

body for accounting in the private sector, the Board's objectives should be considered carefully. However, it should also be recognized that another group might identify somewhat different objectives for financial reporting. The objectives, as well as the other components of the conceptual framework, should, therefore, not be interpreted as "universal truths."

Exhibit 2–2   Objectives of Financial Reporting

General Objective: Provide useful information for decision making

Specific Objectives: Provide information:
                                          a. For assessing cash flow prospects
                                          b. About financial condition
                                          c. About performance and earnings
                                         d. About how funds are obtained and used

Source: *Statement of Financial Accounting Concepts No. 1*

A second and related point is that the objectives of financial reporting are directly connected with the needs of those for whom the information is intended and must be considered in their environmental context. Financial reporting is not an end in itself, but is directed toward satisfying the need for useful information in making business and economic decisions. Thus, the objectives of financial reporting may change due to changes in the information needs of decision makers and because of changes in the economic, legal, political, and social aspects of the total business environment.

Third, the objectives of financial reporting are intended to be broad in nature. The objectives must be broadly based to satisfy a variety of user needs. Thus, they are objectives for general purpose financial reporting, attempting to satisfy the common interests of various potential users rather than to meet the specific needs of any selected group. The list of potential users includes:[5]

1. owners
2. lenders
3. suppliers
4. potential investors
5. creditors
6. employees
7. management
8. directors
9. customers
10. financial analysts
11. advisors
12. brokers
13. underwriters
14. stock exchanges
15. lawyers
16. economists
17. taxing authorities
18. regulatory authorities
19. legislators
20. financial press and reporting agencies
21. labor unions
22. trade associations
23. business researchers
24. teachers and students
25. the public

While there are many potential users of financial reports, the objectives are directed primarily toward the needs of those external users of accounting data who lack the authority to prescribe the information they desire. For example, the Internal Revenue Service or the Securities and Exchange Commission can require selected information from individuals and companies. Investors and creditors, however, must rely to a significant extent on the information contained in the periodic financial reports supplied by management and, therefore, are the major users toward which financial reporting is directed.

A fourth point is that the objectives pertain to financial reporting in general, which encompasses not only disclosures in financial statements, but also other information concerning an enterprise's financial condition and earnings ability. While financial statements are a primary means of communicating information to external parties, other forms and sources are also used for decision making. The total information spectrum relative to investment, credit, and similar decisions is presented in Exhibit 2–3. This illustrates the overall focus of financial reporting and, more specifi-

[5]*Statement of Financial Accounting Concepts No. 1*, "Objectives of Financial Reporting by Business Enterprises" (Stamford: Financial Accounting Standards Board, November, 1978), par. 24.

cally, the areas of primary concern for financial accounting—the financial statements, the notes to financial statements, and supplementary disclosures directly affected by generally accepted accounting principles.

Information for Decision Making

As discussed in Chapter 1, the **overall objective** of financial reporting is **to provide information that is useful for decision making.** The FASB states:

> Financial reporting should provide information that is useful to present and potential investors and creditors and other users in making rational investment, credit, and similar decisions. The information should be comprehensible to those who have a reasonable understanding of business and economic activities and are willing to study the information with reasonable diligence.[6]

The emphasis in this overall objective is on investors and creditors as the primary external users, because in satisfying their needs most other general-purpose needs of external users will be met. The objective also recognizes a fairly sophisticated user of financial reports, one who has a reasonable understanding of accounting and business and who is willing to study and analyze the information presented.

Cash Flow Prospects

Investors and creditors are interested primarily in future cash flows. Thus, financial reporting should **provide information that is useful in assessing cash flow prospects.** Investment and lending decisions are made with the expectation of eventually increasing cash resources. An investor hopes to receive a return on the investment in the form of cash dividends and ultimately to sell the investment for more than it cost. Creditors seek to recover their cash outlays by repayments of the loans and to increase cash resources from interest payments. In making decisions, investors and creditors must consider the amounts, timing, and uncertainty (risk) of these prospective cash flows.

A company is similar to an investor in desiring to recover its investment plus receive a return on that investment. A company invests cash in noncash resources in order to produce a product or service that it expects to sell for an amount greater than the amount invested, thereby increasing cash resources. To the extent that a company is successful in generating favorable cash flows, it can pay dividends and interest, and the market price of its securities will increase. Thus, as illustrated in Exhibit 2–4, the cash flows to investors and creditors are directly related to the cash flows of business enterprises, and financial reporting should provide information that is useful in assessing the enterprise's prospective cash flows.

[6]*Statement of Financial Accounting Concepts No. 1*, par. 34.

Exhibit 2–3   Information Spectrum

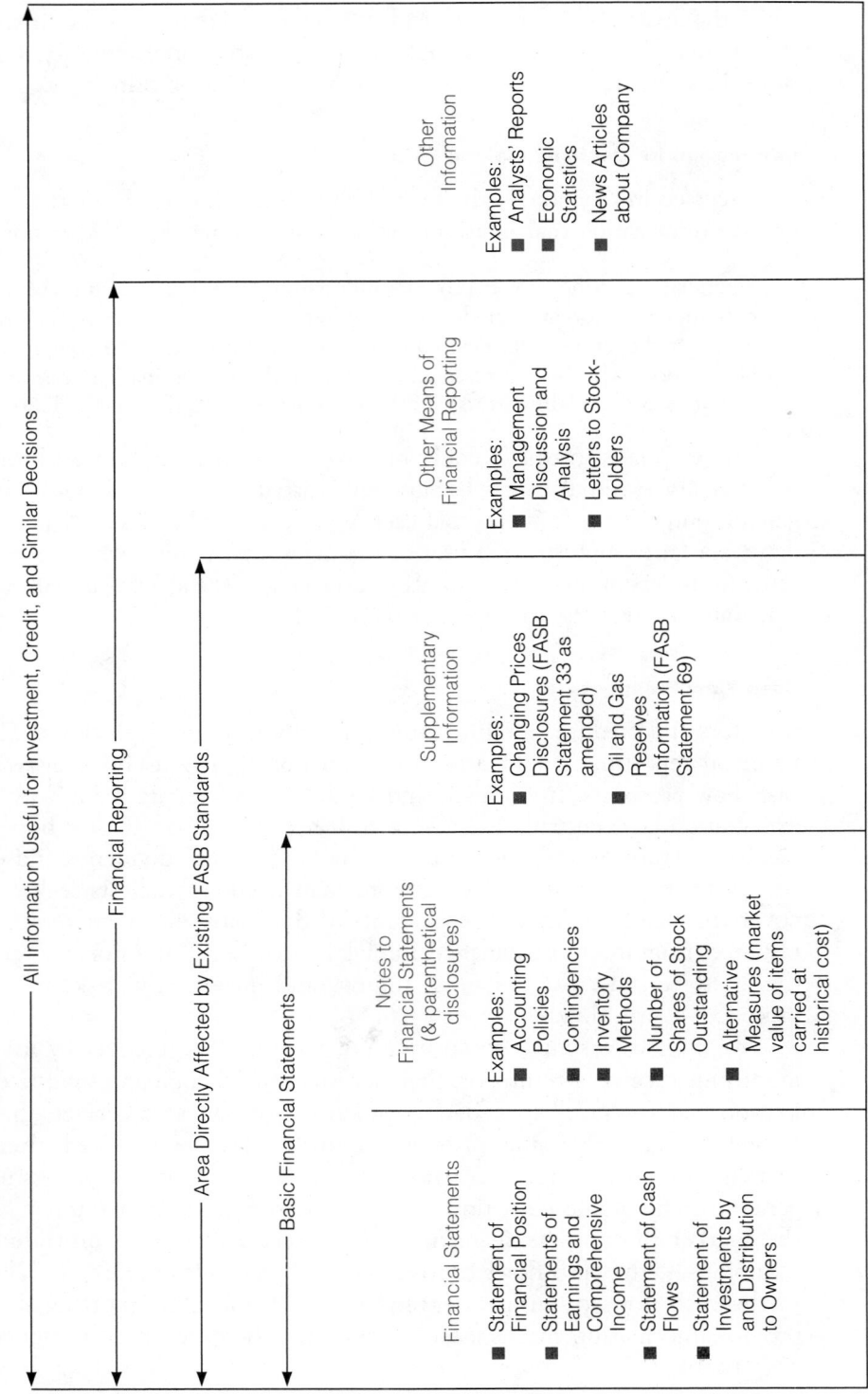

Source: *Adapted from Statement of Financial Accounting Concepts No. 5, p. 5.*

Exhibit 2–4   Enterprise Cash Flows to and from Investors and Creditors

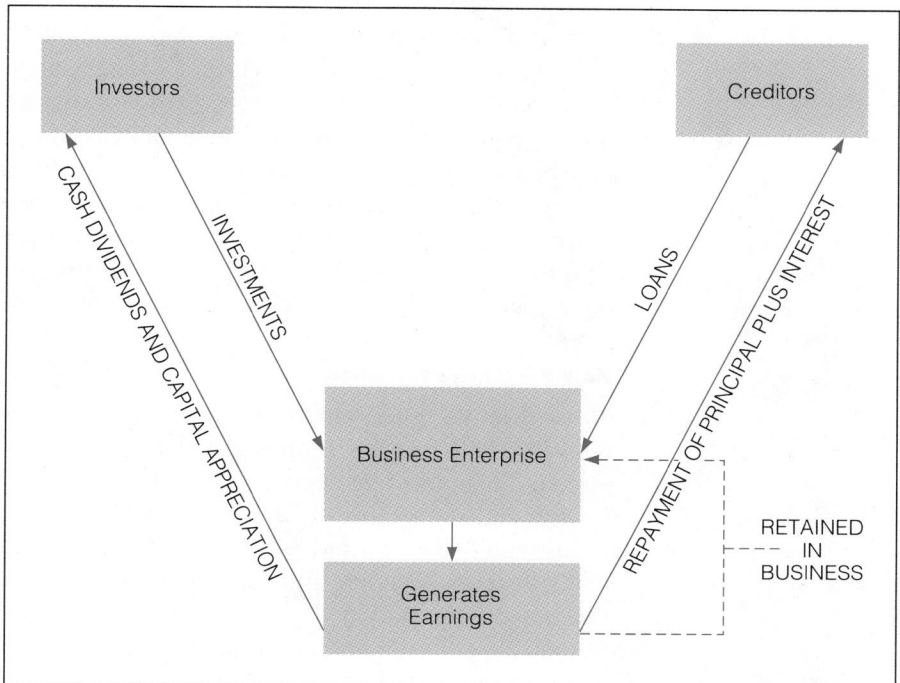

Enterprise Financial Condition

Financial reporting should **provide information about an enterprise's assets, liabilities, and owners' equity** to help investors, creditors, and others evaluate the financial strengths and weaknesses of the enterprise and its liquidity and solvency. Such information will help users determine the financial condition of a company, which, in turn, should provide insight into the prospects of future cash flows. It may also help users who wish to estimate the overall value of a business.

Enterprise Performance and Earnings

Another important objective of financial reporting is to provide **information about an enterprise's financial performance during a period.** Performance is evaluated mainly on the basis of enterprise earnings. In fact, the FASB states that "the primary focus of financial reporting is information about an enterprise's performance provided by measures of earnings and its components."[7] There are several aspects of this important objective. Clearly, investors and creditors are concerned mostly with expectations of future enterprise performance. However, to a large degree, they rely on evaluations of past performance as measures of future performance. The FASB recognizes that investors and creditors want information about earn-

[7]*Statement of Financial Accounting Concepts No. 1*, par. 43.

ings primarily as an indicator of future cash-flow potential. The Board concluded, however, that information about enterprise earnings, measured by accrual accounting, generally provides a better indicator of performance than does information about current cash receipts and disbursements.

Investors and creditors use reported earnings and information concerning the components of earnings in a variety of ways. For example, earnings may be interpreted by users of financial statements as an overall measure of managerial effectiveness, as a predictor of future earnings and long-term "earning power," and as an indicator of the risk of investing or lending. The information may be used to establish new predictions, confirm previous expectations, or change past evaluations.

How Funds Are Obtained and Used

Notwithstanding the emphasis on earnings, another objective of financial reporting is to **provide information about an enterprise's cash flows during a period**. This objective encompasses information about the enterprise's borrowing and repayment of borrowed funds; its capital transactions, such as the issuance of stock and payment of dividends; and any other factors that may affect its liquidity and solvency. Much of the information to satisfy this objective is provided in the statement of cash flows, although information about earnings and about assets, liabilities, and owners' equity is also useful in evaluating the liquidity and solvency of a firm.

Additional Objectives

Although the objectives of financial reporting are aimed primarily at the needs of external users, financial reporting should also **provide information that allows managers and directors to make decisions that are in the best interest of the owners**. A related objective is that sufficient **information should be provided to allow the owners to assess how well management has discharged its stewardship responsibility** over the entrusted resources. This requires an additional objective—**financial reporting should include explanations and interpretations to help users understand the financial information provided**.

In summary, if the objectives discussed in the preceding paragraphs are fully attained, the FASB believes those who make economic decisions will have better information upon which to evaluate alternative courses of action and the expected returns, costs, and risks of each. The result should be a more efficient allocation of scarce resources among competing uses by individuals, enterprises, markets, and the government.

Qualitative Characteristics of Accounting Information

Individuals who are responsible for financial reporting should continually seek to provide the best, i.e., most useful, information possible within reasonable cost constraints. The problem is very complex because of the many choices among acceptable reporting alternatives. For example, what items should be capitalized as assets or reported as liabilities? Which revenues and costs should be assigned to a particular reporting period and on what basis? What are the attributes to be measured: historical costs, current values, or net realizable values? At what level of aggregation or disaggregation should information be presented? Where should specific information be disclosed—in the financial statements, in the notes to the financial statements, or perhaps not at all? These and similar choices must be made by policymakers, such as members of the FASB or SEC; by managements as they fulfill their stewardship roles; and by accountants as they assist management in reporting on a company's activities.

To assist in choosing among financial accounting and reporting alternatives, several criteria have been established by the FASB. These criteria relate to the qualitative characteristics of accounting information. A hierarchy of these qualities is presented in Exhibit 2–5 and will be used as a frame of reference in discussing them.

Exhibit 2–5   A Hierarchy of Accounting Information Qualities

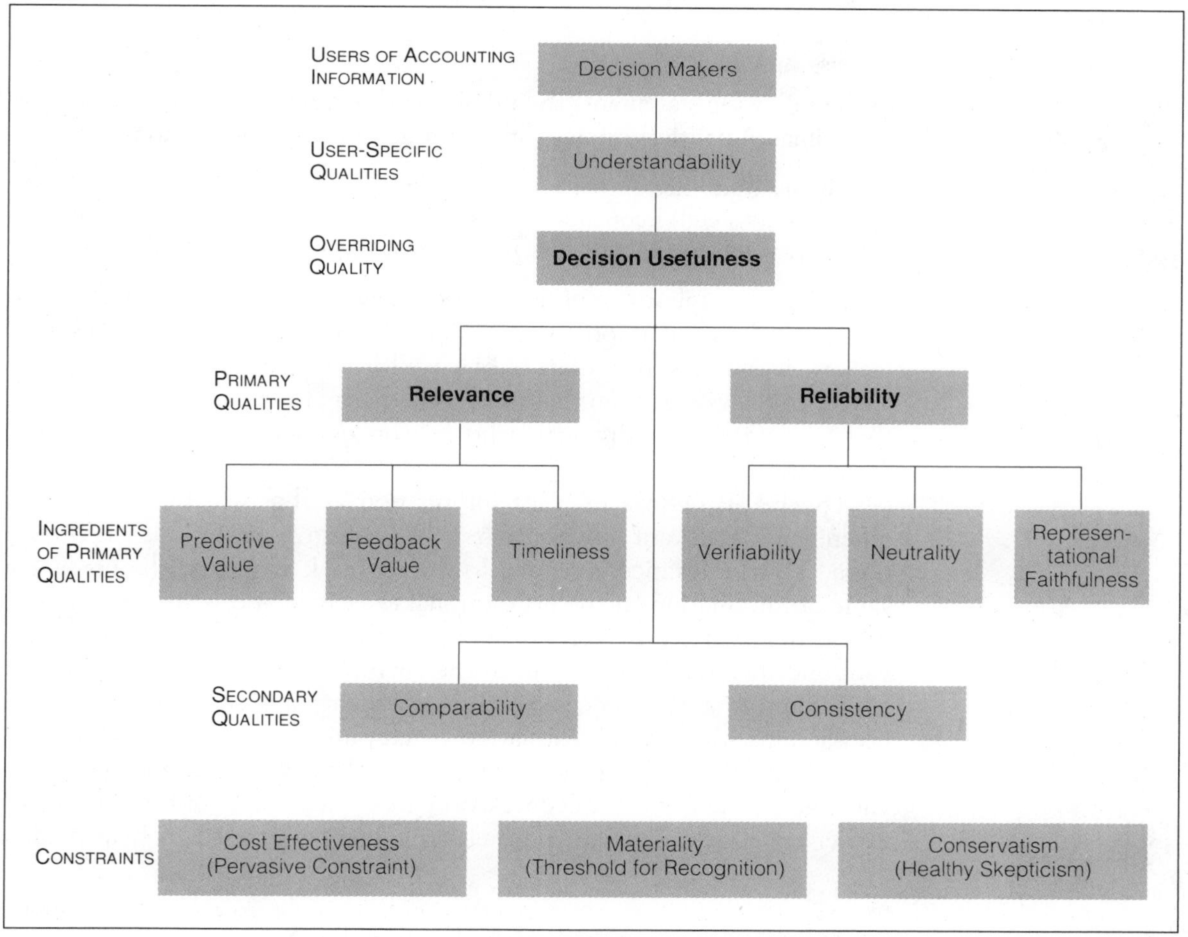

Source: Adapted from FASB *Statement of Financial Accounting Concepts No. 2,* p. 15.

Decision Usefulness

The overriding quality or characteristic of accounting information is **decision usefulness**, which is central to the hierarchy presented in Exhibit 2–5. All other qualities are viewed in terms of their contribution to decision usefulness. The illustrated hierarchy distinguishes user-specific qualities, such as **understandability**, from qualities inherent in accounting information, such as relevance and reliability. The quality of understandability is essential to decision usefulness. Information cannot be useful to decision makers if it is not understood even though the information may be relevant and reliable. The understandability of information depends on the characteristics of users, e.g., their prior knowledge, and also on the inherent characteristics of the information presented. Hence, understandability can be evaluated only with respect to specific classes of decision makers. As indicated earlier, financial reporting is directed toward those users who have a reasonable understanding of business and economic activities and who are willing to study the information provided with reasonable diligence.

Primary Qualities

In the following statement, the FASB identified **relevance** and **reliability** as the primary qualities inherent in useful accounting information:

> The qualities that distinguish "better" (more useful) information from "inferior" (less useful) information are primarily the qualities of relevance and reliability, with some other characteristics that those qualities imply.[8]

Relevance The relevance of information may be judged only in relation to its intended use. If information is not relevant to the needs of decision makers, it is useless regardless of how well it meets other criteria. The objective of relevance, then, is to select methods of measuring and reporting that will aid those individuals who rely on financial statements to make decisions.

The FASB defines relevant information as that which will "make a difference." Relevant information may confirm expectations or change them. Thus, relevance is related to the **feedback value** and the **predictive value** of information. If the decision maker's expectations are neither confirmed nor changed by certain information, that information is not relevant and therefore is not useful to the decision maker. If a user can better predict future consequences based on information about past events and transactions, then such information is relevant.[9]

Relevant information normally provides both feedback and predictive value at the same time. Feedback on past events helps confirm or correct earlier expectations. Such information can then be used to help predict

---

[8]*Statement of Financial Accounting Concepts No. 2*, "Qualitative Characteristics of Accounting Information" (Stamford: Financial Accounting Standards Board, May, 1980), par. 15.

[9]*Ibid.*, pars. 46–50.

future outcomes. For example, when General Motors presents comparative income statements, an investor has information to compare last year's operating results with this year's. This provides a general basis for evaluating prior expectations and for estimating what next year's results might be. The information therefore provides both feedback and predictive value concerning General Motors. As stated by the FASB, "Without a knowledge of the past, the basis for prediction will usually be lacking. Without an interest in the future, knowledge of the past is sterile."[10]

Timeliness is another key ingredient of relevance, relating directly to decision usefulness. Information furnished after a decision has been made is of no value. Again using General Motors as an example, when the company issues interim financial reports, it is attempting to provide information on a timely basis so that the information will be more relevant. Thus, to be relevant, information must offer predictive or feedback value, and it must be presented to users in a timely manner.

Reliability The second primary quality of accounting information is reliability. Accounting information is reliable if users can depend on it to be reasonably free from error or bias and to be a faithful representation of the economic conditions or events that it purports to represent.[11] Reliability does not mean absolute accuracy. Information that is based on judgments and that includes estimates and approximations cannot be totally accurate, but it should be reliable. The objective, then, is to present the type of information in which users can have confidence. Such information must contain the key ingredients of reliability: verifiability, neutrality, and representational faithfulness.

Verifiability implies objectivity and consensus. Accountants seek to base their findings on facts that are determined objectively and that can be verified by other trained accountants using the same measurement methods. For example, assume that the amount of depreciation expense reported in the current year's income statement for the SAVE-ON Company is $125,000. That amount can be verified if it is known that the straight-line method of depreciation was applied to depreciable assets totalling $1,250,000 and that the assets had an estimated useful life of 10 years with no salvage value.

Neutrality relates to information being communicated in an unbiased manner. If financial statements are to satisfy a wide variety of users, the information presented should not be colored in favor of one group of users to the detriment of others. In this sense, the concept of neutrality is similar to the all-encompassing concept of "fairness."

The ingredient of **representational faithfulness** means that there is agreement between the information being reported and the actual results of economic activity being measured. Thus, the amounts and descriptions re-

[10]*Ibid.*, par. 51.

[11]*Ibid.*, par. 63.

ported in the financial statements should reflect the economic reality of what is being represented. For a company to report sales of $3.4 million when they actually had sales of $2.5 million would not be a faithful representation and would cause the information to be unreliable.

Secondary Qualities

In addition to the primary qualities of relevance and reliability, there are two secondary qualities that affect the usefulness of accounting information: comparability and consistency.

Comparability The essence of comparability is that information becomes much more useful when it can be related to a benchmark or standard. The comparison may be with data for other firms or it may be with similar information for the same firm, but for other equivalent periods of time. To illustrate how comparable data can increase the usefulness of information, consider the situation where a company reports current assets of $350,000 and current liabilities of $275,000. The current ratio is 1.27, but does this information reflect a favorable or unfavorable liquidity position? Without knowing comparable data for other companies in the industry or the current ratio of this company for other years, the information is of somewhat limited value. If data were available to show that the average current ratio of all companies in this particular industry is 1.22 and further that this company's current ratio was 1.05 and 1.10, respectively, for the past two years, then it would appear that the company's liquidity position has improved and that it is in relatively good shape.

Given that comparability increases the usefulness of information, financial reports should provide data permitting comparisons among companies and comparison of results of the same company over different time periods. This requires that like things be accounted for in the same manner on the financial statements of different companies and for a particular company for different periods. It should be recognized, however, that uniformity is not always the answer to comparability. Different circumstances may require different accounting treatment.

Still, one of the greatest unsolved problems in accounting is the present acceptance of alternative accounting methods under situations that do not appear to be sufficiently different to warrant different accounting practices. The goal is for basic similarities and differences in the activities of companies to be apparent from the financial statements.

Research in accounting is currently being directed toward identifying circumstances justifying the use of a given method of accounting. If this research is successful, alternative methods can be eliminated where circumstances are found to be the same. In the meantime, current practice requires disclosure of the accounting methods used, as well as the impact of changes in methods when a change can be justified. Although the disclosures currently made do not generally provide enough information for a user to convert the published financial information from one accounting method to another, they do provide information that can assist the user in determining the degree of comparability among enterprises.

Consistency Consistency is another important ingredient of useful accounting information. In view of the number of reporting alternatives, the methods adopted by an enterprise should be consistently employed if there is to be continuity and comparability in the financial statements. In analyzing statements, users seek to identify and evaluate the changes and trends within the enterprise. Conclusions concerning financial position and operations may be materially in error if, for example, accelerated depreciation is applied against the revenue of one year and straight-line depreciation against the revenue of the next year, or if securities are reported under long-term investments in one year and under current assets in the following year.

This is not to suggest that methods once adopted should not be changed. A continuing analysis of the business activities, as well as changing conditions, may suggest changes in accounting methods and presentations leading to more informative statements. These changes should be incorporated in the accounting system and the financial statements. The statements should be accompanied by a clear explanation of the nature of the changes and their effects, where they are material, so that current reporting can be properly interpreted and related to past reporting.

Constraints

Underlying the informational qualities identified in Exhibit 2–5 are three important constraints: (1) cost effectiveness, (2) materiality, and (3) conservatism.

Cost Effectiveness Information is like other commodities in that it must be worth more than the cost of providing it to consumers. This concept is referred to as cost effectiveness. Too often government regulators and others assume that information is a "free" good. Obviously, it is not, and the relationship between costs and benefits must always be kept in mind when selecting or requiring reporting alternatives. To illustrate, in the early 1970s the Federal Trade Commission proposed that large companies be required to disclose information about lines-of-business. A group of companies brought court action to prohibit the proposed requirement. A major argument of the companies was that the information would be very costly to prepare, because it was not normally generated by the accounting system. The companies also argued that the line-of-business disclosures in the form proposed by the FTC would not be beneficial to users, because the reported segments would be artificial and not those the companies normally used to report on a less than company-wide basis. Although the FTC prevailed, primarily because of perceived benefits in regulating anti-trust situations, this case underscores an important point—the cost of producing information (including, for example, modification to the existing accounting system, or even additional printing and mailing costs) must be compared to the extra benefits (generally meaning an improvement in specific decisions of users) to determine if the information should be reported.

The difficulty in assessing cost effectiveness is that the costs and benefits, especially the benefits, are not always evident or easily measured. Notwithstanding this difficulty, cost effectiveness is an important constraint and should be considered when selecting reporting alternatives.

Materiality Contrary to the belief of many readers of financial statements, the amounts reported in the statements are not always complete and are often not exact. While for many decisions completeness and exactness are not required, there is a point at which information that is incomplete or inexact does influence a decision. This point defines the boundary between information that is material and information that is immaterial.

Materiality is an overriding concept related to, but distinguishable from, the primary qualities of relevance and reliability. Materiality determines the threshold for recognition of accounting items and is primarily a quantitative consideration. While relevance is directed toward the nature of the information, materiality focuses on the size of a judgment item in a given set of circumstances. Materiality deals with the specific question: Is the item large enough or the degree of the accuracy precise enough to influence the decision of a user of the information? Of course, the degree of influence caused by the size of an item also depends on the nature of the item and the circumstances in which a judgment must be made. For example, a $1 million loss from a product-related lawsuit might be financially devastating for some enterprises, but may not even warrant separate disclosure on Ford Motor Company's financial statements.

At the present time, there are few guidelines to assist preparers of financial reports in applying the concept of materiality. Where materiality guidelines do exist, they are often not uniform. For example, the materiality guideline for reporting by segments of a company suggests that certain information be disclosed for any major segment that accounts for 10% or more of total company sales. On the other hand, for determining the significance of dilution in earnings per share computations, the materiality guideline is 3%. Thus, for these two different reporting areas the materiality guideline varies from 10% to 3%. Since quantitative guidance concerning materiality is often lacking, managers and accountants must exercise judgment in determining whether a failure to disclose certain data will influence the decisions of the users of financial statements.

Past court cases can help determine what is material by providing examples of where the lack of disclosure of certain information in the financial statements has been considered a material misstatement. The failure to disclose proper inventory values or pending sales of large amounts of assets, the failure to disclose the imminence of a highly profitable transaction or to disclose a significant downward readjustment of reported earnings are a few examples.[12]

In summary, the following point should be kept in mind in making judgments concerning materiality:

> The omission or misstatement of an item in a financial report is material if, in the light of surrounding circumstances, the magnitude of the item is such that it is probable that the judgment of a reasonable person relying upon the report would have been changed or influenced by the inclusion or correction of the item.[13]

Conservatism Another constraint associated with the characteristics of useful information is conservatism. This means that when accountants have genuine doubt concerning which of two or more reporting alternatives should be selected, users are best served by adopting a conservative approach, that is, by choosing the alternative with the least favorable impact on owners' equity. However, conservatism does not mean deliberate and arbitrary understatement of assets and earnings. On the contrary, use of conservative procedures is motivated by not wanting to overstate assets and earnings when dealing in "gray areas."

Conservatism should be used when a degree of skepticism is warranted. For example, generally accepted accounting principles require the expensing of research and development costs on the basis that the future benefits cannot be accurately determined. Since there is often reasonable doubt as to the existence or amount of future benefits, the costs are expensed, and the amount of income reported currently is reduced. Another example of conservatism in accounting practice is reporting short-term marketable equity securities at a lower of cost or market value. If General Mills held short-term marketable equity securities and the market value dropped below cost, the company should report those securities at the lower market value. To continue to report the securities at cost would overstate current assets and might imply to statement users that current assets exceed current liabilities by more than is actually the case.

The constraint of conservatism is a useful one, but one that should be applied carefully and used only as a moderating and refining influence on the information reported. Essentially, conservatism means prudence in financial accounting and reporting.

Elements of Financial Statements Having identified the qualitative characteristics of accounting information, the FASB in Concepts Statement No. 3 established definitions for the ten basic elements of financial statements of business enterprises. In Concepts Statement No. 6, the FASB expanded the scope of Statement No. 3 to encompass not-for-profit organizations as well. These elements comprise

---

[12]For additional examples of quantitative materiality considerations, see *Statement of Financial Accounting Concepts No. 2*, Appendix C, par. 165.

[13]*Ibid.* , par. 132.

the building blocks upon which financial statements are constructed. The elements are interrelated and collectively report the performance and status of an enterprise. For reference purposes, the FASB definitions of the ten basic elements are listed on page 47. These definitions and the issues surrounding them are discussed in detail as the elements are introduced in later chapters.

Recognition,
Measurement, and
Reporting

FASB Concepts Statement No. 5 builds on the foundation laid by the previously issued concepts statements and provides broad guidelines for implementing or applying the objectives and fundamental concepts discussed thus far. It provides guidance in determining *what* information should be formally incorporated into financial statements and *when*. Specifically, Statement No. 5 sets forth recognition criteria and discusses certain measurement issues that are closely related to recognition. In addition, this statement addresses financial reporting and identifies the financial statements that should be presented in light of the objectives of financial reporting.

Recognition Criteria

Recognition is the process of formally recording an item and eventually reporting it as one of the elements in the financial statements. Recognition involves both the initial recording of an item and any subsequent changes related to that item. To qualify for recognition, an item should meet four fundamental criteria: (1) definition, (2) measurability, (3) relevance, and (4) reliability.[14] For an item to be formally recognized, it must meet one of the definitions of the elements of financial statements, as defined in Concepts Statement No. 6. For example, a receivable must meet the definition of an asset to be recorded and reported as such on a balance sheet. The same is true of liabilities, owners' equity, revenues, expenses, and other elements. As an example of a continuing controversy in this area, some accountants question whether deferred income taxes meet the strict definition of a liability and therefore whether they should be recognized as such. For some companies, the amount is significant. For example, IBM reported a deferred tax liability in 1988 of over 4.6 billion. If, in fact, this amount does not represent a future outlay or sacrifice, it is misleading even though it is reported in accordance with GAAP.

In addition to qualifying as an element, an item must be objectively measurable in monetary terms to be recognized. Sometimes an item clearly meets the definition criterion but cannot be measured objectively. For example, the president's letter in the annual report of IBM Corporation mentions the significant value of IBM's more than 400,000 employees. These employees have future benefit to IBM and may be considered assets of high

---

[14]*Statement of Financial Accounting Concepts No. 5*, "Recognition and Measurement in Financial Statements of Business Enterprises" (Stamford: Financial Accounting Standards Board, December, 1984), par. 63.

The 10 Elements of Financial Statements

- **Assets** are probable future economic benefits obtained or controlled by a particular entity as a result of past transactions or events.
- **Liabilities** are probable future sacrifices of economic benefits arising from present obligations of a particular entity to transfer assets or provide services to other entities in the future as a result of past transactions or events.
- **Equity** or **net assets** is the residual interest in the assets of an entity that remains after deducting its liabilities.
- **Investments by owners** are increases in equity of a particular business enterprise resulting from transfers to it from other entities of something valuable to obtain or increase ownership interests (or equity) in it. Assets are most commonly received as investments by owners, but that which is received may also include services or satisfaction or conversion of liabilities of the enterprise.
- **Distributions to owners** are decreases in equity of a particular business enterprise resulting from transferring assets, rendering services, or incurring liabilities by the enterprise to owners. Distributions to owners decrease ownership interests (or equity) in an enterprise.
- **Comprehensive income** is the change in equity of a business enterprise during a period from transactions and other events and circumstances from nonowner sources. It includes all changes in equity during a period except those resulting from investments by owners and distributions to owners.
- **Revenues** are inflows or other enhancements of assets of an entity or settlement of its liabilities (or a combination of both) from delivering or producing goods, rendering services, or other activities that constitute the entity's ongoing major or central operations.
- **Expenses** are outflows or other using up of assets or incurrences of liabilities (or a combination of both) from delivering or producing goods, rendering services, or carrying out other activities that constitute the entity's ongoing major or central operations.
- **Gains** are increases in equity (net assets) from peripheral or incidental transactions of an entity and from all other transactions and other events and circumstances affecting the entity except those that result from revenues or investments by owners.
- **Losses** are decreases in equity (net assets) from peripheral or incidental transactions of an entity and from all other transactions and other events and circumstances affecting the entity except those that result from expenses or distributions to owners.

Source: *Statement of Financial Accounting Concepts No. 6*, pp. ix-x.

value to that company. Yet, that value is not recognized as an asset on IBM's balance sheet, since it cannot be measured in a reliable manner.

Information about an item must be both relevant and reliable in order for the item to be recognized. Since there are often trade-offs between relevance and reliability, consideration of these primary qualities may affect the timing of recognition. For example, information about a pending lawsuit may be relevant, but its recognition usually is delayed until the amounts and circumstances can be determined with sufficient reliability.

The four fundamental recognition criteria apply to all elements of financial statements. However, since one of the major tasks of accounting is to measure and report net income (loss), proper application of the recognition criteria is particularly important when recognizing revenues and expenses. Generally, under the revenue recognition principle, revenues for a period are recorded when two conditions are met: (1) the earnings process is substantially complete, and (2) there is receipt of cash or a near-cash asset, i.e., when revenues are realized or realizable. These two criteria have led to the conventional recognition of revenue at the point of sale, i.e., at the specific point in the earning process when assets are sold or services are rendered. According to the **matching principle**, expenses for a period are determined by association with specific revenues or a particular time period. The revenue recognition and expense matching principles are discussed and illustrated in Chapter 4.

Measurement Attributes

Closely related to recognition is measurement. There are five different measurement attributes currently used in practice.[15]

Historical cost is the cash equivalent price exchanged for goods or services at the date of acquisition. Land, buildings, equipment, and most inventories are common examples of items recognized using the historical cost attribute.

Current replacement cost is the cash equivalent price that would be exchanged currently to purchase or replace equivalent goods or services. Some inventories are recognized at their current replacement costs.

Current market value is the cash equivalent price that could be obtained by selling an asset in an orderly liquidation. Some investments in marketable securities are reported using current market values.

Net realizable value is the amount of cash expected to be received from the conversion of assets in the normal course of business. Generally, this attribute is equal to the sales price less normal costs to sell. Net realizable value is used for recognizing short-term receivables and some inventories.

Present (or discounted) value is the amount of net future cash inflows or outflows discounted to their present value. Long-term receivables and long-term payables use this measurement attribute.

It should be noted that different measurement attributes often have the same monetary value, especially at the point of initial recognition. For example, the historical cost and the current replacement cost of a piece of land are the same at the date of acquisition. The amount would also be the current market value of the land at that point in time, assuming an arm's-length transaction.

The trade-off between relevance and reliability mentioned earlier is also evident in considering which measurement attribute to use. Current accounting practice is said to be based on historical costs since that is the attribute generally used in the initial recording of transactions. Historical cost is used because it is objective (reliable), being based on an exchange that has taken place between presumably independent parties. In effect, the historical cost is the fair market price of the item involved in the transaction at that date. Many accountants feel that current replacement costs or market values are more relevant than historical costs for future-oriented decisions; yet, those attributes often lack reliability. Because it is both reliable and relevant, historical cost has been the valuation basis most com-

---

[15]*Ibid.*, par. 67.

monly used in accounting practice. However, as indicated above, other measurement attributes are used at times and are expected to continue to be used in the future. The "proper" measurement attribute is the one that under the circumstances provides the most useful (relevant and reliable) information at a reasonable cost.

In using historical cost as one (and perhaps the dominant) measurement attribute, the FASB indicated in Concepts Statement No. 5 that it expects nominal units of money to continue to be used in recognizing items in financial reporting. Nominal units of money are unadjusted for general price changes and therefore fluctuate over time in terms of purchasing power. If there is little or no inflation, measurement using nominal dollars is satisfactory. However, if general price levels change significantly, the FASB will probably have to reconsider this decision. The subject of changing prices is discussed fully in a later chapter.

Financial Reporting

For financial reporting to be most effective, all relevant information should be presented in an unbiased, understandable, and timely manner. This is sometimes referred to as the **full disclosure principle**. Because of the cost-benefit constraint discussed earlier, however, it would be impossible to report *all* relevant information. Further, too much information would adversely affect understandability and, therefore, decision usefulness. Those who provide financial information must use judgment in determining what information best satisfies the full disclosure principle within reasonable cost limitations.

Although guidelines in this area are not well defined, Concepts Statement No. 5 indicates that a "full set of financial statements" is necessary to meet the objectives of financial reporting. Included in the recommended set of general-purpose financial statements are reports that would show:[16]

· Financial position at the end of the period
· Earnings (net income) for the period
· Comprehensive income (total nonowner changes in equity) for the period
· Cash flows during the period
· Investments by and distributions to owners during the period

Current practice generally includes a set of financial statements consisting of (1) an **income statement** presenting the results of operations of an entity for a reporting period; (2) a **balance sheet** reporting the financial position of a business at a certain date; and (3) a **statement of cash flows** identifying the net cash flows from operating, investing, and financing activities during the reporting period. The three primary statements are referred to as general-purpose financial statements because they are intended

---

[16]*Statement of Financial Accounting Concepts No. 5*, par. 13.

for use by a wide variety of external users. Although there has been some discussion as to the need for special-purpose statements directed to specific external users, there has been no significant movement toward this in practice.

Sometimes a **retained earnings statement** is provided, or combined with the income statement, showing the changes in retained earnings for the period. When there are changes in owners' equity other than those affecting retained earnings, a supplemental **statement of changes in owners' equity** may be presented to provide a complete reconciliation of the beginning and ending equity balances.

The current general-purpose statements would seem to satisfy the recommendations of Concepts Statement No. 5 with one exception. **Comprehensive income** is a concept specifically defined in Statement No. 5 as including all changes in owners' equity except investments by and distributions to owners. This concept, which is explained and illustrated in Chapter 4, may eventually require a new statement.

In general, the FASB and other standard-setting bodies have been reluctant to specify exact formats for reporting. Instead, they have allowed and encouraged companies to experiment with various reporting (display) techniques. The results are sometimes quite encouraging as companies voluntarily seek new and better ways to present information. For example, many companies present graphic and various types of pictorial displays in their annual reports to assist users in understanding the information provided in financial statements. The graphs reproduced on page 51 were included in the 1987 annual report of Teleflex Incorporated and Subsidiaries to supplement the industry segment data presented in the notes to the financial statements. This is one example of the many ways in which companies are attempting to enhance the usefulness of their financial statements.

Traditional Assumptions of Accounting Model

The FASB's Conceptual Framework described in the preceding sections is influenced by several underlying assumptions. While not addressed explicitly, these traditional assumptions are implicit in the conceptual framework. They too help establish generally accepted accounting practice. The following paragraphs briefly describe the six basic assumptions that were identified in Exhibit 2–1 on page 33.

First, the business enterprise is viewed as a specific **economic entity** separate and distinct from its owners and any other business unit. It is the entity and its activities that receive the focus of attention for accounting and reporting purposes.

Second, in the absence of evidence to the contrary, the entity is viewed as a **going concern.** This continuity assumption provides support for the preparation of a balance sheet that reports costs assignable to future activities rather than market values of properties that would be realized in the event of voluntary liquidation or forced sale. This same assumption

Exhibit 2–6   Teleflex Incorporated

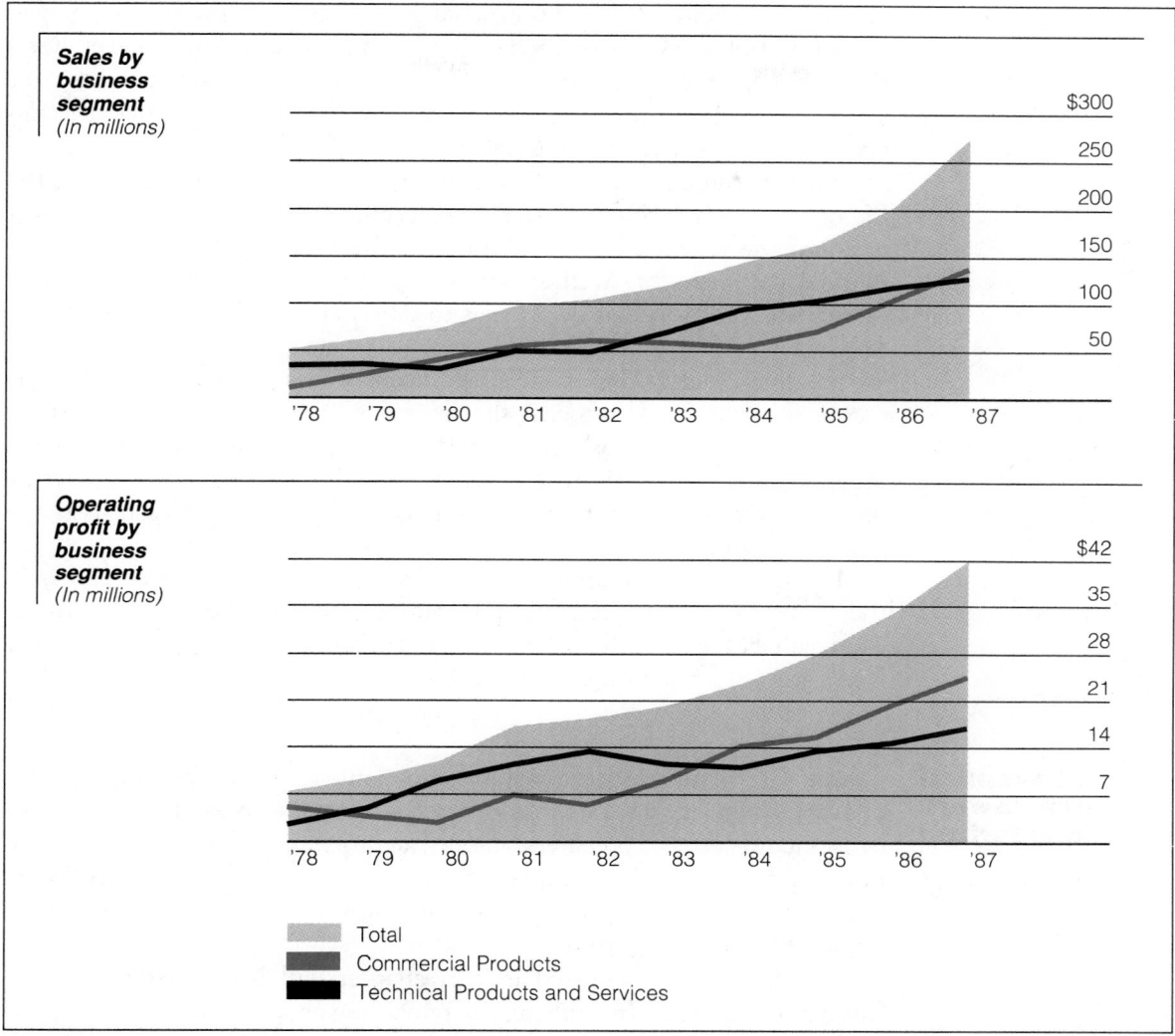

Sales by business segment (In millions)

Operating profit by business segment (In millions)

Total
Commercial Products
Technical Products and Services

calls for the preparation of an income statement reporting only such portions of revenues and costs as are allocable to current activities.

Third, the transactions and events of an entity provide the basis for accounting entries, and any changes in resources and equity values are generally not recorded until a transaction has taken place. Furthermore, transactions are assumed to be **arm's-length transactions**. That is, they occur between independent parties, each of whom is capable of protecting its own interests. If Entity A is selling goods to Entity B, it will try to sell at a sufficiently high price to make a profit. Entity B, on the other hand, will try to purchase those goods at a reasonably low price. The bargained price arrived at in this arm's-length transaction is assumed to be an objective market valuation at that date, and is considered an objective value for measurement purposes.

Fourth, transactions are assumed to be measured in stable monetary units. Because of this assumption, changes in the dollar's purchasing power have traditionally been ignored. Thus, financial statements reflect items that are measured in terms of nominal dollars. To many accountants, this is a serious limitation of the accounting model. As noted earlier, the impact of price changes is discussed in another chapter.

Fifth, because accounting information is needed on a timely basis, the life of a business entity is divided into specific accounting periods. By convention, the year has been established as the normal period for reporting. Annual statements, as well as statements covering shorter intervals, such as quarters, are provided by entities to satisfy the needs of those requiring timely financial information.

Finally, for each time period, an income measure is determined using accrual accounting. This means that revenues are recognized when earned, not necessarily when cash is received; and expenses are recognized when incurred, not necessarily when cash is paid. For most financial reporting purposes, accrual accounting is considered preferable to the cash-basis system of accounting.

In total, these assumptions as well as the concepts discussed earlier in the chapter comprise the current accounting model. They help determine what will be accounted for and in what manner. In effect, they set the boundaries of accounting practice.

Conceptual Framework Summarized

Exhibit 2–7 summarizes the major components of a conceptual framework of accounting. Such a framework provides a basis for consistent judgments by standard-setters, preparers, users, auditors, and others involved in financial reporting. A conceptual framework will not solve all accounting problems, but if used on a consistent basis over time, it should help improve financial reporting.

The framework discussed in this chapter will be a reference source throughout the text. In studying the remaining chapters, you will see many applications and a few exceptions to the theoretical framework established here. An understanding of the overall theoretical framework of accounting should make it easier for you to understand specific issues and problems encountered in practice.

Exhibit 2–7   A Conceptual Framework of Accounting

I. Objectives of Financial Reporting

    A. General—Provide useful information for decision making

    B. Specific—Provide information:
        1. For assessing cash flow prospects
        2. About financial condition
        3. About performance and earnings
        4. About how funds are obtained and used

II. Fundamental Concepts
  A. Qualitative Characteristics of Accounting Information
    1. Overriding quality—decision usefulness
    2. Primary qualities
      a. Relevance
        · predictive value
        · feedback value
        · timeliness
      b. Reliability
        · verifiability
        · neutrality
        · representational faithfulness
    3. Secondary qualities
      a. Comparability
      b. Consistency
    4. Constraints
      a. Cost effectiveness (pervasive constraint)
      b. Materiality (recognition threshold)
      c. Conservatism (healthy skepticism)
  B. Elements of Financial Statements
    1. Assets   6. Comprehensive income
    2. Liabilities   7. Revenues
    3. Equity   8. Expenses
    4. Investments by owners   9. Gains
    5. Distributions to owners   10. Losses

III. Implementation Guidelines
  A. Recognition Criteria
    1. Definition   3. Relevance
    2. Measurability   4. Reliability
  B. Measurement Attributes
    1. Historical cost   4. Net realizable value
    2. Current replacement cost   5. Present (or discounted)
    3. Current market value   value
  C. Financial Reporting
    1. Full disclosure
    2. Set of general-purpose financial statements
      a. Financial Position
      b. Earnings (net income or loss)
      c. Comprehensive Income
      d. Cash flows
      e. Investments by and distributions to owners

IV. Traditional Assumptions of Accounting Model
  A. Economic entity   D. Stable monetary unit
  B. Going concern   E. Accounting periods
  C. Arm's-length transactions   F. Accrual accounting

Key Terms

Accounting periods 52
Accrual accounting 52
Arm's-length transactions 51
Balance sheet 49
Comparability 42
Comprehensive income 50
Conceptual framework 29
Conservatism 45
Consistency 43
Cost effectiveness 43
Current market value 48
Current replacement cost 48
Decision usefulness 40
Economic entity 50
Feedback value 40
Full disclosure principle 49
Going concern 50
Historical cost 48
Income statement 49
Matching principle 48

Materiality 44
Net realizable value 48
Neutrality 41
Predictive value 40
Present (or discounted) value 48
Recognition 46
Relevance 40
Reliability 40
Representational faithfulness 41
Retained earnings statement 50
Revenue recognition principle 47
Stable monetary unit 52
Statement of cash flows 49
Statement of changes in owners'
  equity 50
Statements of financial accounting
  concepts 32
Timeliness 41
Understandability 40
Verifiability 41

Questions

1. List and explain the main reasons why a conceptual framework of accounting is important.
2. Why is judgment required by accountants in fulfilling their role as suppliers of information?
3. The FASB's Conceptual Framework project has received considerable attention. What is the project expected to accomplish? What is it not likely to do?
4. Identify the major objectives of financial reporting as specified by the FASB.
5. The overriding quality of accounting information is decision usefulness. How does the user-specific quality of "understandability" affect decision usefulness?
6. Distinguish between the primary informational qualities of relevance and reliability.
7. Does reliability imply absolute accuracy? Explain.
8. Define comparability. How does comparability relate to uniformity?
9. Of what value is consistency in financial reporting?
10. Why is it so difficult to measure the cost effectiveness of accounting information?
11. What is the current materiality standard in accounting?
12. Is it possible for information to be immaterial and yet relevant? Explain.
13. What is conservatism in accounting? When does it become a relevant issue? What are some examples of conservatism in accounting practice?
14. Identify the criteria that an item must meet to qualify for recognition.
15. Identify and describe five different measurement attributes.
16. FASB Concepts Statement No. 5 indicates that a full set of financial statements is needed to meet the objectives of financial reporting. What should the reports that constitute a set of general-purpose financial statements show?
17. Identify the six traditional assumptions that influence the conceptual framework, and briefly explain how they affect it.

Discussion Cases

Case 2–1   (The establishment of a conceptual framework)

As a student of accounting, you have noticed that a substantial portion of the literature deals with establishing a theoretical framework upon which accounting practice can be based. This is currently the case and has been for the past 50 years. Yet, in discussions with colleagues and friends, you have to admit that the accounting profession has found it difficult to establish an authoritative set of accounting concepts and principles that are universally accepted within the business community. As you think about this problem, at least two questions come to mind: (1) Is an overall conceptual framework of accounting even needed? and (2) What has the FASB done differently, if anything, to succeed in establishing a conceptual framework for accounting where others have failed? Discuss possible answers to these questions.

Case 2–2   (How important are the economic consequences of accounting principles?)

During the 1960s, and again in the 1980s, corporate merger activity increased significantly in the United States. Many of the early mergers involved companies in completely unrelated fields. Sometimes a company in a weak financial position merged with a stronger company. The combined financial statements would then postpone the disclosure of poor management to statement users. In an attempt to clarify the accounting rules and to eliminate financial statement manipulation that did not truly present the entity's financial status, the Accounting Principles Board proposed a change in accounting for mergers. One business executive involved in merger activity commented publicly that the Board had no right to issue such pronouncements. If the accounting requirements were changed, the executive argued, merger activity would decline and economic growth in our economy would stagnate.

More recently, the FASB has issued standards that require companies to account for unfunded pension costs as liabilities. Executives of several large companies have argued that such accounting will seriously limit the ability of many companies to borrow and will have a serious, negative impact on business activity and, therefore, on society.

Recognizing that accounting rules have an impact on business activity and may affect economic growth, should this result influence the decision by accounting standard-setting bodies as to how transactions should be recorded and reported? Should the impact on society be the most important consideration for an accounting principle?

Case 2–3   (Elements of financial statements)

Conserv Corporation, a computer software company, is trying to determine the appropriate accounting procedure to apply to its software development costs. Management is considering capitalizing the development costs and amortizing them over several years. Alternatively, they are considering charging the costs to expense as soon as they are incurred. You, as an accountant, have been asked to help settle this issue. Which definitions of financial statement elements would apply to these costs? Based on this information, what accounting procedure would you recommend and why?

Case 2–4 (Recognition, measurement, and reporting considerations in financial reporting)

Several years ago, the SEC adopted amendments to Regulation S-X, requiring separate disclosure of preferred stock subject to mandatory redemption requirements, often called "redeemable preferred stock." In taking such action, the SEC noted an increase in the use of complex securities—such as redeemable preferred stock—that exhibit both debt and equity characteristics. The question subsequently considered by the FASB was whether or not such securities should be classified as liabilities rather than as equity securities. How might the FASB's guidelines for recognition, measurement, and reporting assist in resolving this or similar issues?

Case 2–5 (Financial reporting: the difficult task of satisfying diverse informational needs)

Teri Green has recently been promoted. She is now the chief financial officer of Teltrex, Inc. and has primary responsibility for the external reporting function. During the past three weeks, Green has met with: Jeff Thalman, the senior vice president of Westmore First National Bank where Teltrex has a $1,000,000 line of credit; Susan Davis, a financial analyst for Stubbs, Jones, and McConkie, a brokerage firm; and Brian Ellis, who is something of a corporate gadfly and who owns 2 percent of the outstanding common stock of Teltrex. Each of these individuals has commented on last year's annual report of Teltrex, pointing out deficiencies and suggesting additional information they would like to see presented in this year's annual report. From Green's point of view, explain the nature of general purpose financial statements and indicate the informational qualities of the accounting data that she must be concerned with in fulfilling the corporation's external reporting responsibility.

Case 2–6   (Responsibility for financial reporting)

It is apparent from reading the *Wall Street Journal* and other financial publications that an increasing number of law suits are being filed each year against independent accountants (CPAs). Most cases involve accountants who audited the financial statements of companies that subsequently went bankrupt. Who is responsible for a company's financial statements? How might a conceptual framework improve the quality of financial reporting?

Case 2–7   (Trade-offs in providing useful accounting information)

The FASB's conceptual framework is intended to provide guidance in selecting from alternative accounting methods those that are most appropriate under the circumstances. Accountants must exercise judgment in applying the general guidelines in each specific set of circumstances. Often trade-offs exist between different qualitative characteristics of accounting information. For each of the following situations, identify the qualitative characteristics involved and discuss the possible trade-offs that exist.
1. Benavides Company charges to expense all items under $1,000.
2. Do-It-Now Company has recently decided to change its depreciation method to straight line from declining balance.
3. Future, Inc. has decided to use the allowance method for bad debts rather than the direct write-off method.

4. Nights Inn is trying to convince its auditors to allow a restatement of all asset values to a current market value.

Exercises   **Exercise 2–1   (Aspects of the FASB's conceptual framework)**

Determine whether the following statements are true or false. If a statement is false, explain why.

1. Comprehensive income includes changes in equity resulting from distributions to owners.
2. Timeliness and predictive value are both characteristics of relevant information.
3. The tendency to recognize favorable events early is an example of conservatism.
4. Objectives of Concepts Statement No. 1 focus primarily on the needs of internal users of financial information.
5. Statements of Financial Accounting Concepts are considered authoritative pronouncements.
6. The overriding objective of financial reporting is to provide information for making economic decisions.
7. Concepts Statement No. 1 seeks to clarify *how* financial statement reporting should be accomplished, and succeeding Concepts Statements clarify *what* should be reported in financial statements.
8. Certain modifying constraints, such as conservatism, can justify departures from GAAP.
9. Under Concepts Statement No. 5, the term "recognized" is synonymous with the term "recorded."
10. Once an accounting method is adopted, it should never be changed.

Exercise 2–2   (Conceptual framework terminology)

Match the statements on the left with the letter of the terms on the right. An answer (letter) may be used more than once and some terms require more than one answer (letter).

1. Key ingredients in quality of relevance.	a. Cost effectiveness
2. Basic assumptions that influence the FASB's Conceptual Framework.	b. Representational faithfulness
3. The idea that information should represent what it purports to represent.	c. Matching principle
	d. Verifiability
4. The most pervasive constraint.	e. Time periods
5. An example of conservatism.	f. Unrealized
6. The availability of information when it is needed.	g. Completeness
7. Associating expense with a particular revenue or time period.	h. Timeliness
8. Determines the threshold for recognition.	i. Materiality
9. Implies objectivity and consensus.	j. Predictive value
10. Transactions between independent parties.	k. Economic entity
	l. Lower of cost or market rule
	m. Accrual accounting
	n. Arm's-length

Exercise 2–3   (Objectives of financial reporting)

For each of the following independent situations, identify the relevant objective(s) of financial reporting that the company may be overlooking. Discuss each of these objectives.

1. The president of Coventry, Inc. feels that the financial statements should be prepared for use by management only, since they are the primary decision makers.
2. Cascade Carpets Co. feels that financial statements should only reflect the present financial standing and cash position of the firm and should not provide any future oriented data.
3. The vice president of Share Enterprises, Inc. believes that the financial statements are to present only current year revenues and expenses and not disclose assets, liabilities and owners' equity.
4. Cruz Co. has a policy of providing disclosures of only its assets, liabilities, and owners' equity.
5. Marty Manufacturing, Inc. always discloses the assets, liabilities, and owners' equity of the firm along with the revenues and expenses. Marty's management believes that these items provide all the information relevant to investing decisions.

Exercise 2–4   (Qualitative characteristics of accounting information)

Identify the qualitative characteristics most likely violated by each of the following situations. (Briefly support your answers.)

a. A prospective purchaser of a company receives only the conventional financial statements.
b. An investor examines the published annual reports of all companies in the steel industry for the purpose of investing in the most profitable one.
c. A company uses the prefix "reserve" for a contra asset, a liability, and a retained earnings appropriation.
d. A company reports all of its land, buildings, and equipment on the basis of a recent appraisal.
e. Management elects to change its method of inventory valuation in order to overcome an unprofitable year from operations. This change enables the company to report a gradual increase in earnings.

Exercise 2–5   (Applications of accounting characteristics and concepts)

For each situation listed, indicate by letter the appropriate qualitative characteristic(s) or accounting concept(s) applied. A letter may be used more than once, and more than one characteristic or concept may apply to a particular situation.

a. Understandability
b. Verifiability
c. Timeliness
d. Representational faithfulness
e. Neutrality
f. Relevance
g. Going concern
h. Economic entity
i. Historical cost
j. Quantifiability
k. Materiality
l. Comparability
m. Conservatism

_____ 1. Goodwill is only recorded in the accounts when it arises from the purchase of another entity at a price higher than the fair market value of the purchased entity's tangible assets.

_____ 2. Marketable securities are valued at the lower of cost or market.

_____ 3. All payments out of petty cash are debited to Miscellaneous Expense.

_____ 4. Plant assets are classified separately as land or buildings, with an accumulated depreciation account for buildings.

_____ 5. Periodic payments of $1,500 per month for services of H. Hay, who is the sole proprietor of the company, are reported as withdrawals.

_____ 6. Small tools used by a large manufacturing firm are recorded as expenses when purchased.

_____ 7. Marketable securities are initially recorded at cost.

_____ 8. A retail store estimates inventory, rather than taking a complete physical count, for purposes of preparing monthly financial statements.

_____ 9. A note describing the company's possible liability in a lawsuit is included with the financial statements even though no formal liability exists at the balance sheet date.

_____10. Depreciation on plant assets is consistently computed each year by the straight-line method.

▌▌▌ Exercise 2–6   (Theoretical support for corrected balance sheet)

G. Nielsen prepared the following balance sheet for Nielsen Inc. as of December 31, 1991. Review each item listed, and considering the additional data given, prepare a corrected, properly classified balance sheet. Where a change is made in reporting an item, disclose in a separate note the theoretical support for your suggested change. Record any offsetting adjustments in the Retained Earnings account, except for possible contributed capital changes.

Assets		Liabilities	
Cash......................	$ 30,000	Accounts payable	$ 85,000
Marketable		Taxes payable	65,000
securities	55,000	Notes payable	120,000
Notes receivable	40,000	Mortgage payable	273,000
Accounts receivable	130,000	Capital stock	300,000
Inventories	195,000	Retained earnings	140,000
Land and buildings	520,000		
Accumulated dep.-			
buildings	(27,000)		
Goodwill..................	40,000		
	$983,000		$983,000

Additional data:

(a) Cash included a bank checking account of $20,000, current checks and money orders on hand of $5,000, and a $5,000 check that could not be cashed. The check was from Davis Co., a customer that had gone out of business. Nielsen feels this $5,000 will probably not be recovered.

(b) Marketable securities are listed at year-end market values. They were purchased early in 1991 for $46,800.

(c) Nielsen estimates that all receivables are collectible except for a three-year-old past-due note of $8,000. Past collection experience indicates that two percent of current notes and accounts prove uncollectible.

(d) Land and buildings are recorded at initial cost. At date of acquisition, land was valued at $70,000 and buildings at $450,000. Building depreciation has been correctly recorded.

(e) Goodwill was recorded when Nielsen received an offer of $40,000 more for the business than the recorded asset values.

(f) Of the notes payable, $30,000 will be due in 1992 with the remainder of the notes coming due in 1993 and 1994.

(g) The mortgage is payable in annual payments of $19,500 plus interest.

(h) The capital stock has a par value of $100 per share; 2,500 shares are issued and outstanding.

Exercise 2–7   (Theoretical support for corrected income statement)

A. Hillstead prepared the following income statement for the calendar year 1991.

Revenues	$80,000
Expenses	50,000
Net income	$30,000

An examination of the records reveals the following:

(a) Hillstead is the sole proprietor.

(b) Business operations include:

   1. A catering service
   2. An equipment rental shop
   3. Rental of a part of Hillstead's home for small receptions

(c) Revenues include:

1. Catering service sales	$50,000
2. Equipment rentals	12,500
3. Reception rental space	17,500
	$80,000

(d) Expenses consisted of:

1. Cost of goods sold (catering)	$15,000
2. Other costs (catering)	11,500
3. Depreciation—equipment rental	1,500
4. Repairs and other costs—equipment rental	2,500
5. Depreciation, $2,000; cleaning, $4,500; and miscellaneous costs, $1,000—reception rental space	7,500
6. Living expenses—family	12,000
	$50,000

Based on the FASB's Conceptual Framework, indicate what changes, if any, you would make in the income statement format and amount of Hillstead's income for 1991 and give theoretical support for your conclusions.

Chapter 3

Review of the Accounting Process

All business enterprises, regardless of size or the nature of their operations, need accurate records of business transactions. Businesses that do not keep accurate records will not operate as efficiently and profitably as they could otherwise. In addition, the Foreign Corrupt Practices Act of 1977 requires publicly held companies to keep accurate books and records that fairly reflect business activity.

A variety of reports are prepared from accounting records to assist users in making better economic decisions. As explained in Chapters 1 and 2, general-purpose financial statements are prepared for external user groups, primarily current or potential investors and creditors, who are involved financially with an enterprise but who are not a part of its management team. User groups within organizations, especially those in managerial positions, receive reports to assist them in planning and controlling the day-to-day operations of their organizations. Tax returns and similar reports must be prepared to comply with Internal Revenue Service (IRS) requirements. Special reports are required by various regulatory agencies such as the Securities and Exchange Commission (SEC).

Each of these reports is based on data that are the result of an accounting system and a set of procedures collectively referred to as the **accounting process,** or the **accounting cycle.** While this process follows a fairly standard set of procedures, the exact nature of the **accounting system** used to collect and report the data will depend on the type of business, its size, the volume of transactions processed, the degree of automation employed, and other related factors. The various routines in each system are developed to meet the special needs of the business unit. Every accounting system, however, should be designed to provide accurate information on a timely and efficient basis. At the same time, the system must provide controls that are effective in preventing mistakes and guarding against dishonesty.

Historically, accounting systems were maintained by hand and referred to as **manual systems.** Such systems continue to be used effectively in many situations. In today's business environment, however, most companies use at least some type of automated equipment, such as cash registers or other special-purpose business machines, and many companies have **electronic data processing (EDP) systems** that utilize the capabilities of high-speed computers. Furthermore, the advent of microcomputers has put EDP systems within the reach of almost all smaller companies that previously had to rely on manual or partially mechanized systems. As explained later in the chapter, an EDP system has many advantages and some disadvantages. The important point is that all accounting systems are designed to serve the same information gathering and processing functions. There is no difference in the underlying accounting concepts involved, only in some mechanical aspects of the process and in the appearance of the records and reports. Since it is easier to understand and to illustrate, a manual system will be used for the examples in this chapter and throughout the text.

The purpose of this chapter is to review the basic steps of the accounting process, including a brief review of the mechanics of double-entry accounting. A number of basic accounting terms are presented in the chapter and are included in the glossary at the end of the book.

Overview of the Accounting Process

The accounting process consists of two interrelated parts: (1) the recording phase and (2) the summarizing phase. The recording phase is concerned with the collection of information about economic transactions and events. For most businesses, the recording function is based on double-entry accounting procedures. In the summarizing phase, the recorded information is organized and summarized, using various formats for a variety of decision-making purposes. There is an overlapping of the two phases, since the recording of transactions is an ongoing activity that does not cease at the end of an accounting period but continues uninterrupted while events of the preceding period are being summarized. The recording and summarizing phases of the accounting process are reviewed and illustrated in this chapter. The form and content of the basic financial statements are discussed in depth and illustrated in Chapters 4 and 5.[1]

The accounting process, illustrated in Exhibit 3–1, generally includes the following steps in well-defined sequence:

Recording Phase

1. Business documents are analyzed. Analysis of the documentation of business activities provides the basis for making an initial record of each transaction.

2. Transactions are recorded. Based on the supporting documents from Step 1, transactions are recorded in chronological order in books of original entry, or journals.

3. Transactions are posted. Transactions, as classified and recorded in the

---

[1]Appendix A at the end of the book provides an illustrated set of financial statements from the 1988 annual report of General Mills, Inc.

Exhibit 3–1 The Accounting Process

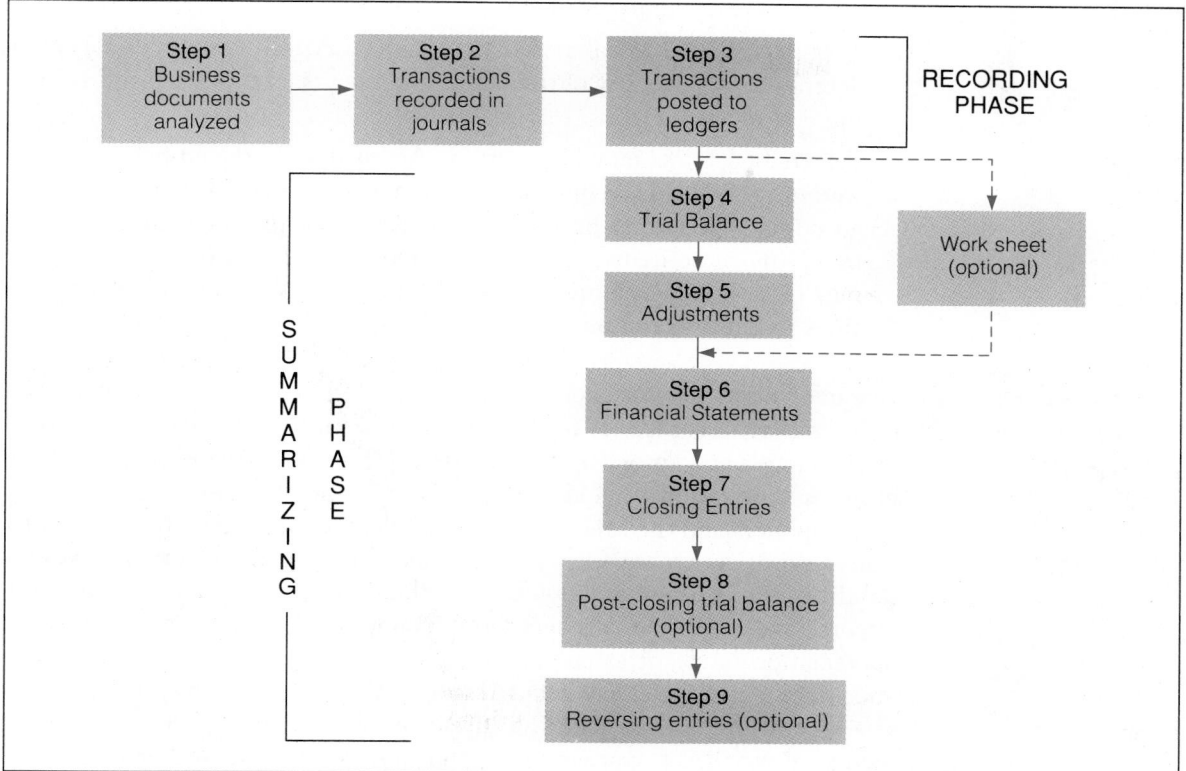

journals, are posted to the appropriate accounts in the general and, where applicable, subsidiary ledgers.

Summarizing Phase

4. A trial balance of the accounts in the general ledger is prepared. The trial balance, usually prepared on a work sheet, provides a summary of the information as classified in the ledger, as well as a general check on the accuracy of recording and posting.

5. Adjusting entries are recorded. Before financial statements can be prepared, all accountable information that has not been recorded must be determined. Often adjustments are first made on a work sheet, and may be formally recorded and posted at any time prior to closing (Step 7). If a work sheet is not used, the adjusting entries must be recorded and posted at this point so the accounts are current prior to the preparation of financial statements.

6. Financial statements are prepared. Statements summarizing operations and showing the financial position and cash flows are prepared from the information on the work sheet or directly from the adjusted accounts.

7. Nominal accounts are closed. Balances in the nominal (temporary) accounts are closed into appropriate summary accounts. As determined in

summary accounts, the results of operations are transferred to the appropriate owners' equity accounts.

8. A post-closing trial balance may be taken. A trial balance is taken to determine the equality of the debits and credits after posting the adjusting and closing entries.

9. Selected accounts may be reversed. Accrued and prepaid balances that were established by adjusting entries may be returned to the nominal accounts that are to be used in recording and summarizing activities involving these items in the new period. This step is not required, but may be desirable as a means of facilitating recording and adjusting routines in the succeeding period.

Recording Phase   Accurate financial statements can be prepared only if transactions have been properly recorded. A transaction is an event that involves the transfer or exchange of goods or services between two or more entities. Examples of business transactions include the purchase of merchandise or other assets from suppliers and the sale of goods or services to customers. In addition to transactions, other events and circumstances may affect the assets, liabilities, and owners' equity of the business. Such events and circumstances also must be recorded. Examples include the recognition of depreciation on plant assets, a decline in the market value of inventories and investments, or a loss suffered from a flood or an earthquake.

As indicated, the recording phase involves analyzing business documents, journalizing transactions, and posting to the ledger accounts. Before discussing these steps, the system of double-entry accounting will be reviewed, since most businesses use this procedure in recording their transactions.

Double-Entry Accounting

As explained in Chapters 1 and 2, financial accounting rests on a foundation of basic assumptions, concepts, and principles that govern the recording, classifying, summarizing, and reporting of accounting data. Double-entry accounting is an old and universally accepted system for recording accounting data. With double-entry accounting, each transaction is recorded in a way that maintains the equality of the basic accounting equation:

$$\text{Assets} = \text{Liabilities} + \text{Owners' Equity}$$

To review how double-entry accounting works, recall that a debit is an entry on the left side of an account and a credit is an entry on the right side. The debit/credit relationships of accounts were explained in detail in your introductory accounting course. Exhibit 3–2 summarizes these relationships for a corporation. You will note that assets, expenses, and dividends are increased by debits and decreased by credits. Liabilities, owners' equity accounts (capital stock and retained earnings), and revenues are increased by credits and decreased by debits.

Exhibit 3–2   Debit and Credit Relationships of Accounts

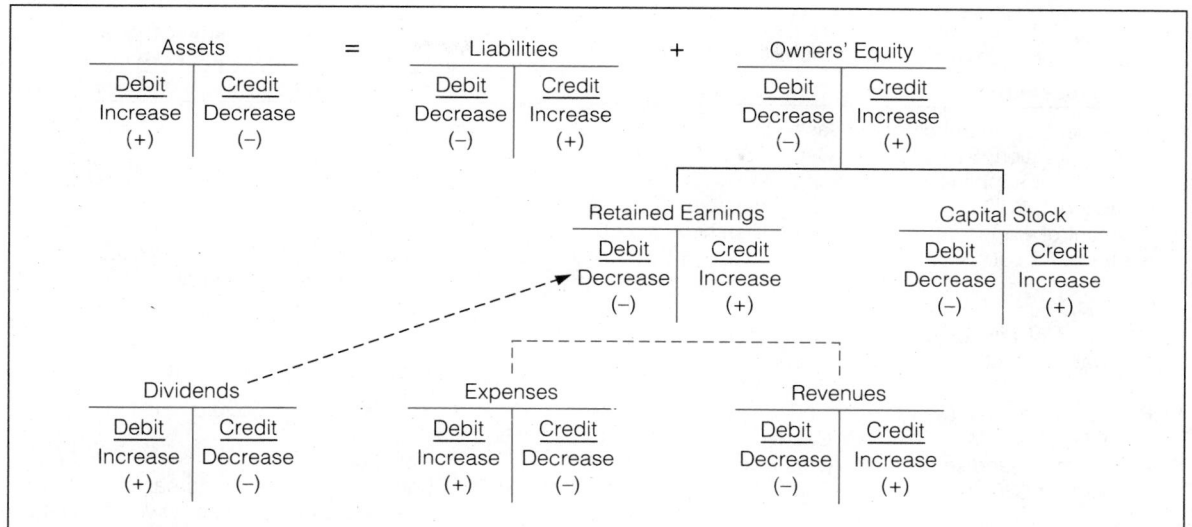

To illustrate double-entry accounting, consider the transactions and journal entries shown in Exhibit 3–3 and their impact on the accounting equation. In studying this illustration, you should note that for each transaction, total debits equal total credits and the equality of the accounting equation is maintained.

To summarize, you should remember the following important features of double-entry accounting:

1. Assets are always increased by debits and decreased by credits.
2. Liability and owners' equity accounts are always increased by credits and decreased by debits.
3. Owners' equity for a corporation includes capital stock accounts and the retained earnings account.
4. Revenues, expenses, and dividends relate to owners' equity through the retained earnings account.
5. Expenses and dividends are increased by debits and decreased by credits.
6. Revenues are increased by credits and decreased by debits.
7. The difference between total revenues and total expenses for a period is net income (loss), which increases (decreases) owners' equity through Retained Earnings.

Analyzing Business Documents

The basic accounting records of a business consist of:

1. Original source material evidencing transactions, called business documents or source documents,

Exhibit 3–3   Double-Entry Accounting: Illustrative Transactions and Journal Entries

Transaction	Journal Entry		Impact of Transaction on Accounting Equation
			Assets = Liabilities + Owners' Equity
1. Investment by shareholder in a corporation, $10,000	Cash Capital Stock	10,000 10,000	+10,000 = +10,000
2. Purchase of supplies on account, $5,000	Supplies Accts Payable	5,000 5,000	+ 5,000 = + 5,000
3. Payment of wages expense, $2,500	Wages Expense Cash	2,500 2,500	− 2,500 = − 2,500 (Increase in an expense reduces Retained Earnings and, therefore, Owners' Equity)
4. Collection of accounts receivable, $1,000	Cash Accts Receivable	1,000 1,000	+ 1,000 = − 1,000
5. Payment of account payable, $500	Accts Payable Cash	500 500	− 500 = − 500
6. Sale of merchandise on account for $20,000	Accts Receivable Sales	20,000 20,000	+20,000 = +20,000 (Increase in revenue increases Retained Earnings and, therefore, Owners' Equity)

7. Purchase of equipment: $15,000 down payment plus $40,000 long-term note	Equipment
	  Cash
	  Note Payable
		55,000
		15,000
		40,000
			+55,000 = +40,000
			−15,000

8. Payment of cash dividends, $4,000	Dividends Cash	4,000 4,000	− 4,000 = − 4,000 (Dividends reduce Retained Earnings and, therefore, Owners' Equity)

2. Records for classifying and recording transactions, known as journals or "books of original entry" and,

3. Records for summarizing the effects of transactions upon individual accounts, known as ledgers.

The recording phase begins with an analysis of the documentation showing what business activities have occurred. Normally, a business document is the first record of each transaction. Such a document offers detailed information concerning the transaction and also fixes responsibility by naming the parties involved. The business documents provide support for the data to be recorded in the journals. Copies of sales invoices or cash register tapes, for example, are the evidence in support of the sales record; purchase invoices support the purchase record; debit and credit memorandums support adjustments in debtor and creditor balances; check stubs and cancelled checks provide data concerning cash disbursements; the corporation minutes book supports entries authorized by action of the board of directors; journal vouchers prepared and approved by appropriate officers are a source of data for adjustments or corrections that are to be reported in the accounts. Documents underlying each recorded transaction provide a means of verifying the accounting records and thus form a vital part of the information and control system.

Journalizing Transactions

Once the information provided on business documents has been analyzed, transactions are recorded in chronological order in the appropriate journals. In some very small businesses, all transactions are recorded in a single journal. Most business enterprises, however, maintain various special journals, designed to meet their specific needs, as well as a general journal. A special journal is used to record a particular type of frequently recurring transaction. Special journals are commonly used, for example, to record each of the following types of transactions: sales, purchases, cash disbursements, and cash receipts. A general journal is used to record all transactions for which a special journal is not maintained. As illustrated below, a general journal shows the transaction date and the accounts affected, and gives a brief description of each transaction. It also provides debit and credit columns and a posting reference column. When transactions are posted, as explained in the next section, the appropriate ledger account numbers are entered in the posting reference column. Special journals are illustrated and explained in Appendix A at the end of this chapter.

GENERAL JOURNAL

Page 24

Date		Description	Post Ref.	Debit	Credit
1991 July	1	Dividends.....................................	330	25,000	
		Dividends Payable	260		25,000
		Declared semiannual cash dividend on common stock.			
	10	Equipment	180	7,500	
		Notes Payable.............................	220		7,500
		Issued note for new equipment.			
	31	Payroll Taxes Expense	418	2,650	
		Payroll Taxes Payable	240		2,650
		Recorded payroll taxes for month.			

Posting To The Ledger Accounts

An account is used to summarize the effects of transactions on each asset, liability, owners' equity, revenue, and expense element. A ledger is a collection of all the accounts maintained by a business and may be in the form of a book or a computer printout. The specific accounts required by a business unit vary depending on the nature of the business, its properties and activities, the information to be provided on the financial statements, and the controls to be employed in carrying out the accounting functions. The accounts used by a particular business are usually expressed in the form of a chart of accounts. This chart lists all accounts in systematic form with identifying numbers or symbols that provide the framework for summarizing business operations.

Information recorded in the journals is transferred to appropriate accounts in the ledger. This transfer is referred to as posting. Ledger accounts for Equipment and Notes Payable are presented below, illustrating the posting of the July 10 transaction from the general journal on page 69. The posting reference (J24) indicates that the transaction was transferred from page 24 of the general journal. Note that the account numbers for Equipment (180) and Notes Payable (220) are entered in the posting reference column of the journal.

GENERAL LEDGER

Account **Equipment**   *Account No:* **180**

Date		Item	Post Ref.	Debit	Credit	Balance
1991 July	1	Balance				10,550
	10	Purchase Equipment	J24	7,500		18,050

Account **Notes Payable**   *Account No.* **220**

Date		Item	Post Ref.	Debit	Credit	Balance
1991 July	1	Balance				5,750
	10	Purchase Equipment	J24		7,500	13,250

It is often desirable to establish separate ledgers for detailed information in support of balance sheet or income statement items. The general ledger includes all accounts appearing on the financial statements, while separate subsidiary ledgers afford additional detail in support of certain general ledger balances. For example, a single accounts receivable account is usually carried in the general ledger, and individual customers' accounts are recorded in a subsidiary accounts receivable ledger; the capital stock account in the general ledger is normally supported by individual stockholders' accounts in a subsidiary stockholders' ledger. The general ledger account that summarizes the detailed information in a subsidiary ledger is known as a control account. Subsidiary ledger accounts are illustrated in Appendix A at the end of this chapter.

Depending primarily on the number of transactions involved, amounts may be posted to ledger accounts on a daily, weekly, or monthly basis. If a computer system is being used, the posting process may be done automatically as transactions are recorded. At the end of an accounting period, when the posting process has been completed, the balances in the ledger accounts are used for preparing the trial balance.

Summarizing Phase

As noted earlier, the objective of the accounting process is to produce financial statements and other reports that will assist various users in making economic decisions. Once the recording phase is completed, the data must be summarized and organized into a useful format. The remaining steps of the accounting process are designed to accomplish this purpose. These steps will be illustrated using data from Rosi, Inc., a hypothetical merchandising company, for the year ended December 31, 1991.

Preparing a Trial Balance

After all transactions for the period have been posted to the ledger accounts, the balance for each account is determined. Every account will have either a debit, credit, or zero balance. A trial balance is a list of all accounts and their balances. The trial balance, therefore, indicates whether total debits equal total credits and thus provides a general check on the accuracy of recording and posting. A trial balance for Rosi, Inc., is presented on page 72.

Preparing Adjusting Entries

In order to report information on a timely basis, the life of a business is divided into relatively short time periods, such as a year, a quarter, or a month. While this is essential for the information to be useful, it does create problems for the accountant who must summarize the financial operations for the designated period and report on the financial position at the end of that period. Transactions during the period have been recorded in the appropriate journals and posted to the ledger accounts. At the end of the period, many accounts require adjustments to reflect current conditions. At this time, too, other financial data, not recognized previously, must be entered in the accounts to bring the books up to date. This requires analysis of individual accounts and various source documents. Based on this analysis, adjusting entries are made, and financial statements are prepared using the adjusted account balances.

This part of the accounting process is illustrated using the adjusting data for Rosi, Inc. presented on page 73. The data are classified according to the typical areas requiring adjustment at the end of the designated time period, in this case the year 1991. The accounts listed in the trial balance on page 72 do not reflect the adjusting data. The adjusting data must be combined with the information on the trial balance if the resulting financial statements are to appropriately reflect company operating results and financial position.

Asset Depreciation Charges to operations for the use of buildings, furniture, and equipment must be recorded at the end of the period. In recording asset depreciation, operations are charged with a portion of the asset's cost, and the carrying value of the asset is reduced by that amount. A reduction in an asset for depreciation is usually recorded by a credit to a contra account, Accumulated Depreciation. A **contra account** (or offset account) is set up to record subtractions from a related account. Certain accounts relate to others, but must be added rather than subtracted on the statements, and are referred to as **adjunct accounts.** Examples include Freight In, which is added to Purchases, and Additional Paid-In Capital, which is added to the Capital Stock account balance.

Rosi, Inc.
Trial Balance
December 31, 1991

Cash	83,110	
Accounts Receivable	106,500	
Allowance for Doubtful Accounts		1,610
Inventory	45,000	
Prepaid Insurance	8,000	
Interest Receivable	0	
Notes Receivable	28,000	
Land	114,000	
Buildings	156,000	
Accum. Depr.—Buildings		39,000
Furniture & Equipment	19,000	
Accum. Depr.—Furniture & Equipment		3,800
Accounts Payable		37,910
Unearned Rent Revenue		0
Salaries and Wages Payable		0
Interest Payable		0
Payroll Taxes Payable		5,130
Income Tax Payable		0
Dividends Payable		3,400
Bonds Payable		140,000
Common Stock, $15 par		150,000
Retained Earnings		126,770
Dividends	13,600	
Sales		479,500
Purchases	162,600	
Purchase Discounts		3,290
Cost of Goods Sold	0	
Salaries and Wages Expense	172,450	
Heat, Light, and Power	32,480	
Payroll Taxes Expense	18,300	
Advertising Expense	18,600	
Doubtful Accounts Expense	0	
Depr. Exp.—Buildings	0	
Depr. Exp.—Furniture & Equipment	0	
Insurance Expense	0	
Interest Revenue		1,100
Rent Revenue		2,550
Interest Expense	16,420	
Income Tax Expense	0	
Totals	994,060	994,060

Adjusting Data for Rosi, Inc.
December 31, 1991

Asset Depreciation:
(a) Buildings, 5% per year.
(b) Furniture and equipment, 10% per year.
Doubtful Accounts:
(c) The allowance for doubtful accounts is to be increased by $1,100.
Accrued Expenses:
(d) Salaries and wages, $2,150.
(e) Interest on bonds payable, $5,000.
Accrued Revenues:
(f) Interest on notes receivable, $250.
Prepaid Expenses:
(g) Prepaid insurance, $3,800.
Deferred Revenues:
(h) Unearned rent revenue, $475.
Income taxes:
(i) Federal and state income taxes, $8,000.
Inventory:
(j) A periodic inventory system is used; the ending inventory balance is $51,000.

Adjustments at the end of the year for depreciation for Rosi, Inc. are as follows:

(a)	Depreciation Expense-Buildings.....................	7,800	
	Accumulated Depreciation-Buildings................		7,800
	To record depreciation on buildings at 5% per year.		
(b)	Depreciation Expense-Furniture & Equipment	1,900	
	Accumulated Depreciation-Furniture & Equipment		1,900
	To record depreciation on furniture and equipment at 10% per year		

Doubtful Accounts Invariably, when a business allows customers to purchase goods and services on credit, some of the accounts receivable will not be collected, resulting in a charge to income for bad debt expense. Under the accrual concept, an adjustment should be made for the estimated expense in the current period, rather than when specific accounts actually become uncollectible. This produces a better matching of revenues and expenses and therefore a better income measurement. Using this procedure, operations are charged with the estimated expense, and receivables are reduced by means of a contra account, Allowance for Doubtful Accounts. To illustrate, the adjustment for Rosi, Inc. at the end of the year, assuming the allowance account is to be increased by $1,100, would be as follows:

(c)   Doubtful Accounts Expense   1,100
    Allowance for Doubtful Accounts   1,100
      To adjust for estimated doubtful accounts expense.

Throughout the accounting period, when there is positive evidence that a specific account is uncollectible, the appropriate amount is written off against the contra account. For example, if a $150 receivable were considered uncollectible, that amount would be written off as follows:

Allowance for Doubtful Accounts   150
    Accounts Receivable....................................   150
      To write off an uncollectible account.

No entry is made to Doubtful Accounts Expense, since the adjusting entry has already provided for an estimated expense based on previous experience for all receivables.

Accrued Expenses During the period, certain expenses may have been incurred for which payment is not to be made until a subsequent period. At the end of the period, it is necessary to determine and record any expenses not yet recognized. In recording an accrued expense, an expense account is debited and a liability account is credited. The adjusting entries to record accrued expenses for Rosi, Inc. are:

(d)   Salaries and Wages Expense   2,150
    Salaries and Wages Payable   2,150
      To record accrued salaries and wages.

(e)   Interest Expense   5,000
    Interest Payable..................................   5,000
      To record accrued interest on bonds.

Accrued Revenues During the period, certain amounts may have been earned, although collection is not to be made until a subsequent period. At the end of the period, it is necessary to determine and record the earnings not yet recognized. In recording accrued revenues, an asset account is debited and a revenue account is credited. The illustrative entry recognizing the accrued revenue for Rosi, Inc. is as follows:

(f)   Interest Receivable................................   250
    Interest Revenue...................................   250
      To record accrued interest on notes receivable.

Prepaid Expenses During the period, expenditures may have been recorded on the books for commodities or goods that are not to be received or used up currently. At the end of the period, it is necessary to determine the portions of such expenditures that are applicable to subsequent periods and hence require recognition as assets.

The method of adjusting for prepaid expenses depends on how the expenditures were originally entered in the accounts. They may have been recorded originally as debits to (1) an asset account or (2) an expense account.

Original Debit to an Asset Account If an asset account was originally debited, the adjusting entry requires that an expense account be debited for the amount applicable to the current period and the asset account be credited. The asset account remains with a debit balance that shows the amount applicable to future periods. An adjusting entry for prepaid insurance for Rosi, Inc. illustrates this situation as follows:

```
(g)  Insurance Expense ................................    4,200
        Prepaid Insurance ..............................              4,200
        To record expired insurance ($8,000 − $3,800 =
        $4,200).
```

Since the asset account Prepaid Insurance was originally debited, as shown in the trial balance, the amount of the prepayment ($8,000) must be reduced to reflect only the $3,800 that remains unexpired.

Original Debit to an Expense Account If an expense account was originally debited, the adjusting entry requires that an asset account be debited for the amount applicable to future periods and the expense account be credited. The expense account then remains with a debit balance representing the amount applicable to the current period. For example, if Rosi, Inc. had originally debited Insurance Expense for $8,000, the adjusting entry would be:

```
Prepaid Insurance ($8,000 − $4,200) ....................    3,800
    Insurance Expense  ....................................              3,800
```

Deferred Revenues Payments may be received from customers prior to the delivery of goods or services. Amounts received in advance are recorded by debiting an asset account, usually Cash, and crediting either a revenue account or a liability account. At the end of the period, it is necessary to determine the amount of revenue earned in the current period and the amount to be deferred to future periods. The method of adjusting for deferred revenues depends on whether the receipts for undelivered goods or services were recorded originally as credits to (1) a revenue account or (2) a liability account.

Original Credit to a Revenue Account If a revenue account was originally credited, this account is debited and a liability account is credited for the revenue applicable to a future period. The revenue account remains with a credit balance representing the earnings applicable to the current period. As indicated in the trial balance for Rosi, Inc., rent receipts are recorded originally in the Rent Revenue account. Unearned revenue at the end of 1991 is $475 and is recorded as follows:

(h)   Rent Revenue   475
            Unearned Rent Revenue   475
            To record unearned rent revenue.

Original Credit to a Liability Account If a liability account was credited originally, this account is debited and a revenue account is credited for the amount applicable to the current period. The liability account remains with a credit balance that shows the amount applicable to future periods. For example, if Rosi, Inc. had originally credited Unearned Rent Revenue for $2,550, the adjusting entry would be:

Unearned Rent Revenue   2,075
      Rent Revenue ($2,550 − $475)   2,075

Income Taxes When a corporation reports earnings, adjustments must be made for federal and state income taxes. Income Tax Expense is debited and Income Tax Payable is credited. The entry to record income taxes for Rosi, Inc. is as follows:

(i)   Income Tax Expense   8,000
            Income Tax Payable   8,000
            To record income taxes.

Note that the above entry assumes a single year-end accrual of income taxes. Most companies record income taxes monthly when estimated payments are made to federal and state taxing authorities.

Adjusting the Inventory Account The type of adjustment required for the inventory account depends on whether a periodic or perpetual inventory system is used. When the periodic inventory system is used, physical inventories must be taken at the end of the period to determine the inventory to be reported on the balance sheet and the cost of goods sold to be reported on the income statement. When perpetual inventory records are maintained, the ending inventory and the cost of goods sold balances appear in the ledger. An adjustment is necessary only to correct the recorded balances for any spoilage or theft or bookkeeping errors that may have occurred, as determined by a physical count of the inventory. The inventory procedures for merchandising companies are reviewed in the following paragraphs. Accounting for inventories of manufacturers is explained in a later chapter.

Periodic (Physical) Inventories When using the periodic inventory system, all purchases of merchandise during a period are recorded in a Purchases account. At the end of the period, before adjustments are made, the Inventory account still reflects the beginning inventory balance. The ending balance, based on a physical count, may be recorded in the Inventory account by an adjusting entry. At the same time the Inventory account is adjusted, the balance in Purchases and related accounts, such as Purchase Discounts or Freight In, are transferred to Cost of Goods Sold. In this way, the amount of Cost of Goods Sold is established through a single adjusting entry.

Using the method just described, an adjustment for Rosi, Inc. would be made to the inventory account by debiting it for $6,000 ($51,000 − $45,000), debiting Purchase Discounts for $3,290, crediting Purchases for $162,600, and debiting Cost of Goods Sold for the net amount, $153,310. This would increase Inventory to its ending balance of $51,000, close Purchase Discounts and Purchases, and reflect the amount of Cost of Goods Sold to be reported on the income statement. The adjusting entry would be as follows:

(j)	Inventory...	6,000	
	Purchase Discounts	3,290	
	Cost of Goods Sold	153,310	
	Purchases...		162,600
	To adjust inventory, cost of goods sold, and related accounts.		

An alternative to the above procedure is illustrated in Appendix B at the end of this chapter. This alternative is sometimes referred to as the "closing method," while the preceding approach is referred to as the "adjusting method" for a periodic inventory system.

Perpetual Inventories When a perpetual inventory system is maintained, a separate Purchases account is not used. The Inventory account is debited whenever goods are acquired. When a sale takes place, two entries are required: (1) the sale is recorded in the usual manner, and (2) the merchandise sold is recorded by a debit to Cost of Goods Sold and a credit to Inventory. At any time during the period, Inventory reflects the inventory on hand, and Cost of Goods Sold shows the cost of merchandise sold. At the end of the period, no adjustment is needed for inventory, except to adjust for spoilage or theft as noted earlier. Cost of Goods Sold would be debited and Inventory would be credited for the cost of the spoiled or stolen goods.

Preparing Financial Statements Once all accounts have been brought up to date through the adjustment process, **financial statements** may be prepared. The data may be taken directly from the adjusted account balances in the ledger, or a work sheet may be used.

Using a Work Sheet An optional step in the accounting process is to use a work sheet to facilitate the preparation of adjusting entries and financial statements. A work sheet is an accounting tool that is often used in organizing large quantities of data. However, preparing a work sheet is not a required step. As indicated, financial statements can be prepared directly from data in adjusted ledger account balances.

When a work sheet is constructed, trial balance data are listed in the first pair of columns. The adjusting entries are listed in the second pair of columns. Sometimes a third pair of columns is included to show the trial balance after adjustment. Account balances, as adjusted, are carried forward to the appropriate financial statement columns. A work sheet for a merchandising enterprise will include a pair of columns for the Income Statement accounts and a pair for the Balance Sheet accounts. Two columns for a Statement of Changes in Stockholders' Equity may be placed between the Income Statement and the Balance Sheet columns if desired. There are no columns for the statement of cash flows, because this statement requires additional analysis of changes in account balances for the period. The income statement, balance sheet, and statement of cash flows are discussed and illustrated in subsequent chapters. A work sheet for Rosi, Inc. is shown on pages 80 and 81. All adjustments illustrated previously are included.

Closing the Nominal Accounts Once adjusting entries are formally recorded in the general journal and posted to the ledger accounts, the books are ready to be closed in preparation for a new accounting period. During this closing process, the nominal (temporary) account balances are transferred to a real (permanent) account, leaving the nominal accounts with a zero balance. Nominal accounts include all income statement accounts plus the dividends account for a corporation or the drawings account for a proprietorship or partnership. The real account that receives the closing amounts from the nominal accounts is Retained Earnings for a corporation or the respective capital accounts for a proprietorship or partnership. Since they are real accounts, these and all other balance sheet accounts remain open and carry their balances forward to the new period.

The mechanics of closing the nominal accounts are straightforward. All revenue accounts with credit balances are closed by being debited; all expense accounts with debit balances are closed by being credited. This reduces these temporary accounts to a zero balance. The difference between the closing debit amounts for revenues and the credit amounts for expenses is net income (or net loss) and is an increase (or decrease) to Retained Earnings. The closing of Dividends reduces Retained Earnings. Thus, the closing entries for revenues, expenses, and dividends may be made directly to Retained Earnings, as follows:

Revenues	xx	
Retained Earnings		xx
To close revenues to Retained Earnings.		
Retained Earnings	xx	
Expenses		xx
To close expenses to Retained Earnings.		
Retained Earnings	xx	
Dividends		xx
To close the dividends account to Retained Earnings.		

An alternative to the closing method described on page 78 is to use an **Income Summary** account. Income Summary is a temporary "clearing" account that is used only to accumulate amounts from the closing entries for revenues and expenses and therefore summarizes the net income or net loss for the period. After revenues and expenses are closed to Income Summary, the balance in that account is then closed to Retained Earnings. Dividends must still be closed directly to Retained Earnings, since dividends do not affect net income and are not closed to Income Summary. If a work sheet is prepared, the balances in the income statement columns provide the data for closing revenues and expenses. The **closing entries** for Rosi, Inc. are presented below, assuming that an Income Summary account is used. Note that with the adjusting method illustrated for Inventory, Cost of Goods Sold is already computed. It can then be closed to Income Summary (or directly to Retained Earnings if an Income Summary account is not used) just like any other operating expense.

Closing Entries

1991			
Dec. 31	Sales	479,500	
	Interest Revenue	1,350	
	Rent Revenue	2,075	
	Income Summary		482,925
	To close revenue accounts to Income Summary.		
	Income Summary	441,710	
	Cost of Goods Sold		153,310
	Salaries and Wages Expense		174,600
	Heat, Light, and Power		32,480
	Payroll Taxes Expense		18,300
	Advertising Expense		18,600
	Interest Expense		21,420
	Doubtful Accounts Expense		1,100
	Depreciation Expense—Buildings		7,800
	Depreciation Expense—Furniture and Equipment		1,900
	Insurance Expense		4,200
	Income Tax Expense		8,000
	To close expense accounts to Income Summary.		
	Income Summary	41,215	
	Retained Earnings		41,215
	To transfer the balance in Income Summary to Retained Earnings.		
	Retained Earnings	13,600	
	Dividends		13,600
	To close Dividends to Retained Earnings.		

Preparing a Post-Closing Trial Balance After the closing entries are posted, a **post-closing trial balance** may be prepared to verify the equality of the debits and credits for all real accounts. The post-closing trial balance for Rosi, Inc. is presented on page 82.

	Account Title	Trial Balance		
		Debit	Credit	
1	Cash	83,110		1
2	Accounts Receivable	106,500		2
3	Allowance for Doubtful Accounts		1,610	3
4	Inventory	45,000		4
5	Prepaid Insurance	8,000		5
6	Interest Receivable	0		6
7	Notes Receivable	28,000		7
8	Land	114,000		8
9	Buildings	156,000		9
10	Accum. Depr.—Buildings		39,000	10
11	Furniture & Equipment	19,000		11
12	Accum. Depr.—Furniture & Equipment		3,800	12
13	Accounts Payable		37,910	13
14	Unearned Rent Revenue		0	14
15	Salaries and Wages Payable		0	15
16	Interest Payable		0	16
17	Payroll Taxes Payable		5,130	17
18	Income Tax Payable		0	18
19	Dividends Payable		3,400	19
20	Bonds Payable		140,000	20
21	Common Stock, $15 par		150,000	21
22	Retained Earnings		126,770	22
23	Dividends	13,600		23
24	Sales		479,500	24
25	Purchases	162,600		25
26	Purchase Discounts		3,290	26
27	Cost of Goods Sold	0		27
28	Salaries and Wages Expense	172,450		28
29	Heat, Light, and Power	32,480		29
30	Payroll Taxes Expense	18,300		30
31	Advertising Expense	18,600		31
32	Doubtful Accounts Expense	0		32
33	Depr. Exp.—Buildings	0		33
34	Depr. Exp.—Furniture & Equipment	0		34
35	Insurance Expense	0		35
36	Interest Revenue		1,100	36
37	Rent Revenue		2,550	37
38	Interest Expense	16,420		38
39	Income Tax Expense	0		39
40	Totals	994,060	994,060	40
41	Net Income			41
42				42

Inc.
Sheet
31, 1991

#	Adjustments Debit	Adjustments Credit	Income Statement Debit	Income Statement Credit	Balance Sheet Debit	Balance Sheet Credit	#
1					83,110		1
2					106,500		2
3		(c) 1,100				2,710	3
4	(j) 6,000				51,000		4
5		(g) 4,200			3,800		5
6	(f) 250				250		6
7					28,000		7
8					114,000		8
9					156,000		9
10		(a) 7,800				46,800	10
11					19,000		11
12		(b) 1,900				5,700	12
13						37,910	13
14		(h) 475				475	14
15		(d) 2,150				2,150	15
16		(e) 5,000				5,000	16
17						5,130	17
18		(i) 8,000				8,000	18
19						3,400	19
20						140,000	20
21						150,000	21
22						126,770	22
23					13,600		23
24				479,500			24
25		(j) 162,600					25
26	(j) 3,290						26
27	(j) 153,310		153,310				27
28	(d) 2,150		174,600				28
29			32,480				29
30			18,300				30
31			18,600				31
32	(c) 1,100		1,100				32
33	(a) 7,800		7,800				33
34	(b) 1,900		1,900				34
35	(g) 4,200		4,200				35
36		(f) 250		1,350			36
37	(h) 475			2,075			37
38	(e) 5,000		21,420				38
39	(i) 8,000		8,000				39
40	193,475	193,475	441,710	482,925	575,260	534,045	40
41			41,215			41,215	41
42			482,925	482,925	575,260	575,260	42

Rosi, Inc.
Post-Closing Trial Balance
December 31, 1991

Cash	83,110	
Accounts Receivable	106,500	
Allowance for Doubtful Accounts		2,710
Inventory	51,000	
Prepaid Insurance	3,800	
Interest Receivable	250	
Notes Receivable	28,000	
Land	114,000	
Buildings	156,000	
Accumulated Depreciation-Buildings		46,800
Furniture and Equipment	19,000	
Accumulated Depreciation—Furniture and Equipment		5,700
Accounts Payable		37,910
Salaries and Wages Payable		2,150
Interest Payable		5,000
Payroll Taxes Payable		5,130
Income Tax Payable		8,000
Dividends Payable		3,400
Bonds Payable		140,000
Unearned Rent Revenue		475
Common Stock, $15 par		150,000
Retained Earnings		154,385
	561,660	561,660

Reversing Entries At the beginning of a new period, the following types of adjusting entries may be reversed:

1. accrued expenses
2. accrued revenues
3. prepaid expenses when the original debit was to an expense account
4. deferred revenues when the original credit was to a revenue account

Reversing entries are not necessary, but they make it possible to record the expense payments or revenue receipts in the new period in the usual manner. For example, if a reversing entry is not made for accrued expenses, payments in the subsequent period would have to be analyzed as to (1) the amount representing payment of the accrued liability, and (2) the amount representing the expense of the current period. Alternatively, the accrued and deferred accounts could be left unadjusted until the close of the subsequent reporting period when they would be adjusted to their correct balances.

The adjustments establishing accrued and prepaid balances for Rosi, Inc. were illustrated earlier in the chapter. The appropriate reversing entries are shown below.

Reversing Entries

1992			
Jan. 1	Salaries and Wages Payable	2,150	
	Salaries and Wages Expense		2,150
	Interest Payable	5,000	
	Interest Expense		5,000
	Interest Revenue	250	
	Interest Receivable		250
	Unearned Rent Revenue	475	
	Rent Revenue		475

To illustrate accounting for an accrued expense when (1) reversing entries are made and (2) reversing entries are not made, assume that accrued salaries on December 31, 1991, are $350 and on December 31, 1992, are $500. Payment of salaries for the period ending January 4, 1992, is $1,000. Adjustments are made and the books are closed annually on December 31. The possible entries are shown below:

	(1) Assuming Liability Account Is Reversed		(2) Assuming Liability Account Is Not Reversed			
			(a) Transaction in Next Period Is Analyzed.		(b) Transaction in Next Period is Not Analyzed. Adjustment at Close of Next Reporting Period.	
December 31, 1991 Adjusting entry to record accrued salaries.	Salaries Exp. . . 350 Salaries Payable	350	Salaries Exp. . . 350 Salaries Payable	350	Salaries Exp. . . . 350 Salaries Payable	350
December 31, 1991 Closing entry to transfer expense to the income summary account.	Income Summary . . . . . xxx Salaries Exp. . .	xxx	Income Summary . . . . xxx Salaries Exp.	xxx	Income Summary . . . . . xxx Salaries Exp. . .	xxx
January 1, 1992 Reversing entry to transfer balance to the account that will be charged when payment is made.	Salaries Payable . . . . . . 350 Salaries Exp. . .	350	No entry		No entry	
January 4, 1992 Payment of salaries for period ending January 4, 1992.	Salaries Exp. . . 1,000 Cash	1,000	Salaries Payable . . . . . 350 Salaries Exp. . . . 650 Cash	1,000	Salaries Exp. . . . 1,000 Cash	1,000
December 31, 1992 Adjusting entry to record accrued salaries.	Salaries Exp. . . 500 Salaries Payable	500	Salaries Exp. . . 500 Salaries Payable	500	Salaries Exp. . . . 150 Salaries Payable	150

Accrual Versus Cash Basis Accounting

The procedures described in the previous sections are those required in a double-entry system based on accrual accounting. **Accrual accounting** recognizes revenues as they are earned, not necessarily when cash is received. Expenses are recognized and recorded when they are incurred, not necessarily when cash is paid. This provides for a better matching of revenues and expenses during an accounting period and generally results in financial statements that more accurately reflect a company's financial position and results of operations.[2]

Some accounting systems are based on cash receipts and cash disbursements instead of accrual accounting. **Cash basis accounting** procedures frequently are found in organizations not requiring a complete set of double-

---

[2]In Concepts Statement No. 6, the FASB discusses the concept of accrual accounting and relates it to the objectives of financial reporting. *Statement of Financial Accounting Concepts No. 6,* "Elements of Financial Statements" (Stamford: Financial Accounting Standards Board, December 1985).

entry records. Such organizations might include smaller, unincorporated businesses, and some nonprofit organizations. Professionals engaged in service businesses, such as CPAs, dentists, and engineers, also have traditionally used cash accounting systems. Even many of these organizations, however, periodically use professional accountants to prepare financial statements and other required reports on an accrual basis.

A controversy exists currently as to the appropriateness of using cash accounting systems, especially as a basis for determining tax liabilities.[3] The FASB, in Concepts Statement No. 1, indicates that accrual accounting provides a better basis for financial reports than does information showing only cash receipts and disbursements. The AICPA's position, however, is that the cash basis is appropriate for some smaller companies and especially for companies in the service industry. Until this controversy is settled, accountants will continue to be asked to convert cash-based records to generally accepted accrual-based financial statements. The necessary procedures are illustrated and explained in Appendix C at the end of this chapter.

Computers and the Accounting Process

The usual procedures for recording transactions and the sequence of activities leading to the preparation of financial statements have been briefly reviewed in this chapter. These procedures and activities are referred to collectively as the accounting process or accounting cycle. The accounting process begins with the analysis of business documents evidencing the transactions of an entity and concludes with the final summarized financial statements.

As an organization grows in size and complexity, the recording and summarizing processes become more involved, and means are sought for improving efficiency and reducing costs. Some enterprises may find that a system involving primarily manual operations is adequate in meeting their needs. Others find that information processing needs can be handled effectively only through electronic data processing (EDP) equipment.

Companies requiring great speed and accuracy in processing large amounts of accounting data often utilize a computer system capable of storing and recalling data, performing many mathematical functions, and making certain routine decisions based on mathematical comparisons. These systems normally include various other machines that can "read" data from disks, magnetic tapes, or punched cards and print information in a variety of forms, all under the control of a computer.

Modern computer systems have vast capabilities. The individual steps involved in recording and summarizing may be combined into one process. The information traditionally recorded in journals and ledgers may be stored in memory banks or on computer disks and recalled as needed. On-

---

[3]For an argument on retaining the cash basis of accounting, see Ronnie G. Flippo, "The President's Tax Proposals: A View from Capitol Hill," *Journal of Accountancy* (September 1985), pp. 86–88.

line, real-time systems have the capability of continuous updating of all relevant files. This makes it possible for reports to be produced on a much more timely basis.

Since the early 1960s, society has been caught in the midst of an ongoing computer revolution. Technological advances in integrated circuitry and microchips led to one of the most significant phenomena of the 1980s—the development of *personal computers (PCs)*. These compact, relatively inexpensive computers have changed the way in which many companies and individuals keep track of their business activities. These computers are being used for a variety of activities: including financial analysis, accounting functions, word processing, data base management, inventory control, and credit analysis of customers. As uses have expanded, software packages have been developed to meet current and future demand. The impact of PCs is felt not only in business, but in education and in family life. Several colleges now require entering freshmen to purchase their own PCs for use in a variety of business, mathematics, and science courses. Exposure to computers, and especially the PC, is also very common in elementary and secondary school curricula.

This computer revolution is rapidly changing society and, along with it, the way business is conducted and, therefore, the way accounting functions are performed. However, despite their tremendous capabilities, computers cannot replace skilled accountants. In fact, their presence places increased demands on the accountant in directing the operations of the computer systems to assure the use of appropriate procedures. Although all arithmetical operations can be assumed to be done accurately by computers, the validity of the output data depends on the adequacy of the instructions given the computer. Unlike a human accountant, a computer cannot think for itself but must be given explicit instructions for performing each operation. This has certain advantages in that the accountant can be sure every direction will be carried out precisely. On the other hand, this places a great responsibility on the accountant to anticipate any unusual situations requiring special consideration or judgment. Various control techniques also must be developed for checking and verifying data recorded in electronic form.

The significance of the accounting process in our society and its applicability to every business unit, regardless of size, must be appreciated. Although the procedures may be modified to meet special conditions and may be performed through a variety of manual or computer systems, the process reviewed in this chapter is fundamental to the accounting systems of all enterprises.

Appendix A

Special Journals and Subsidiary Ledgers

In recording transactions, many companies use **special journals** in addition to the **general journal**. Special journals eliminate much of the repetitive work involved in recording routine transactions. In addition, they permit the recording functions to be divided among accounting personnel, each individual being responsible for a separate record. This specialization often results in greater efficiency and increased accuracy, as well as a higher degree of control.

Some examples of special journals are the sales journal, the purchases journal, the cash receipts journal, the cash disbursements journal, the payroll register, and the voucher register.

Sales on account are recorded in the **sales journal**. The subsequent collections on account, as well as other transactions involving the receipt of cash, are recorded in the **cash receipts journal**. Merchandise purchases on account are entered in a **purchases journal** or a voucher register. Subsequent payments on account, as well as other transactions involving the payment of cash, are recorded in a **cash payments journal** or a **check register**. A payroll register may be employed to accumulate payroll information, including payroll deductions and withholdings for taxes.

Column headings in the various journals specify the accounts to be debited or credited; account titles and explanations may therefore be omitted in recording routine transactions. A Sundry column is usually provided for transactions that are relatively infrequent, and account titles must be entered in recording such transactions.

The use of special journals facilitates recording and also simplifies the posting process, because the totals of many transactions, rather than separate data for each transaction, can be posted to the ledger accounts. Certain data must be transferred individually—data affecting individual accounts receivable and accounts payable and data reported in the Sundry columns—but the overall volume of posting is substantially reduced.

The format of a particular journal must satisfy the needs of the individual business unit. For example, with an automated or computerized system the general journal, any specialized journals, and subsidiary ledgers may be modified or eliminated. Recognizing that modifications are necessary for individual systems, the following sections discuss a voucher system and illustrate some special journals that are commonly used with manual accounting systems.

Voucher System

Relatively large organizations ordinarily provide for the control of purchases and cash disbursements through adoption of some form of a **voucher system**. With the use of a voucher system, checks may be drawn only upon a written authorization in the form of a **voucher** approved by some responsible official.

A voucher is prepared, not only in support of each payment to be made for goods and services purchased on account, but also for all other transactions calling for payment by check, including cash purchases, retirement of debt, replenishment of petty cash funds, payrolls, and dividends. The voucher identifies the person authorizing the expenditure, explains the nature of the transaction, and names the accounts affected by the transaction. For control purposes, vouchers should be prenumbered, checked against purchase invoices, and compared with receiving reports. Upon verification, the voucher and the related business documents are submitted to the appropriate official for final approval. When approved, the prenumbered voucher is recorded in a voucher register. The voucher register is a book of original entry and takes the place of a purchases journal. Charges on each voucher are classified and recorded in appropriate Debit columns, and the amount to be paid is listed in an Accounts Payable or Vouchers Payable column. After a voucher is entered in the register, it is placed in an unpaid vouchers file together with its supporting documents.

Checks are written in payment of individual vouchers. The checks are recorded in a check register, which is used in place of a cash payments journal, as debits to Accounts Payable or Vouchers Payable and credits to Cash. Since charges to the various asset, liability, or expense accounts were recognized when the payable was recorded in the voucher register, these accounts need not be listed in the payments record. When a check is issued, payment of the voucher is reported in the voucher register by entering the check number and the payment date. Paid vouchers and supporting documents are removed from the unpaid file, marked "paid," and placed in a separate paid vouchers file. The balance of the payable account, after the credit for total vouchers issued and the debit for total vouchers paid, should be equal to the sum of the unpaid vouchers file. The voucher register, while representing a journal, also provides the detail in support of the accounts payable or vouchers payable total.

Illustration of Special Journals and Subsidiary Ledgers

Assume that Central Valley, Inc. maintains the following books of original entry: sales journal, cash receipts journal, voucher register, check register, and general journal. As noted, the format of a particular journal must satisfy the needs of the individual business unit. Those presented for Central Valley, Inc. are illustrative only.

Sales Journal

The sales journal for the month of July, 1991, appears as follows:

SALES JOURNAL
Page 6

	Date	Invoice No.	Account Debited	Post Ref.	Accts. Rec. Dr. Sales Cr.	
1	1991					1
2	July 2	701	The Chocolate Factory	✓	3 4 5 0 00	2
3	6	702	Huffman Company	✓	6 5 1 0 00	3
4	10	703	Stocks and Co.	✓	1 5 2 5 00	4
5	12	704	Bennet, Inc.	✓	4 8 6 0 00	5
6	15	705	The Chocolate Factory	✓	2 0 0 0 00	6
7	18	706	Ridnour Corporation	✓	5 9 4 0 00	7
8	20	707	Hillcrest Sales Co.	✓	1 9 1 0 00	8
9	23	708	Kirstein, Inc.	✓	7 6 5 0 00	9
10	27	709	DataMark Systems Inc.	✓	1 2 8 0 00	10
11	29	710	Fuller Distributing Co.	✓	2 9 2 5 00	11
12	31	711	Stocks and Co.	✓	2 1 0 0 00	12
13					4 0 1 5 0 00	13
14					(116) (41)	14

As illustrated, credit sales are recorded by debits to Accounts Receivable and credits to Sales. The sales invoice number provides a reference to the original source document for each transaction. Debits are posted to individual customers' accounts in the accounts receivable subsidiary ledger as indicated by a check (√) in the Posting Reference column. The total sales for the month ($40,150) are posted to Accounts Receivable and Sales (accounts #116 and #41, respectively).

Cash Receipts Journal   The cash receipts journal for Central Valley, Inc. for July, 1991, appears as follows:

CASH RECEIPTS JOURNAL
Page 8

	Date	Account Credited	Post Ref	Sundry Accounts	Accounts Receivable Cr.	Sales Discounts Dr.	Cash Dr.	
1	1991							1
2	July 3	Hamilton Sign Co.	✓		5 6 5 0 00	1 1 3 00	5 5 3 7 00	2
3	7	DataMark Systems Inc.	✓		1 4 0 0 00	2 8 00	1 3 7 2 00	3
4	8	Sales	41	3 6 5 00			3 6 5 00	4
5	10	The Chocolate Factory	✓		3 4 5 0 00	6 9 00	3 3 8 1 00	5
6	11	Sawyer Co.	✓		2 7 3 5 00		2 7 3 5 00	6
7	14	Rohas, Inc.	✓		4 8 7 5 00		4 8 7 5 00	7
8	16	Milo Company	✓		9 2 0 00		9 2 0 00	8
9	17	Poynter Corp.	✓		6 1 0 0 00		6 1 0 0 00	9
10	21	Earnst Co.	✓		6 8 7 0 00		6 8 7 0 00	10
11	22	Tax Refund Receivable........	120	5 7 8 0 00			5 7 8 0 00	11
12	25	Sales	41	4 4 0 00			4 4 0 00	12
13	29	Hillcrest Sales Co.	✓		1 9 0 0 00	3 8 00	1 8 6 2 00	13
14	31	The Chocolate Factory	✓		2 0 0 0 00		2 0 0 0 00	14
15	31	Notes Receivable.............	113	8 5 0 0 00				15
16		Interest Revenue	72	6 5 00			8 5 6 5 00	16
17				15 1 5 0 00	35 9 0 0 00	2 4 8 00	50 8 0 2 00	17
18				(√)	(116)	(42)	(111)	18

The cash receipts journal records all receipts of cash. Collections of cash from previously recorded credit sales are posted in total as a credit to Accounts Receivable (account #116) and as debits to Sales Discounts (account #42) and Cash (account #111). The credits to Accounts Receivable are posted to the individual customers' accounts in the subsidiary ledger as noted by the check (√) in the Posting Reference column. Cash sales, e.g., as shown for July 8 and July 25, are posted individually as a credit to Sales (account #41) and as a part of the total debit to Cash. Other transactions involving cash receipts, e.g., the collection of a note receivable on July 31, are posted individually as credits and as a part of the total debit to Cash.

Voucher Register   As noted, the voucher register takes the place of a purchases journal, providing a record of all authorized payments to be made by check. A partial voucher register appears below. For illustrative purposes, separate debit columns are provided for two accounts—Purchases and Payroll. Other items are recorded in the Sundry Dr. column. Additional separate columns could be added for other items, such as advertising, if desired. The total amount of each column is posted to the corresponding account, with the exception of the Sundry Dr. and Cr. columns, which are posted individually.

VOUCHER REGISTER

Date	Vou. No.	Payee	Paid Date	Ck. No.	Accounts Payable Cr.	Purchases Dr.	Payroll Dr.	Account	Post. Ref.	Sundry Amount Dr.	Cr.
31	7132	Security National Bank........	7/31	3106	9,120			Notes Payable	211	9,120	
31	7133	Payroll	7/31	3107	1,640		2,130	FICA Tax Payable	215		90
								Income Tax Payable	214		400
31	7134	Far Fabrications			3,290	3,290					
31	7135	Midland Inc.			1,500	1,500					
31	7136	Nyland Supply Co.			5,550	5,550					
31		Total			55,375	24,930	2,130			33,645	5,330
					(213)	(51)	(620)			(√)	(√)

Check Register   A partial check register is illustrated on the next page. It accounts for all the checks issued during the period. Checks are issued only in payment of properly approved vouchers. The payee is designated together with the number of the voucher authorizing the payment.

CHECK REGISTER

Date	Check No.	Account Debited	Vou. No.	Accounts Payable Dr.	Purchase Discounts Cr.	Cash Cr.
31	3106	Security National Bank	7132	9,120		9,120
31	3107	Payroll	7133	1,640		1,640
31	3108	Pat Bunnell	7005	1,500	30	1,470
31		Total		61,160	275	60,885
				(213)	(52)	(111)

General Journal

Regardless of the number and nature of special journals, certain transactions cannot appropriately be recorded in the special journals and are recorded in the general journal. A general journal with an illustrative entry during the month of July is illustrated below. This general journal is prepared in two-column form. A pair of debit and credit columns is provided for the entries that are to be made to the general ledger accounts.

GENERAL JOURNAL   Page 3

Date	Description	Post. Ref.	Debit	Credit
1991 July 31	Allowance for Doubtful Accounts	117	1,270	
	Accounts Receivable	116		1,270
	To write off uncollectible account. (Rit-Z Shop)			

Subsidiary Ledgers

As explained in the chapter, subsidiary ledgers provide the detail of individual accounts in support of a control account in the general ledger. Whenever possible, individual postings to subsidiary accounts are made directly from the business documents evidencing the transactions. This practice saves time and avoids errors that might arise in summarizing and transferring this information. If postings to the subsidiary records and to the control accounts are made accurately, the sum of the detail in a subsidiary record will agree with the balance in the control account. A reconciliation of each subsidiary ledger with its related control account should be made periodically, and any discrepancies found should be investigated and corrected.

As an illustration of the relationship of a general ledger control account to its subsidiary ledger accounts, the Accounts Receivable control account is shown on the next page. Three of the subsidiary accounts are also shown.

GENERAL LEDGER

Account: Accounts Receivable   **Account No.** 116

Date		Item	Post. Ref.	Debit	Credit	Balance
1991						
July	1	Balance				9,200
	31	Sales on account	S6	40,150		49,350
	31	Collections on account	CR8		35,900	13,450
	31	Write off of uncollectible account	J3		1,270	12,180
		(Rit-Z Shop)				

ACCOUNTS RECEIVABLE SUBSIDIARY LEDGER

Name: Stocks and Co.
Address: 546 South Fox Rd, Chicago, IL 60665

Date		Item	Post. Ref.	Debit	Credit	Balance
1991						
July	1	Balance				1,000
	10	Purchase	S6	1,525		2,525
	31	Purchase	S6	2,100		4,025

Name: The Chocolate Factory
Address: 7890 Redwood Dr., Pittsburgh, PA 15234

Date		Item	Post. Ref.	Debit	Credit	Balance
1991						
July	2	Purchase	S6	3,450		3,450
	10	Payment	CR8		3,450	-0-
	15	Purchase	S6	2,000		2,000
	31	Payment	CR8		2,000	-0-

Name: The Rit-Z Dress Shop
Address: 789 Cotton Drive, Phoenix, AZ 85090

Date		Item	Post. Ref.	Debit	Credit	Balance
1991						
July	1	Balance				1,270
	31	Write off of uncollectible account (6 months old)	J3		1,270	-0-

Appendix B

Closing Method for Inventory

In the work sheet presented on pages 94 and 95, Inventory and related accounts are adjusted through a cost of goods sold account. An alternative approach is to "close" beginning and ending inventory amounts to Income Summary. With this procedure, cost of goods sold appears only as a calculated figure in the income statement; it does not appear in the accounts. This method is illustrated in the work sheet on pages 80 and 81. Adjusting entries (a) through (i) are the same as those in the earlier example for Rosi, Inc. Using the closing procedure, however, the following entries would be made for Inventory:

(j)	Income Summary	45,000	
	Inventory		45,000
	Close beginning inventory to Income Summary.		
(k)	Inventory	51,000	
	Income Summary		51,000
	Record ending inventory.		

Note that Income Summary shows both a debit and a credit on the Income Statement section of the work sheet, and no adjustment is made for Purchases and Purchase Discounts. The balances in these accounts are extended to the Income Statement columns in the work sheet. Subsequently, these accounts would be closed to Income Summary as part of the normal closing process.

Other variations of the closing approach to merchandise inventory can be found in practice. Regardless of the approach used, financial statements will reflect the same ending inventory and cost of goods sold amounts.

| | Account Title | Trial Balance | | |
		Debit	Credit	
1	Cash	83,110		1
2	Accounts Receivable	106,500		2
3	Allowance for Doubtful Accounts		1,610	3
4	Inventory	45,000		4
5	Prepaid Insurance	8,000		5
6	Interest Receivable	0		6
7	Notes Receivable	28,000		7
8	Land	114,000		8
9	Buildings	156,000		9
10	Accum. Depr—Buildings		39,000	10
11	Furniture & Equipment	19,000		11
12	Accum Depr—Furniture & Equipment		3,800	12
13	Accounts Payable		37,910	13
14	Unearned Rent Revenue		0	14
15	Salaries and Wages Payable		0	15
16	Interest Payable		0	16
17	Payroll Taxes Payable		5,130	17
18	Income Tax Payable		0	18
19	Dividends Payable		3,400	19
20	Bonus Payable		140,000	20
21	Common Stock, $15 par		150,000	21
22	Retained Earnings		126,770	22
23	Dividends	13,600		23
24	Income Summary		0	24
25	Sales		479,500	25
26	Purchases	162,600		26
27	Purchase Discounts		3,290	27
28	Salaries and Wages Expense	172,450		28
29	Heat, Light and Power	32,480		29
30	Payroll Taxes Expenses	18,300		30
31	Advertising Expense	18,600		31
32	Doubtful Accounts Expense	0		32
33	Depr Exp—Buildings	0		33
34	Depr Exp—Furniture & Equipment	0		34
35	Insurance Expense	0		35
36	Interest Revenue		1,100	36
37	Rent Revenue		2,550	37
38	Interest Expense	16,420		38
39	Income Tax Expense	0		39
40	Totals	994,060	994,060	40
41	Net Income			41
42				42

Inc.
Sheet
31, 1991

#	Adjustments Debit	Adjustments Credit	Income Statement Debit	Income Statement Credit	Balance Sheet Debit	Balance Sheet Credit	#
1					83,110		1
2					106,500		2
3		(c) 1,100				2,710	3
4	(k) 51,000	(j) 45,000			51,000		4
5		(g) 4,200			3,800		5
6	(f) 250				250		6
7					28,000		7
8					114,000		8
9					156,000		9
10		(a) 7,800				46,800	10
11					19,000		11
12		(b) 1,900				5,700	12
13						37,910	13
14		(h) 475				475	14
15		(d) 2,150				2,150	15
16		(e) 5,000				5,000	16
17						5,130	17
18		(i) 8,000				8,000	18
19						3,400	19
20						140,000	20
21						150,000	21
22						126,770	22
23					13,600		23
24	(j) 45,000	(k) 51,000	45,000	51,000			24
25				479,500			25
26			162,600				26
27				3,290			27
28	(d) 2,150		174,600				28
29			32,480				29
30			18,300				30
31			18,600				31
32	(c) 1,100		1,100				32
33	(a) 7,800		7,800				33
34	(b) 1,900		1,900				34
35	(g) 4,200		4,200				35
36		(f) 250		1,350			36
37	(h) 475			2,075			37
38	(e) 5,000		21,420				38
39	(i) 8,000		8,000				39
40	126,875	126,875	496,000	537,215	575,260	534,045	40
41			41,215			41,215	41
42			537,215	537,215	575,260	575,260	42

Appendix C

Comprehensive
Illustration of Accrual
Versus Cash Accounting

The adjustments required in converting from a cash basis to accrual accounting are summarized in Exhibit 3–4, which also illustrates the procedure for computing net sales under the accrual concept. The computation of gross sales requires additional adjustment if sales discounts and returns and allowances exist, or if any accounts have been determined to be uncollectible. For example, assume sales data as follows:

Data from cash records:	
Cash sales	$10,000
Collections on accounts receivable arising from sales	42,000
Data from balance sheets:	
Accounts receivable at the beginning of the period	14,300
Accounts receivable at the end of the period	12,500
Supplementary data from special analysis of records:	
Accounts determined to be uncollectible during the period	600
Sales discounts allowed customers during the period	850
Sales returns and allowances during the period	300

The supplementary data indicate that uncollectible accounts of $600, sales discounts of $850, and sales returns and allowances of $300 are to be recognized. These amounts must be added to cash collections in arriving at gross sales, for there must have been sales equivalent to the reductions in accounts receivable from these sources. Gross sales for the period are computed as follows:

Cash sales		$10,000
Sales on account:		
Accounts receivable at the end of the period	$12,500	
Collections on accounts receivable	42,000	
Uncollectible accounts receivable	600	
Sales discounts	850	
Sales returns and allowances	300	
	$56,250	
Deduct accounts receivable at the beginning of the period	14,300	41,950
Gross sales for the period		$51,950

Similar adjustments would be required for purchase discounts, purchase returns and allowances, and freight in to compute gross purchases on an accrual basis.

To provide a comprehensive illustration of the conversion of cash-based records to accrual-based financial statements, data for Bestor Company, a proprietorship, will be used. In making the conversion from cash to accrual, a

Exhibit 3—4   Converting from Cash Basis to Accrual Accounting

Cash Basis	± Adjust Required	= Accrual Basis
Sales Receipts:		
Cash sales + Cash collections of Accounts Receivable	+ Ending Accounts Receivable − Beginning Accounts Receivable	= Net Sales
Other Receipts: (e.g., rent and interest)		
Cash received for rent	+ Beginning Unearned Rent − Ending Unearned Rent	= Rent Revenue
Cash received for interest	+ Ending Interest Receivable − Beginning Interest Receivable	= Interest Revenue
Payments for Goods:		
Cash purchases + Cash payments for Accounts Payable	+ Ending Accounts Payable − Beginning Accounts Payable + Beginning Inventory − Ending Inventory	= Cost of Goods Sold
Payments for Expenses: Cash paid for rent, utilities, wages, etc.	+ Beginning Prepaid Expenses − Ending Prepaid Expenses + Ending Accrued Expenses − Beginning Accrued Expenses	= Operating Expenses (excludes depreciation and similar noncash expenses)

balance sheet is prepared first. Assets and liabilities at year-end are determined by analysis of the prior year's balance sheet, a review of accounting records and documents, and physical counts of inventories and supplies. Owner's equity is the difference between total assets and total liabilities. Comparative balance sheets for Bestor Company appear on page 98.

After the balance sheet is prepared, the next step is to analyze cash records and prepare a summary of cash receipts and cash disbursements for the period, as illustrated below:

Summary of Cash Receipts and Disbursements

Cash Balance, January 1, 1991		$ 3,200
Receipts:		
Cash sales	$ 9,200	
Collections:		
Accounts receivable arising from sales	42,000	
Notes receivable arising from sales	6,000	
From rental of store space	1,750	
From interest and dividends	400	
From sales of investments (cost $7,500)	6,250	65,600
		$68,800
Disbursements:		
Payments on accounts payable arising from purchases	$40,000	
For salaries	4,200	
For rent	4,400	
For supplies	1,000	
Acquisition of furniture and fixtures	3,500	
For miscellaneous expense	1,500	
Owner's withdrawals	9,000	63,600
Cash balance, December 31, 1991		$ 5,200

Bestor Company
Comparative Balance Sheet Data

	Dec. 31 1991	Dec. 31 1990
Assets		
Current Assets:		
Cash	$ 5,200	$ 3,200
Notes receivable	3,000	2,500
Accounts receivable	4,500	6,000
Interest receivable	50	150
Inventory	24,600	20,000
Supplies	600	400
Prepaid miscellaneous expenses	0	100
Total current assets	$37,950	$32,350
Noncurrent assets:		
Long-term investments	$ 2,200	$ 9,700
Furniture and fixtures (cost less accumulated depreciation)	8,325	5,800
Total noncurrent assets	$10,525	$15,500
Total Assets	$48,475	$47,850
Liabilities and Owner's Equity		
Current liabilities:		
Accounts payable	$ 9,000	$ 7,500
Salaries payable	250	200
Miscellaneous expenses payable	150	0
Unearned rent revenues	125	150
Total liabilities	$ 9,525	$ 7,850
Owner's Equity:		
K. Bestor, capital	38,950	40,000
Total liabilities and owner's equity	$48,475	$47,850

Supplementary data developed from an analysis of business documents and the cash records confirm the following:

1. The net amount reported for Furniture and Fixtures in the December 31, 1991 balance sheet was based on the following information: furniture and fixtures were acquired during the year for cash, $3,500; depreciation expense for 1991 is $975.
2. Long-term investments costing $7,500 were sold in 1991 for $6,250.
3. Purchase discounts of $600 were allowed on the payment of creditor invoices during the year. Sales returns and allowances amounted to $1,480.

Based on the information from the balance sheet, the summary of cash receipts and disbursements, and the supplemental data, an income statement can now be prepared for Bestor Company. Schedules in support of the income statement balances as well as a summary of the changes in owner's equity are also provided.

Bestor Company
Income Statement
For Year Ended December 31, 1991

Revenue from net sales:			
Sales	(A)	$57,680	
Less sales returns and allowances ...		1,480	$56,200
Cost of goods sold:			
Beginning inventory		$20,000	
Purchases	(B) $42,100		
Less purchase discounts	600	41,500	
Cost of goods available for sale		$61,500	
Less ending inventory		24,600	36,900
Gross profit on sales			$19,300
Operating expenses:			
Salaries	(C)	$ 4,250	
Rent expense	(D)	4,400	
Supplies expense	(E)	800	
Depreciation expense—furniture			
and fixtures	(F)	975	
Miscellaneous expenses	(G)	1,750	12,175
Operating income			$ 7,125
Other revenues and gains:			
Interest and dividend revenue	(H)	$ 300	
Rent revenue	(I)	1,775	2,075
Other expenses and losses:			
Loss on sale of investments	(J)		(1,250)
Income from continuing operations			
before income taxes...............			$ 7,950

Bestor Company
Notes to Income Statement
For Year Ended December 31, 1991

(A)	Computation of gross sales:		
	Cash sales		$ 9,200
	Sales on account:		
	Notes and accounts receivable, December 31, 1991	$ 7,500	
	Collections on notes and accounts receivable	48,000	
	Sales returns and allowances	1,480	
		$56,980	
	Deduct notes and accounts receivable, January 1, 1991	8,500	48,480
	Gross sales for the year		$57,680
(B)	Computation of gross purchases:		
	Purchases on account:		
	Accounts payable, December 31, 1991		$ 9,000
	Cash payments on accounts payable		40,000
	Discounts allowed on accounts payable		600
			$49,600
	Deduct accounts payable, January 1, 1991		7,500
	Gross purchases for the year		$42,100

Computation of operating expenses:

(C)	Salaries:	
	Salaries payable, December 31, 1991	$ 250
	Add payments for salaries	4,200
		$ 4,450
	Deduct salaries payable, January 1, 1991	200
	Salaries expense for the year	$ 4,250
(D)	Rent expense:	
	Payments for rent	$ 4,400
(E)	Supplies expense:	
	Supplies, January 1, 1991	$ 400
	Add payments for supplies	1,000
		$ 1,400
	Deduct supplies on hand, December 31, 1991	600
	Supplies used during the year	$ 800
(F)	Depreciation expense:	
	Furniture and fixtures (net), January 1, 1991	$ 5,800
	Add purchases of furniture and fixtures during year	3,500
		$ 9,300
	Deduct furniture fixtures (net), December 31, 1991	8,325
	Depreciation expense for the year	$ 975
(G)	Miscellaneous expenses:	
	Prepaid miscellaneous expenses, January 1, 1991	$ 100
	Add: Miscellaneous expense payments	1,500
	Miscellaneous expenses payable, December 31, 1991	150
	Miscellaneous expenses for the year	$ 1,750
(H)	Computation of interest and divided revenue:	
	Interest receivable, December 31, 1991	$ 50
	Add interest and dividend receipts	400
		$ 450
	Deduct interest receivable, January 1, 1991	150
	Total interest and dividend revenue for the year	$ 300
(I)	Computation of rent revenue:	
	Unearned rent revenue, January 1, 1991	$ 150
	Add rent receipts	1,750
		$ 1,900
	Deduct unearned rent revenue, December 31, 1991	125
	Total rent revenue for the year	$ 1,775
(J)	Computation of loss on sale of investments:	
	Cost of investments sold	$ 7,500
	Proceeds from sale	6,250
	Loss on sale of investments	$ 1,250

Bestor Company
Summary of Changes in Owner's Equity
For Year Ended December 31, 1991

K. Bestor, capital, December 31, 1991	$38,950
K. Bestor, capital, January 1, 1991	40,000
Net decrease in owner's equity	$ (1,050)
Withdrawals by owner during year	9,000
Net income for year	$ 7,950

Key Terms

Account 69
Accounting process (cycle) 63
Accounting system 63
Accrual accounting 83
Adjunct account 72
Adjusting entries 71
Business (source) documents 67
Cash basis accounting 83
Chart of accounts 69
Closing entries 79
Contra account 72
Control account 70
Credit 66
Debit 66
Double-entry accounting 66
General journal 69

General ledger 70
Income summary 79
Journals 68
Ledgers 68
Nominal (temporary) accounts 78
Periodic inventory system 76
Perpetual inventory system 77
Post-closing trial balance 79
Posting 70
Real (permanent) accounts 78
Reversing entries 82
Special journal 69
Subsidiary ledgers 70
Transaction 66
Trial balance 71
Work sheet 77

Questions

1. What type of reports are generated from the accounting system?
2. What are the main similarities and differences between a manual and an automated accounting system?
3. Distinguish between the recording and summarizing phases of the accounting process.
4. List and describe the steps in the accounting process. Why is each step necessary? Which steps are optional?
5. Under double-entry accounting, what are the debit/credit relationships of accounts?
6. Distinguish between: (a) real and nominal accounts, (b) general journal and special journals, and (c) general ledger and subsidiary ledgers.
7. As Beechnut Mining Company's independent certified public accountant, you find that the company accountant posts adjusting and closing entries directly to the ledger without formal entries in the general journal. How would you evaluate this procedure in your report to management?
8. Explain the nature and the purpose of (a) adjusting entries, (b) closing entries, and (c) reversing entries.
9. Give three common examples of contra accounts; explain why contra accounts are used.
10. Payment of insurance in advance may be recorded in either (a) an expense account or (b) an asset account. Which method would you recommend? What periodic entries are required under each method?
11. Distinguish between the procedures followed by a merchandising enterprise using a periodic (physical) inventory system and one using a perpetual inventory system.
12. Describe the nature and purpose of a work sheet.
13. What effect, if any, does the use of a work sheet have on the sequence of the summarizing phase of the accounting process?
14. The accountant for the Miller Hardware Store, after completing all adjustments except for the merchandise inventory, makes the following entry to close the beginning inventory, to set up the ending inventory, to

close all nominal accounts, and to report the net result of operations in the capital account.

Inventory (December 31, 1991)	22,500	
Sales	250,000	
Purchase Discounts	2,500	
Inventory (January 1, 1991)		25,000
Purchases		175,000
Selling Expense		25,000
General and Administrative Expense		18,750
Interest Expense		1,875
M. Mills, Capital		29,375

(a) Would you regard this procedure as being acceptable? (b) What alternate procedure could you have followed to close the nominal accounts?

15. From the following list of accounts, determine which ones should be closed and whether each would normally be closed by a debit or credit entry.

Cash	Retained Earnings
Rent Expense	Capital Stock
Accounts Receivable	Interest Revenue
Land	Advertising Expense
Depreciation Expense	Purchase Discounts
Sales Revenue	Notes Payable
Sales Discounts	Dividends
Purchases	Accounts Payable
Freight In	

16. Distinguish between accrual and cash-basis accounting.

17. Is greater accuracy achieved in financial statements prepared from double-entry, accrual data as compared with cash data? Explain.

18. What are the major advantages of electronic data processing as compared with manual processing of accounting data?

19. One of your clients overheard a computer manufacturer sales representative saying the computer will make the accountant obsolete. How would you respond to this comment?

*20. What advantages are provided through the use of: (a) special journals, (b) subsidiary ledgers, and (c) the voucher system?

*21. The Tantor Co. maintains a sales journal, a voucher register, a cash receipts journal, a cash disbursements journal, and a general journal. For each account listed below, indicate the most common journal sources of

(a) Cash	(k) Capital Stock
(b) Marketable Securities	(l) Retained Earnings
(c) Notes Receivable	(m) Sales
(d) Accounts Receivable	(n) Sales Discounts
(e) Allowance for Doubtful Accounts	(o) Purchases
(f) Merchandise Inventory	(p) Freight In
(g) Land and Buildings	(q) Purchase Returns
(h) Accumulated Depreciation	(r) Purchase Discounts
(i) Notes Payabyle	(s) Salaries
(j) Vouchers Payable	(t) Depreciation

debits and credits.

⋆⋆22. How does the closing method differ from the adjusting method for Inventory and related accounts in periodic inventory system?

⋆⋆⋆23. In developing the sales balance, the owner of a business recognizes cash collections from customers and the change in the receivables balance but ignores the write-off of uncollectible accounts. Indicate the effects, if any, that such omissions will have on net income.

   ⋆Relates to Appendix A
  ⋆⋆Relates to Appendix B
 ⋆⋆⋆Relates to Appendix C

Exercises

Exercise 3–1   (Journal entries)

Alaska Supply Company, a merchandising firm, engaged in the following transactions during October 1991. The company records inventory using the perpetual system.

Oct. 1 Sold merchandise on account to the Plough Corporation for $15,000; terms 2/10, n/30, FOB shipping point. Plough paid $200 freight on the goods. The merchandise cost $7,450.

   5 Purchased inventory costing $8,350 on account; terms n/30.

   7 Received payment from Plough for goods shipped October 1.

  15 The payroll paid for the first half of October was $18,000. (Ignore payroll taxes.)

  18 Purchased a machine for $10,400 cash.

  22 Declared a dividend of $.75 per share on 45,000 shares of common stock outstanding.

  27 Purchased building and land for $150,000 in cash and a $250,000 Mortgage payable, due in 30 years. The land was appraised at $150,000 and the building at $350,000.

Record the above transactions in general journal form.

Exercise 3–2   (Adjusting entries)

In analyzing the accounts of Loma Corporation, the adjusting data listed below and on page 104 are determined on December 31, the end of an annual fiscal period.

(a) The prepaid insurance account shows a debit of $3,600, representing the cost of a 2-year fire insurance policy dated July 1.

(b) On September 1, Rent Revenue was credited for $3,750, representing revenue from subrental for a 5-month period beginning on that date.

(c) Purchase of advertising materials for $2,475 during the year was recorded in the advertising expense account. On December 31, advertising materials costing $275 are on hand.

(d) On November 1, $3,000 was paid on rent for a 6-month period beginning on that date. The rent expense account was debited.

(e) Miscellaneous Office Expense was debited for office supplies of $1,350 purchased during the year. On December 31, office supplies of $320 are on hand.

(f) Interest of $352 is accrued on notes payable.

(1) Give the adjusting entry for each item. (2) What sources would provide the information for each adjustment?

Exercise 3–3   (Adjusting and correcting entries)

Upon inspecting the books and records for Beardall Company for the year ended December 31, 1991, you find the following data.

(a) A receivable of $380 from Clarke Realty is determined to be uncollectible. The company maintains an allowance for doubtful accounts for such losses.
(b) A creditor, E.J. Stanley Co., has just been awarded damages of $2,200 as a result of breach of contract during the current year by Beardall Company. Nothing appears on the books in connection with this matter.
(c) A fire destroyed part of a branch office. Furniture and fixtures that cost $10,200 and had a book value of $7,800 at the time of the fire were completely destroyed. The insurance company has agreed to pay $6,500 under the provisions of the fire insurance policy.
(d) Advances of $1,150 to salespersons have been previously recorded as sales salaries expense.
(e) Machinery at the end of the year shows a balance of $18,460. It is discovered that additions to this account during the year totaled $4,460, but of this amount $800 should have been recorded as repairs. Depreciation is to be recorded at 10% on machinery owned throughout the year, but at one half this rate on machinery purchased or sold during the year.

What entries are required to bring the accounts up to date? (Ignore income tax consequences.)

Exercise 3–4   (Adjusting and closing entries)

Accounts of Pioneer Heating Co. at the end of the first year of operations show the balances below. The end-of-the-year physical inventory is $50,000. Prepaid operating expenses are $4,000 and accrued sales commissions payable are $5,900. Investment revenue receivable is $1,000. Depreciation for the year on buildings is $4,500 and on machinery, $5,000. Federal and state income taxes for the year are estimated at $18,100. Give the entries to adjust and close the books, assuming use of an Income Summary account and the adjusting method for inventory.

Cash	$ 39,000	
Investments	50,000	
Land	70,000	
Buildings	180,000	
Machinery	100,000	
Accounts Payable		$ 65,000
Common Stock		320,000
Additional Paid-In Capital		40,000
Sales		590,000
Purchases	280,000	
Sales Commissions	200,000	
General Operating Expenses	101,000	
Investment Revenue		5,000
	$1,020,000	$1,020,000

Exercise 3–5   (Adjusting entries)

The following accounts were taken from the trial balance of Cristy Company as of December 31, 1991. Given the information below, make the necessary adjusting entries.

Sales Revenue	$90,000
Interest Revenue	5,000
Equipment	46,000
Accumulated Depreciation—Equipment	12,000
Beginning Inventory	20,000
Advertising Expense	2,000
Selling Expense	6,000
Interest Expense	1,000

(a) The equipment has an estimated useful life of 5 years and a salvage value of $1,000. Depreciation is calculated using the straight-line method.
(b) Ending inventory is $28,000. The adjusting method for inventory is used.
(c) $1,000 of selling expense has been paid in advance.
(d) Interest of $500 has accrued on notes receivable.
(e) $400 of advertising expense was incorrectly debited to selling expense.

Exercise 3–6   (Adjusting and reversing entries)

On May 16, 1991 Lisa Anderson paid insurance for a 3-year period beginning June 1. She recorded the payment as follows:

Prepaid Insurance	1,224	
Cash		1,224

(1) What adjustment is required on December 31? What reversing entry, if any, would you make?
(2) What nominal account could be debited instead of Prepaid Insurance? What adjusting entry would be needed under these circumstances? What reversing entry, if any, would you make?

Exercise 3–7   (Adjusting entries)

The data listed below were obtained from an analysis of the accounts of Noble Distributor Company as of March 31, 1991, in preparation of the annual report. Noble records current transactions in nominal accounts and *does not* reverse adjusting entries. What are the appropriate adjusting entries?

(a) Prepaid Insurance has a balance of $14,100. Noble has the following policies in force.

Policy	Date	Term	Cost	Coverage
A	1/1/91	2 years	$ 3,600	Shop Equipment
B	12/1/90	6 months	1,800	Delivery Equipment
C	7/1/90	3 years	12,000	Buildings

(b) Unearned Subscription Revenue has a balance of $56,250. The following subscriptions were collected in the current year. There are no other unexpired subscriptions.

Inception	Amount	Term
July 1, 1990	$27,000	1 year
October 1, 1990.......................	22,200	1 year
January 1, 1991	28,800	1 year
April 1, 1991.........................	20,700	1 year

(c) Interest Payable has a balance of $825. Noble owes a 10%, 90-day note for $45,000 dated March 1, 1991.

(d) Supplies has a balance of $2,190. An inventory of supplies revealed a total of $1,410.

(e) Salaries Payable has a balance of $9,750. The payroll for the 5-day workweek ended April 3 totaled $11,250.

Exercise 3–8   (Analyzing adjusting entries)

Computer Consulting Company uses the asset and liability approach in accounting for prepaid expenses and unearned revenues. Selected account balances at the end of the current and prior year are presented below. The company does not make reversing entries, and accrued expenses and revenues are adjusted only at year end.

	Adjusted Balances Dec. 31, 1990	Adjusted Balances Dec. 31, 1991
Prepaid Rent	$ 4,800	$3,600
Salaries and Wages Payable	2,500	4,500
Unearned Consulting Fees	13,000	6,400
Interest Receivable	1,200	1,800

During 1991 Computer Consulting paid $10,000 for rent and $50,000 for wages. $108,000 was received for consulting fees and $2,400 was received as interest.

(1) Provide the entries that were made at December 31, 1991, to adjust the accounts to the year-end balances above.

(2) Determine the proper amount of Rent Expense, Salaries and Wages Expense, Consulting Fees Revenue, and Interest Revenue to be reported on the current year income statement.

Exercise 3–9   (Closing entries)

An accountant for Jolley, Inc., a merchandising enterprise, has just finished posting all the year-end adjusting entries to the ledger accounts and now wishes to close the appropriate account balances in preparation for the new period.

(1) For each of the accounts listed on the next page, indicate whether the year-end balance should be: (a) carried forward to the new period, (b) closed by debiting the account, or (c) closed by crediting the account. Assume Jolley uses a perpetual inventory system.

(a) Cash	25,000	(k) Accounts Payable	12,000
(b) Sales	50,000	(l) Accounts Receivable	140,000
(c) Dividends	3,000	(m) Prepaid Insurance	16,000
(d) Inventory	7,500	(n) Interest Receivable	2,000
(e) Selling Expenses	3,000	(o) Sales Discounts	3,000
(f) Capital Stock	100,000	(p) Interest Revenue	2,000
(g) Income Summary	0	(q) Supplies	8,000
(h) Wages Expense	10,000	(r) Retained Earnings	6,500
(i) Dividends Payable	4,000	(s) Accumulated Depreciation	2,000
(j) Cost of Goods Sold	22,500	(t) Depreciation Expense	1,000

(2) Give the necessary closing entries.

(3) What was Jolley's net income (loss) for the period?

Exercise 3–10   (Closing entries—proprietorship, partnership, and corporation)

Lennon's Tannery shows a credit balance in the Income Summary account of $67,600 after the revenue and expense items have been transferred to this account at the end of the fiscal year. Give the remaining entries to close the books assuming:

(a) The business is a sole proprietorship: the owner, D.H. Lennon, has made withdrawals of $14,000 during the year, and this is reported in a drawing account.

(b) The business is a partnership: the owners, D.H. Lennon and B.L. Oster, share profits 5:3; they have made withdrawals of $25,000 and $16,000 respectively, and these amounts are reported in drawing accounts.

(c) The business is a corporation: the ledger reports Additional Paid-In Capital, $250,000, and Retained Earnings, $100,000; dividends during the year amounting to $32,500 were recorded in a Dividends account.

Exercise 3–11   (Determining income from equity account analysis)

On November 1, the capital of J. Hale was $85,000 and on November 30 the capital was $95,100. During the month, Hale withdrew merchandise costing $5,000 and on November 25 paid a $10,000 note payable of the business with interest at 10% for three months with a check drawn on a personal checking account. What was Hale's net income or loss for the month of November?

Exercise 3–12   (Determining income from equity account analysis)

An analysis of the records of J.L. Kane disclosed changes in account balances for 1991 and the supplementary data listed below. From these data, calculate the net income or loss for 1991.

Cash	3,000 decrease
Accounts receivable	2,000 increase
Inventory	16,000 increase
Accounts payable	4,000 increase

During the year, Kane borrowed $30,000 in notes from the bank and paid off notes of $20,000 and interest of $1,000. Interest of $375 is accrued as of December 31, 1991. There was no interest payable at the end of 1990.

In 1991, Kane also transferred certain marketable securities to the business and these were sold for $8,000 to finance the purchase of merchandise.

Kane made weekly withdrawals in 1991 of $500.

*Exercise 3–13   (Special journals)

Caddy's Inc. uses a general journal, sales journal, cash receipts journal, cash disbursements journal, and a voucher register. For each transaction below, indicate the appropriate journal(s) or register to be used.

(a) Make a credit sale.
(b) Collect cash on an account receivable.
(c) Record bad debt expense.
(d) Write a check for payroll expense.
(e) Purchase materials on account.
(f) Give a discount on a sale.
(g) Sell equipment on credit.
(h) Make a cash sale.
(i) Borrow $3,000 from the bank.
(j) Record adjusting and closing entries.
(k) Pay a supplier with a check.
(l) Record accrued interest payable.
(m) Sell truck for cash.
(n) Record depreciation expense.
(o) Pay back loan.

*Relates to Appendix A

*Exercise 3–14   (Closing method for inventory)

The unadjusted balances for inventory and related accounts for Button-Down Corporation as of December 31, 1991, are as follows:

Inventory—(Beginning)	$26,750
Inventory—(Ending)	32,425
Purchases	59,400
Purchase Discounts	2,650
Freight-In	3,115

(a) Give the necessary adjusting and closing entries for Inventory and related accounts assuming the "closing method" is used.
(b) Determine the amount of Cost of Goods Sold to be reported on the Income Statement.

*Relates to Appendix B

*Exercise 3–15   (Cash to accrual basis)

The following information is taken from the records of Mario's Tune-up Shop:

	Balance Jan. 1 1991	Balance Dec. 31 1991	Transactions During 1991
Accruals:			
Interest receivable	810	975	
Wages payable	1,650	1,725	
Interest payable	1,200	1,425	
Cash receipts and payments:			
Interest on notes receivable			1,860
Wages			96,000
Interest on notes payable			1,395

Compute the interest revenue, the wages expense, and the interest expense for the year 1991.

*Relates to Appendix C

*Exercise 3–16   (Accrual to Cash Basis)

Benito and Fuentes, Inc. reported the following correct account balances, as shown below.

	1/1/91	12/31/91
Prepaid Insurance	$ 6,400	$ 9,200
Prepaid Rent	1,400	1,000
Wages Payable	3,400	2,400
Income Taxes Payable	20,000	22,000

The correct expense amounts as reported on the 1991 income statement that are associated with the above accounts are listed below.

1. Insurance Expense	$ 8,800
2. Rent Expense	4,200
3. Wages Expense	52,000
4. Income Tax Expense	27,000

Determine the amount of cash paid out during the year for each type of expense, (1) through (4).

*Relates to Appendix C

*Exercise 3–17   (Account analysis—gross sales)

Total accounts receivable for the Bako Company were as follows: on January 1, $6,000; on January 31, $6,300. In January, $9,500 was collected on accounts, $600 was received for cash sales, accounts receivable of $700 were written off as uncollectible, and sales allowances of $100 were made. What amount should be reported for gross sales on the income statement for January?

*Relates to Appendix C

*Exercise 3–18   (Comprehensive cash to accrual basis)

The following information for the first quarter of 1991 is obtained from the cash-basis records of Julie Bradford.

	March 31	January 1
Accounts receivable	$26,400	$13,500
Inventory	3,000	11,400
Prepaid operating expense	660	750
Store equipment (net)	9,000	9,750
Accounts payable	7,500	10,500
Operating expenses payable	1,500	810

The cashbook shows the following:

Balance, January 1		$ 4,500
Receipts: Accounts receivable	$10,800	
Investment by Bradford	1,800	12,600
		$17,100
Payments: Accounts payable	$15,600	
Operating expenses	2,100	17,700
Balance, March, 31—bank overdraft		$ (600)

Prepare an accrual-basis income statement for the 3-month period accompanied by schedules in support of revenue and expense balances.
*Relates to Appendix C

Problems

Problem 3–1   (Adjusting and reversing entries)

The trial balance of Kohler's Diamonds shows, among other items, the following balances on December 31, 1990, the end of a fiscal year:

Accounts Receivable	150,000	
9% Century City Bonds	225,000	
Land	275,000	
Buildings	450,000	
Accumulated Depreciation-Buildings		173,250
8% First-Mortgage Bonds Payable		600,000
Rent Revenue		71,500
Office Expense	7,500	

The following facts are ascertained on this date upon inspection of the company's records.

(a) It is estimated that approximately 2% of accounts receivable may prove uncollectible.

(b) Interest is receivable semiannually on the Century City bonds on March 1 and September 1.

(c) Buildings are depreciated at 5% a year; however, there were building additions of $50,000 during the year. The company computes depreciation on asset acquisitions during the year at one half the annual rate.

(d) Interest on the first-mortgage bonds is payable semiannually on February 1 and August 1.

(e) Rent revenue includes $5,100 that was received on November 1, representing rent on part of the buildings for the period November 1, 1990 to October 31, 1991.

(f) Office supplies of $2,000 are on hand at December 31. Purchases of office supplies were debited to the office expense account.

Instructions:

(1) Prepare the journal entries to adjust the books on December 31, 1990.
(2) Give the reversing entries that may be appropriate at the beginning of 1991.

Problem 3–2 (Account classification and debit credit relationship)

Instructions: Using the format provided, for each account identify:

1. Whether the account will appear on a balance sheet (B/S), income statement (I/S), or neither (N);
2. Whether the account is an asset (A), liability (L), owners' equity (OE), revenue (R), expense (E), or other (O);
3. Whether the account is real or nominal;
4. Whether the account will be "closed" or left "open" at year-end; and
5. Whether the account *normally* has a debit (Dr) or a credit (Cr) balance.

Account Title	(1) B/S I/S N	(2) A,L,OE, R,E,O	(3) Real or Nominal	(4) Closed or Open	(5) Debit (Dr) or Credit (Cr)
Example: Cash	B/S	A	Real	Open	Dr

(a) Unearned Rent Revenue
(b) Accounts Receivable
(c) Inventory
(d) Accounts Payable
(e) Prepaid Rent
(f) Mortgage Payable
(g) Sales
(h) Cost of Goods Sold
(i) Dividends
(j) Dividends Payable
(k) Interest Receivable
(l) Wages Expense
(m) Drawings
(n) Supplies
(o) Income Summary
(p) Accumulated Depreciation
(q) Retained Earnings
(r) Discount on Bonds Payable
(s) Goodwill
(t) Additional Paid-In Capital

Problem 3–3 (Adjusting entries)

On December 31, the Philips Company noted the following transactions that occurred during 1991, some or all of which might require adjustment to the books.

(a) Payment to suppliers of $1,200 was made for purchases on account during the year and was not recorded.

(b) Building and land were purchased on January 2 for $175,000. The building's fair market value was $100,000 at the time of purchase. The building is being depreciated over a 20-year life using the straight-line method, and assuming no salvage value.

(c) Of the $34,000 in accounts receivable, 2.5% is estimated to be uncollectible. Currently, the allowance for doubtful accounts shows a debit balance of $290.

(d) On August 1, $25,000 was loaned to a customer on a 6-month note with interest at an annual rate of 12%.

(e) During 1991, Philips received $2,500 in advance for services, 80% of which will be performed in 1992. The $2,500 was credited to sales revenue.

(f) The interest expense account was debited for all interest charges incurred during the year and shows a balance of $1,100. However, of this amount, $300 represents a discount on a 60-day note payable, due January 30, 1992.

Instructions:

(1) Give the necessary adjusting entries to bring the books up to date.
(2) Indicate the net change in income as a result of the foregoing adjustments.

Problem 3—4   (Analysis of adjusting entries)

The accountant for Save More Company made the following adjusting entries on December 31, 1991:

(a) Prepaid Rent	1,200	
Rent Expense		1,200
(b) Advertising Materials	2,000	
Advertising Expense		2,000
(c) Interest Revenue	500	
Unearned Revenue		500
(d) Office Supplies	1,000	
Office Expense		1,000
(e) Prepaid Insurance	1,050	
Insurance Expense		1,050

Further information is provided as follows:

(a) Rent is paid every October 1.
(b) Advertising materials are paid at one time (June 1) and are used evenly throughout the year.
(c) Interest is received every March 1.
(d) Office supplies are purchased every July 1 and used evenly throughout the year.
(e) Yearly insurance premium is payable each August 1.

Instructions: For each adjusting entry, indicate the original transaction entry that was recorded.

Problem 3—5   (Adjusting entries)

The bookkeeper from the Irwin Wholesale Electric Co. prepares no reversing entries and records all revenue and expense items in nominal accounts during the period. The following balances, among others, are listed on the trial balance at the end of the fiscal period, December 31, 1991, before accounts have been adjusted:

	Dr (Cr)
Accounts Receivable	$152,000
Allowance for Doubtful Accounts	(1,000)
Interest Receivable	2,800
Discounts on Notes Payable	300
Prepaid Real Estate and Personal Property Tax	1,800
Salaries and Wages Payable	(4,000)
Discounts on Notes Receivable	(2,800)
Unearned Rent Revenue	(1,500)

Inspection of the company's records reveals the following as of December 31, 1991.

(a) Uncollectible accounts are estimated at 3% of the accounts receivable balance.
(b) The accrued interest on investments totals $2,400.
(c) The company borrows cash by discounting its own notes at the bank. Discounts on notes payable at the end of 1991 are $1,600.
(d) Prepaid real estate and personal property taxes are $1,800, the same as at the end of 1990.
(e) Accrued salaries and wages are $4,300.
(f) The company accepts notes from customers, giving its customers credit for the face of the note less a charge for interest. At the end of each period, any interest applicable to the succeeding period is reported as a discount. Discounts on notes receivable at the end of 1991 are $1,500.
(g) Part of the company's properties had been sublet on September 15, 1990, at a rental of $3,000 per month. The arrangement was terminated at the end of one year.

Instructions: Give the adjusting entries required to bring the books up to date.

▌▌▌ Problem 3—6   (Preparation of work sheet and adjusting and closing entries)

Account balances taken from the ledger of the Builders' Supply Corporation on December 31, 1991, are listed on page 114.
Information relating to adjustments on December 31, 1991, follows:

(a) The inventory on hand is $87,570. Inventory and related accounts are adjusted through Cost of Goods Sold.
(b) The allowance for doubtful accounts is to be increased to a balance of $3,000.
(c) Buildings are depreciated at the rate of 5% per year.
(d) Accrued selling expenses are $3,840.
(e) There are supplies of $780 on hand.
(f) Prepaid insurance relating to 1992 totals $720.
(g) Accrued interest on long-term investments is $240.
(h) Accrued real estate and payroll taxes are $900.
(i) Accrued interest on the mortgage is $480.
(j) Income tax is estimated to be 20% of the income before income tax.

Accounts Payable	$ 35,000	Land	$ 69,600
Accounts Receivable	72,000	Long-Term Investments	15,400
Accumulated Depreciation-		Mortgage Payable	68,800
Buildings	19,800	Office Expense	21,680
Allowance for Doubtful		Purchases	138,480
Accounts	1,380	Purchase Discounts	2,140
Buildings	72,000	Retained Earnings, December	
Capital Stock, $10 par	180,000	31, 1990	14,840
Cash	24,000	Sales	246,000
Dividends	13,400	Sales Discounts	5,400
Freight In	3,600	Sales Returns	4,360
Insurance Expense	1,440	Selling Expense	49,440
Interest Expense	2,640	Supplies Expense	5,200
Interest Revenue	660	Taxes-Real Estate and Payroll	7,980
Inventory, Dec. 31, 1990	62,000		

Instructions:

(1) Prepare a trial balance.
(2) Journalize the adjustments.
(3) Journalize the closing entries.
(4) Prepare a post-closing trial balance.

Although not required, the use of a work sheet is recommended for the solution of this problem.

Problem 3—7   (Closing entries and post-closing trial balance)

Kwon International Corporation
Adjusted Trial Balance
December 31, 1992

Cash	$ 22,500	
Accounts Receivable	24,000	
Allowance for Doubtful Accounts		$ 240
Inventory	45,300	
Equipment	210,000	
Accumulated Depreciation—Equipment		84,000
Accounts Payable		28,000
Notes Payable		80,000
Wages Payable		10,000
Income Taxes Payable		8,900
Common Stock		50,000
Retained Earnings		27,310
Sales Revenue		270,000
Interest Revenue		8,000
Cost of Goods Sold	171,250	
Wages Expense	28,000	
Interest Expense	1,500	
Utilities Expense	5,000	
Depreciation Expense	42,000	
Insurance Expense	2,000	
Advertising Expense	6,000	
Income Tax Expense	8,900	
	$566,450	$566,450

Instructions: Given the adjusted trial balance for Kwon International Corporation:

(1) Journalize the closing entries using an Income Summary account.
(2) Prepare a post-closing trial balance.

*Problem 3—8 (Preparation of work sheet and adjusting, closing, and reversing entries)

The following account balances are taken from the general ledger of the Whitni Corporation on December 31, 1991, the end of its fiscal year. The corporation was organized January 2, 1988.

Cash	$ 40,250
Notes Receivable	16,500
Accounts Receivable	63,000
Allowance for Doubtful Accounts (credit balance)	650
Inventory, January 1, 1991	88,700
Land	80,000
Buildings	247,600
Accumulated Depreciation—Buildings	18,000
Furniture Fixtures	15,000
Accumulated Depreciation—Furniture and Fixtures	9,000
Notes Payable	18,000
Accounts Payable	72,700
Common Stock, $100 par	240,000
Retained Earnings	129,125
Sales	760,000
Sales Returns and Allowances	17,000
Purchases	479,650
Purchase Discounts	7,850
Heat, Light, and Power	16,700
Property Taxes	10,200
Salaries and Wages Expense	89,000
Sales Commissions	73,925
Insurance Expense	18,000
Interest Revenue	2,600
Interest Expense	2,400

Data for adjustments at December 31, 1991, are as follows:

(a) Merchandise inventory; $94,700.
(b) Depreciation (to nearest month for additions):
    Furniture and fixtures, 10%
    Buildings, 4%. Additions to the buildings costing $150,000 were completed June 30, 1991.
(c) The allowance for doubtful accounts is to be increased to a balance of $2,500.
(d) Accrued expenses:
    Sales commissions, $700
    Interest on notes payable, $45
    Property tax, $6,000
(e) Prepaid expenses: insurance, $3,200.
(f) Accrued revenue: interest on notes receivable, $750.
(g) The following information is also to be recorded:

(1) On December 30, the board of directors declared a quarterly dividend of $1.50 per share on common stock, payable January 25, 1992, to stockholders of record January 15, 1992.

(2) Income tax for 1991 is estimated at $15,000.

(3) The only charges to Retained Earnings during the year resulted from the declaration of the regular quarterly dividends.

Instructions: Using either the adjusting method for inventory or the closing method in Appendix B:

(1) Prepare an eight-column work sheet. There should be a pair of columns each for trial balance, adjustments, income statement, and balance sheet.

(2) Prepare all the journal entries necessary to record the effects of the foregoing information and to adjust and close the books of the corporation.

(3) Prepare the reversing entries that may appropriately be made.

*Closing method (Appendix B) is optional for this problem

*Problem 3—9   (Using special journals)

West Mountain Inc., a fruit wholesaler, records business transactions in the following books of original entry: general journal (J); voucher register (VR); check register (CR); sales journal (SJ); and cash receipts journal (CRJ). West Mountain recorded and filed the following business documents:

(a) Sales invoices for sales on account totaling $4,600.

(b) The day's cash register tape showing receipts for cash sales at $700.

(c) A list of cash received on various customers' accounts totaling $2,930. Sales discounts taken were $30.

(d) The telephone bill for $60 payable in one week.

(e) Vendors' invoices for $5,000 worth of fruit received.

(f) Check stub for payment of last week's purchases from All-Growers Farms, $5,940. Terms were 1/10, n/30 and payment was made within the discount period.

(g) Check stub for repayment of a $10,000, 90-day note to Mercantile Bank, $10,300.

(h) A letter notifying West Mountain that Littex Markets, a customer, has declared bankruptcy. All creditors will receive 10 cents on every dollar due. Littex owes West Mountain $1,300.

Instructions:

(1) Indicate the books of original entry in which West Mountain recorded each of the business transactions. (Use the designated abbreviations.)

(2) Record the debits and credits for each entry as though only a general journal were used. Use account titles implied by the voucher system.

*Relates to Appendix A

*Problem 3—10   (Using special journals)

A fire destroyed Fong Company's journals. However, the general ledger and accounts receivable subsidiary ledger were saved. An inspection of the ledgers reveals the following information:

GENERAL LEDGER

Cash (Acct. No. 11)			Sales (Acct. No. 41)		
May 1	Bal. 8,200			May 31	5,050
31	7,338			31	4,500

Sales Discounts (Acct. No. 42)			Accounts Receivable (Acct. No. 12)			
May 3	12		May 1	Bal. 3,100	May 31	2,850
			31	5,050		

ACCOUNTS RECEIVABLE LEDGER

Customer A			Customer B			
May 1	Bal. 290		May 1	Bal. 1,250	May 13	1,000
5	500		5	400		

Customer C			Customer D		
May 2	1,450		May 1	Bal. 1,560	May 11	650

Customer E				
May 2	1,200	May 3	1,200
12	1,500		

Fong's credit policy is 1/10, n/30.

Instructions: Reconstruct the sales and cash receipts journals from the information given.

*Relates to Appendix A

*Problem 3–11   (Cash to Accrual Basis)

Balance sheets for the Fugal Hardware Stores prepared in 1991 report the balances listed on page 118.
An analysis of cash receipts and disbursements discloses the following:

Receipts		Disbursements	
Capital stock	$ 80,000	Trade creditors—notes and	
Trade debtors—notes and		accounts	$210,000
accounts	230,000	Expenses	70,000
Cash sales	65,000	Dividends	40,000
Notes receivable discounted at		Equipment	28,000
bank:		Bonds retired Jan. 2	50,000
Face value, $20,000,			
proceeds	19,500		
12% note issued to bank, dated			
March 31, 1991	30,000		
Sale of investment	25,000		

Assets	June 30	January 1
Cash	$ 84,500	$ 33,000
Notes receivable	21,000	20,000
Accounts receivable	95,000	74,000
Inventory	150,000	160,000
Prepaid expenses	10,000	12,000
Long-term investments (at cost)	10,000	40,000
Buildings and equipment (net)	120,000	100,000
	$490,500	$439,000

Liabilities and Stockholders' Equity		
Notes payable	$ 58,000	$ 75,000
Accounts payable	75,000	60,000
Interest payable	900	—
Expenses payable	3,000	2,000
Bonds payable	—	50,000
Common stock, $100 par	130,000	100,000
Additional paid-in capital	150,000	100,000
Retained earnings	73,600	52,000
	$490,500	$439,000

Instructions:

(1) Prepare an income statement supported by schedules showing computations of revenue and expense balances for the six-month period ended June 30, 1991.

(2) Prove the net income or loss determined in part (1) by preparing a retained earnings statement.

*Relates to Appendix C

*Problem 3–12   (Cash to accrual basis)

The trial balance for Henry Specialty Foods is presented on page 119. This is a calendar-year sole proprietorship, maintaining its books on the cash basis during the year. At year-end, however, Mabel Henry's accountant adjusts the books to the accrual basis for sales, purchases, and cost of sales and records depreciation to more clearly reflect the business income for income tax purposes.

During 1991, Henry signed a new eight-year lease for the store premises and is in the process of negotiating a loan for remodeling purposes. The bank required Henry to present financial statements for 1991 prepared on the accrual basis. During the course of a compilation engagement, Henry's accountant obtained the following additional information.

(a) Amounts due from customers totaled $7,900 at December 31, 1991.

(b) A review of the receivables at December 31, 1991 disclosed that an allowance for doubtful accounts of $1,100 should be provided. Henry had no bad debt losses from inception of the business through December 31, 1991.

(c) Unpaid vendors' invoices for food purchases totaled $9,650 at December 31, 1991.

(d) On signing the new lease on October 1, 1991, Henry paid $8,400 representing one year's rent in advance for the lease year ending October 1,

1992. The $7,500 annual rental under the old lease was paid on October 1, 1990, for the lease year ended October 1, 1991.

(e) On April 1, 1991, Henry paid $2,400 to renew the comprehensive insurance coverage for one year. The premium was $2,160 on the old policy which expired on April 1, 1991.

(f) Depreciation on equipment was computed at $5,800 for 1991.

(g) The inventory amounted to $23,000 at December 31, 1991, based on physical count of goods priced at cost. No reduction to market was required.

(h) Accrued expenses at December 31, 1990, and December 31, 1991, were as follows:

	12/31/90	12/31/91
Payroll taxes	$250	$400
Salaries	375	510
Utilities	275	450

(i) Accrual purchases are closed to Cost of Goods Sold.

Henry Specialty Foods
Trial Balance
December 31, 1991

Cash	$ 18,500	
Accounts Receivable, 12/31/90	4,500	
Inventory, 12/31/90	20,000	
Equipment	35,000	
Accumulated Depreciation, 12/31/90		$ 9,000
Accounts Payable, 12/31/90		5,650
Mabel Henry, Drawings	24,000	
Mabel Henry, Capital, 12/31/90		33,650
Sales		187,000
Purchases	82,700	
Salaries	29,500	
Payroll Taxes	2,900	
Rent	8,400	
Miscellaneous Expense	3,900	
Insurance	2,400	
Utilities	3,500	
	$235,300	$235,300

Instructions:

(1) Prepare a work sheet with the following columns: Cash Basis, Adjustments, and Accrual Basis. Convert the trial balance of Henry Specialty Foods to the accrual basis for the year ended December 31, 1991. Journal entries are not required to support your adjustments.

(2) Prepare the statement of changes in Mabel Henry's capital for the year ended December 31, 1991. (AICPA Adapted)

*Relates to Appendix C.

Chapter 4

Recognition, Measurement, and Reporting of Income

The title of the newspaper article was eye-catching as all good journalism demands: "Income for X Company Up $1.2 Million Over Prior Year." The article stated that, after three years of losses, X Company was reporting a profit. Further down the newspaper column was some additional information about X Company's profit: "The net income figure includes an extraordinary gain of $.8 million and a credit of $.5 million arising from a gain on disposal of discontinued operations, both after income taxes." With this information, the reader is able to put the headline in perspective. While it is true that income was up $1.2 million, it is also true that $1.3 million of unusual gains were recognized during the year. Income from "normal operations" is actually down by $.1 million. As this case demonstrates, there is more to understanding the income reported by a company than just identifying one number.

Importance of Recognizing, Measuring, and Reporting Income

The recognition, measurement, and reporting (display) of business income and its components are considered by many to be the most important tasks of accountants. The users of financial statements who must make decisions regarding their relationship with the company are almost always concerned with a measure of its success in using the resources committed to its operation. Has the activity been profitable? What is the trend of profitability? Is it increasingly profitable, or is there a downward trend? What is the most probable result for future years? Will the company be profitable enough to pay interest on its debt and dividends to its stockholders and still grow at a desired rate? These and other questions all relate to the basic question: what is income?

For many users, only one figure, the "bottom line," is meaningful. They feel uncomfortable trying to analyze additional information. To others, information about the components of income is important and can be used to help predict future income and cash flows. Not only can this information be helpful to a specific user, but it is also of value to the economy. As discussed in Chapter 1, one of the principal tasks facing accountants is to provide information that will assist in allocating scarce resources to the most efficient and effective organizations. If reported income is overstated when compared with the actual underlying situation, a poor allocation will be made. Resources will flow to inefficient entities, while the more efficient entities will suffer due to a lack of resources.

Income figures are also used for purposes other than resource allocation by creditors and investors. Governments, both federal and state, rely heavily on income taxes as a source of their revenues. The income figure used for assessing taxes is based on laws passed by Congress and regulations applied by the IRS and various courts. The income determined for financial reporting, however, is determined by adherence to accounting standards (GAAP) developed by the profession. Thus, the amount of income reported to creditors and investors may not be the same as the income reported for tax purposes. Many items are the same for both types of reporting, but there are some significant differences. Most of these differences relate to the specific purposes Congress has for taxing income. Governments use an income figure as a base to assess taxes, but they must use one that relates closely with the ability of the taxpayer to pay the computed tax. For example, accrual accounting requires companies to defer recognition of revenues that are received before they are earned. Income tax regulations, however, require these unearned revenues to be reported as income as soon as they are received in cash.

This text focuses on principles of accounting that are the supporting foundation for financial accounting and reporting. Income for tax purposes will be discussed, but only as it is used to determine the income tax expense and other tax-related amounts reported in the financial statements.

Income Determination

Although there are varying ways to measure income, all of them share a common basic concept: that income is a return over and above the investment. One of the more widely accepted definitions of income states that it is the amount that an entity could return to its investors and still leave the entity as well-off at the end of the period as it was at the beginning.[1] But what does it mean to be as "well-off," and how can it be measured? Most measurements are based on some concept of capital or ownership maintenance. Two concepts of capital maintenance were considered by the FASB in its conceptual framework: financial capital maintenance and **physical capital maintenance**.

The financial capital maintenance concept assumes that an enterprise has income "only if the dollar amount of an enterprise's net assets (assets − liabilities, or owners' equity) at the end of a period exceeds the dollar amount of net assets at the beginning of the period **after** excluding the

---

[1]Although many economists and accountants have adopted this view, a basic reference is J. R. Hicks' widely accepted book, *Value and Capital,* 2nd edition (Oxford University Press, 1946).

effects of transactions with owners."[2] To illustrate, assume that Kreidler, Inc. had the following assets and liabilities at the beginning and the end of a period:

	Beginning of Period	End of Period
Total assets	$510,000	$560,000
Total liabilities	430,000	390,000
Net assets (owners' equity)	$ 80,000	$170,000

If there were no investments by owners or distributions to owners during the period, income would be $90,000, the amount of the increase in net assets. Assume, however, that owners invested $40,000 in the business and received distributions (dividends) of $15,000. Income for the period would be $65,000, computed as follows:

Net assets, end of period	$170,000
Net assets, beginning of period	80,000
Change (increase) in net assets	$ 90,000
Deduct investment by owners	(40,000)
Add distributions (dividends) to owners	15,000
Income	$ 65,000

Another way of defining capital maintenance is in terms of physical capital maintenance. Under this concept, income occurs "only if the physical productive capacity of the enterprise at the end of a period . . . exceeds the physical productive capacity at the beginning of the same period, also after excluding the effects of transactions with owners."[3] This concept requires that productive assets (inventories, buildings, and equipment) be valued at current cost. Productive capital is maintained only if the current costs of these capital assets are maintained. Thus, if the beginning net assets value of $80,000 in the above example rose to $100,000 by the end of the year because of rising prices, and new investments and dividends were as shown, income would be $45,000 rather than $65,000. The $20,000 difference would be the amount necessary to "maintain physical productive capacity" and would not be part of income.

The Financial Accounting Standards Board considered carefully these two ways of viewing income, and adopted the financial capital maintenance concept as part of its conceptual framework.

Even with the acceptance of the financial capital maintenance concept, the question of how the net asset balance should be valued must be considered. Many suggest that net assets should be measured

[2]*Statement of Financial Accounting Concepts No. 5*, "Recognition and Measurement in Financial Statements of Business Enterprises" (Stamford: Financial Accounting Standards Board 1984) par. 47.

[3]*Ibid.*

at their unexpired historical cost values as is currently being done. Others feel that replacement values or disposal values should be used. Some would include as assets intangible resources, such as human resources, goodwill, and geographical location, that have been attained over time without specifically identified payments. Others feel that only resources that have been acquired in arm's length exchange activities should be included.

Likewise, controversy has developed over the recognition and measurement of liabilities. Should future claims against the entity for items such as pensions, warranties, and deferred income taxes be valued at their discounted values, at their future cash flow values, or eliminated completely from the financial statements until events clearly define the existence of a specific liability? The reported income under the financial maintenance concept will vary widely depending on when and how the assets, liabilities, and changes in the valuation of assets and liabilities are measured.

Comparing the net assets at two points in time, as was done above, yields a single net income figure. However, no detail concerning the components of income is disclosed. To provide this detail, accountants have adopted a transaction approach to measuring income that stresses the direct computation of revenues and expenses. As long as the same measurement method is used, income will be the same under the transaction approach as with a single income computation.

| Transaction Approach to Income Determination | The **transaction approach**, sometimes referred to as the "**matching method**," focuses on business events that affect certain elements of financial statements, namely, revenues, expenses, gains, and losses. Income is measured as the difference between resource inflows (revenues and gains) and outflows (expenses and losses) over a period of time. Definitions for the four income elements were presented in Chapter 2 and are repeated on page 125 as an aid to the following discussion. |

As can be seen from studying these definitions, by defining gains and losses in terms of changes in equity after providing for revenues, expenses, and investments and distributions to the owners, income determined by the transaction approach will be the same income as that determined under financial capital maintenance. However, by identifying intermediate income components, the transaction approach provides detail to assist in predicting future cash flows.

The key problem in recognizing and measuring income using the transaction approach is deciding when an "inflow or other enhancement of assets" has occurred and how to measure the "outflows or other using up of assets." As discussed in Chapter 2, the first issue is identified as "the revenue recognition" problem, and the second issue is identified as the "expense recognition" or "matching" problem.

Component Elements of Income

- **Revenues** are inflows or other enhancements of assets of an entity or settlements of its liabilities (or a combination of both) from delivering or producing goods, rendering services, or other activities that constitute the entity's ongoing major or central operations.
- **Expenses** are outflows or other using up of assets or incurrences of liabilities (or a combination of both) from delivering or producing goods, rendering services, or carrying out other activities that constitute the entity's ongoing major or central operations.
- **Gains** are increases in equity (net assets) from peripheral or incidental transactions of an entity and from all other transactions and other events and circumstances affecting the entity except those that result from revenues or investments by owners.
- **Losses** are decreases in equity (net assets) from peripheral or incidental transactions of an entity and from all other transactions and other events and circumstances affecting the entity except those that result from expenses or distributions to owners.

Source: *Statement of Financial Accounting Concepts No. 6,* "Elements of Financial Statements" (Stamford: Financial Accounting Standards Board, 1985), p. x.

Revenue and Gain Recognition

The transaction approach requires a clear definition of when income elements should be recognized, or recorded, in the financial statements. Under the generally accepted accounting principle of accrual, revenue recognition does not necessarily occur when cash is received. The conceptual framework identifies two factors that should be considered in deciding when revenues and gains should be recognized: **realization** and the **earnings process**. Revenues and gains are generally recognized when:[4]

1. they are realized or realizable and
2. they have been earned through substantial completion of the activities involved in the earnings process.

In order for revenues and gains to be **realized,** inventory or other assets must be exchanged for cash or claims to cash. Revenues are **realizable** when assets held or assets received in an exchange are readily convertible to known amounts of cash or claims to cash. The **earnings process criterion** relates primarily to revenue recognition. Most gains result from transactions and events, such as the sale of land or a patent, that involve no earnings process. Thus, being realized or realizable is of more importance in recognizing gains.

Application of these two criteria to certain industries and companies within these industries has resulted in recognition of revenue at different points in the revenue-producing cycle. This cycle can be a lengthy one. For a manufacturing company, it begins with the development of proposals for a certain product by an individual or by the research and development department and extends through planning, production, sale, collection, and finally expiration of the warranty period. All of these steps are in-

[4]*Statement of Financial Accounting Concepts No. 5,* par. 83.

volved in generating sales revenue. If there is a failure at any step, revenue may be seriously curtailed or even completely eliminated. Yet, there is only one aggregate revenue amount for the entire cycle, the selling price of the product.

For a service company, the revenue-producing cycle begins with an agreement to provide a service and extends through the planning and performance of the service to the collection of the cash and final proof through the passage of time that the service has been adequately performed. With increasing legal actions being taken against professionals, such as doctors and accountants, one could argue that the revenue-producing cycle does not end until the possibility of legal claims for services performed is remote.

Although some accountants have argued for recognizing revenue on a partial basis over these extended production or service periods, the prevailing practice has been to select one point in the cycle that best meets the revenue recognition criteria. Both of these criteria are generally met at the point of sale, which is generally when goods are delivered or services are rendered to customers. Thus, revenue for automobiles sold to dealers by Ford Motor Company will be recognized when the cars are shipped to the dealers. Similarly, Price Waterhouse and Co. will record its revenue from audit and tax work when the services have been performed and billed. In both examples, the earnings process is deemed to be substantially complete, and the cash or receivable from the customer meets the realization criterion. Although the "point-of-sale" practice is the most common revenue recognition point, there are notable variations to this general rule.

1. If products or other assets are readily realizable because they can be sold at reliably determined prices without significant selling effort, revenues may be recognized at the point of completed production. Examples of this situation may occur with certain precious metals and agricultural products that are supported by Government price guarantees. In these situations, the earnings process is considered to be substantially complete when the mining or production of the goods is complete.

2. If a product or service is contracted for in advance, revenue may be recognized as production takes place or as services are performed, especially if the production or performance period extends over more than one fiscal year. The percentage of completion and proportional performance methods of accounting have been developed to recognize revenue at several points in the production or service cycle rather than waiting until the final delivery or performance takes place. This exception to the general point-of-sale rule is necessary if the qualitative characteristics of relevance and representational faithfulness are to be met. Construction contracts for buildings, roads, and dams and contracts for scientific research are examples of situations where these methods of revenue recognition occur. In all cases where this revenue recognition variation is employed, a firm, enforceable contract must exist to meet

the realizability criterion, and an objective measure of progress toward completion must be attainable.

3. If collectibility of assets received for products or services is considered doubtful, revenues and gains may be recognized as the cash is received. Although the earnings process has been substantially completed, the questionable receivable fails to meet the realization criterion. The installment sales and cost recovery methods of accounting have been developed to recognize revenue under these conditions. Sales of real estate, especially speculative recreational property, are often recorded using this variation of the general rule.

The general point-of-sale rule will be assumed unless specifically stated otherwise. The variations introduced above are discussed fully in a later chapter.

Expense and Loss Recognition

In order to determine income, not only must criteria for revenue recognition be established, but the principles for recognizing expenses and losses must be clearly defined. Some expenses are directly associated with revenues and can thus be recognized in the same period as the related revenues. Other expenses are not associated with specific revenues and are recognized in the time period when paid or incurred. Still other expenditures are not recognized currently as expenses because they relate to future revenues and, therefore, are reported as assets. Expense recognition, then, can be divided into three categories: (1) direct matching, (2) immediate recognition, and (3) systematic and rational allocation.

Direct Matching Relating expenses to specific revenues is often referred to as the "matching" process. For example, the cost of goods sold is clearly a direct expense that can be matched with the revenues produced by the sale of goods and reported in the same time period as the revenues are recognized. Similarly, shipping costs and sales commissions usually relate directly to revenues.[5]

Direct expenses include not only those that have already been incurred, but should also include anticipated expenses related to revenues of the current period. After delivery of goods to customers, there are still costs of collection, bad debt losses from uncollectible receivables, and possible warranty costs for product deficiencies. These expenses are directly related to revenues and should be estimated and matched against recognized revenues for the period.

Immediate Recognition Many expenses are not related to specific revenues, but are incurred to obtain goods and services which indirectly help to generate revenues. Because these goods and services are used almost immediately, their costs are recognized as expenses in the period of acquisition.

[5]*Statement of Financial Accounting Concepts No. 6,* par. 144.

Examples include most administrative costs, such as office salaries, utilities, and general advertising and selling expenses.

Immediate recognition is also appropriate when future benefits are highly uncertain. For example, expenditures for research and development may provide significant future benefits, but they are usually so uncertain that the costs are written off in the period in which they are incurred.

Most losses also fit in the immediate recognition category. Because they arise from peripheral or incidental transactions, they do not relate directly to revenues. Examples include losses from disposition of used equipment, losses from natural catastrophes such as earthquakes or tornadoes, and losses from disposition of investments.

Systematic and Rational Allocation   The third general expense recognition category involves assets that benefit more than one accounting period. The cost of assets such as buildings, equipment, patents, and prepaid insurance are spread across the periods of expected benefit in some systematic and rational way. Generally, it is difficult if not impossible to relate these expenses directly to specific revenues or to specific periods, but it is clear that they are necessary if the revenue is to be earned. Examples of expenses that are included in this category are depreciation and amortization.

The methods adopted for recognizing expenses and losses should appear reasonable to an unbiased observer and should be followed consistently unless the underlying conditions surrounding the asset change. Some expenses are related to the goods being produced, and thus may be deferred in inventory values if the goods are unsold at the end of an accounting period. Examples include depreciation on production machinery and plant insurance. Other expenses are related to periods, and are allocated directly as an expense of the immediate time period. Examples include depreciation of delivery trucks and amortization of bond discount.[6]

Changes in Estimates

In reporting periodic revenues and in attempting to properly match those expenses incurred to generate current period revenues, accountants must continually make judgments. The numbers reported in the financial statements reflect these judgments and are based on estimates of such factors as the number of years of useful life for depreciable assets, the amount of uncollectible accounts expected, or the amount of warranty liability to be recorded on the books. These and other estimates are made using the best available information at the statement date. However, conditions may change subsequently, and the estimates may need to be revised. Naturally, if either revenue or expense amounts are changed, the income statement is affected. The question is whether the previously reported income measures should be revised or whether the changes should impact only on current and future periods.

[6]*Ibid.*, par. 147.

The Accounting Principles Board stated in Opinion No. 20 that changes in estimates should be reflected in the current period (the period in which the estimate is revised) and in future periods, if any, that are affected. No retroactive adjustments are to be made for a change in estimate.[7] These changes are considered a normal part of the accounting process and not errors made in past periods. For example, Murphy Oil Corporation extended the life of its offshore drilling barges from 12 to 16 years. Extending the life increased net income by $13.6 million or $.37 a share in the year of the change.

To illustrate the computations for a change in estimate, assume that Springville Manufacturing Inc. purchased a milling machine at a cost of $100,000. At the time of purchase, it was estimated that the machine would have a useful life of 10 years and no salvage value. Assuming the straight-line method is used, the depreciation expense is $10,000 per year ($100,000 ÷ 10). At the beginning of the fifth year, however, conditions indicated that the machine would only be used for 3 more years. Depreciation expense in the fifth, sixth, and seventh years should reflect the revised estimate, but depreciation expense recorded in the first four years would not be affected. Since the book value at the end of four years is $60,000 ($100,000 − $40,000 accumulated depreciation), annual depreciation charges for the remaining 3 years of estimated life would be $20,000 ($60,000 ÷ 3). The following schedule summarizes the depreciation charges over the life of the asset.

Year	Depreciation
1	$ 10,000
2	10,000
3	10,000
4	10,000
5	20,000
6	20,000
7	20,000
	$100,000

Effects of Changing Prices

The preceding presentation of revenue and expense recognition has not addressed the question of how, if at all, changing prices are to be recognized under the transaction approach. As indicated in Chapter 2, accountants have traditionally ignored this phenomenon, especially when gains would result from recognition. When an economy experiences high rates of inflation, users of financial statements become concerned that the statements do not reflect the impact of these changing prices. When the inflation rates are lower, this user concern decreases.

The Financial Accounting Standards Board in Statement No. 33 required certain large publicly held companies to disclose selected informa-

[7]Opinions of the Accounting Principles Board No. 20, "Accounting Changes" (New York: American Institute of Certified Public Accountants, 1971), par. 31.

tion about price changes on a supplemental basis. The Board did not require this recognition to be reported in the basic financial statements, but in a supplemental note to the financial statements that did not have to be audited. Subsequently, some of the disclosure requirements were eliminated in Statement No. 82, and all price-level disclosures were made voluntary in Statement No. 89.

Generally accepted accounting principles are still based primarily on historical exchange prices, and the transaction approach to income determination recognizes price changes only when losses in value are indicated.

Reporting of Income

After recognition and measurement criteria are established, the manner in which income is to be reported (displayed) must be determined. Although GAAP requires disclosure of many specific items of information, there is no standardized form of the income statement or other general-purpose financial statements. The reporting of income thus raises many questions regarding, for example, the format of the income statement, terminology used to describe the items presented, the level of detail in the statement, and income-related disclosures to be presented in notes to the financial statements. In answering these and other questions regarding the reporting of income, the overriding consideration should be the usefulness of the information for decision making.

In the following sections, current practices in reporting income will be examined and illustrated. Subsequently, the implications of the FASB's conceptual framework for future reporting practices will be considered.

Form of the Income Statement

The income statement traditionally has been prepared in either single-step or multiple-step form. Under the **single-step form,** all revenues and gains that are identified as operating items are placed first on the income statement followed by all expenses and losses that are identified as operating items. The difference between total revenues and total expenses represents income from operations. If there are no nonoperating, irregular, or extraordinary items, this difference is also equal to net income. The income statement for The Procter & Gamble Company, reproduced on page 131, illustrates the single-step form. Note that income taxes are reported separately from other expenses, which is a common variation of the basic single-step form.

Under the **multiple-step form,** the income statement is divided into separate sections (referred to as intermediate components in Concepts Statement No. 5), and various subtotals are reported that reflect different levels of profitability. Some of the sections, especially those reported *after* operating income, are specified by FASB pronouncements. Others have become standardized by wide usage. The income statement of the Coca-Cola Company, reproduced on page 132, illustrates one form of a multiple-step income statement. Since the FASB has chosen not to be too specific

---

Exhibit 4—1   Procter & Gamble Company and Subsidiaries

The Procter & Gamble Company   **Consolidated Statement Of Earnings**
And Subsidiaries

Millions of Dollars Except Per Share Amounts	Years Ended June 30	**1988**	1987	1986
INCOME	Net sales	**$19,336**	$17,000	$15,439
	Interest and other income	**155**	163	127
		19,491	17,163	15,566
COST AND EXPENSES	Cost of products sold	**11,880**	10,411	9,829
	Marketing, administrative, and other expenses	**5,660**	4,977	4,305
	Interest expense	**321**	353	257
	Provision for restructuring	**—**	805	—
		17,861	16,546	14,391
EARNINGS BEFORE INCOME TAXES		**1,630**	617	1,175
INCOME TAXES		**610**	290	466
NET EARNINGS		**$ 1,020**	$ 327	$ 709
Per Common Share	Net earnings	**$5.96**	$1.87	$4.20
	Dividends	**$2.75**	$2.70	$2.625

Average shares outstanding (in millions): 1988—169.3 1987—168.6 1986—167.8

See accompanying Notes To Consolidated Financial Statements.

about display, it is understandable that wide variations of reporting can be found in practice.

A multiple-step income statement for the Suhaka Corporation, a hypothetical company, is illustrated on page 133. It will be referred to in discussing the content of a multiple-step income statement. To comply with SEC requirements, income statements are usually presented in comparative form for three years. To simplify the illustration, only one year is presented. The illustrated income statement contains more detail than is usually found in actual published financial statements. It has become common practice to issue highly condensed statements, with details and supporting schedules provided in notes to the statements. The potential problem with

Exhibit 4—2   The Coca-Cola Company and Subsidiaries

Consolidated Statements of Income (In thousands except per share data)   *The Coca-Cola Company and Subsidiaries*

Year Ended December 31,	1987	1986	1985
		(Restated)	*(Restated)*
NET OPERATING REVENUES	$7,658,341	$6,976,558	$5,879,160
Cost of goods	3,633,159	3,453,891	2,909,496
GROSS PROFIT	4,025,182	3,522,667	2,969,664
Selling, administrative and general expenses	2,665,022	2,445,602	2,162,991
Provisions for restructured operations and disinvestment	36,370	180,000	—
OPERATING INCOME	1,323,790	897,065	806,673
Interest income	207,164	139,348	144,648
Interest expense	279,012	196,778	189,808
Equity income	118,533	155,804	164,385
Other income—net	34	33,014	66,524
Gain on sale of stock by former subsidiaries	39,654	375,000	—
INCOME FROM CONTINUING OPERATIONS BEFORE INCOME TAXES	1,410,163	1,403,453	992,422
Income taxes	494,027	469,106	314,856
INCOME FROM CONTINUING OPERATIONS	916,136	934,347	677,566
Income from discontinued operations (net of applicable income taxes of $7,870)	—	—	9,000
Gain on disposal of discontinued operations (net of applicable income taxes of $20,252)	—	—	35,733
NET INCOME	$ 916,136	$ 934,347	$ 722,299
PER SHARE			
Continuing operations	$ 2.43	$ 2.42	$ 1.72
Discontinued operations	—	—	.12
Net income	$ 2.43	$ 2.42	$ 1.84
AVERAGE SHARES OUTSTANDING	377,372	386,831	393,354

this practice is that the condensed statements may not provide as much predictive and feedback value as statements that provide more detail about the components of income directly on the statement.

Content of a Multiple-Step Income Statement

The Suhaka Corporation Income Statement has two major categories of income and nine separate sections as follows:

I. Income from continuing operations:
  1. Net sales
  2. Cost of goods sold

Suhaka Corporation
Income Statement
For Year Ended December 31, 1991

Revenue from net sales:			
Sales		$800,000	
Less: Sales returns and allowances	$ 12,000		
Sales discounts	8,000	20,000	$780,000
Cost of goods sold:			
Beginning inventory		$125,000	
Net purchases	$430,000		
Freight in	32,000	462,000	
Cost of goods available for sale		$587,000	
Less ending inventory		96,000	491,000
Gross profit on sales			$289,000
Operating expenses:			
Selling expenses:			
Sales salaries	$ 46,000		
Advertising expense	27,000		
Miscellaneous selling expenses	12,000	$ 85,000	
General and administrative expenses:			
Officers' and office salaries	$ 62,000		
Taxes and insurance	26,500		
Depreciation expense	12,000		
Doubtful accounts expense	8,600		
Miscellaneous general expense	9,200	118,300	203,300
Operating income			$ 85,700
Other revenues and gains:			
Interest revenue		$ 8,750	
Gain on sale of investment		37,000	45,750
Other expenses and losses:			
Interest expense		$ (5,200)	
Loss from fire		(14,300)	(19,500)
Income from continuing operations before income taxes			$111,950
Income taxes			44,780
Income from continuing operations			$ 67,170
Discontinued operations:			
Loss from operations of discontinued business segment (net of income tax savings of $14,000)		$(21,000)	
Loss on disposal of business segment (net of income tax savings of $6,400)		(9,600)	(30,600)
Extraordinary gain from early debt extinguishment (net of income taxes of $10,160)			15,240
Cumulative effect of changing inventory method (net of income tax savings of $3,000)			(4,500)
Net income			$ 47,310
Earnings per common share:			
Income from continuing operations			$ 1.34
Discontinued operations			−0.61
Extraordinary gain			0.31
Cumulative effect of accounting change			−0.09
Net income			$ 0.95

3. Operating expenses
4. Other revenues and gains
5. Other expenses and losses
6. Income taxes on continuing operations

II. Irregular or extraordinary items:
7. Discontinued operations
8. Extraordinary items
9. Cumulative effects of changes in accounting principles

There are several important points about this classification. Only one income tax amount is reported for all items included in the income from continuing operations category; it is presented as the last section in the category. In contrast, each item in the irregular or extraordinary items category is reported net of its income tax effect, referred to as "net of tax." This separation of income tax expense into different sections of the income statement is referred to as "intraperiod income tax allocation."

The various types of gains and losses are not reported entirely in one section of the statement. Some are reported as part of income from continuing operations, and others are included in irregular or extraordinary items. If a gain or loss is considered part of the ongoing operations of the company, and if its measurement is not too uncertain, it should be included in the continuing operations category. If a gain or loss relates to operations, but is too irregular to classify with the normal recurring items, it is reported separately in the second category. In addition, some gains and losses have been identified by the FASB as not affecting the income statement at all, but are recorded as direct adjustments to owners' equity. In this category are certain foreign currency translation adjustments and market value declines in long-term securities.

Regardless of where gains and losses are reported, they are usually presented as a net figure, i.e., the difference between gross sales price and cost. This, of course, differs from operating revenues and expenses that are usually reported separately at their gross amounts.

Although the FASB has been very specific about how the irregular and extraordinary items should be displayed, the Board has said little about the display of income from operations. The Suhaka Company illustration, although more detailed than most published statements, demonstrates the use of operating income categories commonly found in practice. As the concepts in the Conceptual Framework project are incorporated into the accounting standards, some increased standardization of an operating income format is likely.

A review of the multiple-step income statement discloses several subtotals, especially in the operating category. These subtotals are identified as follows:

1. Gross profit (Net sales—Cost of goods sold)
2. Operating income (#1—Operating expenses)

3. Income from continuing operations before income tax (#2 + Other revenues and gains − Other expenses and losses)
4. Income from continuing operations (#3 − income tax)
5. Net income (#4 + or − irregular and extraordinary items)

Each of the nine major sections and related subtotals will be discussed separately as a way to better understand current practices in reporting income.

Net Sales

Revenue from net sales reports the total sales to customers for the period. This total should not include additions to billings for sales and excise taxes that the business is required to collect on behalf of the government. These billing increases are properly recognized as current liabilities. Sales returns and allowances and sales discounts should be subtracted from gross sales in arriving at net sales revenue. When the sales price is increased to cover the cost of freight to the customer and the customer is billed accordingly, freight charges paid by the company should also be subtracted from sales in arriving at net sales. Freight charges not passed to the buyer are recognized as selling expenses.

Cost of Goods Sold

In any merchandising or manufacturing enterprise, the cost of goods relating to sales of the period must be determined. As illustrated in the Suhaka Corporation income statement, **cost of goods available for sale** is first determined. This is the sum of the beginning inventory, net purchases, and all other buying, freight, and storage costs relating to the acquisition of goods. The net purchases balance is developed by subtracting purchase returns and allowances and purchase discounts from gross purchases. Cost of goods sold is then calculated by subtracting the ending inventory from the cost of goods available for sale.

When the goods are manufactured by the seller, additional elements enter into the cost of goods sold. Besides material costs, a company incurs labor and overhead costs to convert the material from its raw material state to a finished good. A manufacturing company has three inventories rather than one: raw materials, goods in process, and finished goods. The Suhaka Corporation is a merchandising company. The cost of goods sold for a manufacturing company is illustrated in Chapter 9.

Operating Expenses

Operating expenses may be reported in two parts: (1) selling expenses and (2) general and administrative expenses. **Selling expenses** include such items as sales salaries and commissions and related payroll taxes, advertising and store displays, store supplies used, depreciation of store furniture and equipment, and delivery expenses. **General and administrative expenses** include officers' and office salaries and related payroll taxes, office supplies used, depreciation of office furniture and fixtures, telephone, postage, business licenses and fees, legal and accounting services, contributions, and similar items. For manufacturing companies, charges related jointly to both production and administrative functions should be allocated in some equitable manner between manufacturing overhead and operating expenses.

Other Revenues and Gains

This section usually includes items identified with the peripheral activities of the company. Examples include revenue from financial activities, such as rents, interest, and dividends, and gains from the sale of assets such as equipment or investments.

Other Expenses and Losses

This section is parallel to the previous one, but results in deductions from, rather than increases to, operating income. Examples include interest expense, bond discount amortization, and losses from the sale of assets.

Income Tax on Continuing Operations

As explained earlier in this chapter, total income tax expense for a period is allocated to various components of income. One amount is computed for income from continuing operations, and separate computations are made for any irregular or extraordinary items. In the Suhaka illustration, an income tax rate of 40% was assumed. Thus, the amount of income tax related to continuing operations is $44,780 ($111,950 × .40).

The same tax rate is applied to all income components in the Suhaka illustration. In practice, however, intraperiod income tax allocation may involve different rates for different components of income. This results from graduated tax rates and special or alternative rates for certain types of gains and losses.

Discontinued Operations

An increasingly common irregular item involves the disposition of a major segment of a business either through sale or abandonment. In 1986, 102 of the 600 surveyed companies in *Accounting Trends and Techniques* reported discontinued operations in their statements. The segment of the company disposed of may be a product line, a division, or a subsidiary company. To qualify as discontinued operations for reporting purposes, the assets and related activities of the segment must be clearly distinguishable from other assets, operating results, and general activities of the company, both physically and operationally, as well as for financial reporting purposes. For example, closing down one plant of three making the same product, eliminating *part* of a product line, or shifting the production or marketing functions from one location to another would not be classified as discontinued operations.

There are many reasons why management may decide to dispose of a segment. For example:

1. The segment may be unprofitable.
2. The segment may be too isolated geographically.
3. The segment may not fit into the long-range plans for the company.
4. Management may need funds to reduce long-term debt or to expand into other areas.
5. Management may be fearful of a corporate take-over by new investors desiring to gain control of the company.

In the 1980's, management of many companies adopted anti-takeover strategies to try to protect their companies. One of the more popular techniques was to sell peripheral operational segments, especially unprofitable ones, that had been acquired during earlier conglomerate years, and to consolidate the company around its principal business operations. One of the companies that did this was General Mills, Inc., which adopted a massive restructuring plan in 1985. The plan involved the disposal of various non-food business segments and streamlining of its consumer food and restaurant operations. The 1988 financial statements, reproduced in Appendix A at the end of the text, reflect the disposition of General Mills' specialty retailing and furniture segments as part of the restructuring (see Note Two).

Many successful takeovers are financed by financial institutions willing to lend billions of dollars to support the buyout of current stockholders. After the new management assumes control of the company, a common strategy is to sell parts of the company to reduce the debt incurred in the takeover. For example, Allied Corporation purchased Bendix Corporation, a $4.1 billion (revenues) automotive parts, aerospace, and machine tool conglomerate. Within two years, Allied liquidated a machine tool company, an earthmoving machine business, and a large pipe-bending business. Similarly, in 1985 W. R. Grace & Co. purchased a 26% interest in a West German group and then made plans to sell over $1 billion of assets, including its retail operations that included sporting goods, home centers, and western wear.[8]

Regardless of the reason, the discontinuance of a substantial portion of company operations is a significant event. Therefore, information about discontinued operations should be presented explicitly to readers of financial statements.

Reporting Requirements for Discontinued Operations

When a company discontinues operating a segment of its business, future comparability requires that all elements that relate to the discontinued operation be identified and separated from continuing operations. Thus, in

---

[8]"W. R. Grace Plans Asset Sales in 1986 Totaling $1 Billion," *Wall Street Journal*, February 12, 1986, p. 33.

the Suhaka income statement illustrated on page 133, the first category after Income from Continuing Operations is Discontinued Operations. The category is further separated into two subdivisions: (1) the current year income or loss from operating the discontinued segment, or a $21,000 loss, and (2) disclosure of the gain or loss on the actual disposal of the business segment, or a further $9,600 loss.

As previously indicated, the irregular items are all reported net of their respective tax effects. If the item is a gain, it is reduced by the tax on the gain. If the item is a loss, it is deductible against other income and thus its existence *saves* income taxes. The overall company loss can thus be reduced by the tax savings arising from being able to deduct the loss from otherwise taxable income.

The income statement for the Suhaka Corporation on page 133 discloses both of these subdivisions. The income tax rate is 40% on all items. Analysis of the income statement shows that Suhaka had an operating loss for the current year of $35,000, but that after a tax savings of $14,000 was deducted, only $21,000 is reported as a loss. The second item discloses that the segment was sold and a loss of $16,000 was experienced on the sale. Application of the income tax rate of 40% reduces this loss to $9,600. If comparative statements are prepared, the same separation between continued and discontinued operations for prior years should be made.

Often a company will decide on a particular date (the **measurement date**) to dispose of a business segment, but will have a phase-out period between that date and the date the segment is actually sold (**disposal date**). The gain or loss on disposal will include any income or loss from operating the segment during the phase-out period. To illustrate using the income statement on page 133, assume Suhaka Corporation decided on July 1, 1991 to phase out a segment of its operation. This date is the measurement date and marks the beginning of the phase-out period.

In computing the gain or loss from disposal of the segment, any operating income or loss during the phase-out period should be included in the gain or loss computation. Thus, the $9,600 loss on disposal reflects both the operating results during phase out and the gain or loss on final disposal, net of income taxes. The $21,000 loss represents the operating loss (net of income tax savings of $14,000) for the period January 1, 1991, to July 1, 1991.

Further disclosure of discontinued operations can be made in notes to the statements. For example, the note supporting a $140 million gain from discontinued operations for American Express Company is reproduced on page 139.

The reporting requirements for discontinued operations are contained in APB Opinion No. 30, "Reporting the Results of Operations."[9] The reporting of discontinued operations can become complex, and only a summary of the guidelines provided by APB Opinion No. 30 is covered here. Application of the guidelines requires judgment. The goal should be to

[9]*Opinions of the Accounting Principles Board No. 30*, "Reporting the Results of Operations" (New York: American Institute of Certified Public Accountants, 1973), par. 20.

report information that will assist external users in assessing future cash flows by clearly distinguishing normal, recurring earnings patterns from those activities that are irregular yet significant in assessing the total company results of operations.

Exhibit 4–3   American Express Company

---

3 • Discontinued Operations and Dispositions

In February 1986, the Company completed the sale of its 50 percent interest in Warner Amex Cable Communications Inc. (Warner Amex) to Warner Communications Inc. for $450 million in cash and the assumption of Warner Amex's debt, pursuant to an agreement reached in August 1985, at which time the Company ceased recording its 50 percent share of Warner Amex's results. Upon the consummation of the Warner Amex sale, the Company recognized a net gain of approximately $140 million ($208 million pretax). Corporate charges of $80 million, after taxes, which included expenses to develop new business opportunities and the Company's contribution of its common stock to an employee stock ownership plan, offset this gain in part.

The above gain, as well as the Company's 50 percent share of Warner Amex's operating results prior to August 1985, is recorded in discontinued operations in the accompanying consolidated financial statements and in the notes.

Extraordinary Items

According to APB Opinion No. 30, **extraordinary items** are events and transactions that are both **unusual in nature and infrequent in occurrence.** Thus, to qualify as extraordinary, an item must "possess a high degree of abnormality and be of a type clearly unrelated to, or only incidentally related to, the ordinary and typical activities of the entity . . . (and) be of a type that would not reasonably be expected to recur in the foreseeable future . . ."[10]

The intent of the Accounting Principles Board was to restrict the items that could be classified as extraordinary. The presumption of the Board was that an item should be considered ordinary and part of the company's usual activity unless evidence clearly supported its classification as an extraordinary item. The Board offered certain examples of gains and losses that should *not* be reported as extraordinary items. They include:

1. The write-down or write-off of receivables, inventories, equipment leased to others, or intangible assets.

[10]*Ibid.*, par. 20.

2. The gains or losses from exchanges or translation of foreign currencies, including those relating to major devaluations and revaluations.
3. The gains or losses on disposal of a segment of a business.
4. Other gains or losses from sale or abandonment of property, plant, or equipment used in the business.
5. The effects of a strike.
6. The adjustment of accruals on long-term contracts.

The standard-setting bodies have identified only one major item as extraordinary regardless of whether it meets the dual criteria: gains and losses from debt extinguishment.[11] Since 1980, an increasing number of companies have been reporting extraordinary items. *Accounting Trends and Techniques* reports that of the 600 companies analyzed for its publication, 107 reported extraordinary items in 1986 as compared with 47 in 1980.[12] Besides early extinguishment of debt, companies reported as extraordinary items litigation settlements, write-off of assets in foreign countries where expropriation risks were high, and pension plan terminations.

Some items may not meet both criteria for extraordinary items, but may meet one of them. Although these items do not qualify as extraordinary, they should be disclosed separately as part of income from continuing operations, either before or after operating income. Examples of these items include strike-related costs, obsolete inventory write-downs, and gains and losses from liquidation of investments. Because these items appear before income from operations, they are not adjusted for their income tax effects. Georgia-Pacific Corporation reported unusual items arising from liquidation of an investment in a chemical subsidiary. A partial income statement for Georgia-Pacific and the note describing the unusual items are presented on page 141.

Cumulative Effects of Changes in Accounting Principles

The last item included in the irregular category of the income statement is the effect of changing accounting principles. Although the profession has recognized the desirability of consistency in application of accounting principles, there are occasions where conditions justify a change from one principle to another. Sometimes this condition arises because the standard-setting body issues a new pronouncement requiring a change in principle. If GAAP is to be followed, the company has no choice but to change to conform with the new standard. Sometimes economic conditions change, and a company changes accounting principles so that reporting can be more representative of the actual conditions. For example, when there was double-digit inflation during the late 1970's many companies changed their

---

[11]*Statement of Financial Accounting Standards No. 4*, "Reporting Gains and Losses from Extinguishment of Debt" (Stamford: Financial Accounting Standards Board, 1975).

[12]*Accounting Trends and Techniques—1987* (New York: American Institute of Certified Public Accountants, 1987), p. 322, and *Accounting Trends and Techniques—1984* (New York: American Institute of Certified Public Accountants, 1984), p. 303.

Exhibit 4—4   Georgia-Pacific Corporation and Subsidiaries

Statements of Income

Georgia-Pacific Corporation and Subsidiaries

(Millions, except per share amounts) Year ended December 31	**1987**	1986	1985
Net sales	**$8,603**	$7,223	$6,716
Costs and expenses			
Cost of sales	**6,777**	5,783	5,553
Selling, general and administrative	**583**	511	431
Depreciation and depletion	**387**	339	310
Interest	**124**	138	132
	7,871	6,771	6,426
Income from continuing operations before unusual items, income taxes and extraordinary item	**732**	452	290
Unusual items	**66**	33	19
Income from continuing operations before income taxes and extraordinary item	**798**	485	309
Provision for income taxes	**340**	189	102
Income from continuing operations before extraordinary item	**458**	296	207
(Loss) on disposal of discontinued operations, net of taxes	**—**	—	(30)
Income before extraordinary item	**458**	296	177
Settlement of condemnation suit, net of taxes	**—**	—	10
Net income	**$ 458**	$ 296	$ 187

Note 2. Unusual Items

The Corporation realized certain gains during the last three years which are considered to be unusual items:

(Millions) Year ended December 31	**1987**	1986	1985
Liquidation of investments	**$66**	$33	$ —
Sale of timberlands	**—**	—	19
	$66	$33	$19

During the first and second quarters of 1987, the Corporation received cash proceeds of $82 million and recorded a pre-tax gain of $66 million from the liquidation of its remaining $16 million investment in preferred stock and warrants of Georgia Gulf Corporation, purchaser of the Corporation's commodity chemicals subsidiary in 1984.

In the 1986 fourth quarter, the Corporation received cash proceeds of $92 million and recorded a pre-tax gain of $33 million from the liquidation of portions of its investment in Georgia Gulf Corporation.

The Corporation has completed an agreement with an unrelated third party to sell or exchange approximately 134,000 acres of Oregon timberlands. A pre-tax gain of $19 million was recorded in 1985 from the sale of a portion of the timberlands under this agreement.

inventory methods to LIFO to reduce their income and thus reduce the actual cash payments for income taxes.

When a change in accounting principle occurs, management may have the option of deciding to reflect the new principle retroactively or only in the current and future periods. If the change arises because of a new FASB standard, the Board designates how the change must be implemented. If the change is made at management's discretion, however, the implementation decision is made by management. For example, a company may decide to change its depreciation method from straight-line to declining balance for only new acquisitions. Under this condition, no special accounting entries are required in the period of the accounting change. If, however, the company decides to apply the new depreciation method to all existing assets, an entry is needed in the current year to adjust the statements for the cumulative effect of the change. The Board has recognized two different ways to adjust current statements to reflect a change in accounting principle. (1) Generally, income statements should report the cumulative effect of the change in the current year with no restatement of prior years' figures. (2) Special cases require the restatement of financial statements for all prior years. In these special cases, the beginning balance of retained earnings for the current year reflects the cumulative effect of the prior years' changes. As with discontinued operations and extraordinary items, the adjustment in either case should be net of income taxes.

In the income statement on page 133, the Suhaka Corporation recorded a $4,500 cumulative loss due to changing inventory principles as the last of the irregular or extraordinary items. The pretax loss to Suhaka was $7,500, but income tax savings reduced the reported loss by $3,000.

If Suhaka Corporation had followed the other method of reporting the cumulative effects of the change in accounting principles, there would have been no adjustment to income; instead, the loss would have been recorded as a charge directly to Retained Earnings. The Accounting Principles Board specified different criteria to help accountants determine which approach should be applied under what circumstances. Further discussion of these criteria is included in a later chapter.

To illustrate the reporting of accounting changes, a partial income statement and pertinent note describing an accounting change by Ingersoll Rand Corp. are included on page 143.

Earnings per Share

In 1969, the Accounting Principles Board issued Opinion No. 15 that required all companies to include a section in the income statement converting certain income components to earnings per share. Separate earnings-per-share amounts are computed by dividing income from continuing operations and each irregular or extraordinary item by the weighted

Exhibit 4–5   Ingersoll-Rand Corp.

Consolidated Statement of Income

In thousands except per share amounts
For the years ended December 31

	1987	1986	1985
Earnings before income taxes, extraordinary item and cumulative effect of accounting change	**161,136**	154,334	132,681
Provision for income taxes	**53,200**	53,700	53,100
Earnings before extraordinary item and cumulative effect of accounting change	**107,936**	100,634	79,581
Extraordinary item–(net of income tax benefit of $5,673)	**—**	(6,660)	—
Cumulative effect of accounting change– (net of income tax provision of $9,004)	**9,755**	—	—
Net earnings	**$ 117,691**	$ 93,974	$ 79,581

Notes to Consolidated Financial Statements

Accounting Changes: Effective January 1, 1987, the company changed its method of accounting to include in inventory certain manufacturing overhead costs which were previously charged to operating expense. Among the more significant types of these costs are depreciation of manufacturing facilities and equipment, employee pensions and fringe benefits and certain other product-related costs. The company believes that this change is preferable because it provides a better matching of production costs with related revenues in reported operating results. The cumulative effect of this change for the years prior to January 1, 1987 amounted to a net benefit of $9,755,000. The change did not have a material effect on operating results for 1987.

In the fourth quarter of 1986, the company adopted for all domestic plans, certain provisions of the new accounting rules for pensions effective January 1, 1986. The net effect of this change and plan amendments was to reduce net periodic pension costs for 1986 by $18,963,000 and increase net earnings by $10,240,000. The provisions were adopted prospectively, and accordingly net earnings for 1985 have not been restated.

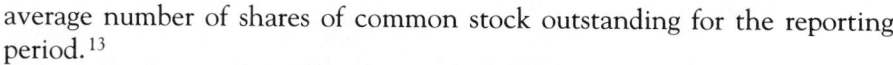

average number of shares of common stock outstanding for the reporting period.[13]

For example, the Suhaka Corporation income statement illustrated on page 133 shows earnings per share of $1.34 for income from continuing operations, $.61 for loss from discontinued operations, $.31 for extraordinary gain, and a loss of $.09 for the cumulative effect of a change in accounting principle, or a total of $.95 for net income. These figures were derived by dividing each identified component of net income by 50,000 shares of common stock outstanding during the period.

Reporting Changes in Retained Earnings   Many corporations include a statement identifying the changes in retained earnings as one of their financial statements. This statement generally begins with the opening balance in the retained earnings account and then shows the additions and deductions to arrive at the ending balance. In

[13]*Opinions of the Accounting Principles Board No. 15*, "Earnings per Share" (New York: American Institute of Certified Public Accountants, 1969), par. 47.

many cases, this statement is very simple. Net income is included as an addition, dividend distributions as a deduction, and any special credits or charges are added or subtracted as appropriate. There are two general types of retained earnings adjustments: (1) prior period adjustments, and (2) as indicated earlier, adjustments arising from some changes in accounting principles. Prior period adjustments arise primarily when an error occurs in one period and is not discovered until a subsequent period.

The retained earnings statement for Suhaka Corporation is illustrated below.

Suhaka Corporation
Retained Earnings Statement
For Year Ended December 31, 1991

Retained earnings, January 1, 1991	$175,000
Add prior period adjustment—correction of inventory under-statement (net of income taxes of $10,000)	15,000
Adjusted retained earnings, January 1, 1991	$190,000
Add net income from income statement	47,310
	$237,310
Deduct dividends declared	40,000
Retained earnings, December 31, 1991	$197,310

Reporting Implications of Conceptual Framework

The Financial Accounting Standards Board recommended new terminology to report the changes in owners' equity. One of the ten elements defined in Concepts Statement No. 6 and presented in Chapter 2 was "Comprehensive Income." The Board defined this term as follows:

> Comprehensive Income is the change in equity of a business enterprise during a period from transactions and other events and circumstances from nonowner sources. It includes all changes in equity during a period except those resulting from investments by owners and distributions to owners.[14]

The Board also defined a new term for the bottom line of an income statement. As discussed in the chapter, the last figure on an income statement is usually labeled "Net Income." The Board did not define net income; however, they did recommend adoption of the term earnings. As defined in the Statement, earnings is identical with net income as that term is used in practice except that the last irregular item discussed, "Cumulative Effects of Changes in Accounting Principles," is not included in earnings. Thus, the earnings amount for the Suhaka Corporation would be $51,810 ($47,310 + $4,500). In addition to an earnings statement, the Board suggested that a new comprehensive income statement should be prepared. This statement would start with the earnings amount and include all other nonowner changes to owners' equity. This statement would include the cumulative effects of changes in accounting principles. Also included

---

[14]*Statement of Financial Accounting Concepts No. 6*, par. 70.

would be any recognized changes in values, such as writedowns of long-term equity investments and foreign translation adjustments.

The Board did not include a display of a suggested statement of comprehensive income in Concepts Statement No. 5, but stated: "This Statement does not consider details of displaying those different kinds of information and does not preclude the possibility that some entities might choose to combine some of that information in a single statement."[15] An example of how a statement of comprehensive income might appear for Suhaka Corporation is included below.

It is important to recognize that the terms "earnings" and "comprehensive income" recommended in the concepts statements are not presently part of GAAP. Not until they are incorporated into a statement of standards will they be required of business management and auditors.

Suhaka Corporation
Statement of Comprehensive Income
For Year Ended December 31, 1991

Earnings per earnings statement	$51,810
Cumulative effect of changing inventory method (net of income tax savings of $3,000)...................................	(4,500)
Prior period adjustment—correction of inventory understatement (net of income taxes of $10,000)	15,000
Foreign translation adjustment	30,000
Comprehensive income	$92,310

A review of *Accounting Trends and Techniques 1987* indicates very little change in terminology has occurred as a result of Concepts Statement No. 5 "Income" is still the most widely used with "earnings" being only half as popular. None of the 600 reporting companies in 1986 adopted the comprehensive income concept terminology.

Summary As indicated in the short case situation that began this chapter, one "bottom line" figure for income can often be misleading and result in an inefficient allocation of resources. Standard-setting bodies have been concerned with the ingredients that enter an income measurement. The FASB has tried to address the related problems of income recognition, measurement, and reporting in their concepts statements. Decision usefulness will be improved if some of these recommendations are incorporated into practice. However, change is always slow, especially when the changes involve entrenched terminology and formats. Many of the income components introduced in this chapter will be explored in greater depth in later chapters of the text. A summary of the treatment of the special items discussed in this chapter is included on page 146.

[15]*Statement of Financial Accounting Concepts No. 5*, par. 14.

Exhibit 4-6   Summary of Procedures for Reporting Irregular, Nonrecurring, or Unusual Items*

Where Reported	Category	Description	Examples
Part of income from continuing operations	Changes in estimates	Normal recurring changes in estimating future. Included in normal accounts.	Changes in building and equipment lives, changes in estimated loss from uncollectible accounts receivable, changes in estimate of warranty liability.
	Unusual gains and losses, not considered extraordinary	Unusual or infrequent, but not both. Related to normal business operations. Material in amount. Shown in other revenues and gains or other expenses and losses.	Gains or losses from sale of assets, investments, or other operating assets. Write-off of receivables as uncollectible, inventories as obsolete.
On income statement, but after income from continuing operations	Discontinued operations	Disposal of completely separate line of business. Include gain or loss from operating segment, and gain or loss from sale or abandonment.	Sale by conglomerate company of separate line of business such as milling company selling restaurant segment.
	Extraordinary items	Both unusual and nonrecurring. Not related to normal business operations. Material in amount.	Material gains and losses from early extinguishment of debt, from some casualties or legal claims if meet criteria.
	Changes in accounting principles— general case	Change from one accepted principle to another.	Change from one method of inventory pricing to another, change in depreciation method.
As adjustment to retained earnings on the balance sheet	Prior period adjustments and special case changes in accounting principles.	Material correction of errors, changes in accounting principles that require retroactive adjustment.	Failure to depreciate fixed assets, mathematical error in computing inventory balance, retroactive adjustment for new standard.

*This chart describes the usual case. Exceptions to the descriptions occasionally do occur.

Key Terms   Comprehensive income 144   Gains 125
Discontinued operations 136   Losses 125
Earnings 144   Physical capital maintenance 123
Expense recognition 127   Prior period adjustments 144
Expenses 125   Revenue recognition 125
Extraordinary items 139   Revenues 125
Financial capital maintenance 122   Transaction approach 124

Questions   1. FASB Concepts Statement No. 1 states, "The primary focus of financial reporting is information about an enterprises's performance provided by measures of earnings and its components." Why is it unwise for users of financial statements to focus too much attention on the income statement?

2. Income as determined by income tax regulations is not necessarily the same as income reported to external users. Why might there be differences?

3. After the necessary definitions and assumptions have been made that support the determination of income, what are the two methods of income measurement that may be used to determine income? How do they differ?

4. What different measurement methods may be applied to net assets in arriving at income under the capital maintenance approach?

5. How are revenues and expenses different from gains and losses?

6. What two factors must be considered in deciding the point at which revenues and gains should be recognized? At what point in the revenue cycle are these conditions usually met?

7. Name three exceptions to the general rule which assumes revenue is recognized at the point of sale. What is the justification for these exceptions?

8. What guidelines are used to match costs with revenues in determining income?

9. What are some possible disadvantages of a multiple-step income statement and a single-step statement?

10. Identify the major sections (components of income) that are included in a multiple-step income statement.

11. What is the meaning of "intraperiod" income tax allocation?

12. The Pop-Up Company has decided to sell its lid manufacturing division even though the division is expected to show a small profit this year. The division's assets will be sold at a loss of $10,000 to another company. What information (if any) should Pop-Up disclose in its financial reports with respect to this division?

13. Which of the following would *not* normally qualify as an extraordinary item?
    (a) The write-down or write-off of receivables.
    (b) Major devaluation of foreign currency.
    (c) Loss on sale of plant and equipment.
    (d) Gain from early extinguishment of debt.
    (e) Loss due to extensive flood damage to asphalt company in Las Vegas, Nevada.
    (f) Loss due to extensive earthquake damage to furniture company in Los Angeles, California.
    (g) Farming loss due to heavy spring rains in the Northwest.

14. Explain briefly the difference in accounting treatment of (a) a change in accounting principle, and (b) a change in accounting estimate.

15. What is the general practice in reporting earnings per share?

16. Define comprehensive income. How does it differ from net income?

Discussion Cases   **Case 4–1 (Are we really better off?)**

The Plath Company Board of Directors finally receives the income statement for the past year from management. Board members are initially pleased to see that after three loss years, the company will be reporting a profit for the current year. Further investigation reveals that depreciation expense is significantly lower than it was last year. Company management, concerned by the losses, decided to change its method of reporting depreciation from an accelerated method to straight-line. If the depreciation method had not been changed, a loss would have resulted for the fourth consecutive year. When questioned by the Board about the accounting change, management replied that the majority of companies in the industry use the straight-line depreciation method, and thus the change makes Plath's income statement more comparable to the other companies. Since comparability is an important qualitative characteristic of accounting information, should the Board accept the explanation of management? How should the information about the change in the depreciation method be displayed in the financial statements?

Case 4–2 (How can my company have income but no cash?)

Max Stevenson owns a local drug store. During the past few years the economy has experienced a period of high inflation. Stevenson has had the policy of withdrawing cash from his business equal to 80% of the company's reported net income. As the business has grown, he has had a CPA prepare the company's financial statements and tax returns. The following is a summary of the company's income statement for the current year:

Revenue........................	$565,000
Cost of goods sold (drugs etc.)	395,000
Gross profit on items sold	$170,000
Operating expenses (including taxes)	110,000
Net income	$ 60,000

Even though the business has reported net income each year, it has experienced severe cash flow shortages. The company has had to pay higher prices for its inventory as the company has tried to maintain the same quantity and quality of its goods. For example, last year's cost of goods sold had a historical cost of $250,000 and a replacement cost of $295,000. The current year's cost of goods sold has a replacement cost of $440,000. Stevenson's personal cash outflows have also grown faster than his withdrawals from the company due to increasing personal demands.

Stevenson asks you as a financial advisor how the company can have income of $60,000, but how he and the company can still have a shortage of cash.

Case 4-3 (When should revenue be recognized?)

Stan Crowfoot is a renowned sculptor who specializes in American Indian sculptures. Typically, a cast is prepared for each work to permit the multiple reproduction of the pieces. A limited number of copies are made for each sculpture, and the mold is destroyed after the number is reached. Limiting the number of pieces enhances the price, and most of the pieces have initially sold for $2,000 to $4,000. To encourage sales, Stan has a liberal return policy that permits customers to return any unwanted piece for a period of up to one year from the date of sale and receive a full refund. Do you think Stan should recognize revenue: (1) when the piece is produced and cast in bronze, (2) when the goods are delivered to the customer, or (3) when the period of return has passed? Justify your answer in terms of the conceptual framework.

Case 4-4 (When should revenue be recognized?)

You are engaged as a consultant to Skyways Unlimited, a manufacturer of satellite dishes for television reception. Skyways sells its dishes to dealers who in turn sell them to customers. As an inducement to carry sufficient inventory, the dealers are not required to pay for the dishes until they have been sold. There is no formal provision for return of the dishes by the dealers; however, Skyways has requested returns when a dealer's sales activity is considered to be too low. Overall, returns have amounted to less than 10% of the dishes sent to dealers. No interest is charged to the dealers on their balances unless they do not remit promptly upon the sale to a customer. At what point would you recommend that Skyways recognize the revenue from the sale of dishes to the dealers?

Case 4-5 (We just changed our minds.)

Management for Marlowe Manufacturing Company decided in 1991 to discontinue one of its unsuccessful product lines. The line was not large enough for it to meet the definition of a business segment. The planned discontinuance involved obsolete inventory, assembly lines, and packaging and advertising supplies. It was estimated that a loss of $250,000 would result from the decision, and this estimate was recorded as a loss in the 1991 income statement. In 1992, new management was appointed and it was decided that maybe the unsuccessful product line could be turned around with a more aggressive marketing policy. The change was made, and indeed, the product began to make money. The new management wants to reverse the adjustment made last year and remove the liability for the estimated loss. How should the 1991 estimated loss be reported in the 1991 income statement? How should the 1992 reversal of the 1991 action be reported in the 1992 financial statements?

Case 4-6 (The sure-fire computer software)

The Flexisoft Company has had excellent success in developing business software for microcomputers. Management has followed the accounting practice of deferring the development costs for the software until sufficient sales have developed to cover the software cost. Because of past successes, management feels it is improper to charge software costs directly to expense as current GAAP requires. What are the pros and cons of deferring or expensing immediately these developmental costs?

Case 4–7 (Deferred initial operating losses)

Small loan companies often experience losses in the operation of newly opened branch loan offices. Such results usually can be anticipated by management prior to making a decision on expansion. It has been recommended by some accountants that the operating losses of newly opened branches should be reported as deferred charges during the first twelve months of operation or until the first profitable month occurs. Such deferred charges would then be amortized over a five-year period. Would you support this recommendation? Justify your answer.

Case 4–8 (What was last year's income?)

The Walesco Corporation has decided to discontinue an entire segment of its business effective November 1, 1991. It hopes to sell the assets involved and convert the physical plant to other uses within the manufacturing division. The CPA auditing the books indicates that GAAP requires separate identification of the revenues and expenses related to the segment to be sold and their removal from the continuing revenue and expense amounts. The controller objects to this change. "We have already distributed widely last year's numbers. If we change them now, one year later, confidence in our financial statements will be greatly eroded." What are the pros and cons of identifying separately the costs related to the discontinued segment?

Case 4–9 (How do you like my display?)

Niewald Company's Statements of Income for the years ended December 31, 1991, and December 31, 1990, are presented at the top of page 151.

Additional facts are as follows:
(a) On January 1, 1990, Niewald Company changed its depreciation method for previously recorded plant machinery from the double-declining-balance method to the straight-line method. The effect of applying the straight-line method for the year of and the year after the change is included in Niewald Company's Statements of Income for the year ended December 31, 1991, and December 31, 1990, in "cost of goods sold."
(b) The loss from operations of the discontinued Nex Division from January 1, 1991, to September 30, 1991, (the portion of the year prior to the measurement date) and from January 1, 1990, to December 31, 1990, is included in Niewald Company's Statements of Income for the year ended December 31, 1991, and December 31, 1990, respectively, in "other, net."
(c) Niewald Company has a simple capital structure with only common stock outstanding and the net income per share of common stock was based on the weighted average number of common shares outstanding during each year.
(d) Niewald Company common stock is listed on the New York Stock Exchange and closed at $13 per share on December 31, 1991, and $15 per share on December 31, 1990.

Niewald Company
Statements of Income
For Years Ended December 31,

	1991	1990
	(000 omitted)	
Net sales	$900,000	$750,000
Costs and expenses:		
Cost of goods sold	$720,000	$600,000
Selling, general and administrative expenses	112,000	90,000
Other, net	11,000	9,000
Total costs and expenses	$843,000	$699,000
Income from continuing operations before income taxes	$ 57,000	$ 51,000
Income taxes current provision	23,000	24,000
Income from continuing operations	$ 34,000	$ 27,000
Loss on disposal of Nex Division, including provision of $1,500,000 for operating losses during phase-out period, less applicable income taxes of $8,000,000	8,000	—
Cumulative effect on prior years of change in depreciation method, less applicable income taxes of $1,500,000	—	3,000
Net income	$ 26,000	$ 30,000
Earnings per share of common stock:		
Income before cumulative effect of change in depreciation method	$ 2.60	$ 2.70
Cumulative effect on prior years of change in depreciation method, less applicable income taxes	—	.30
Net income	$ 2.60	$ 3.00

Instructions: Determine from the additional facts above whether the presentation of those facts in Niewald Company's Statements of Income is appropriate. If the presentation is appropriate, discuss the theoretical rationale for the presentation. If the presentation is not appropriate, specify the appropriate presentation and discuss its theoretical rationale.   (AICPA adapted)

Exercises   **Exercise 4–1   (Calculation of net income)**

Changes in the balance sheet account balances for the Smite Sales Co. during 1991 are shown below.

Dividends declared during 1991 were $40,000. Calculate the net income for the year assuming there were no transactions affecting retained earnings other than the dividends.

	Increase (Decrease)
Cash	$ 95,500
Accounts Receivable	92,000
Inventory	(30,000)
Buildings and Equipment (net)	190,000
Patents	(5,000)
Accounts Payable	(75,000)
Bonds Payable	150,000
Capital Stock	100,000
Additional Paid-In Capital	50,000

Exercise 4–2 (Revenue recognition)

For each of the following transactions, events, or circumstances, indicate whether the recognition criteria for revenues and gains are met and provide support for your answer.

(a) An order of $25,000 for merchandise is received from a customer.
(b) The value of timberlands increases by $40,000 for the year due to normal growth.
(c) Accounting services are rendered to a client on account.
(d) A 1982 investment was made in land at a cost of $80,000. The land currently has a fair market value of $107,000.
(e) Cash of $5,600 is collected from the sale of a gift certificate that is redeemable in the next accounting period.
(f) Cash of $7,500 is collected from subscribers for subscription fees to a monthly magazine. The subscription period is 2 years.
(g) You owe a creditor $1,500 payable in thirty days. The creditor has cash flow difficulties and has agreed to allow you to retire the debt in full with an immediate payment of $1,200.

Exercise 4–3 (Revenue recognition)

Indicate which of the following transactions or events gives rise to the recognition of revenue in 1991 under the accrual basis of accounting. If revenue is not recognized, what is the account that is credited, if any?

(a) On December 15, 1991, Howe Company received $20,000 as rent revenue for the six-month period starting January 1, 1992.
(b) Monroe Tractor Co., on July 1, 1991, sold one of its tractors and received $10,000 in cash and a note for $50,000 at 12% interest, payable in one year. The fair market value of the tractor is $60,000.
(c) Oswald, Inc. issued additional shares of common stock on December 10, 1991 for $30,000 above par value.
(d) Balance Company received a purchase order in 1991 from an established customer for $10,200 of merchandise. The merchandise was shipped on December 20, 1991. The company's credit policy allows the customer to return the merchandise within 30 days, and a 3% discount is allowed if paid within 20 days from shipment.
(e) Gloria, Inc. sold merchandise costing $2,000 for $2,500 in August 1991. The terms of the sale are 15% down on a 12-month conditional sales contract, with title to the goods being retained by the seller until the contract price is paid in full.
(f) On November 1, 1991, Jones & Whitlock entered into an agreement to conduct a 1991 audit for Lehi Mills for $35,000. The audit work began on December 15, 1991 and will be completed about February 15, 1992.

Exercise 4–4   (Classification of income statement items)

Where in a multiple-step income statement would each item be reported?

(a) Purchase discounts
(b) Gain on early retirement of debt
(c) Interest revenue
(d) Loss on sale of equipment

(e) Casualty loss from hurricane
(f) Sales commissions
(g) Loss on disposal of segment
(h) Income tax expense
(i) Gain on sale of land
(j) Sales discounts
(k) Loss from long-term investments written off as worthless
(l) Depletion expense
(m) Cumulative effect of change in depreciation method
(n) Vacation pay of office employee
(o) Ending inventory

Exercise 4—5   (Analysis and preparation of income statement)

The selling expenses of Caribou Inc. for 1991 are 13% of sales. General expenses, excluding doubtful accounts, are 25% of cost of goods sold, but only 15% of sales. Doubtful accounts are 2% of sales. The beginning inventory was $136,000, and it decreased 30% during the year. Income from operations for the year before income tax of 30% is $160,000. Extraordinary gain, net of tax of 30% is $21,000. Prepare an income statement, including earnings per share data, giving supporting computations. Caribou Inc. has 110,000 shares of common stock outstanding.

Exercise 4—6   (Change in estimate)

The Swalberg Corporation purchased a patent on January 2, 1986, for $375,000. The original life of the patent was estimated to be 15 years. However, in December of 1991, the controller of Swalberg received information proving conclusively that the product protected by the the Swalberg patent would be obsolete within three years. Accordingly, the company decided to write off the unamortized portion of the patent cost over four years beginning in 1991. How would the change in estimate be reflected in the accounts for 1991 and subsequent years?

Exercise 4—7   (Intraperiod income tax allocation)

The Brigham Corporation reported the following income items before tax for the year 1991.

Income from continuing operations before income tax	$210,000
Loss from operations of a discontinued business segment	50,000
Gain from disposal of a business segment	20,000
Extraordinary gain on retirement of debt	100,000

The income tax rate is 35% on all items. Prepare the portion of the income statement beginning with "Income from continuing operations before income tax" for the year ended December 31, 1991, after applying proper intraperiod income tax allocation procedures.

Exercise 4—8   (Reporting items on financial statements)

How would you report each of the following items on the financial statements?

(a) Revenue from sale of obsolete inventory.
(b) Loss on sale of the fertilizer production division of a lawn supplies manufacturer.
(c) Material penalties arising from early payment of a mortgage.
(d) Gain resulting from changing asset balances to adjust for the effect of excessive depreciation charged in error in prior years.
(e) Loss resulting from excessive accrual in prior years of estimated revenues from long-term contracts.
(f) Costs incurred to purchase a valuable patent.
(g) Net income from the discontinued dune buggy operations of a custom car designer.
(h) Costs of rearranging plant machinery into a more efficient order.
(i) Error made in capitalizing advertising expense during the prior year.
(j) Gain on sale of land to the government.
(k) Loss from destruction of crops by a hail storm.
(l) Cumulative effect of changing depreciation method.
(m) Additional depreciation resulting from a change in the estimated useful life of an asset.
(n) Gain on sale of long-term investments.
(o) Loss from spring flooding.
(p) Sale of obsolete inventory at less than book value.
(q) Additional federal income tax assessment for prior years.
(r) Loss resulting from the sale of a portion of a line of business.
(s) Costs associated with moving an American business to Japan.
(t) Loss resulting from a patent that was recently determined to be worthless.

Exercise 4–9   (Multiple-step income statement)

From the following list of accounts, prepare a multiple-step income statement in good form showing all appropriate items properly classified, including disclosure of earnings per share data. (No monetary amounts are to be recognized.)

Accounts Payable
Accumulated Depreciation—Office Building
Accumulated Depreciation—Delivery Equipment
Accumulated Depreciation—Office Furniture and Fixtures
Advertising Expense
Allowance for Doubtful Accounts
Cash
Common Stock, $20 par (10,000 shares outstanding)
Delivery Salaries
Depreciation Expense—Office Building
Depreciation Expense—Delivery Equipment
Depreciation Expense—Office Furniture and Fixtures
Dividend Revenue
Dividends Payable
Dividends Receivable
Doubtful Accounts Expense
Extraordinary Gain (net of income taxes)
Freight in

Federal Unemployment Tax Payable
Goodwill
Income Tax
Income Tax Payable
Insurance Expense
Interest Expense—Bonds
Interest Expense—Other
Interest Payable
Interest Receivable
Interest Revenue
Inventory
Loss from Discontinued Operations (net of income taxes)
Miscellaneous Delivery Expense
Miscellaneous General Expense
Miscellaneous Selling Expense
Office Salaries
Office Supplies
Office Supplies Used
Officers' Salaries
Property Taxes
Purchases

Purchase Discounts   Sales
Purchase Returns and Allowances   Sales Discounts
Retained Earnings   Sales Returns and Allowances
Royalties Received in Advance   Sales Salaries and Commissions
Royalty Revenue   Sales Tax Payable
Salaries and Wages Payable

Exercise 4–10 (Correction of retained earnings statement)

M. Taylor has been employed as a bookkeeper for the Losser Corporation for a number of years. With the assistance of a clerk, Taylor handles all accounting duties, including the preparation of financial statements. The following is a "Statement of Earned Surplus" prepared by Taylor for 1991.

Losser Corporation
Statement of Earned Surplus
for 1991

Balance at beginning of year		$ 85,949
Additions:		
Amortization overstatement for 1991	$ 2,800	
Gain on sale of land	18,350	
Interest revenue	4,500	
Profit and loss for 1991	13,680	
Total additions		39,330
Total		$125,279
Deductions:		
Increased depreciation due to change in estimated life	$ 5,000	
Dividends declared and paid	10,000	
Loss on sale of equipment	3,860	
Loss from major casualty (extraordinary)	27,730	
Total deductions		46,590
Balance at end of year		$ 78,689

(1) Prepare a schedule showing the correct net income for 1991. (Ignore income taxes.) (2) Prepare a retained earnings statement for 1991. (3) Explain why you have changed the retained earnings statement.

Exercise 4–11 (Single-step income statement and statement of retained earnings)

The Pensacola Awning Co. reports the following for 1991:

Retained Earnings, January 1	$ 444,500
Selling expenses	287,000
Sales revenue	1,360,000
Interest expense	13,390
General and administrative expenses	236,400
Cost of goods sold	765,000
Dividends declared this year	32,000
Tax rate for all items	35%
Average shares of common stock outstanding during the year	25,000

Prepare a single-step income statement (including earnings per share data) and a statement of retained earnings for Pensacola.

PROBLEMS   **Problem 4–1   (Single-step income statement)**

The Payette Co. on July 1, 1991, reported a retained earnings balance of $1,525,000. The books of the company showed the following account balances on June 30, 1992.

Sales	$2,500,000
Inventory: July 1, 1991	160,000
June 30, 1992	165,000
Sales Returns and Allowances	30,000
Purchases	1,536,000
Purchase Discounts	24,000
Dividends Paid	260,000
Selling and General Expenses	250,000
Income Taxes	249,550

Instructions: Prepare a single-step income statement and a retained earnings statement. The Payette Co. has 400,000 shares of common stock outstanding.

Problem 4–2   (Revenue recognition and preparation of income statement)

The Richmond Company manufactures and sells robot-type toys for children. Under one type of agreement with the dealers, Richmond is to receive payment upon shipment to the dealers. Under another type of agreement, Richmond receives payments only after the dealer makes the sale. Under this latter agreement, toys may be returned by the dealer. The president of Richmond desires to know how the income statement would differ under these two methods over a two-year period.

The following information is made available for making the computations.

Sales price per unit:	
If paid after shipment	$5
If paid after sale, with right of return	$6
Cost to produce per unit (Assume fixed quantity of toys is produced)	$3
Expected bad debt percentage of sales if revenue recognized at time of shipment	5%
Expected bad debt percentage of sales if revenue recognized at time of sale	1/2%
Selling expense—1991	$25,000
Selling expense—1992	$15,000
General and administrative expense 1991 and 1992	$20,000

Quantity shipped and sold	1991	1992
Units shipped to dealers	25,000	30,000
Units sold by dealers ..	14,000	22,000

Instructions: (1) Prepare a comparative income statement for 1991 and 1992 for each of the two types of dealer agreements assuming the company began operations in 1991. (2) Discuss the implications of the revenue recognition method used for each of the dealer agreements.

Problem 4–3 (Intraperiod income tax allocation)

The following information relates to Delaney Manufacturing Inc. for the fiscal year ended July 31, 1991. Assume there are no tax rate changes, a 30% tax rate applies to all items reported in the income statement, and there are no differences between financial and taxable income.

Taxable income, year ending July 31, 1991	$ 975,000
Nonoperating items included in taxable income:	
Extraordinary gain	101,000
Loss from disposal of a business segment	(140,000)
Prior year error resulting in income overstatement for fiscal year 1990; tax refund to be requested	75,000
Retained earnings, August 1, 1990	2,750,000

Instructions: Prepare the income statement for Delaney Manufacturing Inc. beginning with "Income from continuing operations before income taxes" and the retained earnings statement for the fiscal year ended July 31, 1991. Apply intraperiod income tax allocation procedures to both statements.

Problem 4–4 (Reporting special income items)

Radiant Cosmetics Inc. shows a retained earnings balance on January 1, 1991, of $620,000. For 1991, the income from continuing operations was $210,000 before income tax. Following is a list of special items:

Income from operations of a discontinued cosmetic division	$18,000
Loss on the sale of the cosmetics division	50,000
Gain on extinguishment of long-term debt	25,000
Correction of sales understatement in 1990 (net of income taxes of $21,000 to be paid when amended 1990 return is filed)	39,000
Omission of depreciation charges of prior years (a claim has been filed for an income tax refund of $8,000)	20,000

Income tax paid during 1991 was $82,000, which consisted of the tax on continuing operations, plus $8,000 resulting from operations of the discontinued cosmetics division and $10,000 from the gain from extinguishment of debt, less a $20,000 tax reduction for loss on the sale of the cosmetics division. Dividends of $30,000 were declared by the company during the year (50,000 shares of common stock are outstanding).

Instructions: Prepare the income statement for Radiant Cosmetics Inc. beginning with "Income from continuing operations before income taxes." Include an accompanying retained earnings statement.

Problem 4–5 (Income and retained earnings statements)

Selected account balances of Connell Company for 1991 along with additional information as of December 31 are as follows:

Contribution to Employee		Depreciation Expense—	
Pension Fund	$290,000	Office Building	25,000
Delivery Expense	425,000	Depreciation Expense—	
Depreciation Expense—		Office Equipment	10,000
Delivery Trucks	29,000		

Depreciation Expense—		Miscellaneous Selling	
Store Equipment	25,000	Expenses	50,000
Dividends	150,000	Officers' and Office	
Dividend Revenue	5,000	Salaries	850,000
Doubtful Accounts Expense	32,000	Property Taxes	100,000
Freight In	145,000	Purchase Discounts	47,700
Gain on Sale of Office		Purchases	4,133,200
Equipment	10,000	Retained Earnings, January	
Income Taxes, 1991	344,700	1, 1991	550,000
Interest Revenue	1,500	Sales	8,125,000
Loss on Sale of Marketable		Sales Discounts	55,000
Securities	50,000	Sales Returns and	
Loss on Write-Down of		Allowances	95,000
Obsolete Inventory	75,000	Sales Salaries	521,000
Inventory, January 1, 1991	850,000	Stores Supplies Expense	60,000
Miscellaneous General			
Expenses	45,000		

(a) Inventory was valued at year-end as follows:

Cost	$825,000
Write-down of obsolete inventory	75,000
	$750,000

(b) Number of Connell shares of stock outstanding   50,000

Instructions: Prepare statements of income and retained earnings in multiple-step format for the year ended December 31, 1991.

Problem 4–6   (Corrected income statement)

The following is the pre-audit statement for 10 months ended December 31, 1991, of Jericho Recreation Incorporated, a firm which started operations March 4, 1991.

JERICHO RECREATION INC.
Income Statement
For the Period Ended December 31, 1991

Sales	$497,000	
Less sales returns and allowances	0	$497,000
Cost of goods sold:		
Completed units—5000	$401,000	
Less ending inventory—1000 units	80,200	320,800
Gross profit on sales		$176,200
Selling expenses:		
Advertising expense	$13,200	
Selling expense	60,000	$ 73,200
General and administrative expenses:		
Salary expense	$32,100	
Depreciation expense	16,900	
Misc. general and administrative expenses	3,300	52,300	125,500
Income from operations before income taxes		$ 50,700
Income taxes		0
Income from continuing operations		$ 50,700
Extraordinary loss on strike (net of income tax		
savings of $6,000)		(14,000)
Net income		$ 36,700

Year-end pre-audit observations: **Amount**

a. Factory depreciation was included in general and administrative
   expenses $11,200
b. Sales returns and allowances were not recorded   2,750
c. Accrued sales commissions were not recorded as of December 31   5,230
d. Advertising expense paid on March 1 was for newspaper ads
   appearing each month for the next 12 months............   13,200
e. Income tax rate 30%
f. Gain due to change in accounting principles was incorrectly
   included as a deduction from miscellaneous general and
   administrative expenses (before income taxes)   12,000
g. Losses from strike were erroneously reported as an extraordinary
   item (after income taxes)   14,000

Instructions: Prepare a corrected income statement for the period ended
December 31, 1991. (Round to the nearest dollar.)

**III Problem 4–7   (Analysis of income items—multiple-step income statement
preparation)**

On December 31, 1991, analysis of the Dille Sporting Goods' operations for
1991 revealed the following:

(a) Total cash collections from customers, $107,770.
(b) December 31, 1990, inventory balance, $10,020.
(c) Total cash payments, $96,350.
(d) Accounts receivable, December 31, 1990, $20,350.
(e) Accounts payable, December 31, 1990, $9,870.
(f) Accounts receivable, December 31, 1991, $10,780.
(g) Accounts payable, December 31, 1991, $5,175.
(h) General and administrative expenses total 20% of sales. This amount
    includes the depreciation on store and equipment.
(i) Selling expenses of $11,661 total 30% of gross profit on sales.
(j) No general and administrative or selling expense liabilities existed at
    December 31, 1991.
(k) Wages and salaries payable at December 31, 1990, $3,750.
(l) Depreciation expense on store and equipment total 13.5% of general and
    administrative expenses.
(m) Shares of stock issued and outstanding, 6,000.
(n) The income tax rate is 30%.

Instructions: Prepare a multiple-step income statement for the year ended
December 31, 1991.

Problem 4–8   (Corrected income and retained earnings statements)

Selected account balances and adjusting information of Sunset Cosmetics Inc.
for the year ended December 31, 1991, follow:

Retained Earnings, January 1, 1991	$440,670
Sales Salaries and Commissions	25,000
Advertising Expense	16,090
Legal Services	2,225
Insurance and Licenses	7,680
Travel Expense—Sales Representatives	4,560
Depreciation Expense—Sales/Delivery Equipment	6,100
Depreciation Expense—Office Equipment	4,200
Interest Revenue	550
Utilities	6,400
Telephone and Postage	1,475
Supplies Inventory	2,180
Miscellaneous Selling Expenses	2,740
Dividends	33,000
Dividend Revenue	5,150
Interest Expense	4,520
Allowance for Doubtful Accounts (Cr Bal)	160
Officers' Salaries	36,600
Sales	451,000
Sales Returns and Allowances	3,900
Sales Discounts	880
Gain on Sale of Assets	7,820
Inventory, January 1, 1991	89,700
Inventory, December 31, 1991	20,550
Purchases	141,600
Freight In	5,525
Accounts Receivable, December 31, 1991	261,000
Gain from Discontinued Operations (before income taxes)	40,000
Extraordinary Loss (before income taxes)	72,600
Shares of Common Stock Outstanding	39,000

Adjusting information:

(a) Cost of inventory in the possession of consignees as of December 31, 1991, was not included in the ending inventory balance $18,600

(b) After preparing an analysis of aged accounts receivable, a decision was made to increase the allowance for doubtful accounts to a percentage of the ending accounts receivable balance 2%

(c) Purchase returns and allowances were unrecorded. They are computed as a percentage of purchases (not including freight in)... 6%

(d) Sales commissions for the last day of the year had not been accrued. Total sales for the day .... $ 3,050
    Average sales commissions as a percent of sales 3%

(e) No accrual had been made for a freight bill received on January 3, 1992, for goods received on December 29, 1991.. $ 570

(f) An advertising campaign was initiated November 1, 1991. This amount was recorded as "prepaid advertising" and should be amortized over a six-month period. No amortization was recorded .... $ 1,818

(g) Freight charges paid on sold merchandise were netted against sales. Freight charge on sales during 1991 .... $ 3,500

(h) Interest earned but not accrued .... $ 560

(i) Depreciation expense on new forklift purchased March 1, 1991 had not been recognized. (Assume all equipment will have no salvage value and the straight-line method is used. Depreciation is calculated to the nearest month.)

Purchase price	$ 7,800
Estimated life in years	10

A "real" account is debited upon the receipt of supplies.

(j) Supplies on hand at year end	$ 1,225
(k) Income tax rate (on all items)	30%

Instructions: Prepare a corrected multiple-step income statement and a retained earnings statement for the year ended December 31, 1991. Assume all amounts are material.

Problem 4—9   (Comprehensive income statement)

The Blacksburg Company decides to follow the FASB recommendations and prepare both an earnings statement and a statement of comprehensive income. The following information for the year ending December 31, 1991, has been provided for the preparation of the statements.

Sales	$450,000
Cost of goods sold	263,000
Foreign translation adjustment (net of income taxes)	33,000 (cr.)
Selling expenses	63,900
Extraordinary gain (net of income taxes)	39,400
Correction of inventory error (net of income taxes)	28,680 (cr.)
General and administrative expenses	58,720
Cumulative effect of change in depreciation method (net of income tax savings)	18,380 (dr.)
Income tax expense	21,500
Gain on sale of investment	6,700
Proceeds from sale of land at cost	75,000
Dividends	8,900

Instructions: Prepare the two statements for the company. Use a single-step approach for the earnings statement.

Chapter 5

The Balance Sheet and Statement of Cash Flows

The questions posed by the investor were intriguing ones. How can a company go bankrupt when it has continued to report net income every year? If it is profitable, why isn't it successful? The answer, of course, depends on the circumstances in a particular case. One thing is certain, however; net income is not the only measure of success.

For many years, the income statement has been the dominant financial statement for external decision making. Earnings per share, placement of extraordinary items, and revenue recognition have all been topics of great interest to standard-setting bodies. The financial press has regularly reported quarterly earnings of large corporations as newsworthy events. The income statement, however, tells only part of the financial story. It does not answer questions such as: What is the company doing with the income? How is the company being financed? How far in debt is the company? How liquid are its assets? What are the prospects for cash flows over the next six months? To answer these questions, an external user has to consider two other financial statements: the balance sheet and the statement of cash flows. These statements report information that is very important for a user in evaluating the ability of a company to continue in operation.

Over the past several years the financial community has expressed increased interest in the financial conditions of reporting entities, especially their liquidity. The Financial Accounting Standards Board also has devoted considerable attention to evaluating how its standards affect the balance sheet.[1] As indicated in Chapter 2, the Conceptual Framework stresses that a primary objective of financial reporting is to help users predict the future cash flows of a company. To meet this objective, in 1987 the FASB issued a new standard which requires companies to present a statement of cash flows as one of the basic financial statements.[2] The statement of cash flows replaces the more general statement of changes in financial position.

[1]See for example David E. Hawkins, "Toward the New Balance Sheet," *Harvard Business Review* (November-December 1984), pp. 156–163.

[2]*Statement of Financial Accounting Standards No. 95,* "Statement of Cash Flows" (Stamford: Financial Accounting Standards Board, 1987).

The increased interest in the balance sheet and statement of cash flows is partially related to the significant number of companies that have been experiencing financial difficulty. By concentrating too much on profitability at the expense of financial strength, some companies find they have insufficient cash to pay their debts. This chapter focuses on the strengths and limitations of the balance sheet and describes how companies report their assets, liabilities, and owners' equity. It also provides an overview of the statement of cash flows.

Usefulness of the Balance Sheet

The balance sheet, also known as the statement of financial position, reports as of a given point in time the resources of a business (assets), its obligations (liabilities), and the residual ownership claims against its resources (owners' equity). By analyzing the relationships among these items, investors, creditors, and others can assess a firm's liquidity, i.e., its ability to meet short-term obligations, and solvency, i.e., its ability to pay all current and long-term debts as they come due. The balance sheet also shows the composition of assets and liabilities, the relative proportions of debt and equity financing, and how much of a firm's earnings have been retained in the business. Collectively, this information can be used by external parties to help assess the financial status of a firm at a particular date.

Following the traditional accounting model, the balance sheet is a historical report presenting the cumulative results of all past transactions of a business measured in terms of historical costs. It is an expression of the basic accounting equation: **Assets = Liabilities + Owners' Equity.** The balance sheet shows both the character and the amount of the assets, liabilities, and owners' equity.

Balance sheets, especially when compared over time and with additional data, provide a great deal of useful information to those interested in analyzing the financial well-being of a company. Specific relationships, such as a company's current ratio, its debt to equity ratio, and its rate of return on investment can be highlighted.[3] Future commitments, favorable and unfavorable trends, problem areas in terms of collection patterns, and the relative equity positions of creditors and owners can also be analyzed, all of which assist in evaluating the financial position of a company.

Of special interest to both creditors and investors in analyzing the balance sheet is the company's **financial flexibility**. For example, how well could the company weather unexpected losses in assets, damage claims arising from its operations, or significant reductions in sales? Often, the negative impact on net assets from such events is so material that the existence of the company is threatened unless it can enter the capital markets for additional funds from either creditors or investors. The problem is that obtaining funds becomes difficult once a company is in trouble. Terms for

---

[3]These ratios and relationships are discussed in detail in the last chapter of the text.

borrowing, including high interest rates, may be so unfavorable that they create further difficulty for a company. Additional stock issues may only sell at decreased prices, diluting the equity of existing shareholders.

Even large companies are not immune to financial crisis. The names of prominent companies that have had significant shocks to their balance sheets in recent years include Chrysler Corporation, Manville Corporation, and Union Carbide. In the case of Chrysler Corporation, the U.S. Government had to guarantee a sizeable loan in order for the company to be able to continue operations. The loan saved the company and enabled it to become solvent once again. Manville and Union Carbide were both subjected to heavy litigation claims that drained their capital and, in the case of Manville, resulted in bankruptcy and reorganization.

Elements of the Balance Sheet

The three elements found on the balance sheet were defined in Chapter 2. These definitions, which are part of FASB Concepts Statement No. 6, are repeated below.[4]

Elements Related to Balance Sheet

- **Assets** are probable future economic benefits obtained or controlled by a particular entity as a result of past transactions or events.
- **Liabilities** are probable future sacrifices of economic benefits arising from present obligations of a particular entity to transfer assets or provide services to other entities in the future as a result of past transactions or events.
- **Equity** or **net assets** is the residual interest in the assets of an entity that remains after deducting its liabilities. In a business enterprise, the equity is the ownership interest.

Assets are the resources owned or controlled by an entity. They include cash and other highly liquid resources, such as claims against others (receivables) and temporary investments. Assets also include costs that are expected to provide future economic benefits. For example, expenditures made for inventories, prepaid insurance, equipment, and patents are recoverable costs that will be recognized as expenses and matched against revenues of future periods.

Liabilities measure the claims of creditors against entity resources. As indicated by the FASB's definition, the method for settlement of liabilities varies. A liability may call for settlement by cash payment or settlement through goods to be delivered or services to be performed.

Owners' equity measures the interest of the ownership group in the total resources of the enterprise. It equals the net assets of an enterprise, or the difference between total assets and total liabilities. This interest arises from investment by owners, and is increased by net income and

[4]*Statement of Finanncial Accounting Concepts No. 6*, "Elements of Financial Statements" (Stamford: Financial Accounting Standards Board, 1985), p. ix.

decreased by net losses and distributions to owners. An ownership interest does not call for settlement on a certain date; in the event of business dissolution, it represents a claim on assets only after creditors have been paid in full.

Classified Balance Sheets

Balance sheet items are generally classified in a manner that facilitates analysis and interpretation of financial data. Information of primary concern to all parties is the business unit's liquidity and solvency—its ability to meet current and long-term obligations. Accordingly, assets and liabilities are classified as (1) **current** or **short-term** items and (2) **noncurrent** or **long-term** items. When assets and liabilities are so classified, the difference between current assets and current liabilities may be determined. This is referred to as the company's **working capital**—the liquid buffer available in meeting financial demands and contingencies of the future.

The importance of an adequate working capital position cannot be minimized. A business may not be able to survive in the absence of a satisfactory relationship between current assets and current liabilities. Furthermore, its ability to prosper is largely determined by the composition of the current asset pool. There must be a proper balance between liquid assets in the form of cash and temporary investments, and receivables and inventories. Activities of the business center around these assets. Cash and temporary investments, representing immediate purchasing power, are used to meet current claims and purchasing, payroll, and expense requirements; receivables are the outgrowth of sales effort and provide cash in the course of operations; inventory is also a source of cash as well as the means of achieving a profit. Management, in setting policies with respect to selling, purchasing, financing, expanding, and the paying of dividends, must work within the limitations set by the company's working capital position.

Some writers have questioned the usefulness of the current/noncurrent distinction for all companies. For example, Loyd Heath argues that since any classification scheme is arbitrary, the classification between current and noncurrent should be abolished. Assets and liabilities could then be listed in the order of their liquidity without arbitrary subtotals.[5] Although there is some arbitrariness in the detailed classifications, the popularity among users of the current ratio (current assets divided by current liabilities) as a measure of liquidity suggests that the classification does meet the test of decision usefulness and should be retained.

Although there are no standard categories that must be used, the following general framework for a balance sheet is representative, and will be used in this text.

---

[5]Loyd Heath, "Is Working Capital Really Working?" *Journal of Accountancy* (August 1980), pp. 55–62.

Assets
Current assets
Investments
Land, buildings, and equipment
Intangible assets
Other noncurrent assets
Liabilities
Current liabilities
Long-term debt
Long-term lease obligations
Deferred income tax liability
Other noncurrent liabilities
Owners' Equity
Contributed capital
Retained earnings

Current Assets and Current Liabilities
Current assets include cash and resources that are reasonably expected to be converted into cash during the normal operating cycle of a business or within one year, whichever period is longer. As depicted below, the normal operating cycle is the time required for cash to be converted to inventories, inventories into receivables, and receivables ultimately into cash. When the operating cycle exceeds twelve months, for example, in the tobacco, distillery, and lumber industries, the longer period is used.

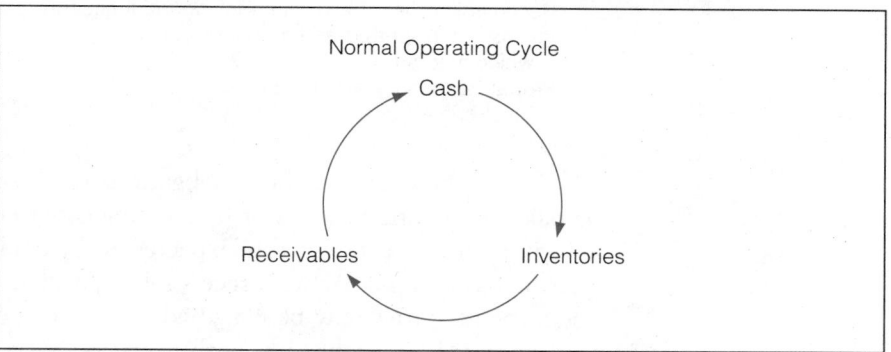

Some exceptions to the general definition of current assets should be noted. Cash that is restricted as to use, e.g., designated for the acquisition of noncurrent assets or segregated for the liquidation of noncurrent debts, should not be included in current assets. Also, in classifying assets not related to the operating cycle, a one-year period is always used as the basis for current classification. For example, a note receivable due in 15 months that arose from the sale of land previously held for investment would be classified as noncurrent even if the normal operating cycle exceeds 15 months.

In addition to cash, receivables, and inventories, current assets typically include such resources as prepaid expenses and marketable securities. Prepayments of such items as insurance and rent are not current assets in the sense that they will be converted into cash but on the basis that, if they had not been prepaid, the use of cash or other current assets during the operating cycle period would have been required. Long-term prepayments should be reported as noncurrent assets and charged to the operations of several years. If securities of companies, whether marketable or not, are acquired for purposes of control rather than conversion back to cash during the normal operating cycle, they should not be designated as current assets. Other items that might be converted into cash, but are not expected to be converted and therefore should not be classified as current assets, include the cash surrender value of life insurance policies, land, and depreciable assets.

Current assets are normally listed on the balance sheet in the order of their liquidity. These assets, with the exception of marketable securities and inventories, are usually reported at their estimated realizable values. Thus, current receivable balances are reduced by allowances for estimated uncollectible accounts. Marketable equity securities should be reported at the lower of aggregate cost or market.[6] Inventories may be reported at cost or on the basis of "cost of market, whichever is lower."

The current asset section of the balance sheet for Metropolitan, Inc., a hypothetical company, is illustrated below.

Current assets:	
Cash	$ 52,650
Marketable securities (reported at market; cost, $72,600)	67,350
Receivables (net of allowance for doubtful accounts)	363,700
Inventories (reported at fifo cost or market, whichever is lower)	536,100
Prepaid expenses and other	32,900
Total current assets	$1,052,700

Current liabilites are those obligations that are reasonably expected to be paid using current assets or by creating other current liabilities. Generally, if a liability is reasonably expected to be paid within 12 months, it is classified as current. As with receivables, payables arising from the normal operating activities may be classified as current even if they are not to be paid within 12 months, but within the operating cycle if it exceeds 12 months. Items commonly reported as current liabilities include:

1. Short-term borrowings
2. Accounts payable
3. Accrued salaries and wages
4. Accrued rental expense
5. Accrued interest expense
6. Accrued taxes
7. Current portion of long-term obligations

[6]*Statement of Financial Accounting Standards No. 12*, "Accounting for Certain Marketable Securities" (Stamford: Financial Accounting Standards Board, 1975), par. 8.

The current liability classification, however, generally does not include the following items, since these do not require the use of resources classified as current.

1. Short-term obligations expected to be refinanced.[7]
2. Debts to be liquidated from funds that have been accumulated and are reported as noncurrent assets.
3. Loans on life insurance policies made with the intent that these will not be paid but will be liquidated by deduction from the proceeds of the policies upon their maturity or cancellation.
4. Obligations for advance collections on contracts that will not be completed within one year.[8]

With respect to short-term obligations that normally would come due within the operating cycle but are expected to be refinanced, i.e., discharged by means of the issuance of new obligations in their place, the FASB has concluded that such obligations should be excluded from current liabilities if the following conditions are met: (1) the intent of the company is to refinance the obligations on a long-term basis, and (2) the company's intent is supported by an ability to consummate the refinancing as evidenced by a post-balance-sheet-date issuance of long-term obligations or equity securities or an explicit financing agreement.[9] In effect, the FASB is recognizing that certain short-term obligations will not require the use of working capital during a period even though they are scheduled to mature during that period. Thus, they should not be classified as current liabilities.

Classification problems can arise when an obligation is **callable** by a creditor because it is difficult to determine exactly when the obligation will be paid. A **callable obligation** is one that is either (1) payable on demand (has no specified due date), or (2) has a specified due date, but is callable if the debtor violates the provisions of the debt agreement. Any obligation that is due on demand or will become due on demand within one year from the balance sheet date (or operating cycle if longer) should be classified as current.[10]

In addition, a long-term obligation should be classifed as current if it is callable at the balance sheet date because the debtor is in violation of a contract provision. For example, some instruments have a specific clause identifying conditions that can cause the debt to be immediately callable, e.g. failure to earn a certain return on assets or failure to make an interest payment. These clauses are referred to as **objective acceleration clauses.** The FASB has stated that if conditions that make the obligation callable have

---

[7]*Statement of Financial Accounting Standards No. 6,* "Classification of Short-Term Obligations Expected to be Refinanced" (Stamford: Financial Accounting Standards Board, 1975).

[8]*Accounting Research and Terminology Bulletins—Final Edition, No. 43,* "Restatement and Revision of Accounting Research Bulletins" (New York: American Institute of Certified Public Accountants, 1961), Chapter 3, par. 8 and footnotes 2 and 3.

[9]*Statement of Financial Accounting Standards No. 6,* par. 9–11.

[10]*Statement of Financial Accounting Standards No. 78,* "Classification of Obligations That Are Callable by the Creditor" (Stamford: Financial Accounting Standards Board, 1983), par. 5.

occurred, the debt should be classified as a current debt unless (1) the creditor has waived the right to demand payment for more than one year (or normal operating cycle if longer) from the balance sheet date, or (2) the debtor has cured the deficiency after the balance sheet date but before the statements are issued, and the debt is not callable for a period that extends beyond the debtor's normal operating cycle.[11]

In some cases, the contract does not specifically identify the circumstances under which a payment will be accelerated, but it does indicate some general conditions that permit the lender to unilaterally accelerate the due date. This type of provision is known as a subjective acceleration clause because, although the clause may specify certain conditions under which the obligation may be called, the violation of the conditions cannot be objectively determined. Examples of the wording in such clauses might be, "if the debtor fails to maintain satisfactory operations," or "if a material adverse change occurs." The FASB has recommended that if invoking of the clause is deemed probable, the liability should be classified as a current liability. If invoking of the clause is considered to be reasonably possible, but not probable, only a footnote disclosure is necessary, and the liability continues to be classified as noncurrent.[12]

The current liability section of the balance sheet for Metropolitan, Inc. is illustrated below:

Current liabilities:	
Notes payable	$ 75,000
Accounts payable	312,700
Accrued expenses	86,300
Current portion of long-term debt	62,000
Other current liabilities	28,600
Total current liabilities	$564,600

Noncurrent Assets and Noncurrent Liabilities

Assets and liabilities not qualifying for presentation under the current headings are classified under a number of noncurrent headings. Noncurrent assets may be listed under separate headings, such as "Investments," "Land, buildings, and equipment," "Intangible assets," "Deferred income tax assets," and "Other long-term assets." Noncurrent liabilities are generally listed under separate headings, such as "Long-term debt," "Deferred income tax liabilities," and "Other noncurrent liabilities."

Investments

Investments held for such long-term purposes as regular income, appreciation, or ownership control are reported under the heading "Investments." Examples of items properly reported under this heading are stocks, bonds, and mortgage holdings; securities of affiliated companies and advances to such companies; sinking fund assets consisting of cash and securities held

---

[11]*Ibid.*

[12]*FASB Technical Bulletin, 79–3,* "Subjective Acceleration Clauses in Long-Term Debt Agreements" (New York: American Institute of Certified Public Accountants, December, 1979), par. 003.

for the redemption of bonds or stocks, the replacement of buildings, or the payment of pensions; land held for investment purposes; the cash surrender value of life insurance; and other miscellaneous investments not used directly in the operations of the business. Although many long-term investments are reported at cost, there are modifications to the valuation of some investments that will be discussed in later chapters.

Land, Buildings, and Equipment

Properties of a tangible and relatively permanent character that are used in the normal business operations are reported under "Land, buildings, and equipment" or other appropriate headings, such as property and equipment. Land, buildings, machinery, tools, furniture, fixtures, and vehicles are included under this heading. Most tangible properties except land are normally reported at cost less accumulated depreciation.

Intangible Assets

The long-term rights and privileges of a nonphysical nature acquired for use in business operations are often reported under the heading "Intangible assets." Included in this class are such items as goodwill, patents, trademarks, franchises, copyrights, formulas, leaseholds, and organization costs. Intangible assets are normally reported at cost less amounts previously amortized.

Other Noncurrent Assets

Those noncurrent assets not suitably reported under any of the previous classifications may be listed under the general heading "Other noncurrent assets" or may be listed separately under special descriptive headings. Such assets include, for example, long-term advances to officers, long-term receivables, deposits made with taxing authorities and utility companies, and deferred income tax assets.

Prepayments for services or benefits to be received over a number of periods are properly regarded as noncurrent. Among these are such items as plant rearrangement costs and developmental and improvement costs. These long-term prepayments are frequently reported under a "Deferred costs" or "Deferred charges" heading. However, objection can be raised to a deferred costs category since this designation could be applied to all costs assignable to future periods including inventories, buildings and equipment, and intangible assets. The deferred costs heading may be avoided by reporting long-term prepayments within the other noncurrent assets section or under separate descriptive headings.

A deferred income tax asset account may be shown under "Other noncurrent assets" or may be reported separately. Deferred income tax assets arise when taxable income exceeds reported income because of temporary differences, and the analysis of the future periods indicates that the advance payment can be recovered against other income tax liabilities.

The noncurrent assets section of the balance sheet for Metropolitan, Inc. is illustrated below:

Noncurrent assets:	
Investments..............................	$ 128,000
Land......................................	76,300
Buildings and equipment (net of accumulated	
depreciation of $228,600)	732,900
Intangible assets	165,000
Other noncurrent assets	37,800
Total noncurrent assets.................	$1,140,000

Long-Term Debt

Long-term notes, bonds, mortgages, and similar obligations not requiring the use of current funds for their retirement are generally reported on the balance sheet under the heading "Long-term debt."

When an amount borrowed is not the same as the amount ultimately required in settlement of the debt, and the debt is stated in the accounts at its maturity amount, a debt discount or premium is reported. The discount or premium should be related to the debt item; a discount, then, should be subtracted from the amount reported for the debt, and a premium should be added to the amount reported for the debt. The debt is thus reported at its present value as measured by the proceeds from its issuance.

To illustrate, bond premiums and discounts could be reported as follows:

	Premium	Discount
Bonds Payable..........	$10,000,000	$10,000,000
Plus Premium	550,000	
Less Discount...........		600,000
Net obligation	$10,550,000	$ 9,400,000

In many cases, only the net obligation is reported.

Amortization of the discount or premium brings the obligation to the maturity amount by the end of its normal term. When a note, a bond issue, or a mortgage formerly classified as a long-term obligation becomes payable within a year, it should be reclassified and presented as a current liability, except when the obligation is to be refinanced, as discussed earlier, or is to be paid out of a sinking fund.

Long-Term Lease Obligations

Some leases of land, buildings, and equipment are financially structured so that they are in substance a debt-financed purchase. The FASB has established criteria to determine which leases are in effect purchases, or capital leases, rather than ordinary operating leases. In accounting for capital leases, the present value of the future minimum lease payments is recorded as a long-term liability. That portion of the present value due within the next year, or normal operating cycle, whichever is longer, is classified as a current liability. As capital leases have become more common, this category appears more often on company balance sheets. The 1987 *Accounting Trends and Techniques* reports that 448 of the 600 companies surveyed reported capital lease obligations on the balance sheet.[13]

Deferred Income Tax Liability

The credit balance in this account indicates that, due to temporary differences between taxable income and financial income, a future tax liability may have to be paid. The most common temporary difference occurs in computing depreciation expense for book and tax purposes. Generally, the tax regulations permit a faster write-off than is allowable for financial reporting purposes.

Almost all major companies include a deferred income tax liability category in their statements. Over the past twenty years, the amounts included in this category have greatly expanded. As companies grow, the cumulative temporary differences also grow. In order to compute this liability, a schedule of the expected future reversals of the temporary differences must be prepared. Because tax laws may change before the taxes must be paid, and because the liability is not reported at its present (discounted) value, some analysts disregard the balance in this account when analyzing the company's debt position.

Other Noncurrent Liabilities

Those noncurrent liabilities not suitably reported under the separate headings may be listed under this general heading or may be listed separately under special descriptive headings. Such liabilities could include long-term obligations to company officers or affiliated companies, matured but unclaimed bond principal and interest obligations, long-term liabilities under pension plans, and unearned revenues.

Contingent Liabilities

Past activities or circumstances may give rise to possible future liabilities, although legal obligations do not exist on the date of the balance sheet. These possible claims are known as contingent liabilities. They are potential obligations involving uncertainty as to possible losses. As future events occur or fail to occur, this uncertainty will be resolved. Thus, a contingent liability is distinguishable from an **estimated liability**. The latter is a definite obligation with only the amount of the obligation in question and subject to estimation at the balance sheet date. There may not be any doubt as to the amount of a contingent liability, for example,

---

[13]*Accounting Trends and Techniques—1987* (New York: American Institute of Certified Public Accountants, 1987), p. 199.

a pending lawsuit, but there is considerable uncertainty as to whether the obligation will actually materialize.

In the past, contingent liabilities were not recorded in the accounts nor presented on the balance sheet. When they were disclosed, it was in the notes to the financial statements. As indicated in Chapter 1, since the issuance of FASB Statement No. 5, if a future payment is considered probable, the liability should be recorded by a debit to a loss account and a credit to a liability account.[14] Otherwise, the contingent nature of the loss may be disclosed in a note to the financial statements as discussed on page 181. The noncurrent liabilities section of Metropolitan, Inc.'s balance sheet is illustrated below.

Noncurrent liabilities:	
Long-term debt:	
Notes payable	$ 75,000
Bonds payable	365,000
Long-term lease obligations	135,000
Deferred income tax liability	126,700
Other noncurrent liabilities	72,500
Total noncurrent liabilities	$774,200

Owners' Equity   The method of reporting the owners' equity varies with the form of the business unit. Business units are typically divided into three categories: (1) **proprietorships**, (2) **partnerships**, and (3) **corporations**. In the case of a proprietorship, the owner's equity in assets is reported by means of a single capital account. The balance in this account is the cumulative result of the owner's investments and withdrawals as well as past earnings and losses. In a partnership, capital accounts are established for each partner. Capital account balances summarize the investments and withdrawals and shares of past earnings and losses of each partner, and thus measure the partners' individual equities in the partnership assets.

In a corporation, the difference between assets and liabilities is referred to as **owners' equity**, **shareholders' equity**, or simply, **capital**. In presenting the owners' equity on the balance sheet, a distinction is made between the equity originating from the stockholders' investments, referred to as contributed capital or paid-in capital, and the equity originating from earnings, referred to as retained earnings.

The relationship and distinction between the amount of capital contributed or paid in by the owners of the corporation relative to the amount the company has earned and retained in the business is a significant one. Such disclosure helps creditors and investors assess the long-term ability of a company to internally finance its own operations. If the contributed capital of a corporation is large relative to the total owners' equity, it means the corporation has been financed primarily from external sources, usually from

---

[14]*Statement of Financial Accounting Standards No. 5*, "Accounting for Contingencies" (Stamford: Financial Accounting Standards Board, 1975), par. 8–13.

the sale of stock to investors. If the earned capital of a corporation is large relative to the total owners' equity, it means the company has been profitable in the past and has retained those earnings in the business to help finance its activities. This distinction between earned and contributed capital is not as important for a proprietorship or partnership because the owners of those types of businesses generally are also involved in their management and therefore are aware of how the company activities are being financed.

Contributed Capital

Contributed (or paid-in) capital is generally reported in two parts: (1) **capital stock** and (2) **additional paid-in capital**. The amount reported on the balance sheet as capital stock usually reflects the number of shares issued multiplied by the par value or stated value per share. When the stock does not have a par or stated value, capital stock is reported at the amount received on its original sale or at some other value as stipulated by law or assigned by the corporation's board of directors. When more than one class of stock has been issued, the stock of each class is reported separately.

Additional paid-in capital represents investments by stockholders in excess of the amounts assignable to capital stock. It may also reflect transactions other than the sale of stock, such as the acquisition of property as a result of a donation or the sale of treasury stock at more than cost. Treasury stock is stock that has been issued but subsequently reacquired by the corporation and is being held for possible future reissuance or retirement.

Additional paid-in capital balances are added to capital stock so that the total amount of contributed capital is reported on the balance sheet. Treasury stock is usually subtracted from the sum of contributed capital and retained earnings balances. Contributed capital is discussed in detail in Chapter 16.

Retained Earnings

The amount of undistributed earnings of past periods is reported as **retained earnings**. The total amount thus shown will probably not represent cash available for payment as dividends since past years' earnings will usually already have been reinvested in other assets. An excess of dividends and losses over earnings results in a negative retained earnings balance called a deficit. The balance of retained earnings is added to the contributed capital total in summarizing the stockholders' equity; a deficit is subtracted.

Portions of retained earnings are sometimes reported as restricted and unavailable as a basis for dividends. Restricted earnings may be designated as *appropriations*. Appropriations are sometimes made for such purposes as sinking funds, plant expansion, loss contingencies, and the reacquisition of capital stock. Often such appropriations are disclosed in a note rather than in the accounts. When appropriations have been made in the accounts, retained earnings on the balance sheet consists of an amount designated as appropriated and a balance designated as *unappropriated* or *free*. The term "reserve" should not generally be used to designate appropriations. Retained earnings is discussed in detail in Chapter 17.

The Owners' Equity section of the balance sheet of Metropolitan, Inc. is illustrated as follows:

Contributed capital:
  Preferred stock, $50 par, 20,000 shares authorized,
    2,500 shares issued and outstanding $125,000
  Common stock, $5 par, 100,000 shares authorized,
    60,000 shares issued and outstanding   300,000
  Additional paid-in capital 120,000 $545,000
Retained earnings . . . . '.   308,900
    Total owners' equity $853,900

Offsets on the Balance Sheet

As illustrated in the preceding discussion, a number of balance sheet items are frequently reported at gross amounts calling for the recognition of offset balances in arriving at proper valuations. Such offset balances are found in asset, liability, and owners' equity categories. In the case of assets, for example, an allowance for doubtful accounts is subtracted from the sum of the customers' accounts in reporting the net amount estimated as collectible; accumulated depreciation is subtracted from the related buildings and equipment balances in reporting the costs of the assets still assignable to future revenues. In the case of liabilities, reacquired bonds or *treasury* bonds, are subtracted from bonds issued in reporting the amount of bonds outstanding; a bond discount is subtracted from the face value of bonds outstanding in reporting the net amount of the debt. In the stockholders' equity section of the balance sheet, treasury stock is deducted in reporting total stockholders' equity.

The types of offsets described above, utilizing contra accounts, are required for proper reporting of particular balance sheet items. Offsets are improper, however, if applied to different asset and liability balances or to asset and owners' equity balances even when there is some relationship between the items. For example, a company may accumulate cash in a special fund to discharge certain tax liabilities; but as long as control of the cash is retained and the liabilities are still outstanding, the company should continue to report both the asset and the liabilities separately. Or a company may accumulate cash in a special fund for the redemption of preferred stock outstanding; but until the cash is applied to the reacquisition of the stock, the company must continue to report the asset as well as the owners' equity item. A company may have made advances to certain salespersons while at the same time reporting accrued amounts payable to others; but a net figure cannot be justified here, just as a net figure cannot be justified for the offset of trade receivables against trade payables.

The offset criteria came under scrutiny in the mid 1980s when a new standard for pension accounting was issued by the FASB. The FASB faced a major question concerning whether pension assets should be reported separately from pension liabilities or whether the past practice of allowing pension assets to be offset against pension liabilities should be continued. The Board elected to allow offsets of pension assets and liabilities, but also decided to add the topic of offsetting to its agenda.

Form of the Balance Sheet

The form of the balance sheet presentation varies in practice. Its form may be influenced by the nature and size of the business, by the character of the business properties, by requirements set by regulatory bodies, or by display preferences in presenting key relationships. The balance sheet is prepared in one of two basic forms: (1) the account form, with assets being reported on the left-hand side and liabilities and owners' equity on the right-hand side, or (2) the report form, with assets, liabilities, and owners' equity sections appearing in vertical arrangement.[15]

The order of asset and liability classifications may vary, but most businesses emphasize working capital position and liquidity, with assets and liabilities presented in the order of their liquidity. An exception to this order is generally found in the Land, Buildings, and Equipment section where the more permanent assets with longer useful lives are listed first. The Balance Sheet for Metropolitan, Inc. reproduced on page 178 illustrates the account form reported in the order of liquidity. The balance sheet of General Mills, Inc., reproduced in Appendix A, is an example of the report form. The categories used by individual companies vary widely; however, the basic format and structure remain the same.

In some industries the investment in plant assets is so significant that they are placed first on the balance sheet. Also, the equity capital and long-term debt obtained to finance plant assets are listed before current liabilities. The utility industry is a good example of this situation. A balance sheet for the Utah Power and Light Company is illustrated on page 179.

Balance sheets are generally presented in comparative form. With comparative reports for two or more dates, information is made available concerning the nature and trend of financial changes taking place within the periods between balance sheet dates. Currently, a minimum of two years of balance sheets and three years of income statements and cash flow statements are required by the SEC to be included in the annual report to shareholders.

Additional Disclosure to the Balance Sheet

Regardless of which form of balance sheet is used, the basic statement does not provide all the information desired by users. Among other things, creditors and investors need to know what methods of accounting were used by the company to arrive at the balances in the accounts. The users often feel they need more information than just account titles and amounts. Sometimes the additional information desired is descriptive and is reported in narrative form. In other cases, additional numerical data are reported.

[15]These two forms have been equally popular; however, the report form has been increasing in popularity. The *Accounting Trends & Techniques* reported that in 1986, 356 of 600 companies used the report form and 241 the account form. p. 109.

Metropolitan, Inc.
Balance Sheet
December 31, 1991

Assets			Liabilities		
Current assets:			**Current liabilities:**		
			Notes payable	$ 75,000	
Cash	$ 52,650		Accounts payable	312,700	
Marketable securities			Accrued expenses	86,300	
(reported at market;			Current portion of long-		
cost, $72,600)	67,350		term debt	62,000	
Receivables (net of			Other current liabilities ..	28,600	$ 564,600
allowance for doubtful					
accounts)	363,700		**Noncurrent liabilities:**		
Inventories (reported at			Notes payable	$ 75,000	
fifo cost or market,			Bonds payable.........	365,000	
whichever is lower)...	536,100		Long-term lease		
Prepaid expenses and			obligations	135,000	
other	32,900	$1,052,700	Deferred income tax		
			liability	126,700	
			Other noncurrent		
			liabilities............	72,500	774,200
			Total liabilities............		$1,338,800
			Owners' Equity		
Noncurrent assets:			**Contributed capital:**		
Investments	$128,000		Preferred stock, $50 par,		
Land	76,300		20,000 shares		
Buildings and equipment			authorized, 2,500		
(net of accumulated			shares issued and		
depreciation of			outstanding	$125,000	
$228,600)..........	732,900		Common stock, $5 par,		
Intangible assets	165,000		100,000 shares		
Other noncurrent assets	37,800	1,140,000	authorized, 60,000		
			shares issued and		
			outstanding	300,000	
			Additional paid-in capital	120,000	$ 545,000
			Retained earnings		308,900
			Total owners' equity		$ 853,900
			Total liabilities and owners'		
Total assets		$2,192,700	equity................		$2,192,700

There are at least three methods commonly used by companies to provide additional disclosure:

1. parenthetical notations in the body of the statement
2. notes to the basic financial statements, and
3. separate schedules furnished by management that supplement the basic financial statements.

It is generally felt that readers of financial statements are more likely to see the additional information if it is included on the face of the financial statement in a parenthetical notation. However, if the data are lengthy or complex, it is generally better to provide the detail in notes recognized as being an integral part of the statements themselves. Unless specifically excluded, notes are covered by the auditor's opinion. In some instances, the

Exhibit 5–1   Utah Power & Light Company and Subsidiary

UTAH POWER & LIGHT COMPANY AND SUBSIDIARY
Consolidated Balance Sheets
(in thousands of dollars)

December 31,	1987
ASSETS	
Utility plant (Notes 2, 3, 4 and 11):	
Electric	**$3,451,857**
Steam heating	**1,423**
Under construction	**37,895**
Total	**3,491,175**
Less accumulated depreciation	**804,493**
Utility plant—net	**2,686,682**
Nonutility property and investments—at cost:	
Pollution control financing proceeds on deposit with trustee (Note 11)	**6,369**
Nonutility property and other investments (Note 6)	**61,822**
Total nonutility property and investments	**68,191**
Current assets:	
Cash—including temporary investments (Notes 11 and 14)	**111,209**
Receivables—principally customers (Note 12)	**110,926**
Unbilled revenues (Note 7)	**42,951**
Fuel—at average cost	**34,559**
Materials and supplies—at average cost	**73,112**
Prepayments	**23,308**
Total current assets	**396,065**
Deferred debits (Notes 5, 6 and 11)	**117,705**
Total	**$3,268,643**
CAPITALIZATION AND LIABILITIES	
Capital paid-in and retained earnings:	
Cumulative preferred stock—outstanding: 1987—2,000,000 shares; 1986—5,400,000 shares (Note 11) (Schedule 1)	**$ 50,000**
Common stock—outstanding: 1987—58,953,462 shares; 1986—57,547,519 shares (Note 9)	**377,302**
Capital paid in excess of par value (Notes 9 and 11)	**584,859**
Retained earnings (Notes 10 and 13)	**126,397**
Total capital paid-in and retained earnings	**1,138,558**
Long-term debt—excluding currently maturing long-term debt (Note 11) (Schedule 2)	**1,317,307**
Other noncurrent liabilities (Note 13)	**40,056**
Current liabilities:	
Currently maturing long-term debt (Schedule 2)	**—**
Notes payable (Note 14)	**—**
Accounts payable	**105,484**
Dividends declared	**34,954**
Taxes accrued	**18,434**
Interest accrued	**26,379**
Tax collections payable	**11,018**
Current portion of accrued fuel adjustment (Note 13)	**12,245**
Other	**4,786**
Total current liabilities	**213,300**
Deferred credits:	
Accumulated investment tax credits (Note 5)	**156,560**
Accumulated deferred income taxes (Note 5)	**339,719**
Other (Note 6)	**63,143**
Total deferred credits	**559,422**
Commitments and contingent liabilities (Note 12)	
Total	**$3,268,643**

See Notes to Financial Statements.

notes include detailed schedules that provide additional information to the serious user. Several parenthetical notations are included in the balance sheet for Metropolitan, Inc. For example, in current assets, there are parenthetical comments concerning valuation. In each case, the same data could have been disclosed in notes.

The following types of notes are typically included by management as support to the basic financial statements.

1. Summary of significant accounting policies.
2. Additional information (both numerical and descriptive) to support summary totals found on the financial statements, usually the balance sheet. This is the most common type of note used.
3. Information about items that are not reported on the basic statements because the items fail to meet the recognition criteria, but are still considered to be significant to users in their decision making.
4. Supplementary information required by the FASB or the SEC to fulfill the full-disclosure principle.

Each of these classifications is briefly discussed in the following paragraphs.

Summary of Significant Accounting Policies

GAAP requires that information about the accounting principles and policies followed in arriving at the amounts in the financial statements be disclosed to the users. The Accounting Principles Board concluded in APB Opinion No. 22:

> . . . When financial statements are issued purporting to present fairly financial position, changes in financial position, and results of operations in accordance with generally accepted accounting principles, a description of all significant accounting policies of the reporting entity should be included as an integral part of the financial statements.[16]

The Board further stated:

> . . . In general, the disclosure should encompass important judgments as to appropriateness of principles relating to recognition of revenue and allocation of asset costs to current and future periods; in particular, it should encompass those accounting principles and methods that involve any of the following: (a) A selection from existing acceptable alternatives; (b) Principles and methods peculiar to the industry in which the reporting entity operates, even if such principles and methods are predominantly followed in that industry; (c) Unusual or innovative applications of generally accepted accounting principles (and, as applicable, of principles and methods peculiar to the industry in which the reporting entity operates).[17]

---

[16]*Opinions of the Accounting Principles Board, No. 22*, "Disclosure of Accounting Policies" (New York: American Institute of Certified Public Accountants, 1972), par. 8.

[17]*Ibid.*, par. 12.

Examples of disclosures of accounting policies required by this opinion would include, among others, those relating to depreciation methods, amortization of intangible assets, inventory pricing methods, the recognition of profit on long-term construction-type contracts, and the recognition of revenue from leasing operations.[18]

The exact format for reporting the summary of accounting policies was not specified by the APB. However, the Board recommended such disclosure be included as the initial note or as a separate summary preceding the notes to the financial statements. The summary of significant accounting policies for General Mills, Inc. is presented in Appendix A.

Additional Information to Support Summary Totals

In order to prepare a balance sheet that is brief enough to be understandable but complete enough to meet the needs of users, notes are sometimes added that provide either quantitative or narrative information to support the statement amounts. The General Mills, Inc. notes in Appendix A include a number of examples of this type of note, e.g., Note Six, Short Term Borrowings; Note Seven, Long-Term Debt; and Note Thirteen, Income Taxes, all provide additional numerical information to support the statement totals. Much of this detail is provided in response to specific disclosure requirements of either the SEC or the FASB. The specific format for the schedules is generally left to management's discretion. Some of the notes that support amounts in the financial statements are primarily descriptive in nature. Examples of this type in the General Mills statements include Note Eleven, Employees' Retirement Plans and Note Twelve, Profit-Sharing Plans.

Information about Items Not Included in Financial Statements

As discussed in Chapter 2, items included in the financial statements must meet certain recognition criteria. Even though an item might not meet the criteria for recognition in the statements, information concerning the item might be relevant to the users. Gain and loss contingencies are good examples of this type of item. **Gain contingencies** relate to possible claims the company has to receive assets, but whose existence is too uncertain to recognize, e.g., a possible favorable court settlement in a lawsuit. **Loss contingencies** relate to possible claims against the company that might require an outflow of assets. In Statement No. 5, the FASB indicated that if the incurrence of a loss is "reasonably possible," the contingency should be disclosed in the notes to the financial statements. The information provided should include as much data as possible to assist the user in evaluating the risk of the loss contingency.[19]

Supplementary Information

The FASB and SEC both require supplementary information that must be reported in separate schedules. For example, the FASB requires the disclo-

---

[18]*Ibid.*, par. 13.

[19]*Statement of Financial Accounting Standards No. 5.* Further discussion of loss contingencies and disclosure examples are presented in Chapter 14.

sure of quarterly information for certain companies. While the information in these notes is important to the users, it may not be covered by the auditors' opinion. A note that is not covered by the opinion should be clearly marked "unaudited." For example, Note 16 in General Mills' statements (Appendix A) presents unaudited quarterly data.

Subsequent Events

Although a balance sheet is prepared as of a given date, it is usually several weeks and sometimes even months after that date before the financial statements are issued and made available to external users. During this time, the accounts are analyzed, adjusting entries are prepared, and for many companies, an independent audit is completed. Events may take place during this "subsequent period" that have an impact upon the balance sheet and the other basic financial statements for the preceding year. Some of these events may even affect the amounts reported in the statements. These events are referred to in the accounting literature as **subsequent events** or **post-balance-sheet events**.

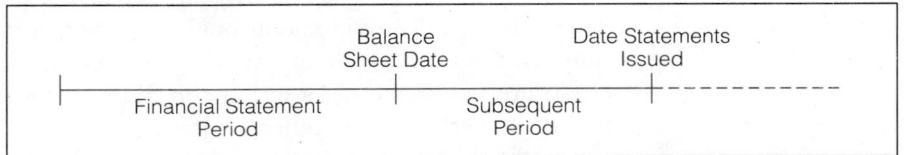

There are two different types of subsequent events that require consideration by management and evaluation by the independent auditor:[20]

1. Those that affect the amounts to be reported in one or more of the financial statements for the preceding accounting period.
2. Those that do not affect the amounts in the financial statements for the preceding accounting period, but that should be reported in the notes to these financial statements.

The first type of subsequent event usually provides additional information that affects the amounts included in the financial statements. The reported amounts in several accounts, such as Allowance for Doubtful Accounts, Warranty Liability, and Income Taxes Payable, reflect estimates of the expected value. These estimates are based on information available as of a given date. If a subsequent event provides information that shows that the conditions existing as of the balance sheet date were different than those assumed when making the estimate, a change in the amount to be reported in the financial statements is required.

To illustrate this type of event, assume that a month after the balance sheet date it is learned that a major customer has filed for bankruptcy. This information was not known as of the balance sheet date, and only ordinary

[20]*AICPA Professional Standards*, AU Section 560, "Subsequent Events" (Chicago: Commerce Clearing House, 1985, par. .02–.05.

provisions were made in determining the Allowance for Doubtful Accounts. In all likelihood, the customer was already in financial difficulty at the balance sheet date, but it was not general knowledge. The filing of bankruptcy reveals that the conditions at the balance sheet date were different than those assumed in preparing the statements, and a further adjustment to both the balance sheet and income statement is indicated.

The second type of subsequent event does not reveal a difference in the conditions as of the balance sheet date, but involves an event that is considered so significant that its disclosure is highly relevant to readers of the financial statements. These events will usually affect the subsequent year's financial statements and thus may affect decisions currently being made by users. Examples of such events include a casualty that destroys material portions of a company's assets, acquisition of a major subsidiary, sale of significant amounts of bonds or capital stock, and losses on receivables when the cause of the loss occurred subsequent to the balance sheet date. Information about this type of event is included in the notes to the financial statements and serves to put the reader on notice that the predictive value of the statements may be affected by the subsequent event. American Express Company reported this type of subsequent event in its 1987 financial statements as follows:

Exhibit 5–2   American Express Company

---

2 • Subsequent Event

In January 1988, Shearson Lehman Brothers Holdings Inc. (Holdings) completed its acquisition of The E. F. Hutton Group Inc. (Hutton). Pursuant to a tender offer commencing December 7, 1987, a wholly owned subsidiary of Holdings purchased 29.6 million shares of Hutton common stock at $29.25 per share in cash. The purchase was financed by borrowings of Shearson Lehman of approximately $800 million in senior subordinated debt at various interest rates and by working capital of Shearson Lehman of $66 million. Subsequently, approximately 3.3 million shares of Hutton common stock will be exchanged for approximately $96.5 million in face value of 10¾% Senior Subordinated Notes of Shearson Lehman. The combined company was renamed Shearson Lehman Hutton Inc.

The transaction will be accounted for as a purchase in January 1988. Accordingly, the acquisition is not reflected in the accompanying financial statements.

There are, of course, many business events that occur during this subsequent period that are related only to the subsequent year and therefore have no impact on the preceding year's financial statements.

The overall objective of note disclosure is clarification of the information presented in the financial statements. Disclosure requirements are so extensive that they cannot be completely discussed in any single chapter. Specific requirements will be noted as appropriate throughout the text.

Limitations of The Balance Sheet

Notwithstanding its usefulness, the balance sheet has some serious limitations. External users often need to know a company's worth. The balance sheet, however, does not generally reflect the current values of a business. Instead, the entity's resources and obligations are usually shown at historical costs based on past transactions and events. The historical cost measurements represent market values existing at the dates the transactions or events occurred. However, when the prices of specific assets increase significantly after the acquisition date, as has certainly been the case recently in the United States, then the balance sheet numbers are not relevant for evaluating a company's current worth.

A related problem with the balance sheet is the instability of the dollar, the standard accounting measuring unit in the United States. Because of general price changes in the economy, the dollar does not maintain a constant purchasing power. Yet the historical costs of resources and equities shown on the balance sheet are not adjusted for changes in the purchasing power of the measuring unit. The result is a balance sheet that reflects assets, liabilities, and equities in terms of unequal purchasing power units. Some elements, for example, may be stated in terms of 1960 dollars and some in terms of 1991 dollars. The variations in purchasing power of the amounts reported in the balance sheet make comparisons among companies and even within a single company less meaningful.

An additional limitation of the balance sheet, also related to the need for comparability, is that all companies do not classify and report all like items similarly. For example, titles and account classifications vary; some companies provide considerably more detail than others; and some companies with apparently similar transactions report them differently. Such differences make comparisons difficult and diminish the potential value of balance sheet analysis.

The balance sheet may be considered deficient in another respect. Due primarily to measurement problems, some entity resources and obligations are not reported on the balance sheet. For example, the employees of a company may be one of its most valuable resources; yet, they are not shown on the balance sheet because their future service potentials are not measurable in monetary terms. Similarly, a company's potential liability for polluting the air would not normally be shown on its balance sheet. The assumptions of the traditional accounting model identified in Chapter 2, specifically the requirements of arm's-length transactions or events measurable in monetary terms, add to the objectivity of balance sheet disclosures but at the same time cause some information to be omitted that is likely to be relevant to certain users' decisions.

One author, reflecting on these limitations, wrote the following:

The current balance sheet published by most corporations is a pathetic financial representation of a company's real resources and obligations. It is a dumping ground for dangling debit and credit entries and a listing of dollar values determined by different, often outmoded, accounting concepts. Users find that the face of such statements often excludes more relevant data than it includes.[21]

This dim view of the balance sheet is not shared by many accountants and users of financial statements. The balance sheet is an important statement for investors and creditors. While its limitations must be understood, it can still provide a user with valuable information for decisions.

The conceptual framework established by the FASB stresses the objective of usefulness of accounting information. During the past few years, the Board has considered several issues that directly affect the balance sheet, using the conceptual framework as a guide in the development of new standards. In some instances, the new standards have a direct impact on the amounts reported on the balance sheet. Notable examples include pensions, receivables with right of return, deferred income tax accounting, and interest capitalization. In other instances, the impact has been on required disclosure in notes, such as the requirement for some companies to disclose segment data and off-balance-sheet financing arrangements. These and other examples will be discussed throughout the text.

Overview of The Statement of Cash Flows

Although the income statement and the balance sheet have historically constituted the primary financial statements for an entity, they do not provide enough information to assess the amounts, timing, and uncertainty of future cash flows, a primary objective of financial reporting.[22] To assist in this assessment, a third general purpose financial statement has been required since 1971. Until 1987, this funds statement was referred to as a statement of changes in financial position, and was most often prepared emphasizing the changes in working capital from period to period. However, in Concepts Statement No. 5, the FASB recommended that the full set of general purpose financial statements should include a statement of "cash flows during the period."

> A statement of cash flows directly or indirectly reflects an entity's cash receipts classified by major uses during a period. It provides useful information about an entity's activities in generating cash through operations to repay debt, distribute dividends, or reinvest to maintain or expand operating activity; about its financing activities, both debt and equity; and about its investing or spending of cash. Important uses of information about an entity's current cash receipts and payments include helping to assess factors such as the entity's liquidity, financial flexibility, profitability, and risk.[23]

[21]David E. Hawkins, "Towards the New Balance Sheet," *Harvard Business Review*, November–December 1984, p. 156.

[22]*Statement of Financial Accounting Concepts No. 1*, "Objectives of Financial Reporting by Business Enterprises" (Stamford: Financial Accounting Standards Board, 1978), par 37.

[23]*Statement of Financial Accounting Concepts No. 5*, "Recognition and Measurement in Financial Statements of Business Enterprises" (Stamford: Financial Accounting Standards Board, December, 1984), par. 63.

In 1987, the FASB acted on this recommendation and issued Statement No. 95 that requires a **statement of cash flows** to replace the more general statement of changes financial position.[24]

Although the statement of cash flows is based on the same data as the balance sheet and income statement, it helps decision makers answer questions that are not addressed directly by the other basic statements. For example, the statement of cash flows helps the reader answer questions such as: How was the income used by the company? Why were dividends not larger in view of increased earnings? How can the company distribute dividends in excess of current earnings? How was the plant expansion financed? Why is cash decreasing when earnings are positive and growing? How was the bond indebtedness repaid even though the company suffered a substantial operating loss? Will the future cash flow be sufficient to meet the debt repayment provisions?

The statement of cash flows is intended to provide a summary of cash inflows and outflows for a period of time. The FASB specified a format in Statement No. 95 that highlights cash flows in three major categories: (1) **operating activities**, (2) **investing activities**, and (3) **financing activities**. Exhibit 5-1 summarizes the major types of cash receipts and cash payments included in each category.

To illustrate the special contribution made by this new statement, consider the needs of a prospective creditor and the means for meeting these needs. An individual or institution asked to make a long-term loan to a company is concerned with the company's prosposed use of the borrowed cash, the ability of the company to meet the periodic interest payments on the loan, and the ability of the company ultimately to repay the loan. Balance sheet analysis will provide answers to questions relative to the cash and near-cash items on hand, the working capital of the business—its amount and composition—present long-term indebtedness, and the implications on financial position if the loan is granted. Income statement analysis will provide answers to questions relative to the earnings of the company, the adequacy of earnings to cover interest charges, and the implications as to earnings and interest charges if the loan is granted. Cash flow statement analysis will indicate the past cash flows from operating, investing, and financing activities. This information can be used to estimate the cash that will be generated in the future if the loan is granted, and add insight into the ability of the company to meet the repayment terms of the added indebtedness.

In requiring a statement of cash flows, the FASB does not specify an exact format to be used, although it does require a classification into the three main categories identified above. The reporting of operating activities may be done in one of two ways. The **direct method** itemizes major

[24]*Statement of Financial Accounting Standards No. 95*, "Statement of Cash Flows (Stamford: Financial Accounting Standards Board, November 1987).

Exhibit 5–3   Major Classifications of Cash Flows

Operating Activities
Cash receipts from:
Sale of goods or services
Interest revenue
Dividend revenue
Cash payments to:
Suppliers for inventory purchases
Employees for services
Governments for taxes
Lenders for interest expense
Others for other expenses (e.g., utilities, rent)
Investing Activities
Cash receipts from:
Sale of plant assets
Sale of a business segment
Sale of investments in debt or equity securities of other entities
Collection of principal on loans made to other entities
Cash payments to:
Purchase plant assets
Purchase debt or equity securities of other entities
Make loans to other entities
Financing Activities
Cash receipts from:
Issuance of own stock
Borrowing (e.g., bonds, notes, mortgages)
Cash payments to:
Stockholders as dividends
Repay principal amounts borrowed
Repurchase an entity's own stock (treasury stock)

cash operating receipts (for example, customer payments) and cash operating expenditures (for example, purchases of materials) and reports the difference as the net cash flow from operating activities. The **indirect method** begins with the reported net income from the income statement, adjusting this amount for revenue and expense items that do not affect cash (such as depreciation and amortization) and for the difference between accrual-based revenues and expenses and cash basis receipts and expenditures. Both methods report the same cash flow from operating activities; however, the indirect method is more popular with accountants preparing the statements because it is more easily generated from the existing accounting system. The illustration of a statement of cash flows on page 188 uses the indirect method.

The statement of cash flows is prepared by analyzing the changes that occurred in all accounts other than cash reported in the enterprise's balance sheet. Usually, additional information must be obtained from the accounting records to prepare the statement at the level of detail considered useful. The techniques for preparing and analyzing the statement of cash flows are discussed in detail in a later chapter.

Staples Corporation
Statement of Cash Flows (Indirect Method)
For the Year Ended December 31, 1991

Cash flows from operating activities:		
Net income	$25,000	
Adjustments:		
Depreciation	10,000	
Amortization of patents and goodwill	10,600	
Increase in notes and accounts receivable	(5,400)	
Decrease in inventory	4,600	
Decrease in notes and accounts payable	(2,500)	
Net cash flow provided (used) by operations		$42,300
Cash flows from investing activities:		
Proceeds from sale of land	$30,000	
Purchase of building and equipment	(42,000)	
Investment in stock of subsidiary	(25,000)	
Purchase of land	(20,000)	
Net cash flow provided (used) by investing activities ..		(57,000)
Cash flows from financing activities:		
Increase in long-term notes payable	$30,000	
Issuance of common stock.......................	20,000	
Payment of dividends	(15,000)	
Net cash flow provided (used) by financing activities ..		35,000
Net increase (decrease) in cash		$20,300
Cash balance, January 1, 1991.....................		15,600
Cash balance, December 31, 1991		$35,900

Key Terms

Account form of balance sheet 177
Additional paid-in capital 175
Assets 165
Balance sheet 164
Callable obligation 169
Capital stock 175
Contingent liabilities 173
Contributed capital 174
Current assets 167
Current liabilities 168
Deferred income tax assets 171
Deferred income tax liability 173
Deficit 175
Direct method 186
Financing activities 186
Indirect method 187
Investing activities 186
Liabilities 165

Liquidity 164
Net assets 165
Normal operating cycle 167
Objective acceleration clause 169
Operating activities 186
Owners' equity 165
Paid-in capital 174
Post-balance-sheet events 182
Report form of balance sheet 177
Retained earnings 174
Solvency 164
Statement of cash flows 186
Statement of financial position 164
Subjective acceleration clause 170
Subsequent events 182
Treasury stock 175
Working capital 166

Questions

1. In what way is the balance sheet useful to decision makers?
2. What three elements are contained in the balance sheet?
3. What are the major classifications of (a) assets, (b) liabilities, and (c) owners' equity? Indicate the nature of the items reported within each major classification.
4. (a) Why is the distinction between current and noncurrent assets and liabilities considered to be important? (b) What arguments are there for not making a distinction?
5. What criteria are generally used (a) in classifying assets as current or noncurrent? (b) in classifying liabilities as current or noncurrent?
6. (a) What is a subjective acceleration clause? (b) An objective acceleration clause? (c) How do these clauses in debt instruments affect the classification of a liability?
7. Barker's Inc. reports the cash surrender value of life insurance on company officials as a current asset in view of its immediate convertibility into cash. Do you support this treatment? Explain.
8. Indicate under what circumstances each of the following can be considered noncurrent: (a) cash, (b) receivables.
9. Distinguish between the following: (a) contingent liabilities and estimated liabilities. (b) appropriated retained earnings and unappropriated retained earnings.
10. Under what circumstances may offset balances be properly recognized on the balance sheet?
11. What are the major types of notes attached to the financial statements?
12. Under what circumstances might a parenthetical notation on the balance sheet be preferred to a note?
13. What are some examples of supplementary information that is included in the notes?
14. Under what circumstances does a subsequent event lead to a journal entry for the previous reporting period?

15. What is the basic purpose of the statement of cash flows and what kind of information does this statement provide that is not readily available from the other general purpose statements?

16. (a) List the three types of activities or functions that provide and use cash. (b) Why is it more informative to separate cash flows into these three activities than to combine all sources and uses together?

Discussion Cases

Case 5–1   (How much are we really worth?)

Daylight, Inc. has been fighting several takeover bids, including one from Proust Industries. The balance sheet of Daylight shows a net asset position of $35 million. This amounts to a $50 per share book value based on 700,000 shares of common stock issued and outstanding. Proust Industries has presented an offer to purchase Daylight's stock from the stockholders for a cash price of $65 per share. Proust will finance the purchase by using Daylight's assets as collateral for a bank loan. Why might Proust be willing to pay more per share of stock than its book value? If Proust Industries is able to purchase Daylight, how would Proust's balance sheet probably be affected?

Case 5–2   (We've got you now!)

The Piedmont Computer Company has brought legal action against ATC Corporation for alleged monopolistic practices in the development of software. The claim has been pending for two years, with both sides accumulating evidence to support their positions. The case is now ready for trial. ATC Corporation has offered to settle out of court for $500,000, but Piedmont is asking for $5,000,000. Piedmont's attorneys feel an award of $2,500,000 from the court is very likely. If financial statements must be issued prior to the court action, how should Piedmont reflect this contingent claim? Support your decision where possible from the conceptual framework.

Case 5–3   (But what is our liability?)

The Ditka Engineering Co. has signed a third-party loan guarantee for Liberty Company. The loan is from the National Bank of Illinois for $500,000. Liberty has recently filed for bankruptcy, and it is estimated by the company's auditors that creditors can expect to receive no more than 40% of their claims from Liberty. The treasurer of Ditka feels that because of the high uncertainty of final settlement, a liability should be recorded for the entire $500,000. The chief accountant, on the other hand, feels the 40% collection figure is reasonable and proposes that a $300,000 liability be recorded. The president of Ditka does not think a reasonable estimate can be made at this time, and proposes that nothing be accrued for the contingent liability, but that a note be added to the financial statements explaining the situation. As an independent outside auditor, what position would you take? Why?

Case 5–4   (Aren't the financial statements enough?)

Excello Corporation's basic financial statements for the year just ended have been prepared in accordance with GAAP. During the current year, management changed the accounting method for computing depreciation; a major competitor constructed a new plant in the area; three separate lawsuits were brought against the corporation that are not expected to be settled for two years or more; and the corporation continued to use an acceptable revenue recognition principle that differs from that used by most other companies in the industry. Also, after the end of the year, but before the statements were issued, Excello issued additional shares of common stock.

Excello has recently applied for a large bank loan, and the bank has requested a copy of the financial statements. The auditors for Excello have prepared several notes, some quite lengthy, to accompany the financial statements, but Excello's management does not think the loan officer at the bank would understand them and therefore submits the statements without the notes. The bank accepts the statements as submitted.

Which of the events described above should be included in notes to the financial statements? Do you think it is acceptable to delete notes when submitting financial statements to third parties? Substantiate your position.

Case 5–5 (Some kind of accountant you are!)

Early in 1992, Laura Dennis, a recent graduate of Southeast State College, delivers the following financial statements to John Roberts of Roberts, Inc. After a quick review, Roberts explains, "What do you mean I had net income of $20,000? I borrowed $40,000 from the bank and my cash balance decreased by $2,000. I must have had a loss! Some kind of accountant you are!" How should Ms. Dennis answer Mr. Roberts?

ROBERTS, INC.
Balance Sheet
December 31, 1991

	1991	1990
ASSETS		
Cash	$ 3,000	$ 5,000
Accounts receivable	18,000	8,000
Inventory	20,000	15,000
Fixed assets (at cost)	52,000	20,000
Accumulated depreciation	(10,000)	(5,000)
Total assets	$83,000	$43,000
LIABILITIES AND STOCKHOLDERS' EQUITY		
Accounts payable	$ 4,000	$ 9,000
Notes payable—long–term	40,000	0
Common stock, $10 par	20,000	20,000
Retained earnings	19,000	14,000
Total liabilities and stockholders' equity	$83,000	$43,000

ROBERTS, INC.
Combined Statements of Income and Retained Earnings
For the Year Ended December 31, 1991

Sales		$240,000
Cost of goods sold	$150,000	
Operating expenses (including depreciation of $5,000)	70,000	220,000
Net income		$ 20,000
Add, retained earnings, January 1, 1991		14,000
Less dividends paid		(15,000)
Retained earnings, December 31, 1991		$ 19,000

Exercises   **Exercise 5–1   (Balance sheet classification)**

A balance sheet contains the following classifications:

(a) Current assets

(b) Investments

(c) Land, buildings, and equipment

(d) Intangible assets

(e) Other noncurrent assets

(f) Current liabilities

(g) Long-term debt

(h) Unearned revenues

(i) Other noncurrent liabilities

(j) Capital stock

(k) Additional paid-in capital

(l) Retained earnings

Indicate by letter how each of the following accounts would be classified. Place a minus sign (−) after all accounts representing offset or contra balances.

_____ (1) Discount on Bonds Payable

_____ (2) Stock of Subsidiary Corporation

_____ (3) 12% Bonds Payable (due in six months)

_____ (4) U.S. Treasury Notes

_____ (5) Income Tax Payable

_____ (6) Sales Tax Payable

_____ (7) Estimated Claims Under Warranties for Service and Replacements

_____ (8) Accounts Payable (debit balance)

_____ (9) Unearned Rental Revenue (three years in advance)

_____ (10) Long-Term Advances to Officers

_____ (11) Interest Receivable

_____ (12) Preferred Stock Retirement Fund

_____ (13) Trademarks

_____ (14) Allowance for Doubtful Accounts

_____ (15) Dividends Payable

_____ (16) Accumulated Depreciation

_____ (17) Petty Cash Fund

_____ (18) Prepaid Rent

_____ (19) Prepaid Insurance

_____ (20) Organization Costs

Exercise 5–2   (Balance sheet classification)

State how each of the following accounts should be classified on the balance sheet.

(a) Accumulated Patent Amortization

(b) Retained Earnings

(c) Vacation Pay Payable

(d) Retained Earnings Appropriated for Loss Contingencies

(e) Allowance for Doubtful Accounts

(f) Liability for Pension Payments

(g) Marketable Securities

(h) Paid-In Capital from Sale of Stock at More Than Stated Value

(i) Leasehold Improvements

(j) Goodwill

(k) Receivables—U.S. Government Contracts

(l) Advances to Salespersons

(m) Customers Accounts with Credit Balances

(n) Inventory

(o) Patents

(p) Unclaimed Payroll Checks

(q) Employees Income Tax Payable

(r) Subscription Revenue Received in Advance

(s) Interest Payable

(t) Deferred Income Tax Asset

(u) Tools

(v) Deferred Income Tax Liability

(w) Loans to Officers

Exercise 5–3   (Balance sheet preparation—account form)

From the following chart of accounts, prepare a balance sheet in account form showing all balance sheet items properly classified. (No monetary amounts are to be recognized.)

Accounts Payable	Income Tax Expense
Accounts Receivable	Income Tax Payable
Accumulated Depreciation—Buildings	Interest Receivable
Accumulated Depreciation—Equipment	Interest Revenue
Advertising Expense	Inventory
Allowance for Decline in Value of	Investment in Bonds
Marketable Securities	Land
Allowance for Doubtful Accounts	Loss on Purchase Commitments
Bonds Payable	Marketable Securities
Buildings	Miscellaneous General Expense
Cash	Notes Payable
Common Stock	Paid-In Capital from Sale of Common
Cost of Goods Sold	Stock at More Than Stated Value
Deferred Income Tax Liability	Paid-In Capital from Sale of Treasury
Depreciation Expense—Buildings	Stock
Dividends	Patents
Doubtful Accounts Expense	Pension Fund
Equipment	Premium on Bonds Payable
Estimated Warranty Expense Payable	Prepaid Insurance
(Current)	Property Tax Expense
Gain on Sale of Land	Purchases
Gain on Sale of Marketable Securities	Purchase Discounts
Goodwill	Retained Earnings
Income Summary	Salaries Payable
	Sales
	Sales Salaries
	Travel Expense

Exercise 5—4   (Computation of working capital)

From the following data, compute the working capital for Benson Equipment Co. at December 31, 1991.

Cash in general checking account	$10,000
Cash in sinking fund to be used to retire	
bonds in 1995	50,000
Cash held to pay sales taxes	18,000
Notes receivable—due February 1993	100,000
Trade accounts receivable	125,000
Inventory	75,000
Prepaid insurance—for 1992 and 1993	15,000
Vacant land held as investment	300,000
Used equipment to be sold—market	
value	25,000
Deferred tax asset—to be recovered in	
1993	10,000
Trade accounts payable	80,000
Note payable July 1992	33,000
Note payable January 1993	10,000
Bonds payable—Maturity date 1995	210,000
Salaries payable	20,000
Sales tax payable	23,000
Goodwill	37,000

Exercise 5–5   (Balance sheet relationships)

For each of the items (a) through (o), indicate the amount that should appear on the balance sheet.

Crosby and Company Inc.
Consolidated Balance Sheet
December 31, 1991

Assets

Current assets:		*473387*
Cash		$ (a)
Marketable securities		25,153
Accounts and notes receivable	$ (b)	
Allowance for doubtful accounts and		
notes receivable......................	9,622	165,693
Inventories		235,813
Other current assets		10,419
Total current assets		$41 (c) 75
Land, buildings, and equipment	$ (d)	
Accumulated depreciation	352,186	419,418
Other noncurrent assets		15,631
Total assets		$885,312

Liabilities and Owners' Equity

Current liabilities:		
Accounts payable		$ 98,670
Payable to banks		22,858
Income taxes payable		8,328
Current installments of long-term debt		(e)
Accrued expenses.....................		6,610
Total current liabilities		$142,186
Long-term debt	$ (f)	
Deferred income tax liability.............	40,406	
Minority interest in subsidiaries	3,309	
Total noncurrent liabilities	*48 2 15*	(g)
Total liabilities.............................		$317,655
Contributed Capital:		
Preferred stock, no par value (authorized		
1,618 shares; issued 1,115 shares)......		$16,596
Common stock, $1 par value per share		
(authorized 60,000 shares, issued		
25,939 shares)	$ (h)	
Additional paid-in capital	(i)	(j)
Total contributed capital		$ (k)
Retained earnings:		
Appropriated	$100,000	
Unappropriated	(l)	504,744
Total contributed capital and retained		
earnings		$ (m)
Less treasury stock, at cost (1,236 shares) ...		26,688
Total owners' equity........................		(n)
Total liabilities and owners' equity		$ (o)

Exercise 5–6   (Corrected balance sheet)

The bookkeeper for Joyner Inc. submitted the following balance sheet as of December 31, 1991.

Joyner Inc.
Balance Sheet
December 31, 1991

Assets		Liabilities and Owners' Equity	
Cash.....................	$ 60,000	Accounts payable—trade ...	$120,000
Accounts receivable—trade	100,000	Salaries payable...........	40,000
Inventories...............	160,000	Owners' equity	300,000
Machinery	80,000		
Goodwill.................	60,000		
	$460,000		$460,000

Reference to the records of the company indicated the following:

(a) Cash included:

Petty cash	$ 2,000
Payroll account	20,000
Savings account for cash to be used for building remodeling	20,000
General checking account	18,000
	$60,000

(b) State and local taxes of $4,800 were accrued on December 31. However, $4,800 had been deposited in a special cash account to be used to pay these and neither cash nor the accrued taxes were reported on the balance sheet.

(c) Twenty-five percent of Joyner Inc.'s inventory is rapidly becoming obsolete. The obsolete portion of the inventory as of the balance sheet date was worth only one half of what Joyner Inc. paid for it.

(d) Goods costing $6,000 were shipped to customers on December 30 and 31, at a sales price of $9,000. Goods shipped were not included in the inventory as of December 31. However, receivables were not recognized for the shipment since invoices were not sent out until January 3.

(e) One of Joyner Inc.'s machines costing $25,000 is located on the Autonomous Island Republic, Tropicana. The dictator of Tropicana nationalized several foreign businesses during 1991 and is almost sure to expropriate Joyner Inc.'s machinery for personal use. All machinery was acquired in July of 1991 and will not be depreciated this year.

(f) The corporation had been organized on January 1, 1991, by exchanging 22,000 shares of stock with a par value of $10 per share for the net assets of the partnership Knight and Cramer.

Prepare a corrected balance sheet in account form as of December 31, 1991.

Exercise 5–7   (Balance sheet schedules)

In its annual report to stockholders, Crantz Inc. presents a condensed balance sheet with detailed data provided in supplementary schedules. From the trial balance of Crantz, prepare the following schedules, properly classifying all accounts as to balance sheet categories:

(a) Current assets

(b) Land, buildings, and equipment

(c) Intangible assets

(d) Total assets

(e) Current liabilities

(f) Noncurrent liabilities

(g) Owners' equity

(h) Total liabilities and owners' equity

Crantz Inc.
Trial Balance
December 31, 1991

Cash	21,500	
Marketable Securities—at cost (market, $23,400)	20,000	
Notes Receivable—trade debtors	30,000	
Accrued Interest on Notes Receivable	1,800	
Accounts Receivable—debit balances	92,000	
Accounts Receivable—credit balances		3,600
Allowance for Doubtful Accounts.....................		4,300
Notes Receivable Discounted		12,000
Inventory	56,900	
Prepaid Expenses	6,100	
Accounts Payable—credit balances		26,500
Accounts Payable—debit balances....................	7,400	
Notes Payable—trade creditors		16,000
Accrued Interest on Notes Payable....................		800
Land	80,000	
Buildings	170,000	
Accumulated Depreciation—Buildings		34,000
Equipment....................................	48,000	
Accumulated Depreciation—Equipment		7,600
Patents	20,000	
Accumulated Amortization—Patents		5,000
Franchises	10,000	
Bonds Payable, 8%—issue 1 (mature 12/31/93)		50,000
Bonds Payable, 12%—issue 2 (mature 12/31/99)		100,000
Accrued Interest on Bonds Payable		8,000
Premium on Bonds Payable—issue 1		1,500
Discount on Bonds Payable—issue 2	10,500	
Mortgage Payable		57,500
Accrued Interest on Mortgage Payable		2,160
Capital Stock, par value $25, 10,000 shares authorized,		
4,000 shares issued................................		100,000
Additional Paid-In Capital		16,800
Retained Earnings Appropriated for Bond Redemption		35,000
Unappropriated Retained Earnings		104,440
Treasury Stock—at cost (500 shares)	11,000	
	585,200	585,200

Exercise 5—8 (Classification of subsequent events)

The following events occurred after the end of the company's fiscal year, but before the annual audit was completed. Classify each event as to its impact on the financial statements, i.e., (1) reported by changing the amounts in the financial statements, (2) reported in notes to the financial statements, (3) does not require reporting. Include support for your classification.

(a) Major customer went bankrupt due to a deteriorating financial condition.
(b) Company sustained extensive hurricane damage to one of its plants.
(c) Company settled a major lawsuit that had been pending for two years.
(d) Increasing U.S. trade deficit may have impact on company's overseas sales.
(e) Company sold a large block of preferred stock.
(f) Preparation of current year's income tax return disclosed an additional $25,000 is due on last year's return.
(g) Company's controller resigned and was replaced by an audit manager from the company's audit firm.

Exercise 5–9   (Preparation of notes to financial statements)

The following information was used to prepare the financial statements for Delta Chemical Company. Prepare the necessary notes to accompany the statements.

Delta uses the LIFO inventory method on its financial statements. If the FIFO method were used, the ending inventory balance would be reduced by $50,000, and net income for the year would be reduced by $35,000 after taxes. Delta depreciates its equipment using the straight-line method. Revenue is generally recognized when inventory is shipped unless it is sold on a consignment basis. The current value of the equipment is $525,000 as contrasted to its depreciated cost of $375,000.

Delta has borrowed $350,000 on 10-year notes at 14% interest. The notes are due on July 1, 1998. Delta's equipment has been pledged as collateral for the loan. The terms of the note prohibit additional long-term borrowing without the express permission of the holder of the notes. Delta is planning to request such permission during the next fiscal year.

The Board of Directors of Delta is currently discussing a merger with another chemical company. No public announcement has yet been made, but it is anticipated that additional shares of stock will be issued as part of the merger. Delta's balance sheet will report receivables of $126,000. Included in this figure is a $25,000 advance to the president of Delta, $30,000 of notes receivable from customers, $10,000 in advances to sales representatives, and $70,000 of accounts receivable from customers. The reported balance reflects a deduction for anticipated collection losses.

Exercise 5–10   (Format of cash flow statement)

From the following information for the Carter Corporation, prepare a statement of cash flows for the year ended December 31, 1991.

Amortization of patent	$ 4,000
Depreciation expense	7,000
Issuance of common stock	25,000
Issuance of new bonds payable	30,000
Net income	55,000
Payment of dividends	22,500
Purchase of equipment	33,200
Retirement of long-term debt	40,000
Sale of land (includes $6,000 gain)	35,000
Decrease in accounts receivable	2,100
Increase in inventory	1,200
Increase in accounts payable	1,500
Increase in cash	56,700
Cash balance, January 1, 1991	62,800

Problems   **Problem 5–1   (Computing balance sheet components)**

Crist Equipment Inc. furnishes you with the following list of accounts.

Accounts Payable	$ 66,000	Investment in Kaine Oil Co. Stock	
Accounts Receivable	40,000	(50% of outstanding stock owned for	
Accumulated Depreciation	44,000	control purposes)	$85,000
Advances to Salespersons	5,000	Investment in Siebert Co. Stock	
Advertising Expense	72,000	(current marketable securities)	21,000
Allowance for Doubtful Accounts	10,000	Paid-In Capital in Excess of Par	42,500
Bonds Payable	70,000	Premium on Bonds Payable	6,000
Cash	22,000	Prepaid Insurance Expense	3,000
Certificates of Deposit	21,000	Rent Revenue	37,000
Common Stock (par)	150,000	Rent Revenue Received in Advance	2,000
Customer Accounts with Credit		Retained Earnings	40,000
Balances	6,000	Retained Earnings Appropriated	
Deferred Income Tax Liability	53,000	for Loss Contingencies	30,000
Equipment	215,500	Taxes Payable	10,000
Inventory	49,000	Tools	68,000

Instructions: From the above list of accounts, determine working capital, total assets, total liabilities, and owners' equity per share of stock (75,000 shares outstanding).

Problem 5–2   (Classified balance sheet)

Below is a list of account titles and balances for Johnson Investment Corporation as of January 31, 1991.

Accounts Payable	$ 75,900	Interest Payable	$ 3,050
Accounts Receivable	116,000	Interest Receivable	900
Accumulated Depreciation—		Inventory	184,300
Buildings	151,700	Investments in Undeveloped	
Accumulated Depreciation—		Properties	197,000
Machinery and Equipment	127,000	Land	188,000
Additional Paid-In Capital—		Machinery and Equipment	145,000
Common Stock	62,000	Miscellaneous Supplies Inventory	6,200
Allowance for Doubtful Notes		Notes Payable (Current)	58,260
and Accounts Receivable	5,800	Notes Payable (due in 1996)	38,000
Buildings	380,000	Notes Receivable	22,470
Cash in Banks	8,880	Preferred Stock $5 par	320,000
Cash on Hand	97,300	Prepaid Insurance	3,500
Cash Surrender Value of Life		Retained Earnings (Debit	
Insurance	17,500	Balance)	11,740
Claim for Income Tax Refund	4,500	Salaries and Wages Payable	9,400
Common Stock $20 par	650,000	Temporary Investment in	
Employees Income Tax Payable	4,780	Marketable Securities	146,800
Income Taxes Payable	24,200		

Instructions: Prepare a properly classified balance sheet in report form.

Problem 5–3   (Classified balance sheet—account form including notes)

Account balances and supplemental information for Brockbank Research Corp. as of December 31, 1991, are as follows:

Accounts Payable	$ 32,160	Furniture, Fixtures, and Store	
Accounts Receivable—Trade	57,731	Equipment	$ 769,000
Accumulated Depreciation—		Inventory	201,620
Leasehold Improvements		Investment in Subsidiary	80,000
and Equipment	579,472	Insurance Claims Receivable	120,000
Additional Paid-In Capital	125,000	Land	6,000

Allowance for Doubtful Accounts	1,731	Leasehold Improvements	65,800
Automobiles	132,800	7½-12% Mortgage Notes	200,000
Cash	30,600	Notes Payable—Banks (due in	
Cash Surrender Value of Life		1992)	17,000
Insurance	3,600	Notes Payable—Trade	63,540
Common Stock	175,000	Patent Licenses	57,402
Deferred Income Tax Liability	45,000	Prepaid Insurance	5,500
Dividends Payable	37,500	Profit Sharing, Payroll, and	
Franchises	12,150	Vacation Payable	40,000
		Retained Earnings	225,800
		Tax Receivable—In Litigation	13,000

Supplemental information:

(a) Depreciation is provided by the straight-line method over the estimated useful lives of the assets.

(b) Common stock is $5 par, and 35,000 of the 100,000 authorized shares were issued and are outstanding.

(c) The cost of an exclusive franchise to import a foreign company's ball bearings and a related patent license are being amortized on the straight-line method over their remaining lives: franchise, 10 years; patents, 15 years.

(d) Inventories are stated at the lower of cost or market: cost was determined by the specific identification method.

(e) Insurance claims based upon the opinion of an independent insurance adjustor are for property damages at the central warehouse. These claims are estimated to be 2/3 collectible in the following year and 1/3 collectible thereafter.

(f) The company leases all of its buildings from various lessors. Estimated fixed lease obligations are $50,000 per year for the next ten years. The leases do not meet the criteria for capitalization.

(g) The company is currently in litigation over a claimed overpayment of income tax of $13,000. In the opinion of counsel, the claim is valid. The company is contingently liable on guaranteed notes worth $17,000.

Instructions: Prepare a properly classified balance sheet in account form. Include all notes and parenthetical notations necessary to properly disclose the essential financial data.

Problem 5–4   (Classification of liabilities)

The bookkeeper for HiTone Corp. prepared the following schedule of liabilities as of December 31, 1991.

Accounts payable	$ 56,000
Notes payable—trade	12,000
Notes payable—bank	70,000
Wages and salaries payable	1,500
Interest payable	16,000
Mortgage note payable—10%	60,000
Mortgage note payable—12%	150,000
Bonds payable	100,000
Total	$465,500

The following additional information pertains to these liabilities:

1. All trade notes payable are due within six months of the balance sheet date.
2. Notes payable—bank includes two separate notes payable to Second City Bank:
   a. A $20,000, 13% note issued March 1, 1989, payable on demand. Interest is payable each six months.
   b. A one-year, $50,000, 11½% note issued January 2, 1991. On December 30, 1991, HiTone negotiated a written agreement with Second City Bank to replace the note with a two-year, $50,000, 12% note to be issued January 2, 1992.
3. The 10% mortgage note was issued October 1, 1988, with a term of 10 years. Terms of the note give the holder the right to demand immediate payment if the company fails to make a monthly interest payment within 10 days of the date the payment is due. As of December 31, 1991, HiTone is three months behind in paying its required interest payment.
4. The 12% mortgage note was issued May 1, 1985, with a term of 20 years. The current principal amount due is $150,000. Principal and interest are payable annually on April 30. A payment of $22,000 is due April 30, 1992. The payment includes interest of $18,000.
5. The bonds payable are 10-year, 8% bonds, issued June 30, 1982.

Instructions: Prepare the liabilities section of the December 31, 1991, classified balance sheet for HiTone Corp. Include notes as appropriate. Assume the interest payable accrual has been computed correctly.

Problem 5–5   (Corrected balance sheet)

The following balance sheet was prepared by the accountant for Rowley Company.

Rowley Company
Balance Sheet
June 30, 1991

Assets

Cash	$ 25,500
Marketable securities (includes 30% ownership in stock of Oak Mountain Developers, at cost of $250,000)	312,000
Inventories (net of amount still due suppliers of $85,000)	624,600
Prepaid expenses (includes a deposit of $10,000 made on inventories to be delivered in 18 months)	33,000
Plant assets (excluding $60,000 of equipment still in use, but fully depreciated)	220,000
Goodwill (based upon estimate of President of Rowley Company)...	70,000
Total assets	$1,285,100

Liabilities and Owners' Equity

Notes payable ($75,000 due in 1993)	$135,000
Accounts payable (not including amount due to suppliers of inventory—see above)	142,000
Long-term liability under pension plan	60,000
Appropriation for building expansion	105,000
Accumulated depreciation—fixed assets....................	73,000
Taxes payable...	44,500
Bonds payable (net of discount of $10,000)	290,000
Deferred income tax liability	68,000

Common stock ($10,000 shares @ $20 par)	200,000
Additional paid-in capital	50,500
Unappropriated retained earnings	117,100
Total liabilities and owners' equity	$1,285,100

Instructions: Prepare a corrected statement in report form using appropriate account titles.

Problem 5–6 (Classified balance sheet—report form)

The financial position of St. Charles Ranch is summarized in the following letter to the corporation's accountant.

Dear Dallas:

The following information should be of value to you in preparing the balance sheet for St. Charles Ranch as of December 31, 1991. The balance of cash as of December 31 as reported on the bank statement was $43,825. There were still outstanding checks of $9,320 that had not cleared the bank, and cash on hand of $5,640 was not deposited until January 4, 1992.

Customers owed the company $40,500 at December 31. We estimated 6% of this amount will never be collected. We owe suppliers $32,000 for poultry feed purchased in November and December. About 75% of this feed was used before December 31.

Because we think the price of grain will rise in 1992, we are holding 10,000 bushels of wheat and 5,000 bushels of oats until spring. The market value at December 31 was $3.50 per bushel of wheat and $1.50 per bushes of oats. We estimate that both prices will increase 15% by selling time. We are not able to estimate the cost of raising this product.

St. Charles Ranch owns 1,850 acres of land. Two separate purchases of land were made as follows: 1,250 acres at $200 per acre in 1974, and 600 acres at $400 per acre in 1979. Similar land is currently selling for $800 per acre. The balance of the mortgage on the two parcels of land is $250,000 at December 31; 10% of this mortgage must be paid in 1992.

Our farm buildings and equipment cost us $176,400 and on the average are 40% depreciated. If we were to replace these buildings and equipment at today's prices, we believe we would be conservative in estimating a cost of $300,000.

We have not paid property taxes of $5,500 for 1992 billed us in late November. Our estimated income tax for 1991 is $18,500. A refund claim for $2,800 has been filed relative to the 1989 income tax return. The claim arose because of an error made on the 1989 return.

The operator of the ranch will receive a bonus of $9,000 for 1991 operations. It will be paid when the entire grain crop has been sold.

As you will recall, we issued 14,000 shares of $10 par stock upon incorporation. The ranch received $290,000 as net proceeds from the stock issue. Dividends of $30,000 were declared last month and will be paid on February 1, 1992.

The new year appears to hold great promise. Thanks for your help in preparing this statement.

Sincerely,
Frank K. Santiago
President—St. Charles Ranch

Instructions: Based on this information, prepare a properly classified balance sheet in report form as of December 31, 1991.

Problem 5–7 (Corrected balance sheet—report form)

The bookkeeper for Dependable Computers Inc. reports the following balance sheet amounts as of June 30, 1991:

Current Assets	$264,050
Other Assets	628,550
Current Liabilities	158,600
Other Liabilities	90,000
Capital	644,000

A review of account balances reveals the following data:

(a) An analysis of current assets discloses the following:

Cash	$ 62,250
Marketable securities held as temporary investment	60,000
Trade accounts receivable	56,800
Inventories, including advertising supplies of $2,000	85,000
	$264,050

(b) Other assets include:

Land, buildings, and equipment:	
Depreciated book value (cost, $656,000)	$549,000
Deposit with a supplier for merchandise ordered for August delivery	2,150
Goodwill recorded on the books to cancel losses incurred by the company in prior years	77,400
	$628,550

(c) Current liabilities include:

Payroll payable		$ 7,150
Taxes payable		4,150
Rent payable		11,400
Trade accounts payable:		
Balance	$101,400	
Less debit balance in vendor account due to merchandise return	1,500	99,900
Notes payable		36,000
		$158,600

(d) Other liabilities include:

9% mortgage on land, buildings and equipment, payable in semiannual installments of $9,000 through June 30, 1996	$90,000

(e) Capital includes:

Preferred stock: 19,000 shares outstanding ($20 par value)	$380,000
Common stock: 160,000 shares at stated value	264,000
	$644,000

(f) Common shares were originally issued for full consideration, but the losses of the company for the past years were charged against the common stock balance.

Total consideration at time of issuance	$391,000

Instructions: Using the account balances and related data, prepare a corrected balance sheet in report form showing individual asset, liability, and capital balances properly classified.

III Problem 5–8   (Corrected balance sheet—report form)

The following balance sheet is submitted to you for inspection and review.

Appalachian Freight Company
Balance Sheet
December 31, 1991

Assets		Liabilities and Owners' Equity	
Cash....................	$ 45,050	Miscellaneous liabilities	$ 3,600
Accounts receivable	112,500	Loan payable	76,200
Inventories...............	204,000	Accounts payable	75,250
Prepaid insurance	8,800	Capital stock..............	215,000
Lands, bldgs, & equip.	376,800	Paid-in capital.............	377,100
	$747,150		$747,150

In the course of the review you find the data listed below:

(a) The possibility of uncollectible accounts on accounts receivable has not been considered. It is estimated that uncollectible accounts will total $4,800.

(b) $45,000 representing the cost of a large-scale newspaper advertising campaign completed in 1991 has been added to the inventories, since it is believed that this campaign will benefit sales of 1992. It is also found that inventories include merchandise of $16,250 received on December 31 that has not yet been recorded as a purchase.

(c) Prepaid insurance consists of $1,300, the cost of fire insurance for 1992, and $7,500, the cash surrender value on officers' life insurance policies.

(d) The books show that land, buildings, and equipment have a cost of $556,800 with depreciation of $180,000 recognized in prior years. However, these balances include fully depreciated equipment of $85,000 that has been scrapped and is no longer on hand.

(e) Miscellaneous liabilities of $3,600 represent salaries payable of $9,500, less noncurrent advances of $5,900 made to company officials.

(f) Loan payable represents a loan from the bank that is payable in regular quarterly installments of $6,250.

(g) Tax liabilities not shown are estimated at $18,250.

(h) Deferred income tax liability arising from temporary differences totals $44,550. This liability was not included in the balance sheet.

(i) Capital stock consists of 6,250 shares of preferred 6% stock, par $20, and 9,000 shares of common stock, stated value $10.

(j) Capital stock had been issued for a total consideration of $283,600, the amount received in excess of the par and stated values of the stock being reported as paid-in capital.

(k) Net income and dividends were recorded in Paid-In Capital.

Instructions: Prepare a corrected balance sheet in report form with accounts properly classified.

Problem 5–9   (Corrected balance sheet—report form)

The accountant for the Delicious Bakery prepares the following condensed balance sheet.

Delicious Bakery
Condensed Balance Sheet
December 31, 1991

Current assets	$53,415
Less current liabilities	29,000
Working capital	$24,415
Add other assets	75,120
	$99,535
Deduct other liabilities	3,600
Investment in business	$95,935

A review of the account balances disclosed the following data:

(a) An analysis of the current asset grouping revealed the following:

Cash	$10,600
Trade accounts receivable (fully collectible)	12,500
Notes receivable (notes of customer who has been declared bankrupt and is unable to pay anything on the obligations)	1,000
Marketable securities, at cost (market value $2,575)	4,250
Inventory	20,965
Cash surrender value of insurance on officers' lives	4,100
Total current assets	$53,415

The inventory account was found to include the cost of supplies of $425, a delivery truck acquired at the end of 1991 at a cost of $2,100, and fixtures at a depreciated value of $10,400. The fixtures had been acquired in 1988 at a cost of $12,500.

(b) The total for other assets was determined as follows:

Land and buildings at cost of acquisition, July 1, 1989	$92,000
Less balance due on mortgage, $16,000, and accrued interest on mortgage, $880 (mortgage is payable in annual installments of $4,000 on July 1 of each year together with interest for the year at that time at 11%)	16,880
Total other assets	$75,120

It was estimated that the land, at the time of the purchase, was worth

$30,000. Buildings as of December 31, 1991, were estimated to have a remaining life of 17½ years.

(c) Current liabilities represented balances that were payable to trade creditors.

(d) Other liabilities consisted of withholding, payroll, real estate and other taxes payable to the federal, state, and local governments. However, no recognition was given the accrued salaries, utilities, and other miscellaneous items totaling $350.

(e) The company was originally organized in 1987 when 5,000 shares of no-par stock with a stated value of $5 per share were issued in exchange for business assets that were recognized on the books at their fair market value of $55,000.

Instructions: Prepare a corrected balance sheet in report form with the items properly classified.

III Problem 5–10   (Classified balance sheet—account form)

Tony Akea incorporated his concrete manufacturing operations on January 1, 1991, by issuing 10,000 shares of $10 par common stock to himself. The following balance sheet for the new corporation was prepared.

Cornish Corporation
Balance Sheet
January 1, 1991

Cash.....................	$ 10,000	Accounts payable—suppliers	$ 75,000
Accounts receivable	75,000	Capital stock, $10 par	100,000
Inventory	75,000	Additional paid in capital ...	100,000
Equipment	115,000		
	$275,000		$275,000

During 1991, Cornish Corporation engaged in the following transactions:

(a) Cornish Corporation produced concrete costing $270,000. Concrete costs consisted of $200,000, raw materials purchased; $25,000, labor; and $45,000, overhead. Cornish Corporation paid the $45,000 owed to suppliers as of January 1, and $130,000 of the $200,000 of raw materials purchased during the year. All labor, except for $1,500, and recorded overhead were paid in cash during the year. Other operating expenses of $15,000 were incurred and paid in 1991.

(b) Concrete costing $290,000 was sold during 1991 for $380,000. All sales were made on credit, and collections on receivables were $365,000.

(c) Cornish Corporation purchased machinery (fair market value = $190,000) by trading in old equipment costing $50,000 and paying $140,000 in cash. There is no accumulated depreciation on the old equipment as it was revalued when the new corporation was formed.

(d) Cornish Corporation issued an additional 4,000 shares of common stock for $25 per share and declared a dividend of $3 per share to all stockholders of record as of December 31, 1991, payable on January 15, 1992.

(e) Depreciation expense for 1991 was $27,000. The allowance for doubtful accounts after year-end adjustments is $2,500.

Instructions: Prepare a properly classified balance sheet in account form for the Cornish Corporation as of December 31, 1991.

Problem 5-11   (Preparation of cash flow statement)

The following data were taken from the records of Alderman Produce Company for the year ended June 30, 1991.

Borrowed on long-term notes	$20,000
Issued capital stock	50,000
Purchased equipment	27,000
Net income	47,000
Purchased treasury stock	2,000
Paid dividends	30,000
Depreciation expense	12,000
Retired bonds payable	70,000
Goodwill amortization	2,000
Sold long-term investment (at cost)	5,000
Increase in cash	11,000
Decrease in inventories	8,000
Increase in accounts receivable	8,000
Increase in accounts payable	4,000
Cash balance, July 1, 1990	20,000

Instructions:

(1) From the information given, prepare in the form illustrated in the chapter a statement of cash flows.

(2) Briefly explain what an interested party would learn from studying the cash flow statement for Alderman Produce Company.

Problem 5-12   (Preparation of cash flow statement)

The following changes occurred in selected accounts of Orlando Co. for the year ended December 31, 1991.

Increase in long-term debt	$ 57,000
Purchase of treasury stock	52,000
Depreciation and amortization	197,000
Gain on sale of equipment (included in net income)	6,000
Proceeds from issuance of common stock	184,000
Purchase of equipment	434,000
Proceeds from sale of equipment	20,000
Payment of dividends	49,000
Net income	375,000
Increase (decrease) in working capital accounts	
Inventories	275,000
Accounts receivable	229,000
Accounts payable	124,000
Taxes payable	(34,000)
Trade notes payable	167,000
Decrease in cash	45,000
Cash balance, January 1, 1991	120,000

Instructions: From the information given, prepare in the form illustrated in the chapter a statement of cash flows.

Chapter 6

The Time Value of Money: Accounting Applications

A noted leader in the accounting profession recently observed that the traditional accounting model is badly in need of a tune-up, or perhaps a major overhaul.[1] One recommended change is more complete acceptance and broader use of the **time value of money** concept. This concept is becoming increasingly important in the business world as decision makers try to adjust for the impact of interest and changing economic prices.[2] Consider the following illustrative situations:

- The management of Wheeler Manufacturing Company intends to purchase a new machine. The supplier will accept a $10,000 cash down payment plus a 3-year, 12% note that calls for annual payments of $11,000. Alternatively, the supplier will accept $38,000 cash for the machine. Which alternative purchase plan should Wheeler choose?
- Telluride, Inc. is considering a long-term investment in Sunset Corporation bonds. What is the maximum amount that Telluride will pay for the bonds if they are $20,000 face, 10%, 5-year bonds and if Telluride must earn at least 11% on the investment to meet its corporate investment objectives?
- Pro Shop, Inc. is considering a pension fund for its employees. Management needs to know how much it must invest now in order to establish a fund large enough to pay for the retirement of employees beginning 12 years from now.
- Med-Cal Corporation, organized by a group of doctors, has entered into a 30-year lease contract on a building. Since this transaction met the requirements of a capital lease, the building and corresponding long-term lease obligation were recorded on the books at a value of $150,000. The controller for Med-Cal now needs to prepare a depreciation schedule for the building and an amortization schedule for the lease obligation. What

[1]Comment by Art Wyatt, member of the Financial Accounting Standards Board, at the Ninth Annual Intermountain Accounting Seminar, Utah State University, Logan, Utah, October 16, 1985.

[2]In October 1988 the FASB added to its agenda a project that will consider the use of present values and interest in accounting measurements.

are the procedures for determining the interest and principal portions of the lease payments over the 30-year lease period?

In each of the preceding situations, decisions must be made regarding inflows and outflows of money over an extended period of time. Making correct financial decisions requires that the time value of money be taken into account. This means that dollars to be received or paid in the future must be "discounted" or adjusted to their present values; alternatively, current dollars may be "accumulated" or adjusted to their future values so that comparisons of dollar amounts at different time periods can be meaningful.

In the first example, Wheeler must decide whether to pay $38,000 cash now or pay only $10,000 now and pay $11,000 at the end of each year for 3 years. Assuming Wheeler has sufficient cash, wouldn't it be better to pay $38,000 for the machine instead of $43,000 under the time-payment plan ($10,000 down plus 3 payments of $11,000)? The answer to that question is "not necessarily." This decision requires that the alternatives be made comparable in terms of the time value of money, that is, the two alternatives must be stated at their respective present values.

The present value of the first alternative, the cash purchase, is simply the amount of cash paid, or $38,000. The present value of the second alternative is equal to the $10,000 down payment plus the present values of the three $11,000 payments, as illustrated below.

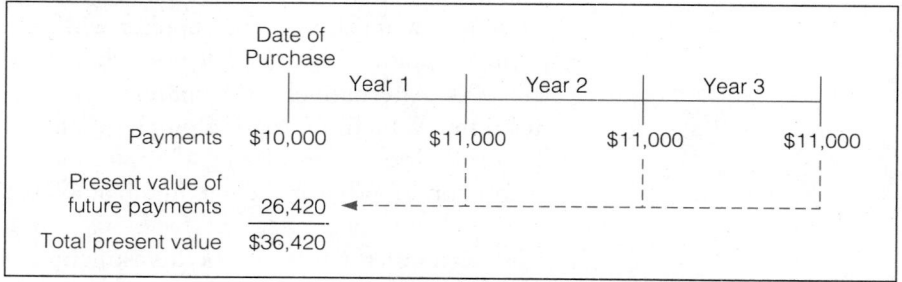

The total present value of three $11,000 payments discounted to the date of purchase at 12% interest is approximately $26,420.[3] This amount plus the down payment of $10,000 equals $36,420, which is less than the $38,000 cash price the supplier is willing to accept. Therefore, assuming other factors equal, Wheeler should purchase the machine with the time-payment plan. This conclusion and the other examples in the chapter ignore any tax implications, which may modify the decision in actual practice.

As suggested by the previous examples, there are many business situations where present or future value techniques must be used in making financial decisions. Common applications in accounting include the following categories.

1. Valuing long-term notes receivable and payable where there is no stated rate of interest or an inappropriate stated rate of interest.

---

[3]As will be explained later, the $26,420 is determined by discounting an annuity of $11,000 for 3 years at 12% interest ($11,000 × P.V. factor of 2.4018 from Table IV = $26,420).

2. Determining bond prices and using the effective-interest method for amortizing bond premiums or discounts.
3. Determining appropriate values for long-term capital leases and measuring the amount of interest expense and principal amortization applicable to the periodic lease payments.
4. Accounting for pension funds, including interest accruals and amortization entries.
5. Accounting for sinking funds.
6. Analyzing capital budgeting alternatives.
7. Establishing amortization schedules for mortgages and measuring periodic payments on long-term purchase contracts.
8. Determining appropriate asset, liability, and equity values in mergers and business combinations.

Since future and present value techniques are commonly used in business and have become increasingly important for accountants, this chapter explains these techniques and provides several illustrations of their use. The emphasis in the chapter is on present value techniques, since most applications in accounting require future amounts to be discounted to the present. The material presented may be a review for some students; for others, it will add to the theoretical foundation underlying current accounting practice. The techniques explained will be used throughout the text, expecially in the chapters dealing with long-term investments and long-term liabilities. Before future and present value techniques can be explained, however, the concept of interest must first be defined.

Simple and Compound Interest

Money, like other commodities, is a scarce resource, and a payment for its use is generally required. This payment (cost) for the use of money is interest. For example, if $100 is borrowed, whether from an individual, a business, or a bank, and $110 is paid back, $10 interest has been paid for the use of the $100. Thus, interest represents the excess cash paid or received over the amount of cash borrowed or loaned.

Generally interest is specified in terms of a percentage rate for a period of time, usually a year. For example, interest at 8% means the annual cost of borrowing an amount of money, called the principal, is equal to 8% of that amount. If $100 is borrowed at 8% annual interest, the total to be repaid is $108—the amount of the principal, $100, and the interest for a year, $8 ($100 × .08 × 1). Interest on a $1,000 note for 6 months at 8% is $40 ($1,000 × .08 × 6/12). Thus, the formula for computing simple interest is

$$i = p \times r \times t,$$

where:

i = Amount of simple interest
p = Principal amount
r = Interest rate (per period)
t = Time (number of periods)

The preceding formula relates to simple interest. Many transactions involve compound interest. This means that the amount of interest earned for a certain period is added to the principal for the next period. Interest for the subsequent period is computed on the new amount, which includes both principal and accumulated interest. As an example, assume $100 is deposited in a bank and left for two years at 6% annual interest. At the end of the first year, the $100 has earned $6 interest ($100 × .06 × 1). At the end of the second year, $6 has been earned for the first year, plus another $6.36 interest (6% on the $106 balance at the beginning of the second year). Thus, the total interest earned is $12.36 rather than $12 because of the compounding effect. The table below, based on the foregoing example, illustrates the computation of simple and compound interest for four years.

Year	Simple Interest Computation	Interest	Total	Compound Interest Computation	Interest	Total
1	($100 × .06)	$6	$106	($100.00 × .06)	$6.00	$106.00
2	(100 × .06)	6	112	(106.00 × .06)	6.36	112.36
3	(100 × .06)	6	118	(112.36 × .06)	6.74	119.10
4	(100 × .06)	6	124	(119.10 × .06)	7.15	126.25

The interest rate used in compound interest problems is the effective rate of interest and is generally stated as an annual rate, sometimes called per annum. However, if the compounding of interest is for periods other than a year, the stated rate of interest must be adjusted. A comparable adjustment must be made to the number of periods. The adjustments required to the interest rate (i) and to the number of periods (n) for semiannual, quarterly, and monthly compounding of interest are as follows:

Example	Annual Compounding	Semiannual Compounding	Quartely Compounding	Monthly Compounding
1.	i=6%, n=10	i=3%, n=20	i=1.5%, n=40	i=.5%, n=120
2.	i=12%, n=5	i=6%, n=10	i=3%, n=20	i=1%, n=60
3.	i=24%, n=3	i=12%, n=6	i=6%, n=12	i=2%, n=36

As shown in the table, the semiannual compounding of interest requires the annual interest rate to be reduced by half and the number of periods to be doubled. Quartely compounding of interest requires use of one-fourth the annual rate and 4 times the number of periods, and so forth. Because of this compounding effect, more interest is earned by an investor with semiannual interest than with annual interest, and more is earned with quarterly compounding than with semiannual compounding.

Future and Present Value Techniques

Since money earns interest over time, $100 received today is more valuable than $100 received one year from today. Future and present value analysis is a method of comparing the value of money received or expected to be received at different time periods.

Analyses requiring alternative computations in terms of present dollars relative to future dollars may be viewed from one of two perspectives, the future or the present. If a future time frame is chosen, all cash flows must be **accumulated** to that future point. In this instance, the effect of interest is to increase the amounts or values over time so that the future amount is greater than the present amount. For example, $500 invested today will accumulate to a *future value* of $1,079 (rounded) in 10 years if 8% annually compounded interest is paid on the investment.

If, on the other hand, the present is chosen as the point in time at which to evaluate alternatives, all cash flows must be **discounted** from the future to the present. In this instance, the discounting effect reduces the amounts or values. To illustrate, if an investor is earning 10% annual interest on a note receivable that will pay $10,000 in 3 years, what might the investor accept today in full payment, i.e., what is the *present value* of that note? The amount the investor should be willing to accept, assuming a 10% interest rate is satisfactory and that other considerations are held constant, is $7,513 (rounded), which is the discounted present value of the note. The rationale for the investor is that the $7,513 could be invested at 10%, compounded annually, and it would accumulate to $10,000 in 3 years.

As just illustrated, the future and present value situations involving lump-sum amounts are essentially reciprocal relationships, and both future and present values are based on the concept of interest. Thus, if interest can be earned at 8% per year, the future value of $100 one year from now is $108 [$100 (1 + .08)]. Conversely, assuming the same rate of interest, the present value of a $108 payment due in one year is $100 [$108 ÷ (1 + .08)]. Similarly, $100 to be received in one year, at a 10% annual interest rate, is worth $90.91 today ($100 ÷ 1.10), because $90.91 invested at 10% will grow to $100 [$90.91(1 + .10)] in one year.

Use of Formulas   There are four common future and present value situations, each with a corresponding formula. Two of the situations deal with one-time, lump-sum payments or receipts[4] (either future or present values), and the other two involve annuities (either future or present values). An **annuity** consists of a **series of equal payments** over a specified number of periods. For example, a contract calling for three annual payments of $3,000 each would be an annuity. However, a similar contract requiring three annual payments of $2,000, $3,000, and $4,000, respectively, would not be an annuity since the payments are not equal.

Without going into the derivation of the formulas, the four common situations are as follows:

---

[4]Hereafter in this chapter, the terms *payments* and *receipts* will be used interchangeably. A payment by one party in a transaction becomes a receipt to the other party and vice versa. The term *rent* is used to designate either a receipt or a payment.

1. Future Value of a Lump-Sum Payment: $FV = P(1 + i)^n$
   where:

$$
\begin{aligned}
FV &= \text{Future value} \\
P &= \text{Principal amount to be accumulated} \\
i &= \text{Interest rate per period} \\
n &= \text{Number of periods}
\end{aligned}
$$

Example

Future value of \$1,500 to be accumulated at 10% annual interest for 5 years.

$$
\begin{aligned}
FV &= \$1,500(1 + .10)^5 \\
FV &= \underline{\$2,416} \text{ (rounded)}
\end{aligned}
$$

2. Present Value of a Lump-Sum Payment: $PV = A\left[\dfrac{1}{(1 + i)^n}\right]$
   where:

$$
\begin{aligned}
PV &= \text{Present value} \\
A &= \text{Accumulated amount to be discounted} \\
i &= \text{Interest rate per period} \\
n &= \text{Number of periods}
\end{aligned}
$$

Example

Present value of \$2,416 to be discounted at 10% annual interest for 5 years.

$$
\begin{aligned}
PV &= \$2,416\left[\dfrac{1}{(1 + .10)^5}\right] \\
PV &= \underline{\$1,500} \text{ (rounded)}
\end{aligned}
$$

3. Future Value of an Annuity: $FV_n = R\left[\dfrac{(1 + i)^n - 1}{i}\right]$
   where:

$$
\begin{aligned}
FV_n &= \text{Future value of an annuity} \\
R &= \text{Annuity payment or periodic rent to be accumulated} \\
i &= \text{Interest rate per period} \\
n &= \text{Number of periods}
\end{aligned}
$$

Example

Future value of annuity of \$2,000 for 10 years to be accumulated at 12% annual interest.

$$
\begin{aligned}
FV_n &= \$2,000\left[\dfrac{(1 + .12)^{10} - 1}{.12}\right] \\
FV_n &= \underline{\$35,097} \text{ (rounded)}
\end{aligned}
$$

4. Present Value of an Annuity: $PV_n = R\left[\dfrac{1 - \dfrac{1}{(1 + i)^n}}{i}\right]$

where:

PV_n = Present value of an annuity
R   = Annuity payment or periodic rent to be discounted
i   = Interest rate per period
n   = Number of periods

Example

Present value of an annuity of $5,000 for 3 years to be discounted at 11% annual interest.

$$PV_n = \$5,000 \left[\dfrac{1 - \dfrac{1}{(1 + .11)^3}}{.11}\right]$$

$$PV_n = \underline{\$12,219} \text{ (rounded)}$$

Use of Tables   In the previous examples, formulas were used to make the computations. This is easily accomplished with most modern-day calculators or with microcomputers. Without such tools, however, use of the formulas may be time consuming. Because of this, future and present value tables have been developed for each of the four situations. These tables, such as those provided on pages 231-234, are based on computing the value of $1 for various interest rates and periods of time. Consequently, future and present value computations can be made by multiplying the appropriate table value factor for $1 by the applicable lump-sum or annuity amount involved in the particular situation. Thus, the formulas for the four situations may be rewritten as follows:

1. Future Value of a Lump-Sum Payment:

$$FV = P(1 + i)^n \text{ or } FV = P(FVF_{\overline{n}i}) \text{ or simply}$$
$$FV = P(\text{Table I factor})$$
where:

$FVF_{\overline{n}i}$ = Future value factor for a particular interest rate (i) and for a certain number of periods (n) from Table I.

Example (from page 214):

FV = $1,500 (1.6105 = Factor from Table l; n = 5; i = 10%)
FV = $\underline{\$2,416}$ (rounded)

2. Present Value of a Lump-Sum Payment:

$$PV = A\frac{1}{(1 + i)^n} \text{ or } PV = A(PVF_{\overline{n}|i}) \text{ or simply}$$

$$PV = A \text{ (Table II factor)}$$

where:

$PVF_{\overline{n}|i}$ = Present value factor for a particular interest rate (i) and for a certain number of periods (n) from Table II.

Example (from page 214):

PV = $2,416 (0.6209 = Factor from Table II; n = 5; i = 10%)

PV = $1,500 (rounded)

3. Future Value of an Annuity:

$$FV_n = R\left[\frac{(1 + i)^n - 1}{i}\right] \text{ or } FV_n = R(FVAF_{\overline{n}|i}) \text{ or simply}$$

$$FV_n = R(\text{Table III factor})$$

where:

$PVAF_{\overline{n}|i}$ = Future value factor for a particular interest rate (i) and for a certain number of periods (n) from Table III.

Example (from page 214):

FV_n = $2,000 (17.5487 = Factor from Table III; n = 10; i = 12%)

FV_n = $35,097 (rounded)

4. Present Value of an Annuity:

$$PV_n = R\left[\frac{1 - \frac{1}{(1 + i)^n}}{i}\right] \text{ or } PVn = R(PVAF_{\overline{n}|i}) \text{ or simply}$$

$$PV_n = R(\text{Table IV factor})$$

where:

$PVAF_{\overline{n}|i}$ = Present value factor for a particular interest rate (i) and for a certain number of periods (n) from Table IV.

Example (from page 215):

PV_n = $5,000 (2.4437 = Factor from Table IV; n = 3; i = 11%)

PV_n = $12,219 (rounded)

Note that the answers obtained in the examples by using the tables are the same as those obtained using the formulas with a calculator or microcomputer.

Business Applications

The following examples demonstrate the application of future and present value computations in solving business problems, including each of the four situations just described. Additional applications are provided in later sections as well as in the excercises and problems at the end of the chapter.

Example 1   **Future Value of a Lump Sum**

Marywhether Company loans its president, Celia Phillips, $15,000 to purchase a car. Marywhether accepts a note due in 4 years with interest at 10% compounded semiannually. How much cash does Marywhether expect to receive from Phillips when the note is paid at maturity?

Solution:

This problem involves a lump-sum payment to be accumulated 4 years into the future. In many present and future value problems, a time line is helpful in visualizing the problem:

		(10% compounded semiannually)						
$15,000 ----	---------	-- $16,538 ----	$18,233 ---		$20,102 ---	--------	►	$22,162
Interest Amounts	$15,750		$17,365		$19,145		$21,107	
	$750	$788	$827	$868	$912	$957	$1,005	$1,055
Interest Periods	1	2	3	4	5	6	7	8
	Year 0							Year 4

The $15,000 must be accumulated for 4 years at 10% compounded semiannually. Table I may be used, and the applicable formula is:

$$FV = P(FVF_{\overline{n}|i})$$

where:

FV = The future value of a lump sum
P = $15,000
n = 8 periods (4 years × 2)
i   = 5% effective interest rate per period (10% ÷ 2)

FV = $15,000 (Table I$_{\overline{8}|5\%}$)
FV = $15,000 (1.4775)
FV = $22,162 (rounded)

In 4 years, Marywhether will expect to receive $22,162, consisting of $15,000 principal repayment and $7,162 interest.

Example 2   **Present Value of a Lump Sum**

Edgemont Enterprises holds a note receivable from a steady customer. The note is for $22,000, which includes principal and interest, and is due to be paid in exactly 2 years. The customer wants to pay the note now, and both parties agree that 10% is a reasonable annual interest rate to use in discounting the note. How much will the customer pay Edgemont Enterprises today to settle the obligation?

Solution:

The lump-sum future payment must be discounted to the present at the agreed upon annual rate of interest of 10%. Since this involves a present-value computation of a lump-sum amount, Table II is used, and the applicable formula is:

$$PV = A(PVF_{\overline{n}|i})$$

where:

PV = The present value of a lump sum
A = $22,000
n = 2 periods
i = 10% effective interest rate per period

PV = $22,000 (Table II$_{\overline{2}|10\%}$)
PV = $22,000 (0.8264)
PV = $\underline{18,181}$ (rounded)

The customer will pay approximately $18,181 today to settle the obligation.

<table>
<tr><td>**Example 3**</td><td>**Present Value of Series of Unequal Payments**</td></tr>
</table>

Casper Sporting Goods Co. is considering a $1 million capital investment that will provide the following expected net receipts at the *end* of each of the next six years.

Year	Expected Net Receipts
1	$195,000
2	457,000
3	593,000
4	421,000
5	95,000
6	5,000

Casper will make the investment only if the rate of return is greater than 12%. Will Casper make the investment?

Solution:

A series of unequal future receipts must be compared with a present lump-sum investment. For such a comparison to be made, all future cash flows must be discounted to the present.

If the rate of return on the investment is greater than 12%, then the total of all yearly net receipts discounted to the present at 12% will be greater than the amount invested. Since the future receipts are not equal, this situation does *not* involve an annuity. Each receipt must be discounted individually. Table II is used, and the applicable formula is:

$$PV = A(PVF_{\overline{n}|i}) \text{ where:}$$

(1) Year = n	(2) A (Net Receipts)	(3) Table II $_{\overline{n}|12\%}$	(2) × (3) = (4) PV (Discounted Amount)
1	$195,000	.8929	$ 174,116
2	457,000	.7972	364,320
3	593,000	.7118	422,097
4	421,000	.6355	267,546
5	95,000	.5674	53,903
6	5,000	.5066	2,533
		Total	$1,284,515 (Rounded)

The total discounted receipts are greater than the $1 million investment; thus, the rate of return is more than 12%. Therefore, other things being equal, Casper will invest.

Example 4   Future Value of an Annuity

Boswell Co. owes an installment debt of $1,000 per quarter for 5 years. The creditor has indicated a willingness to accept an equivalent lump-sum payment at the end of the contract period instead of the series of equal payments made at the end of each quarter. If the money is worth 16% compounded quarterly, what is the equivalent lump-sum payment at the end of the contract period?

Solution:

The equivalent lump-sum payment can be found by accumulating the quarterly $1,000 payments to the end of the contract period. Since the payments are equal, this is an annuity. Table III is used, and the applicable formula is:

$$FV_n = R(FVAF_{\overline{n}|i})$$
where:

FV_n = The unknown equivalent lump-sum payment
R = $1,000 quartely installment to be accumulated
n = 20 periods (5 years × 4 quarters)
i = 4% effective interest rate per period
     (16% ÷ 4)

FV_n = $1,000 (Table III $_{\overline{20}|4\%}$)
FV_n = $1,000 (29.7781)
FV_n = $29,778 (rounded)

$29,778 paid at the end of 5 years is approximately equivalent to the 20 quarterly payments of $1,000 each plus interest.

Example 5   Present Value of an Annuity

Mary Sabin, proprietor of Sabin Appliance, received two offers for her last, used, deluxe-model refrigerator. Jerry Sloan will pay $650 in cash. Elise Jensen will pay $700 consisting of a down payment of $100 and 12 monthly payments of $50. If the installment interest rate is 24% compounded monthly, which offer should Sabin accept?

Solution:

In order to compare the two alternative methods of payment, all cash flows must be accumulated or discounted to one point in time. As illustrated by the time line, the present is selected as the point of comparison.

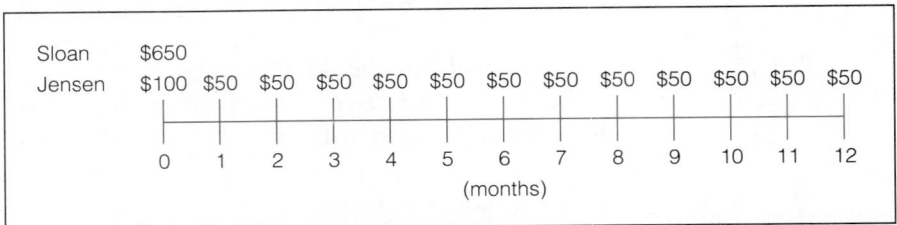

Sloan's offer is $650 today. The present value of $650 today is $650.

Jensen's offer consists of an annuity of 12 payments, plus $100 paid today, which is not part of the annuity. The annuity may be discounted to the present by using Table IV and the applicable formula:

$$PV_n = R(PVAF_{\overline{n}|i})$$

where:

PV_n = Unknown present value of 12 payments
R = $50 monthly payment to be discounted
n = 12 periods (1 year × 12 months)
i = 2% effective interest rate per period (24% ÷ 12)

PV_n = $50 (Table IV$_{\overline{12}|2\%}$)
PV_n = $50 (10.5753)
PV_n = $529

Present value of Jensen's payments	$529
Present value of Jensen's $100 down payment	100
Total present value of Jensen's offer	$629

Therefore, Sloan's offer of $650 cash is more desirable than Jensen's offer.

Determining the Number of Periods, the Interest Rate, or the Rental Payment

So far, the examples and illustrations have required solutions for the future or present values, with the other three variables in the formulas being given. Sometimes business problems require solving for the number of periods, the interest rate,[5] or the rental payment instead of the future or

---

[5]When the interest rate is not known, it is properly called the **implicit rate of interest**, that is, the rate of interest implied by the terms of a contract or situation. (See Examples 7 and 10 in this chapter.)

present value amounts. In each of the formulas, there are four variables. If information is known about any three of the variables, the fourth (unknown) value can be determined. The following examples illustrate how to solve for these other variables.

| Example 6 | **Determining the Number of Periods** |

Rocky Mountain Survey Company wants to purchase new equipment at a cost of $100,000. The company has $88,850 available in cash but does not want to borrow the other $11,150 for the purchase. If the company can invest the $88,850 today at an interest rate of 12% compounded quarterly, how many years will it be before Rocky Mountain will have the $100,000 it needs to buy the equipment?

Solution:

As illustrated below, Rocky Mountain Survey Company can invest $88,850 now at 12% interest compounded quarterly and needs to know how long it will take for this amount to accumulate to $100,000.

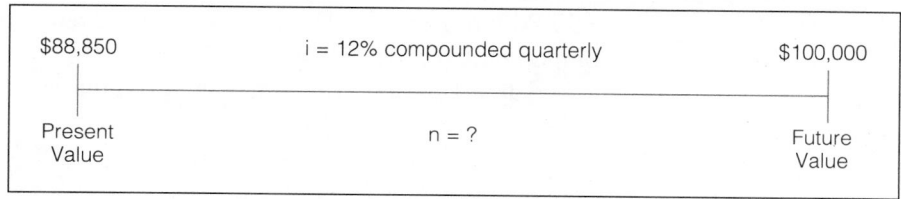

In this situation, involving both present values and future values, either Table I or Table II may be used. If Table I is used, the applicable formula is:

$$FV = PVF_{\overline{n}|i}$$
$$FV = P(\text{Table I factor})$$

The problem would be solved as follows:

$$\frac{FV}{P} = \text{Table I factor}$$

$$\frac{\$100,000}{\$88,850} = 1.1255$$

Reading down the 3% column (12% ÷ 4) in Table I, the factor value of 1.1255 is shown for n = 4. Therefore, it would take 4 periods (quarters) or 1 year for Rocky Mountain to earn enough interest to have $88,850 accumulate to a future value of $100,000.

If Table II is used, the applicable formula is:

$$PV = FVF_{\overline{n}|i}$$
$$PV = A (\text{Table II factor})$$

Solving,

$$\frac{PV}{A} = \text{Table II factor}$$

$$\frac{\$88,850}{\$100,000} = .8885$$

Reading down the 3% column in Table II, the factor of 0.8885 corresponds with n = 4 (quarters) or 1 year. This illustrates again the reciprocal nature of furture and present values for lump-sum amounts.

Example 7   Determining the Interest Rate

The Hughes family wishes to puchase a baby-grand piano. The cost of the piano one year from now will be $5,800. If the family can invest $5,000 now, what annual interest rate must they earn on their investment to have $5,800 at the end of one year?

Solution:

The Hughes family can invest $5,000 now and needs it to accumulate to $5,800 in one year. The rate of annual interest they need to earn can be computed as shown below.

If Table I is used, the applicable formula is:

$$FV = PVF_{\overline{n}|i}$$
$$FV = P(\text{Table I factor})$$
$$\frac{FV}{P} = \text{Table I factor}$$
$$\frac{\$5,800}{\$5,000} = 1.1600$$

Reading across the n = 1 row, the factor value 1.1600 corresponds to an annual effective interest rate of 16%. Therefore, the Hughes family would have to earn 16% annual interest to accomplish their goal. The same result is obtained if Table II is used to solve this problem.

Example 8   Determining the Rental Payment

Provo 1st National Bank is willing to lend a customer $75,000 to buy a warehouse. The note will be secured by a 5-year mortgage and carry an annual interest rate of 12%. Equal payments are to be made at the end of each year over the 5-year period. How much will the yearly payment be?

Solution:

This is an example of an unknown annuity payment. Since the present value ($75,000) is known, as well as the interest rate (12%) and the number of periods (5), the annuity payment can be determined using Table IV. The applicable formula is:

$$PV_n = R(PVAF_{\overline{n}|i})$$
$$PV_n = R(\text{Table IV factor})$$
$$\$75{,}000 = R(3.6048) \ (\text{for } n = 5 \text{ and } i = 12\%)$$

$$\frac{\$75{,}000}{3.6048} = R$$

$$\underline{\$20{,}806} \ (\text{rounded}) = R$$

The payment on this 5-year mortgage would be approximately $20,806 each year.

Additional Complexities

The illustrations up to this point have been fairly straightforward. In practice, however, complexities can arise that make it somewhat more difficult to use the future and present value tables. Two of these complexities involve: (1) converting ordinary annuity tables to annuity due factor values, and (2) interpolation.

Ordinary Annuity vs. Annuity Due

Annuities are of two types: ordinary annuities (annuities in arrears) and annuities due (annuities in advance). The periodic rents or payments for an ordinary annuity are made at the *end of each period*, and the last payment coincides with the end of the annuity term. The periodic rents or payments for an annuity due are made at the *beginning of each period*, and one period of the annuity term remains after the last payment. These differences are illustrated below:

Ordinary Annuity of $1 for 3 Years (10% annual interest)

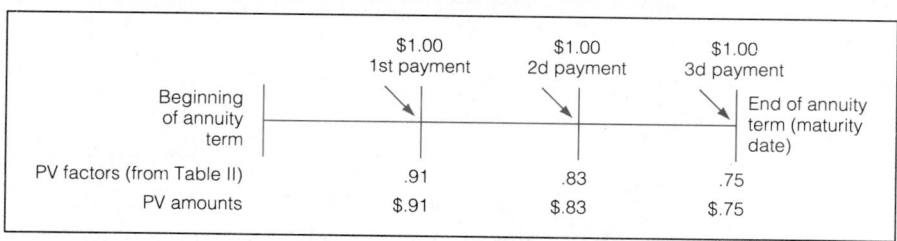

Therefore, assuming a 10% annual interest rate, the present value of an annuity of $1 per year to be received at the *end* of each of the next 3 years is $2.49 ($.91 + $.83 + $.75). Notice that the last $1 is received on the maturity date, or the end of the annuity term.

Again assuming a 10% annual interest rate, the present value of an annuity of $1 per year to be received at the *beginning* of each of the next 3 years is $2.74 ($1.00 + $.91 + $.83). Notice here that the last payment is received 1 year prior to the maturity date.

The difference in the two annuities is in the timing of the payments,

Annuity Due of $1 for 3 Years (10% annual interest)

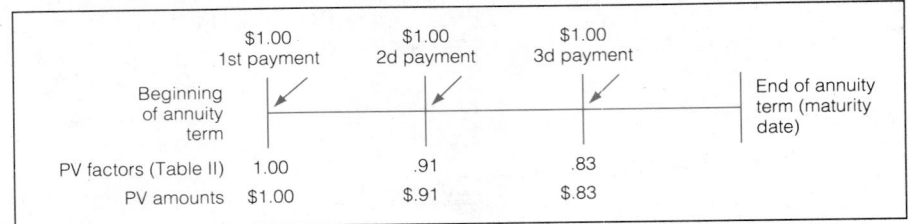

and, therefore, how many interest periods are involved. As shown below, both annuities require 3 payments. However, the ordinary annuity payments are at the end of each period so there are only 2 periods of interest accumulation while the annuity due payments are in advance or at the beginning of the period so there are 3 periods of interest accumulation.

Accumulation of Ordinary Annuity for 3 Years

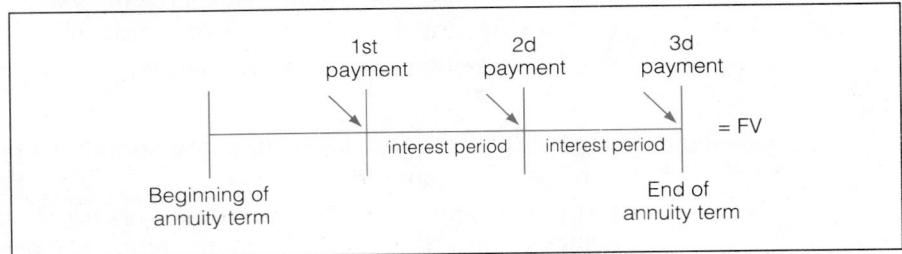

Accumulation of Annuity Due for 3 Years

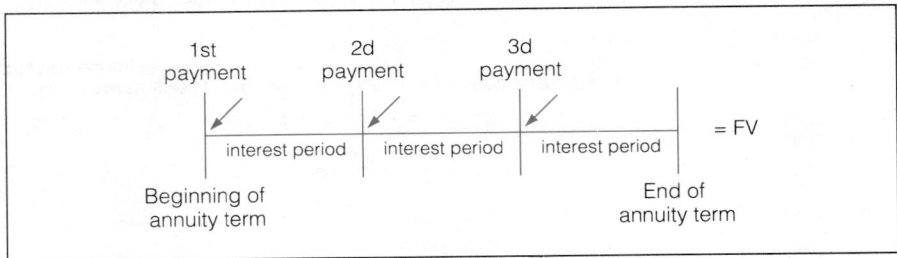

The preceding situation is exactly reversed when viewed from a present-value standpoint. The ordinary annuity has 3 interest or discount periods, while the annuity due has only 2 periods, as shown on page 225.

Even though most future and present value annuity tables are computed for ordinary annuities (payments at the end of the periods), these

Present Value of Ordinary Annuity for 3 Years

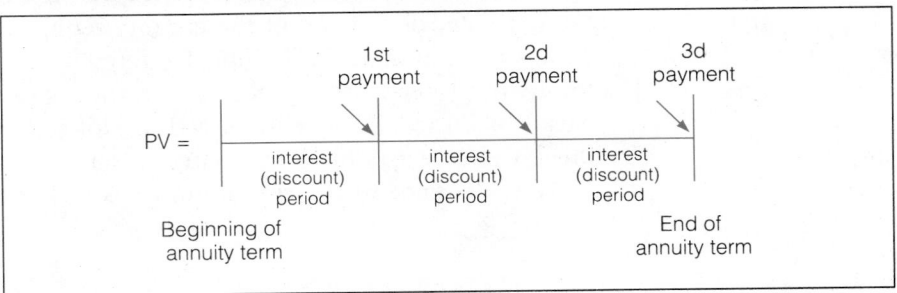

Present Value of Annuity Due for 3 Years

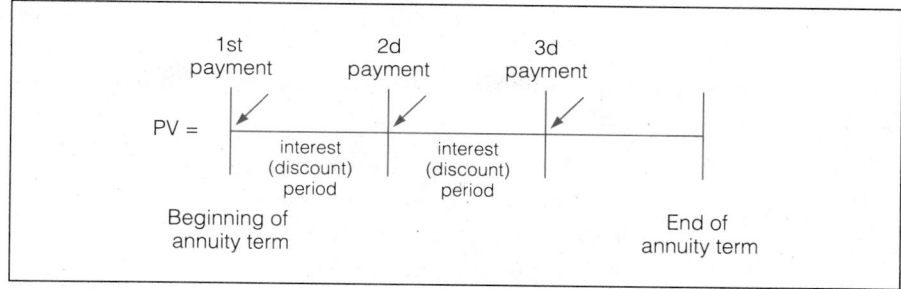

tables can be used for solving annuity due problems where the payments are in advance. However, the following adjustments would be required.

1. To find the **future value of an annuity due** using ordinary annuity table values (Table III), select the appropriate table value for an ordinary annuity for one additional period (n + 1) and subtract the extra payment (which is 1.0000 in terms of the table value for rents of $1.00). The formula is

$$FV_n = R(FVAF_{\overline{n+1}|i} - 1).$$

2. To find the **present value of an annuity due** using ordinary annuity table values (Table IV), select the appropriate table value for an ordinary annuity for one less period (n − 1) and add the extra payment (1.0000). The formula is

$$PV_n = R(PVAF_{\overline{n-1}|i} + 1)$$

By making the above adjustments, when payments are in advance, ordinary annuity tables may be used for all annuity situations. There are special annuity due tables available, but they are not needed if one understands how to convert from ordinary annuity factor values to annuity due factor values.

For example, the table value (Table III) for the future amount of an annuity due for 3 periods at 10% is:

(1) Factor for future value of an ordinary annuity of $1 for 4 perids (n + 1) at 10%	4.6410
(2) Less one payment	1.0000
(3) Factor for future value of an annuity due of $1 for 3 periods at 10%	3.6410

The table value (Table IV) for the present value of an annuity due for 3 periods at 10% is:

(1) Factor for present value of an ordinary annuity of $1 for two periods (n − 1) at 10%	1.7355
(2) Plus one payment	1.0000
(3) Factor for present value of an anuity due of $1 for 3 periods at 10%	2.7355

The following examples illustrate the application of converting from ordinary annuity table values to annuity due table values.

Example 9   **Converting from Ordinary Annuity to Annuity Due Table Values for Future Amounts**

The Porter Corporation desires to accumulate funds to retire a $200,000 bond issue at the end of 15 years. Funds set aside for this purpose can be invested to yield 8%. What annual payment starting immediately would provide the needed funds?

Solution:

Annuity payments of an unknown amount are to be accumulated toward a specific dollar amount at a known interest rate. Therefore, Table III is used. Because the first payment is to be made immediately, all payments will fall due at the beginning of each period and an annuity due is used. The appropriate formula is:

$$FV_n = R(FVAF_{\overline{n+1}|i})$$

where:

FV_n = $200,000
R = Unknown annual payment
n = 15 periods
i = 8% annual interest

$200,000 = R (Table III $_{\overline{16}|8\%}$ − 1)
$200,000 = R(29.3243)
$\dfrac{\$200,000}{29.3243}$ = R
$\underline{\$6,820}$ = R

Porter Corporation must deposit $6,820 annually, starting immediately, to accumulate $200,000 in 15 years at 8% annual interest.

Example 10   **Converting from Ordinary Annuity to Annuity Due Table Values for Present Values**

Utah Corporation has completed negotiations to lease equipment with a fair market value of $45,897. The lease contract specifies semiannual payments of $3,775 for 10 years beginning immediately. At the end of the lease, Utah Corporation may purchase the equipment for a nominal amount. What is the implicit annual rate of interest on the lease purchase?

Solution:

This is a common application of an annuity due situation in accounting since most lease contracts require payments in advance, i.e., at the beginning of the period rather than at the end of the period. The implicit interest rate must be computed for the present value of an annuity due. The present value is the fair market value of the equipment, and the payment is the lease payment. Table IV is used, and the applicable formula is:

$$PV_n = R(PVAF_{\overline{n-1}|i} + 1)$$
where:

$$PV_n = \$45,897$$
$$R \quad = \$3,775$$
$$n \quad = 20 \text{ periods (10 years} \times 2 \text{ payments per year)}$$
$$i \quad = \text{The unknown semiannual interest rate}$$

$$\$45,897 = \$3,775 \ (Table \ IV_{\overline{19}|i} + 1)$$
$$\frac{\$45,897}{\$3,775} = 12.1581 = Table \ IV_{\overline{19}|i} + 1$$
$$11.1581 = Table \ IV_{\overline{19}|i}$$

Examination of Table IV for 19 periods and a factor of 11.1581 shows Table $IV_{\overline{19}|6\%} = 11.1581$. Therefore, $i = 6\%$. The implicit annual interest rate is twice the semiannual rate, or $2 \times 6\% = 12\%$.

Interpolation   A difficulty in using future and present value tables arises when the exact factor does not appear in the table. One solution is to use the formula. Interpolation is another solution. Interpolation assumes the change between two table values is linear. Although such an assumption is not totally correct, the margin of error is often insignificant, especially if the table value ranges are not too wide.

For example, determine the table value for the present value of $1 due in 9 periods at 4½%. The appropriate factor does not appear in Table II. However, the two closest values are Table $II_{\overline{9}|4\%} = .7026$ and Table $II_{\overline{9}|5\%} = .6446$. Interpolation relates the unknown value to the change in the known values. This relationship may be shown as a proportion:

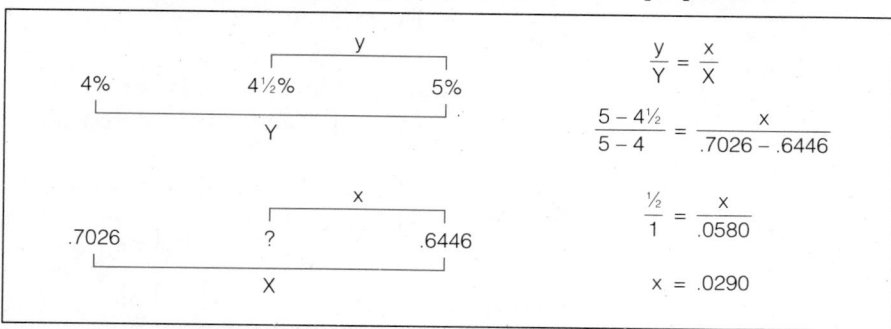

The .0290 is the difference between the value for 5% and the value for 4½%. Therefore, the value needed is $.0290 + .6446 = .6736$. Using the mathematical formula for Table II

$$\left\{ PV = A\left[\frac{1}{(1+i)^n} \right] \right\},$$

the present value of $1 at 4½% interest for 9 periods is .6729

$$\left\{ PV = 1 \left[\frac{1}{(1 + .045)^9} \right] \right\}.$$

The difference (.6736 − .6729 = .0007) is insignificant for most business purposes.

Interpolation is useful in finding a particular unknown table value that lies between two given values. This procedure is also used in approximating the number of periods or unknown interest rates when the table value is known. The following examples illustrate the determination of these two variables.

Example 11   Interpolation: Unknown Number of Periods

The Newbold Foundation contributes $600,000 to a university for a new building on the condition that construction will not begin until the gift, invested at 10% per year, amounts to $1,500,000. How long before construction may begin?

Solution:

This problem involves finding the time (number of periods) required for a lump-sum payment to accumulate to a specified future amount. Table I is used and the applicable formula is:

$$FV = P(FVF_{\overline{n}|}i)$$
where:

FV = $1,500,000
P = $600,000
n = Unknown number of periods
i = 10% effective interest rate per year

$$\$1,500,000 = \$600,000 \ (\text{Table } I_{\overline{n}|10\%})$$
$$\frac{\$1,500,000}{\$\ 600,000} = \text{Table } I_{\overline{n}|10\%}$$
$$2.5 = \text{Table } I_{\overline{n}|10\%}$$

Referring to Table I, reading down the i = 10% column:

n	Table Factor
9 =	2.3579
10 =	2.5937

Interpolating:

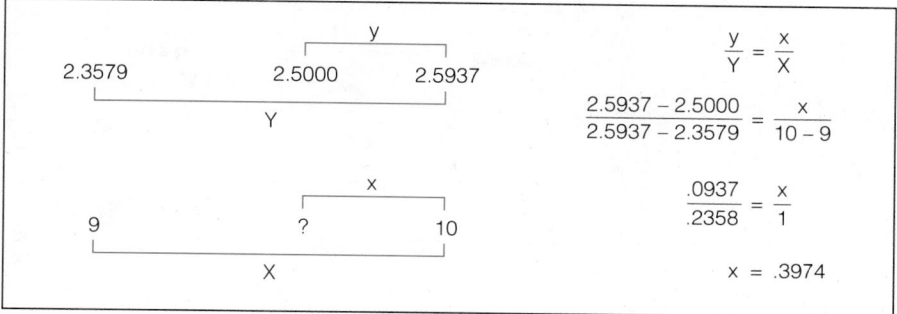

The .3974 is the difference between the number of periods at table factor 2.5937 and the number of periods at table factor 2.5000. Therefore, the number of periods needed is 10.0000 − .3974 = 9.6026. In other words, about 9.6 periods (in this case, years) are required for $600,000 to amount to $1,500,000 at 10% annual interst.

Example 12	Interpolation: Implicit Rate of Interest

Fellmar, Inc. has entered into an automobile lease arrangement. The fair market value of the leased automobile is $15,815 and the contract calls for quarterly payments of $1,525 due at the end of each quarter for 3 years. What is the implicit rate of interest on the lease arrangement?

Solution:

The implicit interest rate must be computed for the present value of an ordinary annuity. The present value is the fair market value of the automobile, and the payment is the lease payment. Table IV is used, and the appropriate formula is given below.

$$PV_n = R(PVAF_{\overline{n}|i})$$

where:

PV_n = $15,815
R = $1,525
n = 12 (3 years − 4 payments per year)
i = The unknown quarterly interest rate

$$\$15,815 = \$1,525 \, (\text{Table IV}_{\overline{12}|i})$$

$$\frac{\$15,815}{\$1,525} = \text{Table IV}_{\overline{12}|i}$$

$$10.3705 = \text{Table IV}_{\overline{12}|i}$$

Reading across the $n = 12$ row of Table IV:

i	Table Factor
2% =	10.5753
3% =	9.9540

Interlopating:

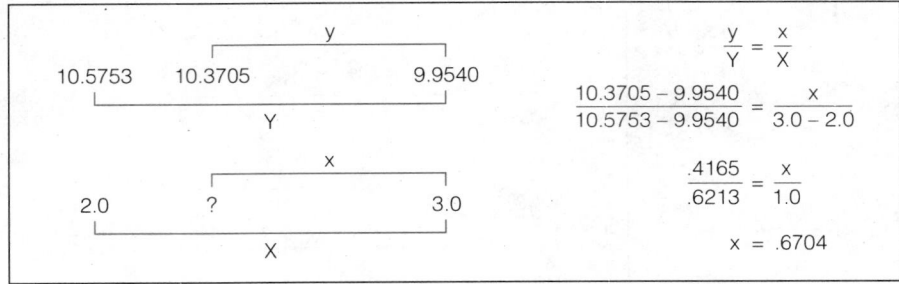

The .6704 is the difference between the interest rate at the table factor 9.9540 and the interest rate at the table factor 10.3705. Therefore, the quarterly implicit interest rate is 3.0000 − .6704 = 2.3296%; and the annual implicit interest rate is 9.3184% (2.3296% × 4).

Concluding Comment   As noted in Chapter 2, the FASB's conceptual framework allows for various measurement attributes, one of which is discounted present values. This chapter has illustrated a few of the many business applications of present and future value measurement techniques. As interest rates continue to fluctuate in the world economy, many times reaching double-digit levels, the importance of the time value of money concept will increase. In the remaining chapters of this text, additional illustrations of this important concept will be presented.

TABLE I
Amount of $1 Due in n Periods

n	1%	2%	3%	4%	5%	6%	7%	8%	9%	10%	11%	12%	14%	16%	20%
1	1.0100	1.0200	1.0300	1.0400	1.0500	1.0600	1.0700	1.0800	1.0900	1.1000	1.1100	1.1200	1.1400	1.1600	1.2000
2	1.0201	1.0404	1.0609	1.0816	1.1025	1.1236	1.1449	1.1664	1.1881	1.2100	1.2321	1.2544	1.2996	1.3456	1.4400
3	1.0303	1.0612	1.0927	1.1249	1.1576	1.1910	1.2250	1.2597	1.2950	1.3310	1.3676	1.4049	1.4815	1.5609	1.7280
4	1.0406	1.0824	1.1255	1.1699	1.2155	1.2625	1.3108	1.3605	1.4116	1.4641	1.5181	1.5735	1.6890	1.8106	2.0736
5	1.0510	1.1041	1.1593	1.2167	1.2763	1.3382	1.4026	1.4693	1.5386	1.6105	1.6851	1.7623	1.9254	2.1003	2.4883
6	1.0615	1.1262	1.1941	1.2653	1.3401	1.4185	1.5007	1.5869	1.6771	1.7716	1.8704	1.9738	2.1950	2.4364	2.9860
7	1.0712	1.1487	1.2299	1.3159	1.4071	1.5036	1.6058	1.7138	1.8280	1.9487	2.0762	2.2107	2.5023	2.8262	3.5832
8	1.0829	1.1717	1.2668	1.3686	1.4775	1.5938	1.7182	1.8509	1.9926	2.1436	2.3045	2.4760	2.8526	3.2784	4.2998
9	1.0937	1.1951	1.3048	1.4233	1.5513	1.6895	1.8385	1.9990	2.1719	2.3579	2.5580	2.7731	3.2519	3.8030	5.1598
10	1.1046	1.2190	1.3439	1.4802	1.6289	1.7908	1.9672	2.1589	2.3674	2.5937	2.8394	3.1058	3.7072	4.4114	6.1917
11	1.1157	1.2434	1.3842	1.5395	1.7103	1.8983	2.1049	2.3316	2.5804	2.8531	3.1518	3.4785	4.2262	5.1173	7.4301
12	1.1268	1.2682	1.4258	1.6010	1.7959	2.0122	2.2522	2.5182	2.8127	3.1384	3.4985	3.8960	4.8179	5.9360	8.9161
13	1.1381	1.2936	1.4685	1.6651	1.8856	2.1329	2.4098	2.7196	3.0658	3.4523	3.8833	4.3635	5.4924	6.8858	10.6993
14	1.1495	1.3195	1.5126	1.7317	1.9799	2.2609	2.5785	2.9372	3.3417	3.7975	4.3104	4.8871	6.2613	7.9875	12.8392
15	1.1610	1.3459	1.5580	1.8009	2.0789	2.3966	2.7590	3.1722	3.6425	4.1772	4.7846	5.4736	7.1379	9.2655	15.4070
16	1.1726	1.3728	1.6047	1.8730	2.1829	2.5404	2.9522	3.4259	3.9703	4.5950	5.3109	6.1304	8.1372	10.7480	18.4884
17	1.1843	1.4002	1.6528	1.9479	2.2920	2.6928	3.1588	3.7000	4.3276	5.0545	5.8951	6.8660	9.2765	12.4677	22.1861
18	1.1961	1.4282	1.7024	2.0258	2.4066	2.8543	3.3799	3.9960	4.7171	5.5599	6.5436	7.6900	10.5752	14.4625	26.6233
19	1.2081	1.4568	1.7535	2.1068	2.5270	3.0256	3.6165	4.3157	5.1417	6.1159	7.2633	8.6128	12.0557	16.7765	31.9480
20	1.2202	1.4859	1.8061	2.1911	2.6533	3.2071	3.8697	4.6610	5.6044	6.7275	8.0623	9.6463	13.7435	19.4608	38.3376
21	1.2324	1.5157	1.8603	2.2788	2.7860	3.3996	4.1406	5.0338	6.1088	7.4002	8.9492	10.8038	15.6676	22.5745	46.0051
22	1.2447	1.5460	1.9161	2.3699	2.9253	3.6035	4.4304	5.4365	6.6586	8.1403	9.9336	12.1003	17.8610	26.1864	55.2061
23	1.2572	1.5769	1.9736	2.4647	3.0715	3.8197	4.7405	5.8715	7.2579	8.9543	11.0263	13.5523	20.3616	30.3762	66.2474
24	1.2697	1.6084	2.0328	2.5633	3.2251	4.0489	5.0724	6.3412	7.9111	9.8497	12.2392	15.1786	23.2122	35.2364	79.4968
25	1.2824	1.6406	2.0938	2.6658	3.3864	4.2919	5.4274	6.8485	8.6231	10.8347	13.5855	17.0001	26.4619	40.8742	95.3962
26	1.2953	1.6734	2.1566	2.7725	3.5557	4.5494	5.8074	7.3964	9.3992	11.9182	15.0799	19.0401	30.1666	47.4141	114.4755
27	1.3082	1.7069	2.2213	2.8834	3.7335	4.8223	6.2139	7.9881	10.2451	13.1100	16.7386	21.3249	34.3899	55.0004	137.3706
28	1.3213	1.7410	2.2879	2.9987	3.9201	5.1117	6.6488	8.6271	11.1671	14.4210	18.5799	23.8839	39.2045	63.8004	164.8447
29	1.3345	1.7758	2.3566	3.1187	4.1161	5.4184	7.1143	9.3173	12.1722	15.8631	20.6237	26.7499	44.6931	74.0085	197.8136
30	1.3478	1.8114	2.4273	3.2434	4.3219	5.7435	7.6123	10.0627	13.2677	17.4494	22.8923	29.9599	50.9502	85.8499	237.3763
35	1.4166	1.9999	2.8139	3.9461	5.5160	7.6861	10.6766	14.7853	20.4140	28.1024	38.5749	52.7996	98.1002	180.3141	590.6682
40	1.4889	2.2080	3.2620	4.8010	7.0400	10.2857	14.9745	21.7245	31.4094	45.2593	65.0009	93.0510	188.8835	378.7212	1,469.7716
45	1.5648	2.4379	3.7816	5.8412	8.9850	13.7646	21.0025	31.9204	48.3273	72.8905	109.5302	163.9876	363.6791	795.4438	3,657.2620
50	1.6446	2.6916	4.3839	7.1067	11.4674	18.4202	29.4570	46.9016	74.3575	117.3909	184.5648	289.0022	700.2330	1,670.7038	9,100.4382

TABLE II
Present Value of $1 Due in n Periods

n	1%	2%	3%	4%	5%	6%	7%	8%	9%	10%	11%	12%	14%	16%	20%
1	0.9901	0.9804	0.9709	0.9615	0.9524	0.9434	0.9346	0.9259	0.9174	0.9091	0.9009	0.8929	0.8772	0.8621	0.8333
2	0.9803	0.9612	0.9426	0.9246	0.9070	0.8900	0.8734	0.8573	0.8417	0.8264	0.8116	0.7972	0.7695	0.7432	0.6944
3	0.9706	0.9423	0.9151	0.8890	0.8638	0.8396	0.8163	0.7938	0.7722	0.7513	0.7312	0.7118	0.6750	0.6407	0.5787
4	0.9610	0.9238	0.8885	0.8548	0.8227	0.7921	0.7629	0.7350	0.7084	0.6830	0.6587	0.6355	0.5921	0.5523	0.4823
5	0.9515	0.9057	0.8626	0.8219	0.7835	0.7473	0.7130	0.6806	0.6499	0.6209	0.5935	0.5674	0.5194	0.4761	0.4019
6	0.9420	0.8880	0.8375	0.7903	0.7462	0.7050	0.6663	0.6302	0.5963	0.5645	0.5346	0.5066	0.4556	0.4104	0.3349
7	0.9327	0.8706	0.8131	0.7599	0.7107	0.6651	0.6227	0.5835	0.5470	0.5132	0.4817	0.4523	0.3996	0.3538	0.2791
8	0.9235	0.8535	0.7894	0.7307	0.6768	0.6274	0.5820	0.5403	0.5019	0.4665	0.4339	0.4039	0.3506	0.3050	0.2326
9	0.9143	0.8368	0.7664	0.7026	0.6446	0.5919	0.5439	0.5002	0.4604	0.4241	0.3909	0.3606	0.3075	0.2630	0.1938
10	0.9053	0.8203	0.7441	0.6756	0.6139	0.5584	0.5083	0.4632	0.4224	0.3855	0.3522	0.3220	0.2697	0.2267	0.1615
11	0.8963	0.8043	0.7224	0.6496	0.5847	0.5268	0.4751	0.4289	0.3875	0.3505	0.3173	0.2875	0.2366	0.1954	0.1346
12	0.8874	0.7885	0.7014	0.6246	0.5568	0.4970	0.4440	0.3971	0.3555	0.3186	0.2858	0.2567	0.2076	0.1685	0.1122
13	0.8787	0.7730	0.6810	0.6006	0.5303	0.4688	0.4150	0.3677	0.3262	0.2897	0.2575	0.2292	0.1821	0.1452	0.0935
14	0.8700	0.7579	0.6611	0.5775	0.5051	0.4423	0.3878	0.3405	0.2992	0.2633	0.2320	0.2046	0.1597	0.1252	0.0779
15	0.8613	0.7430	0.6419	0.5553	0.4810	0.4173	0.3624	0.3152	0.2745	0.2394	0.2090	0.1827	0.1401	0.1079	0.0649
16	0.8528	0.7284	0.6232	0.5339	0.4581	0.3936	0.3387	0.2919	0.2519	0.2176	0.1883	0.1631	0.1229	0.0930	0.0541
17	0.8444	0.7142	0.6050	0.5134	0.4363	0.3714	0.3166	0.2703	0.2311	0.1978	0.1696	0.1456	0.1078	0.0802	0.0451
18	0.8360	0.7002	0.5874	0.4936	0.4155	0.3503	0.2959	0.2502	0.2120	0.1799	0.1528	0.1300	0.0946	0.0691	0.0376
19	0.8277	0.6864	0.5703	0.4746	0.3957	0.3305	0.2765	0.2317	0.1945	0.1635	0.1377	0.1161	0.0829	0.0596	0.0313
20	0.8195	0.6730	0.5537	0.4564	0.3769	0.3118	0.2584	0.2145	0.1784	0.1486	0.1240	0.1037	0.0728	0.0514	0.0261
21	0.8114	0.6598	0.5375	0.4388	0.3589	0.2942	0.2415	0.1987	0.1637	0.1351	0.1117	0.0926	0.0638	0.0443	0.0217
22	0.8034	0.6468	0.5219	0.4220	0.3418	0.2775	0.2257	0.1839	0.1502	0.1228	0.1007	0.0826	0.0560	0.0382	0.0181
23	0.7954	0.6342	0.5067	0.4057	0.3256	0.2618	0.2109	0.1703	0.1378	0.1117	0.0907	0.0738	0.0491	0.0329	0.0151
24	0.7876	0.6217	0.4919	0.3901	0.3101	0.2470	0.1971	0.1577	0.1264	0.1015	0.0817	0.0659	0.0431	0.0284	0.0126
25	0.7798	0.6095	0.4776	0.3751	0.2953	0.2330	0.1842	0.1460	0.1160	0.0923	0.0736	0.0588	0.0378	0.0245	0.0105
26	0.7720	0.5976	0.4637	0.3607	0.2812	0.2198	0.1722	0.1352	0.1064	0.0839	0.0663	0.0525	0.0331	0.0211	0.0087
27	0.7644	0.5859	0.4502	0.3468	0.2678	0.2074	0.1609	0.1252	0.0976	0.0763	0.0597	0.0469	0.0291	0.0182	0.0073
28	0.7568	0.5744	0.4371	0.3335	0.2551	0.1956	0.1504	0.1159	0.0895	0.0693	0.0538	0.0419	0.0255	0.0157	0.0061
29	0.7493	0.5631	0.4243	0.3207	0.2429	0.1846	0.1406	0.1073	0.0822	0.0630	0.0485	0.0374	0.0224	0.0135	0.0051
30	0.7419	0.5521	0.4120	0.3083	0.2314	0.1741	0.1314	0.0994	0.0754	0.0573	0.0437	0.0334	0.0196	0.0116	0.0042
35	0.7059	0.5000	0.3554	0.2534	0.1813	0.1301	0.0937	0.0676	0.0490	0.0356	0.0259	0.0189	0.0102	0.0055	0.0017
40	0.6717	0.4529	0.3066	0.2083	0.1420	0.0972	0.0668	0.0460	0.0318	0.0221	0.0154	0.0107	0.0053	0.0026	0.0007
45	0.6391	0.4102	0.2644	0.1712	0.1113	0.0727	0.0476	0.0313	0.0207	0.0137	0.0091	0.0061	0.0027	0.0013	0.0003
50	0.6080	0.3715	0.2281	0.1407	0.0872	0.0543	0.0339	0.0213	0.0134	0.0085	0.0054	0.0035	0.0014	0.0006	0.0001

Wait to Purchase

TABLE III
Amount of an Ordinary Annuity of $1 per Period

	1%	2%	3%	4%	5%	6%	7%	8%	9%	10%	11%	12%	14%	16%	20%
1	1.0000	1.0000	1.0000	1.0000	1.0000	1.0000	1.0000	1.0000	1.0000	1.0000	1.0000	1.0000	1.0000	1.0000	1.0000
2	2.0100	2.0200	2.0300	2.0400	2.0500	2.0600	2.0700	2.0800	2.0900	2.1000	2.1100	2.1200	2.1400	2.1600	2.2000
3	3.0301	3.0604	3.0909	3.1216	3.1525	3.1836	3.2149	3.2464	3.2781	3.3100	3.3421	3.3744	3.4396	3.5056	3.6400
4	4.0604	4.1216	4.1836	4.2465	4.3101	4.3746	4.4399	4.5061	4.5731	4.6410	4.7097	4.7793	4.9211	5.0665	5.3680
5	5.1010	5.2040	5.3091	5.4163	5.5256	5.6371	5.7507	5.8666	5.9847	6.1051	6.2278	6.3528	6.6101	6.8771	7.4416
6	6.1520	6.3081	6.4684	6.6330	6.8019	6.9753	7.1533	7.3359	7.5233	7.7156	7.9129	8.1152	8.5355	8.9775	9.9299
7	7.2135	7.4343	7.6625	7.8983	8.1420	8.3938	8.6540	8.9228	9.2004	9.4872	9.7833	10.0890	10.7305	11.4139	12.9159
8	8.2857	8.5830	8.8923	9.2142	9.5491	9.8975	10.2598	10.6366	11.0285	11.4359	11.8594	12.2997	13.2328	14.2401	16.4991
9	9.3685	9.7546	10.1591	10.5828	11.0266	11.4913	11.9780	12.4876	13.0210	13.5795	14.1640	14.7757	16.0853	17.5185	20.7989
10	10.4622	10.9497	11.4639	12.0061	12.5779	13.1808	13.8164	14.4866	15.1929	15.9374	16.7220	17.5487	19.3373	21.3215	25.9587
11	11.5668	12.1687	12.8078	13.4864	14.2068	14.9716	15.7836	16.6455	17.5603	18.5312	19.5614	20.6546	23.0445	25.7329	32.1504
12	12.6825	13.4121	14.1920	15.0258	15.9171	16.8699	17.8885	18.9771	20.1407	21.3843	22.7132	24.1331	27.2707	30.8502	39.5805
13	13.8093	14.6803	15.6178	16.6268	17.7130	18.8821	20.1406	21.4953	22.9534	24.5227	26.2116	28.0291	32.0887	36.7862	48.4966
14	14.9474	15.9739	17.0863	18.2919	19.5986	21.0151	22.5505	24.2149	26.0192	27.9750	30.0949	32.3926	37.5811	43.6720	59.1959
15	16.0969	17.2934	18.5989	20.0236	21.5786	23.2760	25.1290	27.1521	29.3609	31.7725	34.4054	37.2797	43.8424	51.6595	72.0351
16	17.2579	18.6393	20.1569	21.8245	23.6575	25.6725	27.8881	30.3243	33.0034	35.9497	39.1899	42.7533	50.9804	60.9250	87.4421
17	18.4304	20.0121	21.7616	23.6975	25.8404	28.2129	30.8402	33.7502	36.9737	40.5447	44.5008	48.8837	59.1176	71.6730	105.9306
18	19.6147	21.4123	23.4144	25.6454	28.1324	30.9057	33.9990	37.4502	41.3013	45.5992	50.3959	55.7497	68.3941	84.1407	128.1167
19	20.8190	22.8406	25.1169	27.6712	30.5390	33.7600	37.3790	41.4463	46.0185	51.1591	56.9395	63.4397	78.9692	98.6032	154.7400
20	22.0190	24.2974	26.8704	29.7781	33.0660	36.7856	40.9955	45.7620	51.1601	57.2750	64.2028	72.0524	91.0249	115.3797	186.6880
21	23.2392	25.7833	28.6765	31.9692	35.7193	39.9927	44.8652	50.4229	56.7645	64.0025	72.2651	81.6987	104.7684	134.8405	225.0256
22	24.4716	27.2990	30.5368	34.2480	38.5052	43.3923	49.0057	55.4568	62.8733	71.4027	81.2143	92.5026	120.4360	157.4150	271.0307
23	25.7163	28.8450	32.4529	36.6179	41.4305	46.9958	53.4361	60.8933	69.5319	79.5430	91.1479	104.6029	138.2970	183.6014	326.2369
24	26.9735	30.4219	34.4265	39.0826	44.5020	50.8156	58.1767	66.7648	76.7898	88.4973	102.1742	118.1552	158.6586	213.9776	392.4842
25	28.2432	32.0303	36.4593	41.6459	47.7271	54.8645	63.2490	73.1059	84.7009	98.3471	114.4133	133.3339	181.8708	249.2140	471.9811
26	29.5256	33.6709	38.5530	44.3117	51.1135	59.1564	68.6765	79.9544	93.3240	109.1818	127.9988	150.3339	208.3327	290.0883	567.3773
27	30.8209	35.3443	40.7096	47.0842	54.6691	63.7058	74.4838	87.3508	102.7231	121.0999	143.0786	169.3740	238.4993	337.5024	681.8528
28	32.1291	37.0512	42.9309	49.9676	58.4026	68.5281	80.6977	95.3388	112.9682	134.2099	159.8173	190.6989	272.8892	392.5028	819.2233
29	33.4504	38.7922	45.2189	52.9663	62.3227	73.6398	87.3465	103.9659	124.1354	148.6309	178.3972	214.5828	312.0937	456.3032	984.0680
30	34.7849	40.5681	47.5754	56.0849	66.4388	79.0582	94.4608	113.2832	136.3075	164.4940	199.0209	241.3327	356.7868	530.3117	1181.8816
35	41.6603	49.9945	60.4621	73.6522	90.3203	111.4348	138.2369	172.3168	215.7108	271.0244	341.5896	431.6635	693.5727	1120.7130	2948.3411
40	48.8864	60.4020	75.4013	95.0255	120.7998	154.7620	199.6351	259.0565	337.8824	442.5926	581.8261	767.0914	1342.0251	2360.7572	7343.8578
45	56.4811	71.8927	92.7199	121.0294	159.7002	212.7435	285.7493	386.5056	525.8587	718.9048	986.6386	1358.2300	2590.5648	4965.2739	18281.3099
50	64.4632	84.5794	112.7969	152.6671	209.3480	290.3359	406.5289	573.7702	815.0836	1163.9085	1668.7712	2400.0182	4994.5213	10435.6488	45497.1908

TABLE IV
Present Value of an Ordinary Annuity of $1 per Period

	1%	2%	3%	4%	5%	6%	7%	8%	9%	10%	11%	12%	14%	16%	20%
1	0.9901	0.9804	0.9709	0.9615	0.9524	0.9434	0.9346	0.9259	0.9174	0.9091	0.9009	0.8929	0.8772	0.8621	0.8333
2	1.9704	1.9416	1.9135	1.8861	1.8594	1.8334	1.8080	1.7833	1.7591	1.7355	1.7125	1.6901	1.6467	1.6052	1.5278
3	2.9410	2.8839	2.8286	2.7751	2.7232	2.6730	2.6243	2.5771	2.5313	2.4869	2.4437	2.4081	2.3216	2.2459	2.1065
4	3.9020	3.8077	3.7171	3.6299	3.5460	3.4651	3.3872	3.3121	3.2397	3.1699	3.1024	3.0373	2.9137	2.7982	2.5887
5	4.8534	4.7135	4.5797	4.4518	4.3295	4.2124	4.1002	3.9927	3.8897	3.7908	3.6959	3.6048	3.4331	3.2743	2.9906
6	5.7955	5.6014	5.4172	5.2421	5.0757	4.9173	4.7665	4.6229	4.4859	4.3553	4.2305	4.1114	3.8887	3.6847	3.3255
7	6.7282	6.4720	6.2303	6.0021	5.7864	5.5824	5.3893	5.2064	5.0330	4.8684	4.7122	4.5638	4.2883	4.0386	3.6046
8	7.6517	7.3255	7.0197	6.7327	6.4632	6.2098	5.9713	5.7466	5.5348	5.3349	5.1461	4.9676	4.6389	4.3436	3.8372
9	8.5660	8.1622	7.7861	7.4353	7.1078	6.8017	6.5152	6.2469	5.9952	5.7590	5.5370	5.3282	4.9464	4.6065	4.0310
10	9.4713	8.9826	8.5302	8.1109	7.7217	7.3601	7.0236	6.7101	6.4177	6.1446	5.8892	5.6502	5.2161	4.8332	4.1925
11	10.3676	9.7868	9.2526	8.7605	8.3064	7.8869	7.4987	7.1390	6.8052	6.4951	6.2065	5.9377	5.4527	5.0286	4.3271
12	11.2551	10.5753	9.9540	9.3851	8.8633	8.3838	7.9427	7.5361	7.1607	6.8137	6.4924	6.1944	5.6603	5.1971	4.4392
13	12.1337	11.3484	10.6350	9.9856	9.3936	8.8527	8.3577	7.9038	7.4869	7.1034	6.7499	6.4235	5.8424	5.3423	4.5327
14	13.0037	12.1062	11.2961	10.5631	9.8986	9.2950	8.7455	8.2442	7.7862	7.3667	6.9819	6.6282	6.0021	5.4675	4.6106
15	13.8651	12.8493	11.9379	11.1184	10.3797	9.7122	9.1079	8.5595	8.0607	7.6061	7.1909	6.8109	6.1422	5.5755	4.6755
16	14.7179	13.5777	12.5611	11.6523	10.8378	10.1059	9.4466	8.8514	8.3126	7.8237	7.3792	6.9740	6.2651	5.6685	4.7296
17	15.5623	14.2919	13.1661	12.1657	11.2741	10.4773	9.7632	9.1216	8.5436	8.0216	7.5488	7.1196	6.3729	5.7487	4.7746
18	16.3983	14.9920	13.7535	12.6593	11.6896	10.8276	10.0591	9.3719	8.7556	8.2014	7.7016	7.2497	6.4674	5.8178	4.8122
19	17.2260	15.6785	14.3238	13.1339	12.0853	11.1581	10.3356	9.6036	8.9501	8.3649	7.8393	7.3658	6.5504	5.8775	4.8435
20	18.0456	16.3514	14.8775	13.5903	12.4622	11.4699	10.5940	9.8181	9.1285	8.5136	7.9633	7.4694	6.6231	5.9288	4.8696
21	18.8570	17.0112	15.4150	14.0292	12.8212	11.7641	10.8355	10.0168	9.2922	8.6487	8.0751	7.5620	6.6870	5.9731	4.8913
22	19.6604	17.6580	15.9369	14.4511	13.1630	12.0416	11.0612	10.2007	9.4424	8.7715	8.1757	7.6446	6.7429	6.0113	4.9094
23	20.4558	18.2922	16.4436	14.8568	13.4886	12.3034	11.2722	10.3711	9.5802	8.8832	8.2664	7.7184	6.7921	6.0442	4.9245
24	21.2434	18.9139	16.9355	15.2470	13.7986	12.5504	11.4693	10.5288	9.7066	8.9847	8.3481	7.7843	6.8351	6.0726	4.9371
25	22.0232	19.5235	17.4131	15.6221	14.0939	12.7834	11.6536	10.6748	9.8226	9.0770	8.4217	7.8431	6.8729	6.0971	4.9476
26	22.7952	20.1210	17.8768	15.9828	14.3752	13.0032	11.8258	10.8100	9.9290	9.1609	8.4881	7.8957	6.9061	6.1182	4.9563
27	23.5596	20.7069	18.3270	16.3296	14.6430	13.2105	11.9867	10.9352	10.0266	9.2372	8.5478	7.9426	6.9352	6.1364	4.9636
28	24.3164	21.2813	18.7641	16.6631	14.8981	13.4062	12.1371	11.0511	10.1161	9.3066	8.6016	7.9844	6.9607	6.1520	4.9697
29	25.0658	21.8444	19.1885	16.9837	15.1411	13.5907	12.2777	11.1584	10.1983	9.3696	8.6501	8.0218	6.9830	6.1656	4.9747
30	25.8077	22.3965	19.6004	17.2920	15.3725	13.7648	12.4090	11.2578	10.2737	9.4269	8.6938	8.0552	7.0027	6.1772	4.9789
35	29.4086	24.9986	21.4872	18.6646	16.3742	14.4982	12.9477	11.6546	10.5668	9.6442	8.8552	8.1755	7.0700	6.2153	4.9915
40	32.8347	27.3555	23.1148	19.7928	17.1591	15.0463	13.3317	11.9246	10.7574	9.7791	8.9511	8.2438	7.1050	6.2335	4.9966
45	36.0945	29.4902	24.5187	20.7200	17.7741	15.4558	13.6055	12.1084	10.8812	9.8628	9.0079	8.2825	7.1232	6.2421	4.9986
50	39.1961	31.4236	25.7298	21.4822	18.2559	15.7619	13.8007	12.2335	10.9617	9.9148	9.0417	8.3045	7.1327	6.2463	4.9995

Key Terms
Annuity 213
Annuity due 223
Compound interest 212
Effective rate of interest 212
Future value 213
Interest 211

Interpolation 227
Ordinary annuity 223
Present value 213
Principal 211
Simple interest 211

Questions

1. Explain what is meant by the time value of money concept and describe its impact on business decisions.
2. Identify some common accounting applications of the time value of money concept.
3. Explain the difference between simple interest and compound interest.
4. Determine the amount of interest earned on the following:
   a. $9,000 borrowed from a bank at 10% simple annual interest for 8 months.
   b. $15,000 invested for 2 years at 15% simple annual interest.
   c. $1,500 invested for 26 days at 12% simple annual interest. (Use a 360-day year.)
5. Indicate the rate per period and the number of periods for each of the following:
   a. 10% per year, for 3 years, compounded annually.
   b. 10% per year, for 3 years, compounded semiannually.
   c. 10% per year, for 3 years, compounded quarterly.
   d. 10% per year, for 3 years, compounded monthly.
6. What is meant by *discounting* cash flows?
7. Indicate the table and the table value that would be used in calculating the following:
   a. The value today of $5,000 due in 3 years at 16% interest per year, compounded semiannually.
   b. The value today of 5 future annual payments of $4,000 at 12% interest per year, compounded annually.
   c. The value in ten years of $6,000 deposited today at 10% interest per year, compounded semiannually.
   d. The value in 5 years of quarterly payments of $1,500 for 5 years at 16% interest per year, compounded quarterly.
8. How much interest is earned on the following (round to nearest dollar):
   a. $10,500 invested for 5 years at 8% per year, compounded annually.
   b. $7,500 invested for 10 years at 20% per year, compounded semiannually.
   c. $12,000 invested for 4 years at 16% per year, compounded quarterly.
   d. $1,750 invested for 1 year at 24% per year, compounded monthly.
9. Determine the table values that would be used for the following:
   a. Present value of a single amount to be received at the end of 2 years at 10% interest compounded annually.
   b. Present value of 14 semiannual payments made at the end of the period at 10% interest compounded semiannually.
   c. Future value of a single amount invested for 5 years at 12% interest compounded annually.
   d. Future value of 6 equal quarterly payments made at the end of the period at 16% interest compounded quarterly.
10. An accounting student bought an inexpensive computer for $260 to assist in

homework assignments. The student bought the computer on time, agreeing to pay $26.12 at the end of each month for 12 months. What approximate monthly interest rate did the student pay?

11. Define an annuity. What is the difference between an "ordinary annuity" and an "annuity due?"

12. Explain how the table values for the future value ordinary annuity table are converted to annuity due values.

13. Explain how the table values for the present value ordinary annuity table are converted to annuity due values.

14. For each of the following, compute the future amount of an ordinary annuity (round to nearest dollar):
   a. 12 annual payments of $100 at 6% per annum, compounded annually.
   b. 8 semiannual payments of $50 at 8% per annum, compounded semiannually.
   c. 19 quarterly payments of $125 at 12% per annum, compounded quarterly.

15. What are the future amounts in Question 14 if the annuities are annuities due?

16. For each of the following, compute the present value of an ordinary annuity:
   a. $1,000 annually for 10 years at 8% per annum, compounded annually.
   b. $2,050 semiannually for 6 years at 6% per annum, compounded semiannually.
   c. $5,600 quarterly for 3 years at 8% per annum, compounded quarterly.

17. What are the present values in Question 16 if the annuities are annuities due?

18. What is interpolation, when is it used, and is it 100% accurate (explain)?

19. Determine by interpolation the table value that would be used for the following:
   a. Future value of $1 in 6 years at 13% interest per year, compounded semiannually.
   b. Future value of $1 paid annually for 10 years at 13% interest per year, compounded annually.
   c. Present value of $1 due in 10 years at 9% interest per year, compounded quarterly.
   d. Present value of semiannual payments of $1 for 10 years at 9% interest per year, compounded semiannually.

20. At what annual rate of interest would an investment of $20,000 accumulate to $38,000 at the end of 5 years? (Hint: Interpolation is needed.)

Exercises   **Exercise 6-1   (Simple and compound interest)**

Dietrick Corporation borrowed $30,000 from its major shareholder, the president of the company, at 12% simple interest. The loan is to be repaid in 18 months. (a) How much will Dietrick have to pay to settle its obligation? (b) How much of the payment is interest? (c) If Dietrick Corporation has to borrow the $30,000 from the First State Bank at 16% annual interest compounded quarterly, how much interest would it have to pay?

Exercise 6-2   (Unknown annuity amount)

Ryan Henry wants to buy his son a BMW for his 21st birthday. If Henry's son is 16 now, and interest is 8% per annum, compounded semiannually, what would Henry's semiannual investment need to be if the car will cost $26,000?

Exercise 6-3   (Reciprocal relationships: future and present values)

Determine the amount that must be deposited now at compound interest to provide the desired sum for each of the following:

a. Amount to be invested for 10 years at 6% per annum, compounded semiannually, to equal $17,000.
b. Amount to be invested for 2½ years at 8% per annum, compounded quarterly, to equal $5,000.
c. Amount to be invested for 15 years at 12% per annum, compounded semiannually, then reinvested at 16% per annum, compounded quarterly, for 5 more years to equal $25,000.
d. Amount to be invested at 8% per annum, compounded semiannually, for 3 years then $5,000 more added and reinvested at the same rate for another 3 years to equal $12,500.

Exercise 6-4   (Unknown investment periods)

Determine the number of periods the following would have to be invested to accumulate to $10,000. Convert the periods to years.

a. $5,051 at 10% per annum, compounded semiannually.
b. $5,002 at 8% per annum, compounded annually.
c. $5,134 at 16% per annum, compounded quarterly.

Exercise 6-5   (Unknown interest rates)

Determine the annual interest rate that is needed for the following to accumulate to $50,000:

a. $10,414 for 20 years, interest compounded semiannually.
b. $7,102 for 10 years, interest compounded quarterly.
c. $33,778 for 10 years, interest compounded annually.

Exercise 6-6   (Reciprocal relationships: future and present values)

Determine the amount that would accumulate for the following investments:

a. $10,050 at 10% per annum, compounded annually, for 6 years.
b. $650 at 12% per annum, compounded quarterly, for 10 years.
c. $5,000 at 16% per annum compounded annually, for 4 years, and then reinvested at 16% per annum, compounded semiannually, for 4 more years.
d. $1,000 at 8% per annum, compounded semiannually, for 5 years, an additional $1,000 added and then reinvested at 12% per annum, compounded quarterly for 3 more years.

Exercise 6-7   (Choosing between alternative investments)

Heather Company has $10,000 to invest. One alternative will yield 10% per year for 4 years. A second alternative is to deposit the $10,000 in a bank that will pay 8% per year, compounded quarterly. Which alternative should Heather select?

Exercise 6-8   (Future values of ordinary annuity payments)

Compute the amounts to which the following periodic investments would accumulate:

a. $1,500 semiannual payments for 6 years at 10% per annum, compounded semiannually.
b. $800 monthly payments for 1 year at 24% interest per annum, compounded monthly.
c. $1,705 quarterly payments for 4 years at 16% per annum, compounded quarterly.

Exercise 6-9   (Future values of annuity due payments)

Compute the amounts in Exercise 8 if the payments are made at the beginning of the period.

Exercise 6-10   (Determining ordinary annuity payments)

Determine the amount of the periodic investment for the following. Investments are made at the end of the period.

a. $500,000 at the end of 1 year with monthly payments invested at 24% per annum, compounded monthly.
b. $1,050 at the end of 2 years with quarterly payments invested at 8% per annum, compounded quarterly.
c. $50,500 at the end of 4 years with annual payments invested at 6% per annum, compounded annually.

Exercise 6-11   (Determining annuity due payments)

Compute the amount of the periodic investments in Exercise 10 if investments are made at the beginning of the period.

Exercise 6-12   (Determining ordinary annuity payments)

Determine the amount of the periodic payments needed to pay off the following purchases. Payments are made at the end of the period.

a. Purchase of a waterbed for $1,205. Monthly payments are to be made for 1 year with interest at 24% per annum, compounded monthly.
b. Purchsase of a motor boat for $26,565. Quarterly payments are to be made for 4 years with interest at 8% per annum, compounded quarterly.
c. Purchase of a condominium for $65,500. Semiannual payments are to be made for 10 years with interest at 10% per annum, compounded semiannually.

Exercise 6-13   (Determing annuity due payments)

Compute the amount of the periodic payments for Exercise 12 if the payments are made at the beginning of the period.

Exercise 6-14   (Unknown purchase price for ordinary annuity payments)

Determine the purchase price for the different payment plans. Payments are at the end of the period.

a. $25.12 monthly payments for 1 year, with 36% interest per annum, compounded monthly.

b. $1,010.75 semiannual payments for 8 years, with 8% interest per annum, compounded semiannually.

c. $5,801.69 annual payments for 20 years with 12% interest per annum, compounded annually.

Exercise 6-15   (Unknown purchase price for ordinary annuity payments)

Determine the purchase price for the payment plans in Exercise 14 if payments are made at the beginning of the period.

Exercise 6-16   (Interpolation—unknown interest rate)

On July 17, 1990, Jerry Sloan borrowed $40,000 from his rich Uncle George to open a sporting goods store. Starting July 17, 1991, Jerry has to make 5 equal annual payments of $10,500 each to repay the loan. What interest rate is Jerry paying?

Exercise 6-17   (Interpolation—unknown interest rate)

Demo Company has decided to purchase a new office building. Management signs a bank note to pay the Second State Bank $10,000 every 6 months for 10 years. At the date of purchase, the office building costs $120,000. The first payment is 6 months later. What is the approximate annual rate of interest on the note?

Exercise 6-18   (Interpolation—unknown interest rate)

If the payments in Exercise 17 began on the date the papers were signed, what would the annual interest rate be?

Problems   **Problem 6-1   (Determining unknown quantities)**

Determine the unknown quantity for each of the following independent situations using the appropriate interest tables:

a. Jeff and Nancy want to start a trust fund for their newborn son, Mark. They have decided to invest $5,000. If interest is 8% compounded semiannually, how much will be in the fund when Mark turns 20?

b. Nixon Corporation wants to establish a retirement fund. Management wants to have $1,000,000 in the fund in 40 years. If fund assets will earn 12%, compounded annually, how much will need to be invested now?

c. How many payments would Star, Inc. need to make if it purchases a new building for $100,000 with annual payments of $16,401.24 and interest of 16%, compounded annually?

d. An investment broker indicates that an investment of $10,000 in a CD for 10 years at the current interest rate will earn $21,589. What is the current annual rate of interest if interest is compounded annually?

Problem 6-2   (Determining unknown quantities)

Determine the unknown quantity for each of the following independent situations using the appropriate interest tables:

a. Sue wants to have $10,000 saved when she begins college. If Sue enters college in 4 years and interest is 8% compounded annually, how much will Sue need to save each year assuming equal payments?

b. XYZ Company has obtained a bank loan to finance the purchase of an automobile for one of its executives. The terms of the loan require monthly payments of $585. If the interest rate is 18% compounded monthly, and the car costs $15,850, for how many months will XYZ have to make payments?

c. Diaz Company is offering the following investment plan. If deposits of $250 are made semiannually for the next 9 years, $7,726 will accure. If interest is compounded semiannually, what is the approximate annual rate of interest on the investment?

d. Jack wants to buy a beanstalk. How long will he have to invest $5,000 in order to accumulate $50,445, the price of the beanstalk, if interest is 12 percent compounded annually?

Problem 6-3   (Determining the effective interest rate)

Valley Technical College needs to purchase some computers. Because the college is short of cash, Computer Sales Company has agreed to let Valley have the computers now and pay $2,500 per computer 6 months from now. If the current cash price is $2,404, what is the rate of interest Valley would be paying?

Problem 6-4   (Choosing between purchase alternatives)

Foot Loose, Inc. needs to purchase a new shoelace making machine. Machines Ready has agreed to sell them the machine for $22,000 down and 4 payments of $5,700 to be paid in semiannual installments for the next 2 years. Do-It-Yourself Machines has offered to sell Foot Loose a comparable machine for $10,000 down and 4 semiannual payments of $9,000. If the current interest rate is 16 percent, compounded semiannually, which machine should Foot Loose purchase?

Problem 6-5   (Choosing between rent payment alternatives)

Park City Construction is building a new office building, and management is trying to decide how rent payments for the office space should be structured. The alternatives are:

a. Annual payment of $15,000 at the end of each year.
b. Monthly payments of $1,200 at the end of each month.

Assuming an interest rate of 12% compounded monthly, which payment schedule should Park City use?

Problem 6-6   (Future value of annuity due deposits)

Rose Sanchez plans to save $1,000 each year to pay for a two-week trip to Mexico. If Rose makes her first deposit on July 1, 1990, and her last deposit on

July 1, 1992, how much will she have for her trip on July 1, 1993? Assume that the annual interest rate is 8%.

Problem 6-7   (Determining number and amount of payments on retirement plan)

Ed Anderson has $250,000 accumulated in a Keogh investment and plans to receive annual payments of $40,360 at the end of each year. (a) If interest is 12% annually, how many payments will Ed receive? (b) If payments are made at the beginning of the year, how many full payments would he receive, and how much would the last payment be? (c) What would the payments have to be if Ed wants to receive 20 payments, each at the end of the year? (d) At the beginning of the year?

Problem 6-8   (Choosing among alternative payment plans)

The following payment plans are offered on the purchase of a new freezer.

a. $375 cash.
b. 8 monthly payments of $55.
c. $100 cash down and 6 monthly payments of $50.

Which payment plan would you choose if interest is 24 percent annually, compounded monthly, if you are the purchaser? the seller? (Assume ordinary annuities where applicable.)

Problem 6-9   (Determining sinking fund payments)

Payback Company wants to start a sinking fund to cover the retirement of a serial bond issuance. The bonds begin maturing in 15 years at a rate of $30,000 per year for 15 years. Payback Company can earn annual interest of 6 percent for the first 15 years and 10% for the remaining years. How much will Payback Company have to deposit annually under the following assumptions?

a. Payments into the fund are made at the end of the year and bonds are retired at the end of the year.
b. Payments into the fund are made at the beginning of the year and bonds are retired at the beginning of the year.
c. Payments into the fund are made at the beginning of the year and bonds are retired at the end of the year.

Problem 6-10   (Determining amount of annuity due payments and interest)

Briercliff Inc. borrowed $4,000 on a 10%, one-year note due on August 1, 1991. On that date, Briercliff was unable to pay the obligation but arranged for Western Loan Company to pay the holder $4,000. Briercliff agreed to pay Western Loan Company a series of 5 equal annual payments beginning August 1, 1991. Each payment is in part a reduction of principal and in part a payment of interest at 12% annually. (a) What is the amount of each payment? (b) What is the total amount of interest on the obligation?

Problem 6-11   (Determing purchase price)

Big Company purchased a machine on February 1, 1991 and will make 7 semiannual payments of $14,000 beginning 5 years from the date of purchase.

The interest rate will be 12%, compounded semiannually. Determine the purchase price of the machine.

Problem 6-12   (Estimating the value of a company)

Cline Corporation is considering the acquisition of a company and wants to determine the value of the company based on the following information. (Assume revenues and expenses are received and incurred evenly throughout the year.)

Years	Estimated Interest Rate	Estimated Annual Revenues	Estimated Annual Expenses
1-5	16% compounded annually	$170,000	$140,000
6-10	12% compounded quarterly	215,000	155,000
11-15	14% compounded semiannually	245,000	185,000

Based on estimated net profit, discounted to the present, what is the value of the company?

Problem 6-13   (Choosing among insurance options)

Dr. Philips is considering the purchase of an insurance policy. The following options are available for payment to the beneficiary upon the death of Dr. Philips.

a. $100,000 immediately.
b. $8,000 at the end of each quarter for 4 years.
c. $30,000 immediately and $5,000 in quarterly payments for 4½ years.
d. Quarterly payments of $4,350 for the next 10 years.

Given an annual interest rate of 12%, compounded quarterly, which option would you recommend to Dr. Philips?

Problem 6-14   (Buy or lease—implicit interest rate)

An office equipment company representative has a machine for sale or lease. If you buy the machine, the cost is $7,596. If you lease the machine, you will have to sign a noncancellable lease and make 5 annual payments of $2,000 each. The first payment will be paid on the first day of the lease. At the time of the last payment, you will receive title to the machine. Determine the implicit interest rate.   (AICPA adapted)

Problem 6-15   (Imputing interest)

On January 1, 1991, Jorgenson Company lent $120,000 cash to McAllister Company. The promissory note made by McAllister did not bear interest and was due on December 31, 1992. No other rights or privileges were exchanged. The prevailing interest for a loan of this type was 12%. What amount of interest income should Jorgenson recognize for 1991.   (AICPA adapted)

PART TWO

Assets

Chapter 7

Cash and Temporary Investments

The first part of this book has established a perspective of accounting and its theoretical foundation. Part II explores items classified as **assets**, beginning with the most liquid assets: cash and temporary investments.

Cash   Cash is perhaps the single most important item on a balance sheet. Since it serves as the medium of exchange in our economy, cash is involved directly or indirectly in almost all business transactions. Even when cash is not involved directly in a transaction, it provides the basis for measurement and accounting for all other items.

Another reason why cash is so important is that individuals, businesses, and even governments must maintain an adequate liquidity position; that is, they must have a sufficient amount of cash on hand to pay obligations as they come due if they are to remain viable operating entities. In the early stages of its conceptual framework project, the FASB identified the need to report information on cash and liquidity as one of the key objectives of financial reporting. This emphasis eventually led to the requirement of providing a statement of cash flows as one of the primary financial statements.[1]

In striking contrast to the importance of cash as a key element in the liquidity position of an entity is its unproductive nature. Since cash is the measure of value, it cannot expand or grow unless it is converted into other properties. Cash kept under a mattress, for example, will not grow or appreciate, whereas land may increase in value if held. Excessive balances of cash on hand are often referred to as **idle cash**. Efficient cash management requires available cash to be continuously working in one of several ways as part of the operating cycle or as a short-term or long-term investment. The management of cash is therefore a critical business function.

---

[1]*Statement of Financial Accounting Standards No. 95*, "Statement of Cash Flows" (Stamford: Financial Accounting Standards Board, November 1987).

Composition of Cash

Cash is the most liquid of current assets and consists of those items that serve as a medium of exchange and provide a basis for accounting measurement. To be reported as "cash," an item must be readily available and not restricted for use in the payment of current obligations. A general guideline is whether an item is *acceptable for deposit at face value* by a bank or other financial institution.

Items that are classified as cash include coin and currency on hand, and unrestricted funds available on deposit in a bank, which are often called demand deposits since they can be withdrawn upon demand. Demand deposits would include amounts in checking, savings, and money market deposit accounts. Petty cash funds or change funds and negotiable instruments, such as personal checks, travelers' checks, cashiers' checks, bank drafts, and money orders are also items commonly reported as cash. The total of these items plus undeposited coin and currency is sometimes called **cash on hand**. Also included as cash would be any company checks that have been written but that have not been mailed or delivered. Deposits that are not immediately available due to withdrawal or other restrictions are sometimes referred to as time deposits. These deposits are often separately classified as "restricted cash" or "temporary investments." Examples of time deposits include certificates of deposit (CDs) and money market savings certificates. CDs, for example, generally may be withdrawn without penalty only at specified maturity dates.

Deposits in foreign banks that are subject to immediate and unrestricted withdrawal generally qualify as cash and are reported at their U.S. dollar equivalents as of the date of the balance sheet. However, cash in foreign banks that is restricted as to use or withdrawal should be designated as receivables of a current or noncurrent character and reported subject to appropriate allowances for estimated uncollectible losses.

Some items do not meet the "acceptance at face value on deposit" test and should not be reported as cash. Examples include postage stamps (which are office supplies) and post-dated checks, IOUs, and not-sufficient-funds (NSF) checks (all of which are in effect receivables).

Cash balances specifically designated by management for special purposes should be reported separately. Those cash balances to be applied to some current purpose or current obligation are properly reported in the current section on the balance sheet. For example, cash funds for employees' travel may be reported separately from cash but still be classified as a current asset. However, restricted cash should be reported as a current item only if it is to be applied to some current purpose or obligation. Classification of the cash balance as current or noncurrent should parallel the classification applied to the liability. Cash balances not available for current purposes require separate designation and classification under a noncurrent heading on the balance sheet.

A credit balance in the cash account resulting from the issuance of checks in excess of the amount on deposit is known as a cash overdraft and should be reported as a current liability. When a company has two or more accounts with a single bank, an overdraft can be offset against an account with a positive balance. If the depositor fails to cover the overdraft, the bank has the legal right to apply funds from one account to cover the overdraft in another. However, when a company has accounts with two different banks and there is a positive balance in one account and an overdraft in the other, both an asset balance and a liability balance should be recognized in view of the claim against one bank and the obligation to the other; if recognition of an overdraft is to be avoided, cash should be transferred to cover the deficiency, because the legal right of offset does not exist between two banks.

In summary, cash is a current asset comprised of coin, currency, and other items that (1) serve as a medium of exchange and (2) provide the basis for measurement in accounting. Most negotiable instruments (e.g., checks, bank drafts, and money orders) qualify as cash because they can be converted to currency on demand or are acceptable for deposit at face value by a bank. Components of cash restricted as to use or withdrawal should be disclosed or reported separately and classified as an investment, a receivable, or other asset. Exhibit 7-1 summarizes the classification of various items that have been discussed. The objective of disclosure is to provide the user of financial statements with information to assist in evaluating the entity's ability to meet obligations (its liquidity and solvency) and in assessing the effectiveness of cash management.

Exhibit 7-1   Classification of Cash and Noncash Items

Item	Classification
Undeposited coin & currency	Cash
Unrestricted funds on deposit at bank (demand deposits)	Cash
Petty cash & change funds	Cash
Negotiable instruments, such as checks, bank drafts, and money orders	Cash
Company checks written but not yet mailed or delivered	Cash
Restricted deposits, such as CDs and money market savings certificates (time deposits)	Temporary Investments
Deposits in foreign banks:	
Unrestricted	Cash
Restricted	Receivables
Postage stamps	Office Supplies
IOUs, post-dated checks, and not-sufficient-funds (NSF) checks	Receivables
Cash restricted for special purposes	*Restricted Cash
Cash overdraft	Current Liability

*Separately reported as current or noncurrent asset depending on the purpose for which it is restricted.

Since the concept of cash embodies the standard of value, few valuation problems are encountered in reporting those items qualifying as cash.

When cash is comprised solely of cash on hand and unrestricted demand deposits, the total generally appears on the balance sheet as a single item "Cash." When other components of cash are significant, they should be disclosed or reported as separate items.

Compensating Balances

In connection with financing arrangements, it is common practice for a company to agree to maintain a minimum or average balance on deposit with a bank or other lending institution. These **compensating balances** are defined by the SEC as ". . . that portion of any demand deposit (or any time deposit or certificate of deposit) maintained by a corporation . . . which constitutes support for existing borrowing arrangements of the corporation . . . with a lending institution. Such arrangements would include both outstanding borrowings and the assurance of future credit availability."[2]

Compensating balances provide a source of funds to the lender as partial compensation for credit extended. In effect, such arrangements raise the interest rate of the borrower because a portion of the amount on deposit with the lending institution cannot be used. These balances present an accounting problem from the standpoint of disclosure. Readers of financial statements are likely to assume the entire cash balance is available to meet current obligations, when, in fact, part of the balance is restricted.

The solution to this problem is to disclose the amount of compensating balances. The SEC recommends that any "legally restricted" deposits held as compensating balances be segregated and reported separately. If the balances are the result of short-term financing arrangements, they should be shown separately among the "cash items" in the current asset section; if the compensating balances are in connection with long-term agreements, they should be classified as noncurrent, either as investments or "other assets." In many instances, deposits are not legally restricted, but compensating balance agreements still exist as business commitments in connection with lines of credit. In these situations, the amounts and nature of the arrangements should be disclosed in the notes to the financial statements, as illustrated on page 249 for Patten Corporation.

Management and Control of Cash

As noted earlier, a business enterprise must maintain sufficient cash for current operations and for paying obligations as they come due. Any excess cash should be invested temporarily to earn an additional return for the shareholders. Effective cash management also requires controls to protect cash from loss by theft or fraud. Since cash is the most liquid asset, it is particularly susceptible to misappropriation unless properly safeguarded. When computerized accounting systems are used, controls are still necessary, and are perhaps even more important than with a strictly

[2]Securities and Exchange Commission, *Accounting Series Release No. 148,* "Disclosure of Compensating Balances and Short-Term Borrowing Arrangements" (Washington: U.S. Government Printing Office, 1973).

manual system, in properly accounting for all inflows, outflows, and balances of cash.

Exhibit 7-2   Patten Corporation

---

5   Notes Payable, Lines of Credit and Commercial Paper

The Company has borrowings with various banks and commercial paper which are used to finance inventory purchases and the carrying of notes receivable and to fund operations. Significant financial data related to the Company's notes payable to banks and commercial paper are as follows:

	Years ended		
	April 3, 1988	March 31, 1987	March 31, 1986
Short-term lines of credit available	$53,748,000	$31,475,000	$ 8,400,000
Long-term lines of credit available	41,500,000	29,500,000	8,000,000
Total lines of credit available	$95,248,000	$60,975,000	$16,400,000

The Company's lines of credit constitute business commitments and, accordingly, are subject to continued creditworthiness and review by the lending banks. Approximately 50% of the aggregate amount available under the lines of credit requires the security of existing notes receivable and inventory. Borrowings outstanding under long-term lines of credit are secured by notes receivable held by the Company with total outstanding principal aggregating $11,579,139 and $7,386,000 at March 31, 1987 and 1986, respectively. The Company is required to maintain average compensating balances of 2.60% of the available lines.

The system for controlling cash must be adapted to a particular business. It is not feasible to describe all the features and techniques employed in businesses of various kinds and sizes. In general, however, systems of cash control deny access to the accounting records to those who handle cash. This reduces the possibility of improper entries to conceal the misuse of cash receipts and cash payments. The probability of misappropriation of cash is greatly reduced if two or more employees must conspire in an embezzlement. Further, systems normally provide for separation of the receiving and paying functions. The basic characteristics of a system of cash control are:

1. Specifically assigned responsibility for handling cash receipts.
2. Separation of handling and recording cash receipts.
3. Daily deposit of all cash received.
4. Voucher system to control cash payments.
5. Internal audits at irregular intervals.
6. Double record of cash—bank and books, with reconciliations performed by someone outside the accounting function.

These controls are more likely to be found in large companies with many employees. Small companies with few employees generally have difficulty in totally segregating accounting and cash-handling duties. Even small companies, however, should incorporate as many control features as possible.

To the extent that a company can incorporate effective internal controls, it can reduce significantly the chances of theft, loss, or inadvertent errors in accounting for and controlling cash. Even the most elaborate control system, however, cannot totally eliminate the possibilities of misappropriations or errors. The use of a petty cash fund can facilitate control over small cash payments, and periodic bank reconciliations can help identify any cash shortages or errors that may have been made in accounting for cash.

Petty Cash Fund   Immediate cash payments and payments too small to be made by check may be made from a petty cash fund. Under an imprest petty cash system, the petty cash fund is created by cashing a check for the amount of the fund. In recording the establishment of the fund, Petty Cash is debited and Cash is credited. The cash is then turned over to a cashier or some person who is solely responsible for payments made out of the fund. The cashier should require a signed receipt for all payments made. These receipts may be printed in prenumbered form. Frequently, a bill or other memorandum is submitted when a payment is requested. A record of petty cash payments may be kept in a *petty cash journal*.

Whenever the amount of cash in the fund runs low and also at the end of each fiscal period, the fund is replenished by writing a check equal to the payments made. In recording replenishment, expenses and other appropriate accounts are debited for petty cash disbursements and Cash is credited. When the fund fails to balance, an adjustment is usually made to a miscellaneous expense or revenue account, sometimes called "Cash Short and Over." Unless theft is involved, this will usually involve only a nominal amount arising, for example, from errors in making change.

As noted above, a petty cash fund is usually replenished at the end of each fiscal period. If replenishment does not occur at year-end, however, an adjustment to Petty Cash is required to properly record all expenditures from the fund during the period. The debit entries would be the same as those to record replenishment; the credit entry would be to Petty Cash, reflecting a reduction in that account.

To illustrate the appropriate entries in accounting for petty cash, assume that Keat Company establishes a petty cash fund on January 1 in the amount of $500. The following entry would be made.

Petty Cash	500	
Cash		500
To establish a $500 petty cash fund.		

During the next six months, the person responsible for the fund made payments for office supplies ($245), postage ($110), and office equipment repairs ($25). Receipts for these items are maintained as evidence supporting the petty cash disbursements. On July 1 the fund is replenished. At that time the coin and currency in the fund totaled $115. The entry to record the expenses and replenish the fund would be:

Office Supplies Expense	245	
Postage Expense	110	
Repair Expense	25	
Cash Short and Over (or Misc. Expense)	5	
Cash		385
To record expenses and replenish the petty cash fund.		

After this entry the fund would be restored to its original amount, $500. If Keat Company decided to reduce the fund to $400, an entry would be required as follows:

Cash	100	
Petty Cash		100
To reduce the petty cash fund from $500 to $400.		

Assume further that during the next six months, Keat Company used its petty cash fund to purchase additional office supplies ($136), purchase decorations and refreshments for an office party ($89), and pay freight charges ($55). Even though the fund was not replenished on December 31, an entry would be required to properly record the expenditures from the fund for that period, as follows:

Office Supplies Expense	136	
Misc. Expenses	89	
Freight	55	
Petty Cash		280
To record expenses paid from the petty cash fund.		

The entry to increase a petty cash fund is the same as to establish the fund initially—a debit to Petty Cash and a credit to Cash. However, petty cash funds should only be large enough to cover small expenditures. Large amounts should be disbursed through an authorized voucher system.

Bank Reconciliations   When daily receipts are deposited and payments other than those from petty cash are made by check, the bank's statement of its transactions with the depositor can be compared with the record of cash as reported on the depositor's books. A comparison of the bank balance with the balance reported on the books is usually made monthly by means of a summary known as a **bank reconciliation statement**. The bank reconciliation statement is prepared to disclose any errors or irregularities in either the records of the bank or those of the business unit. It is developed in a form that points out the reasons for discrepancies in the two balances. It should be prepared by an individual who neither handles nor records cash. Any discrepancies should be brought to the immediate attention of appropriate company officials.

When the bank statement and the depositor's records are compared, certain items may appear on one and not the other, resulting in a difference in the two balances. Most of these differences result from temporary timing lags, and are thus normal. Four common types of differences arise in the following situations:

1. A deposit made near the end of the month and recorded on the depositor's books is not received by the bank in time to be reflected on the bank statement. This amount, referred to as a **deposit in transit**, has to be added to the bank statement balance to make it agree with the balance on the depositor's books.

2. Checks written near the end of the month have reduced the depositor's cash balance, but have not cleared the bank as of the bank statement date. These **outstanding checks** must be subtracted from the bank statement balance to make it agree with the depositor's records.

3. The bank normally charges a monthly fee for servicing an account. The bank automatically reduces the depositor's account balance for this **bank service charge** and notes the amount on the bank statement. The depositor must deduct this amount from the recorded cash balance to make it agree with the bank statement balance. The return of a customer's check for which insufficient funds are available, known as a **not-sufficient-funds (NSF) check**, is handled in a similar manner.

4. An amount owed to the depositor is paid directly to the bank by a third party and added to the depositor's account. Upon receipt of the bank statement (assuming prior notification has not been received from the bank), this amount must be added to the cash balance on the depositor's books. Examples include a direct payroll deposit by an individual's employer and interest added by the bank on a savings account.

If, after considering the items mentioned, the bank statement and the book balances cannot be reconciled, a detailed analysis of both the bank's records and the depositor's books may be necessary to determine whether errors or irregularities exist on the records of either party.

A common form of bank reconciliation is illustrated on page 253. This form is prepared in two sections, the bank statement balance being adjusted to the corrected cash balance in the first section, and the book balance being adjusted to the same corrected cash balance in the second section. Any items not yet recognized by the bank (e.g., deposits in transit or outstanding checks) as well as any errors made by the bank are recorded in the first section. The second section contains any items the depositor has not yet recognized (e.g., direct deposits, NSF checks, or bank service charges) and any corrections for errors made on the depositor's books.

The reconciliation of bank and book balances to a corrected balance has two important advantages: it develops a corrected cash figure, and it shows separately all items requiring adjustment on the depositor's books.

An alternative form of reconciliation would be to reconcile the bank statement balance to the book balance. This form would not develop a corrected cash figure, however, and would make it more difficult to determine the adjustments needed on the depositor's books.

Reconciliation of Bank and Book Balances to Corrected Balance

Svendsen, Inc.
Bank Reconciliation Statement
November 30, 1991

Balance per bank statement, November 30, 1991		$2,979.72
Add: Deposits in transit	$658.50	
Charge for interest made to depositor's account by bank in error	12.50	671.00
		$3,650.72
Deduct outstanding checks:		
No. 1125...	$ 58.16	
No. 1138...	100.00	
No. 1152...	98.60	
No. 1154...	255.00	
No. 1155...	192.07	703.83
Corrected bank balance		$2,946.89
Balance per books, November 30, 1991		$2,952.49
Add: Interest earned during November	$ 98.50	
Check No. 1116 to Ace Advertising for $46 recorded by depositor as $64 in error	18.00	116.50
		$3,068.99
Deduct: Bank service charges	$ 3.16	
Customer's check deposited November 25 and returned marked NSF	118.94	122.10
Corrected book balance		$2,946.89

After preparing the reconciliation, the depositor should record any items appearing on the bank statement and requiring recognition on the company's books as well as any corrections for errors discovered on its own books. The bank should be notified immediately of any bank errors. The following entries would be required on the books of Svendsen, Inc. as a result of the November 30 reconciliation:

Cash	98.50	
Interest Revenue		98.50
To record interest earned during November.		
Cash	18.00	
Advertising Expense		18.00
To record correction for check in payment of advertising recorded as $64 instead of the actual amount, $46.		
Accounts Receivable	118.94	
Miscellaneous General Expense	3.16	
Cash		122.10
To record customer's uncollectible check and bank charges for November.		

After these entries are posted, the cash account will show a balance of $2,946.89. If financial statements were prepared at November 30, this is the amount that would be reported on the balance sheet. It should be noted that the bank reconciliation statement is not presented to external users. It is used as a control procedure and as an accounting tool to determine the adjustments required to bring the cash account and related account balances up to date.

A bank reconciliation is sometimes expanded to incorporate a proof of both receipts and disbursements as separate steps in the reconciliation process. This is often referred to as a **four-column bank reconciliation** or a **proof of cash**.

In a four-column reconciliation, columns are provided for the beginning reconciliation, deposits or receipts, withdrawals or disbursements, and the ending reconciliation. Thus, the four-column approach is really two reconciliations in one. The first column contains a reconciliation as of the end of the preceding period. The deposits per bank statement or receipts per books for the period are added to the beginning balances, and the withdrawals per bank statement or disbursements per books are subtracted to arrive at the ending balances. Deposits/receipts are reconciled in the second column and withdrawals/disbursements in the third column. The

Reconciliation of Bank and Book Balances to Corrected Balance

Svendsen, Inc.
Proof of Cash
November 30, 1991

	Beginning Reconciliation October 31	Deposits/ Receipts	Withdrawals/ Disbursements	Ending Reconciliation November 30
Balance per bank statement	$5,895.42	$21,312.40	$24,228.10	$2,979.72
Deposits in transit:				
October 31	425.40	(425.40)		
November 30		658.50		658.50
Outstanding checks:				
October 31	(810.50)		(810.50)	
November 30			703.83	(703.83)
NSF check redeposited during November; no entry made on books for return or redeposit		(100.00)	(100.00)	
Charge for interest made by bank in error			(12.50)	12.50
Corrected bank balance	$5,510.32	$21,445.50	$24,008.93	$2,946.89
Balance per books	$5,406.22	$21,457.00	$23,910.73	$2,952.49
Bank service charges:				
October	(5.90)		(5.90)	
November			3.16	(3.16)
Customer's check deposited November 25 found to be uncollectible (NSF)			118.94	(118.94)
Interest earned:				
October	110.00	(110.00)		
November		98.50		98.50
Check No. 116 for $46 recorded by depositor as $64 in error			(18.00)	18.00
Corrected book balance	$5,510.32	$21,445.50	$24,008.93	$2,946.89

amounts must reconcile both vertically and horizontally for the ending bank and book balances to agree.

In order to complete this type of reconciliation, each adjustment must be carefully analyzed. Note that two columns are always affected for each adjustment. For example, a deposit of $425.40 on October 31, 1991, was recorded by the bank in November and is included in the total bank deposits of $21,312.40 for November. However, the deposit was properly recorded on the books as a receipt in October; thus, the $425.40 is not included in the book receipts of $21,457 for November, but is included in the beginning book balance of $5,406.22. The reconciliation accounts for this by deducting the in-transit deposit from the total bank deposits for November and by adding the deposit to the beginning October 31 bank statement balance. This is the same type of analysis that would have been made on October 31 for a regular bank reconciliation on that date. Similarly, the $658.50 deposit in transit at the end of November is already recorded in the book receipts and ending cash balance as of November 30, but must be added to the bank deposits and ending balance to reconcile to the correct balances as of November 30.

A similar analysis is needed for reconciling the timing differences for outstanding checks. Checks totaling $810.50 were outstanding (had not cleared the bank) on October 31 and therefore should be deducted from the October 31 bank balance. The bank records include those checks as withdrawals for November (that is, the $810.50 is included in the total bank withdrawals of $24,228.10), and so the $810.50 must be subtracted from the November withdrawals to reconcile with the corrected balances. On the other hand, the outstanding checks at the end of November are valid withdrawals for November, and so the $703.83 must be added to the bank withdrawals for November and subtracted from the bank cash balance as of November 30.

The adjustment for a "not-sufficient-funds" (NSF) check depends on how the company and bank records are kept. Typically, a company will periodically deposit its checks, recording them as receipts and additions to the cash balance. The bank will similarly record the deposits as increases in cash for the company. However, when the bank determines that a particular check is not collectible from the maker (an NSF check), it usually will show the check as a withdrawal and thus a reduction in the company's cash balance. If, after checking with the customer, the company determines the check is now good, it may merely redeposit the check without making any entries on the books for the bank's return of the check or the redeposit. The bank, however, will again show the check as a deposit and an increase in the cash balance. After the redeposit, the bank will show the correct cash balance. However, the bank deposits included the check twice, once when originally deposited and a second time upon redeposit, and the bank withdrawals included the check once, when it became an NSF check. Therefore, to reconcile the bank and book deposits/receipts and withdrawals/disbursements, the NSF check ($100 in the example) is subtracted from both the bank deposits and withdrawals. (Alternatively, the $100 NSF check could be added to the book receipts and disbursements to make the books reconcile with the bank records.) The preceding discussion is illustrated in Exhibit 7-3 using $(+)$ and $(-)$ designations to reinforce this point.

Exhibit 7-3   Typical Treatment in Reconciling NSF Check

Bank	Balance (Oct. 31)	Deposits/ Receipts	Withdrawals/ Disbursements	Balance (Nov. 30)
1. Original deposit		+		+
2. Check becomes NSF			+	−
3. Check redeposited		+		+
4. Adjustment to reconcile		−	−	
Correct balance		+		+
Books				
1. Original deposit		+		+
2. Check returned by bank (no book entry)				
3. Check redeposited (no book entry)				
Correct balance		+		+

If a company finds that an NSF check cannot be collected immediately, then instead of redepositing the check, it must record the check amount in accounts receivable on the books. Such is the case for the $118.94 check for Svendsen, Inc. in the illustration. Since the bank will have already shown the check as a withdrawal and a reduction in the cash balance, a similar adjustment must be made to the company records.

Another common type of adjustment may be required for errors made either on the bank or book records. These have to be corrected as illustrated for Svendsen, Inc. Once all adjustments are made, the total corrected balances will be the same for both the bank and book records for all four columns.

The illustrations for Svendsen, Inc. assume adjustments of the book amounts are made in the month subsequent to their discovery. If the adjustments were made in the same month, as might be true at year-end, there would be no adjustments in the first column for the book amounts. For example, the $5.90 October bank service charge in the illustration is recognized on the books in November. If the adjustment had been made at the end of October, the beginning book balance would have already shown $5,400.32 ($5,406.22 − $5.90), and the total book disbursements for November would have been $5.90 less. A similar rationale exists for the $110 interest recorded by the bank for Svendsen in October.

The expanded proof of cash or four-column reconciliation procedure normally reduces the time and effort required to find errors made by either the bank or the depositor. In developing comparisons of both receipts and disbursements, the areas in which errors have been made, as well as the amounts of the discrepancies within each area, are immediately identified. This procedure is frequently used by auditors when there is any question of possible discrepancies in the handling of cash.

Temporary Investments

Temporarily available excess cash can be invested to generate revenue that would not be available if cash were left idle. Investments made during seasonal periods of low activity can be converted into cash needed during periods of expanding operations. Assets acquired as temporary investments are reported in the current assets section of the balance sheet.

As mentioned previously in the chapter, **temporary investments** commonly include time deposit instruments, such as CDs and money market certificates. They also include short-term debt instruments such as **commercial paper** (high-yield notes issued by corporations and generally maturing within 30 days to nine months) and **Treasury Bills** (U.S. government obligations that are sold at a weekly auction and have maturities ranging from 13 weeks to one year).

Companies also invest funds in securities, including **debt securities** (corporate and government bonds) and **equity securities** (common and preferred stocks). Securities may be reported as current (temporary) or noncurrent investments, depending on their nature and the purpose for which they were acquired. Accounting and reporting considerations applicable to noncurrent investments are discussed later in this book.

Criteria for Reporting Securities as Temporary Investments

Investments in securities qualify for reporting as temporary investments if (1) there is a ready market for converting such securities into cash, *and* (2) it is management's intention to sell them if the need for cash arises. As indicated by the first criterion, only **marketable securities** qualify for reporting as temporary investments. Securities are considered marketable when a day-to-day market exists and when they can be sold on short notice. The volume of trading in the securities should be sufficient to absorb a company's holdings without materially affecting the market price. Securities having a limited market and fluctuating widely in price are not suitable for temporary investments.

Marketable securities may be converted into cash shortly after being acquired or they may be held for some time. In either case, however, they are properly classified as temporary investments as long as management intends to sell them if the need for cash arises. The deciding factor is management's intent, not the length of time the securities are held. Therefore, the following securities do not qualify as temporary investments even though they may be marketable: (1) reacquired shares of a corporation's own stock; (2) securities acquired to gain control of a company; (3) securities held for maintenance of business relations; and (4) any other securities that cannot be used or are not intended to be used as a ready source of cash.

Recording Purchase and Sale of Marketable Securities

Stocks and bonds acquired as temporary investments are recorded at cost, which includes brokers' fees, taxes, and other charges incurred in their acquisition. Stocks are normally quoted at a price per single share; bonds are quoted at a price per $100 face value although they are normally issued in $1,000 denominations. The purchase of 100 shares of stock at 5⅛, then, would indicate a purchase price of $512.50; the purchase of a $1,000 bond at 104¼ would indicate a purchase price of $1,042.50.

When interest-bearing securities are acquired between interest payment dates, the amount paid for the security is increased by a charge for accrued interest to the date of purchase. This charge should not be reported as part of the investment cost. Two assets have been acquired—the security and the accrued interest receivable—and should be reported in two separate asset accounts. Upon the receipt of interest, the accrued interest account is closed and Interest Revenue is credited for the amount of interest earned since the purchase date. Instead of recording the interest as a receivable (**asset approach**), Interest Revenue may be debited for the accrued interest paid. The subsequent collection of interest would then be credited in full to Interest Revenue. The latter procedure (**revenue approach**) is usually more convenient.

To illustrate the entries for the acquisition of securities, assume that $100,000 in U.S. Treasury notes are purchased at 104¼, including brokerage fees, on April 1. Interest is 9% payable semiannually on January 1 and July 1. Accrued interest of $2,250 would thus be added to the purchase price. The entries to record the purchase of the securities and the subsequent collection of interest under the alternate procedures would be as follows:

Asset Approach:

Apr. 1 Marketable Securities (9% U.S. Treasury Notes)	104,250	
Interest Receivable..................................	2,250	
Cash		106,500
July 1 Cash	4,500	
Interest Receivable..................................		2,250
Interest Revenue....................................		2,250

Revenue Approach:

Apr. 1 Marketable Securities (9% U.S. Treasury Notes)	104,250	
Interest Revenue....................................	2,250	
Cash		106,500
July 1 Cash	4,500	
Interest Revenue....................................		4,500

The important point is that under either approach, the interest revenue recorded for the period is equal to the interest earned, not the amount received. In this case, the company earned $2,250, representing interest for the period April 1 to June 30.

When debt securities are acquired at a higher or lower price than their maturity value and it is expected that they will be held until maturity, periodic amortization of the premium or accumulation of the discount with corresponding adjustments to interest revenue is required. However, when securities are acquired as a temporary investment and it is not likely they will be held until maturity, such procedures are normally not necessary. When a temporary investment is sold, the difference between the sales proceeds and the cost is reported as a gain or loss on the sale. For example, if the U.S. Treasury notes in the preceding illustration were sold on July 1 for $105,000, and the brokerage fees on the sale were $500, the transaction would be recorded as follows:

July 1 Cash	104,500	
Marketable Securities (9% U.S. Treasury Notes)		104,250
Gain on Sale of Marketable Securities		250

The gain would be reported on the income statement as "Other revenue." Note that the brokerage fees involved in the purchase increase the cost of a temporary investment, while the selling fees reduce the cash proceeds and any recognized gain on the sale.

Valuation of Marketable Securities

Three different methods for the valuation of marketable securities have been advanced: (1) cost, (2) cost or market, whichever is lower, and (3) market.

Cost

Valuation of marketable securities at cost refers to the original acquisition price of a marketable security including all related fees, unless a new cost basis has been assigned to recognize a permanent decline in the value of the security. Cost is to be used unless circumstances require another method as is the case with marketable equity securities, to be explained in the next section. The recognition of gain or loss is deferred until the asset is sold, at which time investment cost is matched against investment proceeds. The cost basis is consistent with income tax procedures, recognizing neither gain nor loss until there is a sale or exchange.

Cost or Market, Whichever is Lower

When using the lower of cost or market (LCM) method, if market is lower than cost, security values are written down to the lower value; if market is higher than cost, securities are maintained at cost, gains awaiting confirmation through sale.

FASB Statement No. 12, "Accounting for Certain Marketable Securities," requires that **marketable equity securities** be carried at the **lower of aggregate cost or market**.[3] An **equity security** is defined by the FASB in Statement No. 12 as:

> . . . any instrument representing ownership shares (e.g., common, preferred, and other capital stock), or the right to acquire (e.g., warrants, rights, and call options) or dispose of (e.g., put options) ownership shares in an enterprise at fixed or determinable prices. The term does not encompass preferred stock that by its terms either must be redeemed by the issuing enterprise or is redeemable at the option of the investor, nor does it include treasury stock or convertible bonds.[4]

FASB Statement No. 12 deals only with marketable *equity* securities. Other marketable securities, primarily marketable debt securities, still may be carried at cost unless there is a substantial decline that is not due to temporary conditions. It seems logical, however, to treat all short-term marketable securities similarly. All temporary investments are acquired for the same reason—utilization of idle cash to generate a short-term return. Both equity securities and debt securities must meet the same criteria to qualify as temporary investments, and their valuation should reflect a similar concept, i.e., the amount of cash that could be realized upon liquidation at the balance sheet date. Therefore, in the illustrations and end-of-chapter material in this text, the lower of cost or market method is used for *all* short-term marketable securities (i.e., stocks and bonds). It should be recognized, however, that actual practice varies. Some companies interpret FASB No. 12 strictly and account for only marketable equity securities on the lower of cost or market basis.

FASB Statement No. 12 requires that the lower of cost or market method be applied to securities in the **aggregate** and not to individual securities. To illustrate the difference between lower of cost or market on an aggregate basis versus an individual item basis, assume marketable securities with cost and market values on December 31, 1991, as follows:

	Cost	Market	Lower of Cost or Market on Individual Basis
1,000 Shares of Carter Co. common	$20,000	$16,000	$16,000
$25,000 10% U.S. Treasury Notes	25,000	26,500	25,000
$10,000 U.S. Government 8% bonds	10,000	7,500	7,500
	$55,000	$50,000	$48,500

The lower of cost or market value on an aggregate basis is $50,000; on an individual basis, $48,500.

An important factor considered by the FASB in choosing the aggregate

---

[3]*Statement of Financial Accounting Standards No. 12,* "Accounting for Certain Marketable Securities" (Stamford: Financial Accounting Standards Board, 1975), par. 8.

[4]Ibid, par. 7a.

basis is that many companies view their marketable securities portfolios as collective assets. Further, the Board felt that applying the lower of cost or market procedure on an individual security basis would be unduly conservative.

However, the FASB did recognize that many companies classify separately their current and noncurrent securities portfolios. Therefore, when a classified balance sheet is presented, the lower of aggregate cost or market is to be applied to the separate current and noncurrent portfolios. When an unclassified balance sheet is presented, the entire marketable equity securities portfolio is to be considered a noncurrent asset. The application of FASB Statement No. 12 to long-term marketable equity securities is discussed in detail in a later chapter.

In adopting the lower of aggregate cost or market method for marketable equity securities, the FASB chose to recognize declines in the realizable value of short-term marketable equity securities portfolios as a charge against income of the current period. The possibility of a future recovery in the market value was not considered sufficient reason to maintain the carrying value at cost.

Recognition of a decline in value on the books calls for a reduction of the asset and a debit to a loss account. Various titles are used for the loss account: Unrealized Loss on Marketable Securities; Loss on Valuation of Marketable Equity Securities; Recognized Decline in Value of Current Marketable Securities. The authors prefer the last title to avoid confusion with the entry required upon the final sale of the securities or with the title used in accounting for long-term marketable equity securities. It should also be noted that the basis of the securities for measurement of the ultimate gain or loss on final disposition continues to be cost. Cost can be preserved on the books by the use of a valuation account to reduce the securities to market. The following entry illustrates this procedure:

Recognized Decline in Value of Current Marketable Securities	5,000	
Allowance for Decline in Value of Current Marketable Securities . .		5,000

The balance sheet would show:

Current assets:		
Marketable securities (at cost)	$55,000	
Less allowance for decline in value of current marketable securities.	5,000	
Marketable securities (at market, December 31, 1991)		$50,000

In practice a shorter form is often used, such as the following:

Current assets:	
Marketable securities (reported at market; cost, $55,000) . . .	$50,000

The $5,000 loss in the above example would be reported on the current income statement as an "other expense" after operating income. If in the future there is an increase in the market value of the short-term marketable securities portfolio, the write-down should be reversed to the extent that the resulting carrying value does not exceed original cost. The original write-down is viewed as a valuation allowance, representing an estimated decrease in the realizable value of the portfolio. Any subsequent market increase reduces or eliminates this valuation allowance. The reversal of a write-down is considered a change in accounting estimate of an unrealized loss, as was noted in Chapter 4.[5]

In subsequent periods, the portfolio of temporary investments will change through purchases and sales of individual securities. Because cost is the accepted basis for recognition of gain or loss on final disposition, the sale of marketable securities is recorded as though no valuation account existed, i.e., on a cost basis. At the end of each accounting period, an analysis can then be made of cost and aggregated market values for the securities held and the allowance account adjusted to reflect the new difference between cost and market. If market exceeds cost at a subsequent valuation date, the allowance account would be eliminated, and the securities would be valued at cost, the lower of the two values. The offsetting revenue account for the adjustment may be titled Recovery of Recognized Decline in Value of Current Marketable Securities.

To illustrate accounting for subsequent years' transactions, assume in the preceding example that in 1992 the Carter Co. stock is sold for $17,000 and $25,000 of 9% U.S. Treasury notes are purchased for $24,500. The following entries are made.

Cash	17,000	
Loss on Sale of Marketable Securities	3,000	
Marketable Securities (Carter Co. Common)		20,000
Marketable Securities (9% U.S. Treasury Notes)	24,500	
Cash		24,500

Assuming the market value of the remaining securities in the porfolio is unchanged and the market value of the U.S. Treasury notes remains at cost, the aggregate market value of the temporary investments is $58,500 ($26,500 + $7,500 + $24,500). When comparing the aggregate market value to the aggregate cost value of $59,500 ($25,000 + $10,000 + $24,500), the following adjusting entry would be made at the end of 1992:

Allowance for Decline in Value of Current Marketable Securities	4,000	
Recovery of Recognized Decline in Value of Current Marketable Securities		4,000

This entry leaves the valuation account with a balance of $1,000

[5]See *FASB Statement No. 5*, par. 2, and *APB Opinion No. 20*, par. 10.

which, when subtracted from cost of $59,500, will report the marketable securities at their aggregate market value of $58,500.

If the aggregate market value of the securities portfolio had fallen during 1992 to $53,000 (compared to cost of $59,500), the adjusting entry would be:

Recognized Decline in Value of Current Marketable Securities	1,500	
Allowance for Decline in Value of Current Marketable Securities . .		1,500

This entry increases the allowance account to $6,500 which, when subtracted from cost of $59,500, will report marketable securities at their aggregate market value of $53,000.

On the other hand, if the aggregate market value of the securities portfolio had risen to $60,000 (compared to cost of $59,500), the adjusting entry at year end would be:

Allowance for Decline in Value of Current Marketable Securities	5,000	
Recovery of Recognized Decline in Value of Current		
Marketable Securities		5,000

This entry cancels the allowance account since the $59,500 original cost of securities is lower than their current $60,000 aggregate market value.

If the classification of a marketable equity security changes from current to noncurrent or vice versa, the security must be transferred to the applicable portfolio at the lower of cost or market value at date of transfer. If the market value is lower than cost, the market value becomes the new cost basis and a realized loss is to be included in determining net income.[6] In essence, this procedure recognizes the loss upon transfer as though it had been realized. This should reduce the likelihood of income being manipulated through the transfer of securities between current and long-term portfolios.

To summarize the accounting for current marketable equity securities under FASB Statement No. 12, securities are originally recorded at cost. Subsequent valuation is at lower of cost or market on an aggregate basis. Any necessary adjustment is made at year-end through a valuation allowance account. A reduction in value is recognized as a current period loss in the income statement; a recovery of a previous write-down, up to the original cost but no higher, is recognized as a current period gain in the income statement. These gains or losses are usually presented after operating income as "other revenues" or "other expenses." The amount of gain or loss on the ultimate sale of a marketable security is measured as the difference between the sales price and the original cost of the security without consideration for any previous year-end allowance adjustments. Then, at year-

[6]*Statement of Financial Accounting Standards No. 12, op. cit.*, par. 10.

end, the allowance account is adjusted once again to reflect the lower of cost or market amount for the remaining securities in the portfolio.

Any permanent declines in securities values are to be recognized as losses currently, just like any other asset, with the new value being considered cost from that time forward. No subsequent partial recovery is allowed.

FASB Statement No. 12 requires disclosure of specific information with respect to marketable equity securities, including aggregate cost and market values, gross unrealized gains and losses, and the amount of net realized gain or loss included in net income.[7] The information included by Masco Industries in its 1987 annual report, and reproduced on page 265, provides an example of the required disclosures for marketable securities.

Market

Market value refers to the current market price of a marketable security. In applying the market value method, permanent declines in market prices of securities are recognized as losses in the current period. Temporary declines in market values are treated the same as under the lower of cost or market method. That is, security values are written down to market through a valuation adjustment at the end of the accounting period. Where the market method differs is in the valuation of securities whose prices have increased above cost. With the market method, current market prices are recognized as affording an objective basis for the valuation of marketable securities; therefore, such securities would be reported on the balance sheet at their current values, whether higher or lower than cost.

Market value has been and continues to be an acceptable method for valuing marketable securities within certain industries that follow specialized accounting practices with respect to marketable securities. Enterprises within these industries, such as securities brokers and dealers who carry marketable equity securities at market value, are not required by FASB Statement No. 12 to change to lower of cost or market. *For most companies, however, the market value method is not presently considered generally accepted accounting practice, and the lower of cost or market method should be used.*

Evaluation of Methods

Valuation at cost finds support on the grounds that it is an extension of the cost principle; the asset is carried at cost until a sale or exchange provides an alternative asset and confirms a gain or loss. The cost method offers valuation on a consistent basis from period to period. It is the simplest method to apply and adheres to income tax requirements. However, certain objections to cost can be raised. The use of cost means investments may be carried at amounts differing from values objectively determinable at the balance sheet date, and the integrity of both balance sheet and income

[7]Ibid., par. 12.

statement measurements can be challenged. The use of cost also means identical securities may be reported at different values because of purchases at different prices. A further objection is that management, in controlling the sale of securities, can determine the periods in which gains or losses are to be recognized even though the changes in values may have accrued over a number of periods.

The use of market value is advocated on the basis that there is evidence of the net realizable value of the marketable securities held at the balance sheet date and any changes from previous carrying values should be recognized as gains or losses in the current period. Assuming marketable securities are defined as having a readily available sales price or bid and ask price from one of the national securities exchanges or over-the-counter markets, this method is objective and relatively simple to apply. The major drawback of this method is that gains or losses may be recognized prior to realization, i.e., prior to the actual sale of the securities. In addition, market values fluctuate, often significantly, which would require continual changing of the carrying value of marketable securities on the balance sheet. Market is also challenged as a departure from the cost principle and as lacking in conservatism. Furthermore, market is not acceptable for general accounting or income tax purposes.

Exhibit 7-4   Masco Industries

MARKETABLE SECURITIES

As a result of the significant decline in the equity markets in late 1987, the market value of the Company's marketable securities portfolio incurred a substantial unrealized decline and the Company realized substantial losses from the disposition of certain investments in the fourth quarter. Although the realization of actual losses (or gains) related to marketable securities portfolio transactions ultimately occurs only upon disposition of the underlying individual securities, the Company charged income in the fourth quarter of 1987 by establishing a valuation allowance at December 31, 1987 to reflect then current market levels. The Company charged income in the fourth quarter of 1986 to establish a valuation allowance to reflect December 31, 1986 market levels.

| | (In Thousands) At December 31 | |
	1987	**1986**
Marketable securities, principally equity, at cost	$266,240	$190,520
Valuation allowance	(44,750)	(16,610)
Marketable securities at carrying value	$221,490	$173,910

Marketable securities (principally equity) had unrealized gains of approximately $7.8 million and $2.2 million, and unrealized losses of approximately $52.6 million and $18.8 million before application of a valuation allowance at December 31, 1987 and 1986, respectively.

The lower of cost or market procedure provides for recognizing market declines and serves to prevent potential mistakes arising in analyzing statements when these declines are not reported. The lower of cost or market is supported as a conservative procedure. This approach may be challenged on the basis that it may be the most complicated method to follow, and it fails to apply a single valuation concept consistently. Securities carried at cost at the end of one period may be reported at market value in the subsequent period. Critics argue that if net realizable value is a desirable measurement concept, its use should not depend on whether portfolio values are greater or less than original cost.

Regardless of the theoretical merits of the three methods, generally accepted accounting principles currently require use of the lower of cost or market method for marketable equity securities and valuation at cost for other temporary investments. With the emphasis in the conceptual framework on decision usefulness, the market valuation method may gain broader acceptance in the future.

Reporting Cash and Temporary Investments on the Balance Sheet

In reporting cash and temporary investments, many companies follow the guidelines described in the chapter and report cash separately from restricted cash items and marketable securities. Other companies combine cash with time deposits or with marketable securities. When cash and certain types of temporary investment items are combined, an increasingly popular title is "cash and cash equivalents."[8] **Cash equivalents** include time deposits and highly liquid debt instruments, usually having maturities of three months or less. Some examples of the varying methods used for reporting cash and temporary investments follow.

Exhibit 7-5   Procter & Gamble Company and Subsidiaries

The Procter & Gamble Company And Subsidiaries

Consolidated Balance Sheet

Assets

Millions of Dollars	June 30	1988	1987
CURRENT ASSETS	Cash	$ 50	$ 76
	Marketable securities	1,015	665

---

[8]Use of this term as a balance sheet caption will become increasingly common as companies implement FASB Statement No. 95, "Statement of Cash Flows," which requires that the cash flow statement report changes in cash and cash equivalents.

Exhibit 7-6   Centel Corporation

CONSOLIDATED BALANCE SHEETS

Centel Corporation

Thousands of Dollars December 31,	**1987**	1986
Assets		
Current Assets		
Cash and Temporary Investments	**$ 47,757**	$ 41,886

Exhibit 7-7   Ametek, Inc.

AMETEK, Inc.

CONSOLIDATED BALANCE SHEET

		December 31,	
Assets		1987	1986
Current assets:			
Cash (including $166,823,315 in 1987 and $162,925,506 in 1986 of marketable securities-primarily U. S. Government securities)		**$174,958,047**	$173,533,703

Exhibit 7-8   Hon Industries Inc. and Subsidiaries

HON INDUSTRIES Inc. and Subsidiaries

Consolidated Balance Sheets

As of Year-End	**1987**	1986	1985
Assets			
Current Assets			
Cash and cash equivalents	**$ 25,930,000**	$ 33,452,000	$ 22,353,000
Short-term investments	**2,404,000**	2,958,000	2,103,000

Key Terms

Questions

1. Why is cash on hand both necessary and yet potentially unproductive?
2. The following items were included as cash on the balance sheet for the Lawson Co. How should each of the items have been reported?
   (a) Demand deposits with bank
   (b) Restricted cash deposits in foreign banks
   (c) Bank account used for payment of salaries and wages
   (d) Cash in a special cash account to be used currently for the construction of a new building
   (e) Customers' checks returned by the bank marked "Not Sufficient Funds"
   (f) Customers' postdated checks
   (g) IOUs from employees
   (h) Postage stamps received in the mail for merchandise
   (i) Postal money orders received from customers and not yet deposited
   (j) Notes receivable in the hands of the bank for collection
   (k) Special bank account in which sales tax collections are deposited
   (l) Customers' checks not yet deposited
3. On reconciling the cash account with the bank statement, it is found that the general cash fund is overdrawn $436 but the bond redemption account has a balance of $5,400. The treasurer wishes to show cash as a current asset at $4,964. Discuss.
4. The Melvin Company shows in its accounts a cash balance of $66,500 with Bank A and an overdraft of $1,500 with Bank B on December 31. Bank B regards the overdraft as in effect a loan to the Melvin Company and charges interest on the overdraft balance. How would you report the balances with Banks A and B? Would your answer be any different if the overdraft arose as a result of certain checks which had been deposited and proved to be uncollectible and if the overdraft was cleared promptly by the Melvin Company at the beginning of January?
5. Mills Manufacturing is required to maintain a compensating balance of $15,000 with its bank to maintain a line of open credit. The compensating balance is legally restricted as to its use. How should the compensating balance be reported on the balance sheet and why?
6. (a) What are the major advantages in using imprest petty cash funds? (b) What dangers must be guarded against when petty cash funds are used?
7. (a) Give at least four common sources of differences between depositor and bank balances. (b) Which of the differences in (a) require an adjusting entry on the books of the depositor?
8. (a) What purposes are served by preparing a four-column reconciliation of receipts and disbursements? (b) Why might this form be used by auditors?

9. Define *temporary investments*. What criteria must be met for a security to be considered a temporary investment?

10. What two methods may be used to record the payment for accrued interest on interest-bearing securities? Which method is preferable?

11. (a) What positions are held with respect to the valuation of marketable securities? (b) What arguments can be advanced in support of each and which position do you feel has the greatest merit?

12. Cintech International reports marketable securities on the balance sheet at the lower of cost or market. What adjustments are required on the books at the end of the year in each situation below:

    (a) Securities are purchased early in 1990 and at the end of 1990 their market value is more than cost.

    (b) At the end of 1991, the market value of the securities is less than cost.

    (c) At the end of 1992, the market value of the securities is greater than at the end of 1991, but is still less than cost.

    (d) At the end of 1993, the market value of the securities is more than the amount originally paid.

13. FASB Statement No. 12 requires the use of lower of cost or market (LCM) valuation for marketable *equity* securities. Why might companies choose to apply LCM to *all* short-term marketable securities? If LCM is not used to value non-equity securities, what is the appropriate basis of valuation for those securities: cost, market, or some other basis?

Discussion Cases   **Case 7–1   (Cash management)**

Jack Wilson, manager of Expert Building Company, is a valued and trusted employee. He has been with the company from its start two years ago. Because of the demands of his job, he has not taken a vacation since he began working. He is in charge of recording collections on account, making the daily bank deposits, and reconciling the bank statement.

Late last year, clients began complaining to you, the president, about incorrect statements. As president, you check into this matter. Wilson tells you there is nothing to worry about. The problem is due to the slow mail; customers' payments and statements are crossing in the mail.

Because clients were not complaining last year, you doubt the mail is the primary reason for the problem. What might be some of the reasons for the delay? What are some other problems that might begin to occur? What can be done to remedy the problem? What should be done to make sure the problems are avoided in the future?

Case 7–2   (Accounting for petty cash)

You have just accepted a job with Philodendron Co. Your duties include being cashier of the petty cash fund. Upon inspection of the fund, you find that it includes $143 in currency, $5 in postage stamps, $21 in I.O.U.'s, and $37 in various receipts. Since no written records are kept of the petty cash fund, you had to find out from the previous cashier that the approved amount of the fund is $215.

Required:

1. Discuss the elements of control necessary for effective maintenance of a petty cash fund.
2. Suggest changes that Philodendron Co. can make to improve the effectiveness of its petty cash fund.

Case 7–3 (Accounting for marketable securities)

Part A:

The Financial Accounting Standards Board issued its Statement No. 12 to clarify accounting methods and procedures with respect to certain marketable securities.

Required:

1. Why does a company maintain an investment portfolio of current securities?
2. What factors should be considered in determining whether investments in marketable equity securities should be classified as current or noncurrent?

Part B:

Presented below are three unrelated situations involving marketable equity securities.

Situation 1. A current portfolio with an aggregate market value in excess of cost includes one particular security whose market value has declined to less than one-half of the original cost. The decline in value is considered to be permanent.

Situation 2. A marketable equity security, whose market value is currently less than cost, is classified as noncurrent but is to be reclassified as current.

Situation 3. A company's current portfolio of marketable equity securities consists of the common stock of one company. At the end of the prior year, the market value of the security was fifty percent of original cost. However, at the end of the current year, the market value of the security had appreciated to twice the original cost. The security is still considered current at year end.

Required: What is the effect upon classification, carrying value, and earnings for each of the above situations. Complete your response to each situation before proceeding to the next situation.   (AICPA Adapted)

Exercises   **Exercise 7–1 (Reporting cash on the balance sheet)**

1. Indicate how each of the items below should be reported using the following classifications: (a) cash, (b) restricted cash, (c) temporary investment, (d) receivable, (e) liability, or (f) office supplies.

1. Checking account at First Security	$ (20)
2. Checking account at Second Security	350
3. United States savings bonds	650
4. Payroll account	100
5. Sales tax account	150

6. Foreign bank account—restricted (in equivalent U.S. Dollars)   750
7. Postage stamps   22
8. Employee's postdated check   30
9. IOU from President's brother   75
10. A wristwatch (reported at market value; surrendered as security by a customer who forgot his wallet)   30
11. Credit memo from a vendor for a purchase return   87
12. Traveler's check   50
13. Not-sufficient-funds check   18
14. Petty cash fund ($16 in currency and expense receipts for $84)   100
15. Money order   36

2. What amount would be reported as unrestricted Cash on the balance sheet?

Exercise 7–2 (Accounting for petty cash)

An examination on the morning of January 2 by the auditor for the Pearson Lumber Company discloses the following items in the petty cash drawer:

Stamps		$ 22.00
Currency and coin		115.66
IOUs from members of the office staff		121.00
An envelope containing collections for a football pool, with office staff names attached		35.00
Petty cash vouchers for:		
Typewriter repairs	$13.00	
Stamps	45.00	
Telegram charges	28.50	
Delivery fees	12.00	98.50
Employee's check postdated January 15		150.00
Employee's check marked "NSF"		189.00
Check drawn by Pearson Lumber Company to Petty Cash		345.00
		$1,076.16

The ledger account discloses a $1,050 balance for Petty Cash. (1) What adjusting entries should be made so that petty cash is correctly stated on the balance sheet? (2) What is the correct amount of petty cash for the balance sheet? (3) How could the practice of borrowing by employees from the fund be discouraged?

Exercise 7–3 (Compensating balances)

Greenfield Company had the following cash balances at December 31, 1991.

Cash in banks	$1,500,000
Petty cash funds (all funds were reimbursed on December 31, 1991)	20,000
Cash legally restricted for additions to plant (expected to be disbursed in 1992)	2,000,000

Cash in banks includes $500,000 of compensating balances against short-term borrowing arrangements at December 31, 1991. The compensating balances are not legally restricted as to withdrawal by Greenfield. In the current asset

section of Greenfield's December 31, 1991 balance sheet, what total amount
should be reported as cash?   (AICPA adapted)

Exercise 7–4   (Bank reconciliation)

In preparing the bank reconciliation for the month of March, Sanford
Company has available the following information:

Balance per bank statement 3/31	$35,176 ✓
Deposits in transit 3/31	4,576 ✓
Outstanding checks 3/31	3,985
Deposit erroneously recorded by bank in	
Sanford's account 3/12	465
Bank service charge for March	21

What is the correct cash balance at March 31?   (AICPA adapted)

Exercise 7–5   (Correct cash balance)

Lee Corporation's checkbook balance on December 31, 1991, was $5,980. In
addition, Lee held the following items in its safe on December 31:

Check payable to Lee Corporation, dated January 2, 1992, not included in December 31 checkbook balance	$1,000
Check payable to Lee Corporation, deposited December 20, 1991, and included in December 31 checkbook balance but returned by bank on December 31, marked "NSF". The check was redeposited January 2, 1992, and cleared January 7	400
Postage stamps received from mail order customer	75
Check drawn on Lee Corporation's account, payable to vendor, dated and recorded December 31, but not mailed until January 15, 1992	565

What is the proper amount to be shown as cash on Lee's balance sheet at
December 31, 1991?   (AICPA adapted)

Exercise 7–6   (Adjusting the cash account)

The accounting department supplied the following data in reconciling the bank
statement for Thalman Auto:

Cash balance per books	$14,692.71
Deposits in transit	2,615.23
Bank service charge	25.00
Outstanding checks	3,079.51
Note collected by bank including $45 interest (Thalman not yet notified)	1,045.00
Error by bank—check drawn by Thalerman Corp. was charged to Thalman's account	617.08
Sale and deposit of $1,729.00 was entered in the sales journal and cash receipts journal as $1,792.00	

Give the journal entries required on the books to adjust the cash account.

Exercise 7–7   (Bank reconciliation statement)

The Minnesota Manufacturing Co. received its bank statement for the month ending June 30 on July 2. The bank statement indicates a balance of $5,680. The cash account as of the close of business on June 30 has a balance of $3,275. In reconciling the balances, the auditor discovers the following:

(a) Receipts on June 30 of $9,500 were not deposited until July 1.
(b) Checks outstanding on June 30 were $12,310.
(c) Collection by bank of note for $150 less collection fees of $25, not recorded on the books.
(d) The bank has charged the depositor for overdrafts, $80.
(e) A canceled check to W. E. Lee for $9,618 was entered in cash payments in error as $9,168.

Prepare a bank reconciliation statement.

Exercise 7–8   (Bank reconciliation—analysis of outstanding checks)

The following information was included in the bank reconciliation for Rylton, Inc. for June. What was the total of outstanding checks at the beginning of June? Assume all other reconciling items are listed below.

Checks and charges returned by bank in June, including a June service charge of $10	$16,435
Service charge made by bank in May and recorded on the books in June	5
Total of credits to Cash in all journals during June	19,292
Customer's NSF check returned as a bank charge in June (no entry made on books)	100
Customer's NSF check returned in May and redeposited in June (no entry made on books in either May or June)	250
Outstanding checks at June 30	8,060
Deposit in transit at June 30	600

Exercise 7–9   (Four-column bank reconciliation)

Tyler Corporation began doing business with Security Bank on October 1. On that date the correct cash balance was $4,000. All cash transactions are cleared through the bank account. Subsequent transactions during October and November relating to the records of Tyler and Security are summarized below.

	Tyler Company Books	Security Bank Books
October deposits	$7,360	$7,110
October checks	6,290	6,130
October service charge	—	10
October 31 balance	5,070	4,970
November deposits	8,220	8,280
November checks	9,410	9,220
November service charge	—	15
Note collected by bank (included $15 interest)	—	1,015
October service charge recorded in November	10	—
November 30 balance	3,870	5,030

On the basis of the foregoing data: (1) prepare a four-column reconciliation for the month ended November 30, reconciling both bank and book balances to a corrected balance, and (2) give entries that would be required on Tyler's books to adjust the cash account as of November 30.

Exercise 7–10   (Journalizing marketable securities transactions)

Give the entries necessary to record these transactions of Rexton, Inc.

(a) Purchased $80,000 U.S. Treasury 8% bonds, paying 102½ plus accrued interest of $1,500. Broker's fees were $590. Rexton, Inc. uses the revenue approach to record accrued interest on purchased bonds.
(b) Purchased 1,000 shares of Agler Co. common stock at 175 plus brokerage fees of $1,200.
(c) Received semiannual interest on the U.S. Treasury bonds.
(d) Sold 150 shares of Agler at 185.
(e) Sold $20,000 of U.S. Treasury 8% bonds at 103 plus accrued interest of $275.
(f) Purchased a $15,000, 6-month certificate of deposit.

Exercise 7–11   (Valuation of marketable securities)

During 1991, Loveless Company purchased marketable equity securities as a short-term investment. Pertinent data are as follows:

Security	Cost	Market Value (12/31/91)
A	$40,000	$ 36,000
B	80,000	60,000
C	180,000	186,000

Loveless appropriately carries these securities at lower of aggregate cost or market value. What is the amount of loss to be reported in Loveless Company's income statement in 1991?   (AICPA adapted)

Exercise 7–12   (Accounting for marketable securities)

During 1991, Sunshine Inc. purchased the following marketable securities:

	Cost	Year-End Market
Wexler Co. Common	$12,000	$14,000
10% U.S. Treasury Notes	18,000	11,000
TexCo Bonds	25,000	27,000

All marketable securities are to be reported on the balance sheet at the lower of aggregate cost or market. (1) What entry would be made at year-end assuming the above values? (2) What entry would be made during 1992 assuming one half of the Wexler Co. common stock is sold for $7,000? (3) What entry would be made at the end of 1992 assuming (a) the market value of remaining securities is $45,000? (b) The market value of remaining securities is $48,000? (c) The market value of remaining securities is $55,000?

Exercise 7–13   (Reporting marketable securities)

International Corporation reports on a calendar-year basis. Its December 31, 1991, financial statements were issued on February 3, 1992. The auditor's report was dated January 22, 1992. The following information pertains to International's aggregate marketable equity securities portfolio:

Cost	$500,000
Market value (12/31/91)	400,000
Market value (1/22/92)	350,000
Market value (2/3/92)	300,000

How much should be reported on International's balance sheet at December 31, 1991, for marketable equity securities?   (AICPA adapted)

Exercise 7–14   (Valuation of marketable securities)

American Steel Corp. acquires marketable securities in 1990 at a cost of $200,000. Market values of the securities at the end of each year are as follows: 1990, $195,500; 1991, $219,000; 1992, $211,000. Give the entries at the end of 1990, 1991, and 1992 indicating how the securities would be reported on the balance sheet at the end of each year under each of the following assumptions:

(a) Securities are reported at cost.
(b) Securities are reported at the lower of cost or market on an aggregate basis.

Problems   Problem 7–1   (Composition of cash and marketable securities)

The balance of $192,200 in the cash account of Thomson Inc. consists of these items:

Petty cash fund	$ 1,000
Receivable from an employee	200
Cash in bond sinking fund	15,000
Cash in a foreign bank unavailable for withdrawal	40,000
Cash in First Bank	120,000
Currency on hand	16,000

The balance in the marketable securities account consists of:

U.S. Treasury bonds	$52,600
Voting stock of a subsidiary company (70% interest)	425,000
Advances to a subsidiary company (no maturity date specified)	115,000
A note receivable from a customer	20,500
The company's own shares held as treasury stock	25,000
Stock of Midwest Telephone Co.	64,000

Instructions: Calculate the correct Cash and Marketable Securities balances and state what accounts and in what sections of the balance sheet the other items would be properly reported.

Problem 7–2　(Accounting for petty cash)

On December 1, 1991, LGA Corporation established an imprest petty cash fund. The operations of the fund for the last month of 1991 and the first month of 1992 are summarized below:

Dec.　1　The petty cash fund was established by cashing a company check for $1,500 and delivering the proceeds to the fund cashier.

　　　21　A request for replenishment of the petty cash fund was received by the accounts payable department, supported by appropriate signed vouchers, summarized as follows:

Selling expenses	$ 324
Administrative expenses	513
Special equipment	122
Telephone, telegraph, and postage	48
Miscellaneous expenses	260
Total	$1,267

A check for $1,294 was drawn payable to the petty cash cashier.

　　　31　The company's independent certified public accountant counted the fund in connection with the year-end audit work and found the following:

Cash in petty cash fund		$655
Employees' checks with January dates (postdated)		85
Expense vouchers properly approved as follows:		
Selling expenses	$146	
Administrative expenses	412	
Office supplies	28	
Telephone, telegraph, and postage	48	
Miscellaneous expenses	120	754
Total		$1,494

The petty cash fund was not replenished at December 31, 1991.

Jan.　15　The employees' checks held in the petty cash fund at December 31 were cashed and the proceeds retained in the fund.

　　　31　A request for replenishment was made and a check was drawn to restore the fund to its original balance of $1,500. The support vouchers for January expenditures are summarized below.

Selling expenses	$ 85
Administrative expenses	312
Telephone, telegraph, and postage	35
Miscellaneous expenses	220
Total	$652

Instructions: Record the transactions in general journal form.

Problem 7–3　(Bank reconciliation statement)

The cash account of Delta, Inc. disclosed a balance of $17,056.48 on October 31. The bank statement as of October 31 showed a balance of $21,209.45.

Upon comparing the statement with the cash records, the following facts were developed:

(a) Delta's account had been charged on October 26 for a customer's uncollectible check amounting to $1,143.

(b) A 2-month, 9%, $3,000 customer's note dated August 25, discounted on October 12, had been dishonored October 26, and the bank had charged Delta for $3,050.83, which included a protest fee of $5.83.

(c) A customer's check for $725 had been entered as $625 by both the depositor and the bank but was later corrected by the bank.

(d) Check No. 661 for $1,242.50 had been entered in the cash disbursements journal at $1,224.50 and check No. 652 for $32.90 had been entered as $329. The company uses the voucher system.

(e) There were bank service charges for October of $39.43 not yet recorded on the books.

(f) A bank memo stated that M. Sear's note for $2,500 and interest of $62.50 had been collected on October 29, and the bank had made a charge of $12.50 (No entry had been made on the books when the note was sent to the bank for collection.)

(g) Receipts of October 29 for $6,850 were deposited November 1.

The following checks were outstanding on October 31:

No. 620	$1,250.00	No. 671	$ 732.50
621	3,448.23	673	187.90
632	2,405.25	675	275.72
670	1,775.38	676	2,233.15

Instructions:

(1) Prepare a bank reconciliation statement.

(2) Give the journal entries required as a result of the preceding information.

Problem 7—4   (Bank reconciliation statement)

The books of Hawkins Company show a cash balance of $23,383 as of July 31. Hawkins' bank statement shows a cash balance for the company of $21,432. Additional information which might be useful in reconciling the disparity between the two balances follows.

(a) A deposit of $800 was recorded by the bank on July 3, but it should have been recorded for Hawker Company rather than Hawkins Company.

(b) $425 of Petty Cash was included in the cash balance, but an actual count reveals $516 on hand.

(c) Check No. 315 in payment of electric bill for $125 was correctly recorded by the bank but was recorded in the cash disbursements journal of Hawkins as $215.

(d) The bank statement does not show receipts of $1,250 which were deposited on July 31.

(e) The bank statement indicated a monthly service charge of $35.

(f) A check for $372 was returned marked NSF. The check had been included in the July 24 deposit.

(g) Proceeds from cash sales of $1,530 for July 19 were stolen. The company expects to recover this amount from the insurance company. The cash receipts were recorded in the books, but no entry was made for the loss.

(h) A check for $2,560 cleared the bank on July 29. It was a transfer to the payroll account at the same bank. On July 31, all but $1,255 of payroll checks had been processed at the bank.

(i) Interest of $56 has accrued on funds the bank had invested for Hawkins for the month of July.

(j) Outstanding checks totaled $1,420 as of July 31.

(k) The July 22 deposit included a check for $705 that had been returned on July 15 marked NSF. Hawkins Company made no entry upon return of the check.

Instructions:

(1) Prepare a bank reconciliation statement.
(2) Make the necessary journal entries for Hawkins Company with the information provided on the bank reconciliation.

Problem 7–5   (Four-column bank reconciliation)

The following data are applicable to the Morgan Building Co.

(a) The July 31 bank statement balance of $74,875 included a bank service charge of $235 not previously reported to the company but recorded on the company's books in August.

(b) The cash account balance in the general ledger on July 31 was $66,715.

(c) Outstanding checks at July 31 were $13,475. Deposits in transit on July 31 were $5,080.

(d) The bank statement on August 31 had a balance of $78,265, recognizing deposits of $105,360 and withdrawals of $101,970. The withdrawals included a service charge for August of $270 not yet reported to Morgan Building Co.

(e) The cash account balance in the general ledger on August 31 was $80,435, recognizing receipts of $104,405 for August and checks written during August of $90,450. Deposits in transit on August 31 were $4,125, and checks of $2,225 were outstanding as of that date.

Instructions:

(1) Prepare a four-column bank reconciliation as of August 31.
(2) Give any entries at August 31 that may be required on the company's books.

▌▌▌ Problem 7–6   (Four-column bank reconciliation)

The following information is related to Downtown Company:

	August	September
Bank statement balance—at month end	$ 2,412	$ 2,782
Cash account balance—at month end	1,975	2,296
Bank charges for NSF check returned (normally written off in month following return)	38	80
Outstanding checks—at month end	600	865

Deposits in transit—at month end	300	470
Bank service charges (normally recorded in month following bank charge)	25	29
Drafts collected by bank (not recorded by company until month following collection)	200	150
Total credits to cash account	14,853	17,979
Total deposits on bank statement	?	18,080

Check #411 was erroneously recorded in the company checkbook and journal as $286; the correct amount is $236. (This check was not outstanding on September 30.)

All disbursements were made by check.

Instructions: Prepare a four-column bank reconciliation for the month of September.

Problem 7–7 (Four-column bank reconciliation with adjusting entries)

Asil Corporation received the following bank statement on August 1, 1991:

Date	Withdrawals	Deposits	Balance
July 1			66,405
2	2,502		63,903
3	2,240	1,050	62,713
5		2,106	64,819
6		5,535	70,354
8		5,817	76,171
9	8,181		67,990
10		4,317	72,307
11	6,819		65,488
12	7,425	4,926	62,989
13			62,989
15		3,509	66,498
16	9,777		56,721
17	6,221	7,702	58,202
18	6,484		51,718
19		3,418	55,136
20		8,470	63,606
22		6,492	70,098
23	5,546		64,552
24			64,552
25	8,735		55,817
26		8,246	64,063
27		9,385	73,448
29	7,060		66,388
30		5,827	72,215
31	6,405		65,810
Totals	$77,395	$76,800	

Asil's cash account shows the following information for the month of July, 1991: June 30, 1991 balance, $62,150

Date	Disbursements	Receipts
July 1	165	3,729
2		5,535
3	8,181	
5		5,817
6		4,317

8	6,819	
9	7,425	4,926
10		
11		
12		3,509
13	9,391	
15		7,702
16	6,221	
17	6,484	3,418
18		5,310
19		6,492
20	5,074	
22	8,735	
23		8,246
24		
25		
26	6,885	8,913
27		
29	5,913	5,152
30		2,238
31	5,857	
	$77,150	$75,304

Additional information:

1. Asil makes a journal entry for service charges, direct deposits, and interest earned in the month subsequent to the month the items are reflected on the bank statement.
2. Casper Co. makes a direct deposit of $675 to Asil's account at the bank on the 30th of every month. This payment, which is rent revenue to Asil, is not recorded by Asil until the bank statement is received.
3. On the 23rd of July an NSF check for $472 was returned by the bank. The check was redeposited on July 27th, and no entry was made by Asil.
4. Check no. 1145 dated July 29 was written for $1,492 of wages, but recorded by Asil on its books as $1,000.
5. On July 16, the bank recorded a withdrawal of $386 for Asil that should have been for Azil Company.
6. The bank service charge for June was $165 and for July was $175.
7. The interest earned in June was $3,054 and in July was $3,160.
8. During June Asil wrote check no. 1095 for $9,850 for rent expense but recorded the check on its books as $8,955. Asil discovered the mistake in July, when the canceled checks were returned with the June bank statement, but neglected to correct the error on the books at that time.
9. At the end of June Asil had $3,156 of deposits in transit, and checks totaling $4,742 that had not cleared the bank. In addition, all of Asil's transactions with the bank after July 29 have not cleared the bank.

Instructions:

1. Prepare a four column bank reconciliation.
2. Prepare any necessary adjusting journal entries on the books of Asil Corporation.
3. Prepare any necessary notation to the bank for errors that should be corrected by the bank.

Problem 7–8   (Accounting for marketable equity securities)

During 1991 Upstart Company engaged in the following transactions involving marketable equity securities.

Jan.   1   Purchased 1,200 shares in Corporation X for $6 per share.

May 14   Purchased 2,700 shares in Corporation Y for $12 per share.

Sep. 12   Purchased 1,600 shares in Corporation X for $8.50 per share.

Dec. 31   Sold 1,400 shares in Corporation X for $9 per share.

At the end of 1991, the shares in Corporation Y were selling for $7 per share.

On May 13, 1992, all of Corporation Y shares were sold for $8 each. The shares of Corporation X still on hand at December 31, 1992, were selling for $7 per share.

Assume that all the shares are considered to be current assets, and that Upstart Company is *not* part of an industry having specialized accounting for marketable securities.

The company assumes a FIFO flow of marketable securities.

Instructions: Provide the journal entries to be made on December 31, 1991, May 13, 1992, and December 31, 1992.   (AICPA adapted)

Problem 7–9   (Recording and valuing temporary investments)

Myers & Associates reports the following information on the December 31, 1990 balance sheet:

Marketable securities (at cost)	$225,850	
Less allowance for decline in value of marketable securities	2,260	$223,590

Supporting records of Myers' temporary holdings show marketable securities as follows:

	Cost	Market
200 shares of Conway Co. common	$25,450	$24,300
$80,000 U.S. Treasury 7% bonds	79,650	77,400
$120,000 U.S. Treasury 7½% bonds	120,750	121,890
	$225,850	$223,590

Interest dates on the Treasury bonds are January 1 and July 1. Myers & Associates makes reversing entries and uses the revenue approach to recording the purchase of bonds with accrued interest.

During 1991 and 1992 Myers & Associates completed the following transactions related to temporary investments:

1991

Jan.   1   Received semiannual interest on U.S. Treasury bonds. (The entry to reverse the interest accrual at the end of the last year has already been made.)

Apr.   1   Sold $60,000 of the 7½% U.S. Treasury bonds at 102 plus accrued interest. Brokerage fees were $200.

May 21   Received dividends of 25 cents per share on the Conway Co. common stock. The dividend had not been recorded on the declaration date.

July   1   Received semiannual interest on U.S. Treasury bonds, then sold the 7% treasury bonds at 97½. Brokerage fees were $250.

Aug. 15   Purchased 100 shares of Nieman Inc. common stock at 116 plus broker-
          age fees of $50.
Nov.   1 Purchased $50,000 of 8% U.S. Treasury bonds at 101 plus accrued in-
          terest. Brokerage fees were $125. Interest dates are January 1 and July 1.
Dec. 31   Market prices of securities were: Conway Co. common, 110; 7½% U.S.
          Treasury bonds, 101¾; 8% U.S. Treasury bonds, 101; Nieman Inc.
          common, 116¾. Myers & Associates reports all marketable securities at
          the lower of aggregate cost or market.
1992
Jan.   2 Recorded the receipt of semiannual interest on the U.S. Treasury
          bonds.
Feb.   1 Sold the remaining 7½% U.S. Treasury bonds at 101 plus accrued inter-
          est. Brokerage fees were $300.

Instructions:

(1) Prepare journal entries for the foregoing transactions and accrue required
    interest on December 31. Give computations in support of your entries.
(2) Show how marketable securities would be presented on the December 31,
    1991 balance sheet.

Problem 7—10   (Accounting for marketable equity securities)

Feitz Corporation invested idle cash resources in acquiring 5,000 shares of
common stock in another company on May 12, 1990 at a price of $18 per
share. By the end of 1990, the shares had dropped to a market price of $10
each. On March 3, 1991, the corporation sold 1,000 of the shares for $12,000;
by the end of the year, the shares were selling for $14 each. The price of the
shares recovered dramatically during 1992. The corporation sold 1,500 shares
for $30,000 on September 5, 1992, and by the end of the year, the shares had
a market price of $22 each.

Instructions: Assume that the shares are marketable equity securities and that at
all times they are classified as current assets. In accordance with FASB
Statement No. 12, give the journal entries to be made for the years 1990,
1991, and 1992.   (AICPA adapted)

Problem 7—11   (Journal Entries and balance sheet presentation for marketable securities)

On December 31, 1990, Durst Company's balance sheet showed the following
balance in its marketable securities account.

Current Assets:		
Marketable Securities (at Cost)		$155,000
Less allowance for decline in value of current marketable securities		7,250
Marketable Securities		$147,750

Durst's marketable securities portfolio on Dec. 31, 1990, was made up of the
following securities:

	Cost	Market
1000 shares of Herzog Corp. Stock	$ 75,000	$ 76,250
800 shares Taylor, Inc. stock	55,000	52,825
10% New York City Water bonds (Interest payable semiannually on January 1 and July 1)	25,000	18,675
	$155,000	$147,750

During 1991, the following transactions took place:

Jan.   3   Received interest on the New York City Water bonds.
March 1   Purchased 300 additional shares of Herzog Corp. stock for $22,950.
April 15   Sold 400 shares of the Taylor, Inc. stock for $69.00 per share.
July   3   Received interest on the New York City Water bonds.
Oct. 30   Purchased 1,500 shares of Cook Co. stock for $83,250.

Durst makes reversing entries on January 2 for all year-end accrual entries. The value of the stocks and bonds on December 31, 1991, is as follows:

Herzog Corp. stock	$76.60/share
Taylor, Inc. stock	$68.50/share
Cook Co. stock	$55.25/share
New York City Water bonds	$20,555

Required:

1. Make all necessary journal entries for 1991, including any year-end accrual or adjusting entries.
2. Show how the marketable securities would be presented on the balance sheet at December 31, 1991.

Problem 7–12   (Alternative methods of valuing marketable securities)

Dextron Co. made the following investments in marketable securities in 1990:

Martin Inc., 1,400 shares @ 45¾	$ 64,050
Smith Corp., 1,750 shares @ 22½	39,375
Walker Bros. first-mortgage 8% bonds, 105 $1000 bonds at par	105,000
	$208,425

Smith Corp. shares were sold at the end of 1992 for $29,750. The market values of the securities at the end of 1990, 1991, and 1992 were as follows:

	1990	1991	1992
Martin Inc.	$ 68,250	$ 55,650	$ 60,375
Smith Corp.	35,700	30,100	—
Walker Bros.	108,500	110,250	105,350

Instructions: Prepare the necessary entries for 1990, 1991, and 1992 for the valuation and the sale of securities and show how the securities would be reported on the balance sheets prepared at the end of 1990, 1991, and 1992 under each of the following assumptions.

(a) Securities are valued at cost.
(b) Securities are valued at the lower of cost or market (aggregate basis).

Problem 7–13   (Journal entries for temporary investments)

During 1991 and 1992, the Kopson Co. made the following journal entries to account for transactions involving temporary investments.

1991
(a) Nov. 1	Marketable Securities	106,883	
	Cash		106,883
	To record the purchase of $100,000 of U.S. Treasury bonds at 103¼. Brokerage fees were $300. Interest is payable semiannually on January 1 and July 1.		
(b) Dec. 31	Marketable Securities	4,283	
	Allowance for Decline in Value of Current Marketable Securities		4,283
	To record the decrease in market value of the current marketable securities based on the following data:		

	Cost	Market
Fleming Co. stock	$ 25,250	$ 23,350
Dobson Co. stock	32,450	33,950
10% U.S. Treasury bonds	106,883	103,000
	$164,583	$160,300

The beginning allowance account balance was $500. There were no other entries in 1991.

1992
(c) Jan. 1	Cash	5,000	
	Interest Revenue		5,000
	To record interest revenue for six months		
(d) July 1	Cash	5,000	
	Interest Revenue		5,000
	To record interest revenue for six months		
(e) Dec. 6	Marketable Securities	50,000	
	Long-Term Investment in Equity Securities		50,000
	To record the reclassification of 10,000 shares of Braxton Co. stock, which was selected by management for sale in 1993. Market price was $4.80 per share at the date of reclassification.		
(f) Dec. 31	Recognized Decline in Value of Current Marketable Securities	5,483	
	Allowance for Decline in Value of Current Marketable Securities		5,483
	To record the decrease in the market value of the current marketable securities based on the following data:		

	Cost	Market
Fleming Co. stock	$ 25,250	$ 24,950
Dobson Co. stock	32,450	32,650
10% U.S. Treasury bonds	106,883	103,500
Braxton Co. stock	50,000	48,000
	$214,583	$209,100

There were no other entries.

Instructions: For each incorrect entry, give the entry that should have been made. Assume the revenue approach and the lower of cost or market method.

Chapter 8

Receivables

For most businesses receivables are a significant item, often representing a major portion of the liquid assets of a company. Retail and merchandising companies, such as Sears, Roebuck or J C Penney, typically have 50% to 70% of total current assets tied up in receivables. For some service-type businesses, the percentage is even higher. Receivables also can provide a significant source of revenues from finance charges. In 1987, for example, Sears collected over $2 billion in finance charges from its customers. On the other hand, a lack of control of receivables can result in substantial losses from uncollectible accounts. Even with good credit policies and collection procedures, bad debt losses often range from one to five percent of total credit sales. Finally, receivables can be used as collateral for a loan or sold to generate funds for operating purposes. During 1987, for example, Goodyear Tire Company sold $1.2 million of receivables.

As the above examples illustrate, receivables can affect the profitability of company operations in a number of ways. This makes the management, control, and accounting for receivables important tasks. The major considerations in accounting for receivables involve their recognition, classification, valuation, and reporting. Collection of receivables and the use of receivables in financing company operations are also important considerations. These issues are addressed in this chapter.

Classification of Receivables

In its broadest sense, the term receivables is applicable to all claims against others for money, goods, or services. For accounting purposes, however, the term is generally employed in a narrower sense to designate claims expected to be settled by the receipt of cash.

In classifying receivables, an important distinction is made between trade and nontrade receivables. Usually, the chief source of receivables is the normal operating activities of a business, i.e., credit sales of goods or services to customers. These trade receivables may be evidenced by a formal written promise to pay and classified as notes receivable. In most cases, however, trade receivables are unsecured "open accounts," often referred to simply as **accounts receivable**.

Accounts receivable represent an extension of short-term credit to customers. Payments are generally due within 30 to 90 days. The credit arrangements are typically informal agreements between seller and buyer supported by such business documents as invoices, sales orders, and delivery contracts. Normally trade receivables do not involve interest, although an interest or service charge may be added if payments are not made within a specified period. Trade receivables are the most common type of receivable and are generally the most significant in total dollar amount.

Nontrade receivables include all other types of receivables. They arise from a variety of transactions such as: (1) the sale of securities or property other than inventory; (2) advances to stockholders, directors, officers, employees, and affiliated companies; (3) deposits with creditors, utilities, and other agencies; (4) purchase prepayments; (5) deposits to guarantee contract performance or expense payment; (6) claims for losses or damages; (7) claims for rebates and tax refunds; (8) subscriptions for capital stock; and (9) dividends and interest receivable. Nontrade receivables should be summarized in appropriately titled accounts and reported separately in the financial statements.

Another way of classifying receivables relates to the **current** or short-term versus **noncurrent** or long-term nature of receivables. As indicated in Chapter 5, the "Current assets" classification, as broadly conceived, includes all receivables identified as collectible within one year or the normal operating cycle, whichever is longer. Thus, for classification purposes, all trade receivables are considered **current receivables**; each nontrade item requires separate analysis to determine whether it is reasonable to assume that it will be collected within one year. **Noncurrent receivables** are reported under the "Investments" or "Other noncurrent assets" caption, or as a separate item with an appropriate description.

In summary, receivables are classified in various ways, e.g., as accounts or notes receivable, as trade or nontrade receivables, and as current or noncurrent receivables. These categories are not mutually exclusive. For example, accounts receivable are trade receivables and are current; notes receivable may be trade receivables and therefore current in some circumstances, but may be nontrade receivables, either current or noncurrent, in other situations. The classifications used most often in practice and throughout this book will be simply *accounts receivable, notes receivable,* and *other receivables.*

Accounts Receivable

As indicated earlier, accounts receivable include all trade receivables not supported by a written agreement or "note." The following sections discuss the major accounting problems associated with accounts receivable: (1) when they are to be recognized; (2) how they are to be valued and reported; and (3) how they may be used as a source of cash in financing company operations.

Recognition of Accounts Receivable

The recognition of accounts receivable is related to the recognition of revenue. Since revenues are generally recorded when the earning process is complete and cash is realized or realizable, it follows that a receivable arising from the sale of goods is generally recognized when title to the goods passes to the buyer. Because the point at which title passes may vary with the terms of the sale, it is normal practice to recognize the receivable when goods are shipped to the customer. It is at this point in time that the revenue recognition criteria are normally satisfied. Receivables should not be recognized for goods shipped on approval where the shipper retains title until there is a formal acceptance, or for goods shipped on consignment, where the shipper retains title until the goods are sold by the consignee. Receivables for service to customers are properly recognized when the services are performed. The entry for recognizing a receivable from the sale of goods or services is:

Accounts Receivable XXX
   Sales XXX

When the account is collected, Accounts Receivable is credited and Cash is debited.

For department stores and major oil and gas companies, a significant portion of receivables arise from *credit card sales*.[1] The recognition of such receivables is similar to recognition of other trade receivables.

The treatment of credit card sales for other companies, such as American Express or banks that handle VISA or MasterCard, is somewhat different. These companies are generally responsible for approving customers' credit and collecting the receivables. Consequently, they usually charge a service fee, normally 2% to 5% of net credit card sales. These companies generally follow one of two procedures in reimbursing the retail companies that accept their cards: (1) the retailer must submit the credit card receipts in order to receive payments, or (2) they allow retailers to deposit the receipts directly into a checking account. American Express, Diners Club, Carte Blanche, and other travel and entertainment card companies generally follow the first procedure; bank cards are accounted for with the second method.

As an example of how a retail company would account for credit card sales under these two approaches, assume that Little Italy's Pizza Parlor has American Express drafts that total $1,200 on November 20. The entry to record the sales would be:

---

[1] It is estimated that annual credit card sales amount to over $170 billion in the United States alone. There are over 200 million credit-card holders of nationally available cards such as VISA, MasterCard, American Express, and Diners Club, not even counting the cards of major retailers, such as Sears and Penneys, or the large oil companies.

Accounts Receivable-American Express.................	1,200	
Sales		1,200
To record American Express credit card sales for November 20.		

Little Italy would then send the receipts to American Express, which would send a check to Little Italy for $1,200 less its service fees. Assuming a 5% service charge, which Little Italy would recognize as a selling expense, the entry to record the payment from American Express would be:

Cash	1,140	
Credit Card Service Charge	60	
Accounts Receivable		1,200
To record payment from American Express on credit card sales.		

Continuing the example, assume Little Italy also had VISA charge sales of $2,000. These sales are handled under the second method and are treated like a cash sale. In effect, bank credit card sales, such as VISA and Master-Card, are a form of factoring receivables, which is discussed later in the chapter. The retail company makes out a regular, but separate, bank deposit slip and deposits the credit card receipts as though they were cash. The bank receives the deposit slip and credit card receipts and increases the retailer's checking account balance for the total amount less the bank credit card service charge. Assuming a 4% bank service charge, in our example Little Italy would make the following entry:

Cash	1,920	
Credit Card Service Charge	80	
Sales		2,000
To record VISA credit card sales for November 20.		

Note that under this method a receivable is never established by the retail companies. The receivables from the customers are the responsibility of the bank that issued the credit card. The customers pay the bank directly and any uncollectibles are losses for the bank.

Valuation and Reporting of Accounts Receivable

Theoretically, all receivables should be valued at an amount representing the present value of the expected future cash receipts. As explained in Chapter 6, the present value of a $1,000 receivable due in 1 year at a 10% interest rate is $909.10 ($1,000 × the present value factor of .9091 from Table II in Chapter 6). The difference in the present value and the amount to be received in the future ($90.90 in the example) is the implicit interest. Since accounts receivable are short term, usually being collected within 30 to 90 days, the amount of interest is insignificant. Consequently, the accounting profession has chosen to ignore the interest element for these trade receivables.[2]

Instead of valuing accounts receivable at a discounted present value, they are reported at their **net realizable value**, i.e., their expected cash value. This means that accounts receivable should be recorded net of estimated uncollectible items and trade discounts. The objective is to report the receivables at the amount of claims from customers actually expected to be collected in cash.

Uncollectible Accounts Receivable

Invariably, some receivables will prove uncollectible. The simplest method for recognizing the loss from these uncollectible accounts is to debit an expense account, such as Bad Debt Expense or Uncollectible Accounts Expense, and credit Accounts Receivable at the time it is determined that an account cannot be collected. This approach is called the **direct write-off method** and is often used by small businesses because of its simplicity. While the recognition of uncollectibles in the period of their discovery is simple and convenient, this method does not provide for the matching of current revenues with related expenses and does not report receivables at their net realizable value. Therefore, use of the direct write-off method is considered a departure from generally accepted accounting principles. The following sections describe the procedures used in estimating uncollectibles with the **allowance method**, which is required by GAAP.[3]

Establishing an Allowance for Doubtful Accounts When using the allowance method, the amount of receivables estimated to be uncollectible is recorded by a debit to Doubtful Accounts Expense and a credit to Allowance for Doubtful Accounts. The terminology for these account titles may vary somewhat. Other possibilities, besides Allowance for Doubtful Accounts, include Allowance for Uncollectible Accounts and Allowance for Bad Debts. The expense account title usually is consistent with that of the allowance account. A typical entry, normally made as an end-of-the-period adjustment, would be as follows:

```
Doubtful Accounts Expense ...............................   XXX
   Allowance for Doubtful Accounts .........................          XXX
      To record estimated uncollectible accounts receivable for
      the period.
```

The expense would be reported as a selling or general and administrative expense, and the allowance account would be shown as a deduction from

---

[2]See *Opinions of the Accounting Principle Board No. 21*, "Interest on Receivables and Payables" (New York: American Institute of Certified Public Accountants, 1971), par. 3(a).

[3]It should be noted that as a result of recent changes in the tax laws, the allowance method is no longer acceptable for tax purposes.

Accounts Receivable, thereby reporting the net realizable amount of the receivables.

Writing Off an Uncollectible Account under the Allowance Method When positive evidence is available concerning the partial or complete worthlessness of an account, the account is written off by a debit to the allowance account, which was previously established, and a credit to Accounts Receivable. Positive evidence of a reduction in value is found in the bankruptcy, death, or disappearance of a debtor, failure to enforce collection legally, or barring of collection by the statute of limitations. Write-offs should be supported by evidence of the uncollectibility of the accounts from appropriate parties, such as courts, lawyers, or credit agencies, and should be authorized in writing by appropriate company officers. The entry to write off an uncollectible receivable would be:

```
Allowance for Doubtful Accounts .........................    XXX
    Accounts Receivable ..................................           XXX
        To record the write-off of an uncollectible account.
```

Note that no entry is made to Doubtful Accounts Expense at this time. That entry was made when the allowance was established. The expense was thus recorded in the period when the sale was made, not necessarily in the period when the account became uncollectible, as with the direct write-off method.

Occasionally, an account that has been written off as uncollectible is unexpectedly collected. Entries are required to reverse the write-off entry and to record the collection. Assuming an account of $1,500 was written off as uncollectible but was subsequently collected, the following entries would be made at the time of collection:

```
Accounts Receivable ..................................    1,500
    Allowance for Doubtful Accounts ......................           1,500
        To reverse the entry made to write off the account.
Cash ................................................    1,500
    Accounts Receivable ..................................           1,500
        To record collection of the account.
```

Estimating Uncollectibles Based on Sales Percentage The estimate for uncollectible accounts may be based on sales for the period or the amount of receivables outstanding at the end of the period. When a sales basis is used, the amount of uncollectible accounts in past years relative to total sales provides a percentage of estimated uncollectibles. This percentage may be modified by expectations based on current experience. Since doubtful accounts occur only with credit sales, it would seem logical to develop a percentage of doubtful accounts to credit sales of past periods. This percentage is then applied to credit sales of the current period. However, since extra work may be required in maintaining separate records of cash and credit sales or in analyzing sales data, the percentage is frequently developed in terms of total sales. Unless there is considerable periodic fluctuation in the proportion of cash and credit sales, the **percentage of total sales** method will normally give satisfactory results.

To illustrate, if 2% of sales are considered doubtful in terms of collection and sales for the period are $100,000, the charge for doubtful accounts expense would be 2% of the current period's sales, or $2,000. Note that any existing balance in the allowance account resulting from past period charges to Doubtful Accounts Expense is ignored. The entry for this period would be simply: .

Doubtful Accounts Expense	2,000	
Allowance for Doubtful Accounts		2,000
($100,000 × .02 = $2,000)		

The sales percentage method for estimating doubtful accounts is widely used in practice because it is simple to apply. Companies often use this method to estimate doubtful accounts periodically during the year and then adjust the allowance account at year-end in relationship to the accounts receivable balance, as explained in the next section.

Estimating Uncollectibles Based on Accounts Receivable Balance Instead of using a percentage of sales to estimate uncollectible accounts, companies may base their estimates on a **percentage of total accounts receivable outstanding**. This method emphasizes the relationship between the Accounts Receivable balance and the Allowance for Doubtful Accounts. For example, if total Accounts Receivable are $50,000 and it is estimated that 3% of those accounts will be uncollectible, then the allowance account should have a balance of $1,500 ($50,000 × .03). If the allowance account already has a $600 credit balance from prior periods, then the current period adjusting entry would be:

Doubtful Accounts Expense	900	
Allowance for Doubtful Accounts		900

After posting the preceding entry, the balance in the allowance account would be $1,500, or 3% of total accounts receivable. Note that this method adjusts the existing balance to the desired balance based on a percentage of total receivables outstanding. If, in the example, the allowance account had a $200 debit balance caused by writing off more bad debts than had been estimated previously, the adjusting entry would be for $1,700 in order to bring the allowance account to the desired credit balance of $1,500, or 3% of total receivables.

The most commonly used method for establishing an allowance based on outstanding receivables involves aging receivables. Individual accounts are analyzed to determine those not yet due and those past due. Past-due accounts are classified in terms of the length of the period past due. An analysis sheet used in aging accounts receivable is shown on page 294.

ICO Products, Inc.
Analysis of Receivables—December 31, 1991

Customer	Amount	Not Yet Due	Not More Than 30 Days Past Due	31-60 Days Past Due	61-90 Days Past Due	91-180 Days Past Due	181-365 Days Past Due	More Than One Year Past Due
A. B. Andrews	$ 450			$ 450				
B. T. Brooks	300				$100	$200		
B. Bryant	200		$ 200					
L. B. Devine	2,100	$ 2,100						
K. Martinez	200							$ 200
M. A. Young	1,400	1,000			100	300		
Total	$47,550	$40,000	$3,000	$1,200	$650	$500	$800	$1,400

Overdue balances can be evaluated individually to estimate the collectibility of each item as a basis for developing an overall estimate. An alternative procedure is to develop a series of estimated loss percentages and apply these to the different receivables classifications. The calculation of the allowance on the latter basis is illustrated below.

ICO Products, Inc.
Estimated Amount of Uncollectible Accounts—December 31, 1991

Classification	Balances	Uncollectible Accounts Experience Percentage	Estimated Amount of Uncollectible Accounts
Not yet due	$40,000	2%	$ 800
Not more than 30 days past due	3,000	5%	150
31-60 days past due	1,200	10%	120
61-90 days past due	650	20%	130
91-180 days past due	500	30%	150
181-365 days past due	800	50%	400
More than one year past due	1,400	80%	1,120
	$47,550		$2,870

Just as with the previous method based on a percentage of total receivables outstanding, Doubtful Accounts Expense is debited and Allowance for Doubtful Accounts is credited for an amount bringing the allowance account to the required balance. Assuming uncollectibles estimated at $2,870 as shown in the schedule above and a credit balance of $620 in the allowance account before adjustment, the following entry would be made:

Doubtful Accounts Expense	2,250	
Allowance for Doubtful Accounts		2,250

The aging method provides the most satisfactory approach to the valuation of receivables at their net realizable amounts. Furthermore, data developed through aging receivables may be quite useful to management for purposes of credit analysis and control. On the other hand, application of this method may involve considerable time and cost. This method still involves estimates, and the added refinement achieved by the aging process may not warrant the additional cost. With computer programs, however, the time and cost factors are not as significant as they once were.

Corrections to Allowance for Doubtful Accounts. As previously indicated, the allowance for doubtful accounts balance is established and maintained by means of adjusting entries at the close of each accounting period. If the allowance provisions are too large, the allowance account balance will be unnecessarily inflated and earnings will be understated; if the allowance provisions are too small, the allowance account balance will be inadequate and earnings will be overstated.

Care must be taken to see that the allowance balance follows the credit experience of the particular business. The process of aging receivables at different intervals may be employed as a means of checking the allowance balance to be certain that it is being maintained satisfactorily. Such periodic reviews may indicate a need for a correction in the allowance as well as a change in the rate or in the method employed.

When the uncollectible accounts experience approximates the estimated losses, the allowance procedure may be considered satisfactory, and no adjustment is required. When it appears that there has been a failure to estimate uncollectible accounts accurately, resulting in an allowance balance that is clearly inadequate or excessive, an adjustment is in order. Such an adjustment would be considered a change in accounting estimate under APB Opinion No. 20, and the effect would be reported in the current and future periods as an ordinary item on the income statement, usually as an addition to or subtraction from Doubtful Accounts Expense.

The actual write-off of receivables as uncollectible by debits to the allowance account and credits to the receivables account may result temporarily in a debit balance in the allowance account. A debit balance arising in this manner does not mean necessarily that the allowance is inadequate; debits to the allowance account simply predate the end-of-period adjustment for uncollectible accounts. The adjustment, when recorded, should cover uncollectibles already determined as well as those yet to be identified.

Discounts

Many companies bill their customers at a gross sales price less an amount designated as a trade discount. The discount may vary by customer depending on the volume of business or size of order from the customer. In effect, the trade discount reduces the "list" sales price to the "net" sales price actually charged the customer. This net price is the amount at which the receivable and corresponding revenue should be recorded.

Another type of discount is a cash discount or sales discount offered to customers by some companies to encourage prompt payment of bills. Cash discounts may be taken by the customer only if payment is made within a specified period of time, generally thirty days or less. Receivables are generally recorded at their gross amounts, without regard to any cash discount offered. If payment is received within the discount period, Sales Discounts (a contra account to Sales) is debited for the difference between the recorded amount of the receivable and the total cash collected. This method, which is simple and widely used, is illustrated below with credit terms of "2/10, n/30" (2% discount if paid within 10 days, net amount due in 30 days):

Cash Discounts—Gross Method

Sales of $1,000; terms 2/10, n/30:

Accounts Receivable	1,000	
Sales		1,000

Payments of $300 received within discount period:

Cash	294	
Sales Discounts	6	
Accounts Receivable		300

Payments of $700 received after discount period:

Cash	700	
Accounts Receivable		700

Sales Returns and Allowances

In the normal course of business, some goods will be returned by customers and some allowances will have to be made for such factors as goods damaged during shipment, spoiled or otherwise defective goods, or shipment of an incorrect quantity or type of goods. When goods are returned or an allowance is necessary, net sales and accounts receivable are reduced. To illustrate, assume merchandise costing $1,000 is sold and later returned. The return would be recorded in the following manner:

Sales Returns and Allowances	1,000	
Accounts Receivable		1,000

While the charge could be made directly to Sales, the use of a separate contra account preserves information that may be useful to management.

Accounts Receivable as a Source of Cash

Accounts receivable are a part of the normal operating cycle of a business. Cash is used to purchase inventory, which in turn is often sold on account. The receivables are then collected, providing cash to start the cycle over.

Frequently the operating cycle takes several months to complete. Sometimes companies need immediate cash and cannot wait for completion of the normal cycle. At other times companies are not in financial stress but want to accelerate the receivable collection process, shift the risk of credit and the effort of collection to someone else, or merely use receivables from customers as a source of financing.

Receivables financing was once looked upon as a desperate measure. In recent years, however, receivables financing has become quite popular for financing leveraged buyouts and for business expansion. As one executive put it, "receivables financing is no longer viewed as last-resort financing but as a legitimate business tool."[4]

Accounts receivable may be converted to cash in one of three ways: (1) assignment of receivables, which is a borrowing arrangement with receivables pledged as security on the loan; (2) factoring receivables, which is a sale of receivables without recourse for cash to a third party, usually a bank or other financial institution; and (3) the transfer of receivables with recourse, which is a hybrid of the other two forms of receivables financing.

Assignment of Accounts Receivable

Loans are frequently obtained from banks or other lending institutions by assigning or pledging accounts receivable as security. The loan is evidenced by a written promissory note that provides for either a general assignment of receivables or an assignment of specific receivables.

With a **general assignment**, all accounts receivable serve as collateral on the note. There are no special accounting problems involved. The books simply report the loan (a debit to Cash and a credit to Notes Payable) and subsequent settlement of the obligation (a debit to Notes Payable and a credit to Cash). However, disclosure should be made on the balance sheet, by parenthetical comment or note, of the amount and nature of receivables pledged to secure the obligation to the lender.

When there is an **assignment of specific receivables** to a lender, the borrower should transfer the balance of those accounts to a special general ledger control account and clearly identify and account for the individual assigned accounts in the subsidiary ledger. The procedures involved are illustrated in the following example. It is assumed that the assignor (the borrower) collects the receivables, which is often the case.

On July 1, 1991, Provo Mercantile Co. assigns specific receivables totalling $300,000 to Salem Bank as collateral on a $200,000, 12% note. Provo Mercantile does not notify its account debtors and will continue to collect the assigned receivables. Salem assesses a 1% finance charge on assigned receivables in addition to the interest on the note. Provo is to make monthly payments to Salem with cash collected on assigned receivables. The following entries would be made:

---

[4] See "Factoring: A Flexible Borrowing Tool," *Small Business Report* (March 1987), p. 50.

Illustrative Entries for Assignment of Specific Receivables

Provo Mercantile Co.		**Salem Bank**	

Issuance of note and assignment of specific receivables on July 1, 1991.

Cash	197,000		Notes Receivable.....	200,000	
Finance Charge*	3,000		Finance Revenue* ...		3,000
Accounts			Cash..............		197,000
Receivable—					
Assigned...........	300,000				
Notes Payable		200,000			
Accounts					
Receivable		300,000			

*(1% × $300,000)

Collections of assigned accounts during July, $180,000 less cash discounts of $1,000; sales returns in July, $2,000.

Cash	179,000		
Sales Discounts......	1,000		(No Entry)
Sales Returns........	2,000		
Accounts			
Receivable—			
Assigned..........		182,000	

Paid Salem Bank amounts owed for July collections plus accrued interest on note to August 1.

Interest Expense*	2,000		Cash..............	181,000	
Notes Payable	179,000		Interest Revenue		2,000
Cash		181,000	Notes Receivable....		179,000

*($200,000 × .12 × 1/12)

Collections of remaining assigned accounts during August less $800 written off as uncollectible:

Cash	117,200		(No Entry)
Allowance for			
Doubtful Accounts ...	800		
Accounts			
Receivable—			
Assigned*		118,000	

*($300,000 − $182,000)

Paid Salem Bank remaining balance owed plus accrued interest on note to September 1:

Interest Expense*	210		Cash..............	21,210	
Notes Payable**	21,000		Interest Revenue* ...		210
Cash		21,210	Notes Receivable** ..		21,000

* ($21,000 × .12 × 1/12)
**($200,000 − $179,000)

If in the preceding example Salem Bank assumes responsibility for collecting the assigned receivables, the account debtors would have to be notified to make their payments to the bank. Salem would then use a liability account (e.g., Payable to Provo Mercantile) to account for cash collections during the period. Since the receivables are still owned by Provo Mercantile, the bank would not record them as assets. Upon full payment of the note plus interest, the bank would remit to Provo Mercantile any cash collections in excess of the note along with any uncollected accounts.

In disclosing the specifically assigned accounts receivable, Provo Mercantile should report them separately as a current asset if they are material. In addition, the equity in assigned accounts should be disclosed parenthetically or in a note. For example, on July 1, Provo Mercantile had $100,000 equity in its assigned receivables ($300,000 − $200,000).

Factoring Accounts Receivable

Certain banks, dealers, and finance companies purchase accounts receivable outright on a nonrecourse basis. A **sale of accounts receivable without recourse**[5] is commonly referred to as accounts receivable **factoring**, and the buyer is referred to as a "factor." Customers are usually notified that their bills are payable to the factor, and this party assumes the burden of billing and collecting accounts. The flow of activities involved in factoring is presented below.

Exhibit 8-1 Flow of Activities Involved in Factoring

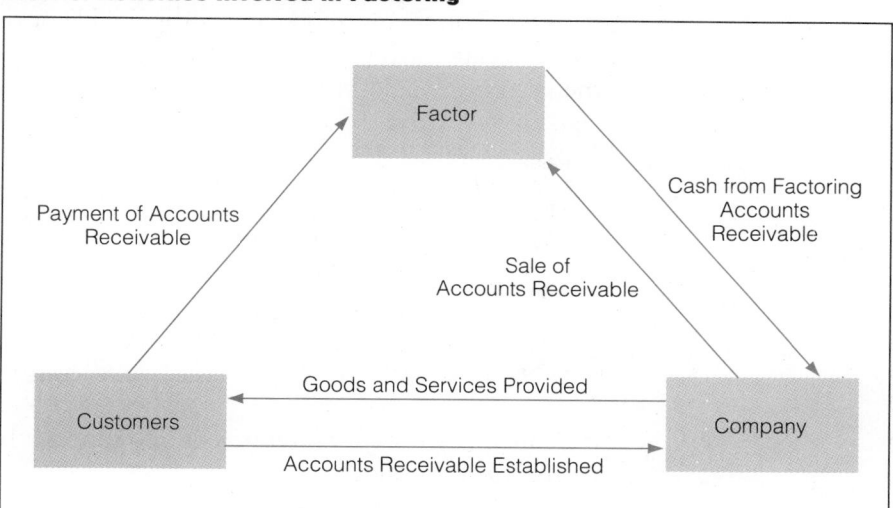

In many cases, factoring involves more than the purchase and collection of accounts receivable. Factoring frequently involves a continuing

[5]Recourse is defined by the FASB as "the right of a transferee of receivables to receive payment from the transferor of those receivables for (a) failure of the debtors to pay when due, (b) the effects of prepayments, or (c) adjustments resulting from defects in the eligibility of the transferred receivables." *Statement of Financial Accounting Standards No. 77*, "Reporting by Transferors for Transfers of Receivables with Recourse" (December, 1983), p. 7.

agreement whereby a financing institution assumes the credit function as well as the collection function. Under such an arrangement, the factor grants or denies credit, handles the accounts receivable records, bills customers, and makes collections. The business unit is relieved of all these activities, and the sale of goods provides immediate cash for business use. Because the factor absorbs the losses from bad accounts and frequently assumes credit and collection responsibilities, the charges associated with factoring generally exceed the interest charges on a loan with an assignment of receivables. Typically the factor will charge a fee of 10% to 30% of the net amount of receivables purchased, except for credit card factoring where the rate is 3% to 5%. The factor may withhold a portion of the purchase price for possible future charges for customer returns and allowances or other special adjustments. Final settlement is made after receivables have been collected.

When receivables are sold outright, without recourse, cash is debited, receivables and related allowance balances are closed, and an expense account is debited for factoring charges. When part of the purchase price is withheld by the factor, a receivable from the factor is established pending final settlement. Upon receipt of the total purchase price from the bank or finance company, the factor receivable account is eliminated. To illustrate, assume that $10,000 of receivables are factored, i.e., sold without recourse, to a finance company for $8,500. An allowance for doubtful accounts equal to $300 was previously established for these accounts. This amount will need to be written off along with the accounts receivable being sold. The finance company withheld 5% of the purchase price as protection against sales returns and allowances. The entry to record the sale of the accounts would be:

Cash	8,075	
Receivable from Factor	425	
Allowance for Doubtful Accounts	300	
Loss from Factoring Receivables	1,200	
Accounts Receivable		10,000

Computations:
Cash = $8,500 − $425 = $8,075;
Factor receivable = $8,500 × 5% = $425;
Factoring loss = ($10,000 − $300) − $8,500 = $1,200

Assuming there were no returns or allowances, the final settlement would be recorded as follows:

Cash	425	
Receivable from Factor		425

Transfer of Accounts Receivable with Recourse

The third way that cash can be obtained from accounts receivable financing is by **transferring accounts receivable with recourse**. This is different from factoring, which generally is on a nonrecourse basis. Transferring with recourse means that a transferee (bank or finance company) advances cash in return for accounts receivable, but retains the right to collect from the transferor if debtors (transferor's customers) fail to make payments when due. An important accounting question is whether this type of transaction is a **borrowing transaction** (like an assignment with the receivables as collateral) or a **sale transaction** (like a factoring arrangement). If viewed as a borrowing transaction, a liability should be reported and the difference between the proceeds received and the net receivables transferred is a financing cost (interest). If viewed as a sale, the difference between the amount received from the finance company (the transfer price) and the net amount of the receivables transferred (the gross amount of the receivables adjusted for allowance for doubtful accounts and any finance and service charges) is to be recognized as a gain or loss on the sale, as illustrated previously in the factoring example.

The FASB in Statement No. 77 has concluded that a transfer of receivables with recourse should be accounted for and reported as a sale if all the following conditions are met:

1. The transferor surrenders control of the future economic benefit embodied in the receivables.
2. The transferor's obligation under the recourse provisions can be reasonably estimated.
3. The transferee cannot require the transferor to repurchase the receivables except pursuant to the recourse provisions.[6]

If these conditions are not met, the transfer is reported as a secured loan, i.e., in the same manner as an assignment of receivables discussed previously.

In summary, accounts receivable provide an important source of cash for many companies. The transfer of receivables to third parties in return for cash generally takes the form of an assignment (borrowing with the receivables pledged as collateral) or factoring (a sale without recourse). The financing arrangements are often complex and may involve a transfer of receivables on a recourse basis. Each transaction must be analyzed carefully to see if in form and substance it is a borrowing transaction or a sale transaction, and treated accordingly.

Notes Receivable

A promissory note is an unconditional written promise to pay a certain sum of money at a specified time. The note is signed by the **maker** and is payable to the order of a specified payee or to bearer. Notes usually involve interest, stated at an annual rate and charged on the face amount of the

---

[6]*Statement of Financial Accounting Standards No. 77*, "Reporting by Transferors of Transfers of Receivables with Recourse" (December, 1983), par. 5.

note. Most notes are negotiable notes that are legally transferable by endorsement and delivery.

For reporting purposes, **trade notes receivable** should include only negotiable short-term instruments acquired from trade debtors and not yet due. Trade notes generally arise from sales involving relatively high dollar amounts where the buyer wants to extend payment beyond the usual trade credit period of 30 to 90 days. Also, sellers sometimes request notes from customers whose accounts receivable are past due. Most companies, however, have relatively few trade notes receivable.

Nontrade notes receivable should be separately designated on the balance sheet under an appropriate title. For example, notes arising from loans to customers, officers, employees, and affiliated companies should be reported separately from trade notes.

Valuation of Notes Receivable

Notes receivable are initially recorded at their present value, which may be defined as the sum of future receipts discounted to the present date at an appropriate rate of interest.[7] In a lending transaction, the present value is the amount of cash received by the borrower. When a note is exchanged for property, goods, or services, the present value equals the current cash selling price of the items exchanged. The difference between the present value and the amount to be collected at the due date or maturity date is a charge for interest.

All notes arising in arm's-length transactions between unrelated parties involve an element of interest. However, a distinction as to form is made between interest-bearing and non-interest-bearing notes. An interest-bearing note is written as a promise to pay a principal or face amount plus interest at a specified rate. In the absence of special valuation problems discussed in the next section, the face amount of an interest-bearing note is the present value upon issuance of the note.

A non-interest-bearing note does not specify an interest rate, but the face amount includes the interest charge. Thus, the present value is the difference between the face amount and the interest included in that amount, sometimes called the implicit or effective interest.

In recording receipt of a note, Notes Receivable is debited for the face amount of the note. When the face amount differs from the present value, as is the case with non-interest-bearing notes, the difference is recorded as a premium or discount and amortized over the life of the note. In the example to follow, a note receivable is established with credits to Sales and a Discount on Notes Receivable account. The amount of discount is the implicit interest on the note and will be recognized as interest revenue as the note matures.

To illustrate, assume that High Value Corporation sells goods on January 1, 1991, with a price of $1,000. The buyer gives High Value a promis-

---

[7]See Chapter 6 for a discussion of present value concepts and applications.

sory note due December 31, 1992. The maturity value of the note includes interest at 10 percent. Thus, High Value will receive $1,210 ($1,000 × 1.21)[8] when the note is paid. The following entries show the accounting procedures for an interest-bearing note and one written in a non-interest-bearing form.

	Interest-Bearing Note Face Amount = Present Value = $1,000 Stated Interest Rate = 10%			Non-Interest-Bearing Note Face Amount = Maturity = $1,210 No Stated Interest Rate	
1991					
Jan. 1	Notes Receivable ..	1,000		Notes Receivable ..	1,210	
	Sales		1,000	Sales		1,000
				Discount on Notes		
				Receivable		210

To record note received in exchange for goods selling for $1,000.

				Discount on Notes		
Dec. 31	Interest Receivable	100		Receivable	100	
	Interest Revenue ..		100	Interest Revenue ..		100

To recognize interest earned for one year; $1,000 × .10.

1992						
Dec. 31	Cash	1,210		Cash	1,210	
	Notes Receivable		1,000	Discount on Notes		
	Interest Receivable		100	Receivable	110	
	Interest Revenue ..		110	Notes Receivable		1,210
				Interest Revenue ..		110

To record settlement of note at maturity and recognize interest earned for one year: ($1,000 + $100) × .10.

At December 31, 1991, the unamortized discount of $110 on the non-interest-bearing note would be deducted from notes receivable on the balance sheet. If the non-interest-bearing note were recorded at face value with no recognition of the interest included therein, the sales price and profit to the seller would be overstated. In subsequent periods interest revenue would be understated. Failure to record the discount would also result in an overstatement of assets.

Although the proper valuation of receivables calls for the amortization procedure just described, exceptions may be appropriate in some situations due to special limitations or practical considerations. The Accounting Principles Board in Opinion No. 21 provided guidelines for the recognition of interest on receivables and payables and the accounting subsequently to be employed. However, the Board indicated that this process is not to be regarded as applicable under all circumstances. Among the exceptions are the following:

. . . receivables and payables arising from transactions with customers or sup-

[8]The amount of $1 due in two years at an annual rate of 10% is $1.21. See Table I, Chapter 6.

pliers in the normal course of business which are due in customary trade terms not exceeding approximately one year.[9]

Accordingly, as mentioned earlier, short-term notes and accounts receivable arising from trade sales may be properly recorded at the amounts collectible in the customary sales terms.

Notes, like accounts receivable, are not always collectible. If notes receivable comprise a significant portion of regular trade receivables, a provision should be made for uncollectible amounts and an allowance account established using procedures similar to those for accounts receivable already discussed.

Special Valuation Problems

APB Opinion No. 21 was issued to clarify and refine existing accounting practice with respect to receivables and payables. The opinion is especially applicable to nontrade, long-term notes, such as secured and unsecured notes, debentures (bonds), equipment obligations, and mortgage notes. Examples are provided below for notes exchanged for cash and for property, goods, or services.

Notes Exchanged for Cash When a note is exchanged for cash, and there are no other rights or privileges involved, the present value of the note is presumed to be the amount of the cash proceeds. The note should be recorded at its face amount and any difference between the face amount and the cash proceeds should be recorded as a premium or discount on the note. The premium or discount should be amortized over the life of the note as illustrated previously for High Value Corporation. The total interest is measured by the difference in actual cash received by the borrower and the total amount to be received in the future by the lender. Any unamortized premium or discount on notes is reported on the balance sheet as a direct addition to or deduction from the face amount of the receivables, thus showing their net present value.

Notes Exchanged for Property, Goods, or Services When a note is exchanged for property, goods, or services in an arm's-length transaction, the present value of the note is usually evidenced by the terms of the note or supporting documents. There is a general presumption that the interest specified by the parties to a transaction represents fair and adequate compensation for the use of borrowed funds.[10] Valuation problems arise, however, when one of the following conditions exists:[11]

1. No interest rate is stated.
2. The stated rate does not seem reasonable, given the nature of the transaction and surrounding circumstances.

---

[9]*Opinions of the Accounting Principles Board, No. 21*, "Interest on Receivables and Payables" (New York: American Institute of Certified Public Accountants, 1971), par. 3(a).

[10]*Ibid., No. 21*, par. 12.

[11]*Ibid.*

3. The stated face amount of the note is significantly different from the current cash equivalent sales price of similar property, goods, or services or from the current market value of similar notes at the date of the transaction.

Under any of the preceding conditions, APB No. 21 requires accounting recognition of the economic substance of the transaction rather than the form of the note. The note should be recorded at (1) the fair market value of the property, goods, or services exchanged or (2) the current market value of the note, whichever is more clearly determinable. The difference between the face amount of the note and the present value is recognized as a discount or premium and amortized over the life of the note.

To illustrate, assume that on July 1 Timberline Corporation sells a tract of land purchased three years ago at a cost of $250,000. The buyer gives Timberline a 1-year note with a face amount of $310,000 bearing interest at a stated rate of 8%. An appraisal of the land prior to the sale indicated a market value of $300,000, which in this example is considered to be the appropriate basis for recording the sale as follows:

```
1991
July 1  Notes Receivable ...............................   310,000
           Discount on Notes Receivable ...................              10,000
           Land .........................................             250,000
           Gain on Sale of Land ...........................              50,000
```

When the note is paid at maturity, Timberline will receive the face value ($310,000) plus stated interest of $24,800. ($310,000 × .08) or a total of $334,800. The interest to be recognized, however, is $34,800—the difference between the maturity value of the note and the market value of the land at the date of the exchange. Thus, the effective rate of interest on the note is 11.6% ($34,800 ÷ $300,000).

Assuming straight-line amortization of the discount and that Timberline's year-end is December 31, the following entries would be made to recognize interest revenue and to record payment of the note at maturity.

```
1991
Dec. 31  Interest Receivable ...............................   12,400*
            Discount on Notes Receivable ....................    5,000
               Interest Revenue ...............................             17,400
               *($310,000 × .08 × 6/12 = $12,400)


1992
June 30  Cash .........................................   334,800
            Discount on Notes Receivable ....................    5,000
               Notes Receivable ...........................             310,000
               Interest Receivable ...........................              12,400
               Interest Revenue ...............................              17,400
```

The unamortized discount balance of $5,000 would be subtracted from Notes Receivable on the December 31, 1991, balance sheet.

Imputing an Interest Rate

If there is no current market price for either the property, goods or services, or the note, then the present value of the note must be determined by selecting an appropriate interest rate and using that rate to discount future receipts to the present. The imputed interest rate is determined at the date of the exchange and is not altered thereafter.

The selection of an appropriate rate is influenced by many factors, including the credit standing of the issuer of the note and prevailing interest rates for debt instruments of similar quality and length of time to maturity. APB Opinion No. 21 states:

> In any event, the rate used for valuation purposes will normally be at least equal to the rate at which the debtor can obtain financing of a similar nature from other sources at the date of the transaction. The objective is to approximate the rate which would have resulted if an independent borrower and an independent lender had negotiated a similar transaction under comparable terms and conditions with the option to pay the cash price upon purchase or to give a note for the amount of the purchase which bears the prevailing rate of interest to maturity.[12]

To illustrate the process of imputing interest rates, assume that Horrocks & Associates surveyed 800,000 acres of mountain property for the Mountain Meadow Ranch. On December 31, 1991, Horrocks accepted a $45,000 note as payment for services. The note is non-interest-bearing and comes due in three yearly installments of $15,000 each beginning December 31, 1992. Assume there is no market for the note and no basis for estimating objectively the fair market value of the services rendered. After considering the current prime interest rate, the credit standing of the ranch, the collateral available, the terms for repayment, and the prevailing rates of interest for the issuer's other debt, a 10% imputed interest rate is considered appropriate. The note should be recorded at its present value and a discount recognized. The computation is based on Present Value Table IV, Chapter 6, as follows:

Face amount of note	$45,000
Less present value of note:	
$PV_n = R(PVAF)_{\overline{3}\,10\%}$	
$PV_n = \$15,000(2.4869)$	37,303*
Discount on note	$ 7,697

*Rounded to nearest dollar.

The entry to record the receipt of the note would be:

---

[12] *Ibid.*, par. 13.

```
1991
Dec. 31  Notes Receivable ...................................    45,000
              Discount on Notes Receivable ...................              7,697
              Service Revenue ................................             37,303
                   To record a non-interest-bearing note receivable at
                   its present value based on an imputed interest rate
                   of 10% per year.
```

A schedule showing the amortization of the discount on the note is presented below.

	(1) Face Amount Before Current Installment	(2) Unamortized Discount	(3) Net Amount (1) − (2)	(4) Discount Amortization 10% × (3)	(5) Payment Received
December 31, 1992	$45,000	$7,697	$37,303	$3,730	$15,000
December 31, 1993	30,000	3,967*	26,033	2,603	15,000
December 31, 1994	15,000	1,364**	13,636	1,364	15,000
				$7,697	$45,000

* $7,697 − $3,730 = $3,967
** $3,967 − $2,603 = $1,364

At the end of each year, an entry similar to the following would be made.

```
1992
Dec. 31  Cash .........................................    15,000
         Discount on Notes Receivable ...................     3,730
              Interest Revenue ................................              3,730
              Notes Receivable ................................             15,000
                   To record the first year's installment on notes
                   receivable and recognize interest earned during the
                   period.
```

By using these procedures, at the end of the 3 years the discount will be completely amortized to interest revenue, the face amount of the note receivable will have been collected, and the appropriate amount of service revenue will have been recognized in the year it was earned. At the end of each year, the balance sheet will reflect the net present value of the receivable by subtracting the unamortized discount balance from the outstanding balance in Notes Receivable.

It is necessary to impute an interest rate only when the present value of the receivable cannot be determined through evaluation of existing market values of the elements of the transaction. The valuation and income measurement objectives remain the same regardless of the specific circumstances—to report Notes Receivables at their net present values and to record appropriate amounts of interest revenue during the collection period of the receivables.

Notes Receivable as a Source of Cash   As discussed earlier in the chapter, accounts receivable can be a source of immediate cash. A company can also obtain cash by "discounting" notes receivable. The discounting of notes receivable, sometimes called bank discounting, is not to be confused with the discounting of future cash receipts to arrive at present value or with the discount deducted from Notes Receivable on the balance sheet as discussed previously. **Bank discounting** involves the transfer of negotiable notes to a bank or other financial institution willing to exchange such instruments for cash.

When discounting an interest-bearing note, which is the usual situation, the following steps are taken to determine the amount to be received from the bank (the proceeds):[13]

1. Determine the maturity value of the note.
   Maturity value = Face amount + Interest
   Interest = Face amount × Interest rate × Interest period
   Interest period = Date of note to date of maturity

2. Determine the amount of discount.
   Discount = Maturity value × Discount rate × Discount period
   Discount period = Date of discount to Date of maturity

3. Determine the proceeds.
   Proceeds = Maturity value − Discount

Once the proceeds are determined, the transaction can be recorded, recognizing the applicable liability and net interest revenue or expense (if a borrowing transaction) or the gain or loss (if a sale transaction).

If a note is transferred **without recourse**, i.e., the bank assumes the risk of uncollectibility, the transaction should be recorded as a sale, much like the factoring of accounts receivable discussed earlier. If the note is transferred **with recourse**, which is the usual case, the discounting transaction may be recorded as a sale or a borrowing transaction, depending on the terms and conditions. The criteria for classifying a transfer of accounts receivable with recourse, set forth in FASB Statement No. 77 and presented on page 301, also apply to transfers of notes receivable with recourse.

To illustrate the recording of a transfer (discounting) of notes receivable with recourse, assume that Meeker Corporation received a 90-day, $5,000, 10% note from a customer on September 1 to settle a past-due account receivable. The note is discounted at a bank after 10 days at a discount rate of 15%. The transaction would be treated as a sale only if the FASB Statement No. 77 criteria are met. Otherwise, the transfer is recorded as a borrowing transaction. The journal entries for both a sale and borrowing transaction would be as follows:

---

[13]The same procedures apply to the discounting of a non-interest-bearing note, except that the maturity value does not have to be computed (Step 1), since the face amount equals the maturity value.

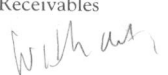

Discounting Notes Receivable With Recourse

Transaction Recorded as Sale	Transaction Recorded as Borrowing

Received a 90-day, $5,000, 10% note from a customer on September 1:

Notes Receivable	5,000		Notes Receivable	5,000	
Accounts Receivable		5,000	Accounts Receivable ..		5,000

Discounted customer's note at bank on September 11 at a discount rate of 15%:

Cash	4,955		Cash	4,955	
Loss on Sale of			Interest Expense	45	
Note	45		Obligation on		
Notes Receivable		5,000	Discounted		
			Notes Receivable		5,000

Computations (rounded to nearest dollar):
Maturity value = $5,000 + Interest ($5,000 × .10 × 90/365 = $123) = $5,123
Discount = $5,123 × .15 × 80/365 = $168
Proceeds = $5,123 − $168 = $4,955
Loss/Interest Expense = $168 − $123 = $45

If maturity value of note paid to bank by customer on due date, November 29:

(No entry)	Obligation on Discounted Notes Receivable	5,000	
	Notes Receivable		5,000

If customer defaults and bank collects from Meeker Corporation on November 29 the maturity value ($5,123) plus a $25 protest fee:

Notes Receivable—			Notes Receivable—		
Past Due	5,148		Past Due	5,148	
Cash		5,148	Cash		5,148
			Obligation on		
			Discounted Notes		
			Receivable	5,000	
			Notes Receivable		5,000

Several important points can be observed in the example. First, the loss or net interest expense recognized at the date of discounting ($45) is the difference between the amount charged by the bank to discount the note (in effect, interest expense of $168) and the amount of interest revenue the company would have earned if it had held the note to maturity ($123). Alternatively, the loss or net interest expense is the difference between the face amount of the note ($5,000) and the proceeds received from the bank ($4,955). Depending on how long the note is held prior to discounting and on the difference between the interest rate on the note and the discount rate charged by the bank, it is possible for the proceeds to be greater than the face amount of the note, which would result in a gain or net interest revenue being recorded. For example, if the Meeker Corporation had held the note for 60 days prior to discounting, the entries on September 11 would be:

Transaction Recorded as Sale			**Transaction Recorded as Borrowing**		
Cash	5,060		Cash	5,060	
Gain on Sale of			Interest Revenue . .		60
Note		60	Obligation on		
Notes Receivable		5,000	Discounted Notes		
			Receivable		5,000

Computations (rounded to nearest dollar):
Maturity value (same) = $5,123
Discount = $5,123 × .15 × 30/365 = $63
Proceeds = $5,123 − $63 = $5,060
Gain/Interest Revenue = $123 − $63 = $60

As indicated in the Meeker example, when a note is discounted with recourse, the bank will require payment from the company that discounted the note if the maker of the note defaults on payment at maturity (often referred to as **dishonoring** the note). In addition, the bank generally will charge a protest fee, which in the example is $25. Subsequently, the company will attempt to collect from the customer and, if unsuccessful, will eventually write off the note as uncollectible.

If the note had been discounted without recourse, the transaction would have been recorded in exactly the same manner as shown for a sale in the example. However, no entries would be required after the discounting transaction is recorded on September 30, since the company has no liability with regard to the note after the transfer.

Presentation of Receivables on the Balance Sheet

The receivables qualifying as current items may be grouped for presentation on the balance sheet in the following classes: (1) notes receivable—trade debtors, (2) accounts receivable—trade debtors, and (3) other receivables. Alternatively, trade notes and accounts receivable can be reported as a single amount. The detail reported for other receivables depends on the relative significance of the various items included. Valuation accounts are deducted from the individual receivable balances or combined balances to which they relate. Any long-term trade and nontrade receivables would be reported as "Other noncurrent assets" on the balance sheet.

When notes receivable have been discounted with recourse, a liability (e.g., Obligation on Discounted Notes Receivable) is reported in the balance sheet if the discounting is treated as borrowing. If treated as a sale, no liability is recognized, but a contingent liability should be disclosed in the notes to the financial statements or parenthetically on the balance sheet with notes receivable. If notes are discounted without recourse, there is no contingent liability. If notes or accounts receivable have been pledged to secure a loan, the amount should be disclosed.

Accounts and notes receivable as presented by Holiday Corporation in its 1988 annual report are shown below. An alternative disclosure method would be to show net trade receivables on the balance sheet and present the detailed information in a note to the financial statements. This latter approach is illustrated below for Cincinnati Milacron Inc.

Exhibit 8-2   Holiday Corporation and Consolidated Subsidiaries

Balance Sheets   Holiday Corporation and Consolidated Subsidiaries

(In thousands, except share amounts)	January 1, 1988	January 2, 1987
Assets		
Current assets		
Cash	$ 65,409	$ 59,822
Temporary cash investments, at cost which approximates market	265,925	14,355
Receivables, including notes receivable of $15,621 and $16,076, less allowance for doubtful accounts of $24,672 and $24,416	128,050	180,102

Exhibit 8-3   Cincinnati Milacron Inc. and Subsidiaries

Consolidated Balance Sheet
Cincinnati Milacron Inc. and Subsidiaries

Fiscal year ends on Saturday closest to December 31

(In thousands)	1987	1986
Assets		
Current Assets		
Cash and marketable securities	$ 13,611	$ 13,446
Notes and accounts receivable less allowances	190,426	197,507

Receivables and Inventories

Notes and accounts receivable less allowances and the components of inventories are shown in the respective tables.

Notes and Accounts Receivable Less Allowances		
(In thousands)	1987	1986
Notes receivable	$ 22,730	$ 13,292
Accounts receivable	176,064	191,470
	198,794	204,762
Less allowances for doubtful accounts	8,368	7,255
	$190,426	$197,507

Key Terms

Accounts receivable 288
Aging receivables 293
Allowance method 291
Assignment of receivables 297
Bank discounting 308
Cash or sales discount 295
Direct write-off method 291
Factoring receivables 297
Implicit or effective interest 302
Imputed interest rate 306
Interest-bearing note 302
Negotiable note 302

Net realizable value 291
Non-interest-bearing note 302
Nontrade receivables 288
Notes receivable 287
Present value 302
Principal or face amount 302
Promissory note 301
Receivables 287
Trade discount 295
Trade receivables 287
Transfer of receivables with recourse
   297

Questions

1. Explain how each of the following factors affects the classification of a receivable (a) the form of a receivable, (b) the source of a receivable, and (c) the expected length of time to maturity or collection.

2. (a) Describe the methods for establishing and maintaining an allowance for doubtful accounts. (b) How would the percentages used in estimating uncollectible accounts be determined under each of the methods?

3. In accounting for uncollectible accounts receivable, why is the allowance method, rather than the direct write-off method, required by generally accepted accounting principles?

4. An analysis of the accounts receivable balance of $8,702 on the records of Jorgenson, Inc. on December 31 reveals the following:

Accounts from sales of last three months (appear to be fully collectible)	$7,460
Accounts from sales prior to October 1 (of doubtful value)	1,312
Accounts known to be worthless	320
Dishonored notes charged back to customers' accounts	800
Credit balances in customers' accounts	1,190

(a) What adjustments are required?

(b) How should the various balances be shown on the balance sheet?

5. In what section of the income statement would you report (a) doubtful accounts expense, (b) sales discounts?

6. How are attitudes regarding the financing of accounts receivable changing? Why do you think this is so?

7. Explain the difference between the general assignment of accounts receivable and specific assignment of accounts receivable with regard to (a) collateral and (b) disclosure on financial statements.

8. (a) Distinguish between the practices of (1) assignment of accounts receivable, (2) transfer of accounts receivable with recourse, and (3) factoring accounts receivable. (b) Describe the accounting procedures to be followed in each case.

9. According to FASB Statement No. 77, what three conditions must be met to record the transfer of receivables with recourse as a sale?

10. The Bockweg Co. enters into a continuing agreement with Goessling Financial Services, whereby the latter company buys without recourse all of the trade receivables as they arise and assumes all credit and collection

functions. (a) Describe the advantages that may accrue to Bockweg Co. as a result of the factoring agreement. (b) Are there any disadvantages? Explain.

11. Comment on the statement, "There is no such thing as a non-interest-bearing note."

12. (a) When should a note receivable be recorded at an amount different from its face amount? (b) Describe the procedures employed in accounting for the difference between a note's face amount and its recorded value.

13. What is meant by imputing a rate of interest? How is such a rate determined?

14. The Lambert Optical Co. discounts at 20% the following three notes at the Security First Bank on July 1 of the current year. Compute the proceeds on each note, rounding amounts to the nearest dollar.

    (a) A 90-day, 13% note receivable for $24,000 dated June 1.

    (b) A 6-month, 11% note receivable for $16,000 dated May 13.

    (c) Its own 4-month note payable dated July 1 with face value of $8,000 and no stated interest rate.

15. Distinguish between accounting procedures for (a) a note receivable discounted with recourse that is subsequently dishonored, and (b) a note receivable discounted without recourse that is subsequently dishonored.

16. Identify alternative methods for presenting information on the balance sheet relating to (a) notes receivable discounted, and (b) assigned accounts receivable.

Discussion Cases

Case 8-1 (Accounting for uncollectibles)

During the audit of accounts receivable of Montana Company, the new CEO, Joe Frisco, asked why the company had debited the current year's expense for doubtful accounts on the assumption that some accounts will become uncollectible next year. Frisco believes that the financial statements should be based on verifiable, objective evidence. In his opinion it would be more objective to wait until specific accounts become uncollectible before the expense is recorded. What accounting issues are involved? Which method of accounting for uncollectible accounts would you recommend and why?

Case 8-2 (Accounts receivable as a source of cash)

Assume you are the treasurer for Fullmer Products Inc., and one of your responsibilities is to ensure that the company always takes available cash discounts on purchases. The corporation needs $150,000 within one week in order to take advantage of current cash discounts. The lending officer at the bank insists on adequate collateral for a $150,000 loan. For various reasons, your plant assets are not available as collateral, but your accounts receivable balance is $205,000. What alternatives would you consider for obtaining the necessary cash?

Case 8-3 (Selling receivables instead of merchandise)

The following excerpts are from an article printed in the *Wall Street Journal.*

Sears, Roebuck & Co. said it arranged to sell $550 million of customer accounts receivable to a group of 16 institutional investors headed by Continental Illinois National Bank & Trust Co.

Under the plan, the investors will assume ownership of the receivables, representing about 8% of Sears' total receivables outstanding as well as additions resulting from new purchases. The receivables will be sold to the institutional investors without recourse. And they will receive subsequent finance charge income on the accounts.

Edward R. Telling, Sears chairman, said the agreement calls for the sale by Sears of additional receivables each month with the total to be sold expected to reach $625 million by February 1, 1979. Subject to further negotiations, the total could reach $1 billion by 1983, he added.

The initial $550 million will be sold at 99.015% of face value with Sears receiving an administrative fee from the institutional buyers for handling the accounts. Initially, the fee will equal 5.62% of the unpaid balance.

What aspects appear to be unique in this actual example of the sale of receivables?

Exercises   **Exercise 8-1   (Classifying receivables)**

Classify each of the items listed below as:

A. Accounts Receivable
B. Notes Receivable
C. Trade Receivable
D. Nontrade Receivable
E. Other (Indicate nature of item)

Since the classifications are not mutually exclusive, more than one classification may be appropriate. Also indicate whether the item would normally be reported as a current or non-current asset assuming a 6-month operating cycle.

1. MasterCard or Visa credit card sale of merchandise to customer.
2. Overpayment to supplier for inventory purchased on account.
3. Insurance claim on automobile accident.
4. Charge sale to regular customer.
5. Advance to sales manager.
6. Interest due on 5-year note from company president.
7. Acceptance of 3-year note on sale of land held as investment.
8. Acceptance of 6-month note for past due account arising from the sale of inventory.
9. Eight-month subscription for the sale of common stock.
10. Claim for a tax refund from last year.
11. Prepaid insurance—four months remaining in the policy period.
12. Overpayment by customer of an account receivable.

Exercise 8-2   (Computing the accounts receivable balance)

The following information, pertaining to the Jumbo Company's first year of operations, is to be used in testing the accuracy of Accounts Receivable, which has a balance of $21,000 at December 31, 1991.

(a) Collections from customers, $72,000
(b) Merchandise purchased, $91,000
(c) Ending merchandise inventory, $26,000
(d) Goods sell at 50% above cost
(e) All sales are on account

Compute the balance that Accounts Receivable should show and determine the amount of any shortage or overage.

Exercise 8-3   (Recording credit card sales)

Sue Milano owns a gift shop at the airport. She accepts only cash or Visa and MasterCard credit cards. During the last month the gift shop had a total of $76,000 in sales. Of this amount 75% were credit card sales. The bank charges a 3% fee on net credit card sales. Make the monthly summary entry to reflect the above transactions.

Exercise 8-4   (Estimating doubtful accounts)

Accounts Receivable of the Fakler Manufacturing Co. on December 31, 1991, had a balance of $200,000. The Allowance for Doubtful Accounts had a $7,500 debit balance. Sales in 1991 were $1,725,000 less sales discounts of $14,000. Give the adjusting entry for estimated doubtful accounts expense under each of the following assumptions:

(1) One half of 1% of 1991 net sales will probably never be collected.
(2) Two percent of outstanding accounts receivable are doubtful.
(3) An aging schedule shows that $9,500 of the outstanding accounts receivable are doubtful.

Exercise 8-5   (Journal entries for doubtful accounts)

Health Care Inc. had gross sales of $155,000 during 1991, 30% of which were on credit. Accounts receivable outstanding at December 31, 1991, totaled $2,800, and the allowance for doubtful accounts had a $200 debit balance. Cash discounts taken by credit customers who paid within the discount period amounted to $12,000. $2,000 of merchandise was returned by dissatisfied customers, 30% of which were by credit customers.

Give the adjusting entry for doubtful accounts expense, assuming:

(1) 1% of net credit sales will be uncollectible.
(2) 2½% of current accounts receivable are doubtful.   270

Exercise 8-6   (Estimating doubtful accounts—percentage of sales method)

Prior to 1991, Jenkins, Inc. followed the percentage-of-sales method of estimating doubtful accounts. The following data are gathered by the accounting department:

	1988	1989	1990	1991
Total sales	$1,050,000	$2,100,000	$3,600,000	$6,300,000
Credit sales	600,000	960,000	1,950,000	3,600,000
Accounts receivable (end-of-year balance)	186,000	234,000	360,000	750,000
Allowance for doubtful accounts (end-of-year credit balance)	3,000	18,000	12,000	66,000
Accounts written off	27,000	6,000	42,000	9,000

(1) What amount was debited to expense for 1989, 1990, and 1991?

(2) Compute the balance in the valuation account at the beginning of 1988 assuming there has been no change in the percentage of sales used over the four-year period.

(3) What explanation can be given for the fluctuating amount of write-off?

(4) Why do the actual write-offs fail to give the correct charge to expense?

▌▌▌ Exercise 8-7   (Aging accounts receivable)

Blanchard Company's accounts receivable subsidiary ledger reveals the following information:

Customer	Account Balance December 31, 1991	Invoice Amounts and Dates	
Allison, Inc.	$ 8,795	$3,500	12/6/91
		5,295	11/29/91
Banks Bros.	5,230	3,000	9/27/91
		2,230	8/20/91
Barker & Co.	7,650	5,000	12/8/91
		2,650	10/25/91
Marrin Co.	11,285	5,785	11/17/91
		5,500	10/9/91
Ring, Inc.	7,900	4,800	12/12/91
		3,100	12/2/91
West Corp.	4,350	4,350	9/12/91

Blanchard Company's receivable collection experience indicates that, on the average, losses have occurred as follows:

Age of Accounts	Uncollectible Percentage
0-30 days	.7%
31-60 days	1.4%
61-90 days	3.5%
91-120 days	10.2%
121 days and over	60.0%

The Allowance for Doubtful Accounts credit balance on December 31, 1991, was $2,245 before adjustment.

(1) Prepare an accounts receivable aging schedule.

(2) Using the aging schedule from part (1), compute the Allowance for Doubtful Accounts balance as of December 31, 1991.

(3) Prepare the end-of-year adjusting entry.

(4) (a) Where accounts receivable are few in number, such as in this exercise, what are some possible weaknesses in estimating doubtful accounts by the aging method? (b) Would the other methods of estimating doubtful accounts be subject to these same weaknesses? Explain.

Exercise 8-8   (Analysis of allowance for doubtful accounts)

The Transtech Publishing Company follows the procedure of debiting Doubtful Accounts Expense for 2% of all new sales. Sales for four consecutive years and year-end allowance account balances were as follows:

Year	Sales	Allowance for Doubtful Accounts End-of-Year Credit Balance
1988	$2,100,000	$21,500
1989	1,975,000	35,500
1990	2,500,000	50,000
1991	2,350,000	66,000

(1) Compute the amount of accounts written off for the years 1989, 1990, and 1991.

(2) The external auditors are concerned with the growing amount in the allowance account. What action do you recommend the auditors take?

Exercise 8-9   (Accounts receivable as a source of cash)

The Alpha Corporation decides to use accounts receivable as a basis for financing. Its current position is as follows:

Accounts receivable	$80,000	Cash overdraft	$	400
Inventories	81,000	Accounts payable		57,500

Prepare a statement of its current position, assuming cash is obtained as indicated in each case below:

(1) Cash of $60,000 is borrowed on short-term notes and $35,000 is applied to the payment of creditors; accounts of $70,000 are assigned to secure the loan.

(2) Cash of $60,000 is advanced to the company by Beta Finance Co., the advance representing 80% of accounts transferred on a recourse basis. (Assume the transfer meets the FASB conditions to be accounted for as a sale.)

(3) Cash of $60,000 is received on factoring of $78,000 of accounts receivable.

Exercise 8-10   (Accounting for a non-interest-bearing note)

Zobell Corporation sells equipment with a book value of $8,000, receiving a non-interest-bearing note due in three years with a face amount of $10,000. There is no established market value for the equipment. The interest rate on similar obligations is estimated at 12%. Compute the gain or loss on the sale and the discount on notes receivable, and make the necessary entry to record the sale. Also, make the entries to record the amortization of the discount at the end of the first, second, and third year using effective-interest amortization. (Round to the nearest dollar.)

Exercise 8-11   (Accounting for an interest-bearing note)

High Country, Inc. purchased inventory costing $50,000. Terms of the purchase were 5/10; n/30. In order to take advantage of the cash discount, High Country borrowed $45,000 from Downtown 1st National, signing a 2-month, 12% note. The bank requires monthly interest payments. Make the entries to record: (1) The initial purchase of inventory on account; (2) the payment to the supplier within the discount period; (3) the loan from the bank; (4) the first month's payment to the bank; and (5) the second and final payment to the bank.

Exercise 8-12   (Discounting notes—computations)

On December 21, the following notes are discounted by the bank at 15%. Determine the cash proceeds, rounded to the nearest dollar, from discounting each note.

(1) 30-day, $4,500, non-interest-bearing note dated December 15.
(2) 60-day, $3,380, 9% note dated December 1.
(3) 60-day, $15,000, 13% note dated November 6.
(4) 90-day, $6,775, 10% note dated November 24.

Exercise 8-13   (Accounting for notes receivable discounted)

Tandy Company accepted a $20,000, 90-day, 12% interest-bearing note dated September 1, 1991, from a customer for the sale of a piece of machinery. The machinery cost $25,000 and was 50% depreciated. On October 15, 1991, Tandy discounted the note, with recourse, at First National Bank at a 15% discount rate. The customer paid the note at maturity. Make the entries necessary to record the above transactions on Tandy Company's books. Assume the transfer of the note to the bank does not meet FASB criteria for recording as a sale. (Round amounts to the nearest dollar.)

Exercise 8-14   (Accounting for notes receivable discounted)

S. Atwater received from K. Rogers, a customer, a 90-day, 12% note for $8,000, dated June 6, 1991. On July 6, Atwater discounted the note, with recourse, at 15% and recorded the discounting as a sale in accordance with FASB Statement No. 77. The note was not paid at maturity, and the bank charged Atwater with protest fees of $25 in addition to the maturity value of the note. On September 28, 1991, the note was collected by Atwater with interest at 15% from the maturity date to the date of collection. What entries would appear on Atwater's books as a result of the foregoing? (Round amounts to the nearest dollar.)

Exercise 8-15   (Discounting a note receivable)

On June 1, 1991, Flint Company received a $5,200, 90-day, 11% interest-bearing note from a customer on an overdue account receivable. Flint discounted the note, with recourse, immediately at State Bank at a discount rate of 15%. The discounting transaction did not meet FASB criteria for recording as a sale. At the date of maturity the bank notified Flint that the note had not been paid and that the amount of the note plus a $25 protest fee had been charged to its account. Flint is unable to collect from the customer. (1) How much money will Flint receive upon discounting the note? (2) What is the effective rate of interest the bank will earn on the note? (3) Prepare the journal entries to record the events described above. (Round amounts to the nearest dollar).

Problems   **Problem 8-1   (Journal entries and balance sheet presentation)**

The balance sheet for the Itex Corporation on December 31, 1990, includes the following receivables balances:

Notes receivable (including notes discounted with recourse, $15,500)		$36,500
Accounts receivable	$85,600	
Less allowance for doubtful accounts	4,150	81,450
Interest receivable		525

Current liabilities reported in the December 31, 1990 balance sheet included:

Obligation on discounted notes receivable	$15,500

Transactions during 1991 included the following:

(a) Sales on account were $767,000.

(b) Cash collected on accounts totaled $576,500, which included accounts of $93,000 on which cash discounts of 2% were allowed.

(c) Notes received in settlement of accounts totaled $82,500.

(d) Notes receivable discounted as of December 31, 1990, were paid at maturity with the exception of one $3,000 note on which the company had to pay the bank $3,090, which included interest and protest fees. It is expected that recovery will be made on this note early in 1992.

(e) Customers' notes of $60,000 were discounted with recourse during the year, proceeds from their transfer being $58,500. (All discounting transactions were recorded as loans.) Of this total, $48,000 matured during the year without notice of protest.

(f) Customers' accounts of $8,720 were written off during the year as worthless.

(g) Recoveries of doubtful accounts written off in prior years were $2,020.

(h) Notes receivable collected during the year totaled $27,000 and interest collected was $2,450.

(i) On December 31, accrued interest on notes receivable was $630.

(j) Uncollectible accounts are estimated to be 5% of the December 31, 1991, Accounts Receivable balance.

(k) Cash of $35,000 was borrowed from the bank, accounts receivable of $40,000 being pledged on the loan. Collections of $19,500 had been made on these receivables (included in the total given in transaction [b]) and this amount was applied on December 31, 1991, to payment of accrued interest on the loan of $600, and the balance to partial payment of the loan.

Instructions:

1. Prepare journal entries summarizing the transactions and information given above.

2. Prepare a summary of current receivables for balance sheet presentation.

Problem 8-2   (Accounting for receivables—journal entries)

The following transactions affecting the accounts receivable of Olympic Corporation took place during the year ended January 31, 1991:

Sales (cash and credit)	$591,050
Cash received from credit customers (customers who paid $298,900 took advantage of the discount feature of the corporation's credit terms 2/10, n/30)	302,755
Cash received from cash customers	205,175
Accounts receivable written off as worthless	4,955
Credit memoranda issued to credit customers for sales returns and allowances	56,275
Cash refunds given to cash customers for sales returns and allowances	16,972
Recoveries on accounts receivable written off as uncollectible in prior periods (not included in cash amount stated above)	10,615

The following two balances were taken from the January 31, 1990 balance sheet:

| Accounts receivable | $95,842 |
| Allowance for doubtful accounts | 9,740 (credit) |

The corporation provides for its net uncollectible account losses by crediting Allowance for Doubtful Accounts for 1½% of net credit sales for the fiscal period.

Instructions:

1. Prepare the journal entries to record the transactions for the year ended January 31, 1991.
2. Prepare the adjusting journal entry for estimated uncollectible accounts on January 31, 1991.

Problem 8-3 (Estimating doubtful accounts expense: sales method vs. receivables method)

During 1991, Lacee Enterprises had gross sales of $247,000. At the end of 1991, Lacee had accounts receivables of $83,000, and a credit balance of $5,600 in the Allowance for Doubtful Accounts. Lacee has used the percent of gross sales method to estimate the Allowance for Doubtful Accounts Expense. For the past several years, the amount estimated to be uncollectible has been 3%.

Instructions:

1. Using the percent of gross sales method, estimate the doubtful accounts expense and make any necessary adjusting entries.
2. Assuming that 6% of receivables are estimated to be uncollectible and that Lacee decides to use the percent of receivables method to estimate doubtful accounts expense, estimate the doubtful accounts expense and make any adjusting entries.
3. Which of the two methods more accurately reflects the net realizable value of receivables? Explain.

III Problem 8-4 (Estimating uncollectible accounts by aging receivables)

Rainy Day Company, a wholesaler, uses the aging method to estimate bad debt losses. The following schedule of aged accounts receivable was prepared at December 31, 1991.

Age of Accounts	Amount
0-30 days	$561,600 ,38
31-60 days	196,100
61-90 days	88,400
91-120 days	18,500
More than 120 days	9,600
	$874,200

The following schedule shows the year-end receivables balances and uncollectible accounts experience for the previous five years:

Loss Experience—Percent of Uncollectible Accounts

Year	Year-End Receivables	0-30 days	31-60 days	61-90 days	91-120 days	Over 120 days
1990	$780,700	.5%	1.0%	10.2%	49.1%	78.2%
1989	750,400	.4	1.1	10.0	51.2	77.3
1988	681,400	.6	1.2	11.0	51.7	79.0
1987	698,200	.5	.9	10.1	52.3	78.5
1986	723,600	.4	1.0	8.9	49.2	77.6

The unadjusted Allowance for Doubtful Accounts balance on December 31, 1991, is $32,796.

Instructions: Compute the correct balance for the allowance account based on the average loss experience for the last five years and prepare the appropriate end-of-year adjusting entry.

Problem 8-5   (Accounting for assignment of specific accounts receivable)

On July 1, 1991, Balmforth Company assigns specific receivables totaling $200,000 to Rocky Mountain Bank as collateral on a $150,000, 16% note. Balmforth will continue to collect the assigned receivables. Besides the interest on the note, Rocky Mountain also receives a 2% finance charge, deducted in advance on the $150,000 value of the note. Additional information for Balmforth Company is as follows:

(a) July collections amounted to $145,000, less cash discounts of $750.
(b) On August 1, paid the bank the amount owed for July collections plus accrued interest on note to August 1.
(c) Balmforth collected the remaining assigned accounts during August except for $550 written off as uncollectible.
(d) On September 1, paid bank the remaining amount owed plus accrued interest.

Instructions: Prepare the journal entries necessary to record the above information on the books of both Balmforth Company and Rocky Mountain Bank.

Problem 8-6   (Assigning and factoring accounts receivable)

During its second year of operations, Shank Corporation found itself in financial difficulties. Shank decided to use its accounts receivable as a means of obtaining cash to continue operations. On July 1, 1991, Shank factored $75,000 of accounts receivable for cash proceeds of $69,500. On December 27,

1991, Shank assigned the remainder of its accounts receivable, $250,000 as of that date, as collateral on a $125,000, 12% annual interest rate loan from Sandy Finance Company. Shank received $125,000 less a 2% finance charge. Additional information is as follows:

Allowance for Doubtful Accounts, 12/31/91	$3,200 (credit)
Estimated uncollectibles, 12/31/91	3% of Accounts Receivable
Accounts Receivable (not including fac-tored and assigned accounts) 12/31/91	$50,000

None of the assigned accounts had been collected by the end of the year.

Instructions:

1. Prepare the journal entries to record the receipt of cash from (a) factoring and (b) general assignment of the accounts receivable.
2. Prepare the journal entry necessary to record the adjustment to Allowance for Doubtful Accounts.
3. Prepare the accounts receivable section of Shank's balance sheet as it would appear after the above transactions.
4. What entry would be made on Shank's books when the factored accounts have been collected?

Problem 8-7   (Discounting notes)

Dival Marketing Corporation completed the following transactions, among others:

May 5 Received a $5,000, 60-day, 10% note dated May 5 from R. D. Spears, a customer.

24 Received an $1,800, 90-day, non-interest-bearing note dated May 23 from B. Collins as settlement for unpaid balance of $1,752.

25 Had Spears' note discounted at the bank at 13%.

June 7 Had Collins' note discounted at the bank at 15%.

25 Received from J. L. Smith, a customer, a $7,000, 90-day, 12% note dated June 5, payable to J. L. Smith and signed by the Racine Corp. Upon endorsement, gave the customer credit for the maturity value of the note less discount at 13%.

29 Received a $3,500, 60-day, 9% note dated June 29 from B. Grady, a customer.

July 5 Received notice from the bank that Spears' note was not paid at maturity. Protest fees of $15 were charged by the bank.

21 Received payment from Spears on the dishonored note, including interest at 16% on the balance from maturity date to payment date.

Instructions:

1. Give the journal entries to record the above transactions. Assume notes are discounted with recourse and do not meet the FASB criteria for recording as a sale. (Show data used in calculations with each entry; round to the nearest dollar.)
2. Give the adjusting entries required on July 31.

Problem 8-8   (Accounting for discounted notes)

The following transactions were completed by M. D. Ellis over a three-month period:

Nov. 10 Received from G. R. Kack, a customer, a $5,000, 60-day, 9% note dated Nov. 9.

11 Received from M. C. Leckner on account, a $2,100, 60-day, 12% note dated Nov. 10.

20 Discounted Leckner's note, without recourse, at the bank at 11%.

24 Discounted Kack's note, with recourse, at the bank at 10%.

Dec. 3 Received a $2,950, 30-day, non-interest-bearing note dated Dec. 1 from M. Ichtemple, crediting Ichtemple's account at face value.

7 Discounted Ichtemple's note, with recourse, at the bank at 12%.

28 Received from S. E. Dillhunt, a $500, 90-day, 12% note dated Dec. 14 and made by Bell Realty Inc. Gave the customer credit for the maturity value of the note less discount at 10%.

29 Received a $4,000, 10-day, 8% note dated Dec. 29 from M. L. Reinhard, a customer.

Jan. 10 Received notice from the bank that Kack's note was not paid at maturity. A protest fee of $15 was charged by the bank.

22 Received a $25,000, 120-day, 9% note dated Jan. 22 from V. M. Cherry, a customer.

28 Received payment on Reinhard's note, including interest at 10%, the legal rate, on the face value from the maturity date.

Instructions:

1. Give the entries to record the preceding transactions. Assume that notes discounted with recourse do not meet FASB criteria for recording as a sale. (Show data used in calculations with each entry; round amounts to nearest dollar.)

2. Give the necessary adjusting entries on January 31. Assume all notes discounted are paid when due unless otherwise indicated.

Problem 8-9   (Discounting notes with and without recourse)

Ladd, Inc. has $162,000 of accounts receivable on July 1, 1990. On that date, Ladd accepts a one year, $27,000, 11% note from Travis Corporation in settlement of Travis' $27,000 accounts receivable balance. The note and interest are due June 30, 1991.

Additional information:

1. On November 30, 1990, Ladd discounts the note with First Valley National Bank at 12% interest.

2. On June 30, 1991, Travis Corporation dishonors the note and the bank collects the maturity value plus a $150 protest fee from Ladd.

3. On August 31, 1991, Travis pays the amount outstanding, including interest since the dishonor date at 11%.

Instructions:

1. Prepare the necessary journal entries assuming the note is considered a borrowing with recourse. (Round to the nearest dollar and compute interest using months rather than days.)

2. Prepare the necessary journal entries assuming the note is discounted without recourse. (Round to the nearest dollar and compute interest using months rather than days.)

Problem 8-10 (Accounting for non-interest-bearing note)

On January 1, 1990, Cache Valley Realty sold a tract of land to three doctors as an investment. The land, purchased ten years ago, was carried on Cache Valley's books at a value of $110,000. Cache Valley received a non-interest-bearing note for $220,000 from the doctors. The note is due December 31, 1991. There is no readily available market value for the land, but the current market rate of interest for comparable notes is 12%.

Instructions:

1. Give the journal entry to record the sale of land on Cache Valley's books.
2. Prepare a schedule of discount amortization for the note with amounts rounded to the nearest dollar.
3. Give the adjusting entries to be made at the end of 1990 and 1991 to record the effective interest earned.

Problem 8-11 (Non-interest-bearing note)

On January 1, 1990, the Denver Company sold land which originally cost $400,000 to the Boise Company. Boise gave Denver a $600,000, non-interest-bearing note payable in six equal annual installments of $100,000, with the first payment due and paid on December 31, 1990. There was no established exchange price for the property and the note has no ready market. The prevailing rate of interest for a note of this type is 12%.

Instructions:

1. Prepare a schedule computing the balance in Denver's net receivable (face amount of note less unamortized discount) from Boise at December 31, 1991, based on the above facts. Show supporting computations in good form.
2. Give the entries required on Denver's books for the life of the note.

(AICPA adapted)

Problem 8-12 (Factoring receivables)

Freemont Factors Inc. was incorporated December 31, 1990. The capital stock of the company consists of 200,000 shares of $10 par value common, all of which were sold at par. The company was organized for the purpose of factoring the accounts receivable of various businesses requiring this service.
Freemont Factors Inc. charges a commission to its clients of 15% of all receivables factored and assumes all credit risks. Besides the commission, an additional 10% of gross receivables is withheld on all purchases and is credited to Client Retainer. This retainer is used for merchandise returns, etc., made by customers of the clients for which a credit memo would be due. Payments are made to the clients by Freemont Factors Inc. at the end of each month to adjust the retainer so that it equals 10% of the unpaid receivables at month end.

Based on the collection experience of other factoring companies in this area, officials of Freemont Factors Inc. have decided to make monthly provisions to Allowance for Doubtful Accounts based on 2% of all receivables purchased. The company also decided to recognize commission revenue on only the factored receivables which have been collected; however, for bookkeeping simplicity, all commissions are originally credited to Commission Revenue and an adjustment is made to Unearned Commissions at the end of each quarter based on 3% of receivables then outstanding.

Operations of the company during the first quarter of 1991 resulted in the following:

Accounts receivable factored:

January	$500,000
February	400,000
March	600,000

Collections on the above receivables totaled $1,200,000.

General and administrative expenses paid during the period:

Salaries	$18,000
Office rent	9,000
Advertising	2,500
Equipment rent	6,600
Miscellaneous	4,000

On February 1, 1991, a 3-month 10% bank loan was obtained for $800,000 with interest payable at maturity.

For the first 3 months of the year, the company rented all of its office furniture and equipment; however, on March 31, 1991, it purchased various equipment on account, terms n/30, at a cost of $60,000, the liability for which had not been recorded as of March 31.

Instructions:

1. Give all entries necessary to record the above transactions and to close the books as of March 31, 1991. (Disregard all taxes.)
2. Prepare a balance sheet and an income statement as of March 31, 1991.

(AICPA adapted)

Chapter 9

Inventories—Cost Allocation and Valuation

The primary source of revenue for a nonservice enterprise is from the sale of inventory. Because there is normally a period of time that elapses between the purchase and sale of inventory, unsold inventory is frequently a significant element on the balance sheet. Sold inventory, on the other hand, is reported as cost of goods sold on the income statement. The valuation and allocation of inventory usually has a very material effect on these two primary financial statements.

The principal valuation problems for inventory relate to which costs should be included in inventory and under what circumstances a deviation from incurred cost should be used for balance sheet valuation. The marketplace generally determines the sales price of inventory held for sale. Until revenue is recognized, usually at time of sale, inventory is valued at cost. When a sale occurs, the inventory cost is allocated to cost of sales. If the inventory cost is the same for all units, the allocation presents no problems. However, if the inventory units were acquired or produced at different costs, a decision must be made as to which costs are charged to cost of goods sold and which costs remain as the valuation of the asset. If there has been a reduction in the costs of inventory, a reduced valuation for the inventory may be required.

This chapter focuses on the various components of cost that are assigned to the asset and also on a discussion of the allocation methods that are employed in practice. Some of these are unique to the United States, and have developed in the economic circumstances of changing prices and income tax laws. Chapter 10 presents some additional valuation issues relating to inventory, including the lower of cost or market rule for adjusting cost valuation downward.

Nature of Inventory

The term inventory designates goods held for sale in the normal course of business and, in the case of a manufacturer, goods in production or to be placed in production. The nature of goods classified as inventory varies widely with the nature of business activities, and in some cases includes assets not normally thought of as inventory. For example, land and buildings held for resale by a real estate firm, partially completed buildings to be sold in the future by a construction firm, and marketable securities held for resale by a stockbroker are all properly classified as inventory by the respective firms.

Inventory represents one of the most active elements in business operations, being continuously acquired or produced and resold. A large part of a company's resources is frequently invested in goods purchased or manufactured.

The term **inventory** or **merchandise inventory** is generally applied to goods held by a merchandising firm, either wholesale or retail, when such goods have been acquired in a condition for resale. The terms **raw materials, goods in process,** and **finished goods** refer to the inventories of a manufacturing enterprise. The latter items require description.

Raw Materials

Raw materials are goods acquired for use in the production process. Some raw materials are obtained directly from natural sources. More often, however, raw materials are acquired from companies and represent the finished products of the suppliers. For example, newsprint is the finished product of the paper mill but represents raw material to the printer who acquires it.

Although the term raw materials can be used broadly to cover all materials used in manufacturing, this designation is frequently restricted to materials that will be physically incorporated in the products being manufactured. The term **factory supplies**, or **manufacturing supplies,** is then used to refer to auxiliary materials, i.e., materials that are necessary in the production process but are not directly incorporated in the products. Oils and fuels for factory equipment, cleaning supplies, and similar items fall into this grouping since these items are not incorporated in a product but simply facilitate production as a whole. Raw materials directly used in the production of certain goods are frequently referred to as **direct materials**; factory supplies are referred to as **indirect materials**.

Although factory supplies may be summarized separately, they should be reported as a part of a company's inventories since they will ultimately be consumed in the production process. Supplies purchased for use in the delivery, sales, and general administrative functions of the enterprise should not be reported as part of the inventories, but as prepaid expenses.

Goods in Process

Goods in process, alternately referred to as **work in process,** consists of materials partly processed and requiring further work before they can be sold. This inventory includes three cost elements: (1) **direct materials**, (2) **direct labor**, and (3) **factory overhead** or **manufacturing overhead**. The cost of materials directly identified with the goods in production is included under (1). The cost of labor directly identified with goods in production is included under (2). The portion of factory overhead assignable to goods still in production forms the third element of cost.

Factory overhead consists of all manufacturing costs other than direct materials and direct labor. It includes factory supplies used and labor not directly identified with the production of specific products. It also includes general manufacturing costs such as depreciation, maintenance, repairs, property taxes, insurance, and light, heat, and power, as well as a reasonable share of the managerial costs other than those relating solely to the selling and administrative functions of the business.

Finished Goods Finished goods are the manufactured products awaiting sale. As products are completed, the costs accumulated in the production process are transferred from Goods in Process to the finished goods inventory account. The diagram below illustrates the basic flow of product costs through the inventory accounts of a manufacturer.

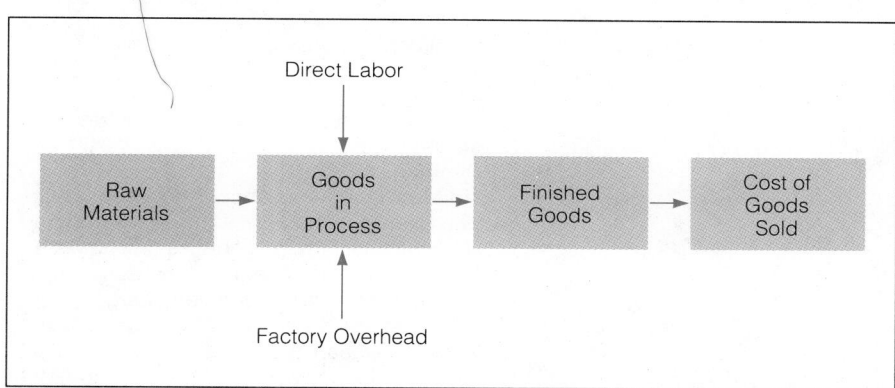

Inventory Systems Inventory records may be maintained on either a periodic or perpetual basis. A periodic inventory system requires a physical inventory, i.e., a counting, measuring, or weighing of goods, at the end of the accounting period to determine the quantities on hand. Values are then assigned to the quantities to determine the portion of the recorded costs to be carried forward. The entries to adjust the inventories under a periodic inventory system are illustrated in Chapter 3, page 77.

The perpetual inventory system requires the maintenance of records that provide a continuous summary of inventory items on hand. Individual accounts are kept for each class of goods. Inventory increases and decreases are recorded in the individual accounts, the resulting balances representing the amounts on hand. Perpetual records may be kept in terms of quantities only or in terms of both quantities and costs. In a manufacturing organization, a perpetual system applied to inventories requires recording the full movement of goods through individual accounts for raw materials, goods in process, and finished goods. To illustrate, assume the following data for the Bartlett Corporation, a manufacturing company that uses a perpetual inventory system:

Inventories, January 1, 1991:	
Finished goods	$45,000
Goods in process	29,400
Raw materials	21,350
Charges incurred during 1991:	
Raw materials purchased	107,500
Raw materials used	106,500
Direct labor	96,850
Factory overhead	134,055
Cost of goods completed in 1991	340,305
Cost of goods sold in 1991	334,305
Inventories, December 31, 1991:	
Finished goods	51,000
Goods in process	26,500
Raw materials	22,350

Summary entries to record the preceding data for 1991 would be as follows:

(a)	Raw Materials...............................	107,500	
	Accounts Payable		107,500
	To record purchases of raw materials.		
(b)	Goods in Process	106,500	
	Raw Materials................................		106,500
	To record raw materials used in production.		
(c)	Goods in Process	96,850	
	Payroll		96,850
	To distribute direct labor to goods in process.		
(d)	Factory Overhead	134,055	
	Various accounts (e.g., liabilities, accumulated depreciation, and prepaid expenses)		134,055
	To record factory overhead charges.		
(e)	Goods in Process	134,055	
	Factory Overhead		134,055
	To apply factory overhead to goods in process.		
(f)	Finished Goods	340,305	
	Goods in Process		340,305
	To transfer completed goods.		
(g)	Cost of Sales	334,305	
	Finished Goods		334,305
	To record the cost of goods sold.		

After posting, the inventory and cost of sales accounts would appear in the ledger as follows:

Raw Materials					Goods in Process		
Jan. 1	21,350	(b) 106,500		Jan. 1	29,400	(f) 340,305	
(a)	107,500	_____		(b)	106,500		
Dec. 31	22,350			(c)	96,850		
				(e)	134,055	_____	
				Dec. 31	26,500		

Finished Goods					Cost of Goods Sold		
Jan. 1	45,000	(g) 334,305		(g)	334,305		
(f)	340,305	_____					
Dec. 31	51,000						

When preparing the income statement for a manufacturing company, it is useful to prepare a separate manufacturing schedule that shows the detail supporting the cost of goods completed and transferred to Finished Goods. An illustration of this schedule, based on the preceding data and additional factory overhead detail, follows:

Bartlett Corporation
Schedule of Cost of Goods Manufactured
For Year Ended December 31, 1991

Direct materials:		
Raw materials inventory, January 1, 1991	$21,350	
Purchases	107,500	
Cost of raw materials available for use	$128,850	
Less raw materials inventory, December 31, 1991	22,350	
Raw materials used in production		$106,500
Direct labor		96,850
Factory overhead:		
Indirect labor	$ 40,000	
Factory supervision	29,000	
Depreciation expense—factory buildings and equipment	20,000	
Light, heat, and power	18,000	
Factory supplies expense	15,000	
Miscellaneous factory overhead	12,055	134,055
Total manufacturing costs		$337,405
Add goods in process inventory, January 1, 1991		29,400
		$366,805
Less goods in process inventory, December 31, 1991 . . .		26,500
Cost of goods manufactured		$340,305

Even when a perpetual system is employed, physical counts of the units on hand should be made at least once a year to confirm the balances on the books. The frequency of physical inventories will vary depending on the nature of the goods, their rate of turnover, and the degree of internal control. A plan for continuous counting of inventory items on a rotation basis is frequently employed. Variations may be found between the recorded amounts and the amounts actually on hand as a result of recording errors, shrinkage, breakage, theft, and other causes. The inventory accounts should be adjusted to agree with the physical count when a discrepancy exists. To illustrate, assume that a physical inventory of raw materials resulted in a value that is $2,500 less than the recorded inventory. The entry to adjust the inventory account would be:

Inventory Adjustment	2,500	
Raw Materials Inventory		2,500

Normal inventory adjustments for shrinkage and breakage are reported as adjustments to cost of goods sold. Abnormal shortages or thefts may be reported separately as operating expenses.

Practically all large trading and manufacturing enterprises and many relatively small organizations have adopted the perpetual inventory system as an integral part of their record keeping and internal control. This system offers a continuous check and control over inventories. Purchasing and production planning are facilitated, adequate inventories on hand are assured, and losses incurred through damage and theft are fully disclosed. The additional costs of maintaining such a system are usually well repaid by the benefits provided to management.

Items to Be Included in Inventory

As a general rule, goods should be included in the inventory of the party holding title. The passing of title is a legal term designating the point at which ownership changes. In some situations, the legal rule may be waived for practical reasons or because of certain limitations in its application. When the rule of passing title is not observed, there should be appropriate disclosure on the statements of the special practice followed and the factors supporting such practice. Application of the legal test under a number of special circumstances is described in the following paragraphs.

Goods in Transit

When terms of sale are FOB (free on board) shipping point, title passes to the buyer with the loading of goods at the point of shipment. Under these terms, application of the legal rule to a year-end shipment calls for recognition of a sale and an accompanying decrease in goods on hand on the books of the seller. Since title passes at the shipping point, goods in transit at year-end should be included in the inventory of the buyer despite the lack of physical possession. A determination of the goods in transit at year-end is made by a review of the incoming orders during the early part of the new period. The purchase records may be kept open beyond the fiscal period to permit the recognition of goods in transit as of the end of the period, or goods in transit may be recorded by means of an adjusting entry.

When terms of a sale are FOB destination, application of the legal test calls for no recognition of the transaction until goods are received by the buyer. In this case, because of the difficulties involved in ascertaining whether goods have reached their destination at year-end, the seller may prefer to ignore the legal rule and employ shipment as a basis for recognizing a sale and the accompanying inventory decrease. In some cases, title to goods may pass before shipment takes place. For example, if goods are produced on special customer order, they may be recorded as a sale as soon as they are completed and segregated from the regular inventory. If the sale is recognized upon segregation by the seller, care must be taken to exclude such goods from the seller's inventory. The buyer, on the other hand, could recognize the in-transit goods as a purchase and thus as part of its inventory.

Goods on Consignment

Goods are frequently transferred to a dealer (consignee) on a consignment basis. The shipper (consignor) retains title and includes the goods in inventory until their sale by the consignee. Consigned goods are properly reported at the sum of their cost and the handling and shipping costs incurred in their transfer to the consignee. The goods may be separately designated on the balance sheet as merchandise on consignment. The consignee does not own the consigned goods; hence neither consigned goods nor obligations for such goods are reported on the consignee's financial statements. Accounting for consignments is discussed in a later chapter. Other merchandise owned by a business but in the possession of others, such as goods in the hands of salespersons and agents, goods held by customers on approval, and goods held by others for storage, processing, or shipment, should also be shown as a part of the owner's ending inventory.

Conditional and Installment Sales

Conditional sales and installment sales contracts may provide for a retention of title by the seller until the sales price is fully recovered. Under these circumstances, the seller, who retains title, may continue to show the goods, reduced by the buyer's equity in such goods as established by collections; the buyer, in turn, can report an equity in the goods accruing through payments made. However, in the usual case when the possibilities of returns and defaults are very low, the test of passing of title should be relinquished and the transaction recorded in terms of the expected outcome: the seller, anticipating completion of the contract and the ultimate passing of title, recognizes the transaction as a regular sale involving deferred collections; the buyer, intending to comply with the contract and acquire title, recognizes the transaction as a regular purchase. Installment sales are discussed in detail in a later chapter.

Determination of Inventory Cost

After the goods to be included as inventory have been identified, the accountant must assign a dollar value to the physical units. As indicated earlier, the profession has historically favored retention of some measure of cost, generally historical cost for this purpose. Attention is directed in this chapter to identifying the elements that comprise cost, and to a consideration of how to determine the portion of historical costs to be retained as the inventory amount reported on the balance sheet and the amount to be charged against current revenues.

Items Included in Cost

Inventory costs consist of all expenditures, both direct and indirect, relating to inventory acquisition, preparation, and placement for sale. In the case of raw materials or goods acquired for resale, cost includes the purchase price, freight, receiving, storage, and all other costs incurred to the time goods are ready for sale. Certain expenditures can be traced to specific acquisitions or can be allocated to inventory items in some equitable manner. Other expenditures may be relatively small and difficult to allocate. Such items are normally excluded in the calculation of inventory cost and are thus charged in full against current revenue as period costs.

The charges to be included in the cost of manufactured products have already been mentioned. Proper accounting for materials, labor, and factory overhead items and their identification with goods in process and finished good inventories is best achieved through adoption of a cost accounting system designed to meet the needs of a particular business unit. Certain costs relating to the acquisition or the manufacture of goods may be considered abnormal and may be excluded in arriving at inventory cost. For example, costs arising from idle capacity, excessive spoilage, and reprocessing are normally considered abnormal items chargeable to current revenue. Only those portions of general and administrative costs that are clearly related to procurement or production should be included in inventory cost.

In practice, companies take different positions in classifying certain costs. For example, costs of the purchasing department, costs of accounting for manufacturing activities, and costs of pensions for production personnel may be treated as inventoriable costs by some companies and period costs by others.

Uniform Cost Capitalization

The Tax Reform Act of 1986 introduced a change in the way costs are considered for income tax purposes. Basically, the tax laws increased the types of costs that must be included as the cost of inventory. The new laws swept aside prior rules that identified costs differently for various industries and circumstances, and replaced them with one set of capitalization[1] rules applicable to all taxpayers and all types of activities. In many instances, the uniform cost capitalization rules differ from what has become generally accepted for financial accounting purposes. Many period costs, including certain general and administrative costs, are included in inventory under the uniform rules. If a company's inventory turns over quite rapidly, the effect on income of the difference between the valuation of inventory for tax purposes and for accounting purposes will not be great. However, if the turnover rate is slow, the impact on net income could be significant. The adoption of these rules is another example of temporary differences between tax and accounting income, and is subject to interperiod income tax allocation as described in Chapter 20. Because of the difference between the uniform cost-capitalization rules and generally accepted accounting principles, companies must adjust their record-keeping systems to provide dual valuation figures. This is another example of the increased complexity that exists in information systems. Further changes in the definition of taxable income can be anticipated in the future as Congress attempts to raise additional revenues without directly increasing the tax rates.

---

[1]*Capitalization* is a term frequently used in the accounting literature to describe the inclusion of a cost as an asset rather than as an expense.

Discounts as Reductions in Cost

Discounts treated as a reduction of cost in recording the acquisition of goods should similarly be treated as a reduction in the cost assigned to the inventory. Trade discounts are discounts converting a catalog price list to the prices actually charged to a buyer. The discount available may vary with such factors as the quantity purchased. Thus, trade discounts are frquently stated in a series. For example, given trade discount terms based on the quantity ordered of 30/20/10, a customer would be entitled to a discount of either 30%, 30% and 20%, or 30% and 20% and 10%, depending on the size of the order. Each successive discount is applied to the net invoice cost after deducting any earlier discounts. To illustrate, assume that an inventory item is listed in a catalog for $5,000 and a buyer is given terms of 20/10/5. The net invoice price is calculated as follows:

	Discount	Net Invoice Amount
$5,000 × 20%	$1,000	$5,000 − $1,000 = $4,000
$4,000 × 10%	$ 400	$4,000 − $ 400 = $3,600
$3,600 × 5%	$ 180	$3,600 − $ 180 = $3,420

An alternative approach to the preceding computation is to compute a composite discount rate which can be applied to the initial gross amount. The following computation could be made for the above invoice:

Discount Rate	×	Percentage of Original Invoice Cost	=	Composite Discount Rate
20%		100%		20.00%
10%		80%(100% − 20%)		8.00
5%		72%(80% − 8%)		3.60
		Composite rate		31.60%

Computation of discount: $5,000 × 31.6% = $1,580 discount
Net price = $5,000 − $1,580 = $3,420

The advantage of the composite approach is that once a composite rate is computed, it can be used directly for all purchases that have the same trade discount terms.

Cost is defined as the list price less the trade discount. No record needs to be made of the discount, and the purchases should be recorded at the net price of $3,420.

Cash discounts are discounts granted for payment of invoices within a limited time period. Business use of such discounts has declined in popularity over the past years, although they are still found in some industries. Cash discounts are usually stated as a certain percentage rate to be allowed if the invoice is paid within a certain number of days, with the full amount due within another time period. For example, 2/10, n/30 (two ten, net thirty) means that 2% is allowed as a cash discount if the invoice is paid within 10 days after the invoice date, but that the full or "net" amount is due within 30 days. Terms of 3/10 eom mean a 3% discount is allowed if the invoice is paid within 10 days after the end of the month in which the invoice is written.

Theoretically, inventory should be recorded at the discounted amount, i.e., the gross invoice price less the allowable discount. This net method reflects the fact that discounts not taken are in effect credit-related expenditures incurred for failure to pay within the discount period. They are recorded in the discounts lost account and reported as a separate item on the income statement. Discounts lost usually represent a relatively high rate of interest. To illustrate, assume a purchase of $10,000 provides for payment on a 2/10, n/30 basis. This means that if the buyer pays for the purchase by the tenth day, only $9,800 must be paid. Twenty days later the full $10,000 is due. Thus, a discount of $200 is earned for 20 days advance payment. The implicit annual interest rate in this arrangement is 36%,[2] clearly a desirable rate even if a loan is necessary to obtain the cash for the advance payment. Failure on the part of financial management to take a cash discount usually represents carelessness in considering payment alternatives.

The inefficiency of not taking cash discounts is not reflected when inventory records are maintained at the gross unit price for convenience, as is often the case. Under the gross method cash discounts taken are reflected through a contra purchases account, Purchase Discounts, when a periodic inventory system is used. With a perpetual inventory system, discounts are credited directly to Inventory.

Because of its control features, the net method of accounting for purchases is strongly preferred; however, many companies still follow the historical practice of recognizing cash discounts only as payments are made. If the payment is made in the same period the inventory is sold, use of either method will result in the same net income. However, if inventory is sold in one period and payment is made in a subsequent period, net income is affected and a proper matching of costs against revenue will not take place. If the net method is used, an adjusting entry should be made at the end of each period to record the discounts lost on unpaid invoices for which the discount period has passed.

The entries required for both the gross and net methods are illustrated at the top of page 337. A perpetual inventory method is assumed.

Purchase Returns and Allowances

Adjustments to invoice cost are also made when merchandise either is damaged or is of a lesser quality than ordered. Sometimes the merchandise is physically returned to the supplier. In other instances, a credit is allowed to the buyer by the supplier to compensate for the damage or the inferior quality of the merchandise. In either case, the liability is reduced and a

---

[2] $I = P \times R \times T$
$$\$200 = \$10,000 \times R \times 20/360$$
$$\$200 = \$556 \times R$$
$$R = 200/556$$
$$R = 36\%$$

credit is made directly to the inventory account under a perpetual inventory system, or to a contra purchases account, Purchase Returns and Allowances, under a periodic inventory system.

Transaction	Purchases Reported Net		Purchases Reported Gross	
Purchase of merchandise priced at $2,500 less trade discount of 30/20 and and a cash discount of 2% $2,500 less 30% = $1,750 $1,750 less 20% = $1,400 $1,400 less 2 % = $1,372	Inventory .... 1,372 Accounts Payable....	1,372	Inventory .... 1,400 Accounts Payable ...	1,400
(a) Assuming payment of the invoice within discount period.	Accounts Payable .... 1,372 Cash	1,372	Accounts Payable .... 1,400 Inventory .... Cash	28 1,372
(b) Assuming payment of the invoice after discount period.	Accounts Payable .... 1,372 Discounts Lost .... 28 Cash	1,400	Accounts payable .... 1,400 Cash	1,400
(c) Required adjustment at the end of the period assuming that the invoice was not paid and the discount period has lapsed.	Discounts Lost .... 28 Accounts Payable....	28	No entry required	

Traditional Historical Cost Allocation Methods

One of the more difficult issues facing the user of financial statements is understanding the effect of the allocation of specific unit prices, measured at the unit's historical cost at the time of purchase, to cost of goods sold and to inventory. Several methods have evolved to make this allocation between expense and inventory. The methods discussed in this section of the chapter are (1) **specific identification**, (2) **first-in, first-out (FIFO)**, (3) **average cost**, and (4) **last-in, first-out (LIFO)**. Each has certain characteristics that make it preferable under certain conditions. One of them, the last-in, first-out method, was specifically developed as an attempt to reduce the impact of changing prices on net income. All four methods have in common the fact that inventory cost, as defined in this chapter, is allocated between the income statement and the balance sheet. No adjustment for price changes is made to the total amount to be allocated.

Except for specific identification, all the cost methods are frequently encountered in practice. Many companies use more than one method, applying different methods to different classes of inventory. *Accounting Trends and Techniques* reported the following data regarding the inventory methods used by the 600 companies surveyed.[3]

[3]*Accounting Trends and Techniques*—1988, (New York: American Institute of Certified Public Accountants, 1988), p. 110.

Method	Number of Companies—1987
Last-in, first-out (LIFO)	393
First-in, first-out (FIFO)	392
Average cost	216
Other	49
Total	1,050

A significant increase in the number of companies using LIFO occurred in the 1970s and 1980s. A survey of LIFO users reported that of 206 respondents using LIFO, only 29 companies adopted LIFO before 1970. The other 177 adopted LIFO between 1970 and 1982.[4]

There have been few guidelines developed by the profession to assist companies in choosing among these alternative cost allocation methods. Some accountants have suggested that, conceptually, costs attach to the inventory as they are incurred and thus should follow the inventory to its disposition. This argument suggests that methods that allocate the cost of inventory sold according to the physical flow of goods would be preferred. Other writers have emphasized capital maintenance concepts and suggest the use of methods that provide for maintenance of a physical quantity of inventory before recognizing income from its sale. The following discussion of the allocation methods demonstrates how each method relates to these different viewpoints.

Specific Identification

Costs may be allocated between goods sold during the period and goods on hand at the end of the period according to the actual cost of specific units. This specific identification method requires a means of identifying the historical cost of each unit of inventory up to the time of sale. With specific identification, the flow of recorded costs matches the physical flow of goods.

The specific identificaiton method is a highly objective approach to matching historical costs with revenues. As stated in Accounting Research Study No. 13, "There appears to be little theoretical argument against the use of specific identification of cost with units of product if that method of determining inventory cost is practicable."[5] Application of this method, however, is often difficult or impossible. When inventory is composed of a great many items or identical items acquired at different times and at different prices, cost identification procedures are likely to be slow, burdensome, and costly. Furthermore, when units are identical and interchangeable, this method opens the doors to possible profit manipulation through the selection of particular units for delivery. Finally, significant changes in costs during a period may warrant charges to expense on a basis other than

---

[4]James M. Reeve and Keith G. Stanga, "Balance Sheet Impact of Using LIFO: An Empirical Study," *Accounting Horizons*, September 1987, p. 11.

[5]Horace G. Barden, *Accounting Research Study No. 13*, "The Accounting Basis of Inventories" (New York: American Institute of Certified Public Accountants, 1973) p. 83.

past identifiable costs. Interstate Bakeries Corporation uses specific identi-fication for part of its inventories as shown below.

Exhibit 9-1   **Interstate Bakeries Corporation**

	May 30, 1987	May 31, 1986
ASSETS		
Current Assets:		
Cash and short-term investments	$ 46,525,000	$ 9,332,000
Accounts and notes receivable, less allowance for doubtful accounts of $1,708,000 ($1,735,000 in 1986)	52,281,000	51,169,000
Inventories	17,817,000	15,056,000
Prepaid expenses	1,898,000	2,225,000
Recoverable federal income tax	—	2,397,000
Total current assets	$118,521,000	$ 80,179,000

NOTES TO CONSOLIDATED FINANCIAL STATEMENTS

Inventories—Inventories are stated at the lower of cost or market. Specific invoiced costs are used with respect to ingredients such as flour and sugar and average costs are used for other inventory items.

First-In, First-Out Method   The first-in, first-out (FIFO) method is based on the assumption that costs should be charged to expense (cost of goods sold) in the order in which incurred. Inventories are thus stated in terms of the most recent costs. To illustrate the application of this method, assume the following data:

Jan.	1	Inventory	200 units at $10	$ 2,000
	12	Purchase	400 units at 12	4,800
	26	Purchase	300 units at 11	3,300
	30	Puchase	100 units at 12	1,200
		Total	1,000	$11,300

A physical inventory on January 31 shows 300 units on hand. The most recent costs would be assigned to the units as follows:

Most recent purchase, Jan. 30	100 units at $12	$1,200
Next most recent purchase, Jan. 26	200 units at 11	2,200
Total	300	$3,400

If the ending inventory is recorded at $3,400, cost of goods sold is $7,900 ($11,300 − $3,400). Thus, expense is charged with the earliest costs incurred.

When perpetual inventory accounts are maintained, a form similar to that illustrated below is used to record the cost assigned to units issued and the cost relating to the goods on hand. The columns show the quantities and values of goods acquired, goods issued, and balances on hand. It should be observed that identical values for physical and perpetual inventories are obtained when FIFO is applied.

FIFO can be supported as a logical and realistic approach to the flow of costs when it is impractical or impossible to achieve specific cost identification. FIFO assumes a cost flow closely paralleling the usual physical flow of goods sold. Expense is charged with costs considered applicable to the goods actually sold; ending inventories are reported in terms of most recent costs—costs closely approximating the current value of inventories at the balance sheet date. FIFO affords little opportunity for profit manipulation because the assignment of costs is determined by the order in which costs are incurred.

COMMODITY: x (FIFO)

DATE	RECEIVED			ISSUED			BALANCE		
	Quantity	Unit Cost	Total Cost	Quantity	Unit Cost	Total Cost	Quantity	Unit Cost	Total Cost
Jan. 1							200	$10	$2,000
12	400	$12	$4,800				200	10	2,000
							400	12	4,800
16				200	$10	$2,000			
				300	12	3,600	100	12	1,200
26	300	11	3,300				100	12	1,200
							300	11	3,300
29				100	12	1,200			
				100	11	1,100	200	11	2,200
30	100	12	1,200				200	11	2,200
							100	12	1,200

Average Cost Method   Some companies value inventories using an **average cost method** that assigns the same average cost to each unit. This cost is computed using a weighted average technique for a periodic system or a moving average technique for a perpetual system.

The **weighted average technique** is based on the assumption that goods sold should be charged at an average cost, such average being influenced or *weighted* by the number of units acquired at each price. Inventories are stated at the same weighted average cost per unit. Using the cost data in the preceding section, the weighted average cost of a physical inventory of 300 units on January 31 would be as follows:

Jan.	1	Inventory	200 units at $10	$ 2,000
	12	Purchase	400 units at 12	4,800
	26	Purchase	300 units at 11	3,300
	30	Purchase	100 units at 12	1,200
		Total	1,000	$11,300

Weighted average cost $11,300 ÷ 1,000 = $11.30.
Ending inventory   300 units at $11.30 = $3,390.

The ending inventory is recorded at a cost of $3,390; cost of goods sold is $7,910 ($11,300 − $3,390), thus charging expense with a weighted average cost. The calculations above were made for costs of one month. Similar calculations could be developed for a periodic inventory system in terms of data for a quarter or for a year.

When a perpetual inventory system that records both quantities and amounts is used, a variation of the weighted average technique is required. A new weighted average amount is calculated after each new purchase, and this amount is used to cost each subsequent sale until another purchase is made. Because this method results in continuous updating of the average, it is referred to as the **moving average technique**. The use of this approach is illustrated below.

COMMODITY: X (moving average)

DATE	RECEIVED			ISSUED			BALANCE		
	Quantity	Unit Cost	Total Cost	Quantity	Unit Cost	Total Cost	Quantity	Unit Cost	Total Cost
Jan. 1							200	$10.00	$2,000
12	400	$12	$4,800				600	11.33	6,800
16				500	$11.33	$5,665	100	*11.35	1,135
26	300	11	3,300				400	11.09	4,435
29				200	11.09	2,218	200	11.09	2,217
30	100	12	1,200				300	11.39	3,417

*Increase in unit cost due to rounding.

On January 12 the new unit cost of $11.33 was found by dividing $6,800, the total cost, by 600, the number of units on hand. Then on January 16, the balance of $1,135 represented the previous balance of $6,800, less $5,665, the cost assigned to the 500 units issued on this date. New unit costs were calculated on January 26 and 30 when additional units were acquired.

With successive recalculations of cost and the use of such different costs during the period, the cost identified with the ending inventory will differ from that determined when cost is assigned to the ending inventory in terms of average cost for all goods available during the period. A physical inventory and use of the weighted average method resulted in a value for the ending inventory of $3,390; a perpetual inventory and use of the moving average method resulted in a value for the ending inventory of $3,417.

The average cost method can be supported as realistic and as paralleling the physical flow of goods, particularly where there is an intermingling of identical inventory units. Unlike the other inventory methods, the average approach provides the same cost for similar items of equal utility. The method does not permit profit manipulation. Limitations of the average method are inventory values that perpetually contain some degree of influence of earliest costs and inventory values that may lag significantly behind current prices in periods of rapidly rising or falling prices.

Last-In, First-Out Method—Specific Goods

The last-in, first-out (LIFO) method is based on the assumption that the latest costs of a specific item should be charged to cost of goods sold. Inventories are thus stated at earliest costs. Using the cost data in the preceding section, a physical inventory of 300 units on January 31 would have a cost as follows:

Earliest costs relating to goods, Jan. 1	200	units at $10	$2,000
Next earliest cost, Jan. 12	100	units at 12	1,200
Total	300		$3,200

The ending inventory is recorded at a cost of $3,200 and cost of goods sold is $8,100 ($11,300 − $3,200). Thus, expense is charged with the most recently incurred costs.

When perpetual inventories are maintained, it is necessary to calculate costs on a last-in, first-out basis using the cost data on the date of each issue as illustrated below.

COMMODITY: X (LIFO)

DATE	RECEIVED			ISSUED			BALANCE		
	Quantity	Unit Cost	Total Cost	Quantity	Unit Cost	Total Cost	Quantity	Unit Cost	Total Cost
Jan. 1							200	$10	$2,000
12	400	$12	$4,800				200	10	2,000
							400	12	4,800
16				400	$12	$4,800			
				100	10	1,000	100	10	1,000
26	300	11	3,300				100	10	1,000
							300	11	3,300
29				200	11	2,200	100	10	1,000
							100	11	1,100
30	100	12	1,200				100	10	1,000
							100	11	1,100
							100	12	1,200

It should be noted that LIFO values obtained under a periodic system will usually differ from those determined on a perpetual basis. In the example, a cost of $3,200 was obtained for the periodic inventory, whereas $3,300 was obtained when costs were calculated as goods were issued. This difference results because it was necessary to "dip into" the beginning inventory layer and charge 100 units of the beginning inventory at $10 to the issue of January 16. The ending inventory thus reflects only 100 units at the beginning unit cost.

These temporary liquidations of inventory frequently occur during the year, especially for companies with seasonal business. These liquidations cause monthly reports prepared on the LIFO basis to be unrealistic and meaningless. Because of this, most companies using LIFO maintain their internal records using other inventory methods, such as FIFO or weighted average, and adjust the statements to LIFO at the end of the year with a LIFO allowance account. Companies frequently refer to this account as the LIFO *reserve* account. Because the profession has recommended that the word *reserve* not be used for asset valuation accounts, the term allowance is used in this text. Burlington Industries, Inc. includes a note to its balance sheet that itemizes its inventories at average cost, and then includes a separate allowance account, identified as "excess of average cost over LIFO," to reduce the inventory to LIFO cost.

Exhibit 9-2   Burlington Industries, Inc.

Inventories: Inventories are valued at the lower of cost or market. Cost of substantially all components of textile inventories in the United States is determined using the dollar value Last-in, First-out (LIFO) method. All other inventories are valued principally at average cost.

Note C. Inventories

Inventories are summarized as follows (in thousands):

	1986	1985
Inventories at average cost:		
Raw materials	$ 54,124	$ 66,248
Stock in process	124,599	131,359
Produced goods	259,576	325,575
Dyes, chemicals and supplies	33,024	37,389
	471,323	560,571
Less excess of average cost over LIFO	144,037	192,241
Total	$327,286	$368,330

Assuming the allowance was used by Burlington Industries for the first time in 1985, the entry to record the allowance would be as follows:

Cost of Goods Sold	192,241	
Excess of average cost over LIFO		192,241

In 1986, the difference was less, therefore, the adjusting entry would reduce the allowance account to its new difference.

Excess of average cost over LIFO   48,204
Cost of Goods Sold   48,204

Each year, the allowance would be adjusted in this manner to properly record the LIFO inventory on the financial statements.

LIFO Conformity Rule

The LIFO inventory method was developed in the United States during the late 1930s as a method of permitting deferral of illusory inventory profits during periods of rising prices. Petition was made to Congress by companies desiring to use this method for tax purposes, and in the Revenue Act of 1938, it became an acceptable tax method. There was, however, a unique provision attached to the use of the LIFO inventory method. It has become known as the **LIFO conformity rule** and specifies that only those taxpayers who use LIFO for financial reporting purposes may use it for tax purposes. LIFO inventory is the only accounting method that must be reported the same way for tax and book purposes. In the early years, the rule was strictly applied. Companies were not permitted to report inventory values using any other method either in the body of the financial statements or in the attached notes. This provision was to avoid the implication that some value other than LIFO was really a better one. Over time, the IRS has gradually relaxed the conformity rule. In 1981, the IRS regulations were further relaxed by (1) permitting companies to provide non-LIFO disclosures such as those presented by Burlington as long as they are not presented on the face of the income statement, and (2) allowing companies to apply LIFO differently for book purposes than for tax purposes as long as they use some acceptable form of LIFO.[6] Differences between book and tax LIFO inventories arise from different definitions of "LIFO pools" or from different application of market values that are lower than LIFO cost.

Prior to the relaxation of the LIFO conformity rule, the income tax regulations became the governing rules for book purposes. The accounting standards bodies elected not to address the method except to recognize that LIFO was an acceptable inventory method.[7] Now that companies may apply LIFO differently for book and tax purposes, both the SEC and the AICPA have addressed the LIFO issue for financial statement reporting purposes. In July 1981, the SEC issued ASR No. 293 that provided guidelines for companies to follow in making supplemental non-LIFO income disclosures. They also included several examples of what they labeled inappropriate use of the LIFO method. Their concern with LIFO as applied was stated as follows:

> For too long, the application of the LIFO method for financial accounting and reporting has been unduly influenced by the tax application. Most explanations or analyses of LIFO in textbooks and articles have been oriented toward

---

[6]Treasury Decision 7756, Title 26 CFR 1.472-2(e), (Washington, D.C.: U.S. Government Printing Office, 1981).

[7]*Accounting Research Bulletin No. 43*, "Restatement and Revision of Accounting Research Bulletins" (New York: American Institute of Certified Public Accountants, 1953), Chapter 4, par. 6.

tax implications, rather than financial accounting and reporting. With few exceptions, the accounting profession has deferred to the IRS in this area; indeed many accountants appear to view IRS LIFO regulations as if they were generally accepted accounting principles ("GAAP"). The Commission disagrees with this approach and believes that since LIFO may now be applied differently for book accounting and tax accounting, it is appropriate for the current practices used in the application of LIFO to be examined.[8]

The AICPA responded to this request, and under the direction of the Accounting Standards Executive Committee, appointed a nine-person Task Force on LIFO Inventory Problems to study the area. Their study resulted in the publication in November 1984 of an Issues Paper, "Identification and Discussion of Certain Financial Accounting and Reporting Issues Concerning LIFO Inventories." The task force addressed over fifty separate issues and reported by vote their views on the topic. Although the task force did not have the power to establish definitive accounting standards, the SEC has accepted their report as authoritative pending review of this area by the FASB. Where applicable, the views of the task force will be referenced in the detailed discussion of LIFO that follows.

Specific-Goods LIFO Pools

With large and diversified inventories, application of the LIFO precedures to specific goods is extremely burdensome. Because of the complexity and cost involved, companies frequently selected only a few very important inventory items, usually raw materials, for application of the LIFO method. As a means of of simplifying the valuation process and extending its applicability to more items, an adaptation of LIFO applied to specific goods was developed and approved by the IRS. This adaptation permitted the establishment of LIFO inventory pools of substantially identical goods. At the end of a period, the quantity of items in the pool is determined, and costs are assigned to those items. Units equal to the beginning quantity in the pool are assigned the beginning unit costs. If the number of units in ending inventory exceeds the number of beginning units, the additional units are regarded as an incremental layer within the pool.

The unit cost assigned to the items in the new layer may be based on one of three measurements:

1. actual costs of earliest acquisitions within the period (LIFO),
2. the weighted average cost of acquisitions within the period, or
3. actual costs of the latest acquisitions within the period (FIFO).

Increments in subsequent periods form successive inventory layers. A decrease in the number of units in an inventory pool during a period is regarded as a reduction in the most recently added layer, then in successively

[8]*Accounting Series Release No. 293*, "The Last-In, First-Out Method of Accounting for Inventories" (Washington, D.C.: US Printing Office, 1981), section II.

lower layers, and finally in the original or base quantity. Once a specific layer is reduced or eliminated, it is not restored.

To further illustrate the LIFO valuation process, assume that a company uses three inventory pools. The changes in the pools are as listed below. The inventory calculations that follow the listing are based on the assumption that weighted average costs are used in valuing annual incremental layers.

Inventory pool increments and liquidations:

	Inventory Pool A	Inventory Pool B	Inventory Pool C
Inv., Dec. 31, 1990	3,000 @ $6	3,000 @ $5	2,000 @ $10
Purchases—1991	3,000 @ $7	2,000 @ $6	3,000 @ $11
	1,000 @ $9		
Total available for sale	7,000	5,000	5,000
Sales—1991	3,000	1,000	3,500
Inv., Dec. 31, 1991	4,000	4,000	1,500
Purchases—1992	1,000 @ $8	2,000 @ $6	3,000 @ $11
	3,000 @ $10		
Total available for sale	8,000	6,000	4,500
Sales—1992	3,500	2,500	2,000
Inv., Dec. 31, 1992	4,500	3,500	2,500

Inventory valuations using specific-goods LIFO pools:

	Inventory Pool A		Inventory Pool B		Inventory Pool C	
Inv., Dec. 31, 1990	3,000 @ $6	$18,000	3,000 @ $5	$15,000	2,000 @ $10	$20,000
Inv., Dec. 31, 1991	3,000 @ $6	$18,000	3,000 @ $5	$15,000	1,500 @ $10	$15,000
	1,000 @ $7.50[1]	7,500	1,000 @ $6	6,000		
	4,000	$25,500	4,000	$21,000	1,500	$15,000
Inv., Dec. 31, 1992	3,000 @ $6	$18,000	3,000 @ $5	$15,000	1,500 @ $10	$15,000
	1,000 @ $7.50	7,500	500 @ $6	3,000	1,000 @ $11	11,000
	500 @ $9.50[2]	4,750				
	4,500	$30,250	3,500	$18,000	2,500	$26,000

[1]Cost of units acquired in 1991, $30,000, divided by number of units acquired, 4,000, or $7.50.
[2]Cost of units acquired in 1992, $38,000, divided by number of units acquired, 4,000, or $9.50.

The layer process for LIFO inventories may be further illustrated as shown on page 347.

A new layer was added to Inventory Pool A each year. Previously established layers were reduced in 1992 for Inventory Pool B and in 1991 for Inventory Pool C.

Last-In, First-Out Method—Dollar Value

Even the grouping of substantially identical items into quantity pools does not produce all the benefits desired from the use of the LIFO method. Technological changes sometimes introduce new products thus requiring the elimination of inventory in old pools, and requiring the establishment of new pools for the new product that no longer qualifies as being substantially identical. For example, the introduction of synthetic fabrics to replace cotton meant that "cotton" pools were eliminated and new "synthetic fabric" pools established. This change resulted in the loss of

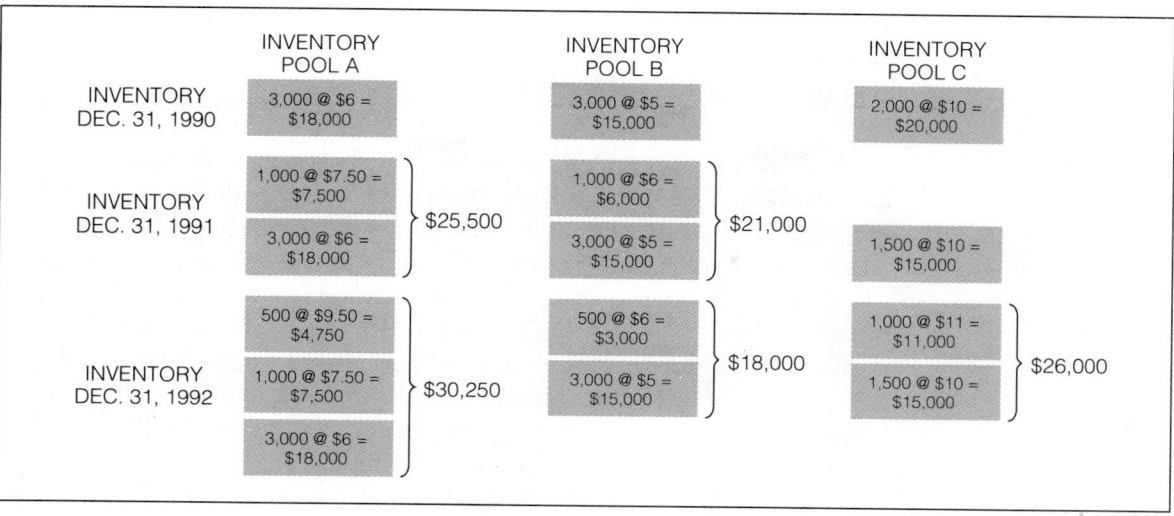

lower LIFO bases by companies changing the type of fabrics they used. To overcome this type of problem and to further simply the clerical work involved, the **dollar-value LIFO inventory method** was developed.[9] Under this method, the unit of measurement is the dollar rather than the quantity of goods. All similar items, such as all raw materials for a given line of business, are grouped into a pool, and layers are determined based on total dollar changes. The dollar-value method has become the most widely used adaptation of the LIFO concept. In a survey of LIFO users, Reeve and Stanga found that 95% of the 206 companies responding to their survey used some version of the dollar value method.[10]

General Procedures—Dollar-Value LIFO

All goods in the inventory pool to which dollar-value LIFO is to be applied are viewed as though they are identical items. To determine if the dollar quantity of inventory has increased during the year, it is necessary to value the ending inventory in a pool at the base-year prices and compare the total with that at the beginning of the year, also valued at base-year prices. If the end-of-year inventory at base-year prices exceeds the beginning-of-year inventory at base-year prices, a new LIFO layer is created. If there has been a decrease, a LIFO layer is reduced.

The following four techniques are applied in practice to determine the ending inventory at base-year prices:

1. Double extension (100% of inventory)
2. Double extension index (sample of inventory)

---

[9]When new items are introduced, the dollar-value LIFO method does not give the same result as the specific-goods LIFO method. See D. R. Bainbridge, "Is Dollar-Value LIFO Consistent with Authoritative GAAP?" *Journal of Accounting, Auditing, and Finance* (Summer 1984), pp. 334-346, for a discussion as to why dollar-value LIFO may violate the historical cost principle and the concept of financial capital maintenance.

[10]James M. Reeve and Keith G. Stanga, "The LIFO Pooling Decision: Some Empirical Results from Accounting Practice," *Accounting Horizons*, June 1987, p. 27.

3. Link-chain index (sample of inventory)
4. Externally published index

The income tax regulations specify that the preferred technique is double extension. This technique results in a direct computation of the ending inventory at base-year prices because it requires extending *all* items in the ending inventory at both the base-year and the end-of-year prices. Because the double extension technique is time consuming when there are many inventory items, the IRS has permitted the use of an index approach to compute the ending inventory at base-year prices. The IRS has ruled that the preferred index is an internal one developed from a sample of items from the company inventory. Under certain conditions, the IRS has permitted the use of an externally published index.

In practice, most companies have adopted some form of an index method, therefore, the examples and discussion that follow are based on the use of indexes. A further discussion of different types of indexes is included in the Appendix to this chapter.

Assume the index numbers and inventories at end-of-year prices for Ahlander Wholesale Co. are as follows:

Date	Year-End Price Index[1]	Inventory at End-of-Year Prices
December 31, 1988	1.00	$38,000
December 31, 1989	1.20	54,000
December 31, 1990	1.32	66,000
December 31, 1991	1.40	56,000
December 31, 1992	1.25	55,000

[1]Many published indexes appear as percentages without decimals, e.g., 100, 120, 132, 140, 125.

The effects of adding or deleting inventory layers in this situation can be most easily observed by preparing a work sheet that includes the following steps:

1. Determine the ending inventory in the pool at year-end prices.
2. Convert the ending inventory to base-year prices using the year-end price index.
3. Determine the inventory layers in base-year dollars.
4. Adjust the inventory to dollar value LIFO layers by applying appropriate indexes to each base-year layer.

The work sheet on page 349 follows these steps and is based on the assumed data for Ahlander.

Date	Inventory at End-of-Year Prices		Year-End Price Index		Inventory at Base-Year Prices	Layers in Base-Year Prices		Incremental Layer Index		Dollar-Value LIFO Cost
December 31, 1988	$38,000	÷	1.00	=	$38,000	$38,000	×	1.00	=	$38,000
December 31, 1989	$54,000	÷	1.20	=	$45,000	$38,000	×	1.00	=	$38,000
						7,000	×	1.20	=	8,400
						$45,000				$46,400
December 31, 1990	$66,000	÷	1.32	=	$50,000	$38,000	×	1.00	=	$38,000
						7,000	×	1.20	=	8,400
						5,000	×	1.32	=	6,600
						$50,000				$53,000
December 31, 1991	$56,000	÷	1.40	=	$40,000	$38,000	×	1.00	=	$38,000
						2,000	×	1.20	=	2,400
						$40,000				$40,400
December 31, 1992	$55,000	÷	1.25	=	$44,000	$38,000	×	1.00	=	$38,000
						2,000	×	1.20	=	2,400
						4,000	×	1.25	=	5,000
						$44,000				$45,400

The following items should be observed in the example:

December 31, 1989—With an ending inventory of $45,000 in terms of base prices, the inventory has increased in 1989 by $7,000; however, the $7,000 increase is stated in terms of the base year and needs to be restated in terms of 1989 year-end prices which are 120% of the base level.

December 31, 1990—With an ending inventory of $50,000 in terms of base prices, the inventory has increased in 1990 by another $5,000; however, the $5,000 increase is stated in terms of the pricing when LIFO was adopted and needs to be restated in terms of 1990 year-end costs which are 132% of the base level.

December 31, 1991—When the ending inventory of $40,000 (expressed in base-year dollars) is compared to the beginning inventory of $50,000 (also expressed in base-year dollars), it is apparent that the inventory has been decreased by $10,000, in base-year terms. Under LIFO procedures, the decrease is assumed to take place in the most recently added layers, reducing or eliminating them. As a result, the 1990 layer, priced at $5,000 in base-year terms, is completely eliminated, and $5,000 of the $7,000 layer from 1989 is eliminated. This leaves only $2,000 of the 1989 layer, plus the base-year amount. The remaining $2,000 of the 1989 layer is multiplied by 1.20 to restate it to 1989 dollars, and is added to the base-year amount to arrive at the ending inventory amount of $40,400.

December 31, 1992—The ending inventory of $44,000 in terms of the base prices indicates an inventory increase for 1992 of $4,000; this increase requires restatement in terms of 1992 year-end prices which are 125% of the base level.

As discussed earlier, the Internal Revenue Service allows the incremental LIFO layer to be valued using FIFO, average, or LIFO costing. Thus, the incremental index used to compute the new layer may be (1) a beginning-of-year index representing costs in the order of acquisition during the year (LIFO costing); (2) an average index, based on an average purchase price during the year (average costing); or (3) a year-end index, based on the latest acquisition price (FIFO costing). [11]

When FIFO costing is used to value the incremental layer, as in the previous example, the incremental index is the same as the year-end index used to determine if a new layer exists. However, if average or LIFO costing is used to compute the new layer, the incremental index will differ from the year-end index. To illustrate, using data from the preceding example, assume that LIFO costing is used to value incremental inventory layers. The beginning-of-year indexes, representing the earliest purchases in each year, are follows:

Date	Price Index Beginning-of-Year Purchases
December 31, 1989	1.02
December 31, 1990	1.21
December 31, 1991	1.35
December 31, 1992	1.38

The computation of year-end inventories would then be made as follows:

Date	Inventory at End-of-Year Prices		Year-End Price Index		Inventory at Base-Year Prices	Layers in Base-Year Prices		Incremental Layer Index		Dollar-Value LIFO Cost
December 31, 1988	$38,000	÷	1.00	=	$38,000	$38,000	×	1.00	=	$38,000
December 31, 1989	$54,000	÷	1.20	=	$45,000	$38,000	×	1.00	=	$38,000
						7,000	×	1.02	=	7,140
						$45,000				$45,140
December 31, 1990	$66,000	÷	1.32	=	$50,000	$38,000	×	1.00	=	$38,000
						7,000	×	1.02	=	7,140
						5,000	×	1.21	=	6,050
						$50,000				$51,190
December 31, 1991	$56,000	÷	1.40	=	$40,000	$38,000	×	1.00	=	$38,000
						2,000	×	1.02	=	2,040
						$40,000				$40,040
December 31, 1992	$55,000	÷	1.25	=	$44,000	$38,000	×	1.00	=	$38,000
						2,000	×	1.02	=	2,040
						4,000	×	1.38	=	5,520
						$44,000				$45,560

In some cases, the index for the first year of the LIFO layers is not 1.00. This is especially true when an externally generated index is used. When this occurs, it is simpler to convert all inventories to a base of 1.00 rather than to use the index for the initial year of the LIFO layers. The computations are done in the same manner as in the previous example except the inventory is

[11]The Task Force on LIFO Inventory Problems considered this issue from an accounting principles standpoint and unanimously agreed that "the order of acquisition approach (LIFO costing) generally is most compatible with the LIFO objective but as a practical matter, any of the three pricing approaches consistently applied may be used for financial reporting purposes." *Issues Paper*, "Identification and Discussion of Certain Financial Accounting and Reporting Issues Concerning LIFO Inventories." (New York: American Institute of Certified Public Accountants, 1984), p. 9.

stated in terms of the base year of the index, not the first year of the inventory layers. To illustrate, assume the same facts as stated for the example on page 348 except that the base year of the external index is 1984; in 1988, the index is 1.20; and, in 1989, it is 1.44. The schedule showing the LIFO inventory computations would be modified as follows for the first two years. Note that the inventory cost is the same under either situation.

Date	Inventory at End-of-Year Prices		Year-End Price Index		Inventory at Base = 1.00 (1984 Prices)	Layers in Base = 1.00 (1984 Prices)		Incremental Layer Index		Dollar-Value LIFO Cost
December 31, 1988	$38,000	÷	1.20	=	$31,667	$31,667	×	1.20	=	$38,000
December 31, 1989	$54,000	÷	1.44	=	$37,500	$31,667	×	1.20	=	$38,000
						5,833	×	1.44	=	8,400
						$37,500				$46,400

Selection of Pools

The selection of inventory pools is critical in dollar value LIFO. A company should have a minimum number of pools to benefit most by the use of the LIFO method. For manufacturers and processors, **natural business unit pools** are recommended. If it can be shown that a business has only one natural business unit, one pool may be used for all its inventory, including raw materials, goods in process, and finished goods. If, however, a business enterprise is composed of more than one natural business unit, more than one pool will be required. If the company maintains separate divisions for internal management purposes, has distinct production facilities and processes, or maintains separate income records for different units, more than one business unit pool is inferred. The Income Tax Regulations give the following example of a company with more than one natural business unit pool:

> A corporation manufactures, in one division, automatic clothes washers and driers of both commercial and domestic grade as well as electric ranges, mangles, and dishwashers. The corporation manufactures, in another division, radios and television sets. The manufacturing facilities and processes used in manufacturing the radios and television sets are distinct from those used in manufacturing the automatic clothes washers, etc. Under these circumstances, the enterprise would consist of two business units and two pools would be appropriate, one consisting of all of the LIFO inventories entering into the manufacture of clothes washers and driers, electric ranges, mangles, and dishwashers and the other consisting of all of the LIFO inventories entering into the production of radio and television sets.[12]

A manufacturer or processor may choose to use **multiple pools** rather than include all inventory in natural business units. Each pool should consist of inventory items that are substantially similar, including raw materials.

Pools for wholesalers, retailers, etc., are usually defined by major lines, types, or classes of goods. The departments of a retail store are examples of

---

[12]*Ibid.*, Sec. 1.472.8(b) (2) (ii).

separate pools for these entities. The number and propriety of inventory pools is reviewed periodically by the IRS, and continued use of established pools is subject to the results of the evaluation.

Although it is not necessary for companies to use the same pools for tax and accounting purposes, Reeve and Stanga found that most companies do, even when the IRS regulations require more pools than might be necessary for accounting purposes.[13] In some cases, companies have increased the number of pools to increase income. For example, in 1982 Stauffer Chemical Co. increased its number of LIFO pools for accounting purposes from 8 to 280. In general, the fewer the pools, the lower the ending inventory due to the ability to retain older costs in inventory layers through substitution of decreased inventory for one product with an increase in another. As the number of pools increase, more dipping into layers occurs with a resulting increase in income. In Stauffer's case, the increase in pools resulted in an increase of $16,515,000 in net income, or 13% of earnings.[14] The SEC objected to the change and, in 1984, required Stauffer to restate its financial statements using fewer pools.

The Economic Recovery Tax Act of 1981, and later the Tax Reform Act of 1986, simplified the selection and use of pools for smaller businesses. Any business with average gross receipts not in excess of $5 million for the three most recent taxable years may group their pools in accordance with the 11 major categories of the Consumer Price Index (CPI) or the 15 major categories of the Producer Price Indexes. The company may then use the published index for the category into which its goods are classified to determine its LIFO inventory values.

Comparison of Cost Allocation Methods

In using first-in, first-out, inventories are reported on the balance sheet at or near current costs. With last-in, first-out, inventories not changing significantly in quantity are reported at more or less fixed amounts relating back to the earliest purchases. Use of the average method generally provides inventory values closely paralleling first-in, first-out values, since purchases during a period are normally several times the opening inventory balance and average costs are thus heavily influenced by current costs. Specific identification can produce any variety of results depending on the desires of management. When the prices paid for merchandise do not fluctuate significantly, alternative inventory methods may provide only minor differences on the financial statements. However, in periods of steadily rising or falling prices, the alternative methods may produce material differences.

Differences in inventory valuations on the balance sheet are accompanied by differences in earnings on the income statement for the period. Use of first-in, first-out in a period of rising prices matches oldest low-cost inventory with rising sales prices, thus expanding the gross profit margin. In a period of de-

---

[13]For additional insight into how the selection of pools can be used for tax planning and income determination, see Reeve and Stanga, *op. cit.*, pp. 25-33.

[14]Stauffer Chemical Company, *1982 annual report.*

clining prices, oldest high-cost inventory is matched with declining sales prices, thus narrowing the gross profit margin. Using an average method, the gross profit margin tends to follow a similar pattern in response to changing prices. On the other hand, use of last-in, first-out in a period of rising prices relates current high costs of acquiring goods with rising sales prices. Thus LIFO tends to have a stabilizing effect on gross profit margins.

The application of the different methods, excluding specific identification, in periods of rising and falling prices is illustrated in the following example. Assume that the Wisconsin Sales Co. sells its goods at 50% over prevailing costs from 1989 to 1992. The company sells its inventories and terminates activities at the end of 1992. Sales, costs, and gross profits using each of the three methods are shown in the following tabulation.

	FIFO		Weighted Average[1]		LIFO	
1989:						
Sales, 500 units @ $9		$4,500		$4,500		$4,500
Inventory, 200 units	@ $5 $1,000		200 @ $5 $1,000		200 @ $5 $1,000	
Purchases, 500 units	@ $6 3,000		500 @ $6 3,000		500 @ $6 3,000	
Goods available for sale		$4,000		$4,000		$4,000
			200 @ $5.71			
Ending Inv., 200 units	@ $6 1,200		($4,000 ÷ 700) 1,142		200 @ $5 1,000	
Cost of goods sold		2,800		2,858		3,000
Gross profit on sales		$1,700		$1,642		$1,500
1990:						
Sales, 450 units @ $12		$5,400		$5,400		$5,400
Inventory, 200 units	@ $6 $1,200		200 @ $5.71 $1,142		200 @ $5 $1,000	
Purchases, 500 units	@ $8 4,000		500 @ $8 4,000		500 @ $8 4,000	
Goods available for sale		$5,200		$5,142		$5,000
			250 @ $7.35		200 @ $5⎱	
Ending Inv., 250 units	@ $8 2,000		($5,142 ÷ 700) 1,838		50 @ $8⎰ 1,400	
Cost of goods sold		3,200		3,304		3,600
Gross Profit on Sales		$2,200		$2,096		$1,800
1991:						
Sales, 475 units @ $10.50		$4,988		$4,988		$4,988
Inventory, 250 units	@ $8 $2,000		250 @ $7.35 $1,838		200 @ $5⎱	
					50 @ $8⎰$1,400	
Purchases, 450 units	@ $7 3,150		450 @ $7 3,150		450 @ $7 3,150	
Goods available for sale		$5,150		$4,988		$4,550
			225 @ $7.13		200 @ $5⎱	
Ending Inv., 225 units	@ $7 1,575		($4,988 ÷ 700) 1,604		25 @ $8⎰ 1,200	
Cost of goods sold		3,575		3,384		3,350
Gross profit on sales		$1,413		$1,604		$1,638
1992:						
Sales, 625 units @ $7.50		$4,688		$4,688		$4,688
Inventory, 225 units	@ $7 $1,575		225 @ $7.13 $1,604		200 @ $5⎱	
					25 @ $8⎰$1,200	
Purchases, 400 units	@ $5 2,000		400 @ $5 2,000		400 @ $5 2,000	
Cost of goods sold		3,575		3,604		3,200
Gross profit on sales		$1,113		$1,084		$1,488

[1]Totals in the illustration are calculated to the nearest dollar.

The foregoing transactions are summarized in the table below.

		FIFO			Weighted Average			LIFO		
Year	Sales	Cost of Goods Sold	Gross Profit on Sales	Gross Profit % to Sales	Cost of Goods Sold	Gross Profit on Sales	Gross Profit % to Sales	Cost of Goods Sold	Gross Profit on Sales	Gross Profit % to Sales
1989	$ 4,500	$ 2,800	$1,700	37.8%	$ 2,858	$1,642	36.5%	$ 3,000	$1,500	33.3%
1990	5,400	3,200	2,200	40.7	3,304	2,096	38.8	3,600	1,800	33.3
1991	4,988	3,575	1,413	28.3	3,384	1,604	32.2	3,350	1,638	32.8
1992	4,688	3,575	1,113	23.7	3,604	1,084	23.1	3,200	1,488	31.7
	$19,576	$13,150	$6,426	32.8%	$13,150	$6,426	32.8%	$13,150	$6,426	32.8%

Although the different methods give the same total gross profit on sales for the four-year period, use of first-in, first-out resulted in increased gross profit percentages in periods of rising prices and a contraction of gross profit percentages in periods of falling prices, while last-in, first-out resulted in relatively steady gross profit percentages in spite of fluctuating prices. The weighted average method offered results closely comparable to those obtained by first-in, first-out. Assuming operating expenses at 30% of sales, use of last-in, first-out would result in a net income for each of the four years; first-in, first-out would result in larger net incomes in 1989 and 1990, but net losses in 1991 and 1992. Inventory valuation on the last-in, first-out basis tends to smooth the peaks and fill the troughs of business fluctuations.

Income Tax Considerations

The preceding comparison of cost methods was made without considering the income tax impact of the method used. As indicated earlier, if a company elects to use LIFO for tax purposes, it must also use some form of LIFO in its financial reports. In a period of inflation, the lower reported profit using LIFO results in lower income taxes. Thus, the tax liability on gross profit, assuming a 45% tax rate, for the three illustrated methods over the four-year period would be as follows:

	FIFO	Weighted Average	LIFO
1989	$ 765	$ 739	$ 675
1990	990	943	810
1991	636	722	737
1992	501	488	670
Total	$2,892	$2,892	$2,892

In this example, a complete cycle of price increases and decreases occurred over the four-year period; thus the total income tax liability for the four years was the same under each method. However, by using LIFO to defer part of the tax during 1989 and 1990, more cash was available to the company for operating purposes. In periods of constantly increasing inflation, the deferral tends to become permanent and is a condition sought by many companies. When inflation started to accelerate in the United States in the mid 1970's, many companies began to report larger net incomes primarily caused by the illusory influence of holding gains. To protect their cash flows, a significant number of companies changed to LIFO inventory to reduce their present and future tax liabilities. These changes had to be approved by the Internal Revenue Service, and were subject to specific rules governing adoption of the LIFO method. The complexity of some of these rules deterred other companies from making the change even though the tax consequences promised to be favorable.[15]

When a company changes its method of valuing inventory, the change is accounted for as a change in accounting principle. If the change is *to* average cost or FIFO, both the beginning and ending inventories can usually be computed on the new basis. Thus, the effect of changing inventory methods can be determined and reported in the financial statements as explained in Chapter 23. If the change is *to* LIFO from another method, however, a company's records are generally not complete enough to reconstruct the prior years' inventory layers. Therefore, the base-year layer for the new LIFO inventory is the opening inventory for the year in which LIFO is adopted (also the ending inventory for the year *before* LIFO is adopted). There is no adjustment to the financial statements to reflect the change to LIFO. However, the impact of the change on income for the current year must be disclosed in a note to the statements. In addition, the note should explain why there is no effect on the financial statements. Required disclosures for a change to LIFO are illustrated in the following note from the 1986 annual report of Elcor Corporation.

Exhibit 9-3	**ELCOR Corporation**

Change to LIFO Method of Inventory Pricing

Effective July 1, 1985, the Company adopted the last-in, first-out (LIFO) method of determining inventory costs. In previous years, the Company used the first-in, first-out (FIFO) method. Management believes the LIFO method is preferable because it more closely matches revenues and expenses during periods of price-level changes. The consolidated financial statements for fiscal years prior to 1986 have not been restated to reflect this change as it is not required under generally accepted accounting principles to state the cumulative effect on Retained Earnings of this change in accounting principle. The effect of this change for the year ended June 30, 1986, was to increase income from continuing operations by $524,000 ($.15 per share), and increase net income by $970,000 ($.28 per share).

---

[15]A survey in 1980 of 213 companies who were not using LIFO indicated many different reasons for their decision. Principal among them were (1) the company had no tax liability, (2) prices were declining in their industry, and (3) the change to LIFO would have an immaterial impact because of rapid inventory turnover. Michael H. Granof and Daniel G. Short, "Why Do Companies Reject Lifo?" *Journal of Accounting, Auditing, and Finance* (Summer 1984), pp. 323-333.

Evaluation of LIFO As a Cost Allocation Method

Because so many companies have resorted to LIFO as a means of reducing reported income and, consequently, their income tax liability, it is important to identify the advantages and disadvantages of this unique inventory method. It should be noted once again that LIFO is a historical cost allocation method; it assigns the most recent historical cost to expense (cost of goods sold) and the oldest relevant historical cost to inventory. Its ability to match recent historical cost, which approximates current cost, to revenue depends upon the rate of price change, inventory turnover, and frequency of purchase. For example, if the most recent purchase of inventory was two years ago, LIFO, at best, can only assign two-year-old historical cost figures to expense. Because LIFO allocates only historical cost between the balance sheet and income statement, it can not adjust for changes in the general price level and in specific prices since the acquisition date. This topic is covered in Chapter 25.

Major Advantages of LIFO

The advantages of LIFO may be summarized as follows:

Tax Benefits

Temporary or permanent deferrals of income taxes can be achieved with LIFO, resulting in current cash savings. These deferrals continue as long as the price level is increasing and inventory quantities do not decline. The improved cash flow enables a company to either decrease its borrowing and reduce interest cost, or invest the savings to produce revenue.

Better Measurement of Income

Because LIFO allocates the most recently incurred costs to cost of sales, this method produces an income figure that tends to report only the operating income and defers recognition of the holding gain until prices or quantities decline. The illusory inflation profits discussed earlier tend not to appear as part of net income when LIFO inventory is used.

Major Disadvantages of LIFO

The disadvantages of LIFO are more subtle than the advantages. Companies adopting LIFO sometimes realize too late that LIFO can produce some severe side effects.

Reduced Income

The application of the most recent prices against current revenue produces a decrease in net income in an inflationary period. If management's goal is to maximize reported income, the adoption of LIFO will produce results that are in opposition to that goal.

Investors and other users of financial statements frequently base their evaluations of a company's performance on the "bottom line" or net income. Failure on the part of users to recognize that a lower net income is due to the use of LIFO rather than a decline in operating proficiency may have a depressing effect on the market price of a company's stock. The reduced income may be perceived as a failure on the part of management. Further, the use of LIFO will reduce bonus payments to employees that are based on net income and could reduce the amount of dividends distributed to shareholders.

Unrealistic Inventory Balances on the Balance Sheet

The allocation of older inventory costs to the balance sheet can cause a serious understatement of inventory values. Depending on the length of time the LIFO layers have been developing and the severity of the price increase, the reported inventory values can be substantially lower than current replacement values. For example, Note 5 to the General Mills statements reproduced in Appendix A at the end of the text shows that if the FIFO method had been used, inventories would be $53 million higher in 1988 than the reported LIFO inventory. This is approximately 13% of the LIFO valued inventory. Because inventory costs enter into the determination of working capital, the current ratio can be seriously distorted under a LIFO inventory system. Although this discussion of LIFO assumes an inflationary economy, if prices were to decrease, LIFO would produce inventory values higher than current replacement costs. It is fair to assume that should this occur, there would be strong pressure for special action to permit the write-down of inventory balances to replacement cost.

Unanticipated Profits Created by Failing to Maintain Inventory Quantities

The income advantages summarized previously will be realized only if inventory quantity levels are maintained. If the ending inventory quantities decline, the old layers of cost eliminated are charged against current revenue. If the inventory costs of these layers are significantly less than the current replacement costs, the reported profit will be artificially increased by the failure to maintain inventory levels.

Two specific examples may clarify this weakness.

1. Many companies who rely on steel as a basic raw material for their production processes use the LIFO inventory method. Assume that during an extended steel strike many manufacturing companies find their steel stock dwindling as their fiscal year-end approaches. Unless they can restock their inventories, they will be forced to match lower inventory costs against current revenue, thus reporting a substantial holding gain in current profit. Assume, for instance, that company sales for the year are $6,000,000 and that the cost of goods sold using current year prices is $5,000,000 but using a mixture of current year and earlier years' lower priced LIFO layers, the cost of goods sold is $4,000,000. The resulting increase in profit of $1,000,000 is caused solely by the inability of the company to replace its normal stock.

2. The failure to protect LIFO layers may be caused by a timing error in requesting shipments of purchases. Assume that a lumber company normally received its lumber by ship, but that at year-end orders were mishandled and a boat load was not received as planned. The company, in failing to record the boat load of lumber as a current year purchase, would have to apply older LIFO costs against sales. The resulting profit could lead to conclusions that would not be justified by the facts.

To avoid the distortion caused by a temporary reduction of LIFO layers at the end of a year, some accountants advocate establishing a replacement allowance that charges the current period for the extra replacement cost expected to be incurred in the subsequent period when the inventory is replenished. However, the use of an allowance for temporary liquidation of LIFO layers, sometimes referred to as the **base-stock method**, is not currently acceptable for financial reporting or tax purposes. The use of this type of allowance on the books could disqualify a company from filing its tax returns on the LIFO basis, and therefore, it is seldom used in practice.

Unrealistic Flow Assumptions

The cost assignment resulting from the application of LIFO does not normally approximate the physical movement of goods through the business. One would seldom encounter in practice the actual use or transfer of goods on a last-in, first-out basis.

Selection of an Inventory Method

As indicated in this chapter, companies have many alternative ways to value inventories. Guidelines for the selection of a proper method are very broad, and a company may justify almost any accepted method. After a lengthy study of inventory practices, Horace Barden, retired partner of Ernst and Whinney, concluded his Research Study by stating:

> . . . one must recognize that no neat package of principles or other criteria exists to substitute for the professional judgment of the responsible accountant. The need for the exercise of judgment in accounting for inventories is so great that I recommend to authoritative bodies that they refrain from establishing rules that, in isolation from the conditions and circumstances that may exist in practice, attempt to determine the accounting treatment to be applied under any and all circumstances.[16]

Many companies use more than one method. For example, General Mills values some domestic inventories at the lower of LIFO cost or market and other inventories at the lower of FIFO cost or market[17] The decision as to which method to use depends on not only the tax consequences but also the nature of the inventories themselves. Except for LIFO, a company may

[16]Horace G. Barden, *Accounting Research Study No. 13*, ''The Accounting Basis of Inventories'' (New York: American Institute of Certified Public Accountants, 1973) p. 141.
[17]See Appendix A at the end of the text. Note 1C and Note 5.

use a different inventory method for tax purposes than it uses for reporting purposes. This creates a temporary difference with respect to cost of goods sold and the resulting net income, which leads to a need for interperiod income tax allocation. (See Chapter 20.)

Companies sometimes change their inventory methods, especially as economic conditions change. For instance, several recent research studies have shown that the stock market reacts favorably to companies that elect to adopt the LIFO method.[18] When inventories are a material item, a change in the inventory method by a company may impair comparability of that company's financial statements with prior years' statements and with the financial statements of other entities. Such changes require careful consideration and should be made only when management can clearly demonstrate the preferability of the alternative method. This position was emphasized by the Accounting Principles Board in Opinion No. 20 with the statement, "The burden of justifying other changes rests with the entity proposing the change."[19] If a change is made, complete disclosure of the impact of the change is encouraged by the FASB.

[18]For example, see Francis L. Stevenson, "New Evidence on LIFO Adoption: The Effects of More Precise Event Dates." *Journal of Accounting Research*, Autumn 1987, pp. 306-316.

[19]*Opinions of the Accounting Principles Board, No. 20*, "Accounting Changes" (New York: American Institute of Certified Public Accountants, 1971), par. 16.

Appendix

Determination of Price Indexes

The chapter illustrated the use of an index method to compute the ending inventory at base-year prices. There are two common approaches for determining price indexes for a particular inventory: (1) developing a specific internal index from the company's inventory records; or (2) using a published external index relating to the inventory.

Internal Indexes

A widely used technique for developing internal indexes for dollar-value LIFO is double extension. A **double extension index** is computed by extending a representative sample of a specific ending inventory pool at both base-year and end-of-year prices. An index can then be computed applying the following formula:

$$\text{Double extension index} = \frac{\text{Inventory extended at year-end prices}}{\text{Inventory extended at base-year prices}}$$

To illustrate, assume an inventory pool contained ten items. The following sample of four items was drawn to compute a double-extension index.

Item	Ending Quantity	Year-End Price	Base-Year Price	Extended Year-End	Extended Base-Year
A	200	$ 50	$30	$10,000	$ 6,000
B	500	70	40	35,000	20,000
C	150	30	25	4,500	3,750
D	200	100	60	20,000	12,000
			Total	$69,500	$41,750

$$\text{Double extension index} = \frac{\$69,500}{\$41,750} = 1.66$$

The Internal Revenue Service has stated that a nonstatistical sample must include at least 50% of the items and represent 70% or more of the dollar value. Fewer items are necessary if a carefully constructed random sample is used.

The double extension index has two principal disadvantages: (1) it is time consuming and costly for companies having a large number of different inventory items; and (2) if new inventory items are being added, it may be difficult to determine base year prices for them. This latter disadvantage is overcome with the **link-chain index**. This modification of the double extension index requires extending a statistically representative portion of the ending inventory at end-of-year prices and beginning-of-year, rather than base-year prices. The index computed from this valuation is then multiplied by a cumulative index carried forward from previous years to determine the current index.

Using the inventory data on page 360, assume that the cumulative link-chain index at the beginning of the current year was 1.51. The following illustrates the computation of the yearly index, i.e., the new "link," and a new cumulative index to use for dollar-value LIFO purposes.

Item	Ending Quantity	Year-End Price	Beginning-of-Year Price	Extended Year-End	Extended Beginning-of-Year
A	200	$ 50	$46	$10,000	$ 9,200
B	500	70	65	35,000	32,500
C	150	30	30	4,500	4,500
D	200	100	85	20,000	17,000
			Total	$69,500	$63,200

$$\text{Yearly Index} = \frac{\$69,500}{\$63,200} = 1.10 \text{ (new link)}$$

$$\text{Link-Chain Index} = 1.51 \times 1.10 = 1.66$$

This approach has the advantage of simplicity because historical records of base-year costs are not necessary. It permits adding new inventory items without causing difficulty in computing base-year prices for the new items. A company may change from the double extension index method to the link-chain index if it has had at least a 90% turnover of inventory items in the preceding five-year period.

External Indexes

Although many price-level indexes are published by governmental and private agencies, only the Bureau of Labor Statistics' (BLS) department store indexes were automatically acceptable for income tax purposes until the Economic Recovery Tax Act of 1981 was passed. This Act directed the IRS to prescribe regulations providing for an expansion of external indexes for use by LIFO companies. As a result, regulations were issued permitting small businesses with annual sales of $5 million or less to use either monthly consumer price indexes (CPI) or monthly producer price indexes (PPI).[20] Companies that do not qualify as small businesses may use these same indexes, but they may only incorporate in their inventory calculations 80 percent of the reported change in the index being used. A separate index must be used for each inventory item that comprises more than 10 percent of the total inventory value. However, aggregation is permitted of each item comprising less than 10 percent of the total inventory value.

The BLS department store indexes that are still acceptable for retail

[20]*IRS Income Tax Regulations*, Section 1.472-8(e)(3)

department stores are divided into twenty groups, and each group becomes a separate dollar-value pool.

The increased number of external indexes available was intended to make the LIFO method more feasible for smaller companies by reducing the cost of implementation required if an internal index must be developed. For this reason, the use of the additional external indexes is referred to as "simplified LIFO." The IRS has decided that adoption of these external indexes in place of internal indexes is a change in accounting method. Except for limited situations, companies making the change must obtain prior approval from the Commissioner of Internal Revenue.

The AICPA Task Force on LIFO Inventory considered the use of external indexes and recommended that the IRS regulations concerning their use be accepted for financial reporting except for the limitation on companies that do not qualify as small businesses and thus can incorporate only 80% of the index change in the inventory. By a vote of 5 to 3, the Task Force did not accept the limitation on the use of the external index for reporting purposes.[21]

[21]Issues Paper, Task Force on LIFO Inventory, Accounting Standards Division, AICPA, "The Acceptability of 'Simplified LIFO' for Financial Reporting Purposes" (New York: American Institute of Certified Public Accountants, 1982), p. 9.

Key Terms

Average cost method 340
Consigned goods 333
Dollar-value LIFO inventory method
    346
Double extension 348
Double extension index 360
FOB destination 332
FOB shipping point 328
Factory overhead 329
Finished goods 329
First-in, First-out (FIFO) method 339
Goods in process 328
Gross method 336
Inventory 327

Last-in, First-out (LIFO) method 342
LIFO allowance 343
LIFO conformity rule 344
LIFO inventory pools 345
Link-chain index 361
Net method 336
Period costs 334
Periodic inventory system 329
Perpetual inventory system 329
Raw materials 328
Specific identification method 338
Trade discounts 335
Work in process 328

Questions

1. What economic conditions make the allocation of inventory costs most difficult?
2. (a) What are the three cost elements entering into goods in process and finished goods? (b) What items enter into factory overhead?
3. Distinguish between raw materials and factory supplies. Why are the terms direct and indirect materials often used to refer to raw materials and factory supplies, respectively?
4. What is the uniform cost capitalization rule? In what ways does it affect financial reporting?
5. Does the adoption of a perpetual inventory system eliminate the need for a physical count or measurement of inventories? Explain.
6. Would you expect to find a perpetual or periodic inventory system used in each of the following situations?
   (a) Diamond ring department of a jewelry store.
   (b) Computer department of a college bookstore.
   (c) Candy department of a college bookstore.
   (d) Automobile dealership—new car department.
   (e) Automobile dealership—parts department.
   (f) Wholesale dealer small tools.
   (g) A plumbing supply house—brass fittings department.
7. Under what conditions is merchandise in transit legally reported as inventory by the (a) seller? (b) buyer?
8. How should the following items be treated in computing year-end inventory costs: (a) segregated goods? (b) conditional sales?
9. State how you would report each of the following items on the financial statements.
   (a) Manufacturing supplies.
   (b) Goods on hand received on a consignment basis.
   (c) Materials of a customer held for processing.
   (d) Goods received without an accompanying invoice.
   (e) Goods in stock to be delivered to customers in subsequent periods.
   (f) Goods in hands of agents and consignees.
   (g) Deposits with vendors for merchandise to be delivered next period.
   (h) Goods in hands of customers on approval.
   (i) Defective goods requiring reprocessing.

10. (a) What are the two methods of accounting for cash discounts? (b) Which method is generally preferred? Why?

11. Theoretically, there is little wrong with inventory costing by the specific cost identification method. What objections can be raised to the use of this method?

12. Would you expect to find the specific identification method or some other historical cost flow assumption, such as average cost or LIFO, used for the items noted in question 6 above.

13. What advantages are there to using the average cost method of inventory pricing?

14. The Wallace Co. decides to adopt specific goods LIFO as of the beginning of 1991, and determines the cost of the different kinds of merchandise carried as of this date. (a) What three different methods may be employed at the end of a period in assigning costs to quantity increases in specific pools? (b) What procedure is employed at the end of each period for quantity decreases of specific items?

15. (a) What is the LIFO conformity rule? (b) How has the rule changed since it was first adopted? (c) How might the changes in the conformity rule affect LIFO inventories reported on the financial statements?

16. Assume a car manufacturer and a discounting retail firm have identical sales and income and that price changes affecting the various factors of production increase at the same rate. The car manufacturer has an inventory turnover rate of 2 times a year and the discounting firm an inventory turnover of 15 times per year. Assume that each firm wants to match an historical cost which approximates current cost against revenue. Which firm will benefit more by changing from FIFO to LIFO?

17. Assume there is no change in the physical quantity of inventory for the current accounting period. During a period of rising prices, which historical cost flow (LIFO or FIFO) will result in the greater dollar value of ending inventory and the greater dollar value of cost of goods sold? Will the beginning and ending inventory value under LIFO and FIFO be equal? Why or why not?

18. What are the major advantages of dollar-value LIFO over specific goods LIFO?

19. Indexes are used for two different purposes in computing the layers of a dollar-value LIFO pool. Clearly distinguish between these uses and describe how the indexes are applied.

20. The selection of inventory pools is very important in using the dollar-value LIFO method of inventory costing. What factors should be considered in identifying the pools for a specific company.

21. Discuss the advantages and disadvantages of LIFO as a cost allocation method.

*22. Identify the three different types of indexes that can be used in applying dollar-value LIFO. What are the advantages and disadvantages of each?

*Relates to Appendix

Discussion Cases   **Case 9-1   (Should we adopt LIFO?)**

You are the controller of the Ford Steel Co. Assume the economy enters a period of rapidly increasing inflation. The turnover of inventory in your company occurs about once every nine months. The inflation is causing revenue to rise more rapidly than the historical cost of the goods sold. Although profits are higher this year than last, you realize that the cost to replace the sold inventory is also higher. You are aware that many companies are changing to the LIFO inventory method, but you are concerned that what goes up will eventually come down, and when prices decline, the LIFO method will result in high profits and taxes. Since declining prices are usually equated with economic recession, it is likely that the higher taxes will have to be paid at a time when revenues are declining.

What factors should you consider before making a change to LIFO? Based on the above considerations, what would you recommend?

Case 9-2 (What is an inventoriable cost?)

You have been hired by Midwestern Products Co. to work in their accounting department. As part of your assignment, you have been asked to review the inventory costing procedures. In the past, the company has attempted to keep its inventory as low as possible to hedge against future declines in demand. One way of doing this has been to charge off as many costs as can be justified as expenses of the current period. Sales have declined, however, and the controller wants to include as high an ending inventory valuation as possible to show the stockholders a better income figure for the current year. Your study shows the following costs have been consistently treated as period costs for financial reporting purposes:

> Depreciation of plant
> Fringe payroll benefits for factory personnel
> Repairs of equipment
> Salaries of foremen
> Warehouse rental for storage of finished products
> Pension costs for factory personnel
> Training program—all employees
> Cafeteria costs—all employees
> Interest expense
> Depreciation and maintenance of fleet of delivery trucks

Which of the items do you suggest could be deferred by including them as inventoriable costs? Evaluate the wisdom and propriety of making the suggested changes.

Case 9-3 (How do we record cash discounts?)

Taylor Company, a household appliances dealer, purchases its inventories from various suppliers. Taylor has consistently stated its inventories at the lower of cost (FIFO) or market. Taylor is considering alternate methods of accounting for the cash discounts it takes when paying its suppliers promptly. From a theoretical standpoint, discuss the acceptability of each of the following methods:

(a) Financial income when payments are made.
(b) Reduction of cost of goods sold for period when payments are made.
(c) Direct reduction of purchase cost.   (AICPA adapted)

Case 9-4   (Which method shall we use?)

The White Wove Corporation began operations in 1991. A summary of the first quarter appears below:

	Purchases	
	Units	Total Cost
January 2	250	$23,250
February 11	100	9,500
February 20	400	38,400
March 21	200	19,600
March 27	225	22,275

	Other Data		
	Sales in Units	Sales Price per Unit	Operating Expenses
January	200	$140	$9,575
February	225	142	7,820
March	350	145	7,905

The White Wove Corporation used the LIFO perpetual inventory method and computed an inventory value of $38,300, at the end of the first quarter. Management is considering changing to a FIFO costing method. They have also considered using a periodic system instead of the perpetual system presently being used. You have been hired to assist management in making the decision. What would you advise?

*Case 9-5   (Should we switch to dollar-value LIFO?)

The Innovative Production Co. has used the LIFO method of valuing its inventories for several years. Layers for some of the inventory items are valued at amounts ⅓ to ½ of the current market price. The products manufactured and marketed by the company are subject to rapid technological obsolescence, and the company is continually developing new products and phasing out old ones. As items are discontinued, the company finds its income and taxes increasing as old costs are matched against current revenues. However, since new products must be produced at higher costs, it has been difficult to maintain a positive cash flow for the company. The president of Innovative Production, having heard a competitor mention dollar-value LIFO, approaches you, the chief accountant, with the following questions. "Would this help us? What differences are there between our LIFO system and dollar-value LIFO?"
˙ Relates to appendix

Exercises   ### Exercise 9-1   (Passage of title)

The management of Kauer Company has engaged you to assist in the preparation of year-end (December 31) financial statements. You are told that on November 30, the correct inventory level was 150,000 units. During the month of December sales totaled 50,000 units including 25,000 units shipped on consignment to Towsey Company. A letter received from Towsey indicates that as of December 31, they had sold 12,000 units and were still trying to sell the remainder. A review of the December purchase orders, to various suppliers, shows the following:

Date of Purchase Order	Invoice Date	Quantity in Units	Date Shipped	Date Received	Terms
12-2-91	1-3-92	10,000	1-2-92	1-3-92	FOB shipping point
12-11-91	1-3-92	8,000	12-22-91	12-24-91	FOB destination
12-13-91	1-2-92	13,000	12-28-91	1-2-92	FOB shipping point
12-23-91	12-26-91	12,000	1-2-92	1-3-92	FOB shipping point
12-28-91	1-10-92	10,000	12-31-91	1-5-92	FOB destination
12-31-91	1-10-92	15,000	1-3-92	1-6-92	FOB destination

Kauer Company uses the "passing of legal title" for inventory recognition. Compute the number of units which should be included in the year-end inventory.

Exercise 9-2   (Passage of title)

The Young Manufacturing Company reviewed its in-transit inventory and found the following items. Indicate which items should be included in the inventory balance at December 31, 1991. Give your reasons for the treatment you suggest.

(a) Merchandise costing $2,350 was received on January 3, 1992, and the related purchase invoice was recorded January 5. The invoice showed the shipment was made on December 29, 1991, FOB destination.

(b) Merchandise costing $625 was received on December 28, 1991, and the invoice was not recorded. The invoice was in the hands of the purchasing agent; it was marked "on consignment."

(c) A packing case containing a product costing $816 was standing in the shipping room when the physical inventory was taken. It was not included in the inventory because it was marked "Hold for shipping instructions." The customer's order was dated December 18, but the case was shipped and the customer billed on January 10, 1992.

(d) Merchandise received on January 6, 1992, costing $720 was entered in the purchase register on January 7. The invoice showed shipment was made FOB shipping point on December 31, 1991. Since it was not on hand during the inventory count, it was not included.

(e) A special machine, fabricated to order for a particular customer, was finished and in the shipping room on December 30. The customer was billed on that date and the machine was excluded from inventory although it was shipped January 4, 1992.   (AICPA adapted)

Exercise 9-3   (Trade and cash discounts)

Olavssen Hardware regularly buys merchandise from Dawson Suppliers and is allowed a trade discount of 20/10/10 from the list price. Olavssen uses the net method to record purchases and discounts. On August 15, Olavssen Hardware purchased material from Dawson Suppliers. The invoice received from Dawson showed a list price of $5,000, and terms of 2/10, n/30. Payment was sent to Dawson Suppliers on August 28. Prepare the journal entries to record the purchase and subsequent payment. (Round to nearest dollar).

Exercise 9-4   (Net and gross methods-entries)

On December 3, Hakan Photography purchased inventory listed at $8,600 from Mark Photo Supply. Terms of the purchase were 3/10, n/20. Hakan Photography also purchased inventory from Erickson Wholesale on December 10, for a list price of $7,500. Terms of the purchase were 3/10 eom. On December 16, Hakan paid both suppliers for these purchases. Hakan does not use a perpetual inventory system.

1. Give the entries to record the purchases and invoice payments assuming that (a) the net method is used, (b) the gross method is used.
2. Assume that Hakan has not paid either of the invoices at December 31. Give the year-ending adjusting entries, if the net method is being used. Also assume that Hakan plans to pay Erickson Wholesale within the discount period.

Exercise 9-5   (Computing cash expenditure for inventory)

Using the following data, compute the total cash expended for inventory in 1991.

Accounts payable	
January 1, 1991	$200,000
December 31, 1991	$240,000
Cost of goods sold—1991	$900,000
Inventory balance	
January 1, 1991	$300,000
December 31, 1991	$200,000

Exercise 9-6   (Inventory computation using different cost flows)

The Webster Store shows the following information relating to one of its products.

Inventory, January 1	300 units @ $17.50
Purchases, January 10	900 units @ $18.00
Purchases, January 20	1200 units @ $18.25
Sales, January 8	200 units
Sales, January 18	600 units
Sales, January 25	1000 units

What are the values of ending inventory under (a) perpetual and (b) periodic methods assuming the cost flows below? (Carry your unit costs to four places and round to three.)

(1) FIFO
(2) LIFO
(3) Average

Exercise 9-7   (Inventory computation using different cost flows)

Richmond Corporation had the following transactions relating to Product AB during September.

Date		Units	Unit Cost
September 1	Balance on hand	500 units	$5.00
September 6	Purchase	100 units	4.50
September 12	Sale	300 units	
September 13	Sale	200 units	
September 18	Purchase	200 units	6.00
September 20	Purchase	200 units	4.00
September 25	Sale	200 units	

Determine the ending inventory value under each of the following costing methods:

(1) FIFO (perpetual)
(2) FIFO (periodic)
(3) LIFO (perpetual)
(4) LIFO (periodic)

Exercise 9-8   (LIFO inventory computation)

White Farm Supply's records for the first three months of its existence show purchases of Commodity Y2 as follows:

	Number of Units	Cost
August	5,500	$29,975
September	8,000	41,600
October	5,100	27,030

The inventory at the end of October of Commodity Y2 using FIFO is valued at $36,390. Assuming that none of Commodity Y2 was sold during August and September, what value would be shown at the end of October if LIFO cost was assumed?

Exercise 9-9   (Dollar-value LIFO inventory method)

The Johnson Manufacturing Company manufactures a single product. The management, Ron and Ken Johnson, decided on December 31, 1989 to adopt the dollar-value LIFO inventory method. The inventory value on that date using the newly adopted dollar-value LIFO method was $500,000. Additional information follows:

Date	Inventory at End-of-Year Prices	Year-End Price Index
Dec. 31, 1990	$605,000	1.10
Dec. 31, 1991	597,360	1.14
Dec. 31, 1992	700,000	1.25

Compute the inventory value at December 31 of each year using the dollar-value method, assuming incremental layers are costed at year-end prices.

Exercise 9-10   (Dollar-value LIFO inventory method)

Jennifer Inc. adopted dollar-value LIFO on December 31, 1989. Data for 1989-1992 follow:

Inventory and index on the adoption date, December 31, 1989:

Dollar-value LIFO inventory	$250,000
Price index at year end (the base year)	1.00

Inventory information in succeeding years:

Date	Inventory at End-of-Year Prices	Year-End Index	Incremental Layer Index
Dec. 31, 1990	$314,720	1.12	1.04
Dec. 31, 1991	361,800	1.20	1.14
Dec. 31, 1992	353,822	1.27	1.20

(1) Compute the inventory value at December 31 of each year under the dollar-value method, assuming incremental layers are costed at beginning-of-year prices.

(2) Compute the inventory value at December 31, 1992 assuming that dollar-value procedures were adopted at December 31, 1990 rather than in 1989.

Exercise 9-11   (Inventory computation from incomplete records)

A flood recently destroyed many of the financial records of Riboldi Manufacturing Company. Management has hired you to re-create as much financial information as possible for the month of July. You are able to find out that the company uses a weighted average inventory costing system. You also learn that Riboldi makes a physical count at the end of each month in order to determine monthly ending inventory values. By examining various documents you are able to gather the following information:

Ending inventory at July 31	50,000 units
Total cost of units available for sale in July	$118,800
Cost of goods sold during July	$99,000
Cost of beginning inventory, July 1	35¢ per unit
Gross margin on sales for July	$101,000

July Purchases

Date	Units	Unit Cost	
July 4	60,000	$0.40	24,000
July 11	50,000	0.41	20,500
July 15	40,000	0.42	16,800
July 16	50,000	0.45	22,500

83,800 тот Риу

You are asked to provide the following information:

(1) Number of units on hand, July 1.
(2) Units sold during July.
(3) Unit cost of inventory at July 31.   .40
(4) Value of inventory at July 31.

Exercise 9-12   (Computation of beginning inventory)

A note to the financial statements of Alpine Inc. at December 31, 1991 reads as follows:

Because of the manufacturer's production problems for our Widget Limited line, our inventories were unavoidably reduced. Under the LIFO inventory accounting method currently being used for tax and financial accounting purposes, the net effect of all the inventory changes was to increase pretax income by $1,200,000 over what it would have been had the inventory of Widget Limited been maintained at the normal physical levels on hand at the start of the year.

The unit purchase price of the merchandise was $20 per unit during the year. Alpine Inc. uses the periodic inventory system. Additional data concerning Alpine's inventory were as follows:

Date	Physical Count of Inventory	LIFO Cost of Inventory
January 1, 1991	400,000 units	$?
December 31, 1991	300,000 units	$2,900,000

(1) What was the unit average cost for the 100,000 units that were sold from the beginning inventory?
(2) What was the reported value for the January 1, 1991 inventory?

Exercise 9-13   (Computation of beginning inventory from ending inventory)

The Killpack Company sells Product N. During a move to a new location, the inventory records for Product N were misplaced. The bookkeeper has been able to gather some information from the sales records, and gives you the data shown below:

July sales: 53,500 units at $10.00
July purchases:

Date	Quantity	Unit Price
July 5	10,000	$6.50
July 9	12,500	6.25
July 12	15,000	6.00
July 25	14,000	6.20

On July 31, 15,000 units were on hand with a total value of $92,800. Killpack has always used a periodic FIFO inventory costing system. Gross profit on sales for July was $205,875. Reconstruct the beginning inventory (quantity and dollar value) for the month of July.

Exercise 9-14   (Impact on profit of failure to replace LIFO layers)

Harrison Lumber Company uses a periodic LIFO method for inventory costing. The following information relates to the plywood inventory carried by Harrison Lumber.

Plywood Inventory

	Quantity	LIFO Costing Layers
May 1	600 Sheets	300 Sheets at $ 8.00
		225 Sheets at 11.00
		75 Sheets at 13.00

Plywood Purchases

May 8	115 Sheets at $14.00
May 17	95 Sheets at $15.00
May 29	200 Sheets at $14.50

All sales of plywood during May were at $20 per sheet. On May 31, there were 360 sheets of plywood in the storeroom.

(1) Compute the gross profit on sales for May, as a dollar value and as a percent of sales.
(2) Assume that because of a lumber strike, Harrison Lumber is not able to purchase the May 29 order of lumber until June 10. If sales remained the same, recompute the gross profit on sales for May, as a dollar value and as a percent of sales.
(3) Compare the results of part (1) and part (2) and explain the difference.

Exercise 9-15 (Gross margin differences—FIFO vs. LIFO)

Assume the Bullock Corporation had the following purchases and sales of its single product during its first 3 years of operation.

	Purchases		Sales	
Year	Units	Unit Cost	Units	Unit Price
Year 1	10,000	$10	8,000	$14
Year 2	9,000	$12	9,000	$17
Year 3	8,000	$15	10,000	$18
	27,000		27,000	

(1) Determine the gross margin for each of the three years assuming FIFO historical cost flow.
(2) Determine the gross margin for each of the three years assuming LIFO historical cost flow.
(3) Compare the total gross margin over the life of the business. How do the different cost flow assumptions affect the gross margin and cash flows over the life of the business? Does it matter which assumption of cash flow is used?

Exercise 9-16 (Income differences—FIFO vs. LIFO)

First-in, first-out has been used for inventory valuation by the Atwood Co. since it was organized in 1989. Using the data that follow, redetermine the net incomes for each year on the assumption of inventory valuation on the last-in, first-out basis:

	1989	1990	1991	1992
Reported net income (FIFO basis)	$15,500	$ 40,000	$ 34,250	$ 44,000
Reported ending inventories—				
FIFO basis	61,500	102,000	126,000	120,000
Inventories—LIFO basis	56,500	75,100	95,000	105,000

*Exercise 9-17   (Double extension and link-chain indexes)

On December 31, 1991, the controller of Hardman Enterprises selected six items to use as a representative sample of the company's inventory. Information relative to these products was compiled and summarized in the following schedule.

Base year	1986
January 1, 1991 cumulative index	1.15

	Products in Sample Inventory					
	1	2	3	4	5	6
Historical cost	$ 20	$ 45	$10	$ 60	$100	$85
January 1, 1986 price	20	50	8	50	92	60
January 1, 1991 price	24	51	13	60	102	71
December 31, 1991 price	26	55	17	62	111	78
December 31, 1991 quantity	300	530	60	180	780	30

(1) Compute a price index for use in determining the December 31, 1991 inventory:
  (a) at base-year prices assuming the use of double extension.
  (b) at beginning-of-year prices assuming the use of link-chain.
(2) Compute the link-chain index at January 1, 1992.
*Relates to Appendix

*Exercise 9-18   (Link-chain indexes)

On December 31, 1991, Kristen's Toy Store took a statistical sample of its inventory. The inventory revealed the following information:

	Quantity		Cost	
	Dec. 31, 1990	Dec. 31, 1991	Dec. 31, 1990	Dec. 31, 1991
Electronic games	600	750	$20.00	$22.60
Dolls	290	250	4.50	5.75
Stuffed animals	260	140	7.10	7.80
Puzzles	440	376	3.50	3.90

The link-chain cumulative price index at December 31, 1990 was 1.51. Compute the cumulative index at December 31, 1991.
*Relates to Appendix

*Exercise 9-19   (Dollar-value LIFO inventory; link-chain indexes)

LaRae's Fashion Clothing Store has hired you to assist with some year-end financial data preparation. The company's accountant quit three weeks ago and left many items incomplete. Information for computation of yearly price indexes and the inventory summary is in the table below. LaRae's uses the link-chain index for LIFO inventory valuation.

	1990	1991	1992
Ending inventory at beginning-of-year prices (December 31)	$155,000	?	$191,500
Ending inventory at end-of-year prices	?	$188,600	?
Beginning cumulative index at January 1	?	?	1.775
Yearly price index	1.100	1.060	?
Cumulative index at end of current year	?	1.775	1.955

Determine the inventory data that are missing from the table. Carry each index to three decimal places.

*Relates to Appendix

Problems   **Problem 9-1   (Inventory computation using different cost flows)**

The Gidewall Corporation uses Part 210 in a manufacturing process. Information as to balances on hand, purchases, and requisitions of Part 210 are given in the following table:

	Quantities			Unit Price
Date	Received	Issued	Balance	of Purchase
January 8	—	—	200	$1.55
January 29	200	—	400	1.70
February 8	—	80	320	—
March 20	—	160	160	—
July 10	150	—	310	1.75
August 18	—	110	200	—
September 6	—	75	125	—
November 14	250	—	375	2.00
December 29	—	200	175	—

Instructions: What is the closing inventory under each of the following pricing methods? (Carry unit costs to four places and round.)

(1) Perpetual FIFO
(2) Periodic FIFO
(3) Perpetual LIFO

(4) Periodic LIFO
(5) Moving average
(6) Weighted average

‖ Problem 9-2   (Inventory computation using different cost flows)

Records of the Schwab New Products Co. show the following data relative to Product C:

March	2	Inventory	325 units at $25.50	March	3	Sales	300 units at $37.50
	6	Purchase	300 units at 26.00		20	Sales	200 units at 35.70
	13	Purchase	350 units at 27.00		28	Sales	125 units at 36.00
	25	Purchase	50 units at 27.50				

Instructions: Calculate the inventory balance and the gross profit on sales for the month on each of the following bases:

(1) First-in, first-out. Perpetual inventories are maintained and costs are charged out currently.
(2) First-in, first-out. No book inventory is maintained.
(3) Last-in, first-out. Perpetual inventories are maintained and costs are charged out currently.
(4) Last-in, first-out. No book inventory is maintained.
(5) Moving average. Perpetual inventories are maintained and costs are charged out currently. (Carry calculations to four places and round to three.)
(6) Weighted average. No book inventory is maintained.

Problem 9-3 (Inventory calculation—LIFO and FIFO)

The Zerbel Manufacturing Co. was organized in 1990 to produce a single product. The company's production and sales records for the period 1990-1992 are summarized below:

	Units Produced		Sales	
	No. of Units	Production Costs	No. of Units	Sales Revenue
1990	340,000	$142,800	200,000	$187,000
1991	310,000	161,200	290,000	230,000
1992	270,000	153,900	260,000	221,000

Instructions: Calculate the gross profit for each of the three years assuming that inventory values are calculated in terms of:

(1) Last-in, first-out. (Average cost used for incremental layers.)
(2) First-in, first-out.

Problem 9-4 (Computation of LIFO inventory with LIFO pools)

The Bergman Company sells three different products. Five years ago management adopted the LIFO inventory method and established three specific pools of goods. Bergman values all incremental layers of inventory at the average cost of purchases within the period. Information relating to the three products for the first quarter of 1992 is given below.

	Product 400	Product 401	Product 402
Purchases:			
January	1,000 @ $12.00	500 @ $25	5,000 @ $5.30
February	1,500 @ $12.50	250 @ $26	4,850 @ $5.38
March	1,200 @ $12.25	—	3,500 @ $5.45
First quarter sales (units)	2,850	775	10,750
January 1, 1992 inventory	950 @ $11.50	155 @ $24	3,760 @ $5.00

Instructions: Compute the ending inventory value for the first quarter of 1992. (Round unit inventory values to the nearest cent and final inventory values to the nearest dollar.)

Problem 9-5 (Computation of inventory from balance sheet and transaction data)

A portion of the Stark Company's balance sheet appears as follows:

	December 31, 1992	December 31, 1991
Assets:		
Cash	$353,300	$100,000
Notes receivable	-0-	25,000
Inventory	To be determined	199,875
Liabilities:		
Accounts payable	To be determined	$ 75,000

Stark Company pays for all operating expenses with cash, and purchases all inventory on credit. During 1992, cash totaling $471,700 was paid on accounts payable. Operating expenses for 1992 totaled $220,000. All sales are cash sales. The inventory was restocked by purchasing 1,500 units per month and valued by using periodic FIFO. The unit cost of inventory was $32.60 during January 1992 and increased $.10 per month during the year. All sales are made for $50 per unit. The ending inventory for 1991 was valued at $32.50 per unit.

Instructions:

(1) Compute the number of units sold during 1992.
(2) Compute the December 31, 1992 accounts payable balance.
(3) Compute the beginning inventory quantity.
(4) Compute the ending inventory quantity and value.
(5) Prepare an income statement for 1992 (including a detailed cost of goods sold section). Ignore income tax.

Problem 9-6   (Impact of LIFO inventory system)

The Manuel Corporation sells household appliances and uses LIFO for inventory costing. The inventory contains ten different products, and historical LIFO layers are maintained for each of them. The LIFO layers for one of their products, Easy Chef, were as follows at December 31, 1991:

1990 layer	4,000 @ $90
1985 layer	3,500 @ $85
1981 layer	1,000 @ $75
1979 layer	3,000 @ $48

Instructions:

(1) What was the value of the ending inventory of Easy Chefs at December 31, 1991?
(2) How did the December 31, 1991 quantity of Easy Chefs compare with the December 31, 1990 quantity?
(3) What was the value of the ending inventory of Easy Chefs at December 31, 1992, assuming that there were 10,800 units on hand?
(4) How would income in part (3) be affected if, in addition to the quantity on hand, 1,250 units were in transit to Manuel Corporation at December 31, 1992? The shipment was made on December 26, 1992, terms FOB shipping point. Total invoice cost was $131,250.

Problem 9-7   (Dollar-value LIFO inventory method)

Steve's Repair Shop began operations on January 1, 1987. After discussing the matter with his accountant, Steve decided dollar-value LIFO should be used for inventory costing. Information concerning the inventory of Steve's Repair Shop is shown at the top of page 377.

Date	Inventory at End-of-Year Prices	Year-End Index
Dec. 31, 1987	$20,500	1.00
Dec. 31, 1988	34,000	1.18
Dec. 31, 1989	55,600	1.36
Dec. 31, 1990	37,800	1.14
Dec. 31, 1991	72,250	1.72
Dec. 31, 1992	53,900	2.05

Instructions: Compute the inventory value at December 31 of each year under the dollar-value LIFO inventory method, assuming incremental layers are costed at end-of-year prices.

▌▌▌ Problem 9-8   (Dollar-value LIFO inventory method)

The Mietus Company manufactures a single product. The company adopted the dollar-value LIFO inventory method on December 31, 1987. More information concerning Mietus Company is shown below:

Inventory and index on the adoption date, December 31, 1987

Dollar-value LIFO inventory	$300,900
Price index at year end (the base year)	1.18

Inventory information in succeeding years:

Date	Inventory at End-of-Year Prices	Year-End Price Index	Incremental Layer Index
Dec. 31, 1988	$369,600	1.320	1.240
Dec. 31, 1989	420,206	1.420	1.368
Dec. 31, 1990	435,095	1.505	1.452
Dec. 31, 1991	417,073	1.543	1.515
Dec. 31, 1992	451,627	1.588	1.552

Instructions: Compute the inventory value at December 31 of each year under the dollar-value LIFO inventory method.

Problem 9-9   (LIFO inventory pools—unit LIFO)

On January 1, 1988, Nolder Company changed its inventory cost flow method from FIFO to LIFO for its raw material inventory. The change was made for both financial statement and income tax reporting purposes. Nolder uses the multiple-pools approach under which substantially identical raw materials are grouped into LIFO inventory pools; weighted average costs are used in valuing annual incremental layers. The composition of the December 31, 1990, inventory for the Class F inventory pool is as follows:

	Units	Weighted Average Unit Cost	Total Cost
Base year inventory—1988	9,000	$10.00	$ 90,000
Incremental layer—1989	3,000	11.00	33,000
Incremental layer—1990	2,000	12.50	25,000
Inventory, December 31, 1990	14,000		$148,000

Inventory transactions for the Class F inventory pool during 1991 and 1992 were as follows:

1991

Mar. 1   4,800 units were purchased at a unit cost of $13.50 for $64,800.
Sept. 1   7,200 units were purchased at a unit cost of $14.00 for $100,800.
A total of 15,000 units were used for production during 1991.

1992

Jan. 10   7,500 units were purchased at a unit cost of $14.50 for $108,750.
May 15   5,500 units were purchased at a unit cost of $15.50 for $85,250.
Dec. 29   7,000 units were purchased at a unit cost of $16.00 for $112,000.
A total of 16,000 units were used for production during 1992.

Instructions:

(1) Prepare a schedule to compute the inventory (unit and dollar amounts) of the Class F inventory pool at December 31, 1991. Show supporting computations in good form.
(2) Prepare a schedule to compute the cost of Class F raw materials used in production for the year ended December 31, 1991.
(3) Prepare a schedule to compute the inventory (unit and dollar amounts) of the Class F inventory pool at December 31, 1992. Show supporting computations in good form.   (AICPA adapted)

Problem 9-10   (Change from FIFO to LIFO inventory)

The Greenriver Manufacturing Company manufactures two products: Raft and Float. At December 31, 1991, Greenriver used the first-in, first-out (FIFO) inventory method. Effective January 1, 1992, Greenriver changed to the last-in, first-out (LIFO) inventory method. The cumulative effect of this change is not determinable and, as a result, the ending inventory of 1991 for which the FIFO method was used, is also the beginning inventory for 1992 for the LIFO method. Any layers added during 1992 should be costed by reference to the first acquisitions of 1992 and any layers liquidated during 1992 should be considered a permanent liquidation.

The following information was available from Greenriver inventory records for the two most recent years:

	Raft		Float	
	Units	Unit Cost	Units	Unit Cost
1991 purchases:				
January 7	5,000	$4.00	22,000	$2.00
April 16	12,000	4.50		
November 8	17,000	5.00	18,500	2.50
December 13	10,000	6.00		
1992 purchases:				
February 11	3,000	7.00	23,000	3.00
May 20	8,000	7.50		
October 15	20,000	8.00		
December 23			15,500	3.50
Units on hand:				
December 31, 1991	15,000		14,500	
December 31, 1992	16,000		13,000	

Instructions: Compute the effect on income before income taxes for the year ended December 31, 1992, resulting from the change from the FIFO to the LIFO inventory method.   (AICPA adapted)

*Problem 9-11   (Link-chain index)

On December 31, 1992 Lelegren Architectural Supply took a statistical inventory of items for the sample of its inventory. The inventory revealed the following information:

	Dec. 31, 1990		Dec. 31, 1991		Dec. 31, 1992	
	Quantity	Cost	Quantity	Cost	Quantity	Cost
Pencil leads	2,000	$ 5.00	2,000	$ 5.50	2,200	$ 5.40
Masking tape	1,000	3.00	1,000	3.30	800	3.50
Pink erasers	5,000	4.00	5,000	4.40	5,500	4.75
Vellum paper	3,000	12.00	3,000	13.20	3,200	14.00
Sketch pads	6,000	8.00	6,000	8.80	5,000	9.00
Triangles	1,000	8.00	1,000	8.80	1,000	8.50
Cost of total Inventory at year-end prices		$750,000		$950,000		$1,020,000

Instructions:

(1) Compute the cumulative index for Lelegren Architectural Supply at December 31, 1991 and 1992 using the link-chain method. Assume the cumulative index at December 31, 1990 was 1.5.

(2) Compute the LIFO inventory at December 31, 1992. Assume the December 1990 LIFO inventory at base-year prices was $500,000, and the balance reported on the balance sheet was $625,000.

*Relates to Appendix

*Problem 9-12   (Double extension index)

Kristy's Cosmetics Supply is interested in generating price indexes for inventory. To aid in accomplishing this task, on December 31, 1991, the controller assembled information on various inventory items.

	Dec. 31, 1988	Dec. 31, 1989		Dec. 31, 1990		Dec. 31, 1991	
	Cost	Quantity	Cost	Quantity	Cost	Quantity	Cost
Base make up	$ 8.00	2,000	$8.80				
Body lotion	4.50	1,000	4.80	1,500	$ 5.25		
Eye shadow	6.00	5,000	6.15	5,025	6.35		
Bath oil	5.50	3,000	5.70	3,200	5.90	3,500	$ 5.85
Blush	8.50	6,000	8.55	6,600	8.80	6,200	9.00
Facial cream	6.20	1,000	6.60	1,200	6.80	1,600	7.40
Carrying cases	14.00			2,000	14.80	2,200	15.75
Compacts	17.50					3,100	19.00
Mascara	3.25					5,500	3.95

The controller indicated that 1988 is the base year.

Instructions: Using the double extension method, compute the year-end price index at December 31, 1989, 1990, and 1991.

*Relates to Appendix

Chapter 10

Inventories— Estimation and Noncost Valuation Procedures

This chapter introduces the gross profit and retail inventory methods, both inventory estimation techniques. Inventory estimation may be necessary whenever it is too costly or it is not possible to physically count the inventory. This may occur when there is a fire, a theft, or when monthly financial statements are prepared. The valuation of inventory at the lower of cost or market is also discussed.

Gross Profit Method

The **gross profit method** of estimating inventory costs is based on an assumed relationship between gross profit and sales. A gross profit percentage is applied to sales to determine cost of goods sold; then cost of goods sold is subtracted from the cost of goods available for sale to arrive at an estimated inventory balance.

The gross profit method is useful when:

1. A periodic system is in use and inventories are required for interim statements or for the determination of the week-to-week or month-to-month inventory position, and the cost of taking physical inventories would be excessive for such purposes.
2. Inventories have been destroyed or lost by fire, theft, or other casualty, and the specific data required for inventory valuation are not available.
3. It is desired to test or check the validity of inventory figures determined by other means. Such application is referred to as the **gross profit test**.

The gross profit percentage used must be a reliable measure of current experience. In developing a reliable rate, reference is made to past rates and these are adjusted for variations considered to exist currently. Past gross profit rates, for example, may require adjustment when inventories are valued at last-in, first-out, and significant fluctuations in inventory position and/or prices have occurred. Current changes in cost-price relationships or in the sales mix of specific products also create a need for modifying past rates.

The calculation of cost of goods sold and inventory depends on whether the gross profit percentage is developed and stated in terms of sales or in terms of cost. The procedures to be followed in each case are shown below.

Example 1   Gross profit as a percentage of sales

Assume sales are $100,000 and goods are sold at a gross profit of 40% of sales.

If gross profit is 40% of sales, then cost of goods sold must be 60% of sales.

Sales	100%		Sales	100%
Cost of goods sold	?	=	Cost of goods sold	60%
Gross profit	40%		Gross profit	40%

Cost of goods sold, then, is 60% of $100,000, or $60,000. Goods available for sale less the estimated cost of goods sold gives the estimated cost of the remaining inventory. Assuming the cost of goods available for sale is $85,000, this balance less the estimated cost of goods sold, $60,000, gives an estimated inventory of $25,000.

Example 2   Gross profit as a percentage of cost (or markup on cost)

Assume sales are $100,000 and goods are sold at a gross profit that is 60% of their cost.

If sales are made at a gross profit that is 60% of cost, then sales must be equal to the sum of cost, considered 100%, and the gross profit on cost, 60%. Sales, then, are 160% of cost:

Sales	?		Sales	160%
Cost of goods sold	100%	=	Cost of goods sold	100%
Gross profit	60%		Gross profit	60%

To find cost, or 100%, sales may be divided by 160 and multiplied by 100, or sales may simply be divided by 1.60. Cost of goods sold, then, is $100,000 ÷ 1.60 = $62,500. This amount is subtracted from the cost of goods available for sale to determine the estimated inventory.

When various lines of merchandise are sold at different gross profit rates, it may be possible to develop a reliable inventory value only by making separate calculations for each line. Under such circumstances, it is necessary to develop summaries of sales, goods available for sale, and gross profit data for the different merchandise lines.

In order to use the gross profit method, four elements must be determinable: (1) cost of the beginning inventory, (2) cost of net purchases for the period, (3) sales, and (4) a gross profit rate. Given these four elements, an estimate of the ending inventory can be made. A common application of the gross profit method is the estimation of inventory when a physical count is impossible because of the loss or destruction of goods. For example, assume that on October 31, 1991, a fire in the warehouse of a wholesale distributing company totally destroyed the contents, including many accounting records. Remaining records indicated that the last physical inventory was taken on December 31, 1990, and that the inventory at that date was $329,500. Microfilm bank records of canceled checks disclosed that during 1991 payments to suppliers for inventory items were $1,015,000. Unpaid invoices at the beginning of 1991 amounted to $260,000, and communication with suppliers indicated a balance due at the time of the fire of $315,000. Bank deposits for the ten months amounted to $1,605,000. All deposits came from customers for goods purchased except for a loan of $100,000 obtained from the bank during the year. Accounts receivable at the beginning of the year were $328,000, and an analysis of the available records indicated that accounts receivable on October 31 totaled $275,000. Gross profit percentages on sales for the preceding four years were:

1987	28%	1989	23%
1988	25%	1990	24%

From these facts, the inventory in the warehouse at the time of the fire could be estimated as follows:

Estimate of sales January 1 to October 31, 1991

Collection of accounts receivable ($1,605,000 − $100,000)	$1,505,000
Add accounts receivable balance at October 31, 1991	275,000
	$1,780,000
Deduct accounts receivable balance at January 1, 1991	328,000
Estimate of sales January 1 to October 31, 1991	$1,452,000
Average gross profit percentage on sales for past 4 years	

$$\left(\frac{.28 + .25 + .23 + .24}{4}\right)$$

	25%
Average cost percentage on sales for past 4 years	75%
Estimate of cost of goods sold to October 31, 1991 ($1,452,000 × 75%)	$1,089,000

Estimate of inventory on October 31, 1991

Inventory January 1, 1991		$ 329,500
Add: Payments to suppliers—1991	$1,015,000	
Amounts payable to suppliers, October 31, 1991	315,000	
	$1,330,000	
Deduct accounts payable to suppliers, January 1, 1991	260,000	
Estimate of purchases January 1 to October 31, 1991		1,070,000
Goods available for sale		$1,399,500
Estimate of cost of goods sold for 1991 (from above)		1,089,000
Estimated inventory, October 31, 1991		$ 310,500

Retail Inventory Method

The retail inventory method is widely employed by retail concerns, particularly department stores, to arrive at reliable estimates of inventory position whenever desired. This method, like the gross profit method, permits the calculation of an inventory amount without the time and expense of taking a physical inventory or maintaining a detailed perpetual inventory record for each of the thousands of items normally included in a retail inventory. When this method is used, records of goods purchased are maintained at two amounts—cost and retail. The computer has now made it feasible to maintain cost records for the thousands of items normally included in a retail inventory. A cost percentage is computed by dividing the goods available for sale at cost by the goods available for sale at retail. This cost percentage can then be applied to the ending inventory at retail, an amount that can be readily calculated by subtracting sales for the period from the total goods available for sale at retail.

The computation of retail inventory at the end of a month is illustrated by the following example:

	Cost	Retail
Inventory, January 1	$30,000	$45,000
Purchases in January	20,000	35,000
Goods available for sale	$50,000	$80,000
Cost percentage ($50,000 ÷ $80,000) = 62.5%		
Deduct sales for January		25,000
Inventory, January 31, at retail		$55,000
Inventory, January 31, at estimated cost		
($55,000 × 62.5%)	$34,375	

The effect of the above procedure is to provide an inventory valuation in terms of average cost. No cost sequence, such as LIFO or FIFO, is recognized in the preceding computation; the percentage of cost to retail for the ending inventory is the same as the percentage of cost to retail for goods sold.

Use of the retail inventory method offers the following advantages:

1. Estimated interim inventories can be obtained without a physical count.
2. When a physical inventory is actually taken for financial statement purposes, it can be taken at retail and then converted to cost without reference to individual costs and invoices, thus saving time and expense.
3. Shoplifting losses can be determined and monitored. Since physical counts of inventory costed at retail should agree with the calculated retail inventory, any difference not accounted for by clerical errors in the company records must be attributable to actual physical loss by shoplifting or employee theft.

Although this method permits the estimation of a value for inventory, errors can occur in accounting for the dual prices and in applying the retail method. Thus, a physical count of the inventory to be reported on the annual financial statements is required at least once a year. Retail inventory records should be adjusted for variations shown by the physical count so that records reflect the actual status of the inventory for purposes of future estimates and control.

The accounting entries for the retail inventory method are similar to those made using a periodic inventory system. The retail figures are part of the analysis necessary to compute the cost of the inventory; however, they do not actually appear in the accounts. Thus, the following entries would be made to record the inventory data included in the preceding example.

Purchases	20,000	
Accounts Payable		20,000
Accounts Receivable	25,000	
Sales		25,000
Inventory	4,375	
Cost of Goods Sold	15,625	
Purchases		20,000
To adjust inventory, cost of goods sold, and		
related accounts.		

Markups and Markdowns— Conventional Retail

In the earlier inventory calculations, it was assumed that there were no changes in retail prices after the goods were originally recorded. Frequently, however, retail prices do change because of changes in the price level, shifts in consumer demand, or other factors. The following terms are used in discussing the retail method:

1. **Original retail**—the initial sales price, including the original increase over cost referred to as the **initial markup**.
2. **Additional markups**—increases that raise sales prices above original retail.
3. **Markup cancellations**—decreases in additional markups that do not reduce sales prices below original retail.
4. **Net markups**—Additional markups less markup cancellations.
5. **Markdowns**—decreases that reduce sales prices below original retail.
6. **Markdown cancellations**—decreases in the markdowns that do not raise the sales prices above original retail.
7. **Net markdowns**—markdowns less markdown cancellations.

To illustrate the use of these terms, assume that goods originally placed for sale are marked at 50% above cost. Merchandise costing $4 a unit, then, is marked at $6, which is the **original retail**. The **initial markup** of $2 is referred to as a "50% markup on cost" or a "33⅓% markup on sales price." In anticipation of a heavy demand for the article, the retail price is subsequently increased to $7.50. This represents an **additional markup** of $1.50. At a later date the price is reduced to $7. This is a **markup cancellation** of 50 cents and not a markdown since the retail price has not been reduced below the original sales price. But assume that goods originally marked to sell at $6 are subsequently reduced to a sales price of $5. This represents a **markdown** of $1. At a later date the goods are marked to sell at $5.25. This is a **markdown cancellation** of 25 cents and not a markup, since sales price does not exceed the original retail.

Retail inventory results will vary depending on whether net markdowns are used in computing the cost percentage. When applying the most commonly used retail method, net markups are added to goods available for sale at retail before calculating the cost percentage; net markdowns, however, are not deducted in arriving at the percentage. This method, sometimes referred to as the **conventional retail inventory method**, is illustrated in the following example:

Net markdowns not deducted to calculate cost percentage (Conventional retail):

	Cost	Retail
Beginning inventory	$ 8,600	$ 14,000
Purchases	72,100	110,000
Additional markups		13,000
Markup cancellations		(2,500)
Goods available for sale	$80,700	$ 134,500
Cost percentage ($80,700 ÷ $134,500) = 60%		
Deduct: Sales		$ 108,000
Markdowns		4,800
Markdown cancellations		(800)
		$ 112,000
Ending inventory at retail		$ 22,500
Ending inventory at estimated cost ($22,500 × 60%)	$13,500	

The conventional retail method results in a lower cost percentage and, correspondingly, a lower inventory amount and a higher cost of goods sold than would be obtained if net markdowns were deducted before calculating the cost percentage. This latter approach, the **average cost retail inventory method**, is illustrated at the top of page 387.

The lower inventory obtained with the conventional retail method approximates a **lower of average cost or market** valuation. The lower of cost or market concept, discussed in detail later in this chapter, requires recognition of declines in the value of inventory in the period such declines occur. Under the conventional retail method, markdowns are viewed as indicating a decline in the value of inventory and are deducted as a current cost of sales. When markdowns are included in the cost percentage computation, the result is an average cost allocated proportionately between cost of sales and ending inventory. Thus, only a portion of the decline in value is charged in the current period. The remainder is carried forward in ending inventory to be charged against future sales.

Net markdowns deducted to calculate cost percentage (average cost retail):

	Cost	Retail
Goods available for sale (conventional retail)	$80,700	$134,500
Deduct net markdowns		4,000
Goods available for sale (average cost retail)		$130,500
Cost percentage ($80,700 ÷ $130,500) = 61.84%		
Deduct sales		108,000
Ending inventory at retail		$ 22,500
Ending inventory at estimated cost ($22,500 × 61.84%)	$13,914	

Markdowns may be made for special sales or clearance purposes, or they may be made as a result of market fluctuations and a decline in the replacement cost of goods. In either case their omission in calculating the cost percentage is necessary in order to value the inventory at the lower of cost or market. This is illustrated in the two examples that follow:

Example 1   Markdowns for special sales purposes

Assume that merchandise costing $50,000 is marked to sell for $100,000. To dispose of part of the goods immediately, one fourth of the stock is marked down $5,000 and is sold. The cost of the ending inventory is calculated as follows:

	Cost	Retail
Purchases	$50,000	$100,000
Cost percentage ($50,000 ÷ $100,000) = 50%		
Deduct: Sales		$ 20,000
Markdowns		5,000
		$ 25,000
Ending inventory at retail		$ 75,000
Ending inventory at estimated cost ($75,000 × 50%)	$37,500	

If cost, $50,000, had been related to sales price after markdowns, $95,000, a cost percentage of 52.6% would have been obtained, and the inventory, which is three fourths of the merchandise originally acquired, would have been reported at 52.6% of $75,000, or $39,450. The inventory would thus be stated above the $37,500 cost of the remaining inventory and cost of goods sold would be understated by $1,950. A markdown relating to goods no longer on hand would have been recognized in the development of a cost percentage to be applied to the entire inventory. Reductions in the goods available at sales prices resulting from shortages or damaged goods should likewise be disregarded in calculating the cost percentage.

Example 2   Markdowns as a result of market declines

Assume that merchandise costing $50,000 is marked to sell for $100,000. With a drop in replacement cost of merchandise to $40,000, sales prices are marked down to $80,000. Three fourths of the merchandise is sold. The cost of the ending inventory is calculated as follows:

	Cost	Retail
Purchases	$50,000	$100,000
Cost percentage ($50,000 ÷ $100,000) = 50%		
Deduct: Sales		$ 60,000
Markdowns		20,000
		$ 80,000
Ending inventory at retail		$ 20,000
Ending inventory at estimated cost ($20,000 × 50%)	$10,000	

If cost, $50,000, had been related to sales price after markdowns, $80,000, a cost percentage of 62.5% would have been obtained and the inventory would have been reported at 62.5% of $20,000, or $12,500. The use of the 50% cost percentage in the example reduces the inventory to $10,000, a balance providing the usual gross profit in subsequent periods if current prices and relationships between cost and retail prices prevail.

Freight, Discounts, Returns, and Allowances

In calculating the cost percentage, freight in should be added to the cost of the purchase; purchase discounts and returns and allowances should be deducted. A purchase return affects both the cost and the retail computations, while a purchase allowance affects only the cost total unless a change in retail price is made as a result of the allowance. Sales returns are proper adjustments to gross sales since the inventory is returned; however, sales discounts and sales allowances are *not* deducted to determine the estimated ending retail inventory. The deduction is not made because the sales price of an item is added into the computation of the retail inventory when it is purchased and deducted when it is sold, all at the gross sales price. Subsequent price adjustments included in the computation would leave a balance in the inventory account with no inventory on hand to represent it. For example, assume the sales price for 100 units of Product A is $5,000. When these units are sold for $5,000, the retail inventory balance would be zero. Subsequently, if an allowance of $100 is granted to the customer, the allowance would not be included in the computation of the month-end retail inventory balance. It would be recorded on the books, however, in the usual manner: debit Sales Allowances and credit Accounts Receivable.

Retail Method with Varying Profit Margin Inventories

The calculation of a cost percentage for all goods carried in inventory is valid only when goods on hand can be regarded as representative of the total goods handled. Varying markup percentages and sales of high-margin and low-margin items in proportions that differ from purchases will require separate records and the development of separate cost percentages for different classes of goods. For example, assume that a store operates three departments and that for July the following information pertains to these departments:

	Department A		Department B		Department C		Total	
	Cost	Retail	Cost	Retail	Cost	Retail	Cost	Retail
Beginning inventory	$20,000	$ 28,000	$10,000	$15,000	$16,000	$ 40,000	$ 46,000	$ 83,000
Net purchases	57,000	82,000	20,000	35,000	20,000	60,000	97,000	177,000
Goods available for sale	$77,000	$110,000	$30,000	$50,000	$36,000	$100,000	$143,000	$260,000
Cost percentage	70%		60%		36%		55%	
Sales		80,000		30,000		40,000		150,000
Inventory at retail		$ 30,000		$20,000		$ 60,000		$110,000
Inventory at cost		$ 21,000		$12,000		$ 21,600		$ 60,500

$54,600

Because of the range in cost percentages from 36% to 70% and the difference in mix of the purchases and ending inventory, the ending inventory balance, using an overall cost percentage, is $5,900 higher ($60,500 − $54,600) than when the departmental rates are used. When material variations exist in the cost percentages by departments, separate departmental rates should be computed and applied.

The retail method is acceptable for income tax purposes, provided the taxpayer maintains adequate and satisfactory records supporting inventory calculations and applies the method consistently on successive tax returns.

Dollar-Value LIFO Retail Method

The dollar-value LIFO procedures described in Chapter 9 can be applied to the retail inventory method in developing inventory values reflecting a last-in, first-out valuation approach.[1] The **dollar-value LIFO retail method** requires that index numbers be applied to inventories stated at retail in arriving at the quantitative changes in inventories. After the LIFO retail layers have been identified and priced at the incremental layer index, a further adjustment is needed to state the inventory at cost. This is done by multiplying the retail inventory of each layer by the incremental cost percentage.

The incremental cost percentages for the dollar-value LIFO retail method are computed in a slightly different manner from that done for the conventional retail method. The two principal differences are:

1. Beginning inventory values are disregarded. The LIFO inventory is composed of a base cost and subsequent cost layers that have not been assigned to revenues. Because costs for prior periods remain unchanged, only the cost of a current incremental layer requires calculation.

2. Markdowns, as well as markups, are recognized in calculating the cost percentage applicable to goods stated at retail. Markdowns were not recognized in arriving at the cost percentage when the objective was to

---

[1] Reeve and Stanga found that 195 retail companies in the U.S. used LIFO, and that over 95% of those used the dollar-value LIFO retail method. James M. Reeve and Keith G. Stanga, "The LIFO Pooling Decision: Some Empirical Results from Accounting Practice," *Accounting Horizons* (June 1987), p. 27.

arrive at a lower of cost or market valuation. However, because LIFO measurements require inventory valuation in terms of cost, the recognition of both markups and markdowns is appropriate.

Even though the beginning inventories are not included in the computation of the cost percentage, they are used to determine the amount of retail inventory that should be on hand at the end of the period. Because the retail inventory is adjusted for markups and markdowns, the ending inventory is automatically stated at year-end retail prices.

To illustrate the computation of the LIFO retail incremental cost percentage, the ending inventory at year-end retail prices, and the inventory at dollar-value LIFO retail, assume that the following LIFO retail layer data apply to Morris Department Stores Inc. as of December 31, 1991.

Layer Year	Year-End and Incremental Price Index	Incremental Cost Percentage	Inventory at End-of-Year Retail Prices
1987	1.00	.60	$60,000
1988 (no layer)			
1989	1.05	.62	69,300
1990	1.10	.64	77,000
1991	1.12	.65	77,280

Assume that the 1992 year-end price index is 1.08. The incremental cost percentage and 1992 ending inventory at end-of-year retail prices are computed as follows:

	Cost	Retail
Beginning inventory—December 31, 1991		$ 77,280
Purchases	$ 63,000	$ 98,000
Purchase returns	(2,000)	(3,000)
Purchase discounts	(1,000)	
Freight in	2,220	
Markups, net of cancellations		8,000
Markdowns, net of cancellations		(1,000)
Totals to determine incremental cost percentage—retail-LIFO	$ 62,220	$ 102,000
Incremental cost percentage ($62,220 ÷ $102,000) = 61%		
Goods available for sale		$ 179,280
Deduct: Sales		100,980
Ending inventory at retail (year-end prices)		$ 78,300

From these data, a worksheet similar to that illustrated in Chapter 9 for dollar-value LIFO can be constructed to determine the LIFO retail inventory layers. One additional column is necessary to record the incremental cost percentage that will reduce the retail inventory to cost. It is important to note that the incremental cost percentage is used only if an incremental layer is added to the inventory in the current period. In the example, this situation occurred in 1991 when no layer was added. If the inventory level has declined, previous inventory levels will be reduced using the respective years' incremental layer index and incremental cost percentage.

Dollar-Value LIFO Retail

Date	Inventory at End-of-Year Retail Prices		Year-End Price Index		Inventory at Base-Year Retail Prices	Layers		Incremental Layer Index		Incremental Cost Percentage		Dollar-Value LIFO Retail Cost
December 31, 1988	$60,000	÷	1.00	=	$60,000	$60,000	×	1.00	×	.60	=	$36,000
December 31, 1989	$69,300	÷	1.05	=	$66,000	$60,000	×	1.00	×	.60	=	$36,000
						6,000	×	1.05	×	.62	=	3,906
						$66,000						$39,906
December 31, 1990	$77,000	÷	1.10	=	$70,000	$60,000	×	1.00	×	.60	=	$36,000
						6,000	×	1.05	×	.62	=	3,906
						4,000	×	1.10	×	.64	=	2,816
						$70,000						$42,722
December 31, 1991	$77,280	÷	1.12	=	$69,000	$60,000	×	1.00	×	.60	=	$36,000
						6,000	×	1.05	×	.62	=	3,906
						3,000	×	1.10	×	.64	=	2,112
						$69,000						$42,018
December 31, 1992	$78,300	÷	1.08	=	$72,500	$60,000	×	1.00	×	.60	=	$36,000
						6,000	×	1.05	×	.62	=	3,906
						3,000	×	1.10	×	.64	=	2,112
						3,500	×	1.08	×	.61	=	2,306*
						$72,500						$44,324

*rounded to nearest dollar

Inventory Valuations at Other Than Cost

The basic cost procedures for determining inventory values have been discussed in this and the previous chapter. In some cases, generally accepted accounting principles permit deviations from cost, especially if a write-down of inventory values is warranted. The following sections of this chapter discuss some of these departures from historical cost and the circumstances under which they are appropriate.

Inventory Valuation at Lower of Cost or Market

The conceptual framework establishes and defines recognition criteria for the elements of the financial statements. The definition of an asset requires that it produce future benefits to the owner. If at any time the monetary value assigned to an asset overstates these future benefits, an adjustment should be made to reflect a loss. Recognition criteria limit the adjustment to situations where the asset value can be estimated and a probable loss exists. The application of these accounting concepts to inventory is known as valuation at the lower of cost or market (LCM).

Currently, generally accepted accounting principles permit recognition of increases in the value of assets above cost only after the increase is realized and/or earned. The current practice of recognizing inventory write-downs before realization but not inventory writeups until after realization results in inconsistent treatment of value changes.

The American Institute of Certified Public Accountants (AICPA) sanctioned lower of cost or market valuation in the following statement:

> A departure from the cost basis of pricing the inventory is required when the utility of the goods is no longer as great as its cost. Where there is evidence that the utility of goods, in their disposal in the ordinary course of business, will be less than cost, whether due to physical deterioration, obsolescence, changes in price levels, or other causes, the difference should be recognized as a loss of the current period. This is generally accomplished by stating such goods at a lower level commonly designated as market.[2]

In applying the lower of cost or market rule, the cost of the ending inventory, as determined under an appropriate cost allocation method, is compared with market value at the end of the period. If market is less than cost, an adjusting entry is made to record the loss and restate ending inventory at the lower value. It should be noted that no adjustment to LIFO cost is permitted for tax purposes; however, for financial reporting purposes, the lower of cost or market rule applies to all inventories. Application of LCM to LIFO inventories for financial reporting purposes does not violate the "LIFO conformity" rules if IRS approval is obtained.

Definition of Market

The term **market** in "lower of cost or market" is interpreted as replacement cost with upper and lower limits that reflect estimated realizable values. This concept of market was stated by the AICPA as follows:

> As used in the phrase *lower of cost or market*, the term *market* means current replacement cost (by purchase or by reproduction, as the case may be) except that:
> (1) Market should not exceed the net realizable value (i.e., estimated selling price in the ordinary course of business less reasonably predictable costs of completion and disposal); and
> (2) Market should not be less than net realizable value reduced by an allowance for an approximately normal profit margin.[3]

Replacement cost, sometimes referred to as **entry cost**, includes the purchase price of the product or raw materials plus all other costs incurred in the acquisition or manufacture of goods. Because wholesale and retail prices are generally related, declines in entry costs usually indicate declines in selling prices or **exit values**. However, exit values do not always respond immediately and in proportion to changes in entry costs. If selling price does not decline, there is no loss in utility and a write-down of inventory values would not be warranted. On the other hand, selling prices may decline in response to factors unrelated to replacement costs. Perhaps an inventory item has been used as a demonstrator which reduces its

---

[2]*Accounting Research and Terminology Bulletins—Final Edition*, No. 43, "Restatement and Revision of Accounting Research Bulletins" (New York: American Institute of Certified Public Accountants, 1961), Ch. 4, statement 5.

[3]*Ibid.*, statement 6.

marketability as a new product. Or perhaps an item is damaged in storage or becomes shopworn from excessive handling.

The AICPA definition considers exit values as well as entry costs by establishing a ceiling for the market value at sales price less costs of completion and disposal and a floor for market at sales price less both the costs of completion and disposal and the normal profit margin. The **ceiling limitation** is applied so the inventory is not valued at more than its net realizable value (NRV). Failure to observe this limitation would result in charges to future revenue that exceed the utility carried forward and an ultimate loss on the sale of the inventory. The **floor limitation** is applied so the inventory is not valued at less than its net realizable value minus a **normal profit**. The concept of normal profit is a difficult one to measure objectively. Profits vary by item and over time. Records are seldom accurate enough to determine a normal profit by individual inventory item. Despite these difficulties, however, the use of a floor prevents a definition of market that would result in a write-down of inventory values in one period to create an abnormally high profit in future periods.

Applying Lower of Cost or Market Method

Application of the LCM rule to determine the appropriate inventory valuation may be summarized in the following steps:

1. Define pertinent values: cost, replacement cost, upper limit (NRV), lower limit (NRV — normal profit).
2. Determine "market" (replacement cost as modified by upper or lower limits).
3. Compare cost with market (as defined in 2 above), and select the lower amount.

To illustrate these steps, assume that a certain commodity sells for $1; selling expenses are $.20; the normal profit is 25% of sales or $.25. The lower of cost or market as modified by the upper and lower limits is developed in each case as shown in the illustration below.

				Market		
Case	Cost	Replacement Cost	Lower Limit—Floor (Estimated sales price less selling expenses and normal profits)	Upper Limit— Ceiling (Estimated sales price less selling expenses)	Market (Limited by floor and ceiling values)	Lower of Cost or Market
A	$.65	$ .70	$.55	$.80	$.70	$.65
B	.65	.60	.55	.80	.60	.60
C	.65	.50	.55	.80	.55	.55
D	.50	.45	.55	.80	.55	.50
E	.75	.85	.55	.80	.55	.50
F	.90	1.00	.55	.80	.80	.80

A: Market is not limited by floor or ceiling; cost is less than market.
B: Market is not limited by floor or ceiling; market is less than cost.
C: Market is limited to floor; market is less than cost.
D: Market is limited to floor; cost is less than market.
E: Market is limited to ceiling; cost is less than market.
F: Market is limited to ceiling; market is less than cost.

The following dollar line graphically illustrates the floor and ceiling range. B and A replacement costs clearly are within bounds and therefore are defined as market. D and C are below the floor and thus the market is the floor; E and F are above the ceiling and market therefore is the ceiling.

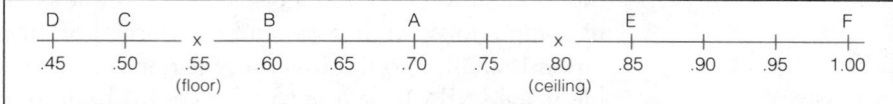

Note that the market value is always the middle value of three amounts: replacement cost, floor, and ceiling.

The lower of cost or market method may be applied to each inventory item, to the major classes or categories of inventory items, or to the inventory as a whole. Application of this procedure to the individual inventory items will result in the lowest inventory value and is the most commonly used application because it is required for income tax purposes. Once an individual item is reduced to a lower market price, the new market price is considered to be the item's cost for future inventory valuations; cost reductions once made are not restored. Thus, detailed inventory records must be adjusted to reflect the new values.

Application of the lower of cost or market method to inventory classes or to the inventory as a whole produces a more representative valuation and avoids the necessity of adjusting individual inventory items. Because declines in the value of some items are offset by increases in value of other items, the value of the items in the detailed inventory records are not adjusted. To assure that the detailed records agree with the inventory control account, an allowance system similar to that described in Chapter 8 for marketable securities would have to be used.

To illustrate the difference in valuation applications, assume Clarks Men's Store classifies its inventories into three categories: (1) formal wear, (2) casual wear and (3) sports wear. As shown on page 395, the inventory, on an individual item basis, the inventory would be valued at $360,300, a reduction from cost of $29,500. The valuation based on categories and on the total inventory would be $371,300 and $377,300 respectively.

The entry to record the writedown of the inventory on an individual item basis is usually made directly to the inventory control account as follows:

```
Loss from Decline in Value of Inventory . . . . . . . . . . . .    29,500
     Inventory  . . . . . . . . . . . . . . . . . . . . . . . . . . . . . . . . . . . . . . .    29,500
        Write down of inventory to market.
```

Any subsidiary inventory records would also be reduced for the decline. The loss on the decline in market value may be shown as a separate item in the income statement after cost of goods sold. Alternatively, the loss may be reflected directly in the cost of goods sold section by reporting the ending inventory at market rather than cost. To illustrate the two reporting

Clarks Men's Store
Applications of Lower of Cost or Market

| Classes and Items | Cost | Market | Cost or Market Whichever is Lower | | |
			Individual Items	Inventory Categories	Total Inventory
Formal wear:					
Tuxedos	$ 75,000	$ 70,000	$ 70,000		
Suits	120,000	130,000	120,000		
Dress shirts	30,000	28,000	28,000		
Dress shoes	18,000	21,000	18,000		
Total formal wear	$243,000	$249,000	$236,000	$243,000	
Casual wear:					
Slacks	$ 39,500	$ 32,000	$ 32,000		
Casual shirts	26,000	23,000	23,000		
Sweaters	15,000	17,000	15,000		
Total casual wear	$ 80,500	$ 72,000	$ 70,000	$ 72,000	
Sports wear:					
Sport shirts	$ 39,000	$ 29,000	$ 29,000		
Swimming wear	10,000	8,000	8,000		
Warm-ups	17,300	19,300	17,300		
Total sports wear	$ 66,300	$ 56,300	$ 54,300	$ 56,300	
Total inventory	$389,800	$377,300			377,300
			$360,300	$371,300	$377,300

alternatives, assume that sales for the period totaled $1.2 million and beginning inventory and net purchases were $280,000 and $855,000, respectively.

Inventory Loss Reported Separately

Sales		$1,200,000
Cost of goods sold:		
Beginning inventory	$ 280,000	
Purchases	855,000	
Cost of goods available for sale	$1,135,000	
Ending inventory (at cost)	389,800	745,200
Gross profit		$ 454,800
Inventory loss due to writedown of cost to market		29,500
		$ 425,300

Inventory Loss Included in Cost of Goods Sold

Sales		$1,200,000
Cost of goods sold:		
Beginning inventory	$ 280,000	
Purchases	855,000	
Cost of goods available for sale	$1,135,000	
Ending inventory (at market which is lower than cost)	360,300	774,700
Gross profit		$ 425,300

Separate reporting of the loss has the advantage of providing readers with increased information to forecast operations and cash flows.

Rather than reducing the inventory directly, the inventory control account could be maintained at cost, and an allowance for inventory decline used to record the decline in value. This method would generally be used when inventory is valued on a category or entire inventory basis. The entry to record the writedown using an allowance for the categories of Clarks Men's Store would be as follows:

Loss from Decline in Value of Inventory	18,500	
Allowance for Decline in Value of Inventory		18,500

The allowance account would be reported as an offset to the inventory account on the balance sheet. In subsequent years, it will be adjusted upward or downward depending on the amount required to adjust cost to market. If the required allowance declines, a recovery or gain entry would be recorded. Assume the difference between cost and market for the three categories in the next year is only $9,500. The adjusting entry to record this information in the next year would be as follows:

Allowance for Decline in Value of Inventory	9,000	
Recovery of Decline in Value of Inventory		9,000

As is true for marketable securities, the recovery is limited by the amount in the allowance account. The category and total inventory applications are not acceptable for income tax purposes.[4]

Evaluation of Lower of Cost or Market Rule

As mentioned earlier, the lower of cost or market rule is evidence of the concept of accounting conservatism. Its strict application has been applied to avoid valuing inventory on the balance sheet at more than replacement cost. Also as discussed earlier, the AICPA replaced this strict entry valuation with a utility measure that relies partially upon exit prices. If selling prices for the inventory have declined and the decline is expected to hold until the inventory is sold, the adjustment of income in the period of the decline seems justified. The value of the inventory has been impaired, which requires current adjustment. However, care must be taken in using this method not to manipulate income by allowing excessive charges against income in one period to be offset by excessive income in the next period.

Some accountants have argued against the use of cost or market because it violates the cost concept. Market valuations are often subjective

---

[4]Many disputes have arisen through the years between taxpayers and the IRS as to what constitutes a recognizable decline in inventory value. An important tax case in this area was settled by the U.S. Supreme Court in 1979. The taxpayer, Thor Power Tool Co., had followed the practice of writing down the value of spare parts inventories that were being held to cover future warranty requirements. Although the sales prices did not decline, the probablity of the parts being sold, and thus their net realizable value, decreased as time passed. The write-down to reflect the current decline in value is consistent with the accounting principle of recognizing declines in value as they occur. The Supreme Court, however, ruled that for tax purposes the reduction must await the actual decline in the sales price for the parts in question.

and based on expectations. To the extent these expectations are not realized, misleading financial statements will be produced. To illustrate, assume that activities summarized in terms of cost provide the following results over a three year period:

	1990		1991		1992	
Sales		$200,000		$225,000		$250,000
Cost of goods sold:						
Beginning inventory	$ 60,000		$ 80,000		$127,500	
Purchases	120,000		160,000		90,000	
Goods available for sale	$180,000		$240,000		$217,500	
Less ending inventory	80,000	100,000	127,500	112,500	92,500	125,000
Gross profit on sales		$100,000		$112,500		$125,000
Operating expenses		80,000		90,000		100,000
Net income		$ 20,000		$ 22,500		$ 25,000
Rate of income to sales		10%		10%		10%

Assume estimates as to the future utility of ending inventories indicated market values as follows:

1990	1991	1992
$75,000	$110,000	$92,500

If the expected decline in selling prices did not occur, inventory valuation at the lower of cost or market would provide the following results.

	1990		1991		1992	
Sales		$200,000		$225,000		$250,000
Cost of goods sold:						
Beginning inventory	$ 60,000		$ 75,000		$110,000	
Purchases	120,000		160,000		90,000	
Goods available for sale	$180,000		$235,000		$200,000	
Less ending inventory	75,000	105,000	110,000	125,000	92,500	107,500
Gross profit on sales		$ 95,000		$100,000		$142,500
Operating expenses		80,000		90,000		100,000
Net income		$ 15,000		$ 10,000		$ 42,500
Rate of income to sales		7.5%		4.4%		17.0%

Reduction of an inventory below cost reduces the net income of the period in which the reduction is made and increases the net income of a subsequent period over what it would have been. In the example just given, total net income for the three-year period is the same under either set of calculations. But the reduction of inventories to lower market values reduced the net income for 1990 and for 1991 and increased the net income for 1992. The fact that inventory reductions were not followed by decreases in the sales prices resulted in net income determinations that varied considerably from those that might reasonably have been expected from increasing sales and costs that normally vary with sales volume.

Objection to valuation at the lower of cost or market is also raised on the grounds it produces inconsistencies in the measurements of both the financial position and the operations of the enterprise. Market decreases are recognized, but increases are not. Although this system does produce some inconsistent application to the upward and downward movement of market, the authors feel that the lower of cost or market concept is preferable to a strict cost measurement. A loss in the utility of any asset should be reflected in the period the impairment is first recognized and a reasonable estimate of its significance can be determined.

Losses on Purchase Commitments

Purchase commitments are contracts made for the future purchase of goods at fixed prices. No entry is required to record the purchase prior to delivery of the goods. However, when price declines take place subsequent to such commitments, it is considered appropriate to measure and recognize these losses on the books just as losses on goods on hand are recognized. A decline is recorded by a debit to a special loss account and a credit to either a contra asset account or an accrued liability account, such as Estimated Loss on Purchase Commitments. Acquisition of the goods in a subsequent period is recorded by a credit to Accounts Payable, a debit canceling the credit balance in the contra asset or accrued liability account, and a debit to Purchases for the difference.

For example, assume that Rollins Manufacturing Company entered into a purchase contract for $120,000 of materials to be delivered in March of the following year. At the end of the current year, the market price for this order had fallen to $100,000. The entries to record this decline and subsequent delivery of the materials would be as follows:

Dec. 31	Loss on Purchase Commitments	20,000	
	Estimated Loss on Purchase Commitments		20,000
Mar. 31	Estimated Loss on Purchase Commitments	20,000	
	Purchases	100,000	
	Accounts Payable		120,000

The loss is thus assigned to the period in which the decline took place, and a subsequent period is charged for no more than the economic utility of the goods it receives. Current loss recognition would not be appropriate when commitments can be canceled, when commitments provide for price adjustment, when hedging transactions[5] prevent losses, or when declines do not suggest reductions in sale prices. No adjustments are customarily made if a recovery occurs prior to delivery.

Valuation of Trade-Ins and Repossessions

When goods are acquired in secondhand condition as a result of repossessions and trade-ins, they should be recorded at their estimated cash purchase price. In some industries, these prices are defined and made

---

[5]Purchases or sales entered into for the purpose of balancing, respectively, sales or purchases already made or under contract in order to offset the effects of price fluctuations.

available to dealers. One of the more organized used markets is that for automobiles. A book, published frequently in the various geographical markets of the country, lists low, medium, and high market values for the different models and makes of cars. It also distinguishes between retail and wholesale values. Similar lists are provided for machinery and equipment in some lines. When these publications exist, the prices listed may be used to value repossessed or trade-in inventory.

When published prices are not available, it is more difficult to measure the equivalent cash purchase price of the inventory. Under these conditions, the consistent use of **floor values**—amounts that, after adding reconditioning charges and selling expenses, will permit the recognition of normal profits—would be appropriate.

Accounting for trade-ins is illustrated by the following example: Christensen Department Store sells a new washing machine to a customer for $350 cash and a trade-in of an old washer. It is estimated that a realistic floor value for the trade-in is $50. Reconditioning costs of $30 are incurred after which the trade-in washer is sold for $120, an amount that provides a normal profit. Perpetual inventory records are maintained for trade-ins but not for the regular inventory. The entries shown below reflect these transactions:

Cash	350	
Trade-In Inventory	50	
Sales		400
Trade-In Inventory	30	
Cash		30
Cash	120	
Sales—Trade-Ins		120
Cost of Trade-Ins Sold	80	
Trade-In Inventory		80

Another approach to valuing trade-in inventories is to establish clearly the sales price of the new inventory being sold, and charge the trade-in inventory for the difference between a cash sales price and the cash required with the trade-in. Assume in the case of the washing machine that the regular cash sales price without a trade-in could be established at $390. The value assigned to the trade-in would thus be $40, the difference between $390 and $350.

Accounting for repossessions requires a slightly different approach. Assume Christensen Department Store sold another washing machine on account for $350 plus interest on the unpaid balance. The customer made principal payments of $200 on the machine and then defaulted on the contract. The machine was repossessed and overhauled at a cost of $40. It was then sold for $150, a price that provided a normal profit of 50% on cost.

The following entries reflect the repossession and subsequent resale.

Loss on Repossession		90	
Repossessed Inventory		60	
Accounts Receivable			150

Computation:
Value of repossession established to permit 50% normal profit on cost.
  (33⅓% on selling price.)

Selling price	$150
Less profit at 33⅓%	50
Cost of repossessed goods sold	$100
Less cost of overhaul	40
Value of repossessed inventory	$ 60

Repossessed Inventory		40	
Cash			40
Cost to overhaul repossessed washing machine.			

Cash		150	
Sales—Repossessed Inventory			150
Sale of repossed washing machine.			

Cost of Repossessed Goods Sold		100	
Repossessed Inventory			100
Cost of repossessed washing machine.			

Effects of Errors In Recording Inventory Position

Failures to report the inventory position accurately result in misstatements on both the balance sheet and the income statement. The effect on the income statement is sometimes difficult to evaluate because of the different amounts that can be affected by an error. Analysis of the impact is aided by recalling the structure of the cost of goods sold section of the income statement:

$$\text{Beginning Inventory}$$
$$+$$
$$\text{Purchases}$$
$$=$$
$$\text{Goods Available for Sale}$$
$$-$$
$$\text{Ending Inventory}$$
$$=$$
$$\text{Cost of Goods Sold}$$

An overstatement of the beginning inventory will thus result in an overstatement of goods available for sale and cost of goods sold. Because the cost of goods sold is deducted from sales to determine the gross profit, the overstated cost of goods sold results in an understated gross profit and finally an understated net income. Sometimes an error may affect two of the amounts in such a way that they offset each other. For example, if a purchase in transit under the FIFO method is neither recorded as a purchase nor included in the ending inventory, the understatement of purchases results in an understatement of goods available for sale; however, the understatement of ending inventory subtracted from goods available for sale off-sets the error and creates a correct cost of goods sold, gross profit, and net income. Inventory and accounts payable, however, will be understated on the balance sheet.

Because the ending inventory of one period becomes the beginning inventory of the next period, undetected accounting errors affect two accounting periods. If left undetected, the errors will offset each other under a FIFO or average method. Errors in LIFO layers, however, may perpetuate themselves until the layer is eliminated.

This type of analysis is required for all inventory errors. It is unwise to try to memorize the impact an error has on the financial statements. It is preferable to analyze each situation. The following analyses of four typical inventory errors, with their impact on both the current and succeeding years, provide additional opportunity for students to practice the above type of analysis.

1. Overstatement of the ending inventory through errors in the count of goods on hand, pricing, or the inclusion in inventory of goods not owned or goods already sold:

   Current year:
   Income statement—overstatement of the ending inventory will cause the cost of goods sold to be understated and the net income to be overstated.
   Balance sheet—the inventory will be overstated and the owners' equity will be overstated.

   Succeeding year:
   Income statement—overstatement of the beginning inventory will cause the cost of goods sold to be overstated and the net income to be understated.
   Balance sheet—the error of the previous year will have been counter-balanced on the succeeding income statement and the balance sheet will be correctly stated.

2. Understatement of ending inventory through errors in the count of goods on hand, pricing, or the failure to include in inventory goods purchased or goods transferred but not yet sold:
   Misstatements indicated in (1) above are reversed.

3. Overstatement of ending inventory accompanied by failure to recognize sales and corresponding receivables at end of period:

   Current year:
   Income statement—sales are understated by the sales price of the goods and cost of goods sold is understated by the cost of the goods relating to the sales; gross profit and net income are thus understated by the gross profit on the sales.

Balance sheet—receivables are understated by the sales price of the goods and the inventory is overstated by the cost of the goods that were sold; current assets and owners' equity are thus understated by the gross profit on the sales.

Succeeding year:
Income statement—sales of the preceding year are recognized in this year in sales and cost of sales; gross profit and net income, therefore, are overstated by the gross profit on such sales.
Balance sheet—the error of the previous year is counterbalanced on the succeeding income statement and the balance sheet will be correctly stated.

4. Understatement of ending inventory accompanied by failure to recognize purchases and corresponding payables at end of period:

Current year:
Income statement—purchases are understated, but this is counterbalanced by the understatement of the ending inventory; gross profit and net income are correctly stated as a result of the counterbalancing effect of the error.
Balance sheet—although owners' equity is reported correctly, both current assets and current liabilities are understated.

Succeeding year:
Income statement—the beginning inventory is understated, but this is counterbalanced by an overstatement of purchases, as purchases at the end of the prior year are recognized currently; gross profit and net income are correctly stated as a result of the counterbalancing effect of the error.
Balance sheet—the error of the previous year no longer affects balance sheet data.

This analysis can be summarized in tabular form as shown on page 403; (+) indicates overstatement, (−) indicates understatement, and (0) indicates no effect.

The correcting entry for each of these errors depends on when the error is discovered. If it is discovered in the current year, adjustments can be made to current accounts, and the reported net income and balance sheet amounts will be correct. If the error is not discovered until the subsequent period, the correcting entry qualifies as a prior period adjustment if the net income of the prior period was misstated. The error to a prior years' income is corrected through retained earnings. To illustrate these entries, assume that error number three has occurred. The correcting entries required, depending on when the error is discovered, would be as follows. Assume the use of a perpetual inventory system.

Error discovered in current year (cost of inventory $1,000; sales price of inventory, $1,500).

Summary of Impact of Inventory Errors on Financial Statements

| | Current year | | | | | | Subsequent Year | | | | | |
| | Income Statement | | | Balance Sheet | | | Income Statement | | | Balance Sheet | | |
	Sales	Cost of goods sold	Net income	Assets	Lia-bili-ties	Equity	Sales	Cost of goods sold	Net income	Assets	Lia-bili-ties	Equity
(1) Overstatement of ending inventory	0	−	+	+	0	+	0	+	−	0	0	0
(2) Understatement of ending inventory	0	+	−	−	0	−	0	−	+	0	0	0
(3) Overstatement of ending inventory and understatement of sales	−	−	−	−	0	−	+	+	+	0	0	0
(4) Understatement of ending inventory and understatement of purchases	0	0	0	−	−	0	0	0	0	0	0	0

Accounts Receivable...............................	1,500	
Cost of Goods Sold	1,000	
Inventory		1,000
Sales..		1,500

Error discovered in subsequent year (sale has been recorded in subsequent year).

Sales	1,500	
Cost of Goods Sold		1,000
Retained Earnings		500

If trend statistics are included in the annual reports, prior years' balances should be adjusted to reflect the correction of the error. Present-day audit techniques can substantially reduce the probability of material inventory errors.

Inventories on the Balance Sheet

It is customary to report both trading and manufacturing inventories as current assets even though in some situations, considerable time will elapse before portions of such inventories are realized in cash. Among the items that are generally reported separately under the inventories heading are merchandise inventory or finished goods, goods in process, raw materials, factory supplies, goods and materials in transit, goods on consignment, and goods in the hands of agents and salespersons. Inventories are normally listed in the order of their liquidity. Any advance payments on purchase commitments should be reported separately and should not be included with inventories. Such advances are preferably listed after inventories in the current asset section since they have not entered the inventory phase of the operating cycle.

The valuation procedures employed must be disclosed in a note to the financial statements outlining all significant accounting policies followed.[6] The basis of valuation (such as cost or lower of cost or market), together with the method of arriving at cost (LIFO, FIFO, average, or other method), should be indicated. The reader of a statement may assume that the valuation procedures indicated have been consistently applied and financial statements are comparable with those of past periods. If this is not the case, a special note should be provided stating the change in the method and the effects of the change upon the financial statements.

If significant inventory price declines take place between the balance sheet date and the date the statement is prepared, such declines should be disclosed by parenthetical remark or note. When relatively large orders for merchandise have been placed by the reporting company in a period of widely fluctuating prices, but the title to such goods has not yet passed, such commitments should be described by special note. Information should also be provided concerning possible losses on purchase commitments. Similar information may be appropriate for possible losses on sales commitments.

Replacement costs of inventories may be disclosed in a note to the financial statements. Until such time as market valuation of inventories becomes generally acceptable for reporting purposes, only supplemental disclosure of current values is permitted.

When inventories or sections of an inventory have been pledged as security on loans from banks, finance companies, or factors, the amounts pledged should be disclosed either parenthetically in the inventory section of the balance sheet or in the notes. The Eastman Kodak Company note reproduced on page 405 illustrates the disclosure requirements for inventories.

[6]*Opinions of the Accounting Principles Board*, No. 22, "Disclosure of Accounting Policies" (New York: American Institute of Certified Public Accountants, 1972), par. 12.

Exhibit 10-1   Eastman Kodak Company

Inventories

Inventories at year-end consisted of the following:

(in millions)	1987	1986
At average cost		
Finished goods	$1,371	$1,336
Work in process.......................	935	899
Raw materials and supplies	806	715
	3,112	2,950
LIFO reserve	(934)	(878)
Total.............................	$2,178	$2,072

During 1986, the valuation of nearly all inventories outside the U.S. was changed from the last-in, first-out (LIFO) method of valuation to the first-in, first-out (FIFO) or average cost valuation method. As a result of the extreme fluctuations of many foreign currencies against the U.S. dollar, use of the LIFO inventory accounting method does not provide the best matching of costs and revenues for such inventories. This change did not have a material impact on earnings.

Inventories valued on the last-in, first-out method are about 60 percent of total inventories (1986—70 percent).

Key Terms   Additional markups 385
Average cost retail inventory method
386
Ceiling limitation 393
Conventional retail inventory method
386
Cost percentage 384
Dollar-value LIFO retail method 389
Entry cost 392
Exit values 392
Floor limitation 393
Freight in 388

Gross profit method 381
Initial markup (markon) 385
Lower of cost or market (LCM) 391
Markdown cancellations 385
Markdowns 385
Market (lower of cost or market) 392
Markup cancellations 385
Net markdowns 385
Net markups 385
Original retail 385
Replacement cost 392
Retail inventory method 384

Questions   1. What is meant by the term "gross profit test"?
2. Distinguish between: (a) gross profit as a percentage of cost and gross profit as a percentage of sales; (b) the gross profit method of calculating estimated inventory cost and the retail inventory method of calculating estimated inventory cost.
3. What effect would the use of the LIFO inventory method have upon the applicability of the gross profit method of valuing inventory?
4. (a) How are markdowns treated under the conventional retail method? (b) What costing method is approximated by this approach?
5. How does the conventional retail inventory method differ from the average cost retail inventory method?
6. How are purchase discounts and sales discounts treated when using the retail inventory method?
7. (a) Describe dollar-value LIFO retail. (b) How does the LIFO retail cost percentage differ from the conventional retail cost percentage?
8. Under what circumstances would a decline in replacement cost of an item not justify a departure from the cost basis of valuing an inventory?
9. The use of lower of cost or market is an archaic continuation of conservative accounting. Comment on this view.
10. Why is a ceiling and floor limitation on replacement cost considered necessary by the AICPA?
11. The Muhlstein Corporation began business on January 1, 1990. Information about inventories, as of December 31 for three consecutive years, under different valuation methods is shown below. Using this information and assuming that the same method is used each year, you are to choose the phrase which best answers each of the following questions:

	LIFO Cost	FIFO Cost	Market	Lower of Cost or Market*
1990	$10,200	$10,000	$ 9,600	$ 8,900
1991	9,100	9,000	8,800	8,500
1992	10,300	11,000	12,000	10,900

*FIFO Cost, item by item valuation.

(a) The inventory basis that would result in the highest net income for 1990 is: (1) LIFO cost, (2) FIFO cost, (3) Market, (4) Lower of cost or market.

(b) The inventory basis that would result in the highest net income for 1991 is: (1) LIFO cost, (2) FIFO cost, (3) Market, (4) Lower of cost or market.

(c) The inventory basis that would result in the lowest net income for the three years combined is: (1) LIFO cost, (2) FIFO cost, (3) Market, (4) Lower of cost or market.

(d) For the year 1991, how much higher or lower would net income be on the FIFO cost basis than on the lower of cost or market basis? (1) $400 higher, (2) $400 lower, (3) $600 higher, (4) $600 lower, (5) $1,000 higher, (6) $1,000 lower, (7) $1,400 higher, (8) $1,400 lower.

12. How does the accounting treatment for losses on purchase commitments differ between actual losses which have already occurred and losses which may occur in the future?

13. What is the justification for valuing trade-ins or repossessions so that a normal profit can be realized upon their sale?

14. How should repossessed goods be valued for inventory purposes? Give reasons for your answers.

15. How would you recommend that the following items be reported on the balance sheet?

(a) Unsold goods in the hands of consignees.
(b) Purchase orders outstanding.
(c) Advance payments on purchase commitments.
(d) Raw materials pledged by means of warehouse receipts on notes payable to bank.
(e) Raw materials in transit from suppliers.
(f) Goods produced by special order and set aside to be picked up by custom·er.
(g) Finished parts to be used in the assembly of final products.
(h) Office supplies.

16. State the effect of each of the following errors made by Clawson Inc. upon the balance sheet and the income statement (1) of the current period and (2) of the succeeding period:

(a) The company fails to record a sale of merchandise on account; goods sold are excluded in recording the ending inventory.
(b) The company fails to record a sale of merchandise on account; the goods sold are included, however, in recording the ending inventory.
(c) The company fails to record a purchase of merchandise on account; goods purchased are included in recording the ending inventory.
(d) The company fails to record a purchase of merchandise on account; goods purchased are not recognized in recording the ending inventory.
(e) The ending inventory is understated as the result of a miscount of goods on hand.

Discussion Cases   **Case 10–1   (Where has the inventory gone?)**

Main Street Department Store uses the retail inventory method. Periodically, a physical count is made of the inventory and compared with the book figure computed from the company sales and purchase records. This year the extended valuation of the physical count resulted in a total inventory value 10% lower than the book figure. Jennifer Strack, the controller, is concerned by the variance. A 2 to 3% loss from shoplifting has been tolerated through the years. But 10% is too much. The branch manager, Bryan Smith, who is summoned to account for the discrepancy, insists that the book figures must be wrong. He is confident that the shortage could not be that high, but that bookkeeping errors must be at fault. Strack, however, is not satisfied with the explanation, and asks Smith to outline specifically what types of errors could have caused such a variance. Prepare Smith's outline for Strack.

Case 10–2   (Inventory valuation without records)

The Ma & Pa Grocery Store has never kept many records. The proceeds from sales are used to pay suppliers for goods delivered. When the owners, Donald and Alicia Wride, need some cash, they withdraw it from the till without any record being made of it. The Wrides realize that eventually tax returns must be filed, but for three years "they just don't get around to it." Finally, the Internal Revenue Service catches up with the Wrides, and an audit of the company records is conducted. The auditor requests the general ledger, special journals, inventory counts, and supporting documentation—very little of which is available. Records of expenditures are extremely sketchy because most expenses are paid in cash. If you were the IRS auditor, what might you do to make a reasonable estimate of income for the company.

Case 10–3   (Have we really had a loss?)

The Destro Company is experiencing an unusual inventory situation. The replacement cost of its principal product has been declining, but because of a unique market condition, Destro has not had to reduce the selling price of the item. Eric Dona, company controller, is aware that GAAP requires the valuation of inventory at the lower of cost or market. He considers market to be replacement cost, and is concerned that to reduce the ending inventory to replacement cost will improperly reduce net income for the current period. Has an inventory loss occurred? Discuss.

Case 10–4   (What value should we place on the clunker?)

The Ritchie Automobile Agency is an exclusive agency for the sales of foreign sports automobiles. As part of its sales strategy, Ritchie allows liberal trade-ins on the sale of its new cars. A used car division of the company sells these trade-ins at a separate location, usually at an amount significantly lower than the trade-in allowance. This division is continually showing large losses because the cars are charged to the division at their trade-in values. John Lund, manager of the used car division, has requested that the costing procedure be changed, and that trade-ins be recorded at a price sufficiently below expected retail to allow a reasonable profit to his division. Janet Perry, controller of the agency, acknowledges that some adjustment needs to be made to the inflated trade-in values, but feels that expected retail value should be used without allowance for a profit. What value should be used on the financial statements for the ending inventory of trade-ins? Discuss the reasonableness of this method for internal management evaluations.

Exercises   **Exercise 10–1   (Inventory loss—gross profit method)**

On August 15, 1991, a hurricane damaged a warehouse of Folkman Merchandise Company. The entire inventory and many accounting records stored in the warehouse were completely destroyed. Although the inventory was not insured, a portion could be sold for scrap. Through the use of microfilmed records, the following data are assembled:

Inventory, January 1	$ 275,000
Purchases, January 1–August 15	1,385,000
Cash sales, January 1–August 15	225,000
Collection of accounts receivable, January 1–August 15	1,932,000
Accounts receivable, January 1	175,000
Accounts receivable, August 15	265,000
Salvage value of inventory	5,000
Gross profit percentage on sales	30%

Compute the inventory loss as a result of the hurricane.

Exercise 10–2   (Inventory loss—gross profit method)

On June 30, 1991, a flash flood damaged the warehouse and factory of Bend Corporation, completely destroying the work-in-process inventory. There was no damage to either the raw materials or finished goods inventories. A physical inventory taken after the flood revealed the following valuations:

Finished goods	$112,000
Work in process	-0-
Raw materials	52,000

The inventory on January 1, 1991, consisted of the following:

Finished goods	$120,000
Work in process	115,000
Raw materials	28,500
	$263,500

A review of the books and records disclosed that the gross profit margin historically approximated 35% of sales. The sales for the first six months of 1991 were $365,000.

Raw material purchases were $96,000. Direct labor costs for this period were $90,000, and factory overhead has historically been applied at 50% of direct labor.

Compute the value of the work-in-process inventory lost at June 30, 1991. Show supporting computations in good form.   (AICPA adapted)

Exercise 10–3   (Retail inventory method)

Hilo Department Store uses the retail inventory method. On December 31, 1991, the following information relating to the inventory was gathered:

	Cost	Retail
Inventory, January 1, 1991	$ 26,550	$ 45,000
Sales		350,000
Purchases	292,000	395,000
Purchase Discounts	(4,200)	
Freight in	5,250	
Net markups		30,000
Net markdowns		10,000
Sales discounts		5,000

Compute the ending inventory value at December 31, 1991, using the conventional retail inventory method.

Exercise 10–4   (Retail inventory method)

The Evening Out Clothing Store values its inventory under the retail inventory method at the lower of cost or market. The following data are available for the month of November 1991:

	Cost	Selling Price
Inventory, November 1	$ 53,800	$ 76,000
Markdowns		5,700
Markups		11,200
Markdown cancellations		2,200
Markup cancellations		5,600
Purchases	157,304	223,600
Sales		244,000
Purchase returns	3,000	3,600
Sale returns		12,000
Sales allowances		6,000

Based upon the data presented above, prepare a schedule in good form to compute the estimated inventory at November 30, 1991, at the lower of cost or market under the retail inventory method.   (AICPA adapted)

Exercise 10–5   (Dollar-Value LIFO retail)

The Paradise Hardware Store began using the LIFO retail method in 1990 for determining inventory values. In 1990, the cost percentage was computed at 62%. Information relating to the inventory for 1991 is given below:

	Cost	Retail
Inventory, January 1	$ 39,680	$ 64,000
Purchases	165,000	270,600
Purchase returns	11,200	18,368
Freight in	26,000	
Sales		269,000
Net markups		26,000
Net markdowns		8,000
Price index:		
1990—All year	1.00	
1991—December 31	1.08	

(1) Compute the cost percentage for 1991. (Round to two decimal places.)
(2) Compute the inventory value to be reported at December 31, 1991, assuming incremental layers are costed at end-of-year prices.

Exercise 10–6   (Dollar-value LIFO retail inventory method)

On July 31, 1992, Rooker, Madras & Associates compiled the following information concerning inventory for five years. They use the dollar-value LIFO retail inventory method.

Date	Year-End Price Index	Incremental Layer Index	Incremental Cost Percentage	Inventory at Retail
Dec. 31, 1987	1.00	1.00	71%	$155,000
Dec. 31, 1988	1.04	1.02	72%	188,600
Dec. 31, 1989	1.14	1.09	64%	192,500
Dec. 31, 1990	1.12	1.11	63%	194,200
Dec. 31, 1991	1.16	1.12	67%	195,800

Compute the inventory cost at the end of each year under the dollar-value LIFO retail method. (Round all dollar amounts to the nearest dollar.)

Exercise 10–7   (Lower of cost or market valuation)

Determine the proper carrying value of the following inventory items if priced in accordance with the recommendations of the AICPA.

Item	Cost	Replacement Cost	Sales Price	Selling Expenses	Normal Profit
Product 561	$1.85	$1.82	$2.30	$.35	$.20
Product 562	.69	.65	1.00	.30	.04
Product 563	.31	.24	.59	.15	.07
Product 564	.92	.84	1.05	.27	.05
Product 565	.84	.82	1.00	.19	.09
Product 566	1.19	1.15	1.43	.13	.09

Exercise 10–8   (Lower of cost or market valuation)

The following inventory data are available for Alpine Ski Shop at December 31.

	Cost	Market
Skis	$60,000	$65,000
Boots	37,500	35,000
Ski Equipment	15,000	14,000
Ski Apparel	12,000	13,500

(1) Determine the value of ending inventory using the lower of cost or market method applied to (a) individual items and (b) total inventory.
(2) Prepare any journal entries required to adjust the ending inventory if lower of cost or market is applied to (a) individual items and (b) total inventory.

Exercise 10–9 (Lower of cost or market valuation)

Newcomer, Inc. values inventories at the lower of cost or market method applied to total inventory. Inventory values at the end of the company's first and second years of operation are presented below.

	Ending Inventory	
	Cost	Market
Year 1	$58,000	$53,000
Year 2	$75,000	$73,800

(1) Prepare the journal entries necessary to reflect the proper inventory valuation at the end of each year. (Assume Newcomer uses an inventory allowance account.)

(2) For Year 1, assume sales were $390,000 and purchases were $320,000. What amount would be reported as cost of goods sold on the income statement for Year 1 if: (a) the inventory decline is reported separately and (b) the inventory decline is not reported separately.

Exercise 10–10   (Loss on purchase commitments)

On October 1, 1991, Bush Electronics, Inc. entered into a six-month $520,000 purchase commitment for a supply of Product A. On December 31, 1991, the market value of this material has fallen so that current acquisition of the ordered quantity would cost $453,000. It is anticipated that a further decline will occur during the next three months and that market at date of delivery will be approximately $412,000. What entries would you make on December 31, 1991, and on March 31, 1992, assuming the expected decline in prices do occur?

Exercise 10–11   (Valuation of trade-in)

Wailea Inc. sells new equipment with a $28,000 list price. Assume that Wailea sells one unit of equipment and accepts a trade-in plus $24,100 in cash. The expected sales price of the reconditioned equipment is $3,500, the reconditioning expenses are estimated to be $500, and normal profit is 30% of the sales price.

(1) Prepare the journal entry to record the sale assuming that floor values are used.

(2) Prepare the journal entry to record the sale assuming that the sale of new equipment is recorded at its normal list price.

(3) Evaluate the entries.

Exercise 10–12   (Repossessed inventory)

Deppe Equipment Inc. sells its inventory on a time basis. In about 5% of the sales, the customer defaults in the payments and the equipment must be repossessed. Assume that equipment was sold for $21,000 which included interest of $2,250 (the company uses an allowance for unearned finance charges account). The customer defaulted after making payments of $10,350 which included $1,350 interest. The equipment was repossessed and overhauled at a cost of $2,700. It was then sold on a thirty day account for $16,500, a price that provided a normal profit of 25% on cost. What journal entries would be required to record the repossession and subsequent resale of the equipment?

Exercise 10–13   (Correction of inventory errors)

Annual income for the Stoker Co. for the period 1987–1991 appears below. However, a review of the records for the company reveals inventory misstatements as listed. Calculate corrected net income for each year.

	1987	1988	1989	1990	1991
Reported net income (loss)	$18,000	$13,000	$2,000	$(5,800)	$16,000
Inventory overstatement, end of year		(5,500)			(3,600)
Inventory understatement, end of year	2,800			10,500	

Exercise 10–14   (Effect on net income of inventory errors)

The Martin Company reported income before taxes of $370,000 for 1990, and $526,000 for 1991. A later audit produced the following information:

(a) The ending inventory for 1990 included 2,000 units erroneously priced at $5.90 per unit. The correct cost was $9.50 per unit.

(b) Merchandise costing $17,500 was shipped to the Martin Company, FOB shipping point, on December 26, 1990. The purchase was recorded in 1990, but the merchandise was excluded from the ending inventory since it was not received until January 4, 1991.

(c) On December 28, 1990, merchandise costing $2,900 was sold to Deluxe Paint Shop. Deluxe had asked Martin to keep the merchandise for them until January 2, when they would come and pick it up. Because the merchandise was still in the store at year-end, the merchandise was included in the inventory count. The sale was correctly recorded in December 1990.

(d) Craft Company sold merchandise costing $1,500 to Martin Company. The purchase was made on December 29, 1990, and the merchandise was shipped on December 30. Terms were FOB shipping point. Because the Martin Co. bookkeeper was on vacation, neither the purchase nor the receipt of goods was recorded on the books until January 1991.

Assuming all amounts are material and a physical count is taken every December 31,

(1) Compute the corrected income before taxes for each year.

(2) By what amount did the total net income change for the two years combined?

(3) Assume all errors were found in January 1992, before the books were closed for 1991; what journal entry would be made?

Exercise 10–15   (Correction of LIFO inventory)

The Cardoza Products Company's inventory record appears below:

	Purchases		Sales
	Quantity	Unit Cost	Quantity
1989	9,000	$5.60	6,500
1990	9,500	5.75	10,000
1991	7,200	5.82	6,000

The company uses a LIFO cost flow assumption. It reported ending inventories as follows for its first 3 years of operations:

1989	$14,000
1990	11,600
1991	18,600

Determine if the Cardoza Products Company has reported its inventory correctly. Assuming that 1991 accounts are not yet closed, make any necessary correcting entries.

Problems

Problem 10–1   (Inventory fire loss)

Bradshaw Manufacturing began operations five years ago. On August 13, 1991, a fire broke out in the warehouse destroying all inventory and many accounting records relating to the inventory. The information available is presented below. All sales and purchases are on account.

	January 1, 1991	August 13, 1991
Inventory	$136,250	
Accounts receivable	130,590	$116,110
Accounts payable	88,140	122,850
Collection on accounts receivable, January 1–August 13		753,800
Payments to suppliers, January 1–August 13		487,500
Goods out on consignment at August 13, at cost		32,500

Summary of previous years sales:

	1988	1989	1990
Sales	$626,000	$675,000	$680,000
Gross profit on sales	194,060	189,000	231,200

Instructions: Determine the inventory loss suffered as a result of the fire.

Problem 10–2   (Interim inventory computation—gross profit method)

The following information was taken from the records of the Prairie Company.

	1/1/90–12/31/90	1/1/91–9/30/91
Sales (net of returns)	$2,500,000	$1,500,000
Beginning inventory	420,000	785,000
Purchases	2,152,000	1,061,000
Freight in	116,000	72,000
Purchase discounts	30,000	15,000
Purchase returns	40,000	13,000
Purchase allowances	8,000	5,000
Ending inventory	785,000	
Selling and general expenses	450,000	320,000

Instructions: Compute by the gross-profit method the value to be assigned to the inventory as of September 30, 1991, and prepare an interim statement summarizing operations for the nine-month period ending on this date.

Problem 10–3 (Inventory theft loss)

In December, 1991 Bullseye Merchandise Inc. had a significant portion of its inventory stolen. The company determined the cost of inventory not stolen to be $45,700. The following information was taken from the records of the company.

	January 1, 1991 to Date of Theft	1990
Purchases	$154,854	$185,375
Purchase returns and allowances	7,225	8,420
Sales	251,882	261,800
Sales returns and allowances	2,882	2,600
Salaries	9,600	10,800
Rent	6,480	6,480
Insurance	1,160	1,178
Light, heat, and water	1,361	1,525
Advertising	5,100	3,216
Depreciation expense	1,506	1,536
Beginning inventory	75,291	59,040

Instructions: Estimate the cost of the stolen inventory.

Problem 10–4 (Retail inventory method)

The Cordon Clothing Store values its inventory under the retail inventory method. The following data are available for 1991:

	Cost	Selling Price
Inventory, January 1	$ 51,053	$ 79,100
Additional markdowns		21,000
Additional markups		40,600
Markdown cancellations		11,000
Markup cancellations		9,000
Purchases	147,179	221,600
Sales		246,500
Purchases returns	4,000	6,000
Sales allowances		12,000
Freight in	14,600	

Instructions:

(1) Prepare a schedule to compute the estimated inventory at December 31, 1991, at the lower of average cost or market under the retail method.
(2) Prepare the summary accounting journal entries to record the above inventory data (include entries to record the purchases, sales, and closing of inventory to cost of goods sold).
(3) What gross profit on sales would be reported on the income statement for 1991?

III Problem 10–5   (Retail inventory method)

The following information was taken from the records of Trump Inc. for the years 1990 and 1991.

	1991	1990
Sales	$138,600	$135,600
Sales discounts	1,840	1,200
Sales returns	2,100	1,600
Freight in	4,000	3,640
Purchases (at cost)	78,000	68,560
Purchases (at retail)	100,500	92,480
Purchase discounts	4,155	1,000
Beginning inventory (at cost)		65,600
Beginning inventory (at retail)		87,520

Instructions: Compute the value of the inventory at the end of 1990 and 1991 using the conventional retail inventory method.

III Problem 10–6   (Dollar-value LIFO retail inventory method)

In 1989, Erdmann Inc. adopted the dollar-value LIFO retail inventory method. The January 1, 1989 price index was 1.00. The following data are available for a four-year period ending December 31, 1992.

		Cost	Retail
1989	Inventory, January 1	$141,750	$235,000
	Purchases	387,500	625,000
	Sales		585,000
	Year-end price index		1.10
1990	Purchases	363,000	550,000
	Sales		593,125
	Year-end price index		1.06
1991	Purchases	377,000	650,000
	Sales		623,000
	Year-end price index		1.09
1992	Purchases	504,000	800,000
	Sales		762,500
	Year-end price index		1.12

Instructions: Calculate the inventories to be reported at the end of 1989, 1990, 1991, and 1992. Incremental layers are costed at end-of-year prices.

Problem 10–7   (Dollar-value LIFO retail inventory method)

The St. George Sports Shop values its inventory on the dollar-value LIFO retail basis. Incremental inventory layers are costed at end-of-year prices. At December 31, 1990, the inventory was valued as follows:

LIFO Layer Year	Cost	Year-End Retail	Year-End Price Index	Retail at Base of 1.00
1984	$14,760	$24,600	1.00	$24,600
1986	9,482	13,545	1.05	12,900
1988	13,442	26,884	1.03	26,100
1989	4,500	6,000	1.10	5,454
	$42,184	$71,029		$69,054

The December 31, 1990, inventory at 1990 retail prices was $77,340. Information relating to 1991 transactions follows:

Purchases—cost	$476,100
Purchases—selling price	673,845
Freight in	9,900
Sales returns	11,220
Sales discounts	1,950
Markups	4,740
Markup cancellations	1,080
Markdowns	2,505
Gross sales	702,000
Year-end price index for 1991	1.08

Instructions: Based on the above information, compute:

(1) The 1991 cost ratio.
(2) The inventory amount that would be reported on the balance sheet at December 31, 1991.

Problem 10—8 **(Lower of cost or market valuation)**

Witte Inc. carries four items in inventory. The following data are relative to such goods at the end of 1991.

	Units	Cost	Per Unit Replacement Cost	Estimated Sales Price	Selling Cost	Normal Profit
Category 1:						
Commodity A	3,000	$5.50	$5.25	$8.00	$. 90	$2.00
Commodity B	1,650	6.00	6.00	9.25	.80	1.25
Category 2:						
Commodity C	5,000	2.50	2.00	4.20	.95	.50
Commodity D	3,250	7.00	7.50	7.50	1.20	1.75

Instructions:

(1) Calculate the value of the inventory under each of the following methods:
    (a) Cost.
    (b) The lower of cost or market applied to the individual inventory items.
    (c) The lower of cost or market applied to the inventory categories.
    (d) The lower of cost or market applied to the inventory as a whole.
(2) Prepare any journal entries necessary to reflect the proper inventory valuation assuming inventory is valued at:
    (a) Cost.
    (b) The lower of cost or market applied to the individual inventory items.
    (c) The lower of cost or market applied to the inventory categories.
    (d) The lower of cost or market applied to the inventory as a whole.

Problem 10—9   **(Lower of cost or market valuation)**

Oriental Sales Co. uses the first-in, first-out method in calculating cost of goods sold for three of the products that Oriental handles. Inventories and purchase information concerning these three products are given for the month of August.

		Product A	Product B	Product C
Aug. 1	Inventory	5,000 units at $6.00	3,000 units at $10,00	6,500 units at $.90
Aug. 1–15	Purchases	7,000 units at $6.50	4,500 units at $10.50	3,000 units at $1.25
Aug. 16–31	Purchases	3,000 units at $8.00		
Aug.	Sales	10,500 units	5,000 units	4,500 units
Aug. 31	Sale Price	$8.00 per unit	$11.00 per unit	$2.00 per unit

On August 31, Oriental suppliers reduced their prices from the most recent purchase prices by the following percentages: Product A, 20%; Product B, 10%; Product C, 8%. Accordingly, Oriental decided to reduce their sales prices on all items by 10% effective September 1. Oriental's selling cost is 10% of sales price. Products A & B have a normal profit (after selling costs) of 30% on sales prices, while the normal profit on Product C (after selling costs) is 15% of sales price.

Instructions:

(1) Calculate the value of the inventory at August 31, using the lower of cost or market method (applied to individual items).
(2) Calculate the FIFO cost of goods sold for August and the amount of inventory write-off due to the market decline.

Problem 10–10   (Trade-ins and repossessed inventory)

The Foutz Appliance Company began business on January 1, 1990. The company decided from the beginning to grant allowances on merchandise traded in as partial payment on new sales. During 1991 the company granted trade-in allowances of $64,035. The wholesale value of merchandise traded in was $40,875. Trade-ins recorded at $39,000 were sold for their wholesale value of $27,000 during the year.

The following summary entries were made to record annual sales and trade-in sales for 1991:

Accounts Receivable	439,890	
Trade-In Inventory	64,035	
Sales		503,925
Cash..	27,000	
Loss on Trade-In Inventory	12,000	
Trade-In Inventory		39,000

When a customer defaults on the accounts receivable contract, the appliance is repossessed. During 1991 the following repossessions occurred:

	Original Sales Price	Unpaid Contract Balance
On 1990 contracts	$37,500	$20,250
On 1991 contracts	24,000	18,750

The wholesale value of these goods is estimated by the trade as follows:

(a) Goods repossessed during year of sale are valued at 50% of original sales price.
(b) Goods repossessed in later years are valued at 25% of original sales price.

Instructions:

(1) At what values should Foutz Appliance report the trade-in and repossessed inventory at December 31, 1991?
(2) Give the entry that should have been made to record the repossessions of 1991.
(3) Give the entry that is required to correct the trade-in summary entries.

Problem 10–11   (Inventory transactions—journal entries)

The Olsen Company values its perpetual inventory at the lower of FIFO cost or market. The inventory accounts at December 31, 1990, had the following balances:

Raw materials	$ 81,000
Allowance to Reduce Raw Materials Inventory from Cost to Market	4,200
Work in Process	131,520
Finished Goods	205,200

The following are some of the transactions that affected the inventory of the Olsen Company during 1991:

Feb. 10   Olsen Company purchases raw materials at an invoice price of $25,000; terms 3/15,n/30. Olsen Company uses the net method of valuing inventories.

Mar. 15   Olsen Company repossesses an inventory item from a customer who was overdue in making payment. The unpaid balance on the sale is $190. The repossessed merchandise is to be refinished and placed on sale. It is expected that the item can be sold for $300 after estimated refinishing costs of $85. The normal profit for this item is considered to be $40.

Apr. 1   Refinishing costs of $80 are incurred on the repossessed item.

Apr. 10   The repossessed item is resold for $300 on account; 20% down.

May 30   A sale on account is made of finished goods that have a list price of $740 and a cost of $480. A reduction of $100 off the list price is granted as a trade-in allowance. The trade-in item is to be priced to sell at $80 as is. The normal profit on this type of inventory is 25% of the sales price.

Nov. 30   Olsen Company orders materials to be delivered January 31, 1992, at a cost of $21,600. No discount terms are included.

Dec. 31   The following information is available to adjust the accounts for the annual statements:

(a) The market value of the items ordered on November 30 has declined to $18,000.
(b) The raw materials inventory account has a cost balance of $110,400. Current market value is $101,400.

(c) The finished goods inventory account has a cost balance of $177,600. Current market value is $189,000.

Instructions: Record this information in journal entry form, including any required adjusting entries at December 31, 1991.

Problem 10–12 (Inventory error correction)

The Sonntag Corporation has adjusted and closed its books at the end of 1991. The company arrives at its inventory position by a physical count taken on December 31 of each year. In March of 1992, the following errors were discovered.

(a) Merchandise which cost $2,500 was sold for $3,400 on December 29, 1991. The order was shipped December 31, 1991, with terms of FOB shipping point. The merchandise was not included in the ending inventory. The sale was recorded on January 12, 1992, when the customer made payment on the sale.

(b) On January 3, 1992, Sonntag Corporation received merchandise which had been shipped to them on December 30, 1991. The terms of the purchase were FOB shipping point. Cost of the merchandise was $1,750. The purchase was recorded and the goods included in the inventory when payment was made in January of 1992.

(c) On January 8, 1992, merchandise which had been included in the ending inventory was returned to Sonntag because the consignee had not been able to sell it. The cost of this merchandise was $1,200 with a selling price of $1,800.

(d) Merchandise costing $750, located in a separate warehouse, was overlooked and excluded from the 1991 inventory count.

(e) On December 26, 1991, Sonntag Corporation purchased merchandise costing $1,175 from a supplier. The order was shipped December 28 (terms FOB destination) and was still "in-transit" on December 31. Since the invoice was received on December 31, the purchase was recorded in 1991. The merchandise was not included in the inventory count.

(f) The corporation failed to make an entry for a purchase on account of $835 at the end of 1991, although it included this merchandise in the inventory count. The purchase was recorded when payment was made to the supplier in 1992.

(g) The corporation included in its 1991 ending inventory merchandise with a cost of $1,350. This merchandise had been custom-built and was being held until the customer could come and pick up the merchandise. The sale, for $1,825, was recorded in 1992.

Instructions: Give the entry in 1992 (1991 books are closed) to correct each error. Assume that the errors were made during 1991 and all amounts are material.

Problem 10–13 (Inventory error correction)

The Collier Corporation adjusted and closed its books on December 31, 1991. Net income of $60,000 was reported for the year. Several months later, the independent auditors discovered the following material errors. Collier used a periodic inventory method.

(a) 3,000 units of Product A, costing $8.59, were recorded at a unit cost of $8.95 in summarizing the ending inventory.

(b) A sale of merchandise shipped on January 3, 1992, was included in the ending inventory count. The cost of this merchandise was $4,750, and the sale was properly recorded at $5,950 on December 31, 1991.

(c) Merchandise costing $5,550 was included in the inventory although it was shipped to a customer on December 31, 1991, with terms of FOB shipping point. The corporation recorded the sale ($7,400) on January 3, 1992.

(d) Merchandise in the storeroom on December 31 (costing $1,500) was included in the 1991 ending inventory although the purchase invoice was not received or recorded until January 5, 1992.

(e) Merchandise in the hands of a consignee, costing $4,000, was included in the inventory; however, $2,400 of the merchandise had been sold as of December 31. The sale was not recorded until January 31, 1992, when the consignee made a full remittance of $3,200 on the merchandise sold.

(f) On December 31, 1991, a purchase of merchandise costing $3,000 was still in a delivery truck parked in the corporation's receiving dock. Because of the rush at year-end, the truck had not been unloaded. The terms of the purchase were FOB destination. The merchandise was not included in the ending inventory, but the purchase was recorded in the books in 1991.

Instructions:

(1) Compute the corrected net income for 1991.
(2) Give the entries that are required in 1992 to correct the accounts.

Problem 10–14   (Inventory error corrections—cut off)

The St. Charles Company is a wholesale distributor of automotive replacement parts. Initial amounts taken from St. Charles' accounting records are as follows:

Inventory at December 31, 1991 (based on physical count of goods in St. Charles' warehouse on December 31, 1991) $1,150,000

Accounts payable at December 31, 1991:

Vendor	Terms	Amount
Holly Company	2% 10 days, net 30	$265,000
Marie Inc.	Net 30	210,000
Durrant Corporation	Net 30	200,000
Call Company	Net 30	125,000
Bob Bottle Company	Net 30	—
		$800,000

Sales in 1991 $8,500,000

Additional information is as follows:

(a) Parts held on consignment from Marie to St. Charles, the consignee, amounting to $125,000, were included in the physical count of goods in

St. Charles' warehouse on December 31, 1991, and in accounts payable at December 31, 1991.

(b) $22,000 of parts which were purchased from Bob Bottle and paid for in December 1991 were sold in the last week of 1991 and appropriately recorded as sales of $28,000. The parts were included in the physical count of goods in St. Charles' warehouse on December 31, 1991, because the parts were on the loading dock waiting to be picked up by customers.

(c) Parts in transit on December 31, 1991, to customers, shipped FOB shipping point on December 28, 1991, amounted to a cost of $34,000. The customers received the parts on January 6, 1992. Sales of $40,000 to the customers for the parts were recorded by St. Charles on January 2, 1992.

(d) Retailers were holding $200,000 at cost ($250,000 at retail) of goods on consignment from St. Charles, the consignor, at their stores on December 31, 1991.

(e) Goods were in transit from Marie to St. Charles on December 31, 1991. The cost of the goods was $25,000, and they were shipped FOB shipping point on December 29, 1991. The transaction was recorded when the goods were received.

(f) A freight bill in the amount of $2,000 specifically relating to merchandise purchases in December 1991, all of which were still in the inventory at December 31, 1991, was received on January 3, 1992. The freight bill was not included in either the inventory or in accounts payable at December 31, 1991.

(g) All of the purchases from Holly occurred during the last seven days of the year. These items have been recorded in accounts payable and accounted for in the physical inventory at cost before discount. St. Charles' policy is to pay invoices in time to take advantage of all cash discounts, adjust inventory accordingly, and record accounts payable, net of cash discounts.

Instructions: Prepare a schedule of adjustments to the initial amounts using the format shown below. Show the effect, if any, of each of the transactions separately and if the transactions would have no effect on the amount shown, state NONE.

	Inventory	Accounts Payable	Sales
Initial amounts	$1,125,000	$ 800,000	$8,500,000
Adjustments			
Total adjustments			
Adjusted amounts	$	$	$

(AICPA adapted)

Problem 10–15   (Gross profit method)

The Wixom Corporation is an importer and wholesaler. Its merchandise is purchased from a number of suppliers and is warehoused by Wixom Corporation until sold to customers.

In conducting the audit for the year ended June 30, 1992, the company's CPA determined that the system of internal control was good. Accordingly, the physical inventory was observed at an interim date, May 31, 1992, instead of at year end.

The following information was obtained from the general ledger:

Inventory, July 1, 1991	$ 87,500
Physical inventory May 31, 1992	95,000
Sales for 11 months ended May 31, 1992	800,000
Sales for year ended June 30, 1992	950,000
Purchases for 11 months ended May 31, 1992 (before audit adjustments)	635,000
Purchases for year ended June 30, 1992 (before audit adjustments)	800,000

The CPA's audit disclosed the following information:

Shipments received in May and included in physical inventory but recorded as June purchases	$7,500
Shipments received in unsalable condition and excluded from physical inventory. Credit memos had not been received nor had chargebacks to vendors been recorded.	
Total at May 31, 1992	1,000
Total at June 30, 1992 (including the May unrecorded chargebacks)	1,500
Deposit made with vendor and charged to purchases in April, 1992. Product was shipped in July, 1992	2,000
Deposit made with vendor and charged to purchases in May 1992. Product was shipped, FOB destination, on May 29, 1992, and was included in May 31, 1992, physical inventory as goods in transit	5,500
Through the carelessness of the receiving department, a June shipment was damaged by rain. This shipment was later sold in June at its cost of $10,000.	

In audit engagements in which interim physical inventories are observed, a frequently used auditing procedure is to test the reasonableness of the year-end inventory by the application of gross profit ratios.

Instructions: Prepare the following schedules:

(1) Computation of the gross profit ratio for 11 months ended May 31, 1992.
(2) Computation by the gross profit method of cost of goods sold during June 1992.
(3) Computation by the gross profit method of the inventory at June 30, 1992.   (AICPA adapted)

Problem 10–16 (Retail and dollar-value LIFO retail inventory methods)

Phillips Department Store converted from the conventional retail method to the dollar-value LIFO retail method on January 1, 1991. Management requested during your examination of the financial statements for the year ended December 31, 1992 that you furnish a summary showing certain computations of inventory costs for the past three years.
Available information follows:

(a) The inventory at January 1, 1990, had a retail value of $45,000 and a cost of $27,500 based on the conventional retail method. (There were no markdowns in 1989.)
(b) Transactions during 1990 were as follows:

	Cost	Retail
Gross purchases	$293,000	$490,000
Purchase returns	6,500	10,000
Purchase discounts	5,000	
Gross sales (exclusive of employee discounts)		492,000
Sales returns		5,000
Employee discounts		3,000
Freight in	26,500	
Net markups		25,000
Net markdowns		10,000

(c) The retail value of the December 31, 1991 inventory was $56,100, the cost percentage for 1991 under the dollar-value LIFO retail method was 62%, and the regional price index was 102% of the January 1, 1991 price level.

(d) The retail value of the December 31, 1992 inventory was $48,300, the cost percentage for 1992 under the dollar-value LIFO retail method was 61%, and the regional price index was 105% of the January 1, 1991 price level.

Instructions:

(1) Prepare a schedule showing the computation of the cost of inventory on hand at December 31, 1990, based on the conventional retail method.

(2) Prepare a schedule showing the computation of the cost of inventory on hand at the store on December 31, 1990, based on the dollar-value LIFO retail method. Assume no price changes occured in 1990.

(3) Without prejudice to your solution to part (2), assume that you computed the inventory on December 31, 1990, (retail value $50,000) under the dollar-value LIFO retail method at a cost of $28,000. Prepare a schedule showing the computations of the cost of the 1991 and 1992 year-end inventories under the dollar-value LIFO retail method.   (AICPA adapted)

Chapter 11

Noncurrent Operating Assets— Acquisition

Many billions of dollars are invested each year in new property, plant, equipment, and intangible assets. Enterprises must continually make choices as to how they will invest their limited resources to acquire the operating assets needed to reach their goals and objectives. Capital budgets are prepared by management to help evaluate the available alternatives and to identify the priorities for implementation.

Many accounting questions are introduced with the acquisition of assets whose lives and economic benefits extend beyond one year, including:

1. How should the various categories of noncurrent operating assets be recorded on the balance sheet?
2. Which costs should be capitalized as assets and which ones should be recognized as expenses in the period of disbursement?
3. At what amounts should the assets be recorded under various methods of purchase?
4. How should expenditures made subsequent to acquisition be recorded?
5. What recognition should be given to changes in either the value of the dollar or the replacement cost of new assets?

These are the central issues concerning the acquisition of noncurrent operating assets that will be explored in this chapter.

Classification of Noncurrent Operating Assets

Assets are probable future economic benefits that are controlled by an economic entity and are the result of past events. While the actual form of an asset is not an essential characteristic, it is common to group noncurrent operating assets according to whether they are tangible or intangible.

Tangible noncurrent operating assets include land, buildings, and equipment used in revenue producing activities. Specific categories of equipment include automobiles and trucks, machinery, patterns and dies, furniture and fixtures, and returnable containers.

Intangible noncurrent operating assets include patents, copyrights, franchises, trademarks, trade names, organization costs, software development costs, and goodwill. While these assets cannot be directly observed, they usually are identified by agreements, contracts, or other documentation.

Valuation of Noncurrent Operating Assets at Acquisition

Noncurrent operating assets are recorded initially at cost—the original bargained or cash sales price. In theory, the maximum price an entity should be willing to pay for an operating asset is the present value of the net benefit the entity expects to obtain from the use and final disposition of the asset. In a competitive economy, the market value, or cost, of an asset at acquisition is assumed to reflect the present value of its future benefits.

The cost of property includes not only the original purchase price or equivalent value, but also any other expenditures required in obtaining and preparing it for its intended use. Any taxes, freight, installation, and other expenditures related to the acquisition should be included in the asset's cost. Post-acquisition costs incurred *after* the asset is placed into service are usually expensed rather than added to the acquisition cost. Exceptions to this general rule apply to some major replacements or improvements, and will be discussed later in the chapter.

Although most noncurrent operating asset categories have similar acquisition costs, over time accounting practice has identified some specific costs that are included for different asset categories. Exhibits 11-1 and 11-2 on pages 429 and 430 summarize the types of cost normally included as acquisition cost for each major noncurrent asset category.

Because land is a nondepreciable asset, costs assigned to land should be those costs that directly relate to land's unlimited life. Together with clearing and grading costs, costs of removing unwanted structures from newly acquired land are considered part of the cost to prepare the land for its intended use and are added to the purchase price of the land. Government assessments for water lines, sewers, roads, and other such items are considered part of the land's cost since maintenance of these items is the responsibility of the government, thus, to the landowner, they have unlimited life. These types of improvements are distinguished from similar costs for landscaping, parking lots, and interior sidewalks that are installed by the owner and must be replaced over time. These owner-responsible improvements are generally classified as land improvements and depreciated.

The cost of purchased buildings includes any reconditioning costs necessary before occupancy. Because self-constructed buildings have many unique costs, a separate discussion of self-constructed assets is included later in this chapter.

Equipment costs include freight and insurance charges while the equipment is in transit and any expenditures for testing and installation. Costs for reconditioning purchased used equipment are also part of the asset cost.

Exhibit 11-1   Acquisition Cost of Tangible Noncurrent Operating Assets

Asset	Description	Examples of Acquisition Costs
Land	Realty used for business purposes.	Purchase price, commissions, legal fees, escrow fees, surveying fees, clearing and grading costs, street and water line assessments.
Land Improvements	Items such as landscaping, paving, fencing that improve the usefulness of property.	Cost of improvements, including expenditures for materials, labor, and overhead.
Buildings	A structure used to house a business operation.	Purchase price, commissions, reconditioning costs.
Equipment	Assets used in the production of goods or in providing services. Examples include automobiles, trucks, machinery, patterns and dies, and furniture and fixtures.	Purchase price, taxes, freight, insurance, installation, and any expenditures incurred in preparing the asset for its intended use, e.g., reconditioning and testing costs.

Intangible assets are also generally recorded at cost; however, acquisition costs differ between externally purchased intangibles and those that are internally developed. Intangible assets arising from exclusive rights granted by the U.S. Government such as copyrights, patents, and trademarks are recorded at their purchase price if externally obtained. Internal research and development costs incurred to generate the items subject to government license are generally expensed as incurred because of the uncertainty as to whether the work will result in a successful product. Only the actual legal and filing costs are included as part of the intangible asset cost for these internally developed items. Any cost to defend the rights in court are added to the intangible asset cost if successful. If not successful, all asset costs related to the rights would be written off as an expense.

Franchise operations have become so common in our everyday life that we often don't realize we are dealing with them. The cost of a franchise includes any sum paid specifically for the franchise right as well as legal fees and other costs incurred in obtaining it. Although the value of a franchise at the time of its acquisition may be substantially in excess of its cost, the amount recorded should be limited to actual outlays. When a franchise is purchased from another company, the amount paid is recorded as the franchise cost.

In forming a corporation, certain organization costs are incurred, including legal fees, promotional costs, stock certificate costs, underwriting costs, and state incorporation fees. The benefits to be derived from these expenditures normally extend beyond the first fiscal period. Because the primary benefits of these start-up costs relate to the first few years of operation, they are usually written off to expense fairly rapidly. Some development stage companies have included such costs as interest, administrative salaries, and taxes as part of organization costs. The Financial Accounting Standards Board concluded that these administrative costs should not be classified as an intangible asset. The same accounting principles should apply to development stage companies as for mature companies. Only the costs related to the actual formation of the company, as mentioned above, should be included as part of organization costs.[1]

In recent years, the tremendous growth in the computer industry, particularly in microcomputers, has raised some significant accounting issues relating to expenditures for the development and production of computer software. Because these costs have been addressed separately by the FASB, the accounting and reporting issues relating to software development expenditures are discussed in detail later in the chapter.

The most frequently reported intangible asset is goodwill. In the 1988 edition of *Accounting Trends and Techniques,* 338 of the 600 surveyed companies reported goodwill. The next most frequent was patents, reported by 59 companies. Goodwill is reported only when it arises from the purchase of another entity for more than the market value of the identifiable net assets. Because of its unique character, it will be discussed in more depth than the other intangibles summarized in Exhibit 11-2.

Exhibit 11-2   Acquisition Cost of Intangible Noncurrent Operating Assets

Asset	Description	Examples of Acquisition Costs
Copyright	An exclusive right granted by the U.S. government that permits an author to sell, license, or control his/her work. Copyright expires 50 years after the death of the author.	Purchase price, filing and registry fees, cost of subsequent litigation to protect right. Does not include internal research and development costs.
Patent	An exclusive right granted by the U.S. government that enables an inventor to control the manufacture, sale, or use of an invention. Legal life 17 years.	
Trademarks and Tradenames	An exclusive right granted by the U.S. government that permits the use of distinctive symbols, labels, and designs, e.g., McDonald's golden arches, Levi's pocket patch, Chrysler's star.	
Franchise	An exclusive right or privilege received by a business or individual to perform certain functions or sell certain products or services.	Expenditures made to purchase the franchise. Legal fees and other costs incurred in obtaining the franchise.
Organization Costs	Costs incurred in forming a corporation.	Expenditures to organize the corporation: cost of stock certificates, underwriting costs, state incorporation fees.
Software Development Costs	Costs incurred in the development of computer software, i.e., programs that may be used with the computer hardware to accomplish specific tasks.	Expenditures made after software is determined to be technologically feasible but before it is ready for commercial production.
Goodwill	The ability of a company to earn above-normal income with its identifiable net assets. Goodwill is recorded only when a business entity is acquired by a purchase.	Portion of purchase price that exceeds the sum of the current market value for all identifiable net assets.

[1]*Statement of Financial Accounting Standards No. 7,* "Accounting and Reporting by Development Stage Enterprises" (Stamford: Financial Accounting Standards Board, 1975), par. 10.

Goodwill   Of all the intangible assets, goodwill is perhaps the most controversial. In a general sense, goodwill is often referred to as that intangible something that makes the whole company worth more than its individual parts. In general, goodwill represents all the special advantages, not otherwise identifiable, enjoyed by an enterprise, such as a good name, capable staff and personnel, high credit standing, reputation for superior products and services, and favorable location. From an accounting point of view, goodwill is recognized as the ability of a business to earn above-normal income with the identifiable assets employed in the business. Above-normal income means a rate of return greater than that normally required to attract investors into a particular type of business.

Goodwill differs from most other assets in that it cannot be exchanged or sold separately from the entity itself. Because goodwill is recorded on the books only as part of an entity acquisition, it is difficult to compare a company that has recorded goodwill with one that hasn't. Merely because a company has not purchased another company does not mean it does not have goodwill as defined above. Thus, current accounting principles may result in misleading users of financial statements as far as goodwill is concerned. On the other hand, to allow companies to place a value on their own goodwill would undoubtedly lead to abuse. These difficulties have led some accountants to suggest that all purchased goodwill should be written off to expense as soon as it is acquired. Advocates of this position include the authors of Accounting Research Study No. 10, "Accounting for Goodwill," whose justification for immediate write-off was given as follows:

1. Goodwill is not a resource or property right that is consumed or utilized in the production of earnings. It is the result of expectations of future earnings by investors and thus is not subject to normal amortization procedures.

2. Goodwill is subject to sudden and wide fluctuations. That value has no reliable or continuing relation to costs incurred in its creation.

3. Under existing practices of accounting, neither the cost nor the value of nonpurchased goodwill is reported in the balance sheet. Purchased goodwill has no continuing, separately measurable existence after the combination and is merged with the total goodwill value of the continuing business entity. As such, its write-off cannot be measured with any validity.

4. Goodwill as an asset account is not relevant to an investor. Most analysts ignore any reported goodwill when analyzing a company's status and operations.[2]

This position has been consistently rejected by the accounting

---

[2]George R. Catlett and Norman O. Olson, "Accounting for Goodwill," *Accounting Research Study No. 10* (New York: American Institute of Certified Public Accountants, 1968).

principles-setting bodies, and the immediate write-off of purchased goodwill is not permitted under GAAP. They maintain that a price has been paid for the excess earnings power, and it should be recognized as an asset. Because of the poor connotative image the term *goodwill* has acquired, some companies use more descriptive titles for reporting purposes, such as "Excess of Cost over Net Assets of Acquired Companies."

In the purchase of a going business, the actual price paid for goodwill usually results from bargaining and compromises between the parties concerned. A basis for negotiation in arriving at a price for goodwill could involve many variables, including:

1. The level of projected future income.
2. An appropriate rate of return.
3. Current valuation of the net business assets other than goodwill.

Several ways in which these variables may be used to aid in the negotiations are presented in the Appendix to this chapter. These are not really accounting methods, but financial models that utilize accounting data.

When a lump-sum amount is paid for an established business and no explicit evaluation is made of goodwill, goodwill may still be recognized. In this case the identifiable net assets require appraisal, and the difference between the full purchase price and the value of identifiable net assets can be attributed to the purchase of goodwill. In appraising properties for this purpose, current market values should be sought rather than the values reported in the accounts. Receivables should be stated at amounts estimated to be realized. Inventories and securities should be restated in terms of current market values. Land, buildings, and equipment may require special appraisals in arriving at their present replacement or reproduction values. Intangible assets, such as patents and franchises, should be included at their current values even though, originally, expenditures were reported as expenses or were reported as assets and amortized against revenue. Care should be taken to determine that liabilities are fully recognized. Assets at their current fair market values less the liabilities to be assumed provide the net assets total that, together with estimated future earnings, are used in arriving at a purchase price.

To the extent possible, the amount paid for any existing company should be related to identifiable assets. If an excess does exist, the use of a term other than goodwill can avoid the implication that only companies that purchase other companies have goodwill.

To illustrate the purchase and recording of an ongoing business, assume that Airnational Corporation purchases the net assets of Speedy Freight Airlines for $675,000 cash. A schedule of net assets for Speedy Freight at the time of acquisition is presented below:

Speedy Freight Airlines
Schedule of Net Assets
December 31, 1992

Assets		
Cash and temporary investments	$ 21,000	
Receivables	146,000	
Inventory	292,000	
Investments	72,000	
Land, buildings, and equipment (net)	489,200	
Patents, trademarks, and trade names	16,500	$1,036,700
Liabilities		
Current liabilities	$286,000	
Long-term debt	183,500	469,500
Net assets		$ 567,200

Analysis of the $107,800 difference between the purchase price ($675,000) and the net asset book value ($567,200) reveals the following differences between the recorded costs and market values of the assets.

	Cost	Market
Inventory	$292,000	$327,000
Investments	72,000	85,000
Land, buildings, and equipment	489,200	504,500
Patents	7,000	12,000
Trademarks and trade names	9,500	10,000
Franchises		5,000
Totals	$869,700	$943,500

The identifiable portion of the $107,800 difference amounts to $73,800 ($943,500 − $869,700), and is allocated to the respective assets. The remaining difference of $34,000 is recorded as an intangible asset, Goodwill.

The entry to record the purchase is as follows:

Cash and Temporary Investments	21,000	
Receivables	146,000	
Inventory	327,000	
Investments	85,000	
Land, Buildings,. and Equipment	504,500	
Patents	12,000	
Trademarks and Trade Names	10,000	
Franchises	5,000	
Goodwill (Excess of market value over cost paid for net assets)	34,000	
Current Liabilities		286,000
Long-Term Debt		183,500
Cash		675,000

Negative Goodwill

Occasionally, the amount paid for another company is less than the fair market value of the net assets of the acquired company. This condition can arise when economic conditions are depressed, and where bargain purchases are possible. The accounting profession has discussed from time to time how such **negative goodwill** should be recorded. Some accountants have suggested that it should be recorded as part of owners' equity.

The APB, however, did not want the total assets to be recorded at an aggregate amount that exceeded cost. The Board decided, therefore, to require the allocation of the excess against all acquired noncurrent assets, except for noncurrent marketable equity securities. If this allocation reduces the noncurrent assets to a zero balance, any remaining excess is credited to a deferred credit account and amortized against revenue over the period benefitted.[3]

For example, assume Goodtime, Inc. purchases the net assets of Funtime, Inc. for $500,000. The fair market value of Funtime's assets are as follows:

Cash and temporary investments	$ 75,000
Receivables	125,000
Inventories	160,000
Property and equipment	250,000
Investment in noncurrent marketable equity securities	75,000
Other investments	50,000
	$735,000

Offsetting the above assets are the following liabilities:

Current liabilities	$ 50,000
Noncurrent liabilities	125,000
	$175,000

The market value of net assets for Funtime is thus $560,000 ($735,000 − $175,000), and the negative goodwill is $60,000 ($560,000 − $500,000). The only noncurrent assets that would meet the Board's criteria for adjustment would be property and equipment and other investments. The allocation of the $60,000 would be performed as follows:

	Book Value	Allocation of Negative Goodwill According to Relative Book Values	Negative Goodwill Assigned to Individual Assets
Property and equipment	$250,000	250,000/300,000 × $60,000	$50,000
Other investments	50,000	50,000/300,000 × $60,000	10,000
	$300,000		$60,000

The $60,000 negative goodwill is thus allocated $50,000 against property and equipment and $10,000 against other investments. The acquisition is then recorded as follows:

---

[3]*Opinions of the Accounting Principles Board No. 16,* "Business Combinations" (New York: American Institute of Certified Public Accountants, 1970), par. 91.

Cash and Temporary Investments	75,000	
Receivables	125,000	
Inventories	160,000	
Property and Equipment	200,000	
Investment in Noncurrent Marketable Equity Securities	75,000	
Other Investments	40,000	
Cash		500,000
Current Liabilities		50,000
Noncurrent Liabilities		125,000
To record acquisition of Funtime, Inc.		

The following note describing an actual negative goodwill transaction was included in the 1984 annual report for Zondervan Corporation:

> On October 1, 1983, the Company also acquired the remaining 49% interest in the Benson Company, Inc. for 66,666 shares of common stock which were recorded at the approximate market value of the stock at that date. This acquisition was accounted for by the purchase method and resulted in negative goodwill of approximately $1,094,000 which was primarily offset against noncurrent assets acquired.

Recording Acquisition of Noncurrent Operating Assets

When an asset is purchased for cash, the acquisition is simply recorded at the amount of cash paid, including all outlays relating to its purchase and preparation for intended use. Assets can be acquired under a number of other arrangements, however, some of which present special problems relating to the cost to be recorded. The acquisition of assets is discussed under the following headings:

1. Assets acquired for a lump-sum purchase price
2. Purchase on deferred payment contract
3. Acquisition under capital lease
4. Acquisition by exchange of nonmonetary assets
5. Acquisition by issuance of securities
6. Acquisition by self-construction
7. Acquisition by donation or discovery

Assets Acquired for a Lump-Sum Purchase Price

In some purchases, a number of assets may be acquired for one lump sum. Some of the assets in the group may be depreciable, others nondepreciable. Depreciable assets may have different useful lives. If there is to be accountability for the assets on an individual basis, the total purchase price must be allocated among the individual assets. When part of a purchase price can be clearly identified with specific assets, such a cost assignment should be made and the balance of the purchase price allocated among the remaining assets. When no part of the purchase price can be related to specific assets, the entire amount must be allocated among the different assets acquired. Appraisal values or similar evidence provided by a competent independent authority should be sought to support such allocation.

To illustrate the allocation of a joint asset cost, assume that land, buildings, and equipment are acquired for $160,000. Assume further that assessed values for the individual assets as reported on the property tax bill are considered to provide an equitable basis for cost allocation. The allocation is made as shown below.

	Assessed Values	Cost Allocation According to Relative Assessed Values	Cost Assigned to Individual Assets
Land	$ 28,000	28,000/100,000 × $160,000	$ 44,800
Buildings	60,000	60,000/100,000 × $160,000	96,000
Equipment	12,000	12,000/100,000 × $160,000	19,200
	$100,000		$160,000

The entry to record this acquisition, assuming a cash purchase, would be as follows:

```
Land .............................................  44,800
Buildings.........................................  96,000
Equipment ......................................  19,200
  Cash ..........................................          160,000
```

Purchase on Deferred Payment Contract

The acquisition of real estate or other property frequently involves deferred payment of all or part of the purchase price. The indebtedness of the buyer is usually evidenced by a note, debenture, mortgage, or other contract that specifies the terms of settlement of the obligation. The debt instrument may call for one payment at a given future date or a series of payments at specified intervals. Interest charged on the unpaid balance of the contract should be recognized as an expense.

To illustrate the accounting for a deferred payment purchase contract, assume that land is acquired for $100,000; $35,000 is paid at the time of purchase and the balance is to be paid in semiannual installments of $5,000, plus interest on the unpaid principal at an annual rate of 10%. Entries for the purchase and for the first payment on the contract are shown below:

Transaction	Entry		
January 2, 1991			
Purchased land for $100,000 paying $35,000 down, the balance to be paid in seminannual payments of $5,000 plus interest at 10%.	Land .... Cash .... Note Payable	100,000	35,000 65,000
June 30, 1991			
Made first payment. Amount of payment: $5,000 + $3,250 (5% of $65,000) = $8,250	Interest Expense ... Note Payable ...... Cash	3,250 5,000	8,250

In the preceding example, the contract specified both a purchase price and interest at a stated rate on the unpaid balance. Sometimes, however, a contract may simply provide for a payment or series of payments without reference to interest, or may provide for a stated interest rate that is unreasonable in relation to the market. As indicated in Chapter 8, APB No. 21, "Interest on Receivables and Payables," requires that in these circumstances, the note, sales price, and cost of the property, goods, or services exchanged for the note should be recorded at the fair market value of the property, goods, or services or at the current market value of the note, whichever value is more clearly determinable.[4] Application of Opinion No. 21 with respect to the seller was illustrated in Chapter 8. The following example illustrates the accounting by the purchaser.

Assume that certain equipment, which has a cash price of $50,000, is acquired under a deferred payment contract. The contract specifies a down payment of $15,000 plus seven annual payments of $7,189.22 each, or a total price, including interest, of $65,324.54. Although not stated, the effective interest rate implicit in this contract is 10%, the rate that discounts the annual payments of $7,189.22 to a present value of $35,000, the cash price less the down payment.[5] As specified in APB Opinion No. 21, if the cash equivalent price, that is, the fair market value of the asset, varies from the contract price because of delayed payments, the difference should be recorded as a discount (contra liability) and amortized over the life of the contract using the implicit or effective interest rate. The entries to record the purchase, the amortization of the discount for the first two years, and the first two payments would be as shown on page 438.

When there is no established cash price for the property, goods, or services, and there is no stated rate of interest on the contract, or the stated rate is unreasonable under the circumstances, an imputed interest rate must be used. A discussion of the determination and application of imputed interest rates is included in Chapter 8.

Property is often acquired under a conditional sales contract whereby legal title to the asset is retained by the seller until payments are completed. The failure to acquire legal title may be disregarded by the buyer and the transaction recognized in terms of its substance—the acquisition of an asset and assumption of a liability. The buyer has the possession and use of the asset and must absorb any decline in its value; title to the asset is retained by the seller simply as a means of assuring payment on the purchase contract.

---

[4]The term *notes* is used by the Board in Opinion No. 21 as a general term for contractual rights to receive money or contractual obligations to pay money at specified or determinable dates.

[5]As illustrated in Chapter 6, the effective or implicit interest rate is computed as follows:

$$PV_n = R(PVAF_{\overline{n}|i}).$$
$$\$50,000 - \$15,000 = \$7,189.22 \ (PVAF_{\overline{n}|i})$$
$$PVAF_{\overline{n}|i} = \frac{\$35,000.00}{\$7,189.22}$$
$$PVAF_{\overline{n}|i} = 4.8684$$

From Table IV, Chapter 6, the interest rate for the present value of 4.8684 when $n = 7$ is 10%. Additional examples of computing an implicit rate of interest are presented in Chapter 6.

Transaction	Entry		
January 2, 1991 Purchased equipment with a cash price of $50,000 for $15,000 down plus seven annual payments of $7,189.22 each, or a total contract price of $65,324.54	Equipment...... Discount on Note Payable .. Note Payable Cash	50,000.00 15,324.54	50,324.54 15,000.00
December 31, 1991 Made first payment of $7,189.22 Amortization of debt discount: 10% × $35,000 = $3,500 ($50,324.54 − $15,324.54 = $35,000)	Note Payable ... Cash .... Interest Expense Discount on Note Payable	7,189.22 3,500.00	7,189.22 3,500.00
December 31, 1992 Made second payment of $7,189.22 Amortization of debt discount: 10% × $31,310.78* = $3,131.08	Note Payable ... Cash .... Interest Expense Discount on Note Payable	7,189.22 3,131.08	7,189.22 3,131.08

*$50,324.54 − $7,189.22 = $43,135.32 Note Payable
$15,324.54 − $3,500.00 = 11,824.54 Discount on note payable
$31,310.78 Present value of note payable end of first year

Acquisition Under Capital Lease

A **lease** is a contractual agreement whereby a **lessee** is granted a right to use property owned by the **lessor** for a specified period of time for a specified periodic cost. Many leases, referred to a **capital leases**, are in effect purchases of property. In such cases, the property should be recorded on the lessee's books as an asset at the present value of the future lease payments. Because lease accounting is a complex area, an entire chapter is devoted to accounting for leases. Even when a lease is not considered to be the same as a purchase and the periodic payments are written off as rental expense, certain lease prepayments or improvements to the property by the lessee may be treated as capital expenditures. Since leasehold improvements, such as partitions in a building, additions, and attached equipment, revert to the owner at the expiration of the lease, they are properly capitalized on the books of the lessee and amortized over the remaining life of the lease. Some lease costs are really expenses of the period and should not be capitalized. This includes improvements that are made in lieu of rent; e.g., a lessee builds partitions in a leased warehouse for storage of its product, and the lessor allows the lessee to offset the cost against rental expense for the period. These costs should be expensed by the lessee.

Acquisition by Exchange of Nonmonetary Assets

In some cases, an enterprise acquires a new asset by exchanging or trading existing nonmonetary assets.[6] Generally, the new asset should be valued at its fair market value or at the fair market value of the asset given up,

[6]Monetary assets are those assets whose amounts are fixed in terms of currency, by contract, or otherwise. Examples include cash and short- or long-term accounts receivable. Nonmonetary assets include all other assets, such as inventories, land, buildings, and equipment.

whichever is more clearly determinable.[7] If the nonmonetary asset is used equipment, the fair market value of the new asset is generally more clearly determinable, and therefore used to record the exchange. It should be observed that determining the fair market value of a new asset can sometimes be difficult.

The quoted or list price for an asset is not always a good indicator of the market value and is often higher than the actual cash price for the asset. An inflated list price permits the seller to increase the indicated trade-in allowance for a used asset. The price for which the asset could be acquired in a cash transaction is the fair market value that should be used to record the acquisition.

To illustrate, assume the sticker on the window of a new car sitting in a dealer's showroom lists a total selling price of $13,500. The sticker includes a base price plus an itemized listing of all the options that have been added. If you, as a buyer, approached the dealer with your old clunker as a trade-in, you might be surprised to be offered $2,000 for a car you know is worth no more than $1,000. If you offered to pay cash for the new car with no trade-in, however, you could probably buy it for approximately $12,500 or the list price reduced by the inflated amount of allowance offered for the trade-in. The fair market value of the new asset is thus not the list price of $13,500, but the true cash price of $12,500.

If the nonmonetary asset given up to acquire the new asset is also property or equipment, a disposition of property occurs simultaneously with the acquisition. Because of the need to first discuss depreciation methods and practices before presenting the disposition of assets, the full discussion of acquisition and disposition by exchange is covered in Chapter 12.

Acquisition by Issuance of Securities

A company may acquire certain property by issuing its own bonds or stocks. When a market value for the securities can be determined, that value is assigned to the asset; in the absence of a market value for the securities, the fair market value of the asset acquired would be used. If bonds or stocks are selling at more or less than par value, Bonds Payable or Capital Stock should be credited at par and the difference recorded as a premium or discount. To illustrate, assume that a company issues 1,000 shares of $25 par stock in acquiring land; the stock is currently selling on the market at $45. An entry should be made as follows:

Land	45,000	
Capital Stock		25,000
Paid-In Capital in Excess of Par		20,000

When securities do not have an established market value, appraisal of the acquired assets by an independent authority may be required to arrive

[7]*Opinions of the Accounting Principles Board, No. 29,* "Accounting for Nonmonetary Transactions" (New York: American Institute of Certified Public Accountants, 1973), par. 18.

at an objective determination of their fair market value. If satisfactory market values cannot be obtained for either securities issued or the assets acquired, values may have to be established by the board of directors for accounting purposes. The source of the valuation should be disclosed on the balance sheet. Assignment of values by the board of directors is normally not subject to challenge unless it can be shown that the board has acted fraudulently. Nevertheless, evidence should be sought to validate the fairness of original valuations, and if, within a short time after an acquisition, the sale of stock or other information indicates that original valuations were erroneous, the affected asset and owners' equity accounts should be adjusted.

Property is frequently acquired in exchange for securities in conjunction with a corporate merger or consolidation. When such combination represents the transfer of properties to a new owner, the combination is designated a *purchase* and the acquired assets are reported at their cost to the new owner. But when such combination represents essentially no more than a continuation of the original ownership in the enlarged entity, the combination is designated a *pooling of interests,* and accounting authorities have approved the practice of recording properties at the original book values as shown on the books of the acquired company. Specific guidelines for distinguishing between a purchase and a pooling of interests are included in APB Opinion No. 16 and are discussed in detail in advanced accounting texts.[8]

Acquisition by Self-Construction

Sometimes buildings or equipment are constructed by a company for its own use. This may be done to save on construction costs, to utilize idle facilities, or to achieve a higher quality of construction.

Self-constructed assets, like purchased assets, are recorded at cost, including all expenditures incurred to build the asset and make it ready for its intended use. Some considerations in determining the cost of self-constructed assets are discussed in the following sections.

Overhead Chargeable to Self-Construction

All costs that can be related to construction should be charged to the assets under construction. There is no question about the inclusion of charges for material and labor directly attributable to the new construction. However, there is a difference of opinion regarding the amount of overhead properly assignable to the construction activity. Some accountants take the position that assets under construction should be charged with no more than the incremental overhead—the increase in a company's total overhead resulting from the special construction activity. Others maintain that overhead should be assigned to construction just as it is assigned to normal opera-

[8]See, for example, Paul M. Fischer, William James Taylor, and J. Arthur Leer, *Advanced Accounting* (Cincinnati: South-Western Publishing Co., 1990).

tions. This would call for the inclusion of not only the increase in overhead resulting from construction activities but also a pro rata share of the company's fixed overhead.

The argument for limiting overhead charges to incremental amounts is that the cost of construction is actually no more than the extra costs incurred. Charges should not be shifted from normal operations to construction activities. Management is aware of the cost of normal operations and decides to undertake a project on the basis of the anticipated added costs. The position that construction should carry a fair share of the fixed overhead if the full cost of the asset is to be reported is based on the premise that overhead has served a dual purpose during the construction period and this is properly reflected in reduced operating costs. The latter argument may be particularly persuasive if construction takes place during a period of subnormal operations and utilizes what would otherwise represent idle capacity cost, or if construction restricts production or other regular business activities.

The assignment to construction of normal overhead otherwise chargeable to current operations will increase net income during the construction period. The recognition of a portion of overhead is postponed and related to subsequent periods through depreciation expense.

The accounting profession has not been successful in coming to an agreement on the issue. Authors of a research study for the AICPA have suggested the following criteria to help resolve the issue.

> . . . in the absence of compelling evidence to the contrary, overhead costs considered to have "discernible future benefits" for the purpose of determining the cost of inventory should be presumed to have "discernible future benefits" for the purpose of determining the cost of a self-constructed depreciable asset.[9]

This criterion would charge both normal and incremental overhead costs to self-constructed fixed assets and has the advantage of providing consistency within a company in the treatment of overhead costs.

Saving or Loss on Self-Construction

When the cost of self-construction of an asset is less than the cost to acquire it through purchase or construction by outsiders, the difference for accounting purposes is not a profit but a savings. The construction is properly reported at its actual cost. The savings will emerge as income over the life of the asset as lower depreciation is charged against periodic revenue. Assume, on the other hand, the cost of self-construction is greater than bids originally received for the construction. There is generally no assurance that the asset under alternative arrangements might have been equal in quality to that which was self-constructed. In recording this transaction, just as in recording others, accounts should reflect those courses of action

[9]Charles Lamden, Dale L. Gerboth, and Thomas McRae, "Accounting for Depreciable Assets," *Accounting Research Monograph No. 1* (New York: American Institute of Certified Public Accountants, 1975), p. 57.

taken, not the alternatives that might have been selected. However, if there is evidence indicating cost has been materially excessive because of certain construction inefficiencies or failures, and the cost exceeds the fair market value of the asset, the excess is properly recognized as a loss; subsequent periods should not be burdened with charges for depreciation arising from costs that could have been avoided.

Interest During Period of Construction

In public utility accounting, interest during a period of construction has long been recognized as a part of asset cost. This practice applies both to interest actually paid and to an implicit interest charge if the public utility uses its own funds. Interest costs, then, are charged to expense through depreciation over the useful life of the asset. Service rates established by regulatory bodies are based on current charges, including depreciation, and thus provide for a recovery of past interest costs.

Generally accepted accounting principles also permit the deferral of certain construction-period interest by nonutility companies. Deferred interest is often referred to as capitalized interest. Only interest costs actually incurred are capitalized, and no implicit interest on internal funds is recognized. The practice of capitalizing interest as part of asset cost is supported on the grounds that interest is a legitimate cost of construction, and the proper matching of revenues and expenses suggests that interest be deferred and charged over the life of the constructed asset. It can also be argued that if buildings or equipment were acquired by purchase rather than by self-construction, a charge for interest during the construction period would be implicit in the purchase price.

Arguments advanced against this practice are:

1. It is difficult to follow cash once it is invested in a firm. Is the interest charge really related to the constructed asset, or is it a payment made to meet general financial needs? Even when a loan is made for specific purposes, it frees cash raised by other means to be used for other projects.
2. To be consistent, implicit interest on all funds used, not just borrowed funds, should be charged to the asset cost. This practice is followed in utility accounting and requires determining a cost of capital for internal funds used, a very difficult task.

Historically, interest capitalization was not a common practice outside the public utility industry. Beginning in the mid 1970s, however, an increasing number of nonutility companies changed their accounting method to a policy of capitalizing interest, an action that tended to increase net income. In 1979, FASB Statement No. 34 was issued recommending limited capitalization of interest cost. If the development of an asset for use or in limited cases, for sale or lease, requires a significant period of time between the initial expenditure related to its development and its readiness for intended use, interest cost on borrowed funds should be capitalized as part of the asset cost.

The amount of interest to be capitalized is

> . . . that portion of the interest cost incurred during the assets' acquisition periods that theoretically could have been avoided (for example, by avoiding additional borrowings or by using the funds expended for the assets to repay existing borrowings) if expenditures for the assets had not been made.[10]

Capitalization of interest is permitted for assets, such as buildings and equipment, that are being self-constructed for an enterprise's own use and assets that are intended to be leased or sold to others that can be identified as **discrete projects**, that is, projects that can be clearly identified as to the assets involved. The construction project should have the following characteristics before interest charges are capitalized:[11]

1. Costs are separately accumulated.
2. Construction covers an extended period of time.
3. Construction costs are substantial.

Interest should not be capitalized for inventories manufactured or produced on a repetitive basis, for assets that are currently being used, or for assets that are idle and are not undergoing activities to prepare them for use. Thus, real property that is being held for future development does not qualify for interest capitalization.[12]

Once it is determined that the construction project qualifies for interest capitalization, the amount of interest to be capitalized must be determined. The following basic principles govern the computation of capitalized interest.[13]

1. Only **interest expense actually incurred** can be capitalized. There is no provision for including an interest cost on equity capital.

2. The **maximum interest** that can be capitalized is the **total interest expense paid or accrued** for the year. In consolidated companies, this includes all interest paid by the parent and subsidiaries.

3. Interest charges begin when the first expenditures are made on the project and continue as long as the activities to get the asset ready for its intended use are in progress, and until the asset is completed and actually ready for use.

4. The average amount of accumulated expenditures is used as the cost on which to compute the interest charge. This can be computed for each expenditure or can be estimated using the assumption that costs are

---

[10]*Statement of Financial Accounting Standards No. 34*, "Capitalization of Interest Cost" (Stamford: Financial Accounting Standards Board, 1979), par. 12.

[11]Alex T. Arcady and Charles Baker, "Interest Cost Accounting: Some Practical Guidance," *Journal of Accountancy* (March 1981), p. 64.

[12]*Statement of Financial Accounting Standards No. 34*, par. 10.

[13]All of the items in the list are included in FASB Statement No. 34 except as otherwise noted.

being incurred evenly over the construction period. Expenditures mean cash disbursements, not accruals.

5. If the construction period covers more than one fiscal period, accumulated expenditures include prior years' capitalized interest.

6. The **interest rates** to be applied to the average accumulated expenditures are applied in a priority order as follows:
   (a) Rate incurred for any debt specifically incurred for funds used on the project.
   (b) Weighted average interest rate from all other enterprise borrowings regardless of the use of funds.

7. If borrowed funds are invested awaiting expenditure on the project, revenue from the investment is not offset against the interest expense in determining the actual interest expense incurred, unless the funds came from tax-exempt borrowings.[14]

8. Disclosure must be made of the total interest expense incurred for the period and the portion that was included as a capitalized cost.

The following illustration demonstrates the application of these guidelines. Cutler Industries, Inc. has decided to construct a new computerized assembly plant. It is estimated that the construction period will be two years, and that the cost of construction will be $6 million. A 12% construction loan for $2 million will be obtained at the beginning of construction.

In addition to the construction loan, Cutler has the following outstanding debt during the construction period:

5-year notes payable, 11% interest	$ 750,000
Mortgage on other plant, 9% interest	$1,200,000

Expenditures on the project are incurred evenly throughout the period, beginning January 1, 1991 and ending on December 31, 1992. The accumulated expenditures at December 31, 1991 amounted to $3,000,000.

Computation of Maximum Interest That Can Be Charged Each Year

Loan	Amount	Interest Rate	Annual Interest
Construction	$2,000,000	12%	$240,000
Notes Payable	750,000	11%	82,500
Mortgage	1,200,000	9%	108,000
Maximum Interest			$430,500

[14]*FASB Technical Bulletin 81-5,* "Offsetting Interest to be Capitalized with Interest Income" (Stamford: Financial Accounting Standards Board, 1981) as amended by *Statement of Financial Accounting Standards No. 62,* "Capitalization of Interest Cost in Situations Involving Certain Tax-Exempt Borrowings and Certain Gifts and Grants" (Stamford: Financial Accounting Standards Board, 1982).

Computation of Weighted-Average Interest Rate

Loan	Principal	Rate	Interest Cost
Notes Payable	$ 750,000	11%	$ 82,500
Mortgage	1,200,000	9%	108,000
	$1,950,000	9.8%*	$190,500

*Weighted average rate = $190,500 ÷ $1,950,000 = 9.8% (rounded)

Computation of Weighted-Average Accumulated Expenditures-1991

Expenditure total, January 1, 1991	0
Expenditure total, December 31, 1991	$3,000,000
	÷ 2
Average accumulated expenditures, 1991	$1,500,000

Computation of Interest Eligible for Capitalization-1991

$1,500,000 × 12% (rate on construction loan) = $180,000

Since $180,000 is less than the actual interest expense, the $180,000 is capitalized as interest cost.

Computation of Weighted-Average Accumulated Expenditures-1992

Expenditure total, December 31, 1991	$3,000,000
1991 capitalized interest	180,000
Adjusted expenditure total, December 31, 1991*	$3,180,000
Average additional expenditures 1992 ($3,000,000 ÷ 2)	1,500,000
Average accumulated expenditures, 1992	$4,680,000

*1991 expenditures are considered incurred for all of 1992.

Computation of Interest Eligible for Capitalization-1992

$2,000,000* × 12%	$240,000
2,680,000** × 9.8%	262,640
	$502,640

*Amount of construction loan
**$4,680,000 − $2,000,000
Since $502,640 is more than the actual interest of $430,500, the actual interest expense is capitalized.

There are several important observations about this example. In 1991, the interest expense actually incurred exceeded the amount of interest computed on the average accumulated expenditures. The computed interest amount was therefore capitalized. In 1992, however, more of the company's internal funds were used for the construction, and the computation of interest that could have been capitalized exceeded the interest actually paid. The interest actually paid was therefore capitalized. The example assumed no new loans during 1992. If additional monies were borrowed specifically for the project, the rate on the new borrowings would have been applied to expended funds before applying the weighted average rate on all other borrowings. If additional general borrowings were made, a new computation of the weighted average rate would have been necessary. The example assumed expenditures were made evenly throughout the construction period. If only a few identifiable payments were made, computation of the weighted averge accumulated expenditures could have been made by weighting each expenditure separately for the portion of the year during which it was outstanding.

FASB Statement No. 34 requires disclosure of the total interest expense for the year and the amount capitalized. This disclosure can be made either in the body of the income statement or in a note to the statements.

To illustrate these two methods, assume that Cutler Industries reported the 1991 interest information in the income statement and the 1992 information in a note as follows:

Cutler Industries Income Statement—1991

Operating income		xxxxx
Other expenses and losses:		
Interest expense	$430,500	
Less capitalized interest	180,000	250,500
Income before income taxes		xxxxx
Income taxes		xxxxx
Net income		xxxxx

Cutler Industries Notes—1992

Note X—Interest expense

Total interest expense of $430,500 was capitalized as part of the cost of construction for the computerized assembly line building in accordance with the requirements of FASB Statement No. 34.

Another example of note disclosure is presented in Note Ten of the 1988 annual report of General Mills, Inc. which appears in Appendix A.

The capitalization of interest costs as part of the cost of self-constructed assets has been subject to much criticism. The initial acceptance vote of the FASB was by a 4 to 3 margin, the minimum acceptable. The conceptual question that still remains is whether the interest added to asset cost truly adds to the expected future benefit of the constructed asset. For now, the profession has specified the conditions where the answer is yes.

Acquisition by Donation or Discovery

When property is received through donation by a governmental unit or other source, there is no cost that can be used as a basis for its valuation. It is classified as a **nonreciprocal transfer of a nonmonetary asset.**[15] Even though certain expenditures may have to be made incident to the gift, these expenditures are generally considerably less than the value of the

---

[15]*Opinions of the Accounting Principles Board, No. 29*, par. 3(d).

property. Here cost obviously fails to provide a satisfactory basis for asset valuation.

Property acquired through donation should be appraised and recorded at its fair market value.[16] A donation increases owners' equity, therefore Donated Capital is credited. To illustrate, if the Beverly Hills Chamber of Commerce donates land and buildings appraised at $400,000 and $1,500,000 respectively, the entry on the books of the donee would be:

Land	400,00	
Buildings	1,500,000	
Donated Capital		1,900,000

Depreciation of an asset acquired by gift should be recorded in the usual manner, the value assigned to the asset providing the basis for the depreciation charge.

If a gift is contingent upon some act to be performed by the donee, no asset should be reported until the conditions of the gift have been met. At that time, both the increase in assets and in owners' equity should be recognized in the accounts and on the financial statements.

Occasionally, valuable resources are discovered on already owned land. The discovery greatly increases the value of the property. However, because the cost of the land is not affected by the discovery, it is common practice to ignore this increase in value. Similarly, the increase in value for assets that change over time, such as growing timber or aging wine, is ignored in common practice. Failure to recognize these discovery or accretion values ignores the economic reality of the situation and tends to materially understate the assets of the entity. More meaningful decisions could probably be made if the user of the statements were made aware of these changes in value.

Classifying Expenditures as Assets or Expenses

The decision as to whether a given expenditure is an asset or an expense is one of the many areas in which an accountant must exercise judgment. If the expenditure is expected to benefit future periods, it is by definition an asset. If the expenditure benefits the current period only, it is an expense.

Income cannot be measured fairly unless expenditures are properly classified. For example, an incorrect charge to an equipment account instead of an expense account results in the overstatement of current earnings on the income statement and the overstatement of assets and owners' equity on the balance sheet. As the charge is assigned to operations in subsequent periods, earnings of such periods will be understated; assets and equity on the successive balance sheets will continue to be overstated, although by lesser amounts each year, until the asset is written off and the original error is fully counterbalanced. On the other hand, an incorrect charge to an

---

[16]*Ibid.*, par. 18.

expense instead of an equipment account results in the understatement of current earnings and the understatement of assets and equity. Earnings of subsequent periods will be overstated in the absence of debits for depreciation or amortization; assets and equity will continue to be understated, although by lesser amounts each year, until the original error is completely offset.

In many companies, not all expenditures for assets that have future benefits are recorded in the noncurrent asset accounts. A lower limit to the definition of an asset expenditure is established to avoid the excessive costs of accounting for relatively small deferred costs. Thus, any expenditure under the established limit is always expensed currently even though future benefits are expected from that expenditure. This practice is justified on the grounds of expediency and materiality. The amount of the limit varies with the size of the company. Limits of $100, $500, and $1,000 are not unusual. This treatment is acceptable as long as it is consistently applied and no material misstatements arise due to unusual expenditure patterns or other causes.

Previous sections of the chapter have described the types of expenditures that are typically recorded as assets and under various types of acquisition arrangements. The remainder of the chapter focuses on areas where some special problems and considerations arise in determining whether an expenditure is an asset or an expense. These areas are: research and development expenditures, computer software development expenditures, and post-acquisition expenditures.

Research and Development Expenditures

Historically, expenditures for **research and development (R & D)** purposes were reported sometimes as assets and sometimes as expenses. The FASB inherited this problem from the Accounting Principles Board and made this area the subject of their first definitive standard.[17] The Board defined **research activities** as those undertaken to discover new knowledge that will be useful in developing new products, services, or processes or that will result in significant improvements of existing products or processes. **Development activities** involve the application of research findings to develop a plan or design for new or improved products and processes. Development activities include the formulation, design, and testing of products, construction of prototypes, and operation of pilot plants.

In general, the FASB concluded that research and development expenditures should be expensed in the period incurred.[18] This decision was reached after much analysis and after many attempts to establish criteria for selectively recording some research and development expenditures as assets and expensing others. Among the arguments for expensing these costs was the frequent inability to find a definite causal relationship between the

[17]*Statement of Financial Accounting Standards No. 2,* "Accounting for Research and Development Costs" (Stamford: Financial Accounting Standards Board, 1974).

[18]*Ibid.,* par. 12.

expenditures and future revenues. Sometimes very large expenditures do not generate any future revenue, while relatively small expenditures lead to significant discoveries that generate large revenues. The Board found it difficult to establish criteria that would distinguish between those research and development expenditures that would most likely benefit future periods and those that would not.

As defined by the FASB in Statement No. 2, research and development costs include those costs of materials, equipment, facilities, personnel, purchased intangibles, contract services, and a reasonable allocation of indirect costs that are specifically related to research and development activities and that have no alternative future uses.[19] Such activities include:

1. Laboratory research aimed at discovery of new knowledge.
2. Searching for applications of new research findings or other knowledge.
3. Conceptual formulation and design of possible product or process alternatives.
4. Testing in search for or evaluation of product or process alternatives.
5. Modification of the formulation or design of a product or process.
6. Design, construction, and testing of pre-production prototypes and models.
7. Design of tools, jigs, molds, and dies involving new technology.
8. Design, construction, and operation of a pilot plant that is not of a scale economically feasible to the enterprise for commercial production.
9. Engineering activity required to advance the design of a product to the point that it meets specific functional and economic requirements and is ready for manufacture.[20]

The Board stipulated, however, that expenditures for certain items having alternative future uses, either in additional research projects or for productive purposes, can be recorded as an asset and allocated against future projects or periods as research and development expenses. This exception permits the deferral of costs incurred for materials, equipment, facilities, and purchased intangibles, but only if an alternative use can be identified.

The Board was very careful to distinguish between research and development expenses and other expenditures that are related to research activities but classified in other categories. These other expenditures are also usually regarded as expenses in the period incurred, but not as research and development expenses. To illustrate how research related expenditures are recorded under current GAAP, assume the Robotics Corporation made the expenditures listed on page 450 during 1991 related to the development of robots for commercial and productive use.

[19]*Ibid.*, par. 11.

[20]*Ibid.*, par. 9.

ROBOTICS CORPORATION

Description of Expenditure	Accounting Treatment per GAAP
1. Purchase of land to construct research facility.	1. Record as land.
2. Self-construction of building to use in all robotic research.	2. Record as building and depreciate as R & D expense.
3. Purchase of special equipment to be used solely for the development of a robot for the space program. The equipment is not expected to have any use beyond this project.	3. Expense immediately as R & D.
4. Purchase of more generalized equipment that can be used for a wide variety of robotic projects.	4. Record as equipment and depreciate as R & D expense.
5. Research salaries dedicated to improvement of general robotic technology.	5. Expense immediately as R & D.
6. Purchase of patent for innovative construction of arm and hand segments.	6. Record as patent and amortize as cost of production.
7. Labor and material costs incurred in building a prototype model of a robot for space travel.	7. Expense immediately as R & D.
8. Costs to produce ten robots to specified design.	8. Include in cost of goods manufactured. Report as inventory on balance sheet until sold.
9. Salary of marketing executive assigned to find customers for the space robot.	9. Expense immediately as marketing expense.
10. Costs of testing the prototype robot under simulated space travel conditions.	10. Expense immediately as R & D.
11. Legal costs to protect patents purchased.	11. Record as patent and amortize as cost of production.
12. Legal costs of filing for patent on space robot.	12. Record as patent and amortize as cost of production.
13. Research costs for Japanese manufacturer who has contracted with Robotics Corporation for research technology.	13. Record as receivable for contracted amount.

Evaluation of FASB Position

Research and development costs vary widely among companies. Many expenditures do have future worth, while others are so highly uncertain as to future worth that recording them as assets is clearly improper. For the FASB to ignore these differences and issue a blanket rule that all research and development expenditures should be handled the same seems arbitrary and without theoretical support. The International Accounting Group studying this area disagreed with the FASB and identified general situations in which they felt deferral of development costs would be justified:

> Development costs of a project may be deferred to future periods if all the following criteria are satisfied:
> (a) the product or process is clearly defined and the costs attributable to the product or process can be separately identified;

(b) the technical feasibility of the product or process has been demonstrated;

(c) the management of the enterprise has indicated its intention to produce and market, or use, the product or process;

(d) there is a clear indication of a future market for the product or process or, if it is to be used internally rather than sold, its usefulness to the enterprise can be demonstrated; and

(e) adequate resources exist, or are reasonably expected to be available, to complete the project and market the product or process.[21]

While guidelines to help distinguish between asset and expense expenditures are desirable, specific rules, such as those issued for research and development expenditures, that mandate by definition the treatment of all expenditures ignore the reality of the great diversity of conditions existing in practice.

Computer Software Development Expenditures

In the best seller, *Megatrends*, John Naisbitt described the significant trend in the United States away from production intensive industries, such as steel, mining, and machine tools, to information processing industries, such as communications, computers, and service.

> The real increase has been in information occupations. In 1950, only about 17 percent of us worked in information jobs. Now more than 65 percent of us work with information as programmers, teachers, clerks, secretaries, accountants, stock brokers, managers, insurance people, bureaucrats, lawyers, bankers, and technicians. And many more workers hold information jobs within manufacturing companies. Most Americans spend their time creating, processing, or distributing information . . . David L. Birch of MIT reports that, as of May 1983, only 12 percent of our labor force is engaged in manufacturing operations today.[22]

As this trend has emerged over the past decade, new accounting issues have arisen that have required special attention. One of these has been accounting for the cost of computer software.

The computer industry has become divided into two major components: hardware and software. Computer hardware consists of the equipment such as consoles, boards, printers, and monitors that are produced and sold by a fairly small number of computer manufacturers. The development of the microcomputer led to the formation of several new hardware manufacturers. However, as the microcomputer explosion spread, the number of computer hardware producing firms decreased through mergers and dissolutions.

Computer software, on the other hand, consists of the programs that have been developed to be used with the hardware to accomplish specific

---

[21]*International Accounting Standard, No. 9,* "Accounting for Research and Development Activities" (London, England: International Accounting Standards Committee, 1978), par. 17.

[22]John Naisbitt, *Megatrends: Ten New Directions Transforming Our Lives,* 6th ed. (New York: Warner Books, 1983), pp. 4–5.

tasks. The development of software requires little in the way of initial capital investment, and thus has led to the formation of hundreds of small software companies, each developing its own special software programs. Scores of computer magazines advertising these programs have emerged in the last decade as businesses and households have purchased their own micros. Software programs such as *Lotus 1-2-3, Wordperfect, Supercalc,* and *Peachtree* have magnified the power of the computer for everyday use. Specialized accounting, tax, architectural, library, medical, educational, and recreational software packages have been developed by these hundreds of companies and marketed throughout the world.

A major accounting question related to the development of computer software has been how to account for the costs of development and production of the finished product. Many companies considered the development costs as research and development and expensed them in the period incurred as required by FASB Statement No. 2, discussed in the previous section. Other companies argued that these costs should be deferred and written off against future revenues. Since these costs were a very significant part of the total expenditures of a software company, the alternate methods used to account for them created considerable differences among the financial statements of the various companies. The FASB, with strong support from the SEC, addressed this issue and in 1985 issued FASB Statement No. 86, "Accounting for the Costs of Computer Software to be Sold, Leased, or Otherwise Marketed."

The Board's conclusions concerning computer software costs are summarized in Exhibit 11-3.

Exhibit 11–3   Development of Successful Software

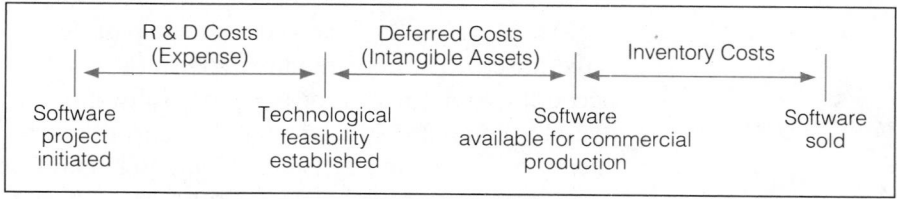

As demonstrated by Exhibit 11–3, all costs incurred up to the point where technological feasibility is established are to be expensed as research and development. They include costs incurred for planning, designing, and testing activities. Costs incurred after this point up until the product is ready for commercial production, such as further coding, testing, and production of masters, are to be recorded as an intangible asset. Additional costs to actually produce software from the masters and package the software for distribution are inventoriable costs and will be charged against revenue as the product is sold.

Considerable judgment is required to determine when technological feasibility has been established. The Board attempted to assist in the judgment with specific definitions and examples as follows:

At a minimum, technological feasibility shall be attained when an enterprise has produced either[23]

1. A **detail program design** of the software establishing that the necessary skills, hardware, and software technology are available to the enterprise to produce the product. (Includes coding and testing necessary to resolve uncertainties for high-risk development issues), or
2. A **working model** of the software has been completed and tested.

If an enterprise purchases computer software externally for further development and resale, it should be accounted for in the same manner as described above for internally developed software. While Statement No. 86 does not directly address accounting for costs of computer software that is to be *used* internally by an enterprise as opposed to being *sold* externally, the Board indicated that the limited deferral of software costs would "likely be applied to costs incurred in developing software for internal use as well as for sale or lease to others."[24]

The treatment of computer software development costs by the FASB demonstrates how the more general research and development guidelines of FASB Statement No. 2 may be applied in future specific situations. By establishing two transitional points (technological feasibility and availability for general release to customers), the Board has recognized a separation between costs that are identified as being expenses and those that are assets to be deferred and amortized against future revenues. This treatment seems more in keeping with the approach used by the International Accounting Group for all research and development costs as described earlier. Of course, such distinctions require enterprises to establish systems and controls that result in a proper accounting. The Board must continue to monitor its standards to determine that the benefits accruing to the users of the statements exceed the cost of implementing the standards.

Post-Acquisition Expenditures

Over the useful lives of plant assets, regular as well as special expenditures are incurred. Certain expenditures are required to maintain and repair assets; others are incurred to increase their capacity or efficiency or to extend their useful lives. Each expenditure requires careful analysis to determine whether it should be charged to an expense account, or whether it should be assigned to revenue of more than one period, which requires a charge to an asset account or to an accumulated depreciation account. In many cases the answer may not be clear, and the procedure chosen may be a matter of judgment.

The terms maintenance, repairs, betterments, improvements, additions, and rearrangements are used in describing expenditures made in the

---

[23]*Statement of Financial Accounting Standards No. 86,* "Accounting for the Costs of Computer Software to Be Sold, Leased, or Otherwise Marketed" (Stamford: Financial Accounting Standards Board, 1985), par. 4.
[24]*Ibid.,* par. 26.

course of asset use. These are described in the following sections. Exhibit 11-4 summarizes the accounting for these subsequent expenditures.

Exhibit 11-4   Summary of Expenditures Subsequent to Acquisition

Type of Expenditure	Definition	Accounting Treatment
Maintenance and repairs	Normal cost of keeping property in operating condition.	Expense as incurred.
Renewals and replacements: 1. No extension of useful life or increase in future cash flows.	Unplanned replacement. Expenditure needed to fulfill original plans.	Expense as incurred.
2. Extends useful life or increases future cash flows.	Improvement resulting from replacement with better component.	Record as an asset by one of two methods: (1) If cost of old component is known: Remove cost of old part and its accumulated depreciation, recognizing gain or loss. Defer cost of new component. (2) If cost of old component is not known: Deduct cost of new component from accumulated depreciation.
Additions and betterments	Expenditures that add to asset usefulness by either extending life or increasing future cash flows. No replacement of component involved.	Add to the cost of an asset.

Maintenance and Repairs

Expenditures to maintain plant assets in good operating condition are referred to as **maintenance**. Among these are expenditures for painting, lubricating, and adjusting equipment. Maintenance expenditures are ordinary and recurring and do not improve the asset or add to its life; therefore, they are recorded as expenses when they are incurred.

Expenditures to restore assets to good operating condition upon their breakdown or to restore and replace broken parts are referred to as **repairs**. These are ordinary and recurring expenditures that benefit only current operations, thus they are also debited to expense immediately.

Renewals and Replacements

Expenditures for the overhauling of plant assets are frequently referred to as **renewals**. Substitutions of parts or entire units are referred to as **replacements**. If these expenditures are necessary to achieve the original plans and do not change the original estimates of useful life or cash flows, they should be expensed. If, however, these expenditures extend the life of the asset or increase the cash flows generated by the asset, they should be capitalized by either adding them to the asset value or deducting them from accumulated depreciation.

Theoretically, if a part is removed and replaced with a superior part, the cost and accumulated depreciation related to the replaced part should be removed from the accounts, a loss recognized for the underpreciated book value, and the expenditure for the replacement added to the asset value. Often it is not possible to identify the cost related to a specific part of an asset. In these instances, by debiting accumulated depreciation, the undepreciated book value is increased without creating a build-up of the gross asset values. When this entry is made, no immediate loss related to the removal of the old asset is recognized.

To illustrate replacements, assume the Mendon Fireworks Company replaces the roof of its manufacturing plant for $40,000 and extends the estimated life of the building by five years. Assume that the original cost of the building was $1,600,000 and it is ¾ depreciated. If the original roof cost $20,000, the following entry could be made to remove the undepreciated book value of the old roof and record the expenditure for the new one.

Buildings (new roof)	40,000	
Accumulated Depreciation (old roof)	15,000	
Loss from Replacement of Roof	5,000	
Buildings (old roof)		20,000
Cash		40,000

If Mendon could not identify the cost of the old roof, the following entry would be made:

Accumulated Depreciation	40,000	
Cash		40,000

The book value of the building after the first entry is $435,000 ($1,600,000 − $1,200,000 + $40,000 − $5,000). Assuming the second entry is made, the book value would be $440,000 ($1,600,000 − $1,200,000 + $40,000). The $5,000 additional cost would be reflected in higher depreciation charges over the remaining life of the building.

Additions and Betterments

Enlargements and extensions of existing facilities are referred to as **additions**. Changes in assets designed to provide increased or improved services are referred to as **betterments**. If the addition or betterment does not involve a replacement of component parts of an existing asset, the expenditure should be deferred by adding it to the cost of the asset. If a replacement is involved, it is accounted for as discussed in the previous section.

Summary   The most challenging issue facing accountants in the area of asset acquisitions is which costs should be deferred and matched against future revenue and which should be expensed immediately. Costs to acquire new property items with lives in excess of one fiscal period should clearly be charged against future periods. Accounting for repairs, additions, and similar costs incurred subsequent to the initial acquisition is less clear, and such expenditures must be individually evaluated in light of existing conditions. The historical acquisition cost of an asset is widely accepted as the basis for the gross investment, whether for tangible or intangible assets. Methods for matching these costs against future revenues will be discussed in the next chapter, as well as accounting for the retirement of assets.

Appendix

Goodwill Estimation

As indicated previously, there are many factors that can be considered in determining the purchase price for a business. In deciding whether more than the current value of identifiable net assets should be paid, management may utilize one or more of the following goodwill valuation methods:

1. Capitalization of average income
2. Capitalization of average excess income
3. Number of years' excess income
4. Present value of future excess income

Variables Used in Goodwill Valuation

Before discussing these methods, two variables that are used in all methods are discussed: (1) an estimate of future income and (2) appropriate rate of return.

Estimating the Level of Future Income

Past earnings ordinarily offer the best basis on which to develop an estimate of the level of future income. In considering past income as a basis for projection into the future, reference should be made to income most recently experienced. A sufficient number of periods should be included in the analysis so a representative measurement of business performance is available and significant trends are observable. In certain instances, it may be considered necessary to restate revenue and expense balances to give effect to alternative depreciation or amortization methods, inventory methods, or other measurement processes considered desirable in summarizing past operations. Irregular or extraordinary gains and losses that cannot be considered a part of regular activities would be excluded from past operating results. Depending on the circumstances, these items may include gains and losses from the sale of investments and land, buildings, and equipment, gains and losses from the retirement of debt, and losses from casualties.

Regular earnings from operations should be analyzed to determine their trend and stability. If earnings over a period of years show a tendency to decline, careful analysis is necessary to determine whether this decline may be expected to continue. There may be greater confidence in possible future income when past income has been relatively stable rather than widely fluctuating.

Any changes in the operations of the business that may be anticipated after the transfer of ownership should also be considered. The elimination of a division, the disposal of substantial property items, or the retirement of long-term debt, for example, could materially affect future income.

The regular income of the past is used as a basis for estimating income of the future. Business conditions, the business cycle, sources of supply, demand for the company's products or services, price structure, competition, and other significant factors must be studied in developing data making it possible to convert past income into estimated future income.

Determining the Appropriate Rate of Return

The existence of above-normal income, if any, can be determined only by reference to a normal rate of return. The **normal income rate** is that which would ordinarily be required to attract investors in the particular type of business being acquired. In judging this rate, consideration must be given to such factors as money market rates, business conditions at the time of the purchase, competitive factors, risks involved, entrepreneurial abilities required, and alternative investment opportunities.

In general, the greater the risk entailed in an investment, the higher the rate of return required. Because most business enterprises are subject to a considerable amount of risk, investors generally expect a relatively high rate of return to justify their investment. A long history of stable income or the existence of certain tangible assets that can be easily sold reduce the degree of risk in acquiring a business and thus reduce the rate of return required by a potential investor.

If goodwill is to be purchased, it should be looked upon as an investment and must offer the prospect of sufficient return to justify the commitment. Special risks are associated with goodwill. The value of goodwill is uncertain and fluctuating. It cannot be separated from the business as a whole and sold, as can most other business properties. Furthermore, it is subject to rapid deterioration and may be totally lost in the event of business sale or liquidation. As a result of the greater risk, a higher rate of return would normally be required on the purchase of goodwill than on the purchase of other business properties.

Methods of Valuing Goodwill

Assume that the following information is available for Company A:

Income after adjustment and elimination of unusual and extraordinary items:

1988	$120,000
1989	80,000
1990	110,000
1991	75,000
1992	115,000
Total	$500,000

Average income 1988-1992: $500,000 ÷ 5 = $100,000. Net assets as appraised on January 2, 1993, before recognizing goodwill, $1,000,000. (Land, buildings, equipment, inventories, and receivables, $1,200,000; liabilities to be assumed by purchaser, $200,000.)

The average income figure of $100,000 for the five-year period 1988-1992 was used in arriving at an estimate of the probable future income.

Different goodwill amounts may be computed using these data depending on which of the four valuation methods listed on page 457 is used. Each of these methods will be described and illustrated with examples.

Capitalization of Average Income

The amount to be paid for a business may be determined by capitalizing expected future income at a rate representing the required return on the investment. Capitalization of income, as used in this sense, means calculation of the principal value that will yield the stated income at the specified rate indefinitely or in perpetuity. This is accomplished by dividing the income by the specified rate.[26] The difference between the amount to be paid for the business as thus obtained and the appraised values of the individual property items may be considered the price paid for goodwill.

If, in the example, a return of 8% were required on the investment and income were estimated at $100,000 per year, the business would be valued at $1,250,000 ($100,000 ÷ .08). Since net assets, with the exception of goodwill, were appraised at $1,000,000, goodwill would be valued at $250,000. If a 10% return were required on the investment, the business would be worth only $1,000,000. In acquiring the business for $1,000,000, there would be no payment for goodwill.

Capitalization of Average Excess Income

In the above method, a single rate of return was applied to the estimated annual income in arriving at the value of the business. No consideration was given to what extent the income was attributable to net identifiable assets and to what extent the income was attributable to goodwill. It would seem reasonable, however, to expect a higher return on a investment in goodwill than on the other assets acquired. To illustrate, assume the following facts:

	Company A	Company B
Net assets as appraised	$1,000,000	$500,000
Estimated future income	100,000	100,000

If the estimated income is capitalized at a uniform rate of 8%, the value of each company is found to be $1,250,000. The goodwill for Company A is then $250,000, and for Company B, $750,000 as shown:

	Company A	Company B
Total net asset valuation (income capitalized at 8%)	$1,250,000	$1,250,000
Deduct net assets as appraised	1,000,000	500,000
Goodwill	$ 250,000	$ 750,000

[26]This may be shown as follows: P = principal amount or the capitalized income to be computed; r = the specified rate of return; E = expected annual income. Then, E = P X r, and P = E ÷ r.

These calculations ignore the fact that the appraised value of the net assets identified with Company A exceed those of Company B. Company A, whose income of $100,000 is accompanied by net assets valued at $1,000,000, would certainly command a higher price than Company B, whose income of $100,000 is accompanied by net assets valued at only $500,000.

Satisfactory recognition of both earnings and asset contributions is generally effected by (1) requiring a fair return on identifiable net assets, and (2) viewing any excess income as attributable to goodwill and capitalizing the excess at a higher rate in recognition of the degree of risk that characterizes goodwill. To illustrate, assume in the previous cases that 8% is considered a normal return on identifiable net assets and that excess income is captialized at 20% in determining the amount to be paid for goodwill. Amounts to be paid in Companies A and B would be calculated as follows:

	Company A	Company B
Estimated income	$ 100,000	$ 100,000
Normal return on net assets:		
Company A—8% of $1,000,000	80,000	
Company B—8% of $500,000		40,000
Excess income	$ 20,000	$ 60,000
Excess income capitalized at 20%	÷.20	÷.20
Value of goodwill	$ 100,000	$ 300,000

	Company A	Company B
Value of net assets offering normal return of 8%	$1,000,000	$ 500,000
Value of goodwill, excess income capitalized at 20%	100,000	300,000
Total net asset valuation	$1,100,000	$ 800,000

Number of Years' Excess Income

Behind each of the capitalization methods just described, there is an implicit assumption that the superior earning power attributed to the existence of goodwill will continue indefinitely. The very nature of goodwill, however, makes it subject to rapid decline. A business with unusually high income may expect the competition from other companies to reduce income over a period of years. Furthermore, the high levels of income may frequently be maintained only by special efforts on the part of the new owners, and they cannot be expected to pay for something they themselves must achieve.

As the goodwill being purchased cannot be expected to last beyond a specific number of years, one frequently finds payment for excess income stated in terms of *years* of excess income rather than capitalization in perpetuity.[27] For example, if excess annual income of $20,000 is expected and payment is to be made for excess income for a five-year period, the

[27]Calculation of goodwill in terms of number of years of excess income will yield results identical to the capitalization method when the number of years used is equal to the reciprocal of the capitalization rate. Payment for the five years' income, for example, is equivalent to capitalizing earnings at a 20% rate (1 ÷ .20 = 5). Payment of four years' income is equivalent to capitalization at a 25% rate (1 ÷ .25 = 4).

purchase price for goodwill would be $100,000. If the excess annual income is expected to be $60,000 and the payment is to be made for four years' excess income, the price for goodwill would be $240,000.

The years of excess earnings method has the advantage of conceptual simplicity. It is related to the common business practice of evaluating investment opportunities in terms of their *payback period*—the number of years expected for recovery of the initial investment.

Present Value Method

The concept of number of years' purchase can be combined with the concept of a rate of return on investment. Excess income can be expected to continue for only a limited number of years, but an investment in this income should provide an adequate return, considering the risks involved. The amount to be paid for goodwill, then, is the discounted or present value of the excess income expected to become available in future periods.

To illustrate the calculation of goodwill by the present value method, assume the income of Company A exceed a normal return on the net identifiable assets used in the business by $20,000 per year. This excess income is expected to continue for a period of five years, and a return of 12% is considered necessary to attract investors in this industry. The amount to be paid for goodwill, then, may be regarded as the discounted value at 12% of five installments of $20,000 to be received at annual intervals. Present value tables may be used in determining the present value of the series of payments. The present value of 5 annual payments of $1 each, to provide a return of 12%, is found to be 3.6048.[28] Goodwill would be computed as the present value of five payments of $20,000 each, or $20,000 × 3.6048 = $72,096.

The principal advantage of the present value method is the explicit recognition of the anticipated duration of excess income together with the use of a realistic rate of return. Thus, it focuses on the factors most relevant to the goodwill evaluation.

[28]See Table IV, Chapter 6.

Key Terms

Additions 455
Average amount of accumulated
  expenditures 443
Betterments 455
Capital leases 438
Capitalized interest 442
Development activities 448
Goodwill 431
Intangible noncurrent operating assets
  427
Lessee 438
Lessor 438
Maintenance 454

Negative goodwill 434
Nonreciprocal transfer of a
  nonmonetary asset 446
Renewals 454
Repairs 454
Replacements 454
Research activities 448
Research and development (R &D)
  448
Tangible noncurrent operating assets
  427
Technological feasibility 453
Weighted average interest rate 444

Questions

1. In the balance sheet of many companies, the largest classification of assets in amount is noncurrent operating assets. Name the items, in addition to the amount paid to the former owner or contractor, that may be properly included as part of the acquisition cost of the following property items: (a) land, (b) buildings, and (c) equipment.

2. What acquisition costs are included in (a) copyrights, (b) franchises, (c) trademarks?

3. How would a trademark worth $5,000,000 be reported on the balance sheet if (a) the trademark were purchased for $5,000,000 or (B) the trademark gradually became identified over the years as a company symbol?

4. How should development stage enterprises report (a) their organization costs and (b) net operating losses?

5. (a) Under what conditions may goodwill be reported as an asset? (b) The Roper Company engages in a widespread advertising campaign on behalf of new products, charging above-normal expenditures to goodwill. Do you approve of this practice? Why or why not?

6. How should negative goodwill be reported in the financial statments?

7. What procedure should be followed to allocate the cost of a lump-sum purchase of assets among specific accounts?

8. What special accounting problems are introduced when a company purchases equipment on a deferred payment contract rather than with cash?

9. (a) Why is the "list price" of an asset often not representatiave of its fair market value? (b) Under these conditions, how should a fair market value be determined?

10. Gaylen Corp. decides to construct a building for itself and plans to use whatever plant facilities it has to further such construciton. (a) What costs will enter into the cost of construction? (b) What two positions can the company take with respect to general overhead allocation during the period of construction? Evaluate each position and indicate your preference.

11. What characteristics must a construction project have before interest can be captialized as part of the project cost?

12. What are the general guidelines for determining the amount of interest that can be capitalized?

13. What are the principal arguments against capitalizing interest as presently mandated by the FASB?

14. The Parkhurst Corporation acquires land and buildings valued at $250,000 as a gift from Industrial City. The president of the company maintains that since there was no cost for the acquisition, neither cost of the facilities nor depreciation needs to be recognized for financial statement purposes. Evaluate the president's position assuming (a) the donation is unconditional, (b) the donation is contingent upon the employment by the company of a certain number of employees for a ten-year period.

15. Why do some companies expense asset expenditures that are under an established monetary amount?

16. Indicate the effects of the following errors on the balance sheet and the income statement in the current year and succeeding years:
    (a) The cost of a depreciable asset is incorrectly recorded as an expense.
    (b) An expense expenditure is incorrectly recorded as an addition to the cost of a depreciable asset.

17. (a) What type of activities are considered to be research and development expenditures? (b) Under what conditions, if any, are research and development costs deferred?

18. What conceptual modification to the FASB standard on research and development costs is apparent in the later standard on accounting for computer software development costs?

19. Which of the following items would be recorded as expenses and which would be recorded as assets?
    (a) Cost of installing machinery
    (b) Cost of unsuccessful litigation to protect patent
    (c) Extensive repairs as a result of a fire
    (d) Cost of grading land
    (e) Insurance on machinery in transit
    (f) Bond discount amortization during construction period
    (g) Cost of major unexpected overhaul on machinery
    (h) New safety guards on machinery
    (i) Commission on purchase of real estate
    (j) Special tax assessment for street improvements
    (k) Cost of repainting offices

20. Why are some asset expenditures made subsequent to acquisition recorded as an increase in an asset account and others recorded as a decrease in accumulated depreciation?

*21. What factors should be considered in estimating the future income of a business in order to develop a fair valuation of goodwill?

*22. (a) Identify and discuss four methods for arriving at a goodwill valuation using estimated future income as a basis for these calculations. (b) Which method do you think would give the most relevant valuation of goodwill?

*Relates to Appendix

Discussion Cases **Case 11-1 (Where should we charge it?)**

Fugate Energy Corp. has recently purchased the assets of a small local company, Gleave Inc., for $556,950 cash. The chief accountant of Fugate has been given the assignment of preparing the journal entry to record the purchase. An investigation disclosed the following information about the assets of Gleave Inc.:

(a) Gleave owned land and a small manufacturing building. The book value of the property on Gleave's records was $115,000. An appraisal for fire insurance purposes had been made during the year. The building was appraised by the insurance company at $175,000. Property tax assessment notices showed that the building's worth was five times the worth of the land.

(b) Gleave's equipment had a book value of $75,000. It is estimated by Gleave that it would take six times the amount of book value to replace the old equipment with new. The old equipment is, on the average, 50% depreciated.

(c) Gleave had a franchise to produce and sell solar energy units from another company in a set geographic area. The franchise was transferred to Fugate as part of the purchase. Gleave carried the asset on its books at $40,000, the unamortized balance of the original cost of $90,000. The franchise is for an unlimited time. Similar franchises are now being sold by the company for $120,000 per geographic area.

(d) Gleave had two excellent research scientists who were responsible for much of the company's innovation in product development. They are each paid $50,000 per year by Gleave. They have agreed to work for Fugate Energy at the same salary.

(e) Gleave held two patents on its products. Both had been fully amortized and were not carried as assets on Gleave's books. Gleave feels they could have been sold separately for $75,000 each.

Evaluate each of the above items and prepare the journal entry that should be made to record the purchase on Fugate's books.

Case 11-2   (How much does it cost?)

The Bakeman Co. decides to construct a piece of specialized machinery using personnel from the maintenance department. This is the first time the maintenance personnel have been used for this purpose, and the cost accountant for the factory is concerned as to the accounting for costs of the machine. Some of the issues raised by the maintenance department management are highlighted below:

(a) The supervisor of the maintenance department has instructed the workers to schedule work so all the overtime hours are charged to the machinery. Overtime is paid at 150% of the regular rate, or at a 50% premium.

(b) Material used in the production of the machine is charged out from the materials storeroom at 125% of cost, the same markup used when material is furnished to subsidiary companies.

(c) The maintenance department overhead rate is applied on maintenance hours. No extra overhead is anticipated as a result of constructing the machine.

(d) The maintenance department personnel are not qualified to test the machine on the production line. This will be done by production employees.

(e) Although the machine will take about one year to build, no extra borrowing of funds will be necessary to finance its construction. The company does, however, have outstanding bonds from earlier financing.

(f) It is expected that the self-construction of the machinery will save the company at least $20,000.

What advice can you give the cost accountant to help in the determination of a proper cost for the machine?

Case 11-3   (But computer software is my inventory)

Strategy, Inc. was organized by Elizabeth Durrant and Ramona Morales, two students working their way through college. Both Elizabeth and Ramona had played with computers while in high school and had become very proficient users. Elizabeth had a special ability for designing computer software games that challenged the reasoning power of players. Ramona could see great potential in marketing Elizabeth's product to other computer buffs, and so the two began Strategy. Sales have exceeded expectations, and they have added ten employees to their company to design additional products, debug new programs, and produce and distribute the final software product.

Because of its growing size, increased capital is needed for the company. The partners decide to apply for a $100,000 loan to support the growing cost of research. As part of the documentation to obtain the loan, the bank asks for audited financial statements for the past year. After some negotiation, Mark Dawson, CPA, is hired. Strategy had produced a preliminary income statement that reported net income of $35,000. After reviewing the statements, Dawson indicates that the company actually had a $10,000 loss for the year. The major difference relates to $45,000 of wage and material costs that Strategy had capitalized as an intangible asset but that Dawson determined should be expensed.

"It's all research and development," Dawson insisted.

"But we'll easily recoup it in sales next year," countered Ramona. "I thought you accountants believed in the matching principle. Why do you permit us to capitalize the equipment we're using, but not our software development costs? We'll never look profitable under your requirements."

What major issues are involved in this case? Which position best reflects the FASB Statement relating to software development costs?

Case 11-4   (Why can't I include the value of that gold on my balance sheet?)

The Ling Company owns several mining claims in Nevada and California. The claims are carried on the books at the cost paid to acquire them ten years ago. At that time, it was estimated that the claims represented ore reserves valued at $250,000, and the price paid for the properties reflected this value. Subsequent mining and exploration activities have indicated values up to four times the original estimate. Additional capital is needed to pursue the claims, and Ling has decided to issue new shares of common stock. The company wants to report the true value of the claims in the financial statements in order to make the stock more attractive to potential investors. The accountant, Jennifer Harrison, realizes that the cost basis of accounting does not permit the recording of discovery values. On the other hand, she believes that to ignore the greatly increased value of the claims would be misleading to users. Isn't there some way the asset values can be increased to better reflect future cash flows arising from the claims?

You are hired as an accounting consultant to assist Ling in its fund raising. What recommendations can you make to them?

Case 11-5   (Is it an asset or not?)

The Hunter Company has developed a computerized machine to assist in the production of appliances. It is anticipated that the machine will do well in the marketplace; however, the company lacks the necessary capital to produce the machine. Rosalyn Finch, the Secretary-Treasurer of the Hunter Company, has offered to transfer land to the company to be used as collateral for a bank loan. Consideration for the transfer is an employment contract for five years and a percentage of any profits earned from sales of the new machine. The title to the land is to be transferred unconditionally. In the event Hunter defaults on the employment contract, a lump-sum cash settlement for lost wages will be paid to Finch.

What are the arguments for and against recording the land as an asset on Hunter's books? Is it a contingent asset? What effect does the provision for a cash settlement in the event of default have on your decision?

Exercises   **‖ Exercise 11-1   (Cost of specific plant items)**

The following expenditures were incurred by the Eagle Food Co. in 1991: purchase of land, $300,000; land survey, $1,500; fees for search of title for land, $350; building permit, $500; temporary quarters for construction crews, $10,750; payment to tenants of old building for vacating premises, $2,000; razing of old building, $20,000; excavation of basement, $10,000; special assessment tax for street project, $2,000; dividends, $5,000; damages awarded for injuries sustained in construction, $8,400 (no insurance was carried; the cost of insurance would have been $500); costs of construction, $750,000; cost of paving parking lot adjoining building, $40,000; cost of shrubs, trees, and other landscaping, $18,000. What is the cost of the land, land improvements, and building?

Exercise 11-2   (Determining cost of patent)

Chen King Enterprises Inc. developed a new machine that reduces the time required to insert the fortunes into their fortune cookies. Because the process is considered very valuable to the fortune cookie industry, Chen King had the machine patented. The following expenses were incurred in developing and patenting the machine:

Research and development laboratory expenses	$15,000
Metal used in the construction of machine	5,000
Blueprints used to design the machine	1,500
Legal expenses to obtain patent	10,000
Wages paid for employees' work on the research, development, and building of the machine (60% of the time was spent in actually building the machine)	30,000
Expense of drawings required by the patent office to be submitted with the patent application	150
Fees paid to government patent office to process application	500

One year later, Chen King Enterprises Inc. paid $12,000 in legal fees to successfully defend the patent against an infringement suit by Dragon Cookie Co.

Give the entries on Chen King's book indicated by the above events. Ignore any amortization of the patent or depreciation of the machine.

Exercise 11-3   (Correcting organization costs account)

The Salt Air Manufacturing Co. was incorporated on January 1, 1991. In reviewing the accounts in 1992, you find the organization costs account appears as follows:

ACCOUNT   Organization Costs

Item	Debit	Credit	Balance	
			Debit	Credit
Incorporation fees..........................	7,500		7,500	
Legal fees relative to organization	21,150		24,900	
Stock certificate cost	6,000		30,900	
Cost of rehabilitating building acquired at end of 1991................................	165,600		196,500	
Advertising expenditures to promote company products in 1991........................	18,000		214,500	
Net loss for 1991	25,000		239,500	

Give the entry or entries required to correct the account.

Exercise 11-4   (Lump-sum acquisition)

The Cowan Shipping Co. acquired land, buildings, and equipment at a lump-sum price of $430,000. An appraisal of the assets at the time of acquisition disclosed the following values:

Land	100,000
Buildings	150,000
Equipment	250,000

What cost should be assigned to each asset?

Exercise 11-5   (Lump-sum acquisition)

The Boswell Corporation purchased land, a building, a patent, and a franchise for the lump sum of $975,000. A real estate appraiser estimated the building to have a resale value of $400,000 (⅔ of the total worth of land and building). The franchise had no established resale value. The patent was valued by management at $250,000. Give the journal entry to record the acquisition of the assets.

Exercise 11-6   (Equipment purchase on deferred payment contract)

Andrews Co. purchases equipment costing $110,000 with a down payment of $20,000 and sufficient semiannual installments of $7,000 (including interest on the unpaid principal at 10% per year) to pay the balance.

(1) Give the entries to record the purchase and the first two semiannual payments.

(2) Assume that there was no known cash price and twenty semiannual installments were to be made in addition to the $20,000 down payment. Give the entries to record the purchase and the first two semiannual payments.

Exercise 11-7   (Exchange of nonmonetary assets)

Baldwin Analysis Inc. purchased a new computer from a dealer. The following data relate to the purchase:

(a) List price of new computer with trade-in—$45,000
(b) Cash price of new computer with no trade-in—$41,000
(c) Baldwin Analysis Inc. received a trade-in allowance (based on list price) of $10,000 on a machine costing $25,000 new and having a present book value of $8,000. The balance of $35,000 was paid in cash.
(d) The Express Delivery Service charged Baldwin $1,200 to deliver the computer.

Determine the cost to be recorded for the new computer.

Exercise 11-8   (Lump-sum acquisition with stock)

On January 31, 1991 Cesarino Corp. exchanged 10,000 shares of its $25 par common stock for the following assets:

(a) A trademark valued at $120,000.
(b) A building, including land, valued at $650,000 (20% of the value is for the land).
(c) A franchise right. No estimate of value at time of exchange.

Cesarino Corp. stock is selling at $91 per share on the date of the exchange. Give the entries to record the exchange on Cesarino's books.

Exercise 11-9   (Purchase of building with bonds and stock)

The Fellingnam Co. enters into a contract with the Dice Construction Co. for construction of an office building at a cost of $710,000. Upon completion of construction, the Dice Construction Co. agrees to accept in full payment of the contract price Fellingham Co. 10% bonds with a face value of $300,000 and common stock with a par value of $300,000 and no established fair market value. Fellingham Co. bonds are selling on the market at this time at 104. How would you recommend the building acquisition be recorded?

Exercise 11-10   (Acquisition of land and building for stock and cash)

Valdilla's Music Store acquired land and an old building in exchange for 50,000 shares of its common stock, par $10, and cash of $80,000. The auditor ascertains that the company's stock was selling on the market at $15 when the purchase was made. The following additional costs were incurred to complete the transaction.

Legal cost to complete transaction	$10,000
Property tax for previous year	30,000
Cost of building demolition	13,000
Salvage value of demolished building	(6,000)

What entry should be made to record the acquisition of the property?

Exercise 11-11 (Cost of self-constructed asset including interest capitalization)

The Brodhead Manufacturing Company has constructed its own special equipment to produce a newly developed product. A bid to construct the equipment by an outside company was received for $620,000. The actual costs incurred by Brodhead to construct the equipment were as follows:

Direct material	$220,000
Direct labor	150,000

It is estimated that incremental overhead costs for construction amount to 125% of direct labor costs. In addition, fixed costs (exclusive of interest) of $700,000 were incurred during the construction period and allocated to production on the basis of total prime costs (direct labor plus direct material). The prime costs incurred to build the new equipment amounted to 20% of the total prime costs incurred for the period. The company follows the policy of captitalizing all possible costs on self-construction projects.

In order to assist in financing the construction of the equipment, a $300,000, 10% loan was acquired at the beginning of the six-month construction period. The company carries no other debt except for trade accounts payable. Assume expenditures were incurred evenly over the six-month period, and interest charges were to be capitalized in accordance with FASB Statement No. 34. Compute the cost to be assigned to the new equipment.

Exercise 11-12 (Capitalization of interest)

Lodi Department Stores, Inc. constructs its own stores. In the past, no cost has been added to the asset value for interest on funds borrowed for construction. Management has decided to change its policy and desires to include interest as part of the cost of a new store just being completed. (a) Based on the following information, how much interest would be added to the cost of the store in 1991? (b) In 1992?

Total construction expenditures:		
January 2, 1991	$200,000	
May 1, 1991	600,000	
November 1, 1991	500,000	
March 1, 1992	700,000	
September 15, 1992	400,000	
December 31, 1992	500,000	
		$2,900,000

Outstanding company debt:		
Mortgage related directly to new store:		
interest rate 12%; term, five years from beginning of construction	$1,000,000	
General bond liability:		
Bonds issued just prior to construction of store;		
interest rate 10% for ten years	$ 500,000	
Bonds issued previously-8%, mature in five years	$1,000,000	
Estimate cost of equity capital	14%	

Exercise 11-13   (Research and development costs)

In 1991 the Jericho Corporation incurred research and development costs as follows:

Materials and equipment	$130,000
Personnel	100,000
Indirect costs	50,000
	$280,000

These cost relate to a product that will be marketed in 1992. It is estimated that these costs will be recouped by December 31, 1995.

(1) What is the amount of research and development costs which should be charged to income in 1991?

(2) Assume that of the above costs, equipment of $90,000 can be used on other research projects. Estimated useful life of the equipment is five years, and it was acquired at the beginning of 1991. What is the amount of research and development costs that should be charged to income in 1991 under these conditions? Assume depreciation on all equipment is computed on a straight-line basis.   (AICPA adapted)

Exercise 11-14   (Classifying expenditures as assets or expenses)

One of the most difficult problems facing an accountant is the determination of which expenditures should be deferred as assets and which should be immediately charged off as expenses. What position would you take in each of the following instances?

(a) Painting of partitions in a large room recently divided into four sections.
(b) Labor cost of tearing down a wall to permit extension of assembly line.
(c) Replacement of motor on a machine. Life used to depreciate the machine is 8 years. The machine is 4 years old. Replacement of the motor was anticipated when the machine was purchased.
(d) Cost of grading land prior to construction.
(e) Assessment for street paving.
(f) Cost of tearing down a previously occupied old building in preparation for new construction; old building is fully depreciated.

*Exercise 11-15   (Calculation of normal pretax income)

In analyzing the accounts of Cabrera in an attempt to measure goodwill, you find pretax income of $550,000 for 1991 after debits and credits for the items listed below. Land, buildings, and equipment are appraised at 40% above cost for purposes of the sale. What is the normal pretax income for purposes of your calculations?

Depreciation of land, buildings, and equipment (at cost)	$75,000
Special year-end bonus to president of company	40,000
Gain on sale of securities	45,000
Gain on revaluation of securities	25,000
Write-off of goodwill	130,000
Amortization of patents and leaseholds	62,500
Income tax refund for 1990	20,000

*Relates to Appendix.

*Exercise 11-16   (Calculation of goodwill—various methods)

The appraised value of net assets of the Hillery Co. on December 31, 1991, was $800,000. Average income for the past 5 years after elimination of unusual or extraordinary gains and losses was $135,000. Calculate the amount to be paid for goodwill under each of the following assumptions.

(a) Income is captialized at 15% in arriving at the business's worth.
(b) A return of 9% is considered normal on net assets at their appraised value; excess income to be capitalized at 15% in arriving at the value of goodwill.
(c) A return of 10% is considered normal on net assets at their appraised value; goodwill is to be valued at 5 years' excess income.
(d) A return of 10% is considered normal on net identifiable assets at their appraised value. Excess income is expected to continue for six years. Goodwill is to be valued by the present value method using a rate of 12%. (Use present value table in Chapter 6.)

*Relates to Appendix.

*Exercise 11-17   (Computation of goodwill—decision)

Because of superior earning power, Caruthers Inc. is considering paying $609,416 for K & M Properties with the following assets and liabilities:

	Cost	Fair Market Value
Accounts receivable	$240,000	$220,000
Inventory	140,000	150,000
Prepaid insurance	10,000	10,000
Buildings and equipment (net)	170,000	300,000
Accounts payable	(160,000)	(160,000)
Net assets	$400,000	$520,000

Estimated future income is expected to exceed normal income by $27,600 for four years. Caruthers Inc. uses, the present value method of valuing goodwill. Caruthers is willing to purchase K & M if the normal rate of return for K & M exceeds 10%. Should Caruthers purchase K & M Properties? (Use present value table in Chapter 6.)

*Relates to Appendix.

*Exercise 11-18   (Computation of goodwill)

The owners of the Summers Clothing Store are contemplating selling the business to new interests. The cumulative income for the past 5 years amounted to $600,000 including extraordinary gains of $40,000. The annual income based on an average rate of return on investment for this industry would have been $76,000. Excess income is to be capitalized at 25%. What is the amount of implied goodwill?   (AICPA adapted)

*Relates to Appendix.

Problems   **Problem 11-1   (Correcting noncurrent operating asset valuation)**

On December 31, 1991, the Fridley Co. shows the following account for machinery it had assembled for its own use during 1991:

ACCOUNT   Machinery (Job Order #962)

Item	Debit	Credit	Balance Debit	Balance Credit
Cost of dismantling old machine	12,480		12,480	
Cash proceeds from sale of old machine		10,000	2,480	
Raw materials used in construction of new machine	63,000		65,480	
Labor in construction of new machine	49,000		114,480	
Cost of installation	11,200		125,680	
Materials spoiled in machine trial runs	2,400		128,080	
Profit on construction	24,000		152,080	
Purchase of machine tools	16,000		168,080	

An analysis of the detail in the account disclosed the following:

(a) The old machine, which was removed in the installation of the new one, had been fully depreciated.
(b) Cash discounts received on the payments for materials used in construction totaled $3,000 and these were reported in the purchase discounts account.
(c) The factory overhead account shows a balance of $292,000 for the year ended December 31,1991; this balance exceeds normal overhead on regular plan activities by approximately $21,200 and is attributable to machine construction.
(d) A profit was recognized on construction for the difference between costs incurred and the price at which the machine could have been purchased.

Instructions:

(1) Determine the machinery and machine tools balances as of December 31, 1991.
(2) Give individuals journal entries necessary to correct the accounts as of December 31, 1991, assuming that the nominal accounts are still open.

Problem 11-2   (Acquisition of land and buildings)

The Excelsior Co. planned to open a new store. The company narrowed the possible sites to two lots and decided to take purchase options on both lots while they studied traffic densities in both areas. They paid $6,000 for the option on Lot A and $14,000 for the option on Lot B. After studying traffic densities, they decided to purchase Lot B. The company opened a single real estate account that shows the following:

Debits:	Option on Lot A	$ 6,000
	Option on Lot B	14,400
	Payment of balance on Lot B	155,000
	Title insurance	2,700
	Assessment for street improvements	5,100
	Recording fee for deed	600
	Cost of razing old building on Lot B	9,000
	Payment for construction of new building	350,000
Credit:	Sale of salvaged materials from old building	5,000

The salvage value of material obtained from the old building and used in constructing the new building was $10,000. The depreciated value of the old building, as shown by the books of the company from which the purchase was made, was $54,000. The old building was razed immediately after the purchase.

Instructions:

(1) Determine the cost of the land, listing the items included in the total.
(2) Determine the cost of the new building, listing the items included in the total.

Problem 11-3 **(Transactions involving property)**

The following transactions were completed by the Space Age Toy Co. during 1991:

Mar. 1   Purchased real property for $628,250 which included a charge of $18,250 representing property tax for March 1-June 30 that had been prepaid by the vendor; 20% of the purchase price is deemed applicable to land and the balance to buildings. A mortgage of $375,000 was assumed by the Space Age Toy Co. on the purchase. Cash was paid for the balance.

Mar. 2-30   Previous owners had failed to take care of normal maintenance and repair requirements on the building, necessitating current reconditioning at a cost of $29,600.

May 15   Garages in the rear of the building were demolished, $4,500 being recovered on the lumber salvage. The company proceeded to construct a warehouse. The cost of such construction was $67,600 which was almost exactly the same as bids made on the construction by independent contractors. Upon completion of construction, city inspectors ordered extensive modifications in the buildings as a result of failure on the part of the company to comply with the Building Safety Code. Such modifications, which could have been avoided, cost $9,600.

June 1   The company exchanged its own stock with a fair market value of $40,000 (par $30,000) for a patent and a new toy making machine. The machine has a market value of $25,000.

July 1   The new machinery for the new building arrived. In addition to the machinery a new franchise was acquired from the manufacturer of the machinery to produce toy robots. Payment was made by issuing bonds with a face value of $50,000 and by paying cash of $18,000. The value of the franchise is set at $20,000 while the fair market value of the machine is $45,000.

Nov. 20   The company contracted for parking lots and landscaping at a cost of $45,000 and $9,600 respectively. The work was completed and billed on November 20.

Dec. 31   The business was closed to permit taking the year-end inventory. During the taking of the inventory, required redecorating and repairs were completed at a cost of $7,500.

Instructions: Give the journal entries to record each of the preceding transactions. (Disregard depreciation.)

Problem 11-4   (Acquisition of land and construction of plant)

The Senger Corporation was organized in June, 1991. In auditing the books of the company, you find a land, buildings, and equipment account with the following details:

ACCOUNT   Land, Buildings, and Equipment

Date		Item	Debit	Credit	Balance Debit	Balance Credit
1991						
June	8	Organization fees paid to the state	20,000		20,000	
	16	Land site and old building . .	315,000		335,000	
	30	Corporate organization costs	30,000		365,000	
July	2	Title clearance fees	18,400		383,400	
Aug	28	Cost of razing old building . .	20,000		403,400	
Sept.	1	Salaries of Senger Corporation executives	36,000		439,400	
	1	Cost to acquire patent for special equipment	60,000		499,400	
Dec.	12	Stock bonus to corporate promoters, 2,000 shares of common stock, $40 par . . .	80,000		579,400	
	15	County real estate tax	14,400		593,800	
	15	Cost of new building completed and occupied on this date	1,500,000		2,093,800	

An analysis of the foregoing account and of other accounts disclosed the following additional information:

(a) The building acquired on June 16, 1991, was valued at $35,000.
(b) The company paid $20,000 for the demolition of the old building, then sold the scrap for $5,000 and credited the proceeds to Miscellaneous Revenue.
(c) The company executives did not paticipate in the construction of the new building.
(d) The county real estate tax was for the six-month period ended December 31, 1991 and was assessed by the county on the land.

Instructions: Prepare journal entries to correct the books of the Senger Corporation. Each entry should include an explanation.

Problem 11-5   (Acquisition of intangible assets)

In your audit of the books of Dyer Corporation for the year ending September 30, 1991 you found the following items in connection with the company's patents account:

(a) The company had spent $120,000 during its fiscal year ended September 30, 1990, for research and development costs and debited this amount to its patent account. Your review of the company's cost records indicated the company had spent a total of $141,500 for the research and development of its patents, of which only $21,500 spent in its fiscal year ended September 30, 1989 had been debited to Research and Development Expense.
(b) The patents were issued on April 1, 1990. Legal expenses in connection

with the issuance of the patents of $14,280 were debited to Legal and Professional Fees.

(c) The company paid a retainer of $15,000 on October 5, 1990, for legal services in connection with an infringement suit brought against it. This amount was debited to Deferred Costs.

(d) A letter dated October 15, 1991 from the company's attorneys in reply to your inquiry as to liabilities of the company existing at September 30, 1991, indicated that a settlement of the infringement suit had been arranged. The other party had agreed to drop the suit and to release the company from all future liabilities for $20,000. Additional fees due to the attorneys amounted to $1,260.

Instructions: From the information given, prepare correcting journal entries as of September 30, 1991.

Problem 11-6 (Acquisition of intangible assets)

Transactions during 1991 of the newly organized Stokes Corporation included the following:

Jan. 2 Paid legal fees of $15,000 and stock certificate costs of $5,100 to complete organization of the corporation.

     15 Hired a clown to stand in front of the corporate office for two weeks and hand out pamphlets and candy to create goodwill for the new enterprise. Clown cost $1,000, candy and pamphlets, $500.

Apr. 1 Patented a newly developed process with the following costs:

Legal fees to obtain patent	$28,600
Patent application and licensing fees	6,350
Total	$34,950

It is estimated that in six years other companies will have developed improved processes making the Stokes Corporation process obsolete.

May 1 Acquired both a license to use a special type of container and a distinctive trademark to be printed on the container in exchange for 600 shares of Stokes Corporation no par common stock selling for $80 per share. The license is worth twice as much as the trademark, both of which may be used for 6 years.

July 1 Constructed a shed for $93,000 to house prototypes of experimental models to be developed in future research projects.

Dec. 31 Salaries for an engineer and a chemist involved in product development totaled $100,000 in 1991.

Instructions:

(1) Give journal entries to record the foregoing transactions. (Give explanations in support of your entries.)

(2) Present in good form the "Intangible assets" section of the Stokes Corporation balance sheet at December 31, 1991.

Problem 11-7 (Lump-sum acquisition of noncurrent operating assets)

The Wenatcher Wholesale Company incurred the following expenses in 1991 for a warehouse acquired on July 1, 1991, the beginning of its fiscal year:

Cost of land	$90,000
Cost of building	510,000
Remodeling and repairs prior to occupancy	67,500
Escrow fee	10,000
Landscaping	25,000
Property tax for period prior to acquisition	15,000
Real estate commission	30,000

The company signed a non-interest-bearing note for $500,000 on July 1, 1991. The implicit interest rate is 10%. Payments of $25,000 are to be made semiannually beginning December 31, 1991 for 10 years.

Instructions: Give the required journal entries to record (1) the acquisition of the land and building (assume that cash is paid to equalize the cost of the assets and the present value of the note), and (2) the first two semiannual payments, including amortization of note discount.

Problem 11-8 **(Income statement for computer software company)**

The Betterword Company is engaged in developing computer software for the small business and home computer market. Most of the computer programmers are involved in developmental work designed to produce software that will perform fairly specific tasks in a user-friendly manner. Extensive testing of the working model is performed before it is released to production for preparation of masters and further testing. As a result of careful preparation, Betterword has produced several products that have been very successful in the marketplace. The following costs were incurred during 1991.

Salaries and wages of programmers doing research	$235,000
Expenses related to projects prior to establishment of technological feasibility	$78,400
Expenses related to projects after technological feasibility has been established but before software is available for production	$49,500
Amortization of captialized software development costs from current and prior years	$26,750
Costs to produce and prepare software for sale	$56,300

Additional data for 1991 include:

Sales of products for the year	$515,000
Beginning inventory	$142,000
Portion of goods available for sale sold during year	60%

Instructions: Prepare an income statement for Betterword for the year 1991. Income tax rate is 30%. (Ignore earnings per share computations.)

Problem 11-9 (Valuation of property)

At December 31, 1990, certain accounts included in the noncurrent operating assets section of the Rodrigo Company's balance sheet had the following balances:

Land	$150,000
Buildings	805,000
Leasehold Improvements	500,000
Machinery and Equipment	600,000

During 1991 the following transactions occurred:

(a) Land site number 653 was acquired for $1,350,000. Additionally, to acquire the land Rodrigo paid a $90,000 commission to a real estate agent. Costs of $25,000 were incurred to clear the land. During the course of clearing the land, timber and gravel were recovered and sold for $10,000.

(b) A second tract of land (site number 654) with a building was acquired for $700,000. The closing statement indicated that the land value was $510,000 and the building value was $190,000. Shortly after acquisition, the building was demolished at a cost of $30,000. A new building was constructed for $600,000 plus the following costs.

Excavation fees	35,000
Architectural design fees	19,000
Building permit fee	15,000
Imputed interest on funds used during construction	42,000

The building was completed and occupied on September 30, 1991.

(c) A third tract of land (site number 655) was acquired for $600,000 and was put on the market for resale.

(d) Extensive work was done to a building occupied by Rodrigo under a lease agreement that expires on December 31, 2000. The total cost of work was $125,000, which consisted of the following:

Painting of ceilings	$10,000 (estimated useful life is one year)
Electrical work	35,000 (estimated useful life is ten years)
Construction of extension to	
current working area	80,000 (estimated useful life is thirty years)
	$125,000

The lessor paid ½ of the costs incurred in connection with the extension to the current working area.

(e) During December 1991 costs of $65,000 were incurred to improve leased office space. The related lease will terminate on December 31, 1993 and is not expected to be renewed.

(f) A group of new machines was purchased under a royalty agreement which provides for payment of royalties based on units of production for the machines. The invoice price of the machines was $90,000, freight costs were $2,000, unloading charges were $2,500, and royalty payments for 1991 were $13,000.

Instructions:

(1) Prepare a detailed analysis of the changes in each of the following balance sheet accounts for 1991. Land, Buildings, Leasehold Improvements, and Machinery and Equipment. (Disregard the related accumulated depreciation accounts.)

(2) List the items in the foregoing information which were not used to determine the answer to (1), and indicate where, or if, these items should be included in Rodrigo's financial statements.   (AICPA adapted)

Problem 11-10   (Aquisition of noncurrent operating assets)

At December 31, 1991, Arnold Company's noncurrent operating asset accounts had the following balances:

Category	Cost
Land	$ 175,000
Buildings	1,500,000
Machinery and Equipment	1,125,000
Automobiles and trucks	172,000
Leasehold improvements	216,000
Land improvements	—

Transactions for 1992 included the following:

Jan.   6 A plant facility consisting of land and a building was acquired from Jesco Corp. in exchange for 25,000 shares of Arnold's common stock. On this date, Arnold's stock had a market price of $50 a share. Current assessed values of land and building for property tax purposes are $187,500 and $562,500, respectively.

Mar. 25 New parking lots, streets, and sidewalks at the acquired plant facility were completed at a total of $192,000.

Jul.   1 Machinery and equipment were purchased at a total invoice cost of $325,000, which included $10,000 of sales tax. Additional costs of $10,000 for delivery and $50,000 for installation were incurred.

Aug. 30 Arnold purchased a new automobile for $12,500.

Nov.   4 Arnold purchased for $350,000 a tract of land as a potential future building site.

Dec. 20 A machine with a cost of $17,000 and a remaining book value of $2,975 at date of disposition was scrapped without cash recovery.

Instructions: Prepare a schedule analyzing the changes in each of the noncurrent operating asset accounts during 1992. This schedule should include columns for beginning balance, increase, decrease, and ending balance for each of the noncurrent operating asset accounts.   (AICPA adapted)

III. Problem 11-11   (Capitalization of interest)

Ocean-Wide Enterprises, Inc. is involved in building and operating cruise ships. Each ship is identified as a separate discrete job in the accounting records, and costs are incurred evenly during the construction period. At the end of 1991, Ocean-Wide correctly reported $5,400,000 as Construction in Progress on the following jobs:

Ship #	Completion date (End of month)	Accumulated costs December 31, 1991
340	October 31, 1991*	$2,300,000
341	June 30, 1992	1,150,000
342	September 30, 1992	1,200,000
343	January 31, 1992	750,000

*Ship #340 was completed and ready for use in October 1991 and will be placed in service May 1, 1992.

Labor, material and overhead costs for 1992 were as follows:

Ship #	Costs	
341	$1,200,000	
342	1,600,000	
343	2,200,000	
344	810,000	(Construction began May 1)
345	360,000	(Construction began Nov. 1)

Ocean-Wide had the following general liabilities at December 31, 1992:

12% 5 year note (Maturity date—1994)	$1,000,000
10% 10 year bonds (Maturity date—1996)	4,000,000

On January 1, 1992, Ocean-Wide borrowed $1,000,000 specifically for the construction projects. The loan was for 3 years with interest at 13%.

Instructions:

(1) Compute the maximum interest that can be capitalized in 1992.
(2) Compute the weighted-average interest rate for the general liabilities for 1992.
(3) Compute the weighted-average accumulated expenditures for 1992.
(4) Compute the interest that Ocean-Wide should capitalize during 1992.

Problem 11-12 (Self-construction of equipment)

American Corporation received a $400,000 low bid from a reputable manufacturer for the construction of special production equipment needed by American in an expansion program. Because the company's own plant was not operating at capacity, American decided to construct the equipment itself and recorded the following production costs related to the construction:

Services of consulting engineer	$10,000
Work subcontracted	20,000
Materials	200,000
Plant labor normally assigned to production	65,000
Plant labor normally assigned to maintenance	100,000
Total	$395,000

Management prefers to record the cost of the equipment under the incremental cost method. Approximately 40% of the corporation's production is devoted to government supply contracts which are all based in some way on cost. The contracts require that any self-constructed equipment be allocated its full share of all costs related to the construction.

The following information is also available:

(a) The above production labor was for partial fabrication of the equipment in the plant. Skilled personnel were required and were assigned from other projects. The maintenance labor amount ($100,000) represents the cost of nonproduction plant employees assigned to the construction project. Had these workers not been assigned to construction, the $100,000 cost would still have been incurred for their idle time.

(b) Payroll taxes and employee fringe benefits are approximately 30% of labor cost and are included in manufacturing overhead cost. Total manufacturing overhead for the year was $5,630,000 including the $100,000 maintenance labor used to construct the equipment.

(c) Manufacturing overhead is approximately 50% variable and is applied on the basis of production labor cost. Production labor cost for the year for the corporation's normal products totaled $6,810,000.

(d) General and administrative expenses include $22,500 of executive salary cost and $10,500 of postage, telephone, supplies, and miscellaneous expenses identifiable with this equipment construction.

Instructions:

(1) Prepare a schedule computing the amount that should be reported as the full cost of the constructed equipment to meet the requirements of the government contracts. Any supporting computations should be in good form.

(2) Prepare a schedule computing the incremental cost of the constructed equipment.

(3) What is the greatest amount that should be capitalized as the cost of the equipment? Why?   (AICPA adapted)

Problem 11-13   (Classifying expenditures as assets or expenses)

The Topp Company completed a program of expansion and improvement of its plant during 1991. You are provided with the following information concerning its buildings account:

(a) On October 31, 1991, a 30-foot extension to the present factory building was completed at a contract cost of $108,000.

(b) During the course of construction, the following costs were incurred for the removal of the end wall of the building where the extension was to be constructed:

(1) Payroll costs during the month of April arising from employees' time spent in removing the wall, $6,940.

(2) Payments to a salvage company for removing unusual debris, $780.

(c) The cost of the original structure allocable to the end wall was estimated to be $26,400 with accumulated depreciation thereon of $11,100. $7,080 was received by Topp Company from the construction company for windows and other assorted materials salvaged from the old wall.

(d) The old flooring was covered with a new type long-lasting floor covering at a cost of $5,290. Cost of old flooring was not available.

(e) The interior of the plant was repainted in new, bright colors for a contract price of $5,375.

(f) New and improved shelving was installed at a cost of $1,212. Cost of old shelving was not determinable.

(g) Old electrical wiring was replaced at a cost of $10,218. Cost of the old wiring was determined to be $4,650 with accumulated depreciation to date of $2,055.

(h) New electrical fixtures using fluorescent bulbs were installed. The new fixtures were purchased on the installment plan; the schedule of monthly payments showed total payments of $9,300, which included interest and carrying charges of $720. The old fixtures were carried at a cost of $2,790 with accumulated depreciation to date of $1,200. The old fixtures has no scrap value.

Instructions: Prepare journal entries including explanations for the above information. Briefly justify the asset vs. expense decision for each item.

*Problem 11-14   (Computation of goodwill)

The Aurora Corp. in considering acquisition of the Payette Company assembles the following information relative to the company.

Payette Company
Balance Sheet
December 31, 1992

Assets	Per Company's Books	As Adjusted by Appraisal and Audit
Current assets	$ 96,000	$ 87,000
Investments......................................	32,000	28,000
Land, buildings, and equipment (net)	279,200	260,000
Goodwill..	79,000	79,000
	$486,200	$454,000

Liabilities and Stockholders' Equity	Per Company's Books	As Adjusted by Appraisal and Audit
Current liabilities..................................	$ 15,000	$ 25,000
Long-term liabilities	160,000	160,000
Capital stock....................................	160,000	160,000
Retained earnings	151,200	109,000
	$486,200	$454,000

An analysis of retained earnings discloses the following information:

	Per Company's Books	As Adjusted by Appraisal and Audit
Retained earnings, January 1, 1990	$115,560	$ 85,600
Add net income, 1990-1992	49,400	64,200
Deduct dividends 1990-1992	(28,800)	(28,800)
Retained earnings, December 31, 1992	$136,200	$121,000
*Loss on sale of plant assets in 1992, included in net income	$ 48,960	$ 52,800

Instructions:

(1) Calculate the amount to be paid for goodwill, assuming that income of the future is expected to be the same as averge normal income of the past three years, 10% is accepted as a reasonable return on net assets other than goodwill as of December 31, 1992, and average income in excess of 10% is capitalized at 16% in determining goodwill.

(2) Give the entry on the books of the Aurora Corp., assuming purchase of the assets of the Payette Company and assumption of its liabilities on the basis as indicated in (1). Cash is paid for net assets acquired.

*Relates to Appendix

*Problem 11-15   (Computation of goodwill)

Southern Industries Inc. assembles the following data relative to the Mendoza Corp. in determining the amount to be paid for the net assets and goodwill of the latter company:

Assets at appraised value (before goodwill)	$1,900,000
Liabilities	825,000
Stockholders' equity	$1,075,000

Income (after elimination of extraordinary items):

1988	$180,000
1989	149,000
1990	194,000
1991	155,000
1992	222,000

Instructions: Calculate the amount to be paid for goodwill under each of the following assumptions:

(1) Average income is capitalized at 16% in arriving at the business' worth.
(2) A return of 12% is considered normal on net assets at appraised values. Goodwill is valued at 5 years' excess income.
(3) A return of 14% is considered normal on net assets at appraised values; excess income is to be capitalized at 20%.
(4) Goodwill is valued at the sum of the income of the last 3 years in excess of a 10% annual yield on net assets at appraised values. (Assume that net assets are the same for the 3-year period.)
(5) A return of 10% is considered normal on net identifiable assets at their appraised values. Excess income is expected to continue for 10 years. Goodwill is to be valued by the present value method using a 20% rate. (Use Chapter 6 present value table.)

*Relates to Appendix

Chapter 12

Noncurrent Operating Assets— Utilization and Retirement

A fundamental characteristic of noncurrent operating assets is that they are used to produce revenues over more than one accounting period. Another characteristic common to these assets is that they have limited economic or useful lives. A notable exception to this generalization is land—even farm land can be kept productive indefinitely with proper fertilization and care. All other noncurrent operating assets, however, have limited lives. The economic benefits provided by intangible assets are, in some cases, limited to a period of time specifed by law or contract. Other intangible assets tend to decline in usefulness with the passage of time.

In order to match costs with related revenues, the cost of an operating asset (other than land) must be allocated in some manner over the estimated useful life of the asset. In practice, three different terms have evolved to describe this cost allocation process depending on the type of asset involved. The allocation of tangible property costs is referred to as depreciation. For mineral and other natural resources, the cost allocation process is appropriately called depletion. For intangible assets, such as patents, copyrights, and goodwill, the process is referred to as amortization. Sometimes the latter term is used generically to encompass all the other terms. Because the principles underlying each of these terms are similar, they are discussed together in this chapter.

Depreciation of Noncurrent Operating Assets

Depreciation is the systematic and rational allocation of tangible asset cost over the periods benefited by the use of the asset. There has been a tendency, however, on the part of many readers of financial statements to interpret depreciation accounting as somehow related to the accumulation of a fund for asset replacement. Terminology used in the past, such as "provision for depreciation" and "reserve for depreciation" has contributed toward this misinterpretation. These have been replaced by more descriptive terms , i.e., "depreciation expense" and "accumulated depreciation."

The charge for depreciation is the recognition of the declining service potential of an asset. The nature of this charge is no different from those made to recognize the expiration of insurance premiums or patent rights. It is true that revenues equal to or in excess of expenses for a period result in a recovery of these expenses; salary expense is thus recovered by revenues, as is insurance expense, patent amortization, and charges for depreciation. But this does not mean that cash equal to the recorded depreciation will be segregated for property replacement. Revenues may be applied to many uses: to the increase in receivables, inventories, or other working capital items; to the acquisition of new property or other noncurrent items; to the retirement of debt or the redemption of stock; or to the payment of dividends. If a special fund is to be established for the replacement of property, specific authorization by management would be required. Such a fund is seldom found, however, because fund earnings would usually be less than the return from alternative uses of the resources.

Factors Affecting the Periodic Depreciation Charge

Four factors must be recognized in determining the periodic charge for depreciation: (1) **asset cost**, (2) **residual or salvage value**, (3) **useful life**, and (4) **pattern of use**.

Asset Cost

The cost of an asset includes all the expenditures relating to its acquisition and preparation for use as described in Chapter 11. The cost of property less the expected residual value, if any, is the depreciable cost or depreciation base, i.e., the portion of asset cost to be charged against future revenues.

Residual or Salvage Value

The residual (salvage) value of property is an estimate of the amount that can be realized upon retirement of the asset. This depends on the retirement policy of the company as well as market conditions and other factors. If, for example, the company normally uses equipment until it is physically exhausted and no longer serviceable, the residual value, represented by the scrap or junk that can be salvaged, may be nominal. But if the company normally replaces its equipment after a relatively short period of use, the residual value, represented by the selling price or trade-in value, may be relatively high. From a theoretical point of view, any estimated residual value should be subtracted from cost in arriving at the portion of asset cost to be charged to depreciation.

In practice, however, residual values are frequently ignored in determining periodic depreciation charges. This practice is not objectionable when residual values are relatively small or not subject to reasonable estimation, and when it is doubtful whether more useful information will be provided through such refinement.

Useful Life

Noncurrent operating assets other than land have a limited useful life as a result of certain physical and functional factors. The **physical factors** that limit the service life of an asset are (1) wear and tear, (2) deterioration and decay, and (3) damage or destruction. Everyone is familiar with the processes of wear and tear that render an automobile, a typewriter, or furniture no longer usable. A tangible asset, whether used or not, is also subject to deterioration and decay through aging. Finally, fire, flood, earthquake, or accident may reduce or terminate the useful life of an asset.

The **functional factors** limiting the lives of these assets are (1) inadequacy and (2) obsolescence. An asset may lose its usefulness when, as a result of altered business requirements or technical progress, it no longer can produce sufficient revenue to justify its continued use. Although the asset is still usable, its inability to produce sufficient revenue has cut short its service life. An example of rapid obsolescence can be observed in the computer industry. The rapid technological changes in this field have rendered perfectly good electronic equipment obsolete for efficient continued use long before the physical asset itself wore out.

Both physical and functional factors must be considered in estimating the useful life of a depreciable asset. This recognition requires estimating what events will take place in the future and requires careful judgment on the part of the accountant.[1] Physical factors are more readily apparent than functional factors in predicting asset life. But when functional factors are expected to hasten the retirement of an asset, these must also be recognized.

In practice, many companies as a matter of policy dispose of certain classes of assets after a predetermined period, without regard to the serviceability of individual assets within a class. Company automobiles, for example, may be replaced routinely every two or three years.

The useful life of a depreciable plan asset may be expressed in terms of either an estimated time factor or an estimated use factor. The **time factor** may be a period of months or years; the **use factor** may be a number of hours of service or a number of units of output. The cost of the asset is allocated in accordance with the lapse of time or extent of use. The rate of cost allocation may be modified by other factors, but basically depreciation must be recognized on a time or use basis.

Pattern of Use

In order to match asset cost against revenues, periodic depreciation charges should reflect as closely as possible the pattern of use. If the asset produces a varying revenue pattern, then the depreciation charges should vary in a corresponding manner. When depreication is measured in terms of a time factor, the pattern of use must be estimated. Because of the difficulty in identifying a pattern of use, several somewhat arbitrary methods have come into common practice. Each method represents a different pattern and is designed to make the time basis approximate the use basis. The time factor is employed in two general classes of methods, **straight-line depreciation and decreasing-charge depreciation.** When depreciation is measured in

---

[1]Although the concept of useful life is generally recognized to be difficult to apply, there has been relatively little written on it in accounting literature. For a thorough discussion of the topic, see Charles Lamden, Dale L. Gerboth, and Thomas McRae, "Accounting for Depreciable Assets," *Accounting Research Monograph No. 1* (New York: American Institute of Certified Public Accountants, 1975), Ch. 5.

terms of a use factor, the units of use must be estimated. The depreciation charge varies periodically in accordance with the services provided by the asset. The use factor is employed in **service-hours depreciation** and in **productive-output depreciation**.

Recording Periodic Depreciation

The periodic allocation of property costs is made by debiting either a production overhead cost account or a selling or administrative expense account, and crediting an allowance or contra asset account. If the charge is made to a production overhead account, it becomes part of the cost of the finished and unfinished goods inventories and is deferred to the extent inventory has not been sold or completed. If the charge is made to selling or administrative expenses, it is considered to be a period cost and is written off against revenue as an operating expense of the current period.

The valuation or allowance account that is credited in recording periodic depreciation is commonly titled Accumulated Depreciation. The accumulation of expired cost in a separate account rather than crediting the asset account directly permits identification of the original cost of the asset and the accumulated depreciation. The FASB requires disclosure of both cost and accumulated depreciation for property on the balance sheet or notes to the financial statements. This enables the user to estimate the relative age of all assets and provides some basis for predicting future cash outflows for the replacement of assets.

Methods of Depreciation

There are a number of different methods for allocating the costs of depreciable assets. The depreciation method used in any specific instance is a matter of judgment and should be selected to most closely approximate the actual pattern of use expected from the asset. The following methods are described in this chapter:

Time-Factor Methods
1. Straight-line depreciation
2. Decreasing-charge (accelerated) methods
   (a) Sum-of-the-years-digits depreciation
   (b) Declining-balance depreciation
3. Accelerated cost recovery system (ACRS)

Use-Factor Methods
1. Service-hours depreciation
2. Productive-output depreciation

Group-Rate and Composite-Rate Methods
1. Group depreciation
2. Composite depreciation

The examples that follow assume the acquisition of a polyurethane plastic molding machine at the beginning of 1991 by Schuss Boom Ski Manufacturing, Inc., at a cost of $100,000 with an estimated residual value of $5,000. The following symbols are used in the formulas for the development of depreciation rates and charges:

C = Asset cost
R = Estimated residual value
n = Estimated life in years, hours of service, or units of output
r = Depreciation rate per period, per hour of service, or per unit of output
D = Periodic depreciation charge

Time-Factor Methods

The most common methods of cost allocation are related to the passage of time. In general, a productive asset is used up over time. Possible obsolescence due to technological changes is also a funtion of time. Of the time-factor depreciation methods, straight-line depreciation has been by far the most popular. Accounting Trends and Techniques reported that 559 of the 600 survey companies used the straight-line method in their 1987 financial statements.[2]

The use of decreasing-charge depreciation methods, sometimes referred to as "accelerated depreciation" methods is based largely on the assumption that there will be rapid reductions in asset efficiency, output, or other benefits in the early years of an asset's life. Such reductions may be accompanied by increased charges for maintenance and repairs. Charges for depreciation decline, then, as the economic advantages afforded through ownership of the asset decline. The most commonly used decreasing-charge methods are sum-of-the-years-digits and some variation of a declining-balance method.

Straight-Line Depreciation

Straight-line depreciation relates cost allocation to the passage of time and recognizes equal periodic charges over the life of the asset. The allocation assumes equal usefulness per time period, and in applying this assumption, the charge is not affected by asset productivity or efficency variations. In developing the periodic charge, an estimate is made of the useful life of the asset in terms of months or years. The difference between the asset cost and residual value is divided by the useful life of the asset in arriving at the cost assigned to each time unit.

Using data for the machine acquired by Schuss Boom Ski Manufacturing (see page 488) and assuming a 5-year life, annual depreciation is determined as follows:

$$D = \frac{C - R}{n}, \text{ or } \frac{\$100,000 - \$5,000}{5} = \$19,000$$

Annual depreciation can also be computed by applying a percentage, or **depreciation rate**, to depreciable cost. The rate is the reciprocal value of the useful life expressed in periods, or r (per period) = 1 ÷ n. In the

[2]*Accounting Trends and Techniques* (New York: American Institute of Certified Public Accountants, 1988), p. 261.

example, the depreciation rate would be 1 ÷ 5 = 20%, and annual depreciation can be computed as follows:

$$\$95,000 \times 20\% = \$19,000$$

A table summarizing the cost allocation process for the asset in the example, using the straight-line method, follows:

Asset Cost Allocation—Straight-Line Method

End of Year	Depreciation Computation		Amount	Accumulated Depreciation	Asset Book Value
					$100,000
1991	$95,000 ÷ 5	=	$19,000	$19,000	81,000
1992	95,000 ÷ 5	=	19,000	38,000	62,000
1993	95,000 ÷ 5	=	19,000	57,000	43,000
1994	95,000 ÷ 5	=	19,000	76,000	24,000
1995	95,000 ÷ 5	=	19,000	95,000	5,000
			$95,000		

It was indicated earlier that residual value is frequently ignored when it is a relatively minor amount. If this were done in the example, depreciation would be recognized at $20,000 per year instead of $19,000.

Sum-of-the-Years-Digits Depreciation The sum-of-the-years-digits depreciation method provides decreasing charges by applying a series of fractions, each of a smaller value, to depreciable asset cost. Fractions are developed in terms of the sum of the asset life periods. The numerators are the years-digits listed in reverse order. The denominator for the fraction is obtained by adding these digits.

For example, given an asset with a 3-year life, the denominator, which is the same each year, would be 6, the 'sum-of-the-years-digits" (1 + 2 + 3). Since the numerators, which decrease each year, are the years-digits in reverse order (3, 2, 1) the fractions would be: 3/6 for the first year; 2/6 for the second year; and 1/6 for the third year. The total of these fractions is 1.00; thus 100% of the depreciable cost is charged to expense at the end of 3 years. The following formula can be used to facilitate computation of the denominator:

$$[(n + 1) \div 2] \times n$$

If useful life is 15 years, the denominator, determined by the formula, is: [(15 + 1) ÷ 2] × 15 = 120. The fraction applied to depreciable cost in the first year would be 15/120, in the second year, 14/120, and so on.

In the Schuss Boom example, useful life is 5 years, and the denominator of the fraction is: [(5 + 1) ÷ 2] × 5 = 15. Alternatively, the denominator can be found by adding the years digits (1 + 2 + 3 + 4 + 5 = 15). Depreciation using the sum-of-the-years-digits method is summarized in the following table:

Asset Cost Allocation—Sum-of-the-Years-Digits Method

End of Year	Decpreciation Computation		Amount	Accumulated Depreciation	Asset Book Value
					$100,000
1991	$95,000 × 5/15	=	$31,667	$31,667	68,333
1992	95,000 × 4/15	=	25,333	57,000	43,000
1993	95,000 × 3/15	=	19,000	76,000	24,000
1994	95,000 × 2/15	=	12,667	88,667	11,333
1995	95,000 × 1/15	=	6,333	95,000	5,000
			$95,000		

Note that under this method, the annual charge to depreciation expense declines by 1/15 of the depreciation asset base each year, or by $6,333.

Declining-Balance Depreciation The declining-balance depreciation methods provide decreasing charges by applying a constant percentage rate to a declining asset book value. The most popular rates are 1.5 times the straight-line rate, often referred to a "150% declining balance," and 2 times the straight-line rate, often referred to as **double-declining-balance depreciation**.[3] Residual value is not used in the computations under this method; however, it is generally recognized that depreciation should not continue once the book value is equal to the residual value. The percentage to be used is a multiple of the straight-line rate, calculated for various useful lives as follows:

Estimated Useful Life in Years	Straight-Line Rate	1.5 times Straight-Line Rate	2.0 times Straight-Line Rate
3	33 1/3%	50%	66 2/3%
5	20	30	40
7	14 2/7	21 3/7	28 4/7
8	12 1/2	18 3/4	25
10	10	15	20
20	5	7 1/2	10

Depreciation using the double-declining-balance method for the asset described earlier is summarized in the table that follows.

End of Year	Depreciation Computation		Amount	Accumulated Depreciation	Asset Book Value
					$100,000
1991	$100,000 × 40%	=	$40,000	$40,000	60,000
1992	60,000 × 40	=	24,000	64,000	36,000
1993	36,000 × 40	=	14,400	78,400	21,600
1994	21,600 × 40	=	8,640	87,040	12,960
1995	12,960 × 40	=	5,184	92,224	7,776
			$92,224		

[3]The pure declining-balance method computes a constant rate that, when applied to a declining book value, will cause the book value to equal the estimated residual value at the end of estimated useful life. The formula to arrive at this rate is $1 - \sqrt[n]{R \div C}$, where R is the residual value, C is cost of the asset, and n is the life of the asset. This method is seldom used in practice because it often exceeds the double-declining-balance rate, a limit imposed in the past through the tax code.

It should be noted that the rate of 40% is applied to the decreasing book value of the asset each year. This results in a declining amount of depreciation expense. In applying this rate, the book value after 5 years exceeds the residual value by $2,776 ($7,776 − $5,000). This condition arises whenever residual values are relatively low in amount. Since it is impossible to bring a value to zero by using a constant multiplier, most adopters of this method switch to the straight-line method when the remaining annual depreciation computed using straight-line exceeds the depreciation computed by continuing to apply the declining-balance rate. In the above example, the depreciation expense for 1995 would be $7,960 if a switch were made from double-declining balance to straight-line. This would reduce the book value of the asset to its $5,000 residual value. In this example, the switch was made in the last year of the asset's life, and the depreciation expense was simply the amount necessary to reduce the asset's book value to its residual value. However, if the asset in the example had a lower residual value, the switch could have been made in the fourth year. For example, assume the asset is expected to have no residual value. The book value under the double-declining-balance method at the end of the third year as shown above is $21,600, thus the straight-line depreciation for years 4 and 5 would be $10,800 ($21,600 ÷ 2). Since the straight-line depreciation of $10,800 exceeds the double-declining depreciation of $8,640, the straight-line amount would be used for years 4 and 5.

Accelerated Cost Recovery System (ACRS) The Economic Recovery Act (ERTA) of 1981 introduced an adaptation of the declining balance depreciation method to be used for income tax purposes. It is referred to as the accelerated cost recovery system (ACRS). Subsequent revisions to the income tax laws have altered the original provisions. Because the Tax Reform Act of 1986 made several significant changes to ACRS, the new system is now referred to as the modified accelerated cost recovery system (MACRS).

The term "cost recovery" was used in the tax regulations to emphasize that ACRS was not a standard depreciation method since the system was not based strictly on asset life or pattern of use. ACRS has largely replaced traditional depreciation accounting for income tax purposes. Its original purpose was to both simplify the computation of tax depreciation and provide for a more rapid write-off of asset cost to reduce income taxes and thus stimulate investment in noncurrent operating assets. Simplification was to be achieved by using one of three cost recovery periods for all assets rather than a specific useful life for each class of asset as previously prescribed by the income tax regulations. More rapid write-off was achieved by allowing companies to write-off most machinery and equipment over 3 to 5 years, and all real estate over 15 years, even though previously prescribed income tax class lives were for much longer periods. The class lives prescribed by the IRS were based on estimates of actual useful lives for specific assets in specific industries.

The subsequent modifications to ACRS by Congress have tended to dampen both of its original objectives, primarily because Congress has become more concerned with increasing tax revenues to offset the rapidly growing federal deficit without increasing income tax rates than with simplification or stimulating growth in the economy. The original three recovery periods have been replaced with six recovery periods for personal property,[4] such as equipment, automobiles, and furniture, and two periods for real property, or buildings. At the same time, the recovery periods for most assets have been extended so that less rapid write-off of asset cost is permitted.

Exhibit 12-1 illustrates the cost recovery periods and depreciation methods uder MACRS. The exhibit applies to assets purchased after December 31, 1986, the date MACRS became effective. For personal property, the appropriate cost recovery period is determined by reference to the IRS class lives defined in the tax regulations. The real property recovery periods relate to the type of real property involved rather than class lives. ACRS initially provided for a 150% declining-balance depreciation. The 1986 Reform Act not only increased the number of asset recovery periods and extended the recovery periods for most assets, but also changed the method of depreciation for most personal property to the 200% declining-balance method.

Exhibit 12-1   **MACRS Cost Recovery Periods and Depreciation Methods**

	IRS Defined Class Lives	MACRS Cost Recovery Period	Depreciation Method	Examples of Business Assets
Personal Property	Less than 4 years	3 years	200% declining balance	Small tools
	4 to < 10 years	5 years	200% declining balance	Cars, trucks, office machinery
	10 to < 16 years	7 years	200% declining balance	Office furniture, most factory machinery
	16 to < 20 years	10 years	200% declining balance	Land improvements
	20 to < 25 years	15 years	150% declining balance	Communication equipment
	More than 25 years	20 years	150% declining balance	Farm buildings
	Type of Property			
Real Property—Buildings	Residential rental	27.5 years	Straight line	
	Nonresidential	31.5 years	Straight line	

Both the AICPA and FASB expressed opposition to the use of ACRS for financial reporting purposes because of the wide disparity between the recovery periods permitted for income tax purposes and the actual useful lives of the assets. The 1986 Reform Act modifications have reduced this disparity, and in

---

[4]Personal property is a general term that encompasses all property other than real property (land and buildings).

many cases, the MACRS recovery periods may represent reasonable estimates of useful life for financial reporting purposes. However, companies should exercise caution in adopting MACRS rules for financial reporting purposes because of the volatility of income tax laws and regulations.

Comparison of Time-Factor Method Exhibit 12-2 illustrates the pattern of depreciation expense for the time-factor methods discussed in the preceding sections. Note that when the straight-line method is used, depreciation is a constant or fixed charge each period. When the life of an asset is affected primarily by the lapse of time rather than by the degree of use, recognition of depreciation as a constant charge is generally appropriate. However, net income measurements become particularly sensitive to changes in the volume of business activity. With above-normal activity, there is no increase in the depreciation charge; with below-normal activity, there is no decrease in the depreciation charge.

Straight-line depreciation is a widely used procedure for financial reporting purposes. It is readily understood and frequently parallels asset use. It has the advantage of simplicity and under normal conditions offers a satisfactory means of cost allocation. Normal asset conditions exist when (1) assets have been accumulated over a period of years so that the total of depreciation plus maintenance is comparatively even from period to period, and (2) service potentials of assets are being steadily reduced by functional as well as physical factors. The absence of either of these conditions may suggest the use of some depreciation method other than straight line.

Decreasing-charge methods can be supported as reasonable approaches to cost allocation when the annual benefits provided by an asset decline as it grows older. These methods, too, are suggested when an asset requires increasing maintenance and repairs over its useful life.[5] When straight-line depreciation is employed, the combined charges for depreciation, maintenance, and repairs will increase over the life of the asset; when the decreasing-charge methods are used, the combined charges will tend to be equalized. Exhibit 12-3 illustrates this relationship.

Other factors suggesting the use of a decreasing-charge method include: (1) the anticipation of a significant contribution in early periods with the extent of the contribution to be realized in later periods being less definite; (2) the possibility that inadequacy or obsolescence may result in premature retirement of the asset.

Depreciation for Partial Periods The discussion thus far has assumed that assets were purchased on the first day of a company's fiscal period. In real-

[5]The AICPA Committee on Accounting Procedure has stated, "The declining-balance method is one of those which meets the requirements of being 'systematic and rational.' In those cases where the expected productivity or revenue-earning power of the asset is relatively greater during the earlier years of its life, or where maintenance charges tend to increase during the later years, the declining-balance method may well provide the most satisfactory allocation of cost." The Committee would apply these conclusions to other decreasing-charge methods, including the sum-of-the-years-digits method, that produce substantially similar results. See *Accounting Research and Terminology Bulletins—Final Edition*, "No. 44 (Revised), Declining-Balance Depreciation" (New York: American Institute of Certified Public Accountants, 1961), par. 2.

Exhibit 12-2   Time-Factor Methods: Depreciation Patterns Compared

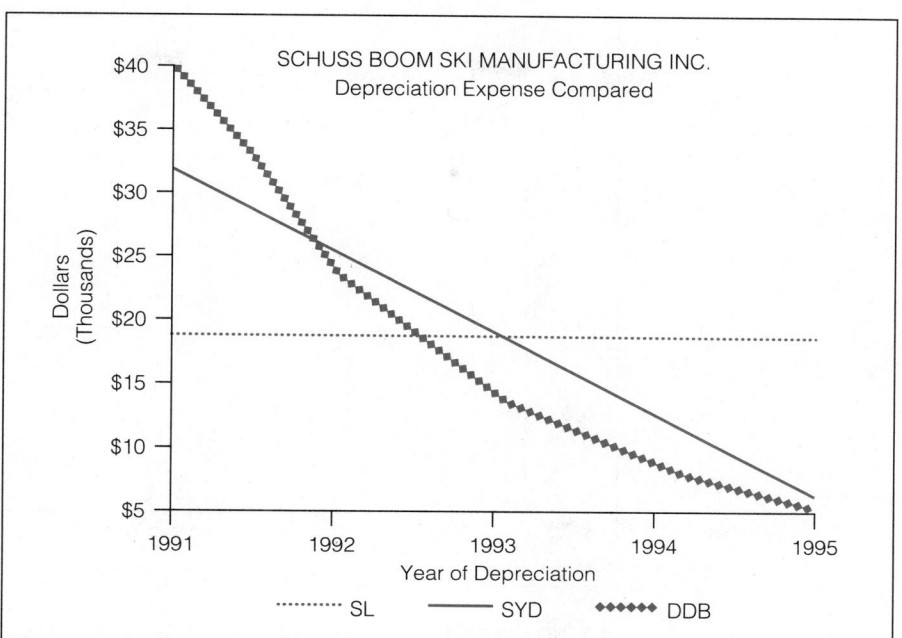

ity, of course, asset transactions occur throughout the year. When a time-factor method is used, depreciation on assets acquired or disposed of during the year may be based on the number of days the asset was held during the period. When the level of acquisitions and retirements is significant, however, companies often adopt a less burdensome policy for recognizing depreciation for partial periods. Some alternatives found in practice include the following:

1. Depreciation is recognized to the nearest whole month. Assets acquired on or before the 15th of the month are considered owned for the entire month; assets acquired after the 15th are not considered owned for any part of the month. Conversely, assets sold on or before the 15th of the month are not considered owned for any part of the month; assets sold after the 15th are considered owned for the entire month.

2. Depreciation is recognized to the nearest whole year. Assets acquired during the first six months are considered held for the entire year; assets acquired during the last six months are not considered in the depreciation computation. Conversely, no depreciation is recorded on assets sold during the first six months and a full year's depreciation is recorded on assets sold during the last six months.

3. One-half year's depreciation is recognized on all assets purchased or sold during the year. A full year's depreciation is taken on all other assets. This approach is required for tax purposes (ACRS and MACRS).

Exhibit 12-3   Decreasing-Charge Depreciation and Repairs and Maintenance Expense

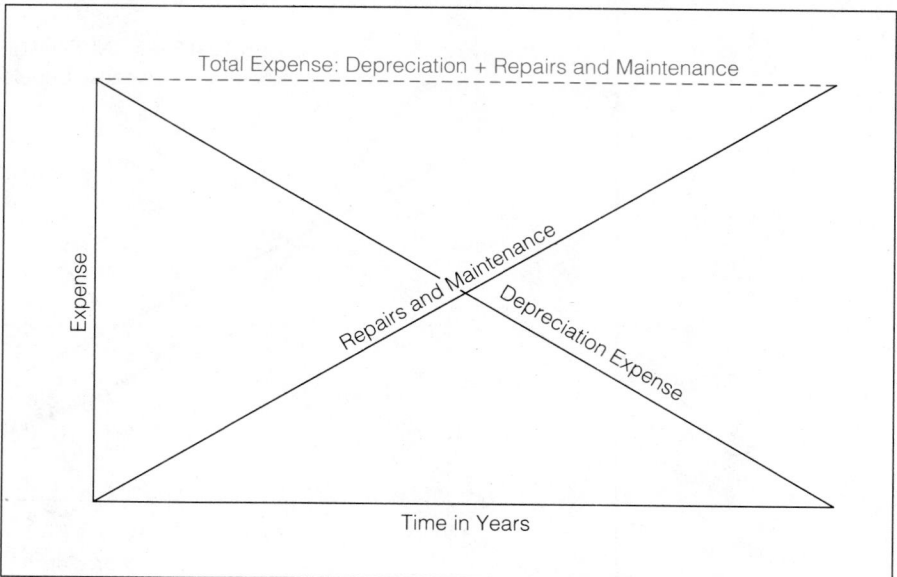

4. No depreciation is recognized on acquisitions during the year but depreciation for a full year is recognized on retirements.

5. Depreciation is recognized for a full year on acquisitions during the year but no depreciation is recognized on retirements.

Alternatives 2 through 5 are attractive because of their simplicity. However, alternative 1 provides greater accuracy and its use is assumed in the examples and problems in the text except for MACRS problems that require alternative 3.

If a company uses the sum-of-the-years-digits method of depreciation and recognizes partial year's depreciation on assets in the year purchased, the depreciation expense for the second year must be determined by the following allocation procedure. Assume that the asset acquired by Schuss Boom Ski Manufacturing (see page 488) was purchased ¾ of the way through the fiscal year. The computation of depreciation expense for the first two years would be as follows:

First year:		
Depreciation for full year (See page 491)	$31,667	
One-fourth year's depreciation ($31,667 ÷ 4)		$ 7,917
Second year:		
Depreciation for balance of first year ($31,667 − $7,917)		$23,750
Depreciation for second full year (See page 491)	$25,333	
One-fourth year's depreciation ($25,333 ÷ 4)		6,333
Total depreciation — second year		$30,083

From this point, each year's depreciation will be 1/15 of the original depreciable asset base ($6,333) less than the previous year. A summary of the depreciation charges for the five-year period is as follows:

	Depreciation	Asset Book Value
Year 1	$ 7,917	$92,083
Year 2	30,083	62,000
Year 3	23,750	38,250
Year 4	17,417	20,833
Year 5	11,083	9,750
Year 6	4,750	5,000
Total	$95,000	

If a company uses a declining-balance method of depreciation, the computation of depreciation when partial years are involved is more straightforward. After the first year's depreciation is computed, the remaining years are calculated in the same manner as illustrated on page 491; a constant percentage is multiplied by a declining book value. Again assuming a purchase ¾ of the way through the fiscal year and the use of alternative 1, the double-declining balance depreciation expense for the asset described on page 488 would be as follows, assuming a switch to straight-line depreciation in year 5.

		Depreciation	Asset Book Value
Year 1	($100,000 × .40 × ¼)	$10,000	$90,000
Year 2	($90,000 × .40)	36,000	54,000
Year 3	($54,000 × .40)	21,600	32,400
Year 4	($32,400 × .40)	12,960	19,440
Year 5	($19,440 × .40 ÷ 1¾)	8,251*	11,189
Year 6	($11,189 − 5,000)	6,189	5,000
	Total	$95,000	

* rounded

In contrast, the MACRS method for personal property requires use of alternative 3, the half-year convention. The cost recovery amounts for the same asset would be as follows:

		Cost Recovery Amount	Asset Book Value
Year 1	($100,000 × .40 × ½)	$20,000	$80,000
Year 2	($80,000 × .40)	32,000	48,000
Year 3	($48,000 × .40)	19,200	28,800
Year 4	($28,800 × .40)	11,520	17,280
Year 5	(($17,280 − $5,000) ÷ 1.5)	8,187	9,093
Year 6	($9,093 − $5,000)	4,093	5,000
	Total	$95,000	

Even though the asset was purchased ¾ of the way through the year, for tax purposes $20,000 is reported as the cost recovery in the first year rather than $10,000 determined by computing depreciation to the nearest month. Note that a switch to the straight-line method was made in year 5. If the double-declining-balance method had been applied to this year, only $6,912 ($17,280 × .40) would have been reported rather than $8,187 using straight-line for the remaining 1.5 years.

Use-Factor Methods

Use-factor depreciation methods view asset exhaustion as related primarily to asset use or output and provide periodic charges varying with the degree of such service. Service life for certain assets can best be expressed in terms of hours of service; for others in terms of units of production.

Service-Hours Method Service-hours depreciation is based on the theory that purchase of an asset represents the purchase of a number of hours of direct service. This method requires an estimate of the life of the asset in terms of service hours. Depreciable cost is divided by total service hours in arriving at the depreciation rate to be assigned for each hour of asset use. The use of the asset during the period is measured, and the number of service hours is multiplied by the depreciation rate in arriving at the periodic depreciation charge. Depreciation charges against revenue fluctuate periodically according to the contribution the asset makes in service hours.

Using asset data previously given and an estimated service life of 20,000 hours, the rate to be applied for each service hour is determined as follows:

$$r \text{ (per hour)} = \frac{C - R}{n}, \text{ or } \frac{\$100,000 - \$5,000}{20,000} = \$4.75$$

Allocation of asset cost in terms of service hours is summarized in the table below.

Asset Cost Allocation—Service-Hours Method

End of Year	Service Hours	Depreciation Computation		Amount	Accumulated Depreciation	Asset Book Value
						$100,000
1991	3,000	3,000 × $4.75	=	$14,250	$14,250	85,750
1992	5,000	5,000 × $4.75	=	23,750	38,000	62,000
1993	5,000	5,000 × $4.75	=	23,750	61,750	38,250
1994	4,000	4,000 × $4.75	=	19,000	80,750	19,250
1995	3,000	3,000 × $4.75	=	14,250	95,000	5,000
	20,000			$95,000		

It is assumed that the original estimate of service hours is confirmed and the asset is retired after 20,000 hours are reached in the fifth year. Such precise confirmation would seldom be found in practice.

It should be observed that straight-line depreciation resulted in an annual charge of $19,000 regardless of fluctuations in productive activity. When asset life is affected directly by the degree of use, and when there are significant fluctuations in such use in successive periods, the service-hours method, which recognizes hours used instead of hours available for use, normally provides the more equitable charges to operations.

Productive-Output Method **Productive-output depreciation** is based on the theory that an asset is acquired for the service it can provide in the form of production output. This method requires an estimate of the total unit output of the asset. Depreciable cost divided by the total estimated output gives the equal charge to be assigned for each unit of output. The measured production for a period multiplied by the charge per unit gives the charge to be made against revenue. Depreciation charges fluctuate periodically according to the contribution the asset makes in unit output.

Using the previous asset data and an estimated productive life of 2,500,000 units, the rate to be applied for each thousand units produced is determined as follows:

$$r \text{ (per thousand units)} = \frac{C - R}{n}, \text{ or } \frac{\$100,000 - \$5,000}{2,500} = \$38.00$$

A table for the productive-output method would be similar to that prepared for the service-hours method.

Evaluation of Use-Factor Methods When quantitative measures of asset use can be reasonably estimated, the use-factor methods provide highly satisfactory approaches to asset cost allocation. Depreciation as a fluctuating charge tends to follow the revenue curve: high depreciation charges are assigned to periods of high activity; low charges are assigned to periods of low activity. When the useful life of an asset is affected primarily by the degree of its use, recognition of depreciation as a variable charge is particularly appropriate.

However, certain limitations in applying the use-factor methods need to be pointed out. Asset performance in terms of service hours or productive output is often difficult to estimate. Measurement solely in terms of these factors could fail to recognize special conditions, such as increasing maintenance and repair costs, as well as possible inadequacy and obsolescence. Furthermore, when service life expires even in the absence of use, a use-factor method may conceal actual fluctuations in earnings; by relating periodic depreciation charges to the volume of operations, periodic operating results may be smoothed out, thus creating a false appearance of stability.

Group and Composite Methods

It was assumed in preceding discussions that depreciation expense is associated with individual assets and is applied to each separate unit. This practice is commonly referred to as **unit depreciation**. However, there may be certain advantages in associating depreciation with a group of assets and applying a single rate to the collective cost of the group at any given time. Group cost allocation procedures are referred to as **group depreciation** and **composite depreciation**.[6]

---

[6]These methods are sometimes referred to as multiple-asset methods of depreciation. See Stephen T. Limberg and Bill N. Schwartz, "Should You Use Multiple Asset Accounts?" *The CPA Journal* (October 1981), pp. 25-31.

Group Depreciation When useful life is affected primarily by physical factors, a group of similar items purchased at one time should have the same expected life, but in fact some will probably remain useful longer than others. In recording depreciation on a unit basis, the sale or retirement of an asset before or after its anticipated lifetime requires recognition of a gain or loss. Such gains and losses, however, can usually be attributed to normal variations in useful life rather than to unforeseen disasters and windfalls.

The **group-depreciation** procedure treats a collection of similar assets as a single group. Depreciation is accumulated in a single valuation account, and the depreciation rate is based on the average life of assets in the group. Because the accumulated depreciation account under the group procedure applies to the entire group of assets, it is not related to any specific asset. Thus, no book value can be calculated for any specific asset and there are no fully depreciated assets. To arrive at the periodic depreciation charge, the depreciation rate is applied to the recorded cost of all assets remaining in service, regardless of age.

When an item in the group is retired, no gain or loss is recognized; the asset account is credited with the cost of the item and the valuation account is debited for the difference between cost and any salvage. With normal variations in asset lives, the losses not recognized on early retirements are offset by the continued depreciation charges on those assets still in service after the average life has elapsed. Group depreciation is generally computed as an adaptation of the straight-line method, and the illustrations in this chapter assume this approach.[7]

To illustrate, assume that 100 similar machines having an average expected useul life of 5 years are purchased at the beginning of 1991 at a total cost of $2,000,000. Of this group, 30 machines are retired at the end of 1994, 40 at the end of 1995, and the remaining 30 at the end of 1996. Based on the average expected useful life of 5 years, a depreciation charge of 20% is reported on those assets in service each year. The charges for depreciation and the changes in the group asset and accumulated depreciation accounts are summarized below, assuming there was no salvage value at retirement.

Asset Cost Allocation—Group Depreciation

End of Year	Depreciation Expense (20% of Cost)	Asset Debit	Asset Credit	Asset Balance	Accumulated Depreciation Debit	Accumulated Depreciation Credit	Accumulated Depreciation Balance	Asset Book Value
		$2,000,000		$2,000,000				$2,000,000
1991	$ 400,000			2,000,000		$ 400,000	$ 400,000	1,600,000
1992	400,000			2,000,000		400,000	800,000	1,200,000
1993	400,000			2,000,000		400,000	1,200,000	800,000
1994	400,000		$ 600,000	1,400,000	$ 600,000	400,000	1,000,000	400,000
1995	280,000		800,000	600,000	800,000	280,000	480,000	120,000
1996	120,000		600,000	—	600,000	120,000	—	—
	$2,000,000	$2,000,000	$2,000,000		$2,000,000	$2,000,000		

[7]The multiple-asset approach may be modified for unusual retirements. In order to preserve the average life computations, retirements arising from involuntary conversion or other such unusual causes may be recorded at a loss. In order to do this, however, there must be enough detail in the records to approximate the book value of the item at the date of the loss.

It should be noted that the depreciation charge is exactly $4,000 per machine-year. In each of the first four years, 100 machine-years of service[8] are utilized, and the annual depreciation charge is $400,000. In the fifth year, when only 70 machines are in operation, the charge is $280,000 (20% of $1,400,000). In the sixth year, when 30 units are still in service, a proportionate charge for such use of $120,000 (20% of $600,000) is made.

If the 30 machines retired in 1994 had been sold for $50,000, the entry to record the sale using the group depreciation method would have been as follows:

Cash	50,000	
Accumulated Depreciation—Equipment	550,000	
Equipment		600,000

Because no gain or loss is recognized, the debit to accumulated depreciation is the difference between the cost of the equipment and the cash received.

The preceding example assumed that no new assets were added to the group. This is referred to as a "closed" group. Companies may create such a group, for example, for all furniture acquired in a given year. The group method may also be applied to an "open-ended" group. In this case, additions are made to the group and, thus, the accounts are never "closed." Assume the previous example is changed to include additions of 20 machines at the end of 1992 at a cost of $425,000, 30 machines at the end of 1995 at a cost of $650,000, and 50 machines at the end of 1996 at a cost of $1,100,000. Assume that all retired machines are from the initial purchase. The charges for the first 6 years under these assumptions are summarized below.

Asset Cost Allocation—Open-Ended Group Depreciation

End of Year	Depreciation Expense (20% of cost)	Asset Debit	Asset Credit	Asset Balance	Accumulated Depreciation Debit	Accumulated Depreciation Credit	Accumulated Depreciation Balance	Asset Book Value
		$2,000,000		$2,000,000				$2,000,000
1991	$400,000			2,000,000		$400,000	$ 400,000	1,600,000
1992	400,000	425,000		2,425,000		400,000	800,000	1,625,000
1993	485,000			2,425,000		485,000	1,285,000	1,140,000
1994	485,000		$600,000	1,825,000	$600,000	485,000	1,170,000	655,000
1995	365,000	650,000	800,000	1,675,000	800,000	365,000	735,000	940,000
1996	335,000	1,100,000	600,000	2,175,000	600,000	335,000	470,000	1,705,000

Application of the group depreciation procedure under circumstances such as the foregoing provides an annual charge that is more closely related to the quantity of productive facilities being used. Gains and losses due solely to normal variations in asset lives are not recognized, and operating results are more meaningfully stated. The convenience of applying a uni-

[8]It should be observed that in the example the original estimates of an average useful life of 5 years is confirmed in the use of the assets. Such precise confirmation would seldom be the case. In instances where assets in a group are continued in use after their cost has been assigned to operations, no further depreciation charges would be recognized. On the other hand, where all of the assets in a group are retired before their cost has been assigned to operations, a special charge related to such retirement would have to be recognized.

form depreciation rate to a number of similar items may also represent a substantial advantage.

Composite Depreciation The basic procedures employed under the group method for allocating the cost of substantially identical assets may be extended to include dissimilar assets. This special application of the group procedure is known as **composite depreciation**. The composite method retains the convenience of the group method, but because assets with varying service lives are aggregated to determine an average life, it is unlikely to provide all the reporting advantages of the group method.

A composite rate is established by analyzing the various assets or classes of assets in use and computing the depreciation as an average of the straight-line annual depreciation as follows:

Asset	Cost	Residual Value	Depreciable Cost	Estimated Life in Years	Annual Depreciation Expense (Straight-line)
A	$ 2,000	$ 120	$ 1,880	4	$ 470
B	6,000	300	5,700	6	950
C	12,000	1,200	10,800	10	1,080
	$20,000	$1,620	$18,380		$2,500

Composite depreciation rate to be applied to cost: $2,500 ÷ $20,000 = 12.5%
Composite or average life of assets: $18,380 ÷ $2,500 = 7.35 years.

It will be observed that a rate of 12.5% applied to the cost of the assets, $20,000, results in annual depreciation of $2,500. Annual depreciation of $2,500 will accumulate to a total of $18,380 in 7.35 years; hence 7.35 years may be considered the composite or average life of the assets. Composite depreciation would be reported in a single accumulated depreciation account. Upon the retirement of an individual asset, the asset account is credited and Accumulated Depreciation is debited with the difference between cost and residual value. As with the group procedure, no gains or losses are recognized at the time individual assets are retired.

After a composite rate has been set, it is ordinarily continued in the absence of significant changes in the lives of assets or asset additions and retirements having a material effect upon the rate. It is assumed in the preceding example that the assets are replaced with similar assets when retired. If they are not replaced, continuation of the 12.5% rate will misstate depreciation charges.

Historical Cost Versus Current Cost Allocation

A difficult problem in accounting for property utilization arises in determining the periodic charges to revenues in periods of changing prices. In accounting practice, depreciation, depletion, and amortization have traditionally been viewed as an allocation of the acquisition cost over the life of the asset. This meaning can be observed in the definition of depreciation accounting adopted by the Committee on Terminology in the 1940's and still accepted today:

Depreciation accounting is a system of accounting which aims to distribute the cost or other basic value of tangible capital assets, less salvage (if any), over the estimated useful life of the unit (which may be a group of assets) in a systematic and rational manner. It is a process of allocation, not of valuation. *Depreciation for the year* is the portion of the total charge under such a system that is allocated to the year. Although the allocation may properly take into account occurrences during the year, it is not intended to be a measurement of the effect of all such occurrences.[9]

Under this allocation view, the total amount charged against revenue is fixed by the acquisition cost less any estimated residual value. While the pattern of charges may vary with the allocation method used, the total amount charged against revenue cannot exceed the historical cost of the asset. For any group of assets at any given time, the cumulative amount charged against past revenues plus the remaining asset carrying or book value will equal the original acquisition cost adjusted by any additions or betterments.

As has been discussed previously, there are many accountants who advocate a charge against revenue based on a current asset value, i.e., the **replacement cost** or **current cost**. This allocation approach matches current rather than past costs against current revenues, resulting in a net income figure that better reflects income available for dividends and that is more useful for estimating future cash flows of a business entity. Noncurrent operating assets, like inventories, must be replaced, and that portion of current and future earnings needed for replacement will not be available for distribution to owners or for payments to creditors.

This problem has been recognized as a particularly serious one for utilities, since they must obtain approval from regulatory commissions for any changes in the rates they charge to customers. One of the significant cost factors used in determining the rate base is depreciation. The tele-communications area has been especially hard hit in the 1980's as the divestitures arising from the court-ordered breakup of American Telephone and Telegraph Company have placed new strains on the pricing structure. The following quotation summarizes the problem as it relates to depreciation:

Traditional Depreciation Can't Keep Up

Depreciation is a big-ticket issue. The problem is that rapid technological advances and competition among telephone companies are making large portions of their plant and equipment obsolete long before the expiration of useful lives that are calculated under traditional depreciation accounting methods.

For more than a decade, the depreciation charges regulators have allowed telephone companies to pass on to their customers have fallen below what the companies need to recover their investment. The growing depreciation expense now represents by far the largest component of rising phone bills—far outstripping the cost added by divestiture. This has created a gap that some estimate as high as $25 billion between the reserves telephone companies have

[9]*Accounting Research and Terminology Bulletins*—Final Edition, "Accounting Terminology Bulletins, No. 1, Review and Résumé" (New York: American Institute of Certified Public Accountants, 1961), par. 56.

set aside for depreciation and the amounts they calculate they should have available to replace outmoded equipment.[10]

Historical cost is still the basis for financial statement reporting. However, various attempts have been made to modify the application of historical cost allocation to partially account for the impact of changing prices. Emphasis in this chapter is on the methods used to allocate the historical acquisition cost against revenue and the modifications made to consider price changes. Supplemental disclosures for price changes are discussed and illustrated in a later chapter.

Amortization of Intangible Assets

The life of an intangible asset is usually limited by the effects of obsolescence, shifts in demand, competition, and other economic factors. Because of the difficulty in estimating such highly uncertain future events, companies sometimes did not amortize the cost of intangible assets, but assumed their value was never used up. This practice was frequently followed for trademarks, goodwill, and some franchises. The Accounting Principles Board, however, felt that eventually all intangible assets became of insignificant worth to the company. The Board, therefore, issued Opinion No. 17, requiring that the recorded costs of all intangible assets acquired after October 31, 1970—the effective date of the Opinion—be amortized over the estimated useful life.[11] Many companies do not amortize certain intangibles, notably goodwill, acquired prior to November 1, 1970, although amortization of these assets was encouraged by the Board.

The useful life of an intangible asset may be affected by a variety of factors, all of which should be considered in determining the amortization period. Useful life may be limited by legal, regulatory, or contractual provisions. These factors, including options for renewal or extension, should be evaluated in conjunction with the economic factors noted above and other pertinent information. A patent, for example, has a legal life of 17 years; but if the competitive advantages afforded by the patent are expected to terminate after 5 years, then the patent cost should be amortized over the shorter period.

Although the life of an intangible asset is to be estimated by careful analysis of the surrounding circumstances, a maximum life of 40 years was established for amortization purposes. APB Opinion No. 17 included this limitation as follows:

The cost of each type of intangible asset should be amortized on the basis of the estimated life of that specific asset and should not be written off in the period of acquisition. . . .

The period of amortization should not, however, exceed forty years. Analysis at the time of acquisition may indicate that the indeterminate lives of some intangible assets are likely to exceed forty years and the cost of those assets

[10]Touche Ross & Co., *Washington Briefing* (January 1986), p. 4.

[11]Opinions of the Accounting Principles Board, No. 17, "Intangible Assets" (New York: American Institute of Certified Public Accountants, 1970).

should be amortized over the maximum period of forty years, not an arbitrary shorter period.[12]

The requirement that the recorded cost of all intangible assets be amortized and the arbitrary selection of a 40-year life are of questionable theoretical merit. An analysis of the expected future benefits to be derived from a particular asset should be the basis for capitalizing and amortizing the cost of any asset, whether tangible or intangible.

The establishment by the APB of a 40-year maximum period for the amortization of intangible assets was not intended to determine the normal write-off period as 40 years. However, for some assets, such as goodwill and franchise costs, 40 years has become the most popular period to use. While it is difficult to determine exactly how long goodwill benefits a company, the amortization period should be established based on sound reasoning, not some arbitrary period of time. Some accountants feel that a five- to ten-year period should be used because after that period, a company has probably built its own goodwill based on expenditures and actions during that period. Others feel that goodwill should be written off immediately against Retained Earnings because of the lack of comparability among companies, some of whom report purchased goodwill and others who do not.

The degree of diversity in the amortization of intangible assets, especially goodwill, suggests that further guidelines are needed in this area.[13]

Amortization, like depreciation, may be charged as an operating expense of the period or allocated to production overhead if the asset is directly related to the manufacture of goods. In practice the credit entry is often made directly to the asset account rather than to a separate allowance account. This practice is arbitrary, and there is no reason why charges for amortization cannot be accumulated in a separate account in the same manner as depreciation. The FASB requires disclosure of both cost and accumulated depreciation for tangible assets, but does not require similar disclosure for intangible assets. When amoritization is recorded in a separate account, such account is typically called Accumulated Amortization.

Amortization of intangible assets is made evenly in most instances, or on a straight-line allocation basis. APB Opinion No. 17 states:

> The Board concludes that the straight-line method of amortization—equal annual amounts—should be applied unless a company demonstrates that another systematic method is more appropriate.[14]

Although practice favors straight-line amortization, analysis of many intangibles such as patents, franchises, and even goodwill suggests that

[12]*Ibid.*, pars. 28-29.

[13]The standard-setting organization for Great Britain considered the goodwill issue in the early 1980's, and issued an official pronouncement in 1984 that recognized two methods of amortizing goodwill: either an immediate write-off against Retained Earnings, which they preferred, or an amortization period of no more than 40 years. The second position agrees with the United States standard. The first position was carefully considered by the APB, and although it was recommended by the authors of Accounting Research Study No. 10, it was rejected as an acceptable alternative.

[14]*Opinions of the Accounting Principles Board, No. 17*, par. 30.

greater benefit is often realized in the early years of the asset's life than in the later years. In those instances, a decreasing-charge amortization seems justified. Monsanto Company summarized its procedures for amortizing intangibles in the following note:

Exhibit 12-4	**Monsanto Company**

NOTES TO FINANCIAL STATEMENTS

Depreciation and Amortization

	1987	1986	1985
Depreciation	$421	$423	$477
Amortization of intangible assets...	225	218	88
Obsolescence	33	139	34
Total	$679	$780	$599

Intangible assets are recorded at cost less amortization. The components of intangible assets, and their estimated remaining useful lives, were as follows:

	Estimated Remaining Life*	1987	1986
Patents	6	$1,057	$1,234
Goodwill	35	639	653
Other intangible assets......	25	257	257
Total		$1,953	$2,144

*Weighted average, in years, at December 31, 1987.

The cost of patents obtained in a business acquisition is initially recorded at the present value of estimated future cash flows resulting from patent ownership. The cost of patents is amortized over their legal lives. Goodwill is the cost of acquired businesses in excess of the fair value of their identifiable net assets, and is amortized over periods of 5 to 40 years. The cost of other intangible assets (principally product rights and trademarks) is amortized over their estimated useful lives.

Depletion of Natural Resources

Natural resources, also called **wasting assets**, move toward exhaustion as the physical units representing these resources are removed and sold. The withdrawal of oil or gas, the cutting of timber, and the mining of coal, sulphur, iron, copper, or silver ore are examples of processes leading to the exhaustion of natural resources. Depletion expense is a charge for the using up of the resources.

Computing Periodic Depletion

The computation of depletion expense is an adaptation of the productive-output method of depreciation. Perhaps the most difficult problem in computing depletion expense is estimating the amount of resources available for economical removal from the land. Generally, a geologist, mining engineer, or other expert is called upon to make the estimate, and it is subject to continual revision as the resource is extracted or removed.

Developmental costs, such as costs of drilling, sinking mine shafts, and constructing roads should be capitalized and added to the original cost of the property in arriving at the total cost subject to depletion. These costs are often incurred before normal activities begin.

To illustrate the computation of depletion expense, assume the following facts: Land containing mineral deposits is purchased at a cost of $5,500,000. The land has an estimated value after removal of the resources of $250,000; the natural resource supply is estimated at 1,000,000 tons. The unit depletion charge and the total depletion charge for the first year, assuming the withdrawal of 80,000 tons are calculated as follows:

Depletion charge per ton: ($5,500,000 − $250,000) ÷ 1,000,000 = $5.25
Depletion charge for the first year; 80,000 tons × $5.25 = $420,000

The following entries should be made to record these events.

Land	250,000	
Mineral Deposits	5,250,000	
Cash		5,500,000
Purchase of mineral rights.		
Depletion Expense	420,000	
Accumulated Depletion (or Mineral Deposits)		420,000
Record depletion expense.		

If the 80,000 tons are sold in the current year, the entire $420,000 would be included as part of the cost of goods sold. If only 60,000 tons are sold, $105,000 is reported as part of ending inventory on the balance sheet.

When buildings and improvements are constructed in connection with the removal of natural resources and their usefulness is limited to the duration of the project, it is reasonable to recognize depreciation on such properties on an output basis consistent with the charges to be recognized for the natural resources themselves. For example, assume buildings are constructed at a cost of $250,000; the useful lives of the buildings are expected to terminate upon exhaustion of the natural resource consisting of 1,000,000 units. Under these circumstances, a depreciation charge of $.25 ($250,000 ÷ 1,000,000) should accompany the depletion charge recognized for each unit. When improvements provide benefits expected to terminate prior to the exhaustion of the natural resource, the cost of such improvements should be allocated on the basis of the units to be removed during the life of the improvements or on a time basis, whichever is considered more appropriate.

Special Problems—Oil and Gas Properties

The preceding discussion relates to depletion of all natural resources. Special problems exist in the oil and gas industry in the determination of the asset cost to be used in computing depletion. Even though apparently valuable property rights are acquired, no one can truly measure their value until exploratory activities have been completed. The nature of oil exploration generally results in several dry wells for each "gusher" that is discovered. The accounting question is, "How should these exploratory costs be recorded? Are they part of the asset cost regardless of their success, or are they a period expense?"

Two methods of accounting have developed to account for exploratory costs. The first method is the full cost approach, and the second method is the successful efforts approach. Under the **full cost approach**, all exploratory costs are deferred and written off against revenues as depletion expense. Under the **successful efforts approach**, exploratory costs for unsuccessful projects are expensed, and only exploratory costs for successful projects are deferred as assets. Most large, successful oil companies follow the second approach. For example, Amoco Corporation included the following explanation of its depletion method in the notes to the 1987 financial statements:

Exhibit 12-5	**Amoco Corporation**

Costs Incurred in oil and gas producing activities—

The corporation follows the successful efforts method of accounting. Costs of property acquisition, successful exploratory wells, all development costs (including CO_2 and certain other injected materials in enhanced recovery projects), and support equipment and facilities are capitalized. Unsuccessful exploratory wells are expensed when determined to be non-productive. Production costs, overhead, and all exploration costs other than exploratory drilling are charged against income as incurred.

For smaller companies, the full cost approach has been popular. This method encourages such companies to continue exploration without the severe penalty of recognizing all costs of unsuccessful projects as immediate expenses. Proponents of the full cost approach argue that often valuable exploratory information is discovered even when a "dry hole" is drilled. The cost of a producing well, therefore, should include these unsuccessful costs. Columbia Gas System, Inc. explains its use of full cost in a note reproduced in Exhibit 12-6.

The issue of how to account for exploratory costs of the oil and gas industry has attracted the attention of the FASB, the SEC, and even the U.S. Congress. When an apparent oil shortage developed in the 1970's, there was strong pressure placed on oil companies to expand their exploration to discover new sources of oil and gas. The Financial Accounting Standards Board was encouraged to identify one of the two alternatives for recording exploratory costs as preferred. In 1977, they selected a form of the successful efforts approach, and issued FASB Statement No. 19, "Financial Accounting and Reporting by Oil and Gas Producing Companies." The smaller companies objected to this standard, arguing that their explo-

Exhibit 12-6   Columbia Gas System, Inc.

Oil and Gas Producing Properties. The Corporation's subsidiaries engaged in exploring for and developing oil and gas reserves follow the full cost method of accounting. Under this method of accounting, all productive and non-productive costs directly identified with acquisition, exploration and development activities are capitalized in country-wide cost centers. If costs exceed the sum of the estimated present value of the cost centers net future oil and gas revenues and the lower of cost or estimated value of un-proved properties, an amount equivalent to the excess is charged to current depletion expense. Gains or losses on the sale or other disposition of oil and gas properties are normally recorded as adjustments to capitalized costs.

ration activities would be less vigorous if they had to immediately expense their drilling costs. In 1979, the SEC issued its own standard that rejected both alternatives, and suggested adoption of a new method they called **Reserve Recognition Accounting (RRA)**. This method was in reality a form of **discovery accounting** that would recognize as an asset the value of the reserves rather than their cost. Under public and congressional pressure, the FASB issued its Statement No. 25 that suspended its earlier standard, and effectively permitted again the use of either the full cost or successful efforts approach.[15]

When oil and gas prices declined, the SEC withdrew its support of RRA. However, the Commission still recommends that current values of reserves be disclosed.

Changes in Estimates of Variables

The allocation of asset costs benefiting more than one period cannot be precisely determined at acquisition because so many of the variables cannot be known with certainty until a future time. Only one factor in determining the periodic charge for depreciation, amortization or depletion is based on historical information—asset cost. Other factors—residual value, useful life or output, and the pattern of use or benefit—must be estimated. The question frequently facing accountants is how adjustments to these estimates, which arise as time passes, should be reflected in the accounts. As indicated in Chapter 4, a change in estimate is normally reported in the current and future periods rather than as an adjustment of prior periods. This type of adjustment would be made for residual value and useful life changes. However, a change in the cost allocation method based on a revised expected pattern of use is a change in accounting principle and is accounted for in a different manner. Changes in accounting principles are discussed in Chapter 23.

[15]*Statement of Financial Accounting Standards No. 25*, "Suspension of Certain Accounting Requirements for Oil and Gas Producing Companies," (Stamford: Financial Accounting Standards Board, 1979).

Change in Estimated Life To illustrate the procedure for a change in estimate affecting allocation of asset cost, assume that a company purchased $50,000 of equipment and estimated a ten-year life for depreciation purposes. Using the straight-line method with no residual value, the annual depreciation would be $5,000. After four years, accumulated depreciation would amount to $20,000, and the remaining undepreciated book value would be $30,000. Early in the fifth year, a re-evaluation of the life indicates only four more years of service can be expected from the asset. An adjustment must therefore be made for the fifth and subsequent years to reflect the change. A new annual depreciation charge is calculated by dividing the remaining book value by the remaining life of four years. In the illustration above, this would result in an annual charge of $7,500 for the fifth through eighth years ($30,000 ÷ 4 = $7,500).

Asset Cost Allocation—Change in Estimated Life (Straight-Line Method)

End of Year	Depreciation Computation	Amount	Accumulated Depreciation
1991	$50,000 ÷ 10	$ 5,000	$ 5,000
1992	$50,000 ÷ 10	5,000	10,000
1993	$50,000 ÷ 10	5,000	15,000
1994	$50,000 ÷ 10	5,000	20,000
1995	($50,000 − $20,000) ÷ 4	7,500	27,500
1996	($50,000 − $20,000) ÷ 4	7,500	35,000
1997	($50,000 − $20,000) ÷ 4	7,500	42,500
1998	($50,000 − $20,000) ÷ 4	7,500	50,000
		$50,000	

A change in the estimated life of an intangible asset is accounted for in the same manner, i.e., the unamortized cost is allocated over the remaining life based on the revised estimate. Because of the uncertainties surrounding the estimation of the life of an intangible asset, frequent evaluation of the amortization period should be made to determine if a change in estimated life is warranted. For example, assume a patent costing $51,000 is being amortized over 17 years. Amortization per year would be $3,000($51,000 ÷ 17). If, at the end of 5 years, the patent is estimated to have a remaining life of 4 years, the book value of $36,000 [$51,000 − ($3,000 × 5)] will be amortized over 4 years at $9,000 per year.

Change in Estimated Units of Production Another change in estimate occurs in accounting for wasting assets when the estimate of the recoverable units changes as a result of further discoveries, improved extraction processes, or changes in sales prices that indicate changes in the number of units that can be extracted profitably. A revised depletion rate is established by dividing the remaining resource cost balance by the estimated remaining recoverable units.

To illustrate, assume the facts used in the example on page 507. Land is purchased at a cost of $5,500,000 with estimated residual value of

$250,000. The original estimated supply of natural resources in the land is 1,000,000 tons. As indicated previously, the depletion rate under these conditions would be $5.25 per ton, and the depletion charge for the first year when 80,000 tons were mined would be $420,000. Assume that in the second year of operation, 100,000 tons of ore are withdrawn, but before the books are closed at the end of the second year, appraisal of the expected recoverable tons indicates a remaining tonnage of 950,000. The new depletion rate and the depletion charge for the second year would be computed as follows:

Cost assignable to recoverable tons at the beginning of the second year:

Original costs applicable to depletable resources	$5,250,000
Deduct depletion charge for the first year	420,000
Balance of cost subject to depletion	$4,830,000

Estimated recoverable tons as of the beginning of the second year:

Number of tons withdrawn in the second year	100,000
Estimated recoverable tons as of the end of the second year	950,000
Total recoverable tons at the beginning of the second year	1,050,000

Depletion charge per ton for the second year: $4,830,000 ÷ 1,050,000 = $4.60
Depletion charge for the second year: 100,000 × $4.60 = $460,000.

Sometimes an increase in estimated recoverable units arises from additional expenditures for capital developments. When this occurs, the additional costs should be added to the remaining recoverable cost and divided by the number of tons remaining to be extracted. To illustrate this situation, assume in the preceding example that $525,000 additional costs had been incurred at the beginning of the second year. The preceeding computation of depletion rate and depletion expense would be changed as follows:

Cost assignable to recoverable tons as of the beginning of the second year:

Original costs applicable to depletable resources	$5,250,000
Add additional costs incurred in the second year	525,000
	$5,775,000
Deduct depletion charge for the first year	420,000
Balance of cost subject to depletion	$5,355,000
Estimated recoverable tons as of the beginning of the second year (as above)	1,050,000

Depletion charge per ton for the second year: $5,355,000 ÷ 1,050,000 = $5.10
Depletion charge for the second year: 100,000 × $5.10 = $510,000

Accounting is made of up many estimates. The procedures outlined in this section are designed to prevent the continual restating of reported income from prior years. Adjustments to prior period income figures are made only if actual errors have occurred, not when reasonable estimates have been made that later prove inaccurate.

Impairment of Tangible and Intangible Asset Values

Events sometimes occur after the purchase of an asset and before the end of its expected life that impair its value and require an immediate writedown of the asset rather than making a normal allocation over a period of time. This type of impairment can occur with any asset, but it occurs with more frequency in relation to goodwill. Excerpts from financial statements for two companies illustrate the varying conditions that can create the need for recording an immediate loss.

Exhibit 12-7   Amoco Corporation

In 1986, the corporation recorded a $300 million pre-tax charge for impairment of unproved oil and gas properties in addition to normal amortization. The charge is included in depreciation, depletion, and amortization expense in the Consolidated Statement of Income. The charge resulted from a reassessment of unproved acreage in light of changed economic conditions and unfavorable drilling results in certain high-cost areas. On an after-tax basis, the special charge reduced net income by $162 million or $0.63 per share.

Exhibit 12-8   Inter-City Gas Corporation

Pursuant to this reorganization and as a result of the losses incurred by KeepRite in the past two years, the Company has re-assessed its investment in KeepRite Inc. As a result of this re-assessment, it has been determined that the value of the underlying assets in KeepRite have been impaired by an amount of $4,697,000. Accordingly, the Company has written off goodwill of $4,697,000 as an extraordinary charge against income.

The timing for recognizing the impairment of an asset value is a matter of judgment. The authoritative accounting literature does not include a clear statement as to when impairment of assets is to be recognized. Since the publication in 1980 of an AICPA Issues paper, *Accounting for the Inability to Fully Recover the Carrying Amounts of Long-Lived Assets*, the FASB has considered adding this topic to its agenda, but work on the conceptual framework and other more pressing issues delayed an asset impairment project until November 1988. At that time, the FASB Staff was directed to prepare a discussion memorandum that would "focus on long-lived, physical assets with consideration of identifiable, intangible assets to be included in the discussion document."[16]

Continued consideration of reported asset values is necessary to assure that there still are future benefits to justify asset amounts. The write-down of an asset may be classified as an extraordinary item or as a special charge to operations depending upon the materiality of the item and the circumstances surrounding the impairment. The write-down of Amoco Corporation assets was a charge against operations, while the write-down of the

---

[16]Memorandum of FAF Trustees from Dennis Beresford, "Agenda Decision—Addition of the Project on Impairment of Assets", November 16, 1988.

goodwill for Inter-City Gas Corporation was an extraordinary charge. In anticipation of more guidance from the FASB on the timing of write-downs for noncurrent operating assets, disclosure of current asset values when they are lower than undepreciated cost would provide important information to users of financial statements. As one writer observed, "I believe such disclosure also would alleviate considerably the surprise that frequently accompanies business failures. A business failure almost always is preceded by a decline in the fair value of the assets of the enterprise."[17]

Asset Retirements

Assets may be retired by sale, exchange, or abandonment. Generally, when an asset is disposed of, any unrecorded depreciation or amortization for the period is recorded to the date of disposition. A book value as of the date of disposition can then be computed as the difference between the cost of the asset and its accumulated depreciation. If the disposition price exceeds the book value, a **gain** is recognized. If the disposition price is less than the book value, a **loss** is recorded. The gain or loss is reported on the income statement as "other revenues and gains" or "other expenses and losses" in the year of asset disposition. As part of the disposition entry, the balances in the asset and accumulated depreciation accounts for the asset are canceled. The following sections illustrate the asset retirement process under varying conditions.

Asset Retirement by Sale

If the proceeds from the sale of an asset are in the form of cash or a receivable (**monetary asset**), the recording of the transaction follows the order outlined in the previous paragraph. For example, assume that on April 1, 1991, Firestone Supply Co. sells for $43,600 manufacturing equipment that is recorded on the books at cost of $83,600 and accumulated depreciation as of January 1, 1991, of $50,600. The company depreciates its manufacturing equipment on the books using a straight-line, 10% rate. It follows the policy of depreciating it assets to the nearest month.

The following entries would be made to record this transaction.

Depreciation Expense—Machinery	2,090	
Accumulated Depreciation—Machinery		2,090
To record depreciation for three months in 1991.		
Cash	43,600	
Accumulated Depreciation—Machinery	52,690	
Machinery		83,600
Gain on Sale of Machinery		12,690
To record sale of machinery at a gain.		

---

[17]Walter Schuetze, "Disclosure and the Impairment Question," *Journal of Accountancy* (December 1987), pp. 26-32.

Computation of gain:
Sales price $43,600
Book value ($83,600 − $52,690)   30,910
Gain on sale $12,690

The preceding entries could be combined in the form of a single compound entry as follows:

Cash   43,600
Depreciation Expense...................   2,090
Accumulated Depreciation—Machinery.....   50,600
    Machinery   83,600
    Gain on Sale of Machinery.............   12,690

Asset Retirement by Exchange for Other Nonmonetary Assets

As indicated in Chapter 11, when operating assets are acquired in exchange for other nonmonetary assets, the new asset acquired is generally recorded at its fair market value or the fair market value of the nonmonetary asset given in exchange, whichever is more clearly determinable. This treatment is referred to as the "general case" and is the more common exchange transaction.

When accounting for exchanges of property, two questions must be asked: (1) Are the assets being exchanged similar in nature? and (2) Are the parties involved in the exchange in the same line of business, i.e., are they both either dealers of the assets or nondealers? If the answers to both of these questions is affirmative, and if the transaction results in a gain, a "special case" approach may be used to record the exchange. The general case will be illustrated first.

The entries required to record the general case for an exchange involving nonmonetary assets are identical to those illustrated in the previous section except that a nonmonetary asset is increased rather than a monetary one. Gains and losses arising from the exchange are recognized when the exchange takes place.

To illustrate, assume in the previous example that the retirement of the described asset was effected by exchanging it for delivery equipment that had a market value of $43,600. The entries would be the same as illustrated except that instead of a debit to Cash, Delivery Equipment would be debited for $43,600. The gain would still be computed by comparing the book value of the machine and the market value of the asset acquired in the exchange.

Delivery Equipment   43,600
Depreciation Expense...................   2,090
Accumulated Depreciation—Machinery.....   50,600
    Machinery   83,600
    Gain on Exchange of Machinery.........   12,690

If the machinery's fair market value were more clearly determinable than the value of the delivery equipment, the value of the machinery would be used to compute the gain or loss and to determine the value for the delivery equipment. Assume the delivery equipment is used and has no readily available market price, but the machinery had a market value of $25,000. Under these circumstances, a loss of $5,910 ($30,910 − $25,000) would be indicated, and the combined entry to record the exchange would be as follows:

Delivery Equipment	25,000	
Depreciation Expense	2,090	
Accumulated Depreciation—Machinery	50,600	
Loss on Exchange of Machinery	5,910	
Machinery		83,600

Often the exchange of nonmonetary assets includes a transfer of cash, since the nonmonetary assets in most exchange transactions do not have equivalent market values. The cash part of the transaction adjusts the market values of the assets received to those of the assets given up. Thus, if in the previous example the exchange of delivery equipment were accompanied by cash of $3,000, the loss would be reduced to $2,910 and the combined entry would be as follows:

Cash	3,000	
Delivery Equipment	25,000	
Depreciation Expense	2,090	
Accumulated Depreciation—Machinery	50,600	
Loss on Exchange of Machinery	2,910	
Machinery		83,600

In this example, the exchange involved assets that were dissimilar in nature: delivery equipment and machinery. If the exchange involved similar assets, i.e., a used truck for a new one, the same accounting entries would be required unless the exchange is between two parties in the same line of business. This special case is discussed in the following section.

Asset Retirement by Exchange of Nonmonetary Assets—Special Case

Not all exchanges of nonmonetary assets have the features to justify the recognition of a gain. Sometimes an exchange of similar assets is made to facilitate one of the parties to the exchange in making a sale to an ultimate consumer. For example, the Tri-City Cadillac dealership has a buyer for a blue Eldorado but has only a red one in stock. Another dealership in a nearby town has a blue Eldorado and is willing to exchange its car for Tri-City's red one. This exchange of similar assets is not intended to be an earnings transaction for either party and, therefore, should not reflect any gain, even if the market values of the cars have increased since they were originally acquired from the manufacturer. Another example of such an exchange would occur if two manufacturing companies exchanged similar equipment which both companies used in the production process.

In both of these illustrations, similar assets were transferred between parties in the same line of business. In the first instance, both parties were dealers of automobiles. In the second example, both parties were nondealers of machines being used in the production process. In neither case was the earning process culminated.

When the Accounting Principles Board studied the exchange of non-monetary assets issue, they determined that an exception to the general rule was needed when the exchange did not culminate the earning process for either party and a gain was otherwise indicated.[18] The exception provided that **no gain** is to be recognized for these special exchanges unless cash (boot) is received as part of the exchange. If a significant amount of cash is involved in the exchange, the transaction becomes a monetary exchange rather than a nonmonetary one. The Emerging Issues Task Force was asked to determine what is significant, and, in its *Bulletin 86-29*, it concluded that if the cash payment is 25% or more of the fair value of the exchange, the transaction should be considered a monetary exchange with the fair values used to determine a gain or loss. If the cash payment is less than 25%, the party paying the cash records no gain, but the party receiving the cash recognizes a proportionate share of the gain.[19] If the transaction indicates that a loss has occurred, the exception does not apply and the exchange is recorded as illustrated in the previous section. Thus, four conditions must exist for the special case to apply:

1. The assets must be similar in nature; i.e., be expected to fulfill similar functions in the entity.
2. The parties to the transaction must be in the same line of business, i.e. both be dealers or both be nondealers.
3. A gain must be indicated in the transaction; i.e., the market value of the assets received must exceed the book value of the assets surrendered.
4. If cash is involved, it is less than 25% of the fair value of the exchange.

To illustrate the special case, two examples are included below. In the first example, no cash is involved in the exchange. In the second example, the exchange includes a transfer of cash.

Example 1   No Cash Involved

The Republic Manufacturing Company owns a special molding machine that it no longers uses because of a change in products being manufactured. The machine still has several years of service remaining. Discussion with other companies in the industry has located a buyer, Logan Square Company. However, Logan Square is low on funds and suggests an

---

[18]*Opinions of the Accounting Principles Board, No. 29*, "Accounting for Nonmonetary Transactions," (New York: American Institute of Certified Public Accountants, 1973), par. 20-23. The "same line of business" test was added by the Emerging Issues Task Force in Issue No. 86-29, "Nonmonetary Transactions: Magnitude of Boot and the Exceptions to the Use of Fair Value." *EITF Abstracts*, October 1, 1987, pp. 275-277.

[19]*EITF Issue NO. 86-29*, "Nonmonetary Transactions: Magnitude of Boot and the Exceptions to the Use of Fair Value," *loc. cit.*

exchange for one of its machines that could be used in Republic's packaging department. It is decided that both machines meet the definition of being similar in use and have the same market values. The following cost and market data relate to the two machines:

	Republic	**Logan**
Costs of machines to be exchanged	$46,000	$54,000
Book values of machines to be exchanged	$14,000	$18,000
Market values of machines to be exchanged	$16,000	$16,000

The entry on Republic's books to record the exchange is as follows:

Machinery (new)	14,000	
Accumulated Depreciation on Machinery ($46,000 − $14,000) . . .	32,000	
Machinery (old)		46,000

The entry on Logan's books to record the exchange is as follows:

Machinery	16,000	
Accumulated Depreciation on Machinery ($54,000 − $18,000) . . .	36,000	
Loss on Exchange of Machines	2,000	
Machinery (old)		54,000

Note that in Republic's entry, the special case is used. All four conditions are present: the machines are similar, both parties are nondealers, the market value of the asset received exceeds the book value of Republic's molding machine, and no cash is involved. Thus, the value assigned to Republic's newly acquired packaging machine is the book value of its old molding machine.

In Logan's entry, however, the general case is used. The market value of the asset exchanged is less than the book value, so a loss is indicated. The molding machine, therefore, is recorded on Logan's books at its market value, the general case solution.

Example 2   Transfer of Cash

Assume the same facts as in Example 1, except that it is decided the molding machine has a market value of $16,000 and the packaging machine is worth $20,000. To make the exchange equal, Republic agrees to pay Logan Square $4,000 cash (20% of the fair value of the exchange) in addition to the molding machine.

The entry on Republic's books for Example 2 is as follows:

Machinery (new)	18,000	
Accumulated Depreciation on Machinery ($46,000 − $14,000) . . .	32,000	
Machinery (old)		46,000
Cash		4,000

As was true for Example 1, the facts of this case require Republic to use the special case. The market value of the machine received ($20,000) exceeds the book value of the molding machine being exchanged plus the cash paid, ($14,000 + $4,000). A $2,000 gain is thus indicated. The machines are similar in use and the parties are both nondealers. The gain, therefore, is deferred and not recognized. The new machine is recorded at $18,000, the market value of the asset received in the exchange ($20,000) less the deferred gain ($2,000).

In Example 2, the book value of the packaging machine on Logan Square's books is less than the market value, indicating a gain ($20,000 − $18,000, or $2,000). The similar assets and similar parties indicate the special case; however, because Logan Square received less than 25% cash as part of the transaction, generally accepted accounting principles specify that a portion of the $2,000 **indicated gain** should be recognized as having been earned. The amount to be recognized is computed using the following formula:

$$\frac{\text{Recognized}}{\text{Gain}} = \frac{\text{Cash Received}}{\text{Cash} + \text{Market Value of Acquired Asset}} \times \frac{\text{Total}}{\text{Indicated Gain}}$$

Using the figures from Example 2, Logan Square, therefore, would recognize $400 of the gain computed as follows:

$$\frac{\$4,000}{\$4,000 + \$16,000} \times \$2,000 = \$400$$

The recorded value of the molding machine on Logan's books is $14,400, the book value of the packaging machine exchanged less the cash received plus the gain recognized, ($18,000 − $4,000 + $400). Another way of computing the recorded value is by deducting the **deferred gain** from the market value of the asset received ($16,000 − $1,600 or $14,400).

The entry on Logan Square's books to record the exchange is as follows:

Cash	4,000	
Machinery (new)	14,400	
Accumulated Depreciation on Machinery ($54,000 − $18,000)	36,000	
Machinery (old)		54,000
Gain on Exchange of Machinery		400

While the exceptions to the general case seem complex, they occur in relatively rare instances. The general effect of the special case is to defer any indicated gain until the new asset is disposed of through sale, trade, or abandonment.[20]

---

[20]For a further discussion of the special case, see James B. Hobbs and D.R. Bainbridge, "Nonmonetary Exchange Transactions: Clarification of APB Opinion No. 29," *Accounting Review* (January 1982), pp. 171-175.

Retirement by Involuntary Conversion

Sometimes retirement of noncurrent operating assets occurs because of extensive damage caused by such events as a fire, earthquake, flood, or condemnation. Retirements caused by these types of uncontrollable events have been classified as **involuntary conversions.** Some of these events are insurable risks, and the occurrence of the event triggers reimbursement from an insurance company. If the proceeds exceed the book value of the destroyed assets, a gain is recognized on the books. If the proceeds are less than the book value, a loss is recorded.

If the loss was either not insurable, or a company failed to carry insurance on the property, the remaining book value of the asset should be recorded as a loss. Because these types of events are unusual and infrequent, the gains and losses realized are often recorded as an extaordinary item. Of course, if the event has a high probability of recurrence, i.e., a factory built in a low area that frequently experiences flooding, the gain or loss may be classifed as an ordinary item.

To illustrate the recording of an involuntary conversion, assume that a flood destroyed a factory building with a $1,200,000 cost and a book value of $350,000. If $400,000 was recovered from the flood insurance policy, the entry to record the loss would be as follows:

Receivable from Insurance Company	400,000	
Accumulated Depreciation—Building	850,000	
Building		1,200,000
Gain on Involuntary Conversion		50,000

Some special problems can arise when provisions of the insurance policy include a coinsurance provision. These complications are addressed in the Appendix to this chapter.

In some cases, the involuntary conversion is caused by government condemnation of private property. Usually such proceedings require the condemning party to pay a fair market value for the assets seized. This generally results in a recognized gain. Some accountants have argued that since these proceeds are often reinvested in similar assets, the gain on such conversion should be deferred by reducing the cost of the new asset. The FASB, however, has indicated that the condemnation and the acquisition of new assets should be viewed as two separate transactions.[21] Thus, the gain is recognized on the condemnation, and the new assets are recorded at their acquisition cost.

For example, assume that the Valley Mining Company had land condemned by the state for a state park. The cost of the land to Valley was $50,000. The agreed upon market value was $260,000. The entry to record the cash receipt would be as follows:

[21]*FASB Interpretation No. 30,* "Accounting for Involuntary Conversions of Nonmonentary Assets to Monetary Assets," (Stamford: Financial Accounting Standards Board, 1979).

Cash......................	260,000
Land....................	50,000
Gain on Condemnation.....	210,000

Balance Sheet Presentation and Disclosure

Tangible noncurrent operating assets, natural resources, and intangible assets are usually shown separately on the balance sheet. As indicated earlier in this chapter, both the gross cost and accumulated depreciation must be disclosed for depreciable assets. Such disclosure is not required for intangible assets and natural resources, and many companies report only net values for these assets. Because of the alternative cost allocation methods available to compute the charges for depreciation, amortization, and depletion, the methods used must be disclosed in the financial statements. Without this information, a user of the statements might be misled in trying to compare the financial results of one company with another. Cost allocation methods are normally reported in the first note to the financial statements, "Summary of Significant Accounting Policies." See General Mills Inc. disclosure of its cost allocation methods in Note 1 (B) and (D) in Appendix A at the end of the text.

Appendix

Insurance Recovery on Involuntary Conversions

Most companies carry insurance to cover losses from many types of involuntary conversions, especially those that are defined as casualty losses.

The most common casualty loss incurred by a business is that from fire. Of all the various types of protection offered by insurance, fire is the risk most widely covered. Because of the importance of fire insurance in business and because of special accounting problems that arise in the event of fire, a discussion of this matter is included in this appendix.

Fire Insurance   Fire insurance policies are usually written in $100 or $1,000 units for a period of three years. Insurance premiums are normally paid annually in advance. The amount of the premium is determined by the conditions prevailing in each case.

The insurance contract may be canceled by either the insurer or the insured. When the insurance company cancels the policy, a refund is made on a pro rata basis. When the policyholder cancels the policy, a refund may be made on what is known as a short-rate basis that provides for a higher insurance rate for the shorter period of coverage.

A **coinsurance clause** is frequently written into a policy by the insurance companies to offset the tendency by the buyer to purchase only a minimum insurance coverage. A business with assets worth $100,000 at fair market value, for example, may estimate that any single loss could not destroy more than one half of these assets and might consider itself adequately protected by insurance of $50,000. With an 80% coinsurance clause, however, the business would have to carry insurance equal to 80% of the fair market value of the property, or $80,000, to recover the full amount on claims up to the face of the policy. When less than this percentage is carried, the insured shares in the risk with the insurer.

To illustrate the calculation of the amount recoverable on a policy failing to meet coinsurance requirements, assume the following: assets are insured for $70,000 under a policy containing an 80% coinsurance clause; on the date of a fire, assets have a fair market value of $100,000. Because insurance of only $70,000 is carried when coinsurance requirements are $80,000, any loss will be borne $\frac{7}{8}$ by the insurance company and $\frac{1}{8}$ by the policyholder; furthermore, whatever the loss, the maximum to be borne by the insurance company is $70,000, the face of the policy. The amount recoverable from the insurance company if a fire loss is $50,000, for example, is calculated as follows:

$$\frac{\$70,000 \text{ (policy)}}{\$80,000 \text{ (coinsurance requirement)}} \times \$50,000 \text{ (loss)} = \$43,750$$

The same calculations are made when the loss is greater than the face of the policy. Assume the same facts given above, but assume a fire loss of $75,000. The amount recoverable from insurance is calculated as follows:

$$\frac{\$70,000 \text{ (policy)}}{\$80,000 \text{ (coinsurance requirement)}} \times \$75,000 \text{ (loss)} = \$65,625$$

In the preceding example, application of the formula gives an amount still less than the face of the policy and hence fully recoverable. But if application of the formula results in an amount exceeding the face value of the policy, the claim is limited to the latter amount. If, for example, the loss is $90,000, the following calculation is made:

$$\frac{\$70,000 \text{ (policy)}}{\$80,000 \text{ (coinsurance requirement)}} \times \$90,000 \text{ (loss)} = \$78,750$$

Recovery from the insurance company, however, is limited to $70,000, the ceiling set by the policy.

When the insurance coverage is equal to or greater than the percentage required by the coinsurance clause, the formula need not be applied since any loss is paid in full up to the face value of the policy. It is important to note that coinsurance requirements are based not on the cost or book value of the insured property but upon the actual market value of the property on the date of a fire. If coinsurance requirements are to be met, a rise in the value of insured assets requires that insurance coverage be increased.

The following general rules may be formulated:

1. In the absence of a coinsurance clause the amount recoverable is the lower of the loss or the face of the policy.
2. When a policy includes a coinsurance clause, the amount recoverable is the lower of the loss as adjusted by the coinsurance formula or the face of the policy.

Insurance policies normally include a **contribution clause** that provides that if other policies are carried on the same property, recovery of a loss on a policy shall be limited to the ratio which the face of the policy bears to the total insurance carried. Such a limitation on the amount to be paid eliminates the possibility of recovery by the insured of amounts in excess of the actual loss. When coinsurance clauses are found on the different policies, the recoverable amount on each is limited to the ratio of the face of the policy to the higher of (a) the total insurance carried, or (b) the total insurance required to be carried by the policy. To illustrate the limitations set by contribution clauses, assume a fire loss of $30,000 on property with a value of $100,000 on which policies are carried as follows: Co. A, $50,000; Co. B, $15,000; Co. C, $10,000.

1. Assuming policies have no coinsurance clauses, amounts that may be recovered from each company are as follows:

$$\text{Co. A: } \frac{\$50{,}000 \text{ (policy)}}{\$75{,}000 \text{ (total policies)}} \times \$30{,}000 \text{ (loss)} \qquad \$20{,}000$$

$$\text{Co. B: } \frac{\$15{,}000 \text{ (policy)}}{\$75{,}000 \text{ (total policies)}} \times \$30{,}000 \text{ (loss)} \qquad 6{,}000$$

$$\text{Co. C: } \frac{\$10{,}000 \text{ (policy)}}{\$75{,}000 \text{ (total policies)}} \times \$30{,}000 \text{ (loss)} \qquad \underline{4{,}000}$$

$$\text{Total amount recoverable} \quad \underline{\underline{\$30{,}000}}$$

2. Assuming each policy includes an 80% coinsurance clause, coinsurance requirements on each policy would exceed the total insurance carried and amounts recoverable from each company are as follows:

$$\text{Co. A: } \frac{\$50{,}000 \text{ (policy)}}{\$80{,}000 \text{ (coinsurance requirement)}} \times \$30{,}000 \text{ (loss)} \qquad \$18{,}750$$

$$\text{Co. B: } \frac{\$15{,}000 \text{ (policy)}}{\$80{,}000 \text{ (coinsurance requirement)}} \times \$30{,}000 \text{ (loss)} \qquad 5{,}625$$

$$\text{Co. C: } \frac{\$10{,}000 \text{ (policy)}}{\$80{,}000 \text{ (coinsurance requirement)}} \times \$30{,}000 \text{ (loss)} \qquad \underline{3{,}750}$$

$$\text{Total amount recoverable} \quad \underline{\underline{\$28{,}125}}$$

3. Assuming each policy includes a 70% coinsurance clause, total insurance carried exceeds coinsurance requirements on each policy and amounts recoverable from each company are the same as in (1).

4. Assuming that coinsurance requirements are Co. A—none, Co. B—70%, and Co. C—80%, recovery on each policy is based on its relationship to the total insurance carried or the coinsurance requirement where this is higher, as follows:

$$\text{Co. A: } \frac{\$50{,}000 \text{ (policy)}}{\$75{,}000 \text{ (total policies)}} \times \$30{,}000 \text{ (loss)} \qquad \$20{,}000$$

$$\text{Co. B: } \frac{\$15{,}000 \text{ (policy)}}{\$75{,}000 \text{ (total policies)}} \times \$30{,}000 \text{ (loss)} \qquad 6{,}000$$

$$\text{Co. C: } \frac{\$10{,}000 \text{ (policy)}}{\$80{,}000 \text{ (coinsurance requirement)}} \times \$30{,}000 \text{ (loss)} \qquad \underline{3{,}750}$$

$$\text{Total amount recoverable} \quad \underline{\underline{\$29{,}750}}$$

Key Terms

Accelerated cost recovery system (ACRS) 492
Amortization 485
Coinsurance clause 521
Composite depreciation 499
Contribution clause 522
Cost recovery periods 492
Current cost 503
Declining-balance depreciation 491
Decreasing-charge depreciation 489
Depletion 485
Depreciation 485
Double-declining-balance depreciation 491
Full cost approach 508
Group depreciation 499
Impairment 512
Involuntary conversions 519

Modified accelerated cost recovery system (MACRS) 492
Natural resources 506
Productive-output depreciation 499
Replacement cost 503
Reserve Recognition Accounting (RRA) 509
Residual (salvage) value 486
Service-hours depreciation 498
Similar assets 515
Straight-line depreciation 489
Successful efforts approach 508
Sum-of-the-years-digits depreciation 490
Time-factor depreciation methods 489
Unit depreciation 499
Use-factor depreciation methods 498
Useful life 486

Questions

1. Distinguish among depreciation, depletion, and amortization expense.
2. What factors must be considered to determine the periodic depreciation charges that should be made for a company's depreciable assets?
3. Distinguish between the functional and physical factors affecting the useful life of a tangible noncurrent operating asset.
4. What role does residual or salvage value play in the various methods of time-factor depreciation?
5. Distinguish between time-factor and use-factor methods of depreciation.
6. The accelerated cost recovery system of depreciation is used for income tax purposes but may not be acceptable for financial reporting. Why is this true?
7. The certified public accountant is frequently called on by management for advice regarding methods of computing depreciation. Although the question arises less frequently, of comparable importance is whether the depreciation method should be based on the consideration of the property items as units, as groups, or as having a composite life.
   (a) Briefly describe the depreciation methods based on recognizing property items as (1) units, (2) groups, or (3) as having a composite life.
   (b) Present the arguments for and against the use of each of these methods.
   (c) Describe how retirements are recorded under each of these methods.
8. What arguments can be made for charging more than an asset's historical cost against revenue?
9. What factors determine the period and method for amortizing intangible assets?
10. What procedures must be followed when the estimate of recoverable natural resources is changed due to subsequent development work?
11. Under what circumstances should an asset's remaining book value be immediately written off as a loss?
12. Why is 40 years used as the maximum number of years for amortizing an intangible asset?

13. (a) Distinguish between the "full cost" and "successful efforts" approaches to recording exploratory costs for oil and gas properties. (b) The SEC recommended a third approach be followed. What were its distinguishing characteristics?

14. Under what circumstances is a gain or loss recognized when a productive asset is exchanged for a similar productive asset?

15. (a) What are some types of involuntary conversions that can take place with property? (b) What are the arguments for and against recognizing gains and losses on such conversions.

16. Machinery in the finishing department of Universal Co., although less than 50% depreciated, has been replaced by new machinery. The company expects to find a buyer for the old machinery, and on December 31 the machinery is in the yards and available for inspection. How should it be reported on the balance sheet?

17. How should property, wasting assets, and intangibles be reported on the balance sheet? What footnote disclosure should be made for these assets?

*18. (a) What is a coinsurance clause and why is it found in fire insurance policies?

(b) What is a contribution clause and how does it affect recovery of a loss?

*Relates to Appendix

Discussion Cases   **Case 12-1   (We don't need depreciation!)**

The managements of two different companies argue that because of specific conditions in their companies, recording depreciation expense should be suspended for 1991. Evaluate carefully their arguments.

(1) The president of Guzman Co. recommends that no depreciation be recorded for 1991 since the depreciation rate is 5% per year, and price indexes show that prices during the year have risen by more than this figure.

(2) The policy of Liebnitz Co. is to recondition its building and equipment each year so that they are maintained in perfect repair. In view of the extensive periodic costs incurred in 1991, officials of the company feel that the need for recognizing depreciation is eliminated.

Case 12-2   (Why write off goodwill?)

The Nevada Corporation purchased the Stardust Club for $500,000, which included $100,000 for goodwill. Nevada Corporation incurs large promotional and advertising expenses to maintain Stardust Club's popularity. As the annual financial statements are being prepared, the CPA of the Nevada Corporation, Emily Teeson, insists that some of the goodwill be amortized against revenue. Teeson cites APB Opinion No. 17 that requires all intangible assets to be written off over a maximum life of 40 years. Mark Stevenson, the Nevada Corporation controller, feels that amortization of the purchased goodwill in the same periods as heavy expenses are incurred to maintain the goodwill in effect creates a double charge against income of the period. Stevenson argues that no write-off of goodwill is necessary. Indeed, goodwill has increased in value and should even be increased on the books to reflect this improvement. Evaluate the logic of these two positions.

Case 12-3   (Is it really worth that much?)

International Enterprises, Inc. owns a building in Des Moines, Iowa that was built at a cost of $5,000,000 in 1980. The building was used as a manufacturing facility from 1981-1990. However, economic conditions have made it necessary to consolidate International's operations, and the building has been leased as of January 1, 1991, as a warehouse for ten years at an annual rental of $240,000. Taxes, insurance, and normal maintenance costs are to be paid by the lessee. At the end of the ten-year period, International may offer the lessee a renewal of the lease, or again use the building in its operations. The building is being depreciated on a straight-line basis over a forty-year life.

Petersen & Sons, CPA, is completing the audit for 1991. Julie Ramos, a new staff auditor, has been assigned to review the building accounts, and raises a question with Alison Crowther, the senior auditor on the job, concerning the carrying value of the Des Moines building. Julie had written a paper in school concerning accounting for the impairment of noncurrent operating assets. She feels the Des Moines building has been impaired and should be written down in value. Alison is unsure about the current position of the FASB on this issue, and invites Julie to prepare a memorandum recommending a specific write-down amount, with supporting justification. Prepare the memorandum, assuming current interest rates are 10%.

Case 12-4   (Should alternative methods of depreciation be eliminated?)

The FASB receives recommendations from its Advisory Board as to areas it should consider for study. Depreciation accounting has not been addressed as a separate topic by the FASB, and several alternative methods are used for recording this expense on the books. Recognizing this situation, a recommendation is made to the Board that a study be made of depreciation accounting with the objective of selecting one method as the only acceptable one. Those making the recommendation reason that only then will comparability in financial statements be achieved. Present the arguments for and against the FASB following the recommendation. If you were a member of the FASB, what would be your position?

Case 12-5   (Which depreciation method should we use?)

The Atwater Manufacturing Company purchased a new machine especially built to perform one particular function on the assembly line. A difference of opinion has arisen as to the method of depreciation to be used in connection with this machine. Three methods are now being considered.

(a) The straight-line method
(b) The productive-output method
(c) The sum-of-the-years-digits method

List separately the arguments for and against each of the proposed methods from both the theoretical and practical viewpoints.

Case 12-6   (Should financial reporting follow tax legislation?)

During the 1960s and 1970s, the United States Congress used a tax measure known as the Investment Tax Credit to encourage companies to expand their investment base. Under these provisions, companies received reductions of their tax liabilities based on a percentage of new investments in noncurrent operating assets. This approach was used in lieu of reducing tax rates as a stimulus to expansion. In 1981, the adoption of the ACRS method of cost allocation for noncurrent operating assets added further stimulation to the economy by permitting companies to write off the cost of their property over a shorter than normal period.

In 1986, Congress passed a massive Tax Reform Act that significantly reduced tax rates for all taxpaying entities. At the same time, the investment Tax Credit was eliminated and the ACRS legislation was replaced by a modified ACRS approach that lengthened the time period for the allocation. These latter provisions reduced the net impact of the reduced tax rates. Because elected government officials do not like to be identified with increased tax rates, there remains the possibility that further modifications to tax accounting for noncurrent operating assets will be made.

Should financial reporting for noncurrent operating assets be affected by tax legislation? Support your answer.

Exercises

Exercise 12-1   (Computation of asset cost and depreciation expense)

A machine is purchased at the beginning of 1991 for $36,000. Its estimated life is 6 years. Freight in on the machine is $2,000. Installation costs are $1,200. The machine is estimated to have a residual value of $2,000 and a useful life of 40,000 hours. It was used 6,000 hours in 1991.

(1) What is the cost of the machine for accounting purposes?
(2) Compute the depreciation charge for 1991 using (a) the straight-line method, and (b) the service-hours method.

Exercise 12-2   (Computation of depreciation expense)

The Feng Company purchased a machine for $180,000 on June 15, 1991. It is estimated that the machine will have a 10-year life and will have a salvage value of $18,000. Its working hours and production in units are estimated at 36,000 and 600,000 respectively. It is the company's policy to take a half-year's depreciation on all assets for which they use the straight-line or double-declining-balance depreciation method in the year of purchase. During 1991, the machine was operated 5,000 hours and produced 70,000 units. Which of the following methods will give the greatest depreciation expense for 1991? (1) double-declining balance; (2) productive-output; or (3) service-hours. (Show computations for all three methods.)

Exercise 12-3   (Computation of depreciation expense)

Ray Construction purchased a concrete mixer on July 15, 1991. Company officals revealed the following information regarding this asset and its acquisition:

Purchase price	$125,000
Residual value	$18,000
Estimated useful life	10 years
Estimated service hours	38,000
Estimated production in units	500,200 yards

The concrete mixer was operated by construction crews in 1991 for a total of 5,225 hours and it produced 77,000 yards of concrete.

It is company policy to take a half-year's depreciation on all assets for which they use the straight-line or double-declining-balance depreciation method in the year of puchase.

Calculate the resulting depreciation expense for 1991 under each of the following methods and specify which method allows the greatest depreciation expense:

(1) double-declining balance
(2) productive-output
(3) service-hours
(4) straight-line

Exercise 12-4   (Computation of book and tax depreciation)

Midwest States Manufacturing purchased factory equipment on March 15, 1990. The equipment will be depreciated for financial purposes over its estimated useful life, counting the year of acquisition as one-half year. The company accountant revealed the following information regarding this machine:

Purchase price	$75,000
Residual value	$9,000
Estimated useful life (class life)	10 years

(1) What amount should Midwest States Manufacturing record for depreciation expense for 1991 using the (a) double-declining-balance method? (b) sum-of-the-years-digits method?
(2) Assuming the equipment is classified as 7-year property under the modified accelerated cost recovery system (MACRS), what amount should Midwest States Manufacturing deduct for depreciation on its tax return in 1991?

Exercise 12-5   (MACRS computation)

The Timpanogas Equipment Company purchases a new piece of factory equipment on May 1, 1991 for $26,500. For income tax purposes, the equipment is classified as a seven-year asset. Because this is similar to the economic life expected for the asset, Timpanogas decides to use the tax depreciation for financial reporting purposes. The equipment is not expected to have any residual value at the end of the seven years. Prepare a depreciation schedule for the life of the asset using the MACRS method of cost recovery.

Exercise 12-6   (Productive-output depreciation and asset retirement)

Equipment was purchased at the beginning of 1989 for $100,000 with an estimated product life of 300,000 units. The estimated salvage value was $4,000. During 1989, 1990, and 1991, the equipment produced 80,000 units, 120,000 units, and 40,000 units respectively. The machine was damaged at the begining of 1992, and the equipment was scrapped with no salvage value.

(1) Determine depreciation using the productive-output method for 1989, 1990, and 1991.
(2) Give the entry to write off the equipment at the begining of 1992.

Exercise 12-7 (Composite depreciaton)

The Gold Crolon Co. records show the following assets:

	Acquired	Cost	Salvage	Estimated Useful Life
Machinery	7/1/90	$105,000	$9,000	8 years
Equipment	1/1/91	33,000	1,500	5 years
Fixtures	1/1/91	45,000	4,500	4 years

For 1991, what is (a) the composite depreciation rate to be applied to cost using the straight-line method and (b) the composite life of the assets?

Exercise 12-8 (Composite depreciation)

A schedule of machinery owned by Delgado Manufacturing Company is presented below:

	Total Cost	Estimated Salvage Value	Estimated Life in Years
Machine A	$700,000	$70,000	12
Machine B	200,000	20,000	8
Machine C	40,000	—	5

Delgado computes depreciation on the stragiht-line method. Based on the information presented, calculate the composite depreciaton rate and the composite life of these assets.

Exercise 12-9 (Group depreciation—closed group)

The NLG International Co. maintains its tools and dies on a closed group basis. A new group is created for each year's purchase of tools and dies. The assets are depreciated at a 25% rate beginning in the year following the acquisition. Any gain or loss is deferred until final disposition of the entire group of assets. Assume that for 1990, $150,000 was spent for tools and dies. Disposition of these tools and dies was made as follows (assume that disposals occurred at the beginning of each year):

Year	Cost	Disposition Cash Price
1991	$ 3,000	$ 1,500
1992	22,000	9,000
1993	53,000	22,000
1994	42,000	17,500
1995	10,000	3,000
1996	20,000	2,000

Prepare all journal entries required to account for tools and dies for the years 1991-1996. All tools and dies are disposed of by the end of 1996.

Exercise 12-10 (Group depreciation entries—open group)

Lundquist, Inc. uses the group depreciation method for its furniture account. The depreciation rate used for furniture is 21%. The balance in the Furniture

account on December 31, 1990, was $125,000, and the balance in
Accumulated Depreciation—Furniture was $61,000. The following purchases
and dispositions of furniture occurred in the years 1991-1993 (assume that
disposals occurred at the beginning of each year):

| | Assets Purchased— | Assets Sold | |
Year	Cost (Cash)	Cost	Selling Price (Cash)
1991	$35,000	$27,000	$8,000
1992	27,600	15,000	6,000
1993	24,500	32,000	8,000

(1) Prepare the summary journal entries Lundquist should make each year
(1991-1993) for the purchase, disposition, and depreciation of furniture.
(2) Prepare a summary of the furniture and accumulated depreciation accounts
for the years 1991-1993.

Exercise 12-11   (Depreciation of special components)

Towsey Manufacturing acquired a new milling machine on April 1, 1986. The
machine has a special component that requires replacement before the end of
the useful life. The asset was originally recorded in two accounts, one
representing the main unit and the other for the special component.
Depreciation is recorded by the straight-line method to the nearest month,
residual values being disregarded. On April 1, 1992, the special component is
scrapped and is replaced with a similar component. This component is expected
to have a residual value of approximately 25% of cost at the end of the useful
life of the main unit and because of its materiality, the residual value will be
considered in calculating depreciation. Specific asset information is as follows:

Main milling machine:	
Purchase price in 1986	$52,400
Residual value	$4,400
Estimated useful life	10 years
First special component:	
Purchase price	$10,000
Residual value	$250
Estimated useful life	6 years
Second special component:	
Purchase price	$15,250

What are the depreciation charges to be recognized for the years (1) 1986, (2)
1992, and (3) 1993?

Exercise 12-12   (Accounting for patents)

The Deep South Co. applied for and received numerous patents at a total cost
of $30,345 at the beginning of 1986. It is assumed the patents will be useful
evenly during their full legal life. At the beginning of 1988, the company paid
$7,875 in successfully prosecuting an attempted infringement of these patent
rights. At the beginning of 1991, $25,200 was paid to acquire patents that
could make its own patents worthless; the patents acquired have a remaining
life of 15 years but will not be used.

(1) Give the entries to record the expenditures relative to patents.

(2) Give the entries to record patent amortization for the years, 1986, 1988, and 1991.

Exercise 12-13   (Depletion and depreciation expense)

On July 1, 1991, Leadville Mining, a calender-year corporation, purchased the rights to a copper mine. Of the total purchase price, $4,500,000 was appropriately allocable to the copper. Estimated reserves were 600,000 tons of copper. Leadville expects to extract and sell 10,000 tons of copper per month. Production began immediately. The selling price is $20 per ton.

To aid production, Leadville also purchased some equipment on July 1, 1991. The equipment cost $750,000 and had an estimated useful life of 8 years. However, after all the copper is removed from this mine, the equipment will be of no use to Leadville and will be sold for an estimated $30,000.

If sales and production conform to expectations, what is Leadville's depletion expense on this mine and depreciation expense on the new equipment for financial accounting purposes for the calender year 1991?

Exercise 12-14   (Computation and recording of depletion expense)

Rich Strike Mining sought to increase reserves of a special mineral resource. During 1989, the company purchased a piece of property that was expected to retain some value after removal of the mineral resources was complete. Company records reveal the following:

In the year 1989:	
Purchase price for property	$4,450,000
Estimated supply of mineral resource	3,640,000 tons
Estimated property value after removal of mineral resource	$650,000
Total resource removal this year	0 tons
In the year 1990:	
Developmental costs	$750,000
Total resource removal this year	0 tons
In the year 1991:	
Total resource removal this year	700,000 tons
In the year 1992:	
Estimated total resources to be recovered in future years	
(based on new discoveries)	3,660,000 tons
Additional developmental costs	$1,195,800
Total resource removal this year	850,000 tons

Show computations and entries made to recognize depletion for (1) 1991, (2) 1992.

Exercise 12-15   (Change in estimated useful life)

Zierbel Corporation purchased a machine on January 1, 1986, for $225,000. At the date of acquisition, the machine had an estimated useful life of 15 years with no salvage value. The machine is being depreciated on a straight-line basis. On January 1, 1991, as a result of Zierbel's experience with the machine, it was decided that the machine had an estimated useful life of 10 years from the date of acquisition. What is the amount of depreciation expense on this machine in 1991 using a new annual depreciation charge for the remaining 5 years?

Exercise 12-16   (Change in estimated useful life)

Pierce Corporation purchased a machine on July 1, 1988, for $180,000. The machine was estimated to have a useful life of 10 years with an estimated salvage value of $10,000. During 1991 it became apparent that the machine would become uneconomical after December 31, 1995, and that the machine would have no scrap value. Pierce uses the straight-line method of depreciation for all machinery. What should be the charge for depreciation in 1991 under a new annual depreciation charge for the remaining life?   (AICPA adapted)

Exercise 12-17   (Recording the sale of equipment with note)

On December 31, 1991, Blodgett Corporation sold for $12,000 an old machine having an original cost of $50,000 and a book value of $6,000. The terms of the sale were as follows: $4,000 down payment, $3,000 payable on December 31 of the next two years. The agreement of sale made no mention of interest; however, 10% would be a fair rate for this type of transaction. Give the journal entries on Blodgett's books to record the sale of the machine and receipt of the two subsequent payments. (Round to the nearest dollar.)

Exercise 12-18   (Recording the sale of equipment)

Schuthess, Inc. puchased equipment costing $220,000 on June 30, 1990, having an estimated life of 5 years and a residual value of $40,000. The company uses the sum-of-the-years-digits method of depreciation and takes one-half year's depreciation on assets in the year of purchase. The asset was sold on December 31, 1992, for $75,000. Give the entry to record the sale of the equipment.

Exercise 12-19   (Exchange of machinery)

Assume that Coaltown Corporation has a machine that cost $52,000, has a book value of $35,000, and has a market value of $40,000. The machine is used in Coaltown's manufacturing process. For each of the following situations, indicate the value at which Coaltown should record the new asset and why it should be recorded at that value.

(a) Coaltown exchanged the machine for a truck with a list price of $43,000.
(b) Coaltown exchanged the machine with another manufacturing company for a similar machine with a list price of $41,000.
(c) Coaltown exchanged the machine for a newer model machine from another manufacturing company. The new machine had a list price of $60,000, and Coaltown paid cash of $15,000.
(d) Coaltown exchanged the machine plus $3,000 cash for a similar machine from Newton Inc., a manufacturing company. The newly acquired machine is carried on Newton's books at its cost of $55,000 with accumulated depreciation of $42,000; its fair market value is $43,000. In addition to determining the value, give the journal entries for both companies to record the exchange.

Exercise 12-20   (Exchange of truck)

On January 2, 1991, Bline Delivery Company traded with a dealer an old delivery truck for a newer model. Data relative to the old and new trucks follow:

Old truck:	
Original cost	$12,000
Accumulated depreciation as of January 2, 1991	$9,000
Average published market price	1,700
New truck:	
List price	$15,000
Cash price without trade-in	14,000
Cash paid with trade-in	12,700

(1) Give the journal entries on Bline's books to record the purchase of the new truck.

(2) Give the journal entries on Bline's books if the cash paid was $10,700.

(AICPA adapted)

Exercise 12-21   (Exchange of assets)

The Laughlin Equipment Company exchanged the following assets during 1991. Prepare the journal entries on Laughlin's books for each exchange.

(a) Exchanged with Loeb Equipment Company (dealer to dealer) a similar machine. Cost of machine exchanged, $25,000; book value of machine exchanged, $13,000; market value of machine exchanged, $16,000. No cash received.

(b) Same as in (a), except received $3,000 cash and machine with market value of $12,000.

(c) Purchased from Baker Manufacturing Company (dealer to nondealer) a new machine with a $50,000 list price. Paid $35,000 cash and a similar used machine; cost of machine exchanged, $40,000; book value of machine exchanged, $12,000; market value of machine exchanged, $10,000.

*Exercise 12-22   (Computation of fire loss and insurance proceeds)

Keener Inc. purchased a building for $600,000 on August 1, 1981. Depreciation was recorded at 3% a year. On October 31, 1991, 50% of the building was destroyed. On this date the building had a fair market value of $1,200,000. A policy for $700,000 was carried on the building, the policy containing an 80% coinsurance clause. What entries would be made to record (a) the loss from destruction of the building and (b) the amount due from the insurance company? (Round the loss percentage to two decimal places. Assume the company's fiscal period is the calendar year.)

*Relates to Appendix

*Exercise 12-23   (Coinsurance computations)

Huefner Corporation had a fire which destroyed its warehouse No. 12 to the extent that it will have to be torn down. The fair market value of the building was $150,000. The contents were valued at $50,000; however, $20,000 was salvaged in a fire-goods sale. The corporation had two insurance polices on the building; one with Springville Mutual for $100,000, and one with Far West, Inc. for $90,000. What amount will each company pay to Huefner assuming; (a) Both companies require 80% coinsurance? (b) Springville Mutual requires 90% coinsurance and Far West Inc. requires 100% coinsurance?

*Relates to Appendix

Problems   ▌▌▌ **Problem 12-1   (Time-factor methods of depreciation)**

A delivery truck was acquired by Navarro Inc. for $20,000 on January 1, 1990. The truck was estimated to have a 3-year life and a trade-in value at the end of that time of $5,000. The following depreciation methods are being considered:

(a) Depreciation is to be calculated by the straight-line method.
(b) Depreciation is to be calculated by the sum-of-the-years-digits method.
(c) Depreciation is to be calculated by the 150% declining-balance method.
(d) Depreciation is to be calculated using the modified accelerated cost recovery system for 5-year recovery property.

Instructions: Prepare tables reporting periodic depreciation and asset book value over a 3-year period for each assumption listed.

Problem 12-2   (Maintenance charges and depreciation of components)

A company buys a machine for $25,400 on January 1, 1989. The maintenance costs for the years 1989-1992 are as follows: 1989, $1,500; 1990, $1,200; 1991, $7,300 (includes $6,100 for cost of a new motor installed in December 1991); 1992, $2,100.

Instructions:

(1) Assume the machine is recorded in a single account at a cost of $25,400. No record is kept of the cost of the component parts. Straight-line depreciation is used and the asset is estimated to have a useful life of 8 years. It is assumed there will be no residual value at the end of the useful life. What are the total expenses related to the machine for each of the first 4 years?
(2) Assume the cost of the frame of the machine was recorded in one account at a cost of $19,600 and the motor was recorded in a second account at a cost of $5,800. Straight-line depreciation is used with a useful life of 10 years for the frame and 4 years for the motor. Neither item is assumed to have any residual value at the end of its useful life. What are the total expenses and losses related to the machine?
(3) Evaluate the two methods.

Problem 12-3   (Group depreciation and asset retirement)

The Wright Manufacturing Co. acquired 20 similar machines at the beginning of 1987 for $75,000. Machines have an average life of 5 years and no residual value. The group-depreciation method is employed in writing off the cost of the machines. Machines were retired as follows:

2 machines at the end of 1989	8 machines at the end of 1991
4 machines at the end of 1990	6 machines at the end of 1992

Assume the machines were not replaced.

Instructions: Give the entries to record the retirement of machines and the periodic depreciation for the years 1987-1992 inclusive.

Problem 12-4   (Composite depreciation)

Machines are acquired by Siegel Inc. on March 1, 1991, as follows:

	Cost	Estimated Residual Value	Estimated Life in Years
Machine 301	$46,000	$6,000	5
302	20,000	2,000	6
303	20,000	4,000	8
304	18,000	1,500	6
305	26,000	None	10

Instructions:

(1) Calculate the composite depreciation rate for this group.
(2) Calculate the composite or average life in years for the group.
(3) Give the entry to record the depreciation for the year ending December 31, 1991.

Problem 12-5   (Computation of asset cost and depreciation)

Geneva Corporation, a manufacturer of steel products, began operations on October 1, 1990. The accounting department of Geneva has started the plant asset and depreciation schedule presented on page 536. You have been asked to assist in completing this schedule. In additon to ascertaining that the data already on the schedule are correct, you have obtained from the company's records and personnel the information shown below and on page 536.

(a) Depreciation is computed from the first of the month of acquisition to the first of the month of disposition.
(b) Land A and Building A were acquired from a predecessor corporation. Geneva paid $812,500 for the land and building together. At the time of acquisition, the land had an appraised value of $72,000 and the building had an appraised value of $828,000.
(c) Land B was acquired on October 2, 1990, in exchange for 3,000 newly issued shares of Geneva's common stock. At the date of acquisition, the stock had a par value of $5 per share and a fair value of $25 per share. During October, 1990, Geneva paid $15,200 to demolish an existing building on this land so it could construct a new building.

Geneva Corporation
Plant Asset and Depreciation Schedule
For Years Ended September 30, 1991, and September 30, 1992

Assets	Acquisition Date	Cost	Salvage	Depreciation Method	Estimated Life in Years	Depreciation Expense Year Ended September 30, 1991	1992
Land A	October 1, 1990	$ (1)	N/A*	N/A	N/A	N/A	N/A
Building A	October 1, 1990	(2)	$47,500	Straight line	(3)	$20,000	(4)
Land B	October 2, 1990	(5)	N/A	N/A	N/A	N/A	N/A
Building B	Under Construction	210,000 to date	—	Straight line	30	—	(6)
Donated Equipment	October 2, 1990	(7)	2,000	Double-declining balance	10	(8)	(9)
Machinery A	October 2, 1990	(10)	5,500	Sum-of-the years-digits	10	(11)	(12)
Machinery B	October 1, 1991	(13)	—	Straight line	12	—	(14)

*N/A—Not Applicable

(d) Construction of Building B on the newly acquired land began on October 1, 1991. By September 30, 1992, Geneva had paid $210,000 of the estimated total construction costs of $300,000. Estimated completion and occupancy are July, 1993.

(e) Certain equipment was donated to the corporation by a local university. An independent appraisal of the equipment when donated placed the fair value at $23,000 and the residual value at $2,000.

(f) Machinery A's total cost of $110,000 includes installation expense of $550 and normal repairs and maintenance of $11,000. Salvage value is estimated at $5,500. Machinery A was sold on April 1, 1992.

(g) On October 1, 1991, Machinery B was acquired with a down payment of $4,000 and the remaining payments to be made in ten annual installments of $4,000 each beginning October 1, 1992. The prevailing interest rate was 10%.

Instructions: For each numbered item on the plant asset and depreciation schedule, determine the correct amount. (Round each answer to the nearest dollar.)

(AICPA adapted)

Problem 12-6　(Accounting for patents)

On January 10, 1984, the Wilkerson Company spent $54,000 to apply for and obtain a patent on a newly developed product. The patent had an estimated useful life of 10 years. At the beginning of 1988, the company spent $18,000 in successfully prosecuting an attempted infringement of the patent. At the beginning of 1989, the company purchased for $40,000 a patent that was expected to prolong the life of its original patent by 5 years. On July 1, 1992, a competitor obtained rights to a patent which made the company's patent obsolete.

Instructions: Give all the entries that would be made relative to the patent for the period 1984-1992, including entries to record the purchase of the patent, annual patent amortization, and ultimate patent obsolescence. (Assume the company's accounting period is the calender year.)

III Problem 12-7   (Financial statements for mining company)

The Findlay Corp. was organized on January 2, 1991. It was authorized to issue 74,000 shares of common stock, par $50. On the date of organization it sold 20,000 shares at par and gave the remaining shares in exchange for certain land bearing recoverable ore deposits estimated by geologists at 900,000 tons. The property is deemed to have a value of $2,700,000 with no residual value.

During 1991, purchases of mine buildings and equipment totaled $250,000. During the year 75,000 tons were mined; 8,000 tons of this amount were on hand unsold on December 31, the balance of the tonnage being sold for cash at $17 per ton. Expenses incurred and paid for during the year, exclusive of depletion and depreciation, were as follows:

Mining	$173,500
Delivery	20,000
General and administrative	19,500

Cash dividends of $2 per share were declared on December 31, payable January 15, 1992.

It is believed that buildings and sheds will be useful only over the life of the mine; hence depreciation is to be recognized in terms of mine output.

Instructions: Prepare an income statement and a balance sheet for 1991. Submit working papers showing the development of statement data. Ignore income taxes.

Problem 12-8   (Computation of depletion and depreciation)

The Delta Mining Company paid $2,700,000 in 1990 for property with a supply of natural resources estimated at 2,000,000 tons. The estimated cost of restoring the land for use after the resources are exhausted is $225,000. After the land is restored, it will have an estimated value of $325,000. Equipment was purchased at a cost of $825,000. Buildings, such as bunk houses and a mess hall, were constructed on the site for $175,000. The useful lives of the buildings and equipment are expected to terminate upon exhaustion of the natural resources. Operations were not begun until January 1, 1991. In 1991, resources removed totaled 500,000 tons. During 1992, an additional discovery was made indicating that available resources subsequent to 1992 will total 1,730,000 tons. 770,000 tons of resources were removed during 1992.

Instuctions: Compute the amount of depletion expense and depreciation expense for 1990, 1991, and 1992.

Problem 12-9   (Computation of depreciation and depletion)

The following independent situations describe facts concerning the ownership of various assets.

(a) The Dewey Company purchased a tooling machine in 1981 for $60,000. The machine was being depreciated on the straight-line method over an estimated useful of 20 years, with no salvage value. At the beginning of 1991, when the machine had been in use for 10 years, Dewey paid $12,000 to overhaul the machine. As a result of this improvement, Dewey estimated that the useful life of the machine would be extended an additional 5 years.

(b) Emerson Manufacturing Co., a calendar year company, purchased a machine for $65,000 on January 1, 1989. At the date of purchase, Emerson incurred the following additional costs:

Loss on sale of old machinery	$1,500
Freight in	500
Installation cost	2,000
Testing costs prior to regular operation	400

The estimated salvage value of the machine was $5,000 and Emerson estimated that the machine would have a useful life of 20 years, with depreciation being computed on the straight-line method. In January 1991, accessories costing $4,860 were added to the machine in order to reduce its operating costs. These accessories neither prolonged the machine's life nor did they provide any additional salvage value.

(c) On July 1, 1991, Lund Corporation purchased equipment at a cost of $34,000. The equipment has an estimated salvage value of $3,000 and is being depreciated over an estimated life of eight years under the double-declining-balance method of depreciation. For the six months ended December 31, 1991. Lund recorded one-half year's depreciation.

(d) The Aiken Company acquired a tract of land containing an extractable natural resource. Aiken is required by its purchase contract to restore the land to a condition suitable for recreational use after it has extracted the natural resource. Geological surveys estimate that the recoverable reserves will be 3,800,000 tons, and that the land will have a value of $500,000 after restoration. Relevant cost information follows:

Land	$9,000,000
Estimated restoration costs	$1,000,000
Tons mined and sold in 1991	700,000

(e) In January 1991, Marcus Corporation entered into a contract to acquire a new machine for its factory. The machine, which had a cash price of $200,000, was paid for as follows:

Down payment	$ 30,000
Notes payable in 10 equal monthly installments, including interest at 10%	150,000
500 shares of Marcus common stock with an agreed value of $50 per share	25,000
Total	$205,000

Prior to the machine's use, installation costs of $7,000 were incurred. The machine has an estimated useful life of 10 years and an estimated salvage value of $10,000. The straight-line method of depreciation is used.

Instructions: In each case, compute the amount of depreciation or depletion for 1991.   (AICPA adapted)

Problem 12-10 (Exchange of assets)

A review of the books of Lakeshore Electric Co. disclosed that there were five transactions involving gains and losses on the exchange of fixed assets. The transactions were recorded as indicated in the following ledger accounts.

Cash		
(2) 5,000	(5) 1,000	
(3) 6,000		

Buildings and Equipment		
(1) 10,000	(3) 118,000	
(2) 25,000	(4) 850,000	
(4) 550,000		

Accum. Depr.—Buildings and Equipment	
(3) 110,000	
(4) 390,000	

Intangible Assets	
(5) 1,000	

Gain on Exchange—Buildings and Equipment	
(1) 10,000	
(2) 30,000	
(4) 90,000	

Loss on Exchange—Buildings and Equipment	
(3) 2,000	

Investigation disclosed the following facts concerning these dealer-dealer transactions:

(1) Exchanged a piece of equipment with a $50,000 original cost, $20,000 book value, and $30,000 current market value for a piece of similar equipment owned by Highlite Electric that had a $60,000 original cost, $10,000 book value, and a $30,000 current market value.

(2) Exchanged a machine, cost $70,000, book value $10,000, current market value $40,000, for a similar machine, market value $35,000, and $5,000 in cash.

(3) Exchanged a building, cost $150,000, book value $40,000, current market value $30,000, for a building with market value of $24,000 plus cash of $6,000.

(4) Exchanged a factory building, cost $850,000, book value $460,000, current market value $550,000, for equipment owned by Romeo Inc. that had an original cost of $900,000, accumulated depreciation of $325,000, and current market value of $550,000.

(5) Exchanged a patent, cost $12,000, book value $6,000, current market value $3,000 and cash of $1,000 for another patent with market value of $4,000.

Instructions: Analyze each recorded transaction as to its compliance with generally accepted accounting principles. Prepare adjusting journal entries where required.

Problem 12-11 (Exchange of assets)

The Mutual Development Co. acquired the following assets in exchange for various nonmonetary assets.

1991

Mar. 15 Acquired from another company a computerized lathe in exchange for 3 old lathes. The old lathes had a total cost of $35,000 and had a remaining book value of $14,000. The new lathe had a market value of $22,000, approximately the same value as the three old lathes.

June 1 Acquired 200 acres of land by issuing 3,000 shares of common stock with par value of $10 and market value of $90. Market analysis reveals that the market value of the stock was a reasonable value for the land.

July 15 Acquired a used piece of heavy earth-moving equipment, market value $120,000, by exchanging a used molding machine with a market value of $20,000 (book value $8,000; cost $40,000) and land with a market value of $110,000 (cost $40,000). Cash of $10,000 was received by Mutual Development Co. as part of the transaction.

Aug. 15 Acquired a patent, franchise, and copyright for 2 used milling machines. The book value of each milling machine was $1,500 and each had originally cost $10,000. The market value of each machine is $12,500. It is estimated that the patent and franchise have about the same market values, and the market value of the copyright is 50% of the market value of the patent.

Nov. 1 Acquired from a dealer a new packaging machine for 4 old packaging machines. The old machines had a total cost of $50,000 and a total remaining book value of $20,000. The new packaging machine has an indicated market value of $30,000, approximately the same value as the four machines.

Instructions: Prepare the journal entries required on Mutual Development Co. books to record the exchanges.

Problem 12-12   (Balance sheet presentation of noncurrent operating assets)

The following account balances pertain to the Liberty Company:

Account Title	Dr.	Cr.
Equipment	675,000	
Goodwill	435,000	
Inventory	90,000	
Land	400,000	
Franchises	260,000	
Cash	65,000	
Accounts Receivable	137,000	
Buildings	1,400,000	
Patents	15,000	
Notes Receivable	456,000	
Accumulated Depreciation-Equipment		365,000
Accounts Payable		147,000
Notes Payable		1,500,000
Accumulated Depreciation-Buildings		385,000

Additional information:

(a) $600,000 of the notes payable are secured by a direct lien on the building.

(b) The company uses the sum-of-the-years-digits method of cost allocation for buildings and equipment and uses straight-line for patents, franchises, and goodwill.

(c) Inventory valuation was made using the retail method.

Instructions: Prepare the land, buildings, and equipment section and the intangible asset section of the balance sheet.

*Problem 12-13   (Computation of fire loss)

The Alfonso Corporation is a small manufacturing company producing a highly flammable cleaning fluid. On May 31, 1991, the company had a fire which completely destroyed the processing building and the in-process inventory; some of the equipment was saved.

The cost of the fixed assets destroyed and their related accumulated depeciation accounts at May 31, 1991, were as follows:

	Cost	Accumulated Depreciation
Buildings	$120,000	$74,000
Equipment	45,000	13,125

At present prices, the cost to reduce the destroyed property would be: building $240,000; equipment, $112,500. At the time of the fire, it was determined that the destroyed building was $62\frac{1}{2}\%$ depreciated, and the destroyed equipment was $33\frac{1}{3}\%$ depreciated.

After the fire a physical inventory was taken. The raw materials were valued at $60,000, the finished goods at $100,000 and supplies at $10,000.

The inventories on January 1, 1991 consisted of:

Finished goods	$140,000
Goods in process	100,000
Raw materials	30,000
Supplies	4,000
Total	$274,000

A review of the accounts showed that the sales and gross profit for the last five years were:

	Sales	Gross Profit
1986	$300,000	$ 86,200
1987	320,000	102,400
1988	330,000	108,900
1989	250,000	62,500
1990	280,000	84,000

The sales for the first five months of 1991 were $150,000. Raw materials purchases were $50,000. Freight on purchases was $5,000. Direct labor for five months was $40,000; for the past five years manufacturing overhead was 50% of direct labor.

Insurance on the property and inventory was carried with three companies. Each policy included an 80% coinsurance clause. The amount of insurance carried with the various companies was:

	Buildings and Equipment	Inventories
Sun Mutual Co.	$90,000	$76,000
Casualty Inc.	60,000	70,000
Fireman's Fund	45,000	70,000

The cost of cleaning up the debris was $21,000. The value of the scrap salvaged from the fire was $1,080.

Instructions:

(1) Compute the value of inventory lost.
(2) Compute the expected recovery from each insurance company.

(AICPA adapted)

*Relates to Appendix.

Problem 12-14   (Computation of depreciation and amortization)

Information pertaining to Hedlund Corporation's property, plant, and equipment for 1991 is presented below:

Account balances at January 1, 1991

	Debit	Credit
Land	$ 150,000	
Building	1,200,000	
Accumulated depreciation		$263,100
Machinery and equipment	900,000	
Accumulated depreciation		250,000
Automotive equipment	115,000	
Accumulated depreciation		84,600

	Depreciation Method	Useful Life
Building	150% declining balance	25 years
Machinery and equipment	Straight-line	10 years
Automotive equipment	Sum-of-the-years' digits	4 years
Leasehold improvements	Straight-line	

The salvage of the depreciable assets is immaterial. Depreciation is computed to the nearest month.

Transactions during 1991 and other information:

(a) On January 2, 1991, Hedlund purchased a new car for $10,000 cash and trade-in of a two-year-old car with a cost of $9,000 and a book value of $2,700. The new car has a cash price of $12,000; the market value of the trade-in is not known.

(b) On April 1, 1991 a machine purchased for $23,000 on April 1, 1986, was destroyed by fire. Hedlund recovered $15,500 from its insurance company.

(c) On May 1, 1991, costs of $168,000 were incurred to improve leased office premises. The leasehold improvements have a useful life of eight years. The related lease, which terminates on December 31, 1997 is renewable for an additional six-year term. The decision to renew will be made in 1997 based on office space needs at that time.

(d) On July 1, 1991, machinery and equipment were puchased at a total invoice cost of $280,000; additional costs of $5,000 for freight and $25,000 for installation were incurred.

(e) Hedlund determined that the automotive equipment comprising the $115,000 balance at January 1, 1991, would have been depreciated at a total amount of $18,000 for the year ended December 31, 1991.

Instructions:

(1) For each asset classification prepare schedules showing depreciation and amortization expense, and accumulated depreciation and amortization that would appear on Hedlund's income statement for the year ended December 31, 1991, and balance sheet at December 31, 1991.

(2) Prepare a schedule showing gain or loss from disposal of assets that would appear in Hedlund's income statement for the year ended December 31, 1991.

(3) Prepare the noncurrent operating assets section of Hedlund's December 31, 1991, balance sheet.   (AICPA adapted)

Problem 12-15   (Comprehensive depreciation and amortization)

At December 31, 1991, Martin Company's noncurrent operating asset and accumulated depreciation and amortization accounts had balances as follows:

Category	Cost of asset	Accumulated depreciation and amortization
Land	$ 130,000	
Buildings	1,200,000	$265,400
Machinery and equipment	775,000	196,200
Automobiles and trucks	132,000	86,200
Leasehold improvements	221,000	110,500

	Depreciation Method	Useful Life
Buildings	150% declining balance	25 years
Machinery and equipment	Straight-line	10 years
Automobiles and trucks	150% declining balance	5 years
Leashold improvements	Straight-line	
Land improvements	Straight-line	

All the autombiles and trucks were acquired after 1988. Depreciation is computed to the nearest month. The salvage values of the depreciable assets are immaterial.

Transactions during 1992 and other information:

(a) On January 6, 1992, a plant facility consisting of land and a building was acquired from Atlas Corp. for $600,000. 20% of this amount was allocated to land.

(b) On April 6, 1992, new parking lots, streets, and sidewalks at the acquired plant facility were completed at a total cost of $192,000. These expenditures had an estimated useful life of 12 years.

(c) The leasehold improvements were completed on December 31, 1988, and had an estimated useful life of eight years. The related lease, which would have terminated on December 31, 1994, was renewable for an additional four-year term. On April 29, 1992, Martin exercised the renewal option.

(d) On July 1, 1992, machinery and equipment were purchased at a total invoice cost of $250,000. Additional costs of $10,000 for delivery and $30,000 for installation were incurred.

(e) On August 30, 1992, Martin purchased a new automobile for $15,000.

(f) On September 30, 1992, a truck with a cost of $24,000 and a carrying amount of $8,100 on the date of sale was sold for $11,500. Depreciation for the 9 months ended September 30, 1992, was $2,650.

(g) On December 20, 1992, a machine with a cost of $17,000 and a carrying amount of $2,975 at date of dispostion was scrapped without cash recovery.

Instructions: For each category, prepare a schedule showing depreciation or amortization expense for the year ended December 31, 1992. Round computations to the nearest whole dollar.   (AICPA Adapted)

Chapter 13

Long-Term Investments in Equity Securities and Other Assets

Chapter Topics   **Accounting for Long-Term Investments in Stocks**

The Cost Method

The Equity Method

Accounting for Long-Term Investments in Funds

Reporting Long-Term Investments on the Balance Sheet

When individuals speak of investments, they generally are referring to such items as stocks and bonds, real estate, certificates of deposit, or other similar items that they have purchased. The investment is made with the intent of receiving the purchase price back (return *of* investment) plus an increase (return *on* investment) in the form of dividends, interest, or gains from appreciation upon sale or maturity of the investment.

Companies also make investments for similar reasons, i.e., to receive a return of the investment as well as to earn a return on the investment. In addition, a company may invest in the stock of another company as a means of diversifying its products or services or to exercise significant influence over that company. For example, if Company A buys most of its raw materials from Company B, Company A may seek to purchase a substantial amount of Company B's stock to insure a source for its raw materials at favorable prices. Another similar reason is to insure a distribution outlet for a company's finished product.

The investment in stock of another company represents an ownership interest in the net operating assets of that company. Sometimes an investment involves the acquisition of all the stock of a company, and therefore represents a 100% ownership interest in the assets and liabilities of the acquired company. For example, in 1988 Kohlberg Kravis Roberts & Co. purchased RJR Nabisco Inc. for over $25 billion in the largest takeover acquisition in U.S. history.

From the standpoint of the owner, investments are either temporary or long-term. As discussed in Chapter 7, investments are classified as temporary or current only where they are (1) readily marketable and (2) it is management's intent to use them in meeting current cash requirements. The general guideline is whether the investment is expected to be converted to cash within a year or the operating cycle, whichever is longer. Investments not meeting these tests are considered **long-term** or **noncurrent investments** and are usually reported on the balance sheet under a separate noncurrent heading, as illustrated in this chapter and in the balance sheet for General Mills, Inc., reproduced in Appendix A.

Long-term investments include a variety of assets. Among the most common are:

1. Equity securities, including both preferred and common stock.
2. Bonds, mortgages, and similar debt instruments.
3. Funds, e.g., for debt retirement, stock redemption, or other special purposes.
4. Miscellaneous items, such as real estate held for appreciation, advances to affiliates, equity in joint ventures and partnerships, and interests in life insurance contracts or in trusts and estates.

The primary emphasis in this chapter will be on accounting for long-term investments in equity securities. Accounting for funds also will be discussed briefly. In addition, the accounting treatment for the cash surrender value of life insurance is explained in an appendix to the chapter. Accounting for investments in bonds and long-term notes is considered in Chapter 15. Investments in stock rights, warrants, and options are covered in Chapter 16.

Long-Term Investments in Equity Securities

One of the characteristics of a free enterprise economy is the considerable level of intercorporate investment. As indicated previously, a corporation may acquire securities of another established corporation for a variety of reasons. Whatever the specific objective, an investment in the securities of another corporate entity is expected to enhance the economic well-being of the acquiring company. The accounting and reporting issues for long-term investments in equity securities (stocks) are discussed in the following sections:

1. Acquisition of stocks
2. Accounting for long-term investments in stocks—consolidation, cost method, and equity method
3. Disclosures for long-term investments in equity securities

Acquisition of Stocks

The acquisition of long-term investments in stocks follows the same general principles as those for temporary investments in stocks, as explained in Chapter 7.

Shares of stock are usually purchased for cash through stock exchanges (e.g., New York, American, or regional exchanges) and from individuals and institutional investors rather than from the corporations themselves. The investment is recorded at the amount paid, including brokers' commissions, taxes, and other fees incidental to the purchase price. Even when part of the purchase price is deferred, the full cost should be recorded as the investment in stock, with a liability account established for the amount yet to be paid. If stock is acquired in exchange for properties or services instead of cash, the fair market value of the consideration given or the value at which the stock is currently selling, whichever is more clearly determinable, should be used as the basis for recording the investment. If two or more securities are acquired for a lump-sum price, the cost should be allocated to each security in an equitable manner, as illustrated in earlier chapters.

Accounting for Long-Term Investments in Stocks

In accounting for long-term investments in stocks, one of three basic methods must be used: consolidation, cost, or equity. Which method is appropriate depends on the **control or degree of influence exercised by the acquiring company (investor) over the acquired company (investee).**

Choosing Among Consolidation, Cost, and Equity Methods

When one company acquires a majority voting interest in another company through the acquisition of **more than 50 percent** of its voting common stock, the acquiring company has **control** over the acquired company. The investor and investee are referred to respectively as the parent company and the subsidiary company. Where control exists, **the** consolidation method is required. This means that the financial statement balances of the parent and subsidiary companies are added together or consolidated for financial reporting purposes even though the companies continue to operate as separate entities. In the consolidation process, any intercompany transactions are eliminated, e.g., any sales and purchases between the parent and subsidiary companies. By eliminating all intercompany transactions, the combined balances or consolidated totals appropriately reflect the financial position and results of operation of the total economic unit. This treatment reflects the fact that majority ownership of common stock assures control by the parent over the decision-making processes of the subsidiary.

Previous accounting standards allowed separate reporting for certain majority-owned subsidiaries if those subsidiaries had "nonhomogeneous" operations, a large minority interest, or a foreign location. Separate reporting by subsidiaries occurred most often when the operations of the subsidiary and parent were significantly different (i.e., nonhomogeneous). Typically, the subsidiary was engaged in finance, insurance, leasing, or real estate, while the parent company was a manufacturer or merchandiser. Examples include General Motors Acceptance Corporation (GMAC) and IBM Credit Corporation, which are finance companies that are wholly owned by General Motors Corp. and IBM Corp., respectively. Traditionally, the financial statements of these subsidiaries were not consolidated with those of their respective parent companies.

With the issuance of Statement of Financial Accounting Standards No. 94, the FASB now requires the consolidation of all majority-owned subsidiaries unless control is temporary or does not rest with the majority owner (as, for instance, where the subsidiary is in legal reorganization or in bankruptcy).[1] Thus, even though a subsidiary has non-homogeneous oper-

---

[1]*Statement of Financial Accounting Standards No. 94,* "Consolidation of All Majority-Owned Subsidiaries," (Stamford: Financial Accounting Standards Board, 1987).

20% or more - Significant influence (equity method)

ations, a large minority interest, or a foreign location, it should be consolidated. The reporting entity is to be the total economic unit consisting of the parent and all its subsidiaries. Accounting for consolidated entities is covered in advanced accounting texts.[2]

Consolidated financial statements are appropriate only when the investor holds a majority voting interest (more than 50%) in the investee. When an investor owns **50 percent or less** of the investee company, the investor may or may not exercise significant influence over the financial and operating decisions of the other company. If conditions indicate that the aquiring company **does exercise significant influence,** the **equity method** of accounting should be used. This method closely parallels the accounting followed when actual control exists, which requires consolidated statements. The equity method is sometimes referred to as a "one-line consolidation."

When the aquiring company **does not exercise significant influence** over the investee, the **cost method** of accounting should be used. This method recognizes the separate identities of the companies.

Since preferred stock is generally nonvoting stock and does not provide for significant influence, the cost method is always used for investments in preferred stock.

The ability of the investor to exercise significant influence over such decisions as dividend distribution and operational and financial administration may be indicated in several ways: e.g., representation on the investee's board of directors, participation in policy-making processes, material intercompany transactions, interchange of managerial personnel, or technological dependency of investee on investor. Another important consideration is the **extent of ownership** by an investor in relation to the concentration of other stockholdings. While it is clear that ownership of over 50% of common stock assures control by the acquiring company, ownership of a lessor percentage may give effective control if the remaining shares of the stock are widely held, and no significant blocks of stockholders are consistently united in their ownership.

The Accounting Principles Board, in Opinion No. 18, recognized that the degree of influence and control will not always be clear and that judgment will be required in assessing the status of each investment. To achieve a reasonable degree of uniformity in the application of its position, the Board set 20% as an ownership standard; the ownership of **20% or more** of the voting stock of the company carries the presumption, in the absence of evidence to the contrary, that an investor has the ability to exercise significant influence over that company. Conversely, ownership of **less than 20%** leads to the presumption that the investor does not have the ability to exercise significant influence unless such ability can be demonstrated.[3]

[2]See, for example, Paul M. Fisher, William James Taylor, and J. Arthur Leer, *Advanced Accounting* (Cincinnati: South-Western Publishing Co., 1990).

[3]*Opinions of the Accounting Principles Board, No. 18,* "The Equity Method of Accounting for Investments in Common Stock" (New York: American Institute of Certified Public Accountants, 1971).

In May 1981, the FASB issued Interpretation No. 35 to emphasize that the 20% criterion is only a guideline and that judgment is required in determining the appropriate accounting method in cases where ownership is 50% or less. Interpretation No. 35 lists five illustrative examples of circumstances that might indicate that the investor does not have significant influence, regardless of the percentage of ownership[4]:

1. Opposition by the investee, such as litigation or complaints to governmental regulatory authorities.

2. An agreement between the investor and investee under which the investor surrenders significant rights as a shareholder.

3. Majority ownership of the investee is concentrated among a small group of shareholders who operate the investee without regard to the views of the investor.

4. The investor needs or wants more financial information to apply the equity method than is available to the investee's other shareholders (for example, the investor wants quarterly financial information from an investee who publicly reports only annually), tries to obtain the information, and fails.

5. The investor tries and fails to obtain representation on the investee's board of directors.

While the FASB examples may be helpful in some cases, evaluating the degree of investor influence is often a very subjective process. As a result, the percentage-of-ownership criterion set forth in APB Opinion No. 18 has been widely accepted as the basis for determining the appropriate method of accounting for long-term investments in equity securities when the investor does not possess absolute voting control. Thus, in the absence of persuasive evidence to the contrary, the **cost method** is used when ownership is **less than 20%**; the **equity method** is used when ownership is **20% to 50%**; the **consolidation method** is used when ownership is **over 50%**. These relationships dealing with the effect of ownership interest and control or influence and the proper accounting method to be used are summarized in Exhibit 13-1 on page 552.[5]

This chapter discusses and illustrates the accounting and reporting issues encountered with the cost and equity methods. The cost method is presented first, followed by the more complex equity method.

The Cost Method   When a long-term investment in another company's stock does not involve either a controlled interest or significant influence, the investment should be accounted for using the cost method. The procedures are

---

[4]*FASB Interpretation No. 35*, "Criteria for Applying the Equity Method of Accounting for Investments in Common Stock" (Stamford: Financial Accounting Standards Board, 1981), par. 4.

[5]It should be noted that the FASB has a project on its agenda to consider the reporting entity. This project will review accounting for consolidations and the equity method.

essentially the same as those described in Chapter 7 for temporary investments in stocks. The investment is initially recorded at cost including commissions and other related expenditures. Revenue is recognized when dividends are received from the investee. Declines in market value are recognized according to the lower-of-cost-or-market (LCM) valuation rule for all marketable equity securities on a portfolio or aggregate basis. Upon sale, the difference between the proceeds received and the cost of the investment is realized as a gain or loss and recorded under "other revenues" or "other expenses" in the income statement.

Exhibit 13–1   **Effect of Ownership Interest and Control or Influence on Accounting for Long-Term Investments in Common Stocks**

Ownership Interest	Control or Degree of Influence	Accounting Method
More than 50%	Control	Consolidated statements
20 to 50%	Significant influence	Equity method
Less than 20%	No significant influence	Cost method

Temporary Changes in Market Value of Noncurrent Marketable Equity Securities

While the above procedures are generally the same as those followed in accounting for temporary investments in equity securities, there is one major difference in the valuation of current versus noncurrent marketable equity securities. To review the valuation discussion in Chapter 7, current marketable equity securities are valued at LCM, and an allowance account is used to reduce the cost to market. If the market value recovers, the securities may be written back up, but not above original cost. Any change in the allowance account is recognized in the income statement in the period of change.

When marketable equity securities are classified as long-term investments because it is not management's intent to use the securities as a current source of cash, a somewhat different treatment is required by FASB Statement No. 12.[6] Temporary declines in value of noncurrent marketable equity securities are still reflected in an allowance account, which is deducted from the long-term investment account on the balance sheet. This is the same as for current marketable equity securities. However, the loss on writedown to LCM is treated differently. Stock prices can fluctuate greatly while the stock is being held, and if the investment is to be retained for a long period, the impact of gains or losses on net income from valua-

---

[6]*Statement of Financial Accounting Standards No. 12,* "Accounting for Certain Marketable Securities" (Stamford: Financial Accounting Standards Board, 1975), par. 9.

tion adjustments could be misleading. Therefore, adjustments for temporary changes in value of noncurrent marketable equity securities are not reflected in current income as are adjustments for current marketable equity securities. Instead a **contra stockholders' equity account** is created for changes in noncurrent securities. This account, which in FASB Statement No. 12 is entitled "Net Unrealized Loss on Noncurrent Marketable Equity Securities," is to be deducted from the total stockholders' equity reported in the balance sheet. Both the allowance account that reduces the investment to market and the contra stockholders' equity account should have the same balance at all times. As the market price of the noncurrent equity securities portfolio fluctuates, these accounts will be adjusted to bring the valuation to the lower of aggregate cost or market. When equity securities are sold, the transaction is recorded on the historical cost basis and a gain or loss recognized. Then at year end, an adjustment is made to the allowance and contra stockholders' equity accounts based on the remaining portfolio of investments. These procedures are illustrated in the following example.

A company carries a noncurrent marketable equity securities portfolio that has a cost of $125,000. At December 31, 1990, the market value of the securities held has fallen to $110,000. The decline is judged to be temporary. The following entries would be required to reduce the securities valuation from cost to market.

Net Unrealized Loss on Noncurrent Marketable Equity Securities . .	15,000	
Allowance for Decline in Value of Noncurrent Marketable Equity Securities		15,000

The applicable disclosures on the balance sheet might be shown as follows:

Investments:		
Noncurrent investments in marketable equity securities (cost)	$125,000	
Less allowance for decline in value of noncurrent marketable equity securities	(15,000)	110,000
Total assets		$xxx,xxx
Stockholders' Equity:		
Total capital stock and retained earnings	$xxx,xxx	
Less net unrealized loss on noncurrent marketable equity securities	(15,000)	
Total stockholders' equity and liabilities		$xxx,xxx

If during 1991 one of the securities costing $25,000 was sold for $30,000, the transaction would be recorded based on the original cost as follows:

Cash	30,000	
Investment in XYZ Stock (original cost)		25,000
Gain on Sale of Investment		5,000

Assume further that during 1991, two other marketable equity securities were purchased as long-term investments at a total cost of $35,000. Assume the aggregate market value of the portfolio at the end of 1991 is $132,000. Therefore, the amount in the allowance account and in the contra equity account would need to be adjusted to $3,000 ($125,000 beginning cost − $25,000 cost of security sold + $35,000 purchases = $135,000 ending cost − $132,000 end-of-year aggregate market value). The entry would be:

Allowance for Decline in Value of Noncurrent Marketable Equity Securities	12,000	
Net Unrealized Loss on Noncurrent Marketable Equity Securities		12,000

The long-term investments would be shown on the balance sheet at the lower of cost or market value, $132,000 (cost of $135,000 less allowance of $3,000), and the stockholders' equity contra account would reduce total stockholders' equity by the $3,000. Note that the $5,000 gain on the actual sale would be reported as additional income for 1991. Also note that the Allowance for Decline and Net Unrealized Loss accounts can be adjusted upward, but only to a zero balance. If market is equal to or exceeds cost, no adjustment is made due to the practice of conservatism in accounting.

Permanent Declines in Market Value

Sometimes the market price of stock declines due to economic circumstances that are unlikely to improve. For example, low oil prices have caused the stocks of some oil companies to decrease significantly without much expectation that they will ever recover. If a decline in the market value of an individual security in a noncurrent investment portfolio is judged to be permanent, the cost basis of that security should be reduced by crediting the investment account rather than an allowance account. In addition, the write-down should be recognized as a loss and charged against current income.[7] The new cost basis for the security may not be adjusted upward to its original cost for any subsequent increases in market value.

To illustrate the accounting for a permanent decline, assume that the portfolio of a company at the end of its first year of operations contains the following noncurrent marketable equity securities:

	Cost	Market
Company A	$ 50,000	$ 40,000
Company B	30,000	35,000
Company C	100,000	60,000
Total	$180,000	$135,000

[7]*Ibid.*, par. 21.

On an aggregate basis, the allowance adjustment would be for the difference between cost and market, or $45,000. However, if evaluation of market conditions for the securities of Company C indicates that the decline in value is permanent, the security should be written down to market, which becomes the new cost basis, and a reevaluation made of the balance of the portfolio to determine the need for an allowance. The write-down entry would be as follows:

Recognized Loss from Permanent Decline in Market Value of
  Noncurrent Marketable Equity Securities 40,000
     Long-Term Investments in Marketable Equity Securities   40,000

The recognized loss account would be closed to Income Summary at the end of the year, reducing net income by $40,000. The portfolio of long-term securities would now appear as follows:

	Cost	Market
Company A	$ 50,000	$ 40,000
Company B	30,000	35,000
Company C	60,000	60,000
Total	$140,000	$135,000

At this point, an adjustment would be required to the Allowance for Decline and Net Unrealized Loss accounts to bring them to a $5,000 balance, which is the remaining difference between total cost and market values.

Change in Classification Between Current and Noncurrent

As noted in Chapter 7, if there is a change in the classification of a marketable equity security between current and noncurrent assets, the transfer should be made at the lower of cost or market value of the security at the date of the reclassification. This amount becomes the new cost basis with any loss being recorded in the current period as was done for permanent declines in value.

Summary of Marketable Equity Securities Valuation

The valuation of marketable equity securities as discussed on the preceding pages is summarized in the flowchart in Exhibit 13–2. By studying the flowchart carefully in conjunction with the discussion and examples, the decision points and accounting treatment can be more clearly understood.

The Financial Accounting Standards Board, in Statement No. 12, places a high premium on the classification of marketable equity securities. Because the classification is determined on the basis of subjective criteria, e.g., the intent of management to hold or sell, there is concern that the classification can be used to manipulate reported net income. In the authors' opinion, the adoption of a consistent valuation approach for all in-

Exhibit 13–2   Flowchart of Valuation for Marketable Equity Securities as Prescribed by FASB Statement No. 12

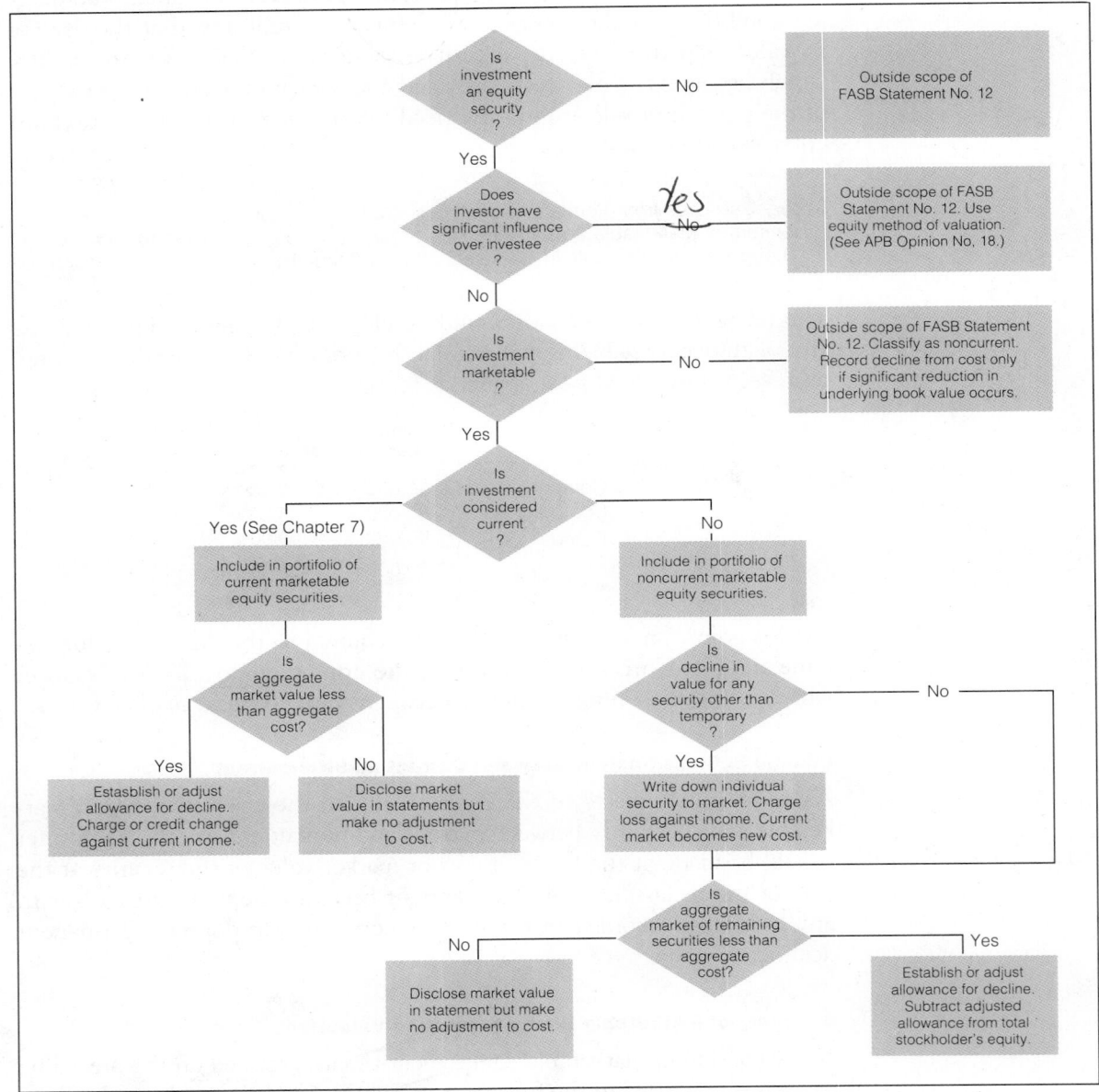

vestments, regardless of their classification, seems preferable to the differentiated treatment for current and noncurrent securities outlined in Statement No. 12.

The Equity Method   The equity method of accounting for long-term investments in common stock reflects the economic substance of the relationship between the investor and investee rather than the legal distinction of the separate entities. The objective of this method is to reflect the underlying claim by the investor on the net assets of the investee company.

Under the equity method, just as under the cost method, the investment is initially recorded at cost. However, with the equity method, the investment account is periodically adjusted to reflect changes in the underlying net assets of the investee. The investment balance is increased to reflect a proportionate share of the earnings of the investee company, or decreased to reflect a share of any losses reported. If preferred stock dividends have been declared by the investee, they must be deducted from income reported by the investee before computing the investor's share of investee earnings or losses. When dividends are received by the investor, the investment account is reduced. Thus, the equity method recognizes that investee earnings increase the investee net assets that underlie the investment; similarly, investee losses and dividends paid out reduce the investee net assets and hence the equity in the investment.

Cost and Equity Methods Compared

To contrast and illustrate the accounting entries under the cost and equity methods, assume that Powell Corporation purchases 5,000 shares of San Juan Company common stock on January 2 at $20 per share, including commissions and other costs. San Juan has a total of 25,000 shares outstanding, thus the 5,000 shares represent a 20% ownership interest. As discussed earlier in the chapter, the equity method is used when ownership is 20% to 50% unless there is persuasive evidence that the investor does not have significant influence over the investee. The appropriate entries under both the cost and equity methods are shown in Exhibit 13–3. The actual method used would depend on the degree of influence exercised by the investor as indicated by a consideration of all relevant factors, as well as the percentage owned. Exhibit 13–3 highlights the basic differences in accounting for long-term investments under the cost and equity methods. Under both methods, the investment is originally recorded at cost. Dividends received are recognized as dividend revenue under the cost method and as a reduction in the investment account under the equity method. The earnings of the investee company are recorded as an increase to the investment account under the equity method, while no entry is required for this event under the cost method. Under the cost method, an adjustment to lower of cost or market may be required, while no entry is needed under the equity method, since the investment value has already been adjusted to reflect the underlying value of the net assets of the investee. The carrying value under the cost method is cost less any applicable allowance for decline in value; under the equity method, the carrying value is original cost plus any increases from the proportionate share of investee earnings less any dividends received.

Complexities Under the Equity Method

When a company is purchased by another company, the purchase price

KNOW!.!

Exhibit 13-3   Comparison of Cost and Equity Methods

COST METHOD			EQUITY METHOD		

Jan. 2   Purchased 5,000 shares of San Juan Company common stock at $20 per share.

Investment in San Juan Company Stock.........	100,000		Investment in San Juan Company Stock	100,000	
Cash		100,000	Cash................		100,000

Oct. 31   Received dividend of $.80 per share from San Juan Company ($.80 × 5,000 shares).

Cash	4,000		Cash.....................	4,000	
Dividend Revenue		4,000	Investment in San Juan Company Stock		4,000

Dec. 31   San Juan Company announces earnings for the year of $60,000.

			Investment in San Juan Company Stock	12,000	
No Entry			Income from Investment in San Juan Company Stock		12,000
			(.20 × $60,000)		

Dec. 31   Market value of San Juan Company common stock is $18.50 per share.

Net Unrealized Loss on Noncurrent Marketable Equity Securities	7,500		No Entry	
Allowance for Decline in Value of Noncurrent Marketable Equity Securities		7,500		
[($20 − $18.50) × 5,000 shares]				

Carrying value (book value) of investment at year-end:

Cost	$100,000	Cost		$100,000
Less allowance for decline in value	7,500	Dividend revenue		(4,000)
	$ 92,500	Share of investee earnings		12,000
				$108,000

usually differs from the recorded book value of the underlying net assets of the acquired company. For example, assume Snowbird Company purchased 100% of the common stock of Ski Resorts International for $8 million, although the book value of Ski Resorts' net assets is only $6.5 million. In effect, Snowbird is purchasing some undervalued assets, above-normal earnings potential, or both.

As explained in Chapter 11, during the consolidation process, if the purchase price exceeds the recorded value, the acquiring company must allocate this purchase price among the assets acquired using their current market values as opposed to the amounts carried on the books of the acquired company. If part of the purchase price cannot be allocated to specific assets, that amount is recorded as goodwill. If the purchase price is less than recorded net asset value, the assets acquired must be recorded at an amount less than their carrying value on the books of the acquired company. Whether assets are increased or decreased as a result of the purchase, future income determination will use the new (adjusted) values to determine the depreciation and amortization charges.

When only a portion of a company's stock is purchased and the equity method is used to reflect the income of the partially owned company, an adjustment to the investee's reported income, similar to that just described, may be required. In order to determine whether such an adjustment is necessary, the acquiring company must compare the purchase price of the common stock with the recorded net asset value of the acquired company at the date of purchase. If the purchase price exceeds the investor's share of book value, the computed excess must be analyzed in the same way as described above for a 100% purchase. Although no entries to adjust asset values are made on the books of either company, an adjustment to the investee's reported income is required under the equity method for the investor to reflect the economic reality of paying more for the investment than the underlying net book value. If depreciable assets had been adjusted to higher market values on the books of the investee to reflect the price paid by the investor, additional depreciation would have been taken by the investee company. Similarly, if the purchase price reflected goodwill, additional amortization would have been required. These adjustments would have reduced the reported income of the investee. To reflect this condition, an adjustment is made by the investor to the income reported by the investee in applying the equity method. This adjustment serves to meet the objective of computing the income reported using the equity method in the same manner as would be done if the company were 100% purchased and consolidated financial statements were prepared.

To illustrate, assume that the book value of common stockholders' equity (net assets) of Stewart Inc. was $500,000 at the time Phillips Manufacturing Co. purchased 40% of its common shares for $250,000. Based on a 40% ownership interest, the market value of the net assets of Stewart Inc. would be $625,000 ($250,000 ÷ .40), or $125,000 more than the book value. Assume that a review of the asset values discloses that the market value of depreciable properties exceeds the carrying value of these assets by $50,000. The remaining $75,000 difference ($125,000 − $50,000) is attributed to goodwill. Assume further that the average remaining life of the depreciable assets is 10 years and that goodwill is amortized over 40 years. Phillips Manufacturing Co. would adjust its share of the annual income reported by Stewart Inc. to reflect the additional depreciation and the amortization of goodwill as follows:

Additional depreciation ($50,000 × 40%) ÷ 10 years = $2,000
Goodwill amortization   ($75,000 × 40%) ÷ 40 years =   750
                                                     $2,750

Each year for the first 10 years, Phillips would make the following entry in addition to entries made to recognize its share of Stewart Inc.'s income and dividends:

Income from Investment in Stewart Inc. Stock....................	2,750	
Investment in Stewart Inc. Stock		2,750
To adjust share of income on Stewart Inc. common stock for proportionate depreciation on excess market value of depreciable property, $2,000, and for amortization of goodwill from acquisition of the stock, $750.		

After the tenth year, the adjustment would be for $750 until the goodwill amount is fully amortized.

To illustrate, assume that the purchase was made January 2, 1991; Stewart Inc. declared and paid dividends of $70,000 to common stockholders during 1991, and Stewart Inc. reported net income of $150,000 for the year ended December 31, 1991. At the end of 1991, the investment in Stewart Inc. common stock would be reported on the balance sheet of Phillips Manufacturing Co. at $279,250, computed as shown below.

This illustration assumes that the fiscal years of the two companies coincide and that the purchase of the stock is made at the first of the year. If a purchase is made at a time other than the beginning of the year, the income earned up to the date of the purchase is assumed to be included in the cost of purchase. Only income earned by the investee subsequent to acquisition should be recognized by the investor.

Investment in Stewart Inc. Common Stock

Acquisition cost		$250,000
Add: Share of 1991 earnings of investee company ($150,000 × .40)		60,000 $310,000
Less: Dividends received from investee ($70,000 × .40)	$ 28,000	
Additional depreciation of undervalued assets	2,000	
Amortization of unrecorded Goodwill	750	30,750
Year-end carrying value of investment (equity in investee company)		$279,250

The adjustment for additional depreciation and goodwill amortization is needed only when the purchase price is greater than the underlying book value at the date of acquisition. If the purchase price is less than the underlying book value at the time of acquisition, it is assumed that specific assets of the investee are overvalued or that there is negative goodwill as discussed in Chapter 11, and an adjustment is necessary to reduce the depreciation or amortization included in the reported income of the investee. The journal entry to reflect this adjustment is the reverse of the one illustrated previously. The computations would also be similar except that the adjustments for overvalued assets would be added to (instead of subtracted from) the carrying value of the investment.

As noted earlier in the chapter, during the consolidation process, adjustments must be made to eliminate any intercompany sales, costs, and profits. Under the equity method, if the investor and investee are engaged in intercompany revenue-producing activities, similar adjustments must be made to the investment account by the investor to eliminate the effects of intercompany transactions. A more complete description of these intercompany problems is found in advanced accounting texts.

Changes Between Cost and Equity Methods

Variations in percentage of ownership caused by additional purchases or sales of stock by the investor or by the additional sale or retirement of stock by the investee may require a change in accounting method. For example, if the equity method has been used but subsequent events reduce the investment ownership below 20%, a change should be made to the cost method effective for the year when the reduced ownership occurs. Similarly, if the cost method has been used but subsequent acquisitions increase the investment ownership to 20% or more, a change should be made to the equity method. The required accounting is different depending on whether the change is from the equity method to the cost method or vice versa.

Change from Equity to Cost Method

If an investment in equity securities has been accounted for under the equity method, but circumstances dictate a change to the cost method, no adjustment to the investment account is needed. At the time of change, the carrying amount of the investment, as determined by the equity method for prior years, becomes the new basis for applying the cost method. From that time forward, the investment account would not be adjusted for a proportionate share of investee earnings, nor would any adjustments be made for additional depreciation or amortization of undervalued or unrecorded assets, and dividends received would be credited to a revenue account, not the investment account. Thus, once the equity method is no longer appropriate, the cost method is applied just as in any other situation where the cost method is used.

Change from Cost to Equity Method

Accounting for a change from the cost method to the equity method is more complex. A **retroactive adjustment** is required for prior years to reflect the income that would have been reported using the equity method. This adjustment modifies the carrying value of the investment, in effect restating it on an equity basis, as if the equity method has been used during the previous periods that the investment was held. The offsetting entry for the adjustment is to Retained Earnings. From the date of change forward, the equity method is applied normally.

To illustrate, assume that MTI Corporation acquired stock of Excellcior Inc. over the three-year period 1989-1991. Purchase, dividend, and income information for these years are as follows (the purchases were made on the first day of each year):

| | Percentage Ownership Acquired | Purchase Price* | Excellcior Inc. | |
			Dividends Paid Dec. 31	Income Earned
Year				
1989	10%	$ 50,000	$100,000	$200,000
1990	5	30,000	120,000	300,000
1991	15	117,000	180,000	400,000

*Purchase price equal to underlying book value at date of purchase.

The following entries would be made on the books of MTI Corporation to reflect the cost method for the years 1989 and 1990.

1989
Jan. 1   Investment in Excellcior Inc. Stock   50,000
         Cash   50,000
           To record purchase of 10% interest.

Dec. 31 Cash   10,000
         Dividend Revenue   10,000
           To record receipt of dividends from Excellcior
           Inc. (10% × $100,000).

1990
Jan. 1   Investment in Excellcior Inc. Stock   30,000
         Cash   30,000
           To record purchase of 5% interest. (Total
           ownership interest is now 15%.)

Dec. 31 Cash   18,000
         Dividend Revenue   18,000
           To record receipt of dividends from Excellcior
           Inc. (15% × $120,000).

The additional acquisition of stock at the beginning of 1991 increases ownership to 30%, and a retroactive adjustment to change to the equity method must be made at the time of acquisition. The adjustment is for the difference between the revenue reported using the cost method and that which would have been reported if the equity method had been used. The adjustment would be computed as follows:

Year	Percentage Ownership	Revenue Recognized- Cost Method	Revenue Recognized- Equity Method	Required Retroactive Adjustment
1989	10%	$10,000	$20,000[1]	$10,000
1990	15%	18,000	45,000[2]	27,000
			Total Adjustment	$37,000

[1]$200,000 × 10%
[2]$300,000 × 15%

The following entries would be made on the books of MTI Corporation to reflect the equity method for 1991:

1991
Jan. 1   Investment in Excellcior Inc. Stock   117,000
         Cash   117,000
           To record purchase of 15% interest. (Total
           ownership interest is now 30%.)

Jan. 1   Investment in Excellcior Inc. Stock   37,000
         Retained Earnings   37,000
           To retroactively reflect revenue for 1989 and 1990
           for investment in Excellcior Inc. as if the equity
           method had been used.

Dec. 31	Investment in Excellcior Inc. Stock	120,000	
	Income from Investment in Excellcior Inc. Stock		120,000
	To record 30% of income earned by Excellcior Inc. using equity method.		
Dec. 31	Cash	54,000	
	Investment in Excellcior Inc. Stock..............		54,000
	To record receipt of dividend from Excellcior Inc. using equity method (30% × $180,000).		

Note that in the above example the retroactive adjustment restates the investment account to an equity basis. From that point on, the equity method is applied in a normal manner. For simplicity, the illustration assumed a purchase price equal to the underlying book value at date of purchase. If this were not the case, an adjustment to income for depreciation and amortization would be needed as discussed in an earlier section.

Required Disclosures for Long-Term Investments in Stock

Since the financial position and operating results of the investor can be significantly affected by the method used in accounting for and reporting long-term investments in stocks, it is important that proper disclosures be made. These disclosures may be included parenthetically in the financial statements or more commonly in a note to the financial statements.

FASB Statement No. 12 sets forth disclosure requirements for equity securities accounted for under the cost method and valued at lower of cost or market. These disclosure requirements were discussed and illustrated in Chapter 7.

Because the equity method is generally more complex than the cost method, the disclosures associated with the equity method are usually more detailed. APB Opinion No. 18 provides some recommendations for disclosures applicable to the equity method, including: names of investees and the related percentages of ownership interest, and the difference, if any, between the carrying value of the investment and the underlying equity in net assets of the investee.[8] In addition, if an investor has more than 20% ownership but chooses not to use the equity method, the reasons for the decision should be disclosed. Similarly, if the equity method is used in cases where there is less than 20% ownership, those reasons also should be disclosed.

An example of the type of disclosure often provided by companies relative to their long-term investments in equity securities is presented in Exhibit 13-3. This example is taken from the notes to the 1987 financial statements of the Norton Company. Another example is provided in note one of the General Mills Annual Report in Appendix A of the text.

Accounting for Long-Term Investments in Stocks Summarized

In summary, the main guidelines for accounting for long-term stock investments are as follows:

---

[8]*Opinions of the Accounting Principles Board, No. 18,* "The Equity Method of Accounting for Investments in Common Stock" (New York: American Institute of Certified Public Accountants, 1971), par. 20.

Exhibit 13–3   The Norton Company

1. Significant Accounting Policies

Principles of Consolidation

The consolidated financial statements of Norton Company include the accounts of all subsidiaries of which the Company owns in excess of 50% of the common stock. Intercompany transactions have been eliminated in consolidation. Investments of 20% to 50% in the common stock of companies and corporate joint ventures are accounted for using the equity method, while investments of less than 20% are accounted for using the cost method.

1. Investments in stock are always initially recorded at cost, which includes commissions and similar expenditures.

2. Revenue is recognized through (a) consolidation when the investor controls the investee or (b) by the cost or equity method, depending on the degree of influence from ownership.

3. If the cost method is used in accounting for long-term marketable equity securities, such securities are valued at the lower of cost or aggregate market, with any write-down reported as a reduction to stockholders' equity rather than charged to income, as is the case for short-term marketable equity securities.

4. If the equity method is used, no valuation adjustment to lower of cost or market is needed, since the investment account is increased to reflect a proportionate share of investee income and decreased to reflect investee losses and dividends received from the investee.

5. As with any asset, significant permanent declines in the value of long-term investments are recognized as a loss in the year they occur.

6. When long-term investments are eventually sold, the difference between the carrying value of the investment and the proceeds from the sale is recognized as a realized gain or loss.

Long-Term Investments in Funds

Cash and other assets set apart for certain designated purposes are called funds. Some funds are to be used for specific current obligations, and are appropriately reported as current assets. Examples of these are petty cash funds, payroll funds, interest funds, dividend funds, and withholding, social security, and other tax funds. Other funds are accumulated over a long term for such purposes as the acquisition or replacement of properties, retirement of long-term debt, the redemption of capital stock, operation of a pension plan, or possible future contingencies. These funds are properly considered noncurrent and are reported under the long-term investment heading.

Establishment and Accumulation of Funds

A fund may be established through the voluntary action of management, or it may be established as a result of contractual requirements. The fund may be used for a single purpose, such as the redemption of preferred stock, or it may be used for several related purposes, such as the periodic payment of interest on bonds, the retirement of bonds at various intervals, and the ultimate retirement of the remaining bond indebtedness.

When a fund is voluntarily created by management, control of the fund and its disposition are arbitrary matters depending on the wishes of management. When a fund is created through some legal requirement, it must be administered and applied in accordance therewith. Such a fund may be administered by one or more independent trustees under an agreement known as a trust indenture. If the trustee assumes responsibility for fulfillment of the requirement, as may be true for a bond retirement or pension program, neither the fund nor the related liability is carried on the company's books. However, if the indenture does not free the company from further obligation, the fund must be accounted for as if there were no trustee.

When a corporation is required by agreement to establish a fund for a certain purpose, such as the retirement of bonds or the redemption of stock, the agreement generally provides that fund deposits (1) shall be fixed amounts, (2) shall vary according to gross revenue, net income, or units of product sold, or (3) shall be equal periodic sums that, together with earnings, will produce a certain amount at some future date. The latter arrangement is based on compound-interest factors, and, as noted in Chapter 6, compound interest or annuity tables may be used to determine the equal periodic deposits. For example, in order to accumulate a fund of $100,000 by a series of 5 equal annual deposits at 8% compounded annually, a periodic deposit of $17,045.65 is required.[9]

A schedule can be developed to show the planned fund accumulation through deposits and earnings. Such a schedule is illustrated below:

Fund Accumulation Schedule

Year	Earnings on Fund Balance for Year	Amount Deposited in Fund	Total Increase in Fund for Year	Accumulated Fund Total
1		$17,045.65	$17,045.65	$ 17,045.65
2	$1,363.65	17,045.65	18,409.30	35,454.95
3	2,836.40	17,045.65	19,882.05	55,337.00
4	4,426.96	17,045.65	21,472.61	76,809.61
5	6,144.74	17,045.65	23,190.39	100,000.00

Assuming deposits at the end of each year, the table shows a fund balance at the end of the first year of $17,045.65 resulting from the first deposit. At the end of the second year, the fund is increased by (1) earnings at 8% on the investment in the fund during the year,

[9]This amount can be determined from Table III in Chapter 6. The rent or annual payment for an annuity of $100,000 at 8% for 5 periods is computed as follows:

$$R = \frac{FV_n}{FVAF_n} = \frac{FV_n}{\text{Table III } \overline{5}|_{8\%}} = \frac{\$100,000}{5.8666} = \$17,045.65$$

$1,363.65, and (2) the second deposit to the fund, $17,045.65. The total in the fund at this time is $35,454.95. Fund earnings in the following year are based on a total investment of $35,454.95 as of the beginning of the year.

The schedule is developed on the assumption of annual earnings of 8%. However, various factors, such as fluctuations in the earnings rate and gains and losses on investments, may provide earnings that differ from the assumed amounts. If the fund is to be maintained in accordance with the accumulation schedule, deposits must be adjusted for earnings that differ from estimated amounts. Smaller deposits, then, can be made in periods when earnings exceed the assumed rate; larger deposits are necessary when earnings fail to meet the assumed rate.

Accounting for Funds   A fund is usually composed of cash and securities, but could include other assets. The accounting for stock held in a fund is the same as that described earlier in this chapter except the securities are reported as part of the fund balance. The accounting for investments in bonds will be discussed in Chapter 15.

To illustrate the accounting for a fund, assume that a preferred stock redemption fund is established with annual payments to the fund of $20,000. The fund administrator invests 90% of its assets in stock and places the remainder in bank certificates of deposit paying 8% interest. Journal entries for the first year's transactions are as follows:

Stock Redemption Fund Cash	20,000	
Cash		20,000
Annual fund contribution.		
Stock Redemption Fund Securities	18,000	
Stock Redemption Fund Cash		18,000
Investment of fund cash in securities.		
Stock Redemption Fund Certificates of Deposit	2,000	
Stock Redemption Fund Cash		2,000
Investment of fund cash in certificates of deposit.		
Stock Redemption Fund Cash	1,400	
Stock Redemption Fund Revenue		1,400
Dividends on fund securities.		
Stock Redemption Fund Cash	160	
Stock Redemption Fund Revenue		160
Interest on certificates of deposit.		
Stock Redemption Fund Expenses	200	
Stock Redemption Fund Cash		200
Expenses to operate fund.		

At the end of the year, the stock redemption fund assets are as follows:

Stock redemption fund cash ($1,400 + $160 − $200)	$ 1,360
Stock redemption fund certificates of deposit	2,000
Stock redemption fund securities	18,000
Total	$21,360

This total amount would be reported under the "investments" heading on the balance sheet.

Stock redemption fund revenue for the year is $1,560 and stock redemption fund expense is $200, resulting in a net income from the fund operation of $1,360. This amount is reported on the income statement as other revenue. When stock is redeemed, the payment is made from Stock Redemption Fund Cash after the securities are converted to cash.

Other Long-Term Investments

In addition to securities and funds, a company may have other long-term investments. Real estate held as an investment; advances to subsidiaries that are of a long-term nature; deposits made to guarantee contract performance; cash surrender values from life insurance policies; and equity interests in partnerships, trusts, and estates are all examples. Most of these assets either produce current revenues or have a favorable effect on the investor's business in some other way. Cost is generally the underlying basis for these miscellaneous investments, and a gain or loss is recognized upon sale equal to the difference between the sales proceeds and the carrying amount of the investment. When available, market or appraised values may be reported parenthetically.

Reporting Long-Term Investments on the Balance Sheet

Long-term investments are generally reported on the balance sheet immediately following the current assets classification. The investment section should include only noncurrent investments, with appropriate headings for different long-term investment categories. Cost data should be supplemented by market quotations in parenthetical or note form if market exceeds cost. Information concerning the pledge of long-term investments as collateral on loans or other relevant information should also be provided.

In reporting funds to be applied to specific purposes or paid to specific parties, disclosure should be made by special note of the conditions relative to their establishment and ultimate application. A fund arrearage or other failure to meet contractual requirements should be pointed out; deposit requirements in the succeeding fiscal period should also be disclosed when material. Offset of a fund balance against a liability item is proper only when an asset transfer to a trustee is irrevocable and actually serves to discharge the obligation.

The "Investments" section of a balance sheet is shown on page 568. In practice, some of the detail is often omitted or reported in the notes to the statements.

Investments:
  Affiliated companies:
    Investment in Salt River Co. common stock, reported
      by the equity method (investment consists of
      90,000 shares representing a 40% interest
      acquired on July 1, 1989, for $1,500,000) $1,548,000
    Advances to Salt River Co. 115,000 $1,663,000
  Miscellaneous stock investments at cost (stock has an
    aggregate quoted market value of $112,000)   100,000
  Stock redemption fund, composed of:
    Cash .... $ 15,000
    Stocks and bonds, at cost (aggregate quoted market
      value, $420,000)   410,500
    Dividends and interest receivable   4,500   430,000
  Investment in land and unused facilities..............   125,000
  Cash surrender value of life insurance carried on
    officers' lives   12,500
Total investments $2,330,500

Appendix

Cash Surrender Value of Life Insurance

Many business enterprises carry life insurance policies on the lives of their executives because the business has a definite stake in the continuing services of its officers. In some cases the insurance plan affords a financial cushion in the event of the loss of such personnel. In other instances the insurance offers a means of purchasing the deceased owner's interest in the business, thus avoiding a transfer of such interest to some outside party or the need to liquidate the business in effecting a settlement with the estate of the deceased. In these cases, the company is the beneficiary.

Insurance premiums normally consist of an amount for insurance protection and the balance for a form of investment. The investment portion is the **cash surrender value** available to the policyholder in the event of policy cancellation. If this cash surrender value belongs to the business, it should be reported as a long-term investment. Insurance expense for a fiscal period is the difference between the insurance premium paid and the increase in the cash surrender value of the policy.

An insurance policy with a cash surrender value also has a **loan value.** The amount an insurance company will lend on a policy is normally limited to the cash surrender value at the end of the policy year less discount from the loan date to the cash surrender value date. For example, assume a cash surrender value of $3,000 at the end of the fifth policy year. The maximum loan value on the policy at the beginning of the fifth year, assuming the insurance premium for the fifth year is paid, is $3,000 discounted for one year. If the discount rate applied by the insurance company is 5%, the policy loan value is calculated as follows: $3,000 ÷ 1.05 = $2,857 (rounded).[10]

When the policyholder uses the policy as a basis for a loan, such a loan may be liquidated by payments of principal and interest, or the loan may be continuing, to be applied against the insurance proceeds upon policy cancellation or ultimate settlement. Although it is possible for the policyholder to recognize policy loan values instead of cash surrender values, the latter values are generally used.

The policyholder may authorize the insurance company to apply any dividends declared on insurance policies to the reduction of the annual pre-

---

[10]The discounted value can also be determined using Table I in Chapter 6 ($3,000 × .9524 = $2,857).

mium payment or to the increase in cash surrender value, or the dividends may be collected in cash. Dividends should be viewed as a reduction in the cost of carrying insurance rather than as a source of supplementary revenue. Hence, if dividends are applied to the reduction of the annual premium, Insurance Expense is simply debited for the net amount paid. If the dividend is applied to the increase in the policy cash surrender value or if it is collected in cash, it should still be treated as an offset to the periodic expense of carrying the policy; the cash surrender value or Cash is debited and Insurance Expense is credited. After a number of years, the periodic dividends plus increases in cash surrender value may exceed the premium payments, thus resulting in revenue rather than expense on policy holdings.

Collection of a policy upon death of the insured requires cancellation of any cash surrender balance. The difference between the insurance proceeds and the balances relating to the insurance policy is recognized as a gain in the period of death. The nature of the insurance policies carried and their coverage should be disclosed by appropriate comment on the balance sheet.

The entries to be made for an insurance contract are illustrated in the following example. The Pro Style Company insured the life of its president, Tom Jolly, on January 1, 1989. The amount of the policy was $50,000; the annual premiums were $2,100 to be paid in advance.

Policy Year	Gross Premium	Dividend	Net Premium	Increase in Cash Value	Insurance Expense
1	$2,100	—	$2,100	—	$2,100
2	2,100	—	2,100	$1,150	950
3	2,100	$272	1,828	1,300	528

The fiscal period for the company is the calendar year. Jolly died on July 1, 1991. The premium rebate for the period July 1 to December 31, 1991 is $1,050, and the dividend accrued as of July 1, 1991 is $210. The entries made in recording transactions relating to the insurance contract are shown on page 571. The procedures illustrated use the asset approach for recording premium payments. The expense approach may be preferred if the entire premium is to be applied during the current year.

Transaction	Entry		
January 1, 1989 Paid first annual premium, $2,100.	Prepaid Insurance . . . . Cash	2,100	 2,100
December 31, 1989 To record insurance expense for 1989.	Life Insurance Expense. . . . . Prepaid Insurance	2,100	 2,100

January 1, 1990
Paid second annual premium, $2,100
  Premium $2,100
  Less cash surrender value 1,150
  Net insurance charge $ 950
	Cash Surrender Value of Life
	  Insurance (as of 12/31/90) . . . . .
	Prepaid Insurance . . . .
	Cash . . . .
		
		1,150
		950
			
			2,100

December 31, 1990 To record insurance expense for 1990.	Life Insurance Expense. . . . . Prepaid Insurance	950	 950

January 1, 1991
Paid third annual premium, $2,100.
  Premium $ 2,100
  Less: Cash Surrender value $1,300
      Dividend   272 1,572
  Net insurance charge $ 528
	Cash Surrender Value of Life
	  Insurance (as of 12/31/91) . . . . .
	Prepaid Insurance . . . .
	Cash . . . .
		
		1,300
		528
			
			1,828

July 1, 1991 To record insurance expense for Jan. 1–July 1: ½ × $528 = $264.	Life Insurance Expense. . . . . Prepaid Insurance	264	 264

July 1, 1991
To record cancellation of policy upon death of insured:
  Amount recoverable on policy:
  Face of policy $50,000
  Premium rebate for period July 1–
    Dec. 31 and current year
    dividend   1,260
          $51,260
 	
Cancellation of asset values:
  Cash surrender values $ 2,450
  Prepaid insurance   264
          $ 2,714
  Gain on policy settlement $48,546
	Receivable from Insurance Co . . .
	  Cash Surrender Value of Life
	    Insurance . . . .
	  Prepaid Insurance . . . .
	  Gain on Settlement of Life
	    Insurance . . . .
		51,260	
			
			2,450
			264
			
			48,546

Key Terms

Cash surrender value 569
Consolidation method 549
Cost method 550
Equity method 550
Funds 564
Loan value 569

Long-term (or noncurrent)
   investments 547
Parent company 549
Subsidiary company 549
Trust indenture 565

Questions

1. (a) Distinguish between long-term (or noncurrent) and short-term (or current) investments.
   (b) List several types of long-term investments.
2. Why might a company invest in the stock of another company?
3. David Giles purchases 1,000 shares of Bart Motors at $90 a share in November, paying his broker $65,000. The market value of the stock on December 31 is $125 a share; Giles has made no further payment to his broker. On this date he shows on his balance sheet Bart Motors stock, $100,000, the difference between market value and the unpaid balance to the broker. Do you approve of this treatment? Explain.
4. What is the general rule used for determining the appropriate method of accounting for investments in equity securities when the investor does not possess absolute voting control?
5. (a) What factors may indicate the ability of an investor owning less than a majority voting interest to exercise significant influence on the investee's operating and financial policies?
   (b) What factors may indicate the investor's inability to exercise significant influence?
6. Distinguish between the method used to account for a temporary decline in the market value of stock under the equity method and under the cost method.
7. How is a permanent decline in the value of long-term stock investments recorded?
8. What adjustment is needed to record the change in classification of an investment in marketable equity securities between current and noncurrent assets?
9. What adjustment is needed when a company switches from (a) the equity method to the cost method and (b) the cost method to the equity method of valuing securities?
10. What disclosures are recommended in APB Opinion No. 18 when using the equity method?
11. Identify and describe examples of funds that would be listed as current assets and those that would be listed as investments.
12. Describe several items properly reported under the "Investments" heading on the balance sheet.

Discussion Cases   **Case 13–1   (Classification of investments)**

Hawkes Systems, Inc., a chemical processing company, has been operating profitably for many years. On March 1, 1991, Hawkes purchased 50,000 shares of Diversified Insurance Company stock for $2,000,000. The 50,000 shares represented 25% of Diversified's outstanding stock. Both Hawkes and Diversified operate on a fiscal year ending August 31.

For the fiscal year ended August 31, 1991, Diversified reported net income of $800,000 earned ratably throughout the year. During November, 1990, and February, May, and August, 1991, Diversified paid its regular quarterly cash dividend of $100,000.

What criteria should Hawkes consider in determining whether its investment in Diversified should be classified as (a) a current asset, or (b) a noncurrent asset? Confine your discussion to the decision criteria for determining the balance sheet classification of the investment.   (AICPA adapted)

Case 13–2   (What is significant influence?)

The Moya Corporation's Board of Directors has been wrestling with a basic decision concerning its involvement with other business entities. Jim Wallace, President, wants to acquire controlling interest (more than 50%) in several companies that serve as suppliers of basic materials used by Moya and other companies that are distributors of its various products. Gail Brewer, Chair of the Board of Directors, feels part of the capital required to obtain more than 50% ownership should be used to expand Moya's working capital. Brewer argues that significant influence over vital operating decisions can be obtained with far less than 50% of the stock. By reducing the investment cost, more funds can be freed for other vital needs. Both Wallace and Brewer are concerned about the impact of stock acquisitions on company profits, especially the effects of different accounting methods, as more substantial investments in other companies are made. They have come to you as the controller of Moya to shed some light on this issue and to obtain your recommendation as to the direction they should go. What factors would you stress in your answer to them?

Case 13–3   (How does increased ownership in another company affect our books?)

For the past five years Apton Corp. has maintained an investment (properly accounted for and reported upon) in Clarke Co. reflecting a 10% interest in the voting common stock of Clarke. The purchase price was $700,000 and the underlying net equity in Clarke at the date of purchase was $620,000. On January 2 of the current year, Apton purchased an additional 15% (total ownership interest is now 25%) of the voting common stock of Clarke for $1,200,000; the underlying net equity of the additional investment at January 2 was $1,000,000. Clarke has been profitable and has paid dividends annually since Apton's initial acquisition.

Discuss how this increase in ownership affects the accounting for and reporting on the investment in Clarke. Include in your discussion adjustments, if any, to the amount shown prior to the increase in investment to bring the amount into conformity with generally accepted accounting principles. Also include how current and subsequent periods would be reported on.

(AICPA adapted)

*Case 13–4   (Cash surrender value)

During your examination of the financial statements of Jones Paint, which

*Relates to Appendix

has never before been audited, you discover that the cash surrender value of a $500,000 life insurance policy on the president, for which Jones is the beneficiary, has not been recorded in the accounting records. The president states that the total premium on the policy was charged to the insurance expense account each year because the company has no intention of "cashing in" the policy or of using the cash surrender value as collateral for a loan from the insurance company or a bank. Therefore, asserts the president, it would be misleading for the company to record as an asset an amount never expected to be realized or used by the company.

Evaluate the position of the president of Jones Paint.

Exercises   **Exercise 13–1   (Accounting methods for long-term investments)**

For each of the following independent situations, determine the appropriate accounting method to be used: consolidation, cost, or equity. Explain the rationale for your decision.

1. ATV Company manufactures and sells four-wheel recreational vehicles. It also provides insurance on its products through its wholly-owned subsidiary, RV Insurance Company.
2. Buy Right Inc. purchased 20,000 shares of Big Supply Company common stock to be held as a long-term investment. Big Supply has 200,000 shares of common stock outstanding.
3. Super Tire Manufacturing Co. holds 5,000 shares of the 10,000 outstanding shares of nonvoting preferred stock of Valley Corporation.
4. Takeover Company owns 15,000 of the 50,000 shares of common stock of Western Supply Company. Takeover has tried and failed to obtain representation on Western's board of directors.
5. Espino Inc. purchased 50,000 shares of Independent Mining Company common stock. Independent has a total of 125,000 common shares outstanding.

Exercise 13–2   (Long-term investments in stocks—cost method)

Prepare journal entries to record the following long-term investment transactions. (Assume that the cost method is used.)

(a) Purchased 4,000 shares of Kat Company common stock at $65.25 per share, including brokerage fees of $800.
(b) Received a cash dividend of $2 per share from Kat Company.
(c) Sold 1,000 shares of Kat Company Stock at $70 per share, less $600 in brokerage fees.
(d) The end-of-year market value of Kat Company stock is $60.25. The decline in market value is considered temporary.

Exercise 13–3   (Long-term investments in stocks—equity method)

On January 1, 1991, Biro Corporation purchased 10,000 shares of JWS Corporation common stock for $30 per share, representing the underlying book value at that date. JWS had a total of 40,000 shares of stock outstanding at the acquisition date. Additional transactions and data for the year are as follows:

Oct. 31   JWS paid a $1 per share dividend
Dec. 31   JWS reported net income for 1991 of $160,000
Dec. 31   The market value of JWS Corporation stock is $25 per share

Record the above transactions on Biro's books and show how Biro would report its investment in JWS stock on its December 31, 1991, balance sheet.

Exercise 13–4   (Investment in common stock—cost and equity methods)
On January 10, 1991, Booker Corporation acquired 16,000 shares of the outstanding common stock of Atlanta Company for $800,000. At the time of purchase, Atlanta Company had outstanding 80,000 shares with a book value of $4 million. On December 31, 1991, the following events took place:

(a) Atlanta reported net income of $180,000 for the calendar year 1991.
(b) Booker received from Atlanta a dividend of $.75 per share of common stock.
(c) The market value of Atlanta Company stock had temporarily declined to $45 per share.

Give the entries that would be required to reflect the purchase and subsequent events on the books of Booker Corporation, assuming (1) the cost method is appropriate; (2) the equity method is appropriate.

Exercise 13–5   (Investment in common stock—unrecorded goodwill)
Alpha Co. acquired 20,000 shares of Beta Co. on January 1, 1990, at $12 per share. Beta Co. had 80,000 shares outstanding with a book value of $800,000. There were no identifiable undervalued assets at the time of purchase. Beta Co. recorded earnings of $260,000 and $290,000 for 1990 and 1991, respectively, and paid per share dividends of $1.60 in 1990 and $2.00 in 1991. Assuming a 40-year straight-line amortization policy for goodwill, give the entries to record the purchase in 1990 and to reflect Alpha's share of Beta's earnings and the receipt of the dividends for 1990 and 1991.

Exercise 13–6   (Valuation of long-term marketable equity securities)
The long-term marketable equity securities portfolio for Hill Top Industries contained the following securities at December 31, 1990 and 1991:

Marketable Equity Securities (Common Stock)	Initial Cost	Market Value 12/31/90	Market Value 12/31/91
Randall Co.	$10,000	$12,000	$15,000
Streuling Co.	7,000	3,000	2,000
Santana Co.	21,000	18,000	22,000

(1) Assuming all declines in market value are considered temporary, what is the effect of the changes in market values on the 1990 and 1991 financial statements? Give the valuation entries for these years.
(2) Assume that at December 31, 1991, management believed that the market value of the Streuling Co. common stock reflected a permanent decline in the value of that stock. Give the entries to be made on December 31, 1991, under this assumption. How would the marketable securities affect the 1991 financial statements?

Exercise 13–7   (Valuation of long-term marketable equity securities)

Bridgeman Paper Co. reported the following selected balances on its financial statements for each of the four years 1988–1991.

	1988	1989	1990	1991
Allowance for Decline in Value of Noncurrent Marketable Equity Securities	0	$25,000	$18,000	$30,000
Recognized Loss from Permanent Decline in Market Value of Noncurrent Marketable Equity Securities	0	0	$ 4,000	0
Allowance for Decline in Value of Current Marketable Equity Securities	0	$ 5,000	$ 8,000	$ 3,000

Based on these balances, reconstruct the valuation journal entries that must have been made each year.

Exercise 13–8   (Accounting for long-term investments)

During January 1991, P&L Company purchased 5,000 shares of Robison Co. common stock for $10 per share, which reflects the underlying book value at the time of purchase. A commission of $1,000 was also paid. In addition, P&L purchased 8,000 shares of Harris Co. preferred stock for $25 per share, including the commission. Robison Co. has 20,000 shares of common stock outstanding and Harris Co. has 24,000 shares of preferred (non-voting) stock outstanding.

The following data were obtained during 1991:

Dividends Paid (Per Share)
Robison Co.	$0.50
Harris Co.	2.00

Net Income
Robison Co.	$ 45,000
Harris Co.	120,000

Market Value (Per Share) at Dec. 31
Robison Co.	$ 9
Harris Co.	22

Give the journal entries required on the books of P&L Company for 1991 to account for the long-term investments in Robison Co. and Harris Co. None of the changes in the market prices of the stocks are considered permanent. Show the balance sheet presentation for the long-term investments.

Exercise 13–9   (Investment in common stock—equity to cost method)

Porter Co. purchased 50,000 shares of Cannon Manufacturing Co. common stock on July 1, 1990, at $16.50 per share, which reflected book value as of that date. Cannon Manufacturing Co. had 200,000 common shares outstanding at the time of the purchase. Prior to this purchase, Porter Co. had no ownership interest in Cannon. In its second quarterly statement, Cannon Manufacturing Co. reported net income of $168,000 for the six months ended June 30, 1990. Porter Co. received a dividend of $21,000 from Cannon on August 1, 1990. Cannon reported net income of $360,000 for the year ended

825.00
+ 48,00
-21,00
-21,00
83,00
÷ 50000 = 16.62
16.62 x 20,00 =
332,400

340,00

December 31, 1990, and again paid Porter Co. dividends of $21,000. On January 1, 1991, Porter Co. sold 20,000 shares of Cannon Manufacturing Co. common stock for $17 per share. Cannon reported net income of $372,000 for the year ended December 31, 1991, and paid Porter Co. dividends of $12,000. Give all entries Porter Co. would make in 1990 and 1991 in regard to the Cannon Manufacturing Co. stock.

Exercise 13–10   (Investment in common stock—cost to equity method)

Devers Corporation purchased 5% of the 100,000 outstanding common shares of Milo Inc. on January 1, 1989, for a total purchase price of $7,500. Net assets of Milo Inc. at the time had a book value of $150,000. Net income for Milo Inc. for the year ended December 31, 1989, was $50,000. Devers received dividends from Milo during the year of $1,500. There was no change of Devers ownership of Milo Inc. during 1990, and Milo reported net income of $70,000 for the year ended December 31, 1990. Devers received dividends of $2,000 from Milo for that year. On January 1, 1991, Devers purchased an additional 20% of Milo Inc.'s common stock or 20,000 shares for a total price of $40,000. Milo Inc.'s net asset book value at the time of the purchase was $200,000. For the year ended December 31, 1991, Milo Inc. reported net income of $100,000; Devers received dividends from Milo Inc. totaling $10,000 for the year ended December 31, 1991.

Prepare journal entries for Devers Corporation to reflect the preceding transactions, including adjusting entries necessary to reflect the change from the cost method to the equity method of accounting for Devers Corporation's investment in Milo Inc.

Exercise 13–11   (Fund investments)

On December 31, 1990, Haws Corporation set up a stock redemption fund, with an initial deposit of $150,000. On February 1, 1991, Haws Corporation invested $127,500 stock redemption fund cash in 10% preferred stock of Mackay Inc., par value of $75,000. Mackay normally declares and pays dividends on the preferred stock semiannually: March 1 and September 1. On April 1, 1991, Haws exchanged the stock with another investor for 4,000 shares of Lamas Corporation common stock. The market value of the common stock at the date of exchange was $35 per share. Give all the entries necessary to record the preceding transactions assuming semiannual dividends were paid.

Exercise 13–12   (Sinking fund accumulation schedule)

Sinking fund tables show that 5 annual deposits of $16,379.75 accruing interest at 10% compounded annually will result in a total accumulation of $100,000 immediately after the fifth payment. (a) Prepare a fund accumulation schedule showing the theoretical growth of a property acquisition fund over the 5-year period. (b) Give all of the entries that would appear on the books for the increases in the property acquisition fund balance for the first 3 years.

*Exercise 13–13   (Cash surrender value)

Case Company follows the practice of taking out whole-life insurance policies

*Relates to Appendix

on its key employees. The annual premium of $8,400 is paid on May 1. The cash surrender value at December 31, 1990 was $39,400. At the end of 1991, the cash surrender value had increased to $41,200. Give the journal entries for 1991.

Problems   **Problem 13—1   (Investments in common stock)**

Arroyo Inc. and the Bell Corp. each have 100,000 shares of no-par common stock outstanding. Universal Inc. acquired 10,000 shares of Arroyo stock and 25,000 shares of Bell stock in 1988. Changes in retained earnings for Arroyo and Bell for 1990 and 1991 are as follows:

	Arroyo Inc.	Bell Corp.
Retained earnings (deficit), January 1, 1990	$200,000	$(35,000)
Cash dividends, 1990	(25,000)	—
	$175,000	$(35,000)
Net income, 1990	40,000	65,000
Retained earnings, December 31, 1990	$215,000	$30,000
Cash dividends, 1991	(30,000)	(10,000)
Net income, 1991	60,000	25,000
Retained earnings, December 31, 1991	$245,000	$45,000

Instructions: Give the entries required on the books of Universal Inc. for 1990 and 1991 to account for its investments.

Problem 13—2   (Long-term investments in stock—equity method)

On January 1, 1991, Compustat Co. bought 30% of the outstanding common stock of Freelance Corp. for $258,000 cash. Compustat Co. accounts for this investment by the equity method. At the date of acquisition of the stock, Freelance Corp.'s net assets had a carrying value of $620,000. Assets with an average remaining life of five years have a current market value that is $130,000 in excess of their carrying values. The remaining difference between the purchase price and the value of the underlying stockholders' equity cannot be attributed to any tangible asset; however, Freelance Corp. is carrying goodwill of $40,000 on its books, which is being amortized at the rate of $1,250 per year for 32 more years. Compustat Co. has a policy of amortizing goodwill over 40 years. At the end of 1991, Freelance Corp. reports net income of $180,000. During 1991, Freelance Corp. declared and paid cash dividends of $20,000.

Instructions: Give the entries necessary to reflect Compustat Co.'s investment in Freelance Corp. for 1991.

Problem 13—3   (Investment in common stock)

On July 1 of the current year, Melissa Co. acquired 25% of the outstanding shares of common stock of International Co. at a total cost of $700,000. The underlying equity (net assets) of the stock acquired by Melissa was only $600,000.

Melissa was willing to pay more than book value for the International stock for the following reasons:

(a) International owned depreciable plant assets (10-year remaining economic life) with a current fair value of $60,000 more than their carrying amount.

(b) International owned land with a current fair value of $300,000 more than its carrying amount.

(c) Melissa believed International possessed enough goodwill to justify the remainder of the cost. International's accounting policy with respect to goodwill is to amortize it over 40 years.

International Co. earned net income of $540,000 evenly over the current year ended December 31. On December 31, International declared and paid a cash dividend of $105,000 to common stockholders. Both companies close their accounting records on December 31.

Instructions:

1. Compute the total amount of goodwill of International Co. based on the price paid by Melissa Co.

2. Prepare all journal entries in Melissa's accounting records relating to the investment for the year ended December 31, under the cost method of accounting.

3. Prepare all journal entries in Melissa's accounting records relating to the investment for the year ended December 31, under the equity method of accounting.

Problem 13-4 (Accounting for long-term investments—cost and equity methods)

On January 2, 1989, Brozo Company acquired 20% of the 200,000 shares of outstanding common stock of Newberry Corp. for $30 per share. The purchase price was equal to Newberry's underlying book value. Brozo plans to hold this stock as a long-term investment.

The following data are applicable for 1989 and 1990:

	1989	1990
Newberry dividends (paid Oct. 31)	$20,000	$24,000
Newberry earnings	70,000	80,000
Newberry stock market price at year end	32	31

On January 2, 1991, Brozo Company sold 10,000 shares of Newberry stock for $31 per share. During 1991, Newberry reported net income of $60,000, and on October 31, 1991, Newberry paid dividends of $10,000. At December 31, 1991, after a significant stock market decline, which is expected to be temporary, Newberry's stock was selling for $22 per share. After selling the 10,000 shares, Brozo does not expect to exercise significant influence over Newberry.

Instructions:

1. Make all journal entries for Brozo Company for 1989, 1990, and 1991 assuming the 20% original ownership interest allowed significant influence over Newberry.

2. Make the year-end valuation adjusting entries for Brozo Company for 1989, 1990, and 1991 assuming the 20% original ownership interest did not allow significant influence over Newberry.

Problem 13–5   (Accounting for marketable equity securities)

The Trans America Trust Co. owns both temporary and long-term investments in marketable equity securities. The following securities were owned on December 31, 1990:

Temporary Investments

Security	Shares	Total Cost	Market Value Dec. 31, 1990
Albert Groceries, Inc.	600	$ 9,000	$11,500
West Data, Inc.	1,000	27,000	18,000
Steel Co.	450	9,900	10,215

Long-Term Investments

Security	Shares	Total Cost	Market Value Dec. 31, 1990
Dairy Products	2,000	$ 86,000	$ 90,000
Vern Movies, Inc.	15,000	390,000	345,000
Disks, Inc.	5,000	60,000	80,000

The following transactions occurred during 1991:

(a) Sold 500 shares of West Data for $9,500.
(b) Sold 200 shares of Disks, Inc. for $3,000.
(c) Transferred all of Albert Groceries to long-term portfolio when the total market value was $12,900.
(d) Transferred the remaining shares of Disks, Inc. to the temporary investment portfolio when the market price was $20 per share. These shares were subsequently sold for $18 per share.

At December 31, 1991, market prices for the remaining securities were as follows:

Security	Market Price Per Share
Albert Groceries	$22
West Data, Inc.	15
Steel Co.	21
Dairy Products	42
Vern Movies, Inc.	28

Instructions: Prepare all journal entries necessary to record Trans America Trust's marketable equity securities transactions and year-end adjustments for 1991. Assume all declines in market value are temporary.

Problem 13–6   (Valuation of long-term marketable equity securities)

The long-term investment portfolio of Morris Inc. at December 31, 1990, contains the following securities:

Opus Co. common, 3% ownership, 5,000 shares;
   cost, $100,000; market value, $95,000.
Garrod Inc. preferred, 2,000 shares; cost, $40,000;
   market value, $43,000.
Sherrill Inc. common, 30% ownership, 20, 000 shares;
   cost, $1,140,000; market value, $1,130,000.
Jennings Co. common, 15% ownership, 25,000 shares;
   cost, $67,500; market value, $50,000.

Instructions:

1. Give the valuation adjustment required at December 31, 1990, assuming market values in the past for the long-term investment portfolio have always exceeded cost and none of the indicated declines in market value are considered permanent.
2. Assume the Jennings Co. common stock market decline is considered permanent. Give the valuation entries required at December 31, 1990, under this change in assumption.
3. Assume the market values for the long-term investment portfolio at December 31, 1991, were as follows:

Opus Co. Common	$ 102,000
Garrod Inc. Preferred	43,000
Sherrill Inc. Common	1,115,000
Jennings Co. Common	45,000

Give the valuation entries at Dec. 31, 1991, assuming all declines in 1990 and 1991 are temporary except for the 1990 decline in Jennings Co. stock.

▌▌▌ Problem 13–7 (Change from cost to equity method)

On January 1, 1990, Loren Inc. paid $700,000 for 10,000 shares of Keller Company's voting common stock, which was a 10% interest in Keller. At this date, the net assets of Keller totaled $6 million. The fair values of all of Keller's identifiable assets and liabilities were equal to their book values. Loren did not have the ability to exercise significant influence over the operating and financial policies of Keller. Loren received dividends of $.90 per share from Keller on October 1, 1990. Keller reported net income of $400,000 for the year ended December 31, 1990.

On July 1, 1991, Loren paid $2,300,000 for 30,000 additional shares of Keller Company's voting common stock, which represents a 30% interest in Keller. The fair value of all Keller's identifiable assets, net of liabilities, was equal to their book values of $6,500,000. As a result of this transaction, Loren has the ability to exercise significant influence over the operating and financial policies of Keller. Loren received a dividend of $.10 per share from Keller on April 1, 1991, and $1.35 per share from Keller on October 1, 1991. Keller reported net income of $500,000 for the year ended December 31, 1991, and $200,000 for the six months ended December 31, 1991. Loren amortizes goodwill over a 40-year period.

Instructions:

(1) Determine the amount of income from the investment in Keller Company

common stock that should be reported in Loren's income statement for the year ended December 31, 1990.

(2) Loren issues comparative financial statements for the years ended December 31, 1991 and 1990. Prepare schedules showing the income or loss that Loren should report from its investment in Keller Company for 1991 and 1990 (restated).   (AICPA adapted)

Problem 13–8   (Investment in common stock—cost to equity to cost method)

Cook Inc. wants to gain a controlling interest in Fox Chemical Co. in order to assure a steady source of a raw material manufactured by Fox. The following transactions occurred with respect to Cook and Fox. Both companies keep their books on a calendar-year basis.

1987

Jan.   2   Cook purchased 5,000 shares (5%) of Fox common stock for $10 per share. The assets of Fox had a net carrying value of $800,000. At that date, certain depreciable equipment owned by Fox had a fair market value $30,000 in excess of its carrying value, with an estimated remaining useful life of 10 years. Fox also carried land on its books that had a fair market value $70,000 in excess of its book value. The balance of the excess of the cost of the stock over the underlying equity in net assets was attributable to goodwill, which is amortized over 40 years. (Unless circumstances indicate otherwise, Cook's policy is to amortize any recognized goodwill evenly over a 40-year period from date of acquisition.)

Feb. 15   Cook received a dividend of $3,000 representing a distribution from income earned in 1986.

July   1   Cook purchased 10,000 additional shares of Fox stock for $11 per share. Fox's net income for the first six months of 1987 was $150,000. The net carrying value of Fox stockholders' equity at July 1, 1987, was $890,000. The difference between the fair market value of Fox's depreciable assets and their carrying value at this date was $30,000, and the equipment had an estimated remaining useful life of 9.5 years from the date of purchase. The market value of the land remained $70,000 over book value. Fox had not issued any new stock during the past six months.

Dec. 31   Fox reported net income for the year of $260,000.

1988

Feb. 15   Cook received a cash dividend from Fox of $18,000.

Dec. 31   Fox reported net income for the year of $320,000.

1989

Jan.   2   Cook purchased 20,000 additional shares of Fox stock for $13 per share, which permitted Cook to exercise significant influence over Fox. At this time Fox was experiencing a boycott of its products that was expected to last indefinitely. Although the difference between the fair market value of its assets and their carrying values remained the same, Fox's boycott problems detracted from the long-term attractiveness of its shares, and no implied goodwill was included in the purchase price. (There has been no change in the estimated useful lives of depreciable assets from the date of the original purchase on January 2, 1987).

Feb. 15 Cook received a cash dividend of $49,000 from Fox Co.

Dec. 31 Fox reported net income of $280,000. In view of Fox's boycott situation, Cook decided to write off remaining goodwill over a period of 10 years, beginning this year.

1990

Feb. 15 Cook received a cash dividend of $39,200 from Fox.

Apr. 1 Cook, after experiencing a series of reversals in the marketplace, ceased manufacturing the product containing the raw material from Fox. On this date, Cook sold 20,000 shares of Fox stock for $12 per share. Cook used the average cost of its investment in Fox in calculating its cost basis per share in the investment. Assume Fox had no income for the first quarter of 1990.

Dec. 31 Fox reported net income of $295,000 for the year ended December 31, 1990.

1991

Feb. 15 Cook received a dividend of $17,700 from Fox.

Mar. 20 Cook sold its remaining 15,000 shares of Fox stock for $11.50 per share.

Instructions: Give all the entries necessary to record these transactions on the books of Cook Inc. (Round computations to the nearest dollar.)

⦀ Problem 13–9   (Fund accumulation)

On December 31, 1989, a fund is set up to redeem $50,000 of preferred stock. The fund is guaranteed to earn 8% compounded annually and must generate enough income to enable the company to retire the stock after four payments. The annual installments paid to the fund trustee are $11,096.07. The first deposit is made immediately.

Instructions:

1. Give the journal entries in connection with the fund for the years 1989 and 1990. (The company keeps its books on the calendar year basis.)
2. Assume that on December 31, 1992, the fund balance of $50,000 consisted of $10,000 cash and $40,000 in securities that were purchased in 1991. The securities are sold at the end of 1992 for $48,000. Give all the journal entries that would be made to record the sale of the securities, retire the $50,000 of preferred stock, and liquidate any balance in the fund account.

*Problem 13–10   (Cash surrender value)

During the course of the audit of Houston Company, which closes its accounts on December 31, you examine the life insurance policies, premium receipts,

*Relates to Appendix

and confirmations returned by the insurance companies in response to your request for information. You find that in 1991 the company had paid premiums on the life of the president, Bill Houston, as shown below:

Sole Owner and Beneficiary	Face of Policy	Billed Premium 1991	Dividend Used to Reduce Premium	Annual Premium Date	Cash Surrender Value December 31	
					1990	1991
(1) Houston Inc.	$500,000	$5,000	$2,000	Aug. 30	$126,000	$130,000
(2) Sue Houston, wife of Bill Houston	200,000	4,500	750	Sept. 30	50,000	53,000
(3) Houston Inc.	50,000	2,500	250	Mar. 1	15,000	16,500

Instructions:

1. Prepare all journal entries required for the year 1991.
2. What balances relating to these insurance policies would appear on the balance sheet prepared on December 31, 1991?

PART THREE

Liabilities and Equity

Chapter 14

Liabilities— Current and Contingent

Part Two focused on the assets of a company, or the debit side of the balance sheet. Liabilities and owners' equity, the credit side of the balance sheet, are considered in Part Three. In this chapter, the general nature of liabilities is discussed as well as how to account for current and contingent liabilities. Subsequent chapters focus on noncurrent liabilities, including bonds, leases, and pensions, that are relatively complex in nature and, in some cases, directly related to asset accounts.

To illustrate the importance of accurately reporting the liabilities of a company, consider the following hypothetical, but realistic, situation.

Judge E. J. Wright is currently deliberating over a type of case that is becoming increasingly common in our society. A suit has been filed by three stockholders against Transcontinental Corporation alleging that Transcontinental's year-end balance sheet was misleading because it did not accurately reflect the financial position of the company at that date. The stockholders relied on the published financial statements and subsequently lost money on their investments in Transcontinental. Two specific points are at issue. First, Transcontinental chose not to estimate its liability under certain warranty provisions, accounting for warranty expenses on a cash basis. The plaintiffs contend that the warranties were in fact liabilities and should have been reported as such under accrual accounting procedures. Second, Transcontinental did not report a contingent liability relating to a significant, pending lawsuit with a supplier, which Transcontinental subsequently lost. Plaintiffs contend again that this information was material and relevant, and should have been disclosed.

Although hypothetical, the above situation is typical of many lawsuits being filed against companies, accountants, underwriters, and financial analysts and advisers. With respect to liabilities, the basic questions are:

· What is a liability?
· When and how should liabilities be measured and disclosed?

These questions relate to definition, recognition, measurement, and reporting addressed by the FASB's Conceptual Framework, as discussed in Chapter 2.

Definition of Liabilities

Liabilities have been defined by the FASB as "probable future sacrifices of economic benefits arising from present obligations of a particular entity to transfer assets or provide services to other entities in the future as a result of past transactions or events."[1] This definition contains significant components that need to be explained before individual liability accounts are discussed.

A liability is a result of **past transactions or events.** Thus, a liability is not recognized until incurred. This part of the definition excludes contractual obligations from an exchange of promises if performance by both parties is still in the future. Such contracts are referred to as **executory contracts.** Determining when an executory contract qualifies as a liability is not always easy. For example, the signing of a labor contract that obligates both the employer and the employee does not give rise to a liability in current accounting practice, nor does the placing of an order for the purchase of merchandise. However, under some conditions, the signing of a lease is recognized as an event that requires the current recognition of a liability even though a lease is essentially an executory contract. Clarification of this area is needed.

A liability must involve a **probable future transfer of assets or services.** Although liabilities result from past transactions or events, an obligation may be contingent upon the occurrence of another event sometime in the future. When occurrence of the future event seems probable, the obligation is defined as a liability. Although the majority of liabilities are satisfied by payment of cash, some obligations are satisfied by transferring other types of assets or by providing services. For example, revenue received in advance requires recognition of an obligation to provide goods or services in the future. Usually, the time of payment is specified by a debt instrument, e.g., a note requiring payment of interest and principal on a given date or series of dates. Some obligations, however, require the transfer of assets or services over a period of time, but the exact dates cannot be determined when the liability is incurred, e.g., obligations to provide parts or service under a warranty agreement.

A liability is the **obligation of a particular entity,** i.e., the entity that has the responsibility to transfer assets or provide services. As long as the payment or transfer is probable, it is not necessary that the entity to whom the obligation is owed be identified. Thus, a warranty to make any repairs necessary to an item sold by an entity is an obligation of that entity even though it is not certain which customers will receive benefits. Generally, the obligation rests on a foundation of legal rights and duties. However, obligations created, inferred, or construed from the facts of a particular situation may also be recognized as liabilities. For example, if a company regularly pays vacation pay or year-end bonuses, accrual of these items as a

---

[1]*Statement of Financial Accounting Concepts No. 6,* "Elements of Financial Statements" (Stamford: Financial Accounting Standards Board, December 1985), par. 35.

liability is warranted even though no legal agreement exists to make these payments.

Although the FASB's definition is helpful, the question of when an item is a liability is still not always easy to answer. Examples of areas where there is continuing controversy include the problems associated with off-balance sheet financing, deferred income taxes, leases, pensions, and even some equity securities such as redeemable preferred stock.[2] Once an item is accepted as having met the definition of a liability, there is still the need to appropriately classify, measure, and report the liability.

Classification and Measurement of Liabilities

For reporting purposes, liabilities are usually classified as **current** or **noncurrent**. The distinction between current and noncurrent liabilities was introduced and explained in Chapter 5, where it was pointed out that the computation of working capital is considered by many to be a useful measure of the liquidity of an enterprise.

Current Versus Noncurrent Classification

As noted in Chapter 5, the same rules generally apply for the classification of liabilities as for assets. If a liability arises in the course of an entity's normal operating cycle, it is considered current if current assets will be used to satisfy the obligation within one year or one operating cycle, whichever period is longer. On the other hand, bank borrowings, notes, mortgages, and similar obligations are related to the general financial condition of the entity rather than directly to the operating cycle, and are classified as current only if they are to be paid with current assets within one year.

When debt that has been classified as noncurrent will mature within the next year, the liability should be reported as a current liability in order to reflect the expected drain on current assets. However, if the liability is to be paid by transfer of noncurrent assets that have been accumulated for the purpose of liquidating the liability, the obligation continues to be classified as noncurrent.

Measurement of Liabilities

The distinction between current and noncurrent liabilities is also an important consideration in the measurement of liabilities. Obviously, before liabilities can be reported on the financial statements, they must be stated in monetary terms. The measurement used for liabilities is the **present value of the future cash outflows** to settle the obligation. Generally, this is the amount of cash required to liquidate the obligation if it were paid today.

If a claim isn't to be paid until sometime in the future, as is the case with noncurrent liabilities, the claim should either provide for interest to be paid on the debt, or the obligation should be reported at the discounted

---

[2]Each of these topics is discussed in a subsequent chapter: off-balance sheet financing, Chapter 15; deferred income taxes, Chapter 20; leases, Chapter 21; pensions, Chapter 22; redeemable preferred stock, Chapter 16.

value of its maturity amount. Current obligations that arise in the course of normal business operations are generally due within a short period, e.g., 30-60 days, and normally are not discounted.[3] Thus, trade accounts payable are not discounted even though they carry no interest provision. However, this is an exception to the general rule; most nonoperating business transactions such as the borrowing of money, purchase of assets over time, and long-term leases, do involve the discounting process. The obligation in these instances is the present value of the future resource outflows.

For measurement purposes, liabilities can be divided into three categories:

1. Liabilities that are definite in amount.
2. Estimated liabilities.
3. Contingent liabilities.

The measurement of liabilities always involves some uncertainty since a liability, by definition, involves a *future* outflow of resources. However, for the first category above, both the existence of the liability and the amount to be paid are determinable because of a contract, trade agreement, or general business practice. An example of a **liability that is definite in amount** is the principal payment on a note.

The second category includes items that are definitely liabilities, i.e., they involve a definite future resource outflow, but the actual amount of the obligation cannot be established currently. In this situation, the amount of the liability is estimated so that the obligation is reflected in the current period, even though at an approximated value. A warranty obligation that is recorded on an accrual basis is an example of an **estimated liability**.

Generally, liabilities from both of the first two categories are reported on a balance sheet as claims against recorded assets, either as current or noncurrent liabilities whichever is appropriate. However, items that resemble liabilities, but are contingent upon the occurrence of some future event, are not recorded until it is probable that the event will occur. Even though the amount of the potential obligation may be known, the actual existence of a liability is questionable since it is contingent upon a future event for which there is considerable uncertainty. An example of a **contingent liability** is a pending lawsuit. Only if the lawsuit is lost, or is settled out of court, will a liability be recorded. While not recorded in the accounts, some contingent liabilities should be disclosed in the notes to the financial statements, as discussed and illustrated later in the chapter.

Liabilities That Are Definite in Amount   Representative of liabilities that are definite in amount and that are reported on the balance sheet are accounts payable, notes payable, and miscellaneous operating payables including salaries, payroll taxes, property

---

[3]*Opinions of the Accounting Principles Board No. 21*, "Interest on Receivables and Payables" (New York: American Institute of Certified Public Accountants, 1971), par. 3.

and sales taxes, and income taxes. Some liabilities accrue as time passes. Most notable in this category are interest and rent, although the latter is frequently paid in advance. Some of the problems arising in determining the balances to be reported for liabilities that are definite in amount are described in the following sections.

Accounts Payable

Most goods and services in today's economic environment are purchased on credit. The term **accounts payable** usually refers to the amount due for the purchase of materials by a manufacturing company or merchandise by a wholesaler or retailer. Other obligations, such as salaries and wages, rent, interest, and utilities are reported as separate liabilities in accounts descriptive of the nature of the obligation. Accounts payable are usually not recorded when purchase orders are placed, but when legal title to the goods passes to the buyer. The rules for the customary recognition of legal passage of title were presented in Chapter 9. If goods are in transit at year-end, the purchase should be recorded if the shipment terms indicate that title has passed. This means that care must be exercised to review the purchase of goods and services near the end of an accounting period to assure a proper cut-off and reporting of liabilities and inventory.

It is customary to report accounts payable at the expected amount of the payment. Because the payment period is normally short, no recognition of interest is required. As indicated in Chapter 9, if cash discounts are available, the liability should be reported net of the expected cash discount. Failure to use the net method in recording purchases usually reports liabilities in excess of the payment finally made, since most companies are careful to take advantage of available cash discounts.

Short-Term Debt

Companies often borrow money on a short-term basis for operating purposes other than for the purchase of materials or merchandise involving accounts payable. Collectively, these obligations may be referred to as **short-term debt**. In most cases, such debt is evidenced by a promissory note, a formal written promise to pay a sum of money in the future, and is usually reflected on the debtor's books as **Notes Payable**.

Notes issued to trade creditors for the purchase of goods or services are called trade notes payable. Notes issued to banks or to officers and stockholders for loans to the company, and those issued to others for the purchase of noncurrent operating assets, are called nontrade notes payable. It is normally desirable to classify current notes payable on the balance sheet as trade or nontrade, since such information would reveal to statement users the sources of indebtedness and the extent to which the company has relied on each source in financing its activities.

The problems encountered in the valuation of notes payable are the same as those discussed in Chapter 8 with respect to notes receivable. Thus, a short-term note payable is recorded and reported at its present value, which is normally the face value of the note. This presumes that the note bears a reasonable stated rate of interest. However, if a note has no stated rate of interest, or if the stated rate is unreasonable, then the face value of the note would need to be discounted to its present value to reflect the effective rate of interest implicit in the note. This is accomplished by debiting Discount on Notes Payable when the note is issued, and by writing off the discount to Interest Expense over the life of the note, in the same manner as was illustrated for the discount on notes receivable in Chapter 8.

Discount on Notes Payable is a contra account to Notes Payable and would be reported on the balance sheet as follows:

Current liabilities:		
Notes payable	$100,000	
Less discount on notes payable	10,000	$90,000

Short-Term Obligations Expected to be Refinanced

As noted at the beginning of the chapter, omissions or misrepresentation in the reporting of liabilities can create serious problems for users of financial statements. A similar problem can result from the misclassification of liabilities. Since the "current" classification is reserved for those obligations that will be satisfied with current assets within a year, a short-term obligation that is expected to be refinanced on a long-term basis should not be reported as a current liability. This applies to the currently maturing portion of a long-term debt and to all other short-term obligations except those arising in the normal course of operations that are due in customary terms. Similarly, it should not be assumed that a short-term obligation will be refinanced, and therefore classified as a noncurrent liability, unless the refinancing arrangements are secure. Thus, to avoid potential manipulation, the refinancing expectation must be realistic and not just a mere possibility.

An example will illustrate this last point and show the importance of proper classification. Assume that a company borrows a substantial amount of money that it expects to pay back at the end of 5 years. The president of the company signs a 6-month note, which the loan officer at the bank verbally agrees will be renewed "automatically" until the actual maturity date in 5 years. The only current obligation expected is payment of the accrued interest each renewal period. Under these circumstances the company reports the obligation as noncurrent, except for the accrued interest obligation. Assume further that the loan officer leaves the bank and that the new bank official will not allow the short-term note to be refinanced. The financial picture of the company is now dramatically changed. What was considered a long-term obligation because of refinancing expectations is suddenly a current liability requiring settlement with liquid assets in the near future. This hypothetical situation is similar to what actually happened to Penn Central Railroad before it went bankrupt.

To assist with this problem, the FASB in 1975 issued Statement No. 6, which contains the authoritative guideline for classifying short-term obligations expected to be refinanced. According to the FASB, *both* of the following conditions must be met before a short-term obligation may be properly excluded from the current liability classification.[4]

1. Management must *intend to refinance* the obligation on a long-term basis.
2. Management must *demonstrate an ability to refinance* the obligation.

Concerning the second point, an ability to refinance may be demonstrated by:

a. Actually refinancing the obligation during the period between the balance sheet date and the date the statements are issued.
b. Reaching a firm agreement that clearly provides for refinancing on a long-term basis.

The terms of the refinancing agreement should be noncancelable as to all parties and extend beyond the current year. In addition, the company should not be in violation of the agreement at the balance sheet date or the date of issuance, and the lender or investor should be financially capable of meeting the refinancing requirements.

If an actual refinancing does occur before the balance sheet is issued, the portion of the short-term obligation that is to be excluded from current liabilities cannot exceed the proceeds from the new debt or equity securities issued to retire the old debt. For example, if a $400,000 long-term note is issued to partially refinance $750,000 of short-term obligations, only $400,000 of the short-term debt can be excluded from current liabilities.

An additional question relates to the timing of the refinancing. If the obligation is paid prior to the actual refinancing, the obligation should be included in current liabilities on the balance sheet.[5] To illustrate, assume that the liabilities of CareFree Inc. at December 31, 1990, include a note payable for $200,000 due January 15, 1991. The management of CareFree intends to refinance the note by issuing 10-year bonds. The bonds are actually issued before the issuance of the December 31, 1990, balance sheet on February 15, 1991. If the bonds were issued prior to payment of the note, the note should be classified as noncurrent on the December 31, 1990, balance sheet. If payment of the note preceded the sale of the bonds, however, the note should be included in current liabilities.

Normally, classified balance sheets are presented that show a total for "current liabilities." If a short-term obligation is excluded from that category due to refinancing expectations, disclosure should be made in the notes to the financial statements. The note should include a general description of the refinancing agreement.

[4]*Statement of Financial Accounting Standards No. 6*, "Classification of Short-Term Obligations Expected to be Refinanced" (Stamford: Financial Accounting Standards Board, 1975), pars. 10 and 11.

[5]*FASB Interpretation No. 8*, "Classification of a Short-Term Obligation Repaid Prior to Being Replaced by a Long-Term Security" (Stamford: Financial Accounting Standards Board, 1976), par. 3.

Miscellaneous Operating Payables

Many miscellaneous payables arise in the course of a company's operating activities. Three of these are specifically discussed in this section. They are indicative of other specific liabilities that could be reported by a given entity. In general, the points made in discussing the definition of liabilities in the opening section of this chapter apply to these miscellaneous operating liabilities.

Salaries and Wages

In an ongoing entity, salaries and wages of officers and other employees accrue daily. Normally, no entry is made for these expenses until payment is made. A liability for unpaid salaries and wages is recorded, however, at the end of an accounting period when a more precise matching of revenues and expenses is desired. An estimate of the amount of unpaid wages and salaries is made, and an adjusting entry is prepared to recognize the amount due. Usually the entire accrued amount is identified as salaries payable with no attempt to identify the withholdings associated with the accrual. When payment is made in the subsequent period, the amount is allocated between the employee and other entities such as government taxing units, unions, and insurance companies.

For example, assume that a company has 15 employees who are paid every two weeks. At December 31, four days of unpaid wages have accrued. Analysis reveals that the 15 employees earn a total of $1,000 a day. Thus the adjusting entry at December 31 would be:

Salaries and Wages Expense	4,000	
Salaries and Wages Payable		4,000

This entry may be reversed at the beginning of the next period, or, when payment is made, Salaries and Wages Payable may be debited for $4,000.

Additional compensation in the form of accrued bonuses or commissions should also be recognized. Bonuses are often based on some measure of the employer's income. (The appendix to this chapter illustrates bonus computations.)

Payroll Taxes

Social security and income tax legislation impose four taxes based on payrolls:

1. Federal old-age, survivors, disability and hospital insurance (tax to both employer and employee)
2. Federal unemployment insurance (tax to employer only)
3. State unemployment insurance (tax to employer only)
4. Individual income tax (tax to employee only, but withheld and paid by employer)

Federal Old-Age, Survivors, Disability, and Hospital Insurance The Federal Insurance Contributions Act (FICA), generally referred to as social security legislation, provides for FICA taxes to both employers and employees to provide funds for federal old-age, survivors, disability, and hospital insurance benefits for certain individuals and members of their families. At one time, only employees were covered by this legislation; however, coverage now includes most individuals who are self-employed.

Provisions of the legislation require an employer of more than one employee, with certain exceptions, to withhold FICA taxes from each employee's wages. The amount of the tax is based on a tax rate and wage base as currently specified in the law. The tax rate and wage base both have increased dramatically since the inception of the social security program in the 1930s. The initial rate of FICA tax was 1% in 1937; the rate in effect for 1989 was 7.51%.[6] During that same period, the annual wages subject to FICA tax increased from $3,000 to $48,000. The taxable wage base is subject to yearly increases based on cost-of-living adjustments in social security benefits.

The employer remits the amount of FICA tax withheld for all employees, along with a matching amount, to the federal government. The employer is required to maintain complete records and submit detailed support for the tax remittance. The employer is responsible for the full amount of the tax even if employee contributions are not withheld.

Federal Unemployment Insurance The Federal Social Security Act and the Federal Unemployment Tax Act (FUTA) provide for the establishment of unemployment insurance plans. Employers with covered workers employed in each of 20 weeks during a calendar year or who pay $1,500 or more in wages during any calendar quarter are affected.

Under present provisions of the law, the federal government taxes eligible employers on the first $7,000 paid to every employee during the calendar year. The rate of tax in effect since 1985 is 6.2%, but the employer is allowed a tax credit limited to 5.4% for taxes paid under state unemployment compensation laws. No tax is levied on the employee. When an employer is subject to a tax of 5.4% or more as a result of state unemployment legislation, the federal unemployment tax, then, is 0.8% of the qualifying wages.

Payment to the federal government is required quarterly. Unemployment benefits are paid by the individual states. Revenues collected by the federal government under the acts are used to meet the cost of administering state and federal unemployment plans as well as to provide supplemental unemployment benefits.

State Unemployment Insurance State unemployment compensation laws are not the same in all states. In most states, laws provide for tax only on employers; but in a few states, taxes are applicable to both employers and

---

[6]In 1990, the rate is scheduled to increase to 7.65%. For illustrative purposes and end-of-chapter exercises and problems, a rate of 7.6% will be used.

employees. Each state law specifies the classes of exempt employees, the number of employees required or the amount of wages paid before the tax is applicable, and the contributions that are to be made by employers and employees. Exemptions are frequently similar to those under the federal act. Tax payment is generally required on or before the last day of the month following each calendar quarter.

Although the normal tax on employers may be 5.4%, states have merit rating or experience plans providing for lower rates based on employers' individual employment experiences. Employers with stable employment records are taxed at a rate in keeping with the limited amount of benefits required for their former employees; employers with less satisfactory employment records contribute at a rate more nearly approaching 5.4% in view of the greater amount of benefits paid to their former employees. Savings under state merit systems are allowed as credits in the calculation of the federal contribution, so the federal tax does not exceed 0.8% even though payment of less than 5.4% is made by an employer entitled to a lower rate under the merit rating system.

Income Tax Federal income tax on the wages of an individual are collected in the period in which the wages are paid. The "pay-as-you-go" plan requires employers to withhold income tax from wages paid to their employees. Most states and many local governments also impose income taxes on the earnings of employees that must be withheld and remitted by the employer. Withholding is required not only of employers engaged in a trade or business, but also of religious and charitable organizations, educational institutions, social organizations, and governments of the United States, the states, the territories, and their agencies, instrumentalities, and political subdivisions. Certain classes of wage payments are exempt from withholding although these are still subject to income tax.

An employer must meet withholding requirements under the law even if wages of only one employee are subject to such withholdings. The amounts to be withheld by the employer are developed from formulas provided by the law or from tax withholding tables made available by the government. Withholding is based on the length of the payroll period, the amount earned, and the number of withholding exemptions claimed by the employee. Taxes required under the Federal Insurance Contributions Act (both employees' and employer's portions) and income tax that has been withheld by the employer are paid to the federal government at the same time. These combined taxes are deposited in an authorized bank quarterly, monthly, or several times each month depending on the amount of the liability. Quarterly and annual statements must also be filed providing a summary of all wages paid by the employer.

Accounting for Payroll Taxes To illustrate the accounting procedures for payroll taxes, assume that salaries for the month of January for a retail store with 15 employees are $16,000. The state unemployment compensation law provides for a tax on employers of 5.4%. Income tax withholdings for the month are $1,600. Assume FICA rates are 7.6% for employer and employee. Entries for the payroll and the employer's payroll taxes follow:

Salaries Expense	16,000	
FICA Taxes Payable		1,216
Employees Income Taxes Payable		1,600
Cash		13,184
To record payment of payroll and related employee withholdings.		

Payroll Tax Expense	2,208	
FICA Taxes Payable		1,216
State Unemployment Taxes Payable		864
Federal Unemployment Taxes Payable		128
To record the payroll tax liability of the employer.		

Computation:

Tax under Federal Insurance Contributions Act: 7.6% × $16,000	$1,216
Tax under state unemployment insurance legislation: 5.4% × $16,000	864
Tax under Federal Unemployment Tax Act: 0.8% (6.2% − credit of 5.4%) × $16,000	128
Total payroll taxes expense	$2,208

When tax payments are made to the proper agencies, the tax liability accounts are debited and Cash is credited.

The employer's payroll taxes, as well as the taxes withheld from employees, are based on amounts paid to employees during the period regardless of the basis employed for reporting income. When financial reports are prepared on the accrual basis, the employer will have to recognize both accrued payroll and the employer's payroll taxes relating thereto by adjustments at the end of the accounting period.

For example, assume that the salaries and wages accrued at December 31 were $9,500. Of this amount, $2,000 was subject to unemployment tax and $6,000 to FICA tax. The accrual entry for the employer's payroll taxes would be as follows:

Payroll Tax Expense	580	
FICA Taxes Payable		456
State Unemployment Taxes Payable		108
Federal Unemployment Taxes Payable		16
To accrue the payroll tax liability of the employer.		

Computation:

Tax under Federal Insurance Contributions Act: 7.6% × $6,000	$456
Tax under state unemployment insurance legislation: 5.4% × $2,000	108
Tax under Federal Unemployment Tax Act: 0.8% × $2,000	16
	$580

As was true with the accrual entry for the salaries and wages discussed on page 597, the preceding entry may be reversed at the beginning of the new period, or the accrued liabilities may be debited when the payments are made to the taxing authorities.

Agreements with employees may provide for payroll deductions and employer contributions for other items, such as group insurance plans, pension plans, savings bonds purchases, or union dues. Such agreements call for accounting procedures similar to those described for payroll taxes.

Other Tax Liabilities

There are many different types of taxes imposed on business entities. In addition to the several payroll taxes discussed in the previous section, a company usually must pay property taxes, federal and state income taxes on their earnings, and serve as an agent for the collection of sales taxes. Each of these liabilities has some unusual features that can complicate accounting for them.

Property Taxes Real and personal property taxes are based on the assessed valuation of properties as of a particular date. This has given rise to the view held by courts and others that taxes accrue as of a particular date. Generally, the date of accrual has been held to be the date of property assessment, or **lien date**, and a liability for the full year's property tax can be established at that date. The offset to the liability is a deferred expense since the tax liability is being established in advance of payment and incurrence of the tax expense. The tax expense is generally recognized as a charge against revenue over the fiscal year of the taxing authority for which the taxes are levied. This procedure relates the tax charge to the period in which the taxes provide benefits through government service. The date for payment of the liability is determined by the taxing authority and is accounted for independently from the monthly recognition of property tax expense.

To illustrate accounting for property taxes, assume that the taxing authority is on a July 1 to June 30 fiscal year, but the entity paying the tax is on a calendar year basis. Property taxes assessed for the period July 1, 1990, to June 30, 1991, are $60,000, and the full year's tax is to be paid on or before November 15, 1990. The following entry is made by the taxpaying entity at the lien date, July 1, 1990, to accrue property taxes for the year:

Deferred Property Taxes	60,000	
Property Taxes Payable		60,000

Each month, the following entry would be made to recognize the expense:

| Property Tax Expense................................. | 5,000 | |
| Deferred Property Taxes .... | | 5,000 |

The entry to record payment of the property taxes on November 15, 1990, would be:

| Property Taxes Payable .... | 60,000 | |
| Cash .... | | 60,000 |

At December 31, 1990, the deferred property tax account would have a debit balance of $30,000, representing the property taxes to be recognized as expenses in 1991. If the tax were due in January, 1991, and no payment had been made as of December 31, 1990, Property Taxes Payable would have a $60,000 credit balance, that would be reported as a current liability on the balance sheet.

Although the preceding approach seems to reflect the current definition of liabilities as established by the FASB, some companies recognize the liability ratably over the year rather than on the assessment or lien date. Under this latter approach a prepaid property tax account is created when the full year's tax is paid before the end of the taxing authority's fiscal year. In the authors' opinion, this practice is not as informative and useful as that illustrated.

Income Taxes Both federal and state governments raise a large portion of their revenue from income taxes assessed against both individuals and corporations. The taxable income of a business entity is determined by applying the tax rules and regulations to the operations of the business. As indicated in Chapter 4, the income tax rules do not always follow generally accepted accounting principles. Thus, the income reported for tax purposes may differ from that reported on the income statement. This difference can give rise to deferred income taxes. The actual amount payable for the current year must be determined after all adjusting entries are made at the close of a fiscal period. Federal and some state income tax regulations require companies to estimate their tax liability, and make periodic payments during the year in advance of the final computation and submission of the tax returns. Thus, the amount of income tax liability at year-end is usually much lower than the total tax computed for the year. Because income tax returns are always subject to government audit, a contingent liability exists for any year within the statute of limitations not yet reviewed by the Internal Revenue Service. If an additional liability arises as a result of an audit, the additional assessment should be reported as a liability until the payment is made.

Sales and Use Taxes With the passage of sales and use tax laws by state and local governments, additional duties are required of a business unit. Laws generally provide that the business unit must act as an agent for the governmental authority in the collection from customers of sales tax on the transfers of tangible personal properties. The buyer is responsible for the payment of sales tax to the seller when both buyer and seller are in the same tax jurisdiction; however, the buyer is responsible for the payment of use tax directly to the tax authority when the seller is outside the jurisdiction of such authority. Provision must be made in the accounts for the liability to the government for the tax collected from customers and the additional tax that the business must absorb.

The sales tax payable is generally a stated percentage of sales. The actual sales total and the sales tax collections are usually recorded separately at the time of sale. Cash or Accounts Receivable is debited; Sales and Sales Tax Payable are credited. The amount of sales tax to be paid to the taxing authority is computed on the recorded sales.

Unearned Revenues

Another category of liabilities that are definite in amount is referred to as **unearned revenues**. Frequently, these liabilities represent an obligation to provide services rather than tangible resources. Examples of unearned revenue include advances from customers, unearned rent, and unearned subscription revenue for publishing companies. Unearned revenue accounts are classified as current or noncurrent liabilities depending on when the revenue will be earned. When the revenue is earned, e.g., when services are performed, the unearned revenue account is debited and an appropriate revenue account is credited. If advances are refunded without providing goods or services, the liability is reduced by the payment, and no revenue is recognized.

Estimated Liabilities

The amount of an obligation is generally established by contract or accrues at a specified rate. There are instances, however, when an obligation clearly exists on a balance sheet date but the amount ultimately to be paid cannot be definitely determined. Because the amount to be paid is not definite does not mean the liability can be ignored or given a contingent status. The claim must be estimated from whatever data are available. Obligations arising from current operations, for example, the cost of meeting warranties for service and repairs on goods sold, must be estimated when prior experience indicates there is a definite liability. Here, uncertainty as to the amount and timing of expenditures is accompanied by an inability to identify the payees; but the fact that there are charges yet to be absorbed is certain.

Representative of liabilities that are estimated in amount and frequently found on financial statements are the following:

1. Refundable deposits, reporting the estimated amount to be refunded to depositors.
2. Warranties for service and replacements, reporting the estimated future claims by customers as a result of past guarantees of services or products or product part replacements.

3. Customer premium offers, reporting the estimated value of premiums or prizes to be distributed as a result of past sales or sales promotion activities.

4. Tickets, tokens, and gift certificates, reporting the estimated obligations in the form of services or merchandise arising from the receipt of cash in past periods.

5. Compensated absences, reporting the estimated future payments attributable to past services of employees.

Refundable Deposits

Liabilities of a company may include an obligation to refund amounts previously collected from customers as deposits. Refundable deposits may be classified as current or noncurrent liabilities depending on the purpose of the deposit. If deposits are made to protect the company against nonpayment for future services to be rendered, and the services are expected to be provided over a long period, the deposit should be reported as a noncurrent liability. Utility companies characteristically charge certain customers, such as those renting their homes, a deposit that is held until a customer discontinues the service, usually because of a move.

Another type of customer deposit is one made for reusable containers, such as bottles or drums, that hold the product being purchased. When a sale is recorded, a liability is recognized for the deposit. When a container is returned, a refund or credit is given for the deposit made. Periodically, an adjustment to recognize revenue is recorded for containers not expected to be returned. The asset "containers" and the related accumulated depreciation account should be reduced to eliminate the book value of containers not expected to be returned, and any gain or loss is recognized on the "sale" of the containers.

Warranties for Service and Replacements

Many companies agree to provide free service on units failing to perform satisfactorily or to replace defective goods. When these agreements, or warranties, involve only minor costs, such costs may be recognized in the periods incurred. When these agreements involve significant future costs and when experience indicates a definite future obligation exists, estimates of such costs should be made and matched against current revenues. Such estimates are usually recorded by a debit to an expense account and a credit to a liability account. Subsequent costs of fulfilling warranties are debited to the liability account and credited to an appropriate account, e.g., Cash or Inventory.

To illustrate accounting for warranties, consider the following example. MJW Video & Sound sells compact stereo systems with a two-year warranty. Past experience indicates that 10% of all sets sold will need repairs in the first year, and 20% will need repairs in the second year. The average repair cost is $50 per system. The number of systems sold in 1990 and 1991 was 5,000 and 6,000, respectively. Actual repair costs were

$12,500 in 1990 and $55,000 in 1991; it is assumed that all repair costs involved cash expenditures.

1990 Warranty Expense	75,000	
Estimated Liability Under Warranties		75,000
Estimated warranty expense based on systems sold:		
5,000 × .30 × $50 = $75,000.		
Estimated Liability Under Warranties	12,500	
Cash		12,500
Repairs actually made in 1990.		
1991 Warranty Expense	90,000	
Estimated Liability Under Warranties		90,000
Estimated warranty expense based on systems sold:		
6,000 × .30 × $50 = $90,000.		
Estimated Liability Under Warranties	55,000	
Cash		55,000
Repairs actually made in 1991.		

Periodically, the warranty liability account should be analyzed to see if the actual repairs approximate the estimate. Adjustment to the liability account will be required if experience differs appreciably from the estimates. These adjustments are changes in estimates and are reported in the period of change. If sales and repairs in the preceding example are assumed to occur evenly through the year, analysis of the liability account at the end of 1991 shows the ending balance of $97,500 ($75,000 + $90,000 − $12,500 − $55,000) is reasonably close to the predicted amount of $100,000 based upon the 10% and 20% estimates.

Computation:

1990 sales still under warranty for 6 months: $50 × [5,000 (½ × .20)]	$ 25,000	
1991 sales still under warranty for 18 months: $50 × [6,000 (½ × .10)		
+ 6,000 (.20)]	75,000	
Total	$100,000	

Assume, however, that warranty costs incurred in 1991 were only $35,000. Then the ending balance of $117,500 would be much higher than the $100,000 estimate. If the $17,500 difference were considered to be material, an adjustment to warranty expense would be made in 1991 as follows:

Estimated Liability Under Warranties	17,500	
Warranty Expense		17,500
Adjustment of estimate for warranty repairs.		

In certain cases, customers are charged special fees for a service or replacement warranty covering a specific period. When fees are collected, an unearned revenue account is credited. The unearned revenue is then recognized as revenue over the warranty period. Costs incurred in meeting the contract requirements are debited to expense; Cash, Inventory, or another appropriate account is credited. The **service contract** is in reality an insurance contract, and the amount charged for the contract is based on the past repair experience of the company for the item sold. The fee usually is set at a rate that will produce a profit margin on the contract if expectations are realized.

To illustrate accounting for service contracts, assume a company sells 3-year service contracts covering its product. During the first year, $50,000 was received on contracts, and expenses incurred for parts and labor in connection with these contracts totaled $5,000. It is estimated from past experience that the pattern of repairs, based on the total dollars spent for repairs, is 25% in the first year of the contract, 30% in the second year, and 45% in the third year. In addition, it is assumed that sales of the contracts are made evenly during the year. The following entries would be made in the first year.

Cash	50,000	
Unearned Revenue from Service Contracts		50,000
Sale of service contracts.		
Unearned Revenue from Service Contracts	6,250	
Revenue from Service Contracts		6,250
Estimated revenue earned from contracts, 12½% (½ of 25%) of $50,000, or $6,250.		
Service Contract Expense	5,000	
Inventory		5,000
Repairs actually made during the year.		

Based on the above entries, a profit of $1,250 on service contracts would be recognized in the first year. If future expectations change, adjustments will be necessary to the unearned revenue account to reflect the change in estimate.

The accounts Estimated Liability Under Warranties and Unearned Revenue from Service Contracts are classified as current or noncurrent liabilities depending on the period remaining on the warranty. Those warranty costs expected to be incurred within one year or unearned revenues expected to be earned within one year are classified as current; the balance as long-term. In the above illustration, the expected revenue percentage for the second year, assuming that sales of the contracts were made evenly during the first year, would be 27½% of the contract price, i.e., 12½% for balance of first year expectations and 15% (½ of 30%) for one-half of the second year expectations, or $13,750. This amount would be classified as current. The remaining 60%, or $30,000, of unearned revenue would be classified as noncurrent.

The method of accounting illustrated above does not recognize any income on the initial sale of the contract, but only as the period of the service contract passes and the actual costs are matched against an estimate of the earned revenue. Alternatively, a company could estimate in advance the cost of the repairs and recognize the difference between the amount of the service contract and the expected repair cost in the period of the contract sale. The choice of which method to use depends on the degree of confidence in the estimated repair cost. As discussed more fully in Chapter 19, revenue recognition varies with the facts involved. When collection is reasonably assured and future costs are known with a high degree of certainty, immediate income recognition is recommended. In the case of service contracts, the uncertainty of future expenses usually dictates use of the deferred revenue method.

Customer Premium Offers

Many companies offer special premiums to customers to stimulate the regular purchase of certain products. These offers may be open for a limited time or may be of a continuing nature. The premium is normally made available when the customer submits the required number of product labels or other evidence of purchase. In certain instances the premium offer may provide for an optional cash payment.

If a premium offer expires on or before the end of the company's fiscal period, adjustments in the accounts are not required; premium obligations are fully met and the premium expense account summarizes the full charge for the period. However, when a premium offer is continuing, an adjustment must be made at the end of the period to recognize the liability for future redemptions—Premium Expense is debited and an appropriate liability account is credited. The expense is thus charged to the period benefitting from the premium plan and current liabilities reflect the claim for premiums outstanding. If premium distributions are debited to an expense account, the liability balance may be reversed at the beginning of the new period.

To illustrate the accounting for a premium offer, assume the following: Good Foods offers a set of breakfast bowls upon the receipt of 20 certificates, one certificate being included in each package of the cereal distributed by this company. The cost of each set of bowls to the company is $2. It is estimated that only 40% of the certificates will be redeemed. In 1990, the company purchased 10,000 sets of bowls at $2 per set; 400,000 packages of cereal containing certificates were sold at a price of $1.20 per package. By the end of 1990, 30% of the certificates had been redeemed. Entries for 1990 are as follows:

Transaction	Entry		
1990:			
Premium purchases:	Premiums—Bowl Sets	20,000	
10,000 sets × $2 = $20,000	Cash		20,000
Sales:	Cash	480,000	
400,000 packages × $1.20 = $480,000	Sales		480,000
Premium claim redemptions:	Premium Expense	12,000	
120,000 certificates, or 6,000 sets × $2 = $12,000	Premiums—Bowl Sets ...		12,000

December 31, 1990:

Coupons estimated redeemable in future periods:		Premium Expense 4,000	
		Estimated Premium	
Total estimated redemptions—		Claims Outstanding	4,000
40% of 400,000	160,000		
Redemptions in 1990	120,000		
Estimated future			
redemptions	40,000		
Estimated claims outstanding:			
40,000 certificates, or			
2,000 sets @ $2	$ 4,000		

January 1, 1991 (optional):

Reversal of accrued liability balance.	Estimated Premium	
	Claims Outstanding 4,000	
	Premium Expense	4,000

The balance sheet at the end of 1990 will show premiums of $8,000 as a current asset and estimated premium claims outstanding of $4,000 as a current liability; the income statement for 1990 will show premium expense of $16,000 as a selling expense.

Experience indicating a redemption percentage that differs from the assumed rate will call for an appropriate adjustment in the subsequent period and the revision of future redemption estimates.

The estimated cost of the premiums may be shown as a direct reduction of sales by recording the premium claim at the time of the sale. This requires an estimate of the premium cost at the time of the sale. For example, in the previous illustration, the summary entry for sales recorded during the year, employing the sales reduction approach, would be as follows:

Cash 480,000	
Sales	464,000
Estimated Premium Claims Outstanding	16,000

The redemption of premium claims would call for debits to the liability account. Either the expense method or the sales reduction method is acceptable, and both are found in practice.

Tickets, Tokens, and Gift Certificates Outstanding

Many companies sell tickets, tokens, and gift certificates that entitle the owner to services or merchandise: for example, airlines issue tickets used for travel; local transit companies issue tokens good for fares; department stores sell gift certificates redeemable in merchandise.

When instruments redeemable in services or merchandise are outstanding at the end of the period, accounts should be adjusted to reflect the obligations under such arrangements. The nature of the adjustment will depend on the entries originally made in recording the sale of the instruments.

Ordinarily, the sale of instruments redeemable in services or merchandise is recorded by a debit to Cash and a credit to a liability account. As instruments are redeemed, the liability balance is debited and Sales or an appropriate revenue account is credited. Certain claims may be rendered void by lapse of time or for some other reason as defined by the sales agreement. In addition, experience may indicate a certain percentage of outstanding claims will never be presented for redemption. These factors must be considered at the end of the period, when the liability balance is reduced to the balance of the claim estimated to be outstanding and a revenue account is credited for the gain indicated from forfeitures. If Sales or a special revenue account is originally credited on the sale of the redemption instrument, the adjustment at the end of the period calls for a debit to the revenue account and a credit to a liability account for the claim still outstanding.

Compensated Absences

Compensated absences include payments by employers for vacation, holiday, illness, or other personal activities. Employees often earn paid absences based on the time employed. Generally, the longer an employee works for a company, the longer the vacation allowed, or the more liberal the time allowed for illnesses. At the end of any given accounting period, a company has a liability for earned but unused compensated absences. The matching principle requires that the estimated amounts earned be charged against current revenue, and a liability established for that amount.[7] The difficult part of this accounting treatment is estimating how much should be accrued. In Statement No. 43, the FASB requires a liability to be recognized for compensated absences that (1) have been earned through services already rendered, (2) vest or can be carried forward to subsequent years, and (3) are estimable and probable.

For example, assume that a company has a vacation pay policy for all employees. If all employees had the same anniversary date for computing time in service, the computations would not be too difficult. However, most plans provide for a flexible employee starting date. In order to compute the liability, a careful inventory of all employees must be made that includes the number of years of service, rate of pay, carryover of unused vacation from prior periods, turnover, and the probability of taking the vacation.

To illustrate the accounting for compensated absences, assume that S&N Corporation has 20 employees that are paid an average of $350 per week. During 1990, a total of 40 vacation weeks were earned by all employees but only 30 weeks of vacation were taken that year. The remaining 10 weeks of vacation were taken in 1991 when the average rate of pay was $400 per week. The entry to record the accrued vacation pay on December 31, 1990, would be:

Wages Expense	3,500	
Vacation Wages Payable		3,500
To record accrued vacation wages ($350 × 10 weeks).		

The above entry assumes that Wages Expense has already been re-

---

[7]*Statement of Financial Accounting Standards No. 43*, "Accounting for Compensated Absences" (Stamford: Financial Accounting Standards Board, 1980), par. 6.

corded for the 30 weeks of vacation taken during 1990. Therefore, the income statement would reflect the total Wages Expense for the entire 40 weeks of vacation earned during the period. On its December 31, 1990, balance sheet, S&N would report a current liability of $3,500 to reflect the obligation for the 10 weeks of vacation pay that is owed. In 1991, when the additional vacation weeks are taken and the payroll is paid, S&N would make the following entry:

Wages Expense	500	
Vacation Wages Payable	3,500	
Cash		4,000
To record payment at current rates of previously earned vacation time ($400 × 10 weeks).		

Since the vacation weeks are now used, the above entry eliminates the liability. An adjustment to Wages Expense is required because the liability was recorded at the rates of pay in effect during the time the compensation (vacation pay) was earned. However, the cash is being paid at the current rate, which requires an adjustment to Wages Expense. If the rate of pay for the 10 hours of vacation taken in 1991 had remained the same as the rate used to record the accrual on December 31, 1990 there would not have been an adjustment to Wages Expense. The entry to record payment in 1991 would simply be a debit to the payable and a credit to Cash for $3,500.

An exception to the requirement for accrual of compensated absences, such as vacation pay, is made for sick pay. The FASB decided that sick pay should be accrued only if it vests with the employee, i.e., the employee is entitled to compensation for a certain number of "sick days" regardless of whether the employee is actually absent for that period. Upon leaving the firm, the employee would be compensated for any unused sick time. If the sick pay does not vest, it is recorded as an expense only when actually paid.[8]

Although compensated absences are not deductible for income tax purposes until the vacation, holiday, or illness occurs and the payment is made, they are required by GAAP to be recognized as liabilities on the financial statements.

Contingent Liabilities

A *contingency* is defined in FASB Statement No. 5 as:

> . . . an existing condition, situation, or set of circumstances involving uncertainty as to possible gain . . . or loss . . . to an enterprise that will ultimately be resolved when one or more future events occur or fail to occur.[9]

As defined, contingencies may relate to either assets or liabilities, and to

---

[8]*Ibid.*, par. 7.

[9]*Statement of Financial Accounting Standards No. 5*, "Accounting for Contingencies" (Stamford: Financial Accounting Standards Board, 1975), par. 1.

either a gain or loss. In this chapter, attention is focused on **contingent losses** that might give rise to a liability. As mentioned previously, contingent liabilities are distinguishable from estimated liabilities.

Historically, when liabilities were classified as contingent, they were not recorded on the books, but were disclosed in notes to financial statements. The distinction between a recorded liability and a **contingent liability** was not always clear. If a legal liability existed and the amount of the obligation was either definite or could be estimated with reasonable certainty, the liability was recorded on the books. If the existence of the obligation depended on the happening of a future event, recording of the liability was deferred until the event occurred. In an attempt to make the distinction more precise, the FASB used three terms in FASB Statement No. 5 to identify the range of possibilities of the event occurring. Different accounting action was recommended for each term. The terms, their definitions, and the accounting actions recommended are as follows:[10]

Term	Definition	Accounting Action
Probable	The future event or events are likely to occur.	Record the probable event in the accounts if the amount can be reasonably estimated. If not estimable, disclose facts in note.
Reasonably possible	The chance of the future event or events occurring is more than remote but less than likely.	Report the contingency in a note.
Remote	The chance of the future event or events occurring is slight.	No recording or reporting unless contingency represents a guarantee. Then note disclosure is required.

If the happening of an event that would create a liability is **probable**, and if the amount of the obligation can be **reasonably estimated**, the contingency should be recognized as a liability. Some of the liabilities already presented as estimated liabilities may be considered probable contingent liabilities because the existence of the obligation is dependent on some event occurring, e.g., warranties are dependent on the need for repair or service to be given, gift certificates are dependent on the certificate being turned in for redemption, and vacation pay is dependent on a person taking a vacation. These liabilities are not included in this section, however, because historically they have been recognized as recorded liabilities. Other liabilities, such as unsettled litigation claims, self insurance, and loan guarantees have more traditionally been considered as unrecorded contingent liabilities, and these will be explored separately in the following pages.

Inasmuch as most liabilities have some element of contingency associated with them, the authors feel that the classification "contingent liabil-

[10]*Ibid.*, par. 3.

ity" should be reserved for those items that fit into one of the latter two terms, i.e., **reasonably possible** or **remote**. If the happening of the event is probable and the amount of the obligation can be estimated, the liability is no longer a contingent liability, but a recorded estimated liability. Such liabilities meet the definition of liabilities established by the FASB. This approach avoids having to say that some contingent liabilities are recorded and others are not. By this definition, a contingent liability would never be recorded but would be either disclosed in a footnote or ignored depending on the degree of remoteness of its expected occurrence.

The FASB statement provided no specific guidelines as to how these three terms should be interpreted in probability percentages. Surveys made of statement preparers and users disclosed a great diversity in the probability interpretations of the terms. It is unlikely, therefore, that FASB Statement No. 5 has greatly reduced the diversity in practice in recording some of these contingent items.

Litigation An increasing number of lawsuits are being filed against companies and individuals. Lawsuits may result in substantial liabilities to successful plaintiffs. Typically, litigation takes a long time to conclude. Even after a decision has been rendered by a lower court, there are many appeal opportunities available. Thus, both the amount and timing of a loss arising from litigation are generally highly uncertain. Some companies carry insurance to protect them against these losses, so the impact of the losses on the financial statements is minimized. For uninsured risks, however, a decision must be made as to when the liability for litigation becomes probable, and thus a recorded loss.

FASB Statement No. 5 identifies several key factors to consider in making the decision. These include:[11]

1. The nature of the litigation.
2. The period when the cause of action occurred. (Liability is not recognized in any period before the cause of action occurred.)
3. Progress of the case in court, including progress between date of the financial statements and their issuance date.
4. Views of legal counsel as to the probability of loss.
5. Prior experience with similar cases.
6. Management's intended response to the litigation.

If analysis of these and similar factors results in the judgment that a loss is probable, and the amount of the loss can be reasonably estimated, the liability should be recorded. A settlement after the balance sheet date but before the statements are issued would be evidence that the loss was probable at the year-end, and would result in a reporting of loss in the current financial statements.

[11]*Ibid.*, par. 36.

Another area of potential liability involves unasserted claims, i.e., a cause of action has occurred but no claim has yet been asserted. For example, a person may be injured on the property of the company, but as of the date the financial statements are issued, no legal action has been taken; or a violation of a government regulation may occur, but no federal action has yet been taken. If it is probable that a claim will be filed, and the amount of the claim can be reasonably estimated, accrual of the liability should be made. If the amount cannot be reasonably estimated, note disclosure is required. If assertion of the claim is not judged to be probable, no accrual or disclosure is necessary.

As a practical matter, it should be noted that a company would be very unlikely to record a loss from unasserted claims or from pending litigation unless negotiations for a settlement had been substantially completed. When that is the case, the loss is no longer a contingency, but an estimated loss.

Some companies do not disclose any information regarding potential liabilities from litigation. Others provide a brief, general description of pending litigation, as illustrated in the following note from the 1987 annual report of Ford Motor Company.

Exhibit 14-1   Ford Motor Company

NOTE 13. Litigation and Claims

Various legal actions, governmental investigations and proceedings, and claims are pending or may be instituted or asserted in the future against the company and its subsidiaries, including those arising out of alleged defects in the company's products, governmental regulations relating to safety, emissions and fuel economy, product warranties, and environmental matters. Certain of the pending legal actions are, or purport to be, class actions. The investigations include a number that are pending before or may be instituted by the National Highway Traffic Safety Administration relating to alleged safety defects or alleged non-compliance with safety standards with regard to motor vehicles made or sold by the company. Some of the foregoing matters involve or may involve compensatory, punitive, or antitrust or other treble damage claims in very large amounts, or recall campaigns or other relief which, if granted, would require very large expenditures.

Litigation is subject to many uncertainties, the outcome of individual litigated matters is not predictable with assurance, and it is reasonably possible that some of the foregoing matters could be decided unfavorably to the company or the subsidiary involved. Although the amount of liability at December 31, 1987 with respect to these matters cannot be ascertained, the company believes that any resulting liability should not materially affect the consolidated financial position of the company and its consolidated subsidiaries at December 31, 1987.

Sometimes companies provide fairly specific information about pending actions and claims. However, companies must be careful not to increase their chances of losing pending lawsuits, and generally do not disclose dollar amounts of potential losses, which might be interpreted as an admission of guilt and a willingness to pay a certain amount. For example, Eastman Kodak disclosed the following information in its 1987 annual report in connection with a lawsuit filed by Polaroid Corporation.

Exhibit 14-2   Eastman Kodak Company

Legal Notes

The action filed by Polaroid Corporation in 1976 in the U.S. District Court in Boston, charging that Kodak's instant cameras and print film infringe certain Polaroid patents and seeking an injunction and treble damages, resulted in a judgment entered on October 11, 1985 holding that Kodak's instant film, PR-10, and EK4 and EK6 instant cameras infringed seven patents of Polaroid Corporation and an injunction, effective January 9, 1986, prohibiting further manufacture or sale of such products in the United States. Kodak's motions to stay the injunction were denied and the injunction accordingly became effective on January 9, 1986. Kodak appealed to the U.S. Court of Appeals for the Federal Circuit, which affirmed the decision of the District Court on April 25, 1986. The United States Supreme Court denied Kodak's petition for certiorari on October 6, 1986. The case has been returned to the U.S. District Court in Boston for trial of the issues of (a) whether Kodak's infringement of any of the patents was willful and deliberate, (b) the amount of damages adequate to compensate Polaroid for Kodak's infringement together with interest and whether such damages should be trebled, (c) whether costs should be imposed against either party, and (d) whether Polaroid is entitled to its reasonable attorneys' fees. Pretrial proceedings are under way. No date has been set for trial of the case. Polaroid, in connection with an informal pretrial conference, included in a submission to the Court a calculation estimating its alleged lost profits from lost sales at $3.2 billion (including interest) and asserted additional lost profits, based on "complex" calculations which Polaroid has "not yet completed," in the range of $1 billion to $2.5 billion because of Polaroid's alleged inability to "pursue the pricing, production and product introduction strategies it would have otherwise chosen." The company is contesting vigorously the amount of damages sought by Polaroid. Based on the advice of counsel retained to represent it in the case, the company does not believe that it is likely the amount of damages awarded will have a material adverse effect on the financial condition of the company. Damages will be charged against earnings of the year of final resolution.

Kodak was involved in other litigation, investigations of a routine nature, and various legal matters during 1987 which are being defended and handled in the ordinary course of business.

Self Insurance   Some large companies with widely distributed risks may decide not to purchase insurance for protection against the normal business risks of fire, explosion, flood, or damage to other persons or their property. These companies in effect insure themselves against these risks. The accounting question that arises in whether a liability should be accrued and a loss recognized for the possible occurrence of the uninsured risk. Sometimes companies have recorded as an expense an amount equal to the insurance premium that would have been paid had commercial insurance been carried. The FASB considered this specific subject in Statement No. 5, and concluded that no loss or liability should be recorded until the loss has occurred. Fires, explosions, or other casualties are random in occurrence, and as such, are not accruable. Further, they stated that

> . . . unlike an insurance company, which has a contractual obligation under policies in force to reimburse insureds for losses, an enterprise can have no such obligation to itself and, hence, no liability.[12]

Thus, although an exposed condition does exist, it is a future period that must bear any loss that occurs, not a current period.

Loan Guarantees   Enterprises sometimes enter into a contract guaranteeing a loan for another enterprise, frequently a subsidiary company, a supplier, or even a favored customer. These guarantees obligate the entity to make the loan payment if the principal borrower fails to make the payment. A similar contingent obligation exists when the payee of a note receivable discounts it at a bank, but is held contingently liable in the event the maker of the note defaults. Discussion of discounted notes receivable was included in Chapter 8. If the default on the loan or the note is judged to be probable based on the events that have occurred prior to the issuance date of the financial statements, the loss and liability should be accrued in accordance with the general guidelines discussed in this section. Otherwise, note disclosure is required even if the likelihood of making the payment is remote. This exception to not disclosing remote contingencies arose because companies have traditionally disclosed guarantees in notes to the financial statements, and the FASB did not want to reduce this disclosure practice.

Balance Sheet Presentation   The liability section of the balance sheet is usually divided between current and noncurrent liabilities as previously discussed. The nature of the detail to be presented for current liabilities depends on the use to be made of the financial statement. A balance sheet prepared for stockholders might report little detail; on the other hand, creditors may insist on full detail concerning current debts.

Assets are normally recorded in the order of their liquidity, and consistency would suggest that liabilities be reported in the order of their maturity. The latter practice may be followed only to the extent it is practical; observance of this procedure would require an analysis of the different classes of obligations and separate reporting for classes with varying maturity dates.

---

[12]*Ibid.*, par. 28.

Liabilities should not be offset by assets to be applied to their liquidation. Disclosure as to future debt liquidation, however, may be provided by an appropriate parenthetical remark or note. Disclosure of liabilities secured by specific assets should also be made by a parenthetical remark or note.

The current liabilities section of a balance sheet prepared on December 31, 1991, might appear as shown below:

Current liabilities:		
Notes payable:		
Trade creditors	$12,000	
Banks (secured by pledge of accounts receivable)	20,000	
Officers	12,500	$ 44,500
Accounts payable		35,250
Current portion of long-term debt		10,000
Salaries and wages payable		1,250
Income taxes payable		6,000
Real and personal property taxes payable		1,550
Dividends payable		4,500
Other current liabilities:		
Advances from customers	$ 7,500	
Estimated warranty costs	2,500	10,000
Total current liabilities		$113,050

Because most of the noncurrent liabilities are discussed in separate chapters that follow, illustration of the details of the noncurrent liabilities section is deferred until Chapter 17 and illustrated with owners' equity. For a further illustration of a liabilities section of a balance sheet, with related notes, see the General Mills financial statements reproduced in Appendix A at the end of this book.

Appendix

Calculation of Bonuses Illustrated

An agreement may provide for a bonus computed on the basis of gross revenue or sales, or on the basis of income. When income is used, the computation will depend on several factors. Three possibilities are illustrated here depending on whether the bonus is based on: (1) income before deductions for bonus or income tax, (2) income after deduction for bonus but before deduction for income tax, or (3) net income after deductions for both bonus and income tax. The degree of difficulty in computing a bonus based on income varies with the measure of income used. To illustrate the computations required in each case, assume the following: Photo Graphics Inc. gives the sales managers of its individual stores a bonus of 10% of store earnings. Income for 1991 for store No. 1 before any charges for bonus or income tax was $100,000. The income tax rate is 40%.

$$\text{Let } B = \text{Bonus}$$
$$T = \text{Income Tax}$$

Example 1   **Bonus Based on Income Before Deductions for Bonus or Income Tax.**

$$B = .10 \times \$100,000$$
$$B = \$10,000$$

Example 2   **Bonus Based on Income After Deduction for Bonus but Before Deduction for Income Tax**

$$B = .10 \, (\$100,000 - B)$$
$$B = \$10,000 - .10B$$
$$B + .10B = \$10,000$$
$$1.10B = \$10,000$$
$$B = \$9,090.91$$

Calculation of the bonus may be proved as follows:

Income before bonus and income tax	$100,000.00
Deduct bonus	9,090.91
Income after bonus but before income tax	$ 90,909.09
Bonus rate	10%
Bonus	$ 9,090.91

Example 3   Bonus Based on Net Income After Deductions for Bonus and Income Tax

$$B = .10 \,(\$100,000 - B - T)$$
$$T = .40 \,(\$100,000 - B)$$

Substituting for T in the first equation and solving for B:

$$B = .10 \,[\$100,000 - B - .40 \,(\$100,000 - B)]$$
$$B = .10 \,(\$100,000 - B - \$40,000 + .40B)$$
$$B = \$10,000 - .1B - \$4,000 + .04B$$
$$B + .1B - .04B = \$10,000 - \$4,000$$
$$1.06B = \$6,000$$
$$B = \$5,660.38$$

Substituting for B in the second equation and solving for T:

$$T = .40 \,(\$100,000 - \$5,660.38)$$
$$T = .40 \times \$94,339.62$$
$$T = \$37,735.85$$

Calculation of the bonus is proved in the following summary:

Income before bonus and income tax		$100,000.00
Deduct: Bonus	$ 5,660.38	
Income tax	37,735.85	43,396.23
Net income after bonus and income tax		$ 56,603.77
Bonus rate		10%
Bonus		$ 5,660.38

The bonus should be reported on the income statement as an expense before arriving at net income regardless of the method employed in its computation.

Key Terms

Compensated absences 606
Contingent liability 608
Liabilities 588
Nontrade notes payable 591
Promissory note 591

Refundable deposits 601
Trade notes payable 591
Unearned revenues 600
Warranties 601

Questions

1. Identify the major components included in the definition of liabilities established by the FASB.
2. (a) What is meant by an executory contract? (b) Do these contracts fit the definition of liabilities included in this chapter?
3. Distinguish between current and noncurrent liabilities.
4. At what amount should liabilities generally be reported?
5. Under what conditions would debt that will mature within the next year be reported as a noncurrent liability?
6. Distinguish between the following categories: (a) liabilities that are definite in amount, (b) estimated liabilities, and (c) contingent liabilities.
7. Gross payroll is taxed by both federal and state governments. Identify these taxes and indicate who bears the cost of the tax, the employer or the employee?
8. How should a company account for revenue received in advance for a service contract?
9. Why should a company normally account for product warranties on an accrual basis?
10. What information must a firm accumulate in order to adequately account for estimated liabilities on tickets, tokens, and gift certificates?
11. How should compensated absences be accounted for?
12. How should contingent liabilities that are reasonably possible of becoming liabilities be reported on the financial statements?
13. What factors are important in deciding whether a pending lawsuit should be reported as a liability on the balance sheet?
14. Why does accounting for self-insurance differ from accounting for insurance premiums with outside carriers?
*15. The sales manager for Off-Road Enterprises is entitled to a bonus equal to 12% of profits. What difficulties may arise in the interpretation of this profit-sharing agreement?

*Relates to Appendix

Discussion Cases

Case 14-1   (How much liability do they have?)

As a consultant for a small CPA firm, you have been asked to provide answers and explanations for each of the following questions:

(a) Under the laws of the state, your client, the Barboza Tile Company, has a choice of methods for paying unemployment insurance contributions. The company may pay a percentatge of gross wages or may reimburse the state employment commission directly for actual claims that may arise. Barboza chose the reimbursement of actual claims method. If no claims against the client are filed, may your client record an expense and a liability for future unemployment claims?

(b) Doyle Company franchises distributorships for oxygen inhalator units. The franchisees lease the units from Doyle and pay an initial leasing fee for each unit before receipt of the unit. The franchise agreement states that the franchisee is entitled to a refund, upon termination of the franchise agreement and return of the units, of a specified amount of the initial leasing fee depending on the length of time the units were leased out. When the units are returned, they are generally redistributed without any repair. Should a liability be recorded by Doyle for the return of a portion of the initial leasing fee?

(c) The Juab County Board of Education employed a teacher for the school year, September through June, at an annual salary of $18,000 payable over a 12-month period. The Board's personnel policy states that the annual salary of a teacher is earned evenly over a 10-month period from September through June. The Board withholds an equal amount from each of the ten paychecks to make it possible for teachers to receive their pay in twelve equal installments. What amount, if any, should be reflected on the Board's statements of financial position at June 30 for the $1,500 per month payable to the teacher for July and August?   (AICPA adapted)

Case 14-2   (Leave my current ratio alone!)

Soto Inc., a closely held corporation, has never been audited and is seeking a large bank loan for plant expansion. The bank has requested audited financial statements. In conference with the president and majority stockholder of Soto, the auditor is informed that the bank looks very closely at the current ratio. The auditor's proposed reclassifications and adjustments include the following:

(a) A note payable issued 4 1/2 years ago matures in six months from the balance sheet date. The auditor wants to reclassify it as a current liability. The controller says no because, "we are probably going to refinance this note with other long-term debt."

(b) An accrual for compensated absences. Again the controller objects because the amount of the pay for these absences cannot be estimated. "Some employees quit in the first year and don't get vacation, and it is impossible to predict which employees will be absent for illness or other causes. Without being able to identify the employees, we can't determine the rate of compensation."

How would you as auditor respond to the controller?

Case 14-3   (When is a loss a loss?)

The following three **independent** sets of facts relate to (a) the possible accrual or (b) the possible disclosure by other means of a loss contingency.

Situation 1. A company offers a one-year warranty for the product that it manufactures. A history of warranty claims has been compiled and the probable amount of claims related to sales for a given period can be determined.

Situation 2. Subsequent to the date of a set of financial statements, but prior to the issuance of the financial statements, a company enters into a contract which, because of a sudden shift in the economy, will probably result in a significant loss to the company. The amount of the loss can be reasonably esimated.

Situation 3. A company has adopted a policy of recording self-insurance for any possible losses resulting from injury to others by the company's vehicles. The premium for an insurance policy for the same risk from an independent insurance company would have an annual cost of $20,000. During the period covered by the financial statements, there were no accidents involving the company's vehicles which resulted to injury to others.

Discuss the accrual and/or type of disclosure necessary (if any) and the reason(s) why such disclosure is appropriate for each of the three independent sets of facts above.   (AICPA adapted)

Case 14-4   (Should a liability be recorded?)

How should the following circumstances affect the presentation of the calendar year-end financial statements for Henderson Corporation? Explain your answer.

(a) There is a suit pending in federal court against Henderson Corporation. Henderson has been accused of dumping toxic wastes in the Cucamonga River which flows through a residential area. The citizens are seeking both compensatory and punitive damages.

(b) The Petrochemical Workers Union, which represents 95% of Henderson's employees, is threatening to strike unless Henderson adopts an employee profit-sharing plan. Negotiations are scheduled for November of the following year.

(c) The Union has pressured Henderson into compensating their employees for a certain number of "sick days" regardless of whether the employee is actually absent for that period.   (AICPA adapted)

Case 14-5   (Is it really self-insurance?)

The auditors of Data Retrieval Systems are concerned with how to account for the insurance premiums on a liability policy carried with a large insurance company. Premiums on the policy are based on the average loss experience of Data Retrieval Systems over the past five years. In some years, no insured loss occurs; however, the company follows the practice of recognizing expenses for the premiums paid to the insurance company regardless of actual loss. The senior auditor, Gary Wells, has read FASB Statement No. 5 and argues that the premiums paid are really deposits with the insurance company. Since the premiums are based on the losses actually incurred, income should be charged only when the losses occur, not when the premiums are paid. By charging the premiums to expense, an artificial smoothing of income results, something FASB Statement No. 5 was designed to prevent. Barbara Orton, controller, argues that the premiums are arm's-length payments, that FASB Statement No. 5 applies only to self-insurance, and that the policy carried by Data Retrieval Systems is obviously with an outside carrier. Thus, Orton believes the premiums should be recognized as a valid period expense. As audit manager, you are asked to render your opinion on the matter.

Exercises   ### Exercise 14-1   (Purchase with non-interest-bearing note)

On September 1, 1990, Perfection Manufacturing Co. purchased two new company automobiles from Top Quality Auto Sales. The terms of the sale called for Perfection to pay $20,111 to Top Quality on September 1, 1991. Perfection gave the seller a non-interest-bearing note for that amount. At the date of purchase, the interest rate for short-term loans was 10.5%.

(a) Prepare the journal entries necessary on September 1, 1990, December 31, 1990, (year-end adjusting), and September 1, 1991.

(b) Show how notes payable would be presented in the December 31, 1990, balance sheet.

Exercise 14-2 (Recording payroll and payroll taxes)

The Express Company paid one week's wages of $10,600 in cash (net pay after all withholdings and deductions) to its employees. Income tax withholdings were equal to 17% of the gross payroll, and the only other deductions were 7.6% for FICA tax and $160 for union dues. Give the entries that should be made on the books of the company to record the payroll and the tax accruals to be recognized by the employer, assuming that the company is subject to unemployment taxes of 5.4% (state) and .8% (federal). Assume that all wages for the week are subject to FICA and unemployment taxes.

Exercise 14-3 (Monthly payroll entries)

Aggie Co. sells agricultural products. Aggie pays its salespeople a salary plus a commission. The salary is the same for each salesperson, $1,000 per month. The commission varies by length of time of employment, and is a percentage of the company's total gross sales. Each salesperson starts with a commission of 1.0%, which is increased an additional 0.5% for each full year of employment with Aggie, to a maximum of 5.0%. The total gross sales for the month of January were $120,000.

Aggie has six salespeople as follows:

	No. of years
Frank	10
Sally	9
Tina	8
Barry	6
Mark	3
Lisa	9 mos.

Assume the FICA rate is 7.6%, the FUTA rate is 6.2% and the state unemployment rate is 5.4%. (Assume the federal government allows the maximum credit for state unemployment tax paid.) The federal income tax withholding rate is 30%. Compute the January salaries and commissions expense and make any necessary entries to record the payroll transactions.

Exercise 14-4 (Accounting for property taxes)

On November 20, 1990, Miranda Floral Shop received a property tax assessment of $14,400 for the taxing unit's fiscal year ending June 30, 1991. No entry was made to record the assessment. Later, Miranda's accountant was preparing the yearly financial statements (based on a February 1 to January 31 fiscal year) and came across the property tax assessment. Give the journal entries to record the tax payment (if any) and any adjusting entries necessary on January 31, 1991, assuming:

(a) The full tax of $14,400 had been paid on January 5, 1991 and charged to expense.
(b) None of the tax had been paid as of January 31, 1991.
(c) A portion of the tax ($9,050) had been paid on January 20, 1991 and charged to expense.

Exercise 14-5   (Warranty liability)

In 1990 Thompson Office Supply began selling a new calculator that carried a two-year warranty against defects. Based on the manufacturer's recommendations, Thompson projects estimated warranty costs (as a percentage of dollar sales) as follows:

First year of warranty	3%
Second year of warranty	8%

Sales and actual warranty repairs for 1990 and 1991 are presented below:

	1990	1991
Sales	$250,000	$475,000
Actual warranty repairs	5,300	18,450

(1) Give the necessary journal entries to record the liability at the end of 1990 and 1991.
(2) Analyze the warranty liability account as of the year ending December 31, 1991, to see if the actual repairs approximate the estimate. Should Thompson revise the manufacturer's warranty estimate? (Assume sales and repairs occur evenly throughout the year.)

Exercise 14-6   (Warranty liability)

Modern Appliance Company's accountant has been reviewing the firm's past television sales. For the past two years, Modern has been offering a special service warranty on all televisions sold. With the purchase of a television, the customer has the right to purchase a three-year service contract for an extra $60. Information concerning past television and warranty contract sales is given below:

Color-All Model II Television		
	1990	1991
Television sales in units	460	550
Sales price per unit	$ 400	$ 500
Number of service contracts sold	300	350
Expenses relating to television warranties	$3,350	$9,630

Modern's accountant has estimated from past records that the pattern of repairs has been 40% in the first year after sale, 36% in the second year, and 24% in the third year. Give the necessary journal entries related to the service contracts for 1990 and 1991. In addition, indicate how much profit on service contracts would be recognized in 1991. Assume sales of the contracts are made evenly during the year.

Exercise 14-7   (Premium liability)

In an effort to increase sales, Pennington Blade Company began a sales promotion campaign on June 30, 1991. Part of this new promotion included placing a special coupon in each package of razor blades sold. Customers were able to redeem 5 coupons for a bottle of shaving lotion. Each premium costs Pennington $.75. Pennington estimated that 60% of the coupons issued will be redeemed. For the six months ended December 31, 1991, the following information is available:

Packages of razor blades sold	1,800,000
Premiums purchased	135,000
Coupons redeemed	605,000

What is the estimated liability for premium claims outstanding at December 31, 1991?   (AICPA adapted)

Exercise 14-8   (Premium liability)

On June 1, 1991, the National Pet Company began marketing a new dog food created specifically to meet the nutritional requirements of puppies. As a promotion, National was offering a free dog house to all customers returning the weight seals from the purchase of 1,000 pounds of the new dog food. National estimates that 30% of the weight seals will be returned. At December 31, 1991, the following information was available:

Sales (1,650,000 pounds × $.40)	$660,000
Dog house purchases (495 × $30)	14,850
Dog house distributed (265 × $30)	7,950

Give the journal entries to record the sales of dog food, purchase of dog house premiums, redemption of weight seals, and the estimated liability for outstanding premium offers as of the end of the year.

Exercise 14-9   (Compensated absence—vacation pay)

The Styles Company employs five people. Each employee is entitled to two weeks' paid vacation every year the employee works for the company. The conditions of the paid vacation are : (a) for each full year of work, an employee will receive two weeks of paid vacation (no vacation accrues for a portion of a year), (b) each employee will receive the same pay for vacation time as the regular pay in the year taken, and (c) unused vacation pay can be carried forward. The following data were taken from the firm's personnel records:

Employee	Starting Date	Cumulative Vacation Taken as of December 31, 1991	Weekly Salary
Norm Racine	December 21, 1984	11 weeks	$375
Michael Smith	March 6, 1989	2 weeks	500
Phyllis Taylor	August 13, 1990	none	350
Brian Hinsman	December 17, 1989	3 weeks	300
Ann Behan	March 29, 1991	none	400

Compute the liability for vacation pay as of December 31, 1991.

Exercise 14-10 (Disclosure of Contingencies)

Sound Wave, Inc., a manufacturer of electronic greeting cards, has had a lawsuit filed against it by Sounds Good, another manufacturer of electronic greeting cards. The suit alleges patent right infringements by Sound Wave and asks for compensatory damages.

For the following situations, determine whether Sound Wave should: (1) report as a liablity on the balance sheet—if so, how much, (2) disclose in a footnote, (3) do nothing. Give reasons for your answers.

(a) Assuming that Sound Wave's legal counsel is convinced that the suit will result in a loss to Sound Wave but isn't sure how much.

(b) Assuming that Sound Wave's legal counsel believes an out-of-court settlement is probable and will cost Sound Wave approximately $600,000.

(c) Assuming that Sound Wave's legal counsel believes it is reasonably possible that the case will result in a $2,000,000 loss to Sound Wave.

(d) Assuming that Sound Wave's legal counsel believes it is probable that the case will result in an undeterminable loss to Sound Wave.

(e) Assuming that Sound Wave's legal counsel believes there is a remote chance for a loss to occur.

(f) Assuming that the suit hasn't been filed but that Sound Wave's legal counsel has informed management that an unintentional patent infringement has occurred.

Exercise 14-11 (Contingent losses)

Conrad Corporation sells motorcycle helmets. In 1990, Conrad sold 4 million helmets before discovering a significant defect in the helmet's construction. By December 31, 1990, two lawsuits had been filed against Conrad. The first lawsuit, which Conrad has little chance of winning, is expected to settle out of court for $900,000 in January of 1991. The second lawsuit, which is for $400,000, Conrad's attorneys think the company has fifty-fifty chance of winning. What accounting treatment should Conrad give the pending lawsuits in the year-end financial statements? (Include any necessary journal entries.)

Exercise 14-12 (Balance sheet reporting of current liabilities)

Prepare the current liabilities section of the balance sheet for the Ilena Company on December 31, 1990, from the information appearing below:

(a) Short-term notes payable: arising from purchases of goods, $62,680; arising from loans from banks, $20,000, on which marketable securities valued at $26,100 have been pledged as security; arising from short-term advances by officers, $22,600.

(b) Accounts payable arising from purchase of goods, $59,300.

(c) Employees income taxes payable, $1,584.

(d) First-mortgage serial bonds, $175,000, payable in semiannual installments of $7,000 due on March 1 and September 1 of each year.

(e) Advances received from customers on purchase orders, $4,140.

(f) Estimated expense of meeting warranty for service requirements on merchandise sold, $6,480.

*Exercise 14-13 (Calculation of bonus)

Illinois Wholesale Company has an agreement with its sales manager whereby the latter is entitled to 8% of company earnings as a bonus. Company income for a calendar year before bonus and income tax is $350,000. Income tax is 40% of income after bonus. Compute the amount of the bonus under each of the conditions below.

(a) The bonus is calculated on income before deductions for bonus and income tax.
(b) The bonus is calculated on income after deduction for bonus but before deduction for income tax.
(c) The bonus is calculated on net income after deductions for both bonus and income tax.

*Exercise 14-14 (Calculation of bonus rate)

The Redwood Furniture Company provides a special bonus for its executive officers based on income before bonus or income tax. Income before bonus and income tax for 1991 was $2,500,000. The combined state and federal income tax rate is 55%, and the total income tax liability for 1991 is $1,278,750. What was the bonus rate?

*Relates to Appendix

Problems   **Problem 14-1 (Miscellaneous operating payables)**

The Collins Corporation closes its books and prepares financial statements on an annual basis. The following information is gathered by the chief accountant to assist in preparing the liability section of the balance sheet:

(a) Property taxes of $54,000 were assessed on the property in May 1990, for the subsequent period of July 1 to June 30. The payment of taxes is divided into three equal installments, November 1, February 1, and May 1. The November 1 payment was made and charged to Property Tax Expense. No other entries have been made for property taxes relative to the 1990-91 assessment.
(b) The estimated 1990 pretax income for Collins is $629,000. The effective state income tax rate is 10% (applied to pretax income). The effective rate for federal income taxes is estimated at 40% (applied to income after deducting state income taxes). Income tax payments of $280,000 were made by Collins during 1990, including $50,000 as the final payment on 1989 federal income taxes, $20,000 for 1990 estimated state taxes, the balance for 1990 estimated federal taxes.
(c) Taxable sales for 1990 were $7,500,000. The state sales tax rate is 5.5%. Quarterly statements have been filed, and the following tax payments were made with the return.

1st Quarter	$ 96,000
2nd Quarter	110,000
3rd Quarter	125,000

The balance in the account Sales Tax Payable is $81,200 at December 31, 1990.

Instructions:

(1) Based on the above data, what amounts should be reported on the balance sheet as liabilities at December 31, 1990?
(2) Prepare the necessary adjusting entries to record the liabilities.

Problem 14-2   (Accrued payroll and payroll taxes)

Martina Clothiers' employees are paid on the 10th and 25th of each month for the period ending the previous 5th and 20th respectively. An analysis of the payroll on Thursday, November 5, 1991, revealed the following data:

	Gross Pay	FICA	Federal Income Tax	State Income Tax	Insurance	Net Pay
Office staff salaries	$11,250	$ 574	$ 1,200	$ 450	$ 270	$ 8,756
Officers' salaries	28,500	364	5,700	1,500	510	20,426
Sales salaries	18,000	712	3,600	750	390	12,548
Total	$57,750	$1,650	$10,500	$2,700	$1,170	$41,730

It is determined that for the November 5 pay period, no additional employees exceeded the wage base for FICA purposes than had done so in prior pay periods. All of the officers' salaries, 70% of the office staff salaries, and 55% of the sales salaries for the payroll period ending November 5 were paid to employees that had exceeded the wage base for unemployment taxes. Assume the rates in force are as follows: FICA, 7.6%; federal unemployment tax, 0.8% and state unemployment tax, 5.4%.

Instructions: Prepare the adjusting entries that would be required at October 31, the end of Martina's fiscal year, to reflect the accrual of the payroll and any related payroll taxes. Separate salary and payroll taxes expense accounts are used for each of the three employee categories: office staff, officers', and sales salaries.

Problem 14-3   (Accounting for payroll)

Bags, Inc., a manufacturer of suitcases, has 10 employees. Five of the employees are paid on a salary basis, and five are hourly employees. The employees and their compensations are as follows.

Ken Scott (President)	$91,500
Tatia Furgins	$57,000
Jennifer Poulins	$48,750
Robyn Meek	$23,800
Kyle Roberts	$13,900
Richard Dean (50 hours per week)	$14.00 per hour
Denise Ray (40 hours per week)	$11.50 per hour
Dale Frank (40 hours per week)	$9.75 per hour
Bryan Leslie (30 hours per week)	$4.50 per hour
Albert Lamb (20 hours per week)	$3.65 per hour

The salaried employees are covered by a comprehensive medical and dental plan. The cost of the plan is $45.00 per employee and is deducted from each pay check. The hourly employees are covered only by a medical plan. The cost is calculated at 3.5% of gross pay and is deducted from each check. The FICA rate is 7.6% and FUTA is 6.2%, with the maximum credit for state unemployment allowed. The state unemployment tax is 5.4%. In addition, each of the hourly employees, except Albert, belongs to the Suitcase Workers of America union. Union dues are $5.65 per month and are deducted and paid on behalf of the hourly employees. The income tax withholding rate is 28% for employees with annual incomes above $29,500 and 15% for employees with annual incomes of $29,500 or less.

Hourly employees are paid weekly on Friday, January 6, 13, 20, and 27. Salaried employees are paid twice a month, on January 13 and 27. Assume that payroll taxes and all employee withholdings and deductions are paid on the 15th and last day of each month.

Instructions:

(1) Make all entries related to Bags, Inc.'s payroll for January 6 and January 13.

(2) Assume the same facts as above, except that on January 14 Jennifer Poulins was given a 10% raise and all the hourly employees were given a raise of $0.20 per hour. Make all entries relating to the payroll for January 20 and January 27.

Problem 14-4 (Tax liability)

Lucille's Cafe, a new business in town, has asked you for help in calculating and recording its property and sales tax liability. On July 1, 1990, Lucille's received notice that property taxes totaling $24,000 were to be paid by October 1, 1990. The property tax was for the period of July 1, 1990, to June 30, 1991. Lucille's Cafe had sales of $89,460 in 1990. This amount included sales tax collections. The sales tax rate in the area is 5%. Sales taxes are due on January 31, 1991.

Instructions:

(1) Give the entries to record the accrual, monthly expensing, and payment of property taxes. (Give only one example of the monthly recognition of property tax.) What is the December 31, 1990, balance in the deferred property tax account?

(2) Calculate the amount of sales tax payable as of December 31, 1990. Make the entry needed to record this liability at year end. Also give the entry to record payment of sales tax on January 31, 1991.

Problem 14-5 (Warranty liability)

High Fidelity Corporation sells stereos under a two-year warranty contract that requires High Fidelity to replace defective parts and provide free labor on all repairs. During 1990, 1,050 units were sold at $900 each. In 1991, High Fidelity sold an additional 900 units at $925. Based on past experience, the estimated two-year warranty costs are $20 for parts and $25 for labor per unit. It is also estimated that 40% of the warranty expenditures will occur in the first year and 60% in the second year.

Actual warranty expenditures were as follows:

| | Warranty Costs | |
	1991	1992
Stereos sold in 1990	$18,300	$26,500
Stereos sold in 1991	—	18,100

Instructions: Assuming sales occurred on the last day of the year for both 1990 and 1991, give the necessary journal entries for the years 1990 through 1992. Analyze the warranty liability account for the year ending December 31, 1992, to see if the actual repairs approximate the estimate. Should High Fidelity revise its warranty estimates?

‖ Problem 14-6   (Warranty liability)

The Monroe Corporation, a client, requests that you compute the appropriate balance for its estimated liability for product warranty account for a statement as of June 30, 1991.

Monroe Corporation manufactures television tubes and sells them with a six-month warranty under which defective tubes will be replaced without a charge. On December 31, 1990, Estimated Liability for Product Warranty had a balance of $510,000. By June 30, 1991, this balance had been reduced to $80,250 by debits for estimated net cost of tubes returned that had been sold in 1990.

The company started out in 1991 expecting 8% of the dollar volume of sales to be returned. However, due to the introduction of new models during the year, this estimated percentage of returns was increased to 10% on May 1. It is assumed that no tubes sold during a given month are returned in that month. Each tube is stamped with a date at time of sale so that the warranty may be properly administered. The following table of percentages indicates the likely pattern of sales returns during the six-month period of the warranty, starting with the month following the sale of tubes.

Month Following Sale	Percentage of Total Returns Expected
First	20%
Second	30
Third	20
Fourth through sixth—10% each month	30
	100%

Gross sales of tubes were as follows for the first six months of 1991:

Month	Amount	Month	Amount
January	$3,600,000	April	$2,850,000
February	3,300,000	May	2,000,000
March	4,100,000	June	1,800,000

The company's warranty also covers the payment of freight cost on defective tubes returned and on the new tubes sent out as replacements. This freight cost runs approximately 10% of the sales price of the tubes returned. The manufacturing cost of the tubes is roughly 80% of the sales price, and the salvage value of returned tubes average 15% of their sales price. Returned tubes on hand at December 31, 1990, were thus valued in inventory at 15% of their original sales price.

Instructions: Using the data given, draw up a suitable working-paper schedule for arriving at the balance of the estimated liability for product warranty account and give the proposed adjusting entry. (AICPA adapted)

Problem 14-7 (Premium liability)

The Village Corp. manufactures a special type of low-suds laundry soap. A dish towel is offered as a premium to customers who send in two proof-of-purchase seals from these soap boxes and a remittance of $2. Data for the premium offer are summarized below:

	1990	1991
Soap sales ($2.50 per package)	$2,500,000	$3,125,000
Dish towel purchases ($2.50 per towel)	$130,000	$176,250
Number of dish towels distributed as premiums	50,000	70,000
Number of dish towels expected to be distributed in subsequent periods	8,500	3,000

Mailing costs are $.26 per package.

Instructions:

(1) Give the entries for 1990 and 1991 to record product sales, premium purchases and redemptions, and year-end adjustments.
(2) Present "T" accounts with appropriate amounts as of the end of 1990 and 1991.

▌▌▌ Problem 14-8 (Compensated absences)

Sandoval Electronics Inc. has a plan to compensate its employees for certain absences. Each employee can receive five days' sick leave each year plus 10 days' vacation. The benefits carry over for two additional years, after which the provision lapses on a FIFO flow basis. Thus, the maximum accumulation is 45 days. In some cases, the company permits vacations to be taken before they are earned. Payments are made based on current compensation levels, not on the level in effect when the absence time was earned.

Employee	Days Accrued Jan. 1, 1991	Daily Rate Jan. 1, 1991	Days Earned 1991	Days Taken 1991	Days Accrued Dec. 31, 1991	Daily Rate Dec. 31
A	10	$38	15	10	15	$40
B	—	$44	15	10	5	$50
C	30	$42	7	37	—	Terminated June 15- Rate = $45
D	−5	$36	15	20	−10	$40
E	40	$58	15	5	50	$70
F	Hired July 1- Rate = $40	—	8	0	8	$40

Instructions:

(1) How much is the liability for compensated absences at December 31, 1991?

(2) Prepare a summary journal entry to record compensation absence payments during the year and the accrual at the end of the year. Assume the payroll liability account is charged for all payments made during the year for both sickness and vacation leaves. The average rate of compensation for the year may be used to value the hours taken except for Employee C who took leaves at the date of termination. The end-of-year rate should be used to establish the ending liability.

Problem 14-9   (Contingent liabilities)

The Western Supply Co. has several contingent liabilities at December 31, 1991. The following brief description of each liability is obtained by the auditor.

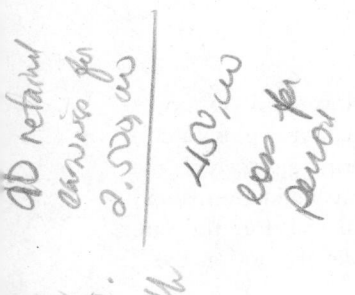

(a) In May 1990, Western Supply became involved in litigation. In December 1991, a judgment for $800,000 was assessed against Western by the court. Western is appealing the amount of the judgment. Attorneys for Western feel it is probable that they can reduce the assessment on appeal by 50%. No entries have been made by Western pending completion of the appeal process, which is expected to take at least a year.

(b) In July 1991, Morgan County brought action against Western for polluting the Jordan River with its waste products. It is reasonably possible that Morgan County will be successful, but the amount of damages Western might have to pay should not exceed $200,000. No entry has been made by Western to reflect the possible loss.

(c) Western Supply has elected to self-insure its fire and casualty risks. At the beginning of the year, the account Reserve for Insurance had a balance of $2,500,000. During 1991, $750,000 was debited to insurance expense and credited to the reserve account. After payment for losses actually sustained in 1991, the reserve account had a balance of $2,800,000 at December 31, 1991. The opening balance was a result of several years of activity similar to 1991.

(d) Western Supply has signed as guarantor for a $50,000 loan by Guaranty Bank to Midwest Parts Inc., a principal supplier to Western. Because of financial problems at Midwest, it is probable that Western Supply will have to pay the $50,000 with only a 40% recovery anticipated from Midwest. No entries have been made to reflect the contingent liability.

Instructions:

(1) What amount should be reported as a liability on the December 31, 1991, balance sheet?

(2) What note disclosure should be included as part of the balance sheet for each of the above items?

(3) Prepare the journal entries necessary to adjust Western's books to reflect your answers in (1) and (2).

Problem 14-10   (Recording and reporting liabilities)

Landon Manufacturing pays its employees on the last day of each month. On December 31, 1991, Landon paid $19,450 in cash to its employees for December salaries and wages. $25,000 of the gross payroll for December is subject to FICA, and $5,000 is subject to unemployment taxes. The FICA tax rate is 7.6%. The FUTA tax rate is 6.2% and the state unemployment tax rate is 5.7%. The federal government allows the maximum credit for state unemployment tax paid. Payroll and withholding taxes for December are to be paid to the taxing authorities in January, 1992. The combined withholding rate for federal, state, and local income taxes is 30%.

Landon has a mortgage of $455,000 for a plant it constructed and completed on September 1, 1988. The entire mortgage balance has been classified as a long-term obligation on the balance sheet. Interest has been paid each September 1, beginning in 1989. The interest is 10% of the outstanding mortgage balance. Beginning September 1, 1992, Landon is required to make annual payments of $46,528, which includes both principal and interest.

In addition, Landon has a $15,000 five-year note payable to First Thrift Bank that matures December 31, 1992. Interest is payable on the note at 12% each January 1. Landon management plans to refinance the note when it comes due. A refinancing agreement has been signed with the bank.

On October 1 of each year, Landon pays property taxes in advance and records the payment as an asset. On October 1, 1991, Landon paid property taxes of $13,500 for the 12-month period ending September 30, 1992. The balance in the asset account as of January 1, 1991 was $9,375.

In August of 1991, a lawsuit was filed against Landon. The plaintiff in the lawsuit has asked for $6 million in damages for injuries allegedly resulting from a defective product manufactured by Landon. Landon's legal counsel believes it is probable that the suit will result in a loss to Landon, but the amount of the potential loss cannot be reasonably estimated as of December 31, 1991.

Instructions:

(1) Make all necessary entries at December 31, 1991, to reflect the above transactions and events.

(2) Prepare the liabilities section of Landon's classified balance sheet.

Problem 14-11   (Adjusting entries and balance sheet presentation)

The unadjusted trial balance of Sunset Company at December 31, 1990, showed the following account balances:

Sales	$427,000
Mortgage Note Payable	80,000
Bank Notes Payable	10,000
Accounts Payable	19,400
Wages Payable	4,000

Additional information:

(a) The Sales account included amounts collected from customers for a 5 percent sales tax. The tax was remitted to the state on January 31, 1991.

(b) The mortgage note is due on March 1, 1991. Interest at 12 percent has been paid through December 31. Sunset intended at December 31, 1990, to refinance the note on its due date with a new 5-year mortgage note. In fact, on March 1, 1991, Sunset paid $20,000 in cash on the principal balance and refinanced the remaining $60,000.

(c) The bank notes are due over the next four years. The current portion of the notes is $2,500 at December 31, 1990. Interest of $500 has not been accrued. It is to be paid during 1991.

(d) On October 1, 1990, a previous employee filed a suit against Sunset, alleging age discrmination and asking for damages of $500,000. At December 31, 1990, Sunset's attorney felt that the likelihood of losing the lawsuit was possible but not probable.

(e) During 1990, Sunset remitted to the federal government estimated income tax payments of $55,000. The actual taxes for 1990 amounted to $75,000. No accrual has been made as of December 31, 1990.

Instructions:

(1) Prepare adjusting journal entries to correct the liability accounts at December 31, 1990. Assume the financial statements will be issued on April 1, 1991.

(2) Prepare the current and noncurrent liability sections of the December 31, 1990, balance sheet.

*Problem 14-12   (Computation of bonus)

Dawn Distributors is considering two different proposals for computing the bonus for its new company president, Sheri Morey. The first plan states that the bonus would be equal to 6% of profits (after the bonus but before taxes have been deducted) exceeding $100,000. The second method bases the bonus on profits after both taxes and the president's bonus have been deducted. It states that the bonus would be 12% of profits above $250,000.

Instructions: Assuming income for 1991 of $975,000 before income tax and bonus and a company tax rate of 40%, compute the bonus under both methods.

*Problem 14-13   (Calculation of bonus)

Nephi Manufacturing Company pays bonuses to its sales manager and two sales agents. The company had income for 1991 of $2,500,000 before bonuses and income tax. Income taxes average 40%.

Instructions: Compute the bonuses assuming:

(1) Sales manager gets 8% and each sales agent gets 6% of income before tax and bonuses.

(2) Each bonus is 12% of net income after income tax and bonuses.

(3) Sales manager gets 12% and each sales agent gets 10% of income after bonuses but before income tax.

*Relates to Appendix

Chapter 15

Accounting for Long-Term Debt Securities

The use of long-term debt securities to finance new products, to expand operations, to acquire other companies, or for a host of other reasons is common practice in today's business environment. This is especially true during periods of low interest rates, allowing companies to use relatively "cheap" money not only for business expansion, but also to retire existing higher-cost debt or, in some cases, to retire equity securities. For example, in 1986, interest rates reached their lowest level in over eight years, resulting in a record number of new corporate bond issues. Large new issues of bonds in recent years have also occurred as a result of the significant increase in debt-financed corporate takeovers, or buyouts.

In addition to bonds, the long-term debt classification includes mortgages, leases, pensions, and other types of long-term obligations. This chapter explains the relative advantages and disadvantages of debt and equity financing, and specifically focuses on how to account for bonds and long-term notes. In discussing bonds, both the liability of the issuer (bonds payable) and the asset of the investor (bond investment) are explained so that the total picture can be seen at one time. Specific issues related to leases and pensions are deferred to Chapters 21 and 22, respectively.

Financing With Long-Term Debt

The long-term financing of a corporation is accomplished either through the issuance of long-term debt instruments, usually bonds or notes, or through the sale of additional stock. The issuance of bonds or notes instead of stock may be preferred by management and stockholders for the following reasons:

1. Present owners continue in control of the corporation.
2. Interest is a deductible expense in arriving at taxable income, while dividends are not.
3. Current market rates of interest may be favorable relative to stock market prices.
4. The charge against earnings for interest may be less than the amount of dividends that might be expected by shareholders.

There are, however, certain limitations and disadvantages of financing with long-term debt securities. Debt financing is possible only when a company is in satisfactory financial condition and can offer adequate security to creditors. Furthermore, interest must be paid regardless of the company's earnings and financial position. If a company has operating losses and is unable ro raise sufficient cash to meet periodic interest payments, debt security holders may take legal action to assume control of company assets.

A complicating factor is that the distinction between debt and equity securities may become fuzzy. Usually, a debt instrument has a fixed interest rate and a definite maturity date when the principal must be repaid. Also, holders of debt instruments generally have no voting privileges. An equity security, on the other hand, has no fixed repayment obligation or maturity date, and dividends on stock become obligations only after being formally declared by the board of directors of a corporation. In addition, common stockholders generally have voting and other ownership privileges. The problem is that certain convertible debt securities have many equity characteristics, and some preferred stocks have many of the characteristics of debt. This makes it important to recognize the distinction between debt and equity and to provide the accounting treatment that is most appropriate under the specific circumstances.

Accounting for Bonds

Conceptually, bonds and long-term notes are similar types of financial instruments. There are some technical differences, however. For example, the trust indenture associated with bonds generally provides more extensive detail than the contract terms of a note, often including restrictions on the payment of dividends or incurrence of additional debt. The length of time to maturity is also generally longer for bonds than for notes. Some bonds do not mature for twenty years or longer, while most notes mature in one to five years. Other characteristics of bonds and notes are similar. Therefore, in the discussion that follows, the accounting principles and reporting practices related to bonds can also be applied to long-term notes.

There are three main considerations in accounting for bonds:

1. Recording their issuance or purchase.
2. Recognizing the applicable interest during the life of the bonds.
3. Accounting for the retirment of bonds, either at maturity or prior to the maturity date.

Before these considerations are discussed, the nature of bonds and the determination of bond market prices will be reviewed.

Nature of Bonds

The power of a corporation to create bond indebtedness is found in the corporation laws of a state and may be specifically granted by charter. In some cases formal authorization by a majority of stockholders is required before a board of directors can approve a bond issue.

Borrowing by means of bonds involves the issuance of certificates of indebtedness. Bond certificates, commonly referred to simply as "bonds," are freqently issued in denominations of $1,000, referred to as the face amount, par value, or maturity value of the bond, although in some cases, bonds are issued in varying denominations.

The group contract between the corporation and the bondholders is known as the bond indenture. The indenture details the rights and obligations of the contracting parties, indicates the property pledged as well as the protection offered on the loan, and names the bank or trust company that is to represent the bondholders.

Bonds may be sold by the company directly to investors, or they may be underwritten by investment bankers or a syndicate. The underwriters may agree to puchase the entire bond issue or that part of the issue which is not sold by the company, or they may agree simply to manage the sale of the security on a commission basis, often referred to as a 'best efforts" basis.

Most companies attempt to sell their bonds to underwriters to avoid incurring a loss after the bonds are placed on the market. As interesting example of this occurred several years ago when IBM Corporation went to the bond market for the first time and issued a record $1 billion worth of bonds and long-term notes. After the issue was released by IBM to the underwriters, interest rates soared as the Federal Reserve Bank sharply increased its rediscount rate. The market price of the IBM securities fell, and the brokerage houses and investment bankers participating in the underwriting incurred a loss in excess of $50 million on the sale of the securities to investors.

Issuers of Bonds

Bonds and similar debt instruments are issued by private corporations, the United States Government, state, county and local governments, school districts, and government sponsored organizations such as the Federal Home Loan Bank and the Federal National Mortgage Association. The total amount of debt issued by these organizations is now well in excess of $1 trillion.

The U.S. debt includes not only Treasury bonds, but also Treasury bills, which are notes with less than one year to maturity date, and Treasury notes, which mature in one to seven years. Both Treasury bills and Treasury notes are in demand in the marketplace, perhaps even more so in recent years than Treasury bonds.

Debt securities issued by state, county, and local governments and their agencies are collectively referred to as **municipal debt**. A unique feature of municipal debt is that the interest received by investors from such securities is exempt from federal income tax. Because of this tax advantage, "municipals" generally carry lower interest rates than debt securities of other issuers, enabling these governmental units to borrow at favorable interest rates. The tax exemption is in reality a subsidy granted by the federal government to encourage capital investment in state and local goverments.

Types of Bonds

Bonds may be categorized in many different ways, depending on the characteristics of a particular bond issue. The major distinguishing features of bonds are identified and discussed in the following sections.

Term Versus Serial Bonds Bonds that mature on a single date are called term bonds. When bonds mature in installments, they are referred to as serial bonds. Serial bonds are much less common than term bonds, and the special considerations in accounting for serial bonds are covered in the appendix to this chapter.

Secured Versus Unsecured Bonds Bonds issued by private corporations may be either secured or unsecured. Secured bonds offer protection to investors by providing some form of security, such as a mortgage on real estate or a pledge of other collateral. A **first-mortgage bond** represents a first claim against the property of a corporation in the event of the company's inability to meet bond interest and principal payments. A **second-mortgage bond** is a secondary claim ranking only after the claim of the first-mortgage bonds or senior issue has been completely satisfied. A **collateral trust bond** is usually secured by stocks and bonds of other corporations owned by the issuing company. Such securities are generally transferred to a trustee who holds them as collateral on behalf of the bondholders and, if necessary, will sell them to satisfy the bondholders' claim.

Unsecured bonds are not protected by the pledge of any specific assets and are frequently termed debenture bonds, or **debentures**. Holders of debenture bonds simply rank as general creditors along with other unsecured parties. The risk involved in these securities varies with the financial strength of the debtor. Debentures issued by a strong company may involve little risk; debentures issued by a weak company whose properties are already heavily mortgaged may involve considerable risk. Quality ratings for bonds are published by both Moody's and Standard and Poor's investment services companies. For example, Moody's bond ratings range from prime, or highest quality (Aaa) to default (C) for a very high risk bond. Standard and Poor's range is from AAA to D.

Registered Versus Bearer (Coupon) Bonds Registered bonds call for the registry of the owner's name on the corporation books. Transfer of bond ownership is similar to that for stock. When a bond is sold, the corporate transfer agent cancels the bond certificate surrendered by the seller and issues a new certificate to the buyer. Interest checks are mailed periodically to the bondholders of record. Bearer or coupon bonds are not recorded in the name of the owner, title to such bonds passing with delivery. Each bond is accompanied by coupons for individual interest payments covering the life of the issue. Coupons are clipped by the owner of the bond and presented to a bank for deposit or collection. The issue of bearer bonds eliminates the need for recording bond ownership changes and preparing and mailing periodic interest checks. But coupon bonds fail to offer the bondholder the protection found in registered bonds in the event the bonds are lost or stolen. In some cases, bonds provide interest coupons but require registry as to principal. Here, ownership safeguards are provided, while the time-consuming routines involved in making interest payments are avoided. Bonds of recent issue are registered rather than coupon bonds.

Zero-Interest Bonds and Bonds with Variable Interest Rates In recent years, some companies have issued long-term debt securities that do not bear interest. Instead, these securites sell at a significant discount that provides an investor with a total interest payoff at maturity. These bonds are known as zero-interest bonds or deep-discount bonds.

Because of potentially wide fluctuations in interest rates, some bonds and long-term notes are issued with **variable (or floating) interest rates**. Over the life of these obligations, the interest rate changes as prevailing market interest rates increase or decrease. A variable interest rate security reduces the risk to the investor when interest rates are rising, and to the issuer when interest rates are falling.

Junk Bonds High-risk, high-yield bonds issued by companies that are heavily in debt or otherwise in weak financial condition are often referred to as junk bonds. These bonds are rated below Baa-3 by Moody's investment service or below triple-B-minus by Standard and Poor's. Junk bonds typically yield at least 12%, and some yield in excess of 20%. Some are zero-interest (deep discount) bonds that pay no interest until maturity or pay no interest for the first few years. While junk bonds are generally not an appropriate investment for individuals due to their high risk, they comprise a significant segment of the corporate bond market.

Junk bonds are issued in at least three types of circumstances. First, they are issued by companies that once had high credit ratings but have fallen on hard times. Several companies in the steel industry are included in this category. Second, junk bonds are issued by emerging growth companies, such as Continental Cablevision, that lack adequate cash flow, credit history, or diversification to permit them to issue higher grade (i.e., lower risk) bonds. The third, and largest, category of junk bonds are those issued by companies undergoing restructuring, often in conjunction with a leveraged buyout (LBO), discussed later in the chapter. Metromedia Inc. is one of many examples of such companies. It is estimated that over $16 billion of junk bonds were issued in connection with corporate takeovers in 1988 alone.

Convertible and Commodity-Backed Bonds Bonds may provide for their conversion into some other security at the option of the bondholder. Such bonds are known as **convertible bonds**. The conversion feature generally permits the owner of bonds to exchange them for common stock. The bondholder is thus able to convert the claim into an ownership interest if corporate operations prove successful and conversion becomes attractive; in the meantime the special rights of a creditor are maintained. Bonds may also be redeemable in terms of commodities, such as oil or precious metals. These types of bonds are sometimes referred to as **commodity-backed bonds** or **asset-linked bonds**.

Callable Bonds Bond indentures frequently give the issuing company the right to call and retire the bonds prior to their maturity. Such bonds are termed **callable bonds** When a corporation wishes to reduce its outstanding indebtedness, bondholders are notified of the portion of the issue to be surrendered, and they are paid in accordance with call provisions. Interest does not accrue after the call date.

Market Price of Bonds   The market price of bonds varies with the saftey of the investment and the current market interest rate for similar instruments. When the financial condition and earnings of a corporation are such that payment of interest and principal on bond indebtedness is virtually assured, the interest rate a company must offer to dispose of a bond issue is relatively low. As the risk factor increases, a higher interest return is necessary to attract investors. The amount of interest paid on bonds is a specified percentage of the face value. This percentage is termed the stated or contract rate. This rate, however, may not be the same as the prevailing or **market rate** for bonds of similar quality and length of time to maturity at the time the issue is sold. Furthermore, the market rate constantly fluctuates. These factors often result in a difference between bond face values and the prices at which the bonds actually sell on the market.

The purchase of bonds at face value implies agreement between the bond stated rate of interest and the prevailing market rate of interest. If the stated rate exceeds the market rate, the bonds will sell at a **premium**; if the stated rate is less than the market rate, the bonds will sell at a **discount**. The **bond premium** or the **bond discount** is the amount needed to adjust the stated rate of interest to the actual market rate of interest for that particular bond. Thus, the stated rate adjusted for the premium or the discount on the purchase gives the actual rate of return on the bonds, known as the **market**, **yield**, or **effective interest rate**. A declining market rate of interest subsequent to issuance of the bonds results in an increase in the market value of the bonds; a rising market rate of interest results in a decrease in their market value.

Bonds are quoted on the market as a percentage of face value. Thus, a bond quotation of 96.5 means the market price is 96.5% of face value, or at a discount; a bond quotation of 104 means the market price is 104% of face value, or at a premium. U.S. Government note and bond quotations are made in 32's rather than 100's. Thus a Government bond selling at 98.16 is selling at 98 $^{16}/_{32}$, or in terms of decimal equivalents, 98.5%.

The market price of a bond at any date can be determined by discounting the maturity value of the bond and each remaining interest payment at the market rate of interest for similar debt on that date. The present value tables in Chapter 6 can be used for computing bond market price.

To illustrate the computation of a bond market price from the tables, assume 10-year, 8% bonds of $100,000 are to be sold on the bond issue date. Further assume that the effective interest rate for bonds of similar quality and maturity is 10%, compounded semiannually.

The computation of the market price of the bonds may be divided into two parts:

Part 1   Present value of principal (maturity value)

Maturity value of bonds after 10 years or 20 semiannual periods =
$100,000

Effective interest rate = 10% per year, or 5% per semiannual period

Present value of $100,000 discounted at 5% for 20 periods:
$PV = R\ (PVF_{\overline{n}i}) = \$100,000\ (\text{Table II }_{\overline{20}|5}) =$
$100,000 (.3769) = $37,690

Part 2   Present value of 20 interest payments

Semiannual payment, 4% of $100,000 = $4,000
Effective interest rate, 10% per year, or 5% per semiannual period

Present value of 20, $4,000 payments, discounted at 5%:
$PV = R\ (PVAF_{\overline{n}i}) = \$4,000\ (\text{Table IV }_{\overline{20}|5}) =$
$4,000 (12.4622) =   49,849

Total present value (market price) of bond $87,539

The market price for the bonds would be $87,539, the sum of the present values of the two parts. Because the effective interest rate is higher than the stated interest rate, the bonds would sell at a $12,461 discount at the issuance date. It should be noted that if the effective rate on these bonds were 8% instead of 10%, the sum of the present values of the two parts would be $100,000, meaning that the bonds would sell at their face amount, or at par. If the effective interest rate were less than 8%, the market price of the bonds would be more than $100,000, and the bonds would sell at a premium.

Specially adapted present value tables are available to determine directly the price to be paid for bonds if they are to provide a certain return. A portion of such a bond table is illustrated below.

Note that the market price from the bond table for 8% bonds sold to yield 10% in 10 years is $87,539, the same amount as computed using present value tables. Also, the bond table shows that if the effective interest rate were 8%, the bonds would sell at par, $100,000. If the effective rate were 7.5%, the market price would be $103,476.

The bond table can also be used to determine the effective rate of interest on a bond acquired at a certain price. To illustrate, assume that a $1,000, 8% bond due in 10 years is selling at $951. Reference to the column "10 years" for $95,070 shows an annual return of 8.75% is provided on an investment of $950.70.

Bond Table
Values to the Nearest Dollar of 8% Bond for $100,000
Interest Payable Semiannually

Yield or Effective Interest	8 years	8½ years	9 years	9½ years	10 years
7.00	$106,046	$106,325	$106,595	$106,855	$107,107
7.25	104,495	104,699	104,896	105,090	105,272
7.50	102,971	103,100	103,232	103,360	103,476
7.75	101,472	101,537	101,595	101,658	101,718
8.00	100,000	100,000	100,000	100,000	100,000
8.25	98,552	98,494	98,437	98,372	98,325
8.50	97,141	97,012	96,893	96,787	96,678
8.75	95,746	95,568	95,398	95,232	95,070
9.00	94,383	94,147	93,920	93,703	93,496
9.25	93,042	92,757	92,480	92,214	91,953
9.50	91,723	91,380	91,055	90,751	90,452
9.75	90,350	89,960	89,588	89,238	88,902
10.00	89,162	88,726	88,310	87,914	87,539

Issuance of Bonds   Bonds may be sold directly to investors by the issuer or they may be sold on the open market through securities exchanges or through investment bankers. Over 50% of bond issues are privately placed with large investors. Regardless of how placed, when bonds are issued (sold), the issuer must record the receipt of cash and recognize the long-term liability. The purchaser must record the payment of cash and the bond investment.

An issuer normally records the bond obligation as its face value—the amount that the company must pay at maturity. Hence, when bonds are issued at an amount other than face value, a bond discount or premium account is established for the difference between the cash received and the bond face value. The premium is added to or the discount is subtracted form the bond face value to report the bonds at their present value. Although an investor could also record the investment in bonds at their face value by using a premium or discount account, traditionally investors record their bond investments at cost, that is, the face value net of any premium or discount. Cost includes brokerage fees and any other costs incident to the purchase.

Bonds issued or acquired in exchange for noncash assets or services are recorded at the fair market value of the bonds, unless the value of the exchanged assets or services is more clearly determinable. A difference between the face value of the bonds and the cash value of the bonds or the value of the property acquired is recognized as bond discount or bond premium. When bonds and other securities are acquired for a lump sum, an apportionment of such cost among the securities is required.

As indicated earlier, bonds may be issued at par, at a discount, or at a premium. They may be issued on an interest payment date or between interest dates, which calls for the recognition of accrued interest. Each of these situations will be illustrated using the following data: $100,000, 8%, 10-year bonds are issued. Semiannual interest of $4,000 ($100,000 × .08 × $\frac{6}{12}$) is payable on January 1 and July 1.

Bonds Issued at Par on Interest Date

When bonds are issued at par, or face value, on an interest date, there is no premium or discount to be recognized nor any accrued interest at the date of issuance. The appropriate entries for the first year, on the issuer's books and on the investor's books, assuming the data in the preceding paragraph and issuance on January 1 at par value, would be:

		Issuer's Books			**Investor's Books**		
Jan.	1	Cash	100,000		Bond Investment . . .	100,000	
		Bonds Payable . . .		100,000	Cash		100,000
July	1	Interest Expense . . .	4,000		Cash	4,000	
		Cash		4,000	Interest Revenue . .		4,000
Dec.	31	Interest Expense . . .	4,000		Interest Receivable	4,000	
		Interest Payable . .		4,000	Interest Revenue . .		4,000

Bonds Issued at Discount on Interest Date

Now assume that the bonds were issued on January 1 but that the effective rate of interest was 10%, requiring recognition of a discount of $12,461 ($100,000 − $87,539). The appropriate entries on January 1 are shown below. The interest entries on July 1 and December 31 are illustrated in a later section that discusses the amortization of discounts and premiums.

		Issuer's Books			**Investor's Books**		
Jan.	1	Cash	87,539		Bond Investment . . .	87,539	
		Bond Discount	12,461		Cash		87,539
		Bonds Payable . . .		100,000			

Bonds Issued at Premium on Interest Date

Again using the data above, assume that the bonds were sold at an effective interest rate of 7%, resulting in a premium of $7,107. In this case the entries on January 1 would be:

Issuer's Books			Investor's Books		
Cash	107,107		Bond Investment . . .	107,107	
Bond Premium . . .		7,107	Cash		107,107
Bonds Payable . . .		100,000			

Bonds Issued at Par Between Interest Dates

When bonds are issued or sold between interest dates, an adjustment is made for the interest accrued between the last interest payment date and the date of the transaction. A buyer of the bonds pays the amount of accrued interest along with the purchase price and then receives the accrued interest plus interest earned subsequent to the purchase date when the next interest payment is made. This practice avoids the problem an issuer of bonds would have in trying to split interest payments for a given period between two or more owners of the securities. To illustrate, if the bonds in the previous example were issued at par on March 1, the appropriate entries would be:

		Issuer's Books			Investor's Books		
Mar.	1	Cash	101,333		Bond Investment . . .	100,000	
		Bonds Payable . . .		100,000	Interest Receivable	1,333	
		Interest Payable . .		1,333*	Cash		101,333
		*($100,000 × .08 × 2/12)					
July	1	Interest Expense . . .	2,667*		Cash	4,000	
		Interest Payable . . .	1,333		Interest Receivable		1,333
		Cash		4,000	Interest Revenue . .		2,667
		*($100,000 × .08 × 4/12)					

Alternatively, as illustrated below, the accrued interest could be initially credited to Interest Expense by the issuer and debited to Interest Revenue by the investor. Then when the full interest payment is made, the proper amount of interest will be recognized.

		Issuer's Books			Investor's Books		
Mar.	1	Cash	101,333		Bond Investment . . .	100,000	
		Bonds Payable . . .		100,000	Interest Revenue . . .	1,333	
		Interest Expense . .		1,333	Cash		101,333
July	1	Interest Expense . . .	4,000		Cash	4,000	
		Cash		4,000	Interest Revenue . .		4,000

Bond Issuance Costs

The issuance of bonds normally involves costs to the issuer for legal services, printing and engraving, taxes and underwriting. Traditionally, these costs have been either (1) summarized separately as **bond issuance costs**, classified as deferred charges, and charged to expense over the life of the bond issue, or (2) offset against any premium or added to any discount arising on the issuance and thus netted against the face value of the bonds. The Accounting Principles Board in Opinion No. 21 recommended that these costs be reported on the balance sheet as deferred charges.[1] However, in Statement of Concepts No. 3, the FASB stated that such costs fail to meet the definition of assets adopted by the Board.[2] The authors agree with the position of the FASB, and favor netting the issuance costs against the bonds payable as part of the premium or discount on the bonds. Concepts Statements do not establish GAAP, however, and until such time as the FASB addresses the issue, the APB Opinion governs generally accepted practice.

Accounting for Bond Interest

With coupon bonds, cash is paid by the issuing company in exchange for interest coupons on the interest dates. Payments on coupons may be made by the company directly to bondholders, or payments may be cleared through a bank or other disbursing agent. Subsidiary records with bondholders are not maintained since coupons are redeemable by bearers. In the case of registered bonds, interest checks are mailed either by the company or its agent. When bonds are registered, the bonds account requires subsidiary ledger support. The subsidiary ledger shows holdings by individuals and changes in such holdings. Checks are sent to bondholders of record as of the interest payment dates.

When bonds are issued at a premium or discount, the market acts to adjust the stated interest rate to a market or effective interest rate. Because of the initial premium or discount, the periodic interest payments made over the bond life by the issuer to the investors do not represent the complete revenue and expense for the periods involved. An adjustment to the cash transfer for the periodic write-off of the premium or discount is necessary to reflect the effective interest rate being incurred or earned on the bonds. This adjustment is referred to as **bond premium** or **discount amortization.** The periodic adjustment of bonds results in a gradual adjustment of the carrying value toward the bond's face value.

A premium on issued bonds recognizes that the stated interest rate is higher than the market interest rate. Amortization of the premium reduces the interest revenue or expense below the amount of cash transferred. A discount on issued bonds recognizes that the stated interest rate is lower than the market interest rate. Amortization of the discount increases the amount of interest revenue or expense above the amount of cash transferred.

Two principal methods are used to amortize the premium or discount: (1) the straight-line method and (2) the effective-interest method.

[1] *Opinions of the Accounting Principles Board, No. 21*, "Interest on Receivables and Payables" (New York: American Institute of Certified Public Accountants, 1971), par. 16.

[2] *Statement of Financial Accounting Concepts No. 3*, "Elements of Financial Statements of Business Enterprises" (Stamford: Financial Accounting Standards Board, December 1980), par. 161.

Straight-Line Method

The straight-line method provides for the recognition of an equal amount of premium or discount amortization each period. The amount of monthly amortization is determined by dividing the premium or discount at purchase or issuance by the number of months remaining to the bond maturity date. For example, if a 10-year, 10% bond issue with a maturity value of $200,000 was sold on the issuance date at 103, the $6,000 premium would be amortized evenly over the 120 months until maturity, or at a rate of $50 per month, ($6,000 ÷ 120). If the bonds were sold three months after the issuance date, the $6,000 premium would be amortized evenly over 117 months, or a rate of $51.28 per month, ($6,000 ÷ 117). The amortization period is always the time from original sale to maturity. The premium amortization would reduce both interest expense on the issuer's books and interest revenue on the investor's books. A discount amortization would have the opposite results: both accounts would be increased.

To illustrate the accounting for bond interest using straight-line amortization, consider again the earlier example of the $100,000, 8%, 10-year bonds issued on January 1. When sold at a $12,461 discount, the appropriate entries to record interest on July 1 and Dec. 31 would be as follows:

	Issuer's Books			Investor's Books		
July 1	Interest Expense...	4,623		Cash	4,000	
	Bond Discount ...		623	Bond Investment ...	623	
	Cash		4,000	Interest Revenue ..		4,623
	($100,000 × .08 × 6/12 = $4,000 cash;					
	$12,461 ÷ 120 × 6 months = $623 (rounded) discount amortization)					
Dec. 31	Interest Expense...	4,623		Interest Receivable	4,000	
	Bond Discount ...		623	Bond Investment ...	623	
	Interest Payable ..		4,000	Interest Revenue ..		4,623

Note that the discount amortization has the effect of increasing the effective interest rate from the 8% stated rate to the 10% market rate of interest that the bonds were sold to yield. Over the life of the bond, the $12,461 discount will be charged to interest expense for the issuer and will be recognized as interest revenue by the investor.

Also note that the amortization of premium or discount may be recognized only once a year prior to preparing financial statements instead of with each interest payment. If this were the case in the preceding illustration, the entries would be:

	Issuer's Books			Investor's Books		
July 1	Interest Expense...	4,000		Cash	4,000	
	Cash		4,000	Interest Revenue ..		4,000
Dec. 31	Interest Expense...	5,246		Interest Receivable	4,000	
	Bond Discount ...		1,246	Bond Investment ...	1,246	
	Interest Payable ..		4,000	Interest Revenue ..		5,246
	($12,461 ÷ 120 × 12 months = $1,246 (rounded) amortization for year)					

Because the results are identical, many companies only make the amortization entry once a year.

To illustrate the entries that would be required to amortize a bond premium, consider again the situation where the 8% bonds were sold to yield 7%, or $107,107. The $7,107 premium would be amortized on a straight-line basis, at year-end, as follows:

		Issuer's Books			**Investor's Books**		
July	1	Interest Expense...	4,000		Cash	4,000	
		Cash		4,000	Interest Revenue ..		4,000
Dec. 31		Interest Expense...	3,289		Interest Receivable	4,000	
		Bond Premium	711		Bond Investment ..		711
		Interest Payable ..		4,000	Interest Revenue ..		3,289

($7,107 ÷ 120 × 12 months = $711 (rounded) premium amortization for year)

The amortization of the premium has the effect of reducing the amount of interest expense or interest revenue to the actual yield or market rate of the bonds, 7%.

Effective-Interest Method

The effective-interest method of amortization uses a uniform interest rate based on a changing investment balance and provides for an increasing premium or discount amortization each period. In order to use this method, the effective interest rate for the bonds must be known. This is the rate of interest at bond issuance that discounts the maturity value of the bonds and the periodic interest payments to the market price of the bonds. This rate is used to determine the effective revenue or expense to be recorded on the books.

To illustrate the amortization of a bond discount using the effective-interest method, consider once again the $100,000, 8%, 10-year bonds sold for $87,539, based on an effective interest rate of 10%.

The discount amortization for the first six months using the effective-interest method would be computed as follows:

Investment balance at beginning of first period	$87,539
Effective rate per semiannual period	5%
Stated rate per semiannual period	4%
Interest amount based on effective rate ($87,539 × .05)	$ 4,377
Interest payment based on stated rate ($100,000 × .04)	4,000
Discount amortization—difference between interest based on effective rate and stated rate	$ 377

This difference is the discount amortization for the first period using the interest method. For the second semiannual period, the bond carrying value increases by the discount amortization. The amortization for the second semiannual period would be computed as follows:

Investment balance at beginning of second period ($87,539 + $377)	<u>$87,916</u>
Interest amount based on effective rate ($87,916) × .05)	$ 4,396
Interest payment based on stated rate ($100,000 × .04)	<u>4,000</u>
Discount amortization—difference between interest based on effective rate and stated rate	<u>$ 396</u>

The amount of interest to be recognized each period is computed at a uniform rate on an increasing balance. This results in an increasing discount amortization over the life of the bonds, which is graphically demonstrated and compared with straight-line amortization below.

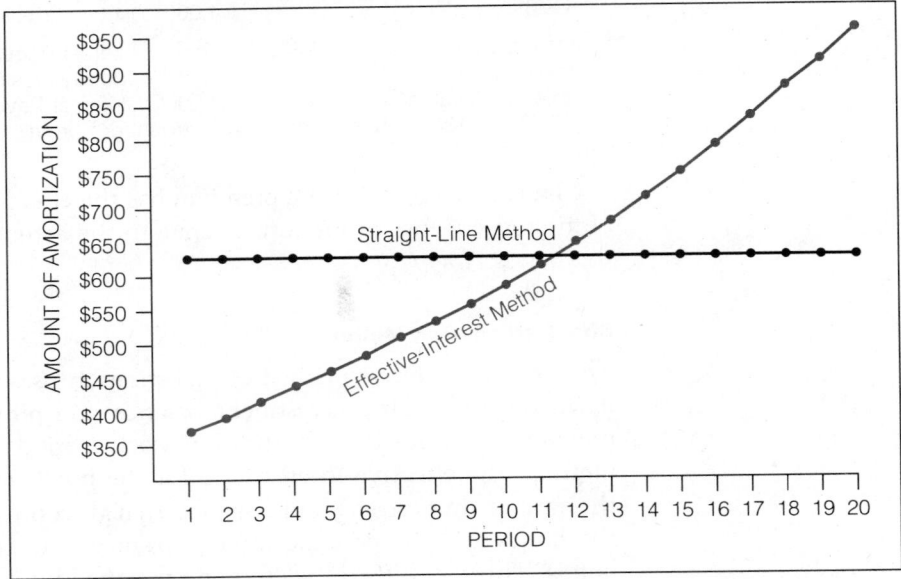

The entries for amortizing the discount would be the same as those shown for straight-line amortization; only the amounts would be different.

Premium amortization would be computed in a similar way except that the interest payment based on the stated interest rate would be higher than the interest amount based on the effective rate. For example, assume that the $100,000, 8%, 10-year bonds were sold on the issuance date for $107,107, thus providing an effective interest rate of 7%. The premium amortization for the first and second six-month periods would be computed as follows (amounts are rounded to the nearest dollar):

Investment balance at beginning of first period	<u>$107,107</u>
Effective rate per semiannual period	3.5%
Stated rate per semiannual period	4.0%
Interest payment based on stated rate ($100,000 × .04)	$ 4,000
Interest amount based on effective rate ($107,107 × .035)	<u>3,749</u>
Premium amortization—difference between interest based on stated rate and effective rate	<u>$ 251</u>
Investment balance at beginning of second period ($107,107 − $251)	<u>$106,856</u>
Interest payment based on stated rate ($100,000 × .04)	$ 4,000
Interest amount based on effective rate ($106,856 × .035)	<u>3,740</u>
Premium amortization—difference between interest based on stated rate and effective rate	<u>$ 260</u>

As illustrated, as the investment or liability balance is reduced by the premium amortization, the interest, based on the effective rate, also decreases. The difference between the interest payment and the effective interest amount increases in a manner similar to discount amortization. Bond amortization tables may be prepared to determine the periodic adjustments to the bond carrying value, i.e., the present value of the bond. A partial bond amortization table is illustrated below.

Amortization of Bond Premium—Effective-Interest Method
$100,000, 10-Year Bonds, Interest at 8% Payable Semiannually,
Sold at $107,107 to Yield 7%

Interest Payment	A Interest Paid (.04 × $100,000)	B Interest Expense (.035 × Bond Carrying Value)	C Premium Amortization (A − B)	D Unamortized Premium (D − C)	E Bond Carrying Value ($100,000 + D)
				$7,107	$107,107
1	$4,000	$3,749 (.035 × $107,107)	$251	6,856	106,856
2	4,000	3,740 (.035 × $106,856)	260	6,596	106,596
3	4,000	3,731 (.035 × $106,596)	269	6,327	106,327
4	4,000	3,721 (.035 × $106,327)	279	6,048	106,048
5	4,000	3,712 (.035 × $106,048)	288	5,760	105,760

Because the effective-interest method adjusts the stated interest rate to an effective interest rate, it is theoretically more accurate as an amortization method than is the straight-line method. Note that the total amortization is the same under either method; only the interim amounts differ. Since the issuance of APB Opinion No. 21, the effective-interest method is the recommended amortization method. However, the straight-line method may be used by a company if the interim results of using it do not differ materially from the amortization using the effective-interest method.[3]

Retirement of Bonds at Maturity

Bonds always include a specified termination or maturity date. At that time, the issuer must pay the current investors the maturity or face value of the bonds. When bond discount or premium and issuance costs have been properly amortized over the life of the bonds, bond retirement simply calls for elimination of the liability or the investment by a cash transaction, illustrated as follows.

Issuer's Books			**Investor's Books**		
Bonds Payable	100,000		Cash	100,000	
Cash		100,000	Bond Investment . .		100,000

There is no recognition of any gain or loss on retirement since the carrying value is equal to the maturity value, which is also equal to the market value of the bonds at that point in time.

---

[3]*APB Opinion No. 21*, par. 15.

Any bonds not presented for payment at their maturity date should be removed from the bonds payable balance on the issuer's books and reported separately as Matured Bonds Payable; these are reported as a current liability except when they are to be paid out of a bond retirement fund. Interest does not accrue on matured bonds not presented for payment. If a bond retirement fund is used to pay off a bond issue, any cash remaining in the fund may be returned to the cash account.

Extinguishment of Debt Prior to Maturity

When debt is retired prior to the maturity date of the obligation, a gain or loss must be recognized for the difference between the carrying value of the debt security and the amount paid.[4] This gain or loss is classified as an **early extinguishment of debt** and, according to FASB Statement No. 4, is to be reported as an extraordinary item on the income statement.[5]

The problems that arise in retiring bonds or other forms of long-term debt prior to maturity are described in the following sections. Bonds may be retired prior to maturity in one of the following ways:

1. Bonds may be **redeemed** by the issuer by purchasing the bonds on the open market or by exercising the call provision that is frequently included in bond indentures;
2. Bonds may be **converted**, i.e., exchanged for other securities; or
3. Bonds may be **refinanced** (sometimes called "refunded") by using the proceeds from the sale of a new bond issue to retire outstanding bonds.

Another form of early extinguishment of debt, called **in-substance defeasance**, will also be discussed. Unlike redemption, conversion, and refinancing, in-substance defeasance does not involve the actual retirement of bonds.

Redemption by Purchase of Bonds on the Market

Corporations frequently purchase their own bonds on the market when prices or other factors make such actions desirable. When bonds are purchased, amortization of bond premium or discount and issue costs should be brought up to date. Purchase by the issuer calls for the cancellation of the bond face value together with any related premium, discount, or issue costs as of the purchase date.

To illustrate a bond purchase prior to maturity, assume that $100,000, 8% bonds of Triad Inc. are not held until maturity, but are sold back to the issuer on February 1, 1991, at 97 plus accrued interest. The book value of the bonds on both the issuer's and investor's books is $97,700 as of January

---

[4]*Opinions of the Accounting Principles Board, No. 26*, "Early Extinguishment of Debt" (New York: American Institute of Certified Public Accountants, 1972), par. 20.

[5]*Statement of Financial Accounting Standards No. 4*, "Reporting Gains and Losses from Extinguishment of Debt" (Stamford: Financial Accounting Standards Board, 1975), par. 8. Note that an exception to the extraordinary classification is made if the early termination is necessary to satisfy bond retirement (sinking) fund requirements within a one-year period; see *Statement of Financial Accounting Standards No. 64*, "Extinguishment of Debt Made to Satisfy Sinking-Fund Requirements" (Stamford: Financial Accounting Standards Board, 1982), par. 3.

1. Discount amortization has been recorded at $50 a month using the straight-line method. Interest payment dates on the bonds are November 1 and May 1; accrued interest adjustments are reversed. Entries on both the issuer's and investor's books at the time of purchase would be as follows:

Issuer's Books

Feb. 1	Interest Expense	50	
	Discount on Bonds Payable		50
	To record discount amortization for January, 1991:		
1	Bonds Payable (or Treasury Bonds)	100,000	
	Interest Expense	2,000	
	Discount on Bonds Payable		2,250
	Cash		99,000
	Gain on Bond Reacquisition		750
	To record purchase of bonds and payment of three months' interest.		

Computation:

Book value of bonds, January 1, 1991	$97,700
Discount amortization for January	50
Book value of bonds, February 1, 1991	$97,750
Purchase price	97,000
Gain on purchase	$ 750

Interest expense for 3 months:
$100,000 × .08 × ¼ = $2,000

Investor's Books

Feb. 1	Investment in Triad Inc. Bonds	50	
	Interest Revenue		50
	To record discount amortization for January, 1991.		
1	Cash	99,000	
	Loss on Sale of Bonds	750	
	Investment in Triad Inc. Bonds		97,750
	Interest Revenue		2,000
	To record sale of bonds and receipt of three months' interest.		

Redemption by Exercise of Call Provision

A call provision gives the issuer the option of retiring bonds prior to maturity. Frequently the call must be made on an interest payment date, and no further interest accrues on the bonds not presented at this time. When only a part of an issue is to be redeemed, the bonds called may be determined by lot.

The inclusion of call provisions in a bond agreement is a feature favoring the issuer. The company is in a position to terminate the bond agreement and eliminate future interest charges whenever its financial position makes such action feasible. Furthermore, the company is protected in the event of a fall in the market interest rate by being able to retire the old issue from proceeds of a new issue paying a lower rate of interest. A bond contract normally requires payment of a premium if bonds are called. A bondholder is thus offered special compensation if the investment is terminated early.

When bonds are called, the difference between the amount paid and the bond carrying value is reported as a gain or a loss on both the issuer's and investor's books. Any interest paid at the time of the call is recorded as a debit to Interest Expense on the issuer's books and a credit to Interest Revenue on the investor's books. The entries to be made are the same as illustrated previously for the purchase of bonds by the issuer.

Convertible Bonds

The issuance of **convertible debt securities**, most frequently bonds, has become increasingly popular.[6] These securities raise specific questions as to the nature of the securities, i.e., whether they should be considered debt or equity securities, the valuation of the conversion feature, and the treatment of any gain or loss on conversion.

Convertible debt securities usually have the following features:[7]

1. An interest rate lower than the issuer could establish for nonconvertible debt.
2. An initial conversion price higher than the market value of the common stock at time of issuance.
3. A call option retained by the issuer.

The popularity of these securities may be attributed to the advantages to both an issuer and a holder. An issuer is able to obtain financing at a lower interest rate because of the value of the conversion feature to the holder. Because of the call provision, an issuer is in a position to exert influence upon the holders to exchange the debt for equity securities if stock values increase; the issuer has had the use of relatively low interest rate financing if stock values do not increase. On the other hand, the holder has a debt instrument that, barring default, assures the return of investment plus a fixed return, and at the same time offers an option to transfer his or her interest to equity capital should such transfer become attractive.

Many convertible bond issues place no restriction on when an issuer can call in bonds, and interest accrued on such bonds is sometimes absorbed in a conversion and not paid to the investor. Thus, a company can have the use of interest-free money as a result of calling in bonds prior to the first interest payment. Widespread use of early call provisions in the early 1980s led some investors to demand a provision restricting exercise of the call provision for a specified time period.[8]

Differences of opinion exist as to whether convertible debt securities

[6]See Leslie Pittel, "Playing Safe—and Sporty, Too," *Forbes* (Oct. 22, 1984), pp. 248–252.

[7]*Opinions of the Accounting Principles Board, No. 14,* "Accounting for Convertible Debt and Debt Issued with Stock Purchase Warrants" (New York: American Institute of Certified Public Accountants, 1969), par. 3.

[8]*See* Ben Weberman, "The Convertible Bond Scam," *Forbes* (January 19, 1981), p. 92.

should be treated by an issuer solely as debt, or whether part of the proceeds received from the issuance of debt should be recognized as equity capital. One view holds that the debt and the conversion privilege are inseparably connected, and therefore the debt and equity portions of a security should not be separately valued. A holder cannot sell part of the instrument and retain the other. An alternate view holds that there are two distinct elements in these securities and that each should be recognized in the accounts: that portion of the issuance price attributable to the conversion privilege should be recorded as a credit to Paid-In Capital; the balance of the issuance price should be assigned to the debt. This would decrease the premium otherwise recognized in the debt or perhaps result in a discount.

These views are compared in the illustration that follows. Assume that 500 ten-year bonds, face value $1,000, are sold at 105, or a total issue price of $525,000 (500 × $1,000 × 1.05). The bonds contain a conversion privilege that provides for exchange of a $1,000 bond for 20 shares of stock, par value $40. The interest rate on the bonds is 8%. It is estimated that without the conversion privilege, the bonds would sell at 96. The journal entries to record the issuance on the issuer's books under the two approaches follow.

Debt and Equity Not Separated

Cash	525,000	
Bonds Payable		500,000
Premium on Bonds Payable		25,000

Debt and Equity Separated

Cash	525,000	
Discount on Bonds Payable	20,000[1]	
Bonds Payable		500,000
Paid-In Capital Arising from Bond Conversion Privilege ..		45,000[2]

Computations:

[1]Par value of bonds (500 × $1,000)	$500,000
Selling price of bonds without conversion feature ($500,000 × .96)	480,000
Discount on bonds without conversion feature	$ 20,000
[2]Total cash received on sale of bonds	$525,000
Selling price without conversion feature	480,000
Amount applicable to conversion feature (equity portion)	$ 45,000

The periodic charge for interest will differ depending on which method is employed. To illustrate the computation of interest charges, assume that the straight-line method is used to amortize bond premium or discount. Under the first approach, the annual interest charge would be $37,500 ($40,000 paid less $2,500 premium amortization). Under the second approach, the annual interest charge would be $42,000 ($40,000 paid plus $2,000 discount amortization).

The Accounting Principles Board stated that when convertible debt is sold at a price or with a value at issuance not significantly in excess of the face amount, ". . . no portion of the proceeds from the issuance . . . should be accounted for as attributable to the conversion feature."[9]

The APB stated that greater weight for this decision was placed on the inseparability of the debt and the conversion option than upon the practical problems of valuing the separate parts. However, the practical problems are considerable. Separate valuation requires asking the question: How much would the security sell for without the conversion feature? In many instances this question would appear to be unanswerable. Investment bankers responsible for selling these issues are frequently unable to separate the two features for valuation purposes; they contend that the cash required simply could not be raised without the conversion privilege.

There would seem to be strong theoretical support for separating the debt and equity portions of the proceeds from the issuance of convertible debt on the issuer's books. Despite these theoretical arguments, current practice follows APB Opinion No. 14, and no separation is usually made between debt and equity. This is true even when separate values are determinable.

When conversion takes place, a special valuation question must be answered. Should the market value of the securities be used to compute a gain or loss on the transaction? If the convertible security is viewed as debt, then the conversion to equity would seem to be a significant economic transaction and a gain or loss would be recognized. If, however, the convertible security is viewed as equity, the conversion is really an exchange of one type of equity capital for another, and the historical cost principle would seem to indicate that no gain or loss would be recognized. In practice, the latter approach seems to be most commonly followed by both the issuer and investor of the bonds. No gain or loss is recognized either for book or tax purposes. The book value of the bonds is transferred to become the book value of the stock issued. However, this treatment seems inconsistent with APB Opinion No. 14 in which convertible debt is considered to be debt rather than equity.

If an investor views the security as debt, conversion of the debt could be viewed as an exchange of one asset for another. The general rule for the exchange of nonmonetary assets is that the market value of the asset exchanged should be used to measure any gain or loss on the transaction.[10] If there is no market value of the asset surrendered or if its value is undeterminable, the market value of the asset received should be used. The market value of convertible bonds should reflect the market value of the stock to be issued on the conversion, and thus the market value of the two securities should be similar.

---

[9]*APB Opinion No. 14*, par. 12.

[10]*Opinions of the Accounting Principles Board*, No. 29, "Accounting for Nonmonetary Transactions" (New York: American Institute of Certified Public Accountants, 1973), par. 18.

To illustrate bond conversion for the investor recognizing a gain or loss on conversion, assume HiTec Co. offers bondholders 40 shares of HiTec Co. common stock, $25 par, in exchange for each $1,000, 8% bond held. An investor exchanges bonds of $10,000 (book value as brought up to date, $9,850) for 400 shares of common stock having a market price at the time of the exchange of $26 per share. The exchange is completed at the interest payment date. The exchange is recorded as follows:

Investment in HiTec Co. Common Stock	10,400	
Investment in HiTec Co. Bonds		9,850
Gain on Conversion of HiTec Co. Bonds		550

If the investor chose not to recognize a gain or loss, the journal entry would be as follows:

Investment in HiTec Co. Common Stock	9,850	
Investment in HiTec Co. Bonds		9,850

Similar differences would occur on the issuer's books depending on the viewpoint assumed. If the issuer desired to recognize the conversion of the convertible debt as a significant culminating transaction, the market value of the securities would be used to record the conversion. To illustrate the journal entries for the issuer using this reasoning, assume 100 bonds, face value $1,000, are exchanged for 2,000 shares of common stock, $40 par value, $55 market value. At the time of the conversion, there is an unamortized premium on the bond issue of $3,000. The conversion would be recorded as follows:

Bonds Payable	100,000	
Premium on Bonds Payable	3,000	
Loss on Conversion of Bonds...........................	7,000	
Common Stock		80,000
Paid-In Capital in Excess of Par......................		30,000

Computation:

Market value of stock issued (2,000 shares at $55)		$110,000
Face value of bonds payable	$100,000	
Plus unamortized premium	3,000	103,000
Loss to company on conversion of bonds		$ 7,000

If the issuer did not consider the conversion as a culminating transaction, no gain or loss would be recognized. The bond carrying value would be transferred to the capital stock account on the theory that the company upon issuing the bonds is aware of the fact that bond proceeds may ultimately represent the consideration identified with stock. Thus, when bondholders exercise their conversion privileges, the value identified with the obligation is transferred to the security that replaces it. Under this assumption, the conversion would be recorded as follows:

Bonds Payable	100,000	
Premium on Bonds Payable	3,000	
Common Stock, $40 par		80,000
Paid-In Capital in Excess of Par		23,000

The profession has not resolved the accounting issues surrounding convertible debt. Although the practice of not recognizing gain or loss on either the issuer's or the investor's books is widespread, it seems inconsistent with the treatment of other items that are transferred by an entity. The economic reality of the transaction would seem to require a recognition of the change in value at least at the time conversion takes place.

Bond Refinancing

Cash for the retirement of a bond issue is frequently raised through the sale of a new issue and is referred to as **bond refinancing**, or **refunding**. Bond refinancing may take place when an issue matures, or bonds may be refinanced prior to their maturity when the interest rate has dropped and the interest savings on a new issue will more than offset the cost of retiring the old issue. To illustrate, assume that a corporation has outstanding 12% bonds of $1,000,000 callable at 102 and with a remaining 10-year term, and similar 10-year bonds can be marketed currently at an interest rate of only 10%. Under these circumstances it would be advantageous to retire the old issue with the proceeds from a new 10% issue since the future savings in interest will exceed by a considerable amount the premium to be paid on the call of the old issue.

The desirability of refinancing may not be so obvious as in the preceding example. In determining whether refinancing is warranted in marginal cases, careful consideration must be given to such factors as the different maturity dates of the two issues, possible future changes in interest rates, changed loan requirements, different indenture provisions, income tax effects of refinancing, and legal fees, printing costs, and marketing costs involved in refinancing.

When refinancing takes place before the maturity date of the old issue, the problem arises as to how to dispose of the call premium and unamortized discount and issue costs of the original bonds. Three positions have been taken with respect to disposition of these items:

1. Such charges are considered a loss on bond retirement.
2. Such charges are considered deferrable and to be amortized systematically over the remaining life of the original issue.
3. Such charges are considered deferrable and to be amortized systematically over the life of the new issue.

Although arguments can be presented supporting each of these alternatives, the Accounting Principles Board concluded that "all extinguishments of debt before scheduled maturities are fundamentally alike. The accounting for such transactions should be the same regardless of the means used to achieve the extinguishment."[11] The first position, immediate recognition of the gain or loss, was selected by the Board for all early extinguishment of debt. The Financial Accounting Standards Board considered the nature of this gain or loss and defined it as being an extraordinary item requiring separate income statement disclosure, as indicated earlier.

In-Substance Defeasance

Another form of early extinguishment of debt is referred to as **in-substance defeasance**, or economic defeasance. This is a technique used by companies to reduce the amount of long-term debt reported on the balance sheet. In-substance defeasance is a process of transferring assets, generally cash and securities, to an irrevocable trust, and using the assets and earnings therefrom to satisfy the long-term obligations as they come due. The transfer of the assets is treated as an extinguishment of debt, and a gain may be recognized on the early retirement, even though the debt has not actually been paid at that point. In some instances, the debt holders are not even aware of these transactions, and continue to rely on the issuer of the debt for settlement of the obligation. In other words, there has been no "legal defeasance" or release of the debtor from the legal liability.

To illustrate the effects of in-substance defeasance and the practical problems associated with these arrangements, assume that Tenax Corporation transfers $350,000 cash to a trust established solely for the retirement of $400,000 of Tenax bonds outstanding. The trust purchases government securities for $350,000. Interest and proceeds from the eventual sale or maturity of the government securities will be used to pay off the principal and interest of the bond indebtedness. Tenax removes the bonds from its balance sheet and recognizes an extraordinary gain of $50,000 on the extinguishment, i.e., the difference between the $400,000 liability to bondholders and the $350,000 cash transferred to the trust. The results of Tenax Corporation's in-substance defeasance are illustrated in the condensed financial statements below and on page 656.

Before In-Substance Defeasance

Tenax Corporation
Balance Sheet

Assets		Liabilities and Equity	
Cash	$ 400,000	Current liabilities	$ 200,000
Other assets	6,000,000	Bonds payable	400,000
Total assets	$6,400,000	Other long-term liabilities	1,200,000
		Equity (400,000 common shares outstanding)	4,600,000
		Total liabilities & equity	$6,400,000

[11]*Opinions of the Accounting Principles Board, No. 26*, par. 19.

Income Statement

Revenues	$8,000,000
Expenses	(6,000,000)
Net income	$2,000,000

Earnings per share ($2,000,000 ÷ 400,000 shares)	$5.00
Debt-to-equity ratio (total liabilities ÷ equity = $1,800,000 ÷ $4,600,000)	.39
Return on assets (net income ÷ total assets = $2,000,000 ÷ $6,400,000)	.31

After In-Substance Defeasance

Tenax Corporation
Balance Sheet

Assets		Liabilities and Equity	
Cash	$ 50,000	Current liabilities	$ 200,000
Other assets	6,000,000	Other long-term liabilities	1,200,000
Total assets	6,050,000	Equity	4,650,000
		Total liabilities & equity . . .	$6,050,000

Income Statement

Revenues	$8,000,000
Extraordinary Gain ($400,000 − $350,000)	50,000
Expenses	(6,000,000)
Net income	$2,050,000)

Earnings per share ($2,050,000 ÷ 400,000 shares)	$5.13
Debt-to-equity ratio ($1,400,000 ÷ $4,650,000)	.30
Return on assets ($2,050,000 ÷ $6,050,000)	.34

As the statements show, the transaction improves both the earnings per share and key financial ratios of Tenax. Earnings are increased by the amount of gain recognized by Tenax, $50,000 or $.13 per share. The debt is removed from the balance sheet, without actually being retired, thereby decreasing the debt-to-equity ratio and increasing the return on assets. In many in-substance defeasance cases, the actual retirement of debt may not be desirable due to market conditions, or may be too costly due to significant call premiums.

To deal with the potential problems of overstating earnings or manipulating financial position, the FASB issued Statement No. 76 as a guideline for in-substance defeasance transactions. For a transaction to qualify as an extinguishment of debt, and therefore for removal of the debt from the balance sheet, the debtor must place cash or risk-free securities (those backed by the U.S. Government) in an irrevocable trust for the sole purpose of retiring the debt principal and interest obligations. In addition, the possibility that the debtor will be required to make further payments on that particular debt security must be remote.[12]

---

[12]*Statement of Financial Accounting Standards No. 76*, "Extinguishment of Debt" (Stamford: Financial Accounting Standards Board, 1983), p. 5. It should be noted that current accounting practice does not allow extinguishment of debt through *instantaneous* in-substance defeasance, which means newly issued debt is immediately "retired" by having assets placed in trust to meet the interest and principal obligations as they come due. Instantaneous defeasance must be accounted for as a borrowing and as an investment, not as an extinguishment. See also *FASB Technical Bulletin No. 84-4*, "In-Substance Defeasance of Debt" (Stamford: Financial Accounting Standards Board, 1984).

Not all accountants agree with the conclusions of FASB Statement No. 76. Some argue that until a debt is actually retired, it should not be removed from the balance sheet under any conditions. Others are skeptical of recognizing a gain or loss on a transaction where the debtor is not legally released from the primary obligation of the debt. On the other hand, supporters of the FASB position claim that the economic reality of in-substance defeasance transactions is essentially the same as a cash settlement. They further maintain that the strict guidelines of having risk-free securities placed in an irrevocable trust and having the probability of additional payments being remote are sufficient to recognize the transaction as an extinguishment of debt. Regardless of individual viewpoints, since FASB Statement No. 76 is generally accepted, transactions that qualify as in-substance defeasance are treated in the same manner as other forms of early retirement. Regardless of the reasons for extinguishment or the means used to accomplish the early retirement, a gain or loss should be recognized as an extraordinary item of that period.

Troubled Debt Restructuring

Another significant accounting problem is created when economic conditions make it difficult for an issuer of long-term debt to make the cash payments required under the terms of the debt instrument. These payments include interest payments, principal payments on installment obligations, periodic payments to bond retirement funds, or even payments to retire debt at maturity. To avoid bankruptcy proceedings or foreclosure on the debt, investors in such situations may agree to make concessions and revise the original terms of the debt to permit the issuer to recover from financial problems. The restructuring may take many different forms. For example, there may be a suspension of interest payments for a period of time, a reduction in the interest rate, an extension of the maturity date of the debt, or even an exchange of assets or equity securities for the debt. The principal accounting question in these cases, on both the books of the issuer and the investor, is whether a gain or loss should be recognized upon the restructuring of the debt.

The issue became critical in the mid 1970's when several issues of municipal bonds, notably New York City bonds, were restructured due to the financial difficulties of the issuing organizations. Investors in the bonds were faced with interest and fund payments in arrears, and a near bankrupt situation for New York City. Most investors felt the decline was only temporary, and so did not recognize any loss on the books. After considerable negotiation, the terms of the bonds were restructured. Changes included a moratorium on interest and fund payments and extended maturity dates. Other municipalities and private companies such as Chrysler and Massey-Ferguson have experienced similar restructuring needs.

The Financial Accounting Standards Board considered this area carefully, and issued Statement No. 15 in 1977. In this statement the Board defined troubled debt restructuring as a situation where "the creditor for economic or legal reasons related to the debtor's financial difficulties grants a concession to the debtor that it would not otherwise consider. That concession either stems from an agreement between the creditor and the debtor or is imposed by law or a court."[13] The key word in this definition is *concession.* If a concession is not made by creditors, accounting for the restructuring follows the procedures discussed for extinguishment of debt prior to maturity.

The major issue addressed by the FASB in Statement No. 15 is whether a troubled debt restructuring agreement should be viewed as a significant economic transaction. It was decided that if it is considered to be a significant economic transaction, entries should be made on both the issuer's and the investor's books to reflect the gain or loss. If the restructuring is not considered to be a significant economic transaction, no entries are required. The accounting treatment thus depends on the nature of the restructuring. The FASB conclusions are summarized in the following table.

Accounting for Different Types of Troubled Debt Restructuring

Type	Restructuring Considered Significant Economic Transaction: Gain or Loss Recognized	Restructuring Not Considered Significant Economic Transaction: No Gain or Loss Recognized
Transfer of assets in full settlement (asset swap)	X	
Grant of equity interest in full settlement (equity swap)	X	
Modification of terms: total payment under new structure exceeds debt carrying value		X
Modification of terms: total payment under new structure in less than debt carrying value	X	

Each type of restructuring is discussed and illustrated in the following sections.

Transfer of Assets in Full Settlement (Asset Swap)

A debtor that transfers assets, such as real estate, inventories, receivables, or investments, to a creditor to fully settle a payable usually will recognize two types of gains or losses: (1) a gain or loss on disposal of the asset, and

---

[13]*Statement of Financial Accounting Standards No. 15,* "Accounting by Debtors and Creditors for Troubled Debt Restructuring" (Stamford: Financial Accounting Standards Board, 1977), par. 2.

(2) **a gain arising from the concession** granted in the restructuring of the debt. The computation of these gains and/or losses is made as follows:

Carrying value of assets being transferred _____

> Difference represents gain or loss on disposal

Market value of asset being transferred _____

> Difference represents gain on restructuring

Carrying value of debt being liquidated _____

The gain or loss on disposal of an asset is usually reported as an ordinary income item unless it meets criteria for reporting it is an unusual or irregular item. However, the gain on restructuring is considered to arise from an early extinguishment of debt and must be reported as an extraordinary item.[14] An investor always recognizes a loss on the restructuring due to the concession granted unless the investment has already been written down in anticipation of the loss. The computation of the loss is made as follows:

Carrying value of investment liquidated _____

> Difference represents loss on restructuring

Market value of asset being transferred _____

The classification of this loss depends on the criteria being used to recognize irregular or extraordinary items. However, usually the loss is anticipated as market values of the investment decline, and it is recognized as an ordinary loss, either prior to the restructuring or as part of the restructuring.

To illustrate these points, assume that Stanton Industries is behind in its interest payments on outstanding bonds of $500,000, and is threatened with bankruptcy proceedings. The carrying value of the bonds on Stanton's books is $545,000 after deducting the unamortized discount of $5,000 and adding unpaid interest of $50,000. To settle the debt, Stanton transfers long-term investments it holds in Worth common stock with a carrying value of $350,000 and a current market value of $400,000, to all investors on a prorata basis. Assume Realty Inc. holds $40,000 face value of bonds. Because of the troubled financial condition of Stanton Industries, Realty Inc. has previously recognized as a loss a $5,000 decline in the value of the debt, and is carrying the investment at $35,000 on its books plus interest receivable of $4,000. The entries to record the asset transfer would be as follows:

[14]*Ibid.*, par. 21.

Stanton Industries (Issuer)

Interest Payable.......................................	50,000	
Bonds Payable	500,000	
Discount on Bonds................................		5,000
Long-Term Investments—Worth Common		350,000
Gain on Disposal of Worth Common		50,000
Gain on Restructuring of Debt		145,000

Computation:

Carrying value of Worth Common	$350,000	
		$50,000 gain on disposal
Market value of Worth Common	400,000	
		$145,000 gain from restructuring
Carrying value of debt liquidated	545,000	

Realty Inc. (Investor)

Long-Term Investments—Worth Common	32,000	
Loss on Restructuring of Debt	7,000	
Long-Term Investments—Stanton Bonds		35,000
Interest Receivable.......................................		4,000

Computation:
Percentage of debt held by Realty Inc.: $40,000/$500,000 = 8\%$
Market value of long-term investment received in settlement of debt:
    $8\% \times \$400,000 = \$32,000$

If an active market does not exist for the assets being transferred, estimates of the value should be made based on transfer of similar assets or by analyzing future cash flows from the assets.[15]

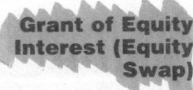
Grant of Equity Interest (Equity Swap)

A debtor that grants an equity interest to the investor as a substitute for a liability must recognize an extraordinary gain equal to the difference between the fair market value of the equity interest and the carrying value of the liquidated liability. A creditor (investor) must recognize a loss equal to the difference between the same fair market value of the equity interest and the carrying value of the debt as an investment. For example, assume that Stanton Industries transferred 20,000 shares of common stock to satisfy the $500,000 face value of bonds. The par value of the common stock per share is $15 and the market value at the date of the restructuring is $20 per share. Assume the other facts described in the illustration of an asset swap on page 659 are unchanged. The entries to record the grant of the equity interest on both sets of books would be as follows:

Stanton Industries (Issuer)

Interest Payable.......................................	50,000	
Bonds Payable	500,000	
Discount on Bonds.....................................		5,000
Common Stock		300,000
Paid-In Capital in Excess of Par.........................		100,000
Gain on Restructuring of Debt		145,000

[15]*Ibid.,* par. 13.

Computation:

Market value of common stock $400,000
                                                            $145,000 gain from restructuring
Carrying value of debt liquidated $545,000

<u>Realty Inc. (Investor)</u>

Long-Term Investments—Stanton Common Stock	32,000	
Loss on Restructuring of Debt	7,000	
Long-Term Investment—Stanton Bonds		35,000
Interest Receivable		4,000

The entry on Stanton's books for an equity swap differs from that made for the asset swap because there can be no gain or loss on disposal of a company's own stock. However, the entry on Realty's books for an equity swap is identical with that for an asset swap except that the investment is in Stanton common stock.

Modification of Debt Terms

There are many ways debt terms may be modified to aid a troubled debtor. Modification may involve either the interest, the maturity value, or both. Interest concessions may involve a reduction of the interest rate, forgiveness of unpaid interest, or a moratorium on interest payments for a period of time. Maturity value concessions may involve an extension of the maturity date or a reduction in the amount to be repaid at maturity. Basically, the FASB decided that most modifications of debt did not result in a significant economic transaction, and thus did not give rise to a gain or loss at the date of restructuring. They argued that the new terms were merely an extension of an existing debt and that the modifications should be reflected in future periods through modified interest charges based on computed implicit interest rates. The only exception to this general rule occurs if the total payments to be made under the new structure, including all future interest payments, are less than the carrying value of the debt or the investment at the time of restructuring. Under this exception, the difference between the total future cash payments required and the carrying value of the debt or investment is recognized immediately as a gain on the debtor's books and a loss on the creditor's books.

To illustrate the accounting for this type of restructuring, assume the interest rate on the Stanton Industries bonds (see page 659) is reduced from 10% to 7%, the maturity date is extended from 3 to 5 years from the restructuring date, and the past interest due of $50,000 is forgiven. The total future payments to be made after this restructuring are as follows:

Maturity value of bonds	$500,000
Interest—7% × $500,000 × 5 years	175,000
Total payments to be made after restructuring	$675,000

Since the $675,000 exceeds the carrying value of $545,000, no gain is recognized on the books of Stanton Industries at the time of restructuring.

A similar computation for Realty Inc. results in total future payments of $54,000 [$40,000 + ($2,800 × 5)] as compared with a carrying value of $39,000. Thus, no further loss is recognized on Realty Inc. books at the time of restructure.

However, if in addition to the preceding changes, $200,000 of maturity value is forgiven, the future payments would be reduced as follows:

Maturity value of bonds	$300,000
Interest—7% × $300,000 × 5 years	105,000
Total payments to be made after restructuring	$405,000

Now the carrying value exceeds the future payments by $140,000, and this gain would be recognized by Stanton as follows:

Interest Payable	50,000	
Bonds Payable	500,000	
Discount on Bonds		5,000
Restructured Debt		405,000
Gain on Restructuring of Debt		140,000
To reclassify restructured debt and recognize a gain of $140,000 on restructuring.		

Similar computations could be made on Realty's books assuming 40% of the debt is cancelled ($200,000/$500,000 = 40%).

Maturity value—($40,000 × 60%)	$24,000
Interest—7% × $24,000 × 5 years	8,400
Total receipts after restructuring	$32,400
Carrying value of investment	39,000
Loss on restructuring	$ 6,600

The entry to record the loss on Realty's books would be as follows:

Loss on Restructuring of Debt	6,600	
Investment in Stanton Bonds		2,600
Interest Receivable		4,000
To recognize a loss of $6,600 on restructuring.		

When terms are modified, the amount recognized as interest expense or interest revenue in the remaining periods of the debt instrument's life is based on a computed implicit interest rate. The implicit interest rate is the rate that equates the present value of all future debt payments to the present carrying value of the debt or investment. The interest expense or interest revenue for each period is equal to the carrying value of the debt for the period involved times the implicit interest rate. The computation of the implicit interest rate can be complex, and usually requires the use of a computer program. However, approximations can be made by using a trial and error approach from the present value tables in Chapter 6.

To illustrate the computation of an implicit interest rate, the restructuring of Stanton Industries described on page 659 will be used. The question to be answered is what rate of interest will equate the total future payments of $675,000 to the present carrying value of $545,000. Trial and error use of Tables II and IV in Chapter 6 shows that the rate is between 4% and 6% per year. The computations are as follows:

	Interest Rate 6% (3% per Semiannual Period)	Interest Rate 4% (2% per Semiannual Period)
Present value of maturity value due in five years (ten semiannual periods).	.7441 × $500,000 = $372,050	.8203 × $500,000 = $410,150
Present value of $17,500 interest payments for ten semiannual payments	8.5302 × $17,500 = 149,279	8.9826 × $17,500 = 157,196
Total present value	$521,329	$567,346

Interpolation indicates that the present value of $545,000 lies almost exactly midway between the present values computed at 6% and 4%; therefore, the approximate interest rate is 5%. For purposes of the illustration, the 5% rate will be used, or 2½% per semiannual payment period.

Using this rate, the recorded interest expense for the first six months would be $13,625, or 2½% of $545,000. Since the actual cash payment for interest is $17,500, the carrying value of the debt will decline by $3,875 ($17,500 − $13,625). The interest expense for the second semiannual period will be less than for the first period because of the decrease in the carrying value of the debt [($545,000 − $3,875) × 2.5% = $13,528 interest expense]. These computations are the same as those required in applying the effective-interest method of amortization described on pages 645-647. If the exact implicit interest rate were used, continuation of the procedure for the 10 periods would leave a balance of $500,000, the maturity value, in the liability account of Stanton Industries. The entries to record the restructuring on Stanton's books and the first two interest payments would be as follows:

Bonds Payable	500,000	
Interest Payable	50,000	
Discount on Bonds		5,000
Restructured Debt		545,000
To reclassify debt into one account.		
Interest Expense	13,625	
Restructured Debt	3,875	
Cash		17,500
Payment of first semiannual interest after restructuring.		
Interest Expense	13,528	
Restructured Debt	3,972	
Cash		17,500
Payment of second semiannual interest after restructuring.		

A similar computation of an implicit interest rate could be made for Realty based on future receipts of $54,000 [$40,000 + ($2,800 × 5)], and the present carrying value of the investment of $39,000. Use of this rate would increase the investment account to $40,000 at the end of the 10 periods, or the maturity value of the investment held.

The preceding discussion covers all situations when bond restructuring reflects a modification of terms except when the cash to be received after the restructuring is less than the carrying value of the debt or investment. Under these conditions the implicit interest rate is negative. In order to raise the rate to zero, the carrying value must be reduced to the cash to be realized and a gain or loss recognized for the difference. All interest payments or receipts in the future are offset directly to the debt or investment account. No interest expense or revenue will be earned or incurred in the future because of the extreme concessions made in the restructuring. By charging or crediting all interest payments to the debt or investment account, the balance remaining at the maturity date will be the maturity value of the debt.

Any combination of these methods of bond restructuring may be employed. Accounting for these multiple restructurings can become very complex, and must be carefully evaluated.

Off-Balance-Sheet Financing

A major issue facing the accounting profession today is how to deal with companies that do not disclose all their debt in order to make their financial position look stronger. This is often referred to as off-balance-sheet financing. Traditionally, leasing has been one of the most common forms of off-balance-sheet financing. (Accounting for leases is covered in detail in Chapter 21.) Other techniques that have been used to borrow money while keeping the debt off the balance sheet are:

1. Sale of receivables with recourse
2. Captive finance companies and other unconsolidated entities
3. Research and development arrangements
4. Project financing arrangements

Sale of Receivables with Recourse

In Chapter 8, the transfer of receivables was identified as a source of financing. It was noted that the transfer of receivables is no longer a "last-ditch" method to prevent bankruptcy, but is a method commonly used by companies to raise needed funds or to avoid the collection and management problems associated with receivables. When receivables are transferred with recourse, and the transaction qualifies as a sale under FASB Statement No. 77, no liability need be recorded on the balance sheet. However, companies are required to disclose the sale of receivables with recourse in notes accompanying the statements. For example, Ingersoll-Rand Company included the following information in a note to its 1987 financial statements:

Exhibit 15-1	**Ingersoll-Rand Company**

During the fourth quarter of 1987, the company entered into an agreement whereby it can sell an undivided interest in a designated pool of accounts and notes receivable up to a maximum of $100,000,000. At December 31, 1987, $100,000,000 of receivables were sold for cash under this agreement. The undivided interest in the designated pool of receivables was sold with limited recourse and the right to continue this arrangement at the company's option on an ongoing basis for a period of up to five years. For receivables sold, the company has retained collection and administrative responsibilities as agent for the purchaser.

Receivables, excluding the designated pool of accounts and notes receivable, sold during 1987 and 1986 with recourse amounted to $18,400,000 and $17,000,000, respectively. At December 31, 1987 and 1986, $14,450,000 and $25,400,000, respectively, of such receivables sold remained uncollected.

Captive Finance Companies and Other Unconsolidated Entities

Several major companies have created wholly owned subsidiaries to assist in the financing activities of the parent company. These are often called **captive finance companies**. Examples include IBM Credit Corporation, Chrysler Finance Corporation, General Motors Acceptance Corporation, and Sears Roebuck Acceptance Corporation. The accounting question has been whether these finance companies should be consolidated with the parent company. Traditionally, generally accepted accounting principles have not required consolidation of these wholly owned finance subsidiaries on the basis that they were involved in nonhomogeneous operations. Therefore, any debt incurred by these finance companies would not get reported on the parent company's balance sheet.

In 1987, the FASB issued Statement No. 94, requiring that all majority-owned subsidiaries be consolidated, whether or not they are involved in nonhomogeneous operations.[16] Thus, the debt from captive finance companies must now be reported on the balance sheet of the parent company. This is an example of an area in which the FASB has eliminated one opportunity that companies have used for off-balance-sheet financing.

Research and Development Arrangements

Another way a company may obtain off-balance-sheet financing is with **research and development arrangements**. These involve situations where an enterprise obtains the results of research and development activities funded partially or entirely by others. The main accounting issue is whether the arrangement is, in essence, a means of borrowing to fund research and development or if it is simply a contract to do research for others.[17] In

---

[16]*Statement of Financial Accounting Standards No. 94,* "Consolidation of all Majority-Owned Subsidiaries" (Stamford: Financial Accounting Standards Board, 1987).

[17]*Statement of Financial Accounting Standards No. 68,* "Research and Development Arrangements" (Stamford: Financial Accounting Standards Board, 1982).

deciding on the appropriate accounting treatment, a major consideration is whether the enterprise is obligated to repay the funds provided by the other parties regardless of the outcome of the research and development activities. If there is an obligation to repay, then the enterprise should estimate and recognize that liability and record the research and development expenses in the current year in accordance with FASB Statement No. 2. If the financial risk associated with the research and development is transferred from the enterprise to other parties and there is no obligation to them, then the liability need not be reported by the enterprise.

Research and development arrangements may take a variety of forms, including a limited partnership. For example, assume Kincher Company formed a limited partnership for the purpose of conducting research and development. Kincher is the general partner and manages the activities of the partnership. The limited partners are strictly investors. The question is—should Kincher record the research and development expenses and the obligation to the investors on its books? The answer depends on an assessment of who is at risk and if Kincher is obligated to repay the limited partners regardless of the results of the research and development. If the limited partners are at risk and have no guarantee or claim against Kincher Company for any of the funds contributed, the debt and related expenses need not be reported on Kincher's books.

Project Financing Arrangements

At times, companies become involved in long-term commitments that are related to **project financing arrangements**. As an example, assume that two oil- and gas-producing companies, Striker Corporation and Jetco, Inc., agree to a joint venture. They form a separate company to construct a refinery in Alaska that both will use. The new company borrows funds for the construction and plans to repay the debt from the proceeds of the project. Striker and Jetco guarantee the repayment of the debt by the new company. The advantage to Striker and Jetco under such an arrangement is that neither of them shows the liability from the borrowing on its balance sheet. Each would report a contingency related to the guarantee of debt repayment in a note to the financial statements. This type of arrangement is another form of off-balance-sheet financing.[18]

Reasons for Off-Balance-Sheet Financing

There are several reasons why companies might use one of the preceding or other techniques to avoid including debt on the balance sheet. It may allow a company to borrow more than it otherwise could due to debt-limit restrictions. Also, if a company's financial position looks stronger, it will usually be able to borrow at a lower cost. Another reason may be that

[18]See *Statement of Financial Accounting Standards, No. 47.* "Disclosure of Long-Term Obligations" (Stamford: Financial Accounting Standards Board, 1981).

inflation tends to understate assets and so companies seek ways to understate liabilities.

Whatever the reasons, the problems of off-balance-sheet financing are serious. Many investors and lenders aren't sophisticated enough to see through the off-balance-sheet borrowing tactics, and so make ill-informed decisions. For example, in periods of economic downturn, a company with hidden debt may find it is not able to meet its obligations, and as a result may suffer severe financial distress or, in extreme cases, business failure. In turn, unsuspecting creditors and investors may sustain substantial losses that could have been avoided had they known the true extent of the company's debt.

The explosion of new financial instruments in recent years has created many accounting issues. Some of these issues arise because the new financial products are not addressed in the accounting literature or because the literature provides conflicting guidance. To address these issues, in May 1986, the FASB added to its agenda a major project on financial instruments and off-balance-sheet financing. This project is expected to develop standards that will aid in resolving issues raised by inconsistent practices that have developed over the years for specialized financial transactions.

The FASB project is divided into phases, and will address several separate, yet related, specific questions including:[19]

1. How to improve disclosures about financial instruments and transactions.
2. Whether financial assets should be considered sold if there is recourse or other continuing involvement with them; whether financial liabilities should be considered settled when assets are dedicated to settle them, and other questions of recognition, nonrecognition, or offsetting of related financial assets and liabilities.
3. How to account for financial instruments and transactions that seek to transfer market and credit risks—for example, futures contracts, interest rate swaps, options, forward commitments, nonrecourse arrangements, and financial guarantees—and for the underlying assets or liabilities to which the risk-transferring items are related.
4. How financial instruments should be measured—for example, at market value, amortized original cost, or the lower of cost or market.
5. How issuers should account for financial instruments that have both liability and equity characteristics.

The FASB and the accounting profession will no doubt continue to deal with the potentially serious problems of off-balance-sheet financing.[20] As the techniques and financial instruments become more complex and

[19]*Status Report,* Financial Accounting Standards Board, October 11, 1988.

[20]See John E. Stewart and Benjamin S. Neuhausen, "Financial Instruments and Transactions: The CPA's Newest Challenge," *Journal of Accountancy* (August 1986), pp. 102–110.

widely used, there is growing concern that the amount of total corporate debt is reaching unhealthy proportions.

Company takeovers, especially debt-financed acquisitions called **leveraged' buy-outs (LBOs)**, and related financial instruments such as junk bonds, are major contributors to the problem of increasing corporate debt. "Hostile" takeovers are sometimes initiated by outsiders (often referred to as corporate raiders) against the wishes of management. In other instances, management or a combination of management and outside investors become the new owners through a "friendly" takeover. During 1988 alone, there were more than 500 buy-outs totaling over $132 billion, including such companies as Tiffany, Levi Strauss, Kraft, and RJR Nabisco.

Traditionally, acquisitions of companies have been paid for mostly with cash or stock. With a leveraged buy-out, often 90 percent or more of the purchase price is debt financed. Thus, the acquiring company has to pay cash of only 10 percent or less of the total purchase price to gain control. After the purchase, the new owners usually sell off parts of the acquired business to raise the money necessary to reduce the company debt. In many cases, the acquired company is later resold, after the debt has been reduced, sometimes at a much higher price than that paid in the LBO. For example, Shearson Lehman Hutton invested $100,000 in Tiffany in 1984 and cashed out with $2.2 million in 1988.

While an LBO may offer advantages to its investors, it frequently is disadvantageous to the acquired company's existing bondholders. The significant amount of new debt created by the LBO often causes the value of existing bonds to fall. In 1988, for example, the $25 billion LBO of RJR Nabisco Inc. by Kohlberg Kravis Roberts & Co. caused the price of RJR bonds to drop over $150 for each $1,000 face amount. The signficant decline in the price of RJR bonds led investing companies such as ITT Corporation's Hartford Insurance Division and Metropolitan Life Insurance Co. to sue RJR Nabisco.

Valuation and Reporting of Long-Term Debt Securities on the Balance Sheet

Thus far, no reference has been made in this chapter to adjusting investments and liabilities when the debt or investment valuation differs from cost. In Chapter 13, accounting for declines in value of long-term equity securities was presented. There it was noted that temporary declines in the market value of equity securities are recognized on the books of the investor by a debit to a contra equity account and by a credit to an allowance account. Permanent declines are recognized by a debit to a recognized loss account on the income statement and a credit to the Investment account. Debt instruments were not explicitly included in FASB Statement No. 12. However, if a market decline in debt securities is deemed to be permanent, and it is probable that the maturity value will not be paid when due, entries similar to those made for permanent declines in equity securities are normally made on the investor's books. If the market declines are considered temporary, no accounting entries are usually made, but the decline in value is recognized in a note to the financial statements. Entries likewise are not made to reflect increases in the market values of bond investments. Changes in the market value of the liability are ignored by the issuer unless a troubled debt restructuring takes place.

Long-term debt securities are frequently very significant items on the balance sheet of both the investor and the issuer. The valuation and reporting problem for the investor and issuer will be considered separately.

Reporting Bonds and Long-Term Notes as Investments

The market value of long-term debt varies with changes in the financial strength of the issuing company, changes in the level of interest rates, and shrinkage in the remaining life of the issue. In the absence of material price declines, bonds held as long-term investments are reported on the balance sheet at book value. This book value approaches maturity value as the bonds move closer to maturity. To this extent, then, the accounting can be considered to follow a similar change that is taking place on the market as the bond life is reduced and a correspondingly lower valuation is attached to the difference between the actual rate and the market rate of remaining interest payments. Although investments are usually reported at book value, parenthetical disclosure of the aggregate market value of the securities makes the financial statements more informative.

Data relative to long-term note and bond investments might be reported as follows:

Long-term investments:

Investment in Golden Corp. Long-Term Note, 11%, $50,000 face value, due July 1, 1992. (Market value, $48,500 at December 31, 1990) ...	$ 50,000
Investment in Wilkins Co. Bonds; 9%, $1,000,000 face value, due July 1, 1998 (reported at cost as adjusted for amortized discount)	982,500

Reporting Bonds and Long-Term Notes as Liabilities

In reporting long-term debt on the balance sheet, the nature of the liabilities, maturity dates, interest rates, methods of liquidation, conversion privileges, sinking fund requirements, borrowing restrictions, assets pledged, dividend limitations, and other significant matters should be indicated. The portion of long-term debt coming due in the current period should also be disclosed.

Bond liabilities are often combined with other long-term debt for balance sheet presentation, with supporting detail disclosed in a note. An example of such a note taken from the 1987 annual report of Avon Corporation is presented on page 670. For another example of disclosure of long-term debt, see Note Seven to General Mills' financial statements in Appendix A at the end of this text.

Exhibit 15-2   Avon Corporation

6. DEBT

Debt consisted of the following at:

		(In millions)
December 31	1987	1986

Short-Term

	1987	1986
International notes payable	$ 45.3	$ 76.3
Current portion of long-term debt	17.1	16.7
Total	$ 62.4	$ 93.0

Long-Term

	1987	1986
Commercial paper, weighted average 8.3%	$213.9	$106.5
8¾% Euronotes, due 1989	100.2	100.3
11¾% Notes, due 1990	100.0	100.0
6¾% Euroyen Notes, due 1991	100.0	100.0
10¼% Euronotes, due 1992	99.7	99.7
5⅜% Swiss Franc Bonds, due 1994	50.0	50.0
Yen Notes, due 1989 to 1991 with interest from 4.4% to 8.8%	36.3	37.5
7½% Deutsche Mark Bonds, due 1988 to 1993	33.3	33.3
9% Euronotes, due 1993	15.0	—
Other, payable to 2016 with interest from 4⅗% to 13½%	85.1	69.7
Less current portion	(17.1)	(16.7)
Total	$816.4	$680.3

Annual maturities for each of the next five years are (in millions): 1988—$17.1; 1989—$120.7; 1990—$128.1; 1991—$127.9; 1992—$131.2.

Avon has $647 million of unused revolving-credit facilities that serve as backing for commercial paper and have annual commitment fees of $1.2 million. Avon also has unused lines of credit, primarily related to international operations, of $350 million with no material compensating balances or commitment fees.

Appendix

Accounting for Serial Bonds

As noted in the chapter, serial bonds mature in installments at various dates. Usually, each bond indicates when it will mature. Because of the difference in time and maturity, the interest rate often varies depending on the due date. In some instances, the stated interest rate remains constant for all maturity dates, but the effective interest rate differs as the selling prices for the different maturity dates vary to reflect the changing risk. When serial bonds are issued at other than par, the premium or discount could be related to the bonds maturing on each specific date, and the amortization of the premium or discount could be made as though each maturity date were a separate bond issue. No new problems related to accounting for interest arise under this approach.

However, an entire serial bond issue is sometimes sold directly to underwriters at a lump-sum price that differs from the total face value of the isuse. When this occurs, the issue price usually cannot be identified with each maturity date. Under these circumstances, the premium or discount on the entire serial bond issue must be amortized as a unit. This requires that either an average effective rate be determined for the entire issue, and the effective-interest method used to determine the amortization; or that a variation of the straight-line method known as the **bonds-outstanding method** be applied. Both methods provide for decreases in the amortization schedule as the principal amounts of the serial bonds mature.

Bonds-Outstanding Method

Amortization by the bonds-outstanding method is illustrated in the example that follows. Assume that bonds with a face value of $100,000, dated January 1, 1990, are issued on this date for a lump-sum price of $101,260. Bonds of $20,000 mature at the end of each year starting on December 31, 1990. The bonds pay interest of 8% annually. The company's accounting period ends on December 31; the accounting period and the bond year thus coincide. A table showing the premium to be amortized each year is developed as shown in the schedule at the top of page 672.

The annual premium amortization is found by multiplying the premium by a fraction whose numerator is the number of bond dollars outstanding in that year and whose denominator is the total number of bond dollars outstanding for the life of bond issue. As bonds are retired, the amounts of premium amortization decline accordingly.

Amortization Schedule—Bonds-Outstanding Method

Year	Bonds Outstanding	Fraction of Premium to be Amortized	Annual Premium Amortization (Fraction × $1,260)
1990	$100,000	100,000/300,000 (or 10/30)	$ 420
1991	80,000	80,000/300,000 (or 8/30)	336
1992	60,000	60,000/300,000 (or 6/30)	252
1993	40,000	40,000/300,000 (or 4/30)	168
1994	20,000	20,000/300,000 (or 2/30)	84
	$300,000	300,000/300,000 (or 30/30)	$1,260

An alternative computation can be made by computing the amount of amortization related to each $1,000 of outstanding bonds. In the preceding example, this would be $4.20 per $1,000 bond ($1,260 ÷ 300). Applying this amount to the number of $1,000 bonds outstanding each year would result in the same amortization shown in the table; e.g., for 1991, 80 × $4.20, or $336. The use of this alternative method of computing the amortization is especially useful when computing the unamortized premium or discount on serial bonds retired early.

Periodic amortization may be incorporated in a table summarizing the interest charges and changes in bond carrying values as follows:

Amortization of Premium—Serial Bonds
Bonds-Outstanding Method

Date	A Interest Payment (8% of Face Value)	B Premium Amortization	C Interest Expense (A − B)	D Principal Payment	E Bond Carrying Value Decrease (B + D)	F Bond Carrying Value (F − E)
Jan. 1, 1990						$101,260
Dec. 31, 1990	$8,000	$420	$7,580	$20,000	$20,420	80,840
Dec. 31, 1991	6,400	336	6,064	20,000	20,336	60,504
Dec. 31, 1992	4,800	252	4,548	20,000	20,252	40,252
Dec. 31, 1993	3,200	168	3,032	20,000	20,168	20,084
Dec. 31, 1994	1,600	84	1,516	20,000	20,084	—

Effective-Interest Method   Tables show that the bonds in the preceding example were sold to return approximately 7½%. Use of this rate results in the following interest charges and premium amortization using the effective-interest method:

Amortization of Premium—Serial Bonds
Effective-Interest Method

Date	A Interest Payment (8% of Face Value)	B Interest Expense (7½% of Bond Carrying Value)	C Premium Amortization (A − B)	D Principal Payment	E Bond Carrying Value Decrease (C + D)	F Bond Carrying Value (F − E)
Jan. 1, 1990						$101,260
Dec. 31, 1990	$8,000	$7,595	$405	$20,000	$20,405	80,855
Dec. 31, 1991	6,400	6,064	336	20,000	20,336	60,519
Dec. 31, 1992	4,800	4,539	261	20,000	20,261	40,258
Dec. 31, 1993	3,200	3,019	181	20,000	20,181	20,077
Dec. 31, 1994	1,600	1,523*	77*	20,000	20,077	—

*The last payment is adjusted because the effective rate was not exactly 7½%. On the final payment the premium balance is closed and interest expense is reduced by this amount.

The bonds-outstanding method of amortization provides for the recognition of uniform amounts of amortization in terms of the par value of bonds outstanding. The effective-interest method provides for the recognition of interest at a uniform rate on the declining debt balance.

Bond Redemption Prior to Maturity—Serial Bonds

When serial bonds are redeemed prior to their maturities, it is necessary to cancel the unamortized premium or discount relating to that part of the bond issue that is liquidated. For example, assume the issuance of serial bonds previously described on pages 671-672 and amortization of the premium by the bonds-outstanding method as shown on page 672. On April 1, 1991, $10,000 of bonds due December 31, 1992, and $10,000 of bonds due December 31, 1993, are redeemed at 100½ plus accrued interest. The premium for the period January 1-April 1, 1991, relating to redeemed bonds affects bond interest for the current period and will be written off as an adjustment to expense. The balance of the premium from the redemption date to the respective maturity dates of the series redeemed must be canceled. The premium balance relating to redeemed bonds is calculated as follows:

Premium identified with 1991: 20,000/80,000 × $336 × 9/12   = $ 63
Premium identified with 1992: 20,000/60,000 × 252   =   84
Premium identified with 1993: 10,000/40,000 × 168   =   42
Premium identifed with redeemed bonds $189

Instead of the foregoing procedure, the premium amortization per year on each $1,000 bond may be applied to bonds of each period that are redeemed. As shown on page 672, the annual amortization per $1,000 bond is $4.20.

The premium to be carried may now be determined as follows:

Year	Number of $1,000 Bonds	Annual Premium Amortization per $1,000 Bond	Fractional Part of Year	Total Premium Cancellation
1991	20	$4.20	9/12	$ 63
1992	20	4.20		84
1993	10	4.20		42
		Premium identified with redeemed bonds		$189

Bonds, carrying value of $20,189, are redeemed at a cost of $20,100 resulting in a gain of $89. Payment is also made for interest on bonds of $20,000 for three months at 8%, or $400. The entry to record the redemption of bonds and the payment of interest on the series retired follows:

Bonds Payable	20,000	
Premium on Bonds Payable	189	
Interest Expense	400	
Cash		20,500
Gain on Bond Redemption		89

The following is a revised schedule for the amortization of bond premium.

Amortization Schedule—Bonds-Outstanding Method
Revised for Bond Retirement

Year	Annual Premium Amortization per Original Schedule	Premium Cancellation on Bond Retirement	Annual Premium Amortization Adjusted for Bond Retirement
1990	$ 420		$ 420
1991	336	$ 63	273
1992	252	84	168
1993	168	42	126
1994	84		84
	$1,260	$189	$1,071

Key Terms

Bearer or coupon bonds 637
Bond certificates 635
Bond discount 638
Bond indenture 635
Bond issuance costs 643
Bond premium 638
Callable bonds 638
Commodity-backed bonds or asset-
  linked bonds 638
Convertible bonds 638
Early extinguishment of debt 648
Effective-interest method 645
Face amount, par value, maturity
  value 635
In-substance defeasance 648
Junk bonds 637

Leveraged buy-out (LBO) 668
Long-term debt 633
Market, yield, or effective interest
  rate 638
Off-balance-sheet financing 664
Registered bonds 636
Secured bonds 636
Serial bonds 636
Stated or contract rate 638
Straight-line method 644
Term bonds 636
Troubled debt restructuring 658
Unsecured (debenture) bonds 636
Zero-interest bonds or deep discount
  bonds 637

Questions

1. What factors should be considered in determining whether cash should be raised by the issue of bonds or by the sale of additional stock?

2. Distinguish between (a) secured and unsecured bonds, (b) collateral trust and debenture bonds, (c) convertible bonds and callable bonds, (d) coupon bonds and registered bonds, (e) municipal bonds and corporate bonds, and (f) term and serial bonds.

3. What is meant by market rate of interest, stated or contract rate, and effective or yield rate? Which of these rates changes during the lifetime of the bond issue?

4. An investor purchases bonds with a face value of $100,000. Payment for the bonds includes (a) a premium, (b) accrued interest, and (c) brokerage fees. How would each of these charges be recorded and what disposition would ultimately be made of each of these charges?

5. How should bond issuance costs be accounted for on the issuer's books?

6. What amortization method for premiums and discounts on bonds is recommended by APB Opinion No. 21? Why? When can the alternative method be used?

7. Under what conditions would the following statement be true? "The effective-interest method of bond premium or discount amortization for the issuer results in higher net income than would be reported using straight-line amortization."

8. List three ways that bonds are commonly retired prior to maturity. How should the early extinguishment of debt be presented on the income statement?

9. What purpose is served by issuing callable bonds?

10. What are the distinguishing features of convertible debt securities? What questions relate to the nature of this type of security?

11. The conversion of convertible bonds to common stock by an investor may be viewed as an exchange involving no gain or loss, or as a transaction for which market values should be recognized and a gain or loss reported. What arguments support each of these views for the investor and for the issuer?

12. Why do companies find the issuance of convertible bonds a desirable method of financing?

13. What is meant by refinancing or refunding a bond issue? When may refinancing be advisable?

14. What is in-substance defeasance, and what action must the debtor take for it to qualify as an early extinguishment of debt?

15. What distinguishes a troubled debt restructuring from other debt restructurings?

16. What is the recommended accounting treatment for bond restructurings effected as:
    a. An asset swap?
    b. An equity swap?
    c. A modification of terms?

17. Why is off-balance-sheet financing popular with many companies? What problems are associated with the use of this method of financing?

18. What is a leveraged-buy-out? Why have they become popular? What is the risk to bondholders if a leverged buy-out occurs?

19. How should long-term investments in bonds be recorded and adjusted for significant price change in periods subsequent to their purchase so that their valuation will be in accordance with GAAP?

*20. (a) Describe the bonds-outstanding method for premium or discount amortization for serial bonds. (b) How does this method differ from the effective-interest method of amortization?

*Relates to Appendix

Discussion Cases

Case 15-1 (Debt or equity financing)

Assume you are a member of the board of directors of Layton Enterprises, a relatively new company in the computer industry. You have just listened to a presentation of the treasurer and an extended discussion among the other board members. The issue is how to raise $13 million of additional funds for company expansion. You must now vote on whether to authorize debt financing through a bond issue or to seek equity financing through additional stock sales. What are the advantages and disadvantages of debt financing versus equity financing? As a member of the board, how would you vote and why?

Case 15-2 (Accounting for bonds)

Startup Company decided to issue $100,000 worth of 10%, 5-year bonds dated January 1, 1990, with interest payable semi-annually on January 1 and July 1 of each year. Due to printing and other delays, Startup was not able to sell the bonds until July 1, 1990. The bonds were sold to yield 12% interest, and they are callable at 102 after January 1, 1992. The company expects interest rates to fall during the next few years and is planning to retire this bond issue and to replace it with a less costly one if the expected decline occurs.

Assume that you have just been hired as the accountant for Startup Company. The Financial Vice President would like you to identify the accounting issues involved with the bond transaction. You are also asked to explain why the company received less than $100,000 on the sale of the bonds, and to compute the anticipated gain or loss on retirement of the bonds, assuming retirement on July 1, 1992, and use of straight-line amortization.

Case 15-3   (Is there a loss on conversion?)

Holton Co. recently issued $1,000,000 face value, 8%, 30-year subordinated debentures at 97. The debentures are callable at 103 upon 30 days' notice by the issuer at any time beginning 10 years after the date of issue. The debentures are convertible into $10 par value common stock of the company at the conversion price of $12.50 per share for each $500 or multiple thereof of the principal amount of the debentures. ($500 ÷ $12.50 = 40 shares for each $500 of face value.)

Assume that no value is assigned to the conversion feature at the date of issue of the debentures. Assume further that 5 years after issue, debentures with a face value of $100,000 and book value of $97,500 are tendered for conversion on an interest payment date when the market price of the debentures is 104 and the common stock is selling at $14 per share and that J.K. Biggs, the company accountant, records the conversion as follows:

Bonds Payable	100,000	
Discount on Bonds Payable		2,500
Common Stock		80,000
Paid-In Capital in Excess of Par		17,500

Julie Robinson, staff auditor for the CPA firm, reviews the transaction and feels the conversion entry should reflect the market value of the stock. According to Robinson's analysis, a loss on the bond conversion of $14,500 should be recognized. Biggs objects to recognizing a loss, so Robinson discusses the problem with the audit manager, K. Ashworth. Ashworth has a different view and recommends using the market value of the debentures as a basis for recording the conversion and recognizing a loss of only $6,500.

Evaluate the various positions. Include in your evaluation the substitute entries that would be made under both Robinson's and Ashworth's proposals.

Case 15-4   (Do we really have income?)

The Jefferson Corporation has $20,000,000 of 10% bonds outstanding. Because of cash flow problems, the company is behind in interest payments and in contributions to its bonds retirement fund. The market value of the bonds has declined until it is currently only 50% of the face value of the bonds. After lengthy negotiations, the principal bondholders have agreed to exchange their bonds for preferred stock that has a current market value of $10,000,000. The accountant for Jefferson Corporation recorded the transaction by charging the bond liability for the entire $20,000,000, and crediting Preferred Stock for the same amount. This entry thus transfers the amount received by the company from debt to equity.

The CPA firm performing the annual audit, however, does not agree with this treatment. The auditors argue that this transfer represents a troubled debt restructuring due to the significant concessions made by the bondholders, and under these conditions, the FASB requires Jefferson to use the market value of the preferred stock as its recorded value. The difference between the $20,000,000 face value of the bonds and the $10,000,000 market value of the preferred stock is a reportable gain.

The controller of Jefferson, L. Rogers, is flabbergasted, "Here we are, almost bankrupt, and you tell us we must report the $10,000,000 as a gain. I don't care what the FASB says; that's a ridiculous situation. You can't be serious."

But the auditor in charge of the engagements is adamant, "We really have no choice. You have had a forgiveness of debt for $10,000,000. You had use of the money, and based on current conditions, you won't have to pay it back. That situation looks like a gain to me."

What position do you think should be taken? Consider the external users of the statement and their needs in your discussion.

Case 15-5 (Can we take a loss today for a gain in the future?)

Northeastern Investment Group follows the policy of borrowing money for relatively long periods of time and lending the money to newly formed companies on a medium-term basis. At December 31, 1991, Northeastern has several loans outstanding, and all but one are current in their interest payments and are living up to the covenant agreements made in conjunction with the loan. However, one loan to Digital Corporation for $10,000,000 made at 14% interest is of much concern to Northeastern. Digital has not been successful in generating a steady cash flow, and thus has fallen behind in its interest payments. The current position of the company is also far below the amount specified in the loan agreement. The president of Digital has asked Northeastern for help and suggests a two-year suspension of interest payments followed by a new rate of 4% on the debt. The owners of Northeastern initially refuse, saying that for the risk now involved, the going interest rate would really be more like 20%. After a somewhat bitter discussion, the president of Digital says that Northeastern leaves them no alternative; they must declare bankruptcy. After renewed discussion, the new terms requested are agreed upon and the past accrued interest is removed from the books by crediting accrued interest expense.

After reviewing the situation, Northeastern's auditor argues that present value accounting for debt requires Northeastern to restate the loan so that it would reflect the present value of the future payments at the 20% effective interest rate. This means that the present value of the $10,000,000 investment would be significantly reduced and the loss recognized in the current year. Future income would then reflect interest revenue at the 20% rate rather than the greatly reduced 4% rate. Now Northeastern's partners are really upset. "Must we take a loss now just to report an increased profit in the future? That is ridiculous accounting!"

Before agreement is reached, the Financial Accounting Standards Board issues its Statement No. 15 that supports Northeastern's position. But Northeastern's auditors are still concerned. "How can we argue for present value accounting and ignore the impact of the changed terms on the indebtedness? The FASB has abandoned the conceptual basis for expediency."

How would you evaluate the situation?

Exercises   Exercise 15-1   (Raising capital with bonds or stock)

Shop Right, Inc. must raise $600,000 for additional working capital.

Management wants to choose the method of financing that will result in the higher return per share to the original shareholders. 10,000 shares of $60 par common stock have already been issued. Assume the company can sell an additional 7,500 shares at $80 or it can issue $600,000 in 8% bonds. Earnings before income taxes have historically been approximately $100,000 annually, and it is expected that they will increase by 15% (before additional interest charges) as a result of the additional funds. Assuming an income tax rate of 40%, which method of financing would you recommend? Why? (Show computations.)

Exercise 15-2   (Computation of market values of bond issues)

What is the market value of each of the following bond issues? (Round to the nearest dollar.)

(a) 10% bonds of $100,000 sold on bond issue date; 10-year life; interest payable semiannually; effective rate, 12%.
(b) 9% bonds of $200,000 sold on bond issue date; 5-year life; interest payable semiannually; effective rate, 8%.
(c) 8% bonds of $150,000 sold 30 months after bond issue date; 15-year life; interest payable semiannually; effective rate, 10%.

Exercise 15-3   (Selling bonds at par, premium or discount)

In each of the following independent cases, state whether the bonds were issued at par, a premium, or a discount. Explain your answers.

(a) Pop-up Manufacturing sold 1,500 of its $1,000, 13% stated-rate bonds when the market rate was 14%.
(b) Splendor, Inc. sold 500 of its $2,000, 8¾% bonds to yield 9%.
(c) Cards Corporation issued 1,000 of its 9%, $100 face amount bonds at an effective rate of 8½%.
(d) Floppy, Inc. sold 3,000 of its 10% bonds with a face value of $2,500 at a time when the market rate was 9%.
(e) Cintron Co. sold 5,000 of its 12% contract rate bonds with stated value of $1,000 at an effective rate of 12%.

Exercise 15-4   (Issuance and reacquisition of bonds)

On December 1, 1989, the Housen Company issued 10-year bonds of $500,000 at 102. Interest is payable on December 1 and June 1 at 10%. On April 1, 1991, the Housen Company reacquires and retires 50 of its own $1,000 bonds at 98 plus accrued interest. The fiscal period for the Housen Company is the calendar year.

Prepare entries to record (a) the issuance of the bonds, (b) the interest payments and adjustments relating to the debt in 1990, (c) the reacquisition and retirement of bonds in 1991, and (d) the interest payments and adjustments relating to the debt in 1991. Assume the premium or discount is amortized at year-end on a straight-line basis. (Round to the nearest dollar.)

Exercise 15-5   (Amortization of bond premium or discount)

On January 1, 1990, Terrel Company sold $100,000 of 10-year, 9% bonds at

93.5, an effective rate of 9%. Interest is to be paid on July 1 and December 31. Compute the premium or discount to be amortized in 1990 and 1991 using (a) the straight-line method and (b) the effective-interest method. Make the journal entries to record the amortization when the effective-interest method is used.

Exercise 15-6   (Bond interest and premium or discount amortization)
Assume that $100,000 Baker School District 6% bonds are sold on the bond issue date for $92,894. Interest is payable semiannually and the bonds mature in 10 years. The purchase price provides a return of 7% on the investment.

1. What entries would be made on the investor's books for the receipt of the first two interest payments, assuming premium or discount amortization on each interest date by (a) the straight-line method and (b) the effective-interest method? (Round to the nearest dollar.)
2. What entries would be made on Baker School District's books to record the first two interest payments, assuming premium or discount amortization on each interest date by (a) the straight-line method and (b) the effective-interest method? (Round to the nearest dollar.)

Exercise 15-7   (Discount and premium amortization)
The Pascuala Corporation issued $200,000 of 8% debenture bonds to yield 10%, receiving $184,556. Interest is payable semiannually and the bonds mature in 5 years.

1. What entries would be made by Pascuala for the first two interest payments, assuming premium or discount amortization on interest dates by (a) the straight-line method and (b) the effective-interest method? (Round to nearest dollar.)
2. Assuming the situation in (1) above, what entries would be made on the books of the investor for the first two interest receipts assuming one party obtained all the bonds and the straight-line method of amortization was used? (Round to the nearest dollar.)
3. If the sale is made to yield 6%, $217,062 being received, what entries would be made by Pascuala for the first two interest payments, assuming premium or discount amortization on interest dates by (a) the straight-line method and (b) the effective-interest method? (Round to nearest dollar.)

Exercise 15-8   (Sale of bond investment)
Jennifer Stack acquired $50,000 of Oldtown Corp. 9% bonds on July 1, 1988. The bonds were acquired at 92; interest is paid semiannually on March 1 and September 1. The bonds mature September 1, 1995. Stack's books are kept on a calendar-year basis. On February 1, 1991, Stack sold the bonds for 97 plus accrued interest. Assuming straight-line amortization recorded on a calendar-year basis, and no reversing entry at January 1, 1991, give the entry to record the sale of the bonds on February 1. (Round to the nearest dollar.)

Exercise 15-9   (Retirement of debt before maturity)
The long-term debt section of Starr Company's balance sheet as of December

31, 1990, included 9% bonds payable of $200,000 less unamortized discount of $16,000. Further examination revealed that these bonds were issued to yield 10%. The amortization of the bond discount was recorded using the effective-interest method. Interest was paid on January 1 and July 1 of each year. On July 1, 1991, Starr retired the bonds at 102 before maturity. Prepare the journal entries to record the July 1, 1991, payment of interest, the amortization of the discount since December 31, 1990, and the early retirement on the books of Starr Company.

Exercise 15-10 (Retirement of bonds)

The December 31, 1990, balance sheet of Stice Company includes the following items:

> 9% bonds payable due December 31, 1999 .... $400,000
> Premium on bonds payable   10,800

The bonds were issued on December 31, 1989, at 103, with interest payable on June 30 and December 31 of each year. The straight-line method is used for premium amortization.

On March 1, 1991, Stice retired $100,000 of these bonds at 98, plus accrued interest. Prepare the journal entries to record retirement of the bonds, including accrual of interest since the last payment and amortization of the premium.

Exercise 15-11 (Retirement and refinancing of bonds)

Chiam Corporation has $300,000 of 12% bonds, callable at 102, with a remaining 10-year term, and interest payable semiannually. The bonds are currently valued on the books at $290,000 and the company has just made the interest payment and adjustments for amortization of any premium or discount. Similar bonds can be marketed currently at 10% and would sell at par.

1. Give the journal entries to retire the old debt and issue $300,000 of new 10% bonds at par.
2. In what year will the reduction in interest offset the cost of refinancing the bond issue?

Exercise 15-12 (Issuance of convertible bonds)

Ignacio Insurance decides to finance expansion of its physical facilities by issuing convertible debenture bonds. The terms of the bonds are: maturity date 20 years after May 1, 1990, the date of issuance; conversion at option of holder after 2 years; 40 shares of $30 par value stock for each $1,000 bond held; interest rate of 12% and call provision on the bonds of 103. The bonds were sold at 101.

1. Give the entry on Ignacio's books to record the sale of $1,000,000 of bonds on July 1, 1990; interest payment dates are May 1 and November 1.
2. Assume the same condition as in (1) except that the sale of the bonds is to be recorded in a manner that will recognize a value related to the conversion privilege. The estimated sales price of the bonds without the conversion privilege is 97.

Exercise 15-13   (Convertible bonds)

Clarkston Inc. issued $500,000 of convertible 10-year 11% bonds on July 1, 1990. The interest is payable semiannually on January 1 and July 1. The discount in connection with the issue was $4,250, which is amortized monthly using the straight-line basis. The debentures are convertible after 1 year into 5 shares of the company's $50 par common stock for each $1,000 of bonds.

On August 1, 1991, $100,000 of the bonds were converted. Interest has been accrued monthly and paid as due. Any interest accrued at the time of conversion of the bonds is paid in cash.

Prepare the journal entries to record the conversion, amortization, and interest on the bonds as of August 1 and August 31, 1991. (Round to the nearest dollar.)

Exercise 15-14   (Troubled-debt restructuring—asset swap)

The Buck Machine Company has outstanding a $150,000 note payable to the Ontario Investment Corporation. Because of financial difficulties, Buck negotiates with Ontario to exchange inventory of machine parts to satisfy the debt. The cost of the inventory transferred is carried on Buck's books at $90,000. The estimated retail value of the inventory is $120,000. Buck uses a perpetual inventory system. The note receivable is carried on Ontario's books at $150,000. Prepare journal entries for the exchange on the books of both Buck Machine Company and Ontario Investment Corporation according to the requirements of FASB Statement No. 15.

Exercise 15-15   (Troubled-debt restructuring—equity swap)

Southwest Enterprises is threatened with bankruptcy due to its inability to meet interest payments and fund requirements to retire $5,000,000 of long-term notes. The notes are all held by Imperial Insurance Company. In order to prevent bankruptcy, Southwest has entered into an agreement with Imperial to exchange equity securities for the debt. The term of the exchange are as follows: 250,000 shares of $5 par common stock, current market value $8 per share, and 20,000 shares of $10 par preferred stock, current market value $70 per share. Imperial has previously written down its investment in Southwest by 20%. Prepare journal entries for the exchange on the books of both Imperial Insurance Company and Southwest Enterprises according to the requirements of FASB Statement No. 15.

Exercise 15-16   (Valuation of bonds used as investment)

Several years ago, Eastern Life Insurance Company bought $1,000,000 of Overland City 6% bonds at par. The bonds are currently selling at 78. Because of recent trouble the bond issuer has had in meeting bond payments, the bondholder has decided to write down the market decline as a permanent decline. It is felt that only 80% of the original bond value will be recovered. Eastern Life Insurance Company also holds $500,000 of Middle School 8% bonds that were bought at par but are selling at 96. They perceive this to be a temporary decline.

1. What journal entries would you make to record the decisions?
2. What disclosure would you make in the financial statements?

Exercise 15-17 (Disclosure of bonds)

For the Ribsey Corporation, arrange the following information as you would present it on the balance sheet dated December 31, 1991.

(a) Items in the possession of a bond retirement fund trustee for the first-mortgage bonds in (c): Cash of $8,000 and stocks of $84,000 (market value $94,500).

(b) Investment in Holder Company 10% bonds, $100,000 face value, due July 1, 1996, (cost as adjusted for unamortized premium $103,000) currently selling at 99.

(c) 20-year, 9% Ribsey Corp. first-mortgage bonds, $500,000 face value, due January 1, 2009 (cost as adjusted for unamortized discount $493,000).

(d) Investment in Stahman Corporation long-term notes, 12%, $60,000 face value, due September 1, 1998 (market value $63,000).

*Exercise 15-18 (Issuance of serial bonds)

On January 1, 1989, JVJ Corporation issued and sold $1,000,000 in five-year, 10% serial bonds to be repaid in the amount of $200,000 on January 1 of 1990, 1991, 1992, 1993, and 1994. Interest is payable at the end of each year. The bonds were sold to yield a rate of 12%. Prepare the entry to record the issuance of the serial bonds on the books of JVJ Corporation.

*Relates to Appendix

▮ *Exercise 15-19 (Bonds-outstanding table)

Rafael Corporation purchased 9% serial bonds on April 1, 1990, face value $2,000,000. The bonds mature in $400,000 lots on April 1 of each of the following years. Interest is payable semiannually; the issue has an overall discount of $50,000. Assuming that Rafael reports on a calendar year, prepare a table summarizing interest charges and bond carrying values by the bonds-outstanding method.

*Relates to Appendix

Problems   ### Problem 15-1 (Bond issuance and adjusting entries)

On January 1, 1991, Bel Air Company issued bonds with a face value of $1,000,000 and a maturity date of December 31, 2000. The bonds have a stated interest rate of 10%, payable on January 1 and July 1. They were sold to Mercur Company for $885,300, a yield of 12%. It cost Bel Air $30,000 to issue the bonds. This amount was deferred and amortized over the life of the issue using the straight-line method. Assume that both companies have December 31 year-ends and that Bel Air uses the effective-interest method to amortize any premium or discount and Mercur uses the straight-line method.

Instructions:

(1) Make all entries necessary to record the sale and purchase of the bonds on the two companies' books.

(2) Prepare the adjusting entries as of December 31, 1991, for both companies. Assume adjusting entries for amortization are made only once each year and that Mercur is carrying the bonds as a long-term investment.

Problem 15-2   (Computation of bond market price and amortization of premium or discount)

Signal Enterprises decided to issue $800,000 of 10-year bonds. The interest rate on the bonds is stated at 7%, payable semiannually. At the time the bonds were sold, the market rate had increased to 8%.

Instructions:

(1) Determine the maximum amount an investor should pay for these bonds. (Round to the nearest dollar.)
(2) Assuming that the amount in (1) is paid, compute the amount at which the bonds would be reported after being held for one year. Use two recognized methods of handling amortization of the difference in cost and maturity value of the bonds, and give support to the method you prefer. (Round to the nearest dollar.)

Problem 15-3   (Premium or discount amortization table)

The Green Co. acquired $20,000 of International Sales Co. 7% bonds, interest payable semiannually, bonds maturing in 5 years. The bonds were acquired at $20,850, a price to return approximately 6%.

Instructions:

(1) Prepare tables to show the periodic adjustments to the investment account and the annual bond earnings, assuming adjustment by each of the following methods: (a) the straight-line method, and (b) the effective-interest method. (Round to the nearest dollar.)
(2) Assuming use of the effective-interest method, give entries for the first year on the books of both companies.

Problem 15-4   (Bond entries—issuer)

On April 1, 1980, the Quality Tool Company issued $8 million of 7% convertible bonds with interest payment dates of April 1 and October 1. The bonds were sold on July 1, 1980, and mature on April 1, 2000. The bond discount totaled $426,600. The bond contract entitles the bondholders to receive 25 shares of $15 par value common stock in exchange for each $1,000 bond. On April 1, 1990, the holders of bonds with total face value of $1,000,000 exercised their conversion privilege. On July 1, 1990, the Quality Tool Company reacquired bonds, face value $500,000, on the open market. The balances in the capital accounts as of December 31, 1989, were:

Common Stock, $15 par, authorized 3 million shares, issued
and outstanding, 250,000 shares $3,750,000
Paid-in capital in excess of par 2,500,000

Market values of the common stock and bonds were as follows:

Date	Bonds (per $1,000)	Common Stock (per share)
April 1, 1990	$1,220	$47
July 1, 1990	1,250	51

Instructions: Prepare journal entries on the issuer's books for each of the following transactions. (Use the straight-line amortization method for the bond discount.)

(1) Sale of the bonds on July 1, 1980.
(2) Interest payment on October 1, 1980.
(3) Interest accrual on December 31, 1980, including bond discount amortization.
(4) Conversion of bonds on April 1, 1990. (Assume that interest and discount amortization are correctly shown as of April 1, 1990. No gain or loss on conversion is recognized.)
(5) Reacquisition and retirement of bonds on July 1, 1990. (Assume that interest and discount amortization are correctly reported as of July 1, 1990.)

Problem 15-5   (Bond entries—issuer)

The Tri Arc Company sold $3,000,000 of 9% first-mortgage bonds on October 1, 1983, at $2,873,640 plus accrued interest. The bonds were dated July 1, 1983; interest payable semiannually on January 1 and July 1; redeemable after June 30, 1988, to June 30, 1991, at 101, and thereafter until maturity at 100; and convertible into $100 par value common stock as follows:

Until June 30, 1988, at the rate of 6 shares for each $1,000 bond.
From July 1, 1988, to June 30, 1991, at the rate of 5 shares for each $1,000 bond.
After June 30, 1991, at the rate of 4 shares for each $1,000 bond.

The bonds mature in 10 years from their issue date. The company adjusts its books monthly and closes its books as of December 31 each year.
The following transactions occur in connection with the bonds:

1989
July 1 $1,000,000 of bonds were converted into stock, with no gain or loss recognized.

1990
Dec. 31 $500,000 face amount of bonds were reacquired at 99¼ plus accrued interest. These were immediately retired.

1991
July 1   The remaining bonds were called for redemption. For purposes of obtaining funds for redemption and business expansion, a $4,000,000 issue of 7% bonds was sold at 97. These bonds are dated July 1, 1991, and are due in 20 years.

Instructions: Prepare in journal form the entries necessary for Tri Arc Company in connection with the preceding transactions, including monthly adjustments where appropriate, as of the following dates. (Round to nearest dollar.)

(1) October 1, 1983	(4) December 31, 1990
(2) December 31, 1983	(5) July 1, 1991
(3) July 1, 1989	(AICPA adapted)

Problem 15-6   (Bond entries—investor)

On June 1, 1990, Sunderland Inc. purchased as a long-term investment 400 of the $1,000 face value, 8% bonds of Stateline Corporation for $369,150. The bonds were purchased to yield 10% interest. Interest is payable semiannually on December 1 and June 1. The bonds mature on June 1, 1995. Sunderland uses the effective-interest method of amortization. On November 1, 1991, Sunderland sold the bonds for $392,500. This amount includes the appropriate accrued interest.

Instructions: Prepare a schedule showing the income or loss before income taxes from the bond investment that Sunderland should record for the years ended December 31, 1990, and 1991.

(AICPA adapted)

Problem 15-7   (Bond entries—investor)

On May 1, 1988, the Alpine Co. acquired $40,000 of ZZX Corp. 9% bonds at 97 plus accrued interest. Interest on bonds is payable semiannually on March 1 and September 1, and bonds mature on September 1, 1991.

On May 1, 1989, the Alpine Co. sold bonds of $12,000 for 103 plus accrued interest. On July 1, 1990, bonds of $16,000 were exchanged for 2,250 shares of ZZX Corp. no-par common, quoted on the market on this date at $8. Interest was received on bonds to date of exchange.

On September 1, 1991, remaining bonds were redeemed.

Instructions: Give journal entries for 1988-1991 to record the foregoing transactions on the books for the Alpine Co., including any adjustments that are required at the end of each fiscal year ending on December 31. Assume bond premium or discount amortization by the straight-line method.

▌▌▌ Problem 15-8   (Note payable entries—investor and issuer)

Fitzgerald Inc. issued $750,000 of 8-year, 11% notes payable dated April 1, 1987. Interest on the notes is payable semiannually on April 1 and October 1. The notes were sold on April 1, 1987, to an underwriter for $720,000 net of issuance costs. The notes were then offered for sale by the underwriter, and on July 1, 1987, L. Baum purchased the entire issue as a long-term investment. Baum paid 101 plus accrued interest for the notes. On June 1, 1990, Baum sold the investment in Fitzgerald notes to J. Gott as a short-term investment. Gott paid 96 plus accrued interest for the notes as well as $1,500 for brokerage fees. Baum paid $1,000 broker's fees to sell the notes. Gott held the investment until April 1, 1991, when the notes were called at 102 by Fitzgerald.

Instructions: Prepare all journal entries required on the books of Fitzgerald Inc. for 1987 and 1991; on the books of Baum for 1987 and 1990; and on the books of Gott for 1990 and 1991. Assume each entity uses the calendar year for reporting purposes and that issue costs are netted against the note proceeds by Fitzgerald. Any required amortization is made using the straight-line method at the end of each calendar-year or when the notes are transferred.

Problem 15-9 (Adjustment of bond investment account)

In auditing the books for the Carmicheal Corporation as of December 31, 1991, before the accounts are closed, you find the following long-term investment account balance:

ACCOUNT   Investment in Big Oil 9% Bonds (Maturity date, June 1, 1995)

Date		Item	Debit	Credit	Balance Debit	Balance Credit
1991						
Jan.	21	Bonds, $200,000 par, acquired at 102 plus accrued interest	206,550		206,550	
Mar.	1	Proceeds from sale of bonds, $100,000 par and accrued interest		106,000	100,550	
June	1	Interest received		4,500	96,050	
Nov.	1	Amount received on call of bonds, $40,000 par, at 101 and accrued interest		41,900	54,150	
Dec.	1	Interest received		2,700	51,450	

Instructions:

(1) Give the entries that should have been made relative to the investment in bonds, including any adjusting entries that would be made on December 31, the end of the fiscal year. (Assume bond premium or discount amortization by the straight-line method.)

(2) Give the journal entries required at the end of 1991 to correct and bring the accounts up to date in view of the entries actually made.

Problem 15-10 (Reacquisition of bonds)

Guerra Company issued $500,000 of 12%, 10-year debentures on January 1, 1986. Interest is payable on January 1 and July 1. The entire issue was sold on April 1, 1986, at 102 plus accrued interest. On April 1, 1991, $250,000 of the bond issue was reacquired and retired at 98 plus accrued interest. On June 30, 1991, the remaining bonds were reacquired at 97 plus accrued interest and refunded with $400,000, 9% bonds issue sold at 100.

Instructions: Give the journal entries for 1986 and 1991 (through June 30) on the Guerra Company books. The company's books are kept on a calendar-year basis. (Round to nearest dollar. Assume straight-line amortization of premium or discount.)

Problem 15-11   (Convertible bonds)

The Robison Co. issued $1,000,000 of convertible 10-year debentures on July 1, 1990. The debentures provide for 9% interest payable semiannually on January 1 and July 1. The discount in connection with the issue was $19,500, which is being amortized monthly on a straight-line basis.

The debentures are convertible after 1 year into 7 shares of the Robison Co.'s $100 par value common stock for each $1,000 of debentures.

On August 1, 1991, $100,000 of debentures were turned in for conversion into common. Interest has been accrued monthly and paid as due. Accrued interest on debentures is paid in cash upon conversion.

Instructions: Prepare the journal entries to record the conversion, amortization, and interest in connection with the debentures as of: August 1, 1991, August 31, 1991, and December 31, 1991—including closing entries for end of year. No gain or loss is to be recognized on the conversion. (Round to nearest dollar.)

(AICPA adapted)

Problem 15-12   (Early extinguishment and conversion of bonds)

On January 1, 1990, Brewster Company issued 2,000 of its five-year, $1,000 face value, 11% bonds dated January 1 at an effective annual interest rate (yield) of 9%. Interest is payable each December 31. Brewster uses the effective-interest method of amortization. On December 31, 1991, the 2,000 bonds were extinguished early through acquisition in the open market by Brewster for $1,980,000.

On July 1, 1990, Brewster issued 5,000 of its six-year, $1,000 face value, 10% convertible bonds dated July 1 at an effective annual interest rate (yield) of 12%. Interest is payable every June 30 and December 31. The bonds are convertible at the investor's option into Brewster's common stock at a ratio of 10 shares of common stock for each bond. On July 1, 1991, an investor in Brewster's convertible bonds tendered 1,500 bonds for conversion into 15,000 shares of Brewster's common stock, which had a fair market value of $105 and a par value of $90 at the date of conversion.

Instructions:

(1) Make all necessary journal entries for the issuer and the investor to record the issuance of both the 11% and the 10% bonds.

(2) Make all necessary journal entries to record the early extinguishment of both debt instruments assuming:

   a) Brewster considered the conversion to be a significant culminating event and the investors considered their investment in convertible bonds to be debt rather than equity.

   b) Brewster considered the conversion to be a nonculminating event and the investors considered their investment in convertible bonds to be equity rather than debt.

Problem 15-13   (Troubled-debt restructuring—modification of terms)

Risky Company, after having experienced financial difficulties in 1989, negotiated with two major creditors and arrived at an agreement to restructure their debts on December 31, 1989. The two creditors were M. Barboza and R. Janeiro. Barboza was owed principal of $300,000 and interest of $60,000 but agreed to accept equipment worth $60,000 and notes receivable from Risky Company's customers worth $250,000. The equipment had an original cost of $80,000 and accumulated depreciation of $30,000. Janeiro was owed $500,000 and agreed to extend the terms and to accept immediate payment of $100,000 and the remaining balance of $424,360 to be paid on December 31, 1991. All payments were made according to schedule.

Instructions: Prepare Risky's journal entries to record the restructuring on December 31, 1989, and the entries necessary to make the adjustments and record payments on December 31, 1990, and 1991. (Note that a reasonable interest rate for Risky is 15%.)

Problem 15-14   (Troubled debt restructuring—modification of terms)

In the latter part of 1990, Caltex Company experienced severe financial pressure and is in default in meeting interest payments on long-term notes of $6,000,000 due on December 31, 1995. The interest rate on the debt is 11% payable semiannually on June 30 and December 31. In an agreement with Modern Investment Corporation, Caltex obtained acceptance of a change in principal and interest terms for the remaining 5-year life of the notes. The changes in terms are as follows:

(a) A reduction of principal of $600,000.
(b) A reduction in the interest rate to 8%.
(c) Caltex agreed to pay on December 31, 1990, both the $660,000 of interest in arrears and the normal interest payment under the old terms.

Instructions:

(1) What is the total dollar difference in cash payments by Caltex over the five-year period as a result of the restatement of terms?
(2) What journal entries for the restructuring of the debt, payment of interest under the old terms, and the first two interest payments under the new terms would Caltex make? (Assume an implicit interest rate of 6%).
(3) What journal entries would Modern Investment make in 1990 and 1991?

*Problem 15-15   (Serial bonds—amortization of premium or discount)

A serial bond issue in the amount of $2,000,000, dated January 1, 1989, bearing 8% interest payable at December 31 each year, is sold by Rural Farm Co. to yield 9% per year. The bonds mature in the amount of $400,000 on January 1 of each year starting in 1990.

Instructions:

(1) Compute the bond price and any premium or discount.
(2) Prepare an amortization schedule using the bonds outstanding method.

*Relates to Appendix

*Problem 15-16   (Bonds-outstanding tables)

The Hanifer Manufacturing Company issued $2,000,000 of 8% serial bonds on January 1, 1983, at 98. The bonds mature in units of $250,000 beginning January 1, 1988, with interest payable semiannually on January 1 and July 1. On June 1, 1991, Hanifer reacquired at 101 plus accrued interest, $200,000 of the bonds due January 1, 1993, and $100,000 due January 1, 1994.

Instructions:

(1) Assuming premium or discount amortization by the bonds-outstanding method and bond retirements as scheduled, prepare a table summarizing interest charges and bond carrying values for the bond life, supported by a schedule showing the calculation of amortization amounts. (Round to the nearest dollar.)

(2) Prepare a similar table summarizing interest charges and bond carrying values for the bond life taking into consideration bond redemptions in advance of maturity dates as indicated. (Round to nearest dollar.)

(3) Record in general journal form the retirement of bonds on June 1, 1991.

*Relates to Appendix

Chapter 16

Owners' Equity—Contributed Capital

Chapter Topics	**Nature and Classifications of Capital Stock**
	Preferred and Common Stock Features
	Issuance of Capital Stock
	Accounting for Treasury Stock
	Accounting for Stock Rights, Warrants, and Options
	Stock Conversions and Stock Splits
	Balance Sheet Disclosure of Contributed Capital

In analyzing the financial position of a company, it is important to understand certain key relationships. For example, the basic accounting equation—**Assets = Liabilities + Owners' Equity**—shows that the assets of an enterprise have been provided by creditors and owners. Assets represent entity resources, while liabilities reflect the creditor claims against those resources. Since the difference between assets and liabilities is owners' equity or capital, the owners' equity of an entity represents the residual interest of the owners in the net assets (total assets less total liabilities) of the enterprise.

The capital of a business originates from two primary sources—investments by owners and business earnings. Reductions in capital result primarily from distributions to owners and business losses. In a proprietorship, the entire owner's equity resulting from investments, withdrawals, and earnings or losses is reflected in a single capital account. Similarly, in a partnership, a single capital account for each partner reports the partner's equity resulting from investments, withdrawals, and earnings or losses. In reporting corporate capital, however, a distinction is made between (1) investments by owners, called contributed (or paid-in) capital and (2) increases in net assets arising from earnings, designated as retained earnings.

The issues surrounding contributed capital are discussed in this chapter, while those relating to retained earnings are considered in Chapter 17. Accounting for corporations is emphasized because they are the dominant form of organization in today's economy. Not only are corporations the major source of our national output, but they also provide the majority of employment opportunities. Millions of people hold equity securities (capital stock) in corporations throughout the world.

Nature and Classifications of Capital Stock

A corporation is an artificial entity created by law that has an existence separate from its owners and may engage in business within prescribed limits just as a natural person. Unless the life of a corporation is limited by law, it has perpetual existence. The modern corporation makes it possible for large amounts of resources to be assembled under one management. These resources are transferred to the corporation by individual owners because they believe they can earn a greater rate of return through the corporation's efficient use of the resources than would be possible from alternative investments. In exchange for these resources, the corporation issues **stock certificates** evidencing ownership interests. Directors elected by stockholders delegate to management responsibility for supervising the use, operation, and disposition of corporate resources.

Business corporations may be created under the incorporating laws of any one of the fifty states or of the federal government. Since the states do not follow a uniform incorporating act, the conditions under which corporations may be created and under which they may operate are somewhat varied.

In most states at least three individuals must join in applying for a corporate charter. Application is made by submitting **articles of incorporation** to the secretary of state or other appropriate official. The articles must set forth the name of the corporation, its purpose and nature, the stock to be issued, those persons who are to act as first directors, and other data required by law. If the articles conform to the state's laws governing corporate formation, they are approved and are recognized as the **charter** for the new corporate entity. When stock of a corporation is to be offered or distributed outside the state in which it is incorporated, registration with the Securities and Exchange Commission may be required. The objective of such registration is to ensure that all facts relative to the business and its securities will be adequately and honestly disclosed. A stockholders' meeting is called at which a code of rules or **bylaws** governing meetings, voting procedures, and other internal operations are adopted; a **board of directors** is elected; and the board appoints company administrative officers. Corporate activities may now proceed in conformance with laws of the state of incorporation and charter authorization. A complete record of the proceedings of both the stockholders' and the directors' meetings should be maintained in a minutes book.

When a corporation is formed, a single class of stock, known as **common stock**, is usually issued. Corporations may later find that there are advantages to issuing one or more additional classes of stock with varying rights and priorities. Stock with certain preferences (rights) over the common stock is called **preferred stock**. All shares within a particular class of stock are identical in terms of ownership rights represented.

Rights of Ownership   Unless restricted or withheld by terms of the articles of incorporation or bylaws, certain basic rights are held by each stockholder. These rights are as follows:

1. To share in distributions of corporate earnings.
2. To vote in the election of directors and in the determination of certain corporate policies.
3. To maintain one's proportional interest in the corporation through purchase of additional capital stock if issued, known as the *preemptive right*. (In recent years, some states have eliminated this right.)

4. To share in distributions of cash or other properties upon liquidation of the corporation.

If both preferred and common stock are issued, the special features of each class of stock are stated in the articles of incorporation or in the corporation bylaws and become a part of the contract between the corporation and its stockholders. One must be familiar with the overall capital structure to understand fully the nature of the equity found in any single class of stock. Frequently, the stock certificate describes the rights and restrictions relative to the ownership interest it represents together with those pertaining to other securities issued. Shares of stock represent personal property and may be freely transferred by their owners in the absence of special restrictions.

Par or Stated Value of Stock

As indicated, the capital of a corporation is divided between contributed capital and retained earnings. This is an important distinction because readers of financial statements need to know the portion of equity derived from investments by owners as contrasted with the portion of equity that has been earned and retained by the business. The invested or contributed capital may be further classified into (a) an amount forming the corporate legal capital, and (b) the balance, if any, in excess of legal capital. The amount of the investment representing the legal capital is reported as capital stock. The remaining balance is recognized as additional paid-in capital. As discussed in this chapter, and elsewhere in the text, additional paid-in capital may arise from several sources, including the sale of stock at more than par or stated value, treasury stock transactions, and donations of assets. Additional paid-in capital includes all sources of contributed capital other than, or in excess of, legal capital.

The major components of owners' equity for a corporation are shown below. It should be recognized, however, that the definitions and clasifications of legal and other capital categories may vary according to state statutes.

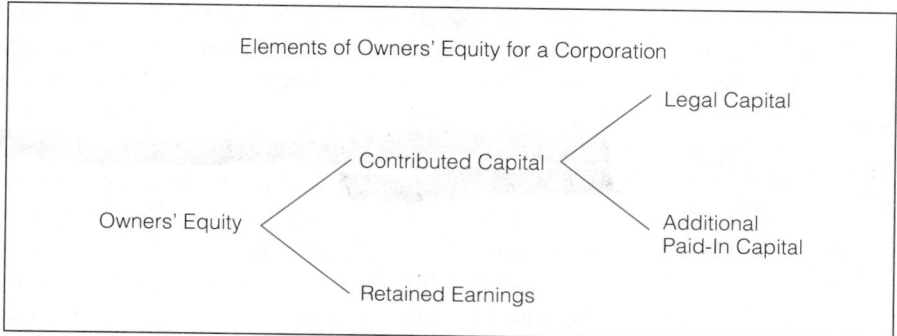

Elements of Owners' Equity for a Corporation

Owners' Equity
— Contributed Capital
  — Legal Capital
  — Additional Paid-In Capital
— Retained Earnings

The significance of legal capital is that most state incorporation laws provide that dividends cannot reduce corporate capital below an amount designated as legal capital. Modern corporation laws normally go beyond these limitations and add that legal capital cannot be impaired by the reacquisition of capital stock. Creditors of a corporation cannot hold individual stockholders liable for claims against the company. But with a portion of the corporate capital restricted as to distribution, creditors can rely on the absorption by the ownership group of losses equal to the legal capital before losses are applied to the creditors' equity. As a practical matter, the legal capital of a corporation is generally small in comparison to total capital and does not strongly influence dividend policy nor provide significant creditor protection.

When a value is assigned to each share of stock, whether common or preferred, and is reported on the stock certificate, the stock is said to have a **par value**; stock without such an assigned value is called **no-par** stock. When shares have a par value, the legal capital is normally the aggregate par value of all shares issued and subscribed. When a corporation is authorized to issue stock with a par value, the incorporation laws of most states permit such issue only for an amount equal to or in excess of par. Par value may be any amount, for example, $100, $5, or 25 cents. An amount received on the sale of stock in excess of its par value is recorded in a separate account, such as Paid-In Capital in Excess of Par. The balance in this account is added to capital stock at par in reporting total contributed capital.

From a financial reporting perspective, the concept of par value has little significance. Par value also has virtually no economic significance. Originally, the par value of stock was equal to the market value of the stock at the date of issue. Today, however, most par value stock has only a nominal value; that is, the par value is significantly below its issue or market price.

Par value does have legal significance in the historical development of common law and statutory law. But the modern trend is away from par value and an emphasis on legal capital. Since passage of the 1984 Revised Model Business Corporation Act, over ten states have eliminated par value as a legal concept.[1]

When shares are no-par, laws of certain states require that the total consideration received for the shares, even when they are sold at different prices, be recognized as legal capital. Laws of a number of states, however, permit the corporate directors to establish legal capital by assigning an arbitrary value to each share regardless of issue price, although in some instances the value cannot be less than a certain minimum amount. The value fixed by the board of directors or the minimum value required by law is known as the share's stated value, and an amount received in excess of stated value is reported in the same manner as an excess over par value, using an appropriate account title, e.g., Paid-In Capital in Excess of Stated Value.

Prior to 1912, corporations were permitted to issue only stock with a par value. In 1912, however, New York state changed its corporation laws

---

[1]For a more complete discussion of the legal significance of par value, see Philip McGough, "The Legal Significance of the Par Value of Common Stock: What Accounting Educators Should Know," *Issues in Accounting Education*, Fall 1988, pp. 330-350.

to permit the issuance of stock without a par value, and since that time all other states have followed with similar statutory provisions. Today, many of the common stocks, as well as some of the preferred stocks, listed on the major securities exchanges are no-par. Usually, no-par stock must have a stated value for reporting purposes. This makes it very similar to par stock and defines a separation of the stock proceeds between stated value and additional paid-in capital.

Preferred Stock   When a corporation issues both preferred and common stock, the preference rights attaching to preferred stock normally consist of prior claims to dividends. A dividend preference does not assure stockholders of dividends on the preferred issue but simply means that dividend requirements must be met on preferred stock before anything may be paid on common stock. Dividends do not legally accrue; a dividend on preferred stock, as on common stock, requires the ability on the part of the company to make such a distribution as well as appropriate action by the board of directors. When the board of directors fails to declare a dividend on preferred stock at the time such action would be called for, the dividend is said to be "passed." Although preferred stockholders have a prior claim on dividends, such preference is usually accompanied by limitations on the amount of dividends they may receive.

Preferred stock is generally issued with a par value. When preferred stock has a par value, the dividend is stated in terms of a percentage of par value. When preferred stock is no-par, the dividend must be stated in terms of dollars and cents. Thus, holders of 5% preferred stock with a $50 par value are entitled to an annual dividend of $2.50 per share before any distribution is made to common stockholders; holders of $5 no-par preferred stock are entitled to an annual dividend of $5 per share before dividends are paid to common stockholders.

A corporation may issue more than one class of preferred stock. For example, preferred issues may be designated first preferred or second preferred with the first preferred issue having a first claim on earnings and the second preferred having a second claim on earnings. In other instances the claim to earnings on the part of several preferred issues may have equal priority, but dividend rates or other preferences may vary. Holders of the common stock may receive dividends only after the satisfaction of all preferred dividend requirements.

Other characteristics and conditions are frequently added to preferred stock in the extension of certain advantages or in the limitation of certain rights. For example, preferred stock may be cumulative, convertible, callable, or redeemable. More than one of these characteristics may be applicable to a specific issue of preferred stock.

Cumulative and Noncumulative Preferred Stock

When a corporation fails to declare dividends on cumulative preferred stock, such dividends accumulate and require payment in the future before any dividends may be paid to common stockholders.

For example, assume that Good Time Corporation has outstanding 100,000 shares of 9% cumulative preferred stock, $10 par. Dividends were last paid in 1988. Total dividends of $300,000 are declared in 1991 by the board of directors. The majority of this amount will be paid to the preferred shareholders as follows:

	Dividends to Preferred Shareholders	Dividends to Common Shareholders	Total Dividends
Cumulative dividend for 1989	$ 90,000	0	$ 90,000
Cumulative dividend for 1990	90,000	0	90,000
Dividends for 1991	90,000	$30,000	120,000
Totals	$270,000	$30,000	$300,000

Dividends on cumulative preferred stock that are passed are referred to as dividends in arrears. Although these dividends are not a liability until declared by the board of directors, this information is of importance to stockholders and other users of the financial statements. Disclosure of the amount of dividends in arrears is made by special note on the balance sheet.

With noncumulative preferred stock, it is not necessary to provide for passed dividends. A dividend omission on preferred stock in any one year means it is irretrievably lost. Dividends may be declared on common stock as long as the preferred stock receives the preferred rate for the current period. Thus, in the previous example, if the preferred stock were noncumulative, the 1991 dividends would be distributed as follows:

	Dividends to Preferred Shareholders	Dividends to Common Shareholders	Total Dividends
Dividend passed in 1989	0	0	0
Dividend passed in 1990	0	0	0
Dividends for 1991	$90,000	$210,000	$300,000
Totals	$90,000	$210,000	$300,000

Preferred stock contracts normally provide for cumulative dividends. Also, courts have generally held that dividend rights on preferred stock are cumulative in the absence of specific provisions to the contrary.

Convertible Preferred Stock

Preferred stock is **convertible** when terms of the issue provide that it can be exchanged by its owner for some other security of the issuing corporation. Conversion rights generally provide for the exchange of preferred stock into common stock. Since preferred stock normally has a prior but limited right to earnings, large earnings resulting from successful operations accrue to the common stockholders. The conversion privilege gives the preferred stockholders the opportunity to exchange their holdings for stock in which the rights to earnings are not limited. In some instances, preferred stock may be convertible into bonds, thus allowing investors the option of changing their positions from stockholders to creditors. Convertible preferred issues have become popular with some companies, as indicated by the following excerpt from an article that appeared in *Barron's*.

> In recent years, a growing number of blue-chip companies have turned to convertibles as a source of cheaper cash than straight debt, and when IBM issued $1.3 billion worth last year to finance its acquisition of Rolm Corp., it symbolized a rite of passage for these securities.
>
> This year, both volume and demand have continued to soar. Some $6.55 billion worth of convertibles was issued by mid-July, more than the $5.05 billion for all of 1984.[2]

The journal entries required for stock conversions are illustrated later in the chapter.

Callable Preferred Stock

Preferred stock is **callable** when it can be called or redeemed at the option of the corporation. Many preferred issues are callable. The **call price** is usually specified in the original agreement and provides for payment of dividends in arrears as part of the repurchase price. When convertible stock has a call provision, the holders of the stock, at the time of the call, are frequently given the option of converting their holdings into common stock rather than accepting the call price. The decision made by the investor will be based on the market price of the common stock.

Redeemable Preferred Stock

Preferred stock is sometimes subject to mandatory redemption requirements or other redemption provisions that give the security overlapping debt and equity characteristics. This type of stock is referred to as redeemable preferred stock and is defined as preferred stock that is redeemable at the option of the holder, or at a fixed or determinable price on a specific date, or upon other conditions not solely within the control of the issuer (e.g., redemption upon reaching a certain level of earnings). The FASB currently requires disclosure of long-term obligations, including the extent of redemption requirements for all issues of capital stock that are redeemable at fixed or determinable prices on fixed or determinable dates. Redemption requirements may be disclosed separately for each issue or for all issues combined.[3]

---

[2]Jaye Scholl, "Convertibles Come Into Their Own," *Barron's* (November 11, 1985), p. 68.
[3]*Statement of Financial Accounting Standards No. 47*, "Disclosure of Long-Term Obligations" (Stamford: Financial Accounting Standards Board, 1981), par. 10c.

The entries for reacquiring stock by exercising a call or redemption feature are discussed later in the chapter.

Asset and Dividend Preferences upon Corporation Liquidation

Preferred stock generally takes priority over common stock as to assets distributed upon corporate liquidation. Such a preference, however, cannot be assumed but must be specifically stated in the preferred stock contract. The asset preference for stock with a par value is an amount equal to par, or par plus any amount paid in excess of par; in the absence of a par value, the preference is a stated amount. Terms of the preferred contract may also provide for the full payment of any dividends in arrears upon liquidation, regardless of the retained earnings balance reported by the company. When this is the case and there are insufficient retained earnings, i.e., a deficit, such dividend priorities must be met from paid-in capital of the common stock; the common stockholders receive whatever assets remain after settlement with the preferred group.

Common Stock

Strictly speaking, there should be but one kind of common stock, representing the residual ownership equity of a company. In recent years, however, a few companies have begun to issue different classes of common stock with different ownership rights. General Motors, for example, has several classes of common stock to appeal to different types of investors. In many ways, these classes of common stock are similar in nature and purpose to preferred stock. For most companies, there is but one class of common stock.[4]

Common stock carries the greatest risk since common shareholders receive dividends only after preferred dividends are paid. In return for this risk, common stock ordinarily shares in earnings to the greatest extent if the corporation is successful. There is no inherent distinction in voting rights between preferred and common stocks; however, voting rights are frequently given exclusively to common stockholders as long as dividends are paid regularly on preferred stock. Upon failure to meet preferred dividend requirements, special voting rights may be granted to preferred stockholders, thus affording this group a more prominent role in the

[4]In an interesting recent development, four companies have offered investors the opportunity to purchase new securities called "unbundled stock units." These companies (American Express, Dow Chemical, Pfizer, and Sara Lee) argue that the common stock security is undervalued when sold as a single unit. So they propose to "unbundle" the value represented by common stock and sell three new securities as an alternative to the common stock certificate. The new security package would contain a 30-year bond paying interest at the stock's current dividend rate; a preferred stock that initially pays no dividends but matches any dividend increases on the company's common stock over the next 30 years; and a security closely resembling a stock warrant that allows investors to profit from stock appreciation. In effect, the three new securities provide a package that allows investors to profit explicitly in the same way that common stockholders do with a single security, i.e., from dividends, from dividend increases, and from capital appreciation in the value of common stock. What these companies are counting on is that the value of the three new securities will be worth more to investors than common stock sold as a single security. If the tactic works, which critics say is uncertain, it may create another alternative to common stock securities. (See "Package Deal." *Wall Street Journal* 6 December, 1988.)

management. In some states, voting rights cannot be withheld on any class of stock.

Issuance of Capital Stock

In accounting for capital stock, it should be recognized that stock may be:

1. Authorized but unissued.
2. Subscribed for and held for issuance pending receipt of cash for the full amount of the subscription price.
3. Outstanding in the hands of stockholders.
4. Reacquired and held by the corporation for subsequent reissuance.
5. Canceled by appropriate corporation action.

Thus, an accurate record of all transactions involving capital stock must be maintained by a corporation. Separate general ledger accounts are required for each source of capital including each class of stock. In addition, subsidiary records are needed to keep track of individual stockholders and stock certificates.

Capital Stock Issued for Cash

The issuance of stock for cash is recorded by a debit to Cash and a credit to Capital Stock for the par or stated value.[5] When the amount of cash received from the sale of stock is greater than the par or stated value, the excess is recorded separately as a credit to an additional paid-in capital account. This account is carried on the books as long as the stock to which it relates is outstanding. When stock is retired, the capital stock balance as well as any related additional paid-in-capital balance is generally canceled.

To illustrate, assume the Goode Corporation is authorized to issue 10,000 shares of $10 par common stock. On April 1, 1991, 4,000 shares are sold for $45,000 cash. The entry to record the transaction is:

```
1991
April 1   Cash .........................................   45,000
              Common stock ...................................            40,000
              Paid-In Capital in Excess of Par ...................             5,000
                  To record the issuance of 4,000 shares of $10 par
                  common stock for $45,000.
```

If, in the example, the common stock were no-par stock but with a $10 stated value, the entry would be the same except the $5,000 would be designated Paid-In Capital in Excess of Stated Value. Generally, stock is assigned a par or a stated value. However, if there is no such value assigned, the entire amount of cash received on the sale of stock is credited to the capital stock account and there is no additional paid-in capital account associated with the stock. Assuming Goode Corporation's stock were

[5]The term *Capital Stock* is used in account titles in the text when the class of stock is not specifically designated. When preferred and common designations are given, these are used in the account titles.

no-par common without a stated value, the entry to record the sale of 4,000 shares for $45,000 would be:

```
1991
April 1  Cash ............................................  45,000
              Common Stock.................................              45,000
                 To record the issuance of 4,000 shares of no-par,
                 no stated-value common stock for $45,000.
```

Capital Stock Sold on Subscription

Capital stock may be issued on a subscription basis. A **subscription** is a legally binding contract between the subscriber (purchaser of stock) and the corporation (issuer of stock). The contract states the number of shares subscribed, the subscription price, the terms of payment, and other conditions of the transaction. A subscription, while giving the corporation a legal claim for the contract price, also gives the subscriber the legal status of a stockholder unless certain rights as a stockholder are specifically withheld by law or by terms of the contract. Ordinarily, stock certificates evidencing share ownership are not issued until the full subscription price has been received by the corporation.

When stock is subscribed for, Capital Stock Subscriptions Receivable is debited for the subscription price, Capital Stock Subscribed is credited for the amount to be recognized as capital stock when subscriptions have been collected, and a paid-in capital account is credited for the amount of the subscription price in excess of par or stated value.

Capital Stock Subscriptions Receivable is a control account, individual subscriptions being reported in the subsidiary **subscribers ledger**. A special **subscribers journal** may be used in recording capital stock subscriptions. Subscriptions Receivable is regarded as a current asset when the corporation expects to collect the balance within one year, which is the usual situation. Capital Stock Subscribed and any related paid-in capital accounts are reported as contributed capital in the stockholders' equity section of the balance sheet.

Subscriptions may be collected in cash or in other assets accepted by the corporation. When collections are made, the appropriate asset account is debited and the receivable account is credited. Credits are also made to subscribers' accounts in the subsidiary ledger.

The actual issuance of stock is recorded by a debit to Capital Stock Subscribed and a credit to Capital Stock. The following entries illustrate the recording and issuance of capital stock sold on subscription. It is assumed that the Feitz Corporation is authorized to issue 10,000 shares of $10 par value common stock.

Recording and Issuance of Capital Stock Sold on Subscription

November 1-30: Received subscriptions for 5,000 shares of $10 par common at $12.50 per share with 50% down, balance due in 60 days.

Common Stock Subscriptions Receivable	62,500	
Common Stock Subscribed		50,000
Paid-In Capital in Excess of Par		12,500
Cash	31,250	
Common Stock Subscriptions Receivable		31,250

December 1-31: Received balance due on one half of subscriptions and issued stock to the fully paid subscribers, 2,500 shares.

Cash	15,625	
Common Stock Subscriptions Receivable		15,625
Common Stock Subscribed	25,000	
Common Stock		25,000

As a result of the preceding transactions, current assets in the December 31 balance sheet would include subscriptions receivable of $15,625. Contributed capital would be reported in the stockholders' equity section of the balance sheet as follows.

Stockholders' Equity

Contributed capital:	
Common stock, $10 par, 10,000 shares authorized, 2,500 shares issued and outstanding	$25,000
Common stock subscribed, 2,500 shares	25,000
Paid-in capital in excess of par	12,500
Total contributed capital	$62,500

Subscription Defaults   If a subscriber defaults on a subscription by failing to make a payment when it is due, a corporation may (1) return to the subscriber the amount paid, (2) return to the subscriber the amount paid less any reduction in price or expense incurred on the resale of the stock, (3) declare the amount paid by the subscriber as forfeited, or (4) issue to the subscriber shares equal to the number paid for in full. The practice followed will depend on the policy adopted by the corporation within the legal limitations set by the state in which it is incorporated.

To illustrate the entries under these different circumstances, assume in the Feitz Corporation example described earlier (with subscriptions at $12.50 per share) that one subscriber for 100 shares defaults after making the 50% down payment. Defaulted shares are subsequently resold at $11. The entries to record the default by the subscriber and the subsequent resale of the defaulted shares would be as follows:

1. Assuming the amount paid in is returned to the subscriber:

Common Stock Subscribed	1,000	
Paid-In Capital in Excess of Par	250	
Common Stock Subscriptions Receivable		625
Cash		625
Cash	1,100	
Common Stock		1,000
Paid-In Capital in Excess of Par		100

2. Assuming the amount paid in less the price reduction on the resale is returned to the subscriber:

Common Stock Subscribed	1,000	
Paid-In Capital in Excess of Par	250	
Common Stock Subscriptions Receivable		625
Payable to Defaulting Subscriber		
(payment withheld pending stock resale)		625
Cash	1,100	
Payable to Defaulting Subscriber	150	
Common Stock		1,000
Paid-In Capital in Excess of Par		250
Payable to Defaulting Subscriber	475	
Cash		475

3. Assuming the full amount paid in is declared to be forfeited:

Common Stock Subscribed	1,000	
Paid-In Capital in Excess of Par	250	
Common Stock Subscriptions Receivable		625
Paid-In Capital from Forfeited Stock Subscriptions		625
Cash	1,100	
Common Stock		1,000
Paid-In Capital in Excess of Par		100

4. Assuming shares equal to the number paid for in full are issued:

Common Stock Subscribed	1,000	
Paid-In Capital in Excess of Par	125	
Common Stock		500
Common Stock Subscriptions Receivable		625
Cash	550	
Common Stock		500
Paid-In Capital in Excess of Par		50

Capital Stock Issued for Consideration Other Than Cash

When capital stock is issued for consideration in the form of property other than cash or for services received, the fair market value of the stock or the fair market value of the property or services, whichever is more objectively determinable, is used to record the transaction. If a quoted market price for the stock is available, that amount should be used as a basis for recording the exchange. Otherwise, it may be possible to determine the fair market value of the property or services received, e.g., through appraisal by a competent outside party.

To illustrate, assume that AC Company issues 200 shares of $100 par value common stock in return for land. The company's stock is currently selling for $150 per share. The entry on AC Company's books would be:

Land	30,000	
Common Stock		20,000
Paid-In Capital in Excess of Par		10,000

If, on the other hand, the land has a readily determinable market price of $25,000 but AC Company's common stock has no established fair market value, the transaction would be recorded as follows:

Land.	25,000	
Common Stock.		20,000
Paid-In Capital in Excess of Par		5,000

If an objective value cannot be established for either the stock or the property or services received, the board of directors normally has the right to assign values to the securities issued and the assets or services received. These values will stand for all legal purposes in the absence of proof that fraud was involved. However, the assignment of values by the board of directors should be subject to careful scrutiny. There have been cases where directors have assigned excessive values to the consideration received for stock to improve the company's reported financial position. When the value of the consideration cannot be clearly established and the directors' valuations are used in reporting assets and invested capital, the source of the valuations should be disclosed on the balance sheet. When there is evidence that improper values have been assigned to the consideration received for stock, such values should be restated.

Issuance of Capital Stock in Exchange for a Business

A corporation, upon its formation or at some later date, may be combined with another ongoing business, issuing capital stock in exchange for the net assets acquired. This is referred to as a **business combination**. In determining the amount of stock to be issued, the fair market value of the stock, as well as the values of the net assets acquired, must be considered.

Frequently the value of the stock transferred by a corporation will exceed the value of the identifiable assets acquired because of a favorable earnings record of the business acquired. If the exchange is accounted for as a **purchase**, the value of the stock in excess of the values assigned to identifiable assets is recognized as goodwill. Under this approach, the retained earnings of the company acquired *do not* become part of the combined retained earnings. On the other hand, if the exchange is treated as a **pooling of interest**, neither the revaluation of assets nor the recognition of goodwill is recorded. Assets are stated at the amounts previously reported; the retained earnings accounts of the two companies are added together and become the amount of retained earnings for the combined entity. The purchase method assumes that one of the companies is dominant and is acquiring the other company. The pooling of interests method assumes equal status and continuity of common ownership. Accounting for business combinations is dealt with in APB Opinion No. 16, and is discussed in detail in advanced accounting texts.

Capital Stock Reacquisition

For a variety of reasons, a company may find it desirable to reacquire shares of its own stock. In 1988, for example, IBM Corporation announced a $2 billion buy-back program. Over the past few years IBM has completed stock purchase programs totaling about 28 million shares. Companies acquire their own stock to:

1. Finance acquisitions.
2. Provide for incentive compensation and employee savings plans.
3. Improve per-share earnings by reducing the number of shares outstanding.
4. Support the market price of the stock.
5. Increase the ratio of debt to equity.
6. Obtain shares for conversion to other securities.
7. Invest excess cash temporarily.

Whatever the reason, a company's stock may be reacquired by exercise of call or redemption provisions, by repurchase of the stock in the open market, or by donation from stockholders. In reacquiring stock, a company must comply with applicable state laws, which can have a significant impact on transactions involving a company's stock. For example, state laws normally provide that the reacquisition of stock must serve a legitimate corporate purpose and must be made without injury or prejudice to the creditors or to the remaining stockholders. Another general restriction relates to the preserving of sufficient legal capital of the corporation.

In accounting for the reacquisition of stock, it should be emphasized that *reacquisitions do not give rise to income or loss.* A company issues stock to raise capital, which it intends to employ profitably; in reacquiring shares of its stock, the company reduces the capital to be employed in subsequent operations. Income or loss arises from the operating and investing activities of the business, not from transactions with its shareholders.

A company's stock may be reacquired for immediate retirement or reacquired and held as treasury stock for subsequent disposition, either eventual retirement or reissuance. Accounting for immediate retirements will be discussed first, followed by accounting for treasury stock transactions.

Stock Reacquired for Immediate Retirement

If shares of stock are reacquired at par or stated value and then retired, the capital stock account is debited and Cash is credited. However, if the purchase price of the stock exceeds the par or stated value, the excess amount may be: (1) charged to any paid-in capital balances applicable to that class of stock, (2) allocated between paid-in capital and retained earnings, or (3) charged entirely to retained earnings.[6] The alternative used depends on the existence of previously established paid-in capital amounts and on management's preference. To illustrate the application of the alternatives, assume that Interwest Corporation reports the following balances related to an issue of preferred stock:

Preferred Stock (par $10, 10,000 shares outstanding)	$100,000
Paid-In Capital in Excess of Par	10,000

[6]*Opinions of the Accounting Principles Board, No. 6,* "Status of Accounting Research Bulletins" (New York: American Institute of Certified Public Accountants, 1965), par. 12a.

Assume Interwest redeems and retires 2,000 shares, or 20%, of the preferred stock at $12.50 per share, or a total purchase price of $25,000. Reductions are made in the preferred stock account for $20,000 (2,000 shares at par of $10) and in the related paid-in capital account for a pro rata share, 20% of $10,000, or $2,000. The remainder of the purchase price, $3,000, is charged to Retained Earnings. The journal entry would be:

Preferred Stock	20,000	
Paid-In Capital in Excess of Par	2,000	
Retained Earnings	3,000	
Cash		25,000

Alternatively, the entire amount paid over par or stated value of the retired shares can be debited to Retained Earnings. In the above example, the entry would be:

Preferred Stock	20,000	
Retained Earnings	5,000	
Cash		25,000

When a corporation reacquires stock at a price that is less than par or stated value, the difference is credited to a paid-in capital account, not to Retained Earnings. To illustrate, assume Interwest Corporation redeems the 2,000 shares of preferred stock at only $9 per share, or a total of $18,000. The preferred stock account is reduced by the par value of the shares, $20,000, and the difference between the debit to Preferred Stock and the amount paid is credited to a paid-in capital account, as illustrated in the following entry:

Preferred Stock	20,000	
Cash		18,000
Paid-In Capital from Preferred Stock Reacquisition		2,000

If additional shares of preferred stock are subsequently reacquired at amounts in excess of par, the excess can be debited to Paid-In Capital in Excess of Par, Paid-In Capital from Preferred Stock Reacquisition, and/or Retained Earnings.

The preceding discussion and illustrations dealt only with the corporation's books. From the investor's perspective, a stock redemption is recorded by a debit to Cash for the call price received and a credit to the investment account at cost; the difference, if any, is recorded as a gain or loss. Generally, a gain is recognized, since the call price is usually higher than the cost of the investment. Using the first example given for the Interwest Corporation (reacquisition price of $12.50 per share) and assuming only one investor held the 2,000 shares of preferred stock at a cost of $22,000, the entry for the stockholder would be:

Cash	25,000	
Gain on Redemption of Interwest Corporation Preferred		
Stock		3,000
Investment in Interwest Corporation Preferred Stock		22,000

Treasury Stock

When a company's own stock is reacquired and held in the name of the company rather than formally retired, it is referred to as treasury stock. Treasury shares may subsequently be reissued or formally retired. Before discussing how to account for treasury stock, several important features should be noted.

First, treasury stock should not be viewed as an asset; instead, it should be reported as a reduction in total owners' equity. A company cannot have an ownership interest in itself. Furthermore, treasury stock does not confer upon the corporation stockholder rights, e.g., cash dividends or voting rights. Treasury shares may or may not participate in stock dividends or stock splits, depending on the circumstances. The distribution of stock dividends on treasury stock is specifically prohibited by law in some states. In states where such distributions are permitted, stock dividends generally would be distributed on treasury shares only in certain situations, for example when the treasury shares are intended for distribution to employees under a stock option plan. When a stock split alters the par or stated value of all the shares of a particular class of stock, treasury shares would participate in the split.

Legal capital is not affected by the acquisition or reissuance of treasury stock. The acquisition of treasury stock decreases the number of shares outstanding, while reissuance increases the number of shares outstanding, but the legal capital is not changed by either the reacquisition or the subsequent reissuance. Third, as noted earlier, there is no income or loss on the reacquisition, reissuance, or retirement of treasury stock. Finally, as illustrated in the next section, Retained Earnings can be decreased by treasury stock transactions, but is never increased by such transactions.

Accounting for Treasury Stock

Two methods for recording treasury stock transactions are generally accepted: (1) the **cost method**, where the purchase of treasury stock is viewed as giving rise to a capital element whose ultimate disposition remains to be determined; and (2) the **par (or stated) value method**, where the purchase of treasury stock is viewed as effective or "constructive" retirement of outstanding stock.

Cost Method Under the cost method, the purchase of treasury stock is recorded by debiting a treasury stock account for the cost of the purchase and crediting Cash. The cost is determined by the current market price of the stock and is not necessarily tied to the original stock issue price. The balance in the treasury stock account is reported as a deduction from total stockholders' equity on the balance sheet. If treasury stock is subsequently retired, the debit balance in the treasury stock account is eliminated by allocating proportionate amounts to the appropriate capital stock, paid-in capital, and retained earnings accounts, as noted previously. If treasury stock is subsequently sold, the difference between the acquisition cost and the selling price is reported as an increase or decrease in stockholders' equity. If stockholders' equity is increased by the sale of treasury stock, a paid-in capital account, such as Paid-In Capital from Teasury Stock, is credited. If stockholders' equity is decreased, paid-in capital accounts established from previous treasury stock transactions may be debited, or the entire amount may be debited to Retained Earnings.

The cost method of accounting for treasury stock transactions is illustrated in the following example.

Cost Method of Accounting for Treasury Stock

1990   Newly organized corporation issued 10,000 shares of common stock, $10 par, at $15:

Cash	150,000	
Common Stock		100,000
Paid-In Capital in Excess of Par		50,000

Net income for first year of business, $30,000:

Income Summary	30,000	
Retained Earnings		30,000

1991   Reacquired 1,000 shares of common stock at $16 per share:

Treasury Stock	16,000	
Cash		16,000

Sold 200 shares of treasury stock at $20 per share:

Cash	4,000	
Treasury Stock		3,200
Paid-In Capital from Treasury Stock		800

Sold 500 shares of treasury stock at $14 per share:

Cash	7,000	
Paid-In Capital from Treasury Stock	800	
Retained Earnings	200	
Treasury Stock		8,000

Retired 300 shares of treasury stock (3% of original issue of 10,000 shares):

Common Stock	3,000	
Paid-In Capital in Excess of Par	1,500*	
Retained Earnings	300*	
Treasury Stock (300 × $16)		4,800

*As indicated earlier, the entire $1,800 difference between the debit to Common Stock and the cost to acquire the treasury stock may be debited to Retained Earnings.

In the preceding example, if a balance sheet were prepared after the acquisition of the treasury stock but prior to the reissuance and retirement of the stock, the stockholders' equity section would appear as follows:

Stockholders' Equity

Contributed capital:	
Common stock	$100,000
Paid-in capital in excess of par	50,000
Total contributed capital	$150,000
Retained earnings	30,000
Total contributed capital and retained earnings	$180,000
Less treasury stock at cost	16,000
Total stockholders' equity	$164,000

It should be noted that in the example, all treasury stock was acquired at $16 per share. If several acquisitions of treasury stock are made at different prices, the resale or retirement of treasury shares must be recorded using the actual cost to reacquire the shares being sold or retired (specific identification) or on the basis of a cost-flow assumption, such as FIFO or average cost.

Par (or Stated) Value Method If the par (or stated) value method is used, the purchase of treasury stock is regarded as a withdrawal of a group of stockholders. Similarly, the sale or reissuance of treasury stock, under this approach, is viewed as the admission of a new group of stockholders, requiring entries giving effect to the investment by this group. Thus, the purchase and sale are viewed as two separate and unrelated transactions.

Using the data given for the cost method illustration, the following entries would be made for 1991 under the par value method.

Par Value Method of Accounting for Treasury Stock

1991   Reacquired 1,000 shares of common stock at $16 per share:

Treasury Stock	10,000	
Paid-In Capital in Excess of Par	5,000	
Retained Earnings	1,000	
Cash		16,000

Sold 200 shares of treasury stock at $20 per share:

Cash	4,000	
Treasury Stock		2,000
Paid-In Capital in Excess of Par		2,000

Sold 500 shares of treasury stock at $14 per share:

Cash	7,000	
Treasury Stock		5,000
Paid-In Capital in Excess of Par		2,000

Retired 300 shares of treasury stock:

Common Stock	3,000	
Treasury Stock		3,000

Prior to the reissuance or retirement of treasury stock in the example using the par value method, the stockholders' equity section would show:

Stockholders' Equity

Contributed capital:	
Common stock	$100,000
Less treasury stock at par value	10,000
Common stock outstanding	$90,000
Paid-in capital in excess of par	45,000
Total contributed capital	$135,000
Retained earnings	29,000
Total stockholders' equity	$164,000

Evaluating the Cost and Par Value Methods

Neither the AICPA through the Accounting Principles Board, nor the FASB has expressed a preference between the two methods of accounting for treasury stock transactions. Although there is theoretical support for each approach, in practice the cost method is strongly favored because of its simplicity. As noted in the 1988 *Accounting Trends and Techniques*, less than 10% of the companies that reported treasury stock used some form of par or stated value method.[7]

The following comparison shows the impact on stockholders' equity of the two approaches after all treasury stock transactions have occurred in the illustrative example. Note that total stockholders' equity is the same regardless of which method is used. As shown by the example, however, there may be differences in the relative amounts of contributed capital and Retained Earnings reported. Note again that Retained Earnings may be decreased by treasury stock transactions, but can never be increased by buying and selling treasury stock.

Comparison of Stockholders' Equity

	Cost Method	Par Value Method
Contributed capital:		
Common stock	$ 97,000	$ 97,000
Paid-in capital in excess of par	48,500	49,000
Total contributed capital	$145,500	$146,000
Retained earnings	29,500	29,000
Total contributed capital and retained earnings	$175,000	$175,000
Less treasury stock	-0-	-0-
Total stockholders' equity	$175,000	$175,000

Donated Treasury Stock

Treasury stock is occasionally acquired by donation from stockholders. Shares may be donated to enable the company to raise capital by reselling the shares. In other cases, shares may be donated to eliminate a deficit. Ordinarily, all stockholders participate in the donation on a pro rata basis,

[7]*Accounting Trends and Techniques—1988* (New York: American Institute of Certified Public Accountants, 1988), p. 206.

each party donating a certain percentage of holdings so that relative interests in the corporation remain unchanged.

When treasury stock is donated and the market value of the stock is known, the transaction would be recorded normally, using either the cost or the par value method. Instead of a credit to cash, however, the credit entry would be to a paid-in capital account, e.g., Donated Capital.

In the absence of an objective basis for valuation, the acquisition of treasury stock by donation may be reported on a corporation's books by a memorandum entry. Upon sale of the donated stock, the entry would be recorded by a debit to Cash and a credit to a paid-in capital account.

Stock Rights, Warrants, and Options

A corporation may issue rights, warrants, or options that permit the purchase of the company's stock for a specified period (the **exercise period**) at a certain price (the **exercise price**). Although the terms *rights, warrants,* and *options* are sometimes used interchangeably, a distinction may be made as follows:

1. **Stock rights**—issued to existing shareholders to permit them to maintain their proportionate ownership interests when new shares are to be issued. (Some state laws require this preemptive right.)
2. **Stock warrants**—sold by the corporation for cash, generally in conjunction with another security.
3. **Stock options**—granted to officers or employees, sometimes as part of a compensation plan.

A company may offer rights, warrants, or options: (1) to raise additional capital, (2) to encourage the sale of a particular class of securities, or (3) as compensation for services received. The exercise period is generally longer for warrants and options than for rights. Warrants and rights may be traded independently among investors, whereas options generally are restricted to a particular person or specified group to whom the options are granted. The accounting considerations relating to stock rights, warrants, and options are described in the following sections.

Stock Rights

When announcing rights to purchase additional shares of stock, the directors of a corporation specify a date on which the rights will be issued. All stockholders of record on the issue date are entitled to receive the rights. Thus, between the announcement date and the issue date, the stock is said to sell *rights-on*. After the rights are issued, the stock sells *ex-rights,* and the rights may be sold separately by those receiving them from the corporation. An expiration date is also designated when the rights are announced, and rights not exercised by this date are worthless.

Accounting for Stock Rights by the Issuer

When rights are issued to stockholders, only a memorandum entry is made on the issuing company's books stating the number of shares that may be claimed under the outstanding rights. This information is required so the corporation may retain sufficient unissued or reacquired stock to meet the exercise of the rights. Upon surrender of the rights and the receipt of payments as specified by the rights, the stock is issued. At this time a memorandum entry is made to record the decrease in the number of rights outstanding accompanied by an entry to record the stock sale. The entry for the sale is recorded the same as any other issue of stock, with appropriate recognition of the cash received, the par or stated value of the stock issued, and any additional paid-in capital.

Information concerning outstanding rights should be reported with the corporation's balance sheet so that the effects of the future exercise of remaining rights may be determined.

Accounting for Stock Rights by the Investor

The receipt of stock rights by a stockholder is comparable to the receipt of a stock dividend (to be discussed fully in Chapter 17). The corporation has made no asset distribution and stockholders' equity remains unchanged. However, a stockholders' investment is now evidenced by shares of stock previously acquired and by rights that have a value of their own when they permit the purchase of shares at less than the market price. These circumstances call for an **allocation of cost** between the shares of stock and the rights. Since the shares and the rights have different values, an apportionment should be made in terms of the relative market values as of the date the rights are issued. Subsequently, the stock and the rights are accounted for separately. Accounting for stock rights by the shareholder is illustrated in the following example.

Assume that in 1990, Northern Supply Co. acquired 100 shares of Telstar Inc.'s common stock at $180 per share. In 1991, the corporation issues rights to purchase 1 share of common at $110 for every 5 shares owned. Northern thus receives 100 rights—1 right for each share owned. However, since 5 rights are required for the acquisition of a single share, the 100 rights enable Northern to subscribe for only 20 new shares. Northern's original investment cost of $18,000 now applies to 2 assets, the shares and the rights. This cost is apportioned on the basis of the relative market values of each security as of the date that the rights are issued to the stockholders. The cost allocation may be expressed as follows:

$$\text{Cost assigned to rights} = \text{Original Cost of Stock} \times \frac{\text{Market Value of Rights}}{\text{Market Value of Stock Ex-rights} + \text{Market Value of Rights}}$$

$$\text{Cost assigned to stock} = \text{Original Cost of Stock} \times \frac{\text{Market Value of Stock Ex-rights}}{\text{Market Value of Stock Ex-rights} + \text{Market Value of Rights}}$$

Assume that Telstar Inc.'s common stock is selling ex-rights at $131 per share, and rights are selling at $4 each. The cost allocation would be made as follows:

$$\text{To rights: } \$18,000 \times \frac{\$4}{\$131 + \$4} = \$533 \text{ (rounded) } (\$533 \div 100 = \$5.33, \text{ cost per right})$$

$$\text{To stock: } \$18,000 \times \frac{\$131}{\$131 + \$4} = \$17,467 \text{ (rounded) } (\$17,467 \div 100 = \$174.67, \text{ cost per share})$$

The following entry may be made to record the allocation:

Investment in Telstar Inc. Stock Rights	533	
Investment in Telstar Inc. Common Stock		533
Received 100 rights permitting the purchase of 20 shares at $110.		

The cost apportioned to the rights is used in determining any gain or loss arising from the sale of rights. Assume that the rights in the preceding example are sold for $4.50 each. The following entry would be made:

Cash	450	
Loss on Sale of Telstar Inc. Stock Rights	83	
Investment in Telstar Inc. Stock Rights		533
Sold 100 rights at $4.50.		

If the rights are exercised rather than sold, the cost of the new shares acquired consists of the cost assigned to the rights plus the cash that is paid on the exercise of rights. Assume that, instead of selling the rights, Northern Supply Co. exercises its rights to purchase 20 additional shares at $110. The following entry would be made:

Investment in Telstar Inc. Common Stock	2,733	
Investment in Telstar Inc. Stock Rights		533
Cash		2,200
Exercised rights, acquiring 20 shares at $110.		

Upon exercising the rights, Northern's records show an investment balance of $20,200 consisting of two lots of stock as follows:

Lot 1 (1990 acquisition) 100 shares: ($17,467 ÷ 100 = $174.67, cost per share, adjusted for stock rights)	$17,467
Lot 2 (1991 acquisition) 20 shares: ($2,733 ÷ 20 = $136.65, cost per share, acquired through stock rights)	2,733
Total	$20,200

These costs provide the basis for calculating gain or loss on subsequent sale of the stock.

Frequently the receipt of rights includes 1 or more rights that cannot be used in the purchase of a whole share. For example, assume that the owner of 100 shares receives 100 rights; 6 rights are required for the purchase of 1 share. Here the holder uses 96 rights in purchasing 16 shares. Several alternatives are available to the holder: allow the remaining 4 rights to lapse; sell the rights and report a gain or a loss on such sale; or supplement the rights held by the purchase of 2 more rights making possible the purchase of an additional share of stock.

If the owner of valuable rights allows them to lapse, it would appear that the cost assigned to such rights should be written off as a loss. This can be supported on the theory that the issuance of stock by the corporation at less than current market price results in a dilution in the equities identified with original holdings. However, when changes in the market price of the stock make the exercise of rights unattractive to all investors and none of the rights can be sold, no dilution has occurred and any cost of rights reported separately should be returned to the investment account.

Stock Warrants   As noted previously, warrants may be sold in conjunction with other securities as a "sweetener" to make the purchase of the securities more attractive. For example, warrants to purchase shares of a corporation's common stock may be issued with bonds to encourage investors to purchase the bonds. A warrant has value when the exercise price is less than the market value, either present or potential, of the security that can be purchased with the warrants. Warrants issued with other securities may be detachable or nondetachable. **Detachable warrants** are similar to stock rights because they can be traded separately from the security with which they were originally issued. **Nondetachable warrants** cannot be separated from the security they were issued with.

As described in Chapter 15, the Accounting Principles Board in Opinion No. 14 recommended assigning part of the issuance price of debt securities to any detachable stock warrants and classifying it as part of owners' equity.[8] The value assigned to the warrant is determined by a procedure similar to that described for stock rights and is expressed in the following equation:

$$\text{Value assigned to warrants} = \text{Total issue price} \times \frac{\text{Market value of warrant}}{\text{Market value of security without warrant} + \text{Market value of warrant}}$$

Although Opinion No. 14 is directed only to warrants attached to debt, it appears logical to extend the conclusions of that Opinion to warrants attached to preferred stock. Thus, if a market value exists for the warrants at the issuance date, a separate equity account is credited with that portion of the issuance price assigned to the warrants. If the warrants are exercised, the value assigned to the common stock is the value allocated to the warrants plus the cash proceeds from the issuance of the common stock. If the warrants are allowed to expire, the value assigned to the warrants may be transferred to a permanent paid-in capital account.

Accounting for detachable warrants attached to a preferred stock issue

---

[8]*Opinions of the Accounting Principles Board, No. 14*, "Accounting for Convertible Debt and Debt Issued with Stock Purchase Warrants" (New York: American Institute of Certified Public Accountants, 1969), par. 16.

is illustrated as follows: assume the Stewart Co. sells 1,000 shares of $50 par preferred stock for $58 per share. As an incentive to purchase the stock, Stewart Co. gives the purchaser detachable warrants enabling holders to subscribe to 1,000 shares of $20 par common stock for $25 per share. The warrants expire after one year. Immediately following the issuance of the preferred stock, the warrants are selling at $3, and the fair market value of the preferred stock without the warrant attached is $57. The proceeds of $58,000 should be allocated by the Stewart Co. as follows:

$$\text{Value assigned to the warrants} = \$58,000 \times \frac{\$3}{\$57 + \$3} = \$2,900$$

A similar allocation would be made by the investor, and the warrants would subsequently be accounted for in the same manner as stock rights.

The entry on Stewart's books to record the sale of the preferred stock with detachable warrants is:

Cash	58,000	
Preferred Stock, $50 par		50,000
Paid-In Capital in Excess of Par—Preferred Stock		5,100
Common Stock Warrants		2,900

If the warrants are exercised, the entry to record the issuance of common stock would be:

Common Stock Warrants	2,900	
Cash	25,000	
Common Stock, $20 par		20,000
Paid-In Capital in Excess of Par—Common Stock		7,900

This entry would be the same regardless of the market price of the common stock at the issuance date.

If the warrants in the example were allowed to expire, the following entry would be made.

Common Stock Warrants	2,900	
Paid-In Capital from Expired Warrants		2,900

If warrants are nondetachable, the securities are considered inseparable, and no allocation is made to recognize the value of the warrant. The entire proceeds are assigned to the security to which the warrant is attached. Thus, for nondetachable warrants, the accounting treatment is similar to that for convertible securities, such as convertible bonds. Some accountants feel this inconsistency is not justified since the economic value of a warrant exists, even if the warrant cannot be traded separately or "detached." This is essentially the same argument made for recognizing the conversion feature of a convertible security. Notwithstanding this argument, a separate instrument does not exist for a nondetachable warrant, and current practice does not require a separate value to be assigned to these warrants.

**Stock Options Issued
to Employees**

Many corporations have adopted various types of stock option plans giving executives and other employees the opportunity to purchase stock in the employer company. Often these plans are intended as a form of compensation, especially when directed toward or restricted to key executives of a company. These plans are referred to as **compensatory plans**, as contrasted to **noncompensatory plans** that are offered to all full-time employees on an equal basis. Noncompensatory plans generally provide for the purchase of stock at a relatively small discount from the market price of the stock. For example, all employees of IBM Corporation are allowed to purchase IBM stock at a 15% discount.

No special accounting problems arise for noncompensatory stock option plans. Stock issued upon the exercise of the options is recorded normally, as an increase in common or preferred stock including any applicable paid-in capital in excess of par or stated value. The issue price is the amount of cash received, i.e., the exercise price.

The major accounting questions associated with compensatory plans include:

1. What amount of compensation expense, if any, should be recognized?
2. When should the compensation expense be recognized, i.e., what period should be charged with the cost?
3. What information should be disclosed relative to stock option plans?

Measuring Compensation Expense

For a number of years, the accounting standard in this area has been APB Opinion No. 25, "Accounting for Stock Issued to Employees."[9] Even though APB Opinion No. 25 has been generally accepted for some time, its guidelines have been questioned perhaps because of perceived inconsistencies in the treatment of various types of stock option plans. Consequently, this is a topic that has been on the FASB's agenda for some time. Even after several years of studying this complex issue, the FASB has been unable to agree on a conceptually valid and practical improvement to the current guidelines of APB Opinion No. 25. The FASB has now decided that the problems of measuring stock compensation cannot be separated from the broader problem of distinguishing between financial instruments that relate to liabilities and those that are a part of equity. Accordingly, the FASB will now consider accounting for stock compensation as a part of the broader agenda item to distinguish between debt and equity instruments.

One of the key issues regarding compensatory stock option plans concerns an appropriate **measurement date**, i.e., the date on which the value of stock options should be determined. Several possibilities exist: (1) the date of adoption of a plan (**plan date**); (2) the date an option is granted to a

---

[9]*Opinions of the Accounting Principles Board, No. 25*, "Accounting for Stock Issued to Employees" (New York: American Institute of Certified Public Accountants, 1972), par. 7.

specific individual grantee (**grant date**); (3) the date on which the grantee may first exercise an option (**exercisable date**); (4) the date the grantee actually exercises an option (**exercise date**); (5) the date the grantee disposes of the stock acquired (**disposal date**); or (6) when variable factors are involved, the date at which both the number of shares and the option price are first known. These dates are not necessarily mutually exclusive. In some cases, for example, the exercisable date may coincide with the exercise date.

The Accounting Principles Board defined the proper measurement date as the first date on which the following are both known: (1) the number of shares that an individual employee is entitled to receive, and (2) the option or exercise price, if any.[10] For "fixed plans," i.e., plans in which the number of shares and the exercise price are set at the date of grant, the measurement date is generally the date of grant. Plans with variable terms, however, normally use a later measurement date, often the exercisable or exercise date.

The amount of compensation expense to be recognized for a compensatory plan is the amount by which the market price of the stock at the measurement date exceeds the exercise price. Thus, an employer will recognize compensation expense only if the exercise price is less than the market price at the measurement date.

If compensation expense is to be recognized and the amount has been determined, the remaining accounting problem is determining when the compensation expense should be recognized. Generally, the compensation should be charged to the current and future periods in which the employees perform the services for which the options were granted. Past periods should not be adjusted. The grant may specify the period or periods during which the service is to be performed, or it may be inferred from the past patterns of grants or awards. When several periods of employment are involved before the stock is issued, the employer corporation should accrue compensation expense in each period involved. If the measurement date is later than the grant date, the compensation expense for each period prior to the measurement date must be estimated based on the quoted market price of the stock at the end of each period.[11]

As noted, the FASB is currently studying the issues surrounding accounting and reporting for stock option plans in the context of a broader financial reporting issue. As a result, accounting for these plans is in a state of uncertainty. This uncertainty is compounded by frequent changes in the tax laws, some of which make certain types of stock option plans less attractive as a form of compensation. At present, however, the accounting and reporting requirements for stock option plans are those in APB Opinion No. 25. These requirements are illustrated in the following sections. Fixed stock option plans are presented first, followed by variable plans.

[10]*Ibid.*, par. 10b.
[11]*Ibid.*, par. 13.

Recording Compensatory Stock Options—Fixed Plans

To illustrate accounting for compensatory stock options under a fixed plan, assume that on December 31, 1988, the board of directors of the Neff Co. authorized the grant of stock options to supplement the salaries of certain executives. The options permit the purchase of 10,000 shares of $10 par common stock at a price of $47.50. The market price of the stock at the grant date was $50. Options can be exercised beginning January 1, 1991, but only by executives that are still in the employ of the company; the options expire at the end of 1992. All options are exercised on December 31, 1991, when the $10 par common stock is quoted on the market at $60.

The value of the stock options at the date of the grant (compensation expense) is determined as follows:

Market value of common stock on December 31, 1988, 10,000 shares at $50	$500,000
Option price, 10,000 shares at $47.50	475.000
Value of stock options (compensation expense)	$ 25,000

The terms of the grant indicate that the options relate to services to be performed for the period from the grant date to the exercisable date, or for 1989 and 1990.

The following entries are made by the corporation to record the grant of the options, the annual accrual of option rights, and the exercise of the options.

Transaction	Entry		
December 31, 1988 Grant of compensatory stock options.	(Memorandum entry) Granted options to executives for the purchase of 10,000 shares of common stock at $47.50. Options are exercisable beginning January 1, 1991, providing officers are in the employ of the company on that date. Options expire on December 31, 1992. Value of options on December 31, 1988, is $25,000 (market value of stock, $500,000; option price, $475,000).		

December 31, 1989
To record compensation and stock option credit accrual for 1989. Value of stock options, $25,000; period of service covered by plan, 1989 and 1990; cost assigned to 1989: ½ × $25,000 = $12,500.
	Executive Compensation
	  Expense ....
	  Credit Under Stock Option
	    Plan ....
		12,500	12,500

December 31, 1990
To record compensation and stock option credit accrual for 1990: ½ × $25,000 = $12,500.
	Executive Compensation
	  Expense ....
	  Credit Under Stock Option
	    Plan ....
		12,500	12,500

December 31, 1991
To record exercise of stock options: cash received for stock, 10,000 shares at $47.50, or $475,000; par value of stock issued, 10,000 shares at $10, or $100,000.
	Cash ....
	Credit Under Stock Option Plan
	  Common Stock ....
	  Paid-In Capital in Excess of
	    Par ....
		475,000
		25,000
			100,000
			400,000

The accrued compensation reported in Credit Under Stock Option Plan is properly reported as a part of paid-in capital because it represents investments of services made by employees that are expected to be paid for by the issuance of capital stock at a reduced price. If options expire through a failure of employees to meet the conditions of the option or through changes in the price of the stock making exercise of options unattractive, the balance of the account should be eliminated by decreasing compensation expense in the period of forfeiture.[12]

Recording Compensatory Stock Options—Variable Plans

As noted previously, stock option plans with variable terms generally use the exercisable or exercise date as the measurement date instead of the grant date, since this is usually the earliest date that both the number of shares and the option price can be determined. This presents a problem in recording the compensation expense during the period between the grant date and the exercise date. FASB Interpretation No. 28 addressed this problem and requires the accrual of compensation expense for variable plans in the appropriate service periods.[13] The Interpretation indicates that changes in the market value, either up or down, between the grant date and the measurement date result in a change in the measurement of compensation associated with the options. If a quoted market price is not available, the best estimate of the market value should be used. A catch-up adjustment for the changes in values is to be reflected in the period when the change occurs and the new balance spread over current and future periods.

To illustrate, if the grant provisions offered by Neff Co. were variable and the measurement date occurred after the grant date, different entries would be required than those shown on page 719. Assume that on December 31, 1988, the executives of Neff Co. are given the right to purchase 10,000 shares of $10 par stock at 80% of the market price on December 31, 1990, two years after the grant date. December 31, 1990, is the measurement date in this case, since it is the earliest date that the option price is known. To be eligible for the stock, the executives must remain with the company until the exercisable date, December 31, 1991. The market price for the stock is as follows: December 31, 1988, date of grant, $50; December 31, 1989, end of first year of service period, $60; December 31, 1990, end of second year of service period, $65; and December 31, 1991, exercise date, $80.

The following entries and computations would be made to record the annual accruals of option rights and the exercise of the options for the variable stock option plan.

---

[12]*Ibid.*, par. 15.

[13]*FASB Interpretation No. 28*, "Accounting for Stock Appreciation Rights and Other Variable Stock Option or Award Plans" (Stamford: Financial Accounting Standards Board, 1978).

Transaction	Entry

December 31, 1989
To record estimate of compensation expense accrual for 1989, market price of stock, December 31, 1989, $60; estimated option price, 80% of $60, or $48; estimated value of option per share, $12 ($60 − $48); total compensation, $120,000 ($12 × 10,000). Period of services rendered, three years or $40,000 each year.
	Executive Compensation
	  Expense 40,000
	  Credit Under Stock
	    Option Plan.............. 40,000

December 31, 1990
To record estimate of compensation expense accrual for 1990; market price of stock, December 31, 1990, $65; estimated option price, 80% of $65, or $52; estimated value of option per share, $13 ($65 − $52); total compensation, $130,000 ($13 × 10,000). Compensation recognized 1989, $40,000. Compensation as adjusted for changes in market values, to be recognized in 1989, $46,667 = ($130,000 ÷ 3 = $43,333) plus $3,334 catch-up from 1989.
	Executive Compensation
	  Expense 46,667
	  Credit Under Stock
	    Option Plan.............. 46,667

December 31, 1991
To record compensation expense for 1991, as adjusted, and issuance of stock. (See computations above.)
	Executive Compensation
	  Expense 43,333
	  Credit Under Stock
	    Option Plan.............. 43,333
	
	Cash 520,000
	Credit Under Stock
	  Option Plan............... 130,000
	    Common Stock 100,000
	    Paid-In Capital in Excess
	      of Par 550,000

Computations:

			Compensation			Accrual of Expense by Year		
Date	Market Price	Per Share	Aggregate	Percentage Accrued	Accrued to Date	1989	1990	1991
12/31/89	$60	$12	$120,000	33⅓%	$ 40,000	$40,000		
					46,667		$46,667	
12/31/90	$65*	$13	$130,000	66⅔%	$ 86,667			
					43,333			$43,333
12/31/91	$65*	$13	$130,000	100%	$130,000			

*Measurement date value

It should be noted in the example that the compensation expense accrual of $46,667 recognizes the "catch-up" adjustment for changes in market value in 1990, which is in accordance with Interpretation No. 28. Recall that changes in accounting estimates are generally reflected in the current period or "spread" over current and future periods and that no cumulative effect or "catch-up" adjustment is required per APB Opinion No. 20. If the $10,000 change in estimate in the example had been spread only over the current and future periods, the compensation expense entry for 1990 and 1991 would have been $45,000 in each year ($130,000 −

$40,000 = $90,000; $90,000 ÷ 2 = $45,000). Because the example deals with a variable stock option plan and falls specifically under Interpretation No. 28, a catch-up adjustment must be made to the current period, that is, in the period when the change was first determined.

Disclosure of Stock Options

When stock option plans are in existence, disclosure should be made as to the status of the option or plan at the end of the reporting period, including the number of shares under option, the option (exercise) price, and the number of shares that were exercisable. Information on options exercised should also be provided, including the number of options exercised and the option price. Note Nine to the financial statements of General Mills, Inc., reproduced in Appendix A, provides an illustration of disclosures for stock options.

Stock Conversions

As noted earlier, stockholders may be permitted by the terms of their stock agreement or by special action of the corporation to exchange their holdings for stock of other classes. No gain or loss is recognized by the issuer on these conversions because it is an exchange of one form of equity for another. In certain instances, the exchanges may affect only corporate contributed capital accounts; in other instances, the exchanges may affect both capital and retained earnings accounts.

To illustrate the different conditions, assume that the capital of the Sorensen Corporation on December 31, 1991 is as follows:

Preferred stock, $100 par, 10,000 shares	$1,000,000
Paid-in capital in excess of par	100,000
Common stock, $25 stated value, 100,000 shares	2,500,000
Paid-in capital in excess of stated value	500,000
Retained earnings	1,000,000

Preferred shares are convertible into common shares at any time at the option of the shareholder.

Case 1   Converting One Share Preferred for Four Shares Common

Assume the terms of conversion permit the exchange of one share of preferred for 4 shares of common. On December 31, 1991, 1,000 shares of preferred stock are exchanged for 4,000 shares of common. The amount originally paid for the preferred, $110,000, is now the consideration identified with 4,000 shares of common stock with a total stated value of $100,000. The conversion is recorded by the issuer as follows:

Preferred Stock, $100 par	100,000	
Paid-In Capital in Excess of Par	10,000	
Common Stock, $25 Stated Value		100,000
Paid-In Capital in Excess of Stated Value		10,000

Case 2   Converting One Share Preferred for Five Shares Common

Assume terms of conversion permit the exchange of one share of preferred for 5 shares of common. In converting 1,000 shares of preferred for 5,000 shares of common, an increase in common stock of $125,000 must be recognized, although it is accompanied by a decrease in the preferred equity of only $110,000; the increase in the legal capital related to the issue of common stock is generally accomplished by a debit to Retained Earnings. The conversion on Sorensen's books, then, is recorded as follows:

Preferred Stock, $100 par	100,000	
Paid-In Capital in Excess of Par	10,000	
Retained Earnings	15,000	
Common Stock, $25 stated value		125,000

On the investor's books at the conversion date, an entry would be required to eliminate the cost of the investment in preferred stock and to establish the investment in common stock of Sorensen Corporation. The accounting issue here is similar to the one discussed for convertible bonds. That is, should a gain or loss be recognized on the conversion? If the transaction is viewed as a continuation of the previous investment, then it would be appropriate to record the investment in common stock at the same cost as the preferred stock investment. Since no additional cost has been incurred, this approach is consistent with the cost basis of accounting. Using Case 1 as an example, the entry on the investor's books would be:

Investment in Sorensen Corp. Common Stock	110,000	
Investment in Sorensen Corp. Preferred Stock		110,000

If, on the other hand, the transaction is viewed as a culminating event and if the market value of the common stock is known, then it would be appropriate to record the investment in the common stock at its current market price and recognize a gain or loss on the conversion. The gain or loss is the difference between the current market price of the common stock and the investment cost of the preferred stock. Assuming, for example, the situation for Case 2 and an objective market price of $24 per share for Sorensen Corp.'s common stock at the conversion date, the entry on the investor's books would be:

Investment in Sorensen Corp. Common Stock	120,000	
Investment in Sorensen Corp. Preferred Stock		110,000
Gain on Conversion		10,000

The problems relating to the conversion of bonds for capital stock were described in Chapter 15. When either stocks or bonds have conversion rights, the company must be in a position to issue securities of the required class. Unissued or reacquired securities may be maintained by the company for this purpose. Detailed information should be given on the balance sheet or in notes to the financial statements relative to security conversion features as well as the means for meeting conversion requirements.

Stock Splits and Reverse Stock Splits

When the market price of shares is relatively high and it is felt that a lower price will result in more active trading and a wider distribution of ownership, a corporation may authorize the shares outstanding to be replaced by a larger number of shares. For example, 100,000 shares of stock, par value $100, are exchanged for 500,000 shares of stock, par value $20. Each stockholder receives 5 new shares for each share owned. The increase in shares outstanding in this manner is known as a **stock split**. The reverse procedure, replacement of shares outstanding by a smaller number of shares, may be desirable when the price of shares is low and it is felt there may be certain advantages in having a higher price for shares. The reduction of shares outstanding by combining shares is referred to as a **reverse stock split**.

After a stock split or reverse stock split, the capital stock balance for the issue remains the same; however, the change in the number of shares of stock outstanding is accompanied by a change in the par or stated value of the stock. Similarly, the amount of recorded investment for the investor remains the same, but the number of shares and cost per share will be adjusted. The change in the number of shares outstanding, as well as the change in the par or stated value, may be recorded by means of a memorandum entry.

Stock splits are sometimes effected by issuing a large stock dividend. In this case, the par value of the stock is not changed, and an amount equal to the par value of the newly issued shares is transfered to the capital stock account from either additional paid-in capital or from retained earnings. A further discussion of this type of stock split is included in Chapter 17.

Balance Sheet Disclosure of Contributed Capital

Contributed capital and its components should be disclosed separately from Retained Earnings in the balance sheet. Within the contributed capital section, it is important to identify the major classes of stock and the additional paid-in capital. Although it is common practice to report a single amount for additional paid-in capital, separate accounts should be provided in the ledger to identify the individual sources of additional paid-in capital, e.g., paid-in capital in excess of par or stated value, paid-in capital from treasury stock, from forfeited stock subscriptions, or from donations by stockholders.

For each class of stock, a description of the major features should be disclosed, such as par or stated value, dividend preference, or conversion terms. The number of shares authorized, issued, and outstanding should also be disclosed. As an example, the stockholders' equity section and related notes for American Maize-Products Company is presented on page 726. The balance sheet and accompanying notes for General Mills, Inc. in Appendix A also illustrates many of these points.

Exhibit 16-1   American Maize-Products Company

	1987	1986
	in thousands	
Stockholders' equity		
Capital stock (Note 7):		
Common, Class A, $.80 par value; authorized 8,750,000 shares; issued 4,999,585 shares in 1987 and 3,969,455 shares in 1986	$ 4,000	$ 3,176
Common, Class B, $.80 par value; authorized 2,500,000 shares; issued 1,809,282 shares in 1987 and 1986 ..	1,447	1,447
Capital in excess of par value of common stock	39,849	22,506
Retained earnings.........................	110,277	100,801
	155,573	127,930
Less, Common stock in treasury, at cost; Class A, 158,159 shares in 1987 and 134,152 shares in 1986; Class B, 52,425 shares in 1987 and 50,925 shares in 1986 (Note 7)	2,045	1,587
Total stockholders' equity	153,528	126,343

NOTES TO CONSOLIDATED FINANCIAL STATEMENTS

7 (in part): Capital Stock

Class A and Class B Common Stock are identical in all respects except that voting power of the Class A Common Stock is limited to the election of 30% of the Board of Directors, to matters involving stock options and, under certain circumstances, to the acquisition of the stock or assets of another company. All other voting rights are vested in the Class B Common Stock (one vote per share) and the 7% cumulative preferred stock (45 votes per share).

The Company's authorized stock includes 2,500,000 shares of Series Preferred Stock, without par value. The voting rights, dividend rate, redemption price, rights of conversion, rights upon liquidation and other preferences are subject to determination by the Board of Directors. No Series Preferred Stock has been issued.

During 1987, 1986 and 1985 there were 6 shares of 7% cumulative preferred stock outstanding, with a par and liquidating value of $100 per share.

During 1987, the Company purchased a total of 35,800 shares of its Class A Common Stock and 1,500 shares of its Class B Common Stock at a cost of approximately $424,000. An additional 29,600 shares of its Class A Common Stock and 10,700 shares of its Class B Common Stock were purchased through February 29, 1988, at a cost of approximately $513,000.

Key Terms

Business combination 705	Pooling of interest 705
Common stock 694	Preferred stock 694
Compensatory plans 717	Proprietorship 693
Contributed (paid-in) capital 693	Purchase 705
Corporation 693	Redeemable preferred stock 699
Cumulative preferred stock 697	Stated value 696
Dividends in arrears 698	Stock options 712
Noncompensatory plans 717	Stock rights 712
Noncumulative preferred stock 698	Stock splits 724
Owners' equity 693	Stock warrants 712
Par value 696	Treasury stock 708
Partnership 693	

Questions

1. What are the basic rights inherent in the ownership of capital stock? What modifications of these basic rights are usually found in preferred stock?

2. What are the two major classifications of contributed capital?

3. Distinguish between cumulative preferred stock and noncumulative preferred stock. If a company with cumulative preferred stock outstanding fails to declare dividends during the year, what disclosure should be made in the financial statements?

4. What is callable preferred stock? Redeemable preferred stock? Convertible preferred stock?

5. The Merrill Co. treats proceeds from capital stock subscription defaults as miscellaneous revenue. (a) Would you approve of this practice? Explain. (b) What alternatives would the Merrill Co. have when dealing with subscription defaults? (c) What limits the choice between the alternatives in (b)?

6. Explain the accounting principle followed in recording the issuance of capital stock in exchange for nonmonetary assets or services.

7. Why might a company purchase its own stock?

8. The Daytime Co. reports treasury stock as a current asset, explaining that it intends to sell the stock soon to acquire working capital. Do you approve of this reporting?

9. (a) What is the basic difference between the cost method and the par value method of accounting for treasury stock? (b) How will total stockholders' equity differ, if at all, under the two methods?

10. There is frequently a difference between the purchase price and the selling price of treasury stock. Why isn't this difference properly shown as an income statement item, especially in view of accounting pronouncements that restrict entries to Retained Earnings?

11. (a) What entries should be made on both the issuer's books and the investor's books when stock rights are issued to stockholders? (b) What entries should be made by both issuer and investor when stock is issued on the exercise of rights? (c) What information, if any, should appear on the company's balance sheet relative to outstanding rights?

12. Distinguish between a compensatory stock option plan and a noncompensatory stock option plan.

13. What determines the measurement date for purposes of a stock option plan valuation?

14. Preferred stockholders of the Lexus Corporation exchange their holdings for no-par common stock in accordance with terms of the preferred stock issue. How should this conversion be reported on the corporation books?

15. The controller of Williams Company contends that the redemption of preferred stock at less than its issuance price should be reported as an increase in Retained Earnings, since redemption at more than issuance price calls for a decrease in Retained Earnings. How would you answer the controller's argument?

16. Define a stock split and identify the major objectives of this corporate action.

Discussion Cases

Case 16-1   (Should par value be used to determine the amount of contributed capital?)

The Raton Company, in payment for services, issues 5,000 shares of common stock to persons organizing and promoting the company and another 20,000 shares in exchange for properties believed to have valuable mineral rights. The par value of the stock, $10 per share, is used in recording the consideration for the shares. Shortly after organization, the company decides to sell the properties and use the proceeds for another venture. The properties are sold for $265,000. What accounting issues are involved? How would you record the sale of properties and why?

Case 16-2   (Is the sum of the parts worth more than the whole?)

The footnote on page 700 described a new securities package, called "Unbundled Stock Units." Essentially, an offer is being made by a few companies to exchange their common stock for three new securities: a long-term bond, preferred stock, and a stock warrant. Why might investors be willing to pay a premium for such a package, i.e., pay more for the three securities than for the single common stock security? What disadvantages can you see for investors in exchanging their common stock for the unbundled stock units?

Case 16-3   (Giving something for nothing)

Excerpts from an article appearing in the *Wall Street Journal* are presented as follows:

Dividend News

**IBM Holders Vote
4-for-1 Stock Split,
Effective May 10**

By a *Wall Street Journal* Staff Reporter

SAN DIEGO—International Business Machines Corp. shareholders, as expected, authorized a four-for-one split of the company's stock, effective May 10.

At a quiet annual meeting attended by an estimated 1,400 of the computer giant's more than 600,000 shareholders, the split was opposed by less than 1% of the votes cast.

The split which is expected to make IBM's shares more attractive to small investors, will increase the number of authorized shares to 650 million from 162.5 million. About 583 million shares are expected to be outstanding after the split.

IBM has made numerous stock distributions in recent years so that 100 shares from 1958 ballooned to 1,135 shares at the annual meeting, but the forthcoming split is the first distribution since 1958 that will result in a change in the par value of IBM's shares. The par value will be reduced to $1.25 a share, from $5.00.

Regarding the mechanics of the split, IBM said that current stock certificates will remain in effect. Each shareholder of record May 10 will receive new certificates representing three shares for each held. The new certificates will be mailed around May 31.

Why did IBM propose the 4-for-1 stock split and why were the stockholders not opposed to the split? What will the impact be on the owners' equity section of IBM's balance sheet?

Case 16-4   (Conversion of preferred stock)

Colter Corporation suspended dividend payments on all four classes of capital stock outstanding because of a downturn in the economy. The four classes of stock include: 7% preferred stock, cumulative, $50 par; 5% preferred stock, noncumulative, convertible, $35 par; 9% preferred stock, noncumulative, $80 par; and common stock. Fifteen thousand shares of each class of stock were outstanding. Dividends had been paid through 1988. Colter did not pay dividends in 1989 or 1990. In 1991, the economy improved and a proposal to pay a dividend of $1.50 per share of common stock was made.

You own 100 shares of the 5%, noncumulative, convertible preferred stock and have been thinking of converting those 100 shares to common stock at the existing conversion rate of 3 to 1 (3 shares of common for 1 share of preferred). The rate is scheduled drop to 2 to 1 at the end of 1991. Because the price of common stock has been rising rapidly, you are trying to decide between retaining your preferred stock or converting to common stock before the price goes higher and the ratio is lowered.

Assuming there is no conversion of preferred stock, how much cash does Colter need to pay the proposed dividend? What are the merits of converting your stock at this time as opposed to waiting until after the dividend is paid and the conversion ratio decreases. Explain the issues involved.

Exercises   Exercise 16-1   (Issuance of common stock)

The Verdero Company is authorized to issue 100,000 shares of $30 par value common stock. Verdero has the following transactions:

(a) Issued 20,000 shares at par value; received cash.
(b) Issued 250 shares to attorneys for services in securing the corporate charter and for preliminary legal costs of organizing the corporation. The value of the services was $9,000.
(c) Issued 300 shares, valued objectively at $10,000, to the corporate promoters.
(d) Issued 12,500 shares of stock in exchange for buildings valued at $295,000 and land valued at $80,000. (The building was originally acquired by the investor for $250,000 and has $100,000 of accumulated depreciation; the land was acquired for $30,000)
(e) Received cash for 6,500 shares of stock sold at $38 per share.
(f) Issued 8,000 shares at $45 per share; received cash.

(1) Record the above transactions in journal entry form for Verdero Company.
(2) Record the above transactions in journal entry form for the investors.

Exercise 16-2   (Par and stated values)

At the time of formation, the Buck Corporation was authorized to issue

100,000 shares of common stock. Buck later received cash from the issuance of 25,000 shares at $24.50 per share. Record the entries for the issuance of the common stock under each of the following assumptions. (Consider each assumption independently.)

(a) Stock has a par value of $22 per share.
(b) Stock has a stated value of $20 per share.
(c) Stock has no par or stated value.

Exercise 16-3 (Dividends per share; cumulative and noncumulative features)

The Anderson Company paid dividends at the end of each year as follows: 1989, $150,000; 1990, $240,000; 1991, $560,000. Determine the amount of dividends per share paid on common and preferred stock for each year, assuming independent capital structures as follows:

(a) 300,000 shares of no-par common; 10,000 shares of $100 par, 9% non-cumulative preferred.
(b) 250,000 shares of no-par common; 20,000 shares of $100 par, 9% non-cumulative preferred.
(c) 250,000 shares of no-par common; 20,000 shares of $100 par, 9% cumulative preferred.
(d) 250,000 shares of $10 par common; 30,000 shares of $100 par, 9% cumulative preferred.

Exercise 16-4 (Dividends—different classes of stock)

Blank Page Inc. began operations on June 30, 1990, and issued 40,000 shares of $10 par common stock on that date. On December 31, 1990, Blank Page declared and paid $25,600 in dividends. After a vote of the board of directors, Blank Page issued 24,000 shares of 6% cumulative, $12 par, preferred stock on January 1, 1992. On December 31, 1992, Blank Page declared and paid $15,500 in dividends and again on December 31, 1993, Blank Page declared and paid $28,660 in dividends.

Determine the amount of dividends to be distributed to each class of stock for each of Blank Page's dividend payments.

Exercise 16-5 (Computing liquidation amounts)

The stockholders' equity for the Baum Company on July 1, 1991, is given below.

Contributed capital:
Preferred stock, cumulative, $10 stated value, 37,000 shares outstanding,
  entitled upon involuntary liquidation to $12 per share plus dividends in
  arrears amounting to $4 per share on July 1, 1991 . . . . $370,000
Common stock, $2 stated value, 90,000 shares outstanding 180,000
Paid-in capital from sale of common stock at more than stated value 200,000
Retained earnings 56,000
Total stockholders' equity $806,000

Determine the amounts that would be paid to each class of stockholders if the company is liquidated on this date, assuming cash available for stockholders after meeting all of the creditors' claims is (a) $300,000; (b) $500,000; (c) $640,000.

Exercise 16-6   (Issuance of capital stock)

The Mountain View Company was incorporated on January 1, 1991, with the following authorized capitalization:

20,000 shares of common stock, stated value $50 per share.
5,000 shares of 7% cumulative preferred stock, par value $15 per share.

Give the entries required for each of the following transactions

(a) Issued 12,000 shares of common stock for a total of $672,000 and 3,000 shares of preferred stock at $20 per share.
(b) Subscriptions were received for 2,500 shares of common stock at a price of $52. A 30% down payment is received.
(c) One subscriber defaults for 300 shares of common and the down payment is retained pending sale of these shares.
(d) The 300 shares of common are sold at $51 per share. Loss on resale is charged against the account of the defaulting subscriber, and the down payment less the loss is returned to the subscriber.
(e) Collected the remaining amount owed on the stock subscriptions and issued the stock.
(f) The remaining authorized shares of common stock are sold at $57.50 per share.

Exercise 16-7   (Accounting for defaulted subscriptions)

On January 1, 1991, Leslie Corporation received authorization to issue 200,000 shares of common stock with a par value of $22 per share. The stock was offered at a subscription price of $40 per share, and subscriptions were received for 20,000 shares. Subscriptions were recorded by a debit to Common Stock Subscriptions Receivable and credits to Common Stock Subscribed and to a paid-in capital account. Subsequently, a subscriber who had contracted to purchase 1,500 shares defaulted after paying 40% of the subscription price. Identify four methods of accounting for the default, and give the journal entry to record the default under each method.

Exercise 16-8   (Acquisition and retirement of stock)

The Steinbeck Company reported the following balances related to common stock as of December 31, 1990:

Common Stock, $20 par, 100,000 shares issued and outstanding	$2,000,000
Paid-in capital in excess of par	100,000

The company purchased and immediately retired 5,000 shares at $26 on August 1, 1991, and 12,000 shares at $18 on December 31, 1991. Give the entries to record the acquisition and retirement of the common stock. (Assume all shares were originally sold at the same price.)

Exercise 16-9   (Treasury stock: par value and cost methods)

The stockholders' equity of the Thomas Company as of December 31, 1990, was as follows:

Common stock, $15 par, authorized 275,000 shares; issued and outstanding
   240,000 shares $3,600,000
Paid-in capital in excess of par   480,000
Retained earnings   900,000

On June 1, 1991, Thomas reacquired 15,000 shares of its common stock at $16. The following transactions occurred in 1991 with regard to these shares.

    July 1   Sold 5,000 shares at $20.
    Aug. 1   Sold 8,000 shares at $14.
    Sept. 1   Retired 1,000 shares.

(1) Using the *cost method* to account for treasury stock:
    (a) Prepare the journal entries to record all treasury stock transactions in 1991.
    (b) Prepare the stockholders' equity section of the balance sheet at December 31, 1991, assuming retained earnings of $1,005,000.
(2) Using the *par value method* to account for treasury stock:
    (a) Prepare the journal entries to record all treasury stock transactions in 1991.
    (b) Prepare the stockholders' equity section of the balance sheet at December 31, 1991, assuming retained earnings of $1,005,000.

Exercise 16-10   (Stock rights)

J. Matson bought 2,000 shares of Layton Mining Co. common stock for $15 per share on April 3, 1990. On June 22, 1991, Layton Mining Co. issued stock rights to its holders of common stock, one right for each share owned. The terms of the exercise required 4 rights plus $15 for each share purchased. Layton stock was selling ex-rights for $19 per share, and the rights have a market value of $1 each. On September 1, 1991, Matson exercised 1,000 rights, and on October 15, 1991, sold the remaining rights at $1.40 each. What entries would be required to reflect the stock rights transactions in Matson's accounting records?

Exercise 16-11   (Stock rights)

The Jordan Co. holds stock of Caltex Inc. acquired as follows:

	Shares	Total Cost
Lot A, 1989	75	$ 6,000
Lot B, 1990	125	11,000

In 1991, Jordan Co. receives 200 rights to purchase Caltex Inc. stock at $75 per share. The shares have a par value of $70. Five rights are required to purchase one share. At issue date, rights had a market value of $4 each and stock was selling ex-rights at $96. Jordan Co. used rights to purchase 30 additional shares of Caltex Inc. Subsequently, the market price of the stock fell to $92, and Jordan Co. allowed the unexercised rights to lapse. Both companies use the first-in, first-out method of identifying stock rights exercised.

(1) What entries are required to record the preceding events in Jordan's accounting records?
(2) What entries are required to record the preceding events in Caltex's accounting records?

Exercise 16-12   (Accounting for stock warrants)

The Western Company wants to raise additional equity capital. After analysis of the available options, the company decides to issue 1,000 shares of $20 par preferred stock with detachable warrants. The package of the stock and warrants sells for $90. The warrants enable the holder to purchase 1,000 shares of $25 par common stock at $30 per share. Immediately following the issuance of the stock, the stock warrants are selling at $9 per share. The market value of the preferred stock without the warrants is $85.

(1) Prepare a journal entry for Western Company to record the issuance of the preferred stock and the attached warrants.
(2) Assuming that all the warrants are exercised, prepare a journal entry for Western to record the exercise of the warrants.
(3) Assuming that only 80% of the warrants are exercised, prepare a journal entry for Western to record the exercise and expiration of the warrants.

Exercise 16-13   (Accounting for compensatory stock options)

The stockholders of the Johnson Co. on December 24, 1984, approved a plan granting certain officers of the company nontransferable options to buy 100,000 shares of no-par common stock at $32 per share. Stock was selling at this time at $40 per share. The option plan provides that the officers must be employed by the company for the next five years, that options can be exercised after January 1, 1990, and that options will expire at the end of 1991. One of the officers who had been granted options for 20,000 shares left the company at the beginning of 1988; remaining officers exercised their rights under the option plan at the end of 1991. Give the entries that should be made on the books of the corporation at the end of each year for 1984-1991 inclusive. The market price of the stock at January 1, 1990, was $60 per share.

Exercise 16-14   (Accounting for variable stock option plans)

On March 31, 1988, the Board of Directors of Allied Industries approved a stock option plan for its twenty executives to purchase 500 shares of $25 par common stock each. The plan further indicated that the twenty executives must remain with the company until March 31, 1991, at which time they could exercise their options. The exercise price is 90% of the market price of the stock on December 31, 1990. All outstanding options expire on December 31, 1992. Assuming the following stock prices and that all options are exercised on June 27, 1991, give the journal entries for the company for its calendar years 1988, 1989, 1990, and 1991.

Date	Stock Price
March 31, 1988	$30
December 31, 1988	35
December 31, 1989	45
December 31, 1990	42
March 31, 1991	45
June 27, 1991	46

Exercise 16-15   (Convertible preferred stock)

Stockholders' equity for the Damon Co. on December 31 was as follows:

Preferred stock, $15 par, 30,000 shares issued and outstanding	$ 450,000
Paid-in capital in excess of par—preferred stock	90,000
Common stock, $10 par, 150,000 shares issued and outstanding	1,500,000
Paid-in capital in excess of par—common stock	750,000
Retained earnings	1,450,000

Preferred stock is convertible into common stock.

(1) Give the entry made on Damon Co.'s books assuming 2,000 shares of preferred are converted under each assumption listed:
   (a) Preferred shares are convertible into common on a share-for-share basis.
   (b) Each share of preferred stock is convertible into 4 shares of common.
   (c) Each share of preferred stock is convertible into 1.5 shares of common.

(2) Assuming that all the preferred stock is converted into common stock under the conditions in 1a, 1b, and 1c above and that Stadium Inc. owns 45% of Damon Co.'s preferred stock, give the entry made on the books of Stadium Inc. given the following:
   (a) The stock conversion is recorded at the cost of the preferred stock.
   (b) The stock conversion is recorded at the current market price of the common stock. The common stock was selling at $21 per share on the date of conversion.
   (c) The stock conversion is recorded at the current market price of the common stock. The common stock was selling at $11 per share on the date of the conversion.

(Assume all of Damon Co.'s preferred shares were originally acquired by Stadium, Inc. at the same price.)

Exercise 16-16   (Analysis of owners' equity)

From the following information, reconstruct the journal entries that were made by the Rivers Corporation during 1991.

	December 31, 1991		December 31, 1990	
	Amount	Shares	Amount	Shares
Common stock	$175,000	7,000	$150,000	6,000
Paid-in capital in excess of par	54,250		36,000	
Paid-in capital from treasury stock	1,000	200	—	—
Retained earnings	76,500*	—	49,000	—
Treasury stock	15,000	300	—	—

*Includes net income for 1991 of $40,000. There were no dividends.

2,500 shares of common stock issued when the company was formed were purchased at the beginning of 1991 and were retired later in the year. The cost method is used to record treasury stock transactions.

Problems

Problem 16-1   (Journalizing stock transactions)

Vicars Company began operations on January 1. 20,000 shares of $10 par value common stock and 4,000 shares of $100 par value convertible preferred stock were authorized. The following transactions involving stockholders' equity occurred during the first year of operations:

Jan. 1 Issued 500 shares of common stock to the corporation promoters in exchange for property valued at $17,000 and services valued at $6,000. The property had cost the promoters' $9,000 three years before and was carried on the promoters' books at $5,000.

Feb. 23 Issued 1,000 shares of convertible preferred stock with a par value of $100 per share. Each share can be converted to 5 shares of common stock. The stock was issued at a price of $150 per share, and the company paid $6,000 to an agent for selling the shares.

Mar. 10 Sold 3,000 shares of the common stock for $39 per share. Issue costs were $2,500.

Apr. 10 4,000 shares of common stock were sold under stock subscriptions at $45 per share. No shares are issued until a subscription contract is paid in full. No cash was received.

July 14 Exchanged 700 shares of common stock and 140 shares of preferred stock for a building with a fair market value of $51,000. The building was originally purchased for $38,000 by the investors and has a book value of $22,000. In addition, 600 shares of common stock were sold for $24,000 in cash.

Aug. 3 Received payments in full for half of the stock subscriptions and payments on account on the rest of the subscriptions. Total cash received was $140,000. Shares of stock were issued for the subscriptions paid in full.

Sept. 28 Received 10 acres of land from a wealthy stockholder to be used for construction of a new factory. Total cost for Vicars was legal fees of $4,000, but the estimated fair market value of the land was $75,000. The cost of the land to the stockholder was $25,000.

Dec. 1 Declared a cash dividend of $10 per share on preferred stock, payable on December 31 to stockholders of record on December 15, and a $2 per share cash dividend on common stock, payable on January 5 of the following year to stockholders of record on December 15. (No dividends are paid on unissued subscribed stock.)

Dec. 31 Received notice from holders of stock subscriptions for 800 shares that they would not pay further on the subscriptions since the price of the stock had fallen to $25 per share. The amount still due on those contracts was $30,000. Amounts previously paid on the contracts are forfeited according to the agreements.

Net income for the first year of operations was $60,000.

Instructions:

(1) Prepare journal entries to record the preceding transactions on Vicars' books.
(2) Prepare the stockholders' equity section of the balance sheet at December 31 for Vicars.

Problem 16-2   (Stockholders' equity transactions and balance sheet presentation)

The Pacific Basin Corporation was organized on September 1, 1991, with authorized capital stock of 200,000 shares of 9% cumulative preferred with a $40 par value and 1,000,000 shares of no-par common stock with a $30 stated value. During the balance of the year, the following transactions relating to capital stock were completed:

Oct.   1   Subscriptions were received for 300,000 shares of common stock at $42, payable $22 down and the balance in two equal installments due November 1 and December 1. On the same date 16,500 shares of common stock were issued to Jim Williams in exchange for his business. Assets transferred to the corporation were valued as follows: land, $210,000; buildings, $250,000; equipment, $50,000; merchandise, $110,000. Liabilities of the business assumed by the corporation were: mortgage payable, $41,000; accounts payable, $11,000; accrued interest on mortgage, $550. No goodwill is recognized in recording the issuance of the stock for net assets.

Oct.   3   Subscriptions were received for 120,000 shares of preferred stock at $45, payable $15 down and the balance in two equal installments due November 1, and December 1.

Nov. 1   Amounts due on this date were collected from all common and preferred stock subscribers.

Nov. 12   Subscriptions were received for 480,000 shares of common stock at $44, payable $22 down and the balance in two equal installments due December 1, and January 1.

Dec.   1   Amounts due on this date were collected from all common stock subscribers and stock fully paid for was issued. The final installment on preferred stock subscriptions was received from all subscribers except one whose installment due on this date was $9,000. State corporation laws provide that the company is liable for the return to the subscriber of the amount received less the loss on the subsequent resale of the stock. Preferred stock fully paid for was issued.

Dec.   6   Preferred stock defaulted on December 1 was issued for cash at $36. Stock was issued, and settlement was made with the defaulting subscriber.

Instructions:

(1) Prepare journal entries to record the foregoing transactions.
(2) Prepare the contributed capital section of stockholders' equity for the corporation as of December 31.

Problem 16-3   (Reconstruction of equity transactions)

The Fairfield Company had the following account balances on its balance sheet at December 31, 1991, the end of its first year of operations. All stock was issued on a subscription basis, and the state laws permit the company to retain all partial subscriptions paid by defaulting subscribers.

Common Stock Subscriptions Receivable	$150,000
Common Stock, $25 par	75,000
Common Stock Subscribed	225,000
Paid-In Capital in Excess of Par—Common Stock	40,000
8% Preferred Stock, $100 par	100,000
Paid-In Capital in Excess of Par—8% Preferred Stock	50,000
Paid-In Capital from Default on 8% Preferred Stock Subscriptions (200 Shares)	10,000
10% Preferred Stock, $50 par	25,000
Retained Earnings	20,000

The reported net income for 1991 was $55,000.

Instructions: From the data given, reconstruct in summary form the journal entries to record all transactions involving the company's stockholders. Indicate the amount of dividends distributed on each class of stock.

III Problem 16-4   (Comprehensive analysis and reporting of stockholders' equity)

The Gastino Company has two classes of capital stock outstanding: 9%, $20 par preferred and $70 par common. During the fiscal year ending November 30, 1991, the company was active in transactions affecting the stockholders' equity. The following summarizes these transactions:

Type of Transaction	Number of Shares	Price per Share
(a) Issue of preferred stock	10,000	$28
(b) Issue of common stock	35,000	70
(c) Reacquisition and retirement of preferred stock	2,000	30
(d) Purchase of treasury stock—common (reported at cost)	5,000	80
(e) Stock split—common (par value reduced to $35)	2 for 1	
(f) Reissue of treasury stock—common	5,000	52

Balances of the accounts in the stockholders' equity section of the November 30, 1990, balance sheet were:

Preferred Stock, 50,000 shares	$1,000,000
Common Stock, 100,000 shares	7,000,000
Paid-In Capital in Excess of Par—Preferred	400,000
Paid-In Capital in Excess of Par—Common	1,200,000
Retained Earnings	550,000

Dividends were paid at the end of the fiscal year on the common stock at $1.20 per share, and on the preferred stock at the preferred rate. Net income for the year was $850,000.

Instructions: Based on the preceding data, prepare the stockholders' equity section of the balance sheet as of November 30, 1991. (Note: A work sheet beginning with November 30, 1990 balances and providing for transactions for the current year will facilitate the preparation of this section of the balance sheet.)

Problem 16-5   (Accounting for various capital stock transactions)

The stockholders' equity section of Hastings Inc. showed the following data on December 31, 1990: common stock, $30 par, 300,000 shares authorized, 250,000 shares issued and outstanding, $7,500,000; paid in capital on common stock, $300,000; credit under stock option plan, $150,000; retained earnings, $480,000. The stock options were granted to key executives and provided them the right to acquire 30,000 shares of common stock at $35 per share. The stock was selling at $40 at the time the options were granted.

The following transactions occurred during 1991:

Mar. 31   4,500 options outstanding at December 31, 1990 were exercised. The market price per share was $44 at this time.

Apr. 1   The company issued bonds of $2,000,000 at par, giving each $1,000 bond a detachable warrant enabling the holder to purchase 2 shares of stock at $40 for a 1-year period. Market values immediately following issuance of the bonds were: $4 per warrant and $998 per $1,000 bond without the warrant.

June 30   The company issued rights to stockholders (1 right on each share, exercisable within a 30-day period) permitting holders to acquire 1 share at $40 with every 10 rights submitted. Shares were selling for $43 at this time. All but 6,000 rights were exercised on July 31, and the additional stock was issued.

Sept.30   All warrants issued with the bonds on April 1 were exercised.

Nov. 30   The market price per share dropped to $33 and options came due. Since the market price was below the option price, no remaining options were exercised.

Instructions:

(1) Give entries to record the foregoing transactions.

(2) Prepare the stockholders' equity section of the balance sheet as of December 31, 1991, (assume net income of $210,000 for 1991).

Problem 16-6   (Accounting for various capital stock transactions)

Pineview Co., organized on June 1, 1990, was authorized to issue stock as follows:

> 80,000 shares of preferred 9% stock, convertible, $100 par
> 250,000 shares of common stock, $25 stated value

During the remainder of the Pineview Co.'s fiscal year ending May 31, 1991 the following transactions were completed in the order given.

(a) 30,000 shares of preferred stock were subscribed for at $105 and 80,000 shares of the common stock were subscribed for at $26. Both subscriptions were payable 30% upon subscription, the balance in one payment.

(b) The second subscription payment was received, except one subscriber for 6,000 shares of common stock defaulted on payment. The full amount paid by this subscriber was returned, and all of the fully paid stock was issued.

(c) 15,000 shares of common stock were reacquired by purchase at $18. (Treasury stock is recorded at cost.)

(d) Each share of preferred stock was converted into 4 shares of common stock.

(e) The treasury stock was exchanged for machinery with a fair market value of $280,000.

(f) There was a 2:1 stock split and the stated value of the new common stock is $12.50.

(g) A major stockholder donated 100,000 shares of common stock to the company when the market value was $20 per share.

(h) Net income was $83,000.

Instructions:

(1) Give the journal entries to record the foregoing transactions. (For net income, give the entry to close the income summary account to Retained Earnings.)

(2) Prepare the stockholders' equity section as of May 31, 1991.

Problem 16-7   (Issuance, reacquisition, and resale of capital stock)

Tucker Company had the following transactions occur during 1991:

(a) 8,000 shares of common stock were issued to the founders for land valued at $450,000. Par value of the common stock is $30 per share.

(b) 5,000 shares of $100 par preferred stock were issued for cash at $110.

(c) 1,000 shares of common stock were sold to the company president for $60 per share.

(d) 400 shares of outstanding preferred stock (issued in (b)) were purchased for cash at par.

(e) 500 shares of the outstanding common stock issued in (a) were purchased for $55 per share.

(f) 150 shares of repurchased preferred stock were reissued at 102.

(g) 300 shares of reacquired common stock were reissued for $58 per share.

(h) 100 shares of the common stock sold in (g) were repurchased for $53 per share. These same 100 shares were later reissued for $50 per share.

Instructions:

(1) Prepare the necessary entries to record the preceding transactions involving Tucker preferred stock. Assume that the par value method is used for recording treasury stock.

(2) Prepare the necessary entries for the common stock transactions assuming that the cost method is used for recording treasury stock.

Problem 16-8   (Treasury stock transactions)

Transactions which affected Freeland Company's stockholders' equity during 1991, the first year of operations, are given below:

(a) Issued 30,000 shares of 9% preferred stock, $20 par, at $26.

(b) Issued 50,000 shares of $30 par common stock at $33.
(c) Purchased and immediately retired 4,000 shares of preferred stock at $28.
(d) Purchased 6,000 shares of its own common stock at $35.
(e) Reissued 1,000 shares of treasury stock at $37.
(f) Stockholders donated to the company 4,000 shares of common when shares had a market price of $36. One half of these shares were sold for $38.

No dividends were declared in 1991 and net income for 1991 was $185,000.

Instructions:

(1) Record each of the transactions. Assume treasury stock acquisitions are recorded at cost.
(2) Prepare the stockholders' equity section of the balance sheet at December 31, 1991.

Problem 16-9   (Accounting for stock options)

The board of directors of the Crisex Company adopted a stock option plan to supplement the salaries of certain executives of the company. Options to buy common stock were granted as follows:

		Number of Shares	Option Price	Price of Shares at Date of Grant
Jan. 10, 1988	Q. L. Peck	75,000	$20	$21
June 30, 1988	A. G. Byrd	50,000	25	26
June 30, 1988	K. C. Nelson	20,000	25	26

Options are nontransferable and can be exercised 3 years after date of grant providing the executive is still in the employ of the company. Options expire 2 years after the date they can first be exercised.

Nelson left the employ of the company at the beginning of 1990.
Stock options were exercised as follows:

		Number of Shares	Price of Shares at Date of Exercise
Jan. 15, 1991	Q. L. Peck	60,000	$45
Dec. 20, 1991	Q. L. Peck	15,000	36
Dec. 22, 1991	A. G. Byrd	50,000	32

Stock of the company has a $14 par value. The accounting period for the company is the calendar year.

Instructions: Give all entries that would be made on the books of the company relative to the stock option agreement for the period 1988 to 1991 inclusive.

Problem 16-10   (Variable stock options)

The Diablo Manufacturing Company adopted an executive stock option plan on January 1, 1988. The plan states that all executives remaining with the firm until the exercisable date would be eligible for the stock. The options are exercisable beginning January 1, 1991, and will expire on December 31, 1991. The option price is to be 75% of the market price on January 1, 1990. The stock price on December 31, 1988, was $90 and on December 31, 1990, was $120. The following information was given for 1991:

Change in common stock (par $30) from options exercised	$180,000
Change in paid-in capital on common stock from options exercised	450,000
Balance remaining in Credit Under Stock Option Plan	78,750

Instructions:

(1) Compute the following:
   (a) The stock price at January 1, 1990 (b) cash received on options exercised, (c) the total number of shares optioned to the executives, and (d) the executive compensation expense for 1988, 1989, and 1990.
(2) Give the journal entries for 1991.

Problem 16-11   (Analysis of stock transactions)

You have been asked to audit the Greystone Company. During the course of your audit, you are asked to prepare comparative data from the company's inception to the present. You have determined the following:

(a) Greystone Company's charter became effective on January 2, 1987, when 2,000 shares of no-par common and 1,000 shares of 7% cumulative, nonparticipating, preferred stock were issued. The no-par common stock had no stated value and was sold at $120 per share, and the preferred stock was sold at its par value of $100 per share.

(b) Greystone was unable to pay preferred dividends at the end of its first year. The owners of the preferred stock agreed to accept 2 shares of common stock for every 50 shares of preferred stock owned in discharge of the preferred dividends due on December 31, 1987. The shares were issued on January 2, 1988. The fair market value was $100 per share for common on the date of issue.

(c) Greystone Company acquired all of the outstanding stock of Booth Corporation on May 1, 1989, in exchange for 1,000 shares of Greystone common stock.

(d) Greystone split its common stock 3 for 2 on January 1, 1990, and 2 for 1 on January 1, 1991.

(e) Greystone offered to convert 20% of the preferred stock to common stock on the basis of 2 shares of common for 1 share of preferred. The offer was accepted, and the conversion was made on July 1, 1991.

(f) No cash dividends were declared on common stock until December 31, 1989. Cash dividends per share of common stock were declared as follows:

	June 30	Dec 31
1989		$3.19
1990	$1.75	2.75
1991	1.25	1.25

Instructions: Prepare schedules that show the computation of:

(1) The number of shares of each class of stock outstanding on the last day of each year from 1987 through 1991.
(2) Total cash dividends applicable to common stock for each year from 1989 through 1991.   (AICPA adapted)

Problem 16-12   (Auditing stockholders' equity)

You have been assigned to the audit of Belcore Inc., a manufacturing company. You have been asked to summarize the transactions for the year ended December 31, 1991, affecting stockholders' equity and other related accounts. The stockholders' equity section of Belcore's December 31, 1990, balance sheet follows:

Stockholders' Equity

Contributed capital:	
Common stock, $20 par value, 500,000 shares authorized, 90,000 shares issued	$1,800,000
Paid-in capital from treasury stock	22,500
Paid-in capital in excess of par	200,000
Total contributed capital	$2,022,500
Retained earnings	324,689
Total contributed capital and retained earnings	$2,347,189
Less cost of 1,210 shares of treasury stock	72,600
Total stockholders' equity	$2,274,589

You have extracted the following information from the accounting records and audit working papers.

1991

Jan. 15   Six hundred fifty shares of treasury stock were reissued for $40 per share. The 1,210 shares of treasury stock on hand at December 31, 1990, were purchased in one block in 1990. Belcore used the cost method for recording the treasury shares purchased.

Feb.   2   Ninety, $1,000, 9% bonds due February 1, 1994, were sold at 103 with one detachable stock purchase warrant attached to each bond. Interest is payable annually on February 1. The fair market value of the bonds without the stock warrants is 97. The detached warrants have a fair value of $60 each and expire on February 1, 1992. Each warrant entitles the holder to purchase 10 shares of common stock at $40 per share.

Mar.   6   Subscriptions for 1,400 shares of common stock were issued at $44 per share, payable 40% down and the balance by March 20.

Mar. 20   The balance due on 1,200 shares was received and those shares were issued. The subscriber who defaulted on the 200 remaining shares forfeited the down payment in accordance with the subscription agreement.

Nov.   1   Fifty-five stock warrants detached from the bonds were exercised.

Instructions: Give journal entries required to summarize the above transactions.
                                                    (AICPA adapted)

Chapter 17

Owners' Equity— Retained Earnings

Chapter Topics

Factors Affecting Retained Earnings

Prior Period Adjustments

Restrictions on Retained Earnings

Accounting for Dividends

Stock Dividends vs. Stock Splits

Quasi-Reorganizations

Reporting Stockholders' Equity

In the previous chapter, **owners' equity** was defined as the residual ownership interest in the net assets (total assets minus total liabilities) of a business. Owners' equity was further classified into that portion of capital that is contributed by owners and the amount of earnings generated and retained by the enterprise. Chapter 16 discussed the accounting issues associated with contributed capital; the purpose of this chapter is to identify and explain the different types of transactions and events that directly affect retained earnings.

The nature of retained earnings is frequently misunderstood, and this misunderstanding may lead to incorrect impressions in reading and interpreting financial statements. The retained earnings account is essentially the meeting place of the balance sheet accounts and the income statement accounts. In successive periods, retained earnings are increased by income and decreased by losses and dividends. As a result, the retained earnings balance represents the net accumulated earnings of a corporation. If the retained earnings account were affected *only* by income (losses) and dividends, there would be little confusion in its interpretation. A number of other factors, however, can affect retained earnings.

Factors Affecting Retained Earnings

In addition to earnings or losses and dividends, factors that affect retained earnings include: prior period adjustments for corrections of errors, quasi-reorganizations, and treasury stock transactions (discussed in Chapter 16). The transactions and events that increase or decrease retained earnings may be summarized as follows:

Retained Earnings

Decreases	Increases
Prior period adjustments for overstatements of past earnings	Prior period adjustments for understatements of past earnings
Current net loss	Current net income
Dividends	Quasi-reorganizations
Treasury stock transactions	

Prior Period Adjustments

In some situations, errors made in past years are discovered and corrected in the current year by an adjustment to the retained earnings account, referred to as a prior period adjustment. There are several types of errors that may occur in measuring the results of operations and the financial status of an enterprise. Accounting errors can result from mathematical mistakes, a failure to apply appropriate accounting procedures, or a misstatement or omission of certain information. In addition, a change from an accounting principle that is not generally accepted to one that is accepted is considered a correction of an error.[1]

Fortunately, most errors are discovered during the accounting period, prior to closing the books. When this is the case, corrections can be made by adjusting entries directly to the accounts. The corrected balances are then shown on the balance sheet and on the income statement.

Sometimes errors go undetected during the current period, but they are offset by an equal misstatement in the subsequent period; that is, they are **counterbalanced**. When this happens, the under- or overstatement of income in one period is counterbalanced by an equal over- or understatement of income in the next period, and after the closing process is completed for the second year, the retained earnings account is correctly stated. If a counterbalancing error is discovered during the second year, however, it should be corrected at that time.

When errors of past periods are not counterbalancing, retained earnings will be misstated until a correction is made in the accounting records. If the error is material, a prior period adjustment should be made directly to the retained earnings account.[2] If an error resulted in an understatement of income in previous periods, a correcting entry would be needed to increase retained earnings; if an error overstated income in prior periods, then retained earnings would have to be decreased. These adjustments for corrections in net income of prior periods would typically be shown as a part of the total change in retained earnings as follows:

Retained Earnings, unadjusted beginning balance	$xxx
Add or deduct prior period adjustments	xx
Retained Earnings, adjusted beginning balance	$xxx
Add current year's net income or deduct current year's net loss	xx
	$xxx
Deduct dividends	xx
Retained Earnings, ending balance	$xxx

When errors are discovered, the accountant must be able to analyze the situation and determine what action is appropriate under the circumstances. This calls for an understanding of accounting standards as well as

---

[1]*Opinions of the Accounting Principles Board, No. 20,* "Accounting Changes" (New York: American Institute of Certified Public Accountants, 1971) par. 13.

[2]*Ibid.,* par. 36.

good judgment. Chapter 23 covers in detail the techniques for analyzing and correcting errors.

Earnings

The primary source of retained earnings is the net income generated by a business. The retained earnings account is increased by net income and is reduced by net losses from business activities. When operating losses or other debits to Retained Earnings produce a debit balance in this account, the debit balance is referred to as a **deficit**.

Corporate earnings originate from transactions with individuals or businesses outside the company. No earnings are recognized for the construction of buildings or other plant assets for a company's own use, even though the cost of such construction is below the market price for similar assets; self-construction at less than the asset purchase price is regarded simply as a savings in cost. No increases in retained earnings are recognized from transactions with stockholders involving treasury stock; however, as indicated in Chapter 16, decreases may be recognized. The receipt of assets through donation is not recognized as earnings, but as paid-in capital. The earnings of a corporation may be distributed to the stockholders or retained to provide for expanding operations.

Dividends

Dividends are distributions to the stockholders of a corporation in proportion to the number of shares held by the respective owners. Distributions may take the form of (1) cash, (2) other assets, (3) notes or other evidence of corporate indebtedness, in effect, deferred cash dividends, and (4) stock dividends, i.e., shares of a company's own stock. Most dividends involve reductions in retained earnings. Exceptions include (1) some stock dividends issued in the form of stock splits, which involve a transfer from additional paid-in capital to legal capital, and (2) dividends in corporate liquidation, which represent a return to stockholders of a portion or all of their investment and call for reductions in contributed capital.

Use of the term *dividend* without qualification normally implies the distribution of cash. Dividends in a form other than cash, such as property or stock dividends, should be designated by their special form. Distributions from a capital source other than retained earnings should carry a description of their special origin, e.g., *liquidating dividend* or *dividend distribution of paid-in capital*.

"Dividends paid out of retained earnings" is an expression frequently encountered. Accuracy, however, requires recognition that dividends are paid out of cash, which serves to reduce retained earnings. Earnings of the corporation increase net assets or stockholders' equity. Dividend distributions represent no more than asset withdrawals that reduce net assets. The nature and types of dividends are covered in depth later in the chapter.

Other Changes in Retained Earnings

The most common changes in retained earnings result from earnings (or losses) and dividends. Other changes may occur, however, resulting from treasury stock transactions or from a quasi-reorganization, which is effected only under special circumstances in which a business seeks a "fresh start."

The remainder of this chapter focuses on accounting for dividends, followed by a discussion of quasi-reorganizations.

Accounting For Dividends

Among the powers delegated by the stockholders to the board of directors is the power to control the dividend policy. Whether dividends shall or shall not be paid, as well as the nature and the amount of dividends, are matters that the board determines. In setting dividend policy, the board of directors must answer two questions:

1. Do we have the legal right to declare a dividend?
2. Is a dividend distribution financially advisable?

In answering the first question, the board of directors must observe the legal requirements governing the maintenance of legal capital. The laws of different states range from those making any part of capital other than legal capital available for dividends to those permitting dividends only to the extent of retained earnings and under specified conditions. In most states dividends cannot be declared in the event of a deficit; in a few states, however, dividends equal to current earnings may be distributed despite a previously accumulated deficit. The availability of capital as a basis for dividends is a determination to be made by the legal counsel and not by the accountant. The accountant must report accurately the sources of each capital increase or decrease; the legal counsel investigates the availability of such sources as bases for dividend distributions.

The board of directors must also consider the second question, i.e., the financial aspect of dividend distributions. The company's cash position relative to present and future cash requirements is a key factor. For example, a corporation may have retained earnings of $500,000. If it has cash of only $150,000, however, cash dividends must be limited to this amount unless it converts certain assets into cash or borrows cash. If the cash required for regular operations is $100,000, the cash available for dividends is then only $50,000. Although legally able to declare dividends of $500,000, the company would be able to distribute no more than one tenth of that amount at this time. Generally, companies pay dividends that are significantly less than the legal amount allowed or the amount of cash on hand.

When a dividend is legally declared and announced, it cannot be revoked. In the event of corporate insolvency after a dividend declaration but prior to payment of the dividend, stockholders have claims as a creditor group to the dividend, and as an ownership group to any assets remaining after all corporate liabilities have been paid. A dividend that was illegally declared, however, is revocable; in the event of insolvency at the time of declaration, such action is nullified and stockholders participate in asset distributions only after creditors have been paid in full.

Restrictions on Retained Earnings

Although state laws generally permit the distribution of dividends to the extent of retained earnings, other factors may limit the amount of dividends that can be declared. For example, a portion of retained earnings may be restricted as a result of contractual requirements, such as an agreement with creditors that provides for the retention of earnings to ensure repayment of debt at maturity. Retained earnings may also be restricted at the discretion of the board of directors. For example, the board may designate a portion of retained earnings as restricted for a particular purpose, such as expansion of plant facilities.

If restrictions on retained earnings are material, they are generally disclosed in a note to the financial statements. Sometimes, however, the restricted portion of retained earnings is reported on the balance sheet separately from the unrestricted amount that is available for dividends. The restricted portion may be designated as **appropriated retained earnings** and the unrestricted portion as **unappropriated (or free) retained earnings**. When the restrictions are recognized in the accounts, the entry is a debit to the regular retained earnings account and a credit to a special appropriated retained earnings account.

As an example, assume Silverstein Company restricted $100,000 of its $600,000 retained earnings balance for possible plant expansion by making the following entry on January 1, 1991.

Jan. 1, 1991	Retained Earnings..........................	100,000	
	Appropriated Retained Earnings		100,000
	To restrict retained earnings for possible plant expansion.		

The balance sheet subsequent to this entry would reflect both retained earnings accounts.

Appropriated retained earnings	$100,000
Unappropriated retained earnings	500,000
Total retained earnings	$600,000

Once the purpose of the appropriation has been served, the original entry creating the appropriated retained earnings balance is reversed. To illustrate, assume that on June 15, the Silverstein Company decided not to expand its plant and to eliminate the appropriated retained earnings balance. The applicable entry would be

Appropriated Retained Earnings	100,000	
Retained Earnings..................................		100,000
To discontinue the appropriation of retained earnings for plant expansion.		

Note that there is no segregation of funds and no gain or loss involved in the restriction of retained earnings. Whatever the form of disclosure, the main idea behind restrictions on retained earnings is to alert stockholders that some of the assets that might otherwise be available for dividend distribution are being retained within the business for specific purposes. Because the amount of dividends actually paid is usually much less than the retained earnings balance, this is generally not a significant issue.

Recognition and Payment of Dividends

Three dates are essential in the recognition and payment of dividends: (1) date of declaration, (2) date of record, and (3) date of payment. Dividends are made payable to stockholders of record as of a date following the date of declaration and preceding the date of payment. The liability for dividends payable is recorded on the declaration date and is canceled on the payment date. No entry is required on the record date, but a list of the stockholders is made as of the close of business on this date. These are the persons who receive dividends on the payment date. For example, on January 13, 1989, Ford Motor Co. declared a cash dividend payable on March 1 to stockholders of record on January 30.

Stockholders become aware of a forthcoming dividend upon its declaration and announcement. If stock is sold and a new owner is recognized by the corporation prior to the record date, the dividend is paid to the new owner. If a stock transfer is not recognized by the corporation until after the record date, the dividend will be paid to the former owner, i.e., the shareholder of record. After the record date, stock no longer carries a right to dividends and sells at a lower price or ex-dividend.[3] Accordingly, a stockholder is justified in recognizing the corporate dividend action on the record date by debiting a receivable and crediting Dividend Revenue. Upon receipt of the dividend, Cash is debited and the receivable is eliminated. In practice, however, the accrual is frequently omitted, and dividend revenue is recognized when the cash is received.

Cash Dividends

The most common type of dividend is a cash dividend. For the corporation, these dividends involve a reduction in retained earnings and in cash. For the investor, a cash dividend generates cash and is recognized as dividend revenue. Entries to record the declaration and payment of a $100,000 cash dividend by a corporation follow:

Declaration of Dividend

Dividends (or Retained Earnings)	100,000	
Dividends Payable		100,000

Payment of Dividend

Dividends Payable	100,000	
Cash		100,000

[3]Stock on the New York Stock Exchange is normally quoted ex-dividend (or ex-rights) four full trading days prior to the record date because of the time required to deliver the stock and to record the stock transfers.

An investor owning five percent of the outstanding stock would record the dividend as follows:

<u>Receipt of Dividend</u>

Cash	5,000	
Dividend Revenue......................................		5,000

Computation:
$100,000 (total dividends) × .05 (investor's share) = $5,000

As noted previously, the investor could recognize dividend revenue and the corresponding receivable at the date of record. In practice, however, investors typically recognize dividend revenue at the time of receipt.

Property Dividends A distribution to stockholders that is payable in some asset other than cash is generally referred to as a **property dividend**. Frequently the assets to be distributed are securities of other companies owned by the corporation. The corporation thus transfers to its stockholders its ownership interest in such securities. Property dividends occur most frequently in closely held corporations.

This type of transfer is sometimes referred to as a **nonreciprocal transfer to owners** inasmuch as nothing is received by the company in return for its distribution to the stockholders. These transfers should be recorded using the fair market value (as of the day of declaration) of the assets distributed, and a gain or loss recognized for the difference between the carrying value on the books of the issuing company and the fair market value of the assets.[4] Property dividends are valued at carrying value if the fair market value is not determinable.

To illustrate the entries for a property dividend, assume that the Bigler Corporation owns 100,000 shares in the Tri-State Oil Co., cost $2,000,000, fair market value $3,000,000, or $30 per share, which it wishes to distribute to its stockholders. There are 1,000,000 shares of Bigler Corporation stock outstanding. Accordingly, a dividend of 1/10 of a share of Tri-State Oil Co. stock is declared on each share of Bigler Corporation stock outstanding. The entries for Bigler for the dividend declaration and payment are:

<u>Declaration of Dividend</u>

Dividends (or Retained Earnings)	3,000,000	
Property Dividends Payable		2,000,000
Gain on Distribution of Property Dividends		1,000,000

<u>Payment of Dividend</u>

Property Dividends Payable	2,000,000	
Investment in Tri-State Oil Co. Stock		2,000,000

[4]*Opinions of the Accounting Principles Board, No. 29,* "Accounting for Nonmonetary Transactions" (New York: American Institute of Certified Public Accountants, 1973), par. 18.

An investor owning 5,000 shares of Bigler stock would make the following entry to record the receipt of the property (Tri-State Oil stock) dividend:

<u>Receipt of Dividend</u>

Investment in Tri-State Oil Co. Stock	15,000	
Dividend Revenue		15,000

Computation:
5,000 shares × 1/10 = 500 shares
500 shares × $30 per share = $15,000

Stock Dividends A corporation may distribute to stockholders additional shares of the company's own stock as a stock dividend. A stock dividend permits the corporation to retain within the business net assets produced by earnings while at the same time offering stockholders additional ownership shares.

Accounting for Stock Dividends by the Issuer

A stock dividend usually involves (1) the capitalization of retained earnings, and (2) a distribution of common stock to common stockholders. These distributions are sometimes referred to as "ordinary stock dividends." In other instances, common stock is issued to holders of preferred stock or preferred stock is issued to holders of common stock. These distributions are sometimes referred to as "special stock dividends."

A stock dividend decreases retained earnings while increasing the legal capital of a corporation. In recording the dividend, a debit is made to Retained Earnings and credits are made to appropriate paid-in capital balances. A stock dividend has the same effect as the payment by the corporation of a cash dividend and a subsequent return of the cash to the corporation in exchange for capital stock, as illustrated in a subsequent section.

In distributing stock as a dividend, the issuing corporation must meet legal requirements relative to the minimum amounts to be capitalized. If stock has a par or a stated value, an amount equal to the par or stated value of the shares issued will have to be transferred to capital stock; if stock has no par value and no stated value, the laws of the state of incorporation may provide specific requirements as to the amounts to be transferred, or they may leave such determinations to the corporate directors.

Accounting for Stock Dividends by the Investor

From the shareholders' point of view, a stock dividend does not change the proportional ownership interests. Although the number of shares held by each individual stockholder has gone up, there are now a greater total number of shares outstanding, and proportionate interests remain unchanged. This division of equities into a greater number of parts should not be regarded as giving rise to revenue. To illustrate, assume the following for Jeff's Corporation and a shareholder owning 10 shares of stock.

	Prior to 10% Stock Dividend	After 10% Stock Dividend
Common stock outstanding	10,000 shares	11,000 shares
Total stockholders' equity	$330,000	$330,000
Company book value per share	$33	$30
Individual stockholder book value	$330	$330
	(10 shares × $33)	(11 shares × $30)

As indicated above, the book value per share would decrease, but total book value would not change. The market value of the stock may or may not react in a similar manner. Theoretically, the same relative decrease should occur in the market price as occurred in the book value; however, there are many variables that influence the market price of securities. If the percentage of the stock dividend is comparatively low, there is generally less than a pro rata immediate effect on the market price of the stock. This has led the profession to treat small stock dividends somewhat differently than large stock dividends, as explained in the next section. In any event, since there is no effect on the underlying book value of the investment, the investor need only make a memorandum entry noting the receipt of additional shares and the new, lower per-share cost basis of the investment.

Small vs. Large Stock Dividends

In accounting for stock dividends, a distinction is made between a small and a large stock dividend.[5] A **small stock dividend** is one in which the number of shares issued is so small in comparison to the number of shares outstanding that it has little or no impact on the market price per share; therefore, the market value of the shares previously held remains substantially unchanged. As a general guideline, a stock dividend of less than 20-25% of the number of shares previously outstanding is considered a small stock dividend. Stock dividends involving the issuance of more than 20-25% are considered **large stock dividends**.

With a small stock dividend, which is the normal situation, the accounting profession recommends that companies transfer from Retained Earnings to capital stock and additional paid-in capital an amount equal to the fair market value of the additional shares at the declaration date. Such a transfer is consistent with the general public's view of a stock dividend as a distribution of corporate earnings at an amount equivalent to the fair market value of the shares received. When a large stock dividend is involved, however, the transfer from Retained Earnings to contributed capital is made at the stock's par value, stated value, or other value as required

---

[5]See *Accounting Research and Terminology Bulletins—Final Edition. No. 43*, "Restatement and Revision of Accounting Research Bulletins," (New York: American Institute of Certified Public Accountants, 1961), Ch. 7, Sec. B.

by law. The following examples illustrate the entries for the declaration and issuance of stock dividends.

Assume that stockholders' equity for the Fuji Company on July 1 is as follows:

Common stock, $10 par, 100,000 shares outstanding	$1,000,000
Paid-in capital in excess of par	1,100,000
Retained earnings	750,000

The company declares a 10% stock dividend, or a dividend of 1 share of common for every 10 shares held. The stock is selling on the market on this date at $16 per share. The stock dividend is to be recorded at the market value of the shares issued, or $160,000 (10,000 shares at $16). The entries to record the declaration of the dividend and the issue of stock by Fuji Company are:

Declaration of Dividend

Retained Earnings	160,000	
Stock Dividends Distributable		100,000
Paid-In Capital in Excess of Par		60,000

Issuance of Dividend

Stock Dividends Distributable	100,000	
Common Stock, $10 par		100,000

Assume, however, that the company declares a large stock dividend of 50%, or a dividend of 1 share for every 2 held. Legal requirements call for the transfer to capital stock of an amount equal to the par value of the shares issued. Entries for the declaration of the dividend and the issue of stock follow:

Declaration of Dividend

Retained Earnings	500,000	
Stock Dividends Distributable		500,000

Issuance of Dividend

Stock Dividends Distributable	500,000	
Common Stock, $10 par		500,000

Fractional Share Warrants

When stock dividends are issued by a company, it may be necessary to issue **fractional share warrants** to certain stockholders. For example, when a 10% stock dividend is issued, a stockholder owning 25 shares can be given no more than 2 full shares; however, the holdings in excess of an even multiple of 10 shares are recognized by the issue of a fractional share warrant for one-half share. The warrant for one-half share may be sold, or a warrant for an additional half share may be purchased so that a full share may be claimed from the company. In some instances, the corporation may arrange for the payment of cash in lieu of fractional warrants or it may issue a full share of stock in exchange for warrants accompanied by cash for the fractional share deficiency.

Assume that the Fuji Company in distributing a stock dividend issues fractional share warrants equivalent to 500 shares of $10 par common. The entry for the fractional share warrants issued would be as follows:

Stock Dividends Distributable	5,000	
Fractional Share Warrants Issued		5,000

Assuming 80% of the warrants are ultimately turned in for shares and the remaining warrants expire, the following entry would be made:

Fractional Share Warrants Issued	5,000	
Common Stock, $10 par		4,000
Paid-In Capital from Forfeitures of Fractional Share Warrants		1,000

Stock Dividends vs. Stock Splits

As noted in Chapter 16, a corporation may effect a **stock split** by reducing the par or stated value of capital stock and increasing accordingly the number of shares outstanding. For example, a corporation with 1,000,000 shares outstanding may split the stock on a 3-for-1 basis. After the split, the corporation will have 3,000,000 total shares outstanding and each stockholder will have 3 shares for every 1 previously held. However, each share now represents only one third of the capital interest it previously represented; furthermore, each share of stock can be expected to sell for approximately one-third of its previous market price. From an investor's perspective, therefore, a stock split can be viewed the same as a stock dividend. In fact, the accounting for the investor is the same for stock splits as for stock dividends. With an increase in the number of shares, each new share is assigned a portion of the original cost.

Although a stock dividend can be compared to a stock split from the investors' point of view, its effects on corporate capital differ from those of a stock split. A stock dividend results in not only an increase in the number of shares outstanding, but also an increase in the capital stock balance, with no change in the value assigned to each share of stock on the company records; the increase in capital stock outstanding is effected by a transfer from the retained earnings balance, retained earnings available for dividends being permanently reduced by this transfer. A stock split merely divides the existing capital stock balance into more parts, with a reduction in the stated or legal value related to each share; there is no change in the retained earnings balance or the capital stock balance.

Exhibit 17-1 provides a comparative example of the effects of a stock dividend and a stock split, both from the issuing company's perspective and from an investor's perspective.

Exhibit 17-1   Comparative Example—Stock Dividend vs. Stock Split

---

Stockholders' Equity (Prior to Stock Dividend or Stock Split)

Common stock, 200,000 shares authorized, $5 par, 50,000 shares outstanding	$250,000
Paid-in-capital in excess of par	100,000
Retained earnings	200,000
Total stockholders' equity	$550,000

Issuing Company's Perspective

Stockholders' Equity after 10% Stock Dividend*		Stockholders' Equity after 2:1 Stock Split	
Common stock, 200,000 shares authorized, $5 par, 55,000 shares outstanding	$275,000	Common stock, 400,000 shares authorized, $2.50 par, 100,000 shares outstanding . .	$250,000
Paid-in-capital in excess of par	175,000	Paid-in-capital in excess of par	100,000
Retained earnings	100,000	Retained earnings	200,000
Total stockholders' equity	$550,000	Total stockholders' equity	$550,000

*Assume market value of $20 per share at declaration date.

Investor's Perspective**

Effect of 10% Stock Dividend		Effect of 2:1 Stock Split	
Original investment (1,000 × $15)	$15,000	Original investment (1,000 × $15)	$15,000
Investment after 10% stock dividend (1,100 × $13.64)	$15,000	Investment after 2:1 stock split (2,000 × $7.50)	$15,000

**Assume an original investment of 1,000 shares at $15 cost per share.

Stock Dividends on the Balance Sheet

Special disclosure should be provided on the balance sheet when retained earnings have been reclassified as paid-in capital as a result of stock dividends, recapitalizations, or other actions. Information concerning the amount of retained earnings transferred to paid-in capital will contribute to an understanding of the extent to which business growth has been financed through corporate earnings. For example, assume the information for the Fuji Company on page 754 and the transfer to paid-in capital of $500,000 as a result of the 50% stock dividend. The stockholders' equity may be presented as illustrated below.

Contributed capital:		
Common stock, $10 par, 150,000 shares	$1,500,000	
Paid-in capital in excess of par	1,100,000	$2,600,000
Retained earnings	$ 750,000	
Less amount transferred to paid-in capital by stock dividend	500,000	250,000
Total stockholders' equity		$2,850,000

If a balance sheet is prepared after the declaration of a stock dividend but before issue of the shares, Stock Dividends Distributable is reported in the stockholders' equity section as an addition to capital stock outstanding. Through stock dividends, the corporation reduces its retained earnings balance and increases its capital stock.

Liquidating Dividends   A liquidating dividend is a distribution representing a return to stockholders of a portion of contributed capital. Whereas a normal cash dividend provides a return on investment, and is accounted for by reducing Retained Earnings, a liquidating dividend provides a return of investment. A liquidating dividend is accounted for by reducing paid-in capital.

To illustrate, assume the Schwab Corporation declared and paid a cash dividend and a partial liquidating dividend amounting to $150,000. Of this amount, $100,000 represents a regular $10 cash dividend on 10,000 shares of common stock. The remaining $50,000 represents a $5 per share liquidating dividend, which is recorded as a reduction to Paid-in Capital in Excess of Par. The entries would be:

Declaration of Dividend

Dividends (or Retained Earnings)	100,000	
Paid-In Capital in Excess of Par	50,000	
Dividends Payable		150,000

Payment of Dividend

Dividends Payable	150,000	
Cash		150,000

Stockholders should be notified as to the allocation of the total dividend payment so they can determine the amount that represents revenue and the amount that represents a return of investment. An investor owning 500 shares of Schwab Corporation common stock would record receipt of the dividend as follows:

Cash	7,500	
Dividend Revenue (500 shares × $10)		5,000
Investment in Schwab Corp. Common Stock (500 shares × $5)		2,500

Quasi-Reorganizations   As noted earlier, a debit balance in the Retained Earnings account is called a deficit. It may be the result of accumulated losses over a number of years or other significant debits to Retained Earnings. Sometimes a company with a large deficit is forced to discontinue operations and/or enter into bankruptcy proceedings. In some cases, however, where state laws permit, a company may eliminate a deficit through a restatement of invested capital balances. This provides, in effect, a fresh start for the company with a zero Retained Earnings balance. This is known as a quasi-reorganization. The advantage of a quasi-reorganization is that the procedure does not require recourse to the courts as in a formal reorganization or bankruptcy, and there is no change in the legal corporate entity or interruption of business activity.

Quasi-reorganizations are not common, but may be appropriate for a company operating under circumstances that are quite different from those of the past, e.g., a company with new management. Even if operated profitably, the company may take years to eliminate the deficit which was created under a prior management. In the meantime, the corporation generally cannot pay dividends to stockholders. With a quasi-reorganization, however, the accumulated deficit is eliminated. Performance from the reorganization date forward can then be measured and reported without having past mistakes and negative results reflecting unfavorably on the "new" company.

Normally in a quasi-reorganization, assets are revalued to reflect their current market values. This may require significant write-downs of assets against Retained Earnings, thus increasing the deficit. The total deficit is then written off (Retained Earnings is adjusted to a zero balance) against paid-in capital balances, giving the company a new capital structure. The Securities and Exchange Commission provides that any deficit reclassification is to be considered a quasi-reorganization and can only be made if all requisite conditions for a quasi-reorganization are met. Furthermore, the SEC requires that any anticipated accounting changes should be an integral part of the quasi-reorganization, and that the reorganization should not result in a write-up of net assets of the company.[6]

To illustrate the nature of a quasi-reorganization, assume TSS Corporation has suffered operating losses for some time, but is now operating profitably and expects to continue to do so. Current and projected income, however, will not be sufficient to eliminate the deficit in the near term. It also appears that plant assets are overstated considering current prices and economic conditions. After receiving permission from state authorities and approval from the shareholders, the board of directors of TSS Corporation decides to restate company assets and paid-in capital balances in order to remove the deficit and make possible the declaration of dividends from profitable operations. A balance sheet for the company just prior to this action is presented below.

TSS Corporation
Balance Sheet
June 30, 1991

Assets			Liabilities and Stockholders' Equity		
Current assets		$ 250,000	Liabilities		$ 300,000
Land, buildings, and			Common stock, $10 par,		
equipment	$1,500,000		100,000 shares	$1,000,000	
Less accumulated			Less deficit	150,000	850,000
depreciation	600,000	900,000	Total liabillities and		
Total assets		$1,150,000	stockholders' equity		$1,150,000

The quasi-reorganization is to be accomplished as follows:

[6]Staff Accounting Bulletin, No. 78, "Quasi-Reorganizations" (Washington: SEC, August 25, 1988).

1. Land, buildings, and equipment are to be reduced to their present fair market value of $600,000 by reducing the asset and accumulated depreciation balances by 33⅓%.
2. Common stock is to be reduced to a par value of $5, $500,000 in capital stock thus being converted into "additional paid-in capital."
3. The deficit of $450,000 ($150,000 as reported on the balance sheet increased by $300,000 arising from the write-down of land, buildings, and equipment) is to be applied against the capital from the reduction of the par value of stock.

Entries to record the changes follow:

Transaction	Entry		
(1) To write down land, buildings, and equipment and accumulated depreciation balances by 33⅓%.	Retained Earnings . . . . Accumulated Depreciation . . . . Land, Buildings, and Equipment	300,000 200,000	 500,000
(2) To reduce the common stock balance from $10 par to $5 par and to establish paid-in capital from reduction in stock par value.	Common Stock, $10 par . . . . . . Common Stock, $5 par . . . . . Paid-In Capital from Reduction in Stock Par Value	1,000,000	500,000 500,000
(3) To apply the deficit after asset devaluation against paid-in capital from reduction in stock par value.	Paid-In Capital from Reduction in Stock Par Value . . . . Retained Earnings	450,000	 450,000

The balance sheet after the quasi-reorganization is shown below.

TSS Corporation
Balance Sheet
June 30, 1991

Assets			Liabilities and Stockholders' Equity	
Current assets . . .		$250,000	Liabilities	$300,000
Land, buildings,			Common stock, $5 par,	
and equipment	$1,000,000		100,000 shares	500,000
Less accumulated			Paid-in capital from reduction	
depreciation . . .	400,000	600,000	in stock par value	50,000
Total assets		$850,000	Total liabilities and	
			stockholders' equity	$850,000

Following the quasi-reorganization, the accounting for the company's operations is similar to that for a new company. Earnings subsequent to the quasi-reorganization, however, should be accumulated in a **dated retained earnings account**. On future balance sheets, retained earnings dated as of the time of account readjustment will inform readers of the date of such action and of the fresh start in earnings accumulation.

Reporting Stockholders' Equity

In reporting stockholders' equity, it is important to provide readers with information concerning:

1. The sources of stockholders' equity, especially the amount paid in by

stockholders (contributed capital) and the amount representing earnings retained in the business (retained earnings).

2. The classes of capital stock, including par or stated values; number of shares authorized, issued, and outstanding; number of shares of treasury stock.

3. Any restrictions on retained earnings.

In addition to the preceding information, the cost (or par value) of treasury stock should be deducted from stockholders' equity. Similarly, any unrealized loss on noncurrent marketable equity securities is to be reported as a contra-equity item and deducted in determining total stockholders' equity.

As an illustration, the stockholders' equity section of the balance sheet of Hypothetical Corporation as of December 31, 1991, is presented. Many companies do not provide as much detail in the balance sheet as is illustrated for Hypothetical Corporation. A typical presentation is made in the actual financial statements of General Mills, Inc. in Appendix A.

Stockholders' Equity

Contributed capital:			
6% Preferred stock, $100 par, cumulative, callable, 5,000 shares authorized and issued	$500,000		
Common stock, $5 stated value, 100,000 shares authorized, 60,000 shares issued; treasury stock, 5,000 shares—deducted below	300,000	$ 800,000	
Paid-in capital in excess of stated value	$260,000		
Paid-in capital from treasury stock	16,000	276,000	
Total contributed capital		$1,076,000	
Retained earnings:			
Appropriated for contingencies (Note X)	$125,000		
Unappropriated	225,000		
Total retained earnings		350,000	
Total contributed capital and retained earnings		$1,426,000	
Deduct: Common treasury stock, at cost (5,000 shares acquired at $8)	$ 40,000		
Net unrealized loss on noncurrent marketable equity securities	24,000	64,000	
Total stockholders' equity			$1,362,000

Readers of financial statements should be provided with an explanation of the changes in individual equity balances during the period. Frequently, such explanation is provided in notes to the financial statements. When stockholders' equity is composed of numerous accounts, as in the preceding example, a **statement of changes in stockholders' equity** is sometimes presented. An illustrative statement for the Hypothetical Corporation is shown on page 761.

The net ownership equity of a business is an important element. Analyses of the amounts and sources of contributed capital compared to those generated and retained by the company provide useful information for assessing the long-term profitability and solvency of a business. The techniques for analyzing financial statements are discussed in Chapter 26.

Hypothetical Corporation
Statement of Changes in Stockholders' Equity
For the Year Ended December 31, 1991

	Preferred Stock	Common Stock	Paid-In Capital	Appropriated Retained Earnings for Contingencies	Unappropriated Retained Earnings	Contra-Equity Balances	Total
Balances, December 31, 1990	$300,000	$300,000	$260,000*	$ 90,000	$222,500	$ -0-	$1,172,500
Prior period adjustment—correction of 1989 error, net of tax					(25,000)		(25,000)
Adjusted balances, December 31, 1990	$300,000	$300,000	$260,000	$ 90,000	$197,500	$ -0-	$1,147,500
Increase from sale of 1,000 shares of preferred stock in January, 1991, at par value	200,000						200,000
Increase from sale of 25,000 shares of treasury stock, common, in January, 1991, cost $20,000, for $36,000			16,000				16,000
Net income for 1991					120,000		120,000
Cash dividends:							
Preferred stock, $6 on 5,000 shares, $30,000					(57,500)		(57,500)
Common stock 50¢ on 55,000 shares, $27,500							
Retained earnings appropriated for contingencies				35,000	(35,000)		
Purchase of 5,000 shares of common treasury stock @ cost, $8						(40,000)	(40,000)
Net unrealized loss on noncurrent marketable equity securities						(24,000)	(24,000)
Balances, December 31, 1991	$500,000	$300,000	$276,000	$125,000	$225,000	$(64,000)	$1,362,000

*From sale of common stock at more than stated value.

Key Terms   Appropriated retained earnings 749   Retained earnings 745
Cash dividend 750   Statement of changes in stockholders'
Deficit 747   equity 760
Dividends 747   Stock dividend 752
Liquidating dividend 757   Stock split 755
Prior period adjustment 746   Unappropriated (free) retained
Quasi-reorganization 757   earnings 749
Property dividend 751

Questions

1. What is the impact of each of the following transactions or events on retained earnings or total stockholders' equity?
   (a) Operating profits.
   (b) Discovery of an understatement of income in a previous period.
   (c) Release of Retained Earnings Appropriated for Purchase of Treasury Stock upon the sale of treasury stock.
   (d) Issue of bonds at a premium.
   (e) Purchase of a corporation's own capital stock.
   (f) Increase in a company's earning capacity, assumed to be evidence of considerable goodwill.
   (g) Construction of equipment for a company's own use at a cost less than the prevailing market price of identical equipment.
   (h) Donation to a corporation of its own stock.
   (i) Sale of land, buildings, and equipment at a gain.
   (j) Gain on bond retirement.
   (k) Conversion of bonds into common stock.
   (l) Conversion of preferred stock into common stock.

2. What are the two major considerations of a board of directors in making decisions involving dividend declarations?

3. Very few companies pay dividends in amounts equal to their retained earnings. Why?

4. The following announcement appeared on the financial page of a newspaper.

   The Board of Directors of Benton Co., at their meeting on June 15, 1991, declared the regular quarterly dividend on outstanding common stock of $1.40 per share, payable on July 10, 1991, to the stockholders of record at the close of business June 30, 1991.

   (a) What is the purpose of each of the three dates given in the announcement?
   (b) When would the common stock of Benton Co. normally trade "ex-dividend"?

5. Dividends are sometimes said to have been paid "out of retained earnings." What is wrong with such a statement?

6. The directors of The Dress Shoppe are considering issuance of a stock dividend. They have asked you to answer the following questions regarding the proposed action:
   (a) How is a stock dividend different from a stock split?
   (b) How are stock dividends accounted for: (1) by the issuing corporation? (2) by the stockholder?

7. Often, when a company declares a stock dividend, fractional share warrants are issued to certain stockholders. (a) What is a fractional share warrant? (b)

What can the stockholder do with fractional share warrants? (c) If the company does not want to issue fractional share warrants, what alternatives are available?

8. At a regular meeting of the board of directors of the Greenwood Corporation, a dividend payable in the stock of the Mossey Corporation is to be declared. The stock of Mossey Corporation is recorded on the books of the Greenwood Corporation at $190,000; the market value of the stock is $230,000. The question is raised whether the amount to be recorded for the dividend payable should be the book value or the market value. What is the proper accounting treatment?

9. (a) What is a liquidating dividend? (b) Under what circumstances are such distributions made?

10. (a) Why might a company seek a quasi-reorganization? (b) What are the steps in a quasi-reorganization?

11. In reviewing the financial statements of Farmer Inc., a stockholder does not understand the purpose of Appropriation of Retained Earnings for Bond Redemption Fund that has been set up by periodic debits to Retained Earnings. The stockholder is told that this balance will not be used to redeem the bonds at their maturity. (a) What account will be reduced by the payment of the bonds? (b) What purpose is accomplished by the Appropriation of Retained Earnings for Bond Redemption Fund? (c) What disposition is made of the appropriation after the bonds are retired?

Discussion Cases

Case 17-1 (Small stock dividends)

The president of Info Company suggests including the following statement in this year's annual report.

On December 18, a 10% common stock dividend was distributed to stockholders, resulting in a transfer of $1,536,000 from Retained Earnings to Common Stock and Capital in Excess of Par. While the percentage of the stock dividend was the same as the previous year, the sum transferred to stockholders' equity was nearly $80,000 less.

The seeming inconsistency is the result of the requirement of regulatory authorities that the value of stock dividends on the company's books be related to the market value of the stock. As a result, the present year's dividend was valued at $65 per share as compared to $74 per share for last year's stock dividend.

The president feels that this statement would help clarify the apparent inconsistency in the company's dividend policy. As partner for the accounting firm that is performing the annual audit of Info Company, you feel that the president's statement may mislead the readers of the report even though the figures are correct.

State how the stock dividends should be accounted for in a situation such as this one, explaining your reasoning. What criticism, if any, do you have of the terminology used by the president? Explain.

Case 17-2 (How much should our dividend be?)

Seaside Corp. has paid quarterly dividends of $.70 per share for the last three years and is trying to continue this tradition. Seasides' balance sheet is as follows:

Seaside Corp.
Balance Sheet
December 31, 1991

Assets			Liabilities		
Current assets:			**Current Liabilities:**		
Cash..................	$ 50,000		Accounts payable	$ 520,000	
Accounts receivable.....	450,000		Taxes payable	100,000	
Inventory	1,200,000		Accrued liabilities.......	90,000	
Total current assets ...	$1,700,000		Total current liabilities	$ 710,000	
			Bonds payable	1,500,000	
Investments	500,000		Total liabilities	$2,210,000	
Land, buildings and					
equipment (net).......	1,600,000		**Stockholders' Equity**		
			Common stock ($10 par,		
			69,000 shares		
			outstanding)	$ 690,000	
			Retained earnings	900,000	
			Total stockholders'		
			equity	$1,590,000	
Total Assets	$3,800,000		Total liabilities and		
			stockholders' equity ...	$3,800,000	

Discuss Seaside's possibilities concerning the issuance of dividends.

Case 17-3 (Cash or stock dividend?)

Best Ski Manufacturer is considering offering a 10% stock dividend rather than its normal cash dividend of $1 per share in the first quarter of 1991. However, some of Best's stockholders have expressed displeasure at the idea and say they strongly prefer cash dividends.

Discuss the issue of a stock dividend as opposed to a cash dividend from the points of view of (a) a stockholder and (b) the board of directors.

Case 17-4 (Stock splits and stock dividends)

Union and Eastern Corporation has been one of the more popular growth stocks during the past several years. In 1991, its $20 par common stock was selling in the range of $200-$230, with 146,000 shares outstanding. On May 1, 1991, Union and Eastern announced that, effective May 10, 1991, its stock would be split 4-for-1. This was the first time since 1971 that Union and Eastern's stock had been split, although several stock dividends had been issued during the past 20 years. (a) What are the differences between a stock dividend and a stock split both from the standpoint of the investor and the company? (b) What are some possible reasons for Union and Eastern issuing stock dividends prior to 1991?

Exercises   **Exercise 17-1 (Cash and stock dividends)**

On September 30, 1990, White Company issued 4,000 shares of its $5 par common stock in connection with a stock dividend. No entry was made on the stock dividend declaration date. The market value per share on the date of declaration was $10 per share. The stockholders' equity accounts of White Company immediately before issuance of the stock dividend shares were as follows:

Common stock, $5 par; 100,000 shares authorized; 40,000 shares outstanding	$200,000
Additional paid-in capital	300,000
Retained earnings	350,000

On December 30, 1990, White Company declared a cash dividend of $3.50 per share payable January 5, 1991. Give the necessary entries to record the declaration and payment or issuance of the dividends.   (AICPA adapted)

Exercise 17-2   (Property dividends)

WW Company distributed the following dividends to its stockholders:

(a) 400,000 shares of Shell Corporation stock, carrying value of investment $1,200,000, fair market value $2,300,000.
(b) 230,000 shares of Evans Company stock, a closely held corporation. The shares were purchased by WW 3 years ago at $5.60 per share, but no current market price is available.

Give the journal entries to account for the declaration and the payment of the dividends.

Exercise 17-3   (Accounting for property dividends)

Hartz Corporation owned 2,700 shares of Finch Corporation common stock that it had purchased in 1988 for $10 per share. On August 15, 1991, when the value of Finch stock was $25 per share, Hartz declared a property dividend of 1 share of Finch for every 15 shares of Hartz common stock held by stockholders on October 15, 1991. Hartz had 40,500 shares of common outstanding. The Finch shares were distributed on December 15, 1991.

(1) Give the necessary journal entries on Hartz' books to record the property dividend.
(2) Give the necessary journal entry to record the property dividend on the books of an investor who owns 900 shares of Hartz Corporation common stock.

Exercise 17-4   (Dividend computations)

Consistent Company has been paying regular quarterly dividends of $1.50 and wants to pay the same amount in the third quarter of 1991. Given the following information, (1) what is the total amount that Consistent will have to pay in dividends in the third quarter in order to pay $1.50 per share, and (2) what is total amount of dividends to be distributed during the year assuming no equity transactions occur after June 30?

1991
Jan.   1   Shares outstanding, 800,000; $8 par (1,500,000 shares authorized)
Feb.   15   Issued 50,000 new shares at $10.50
Mar.   31   Paid quarterly dividends of $1.50 per share
May   12 $1,000,000 of $1,000 bonds were converted to common stock at the rate
            of 100 shares of stock per $1,000 bond.
June   15   Issued a 15% stock dividend.
       30   Paid quarterly dividends of $1.50 per share.

Exercise 17-5   (Stock dividends)

The balance sheet of the Carmen Corporation shows the following:

Common stock, $5 stated value, 80,000 shares issued and outstanding	$400,000
Paid-in capital in excess of stated value	800,000
Retained earnings	350,000

A 25% stock dividend is declared, the board of directors authorizing a transfer from Retained Earnings to Common Stock at the stated value of the shares.

(a) Give entries to record the declaration and issuance of the stock dividend.
(b) What was the effect of the issue of the stock dividend on the ownership equity of each stockholder in the corporation?
(c) Give entries to record the declaration and issuance of the dividend if the board of directors had elected to transfer amounts from Retained Earnings to Common Stock equal to the market value of the stock ($10 per share).

Exercise 17-6   (Stock dividends and stock splits)

The capital accounts for Shop Right Market on June 30, 1991, are as follows:

Common stock, $15 par, 40,000 shares	$ 600,000
Paid-in capital in excess of par	435,000
Retained earnings	2,160,000

Shares of the company's stock are selling at this time at $25. What entries would you make in each of the following cases?

(a) A 10% stock dividend is declared and issued.
(b) A 50% stock dividend is declared and issued.
(c) A 3-for- 1 stock split is declared and issued.

Exercise 17-7   (Accounting for stock splits)

Effective December 31, 1991, the stockholders of Interstate Corp. approved a 2-for-1 split of the company's common stock, and an increase in authorized common shares from 200,000 (par value $10 per share) to 400,000 shares (par value $5 per share). Interstate's stockholders' equity account immediately before these events is summarized on the following page.

Common stock ($10 par, 200,000 shares authorized, 100,000 issued and outstanding)	$1,000,000	
Additional paid-in capital—common stock	150,000	
Total contributed capital		$1,150,000
Retained earnings		1,350,000
Total stockholders' equity		$2,500,000

(1) Make the necessary entries to record the stock split for both Interstate and the investors.

(2) Prepare the stockholders' equity section of Interstate's December 31, 1991 balance sheet.

Exercise 17-8 (Stock dividend computation)

The directors of Warehouser Inc., whose $80 par value common stock is currently selling at $100 per share, have decided to issue a stock dividend. Warehouser has authorization for 400,000 shares of common, has issued 220,000 shares, all of which are currently outstanding, and desires to capitalize $2,400,000 of the retained earnings account balance. What percent stock dividend should be issued to accomplish this goal?

Exercise 17-9 . (Accounting for dividends)

The following information has been taken from the balance sheet of Kain Company.

Current assets	$371,250
Investments	431,400
Common stock (par value $20)	337,000
Paid-in capital in excess of par	200,000
Retained earnings	385,000

Prepare the journal entries for the following unrelated items:

(a) A 30% stock dividend is declared and distributed when the market value of the stock is $23 per share.

(b) Par value of the common stock is reduced to $5, and the stock is split 4-for-1.

(c) A dividend of 1 share Northern Co. common stock for every share of Kain Company stock is declared and distributed. Northern Co. common stock is carried on the books of Kain Co. at a cost of $.80 per share, and the market value is $1.10 per share.

Exercise 17-10 (Restricting retained earnings)

On January 1, 1989, Northwest Manufacturing Corporation issued $20,000,000 of bonds payable. The bond issue agreement with the underwriters required Northwest Manufacturing to appropriate earnings of $1,250,000 at the end of each year until the bonds are retired. During their June, 1991, board meeting, the directors decided to change the company's financial structure to include only short-term debt and equity and to drop their present insurance policy in favor of a self-insurance plan. On July 1, 1991, the company retired the bond issue and set up the first annual appropriation for self-insurance for $28,000.

(1) Give the entries to record the periodic appropriations under the bond issue agreement for 1989 and 1990 and their cancellation in 1991.

(2) Give the entry to record the appropriation for self-insurance.

Exercise 17-11   (Computation of retained earnings)

The following information has been taken from the accounts of Oviatt Corporation:

Total net income reported since incorporation	$300,000
Total cash dividends paid	80,000
Proceeds from sale of donated stock	60,000
Capitalized value of stock dividends distributed	70,000
Paid-in capital from treasury stock	35,000
Unamoritzed discount on bonds payable	75,000
Appropriation for plant expansion	100,000

Determine the current balance of unappropriated retained earnings.

Exercise 17-12   (Correcting the retained earnings account)

The retained earnings account for Olausson Corp. shows the following debits and credits. Give all entries required to correct the account. What is the corrected amount of retained earnings?

Account   Retained Earnings

Date		Item	Debit	Credit	Balance Debit	Balance Credit
Jan.	1	Balance				263,200
(a)		Loss from fire	2,625			260,575
(b)		Write-off of goodwill	26,250			234,325
(c)		Stock dividend	70,000			164,325
(d)		Loss on sale of equipment ..	24,150			140,175
(e)		Officers compensation related to income of prior periods—accrual overlooked.............	162,750		22,575	
(f)		Loss on retirement of preferred shares at more than issuance price	35,000		57,575	
(g)		Paid-in capital in excess of par		64,750		7,175
(h)		Stock subscription defaults..		4,235		11,410
(i)		Gain on retirement of preferred stock at less than issuance price		12,950		24,360
(j)		Gain on early retirement of bonds at less than book value		7,525		31,885
(k)		Gain on life insurance policy settlement		5,250		37,135
(l)		Correction of prior period error		25,025		62,160

Exercise 17-13   (Quasi-reorganization)

Hard Luck Corporation has incurred losses from operations for many years. At the recommendation of the newly hired president, the board of directors voted to implement a quasi-reorganization, subject to stockholders' approval. Immediately prior to the quasi-reorganization, on June 30, 1991, Hard Luck's balance sheet was as follows:

Current assets	$ 275,000
Property, plant, and equipment (net)	675,000
Other assets	100,000
	$1,050,000
Total liabilities	$ 300,000
Common stock	800,000
Additional paid-in capital	150,000
Retained earnings	(200,000)
	$1,050,000

The stockholders approved the quasi-reorganization effective July 1, 1991, to be accomplished by a reduction in property, plant, and equipment (net) of $175,000, a reduction in other assets of $75,000, and appropriate adjustment to the capital structure.

(1) Prepare the journal entries to record the quasi-reorganization on July 1, 1991.

(2) Prepare a new balance sheet after the quasi-reorganization.

(AICPA adapted)

Exercise 17-14   (Reporting stockholders' equity)

Kenny Co. began operations on January 1, 1990, by issuing at $15 per share one half of the 950,000 shares of $10 par value common stock that had been authorized for sale. In addition, Kenny has 500,000 shares of $5 par value, 6% preferred shares authorized. During 1990, Kenny had $1,025,000 of net income and declared $237,500 of dividends.

During 1991 Kenny had the following transactions:

Jan. 10   Issued an additional 100,000 shares of common stock for $17 per share.

Apr. 1   Issued 150,000 shares of the preferred stock for $8 per share.

July 19   Authorized the purchase of a custom made machine to be delivered in January of 1992. Kenny restricted $295,000 of retained earnings for the purchase of the machine.

Oct. 23   Sold an additional 50,000 shares of the preferred stock for $9 per share.

Dec. 31   Reported $1,215,000 of net income and declared a dividend of $645,000 to stockholders of record on January 15, 1992 to be paid on February 1, 1992.

Prepare the stockholders' equity section of Kenny's balance sheet for December 31, 1990 and December 31, 1991.

Problems   Problem 17-1   (Accounting for stock transactions)

TRX Corporation is publicly owned and its shares are traded on a national stock exchange, TRX has 16,000 shares of $25 stated value common stock authorized. Only 75% of these shares have been issued, and, of the shares issued, only 11,000 are outstanding. On December 31, 1990, the stockholders' equity section revealed that the balance in Paid-In Capital in Excess of Stated Value was $140,000, and the Retained Earnings balance was $110,000. Treasury stock was purchased at an average cost of $37.50 per share.

During 1991, TRX had the following transactions:

Jan. 15   TRX issued, at $55 per share, 800 shares of $50 par, 5% cumulative preferred stock; 2,000 shares are authorized.

Feb. 1   TRX sold 1,500 shares of newly issued $25 stated value common stock at $42 per share.

Mar. 15   TRX declared a cash dividend on common stock of $.15 per share payable on April 30 to all stockholders of record on April 1.

Apr. 15   TRX reacquired 200 shares of its common stock for $43 per share. TRX uses the cost method to account for treasury stock.

Apr. 30   Employees exercised 1,000 options granted in 1989 under a non-compensatory stock option plan. When the options were granted, each option entitled the employee to purchase 1 share of common stock for $50 per share. On April 30, when the market price was $55 per share, TRX issued new shares to the employees.

May 1   TRX declared a 10% stock dividend to be distributed on June 1 to stockholders of record on May 7. The market price of the common stock was $50 per share on May 1. (Assume treasury shares do not participate in stock dividends.)

May 31   TRX sold 150 treasury shares reacquired on March 15 and an additional 200 shares costing $7,500 that had been on hand since the beginning of the year. The selling price was $57 per share.

Sept. 15   The semiannual cash dividend on common stock was declared, amounting to $.15 per share. TRX also declared the yearly dividend on preferred stock. Both are payable on October 15 to stockholders of record on October 1.

Net income for 1991 was $50,000.

Instructions:

(1) Compute the number of shares and dollar amount of treasury stock at the beginning of 1991.

(2) Make the necessary journal entries to record the transactions in 1991 relating to stockholders' equity.

(3) Prepare the stockholders' equity section of TRX Corporation's December 31, 1991 balance sheet.

Problem 17-2   (Accounting for stock transactions)

Brady Company has 30,000 shares of $10 par value common stock authorized and 20,000 shares issued and outstanding. On August 15, 1991, Brady purchased 1,500 shares of treasury stock for $12 per share. (All outstanding shares were issued for $11 per share.) Brady uses the cost method to account for treasury stock. On September 14, 1991, Brady sold 500 shares of the treasury stock for $14 per share.

1000

On October 30, 1991 when the market value of the common stock was $16 per share, Brady declared and distributed 2,000 shares as a "small" stock dividend, 1,500 from unissued shares and 500 from treasury shares. (Assume treasury shares do not participate in stock dividends.)

On December 20, 1991, Brady declared a $1 per share cash dividend, payable on January 10, 1992, to shareholders of record on December 31, 1991.

Instructions:

(1) Make the entries necessary for Brady to record the above transactions.
(2) Assuming that Brady's stockholders' equity consists of only the above mentioned items and that retained earnings were $375,000 as of December 31, 1990 (net income for 1991 was $56,000), prepare the stockholders' equity section of Brady's balance sheet as of December 31, 1991.

(AICPA adapted)

Problem 17-3 (Accounting for stock transactions)

Ellis Corporation was organized on June 30, 1988. After two and one-half years of profitable operations, the equity section of Ellis's balance sheet was as follows:

2 1/2 years

Contributed capital:	
Common stock, $30 par, 600,000 shares authorized, 200,000 shares issued and outstanding	$6,000,000
Paid-in capital in excess of par	600,000
Retained earnings	2,800,000
Total stockholders' equity	$9,400,000

During 1991, the following transactions affected the stockholders' equity:

Jan. 31   10,000 shares of common stock were reacquired at $32; treasury stock is recorded at cost.

Apr. 1   The company declared a 30% stock dividend. (Applies to all issued stock.)

    30   The company declared a $.75 cash dividend. (Applies only to outstanding stock.)

June 1   The stock dividend was issued, and the cash dividend was paid.

Aug. 31   All treasury stock was sold at $35.

Instructions: Give journal entries to record the stock transactions.

Problem 17-4 (Stockholders' equity transactions)

The stockholders' equity of the Seasoned Lumber Co. on June 30, 1991, was as follows:

Contributed capital:	
5% Preferred stock, $50 par, cumulative, 30,000 shares issued, dividends 5 years in arrears	$1,500,000
Common stock, $30 par, 100,000 shares issued	3,000,000
	$4,500,000
Deficit from operations	(600,000)
Total stockholders' equity	$3,900,000

On July 1 the following action was taken:

(a) Common stockholders turned in their old common stock and received in exchange new common stock, 1 share of the new stock being exchanged for every 4 shares of the old. New common stock was given a stated value of $60 per share.

(b) One-half share of the new common stock was issued on each share of preferred stock outstanding in liquidation of dividends in arrears on preferred stock.

(c) The deficit from operations was applied against the paid-in capital arising from the common stock restatement.

Transactions for the remainder of 1991 affecting the stockholders' equity were as follows:

Oct.   1   10,000 shares of preferred stock were called at $55 plus dividends for 3 months at 5%. Stock was formally retired.

Nov. 10   60,000 shares of new common stock were sold at $65.

Dec. 31   Net income for the 6 months ended on this date was $400,000. (Debit Income Summary.) The semiannual dividend was declared on preferred shares and a $.75 dividend was declared on common shares, dividends being payable January 20, 1992.

Instructions:

(1) Record in journal form the foregoing transactions.

(2) Prepare the stockholders' equity section of the balance sheet as of December 31, 1991.

Problem 17-5   (Stockholders' equity transactions)

Seneca Inc. was organized on January 2, 1990, with authorized capital stock consisting of 50,000 shares of 10%, $200 par preferred, and 200,000 shares of no-par, no-stated value common. During the first 2 years of the company's existence, the following selected transactions took place:

1990

Jan.   2   Sold 10,000 shares of common stock at $16.

       2   Sold 3,000 shares of preferred stock at $216.

Mar.   2   Sold common stock as follows: 10,800 shares at $22; 2,700 shares at $25.

July 10   A nearby piece of land, appraised at $400,000, was acquired for 600 shares of preferred stock and 27,000 shares of common. (Preferred stock was recorded at $216, the balance being assigned to common.)

Dec. 16   The regular preferred and a $1.50 common dividend were declared.

      28   Dividends declared on December 16 were paid.

      31   The Income Summary account showed a credit balance of $450,000, which was transferred to Retained Earnings.

1991

Feb. 27   The corporation reacquired 12,000 shares of common stock at $19. The treasury stock is carried at cost. (State law required that an appropriation of retained earnings be made for the purchase price of treasury stock. Appropriations are to be returned to Retained Earnings upon resale of the stock).

June 17   Resold 10,000 shares of the treasury stock at $23.

July 31   Resold all of the remaining treasury stock at $18.

Sept. 30   The corporation sold 11,000 additional shares of common stock at $21.

Dec. 16   The regular preferred dividend and an $.80 common dividend were declared.

28   Dividends declared on December 16 were paid.

31   The income summary account showed a credit balance of $425,000 which was transferred to Retained Earnings.

Instructions:

(1) Give the journal entries to record the foregoing transactions.
(2) Prepare the stockholders' equity section of the balance sheet as of December 31, 1991.

⦀ Problem 17-6   (Accounting for stockholders' equity)

A condensed balance sheet for Sharp Tax Inc. as of December 31, 1988, appears below:

Sharp Tax Inc.
Condensed Balance Sheet
December 31, 1988

Assets		Liabilities and Stockholders' Equity	
Assets	$525,000	Liabilities	$120,000
		8% Preferred stock, $100 par	75,000
		Common stock, $50 par	150,000
		Paid-in capital in excess of	
		par	30,000
		Retained earnings	150,000
		Total liabilities and	
Total assets	$525,000	stockholders' equity	$525,000

Capital stock authorized consists of: 750 shares of 8%, cumulative preferred stock, and 15,000 shares of common stock.

Information relating to operations of the succeeding 3 years follows:

	1989	1990	1991
Dividends declared on Dec. 20, payable on Jan. 10 of the following year:			
Preferred stock	8% cash	8% cash	8% cash
Common stock	$1.00 cash	$1.25 cash	$1.00 cash
	50% stock*		
Net income for year	$67,500	$39,000	$51,000

*Retained earnings is reduced by the par value of the stock dividend.

1990

Feb. 12   Accumulated depreciation was reduced by $72,000 following an income tax investigation. (Assume that this was an error that qualified as a prior period adjustment.) Additional income tax of $22,500 for prior years was paid.

Mar. 3   300 shares of common stock were purchased by the corporation at $54 per share; treasury stock is recorded at cost, and retained earnings are appropriated equal to such costs.

1991

Aug. 10   All the treasury stock was resold at $59 per share and the retained earnings appropriation was canceled.

Sept. 12   By vote of the stockholders, each share of the common stock was exchanged by the corporation for 4 shares of no-par common stock with a stated value of $15.

Instructions:

(1) Give the journal entries to record the foregoing transactions for the 3-year period ended December 31, 1991.

(2) Prepare the stockholders' equity section of the balance sheet as it would appear at the end of 1989, 1990, and 1991.

Problem 17-7   (Adjustments to Retained Earnings)

On March 31, 1991, the Retained Earnings account of Universal Services showed a balance of $19,000,000. The board of directors of Universal made the following decisions during the remainder of 1991 that possibly affect the Retained Earnings account.

Apr. 1   Universal decided to assume the risk for workers' compensation insurance. The estimated liability for 1991 was $120,000. Also, a fund was set up to cover the estimated liability.

30   Universal has not experienced even a small fire since 1949; therefore, the board of directors decided to start a self-insurance plan. They decided to start with a $400,000 appropriation.

May 15   A fire did considerable damage to the outside warehouse. It cost $360,000 to repair the warehouse.

Aug. 20   The board of directors received a report from the plant engineer indicating that the company is possibly in violation of pollution control standards. The fine for such a violation is $800,000. As a result of the engineer's report, the board decided to set up a general contingency appropriation for $800,000.

Sept. 1   The company reacquired 80,000 shares of its own stock at $29; treasury stock is recorded at cost. Due to legal restrictions, Universal has to set up an appropriation to cover the cost of the treasury stock.

Dec. 31   The company had to pay an $800,000 fine for pollution control violations and the treasury stock was sold at $31. No workers' compensation was paid during the year.

Instructions: Prepare all of the necessary entries to record the transactions.

Problem 17-8 (Reporting stockholders' equity)

Accounts of High Country Ranch on December 31, 1991, show the following balances:

	Debits	Credits
Accumulated Depreciation—Buildings		$ 255,000
Allowance for Purchase Discounts...................	$ 4,200	
Bonds Payable		325,000
Bond Retirement Fund...........................	138,000	
Buildings	1,150,000	
Common Stock, $10 par (89,000 shares authorized, 63,200 shares issued and outstanding)		632,000
Common Stock Subscribed (4,000 shares)		40,000
Current Assets	786,000	
Current Liabilities—Other		270,000
Customers' Deposits		17,000
Dividends Payable—Cash.........................		16,000
Income Taxes Payable		43,000
Paid-In Capital from Treasury Stock		32,000
Paid-In Capital in Excess of Par....................		24,000
Retained Earnings Appropriated for Contingencies......		100,000
Retained Earnings Appropriated for Bond Retirement Fund.....................................		138,000
Retained Earnings Appropriated for Purchase of Treasury Stock		56,000
Stock Dividends Distributable (5,040 shares)...........		50,400
Treasury Stock (4,800 shares at cost)................	56,000	
Unappropriated Retained Earnings		135,800
	$2,134,200	$2,134,200

Instructions: From these data prepare the stockholders' equity section as it would appear on the balance sheet.

Problem 17-9 (Quasi-reorganization)

Kennington Copper has experienced several loss years and has plant assets on its books that are overvalued. Kennington plans to revalue its assets downward and eliminate the deficit. At December 31, 1991, the company owns the following plant assets:

	Cost	Accumulated Depreciation	Book Value	Current Value
Land	$ 600,000	—	$ 600,000	$300,000
Buildings	850,000	$350,000	500,000	250,000
Machinery and Equipment	450,000	250,000	200,000	150,000
	$1,900,000	$600,000	$1,300,000	$700,000

The balance sheet on December 31, 1991, reported the following balances in the stockholders' equity section:

Common stock, $25 par, 70,000 shares	$1,750,000
Paid-in capital in excess of par	300,000
Retained earnings (deficit)	(350,000)
Total	$1,700,000

As part of the reorganization, the common stock is to be canceled and reissued at $10 par.

Instructions:

(1) Prepare the journal entries to record the quasi-reorganization.
(2) Give the plant asset section and stockholders' equity section of the company's balance sheet as they would appear after the entries are posted.

||| Problem 17-10   (Balance sheet preparation)

The following trial balance was taken from the books of Miller Manufacturing, a calendar-year corporation, as of April 30, 1991:

Miller Manufacturing
Trial Balance
April 30, 1991

Cash	310,000	
Accounts Receivable	800,000	
Finished Goods	500,000	
Goods in Process	100,000	
Raw Materials	750,000	
Land, Buildings, and Equipment	1,460,000	
Prepaid Expenses	5,400	
Sales Returns and Allowances	25,000	
Administrative Salaries	65,000	
Cost of Goods Sold	2,350,000	
Travel Expense	30,030	
Interest Expense	10,570	
Accounts Payable		175,000
Notes Payable		100,000
Payroll Payable		6,000
Interest Payable on 6% Bonds		10,000
6% Preferred Stock, $50 par		1,000,000
Common Stock, $100 par		1,416,000
6% Bonds Payable (due June 30, 1999)		500,000
Sales		2,500,000
Retained Earnings, December 31, 1990		520
Paid-In Capital		698,480
	6,406,000	6,406,000

The following transactions have been completed by the company:

(a) The company has purchased various lots of its $100 par value common stock, totaling 840 shares, at an average price of $65.50 per share, for $55,020. In recording these transactions, the company has canceled the stock certificates and debited the common stock account with the par value of $84,000 and credited the paid-in capital account with the $28,980 difference between par and the cash paid.

(b) Paid-In Capital was previously credited for $20 per share on the sale of 15,000 shares of common stock at $120.

(c) 6% bonds with a total face amount of $250,000 falling due on December 31, 1997, were issued on January 1, 1973, at a 10% discount. To June 30, 1989, $16,500 of this discount had been charged against revenues and as of this date the entire issue of these bonds was retired at par and the unamortized discount debited to Additional Paid-In Captial.

(d) A new issue of $500,000, 6% 10-year bonds was sold at par on July 1, 1989. Expenses incurred with respect to this issue in the amount of $20,000 were debited to Paid-In Capital.

Instructions: Prepare a balance sheet as of April 30, 1991, making any corrections necessary in view of the company's treatment of the preceding transactions.

(AICPA adapted)

Problem 17-11 (Dividends and stock rights—entries for company and investor)

On April 1, 1990, Estancia Co. purchased 1,000 shares of Cooper Co. common stock, par $10, at $20. On June 1, when the stock was selling for $22 on the open market, Estancia Co. received a 10% stock dividend from Cooper Co. On October 26, Cooper Co. paid Estancia Co. a dividend of $.75 on the stock and granted a stock right to purchase 1 share at $15 for every 5 shares held. On this date stock had a market value ex-rights of $22.50 and each right had a value of $1.70; the stock cost was allocated on this basis. On November 15, Estancia sold 120 rights at $1.25 and exercised the remaining rights. On March 3, 1991, Estancia received a cash dividend from Cooper Co. of $1.50 per share. On October 13, Cooper Co. declared a 2-for-1 stock split and, on October 31, declared dividends of $.40 per share. On December 31, Estancia sold all of its shares in Cooper Co. for $11.50.

Instructions: Prepare all entries for the preceding transactions on the books of (a) Estancia Co. and (b) Cooper Co. Omit explanations but show computations. Assume these are the only equity transactions for Cooper Co.

Problem 17-12 (Reporting stockholders' equity)

The stockholders' equity section of Nilsson Corporation's balance sheet as of December 31, 1990, is as follows:

Common stock ($5 par, 500,000 shares authorized, 275,000 issued and outstanding)	$1,375,000	
Additional Paid-in capital—Common stock	550,000	
Total paid-in capital		$1,925,000
Unappropriated retained earnings	$1,335,000	
Appropriated retained earnings	500,000	
Total retained earnings		1,835,000
Total stockholders' equity		$3,760,000

Nilsson Co. had the following stockholders' equity transactions during 1991:

Jan. 15 Completed the building renovation for which $500,000 of retained earnings had been restricted. Paid the contractor $485,000, all of which is capitalized.

March 3 Issued 100,000 additional shares of the common stock for $8 per share.

May 18 Declared a dividend of $1.50 per share to be paid on July 31, 1991, to stockholders of record on June 30, 1991.

June	19	Approved additional building renovation to be funded internally. The estimated cost of the project is $400,000.
July	31	Paid the dividend.
Nov.	12	Declared a property dividend to be paid on December 31, 1991, to stockholders of record on November 31, 1991. The dividend is to consist of 35,000 shares of Hampton Inc. stock that Nilsson purchased for $9 per share. The fair market value of the stock on November 12 is $13 per share.
Dec.	31	Reported $885,000 of net income on the December 31, 1991 income statement. In addition, the stock was distributed in satisfaction of the property dividend. The Hampton stock closed for $14 per share at the end of the day's trading.

Instructions:

(1) Make all necessary journal entries for Nilsson to account for the stockholders' equity transactions.
(2) Prepare the December 31, 1991 stockholders' equity section of the balance sheet for Nilsson.

PART FOUR

Special Problems in Income Determination and Reporting

Chapter 18

Earnings per Share

As indicated in Chapter 2, a primary objective of financial reporting is to provide information that is useful in making credit and investment decisions. Investors are interested in gaging how well a company is performing in comparison with other companies and with itself over time. When evaluating a company, it is not enough to know that net income is increasing or decreasing. Investors are concerned with how income is changing relative to their investment and to the current stock market valuation.

In an attempt to include both income and investment information in the same measurement, a computation known as earnings per share has been developed. While this measurement has some limitations that will be discussed later in this chapter, its presentation on the income statement has been required by generally accepted accounting principles since 1969.

Potential investors might use the earnings per share figure when choosing between different investment options. For example, by dividing the earnings per share figure into the market price per share, a price-earnings ratio may be computed and compared among different companies. Thus, if Company A earns $3 per share on common stock with a $21 per share market price, and Company B earns $6 per share on common stock with a $54 per share market value, an investor can state that Company A stock is selling at seven times earnings and Company B stock is selling at nine times earnings. Other things being equal between these two companies, Company A's stock would be the better buy since its market price is lower in relation to earnings than is the price of Company B's stock.

Investors are also interested in dividends and can use earnings per share data to compute a dividend payout percentage (or payout rate). This percentage is computed by dividing earnings per share into dividends per share. Thus, if Company A in the previous example pays a dividend of $2 per share, and Company B pays $3 per share, the payout percentage would be 66⅔% for Company A and 50% for Company B.

Earnings per share data receive wide recognition in the annual reports issued by companies, in the press, and in financial reporting publications.

This measurement is frequently regarded as an important determinant of the market price of common stock.

Evolution of Requirements for Earnings per Share Disclosure

Earnings per share figures were historically computed and used primarily by financial analysts. Sometimes the computation was disclosed in the unaudited section of the annual report along with a message from the company's president. However, because this measurement was not reviewed by an independent third party, figures used to develop earnings per share were often different from those attested to by the auditor. The situation became more complex when some companies and analysts began computing earnings per share not only on the basis of common shares actually outstanding, but also on the basis of what shares would be outstanding if certain convertible securities were converted and if certain stock options were exercised. Usually, the conversion or exercise terms were very favorable to the holders of these securities, and earnings per share would decline if common stock were issued upon conversion or exercise. This result, a reduced earnings per share, is referred to as a dilution of earnings. In some cases, however, the exercise of options or conversion of securities might result in an increased earnings per share. This result is referred to as an antidilution of earnings. Securities that would lead to dilution are referred to as dilutive securities, and those that would lead to antidilution are referred to as antidilutive securities. Rational investors would not convert or exercise antidilutive securities because they could do better by purchasing common stock in the market place.

These forward-looking computations of earnings per share attempted to provide information as to what future earnings per share *might* be assuming conversions and exercises took place. Because these "as if" conditions were based on assumptions, they could be computed in several ways. Recognizing the diversity of reporting practices, the Accounting Principles Board became involved in establishing guidelines for the computation and disclosure of earnings per share figures. The result was the issuance in 1969 of APB Opinion No. 15, "Earnings per Share," which concluded:

> The Board believes that the significance attached by investors and others to earnings per share data, together with the importance of evaluating the data in conjunction with the financial statements, requires that such data be presented prominently in the financial statements. The Board has therefore concluded that earnings per share or net loss per share data should be shown on the face of the income statement. The extent of the data to be presented and the captions used will vary with the complexity of the company's capital structure. . . .[1]

For the first few years after Opinion No. 15 was issued, all business

[1] *Opinions of the Accounting Principles Board, No. 15*, "Earnings per Share" (New York: American Institute of Certified Public Accountants, 1969), par. 12

entities were required to include earnings per share data in their income statements. However, in 1978, the FASB issued Statement No. 21, which eliminated this requirement for nonpublic entities. A nonpublic company is defined as any enterprise other than "one (a) whose debt or equity securities trade in a public market on a foreign or domestic stock exchange or in the over-the-counter market, . . . or (b) that is required to file financial statements with the Securities and Exchange Commission."[2]

In the process of establishing rules for computing earnings per share, the Accounting Principles Board felt it necessary to be very specific about how future-orieneted "as if" figures were to be computed. Many interpretations and amendments were issued with the intent to clarify the computations for a variety of securities and under varied circumstances. In some areas the the rules became arbitrary and complex, and the resulting earnings per share computations have received much criticism as to their usefulness. Indeed, for companies with complex capital structures, the historical or simple earnings per share figure based on actual shares of common stock outstanding may not even be reported. In its place the APB substituted two earnings per share amounts: (1) primary earnings per share based on the assumed conversion or exercise of certain securities identified as common stock equivalents and (2) fully diluted earnings per share based on the assumed conversions of all convertible securities or exercise of all stock options that would reduce or dilute primary earnings per share.

Although more than twenty years have passed since APB Opinion No. 15 was issued, there has been little evidence to support the usefulness of these forward-type earnings per share figures. Shortly after APB Opinion No. 15 was issued, in fact, the Canadian Institute of Chartered Accountants reviewed what the APB had done, and concluded that only a historical earnings per share and a fully diluted earnings per share had potential value. They rejected the attempt to define an intermediary figure that was intended to measure the probability of conversion or exercise.[3] A United States survey of investors in 1980 indicated that various return on investment figures have become more popular than earnings per share as a measure of profitability.[4] Of those corporate, government, and accounting executives surveyed, 66% listed return on investment as highly important, while only 49% listed earnings per share as highly important. A majority of 3 to 1 felt that return on investment was a better or more desirable measure of corporate performance than earnings per share. Other writers have argued that earnings per share, as defined by the APB in Opinion No. 15, is

[2]*Statement of Financial Accounting Standards No. 21*, "Suspension of the Reporting of Earnings Per Share and Segment Information by Nonpublic Enterprises" (Stamford: Financial Accounting Standards Board, 1978), par. 13.

[3]*CICA Handbook, Section 3500*, "Earnings per Share" (Toronto: The Canadian Institute of Chartered Accountants, February 1970).

[4]As reported by a Lou Harris survey for the Financial Accounting Foundation in the Alexander Grant Newsletter, July 1980.

neither relevant nor reliable, two characteristics identified by the FASB as being essential to useful information.[5]

However, because earnings per share figures are presently required for all public companies, accountants must understand how they are computed and the rationale for the computations. Only the basic recommendations can be presented here. When Opinion No. 15 fails to state the specific procedures to be followed under special circumstances, the accountant must exercise judgment in developing supportable presentations within the recommended framework.

Simple and Complex Capital Structures

The capital structure of a company may be classified as simple or complex. If a company has only common stock, or common and nonconvertible preferred stock, outstanding and there are no convertible securities, stock options, warrants, or other rights outstanding, it is classified as a company with a **simple capital structure**. Earnings per share is computed by dividing the net income for the period by the weighted average number of common shares outstanding for the period. No future-oriented "as if" conditions need to be considered. If net income includes extraordinary gains or losses or other below-the-line items as discussed in Chapter 4, a separate earnings per share figure is required for each major component of income, as well as for net income.

Even if convertible securities, stock options, warrants or other rights do exist, the capital stucture may be classified as simple if there is no potential material dilution to earnings per share from the conversion or exercise of these items. Potential earnings per share dilution exists if the earnings per share would decrease or the loss per share would increase as a result of the conversion of securities or exercise of stock options, warrants, or other rights based on the conditions existing at the financial statement date. The Accounting Principles Board defined **material dilution** as being a decrease of 3% or more in the simple earnings per share. If a company's capital structure does not qualify as simple, it is classified as a **complex capital structure**, and the two figures identified previously—primary and fully diluted earnings per share—are required if either is materially dilutive.

The Simple Capital Structure— Computational Guidelines

The earnings per share computation presents no problem when only common stock has been issued and the number of shares outstanding has remained the same for the entire period. The numerator is the net income (loss), and the denominator is the number of shares outstanding for the entire period. Frequently, however, either the numerator, the denominator, or both must be adjusted because of the following conditions:

(1) When common shares have been issued or have been reacquired by a company during a period, the resources available to the company have

[5]Lola Woodard Dudley, "A Critical Look at EPS," *Journal of Accountancy* (August 1985): 102-111.

changed and this change should affect earnings. Under these circumstances, a weighted average for shares outstanding should be computed.

The weighted average number of shares may be computed by determining month-shares of outstanding stock and dividing by 12 to obtain the weighted average for the year. For example, if a company has 10,000 shares outstanding at the beginning of the year, issues 5,000 more shares on May 1, and reacquires 2,000 shares on November 1, the weighted average number of shares would be computed as illustrated below. Note that a separate period computation is required each time stock is sold or reacquired.

		Month-Shares
Jan. 1 to May 1	10,000 × 4 months	40,000
May 1 to Nov. 1 (10,000 + 5,000)	15,000 × 6 months	90,000
Nov. 1 to Dec. 31 (15,000 − 2,000)	13,000 × 2 months	26,000
Total month-shares		156,000
Weighted average number of shares:		
156,000 ÷ 12		13,000

The same answer can be obtained by applying a weight to each period equivalent to the portion of the year since the last change in shares outstanding, as follows:

Jan. 1 to May 1	10,000 × 4/12 year	3,333
May 1 to Nov. 1	15,000 × 6/12 year	7,500
Nov. 1 to Dec. 31	13,000 × 2/12 year	2,167
Weighted average number of shares		13,000

If transactions occurred during a month, the weighted average computation could be made either on a daily basis or to the nearest month. In examples and end-of-chapter material, assume computations to the nearest month unless otherwise specified.

(2) When the number of common shares outstanding has changed during a period as a result of stock dividend, a stock split, or a reverse split, a retroactive recognition of this change must be made in arriving at the amount of earnings per share. To illustrate, assume that a company had 2,600 shares outstanding as of January 1, and that the following events affecting common stock occurred during the year:

Date	Economic Event	Change in Shares Outstanding
February 1	Exercise of stock option	+ 400
May 1	10% stock dividend (3,000 × 10%)	+ 300
September 1	Sale of stock for cash	+1,200
November 1	Purchase of treasury stock	− 400
December 15	3-for-1 stock split	+8,200

The computation of the weighted average number of shares for the year would be as follows:

Dates	Outstanding Shares		Stock Dividend		Stock Split		Portion of Year		Weighted Average
Jan. 1 to Feb. 1	2,600	×	1.10	×	3.0	×	1/12	=	715
Feb. 1—option	400								
Feb. 1 to May 1	3,000	×	1.10	×	3.0	×	3/12	=	2,475
May 1—stock dividend	300								
May 1 to Sept. 1	3,300			×	3.0	×	4/12	=	3,300
Sept. 1—sale	1,200								
Sept. 1 to Nov. 1	4,500			×	3.0	×	2/12	=	2,250
Nov. 1—treasury stock	(400)								
Nov. 1 to Dec. 1	4,100			×	3.0	×	1/12	=	1,025
Dec. 1 split	8,200								
Dec. 1 to Dec. 31	12,300					×	1/12	=	1,025
									10,790

Weighted average number of shares

In the illustration above, the outstanding shares for January 1 to May 1 were multiplied by 1.10 to reflect the 10% stock dividend, and the outstanding shares for January 1 to December 1 were multiplied by 3 to reflect the 3-for-1 stock split.

When comparative financial statements are presented, the outstanding common shares for all periods shown must be adjusted to reflect any stock dividend or stock split in the current period.

Only with the retroactive recognition of changes in the number of shares can earnings per share presentations for prior periods be stated on a basis comparable with the earnings per share presentation for the current period. Similar retroactive adjustments must be made even if a stock dividend or stock split occurs after the end of the period but before the financial statements are prepared; disclosure of this situation should be made in a note to the financial statements.

(3) Earnings per share reflects only income available to common stockholders, and does not include preferred stock. It would be inappropriate to report earnings per share on preferred stock in view of the limited dividend rights of such stock. When a capital structure includes preferred stock, dividends on preferred stock should be deducted from net income and also from income before extraordinary or other special items, when such items appear on the income statement, in arriving at the earnings related to common shares. If preferred dividends are not cumulative, only the dividends declared on preferred stock during the period are deducted. If preferred dividends are cumulative, the full amount of dividends on preferred stock for the period, whether declared or not, should be deducted from income before extaordinary or other special items and from net income in arriving at the earnings or loss balance related to the common stock. If there is a loss for the period, preferred dividends for the period, including any un-

declared dividends on cumulative preferred stock, are added to the loss in arriving at the full loss related to the common stock.

To illustrate the computation of earnings per share at December 31, 1992, for a company with a simple capital structure for a comparative two-year period, assume the following data:

Summary of changes in capital balances

	10% Cumulative Preferred Stock $100 Par		Common Stock No Par		Retained Earnings
	Shares	Amount	Shares	Amount	
Dec. 31, 1990 balances	10,000	$1,000,000	200,000	$1,000,000	$4,000,000
June 30,1991 issuance of 100,000 shares of common stock			100,000	600,000	
June 30, 1991 dividend on preferred stock, 8%					(80,000)
June 30, 1991 dividend on common stock, $.30					(90,000)
Dec. 31, 1991 net income for year, including extraordinary gain of $75,000					380,000
Dec. 31, 1991 balances	10,000	$1,000,000	300,000	$1,600,000	$4,210,000
May 1, 1992 50% stock dividend on common stock			150,000	800,000	(800,000)
Dec. 31, 1992 net loss for year					(55,000)
Dec. 31, 1992 balances	10,000	$1,000,000	450,000	$2,400,000	$3,355,000

Because comparative statements are presented, the denominator of weighted shares outstanding for 1991 must be adjusted for the 50% stock dividend issued in 1992 as follows:

1991: Jan. 1-June 30	200,000 × 1.5 (50% stock dividend in 1992) × 6/12 year	150,000		
July 1-Dec. 31	200,000 + 100,000 (issuance of stock on June 30, 1991) × 1.5 (50% stock dividend in 1992) × 6/12 year	225,000	375,000	
1992: Jan. 1-Dec. 31	300,000 × 1.5 (50% stock dividend in 1992) × 1 year		450,000	

Continuing the example, earnings per share for 1991 must be shown separately for income from continuing operations, the extraordinary gain, and net income. The preferred dividends must be deducted from both income from continuing operations and net income in computing earnings per share for these income components. For 1992, the reported net loss must be increased by the full amount of the preferred dividend even though the dividend was not declared. If the preferred stock were noncumulative, no adjustment for the undeclared preferred dividend would be necessary in 1992. The adjusted income (loss) figures for computing earnings per share are determined as follows:

1991:	Income from continuing operations ($380,000 net income − $75,000 extraordinary gain)	$305,000
	Less preferred dividend	80,000
	Income from continuing operations identified with common stock	$225,000
	Net income	$380,000
	Less preferred dividend	80,000
	Net income identified with common stock	$300,000
1992:	Net loss	$ 55,000
	Add preferred dividend	80,000
	Net loss identified with common stock	$135,000

The earnings per share amounts can now be computed as follows:

1991:	Earnings per common share from continuing operations ($225,000 ÷ 375,000)	$.60
	Extraordinary gain ($75,000 ÷ 375,000)	.20
	Net income per share ($300,000 ÷ 375,000)	$.80
1992:	Loss per share ($135,000 ÷ 450,000)	$.30

The Complex Capital Structure— Computational Guidelines

As discussed earlier, complex capital structures call for a dual presentation of earnings per share data on the face of the income statement: (1) primary earnings per share—a presentation based on the number of common shares outstanding plus the shares represented by common stock equivalents that have a dilutive effect on earnings per share; (2) fully diluted earnings per share—a second presentation based on the assumption that all of the contingent issuances of shares of common stock that would dilute earnings per share had taken place. In computing both primary and fully diluted earnings per share, any securities whose exercise or conversion would increase earnings per share or reduce loss per share are referred to as **antidilutive** securities. In general, these securities are not included in the computation of either earnings per share figure.

Computation of dual earnings per share requires application of the procedures for the simple structure previously described as well as special analyses and additional computations described in the following sections. The first section describes the computation of primary earnings per share; the second section describes the computation of fully diluted earnings per share.

Primary Earnings Per Share

The computation of primary earnings per share requires an identification of those securities qualifying as common stock equivalents. A common stock equivalent is a security that is in substance equivalent to common stock due to its terms or the circumstances under which it was issued.[6] Holders of these securities can expect to participate in the appreciation of the value of common stock resulting primarily from present and potential earnings of the issuing company. A security identified as a common stock equivalent

[6]*Opinions of the Accounting Principles Board No. 15*, Appendix D.

enters into the computation of primary earnings per share only if it is dilutive. Once a security is recognized as a common stock equivalent, the Accounting Principles Board indicated that it retains this status. However, depending on its dilutive effect, it could enter into the computation of primary earnings per share in one period and not in another.

Following is a summary of the principal items considered as common stock equivalents for computing earnings per share. A detailed discussion of each item follows the summary.

1. Stock options, warrants, and rights are always considered to be common stock equivalents.
2. Convertible debt or convertible preferred stock is considered to be a common stock equivalent if the security's effective yield, at date of issue, is less than 66⅔% of the Aa corporate bond yield.

Stock Options, Warrants, and Rights

As explained in Chapter 16, stock options, warrants, and rights provide no cash yield to investors, but have value because they permit the acquisition of common stock at specified prices for a certain period of time. By definition of the APB, these items are always regarded as common stock equivalents. However, options, warrants, and rights are included in the computation of primary earnings per share for a particular period only if they are dilutive. If the price for which stock can be acquired (exercise price) is lower than the current market price, the options, warrants, or rights would probably be exercised and their effect would be dilutive. If the exercise price is higher than the current market price, no exercise would take place; thus, there is no potential dilution from these securities.[7]

If it is assumed that exercise of options, warrants, or rights takes place as of the beginning of the year or at the date they are issued, whichever comes later, additional cash resources would have been available for the company's use. In order to compute primary earnings per share when these types of securities exist, either net income must be increased to take into consideration the increase in revenue such additional resources would produce, or the cash must be assumed to be used for some nonrevenue producing purpose. The latter approach was selected by the APB, and they recommended it be assumed that the cash proceeds from the exercise of options, warrants, or rights be used to purchase common stock on the market (treasury stock) at the **average market price** for the period involved. It is further assumed that the shares of treasury stock are issued to those exercising their options, warrants, or rights, and the remaining shares required to be issued will be added to the actual number of shares outstanding to compute primary earnings per share. This method of including warrants,

---

[7] The Board stated that, as a practical matter, no assumption of exercise is necessary until the market price has exceeded the exercise price for substantially all of three consecutive months ending with the last month to which earnings per share relate. "Substantially all" has been defined as 11 of the 13 weeks. This is a one-time test. Once the requirement is met, future computations of primary earnings per share will include the options, warrants, or rights unless they are antidilutive. See APB Opinion No. 15, par. 36.

options, and rights in the EPS computation is known as the **treasury stock method.**

To illustrate, assume that at the beginning of the current year, employees were granted options to acquire 5,000 shares of common stock at $40 per share. The year-end market price of the stock is $50, so exercise would be assumed and the effect will be dilutive. The proceeds received by the corporation from the issuance of stock to the employees would be $200,000 (5,000 shares × $40 exercise price). Assuming the average market price of the stock for the year was also $50, these proceeds would purchase 4,000 shares of treasury stock ($200,000 ÷ $50). If it is assumed that these 4,000 shares are issued to the employees, an additional 1,000 shares would have to be issued, and the number of shares of stock for computing primary earnings per share would be increased by 1,000 shares. The interpretations of Opinion No. 15 refer to these shares as **incremental shares.**[8]

Illustration of Primary EPS with Stock Options

The use of the treasury stock method in computing primary earnings per share is illustrated with the following data for the Tring Corporation:

Summary of relevant information

Net income for the year	$92,800
Common shares outstanding (no change during year)	100,000
Options outstanding to purchase equivalent shares	20,000
Exercise price per share on options	$ 6
Average market price for common shares	$10

Earnings per share without common stock equivalents (simple EPS):

Net income for the year	$92,800
Actual number of shares outstanding	100,000
Simple earnings per share ($92,800 ÷ 100,000)	$.93

Application of proceeds from assumed exercise of options outstanding to purchase treasury stock:

Proceeds from assumed exercise of options outstanding (20,000 × $6)	$120,000
Number of outstanding shares assumed to be repurchased with proceeds from options ($120,000 ÷ $10)	12,000

Number of shares to be used in computing primary earnings per share:

Actual number of shares outstanding		100,000
Incremental shares:		
Issued on assumed exercise of options	20,000	
Less assumed repurchase of shares from proceeds of options	12,000	8,000
Total		108,000
Primary earnings per share ($92,800 ÷ 108,000)		$.86

Percentage dilution: $.93 − $.86 = $.07; $.07 ÷ $.93 = 7.5% (rounded)

---

[8]*Accounting Interpretations of APB Opinion No. 15, Interpretation 51,* "Computing Earnings Per Share" (New York: American Institute of Certified Public Accountants, 1970).

The materiality test of dilution is applied after all dilutive common stock equivalents have been included. In this illustration, there is only one such security; therefore, the test is applied after its inclusion. The dilution of approximately 7.5% exceeds the materiality standard (3% or more), so the common stock equivalent would be used in computing primary earnings per share.

Limitation on Use of Treasury Stock Method

If the number of common shares of stock involved in exercising options, warrants, or rights is large, the market price of the shares may not be a reliable figure, because any attempt to purchase a large block of stock would drive the stock price upward. The Accounting Principles Board recognized this possibility, and declared the treasury stock method inappropriate for proceeds in excess of those required to purchase 20% of the shares outstanding at the end of the year. Proceeds beyond those required to purchase 20% of the common stock are assumed to be applied first to reduce any short-term or long-term borrowings, and any remaining proceeds are assumed to be invested in U.S. Government securities or commercial paper, with appropriate recognition of any income effect, net of tax.

To illustrate the computation of primary earnings per share under these circumstances, assume the following data for the Mirage Corporation:

Summary of relevant information:

Net income for the year	$4,000,000
Common shares outstanding (no change during year)	3,000,000
10% Bonds payable	$5,000,000
Options outstanding to purchase equivalent shares	1,000,000
Limitation on assumed repurchase of shares (3,000,000 × 20%)	600,000
Exercise price per share on options	$15
Average market price for common shares	$20
Income tax rate	40%

Earnings per share without common stock equivalents (simple EPS):

Net income for the year	$4,000,000
Actual number of shares outstanding	3,000,000
Simple earnings per share ($4,000,000 ÷ 3,000,000)	$1.33

Application of proceeds from assumed exercise of options outstanding:

Proceeds from assumed exercise of options outstanding (1,000,000 × $15)	$15,000,000
Maximum applied toward repurchase of outstanding shares (600,000 × $20)	12,000,000
Balance of proceeds applied to retirement of 8% bonds	$ 3,000,000

Net income to be used in computing primary earnings per share:

Net income		$4,000,000
Add interest on 10% bonds assumed retired, net of income tax:		
Interest ($3,000,000 × 10%)	$300,000	
Less income tax savings ($300,000 × 40%)	120,000	180,000
Adjusted net income		$4,180,000

Number of shares to be used in computing primary earnings per share:

Actual number of shares outstanding		3,000,000
Incremental shares:		
Issued on assumed exercise of options	1,000,000	
Less assumed repurchase of shares from proceeds of options	600,000	400,000
Total		3,400,000
Primary earnings per share ($4,180,000 ÷ 3,400,000)		$1.23

Percentage dilution: $1.33 − $1.23 = $.10; $.10 ÷ $1.33 = 7.52% (rounded)

The dilution again is considered material, and options would be included.

Partially paid stock subscriptions are to be considered the equivalent of warrants for purposes of computing earnings per share amounts. The unpaid balance is assumed to be the proceeds used to purchase stock under the treasury stock method. The number of incremental shares for partially paid stock subscriptions is the difference between the number of shares subscribed and the number of shares assumed to be purchased under the treasury stock method.[9]

Convertible Securities

A convertible security, whether bonds or preferred stock, that at the time of its issuance has terms indicating the purchaser is placing a premium on the conversion feature is recognized as a common stock equivalent. Specifically, a convertible security is considered a common stock equivalent if, at the time of issuance, it has an effective yield of less than 66⅔% of the then current average Aa corporate bond yield.[10] The effective yield is the rate that would discount all future cash flows from the security to the issue price. For example, assume that Brown Inc. purchased a $10,000, 14% ten-year convertible bond when the effective market interest yield was 12%. The purchase price of the bond would be $11,130 computed as follows:

Present Value of the Interest	
$1,400 × 5.6502 (Table IV; 12%, 10 years)	$ 7,910
Present Value of the Principal	
$10,000 × .3220 (Table II; 12%, 10 years)	3,220
Market price discounted at the effective interest rate	$11,130

Usually the purchase price is known and the effective yield must be computed. Because the computation involves an annuity and a single payment, a computer or a bond yield table is required to determine the effective yield. If a security has no maturity date, the effective yield is the same as the cash yield, or the annual return divided by the issue price of the secur-

[9]*Accounting Interpretations of APB Opinion No. 15, Interpretation No. 83*, "Stock Subscriptions are Warrants" (New York: American Institute of Certified Public Accountants, 1970).

[10]*Statement of Financial Accounting Standards No. 85*, "Yield Test for Determining Whether a Convertible Security is a Common Stock Equivalent" (Stamford: Financial Accounting Standards Board, 1985).

ity. Most preferred stock fits this situation. Thus if 8%, $100 par preferred stock is sold for $105, the cash yield would be 7.6% ($8 ÷ $105).

The identification of a convertible security as a common stock equivalent is made at the time of its issuance, and it retains this identity as long as it remains outstanding, regardless of changes in the interest rate. Convertible securities are included in primary earnings per share only if they are dilutive.

For example, assume at December 31, 1991, the Aa corporate bond yield is 11%. A $1,000, 20-year, convertible bond with a stated interest rate of 7% is sold at a price providing an effective yield of 6.42%. Since the yield is less than 66⅔% of the Aa corporate bond yield of 11%, or 7⅓%, the bond is recognized as a common stock equivalent. The bond will retain this classification even though future bond interest rates fall and the effective yield exceeds 66⅔% of the Aa yield.

In order to compute primary earnings per share when convertible securities exist, adjustments must be made **both** to net income and to the number of shares of common stock outstanding. These adjustments must reflect what these amounts would have been if the conversion had taken place at the beginning of the current year or at the date of issuance of the convertible securities, whichever comes later. This method of including convertible securities in the EPS computation is referred to as the **if-converted method**. If the securites are bonds, net income is adjusted by adding back the interest expense, net of tax, to net income; the number of shares of common stock outstanding is increased by the number of shares that would have been issued on conversion.[11] Any amortization of initial premium or discount is included in the interest expense added back. If the convertible securities are shares of preferred stock, no reduction is made from net income for preferred dividends, as is done with the computation of earnings per share in a simple capital structure; the number of shares of common stock outstanding is increased by the number of shares that would have been issued upon conversion. If the convertible securities were issued during the year, adjustments would be made for only the portion of the year since the issuance date.

In order to test for dilution, each convertible security that qualifies as a common stock equivalent must be evaluated individually. If there is only one such security, comparison is made between earnings per share before considering the convertible security with the earnings per share after including it. As indicated earlier, if the earnings per share decreases or loss per share increases, the convertible security is defined as dilutive. Antidilutive securities are excluded from the computation of primary earnings per share. The 3% materiality test for dilution is applied by comparing the

---

[11]In addition to adjustments for interest, adjustments to net income for nondiscretionary or indirect items would have to be made in many situations. These items would include profit-sharing bonuses and other payments whose amount is determined by the net income reported. For simplicity, no indirect effects are illustrated in this chapter.

primary earnings per share after considering all dilutive common stock equivalents with the simple earnings per share. A simplified procedure for considering multiple common stock equivalents is included in the appendix to this chapter.

Illustration of Primary EPS with Convertible Securities

The following examples for the Reid Corporation illustrate the computation of primary earnings per share when convertible securities qualifying as common stock equivalents exist.

Summary of relevant information:

8% convertible bonds issued at par	$500,000
Net income for the year	$ 83,000
Common shares outstanding (no change during year)	100,000
Conversion terms of convertible bonds—80 shares for each $1,000 bond	
Assumed tax rate	40%

Earnings per share without common stock equivalents (simple EPS):

Net income	$ 83,000
Actual number of shares outstanding	100,000
Simple earnings per share ($83,000 ÷ 100,000)	$.83

Primary earnings per share including common stock equivalents:

Net income		$ 83,000
Add interest on convertible bonds, net of income tax:		
Interest ($500,000 × 8%)	$40,000	
Less income tax savings ($40,000 × 40%)	16,000	24,000
Adjusted net income		$107,000
Actual number of shares outstanding		100,000
Additional shares issued on assumed conversion of bonds (500 × 80)		40,000
Adjusted number of shares		140,000
Primary earnings per share ($107,000 ÷ 140,000)		$.76

Percentage dilution: $.83 − $.76 = $.07; $.07 ÷ $.83 = 8.4% (rounded)

Computation of Primary EPS for Partial Year

If the convertible bonds had been issued by Reid Corporation on March 31 of the current year, the adjustment would be made to reflect only the period subsequent to the issuance date, or ¾ of a year.

Primary earnings per share including common stock equivalents (¾ year):

Net income		$ 83,000
Add interest on convertible bonds, net of income tax:		
Interest ($500,000 × 8% × ¾ year)	$30,000	
Less income tax ($30,000 × 40%)	12,000	18,000
Adjusted net income		$101,000
Actual number of shares outstanding		100,000
Additional shares issued on assumed conversion of bonds (500 × 80 × ¾)		30,000
Adjusted number of shares		130,000
Primary earnings per share ($101,000 ÷ 130,000)		$.78

Percentage dilution: $.83 − $.78 = $.05; $.05 ÷ $.83 = 6% (rounded)

Convertible preferred stock is treated in the same manner as convertible debt securities (bonds). To illustrate application of the "if-converted" method to preferred stock, assume the same facts as given for the bond example for Reid Corporation on page 749, except that instead of 8% convertible bonds, the company has 8% preferred stock outstanding, par value $500,000, convertible into 40,000 shares of common stock. Note that since Reid would have no bond interest under the change in assumptions, the reported net income would be $107,000 ($83,000 + $24,000 bond interest net of tax savings.) The preferred stock was outstanding for the entire year and qualifies as a common stock equivalent.

Earnings per share without common stock equivalents (simple EPS):

Net income, without the deduction for interest on bonds (as computed on page 749)	$107,000
Less preferred dividends	40,000
Net income identified with common stock	$ 67,000
Actual number of shares outstanding	100,000
Simple earnings per share ($67,000 ÷ 100,000)	$.67

Primary earnings per share including common stock equivalents:

Net income assuming no payment of preferred dividends	$107,000
Actual number of shares outstanding	100,000
Additional shares issued on assumed conversion of preferred stock	40,000
Adjusted number of shares	140,000
Primary earnings per share ($107,000 ÷ 140,000)	$.76

In this example, primary earnings per share ($.76) is greater than simple earnings per share ($.67). Thus the convertible preferred stock is antidilutive and would not be considered in the computation of earnings per share. Assuming the corporation had no other potentially dilutive securities outstanding, only simple earnings per share would be presented on the income statement.

Short-Cut Test for Antidilution

It is possible to determine if a convertible security is antidilutive without actually computing primary or fully diluted earnings per share assuming conversion. If a company has net income rather than losses, the antidilutive test is performed by computing what the conversion contributes to per share earnings. For example, if the 8% bonds are converted, net income to the common shareholders will increase by $24,000, (see page 749) and the number of common shares outstanding will increase by 40,000 shares. The contribution of this conversion to earnings is $.60 per share, ($24,000 ÷ 40,000). Since this amount is less than the preconversion simple earnings per share of $.83, the bonds are dilutive. On the other hand, if the preferred stock is converted, the preferred dividends of $40,000 would no longer be deducted from net income in computing earnings per share, and the number of common shares outstanding will increase by 40,000 shares. The contribution of this conversion to earnings is $1.00 per share, ($40,000 ÷ 40,000). Since the preferred stock conversion contributes more per share than preconversion simple earnings of $.67, the preferred stock is antidilutive.

Multiple Potentially Dilutive Securities

When several potentially dilutive securities exist, the combination of convertible securities and options, warrants, and other rights that produce the lowest primary earnings per share should be determined and reported. This lowest figure is found by computing earnings per share for all possible combinations of potentially dilutive securities that are not antidilutive, and identifying the lowest figure. The use of computers assists greatly in testing for the lowest combination figure. A comprehensive illustration that includes multiple dilutive securities is included in the Appendix to this chapter.

Fully Diluted Earnings per Share

In calculating fully diluted earnings in the dual presentation of earnings per share, it is necessary to consider not only all dilutive common stock equivalents, but all other potentially dilutive securities even though they do not qualify as common stock equivalents. For example, fully diluted earnings per share would include convertible securities whose effective yield equaled or exceeded 66⅔% of the Aa corporate bond yield at the issuance date that were dilutive. As with common stock equivalents, conversion is assumed to have taken place at the beginning of the period or at the time the convertible security was issued, if later. The maximum potential dilution of current earnings per share on a prospective basis is thus determined.

When primary earnings are diluted as a result of the inclusion of outstanding options and warrants, a modification in the application of the treasury stock method may be necessary for purposes of calculating the fully diluted earnings per share. To reflect maximum potential dilution, the market price of the common stock at the close of the period is used in computing the number of shares assumed to be reacquired if the ending market price is higher than the average price used in computing primary earnings per share. As is the case for primary earnings per share, the computation of fully diluted earnings per share should include only dilutive securities.

Illustration of Fully Diluted Earnings Per Share

To illustrate fully diluted earnings per share, assume the following additional facts for the Tring Corporation as presented on page 790:

Additional relevant information:

Tax rate	40%
Ending market price for common shares	$16
9% convertible bonds not qualifying as common stock equivalents	$60,000
Conversion terms for 9% bonds—100 shares for each $1,000 bond	

Test for dilution of 9% convertible bonds:

$$\frac{\text{Interest, net of 40\% tax}}{\text{Additional shares}} = \frac{(\$60{,}000 \times .09 \times .60)}{100 \times 60} = \$.54 \text{ per share}$$

Because the contribution of $.54 is less than the primary earnings per share of $.86 (see page 000), the convertible bonds are potentially dilutive and will be used in computing fully diluted earnings per share.

Net income to be used in computing fully diluted earnings per share:

Net income		$ 92,800
Add interest on convertible bonds net of income tax:		
Interest ($60,000 × 9%)	$5,400	
Less income tax savings ($5,400 × 40%)	2,160	3,240
Adjusted net income		$ 96,040

Application of proceeds from assumed exercise of options outstanding to purchase treasury stock:

Proceeds from assumed exercise of options outstanding (20,000 × $6)	$120,000
Number of outstanding shares assumed to be repurchased with proceeds from options ($120,000 ÷ $16)	7,500

Number of shares to be used in computing fully diluted earnings per share:

Actual number of shares outstanding		100,000
Incremental shares:		
Issued on assumed exercise of options	20,000	
Less assumed repurchase of shares from proceeds of options	7,500	12,500
Additional shares issued on assumed conversion of 9% bonds (100 × 60)		6,000
Total		118,500
Fully diluted earnings per share ($96,040 ÷ 118,500)		$.81

Primary and fully diluted earnings in the Tring example would be reported on the income statement as shown below. This presentation would be accompanied by notes explaining the nature of the calculations:

Primary earnings per share.........	$.86
Fully diluted earnings per share.....	$.81

Effect of Actual Exercise or Conversion If exercise or conversion actually takes place during the year, the weighted average number of shares issued will be included in all earnings per share computations. In addition, however, an adjustment is made to reflect what the earnings per share would have been if conversion or exercise had taken place at the beginning of the period or issuance date whichever comes later. This adjustment is required for all securities actually converted or exercised during the period for computing fully diluted earnings per share whether dilutive or not. However, for computing primary earnings per share, the adjustment is required only if the results are dilutive.

When options or warrants are exercised, the adjustment for the period before exercise for primary earnings per share uses the average market price for the pre-exercise period; the adjustment for fully diluted earnings per share uses the market price at exercise date, regardless of whether it is higher than the average price.

To illustrate the computation of primary and fully diluted earnings per share when stock options are exercised during the year, assume the data that follow for Weatherby, Inc.

Summary of relevant information:

Net income for the year	$2,300,000
Common shares outstanding at beginning of year	400,000
Options outstanding at beginning of year to purchase equivalent shares	100,000
Exercise price per share on options	$9.00
Proceeds from actual exercise of options on October 1 of current year	$900,000
Market prices of common stock during year:	
Average for 9 months ending September 30	$12.50
Market price at exercise date, October 1	$15.00

Number of shares to be used in computing simple earnings per share:

Actual number of shares outstanding for full year	400,000
Weighted shares issued on October 1 (100,000 × ¼ year)	25,000
Weighted average number of shares for simple earnings per share	425,000
Simple earnings per share ($2,300,000 ÷ 425,000)	$5.41

Number of shares to be used in computing primary earnings per share:

Weighted average number of shares for simple earnings per share		425,000
Incremental shares if options had been exercised on January 1 (options are dilutive since average market price of stock exceeds the exercise price):		
Issued on assumed exercise of options	100,000	
Less assumed repurchase of shares with proceeds ($900,000 ÷ $12.50)	72,000	
Incremental shares assumed to be issued	28,000	
Weighted average of incremental shares assumed to be issued (28,000 × ¾ year)		21,000
Weighted average number of shares for primary earnings per share		446,000
Primary earnings per share ($2,300,000 ÷ 446,000)		$5.16

Percentage dilution: $5.41 − $5.16 = $.25; $.25 ÷ $5.41 = 4.6%

Number of shares to be used in computing fully diluted earnings per share:

Weighted average number of shares for simple earnings per share		425,000
Incremental shares if options had been exercised on January 1 (included whether dilutive or not):		
Issued on assumed exercise of options	100,000	
Less assumed repurchase of shares with proceeds ($900,000 ÷ $15)	60,000	
Incremental shares assumed to be issued	40,000	
Weighted average of incremental shares assumed to be issued (40,000 × ¾ year)		30,000
Weighted average number of shares for fully diluted earnings per share		455,000
Fully diluted earnings per share ($2,300,000 ÷ 455,000)		$5.05

Effect of Net Losses

If a company has a net loss, no dual computation of earnings per share is necessary since inclusion of stock options or convertible securities would decrease the loss per share and thus always be antidilutive. To illustrate this situation, assume the following data for the Boggs Co.

Summary of relevant information:

Net loss for the year	($50,000)
Number of shares of stock outstanding—full year	100,000
Number of shares of convertible preferred stock	10,000
Conversion terms—2 shares of common for 1 share of preferred	
Dividends on preferred stock	$8,000

The computation of simple and primary earnings per share would be as follows:

Loss per share without common stock equivalents (simple):

Net loss	($50,000)
Dividends on preferred stock	(8,000)
Total loss to common shareholders	($58,000)
Actual number of shares outstanding	100,000
Loss per share ($58,000 ÷ 100,000)	($.58)

Primary loss per share including common stock equivalents:

Net loss	($50,000)
Actual number of shares outstanding	100,000
Incremental shares on assumed conversion of preferred stock	20,000
Adjusted number of shares	120,000
Primary loss per share ($50,000 ÷ 120,000)	($.42)

Because the primary loss per share is less than the simple loss per share, only the simple loss per share would be reported on the income statement.

If a company has an operating loss, but a positive net income because of net nonrecurring gains, or a negative net income but a positive operating income, the dilutive effect must be computed for each income figure. If inclusion of stock options or convertible securities results in dilution of any one income figure (i.e., operating income, extraordinary gains, gain from discontinued operations, etc.), the securities are included in all earnings per share calculations.

Summary of Earnings per Share Computations

The discussion and illustration of earnings per share computations included in this chapter present only a few of the many provisions included in the accounting standards and their interpretations. The existence of various kinds of dilutive securities has made the accounting standards and their application very complex. Elaborate computer programs have been designed to assist companies and their auditors in computing the various earnings per share figures required. In some instances, the rules appear arbitrary and inconsistent with the objective of showing the most dilutive position. Exhibit 18-1 summarizes the rules for the inclusion of stock options, warrants, rights, and convertible securities in computing primary and fully diluted earnings per share.

APB Opinion No. 15 is frequently cited by accountants who argue that there is an accounting standards overload, and that the standards have become too detailed. Because of the complexity involved in applying the provisions of the opinion, in 1978 the FASB suspended the requirement of reporting earnings per share data for nonpublic companies.[12]

Critics of the complex provisions of the earnings per share pronouncements frequently cite research studies conducted in the early 1970s which showed that neither the effective yield test nor the cash yield test accurately predicted conversion of convertible securities.[13] This led one FASB member, Frank Walter, to dissent to FASB Statement No. 55 in 1982 and another FASB member, Frank Block, to dissent to FASB Statement No. 85 in 1985 stating that primary earnings per share "is not relevant because it furnishes little or no incremental information about the probability, timing or amount of potential dilution. It is not reliable, that is, representationally faithful, because it implies imminent or predictable dilution, whereas research suggests that it has been a poor predictor of dilution."[14] Even though these questions about the usefulness of earnings per share data have been raised frequently, these figures continue to be required as part of the income disclosures for larger companies.

---

[12]*Statement of Financial Accounting Standards No. 21, op. cit.*

[13]Werner G. Frank and Jerry Weygandt, "Convertible Debt and Earnings per Share: Pragmatism vs. Good Theory," *Accounting Review* (April 1970): 280-289; Thomas R. Hofstedt and Richard R. West, "The APB, Yield Indices, and Predictive Ability," *Accounting Review* (April 1971): 329-337; Werner G. Frank and Jerry Weygandt, "The APB, Yield Indices, and Predictive Ability: A Reply," *Accounting Review*, (April 1971): 338-341.

[14]*Statement of Financial Accounting Standard No. 55, op. cit.,* dissent.

Exhibit 18-1   Summary of Earnings Per Share Components

Type of Securities	Simple EPS	Primary EPS	Fully Diluted EPS
Stock Options, Warrants, and Rights	Exclude	Always common stock equivalent. Include if dilutive.	Include if dilutive.
Convertible Securities (Bonds and Preferred Stocks)	Exclude	Include if common stock equivalent, (effective yield at time of issue is less than 66⅔% of the Aa bond rate), and if dilutive.	Include if dilutive.

Financial Statement Presentation

When earnings of a period include extraordinary items, income or loss from discontinued operations, or a cumulative effect of a change in accounting principle, earnings per share amounts should be presented for amounts before these special items, for each of these significant items, and for net income. For a complex capital structure, each of these items should be presented on both a primary and a fully diluted basis.

A schedule or note should be provided for a dual presentation explaining how primary and fully diluted earnings are calculated. Those securities included as common stock equivalents in arriving at primary earnings per share, as well as those included in the computation of fully diluted earnings per share, should be identified. All assumptions made and the resulting adjustments required in developing the earnings per share data should be disclosed. Additional disclosures should be made of the number of shares of common stock issued upon conversion, exercise, or satisfaction of required conditions for at least the most recent annual fiscal period. To illustrate, pertinent sections of the 1988 financial statements of USX Corporation are reproduced on page 802.

A common stock equivalent or other dilutive security may dilute one of the several per share amounts required to be disclosed on the face of the income statement, while increasing another amount. In such a case, the common stock equivalent or other dilutive securities should be recognized for all computations even though they have an antidilutive effect on one or more of the per share amounts.[16]

Earnings per share data should be presented for all periods covered by the income statement. If potential dilution exists in any of the periods presented, the dual presentation of primary and fully diluted earnings per share should be made for all periods presented.[17] Whenever net income of prior periods has been restated as a result of a prior period adjustment, the

---

[16]*Opinions of the Accounting Principles Board, No. 15*, par. 30.

[17]*Ibid.*, par. 17.

Exhibit 18-2   USX Corporation

Income per common share	1988	1987	1986
Primary:			
Weighted average shares, in thousands (Note 21)	*262,154*	*263,571*	*257,821*
Total income (loss) before extraordinary items, cumulative effect of change in accounting principle and preferred stock dividends.........................	$ 2.88	$ .79	$ (6.18)
Extraordinary items	—	—	(.93)
Cumulative effect of change in accounting principle	—	.05	—
Dividends on preferred stock	(.26)	(.30)	(.35)
Net income (loss) per common share...	$ 2.62	$ .54	$ (7.46)
Fully diluted:			
Weighted average shares, in thousands (Note 21)	*262,169*	*268,248*	*257,821*
Total income (loss) before extraordinary items, cumulative effect of change in accounting principle and preferred stock dividends.........................	$ 2.88	$ .77	$ (6.18)
Extraordinary items	—	—	(.93)
Cumulative effect of change in accounting principle	—	.05	—
Dividends on preferred stock	(.26)	(.25)	(.35)
Net income (loss) per common share...	$ 2.62	$ .57	$ (7.46)
Pro forma data, assuming the 1987 change in accounting principle were applied retroactively			
Total income (loss) before extraordinary items		$ 206	$ (1,613)
Per common share (after preferred stock dividends) — primary......................		.49	(6.61)
— fully diluted..............................		.52	(6.61)
Net income (loss)		$ 206	$ (1,853)
Per common share (after preferred stock dividends) — primary......................		.49	(7.54)
— fully diluted..............................		.52	(7.54)

The accompanying notes are an integral part of these consolidated financial statements.

Note 21. Income Per Common Share   Primary net income per share is calculated by adjusting net income for dividend requirements of preferred stock and is based on the weighted average number of common shares outstanding plus common stock equivalents, provided they are not antidilutive. Common stock equivalents result from assumed exercise of stock options and surrender of stock appreciation rights (50% stock — 50% cash) associated with stock options.

Fully diluted net income per share assumes full conversion of the 5¾% Convertible Subordinated Debentures and convertible preferred stock for the applicable periods outstanding and assumes exercise of stock options and surrender of stock appreciation rights (50% stock — 50% cash), provided the effect is not antidilutive. In 1987, the $2.25 convertible preference stock was antidilutive, but was included in fully diluted calculations because it was converted.

earnings per share for these prior periods should be restated and the effect of the restatements disclosed in the current year.[18]

It is important that great care be exercised in interpreting earnings per share data regardless of the degree of refinement applied in the development of the data. These values are the products of the principles and practices employed in the accounting process and are subject to the same limitations found in the net income measurement reported on the income statement.

[18]*Ibid.*, par. 18.

Appendix

Comprehensive Illustration Using Multiple Potentially Dilutive Securities

The illustrations in the chapter dealt primarily with one type of potentially dilutive security at a time. For a company having several different issues of convertible securities and/or stock options and warrants, the APB requires selection of the combination of securities producing the lowest possible earnings per share figure. To avoid having to test a large number of different combinations to find the lowest one, companies can compute the individual impact on earnings per share for each potentially dilutive security, rank them in order from the smallest to the largest in terms of impact on EPS, and introduce each security into the computation until the earnings per share is lower than the next security's individual impact. At that point, all remaining securities in the list would be antidilutive.

To illustrate, assume a company had four convertible securities that would have the following effects on fully diluted earnings per share if each were considered separately.

	Effects of Assumed Conversion		
	Increase in Net Income	Increase in No. of Shares	Individual Impact on EPS
Convertible Security A	$ 75,000	50,000	$1.50
Convertible Security B	150,000	60,000	2.50
Convertible Security C	110,000	20,000	5.50
Convertible Security D	600,000	100,000	6.00

Assume further that simple earnings per share was $6.50 ($2,275,000 income divided by 350,000 outstanding shares). Each of the four securities considered separately result in an earnings per share figure lower than simple earnings per share and would thus be dilutive. However, when considering all four securities together, only the first two (A and B) would be dilutive and therefore included in fully diluted earnings per share. This is determined by adding one security at a time to the simple earnings per share figure as follows:

	Net Income (adjusted)	Number of Shares (adjusted)	Fully Diluted EPS
Simple capital structure	$2,275,000	350,000	$6.50
Convertible Security A	75,000	50,000	
	$2,350,000	400,000	$5.87
Convertible Security B	150,000	60,000	
	$2,500,000	460,000	$5.43
Convertible Security C	110,000	20,000	
	$2,610,000	480,000	$5.44
Convertible Security D	600,000	100,000	
	$3,210,000	580,000	$5.53

It would not be necessary to continue the computation beyond Security B since the EPS at that point ($5.43), is lower than the EPS impact of Security C ($5.50). Inclusion of Securities C and D would be antidilutive as the computations show.

This approach to multiple securities will be used in the comprehensive problem that follows.

The Circle West Transportation Co. has the following outstanding stocks and bonds at January 1, 1992. All securities had been sold at par or face value. Thus the effective yield is equal to the stated interest or dividend rate for each security.

Date of Issue	Type of Security	Par or Face Value	Number of Shares or Total Face Value	Conversion Terms	Aa Bond Rate at Date of Issue
1980-1991	Common stock	$25	200,000	none	
May 1, 1986	12% debentures	$1,000	$750,000	none	9%
Jan. 1, 1990	6% cumulative preferred stock	$100	40,000	4 shares of common for each preferred share	14%
Jan. 1, 1991	8% debentures	$1,000	$1,000,000	15 shares of common for each $1,000 debenture	13%
June 30, 1991	10% debentures	$1,000	$600,000	30 shares of common for each $1,000 debenture	12%
Dec. 31, 1991	8% cumulative preferred stock	$50	12,500	none	11%

Circle West also had stock options outstanding at January 1, 1992, for the purchase of 20,000 shares of common. During 1992, options were granted for an additional 40,000 shares. The terms of these stock options are as follows:

Date of Issue	Exercisable Date	Exercise Price	Number of Options
Jan. 1, 1989	June 30, 1992	$30	20,000
June 30, 1992	June 30, 1994	$62	40,000

Common stock market prices for 1992 were as follows:

Average for year	$60
Average for first ¾ of year	$58
Average for last half of year	$61
October 1 price	$62
December 31 price	$65

(Market price exceeded October 1 price for entire fourth quarter)

During 1992, Circle West issued the following common stock:

Apr. 1   30,000 shares sold at $56
Oct. 1   20,000 shares issued from exercise of Jan. 1, 1989, options

On December 1, 1992, Circle West paid a full year's dividend on the 6% preferred stock and on the 8% preferred stock. Assume that the company had net income of $1,026,000 in 1992, all of which was income from continuing operations. The income tax rate is 40%.

When a company has multiple potentially dilutive convertible securities an orderly approach to computing earnings per share is necessary. The following steps should prove helpful in understanding this illustration and in solving complex earnings per share problems.

1. Compute simple earnings per share using a weighted average number of shares for common stock outstanding during the year.

2. Identify common stock equivalents:
   (a) All stock options, warrants, and rights.
   (b) Convertible securities with an effective yield less than ⅔ of the Aa bond rate at the time the securities were issued.

3. Determine whether common stock equivalents are dilutive.
   (a) Stock options, warrants, and rights:
       Primary: If the exercise price of the option is less than the average market price of the stock.
       Fully diluted: If the exercise price is less than the higher of the ending or average market price of the stock.
   (b) Convertible securities: Compute impact of assumed conversion on earnings per share for each security individually. Those with an impact greater than simple earnings per share are antidilutive and are excluded.

4. Compute primary earnings per share:
   (a) Include dilutive stock options, warrants, and rights first. Use the average market price for the period they were outstanding to compute incremental shares under the treasury stock method.
   (b) Include dilutive common stock equivalent convertible securities one at a time beginning with the security that has the smallest EPS impact. Compute new earnings per share. Continue until the next security in the list has an impact on earnings per share greater than the last computed earnings per share. Discontinue the process at that point. All other securities in the list are antidilutive for pur-

poses of computing the lowest possible primary earnings per share figure.

(c) Test for materiality. If primary earnings per share is 3% or more dilutive when compared with simple earnings per share, primary earnings per share is reported and dual presentation is required.

5. Determine whether convertible securities that are not common stock equivalents are individually dilutive. Rank all dilutive convertible securities, both common stock equivalents and non-common-stock equivalents, in order from lowest to highest impact on earnings per share.

6. Compute fully diluted earnings per share:

(a) Stock options, warrants, and rights: Include all dilutive securities as identified in step 3a. Use ending common stock market price, if higher than average price, to compute incremental shares under the treasury stock method.

(b) Convertible securities: Include convertible securities one at a time, following the same process described in step 4b.

(c) Test for materiality. The 3% materiality test is applied to both primary and fully diluted earnings per share. If either of these earnings per share figures meets the test, dual presentation is required.

These steps will be applied to the data for Circle West Transportation Company to compute the various earnings per share amounts.

Step 1   Compute simple earnings per share

Net income		$1,026,000
Less preferred dividends:		
6% stock (40,000 × $100 × .06)	$240,000	
8% stock (12,500 × $50 × .08)	50,000	290,000
Net income identified with common stock		$ 736,000

Weighted average number of shares:

Jan. 1 to Apr. 1	200,000 × ¼	50,000
Apr. 1 to Oct 1 (200,000 + 30,000)	230,000 × ½	115,000
Oct. 1 to Dec. 31 (230,000 + 20,000)	250,000 × ¼	62,500
Total weighted average number of shares		227,500
Simple earnings per share ($736,000 ÷ 227,500)		$3.24

Step 2   Identify common stock equivalent

Both stock options are common stock equivalents. Circle West has 3 convertible securities. The 6% preferred stock and the 8% debentures both qualify as common stock equivalents, since their effective yields are less than ⅔ of the Aa bond rate at the date of issuance (14% and 13% respectively). The 10% debentures do not qualify as common stock equivalents, since the 10% rate is more than ⅔ of the Aa bond rate of 12%. The 8% preferred stock and 12% debentures are not potentially dilutive securities because they are not convertible.

| Step 3 | **Determine whether common stock equivalents are dilutive** |

(a) Stock options: The options issued on January 1, 1989, are dilutive since the exercise price ($30) is less than the average price for the period in which the options were outstanding ($58). The options issued June 30, 1992 are antidilutive since the exercise price ($62) is more than the average price for the last half of 1992 ($61).

(b) Common stock equivalent convertible securities:

	Net Income Impact	Number of Shares	EPS Impact
6% Preferred stock	$240,000*	160,000	$1.50
8% Debentures	$48,000**	15,000	$3.20

*40,000 × $100 × .06
**$1,000,000 × .08 × .60 (1 − tax rate)

Each security is potentially dilutive, since its impact on EPS is less than the $3.24 simple earnings per share. The 6% preferred stock has a lower impact on earnings per share than the 8% debentures; therefore, it will be used first in computing primary earnings per share.

| Step 4 | **Compute primary earnings per share** |

Description	Net Income	Number of Shares	Part of Year	Weighted Average	EPS
Simple earnings per share	$736,000			227,500	$3.24
Jan. 1, 1989, options— exercised Oct. 1, as if exercised Jan. 1, 1992					
Number of shares assumed issued		20,000	¾	15,000	
Number of treasury shares assumed repurchased [(20,000 × $30) ÷ $58 (average for ¾ year)]		(10,345)	¾	(7,759)	
	$736,000			234,741	$3.14
6% preferred stock	240,000	160,000	1	160,000	
Primary earnings per share	$976,000			394,741	$2.47

Percentage dilution: $3.24 − $2.47 = $.77; $.77 ÷ $3.24 = 24%
8% debentures: Because impact value of $3.20 exceeds latest EPS of $2.47, the debentures are antidilutive and not included in primary EPS.

| Step 5 | **Determine whether options and convertible securities that are not common stock equivalents are dilutive for computing fully diluted earnings per share** |

(a) Stock options: Both stock options are dilutive since the exercise prices ($30 and $62) are less than the applicable ending market prices ($62 on October 1 for the exercised options and $65 at year-end for the unexercised options).

(b) Convertible securities:

	Net Income Impact	Number of Shares	EPS Impact
6% Preferred stock	$240,000	160,000	$1.50
10% Debentures	$36,000*	18,000	$2.00
8% Debentures	$48,000	15,000	$3.20

*$600,000 × .10 × .60 (income tax rate)

All three convertible securities are potentially dilutive since their impact on earnings per share is less than the $3.24 simple earnings per share.

| Step 6 | **Compute fully diluted earnings per share** |

Description	Net Income	Number of Shares	Part of Year	Weighted Average	EPS
Simple earnings per share	$ 736,000			227,500	$3.24
Jan. 1, 1989 options— exercised Oct. 1, as if exercised Jan. 1, 1989					
Number of shares assumed issued		20,000	¾	15,000	
Number of treasury shares assumed repurchased [(20,000 × $30) ÷ $62 (price at exercise date)]		(9,677)	¾	(7,258)	
June 30, 1992 options					
Number of shares assumed issued		40,000	½	20,000	
Number of treasury shares assumed repurchased [(40,000 × $62) ÷ $65 (price at year-end)]		(38,154)	½	(19,077)	
	$ 736,000			236,165	$3.12
6% preferred stock	240,000	160,000	1	160,000	
	$ 976,000			396,165	$2.46
10% debentures	36,000			18,000	
Fully diluted earnings per share	$1,012,000			414,165	$2.44

Percentage dilution: Since primary EPS was materially dilutive, and fully diluted EPS is lower, a dual presentation would be required.

8% debentures: Because impact value of $3.20 exceeds latest EPS of $2.44, the debentures are antidilutive and not included in fully diluted EPS.

Key Terms

Antidilution of earnings 782
Antidilutive securities 782
Common stock equivalent 788
Complex capital structure 784
Convertible securities 792
Dilution of earnings 782
Dilutive securities 782
Dividend payout percentage (or
  payout rate) 781
Earnings per share 781

Fully diluted earnings per share 783
If-converted method 793
Incremental shares 790
Material dilution 784
Price-earnings ratio 781
Primary earnings per share 783
Simple earnings per share 783
Simple capital structure 784
Treasury stock method 790

Questions

1. Earnings per share computations have received increased prominence on the income statement. How would an investor use such information in making investment decisions?

2. Why are earnings per share figures computed on the basis of common stock transactions that have not yet happened rather than on the basis of strictly historical common stock data?

3. An enterprise split its common stock 3-for-1 on July 1. Its accounting year ends December 31. Prior to the split there were 10,000 shares of common stock outstanding. What is the weighted average of shares that should be used to compute earnings per share in the current and preceding year?

4. Why are earnings per share figures adjusted retroactively for stock dividends, stock splits, and reverse stock splits?

5. What is meant by "dilution of earnings per share"?

6. What is an antidilutive security? Why are such securities generally excluded from the comptutation of earnings per share?

7. What distinguishes a simple from a complex capital structure?

8. A dual presentation of earnings per share is required only if the effects of including dilutive securities is material. How does the profession define materiality in this case?

9. What constitutes a common stock equivalent for calculating primary earnings per share?

10. (a) Under what conditions are stock options and warrants recognized as common stock equivalents? (b) Under what conditions is a convertible security recognized as a common stock equivalent?

11. What is the treasury stock method of accounting for outstanding stock options and warrants in computing primary earnings?

12. What modification to the treasury stock method is required if the number of shares obtainable from the exercise of outstanding options and warrants exceeds 20% of the number of shares outstanding?

13. What is the effective interest rate test and when is it applied?

14. Convertible debt that is a common stock equivalent and is dilutive requires an adjustment to income. What is the nature of the adjustment?

15. What is the meaning of the "if converted method" of computing earnings per share?

16. Compare the concept of primary earnings per share with the concept of fully diluted earnings per share.

17. If stock options are actually exercised during the year, how is fully diluted earnings per share affected?

18. How is the treasury stock method for stock options and warrants modified in

computing fully diluted earnings per share as compared with computing primary earnings per share?

19. When convertible debentures are not considered common stock equivalents, how are they handled for purposes of earnings per share computations?

20. Why are all convertible securities and options antidilutive when a company is operating at a loss?

21. What limitations should be recognized in using earnings per share data?

*22. If a company has multiple potentially dilutive securities, how are the computations made to assure obtaining the lowest earnings per share figure?

*Relates to Appendix.

Discussion Cases

Case 18-1   (How does a complex capital structure affect EPS?)

Big Horn Construction Company has gradually grown in size since its inception in 1919. The third generation of Jensens who now manage the enterprise are considering selling a large block of stock to raise capital for new equipment purchases and to help finance several big projects. The Jensens are concerned about how the earnings per share information should be presented on the income statement and have many questions concerning the nature of earnings per share:

(1) Discuss the earnings per share presentation that would be required if Big Horn Construction has (a) a simple capital structure; (b) a complex capital structure. What factors determine whether a capital structure is simple or complex?

(2) Are primary earnings per share for a complex structure with common stock equivalents the same as earnings per share for a simple structure? Discuss why APB Opinion No. 15 does not provide for a simple earnings per share for a complex capital structure.

(3) Assume Big Horn Construction Company has a complex capital structure. Discuss the effect, if any, of each of the following transactions on the computation of earnings per share:

(a) The firm acquires some of its outstanding common stock to hold as treasury stock.

(b) The firm pays a dividend of 50¢ per common stock share.

(c) The firm declares a dividend of 75¢ per share on cumulative preferred stock.

(d) A 3-for-1 common stock split occurs during the year.

(e) Retained earnings are appropriated for a disputed construction contract that may be litigated.

Case 18-2   (Are we in trouble or not?)

Tolman Yacht Company has just completed its determination of earnings per share for the year. As a result of issuing convertible securities during the year, the capital structure of Tolman is now defined as being complex. The primary earnings per share for this year is $2.90, but the fully diluted earnings per share is only $2.50, both figures down from the prior year's $3.25 simple earnings per share figure.

Tony Rice and Martha Chou, two stockholders, have received their financial statements from Tolman, and are discussing the earnings per share figures over lunch. The following dialogue ensues:

Rice I guess Tolman must be having trouble. I see their earnings per share is down significantly.

Chou Maybe so, but this year there are two figures where before there was only one.

Rice Something to do with the convertible bonds and preferred stock they issued during the year making it a complex capital structure. But both of the earnings per share figures are lower than the single figure the year before.

Chou That's true. But income for the current year is higher than last year. I'm confused.

Enlighten the stockholders.

Case 18-3 (But why is EPS different if income is the same?)

Fredrica Brown has $200,000 which she plans to invest in growth common stock. She has narrowed her choice to two companies in the same industry, White Inc. and Adam Inc. Each company has a documented history of growth and has an established, strong position within the industry. Last year each company reported net income of $10 million and a return on owners' investment of 17%; however, White reported earnings per share of $10 and Adam reported earnings per share of $20.

Fredrica requests that you explain why the EPS differs when other measures of activity and profitability are similar. What factors contribute to and limit the comparability of these data?

Case 18-4 (When should common stock equivalency be determined?)

Frank Smith and Kim Morse are discussing the concept of common stock equivalents for convertible securities as defined by APB Opinion No. 15. Smith believes the status of a convertible security should be determined (using the effective yield test) not only at the time of issuance but from time to time thereafter because convertible securities are designed to react to changes in the earnings or earnings potential just as common stock does. Furthermore, although many convertible securities are issued under market and yield conditions that do not emphasize their common stock characteristics, both the issuer and the holder recognize the possibility of these characteristics becoming more significant as the value of the underlying common stock increases. But limiting determination of the common stock equivalent status to "at issuance only" disregards these factors.

Morse believes that for practical simplicity, common stock equivalent status should be determined only by the conditions that exist at time of issuance and that fully diluted earnings per share adequately disclose the potential dilution that may exist.

You are asked to give a third opinion. Which argument is more valid?

Case 18-5 (But let's maintain earnings per share)

On January 1, 1989, Farnsworth Company had 1,000,000 shares of common stock and 100,000 shares of $8 cumulative preferred stock issued and outstanding. A principal goal of Farnsworth's management is to maintain or increase earnings per share.

On January 1, 1990, Farnsworth Company retired 50,000 shares of the preferred stock with excess cash and additional funds provided from the sale of a subsidiary.

At the beginning of 1991, the company borrowed $5,000,000 at 10% and used the proceeds to retire 200,000 shares of common stock. Operating income, before interest and income taxes (income tax rate is 40%), is as follows:

	1991	1990	1989
Operating income	$6,500,000	$7,000,000	$7,500,000

Did Farnsworth Company maintain its earnings per share even though income declined? What was the impact of the preferred and common stock transactions on earnings per share?

Exercises   **Exercise 18-1   (Weighted average number of shares)**

Compute the weighted average number of shares outstanding for Troy Company, which has a simple capital structure, assuming the following transactions in common stock occurred during the year:

Date	Transactions in Common Stock	Number of Shares $10 Par Value
Jan. 1	Shares outstanding	40,000
Feb. 1	Issued for cash	10,000
May 1	Acquisition of treasury stock	(6,000)
July 1	Resold part of treasury stock shares	3,200
Sept. 1	50% stock dividend	50% of shares outstanding
Dec. 1	Issued in exchange for property	13,200

Exercise 18-2   (Weighted average number of shares)

Transactions involving the common stock account of the Higrade Gas Company during the 2-year period, 1991 and 1992 were as follows:

1991
Jan. 1   Balance 200,000 shares of $10 par common stock.
Apr. 1 $2,500,000 of convertible bonds were converted with 50 shares issued for each $1,000 bond.
July 1   A 10% stock dividend was declared.
Oct. 1   Option to purchase 7,000 shares for $20 a share was exercised.
1992
Apr. 1   A 2-for-1 stock split was declared.
Oct. 1   80,000 shares were sold for $30 a share.

From the information given, compute the comparative number of weighted average shares outstanding for 1991 and 1992 to be used for earnings per share computations at the end of 1992. Assume that conversion of bonds and exercise of options at January 1, 1991, would not have resulted in material dilution, and there are no other convertible securities or options outstanding. Thus, only a simple earnings per share is required.

Exercise 18-3   (Weighted average number of shares)

Assume the following transactions affected owners' equity for Cervantes Inc. during 1992.

Feb.	1	20,000 shares of common stock were sold in the market.
Apr.	1	Purchased 5,000 shares of common stock to be held as treasury stock. Paid cash dividends of $.50 per share.
May	1	Split common stock 3-for-1.
July	1	35,000 shares of common stock sold.
Oct.	1	A 5% stock dividend was issued.
Dec. 31		Paid a cash dividend of $.75 per share. The total amount paid for dividends on December 31 was $511,875.

Compute the weighted average number of shares to be used in computing earnings per share for 1992. Because no beginning share figures are available, you must work backwards from December 31, 1992, to compute shares outstanding.

Exercise 18-4   (Earnings per share—simple capital structure)

At December 31, 1991, the Munter Corporation had 50,000 shares of common stock issued and outstanding, 30,000 of which had been issued and outstanding throughout the year and 20,000 of which had been issued on October 1, 1991. Operating income before income taxes for the year ended December 31, 1991, was $703,200. In 1991, and 1992, a dividend of $80,000 was paid on 80,000 shares of 10% cumulative preferred stock, $10 par.

On April 1, 1992, 30,000 additional shares were issued. Total income before income taxes for 1992 was $477,000, which included an extraordinary gain before income taxes of $37,000. Assuming a 30% tax rate, what is Munter's earnings per common share for 1991 and for 1992, rounded to the nearest cent? Show computations in good form.

Exercise 18-5   (Earnings per share—simple capital structure)

The income statement for the Crosby Co. for the year ended December 31, 1992, reported the following:

Income from continuing operations before income taxes	$330,000
Income taxes	132,000
Income from continuing operations	$198,000
Loss from disposal of segment (net of income taxes)	(60,000)
Net income	$138,000

Compute earnings per share amounts for 1992 under each of the following assumptions:

(a) The company has only one class of common stock with 150,000 shares outstanding.

(b) The company has shares outstanding as follows: preferred 8% stock, $50

par, cumulative, 25,000 shares; common, $25 par, 150,000 shares. Only
the current year's preferred dividends are unpaid.

(c) Same as (b) except Crosby Co. *also* has preferred 7% stock, $40 par,
noncumulative, 20,000 shares. Only $30,000 in dividends on the
noncumlative preferred has been declared.

Exercise 18-6   (Common stock equivalents)

Which of the following securities would qualify as common stock equivalents? If
a common stock equivalent, would it be used in computing primary earnings
per share? Give reasons supporting each answer.

(a) Employee stock options to purchase 1,000 shares of common stock in 4
years at $40 are outstanding. The market price of the common stock has
been in excess of $45 throughout the year.
(b) Warrants to purchase 2,000 shares at $30 are issued. The current market
price is $27.
(c) 8%, $1,000 convertible bonds are sold; sales price, to yield 6.67%. The Aa
corporate bond yield is 11½%.
(d) Preferred stock, 7%, convertible, is sold at par. The Aa corporate bond
yield is 10¼%.

Exercise 18-7   (Primary earnings per share—convertible bonds)

On January 2, 1992, Saftner Co. issued at par $30,000 of 10% bonds
convertible in total into 2,000 shares of Saftner's common stock. These bonds
are common stock equivalents for purposes of computing earnings per share. No
bonds were converted during 1992.

Throughout 1992, Saftner had 5,000 shares of common stock outstanding.
Saftner's 1992, net income was $45,000. Saftner's tax rate is 40%.

No other potentially dilutive securities other than the convertible bonds
were outstanding during 1992. For 1992, compute Saftner's primary earnings per
share.

Exercise 18-8   (Dilutive securities)

The Claney Corporation has earnings per common share of $2.09 for the period
ended December 31, 1991. For each of the following examples, decide whether
the convertible security would be dilutive or antidilutive in computing primary
earnings per share. Consider each example individually. All are common stock
equivalents. The tax rate is 30%.

(a) 8½% debentures, $1,000,000 face value, are convertible into common
stock at the rate of 40 shares for each $1,000 bond.
(b) $5 preferred stock is convertible into common stock at the rate of 2 shares
of common for 1 share of preferred. There are 50,000 shares of preferred
stock outstanding.
(c) Options to purchase 200,000 shares of common stock are outstanding. The
exercise price is $25 per share. Current market price is $20 per share.
(d) $400,000 of 10% debentures are convertible at the rate of 25 shares of
common stock for each $1,000 bond.
(e) Preferred 6% stock, $100 par, 5,000 shares outstanding, convertible into 3
shares of common stock for each 1 share of preferred.

Exercise 18-9   (Primary earnings per share—convertible bonds)

The Benton Manufacturing Company reports long-term liabilities and stock-holders' equity balances at December 31, 1991, as follows:

Convertible 8% bonds (par)	$500,000
Common stock, $25 par, 90,000 shares issued and outstanding	2,250,000

Additional information is determined as follows:

Conversion terms of bonds	80 shares for each $1,000 bond
Income before extraordinary gain—1991	$300,000
Extraordinary gain (net of tax)	40,000
Net income—1991	$340,000

What are the primary earnings per share for the company for 1991, assuming that the income tax rate is 35% and the Aa corporate bond yield at the date the bonds were sold was 12½%? No changes occurred in the debt and equity balances during 1991.

Exercise 18-10   (Number of shares—stock options)

On January 1, 1992, Wander Corporation had 56,000 shares of outstanding common stock which did not change during 1992. In 1991 Wander Corporation granted options to certain executives to purchase 9,000 shares of its common stock at $7 each. The market price of common was $10.50 per share on December 31, 1992, and averaged $9 per share during the year. Compute the number of shares to be used in computing primary and fully diluted earnings per share for 1992.

Exercise 18-11   (Number of shares—stock options)

Barone Company has employee stock options outstanding to purchase 40,000 common shares at $12 per share. All options were outstanding during the entire year and are presently exercisable or will become exercisable within 4 years. The average market price of the company's common stock during the year was $20 and the price of the stock at the end of the year was $30. Compute the common stock equivalent incremental shares that would be used in arriving at (1) primary earnings per share, and (2) fully diluted earnings per share. Barone has 80,000 shares outstanding at the date the option is granted.

Exercise 18-12   (Earnings per share—convertible bonds)

At December 31, 1992, the books of Yorke Corporation include the following balances:

Long-term liabilities:	
Bonds payable, 8%, each $1,000 bond is convertible into 50 shares of	
common stock; bonds sold at par and were issued November 3, 1991	$ 500,000
Stockholders' equity:	
Preferred stock, 7%, par $50, cumulative, nonconvertible, 10,000 shares	
outstanding	500,000
Paid-in capital in excess of par, preferred stock	300,000
Common stock, par $10, authorized 300,000 shares; 199,500 outstanding	1,995,000
Paid-in capital in excess of par, common stock	450,000
Retained earnings	519,000

The records of Yorke reveal the following additional information:

(a) 150,000 shares of common stock were outstanding January 1, 1992.
(b) 40,000 shares of common stock were sold for cash on April 30, 1992.
(c) Issued 5% stock dividend on July 2, 1992.
(d) Aa corporate bond yield was 12% when bonds were issued.
(e) Operating income before extraordinary items (after tax) was $715,000.
(f) Extraordinary loss (net of tax), $16,000.
(g) Income tax rate, 40%.
(h) Bond indenture does not provide for increase in shares at conversion due to stock dividends declared subsequent to the bond issue date.

(1) Is this a simple or complex capital structure?
(2) Compute required earnings per share amounts. How should earnings per share data be presented?

Exercise 18-13   (Earnings and loss per share—convertible preferred stock, net loss)

During all of 1991, Malone Inc. had outstanding 100,000 shares of common stock and 5,000 shares of $7 preferred stock. Each share of the preferred stock, which is classified as a common stock equivalent, is convertible into 3 shares of common stock. For 1991, Malone had $230,000 income from operations and $575,000 extraordinary loss, net of income tax effect; no dividends were paid or declared.

Compute the required earnings (loss) per share for income (loss) before extraordinary items and for net income (loss) assuming:

(a) The preferred stock is noncumulative.
(b) The preferred stock is cumulative.

Exercise 18-14   (Earnings per share with actual conversion)

Atlas, Inc. has the following capital structure at January 1, 1992:

	Outstanding
Common stock, $10 par	800,000 shares
11% stated interest rate convertible bonds issued at par. (Aa corporate bond rate at issuance date in 1990 was 13%. Each $1,000 bond is convertible into 80 shares of common stock.)	$5,000,000

During 1992, Atlas had the following stock transactions:
May 1   Issued 50,000 shares of common stock for $30 per share.
Aug. 1   Purchased 100,000 shares of treasury stock at $35 per share.
Oct. 1   Converted $2,000,000 of bonds.
Net income for 1992 was $950,000. The income tax rate was 30%.
Compute the following earnings per share amounts:
(a) Simple earnings per share.
(b) Primary earnings per share.
(c) Fully diluted earnings per share.

*Exercise 18-15   (Earnings per share—convertible securities)

Information relating to the capital structure of the Stantz Corporation at December 31, 1990 and 1991, is as follows:

	Outstanding
Common stock	90,000 shares
Convertible preferred stock noncumulative (issued in 1989)	20,000 shares
9% convertible bonds (issued in 1990)	$1,000,000

Stantz Corporation paid dividends of $4 per share on its preferred stock. The preferred stock is convertible into 60,000 shares of common stock and is considered a common stock equivalent. The 9% convertible bonds are convertible into 25,000 shares of common stock, but are *not* considered to be common stock equivalents. The net income for the year ended December 31, 1991, is $530,000. Assume that the income tax rate is 35%. Compute (a) simple earnings per share, (b) primary earnings per share, and (c) fully diluted earnings per share for the year ended December 31, 1991.

*Relates to appendix.

Problems   **Problem 18-1   (Weighted average number of shares)**

Inman's Wholesale Products Inc. had 75,000 shares of common stock outstanding at the end of 1990. During 1991 and 1992, the following transactions took place:

1991	
Mar. 31	Sold 5,000 shares at $27.
Apr. 26	Paid cash dividend of 50¢ per share.
July 31	Paid cash dividend of 25¢ per share, and issued a 10% stock dividend.
Nov. 1	Sold 7,000 shares at $30.
1992	
Feb. 28	Purchased 5,000 shares of common stock to be held in treasury.
Mar. 1	Paid cash dividend of 50¢ per share.
Apr. 30	Issued 3-for-1 stock split.
Nov. 1	Sold 6,000 shares of treasury stock.
Dec. 20	Declared cash dividend of 25¢ per share.

Inman's Wholesale Products Inc. has a simple capital structure.

Instructions: Compute the weighted average number of shares for 1991 and 1992 to be used in the earnings per share computation at the end of 1992.

Problem 18-2   (Earnings per share—simple capital structure)

The following condensed financial statements for the Daily Corporation were prepared by the accounting department:

Daily Corporation
Income Statement
For Year Ended December 31, 1992

Sales		$10,000,000
Cost of goods sold		8,000,000
Gross profit on sales		$ 2,000,000
Expenses:		
Selling expense	$405,000	
Administrative expense	300,000	
Interest expense	29,000	734,000
Income from continuing operations before income taxes		$ 1,266,000
Income taxes		506,400
Income from continuing operations		$ 759,600
Extraordinary loss, net of tax savings		(65,000)
Net income		$ 694,600

Daily Corporation
Balance Sheet
December 31, 1992

Assets	$4,250,000
Current liabilities	$1,000,000
8% Bonds, due December 31, 1999	600,000
Stockholders' equity:	
Common stock, $5 par, 200,000 shares authorized, issued	
and outstanding	1,000,000
Additional paid-in capital	400,000
Retained earnings	1,250,000
	$4,250,000

Instructions: Compute the earnings per share under each of the following separate assumptions (the company has a simple capital structure):

(1) No change in the capital structure occurred in 1992.
(2) On December 31, 1991, there were 100,000 shares outstanding. On April 1, 1992, 80,000 shares were sold at par and on October 1, 1992, 20,000 shares were sold at par.
(3) On December 31, 1991, there were 160,000 shares outstanding. On July 1, 1992, the company issued a 25% stock dividend.

‖ Problem 18-3   (Earnings per share—simple capital structure)

Great Northern Inc. reported the following comparative information in the stockholders' equity section of its 1992 balance sheet.

	Dec. 31 1992	Dec. 31 1991	Dec. 31 1990
12% Preferred stock, $50 par	$ 82,500	$ 67,500	$ 50,000
Paid-in capital in excess of par—preferred	13,400	9,200	5,000
Common stock, $5 par*	410,600	399,600	325,000
Paid-in capital in excess of par—common	64,300	58,800	35,000
Paid-in capital from treasury stock	1,800	800	800
Retained earnings	471,200	396,460	290,200
Total stockholders' equity	$1,043,800	$932,360	$706,000

*Par value prior to June 1, 1992, stock split.

In addition, company records show that the following transactions involving stockholders' equity were recorded in 1991 and 1992:

1991
May 1	Sold 4,500 shares of common stock for $12, par value $10.
June 30	Sold 350 shares of preferred stock for $62, par value $50.
Aug. 1	Issued an 8% stock dividend on common stock. The market price of the stock was $15.
Sept. 1	Declared cash dividends of 12% on preferred stock and $1.50 on common stock.
Dec. 31	Income from operations for the year totaled $316,200. In addition, Great Northern had an extraordinary gain of $12,500, net of tax.

1992
Jan. 31	Sold 1,100 shares of common stock for $15.
May 1	Sold 300 shares of preferred stock for $64.
June 1	Issued a 2-for-1 split of common stock, reduced par value to $5.
Sept. 1	Purchased 500 shares of common stock for $9 to be held as treasury stock.
Oct. 1	Declared cash dividends of 12% on preferred stock and $2 on common stock.
Nov. 1	Sold 500 shares of treasury stock for $11.
Dec. 31	Net income for the year included an extraordinary loss net of income tax of $19,000.

Instructions: Compute the earnings per share amounts for 1991 and 1992 to be presented in the income statement for 1992.

Problem 18-4 (Earnings per share—stock options)

The records of Mountain Crest Company reveal the following capital structure as of December 31, 1991:

$10 Preferred stock, $80 par, 7,500 shares issued and outstanding	$ 600,000
Additional paid-in capital on preferred stock	90,000
Common stock, $10 par, 200,000 shares issued and outstanding	2,000,000
Additional paid-in capital on common stock	350,000
Retained earnings	886,000

To stimulate work incentive and to bolster trade relations, Mountain Crest on May 1, 1992 issued stock options to select executives, creditors, and others allowing the purchase of 26,000 shares of common stock for $28 a share. Market prices for the stock at various times during 1992 were:

Option issuance date	$25
Year-end	75
Average, May 1 to Dec. 31	50

A dividend on preferred stock was paid during the year, and there are no dividends in arrears at year-end. There are no other capital transactions during the year. Net income for 1992 was $631,000.

Instructions: Compute the earnings per share data required to satisfy generally accepted accounting principles.

Problem 18-5   (Earnings per share—conversion of debentures)

The following information relates to the December 31, 1991, balance sheet for Advance Incorporated:

8% Convertible 10-year debentures issued at par	$ 900,000
Common stock, $12 par, 80,000 shares issued and outstanding	$ 960,000
Retained earnings	882,000
Total stockholders' equity	$1,842,000

(a) The convertible debentures include terms stating that each $1,000 bond can be converted into 40 shares of common stock. The Aa bond interest rate at date of issuance was 13%.

(b) On July 31, 1992, the complete issue of convertible debentures was converted into common stock.

(c) Advance reported net income of $436,000 in 1992. The company's income tax rate was 30%.

(d) No other common stock transactions took place during the year other than the debenture conversion.

Instructions:

(1) Compute earnings per share for Advance for the year ended December 31, 1992.

(2) Assume Advance had a net loss of $180,000. Show why the convertible debentures are antidilutive under loss conditions.

III Problem 18-6   (Earnings per share—stock options)

The Donner Hardware Co. provides the following data at December 31, 1992.

Operating revenue	$875,000
Operating expenses	$450,000
Income tax rate	30%
Common stock outstanding during the entire year	22,000 shares

On January 1, 1992, there were options outstanding to purchase 10,000 shares of common stock at $20 per share. During 1992, the average price per share was $25 but at December 31, 1992, the market price had risen to $30 per share. The balance sheet reports $200,000 of 8% nonconvertible bonds at December 31, 1992. (Interest expense is included in operating expenses.)

Instructions: Compute for 1992:

(1) Primary earnings per share.

(2) Fully diluted earnings per share.

Problem 18-7   (Earnings per share with exercise of stock options)

As of January 1, 1992, the Bayer Corporation had 30,000 shares of $5 par common stock outstanding. The company had issued stock options in 1990 to its management personnel permitting them to acquire 6,000 shares of common stock at $9 per share. At the time of the issuance, common stock was selling for $9 per share. The average price of common stock for the year 1992 was

$21. The market price was $23 on September 1, 1992, and $25 on December 31, 1992. The average price for the first eight months of the year was $20. Income from operations for 1992 was $131,700. The company also had an extraordinary gain of $25,000, net of taxes. Terms of the options make them currently exercisable. On September 1, 1992, options to acquire 2,000 shares were exercised. The other 4,000 options are still outstanding at December 31, 1992.

Instructions: Compute primary and fully diluted earnings per share to be reported on the income statement for the year ended December 31, 1992.

Problem 18-8   (Earnings per share—complex capital structure)

The "Stockholders' equity" section of Alta Company's balance sheet as of December 31, 1992, contains the following:

$2 cumulative preferred stock, $25 par, convertible, 1,600,000 shares authorized, 1,400,000 shares issued. 750,000 converted to common, 650,000 shares outstanding	$16,250,000
Common stock, $.25 par, 15,000,000 shares authorized, 8,800,000 shares issued and outstanding	2,200,000
Additional paid-in capital	32,750,000
Retained earnings	40,595,000
Total stockholders' equity	$91,795,000

Included in the liabilities of Alta Company are 9% convertible subordinated debentures face value $20,000,000, issued at par in 1991. The debentures are due in 2000 and until then are convertible into the common stock of Alta Company at the rate of 50 shares of common stock for each $1,000 debenture. To date none of these have been converted.

On April 2, 1992, Alta Company issued 1,400,000 shares of convertible preferred stock at $40 per share. Quarterly dividends to December 31, 1992, have been paid on these shares. The preferred stock is convertible into common stock at the rate of 2 shares of common for each share of preferred. On October 1, 1992, 150,000 shares and on November 1, 1992, 600,000 shares of the preferred stock were converted into common stock.

During July 1992, Alta Company granted options to its officers and key employees to purchase 500,000 shares of the company's common stock at a price of $20 a share. The options do not become exercisable until 1993.

During 1992 dividend payments and average market prices of the Alta common stock were as follows:

	Dividend per Share	Average Market Price per Share
First quarter	$.10	$20
Second quarter	.15	25
Third quarter	.10	30
Fourth quarter	.15	25
Average for the year		25

The December 31, 1992, closing price of the common stock was $25 a share.

Assume that the Aa corporate bond yield was 12% throughout 1991 and 1992. Alta Company's net income for the year ended December 31, 1992 was $9,750,000. The provision for income tax was computed at a rate of 40%.

Instructions:

(1) Prepare a schedule that shows the evaluation of the common stock equivalency status of the (a) convertible debentures, (b) convertible preferred stock, and (c) employee stock options.
(2) Compute simple earnings per share and test any common stock equivalents for dilution.
(3) Compute primary earnings per share.
(4) Compute fully diluted earnings per share.   (AICPA adapted)

Problem 18-9   (Earnings per share—complex capital structure)

Carrizo Corporation's capital structure is as follows:

	December 31	
	1992	1991
Outstanding shares of:		
Common stock	336,000	280,000
Nonconvertible, noncumulative preferred stock	10,000	10,000
10% convertible bonds	$1,000,000	$1,000,000

The following additional information is available:

(a) On September 1, 1992, Carrizo sold 56,000 additional shares of common stock.
(b) Net income for the year ended December 31, 1992, was $860,000.
(c) During 1992, Carrizo declared and paid dividends of $5 per share on its preferred stock.
(d) The 10% bonds are convertible into 40 shares of common stock for each $1,000 bond, and were not considered common stock equivalents at the date of issuance.
(e) Unexercised options to purchase 30,000 shares of common stock at $22.50 per share were outstanding at the beginning and end of 1992. The average market price of Carrizo's common stock was $36 per share during 1992. The market price was $33 per share at December 31, 1992.
(f) Warrants to purchase 20,000 shares of common stock at $38 per share were attached to the preferred stock at the time of issuance. The warrants, which expire on December 31, 1997, were outstanding at December 31, 1992.
(g) Carrizo's effective income tax rate was 40% for 1991 and 1992.

Instructions: Compute the following earnings per share amounts as of December 31, 1992:

(1) Simple
(2) Primary
(3) Fully diluted   (AICPA adapted)

*Problem 18-10   (Earnings per share—complex capital structure)

At December 31, 1991, the Norbalco Company had 400,000 shares of common stock outstanding. Norbalco sold 100,000 shares on October 1, 1992. Net income for 1992 was $2,565,000; the income tax rate was 30%. In addition, Norbalco had the following debt and equity securities on its books at December 31, 1991.

(a) 20,000 shares of $100 par 10% cumulative preferred stock. Aa corporate bond yield was 11% at time of sale. Stock was sold at 102.

(b) 30,000 shares of 8% convertible cumulative preferred stock, par $100, sold at 110 when Aa corporate bond yield was 11%. Each share of preferred stock is convertible into two shares of common.

(c) $2,000,000 face value of 8% bonds sold at par when Aa corporate bond yield was 10%.

(d) $3,000,000 face value of 6% convertible bonds sold to yield 7% when Aa corporate bond yield was 8%. Unamortized bond discount is $100,000 at December 31, 1991. Each $1,000 bond is convertible into 20 shares of common.

Also, options to purchase 10,000 shares were issued May 1, 1992. Exercise price is $30 per share; market value at date of option was $29; market value at end of year, $40; average market value May 1 to December 31, 1992, $35.

Instructions: For the year ended December 31, 1992,
(1) Compute simple earnings per share.
(2) Compute primary earnings per share.
(3) Compute fully-diluted earnings per share.
*Relates to appendix.

*Problem 18-11 (Earnings per share—multiple convertible securities)

Data for the Dwight Powder Company at the end of 1992 are listed below. All bonds are convertible as indicated and were issued at their face amounts.

Description of Bonds	Amount	Date Issued	Aa Corporate Bond Yield on Date Issued	Conversion Terms
10-year, 6½% convertible bonds	$700,000	1/1/86	9½%	100 shares of common for each $1,000 bond
20-year, 7% convertible bonds	1,000,000	1/1/87	11%	50 shares of common for each $1,000 bond
25-year, 10½% convertible bonds	1,600,000	6/30/91	14¼%	32 shares of common for each $1,000 bond

Common shares outstanding at December 31, 1991	700,000
Net income for 1992	$1,406,000
Income tax rate	40%

Instructions:
(1) Compute primary earnings per share for 1992, assuming that no additional shares of common stock were issued during the year.
(2) Compute fully diluted earnings per share for 1992, assuming that no additional shares of common stock were issued during the year.
(3) Compute both primary and fully diluted earnings per share assuming that the 10-year bonds were converted on July 1, 1992, and that net income for the year was $1,419,650 (reflects reduction in interest due to bond conversion).
*Relates to appendix.

*Problem 18-12   (Earnings per share—multiple convertible securities)

Sawyer Company had the following capital structure at December 31, 1991 and 1992:

	1992	1991
Outstanding Shares:		
Common stock	756,000	600,000
$6 Convertible preferred stock	10,000	20,000
8½% 10-year Convertible bonds	$1,500,000	$2,000,000

The following additional information is available:

(a) The conversion terms of the preferred stock and bonds at January 1, 1992 were as follows:
Preferred stock, 5 shares of common for each share of preferred.
Convertible bonds, 40 shares of common for each $1,000 bond.
These terms are to be adjusted for any issued stock dividends or stock splits.

(b) On May 1, 1992, Sawyer sold an additional 50,000 shares of common stock, and on August 1, 1992 a 5% stock dividend on common shares was declared.

(c) On October 1, 1992, 10,000 shares of preferred stock were converted to 52,500 shares of common stock (5.25 shares common for each 1 share of preferred). The preferred stock was issued at $100 par in 1988 when the Aa corporate interest rate was 9.5%.

(d) On December 1, 1992, 25% of the convertible bonds were converted. The bonds were issued at par in 1991 when the Aa corporate interest rate was 13%.

(e) On December 31, 1992, Sawyer declared and paid a $6.00 per share dividend on outstanding preferred stock. Income for the year was $1,400,000.

(e) Stock options (issued and unexercised) to purchase 60,000 shares of common stock at $25 per share were outstanding at the beginning of 1992. Average market price was $40 and the market price at December 31, 1992 was $48.

(f) Stock warrants to purchase 40,000 shares of common stock at $46 per share were attached to the preferred stock. The warrants expire on December 31, 1996, and were outstanding at December 31, 1992.

(g) The effective tax rate was 35% for both years.

(h) On February 1, 1993, before the 1992 financial statements were issued, Sawyer split its common stock 2 for 1.

Instructions: For the year ended December 31, 1992, compute:

(1) Simple earnings per share
(2) Primary earnings per share
(3) Fully diluted earnings per share
Carry EPS figures to 3 decimal places.
*Relates to Appendix.

Chapter 19

Revenue Recognition

As discussed and illustrated in Chapter 4, both internal and external users of financial information focus considerable attention on how business activities affect the income statement. Because all of the financial statements are interrelated, a study of the measurement and recognition of the elements contained in the income statement is also a study of the measurement and recognition of changes in the elements contained in the balance sheet. Thus, while the focus in this chapter is on the recognition of revenue, it also relates to the recognition of assets and liabilities on the balance sheet.

Recognition refers to the time when transactions are recorded on the books. The FASB's two criteria for recognizing revenues and gains were identified in Chapter 4, and are repeated here for emphasis.

Revenues and gains are generally recognized when:

1. they are realized or realizable, and
2. they have been earned through substantial completion of the activities involved in the earnings process.

Both of these criteria are generally met at the point of sale, which most often occurs when goods are delivered or when services are rendered to customers. Usually, assets and revenues are recognized concurrently. Thus, a sale of inventory results in an increase in Cash or Accounts Receivable and an increase in Sales Revenue. However, assets are sometimes recognized before these revenue recognition criteria are met. In those cases a liability, Unearned Revenue, is recorded. When the criteria are fully met, revenue is recognized and the liability account is reduced.

While the point-of-sale rule has dominated the interpretation of revenue recognition, there have been notable variations to this rule, especially in specific industries such as construction, real estate, and franchising. Special committees of the AICPA, and later the FASB, have studied these and other areas. For several years, these special studies were conducted under the direction of the AICPA, and publications of the committees' results appeared in the form of **Industry Accounting Guides, Industry Audit**

Guides, or Statements of Position (SOP's). These publications have been studied by the FASB, and where deemed desirable, have been incorporated in the literature as Statements of Financial Accounting Standards.[1]

This chapter will explore some of the variations in revenue recognition that have arisen through these special industry studies. The focus of the presentation will be upon the revenue recognition variations and not on the detailed accounting procedures for a specific industry. The discussion focuses first on revenue recognition **prior to delivery** of goods or performance of services; second on revenue recognition **after delivery** of goods or performance of services; and finally upon methods of accounting before revenue recognition occurs. The special industries referred to are construction, real estate, service, and franchising.

Revenue Recognition Prior To Delivery Of Goods Or Performance of Services

Under some circumstances, revenue can be meaningfully reported prior to the delivery of the finished product or completion of a service contract. Usually this occurs when the construction period of the asset being sold or the period of service performance is relatively long; that is, more than one year. If a company waits until the production or service period is complete to recognize revenue, the income statement may not meaningfully report the periodic achievement of the company. Under this approach, referred to as the completed contract method, all income from the contract is related to the year of completion, even though only a small part of the earnings may be attributable to effort in that period. Previous periods receive no credit for their efforts; in fact, they may be penalized through the absorption of selling, general and administrative, and other overhead costs relating to the contract but not considered part of the inventory cost.

Percentage-of-completion accounting, an alternative to the completed-contract method, was developed to relate recognition of revenue on long-term construction-type contracts to the activities of a firm in fulfilling these contracts. Similarly, the proportional performance method has been developed to reflect revenue earned on service contracts under which many acts of service are to be performed before the contract is completed. Examples include contracts covering maintenance on electronic office equipment, correspondence schools, trustee services, health clubs, professional services such as those offered by attorneys and accountants, and servicing of mortgage loans by mortgage bankers. Percentage-of-completion accounting and proportional performance accounting are similar in their application. However, some special problems arise in accounting for service contracts. The discussion and examples in the following sections relate first

---

[1] In the early 1980's, the FASB issued three research reports dealing with revenue recognition. These reports were used by the FASB in its deliberations leading to Concepts Statement No. 5 and several of the special industry standards. The reports were: (1) Yuji Ijiri, *Recognition of Contractual Rights and Obligations* (Stamford: Financial Accounting Standards Board, 1980); (2) Henry R. Jaenicke, *Survey of Present Practice in Recognizing Revenues, Expenses, Gains and Losses* (Stamford: Financial Accounting Standards Board, 1981); (3) L. Todd Johnson and Reed K. Storey, *Recognition in Financial Statements: Underlying Concepts and Practical Conventions* (Stamford: Financial Accounting Standards Board, 1982).

to long-term construction contracts, then to the special problems encountered with service contracts.

General Concepts of Percentage-of-Completion Accounting

Under the percentage-of-completion method, a company recognizes revenues and costs on a contract as it progresses toward completion rather than deferring recognition of these items until the contract is completed. The amount of revenue to be recognized each period is based on some measure of progress toward completion. This requires an estimate of costs yet to be incurred. Changes in estimates of future costs arise normally, and the necessary adjustments are made in the year the estimates are revised. Thus, the revenues and costs to be recognized in a given year are affected by the revenues and costs already recognized. As work progresses on the contract, the actual costs incurred are charged to inventory. The amount of profit earned each period is also charged to this asset account. Thus, the inventory account is valued at its net realizable value—the sales (or contract) price less the cost to complete the contract and less the unearned profit on the unfinished contract. If a company projects a loss on the contract prior to completion, the full amount of the loss should be recognized immediately. This loss recognition results in a write down of the asset to its estimated net realizable value, the sales price less the cost to complete the contract. If only a percentage of the loss were recognized, the asset value would exceed the net realizable value. This would violate the lower-of-cost-or-market rule discussed in Chapter 10.

Necessary Conditions to Use Percentage-of-Completion Accounting

Most long-term construction-type contracts should be reported using the percentage-of-completion method. The guidelines presently in force, however, are not specific as to when a company must use percentage-of-completion and when it must use the alternative completed-contract method. The accounting standards that still govern this area were issued by the Committee on Accounting procedure in 1955.[2] In January 1981, the Construction Contractor Guide Committee of the Accounting Standards Division of the AICPA issued Statement of Position 81-1, "Accounting for Performance of Construction-Type and Certain Production-Type Contracts." In this SOP, the committee strongly recommended which of the two common methods of accounting for these types of contracts should be required, depending on the specific circumstances involved. They further stated that the two methods should not be viewed as acceptable alternatives for the same circumstances. The committee identified several elements that should be present if percentage-of-completion accounting is to be used.[3]

---

[2]Committee on Accounting Procedure, *Accounting Research Bulletin No. 45*, "Long-Term Construction-Type Contracts" (New York: American Institute of Certified Public Accountants, 1955).

[3]Construction Contractor Guide Committee of the Accounting Standards Division, AICPA, *Statement of Position 81-1*, "Accounting for Performance of Construction-Type and Certain Production-Type Contracts" (New York: American Institute of Certified Public Accountants, 1981), par. 23.

Must be present for Ob of Compl. Method.

1. Dependable estimates can be made of the extent of progress towards completion, contract revenues, and contract costs.
2. The contract clearly specifies the enforceable rights regarding goods or services to be provided and received by the parties, the consideration to be exchanged, and the manner and terms of settlement.
3. The buyer can be expected to satisfy obligations under the contract.
4. The contractor can be expected to perform the contractual obligation.

The completed-contract method should be used only when an entity has primarily short-term contracts, when the conditions for using the percentage-of-completion accounting are not met, or when there are inherent uncertainties in the contract beyond the normal business risks.

In February 1982, the FASB issued Statement No. 56 designating the accounting and reporting principles and practices contained in SOP 81-1 and in the *AICPA Audit and Accounting Guide for Construction Contractors* as preferable accounting principles.[4] The Board indicated that they would consider adopting these principles as FASB standards after allowing sufficient time for the principles to be used in practice so that a basis can be provided for determining their usefulness. A critical issue involved in this area is the clear preference in the SOP for using the percentage-of-completion method of accounting.

For many years, the income tax regulations permitted contractors wide latitude in selecting either the percentage-of-completion or completed-contract method. Beginning with the Tax Reform Act of 1986, the tax laws have limited the use of the completed-contract method and have required increased use of the percentage-of-completion method. This results in greater revenues from taxes without increasing the tax rates, and also results in similar revenue recognition treatment for both taxes and financial reporting.

Measuring the Percentage of Completion

Various methods are currently used in practice to measure the earnings process. They can be conveniently grouped in two categories: input and output measures.

Input Measures

Input measures are made in relation to the costs or efforts devoted to a contract. They are based on an established or assumed relationship between a unit of input and productivity. They include the widely used cost-to-cost method and several variations of efforts-expended methods.

Cost-to-Cost Method Perhaps the most popular of the input measures is the cost-to-cost method. Under this method, the degree of completion is deter-

---

[4]*Statement of Financial Accounting Standards No. 56*, "Designation of AICPA Guide and Statement of Position (SOP) 81-1 on Contractor Accounting and SOP 81-2 Concerning Hospital-Related Organizations as Preferable for Purposes of Applying APB Opinion 20" (Stamford: Financial Accounting Standards Board, 1982).

mined by comparing costs already incurred with the most recent estimates of total expected costs to complete the project. The percentage that costs incurred bear to total expected costs is applied to the expected net income on the project in arriving at earnings to date. Some of the costs incurred, particularly in the early stages of the contract, should be disregarded in applying this method because they do not directly relate to effort expended on the contract. These include such items as subcontract costs for work that has yet to performed and standard fabricated materials that have not yet been installed. One of the most difficult problems in using this method is estimating the costs yet to be incurred. However, this estimation is required in reporting income, regardless of how the percentage of completion is computed.

To illustrate, assume that in January, 1990, Strong Construction Company was awarded a contract with a total price of $3,000,000. Strong expected to earn $400,000 profit on the contract or, in other words, total costs on the contract were estimated to be $2,600,000. The construction was completed over a 3-year period, and the following cost data and cost percentages were compiled during that time:

Year	(1) Actual Costs Incurred	(2) Estimated Cost to Complete	(3) Total Cost (1) + (2)	(4) Cost Percentage (1) ÷ (3)
1990	$1,092,000	$1,508,000	$2,600,000*	42%
1991	832,000			
Total	$1,924,000	676,000	2,600,000*	74%
1992	700,000			
Total	$2,624,000	-0-	2,624,000**	100%

*Estimated total contract cost
**Actual total contract cost

Note that the cost percentage is computed by dividing cumulative actual costs incurred by total cost, the amount of which is estimated for the first two years.

Efforts-Expended Methods The efforts-expended methods are based on some measure of work performed. They include labor hours, labor dollars, machine hours, or material quantities. In each case, the degree of completion is measured in a way similar to that used in the cost-to-cost approach: the ratio of the efforts expended to date to the estimated total efforts to be expended on the entire contract. For example, if the measure of work performed is labor hours, the ratio of hours worked to date to the total estimated hours would produce the percentage for use in measuring income earned.

Output Measures

Output measures are made in terms of results achieved. Included in this category are methods based on units produced, contract milestones reached, and values added. For example, if the contract calls for units of output, such as miles of roadway, a measure of completion would be a ratio of the miles completed to the total miles in the contract. Architects or engineers are sometimes asked to evaluate jobs and estimate what percentage of a job is complete. These estimates are in reality output measures and are usually based on the physical progress made on a contract.

Accounting for Long-Term Construction-Type Contracts

For both the percentage-of-completion and the completed contract methods, all direct and allocable indirect costs of the contracts are charged to an inventory account. The difference in recording between the two methods relates to the timing of revenue and expense recognition, that is, when the estimated earned income is recognized with its related effect on the statement of income and the balance sheet. During the construction period, the annual reported income under these two accounting methods will differ. However, after the contract is completed, the combined income for the total construction period will be the same under each method of accounting, assuming no change in income tax rates. The balance sheet at the end of the construction and collection period will also be identical.

Usually, contracts require progress billings by the contractor and payments by the customer on these billings. The billings and payments are accounted for and reported in the same manner under both methods. The amount of these billings is usually specified by the contract terms, and may be related to the costs actually incurred. Generally, these contracts require inspection before final settlement is made. As a protection for the customer, the contract frequently provides for an amount to be held out from the progress payment. This retention is usually a percentage of the progress billings, 10–20%, and is paid upon final acceptance of the construction. The billings, including any amount to be retained, are debited to Accounts Receivable and credited to a deferred credit account, Progress Billings on Construction Contracts, that serves as an offset to the inventory account, Construction in Progress. The billing of the contract thus in reality transfers the asset value from inventory to receivables, but because of the long-term nature of the contract, the construction costs continue to be reflected in the accounts.

To illustrate accounting for a long-term construction contract, assume that a dam was constructed over a two-year period commencing in September 1990, at a contract price of $5,000,000. The direct and allocable indirect costs, billings, and collections for 1990, 1991, and 1992 were as follows:

Year	Direct and Allocable Indirect Costs	Billings Including 10% Retention	Collections
1990	$1,125,000	$1,000,000	$ 800,000
1991	2,250,000	2,300,000	1,900,000
1992	1,125,000	1,700,000	2,300,000

The following entries for the three years would be made on the contractor's books under either the percentage-of-completion or the completed-contract methods.

	1990		1991		1992	
Construction in Progress	1,125,000		2,250,000		1,125,000	
Materials, Cash etc.		1,125,000		2,250,000		1,125,000
To record costs incurred.						
Accounts Receivable	1,000,000		2,300,000		1,700,000	
Progress Billings on						
Construction Contracts		1,000,000		2,300,000		1,700,000
To record billings.						
Cash	800,000		1,900,000		2,300,000	
Accounts Receivable		800,000		1,900,000		2,300,000
To record cash collections.						

No other entries would be required in 1990 and 1991 under the completed-contract method. In both years, the balance of the construction in progress account exceeds the amount in Progress Billings on Construction Contracts, thus the latter account would be offset against the inventory account in the balance sheet. Because the operating cycle of a company that emphasizes long-term contracts is usually more than one year, all of the above balance sheet accounts would be classified as current. The balance sheet at the end of 1991 would disclose the following balances related to the dam construction contract.

Current assets:
Accounts receivable, including 10% retention		
fee of $330,000		$600,000
Construction in progress	$3,375,000	
Less progress billings on construction contracts . .	3,300,000	75,000

If the billings exceeded the construction costs, the excess would be reported in the current liability section of the balance sheet.

At the completion of the contract, the following entries would be made under the completed-contract method to recognize revenue and costs and to close out the inventory and billings accounts.

Progress Billings on Construction Contracts	5,000,000	
Revenue from Long-Term Construction Contracts . .		5,000,000
Cost of Long-Term Construction Contracts	4,500,000	
Construction in Progress		4,500,000

The income statement for 1992 would report the gross revenues and the matched costs, thus recognizing the entire $500,000 profit in one year.

Using Percentage-of-Completion—Cost-to-Cost Method

If the company used the percentage-of-completion method of accounting, the $500,000 profit would be spread over all three years of construction according to the estimated percentage of completion for each year. Assume that the estimated cost from the beginning of construction was $4,500,000, and that the estimate did not change over the three years. Also, assume that the cost-to-cost method of determining percentage of completion is used. The percentage for each year would be calculated as follows:

	1990	1991	1992
(1) Actual cost incurred to date	$1,125,000	$3,375,000	$4,500,000
(2) Estimated cost to complete	3,375,000	1,125,000	-0-
(3) Total estimated cost	$4,500,000	$4,500,000	$4,500,000
Percentage of completion to date [(1) ÷ (3)]	25%	75%	100%

These percentages may be used to determine directly the gross profit that should be recognized on the income statement; that is, the income statement would report only the gross profit from construction contracts in the amount of $125,000 (estimated income—1990, $500,000 × 25% = $125,000). Preferably, however, the percentages should be used to determine both revenues and costs. The income statement will then disclose revenues, costs, and the resulting gross profit, a method more consistent with normal income statement reporting. The AICPA Audit and Accounting Guide for Construction Contractors recommended this proportional procedure, and the presentations in this chapter will reflect those recommendations.[5] The procedures are as follows:

1. Cumulative revenue to date should be computed by multiplying total estimated contract revenue by the percentage of completion. Revenue for the current period is the difference between the cumulative revenue at the end of the current period and the cumulative revenue recognized in prior periods.

2. Cumulative costs to date should be computed in a manner similar to revenue and should be equal to the total estimated contract cost multiplied by the percentage of completion on the contract. Cost for the current period is the difference between the cumulative costs at the end of the current period and the cumulative costs reported in prior periods.

3. Cumulative gross profit is the excess of cumulative revenue over cumulative costs, and the current period gross profit is the difference between current revenue and current costs.

If the cost-to-cost method is used to estimate earned revenue, the proportional cost will equal the actual cost incurred.

---

[5]Construction Contractor Guide Committee of the Accounting Standards Division, AICPA, *Audit and Accounting Guide for Construction Contractors* (New York: American Institute of Certified Public Accountants, 1980), p. 44.

To illustrate, for 1990, 25% of the fixed contract price of $5,000,000 would be recognized as revenue and 25% of the expected total cost of $4,500,000 would be reported as cost. The following revenue recognition entries would be made for each of the three years of contract.

	1986	1987	1988
Cost of Long-Term Construction Contracts	1,125,000	2,250,000	1,125,000
Construction in Progress	125,000	250,000	125,000
Revenue from Long-Term Construction Contracts	1,250,000	2,500,000	1,250,000

Handwritten annotations on the table: "1986" crossed out and replaced with "1996", "1987" crossed out and replaced with "1991", "1988" crossed out and replaced with "1992".

The gross profit recognized each year is added to the construction in progress account. At the conclusion of the construction, the balance in Construction in Progress will be exactly equal to the amount in Progress Billings on Construction Contracts, and the following closing entry would complete the accounting process.

Progress Billings on Construction Contracts	5,000,000	
Construction in Progress		5,000,000

Using Percentage-of-Completion—Other Methods

If the cost-to-cost method is not used to measure progress on the contract, the proportional costs recognized under this method may not be equal to the actual costs incurred. For example, assume in 1990 that an engineering estimate measure was used, and 20% of the contract was assumed to be completed. The gross profit recognized would therefore be computed and reported as follows:

Recognized revenue (20% of $5,000,000)	$1,000,000
Cost (20% of $4,500,000)	900,000
Gross profit (20% of $500,000)	$100,000

Because some accountants felt that the amount of cost recognized should be equal to the costs actually incurred, an alternative to the preceding approach was included in SOP 81-1.[6] Under this **actual cost approach,** revenue is defined as the actual costs incurred on the contract plus the gross profit earned for the period on the contract. Using the data from the previous example, the revenue and costs to be reported on the 1990 income statement would be as follows:

Actual cost incurred to date	$1,125,000
Recognized gross profit (20% of $500,000)	100,000
Recognized revenue	$1,225,000

[6]*SOP 81-1*, par. 80 and 81.

This contrasts with the $1,000,000 revenue using the proportional cost approach.

In a footnote to this discussion in the SOP, the Committee made it clear that these two alternatives are equally acceptable. However, because the actual cost approach results in a varying gross profit percentage from period to period whenever the measurement of completion differs from that which would occur if the cost-to-cost method were used, the authors feel that proportional cost is preferable. Unless a different method is explicitly stated, examples and end-of-chapter material will assume the use of proportional cost.

Revision of Estimates

In the example, it was assumed that the estimated cost did not vary from the beginning of the contract. This would rarely be true. As estimates change, catch-up adjustments are made in the year of the change. To illustrate the impact of changing estimates, assume that at the end of 1991 it was estimated that the remaining cost to complete the contract would be $1,225,000, making a total estimated cost of $4,600,000. Since costs of $3,375,000 had been incurred by the end of 1991, the estimated percentage of completion for 1991 using the cost-to-cost method would be 73.37% ($3,375,000 ÷ $4,600,000).

The following analysis would be made to compute revenues and costs for the three years of the contract assuming actual costs of $1,175,000 were incurred in 1992.

	(A) To Date	(B) Recognized in Prior Years	(C) Recognized in Current Year (A)—(B)
1990—(25% completed)			
Recognized revenue ($5,000,000 × .25)	$1,250,000		$1,250,000
Cost ($4,500,000 × .25)	1,125,000		1,125,000
Gross profit	$ 125,000		$ 125,000
Gross profit rate	10%		10%
1991—(73.37% completed)			
Recognized revenue ($5,000,000 × .7337)	$3,668,500	$1,250,000	$2,418,500
Cost ($4,600,000 × .7337)	3,375,000*	1,125,000	2,250,000
	$ 293,500	$ 125,000	$ 168,500
Gross profit			
Gross profit rate	8%	10%	6.97%
1992—(100% completed)			
Recognized revenue	$5,000,000	$3,668,500	$1,331,500
Cost	4,550,000	3,375,000	1,175,000
Gross profit	$ 450,000	$ 293,500	$ 156,500
Gross profit rate	9%	8%	11.75%

*Made equal to cost incurred, difference due to rounding of completion percentage.

The entries to record revenue and cost for the three years given the assumed estimate revision would be as follows:

	1990	1991	1992
Cost of Long-Term Construction Contracts	1,125,000	2,250,000	1,175,000
Construction in Progress	125,000	168,500	156,500
Revenue from Long-Term Construction Contracts	1,250,000	2,418,500	1,331,500

The computation of gross profit rates shows how sensitive the reporting is to revisions in estimated costs, and why great care is required in making these estimates.

Reporting Anticipated Contract Losses—Completed Contract

The examples thus far have assumed a profit is expected to be realized. If a loss on the total contract is anticipated, however, generally accepted accounting principles require reporting the loss *in its entirety* in the period when the loss is first anticipated. This is true under either the completed-contract or the percentage-of-completion methods. For example, assume that in the earlier dam construction example the estimated cost to complete the contract at the end of 1991 was $1,725,000. This would mean the total estimated cost of the contract would be $5,100,000 or $100,000 more than the contract price. If the completed-contract method were being used, the following entry would be required at the end of 1991.

Anticipated Loss on Long-Term Construction Contracts	100,000	
Construction in Progress		100,000

The inventory account, Construction in Progress, is thus reduced by the anticipated loss.

Reporting Contract Losses—Percentage-of-Completion

When using the percentage-of-completion method of accounting for long-term contracts, a loss may be reported for a given accounting period under two different situations. The first situation is when the total contract is profitable, but because of changes in actual costs and estimated costs to complete the contract, the estimated total gross profit is less than originally expected. If the cumulative gross profit at the end of the current year is less than the cumulative gross profit recognized in prior years, a loss must be reported in the current period.

To illustrate, assume that the cost to complete the dam described on page 832 at the end of 1991 was $1,495,000 rather than $1,125,000. Thus, the total estimated cost would be $4,870,000, the total estimated gross profit at the end of 1991 would be $130,000 rather than $500,000 as estimated at the end of 1990, and the percentage of completion at the end of 1991 would be 69.3% ($3,375,000 ÷ $4,870,000). Although $125,000 gross profit was recognized in 1990, the cumulative gross profit at the end of 1991 would only be $90,090 ($130,000 × 69.3%). Thus, for 1991, a loss of $34,910 would be reported ($125,000 − $90,090).

The second situation which gives rise to a reported loss is when the total contract is expected to result in a loss; that is, when the total estimated costs exceed the contract price. Again referring to the dam construction example, the percentage of completion under the cost-to-cost method would be 66.18% under the changed assumptions ($3,375,000 ÷ $5,100,000). Cumulative earned revenue would be computed as before, 66.18% × $5,000,000, or $3,309,000. However, cumulative construction costs would be computed by adding the anticipated loss to the earned revenue, thus resulting in cumulative recognized costs of $3,409,000. The loss to be recognized in 1991 would thus be not only the $100,000 loss anticipated on the entire contract but also an additional loss of $125,000 to adjust for the 1990 recognized profit that is now not expected to be realized. These computations can be illustrated by reconstructing part of the earlier table as follows:

	(A) To Date	(B) Recognized in Prior Years	(C) Recognized in Current Year (A)—(B)
1991—(66.18% completed)			
Recognized revenue ($5,000,000 × .6618)	$3,309,000	$1,250,000	$2,059,000
Cost ($3,309,000 + $100,000)	3,409,000	1,125,000	2,284,000
Gross profit (loss)	($ 100,000)	$ 125,000	($ 225,000)

The entry to record the revenue, costs, and adjustments to Construction in Progress for the loss would be as follows:

```
Cost of Long-Term Construction Contracts. . . . . . . . . .   2,284,000
    Revenue from Long-Term Construction Contracts . .                    2,059,000
    Construction in Progress  . . . . . . . . . . . . . . . . . . . . . . .                    225,000
```

The construction in progress account under both methods would have a balance of $3,275,000 computed as follows:

Completed-contract method:

Construction in Progress

1990 cost	1,125,000	1991 loss	100,000
1991 cost	2,250,000		
Bal.	3,275,000		

Percentage-of-completion method:

Construction in Progress

1990 cost	1,125,000	1991 loss	225,000
1990 gross profit	125,000		
1991 cost	2,250,000		
Bal.	3,275,000		

Accounting for Contract Change Orders

Long-term construction contracts are seldom completed without change orders that affect both the contract price and the cost of performance. Change orders are modifications of an original contract that effectively change the provisions of the contract. They may be initiated by the contractor or the customer, and include changes in specifications or design, method or manner of performance, facilities, equipment, materials, location, site, etc. If the contract price is changed as a result of a change order, future computations are made with the revised expected revenue and any anticipated cost changes that will arise because of the change order. Change orders are often unpriced, that is, the work to be performed is defined, but the adjustment to the contract price is to be negotiated later. If it is probable that a contract price change will be negotiated to at least recover the increased costs, the increased costs may be included with the incurred costs of the period and the revenue may be increased by the same amount.

Accounting for Long-Term Service Contracts—the Proportional Performance Method

Thus far, the discussion in this chapter has focused on long-term construction contracts. As indicated earlier, another type of contract that frequently extends over a long period of time is a **service contract.** An increasing percentage of sales in our economy are classified as sales of services as opposed to sales of goods. When the service to be performed is completed as a single act or over a relatively short period of time, no revenue recognition problems arise. The revenue recognition criteria previously defined apply, and all direct and indirect costs related to the service are charged to expense in the period the revenue is recognized. However, when several acts over a period of time are involved, the same revenue recognition problems illustrated for long-term construction contracts arise. Although the FASB has not issued a standard dealing with these contracts, the Board did issue an Invitation to Comment on a proposed Statement of Position that had been issued by the AICPA's Accounting Standards Division.[7] The discussion in the following pages reflects the recommendations made by the Accounting Standards Division.

The Division recommends that unless the final act of service to be performed is so vital to the contract that earlier acts are relatively insignificant, e.g., the packaging, loading, and final delivery of goods in a delivery contract, revenue should be recognized under the proportional performance method.[8] Both input and output measures are identified as possible ways of measuring progress on a service contract. If a contract involves a specified number of identical or similar acts, e.g., the processing of monthly mortgage payments by a mortgage banker, an output measure derived by relating the number of acts performed to the total number of acts to be performed over the contract life is recommended. If a contract involves a specified number

---

[7]*FASB Invitation to Comment,* "Accounting for Certain Service Transactions," (Stamford: Financial Accounting Standards Board, 1978).

[8]*Ibid,* pp. 12-13.

of defined but not identical acts, e.g., a correspondence school that provides evaluation, lessons, examinations, and grading, a cost-to-cost input measurement percentage would be applicable. If future costs are not objectively determinable, output measures such as relating sales value of the individual acts to the total sales value of the service contract may be used. If no pattern of performance can be determined, or if a service contract involves an unspecified number of similar or identical acts with a fixed period for performance, e.g., a maintenance contract for electronic office equipment, the Division recommends the use of the straight-line method, i.e., recognizing revenue equally over the periods of performance.

These measures are used to determine what portion of the service contract fee should be recognized as revenue. Generally, the measures are only indirectly related to the pattern of cash collection; however, they are applicable only if cash collection is reasonably assured and if losses from nonpayment can be objectively determined.

The cost recognition problems of service contracts are somewhat different from long-term construction contracts. Most service contracts involve three different types of costs: (1) initial direct costs related to obtaining and performing initial services on the contract, such as commissions, legal fees, credit investigations, and paper processing; (2) direct costs related to performing the various acts of service; and (3) indirect costs related to maintaining the organization to service the contract, e.g., general and administrative expenses. Initial direct costs are generally charged against revenue using the same input or output measure used for revenue recognition. If the cost-to-cost method of input measurement is used, initial direct costs should be excluded from the cost incurred to date in computing the measure. Only direct costs related to the acts of service are relevant. Direct costs are usually charged to expense as incurred because they are felt to relate directly to the acts for which revenue is recognized. Similarly, all indirect costs should be charged to expense as incurred. As is true for long-term construction contracts, any indicated loss on completion of the service contract is to be charged to the period in which the loss is first indicated. If collection of a service contract is highly uncertain, revenue recognition should not be related to performance but to the collection of the receivable using one of the methods described in the latter part of this chapter.

To illustrate accounting for a service contract using the proportional performance method, assume a correspondence school enters into one hundred contracts with students for an extended writing course. The fee for each contract is $500 payable in advance. This fee includes many different services such as providing the text material, evaluations of writing, examinations, and awarding of a certificate. The total initial direct costs related to the contracts are $5,000. Direct costs for the lessons actually completed during the period are $12,000. It is estimated that the total direct costs of these contracts will be $30,000. The facts of this case suggest that the cost-to-cost method is applicable, and the following entries would be made to record these transactions:

Cash	50,000	
Deferred Course Revenue		50,000
Deferred Initial Costs	5,000	
Cash		5,000
Contract Costs	12,000	
Cash		12,000
Deferred Course Revenue	20,000[1]	
Recognized Course Revenue		20,000
Contract Costs	2,000[2]	
Deferred Initial Costs		2,000

Computations:
[1]Cost-to-cost percentage: $12,000 \div \$30,000 = 40\%$; $50,000 \times .40 = \$20,000$
[2]$5,000 \times .40 = \$2,000$

The gross profit reported on these contracts for the period would be $6,000 ($20,000 − $12,000 − $2,000). The deferred initial cost and deferred course revenues would normally be reported as current balance sheet deferrals because the operating cycle of a correspondence school would be equal to the average time to complete a contract or one year, whichever is longer.

The Wang Laboratories, Inc. financial statement and notes illustrate disclosures which relate to service contracts.

Exhibit 19-1   Wang Laboratories Inc.

	1987	1986
	(in millions)	
Current Liabilities		
Notes payable to banks	$ 8.3	$ 10.1
Accounts payable, other payables and accruals	391.0	333.0
Unearned service revenue	148.0	122.1
Income taxes	16.5	12.1
Dividends payable to stockholders	6.4	6.0
Portion of long-term debt due within one year	83.2	54.6
Total Current Liabilities	653.4	537.9

NOTES TO CONSOLIDATED FINANCIAL STATE-MENTS

Note A (in part): Significant Accounting Policies

Revenue Recognition and Related Costs—

Revenues from product sales and noncancellable sales-type leases are recongized at the time products are shipped.

Customer leases having an initial term of one or two years are accounted for as operating leases.

Service revenues are recognized ratably over the contract period or as the services are performed.

Cost of products sold includes all product manufacturing and distribution costs associated with products sold. Costs associated with installation and service and depreciation of rental equipment are included in cost of service and rental income. Service and rental income includes the service contract equivalent of service income during the warranty period.

Evaluation of Proportional Performance Method

The FASB has not issued a standard on service industries. While the proportional performance method has theoretical support for its adoption, it tends to be extremely conservative, especially during a period of rapid growth in a company's revenues. This situation is often encountered with new companies, such as those in the rapidly expanding health-spa industry. Since no revenue is recognized until performance of the service is begun, the proportional performance method recognizes no revenue at the critical point of signing a service contract. Thus, in the growing years of a company, use of the proportional performance method will result in large losses being reported even though the operation might be very profitable over time. This can lead to the questionable conclusion that a company is no better off after service contracts are sold than it was before.

An alternative method of recognizing revenue for service contracts would be to recognize part of the revenue upon the signing of the contract, and then spread the balance of the revenue over the contract life using the proportional performance concept. The decision as to how much revenue should be recognized at the beginning of the contract would depend on the nature and terms of the contract, including any forfeiture or cancellation provisions.

Revenue Recognition After Delivery of Goods or Performance of Services

One of the FASB's two revenue recognition criteria, listed at the beginning of this chapter, states that revenue should not be recognized until the earnings process is substantially complete. Normally, the earnings process is substantially completed by the delivery of goods or performance of services. Collection of receivables is usually routine, and any future warranty costs can be reasonably estimated. In some cases, however, the circumstances surrounding a revenue transaction are such that considerable uncertainty exists as to whether payments will indeed be received. This can occur if the sales transaction is unusual in nature and involves a customer in such a way that default carries little cost or penalty. Under these circumstances, the uncertainty of cash collection suggests that revenue recognition should await the actual receipt of cash. There are at least three different approaches to revenue recognition that depend on the receipt of cash: **installment sales, cost recovery**, and **cash**. These methods differ as to the treatment of costs incurred and the timing of revenue recognition. They are summarized and contrasted with the full accrual method in the table at the top of page 843.

These methods are really not alternatives to each other; however, the guidelines for applying them are not well defined. As the uncertainty of the environment increases, generally accepted accounting principles would require moving from the full accrual method to installment sales, cost recovery and finally, a strict cash approach. The cash method is the most conservative approach because it would not permit the deferral of any costs, but would charge them to expense as incurred. In the following pages, each of these revenue recognition methods will be discussed and illustrated.

Method	Treatment of Product Costs or Initial Costs Under Service Contracts	Timing of Revenue and/ or Income Recognition
Full accrual	Charge against revenue at time of sale or rendering of service.	At point of sale.
Installment sales	Defer to be matched against part of each cash collection. Usually done by deferring the estimated profit.	At collection of cash. Usually a portion of the cash payment is recognized as income.
Cost recovery	Defer to be matched against total cash collected.	At collection of cash, but only after all costs are recovered.
Cash	Charge to expense as incurred.	At collection of cash.

Installment Sales Method

Traditionally, the most commonly applied method for dealing with the uncertainty of cash collections has been the installment sales method. Under this method, income is recognized as cash is collected rather than at the time of sale. This method of accounting was developed after World War II in response to an increasing number of sales contracts that extended the time payment over several years, with full title to the "sold" property being transferred only at the time of final collection. Consumer goods such as electrical appliances, jewelry, automobiles, and recreational equipment were commonly purchased and accounted for in this way. As this method of sales became more popular, and as credit rating evaluations became more sophisticated, the probability of collection on these contracts became more certain. The collection of cash was no longer the critical event, but the point of sale essentially completed the earnings process. Collection costs and the cost of uncollectible accounts could be estimated at the time of sale. Additional protection was afforded the seller because most contracts included a right of repossession. For these reasons, the Accounting Principles Board concluded in 1966 that, except for special circumstances, the installment method of recognizing revenue is not acceptable for reporting purposes.[9]

In more recent years, sales of other types of property, such as developed real estate and undeveloped land, have also been made with greatly extended terms. Commonly, these contracts involve little or no down payment, the payments are spread over ten to thirty or forty years, and the probability of default in the early years is high because of a small investment by the buyer in the contract and because the market prices of the

[9]*Opinions of the Accounting Principles Board, No. 10*, "Omnibus Opinion—1966" (New York: American Institute of Certified Public Accountants, 1967), par. 12.

property are often unstable. Application of the accrual method to these contracts frequently overstates income in the early years due to the failure to realistically provide for future costs related to the contract, including losses from contract defaults. The FASB considered these types of sales and concluded that accrual accounting applied in these circumstances often results in "front-end loading," i.e., a recognition of all revenue at the time of the sales contract with improper matching of related costs. Thus, the Board has established criteria that must be met before real estate and retail land sales can be recorded using the full accrual method of revenue recognition. If the criteria are not fully met, then the use of the installment sales method, or in some cases the cost recovery or deposit methods, is recommended to reflect the conditions of the sale more accurately.[10] Because the installment sales method is often recommended in new sales environments, it is important for accountants to understand its application.

Accounting for installment sales using the deferred gross profit approach requires determining a gross profit rate for the sales of each year, and establishing an accounts receivable and a deferred revenue account identified by the year of the sale. As collections are made of a given year's receivables, a portion of the deferred revenue equal to the gross profit rate times the collections made is recognized as income. The most common application of this method has been for the sale of merchandise. However, any sale of property or services may be recorded using the concept. The following examples of transactions and journal entries will illustrate this method of recognizing revenue.

Installment Sales of Merchandise

Assume that the Riding Corporation sells merchandise on the installment basis, and that the uncertainties of cash collection make the use of the installment sales method acceptable. The following data relate to three years of operations. To simplify the presentation, interest charges are excluded from the example.

	1991	1992	1993
Installment sales	$150,000	$200,000	$300,000
Cost of installment sales	100,000	140,000	204,000
Gross profit	$ 50,000	$ 60,000	$ 96,000
Gross profit percentage	33.3%	30%	32%
Cash collections:			
1991 Sales	$ 30,000	$ 75,000	$ 30,000
1992 Sales		70,000	80,000
1993 Sales			100,000

The entries to record the transactions for 1991 would be as follows:

---

[10]*Statement of Financial Accounting Standards No. 66*, "Accounting for Sales of Real Estate" (Stamford: Financial Accounting Standards Board, October, 1982).

Installment Accounts Receivable—1991	150,000	
Installment Sales		150,000
Cost of Installment Sales	100,000	
Inventory		100,000
Cash	30,000	
Installment Accounts Receivable—1991		30,000
Installment Sales	(150,000)	
Cost of Installment Sales		100,000
Deferred Gross Profit—1991		50,000
Deferred Gross Profit—1991	10,000*	
Realized Gross Profit on Installment Sales		10,000

*$30,000 × 33.3%

The sales and costs related to sales are recorded in a manner identical with the accounting for sales discussed in Chapter 8. At the end of the year, however, the sales and cost of sales accounts are closed to a deferred gross profit account rather than to Income Summary. The realized gross profit is then recognized by applying the gross profit percentage to cash collections. All other general and administrative expenses are normally written off in the period incurred.

Entries for the next two years are summarized in the schedule below.

	1992		1993	
Installment Accounts Receivable—1992	200,000			
Installment Accounts Receivable—1993			300,000	
Installment Sales		200,000		300,000
Cost of Installment Sales	140,000		204,000	
Inventory		140,000		204,000
Cash	145,000		210,000	
Installment Accounts Receivable—1991		75,000		30,000
Installment Accounts Receivable—1992		70,000		80,000
Installment Accounts Receivable—1993				100,000
Installment Sales	200,000		300,000	
Cost of Installment Sales		140,000		204,000
Deferred Gross Profit—1992		60,000		
Deferred Gross Profit—1993				96,000
Deferred Gross Profit—1991	25,000[1]		10,000[3]	
Deferred Gross Profit—1992	21,000[2]		24,000[4]	
Deferred Gross Profit—1993			32,000[5]	
Realized Gross Profit on Installment Sales		46,000		66,000

Computations:
[1] $75,000 × .333 = $25,000
[2] $70,000 × .30 = $21,000
[3] $30,000 × .333 = $10,000
[4] $80,000 × .30 = $24,000
[5] $100,000 × .32 = $32,000

Although this method of recording installment sales is the one most commonly followed, it would also be possible to defer both the gross revenue and the gross costs rather than just the net difference. If this approach is followed, the resulting entries would be more similar to those illustrated for percentage-of-completion accounting. Each year a portion of the gross revenue and gross costs would be recognized with the difference being the realized gross profit. Both methods produce the same net income.

If a company is heavily involved in installment sales, the operating cycle of the business is normally the period of the average installment contract. Thus, the currently accepted definition of current assets and current liabilities requires the receivables and their related deferred gross profit accounts to be reported in the current asset section of classified balance sheets. The deferred gross profit accounts should be reported as an offset to the related accounts receivable. Thus, at the end of 1991 the current asset section would include the following accounts:

Installment accounts receivable	$120,000	
Less deferred gross profit	40,000	$80,000

Complexities of Installment Sales of Merchandise

In the previous example, no provision was made for interest. In reality, however, installment sales contracts always include interest, either expressed or implied. The interest portion of the payments is recognized as income in the period accrued, and the balance of the payment is treated as a collection on the installment sale. Thus, if in the example on pages 844-845 the $75,000 collection of 1991 sales in 1992 included interest of $40,000, only $35,000 would be used it compute the realize gross profit from 1991 sales. A complete example involving interest is illustrated in the next section dealing with real estate installment sales.

Additional complexities can arise in installment sales accounting in providing for uncollectible accounts. Because of the right to repossess merchandise in the event of nonpayment, the provision for uncollectible accounts can be less than might be expected. Only the amount of the receivable in excess of the current value of the repossessed merchandise is a potential loss. Accounting for repossessions was discussed in Chapter 10. Theoretically, a proper matching of estimated losses against revenues would require allocating the expected losses over the years of collection. Practically, however, the provision is made and charged against income in the period of the sale. Thus, the accounting entries for handling estimated uncollectible accounts are the same as illustrated in Chapter 8.

Installment Sales of Real Estate

The installment sales method of accounting is often used for sales of real estate on a long-term contract basis. These sales are frequently characterized by small down payments with long payout periods on the balance. Usually the seller retains title to the real estate until the final payment is made, thus giving the seller the right of repossession. In an inflationary economy, this right is valuable and in most cases means that ultimate collection of the debt, either through payment or repossession, is virtually assured. However, if circumstances reduce the probability of collection or if the market value of the property is unstable, then the installment sales method may be applied, or in extreme cases, the cost recovery method may be required.

To illustrate the accounting for real estate sales using the installment method, assume that Emery Industries Inc. sells land and buildings on January 1, 1991, for $4,000,000. Emery receives a down payment of $300,000 and a promissory note for the remaining $3,700,000 plus interest at 12% to be paid in equal installments of $471,752 at the end of each of the next 25 years. The land has a carrying value on Emery's books at the time of the sale of $200,000, and the buildings have a carrying value of $2,000,000. The sale does not meet the FASB's criteria for the full accrual method of revenue recognition, and the installment method of accounting is assumed to be appropriate. The following entries would be made to record the initial transaction:

1991
Jan. 1

Cash	300,000	
Notes Receivable	11,793,800[1]	
Discount on Notes Receivable (or Unearned		
Interest Revenue)		8,093,800[2]
Real Estate Sales		4,000,000
Cost of Real Estate Sales	2,200,000	
Land		200,000
Building (net of accumulated depreciation)		2,000,000
Real Estate Sales	4,000,000	
Cost of Real Estate Sales		2,200,000
Deferred Gross Profit on Real Estate Sales		1,800,000

Computations:
[1]$471,752 × 25 = $11,793,800
[2]$11,793,800 − $3,700,000 = $8,093,800

The gross profit percentage for this sale is 45% ($1,800,000 ÷ $4,000,000). This percentage is applied to each cash collection reduced by the amount of interest included in the cash receipt. Thus, $135,000 would be recognized immediately upon receipt of the $300,000 down payment (.45 × $300,000) and the following entry would be made to recognize this profit.

1991
Jan. 1

Deferred Gross Profit on Real Estate Sales	135,000	
Realized Gross Profit on Real Estate Sales		135,000

At the end of the first year, cash of $471,752 will be collected in accordance with the contract terms. Included in this amount is interest earned of $444,000 (.12 × $3,700,000). The remainder of the cash collected, $27,752, is payment on the principal amount of the debt; 45% of this portion of the payment, or $12,488 (.45 × $27,752), would also be recognized as realized gross profit in the first year.

1991

Dec. 31	Cash	471,752	
	Discount on Notes Receivable	444,000	
	Notes Receivable		471,752
	Interest Revenue		444,000
	Deferred Gross Profit on Real Estate Sales . .	12,488	
	Realized Gross Profit on Real Estate Sales		12,488

The following T-accounts summarize these transactions for the first year before closing entries.

Notes Receivable

| 11,793,800 | 471,752 |
| Bal.   11,322,048 | |

Discount on Notes Receivable

| 444,000 | 8,093,800 |
| | Bal.   7,649,800 |

Real Estate Sales

| 4,000,000 | 4,000,000 |

Cost of Real Estate Sales

| 2,200,000 | 2,200,000 |

Interest Revenue

| | 444,000 |

Land

| 200,000 | 200,000 |

Building (net of accumulated depreciation)

| 2,000,000 | 2,000,000 |

Deferred Gross Profit on Real Estate Sales

135,000	1,800,000
12,488	
	Bal 1,652,512

Realized Gross Profit on Real Estate Sales

	135,000
	12,488
	Bal. 147,488

Cash collections in subsequent years would be divided between interest and principal in the same manner, and a portion of the deferred profit would be recognized each year. Because the collections are constant, and the interest revenue is declining as the carrying value of the receivable declines, the gross profit recognized would increase each year.

Care must be taken in evaluating a sale of real estate. In some cases, the contract may be in reality a financial arrangement or an operating lease, or it may be a deposit on a possible future sale. Revenue should be recognized only after careful evaluation of the contractual arrangements and application of the criteria in FASB Statement No. 66.

Cost Recovery Method

Under the cost recovery method, no income is recognized on a sale until the cost of the item sold is recovered through cash receipts. Then, all subsequent receipts are reported as revenue. Because all costs have been recovered, the recognized revenue after cost recovery represents income. This method is used only when the circumstances surrounding a sale are so uncertain that earlier recognition is impossible.

To illustrate the accounting entries required under this method, assume that collection on the real estate sales contract for Emery Industries Inc. is felt to be so uncertain that the cost recovery method should be used.

Under this method, the $2,200,000 carrying value of the real estate must be collected before any revenue or income is recognized, including any recognition of interest revenue on the contract. The same entries would be made to record the sale, the cost of the sale, and the deferred gross profit as was done under the installment sales method. The difference between the book value of the property and the down payment received equals the un-recovered cost of $1,900,000 ($2,200,000 — $300,000). Unrecovered cost may also be computed as follows:

Notes receivable		$11,793,800
Less:		
Discount on notes receivable	$8,093,800	
Deferred gross profit	1,800,000	9,893,800
		$ 1,900,000

When the first annual payment of $471,752 is collected, the following entry would be made:

1991		
Dec. 31	Cash	471,742
	Discount on Notes Receivable	444,000
	Notes Receivable	471,752
	Deferred Gross Profit on Real Estate Sales	444,000

The unrecovered cost would be $1,428,248 ($1,900,000—$471,752). This agrees with the balance to be reported on the balance sheet as follows:

Notes receivable		$11,322,048
Less:		
Discount on notes receivable	$7,649,800	
Deferred gross profit	2,244,000	9,893,800
		$ 1,428,248

Note that the deferred gross profit account includes both gross profit and interest revenue that will not be recognized until the cost is recovered.

At the end of 1994, the difference between the receivable and the two offset accounts would be $12,992. The 1995 collection would result in a cost recovery of $12,992 and a recognition of $458,760 revenue. In each of the remaining collection years, the total cash receipt will be recognized as revenue.

The selection of a revenue recognition method has a great impact on revenue and income, especially in the first year of a sales contract. The following summary shows how income would vary on the real estate sale of Emery Industries Inc. depending on which revenue recognition method is used.

Revenue Recognition Method	Income for 1991
Full Accrual	$2,244,000[1]
Installment Sales	591,488[2]
Cost Recovery	—0—

Computations:
[1]$1,800,000 gross profit + $444,000 interest revenue = $2,244,000
[2]$147,488 gross profit + $444,000 interest revenue = $591,488

In subsequent years, only interest revenue is recognized as revenue under the full accrual method, but interest revenue plus a portion of the payment on the principal is recognized under the installment sales method. After four years, all the cash collected is recognized as revenue under the cost recovery method. The graph below illustrates how revenue for the real estate sale would be recognized over the twenty-five years assuming all payments were made as scheduled.

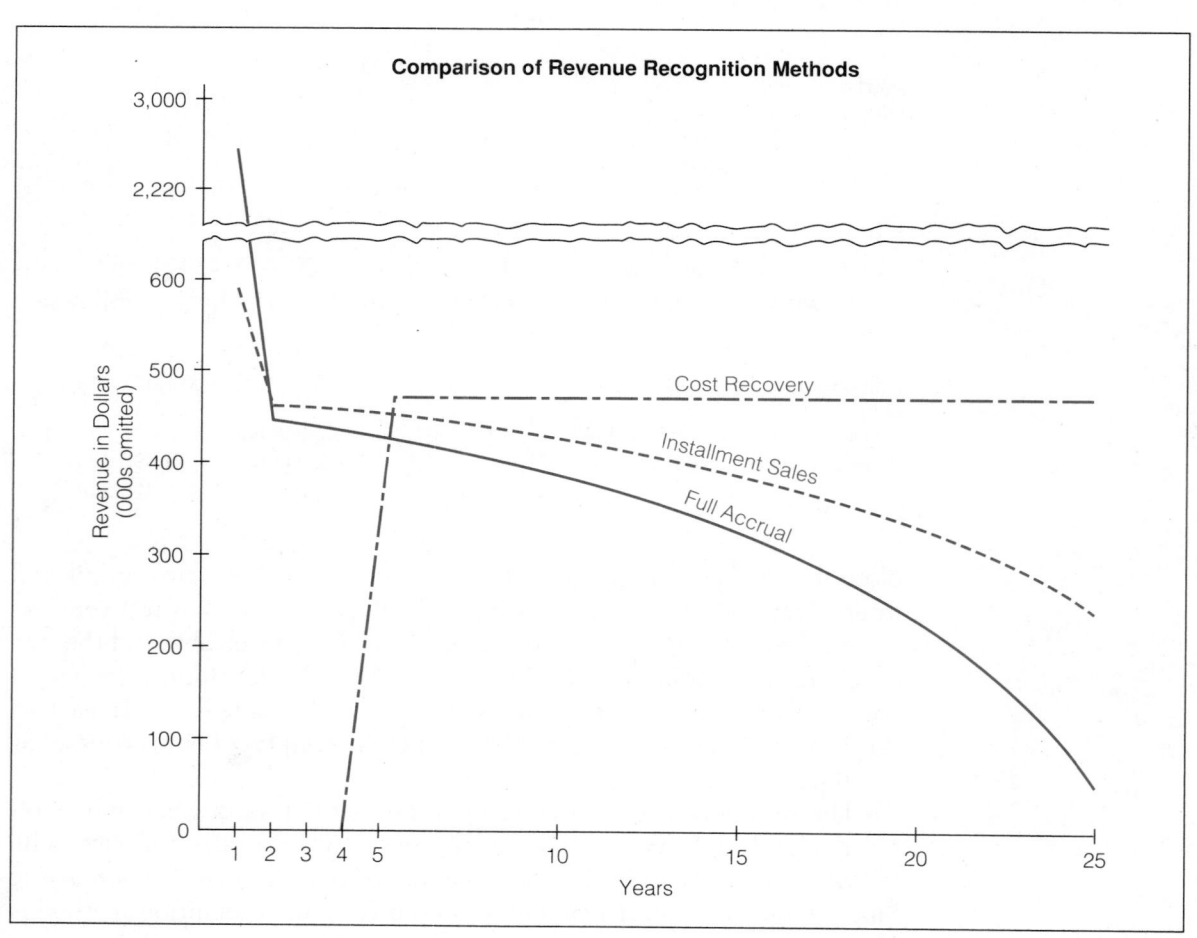

Cash Method   If the probability of recovering product or service costs is remote, the cash method of accounting could be used. Seldom would this method be applicable for sales of merchandise or real estate because the right of repossession would leave considerable value to the seller. However, the cash method might be appropriate for service contracts with high initial costs and considerable uncertainty as to the ultimate collection of the contract price. Under this method, all costs are charged to expense as incurred, and revenue is recognized as collections are made. This extreme method of revenue and expense recognition would be appropriate only when the potential losses on a contract cannot be estimated with any degree of certainty.

Methods of Accounting Before Revenue Recognition   In addition to the revenue recognition methods discussed in this chapter, some sales arrangements involve an exchange of either goods or monetary assets such as cash and notes receivable prior to the point where the earnings process has been completed sufficiently to recognize revenue. Under these circumstances, special accounting procedures must be applied pending the finalization of the sale and subsequent application of one of the methods of revenue recognition. If monetary assets are received prior to finalization of a sale, the deposit method of accounting should be used. If inventory is exchanged in advance of a sale, consignment accounting procedures should be applied. Each of these methods will be discussed briefly.

Deposit Method— General   In some cases, cash is collected before a sales contract is sufficiently defined to recognize revenue. This situation frequently arises in real estate sales contracts. For these cases, a method of accounting referred to as the deposit method has been developed.[11] Pending recognition of a sale, the cash received from a buyer is reported as a deposit on the contract and classified among the liabilities on the balance sheet. The property continues to be shown as an asset of the seller, and any related debt on the property continues to be reported as debt of the seller. No revenue or income should be recognized until the sales contract is finalized. At that time, one of the revenue recognition methods illustrated in this chapter may be used, and the deposit account would be closed. If the deposit is forfeited, it should be credited to income.

Deposit Method— Franchising Industry   A special application of the deposit method is found in the franchising industry, one of the fastest growing retail industries of recent years. Franchisors create faster growth by selling various rights to use a name and/ or a product to operators (franchisees) who manage independent units as separate entrepreneurs from the franchisor.

---

[11]*Statement of Financial Accounting Standards No. 66*, par. 65–67.

Sales of franchises usually include several different services, products, and/or plant assets including: (1) intangible rights to use a trademark or name, (2) property owned by the franchisor, (3) pre-opening services such as helping locate suitable business sites, constructing a building, and training employees, and (4) ongoing services, products, and processes as the operations are carried out. Many revenue recognition problems are present in typical franchises, however, most of them may be solved if the elements are separately identified and accounted for in the same manner as they would be if the sale were a separate transaction. The most troublesome revenue recognition problem has been the initial fee. Typically, the franchisor charges a substantial amount for the right to use the franchise name and to provide for pre-opening services. Sometimes these fees are payable immediately in cash, but typically they include a long-term note receivable. Frequently liberal refund provisions are included in the agreement, especially in the period prior to opening.

In the early days of franchising agreements, franchisors often reported the initial fee as revenue when the monetary assets were received. Future estimated costs were provided as offsets to the revenue. However, this treatment often resulted in questionable front-end loading of revenue similar to that occurring in the real estate and retail land sale industries. As a result, the AICPA issued an Industry Accounting Guide in 1973 that established revenue recognition guidelines for the franchising industry.[12] The essentials of this guide were later incorporated into FASB Statement No. 45.[13] This standard specifies that no revenue be recognized prior to **substantial performance** of the services covered by the initial fee. Until that time, any monetary assets received should be offset by a deposit or deferred credit account, and any costs related to the services rendered should be deferred until revenue is recognized, except that such deferred costs shall not exceed anticipated revenue less estimated additional related costs. Once substantial preformance is achieved, revenue should be recognized using the method that best reflects the probability of cash collection, i.e., accrual, installment sales, or cost recovery method. The latter two methods "shall be used to account for franchise fee revenue only in those exceptional cases when revenue is collectible over an extended period and no reasonable basis exists for estimating collectibility."[14]

To illustrate, assume that a franchisor charges new franchisees an initial fee of $25,000. Of this amount $10,000 is payable in cash when the agreement is signed, and the remainder is to be paid in four annual installments of $3,750 each. This obligation is evidenced by a $15,000, non-interest-bearing note. The agreement provides that the franchisor will assist in locating the site for a building, conduct a market survey to estimate potential income, supervise the construction of a building, and provide

[12]Committee on Franchise Accounting and Auditing, AICPA, *Industry Accounting Guide,* "Accounting for Franchise Fee Revenue" (New York: American Institute of Certified Public Accountants, 1973).

[13]*Statement of Financial Accounting Standards No. 45,* "Accounting for Franchise Fee Revenue" (Stamford: Financial Accounting Standards Board, March, 1981).

[14]*Ibid,* par 6.

initial training to employees. Assume that the franchisee could borrow money at 10%. Thus, the present value of the four $3,750 payments would be $11,887 ($3,750 × 3.1699). The discount of $3,113 represents interest to be earned over the payment period.

If the down payment is refundable, and no services have been rendered at the time the arrangement is made, the deposit method would be used as long as collection on the note is reasonably certain. The following entry would be made to record the transaction:

Cash	10,000	
Notes Receivable	15,000	
Discount on Notes Receivable		3,113
Deposit on Franchise (or Unearned Franchise Fee)		21,887

When the initial services are determined to be substantially performed, the revenue recognition method to be used and the resulting journal entries depend on the probability of future cash collection. If the collection of the note is reasonably assured, the full accrual method would be used. Assume that substantial performance of the initial services costs $15,000. The entries to record this event using the full accrual method would be as follows:

Cost of Franchise Fee Revenue	15,000	
Cash		15,000
Deposit on Franchise (or Unearned Franchise Fee)	21,887	
Franchise Fee Revenue		21,887

If the collection of the note is doubtful, the installment sales method could be used. In addition to the entries used under the full accrual method, the following entries would be required.

Franchise Fee Revenue	21,887	
Cost of Franchise Fee Revenue		15,000
Deferred Gross Profit on Franchise		6,887
Deferred Gross Profit on Franchise	3,147*	
Realized Gross Profit on Franchise		3,147

*Computation:
$6,887 ÷ $21,887 = 31.47% gross profit percentage
.3147 × $10,000 = $3,147

Consignment Sales   Another method of accounting has developed when property is exchanged without a transfer of title and without a sales contract being completed. This type of arrangement is referred to as a **consignment**. Under a consignment, the potential seller, the **consignor**, ships merchandise to another party, the **consignee**, who then acts as an *agent* for the consignor to sell the goods. Title to the merchandise continues to be held by the consignor until a sale is made, at which time title passes to the ultimate purchaser. The consignee is usually entitled to reimbursement for expenses incurred in relation to this arrangement, and is also entitled to a commission if a sale is successfully made.

Because title to the merchandise is held by the consignor, but physical possession is held by the consignee, special accounting records must be maintained by the consignor for control purposes. No revenue is recognized until a sale is made by the consignee. Upon shipment of the merchandise by the consignor, a special inventory account is established on the consignor's books to identify the consigned merchandise. Any consignment expenses paid by the consignor are added to the inventory balance as added costs. The consignee does not make an entry for receipt of the inventory in the general ledger; however, memorandum control records are usually kept. Any reimbursable expense paid by the consignee is charged to a receivable account by the consignee and added to the inventory balance by the consignor. When a sale is made, the consignor recognizes the sale as revenue according to one of the revenue recognition methods, and the consignee recognizes the commission as revenue on the transaction.

To illustrate consignment accounting entries, assume that Harrison Products Inc. sends $500,000 worth of goods on consignment to Benson Industries. Shipping costs of $5,000 are paid by Harrison, and reimbursable advertising costs of $20,000 are paid by Benson Industries. By the end of the year, one half of the goods on consignment are sold for $400,000 cash. A 10% commission is earned by Benson Industries according to the terms of the consignment. The journal entries shown on page 855 would be made on the consignor's and consignee's books.

If the sale by Benson Industries had been on the installment basis, the installment sales entries illustrated earlier in this chapter could have been used in place of the accrual entries illustrated.

Concluding Comments

This chapter has explored some special problems that arise in recognizing revenue. Some industries such as franchising, construction, and real estate, have been used as illustrative of the types of problems that exist in applying the revenue recognition criteria included in currently accepted accounting standards. While recognizing revenue at the point of sale is still the most traditional method, accounting standards provide for flexibility when a different method of revenue recognition provides more meaningful information to users. Percentage-of-completion, proportional performance, installment sales, cost recovery, and deferral through the deposit method are all part of generally accepted accounting principles under specified conditions.

Transaction	Entries on Consignor's Books (Harrison Products Inc.)		Entries on Consignee's Books (Benson Industries)	
(1) Shipment of goods on consignment.	Inventory on Consignment .... Finished Goods Inventory	500,000 500,000	No entry (memorandum control record)	
(2) Payment of expenses by consignor.	Inventory on Consignment .... Cash	5,000 5,000	No entry	
(3) Payment of expenses by consignee.	Inventory on Consignment .... Consignee Payable	20,000 20,000	Consignor Receivable .... Cash	20,000 20,000
(4) Sale of Merchandise.	No entry		Cash .... Consignor Payable	400,000 400,000
(5) Notification of sale to consignor and payment of cash due.	Commission Expense .... Cash .... Consignee Payable .. Consignment Sales Revenue	40,000 340,000 20,000 400,000	Consignor Payable .. Cash .... Commission Revenue .... Consignor Receivable	400,000 340,000 40,000 20,000
	Cost of Goods Sold Inventory on Consignment	262,500* 262,500		
	*Computation: 1/2($500,000 + $25,000) = $262,500			

Key Terms

Change orders 839
Completed contract method 828
Consignment 853
Consignee 853
Consignor 853
Cost recovery method 848
Cost-to-cost method 830
Deposit method 850
Efforts-expended methods 831

Input measures 830
Installment sales method 843
Output measures 831
Percentage-of-completion accounting 828
Proportional performance method 828
Substantial performance 852

Questions

1. Under what conditions is percentage-of-completion accounting recommended for construction contractors?
2. Distinguish between the cost-to-cost method and efforts-expended methods of measuring the percentage of completion.
3. Output measures of percentage of completion are sometimes used in preference to input measures. What are some examples of commonly used output measures?
4. What is the relationship between the construction in progress account and the progress billings on construction contracts account? How should these accounts be reported on the balance sheet?
5. When a measure of percentage of completion other than cost-to-cost is used, the amount of cost charged against revenue using the percentage of completion will usually be different from the costs incurred. How do some AICPA committee members recommend handling this situation so that the costs charged against revenue are equal to the costs incurred?
6. The construction in progress account is used to accumulate all costs of construction. What additional item is included in this account when percentage-of-completion accounting is followed?
7. The gross profit percentage reported on long-term construction contracts often varies from year to year. What is the major reason for this variation?
8. How are anticipated contract losses treated under the completed-contract and percentage-of-completion methods?
9. What input and output measures are usually applicable to the proportional performance method for long-term service contracts?
10. The proportional performance method spreads the profit over the periods in which services are being performed. What arguments could be made against this method of revenue recognition for newly formed service oriented companies?
11. Distinguish among the three different approaches to revenue recognition that await the receipt of cash. How does the treatment of costs incurred vary depending on the approach used?
12. Under what general conditions is the installment sales method of accounting preferred to the full accrual method?
13. The normal accounting entries for installment sales require keeping a separate record by year of receivables, collections on receivables, and the deferred gross profit percentages. Why are these separate records necessary?
14. Installment sales contracts generally include interest. Contrast the method of recognizing interest revenue from the method used to recognize the gross profit on the sale.

15. Under what conditions would the cash method of recognizing revenue be acceptable for reporting purposes?

16. What special recognition problems arise in accounting for franchise fees?

17. Consignment accounting is primarily a method of accounting for transfers of inventory prior to the point of revenue recognition. Describe the essential elements of this method from the standpoint of (a) the consignor and (b) the consignee.

Discussion Cases

Case 19-1   (Recognizing revenue on a percentage-of-completion basis)

As the new controller for Enclave Construction Company, you have been advised that your predecessor classified all revenues and expenses by project, each project being considered a separate venture. All revenues from uncompleted projects were treated as unearned revenue, and all expenses applicable to each uncompleted project were treated as "work in process" inventory. Thus, the income statement for the current year includes only the revenues and expenses related to projects completed during the year. What do you think about the use of the completed-contract method by the previous controller? What alternative approach might you suggest to company management?

Case 19-2   (Let's spread our losses too!)

The Abbott Construction Company has several contracts to build sections of freeways, bridges, and dams. Because most of these contracts require more than one year to complete, the accountant, Dave Allred, has recommended use of the percentage-of-completion method to recognize revenue and income on these contracts. The president, Kathy Bahr, isn't quite sure how it works, and indicates concern about the impact of this decision on income taxes. Bahr also inquires as to what happens when a contract results in a loss. When told by Allred that any estimated loss must be recognized when it is first identified, Bahr becomes upset. "If it is a percentage-of-completion method, and we are recognizing profits as production is finished, why shouldn't we be able to do the same for losses?" How would you as the accountant answer Bahr's concerns?

Case 19-3   (What is the difference between completed-contract and percentage-of-completion accounting?)

In accounting for long-term contracts (those taking longer than one year to complete), the two methods commonly followed are the percentage-of-completion method and the completed-contract method. (a) Discuss how earnings on long-term contracts are recognized and computed under these two methods. (b) Under what circumstances is it preferable to use one method over the other? (c) Why is earnings recognition as measured by interim billings not generally accepted for long-term contracts?   (AICPA adapted)

Case 19-4   (When is the membership fee earned?)

The Superb Health Studio has been operating for 5 years but is presently for sale. It has opened 50 salons in various cities in the United States. The normal pattern for a new opening is to advertise heavily and sell different types of memberships: 1-year, 3-year, and 5-year. For the initial membership fee, members may use the pool, exercise rooms, sauna, and other recreational facilities without charge. If special courses or programs are taken, additional fees are charged; however, members are granted certain priorities and the fees are less than those charged to outsiders. In addition, a minimal $10 a month dues charge is made to all members. Non-members may use the facilities; however, they must pay a substantial daily charge for services they receive.

Your client, Dickson Inc., is considering purchasing the chain of health studios, and asks you to give your opinion on its operations. You are provided with financial statements that show a growing revenue and income pattern over the 5-year period. The balance sheet shows that the physical facilities are apparently owned rather than leased. But you are aware that health studios, like all service institutions, have some challenging revenue recognition problems. What questions would you want answered in preparing your report for Dickson?

Case 19-5   (When is it revenue?)

Hertzel Advertising Agency handles advertising for clients under contracts that require the agency to develop advertising copy and layouts, and place ads in various media, charging clients a commission of 15% of the media cost as its fee. The agency makes advance billings to its clients of estimated media cost plus its 15% commission. Adjustments to these advances are usually small. Frequently both the billings and receipt of cash from these billings occur before the period in which the advertising actually appears in the media.

A conference meeting is held between officers of the agency and the new firm of CPAs recently engaged to perform annual audits. In this meeting, consideration is given to 4 possible points for measuring revenue: (1) at the time the advanced billing is made, (2) when payment is received from the client, (3) in the month when the advertising appears in the media, and (4) when the bill for advertising is received from the media, generally in the month following its appearance. The agency has been following the first method for the past several years on the basis that a definite contract exists and the revenue is earned when billed. When the billing is made, an entry is prepared to record the estimated receivable and liability to the media. Estimated expenses related to the contract are also recorded. Adjusting entries are later made for any differences between the estimated and actual amounts.

As a member of the CPA firm attending this meeting, how would you react to the agency's method of recognizing revenue? Discuss the strengths and weaknesses of each of the 4 methods of revenue recognition and indicate which one you would recommend the agency follow.

Case 19-6   (When is the initial franchise fee really earned?)

Magleby Inn sells franchises to independent operators throughout the western part of the United States. The contract with the franchisee includes the following provisions:

   (a) The franchisee is charged an initial fee of $25,000. Of this amount $5,000 is payable when the agreement is signed and a $4,000 non-interest-bearing note is payable at the end of each of the 5 subsequent years.

(b) All the initial franchise fee collected by Magleby Inn is to be refunded and the remaining obligation canceled if, for any reason, the franchisee fails to open the franchise.

(c) In return for the initial franchise fee, Magleby agrees to: assist the franchisee in selecting the location for the business; negotiate the lease for the land; obtain financing and assist with building design; supervise construction; establish accounting and tax records; and provide expert advice over a 5-year period relating to such matters as employee and management training, quality control, and promotion.

(d) In addition to the initial franchise fee, the franchisee is required to pay to Magleby Inn a monthly fee of 2% of sales for recipe innovations, and the privilege of purchasing ingredients from Magleby Inn at or below prevailing market prices.

Management of Magleby Inn estimates that the value of the services rendered to the franchisee at the time the contract is signed amounts to at least $5,000. All franchisees to date have opened their locations at the scheduled time and none has defaulted on any of the notes receivable.

The credit ratings of all franchisees would entitle them to borrow at the current interest rate of 10%.

Given the nature of Magleby's agreement with its franchisees, when should revenue be recognized? Discuss the question of revenue recognition for both the initial franchise fee and the additional monthly fee of 2% of sales.

(AICPA adapted)

Case 19-7   (I think they're sales!)

The Rain-Soft Water Company distributes its water softeners to dealers upon their request. The contract agreement with the dealers is that they may have 90 days to sell and pay for the softeners. Until the 90-day period is over, any softeners may be returned at the dealer's expense and with no further obligation on the dealer's part. Full payment by the dealer is required after 90 days has elapsed, whether the softeners are sold or not. Past experience indicates that 75% of all softeners distributed on this basis are sold by the dealer. In June, 100 units are delivered to dealers at an average billed price of $800 each. The average cost of the softeners to Rain-Soft is $600. Based on the expected sales, Rain-Soft reports profit of $15,000 [$200 × .75(100)]. You are asked to evaluate the income statement for its compliance with GAAP. What recommendations would you make?

Exercises   **Exercise 19-1   (Completed-contract method)**

On December 1, 1991, bids were submitted for a construction project to build a new municipal building and fire station. The lowest bid was $3,980,000 submitted by the Jessop Construction Company, and they were awarded the contract. Jessop uses the completed-contract method to report gross profit. The following data are given to summarize the activities on this contract for 1991 and 1992. Give the entries to record these transactions using the completed-contract method.

Year	Cost Incurred	Estimated Cost to Complete	Billings on Contract	Collections of Billings
1991	$1,720,000	$2,060,000	$1,350,000	$1,150,000
1992	2,020,000	-0-	2,630,000	2,830,000

Exercise 19-2   (Percentage-of-completion analysis)

Espiritu Construction Co. has used the cost-to-cost percentage-of-completion method of recognizing revenue. Tony Espiritu assumed leadership of the business after the recent death of his father, Howard. In reviewing the records, Espiritu finds the following information regarding a recently completed building project for which the total contract was $2,000,000.

	1990	1991	1992
Gross profit (loss)	$ 40,000	$140,000	$ (20,000)
Cost incurred to date	360,000	?	820,000

Espiritu wants to know how effectively the company operated during the last 3 years on this project and, since the information is not complete, has asked you to help by answering the following questions.

(1) How much cost was incurred in 1991?
(2) What percentage of the project was completed by the end of 1991?
(3) What was the total estimated gross profit on the project by the end of 1991?
(4) What was the estimated cost to complete the project at the end of 1991?

Exercise 19-3   (Percentage of completion using architect's estimates)

Central Iowa Builders Inc. entered into a contract to construct an office building and plaza at a contract price of $10,000,000. Income is to be reported using the percentage-of-completion method as determined by estimates made by the architect. The data below summarize the activities on the construction for the years 1991 through 1993. What entries are required to record this information, assuming the architect's estimate of the percentage completed is used to determine revenue?

Year	Actual Cost Incurred	Estimated Cost to Complete	Percentage Complete— Architect's Estimate	Project Billings	Collections on Billings
1991	$3,200,000	$6,000,000	25%	$3,300,000	$3,100,000
1992	4,300,000	1,600,000	75	4,500,000	4,000,000
1993	1,550,000	0	100	2,200,000	2,900,000

Exercise 19-4   (Percentage-of-completion analysis)

Smokey International Inc. recently acquired the Kurtz Builders Company. Kurtz has incomplete accounting records. On one particular project, only the information on page 861 is available. Because the information is incomplete, you are asked the following questions assuming the percentage-of-completion method is used and an output measure is used to estimate the percentage completed, and revenue is recorded using the costs actually incurred.

	1990	1991	1992
Costs incurred during year	$200,000	$250,000	?
Estimated cost to complete	450,000	190,000	-0-
Contract revenue	240,000	?	?
Gross profit on contract	?	10,000	$(10,000)
Contract price	700,000		

(1) How much gross profit should be reported in 1990?
(2) How much revenue should be reported in 1991?
(3) How much revenue should be reported in 1992?
(4) How much cost was incurred in 1992?
(5) What are the total costs on the contract?
(6) What would the gross profit be for 1991 if the cost-to-cost percentage-of-completion method were used? Ignore the revenue amount shown for 1990 and gross profit amount reported for 1991.

Exercise 19-5 (Reporting construction contracts)

Dolbin Builders Inc. is building a new home for Margaret Mitchell at a contracted price of $120,000. The estimated cost at the time the contract is signed (January 2, 1992) is $97,000. At December 31, 1992, the total cost incurred is $59,000 with estimated costs to complete of $41,000. Dolbin has billed $70,000 on the job and has received a $60,000 payment. This is the only contract in process at year end. Prepare the sections of the balance sheet and the income statement of Dolbin Builders Inc. affected by these events assuming use of (a) the percentage-of-completion method and (b) the completed-contract method.

Exercise 19-6 (Percentage-of-completion accounting)

The Quality Construction Company was the low bidder on an office building construction contract. The contract bid was $7,000,000, with an estimated cost to complete the project of $6,000,000. The contract period was 34 months starting January 1, 1991. The company uses the cost-to-cost method of estimating earnings. Because of changes requested by the customer, the contract price was adjusted downward to $6,500,000 on January 1, 1992.

A record of construction activities for the years 1991-94 follows:

Year	Actual Cost Current Year	Progress Billings	Cash Receipts
1991	$2,500,000	$2,100,000	$1,800,000
1992	3,300,000	3,100,000	3,000,000
1993	410,000	1,800,000	1,500,000
1994			700,000

The estimated cost to complete the contract as of the end of each accounting period is:

1991	$3,500,000
1992	400,000
1993	-0-

Calculate the gross profit for the years 1991-1993 under the percentage-of-completion method of revenue recognition.

Exercise 19-7   (Completed-contract method)

On January 1, 1991, the Ishikawa Construction Company entered into a 3-year contract to build a dam. The original contract price for the construction was $18,000,000 and the estimated cost was $16,100,000. The following cost data relate to the construction period.

Year	Cost Incurred in Year	Estimated Cost to Complete	Billings	Cash Collected
1991	$6,000,000	$10,000,000	$6,300,000	$6,000,000
1992	5,300,000	7,400,000	5,700,000	5,400,000
1993	7,650,000	-0-	6,000,000	6,600,000

Prepare the required journal entries for the 3 years of the contract, assuming Ishikawa uses the completed-contract method.

Exercise 19-8   (Percentage-of-completion method with change orders)

The Build It Construction Company enters into a contract on January 1, 1992, to construct a 20-story office building for $40,000,000. During the construction period, many change orders are made to the original contract. The following schedule summarizes these changes made in 1992.

	Cost Incurred 1992	Estimated Cost to Complete	Contract Price
Basic contract	$8,000,000	$28,000,000	$40,000,000
Change Order #1	50,000	50,000	125,000
Change Order #2	—	50,000	-0-
Change Order #3	300,000	300,000	Still to be negotiated. At least cost.
Change Order #4	125,000	-0-	100,000

Compute the revenue, costs, and gross profit to be recognized in 1992, assuming use of the cost-to-cost method to determine the percentage completed. Round percentage to two decimal places.

Exercise 19-9   (Service industry accounting)

The Fitness Health Spa charges an annual membership fee of $600 for its services. For this fee, each member receives a fitness evaluation (value $100), a monthly magazine (value $32), and 2-hour's use of the equipment each week. The initital direct costs to obtain the membership are estimated to be $120. The direct cost of the fitness evaluation is $50, and the monthly direct costs to provide the services are estimated to be $15 per person. In addition, the monthly indirect costs are estimated to average $8 per person. Give the journal entries to record the transactions in 1992 relative to a membership sold on July 1, 1992. The fitness evaluation is given in the first month of membership, and the initial direct cost is to be spread over all direct costs using the proportional performance method. (Round percentage of performance to two decimal places and journal entries to the nearest dollar.)

Exercise 19-10   (Installment sales accounting—real estate)

On January 1, 1992, the Krystyu Realty Company sold property carried in inventory at a cost of $85,000 for $140,000 to be paid 10% down and the balance in annual installments over a 10-year period at 12% interest. Installment payments are to be made at the end of each year.

(1) What is the equal annual payment necessary to pay for this property under the stated terms. (Round to nearest dollar.)
(2) Give the entries for the first year assuming the installment sales method is used.

Exercise 19-11   (Installment sales accounting)

Denna Corporation had sales in 1991 of $210,000, in 1992 of $270,000, and in 1993 of $350,000. The gross profit percentage of each year, in order, was 25%, 29%, and 27%. Past history has shown that 10% of total sales are collected in the first year, 40% in the second year, and 30% in the third year. Assuming these collections are made as projected, give the journal entries for 1991, 1992, and 1993, assuming use of the installment sales method. Ignore provisions for doubtful accounts and interest.

Exercise 19-12   (Installment sales analysis)

Complete the following table:

	1990	1991	1992
Installment sales	$50,000	$80,000	$ (7)
Cost of installment sales	(1)	(5)	91,800
Gross profit	(2)	(6)	28,200
Gross profit percentage	(3)	25%	(8)
Cash collections:			
1990	(4)	25,000	10,000
1991		20,000	50,000
1992			45,000
Realized gross profit on installment sales	1,100	10,500	(9)

Exercise 19-13   (Cost recovery method)

Pomona Inc. is a land development company. It has acquired 1,000 acres of choice recreational property for $1,200 per acre, and is selling developed recreational building lots for $5,000 per acre. The improvement costs amount to $1,200 per acre. The land cost, including improvements, is carried on Pomona's books as inventory. In the first year, Pomona sold 30 one-acre lots, 10% down, the balance to be paid over 10 years in annual installments at an interest rate of 10%. Assume the lots were sold on January 1, 1991.

(1) Give the entries required for 1991 and 1992 if the cost recovery method is used to recognize revenue.
(2) Prove that the balance reported on the December 31, 1992 balance sheet is equal to the unrecovered cost of the land.

Exercise 19-14   (Franchise accounting)

On September 1, 1992, Jensen Company entered into franchise agreements with three franchisees. The agreements required an initial fee payment of $7,000 plus four $3,000 payments due every 4 months, the first payment due December 31, 1992. The interest rate is 12%. The initial deposit is refundable until substantial performance has been completed. The following table describes each agreement.

Franchisee	Probability of Full Collection	Services Performed by Franchisor at December 31, 1992	Total Cost Incurred to December 31, 1992
A	Likely	Substantially	$ 7,000
B	Doubtful	25%	2,000
C	Doubtful	Substantially	10,000

For each franchisee, identify the revenue recognition method that you would recommend considering the circumstances. What amount of revenue and income would be reported in 1992 for the method selected? Assume $10,000 was received from each franchisee during the year.

Exercise 19-15   (Franchise accounting)

Starbrite Pizzas franchises its name to different people across the country. The franchise agreement requires the franchisee to make an initial payment of $12,000 and sign a $32,000 non-interest-bearing note on the agreement date. The note is to be paid with 4 annual payments of $8,000 each beginning one year from the agreement date. The initial payment is refundable until the date of opening. Interest rates are assumed to be 10%. The franchisor agrees to make market studies, find a location, train the employees, and a few other relatively minor services. The following transactions describe the relationship with Libby Loebig, a franchisee.

1991
July   1   Entered into a franchise agreement.
Sept. 1   Completed a market study at a cost of $5,000.
Nov. 15   Found suitable location. Service cost $3,000.

1992
Jan. 10   Completed training program for employees, cost $5,000.
Jan. 15   Franchise outlet opened.

Give Starbrite Pizzas' journal entries in 1991-1992 to record these transactions, including any adjusting entries at December 31, 1991.

Exercise 19-16   (Consignment accounting)

In 1992, Rawlings Wholesalers transferred goods to a retailer on consignment. The transaction was recorded as a sale by Rawlings. The goods cost $45,000 and were sold at a 30% markup. In 1992, $12,000 (cost) of the merchandise was sold by the retailer at the normal markup, and the balance of the merchandise was returned to Rawlings. The retailer withheld a 10% commission from payment. Prepare the journal entry in 1992 to correct the books for 1991, and prepare the correct entries relative to the consignment sale in 1992.

Problems   **Problem 19-1   (Construction accounting)**

Zamponi's Construction Company reports its income for tax purposes on a completed-contract basis and income for financial statement purposes on a percentage-of-completion basis. A record of construction activities for 1991 and 1992 follows:

		1991			1992
	Contract Price	Cost Incurred 1991	Estimated Cost to Complete	Cost Incurred 1992	Estimated Cost to Complete
Project A	$1,450,000	$840,000	$560,000	$480,000	-0-
Project B	1,700,000	720,000	880,000	340,000	$650,000
Project C	850,000	160,000	480,000	431,500	58,500
Project D	1,000,000			280,000	520,000

General and administrative expenses for 1991 and 1992 were $60,000 for each year and are to be recorded as a period cost.

Instructions:

(1) Calculate the income for 1991 and 1992 that should be reported for financial statement purposes.
(2) Calculate the income for 1992 to be reported on a completed-contract basis.

III Problem 19-2   (Construction accounting)

The Rushing Construction Company obtained a construction contract to build a highway and bridge over the Snake River. It was estimated at the beginning of the contract that it would take 3 years to complete the project at an expected cost of $50,000,000. The contract price was $60,000,000. The project actually took 4 years, being accepted as completed late in 1992. The following information describes the status of the job at the close of production each year.

	1989	1990	1991	1992	1993
Annual costs incurred	$12,000,000	$18,160,000	$14,840,000	$10,000,000	
Estimated cost to complete	38,000,000	27,840,000	10,555,555		
Collections on contract	12,000,000	13,500,000	15,000,000	15,000,000	$4,500,000
Billings on contract	13,000,000	15,500,000	17,000,000	14,500,000	

Instructions:

(1) What is the revenue, cost, and gross profit recognized for each of the years 1989-1993 under (a) the percentage-of-completion method, (b) the completed-contract method?
(2) Give the journal entries for each year assuming that the percentage-of-completion method is used.

Problem 19-3   (Construction accounting)

The Urban Construction Company commenced doing business in January 1992. Construction activities for the year 1992 are summarized as follows:

Project	Total Contract Price	Contract Expenditures to December 31, 1992	Estimated Additional Costs to Complete Contracts	Cash Collections to December 31, 1992	Billings to December 31, 1992
A	$ 310,000	$187,500	$ 12,500	$155,000	$155,000
B	415,000	195,000	255,000	210,000	249,000
C	350,000	310,000	—	300,000	350,000
D	300,000	16,500	183,500	—	4,000
	$1,375,000	$709,000	$451,000	$665,000	$758,000

The company is your client. The president has asked you to compute the amounts of revenue for the year ended December 31, 1992, that would be reported under the completed-contract method and the percentage-of-completion method of accounting for long-term contracts.

The following information is available:

(a) Each contract is with a different customer.
(b) Any work remaining to be done on the contracts is expected to be completed in 1993.
(c) The company's accounts have been maintained on the completed-contract method.

Instructions:

(1) Prepare a schedule computing the amount of revenue, cost, and gross profit (loss) by project for the year ended December 31, 1992, to be reported under (a) the percentage-of-completion method, and (b) the completed-contract method. (Round to two decimal places on percentages.)
(2) Prepare a schedule under the completed-contract method, computing the amount that would appear in the company's balance sheet at December 31, 1992, for (a) costs in excess of billings, and (b) billings in excess of costs.
(3) Prepare a schedule under the percentage-of-completion method that would appear in the company's balance sheet at December 31, 1992, for (a) costs and estimated earnings in excess of billings, and (b) billings in excess of costs and estimated earnings.   (AICPA adapted)

Ⅲ Problem 19-4   (Construction accounting)

The Kurtz Construction Corporation contracted with the City of Port Huron to construct a dam on the Erie River at a price of $16,000,000. The Kurtz Corporation expects to earn $1,520,000 on the contract. The percentage-of-completion method is to be used and the completion stage is to be determined by estimates made by the engineer. The following schedule summarizes the activities of the contract for the years 1990-1992.

Year	Cost Incurred	Estimated Cost to Complete	Engineer's Estimate of Completion	Billings on Contract	Collection on Billings
1990	$4,600,000	$9,640,000	31%	$5,000,000	$4,500,000*
1991	4,500,000	5,100,000	58%	6,000,000	5,400,000*
1992	5,250,000	-0-	100%	5,000,000	6,100,000

*A 10% retainer accounts for the difference between billings and collections.

Instructions:

(1) Prepare a schedule showing the revenue, costs, and the gross profit earned each year under the percentage-of-completion method, using the engineer's estimate as the measure of completion to be applied to revenues and costs.
(2) Prepare all journal entries required to reflect the contract.
(3) Prepare journal entries for 1992, assuming the completed-contract method is used.
(4) How would the journal entries in (2) differ if the actual costs incurred were used to calculate cost for the period instead of the engineer's estimate.

Problem 19-5 (Construction accounting)

Jana Crebs is a contractor for the construction of large office buildings. At the beginning of 1992, 3 buildings were in progress. The following data describe the status of these buildings at the beginning of the year:

	Contract Price	Costs incurred to 1/1/92	Estimated Cost to Complete 1/1/92
Building 1	$ 4,000,000	$2,070,000	$1,380,000
Building 2	9,000,000	6,318,000	1,782,000
Building 3	13,150,000	3,000,000	9,000,000

During 1992 the following costs were incurred:

Building 1 $930,000 (estimated cost to complete as of 12/31/92, $750,000)
Building 2 $1,800,000 (job completed)
Building 3 $7,400,000 (estimated cost to complete as of 12/31/92, $2,800,000)
Building 4 $800,000 (contract price, $2,500,000; estimated cost to complete as of 12/31/92, $1,200,000)

Instructions:

(1) Compute the total revenue, costs, and gross profit in 1992. Assume that Crebs uses the cost-to-cost percentage-of-completion method. (Round to the nearest two decimal places for percentage completed.)
(2) Compute the gross profit for 1992 if Crebs uses the completed-contract method.

Problem 19-6 (Construction accounting)

The Power Construction Company was the low bidder on a specialized equipment contract. The contract bid was $6,000,000 with an estimated cost to complete the project of $5,300,000. The contract period was 33 months, beginning January 1, 1991. The company uses the cost-to-cost method to estimate profits.

A record of construction activities for the years 1991-1994 follows:

Year	Actual Cost Current Year	Progress Billings	Cash Receipts
1991	$3,400,000	$3,200,000	$3,000,000
1992	2,550,000	2,000,000	2,000,000
1993	200,000	800,000	600,000
1994			400,000

The estimated cost to complete the contract at the end of each accounting period is:

1991	$2,100,000
1992	$ 150,000
1993	-0-

Instructions:

(1) What is the revenue, cost, and gross profit recognized for each of the years 1991-1993 under the percentage-of-completion method?
(2) Give the journal entries for each of the years 1991-1993 to record the information from (1).
(3) Give the journal entries in 1994 to record any collections and to close out all construction accounts.

Problem 19-7   (Installment sales accounting)

London Corporation has been using the cash method to account for income since its first year of operation in 1991. All sales are made on credit with notes receivable given by the customer. The income statements for 1991 and 1992 included the following amounts:

	1991	1992
Revenues—collection on principal	$32,000	$50,000
Revenues—interest	3,600	5,500
Cost of goods purchased*	45,200	52,020

*Includes increase in inventory of goods on hand of $2,000 in 1991 and $8,000 in 1992.

The balance due on the notes at the end of each year were as follows:

	1991	1992
Notes receivable 1991	$62,000	$36,000
Notes receivable 1992		60,000
Discount on notes receivable—1991	7,167	5,579
Discount on notes receivable—1992		8,043

Instructions: Give the journal entries for 1991 and 1992 assuming the installment sales method was used rather than the cash method.

Problem 19-8   (Cost recovery accounting)

After a 2-year search for a buyer, Choapas Inc. sold its idle plant facility to

Reeve Company for $700,000 on January 1, 1988. On this date the plant had a depreciated cost on Choapas' books of $500,000. Under the agreement, Reeve paid $200,000 cash on January 1, 1988, and signed a $500,000 note bearing interest at 10%. The note was payable in installments of $100,000, $150,000, $250,000 on January 1, 1989, 1990 and 1991, respectively. The note was secured by a mortgage on the property sold. Choapas appropriately accounted for the sale under the cost recovery method since there was no reasonable basis for estimating the degree of collectibility of the note receivable. Reeve repaid the note with 3 late installment payments, which were accepted by Choapas, as follows:

Date of payment	Principal	Interest
July 1, 1989	$100,000	$90,000
December 31, 1990	150,000	75,000
February 1, 1992	250,000	32,500

Instructions: Prepare the journal entries required for the years 1988-1992 for the sale and subsequent collections.   (AICPA adapted)

Problem 19-9   (Consignment accounting)

Tingey Industries sells merchandise on a consignment basis to dealers. Shipping costs are chargeable to Tingey, although in some cases, the dealer pays them. The selling price of the merchandise averages 25% above cost. The dealer is paid a 10% commission on the sales price for all sales made. All dealer sales are made on a cash basis. The following consignment sales activities occurred during 1992.

Manufacturing cost of goods shipped on consignment		$250,000
Freight costs incurred:		
Paid by Tingey Industries	$15,000	
Paid by dealer	5,000	20,000
Sales price of merchandise sold by dealers		210,000
Payments made by dealers after deducting commission and freight costs		139,000

Instructions:

(1) Prepare summary entries on the books of the consignor for these consignment sales transactions.
(2) Prepare summary entries on the books of the dealer consignee assuming there is only one dealer involved.
(3) Prepare the parts of Tingey Industries financial statements at December 31, 1992, that relate to these consignment sales.

Problem 19-10   (Revenue recognition analysis)

The Wasatch Construction Company entered into a $4,500,000 contract in early 1992 to construct a multipurpose recreational facility for the City of Helper. Construction time extended over a 2-year period. The table on page 870 describes the pattern of progress payments made by the City of Helper and costs incurred by Wasatch Construction by semiannual periods. Estimated costs of $3,600,000 were incurred as expected.

Period	Progress Payments for Period	Progress Cost for Period
(1) (Jan. 1-June 30, 1992)	750,000	$900,000
(2) (July 1-Dec. 31, 1992)	1,050,000	1,200,000
(3) (Jan. 1-June 30, 1993)	1,950,000	1,080,000
(4) (July 1-Dec. 31, 1993)	750,000	420,000
Total	$4,500,000	$3,600,000

The Wasatch Construction Company prepares financial statements twice each year, June 30 and December 31.

Instructions:

(1) Based on the foregoing data, compute the amount of revenue, costs, and gross profit for the 4 semiannual periods under each of the following methods of revenue recognition:
 (a) Percentage of completion.
 (b) Completed contract.
 (c) Installment sales (gross profit only).
 (d) Cost recovery (gross profit only).
(2) Which method do you feel best measures the performance of Wasatch on this contract?

Chapter 20

Accounting for Income Taxes

Accounting for income taxes has become one of the more complex areas addressed by accountants. Governments at all levels levy different types of taxes to raise the revenues necessary to pay for their legislated functions. Most taxes do not cause unusual accounting problems. Property taxes are based on appraised values of property; sales taxes on selling transactions; gasoline taxes on gasoline purchases; excise taxes on selected types of sales. These taxes are levied and the amount paid is charged to expense. But because the tax on income is based on some measure of profitability, it has historically resulted in many complications.

If the income reported on the financial statements were the same as income determined in accordance with income tax regulations, there would be few accounting problems. The income tax expense would be the same as the income tax payment. As discussed in Chapter 1, however, governments use the income tax laws for purposes other than raising revenue. Taxing authorities also use them to encourage investments during periods of recession, to encourage one type of industry over another, and to encourage social policy decisions, such as making charitable contributions and protecting the environment. The income tax laws and regulations have become increasingly complex as the economy has become more complex. The 1986 Tax Reform Act and subsequent revisions were originally intended to result in a fairer and simpler income tax. While they may have resulted in a fairer assessment, it is generally agreed that the Act did *not* simplify the income tax laws.

This chapter discusses the treatment of income taxes for financial accounting and reporting purposes. In 1987, the Financial Accounting Standards Board issued Statement No. 96, *Accounting for Income Taxes*. This statement greatly altered accounting for income taxes because it changed the basic concept underlying the reporting of deferred income taxes. This chapter reflects the new standard. Reference to the former standard, APB Opinion No. 11, is limited to discussion of the conceptual differences among the possible alternative methods.

Two other income tax related topics are discussed in appendixes at the end of this chapter. FASB Statement No. 96 guidelines for intraperiod tax allocation are presented in Appendix A. Accounting for the investment tax credit is discussed in Appendix B.

United States Income Tax Laws

Before discussing accounting for income taxes, it is important to consider briefly some provisions of the tax laws and the underlying concepts that have emerged from legislative action. In the United States, the federal government dominates in the use of income taxes to raise revenues. Many state and local governments also assess income taxes, and they often base their tax legislation on that of the federal government.

Differences Between Financial and Taxable Income

Differences between the financial reporting objectives of business enterprises and the budget and fiscal policy objectives of taxing authorities result in differences between financial income, reported in the financial statements, and taxable income, reported in the tax return. As presented in Chapter 2, the overriding objective of financial reporting by business enterprises is to provide information that is useful to investors, creditors, and others in making economic decisions. In contrast, two principal objectives underlying taxable income are (1) to assess taxes in accordance with the ability to pay the tax and (2) to assist in achieving political and economic goals such as economic growth, full employment, and redistribution of wealth.

Temporary Differences

Most differences between taxable and financial income are only temporary; i.e., in future years the differences reverse and thus over time, aggregate financial income and taxable income are the same. Many of these temporary differences can be identified as timing differences because they arise from recognizing certain types of revenues and expenses in different periods for financial reporting and tax purposes. Because of the interrelationship among the financial statements, the difference between financial and taxable income also creates a difference between the valuation basis of assets and/or liabilities for financial reporting and tax purposes. For example, present income tax laws permit the write-off to expense of depreciable asset cost on a more rapid basis than is acceptable for financial reporting purposes. This results in a higher financial reporting basis (undepreciated cost or book value) than the asset's corresponding tax basis (unrecovered asset cost).

In addition to timing differences, other temporary differences may arise from specific tax laws that create different bases for financial and tax purposes. For example, a depreciable asset donated by a stockholder would by law have a zero basis for tax purposes but would be recorded on the books at the fair market value on the date of donation. This situation creates a temporary difference in basis which will reverse either through depreciation or sale of the asset. Because these latter types of temporary differences relate to more complex provisions of the income tax laws, only timing differences are illustrated in this chapter.

Specific timing differences are discussed in the following sections. Some of the differences arise from the ability to pay tax concept, while others derive from efforts to achieve political and economic goals.

Ability to Pay vs. Accrual Accounting Under accrual accounting, with an emphasis on revenue recognition and expense matching, revenues are recognized when earned and expenses are recognized when incurred rather than when cash is received or paid. For income tax purposes, although the accrual concept is usually followed, the ability to pay concept is applied to some transactions. In these circumstances, revenue is recognized when cash is received rather than when the revenue is earned. The following revenue transactions are examples of temporary differences arising from the ability to pay concept.

Item	Time of revenue recognition	
	Tax	Book
Prepaid rent revenue	When cash is received	When rental period passes
Prepaid subscriptions	When cash is received	When publication is mailed

In both cases, revenue is recognized earlier for tax purposes than it is for book purposes.

The same ability to pay taxation concept leads to the postponement of expense recognition for tax purposes until cash is paid or until receivables are determined to be uncollectible. The following transactions are examples of temporary differences arising from expense postponement:

Item	Time of expense recognition	
	Tax	Book
Vacation pay	When vacation payment is made	When vacation is earned by rendering services
Warranty liability	When warranty payments are made	When sale of product includes warranty provision and it is probable warranty costs will be paid
Doubtful accounts receivable	When specific accounts can be identified as uncollectible	On an estimated (allowance) basis
Losses on current marketable equity securities	When realized through sale or permanent loss of value	When market is lower than cost on aggregate basis

Taxes Used to Control Economic Growth The use of the federal income tax laws by Congress to regulate economic growth and stability has a long and varied history. Often a major contributing factor is a political one, and the national parties use the income tax laws for favors or to achieve platform goals. The regulations change frequently as the economy changes. Some income tax provisions permit immediate reductions in income taxes in the form of tax credits. Others permit accelerated expense recognition or deferred revenue recognition to provide tax breaks for certain segments of the economy. Generally, a company may take advantage of these recognition provisions to postpone payment of taxes while using different recognition principles in preparing financial statements. The major exception is LIFO inventory. If a taxpayer elects to use the LIFO method of inventory costing for tax purposes, that method must also be used for financial reporting purposes. The following table illustrates three examples of temporary differences that arise when companies use one method for determining taxable income and another method for financial reporting.

Item	Method of Recognition	
	Tax	Book
Depreciation expense	An accelerated method, such as ACRS or MACRS	Straight line
Construction contract revenue	Completed contract if certain conditions are met	Percentage of completion
Installment sales	When installment is received (in limited cases)	At time of sale

Nontaxable Revenues and Nondeductible Expenses

In addition to temporary differences, there are some differences that never reverse. These differences may be referred to as permanent differences; that is, some revenues are *never* taxed, while some expenses are *never* deductible for tax purposes. Examples of permanent differences include certain types of nontaxable income, such as proceeds from life insurance policies and revenue from municipal bonds, and certain types of nondeductible expenses, such as fines from violation of laws, amortization of goodwill, and premiums paid for life insurance policies. Laws may change the list of items that are recognized as permanent, and they often vary among tax jurisdictions.

Accounting for Differences Between Financial and Taxable Income

Permanent differences do not create any accounting or reporting problems. Nontaxable revenues are deducted from, and nondeductible expenses are added to, financial income to determine the income that is subject to tax. Temporary differences, however, require an allocation of income taxes among different accounting periods. This interperiod tax allocation process has been a subject of controversy for many years. The concepts and procedures involved are presented later in the chapter. Some of those concepts and procedures are based on the net operating loss provisions of the income tax laws, which are discussed in the following section.

Carryback and Carryforward of Operating Losses

Since income tax is based on the amount of income earned, no tax is payable if a company experiences an operating loss. As an incentive to those businesses that experience alternate periods of income and losses, the income tax regulations provide a way to ease the risk of loss years. This is done through a carryback and carryforward provision that permits a company to apply a net operating loss occurring in one year against income of other years.

The number of years a loss can be carried backward and forward has varied over time. The United States Tax Code provides for either a three-year carryback and a fifteen-year carryforward, or only a fifteen-year carryforward. Many state codes have different terms for state income tax purposes. For example, California allows no carryback, and provides for a fifteen-year carryforward of only 50% of the net operating loss (NOL).[1] Unless otherwise specified, the discussion in this chapter assumes a three-year carryback and a fifteen-year carryforward.

Net Operating Loss Carryback

A net operating loss carryback is applied to the income of the three preceding years in reverse order, beginning with the third year and moving to the first year. If unused net operating losses are still available, they may be carried forward to offset against any future income. Amended income tax returns must be filed for each year to which the carryback is applied to receive refunds of previously paid income taxes. Net operating loss carrybacks result in a journal entry establishing a receivable for the tax refund claim. The benefit that arises from such refunds is used to reduce the loss in the current period. This treatment is supported in theory because it is the current year's operating loss that results in the tax refund.

To illustrate, assume the Prairie Company had the following pattern of income and losses for the years 1991-1994.

Year	Income (Loss)	Income Tax Rate	Income Tax
1991	$15,000	40%	$6,000
1992	10,000	35	3,500
1993	14,000	30	4,200
1994	(29,000)	30	0

The $29,000 net operating loss in 1994 would be carried back to 1991 first, then to 1992, and finally, $4,000 to 1993. An income tax refund claim of $10,700 would be filed for the 3 years ($6,000 + $3,500 + .30(4,000)). The entry to record the income tax receivable would be as follows:

Income Tax Refund Receivable	10,700	
Refund of Income Tax from Net Operating Loss Carryback.		10,700
Refund from applying net operating loss carryback.		

[1]Price Waterhouse & Co., *The New Accounting for Income Taxes: Implementing FAS 96*, 1988, p. 43.

The refund will be reflected on the income statement as a reduction of the operating loss as follows:

Net operating loss before refundable income tax	$29,000
Refund of prior years' income tax arising from carryback of	
operating loss.	10,700
Net Loss	$18,300

The 1994 net operating loss reduces the 1991 and 1992 taxable income to zero and the 1993 income to $10,000 ($14,000 − $4,000). If another net operating loss occurs within the next two years, it may be carried back to the remaining $10,000 from 1993.

Operating Loss Carryforward

As indicated previously, any unused operating loss may be applied against net income earned over the future fifteen years as a **net operating loss carryforward**. In the preceding example, the Prairie Company had $10,000 of income left against which operating losses could be applied. Assume that in 1995, another operating loss of $40,000 was incurred. After applying $10,000 to the 1993 income, $30,000 is left to carry forward against future operating income. The benefit of this carryforward depends on the company having income equal to the carryforward in the next fifteen years. If no income is earned, there is no benefit from having the operating loss carryforward. The ability to carryforward the loss is not considered an asset because currently accepted accounting principles do not allow assets to be recorded in a current year based on possible future revenues.

If income is actually earned in the next year, the prior year loss carryforward may be used to reduce the current year taxes payable. Thus, if Prairie Company reported $20,000 income in 1996, $20,000 of the $30,000 carryforward could be applied to the 1996 income, and no taxes would be paid. Assuming a 30% tax rate, the $6,000 ($20,000 × 30%) tax benefit from the carryover would be reported as a credit adjustment to income tax expense. The following entries would be required to record the tax provisions.

Income Tax Expense—Current Provision	6,000	
Income Taxes Payable		6,000
Income tax liability assuming no carryforward.		
Income Taxes Payable	6,000	
Income Tax Expense—Benefit of NOL Carryforward		6,000

Prairie would report the income and tax effects in its 1996 income statement as follows:

Income from continuing operations before income taxes		$20,000
Income tax expense:		
Current provision	$6,000	
Benefit of NOL Carryforward	(6,000)	0
Income from continuing operations		$20,000

The remaining $10,000 carryforward is available for 1997 and beyond.

Conceptual Basis for Interperiod Tax Allocation

As noted earlier in the chapter, temporary differences between financial and taxable income create the need for interperiod tax allocation. There are many issues involved in accounting for temporary differences. The discussion concerning these issues has a long history, and even though a new standard has been issued and certain conclusions reached, there will still be considerable debate of these issues in the future.

Allocation vs. Nonallocation of Income Tax Expense

Income tax expense differs from most other expenses because the amount of the expense is directly related to the net income of a business enterprise. The easiest way to account for income tax expense is to charge the expense account for the amount of tax paid each period. Under this "nonallocation" approach, the differences between financial income and taxable income would be ignored, and deferred taxes would not be recorded. Following are some of the principal arguments presented in favor of this approach:

1. Income taxes paid are determined by specific laws passed by the legislature of a taxing body. Each year these laws are subject to change. It is the taxable income that determines the amount of income taxes paid, not financial income.

2. Income tax expense based on taxes paid is understandable to users and is less costly to apply than alternative approaches.

3. Income taxes actually paid is a better predictor of future cash flows because deferred taxes may never be paid, or not be paid for many years.

Although these arguments have considerable merit, the accounting standards-setting bodies have argued successfully that an allocation of income tax expense is necessary in order to meet the objectives of financial reporting. Because generally accepted accounting principles are based on the concept of a going concern, temporary differences between financial income and taxable income will affect future periods. Some of the principal arguments that have resulted in the adoption of interperiod tax allocation are as follows:

1. Income taxes are a cost of doing business. Although they are computed on income, other expenses such as officers' bonuses may also be computed on income. All expenses should be subject to the same accrual and deferral procedures.

2. Ultimately, all temporary differences do reverse, and when they do, the tax effects should be related to the period when the transactions that gave rise to the differences occurred, not when the tax payment is made.

3. Failure to allocate income taxes causes net income to fluctuate according to the temporary differences and may make future predictions of net income and cash flows more difficult.

4. Recognition of deferred income tax assets and liabilities is consistent

with the definitions of elements included in the FASB's conceptual framework.

Methods of Allocating Income Taxes

There are two principal methods of allocating income taxes to different periods: (1) the **deferred method,** and (2) the **asset and liability method.** These methods are conceptually very different, and their application can result in materially different deferred tax balances. Under APB Opinion No. 11, issued in 1967, the deferred method was used in accounting for income taxes. In 1987 the FASB issued Statement No. 96, which supersedes Opinion No. 11 and requires the use of the asset and liability method.

Deferred Method of Interperiod Tax Allocation

The deferred method of interperiod tax allocation assumes that income tax expense reported on the income statement should be based on financial income rather than on taxable income. The difference between the income tax that would have been paid based on financial income and the income tax that was actually paid based on taxable income is reported as either a deferred asset or a deferred liability. As temporary differences reverse, the deferred accounts are reduced and each year's income tax expense continues to be based on financial income using the tax rates in effect for each respective year. The deferred account balance is not altered for a change in tax rates or any other legislative changes unless temporary differences cease to exist.

A conceptual problem with the deferred method arises because the deferred tax accounts do not meet the definitions of assets and liabilities included in the FASB's conceptual framework. The amount reported as a deferred tax liability does not necessarily represent the amount to be paid on taxes in the future, because it is related to past temporary differences and rates. Likewise, the amount reported as a deferred tax asset is not based on a tax receivable. The principal emphasis under the deferred method is that of matching and disclosure in the income statement. If income tax expense is related to pre-tax financial income, it will tend to vary more directly with income and avoid the distortions that arise from nonallocation, or from methods that require changing the deferrals as the tax laws change.

Asset and Liability Method of Interperiod Tax Allocation

Unlike the deferred method with its emphasis on the income statement, the asset and liability method of interperiod tax allocation stresses the balance sheet and the computation of deferred tax liabilities and assets based on expected reversals of temporary differences in the future. The stated objective of this method in FASB Statement No. 96 is as follows:

> The objective in accounting for income taxes on an accrual basis is to recognize the amount of current and deferred taxes payable or refundable at the date

of the financial statements (a) as a result of all events that have been recognized in the financial statements and (b) as measured by the provisions of enacted tax laws.[2]

Three basic principles are applied to achieve this objective.

1. A current or deferred tax liability or asset is recognized for the current or deferred tax consequences of all events that have been recognized in the financial statements.
2. The current or deferred tax consequences of an event are measured based on provisions of the enacted law to determine the amount of taxes payable or refundable currently or in future years, and
3. The tax consequences of earning income or incurring losses or expenses in future years or the future enactment of a change in tax laws or rates are not anticipated for purposes of recognition and measurement of a deferred tax liability.[3]

The computation of the deferred tax liability or asset is based on the currently enacted tax rates for the years when the deferred liability is expected to be paid or when the deferred tax asset is to be realized. Changes in tax rates are usually legislated prior to the years in which they become effective. For example, the 1986 Tax Reform Act legislated a phased tax rate reduction over three years. As tax rates change for future years, the balance sheet accounts are adjusted. Under the asset and liability method, each temporary difference must be analyzed and a schedule prepared to determine when it is expected to reverse. By applying the enacted future tax rates to the expected reversals, a liability or asset is computed that meets the conceptual framework definitions. Thus, a deferred tax *liability* represents probable future sacrifices of economic benefits arising from present obligations to transfer assets (cash payments) to other entities (taxing bodies) in the future as a result of past transactions or events (temporary differences). A deferred tax *asset* represents probable future economic benefits (refunds of taxes paid).

The deferred tax expense reported on the income statement is a residual amount. As rates, assumptions, and tax strategies change, the amount reported as income tax expense may fluctuate significantly because of the emphasis placed by the FASB on the amount reported as assets and liabilities.

Application of Deferred Income Taxes—Asset and Liability Method

As indicated in the previous section, the computation of deferred taxes using the asset and liability method requires projecting the timing of future temporary difference reversals by years. FASB Statement No. 96 summarizes the asset and liability method as follows:

[2]Statement of Financial Accounting Standards No. 96, "Accounting for Income Taxes" (Stamford: Financial Accounting Standards Board, 1987), par. 7.
[3]Ibid.

In concept, this Statement [96] requires determination of the amount of taxes payable or refundable in each future year as if a tax return were prepared for the net amount of temporary differences that will result in taxable or deductible amounts in each of those years.[4]

A very basic assumption in applying the asset and liability method is that *all* future years' pretax financial income is zero and the taxable income reflects only the net impact of any temporary difference reversals. By making this assumption, no estimate of future earnings is required or even allowed. This assumption reflects the consistent approach by the FASB of not establishing accounting principles that depend on future income.

If the impact of temporary differences produces a taxable income in future years, the computed income is referred to as a **taxable amount**. The taxable amount multiplied by the enacted tax rate for that future year results in a **deferred tax liability** to be reported on a company's balance sheet. For example, if gross profit is included in financial income at the date of an installment sale, but the profit is included in taxable income only as the revenue is collected, the years when the revenue is collected will create taxable amounts if there are no other offsetting temporary differences. Thus, if $20,000 of gross profit is expected to be collected in the second year after an installment sale and the currently enacted tax rate for that year is 30%, a deferred tax liability of $6,000 (30% × $20,000) would be reported on this year's balance sheet as a noncurrent liability. If the $20,000 is expected to be collected in the next year, the deferred tax liability would be reported as a current liability. In classified balance sheets, the one-year rule for current assets and liabilities applies unless the company has an operating cycle that exceeds one year.

If the impact of temporary difference reversals produces a taxable loss in future years, the loss is referred to as a **deductible amount**. Because future financial income is always assumed to be zero, the deductible amount is reflected as if it were a net operating loss. As discussed earlier in this chapter, tax laws allow companies to carry losses backward and forward to offset them against other income amounts. The same assumption is made for temporary difference deductible amounts. It is only through such offsets that refundable amounts, called **deferred tax assets**, can be generated. Before the amount of a tax asset can be determined, a schedule of deductible amount carrybacks and carryforwards must be completed. If a deductible amount can be carried back to income years already completed within the carryback period, a deferred tax asset may be recorded that reflects the refund that would be obtained if the company has no income or loss except for the deductible amount. If there is no current or prior income, or if there are no taxable amount years in the carryforward period against which to offset the deductible amount, no deferred tax asset may be reported for the deductible amount.

[4]Statement of Financial Accounting Standards No. 96, "Accounting for Income Taxes" (Stamford: Financial Accounting Standards Board, 1987), par. 17.

A summary of the more frequently applied temporary differences, with their general impact on the current and future financial statements, is included in Exhibit 20-1.

Exhibit 20-1   Temporary Differences

General Type	Current Year Income Effect	Current Year Asset/Liability Effect	Future Taxable Income Effect When Reversal Occurs	Specific Examples
A. Revenues or gains that are taxable after they are recognized as financial income	Taxable income lower than financial income	Deferred tax liability	Taxable amount	1. Profit on installment sales—limited 2. Percentage of completion profit on contracts 3. Earnings of investee—equity method
B. Expenses or losses that are deductible for taxable income after they are recognized in financial income	Taxable income higher than financial income	Deferred tax asset	Deductible amount	1. Accrued warranty costs 2. Unrecognized losses on marketable securities 3. Additions to allowance for doubtful accounts 4. Accrued vacation pay 5. Accrued litigation costs
C. Revenues or gains that are taxable before they are recognized in financial income	Taxable income higher than financial income	Deferred tax asset	Deductible amount	1. Prepaid rental revenue 2. Prepaid subscriptions
D. Expenses or losses that are deductible for taxable income before they are recognized in financial income	Taxable income lower than financial income.	Deferred tax liability	Taxable amount	1. Accelerated cost recovery on plant and equipment

As can be seen from the foregoing discussion, the asset and liability method of accounting for deferred income taxes requires the computation of deferred balance sheet tax accounts based on a scheduling of all future temporary difference reversals. The income tax expense reported on the income statement reflects the **current tax provision** that is based on the actual income tax liability for the year plus the **deferred tax provision** that reflects the net changes from the prior reporting period deferred tax asset and tax liability accounts arising from the temporary difference schedules.

If the legislature of the taxing body changes the income tax rates applicable to future years, the deferred accounts are immediately adjusted to reflect the new rates, and the effect of the change is reported as a separate component of income tax expense. Other adjustments, such as the carryforward of actual net operating losses, will also affect the deferred accounts. Some of these other adjustments are discussed in a later section of this chapter.

Because of changing future estimates of reversals and because of additional income data, a new schedule of temporary difference reversals is required for each year for each taxing jurisdiction. From these schedules, the new balances for the deferred tax assets and deferred tax liabilities can be computed.

The preparation of these schedules can become very complicated. The following set of examples begins simply and progresses to the more complex. Specific income tax laws affect the preparation of these schedules. The federal income tax laws have become increasingly complex and this affects the computation of income taxes using the asset and liability method. The following examples have been simplified to focus on the techniques involved. It is assumed in the illustrations that only *one taxing jurisdiction* is involved and that the company is in its first year of operations unless otherwise indicated.

| Example 1 | **Temporary Differences Creating Future Year Taxable Amounts (Deferred Tax Liabilities)** |

If a company's current year taxable income is less than pretax financial income because of temporary differences, the reversal in future years will create **taxable amounts.** The tax on these taxable amounts must be accrued in the current period at the rates legislated to be in effect in the specific future years. Deferred tax liabilities for temporary differences reversing in the next year are classified as a current liability on the firm's financial statements, and all subsequent years' deferrals are classified as noncurrent. As indicated earlier, the only exception occurs if the operating cycle exceeds one year, in which case the longer period is used to distinguish current from noncurrent.

To illustrate the computation of deferred tax liabilities, assume that Delvado Inc. begins operations in 1991. Although Delvado makes most of its sales on a short-term account basis, it occasionally makes installment sales with payments spread over a three year future period. For financial reporting purposes, Delvado recognizes the income on the installment sales on an accrual basis; however, for income tax purposes, income is recognized as the installment collections are made. Assume that Delvado's pretax financial income in the first year is $140,000. Pretax financial income reflects the difference between all revenues and expenses, except income taxes, reported in the income statement. Assume further that the income statement includes goodwill amortization of $10,000, which is never a deductible expense for income tax purposes. Thus, Delvado's taxable financial income, the amount of financial income subject to income tax, is $150,000, or $140,000 plus the nondeductible expense (permanent difference) of $10,000. This $150,000 includes a gross profit of $40,000 on installment sales that will not be reported on the tax return until the installments are collected in future years. This temporary difference results in **taxable income** for 1991 of $110,000 ($150,000 − $40,000). In this case, the $110,000 taxable income is the net amount of revenues and expenses reported in the income tax return and is used to compute the amount of taxes payable for the current year. Thus, of the total taxable financial income of $150,000, only $110,000 is taxed in 1991. The remaining $40,000 will be included in taxable income of subsequent years. Assume that income tax rates have been enacted for 1991 and subsequent years in a declining pattern of 40%, 35%, 32%, and 30%.

Exhibit 20-2 illustrates the schedule of the expected reversals, the calculation of the taxable amounts for the years 1992-1994, and the computation of the deferred tax liabilities. Exhibit 20-2 and all other exhibits in this section of the chapter also include the journal entries required to record the income taxes and the income statement presentation of income tax expense. A careful study of each exhibit will greatly enhance an understanding of deferred income tax accounting under the asset and liability method.

The years 1992-1994 each show assumed taxable amounts equal to the installment sale reversal because it is assumed there is no pre-tax financial income in any future year. The 1991 income tax liability and current income tax provision are computed by multiplying the 1991 taxable income of $110,000 by the enacted tax rate for 1991. The expected reversal of $13,000

Exhibit 20-2   Deferred Tax Liability, Future Taxable Amounts

	1991	1992	1993	1994	
Pretax financial income	$140,000				
Nondeductible expense	10,000				
Taxable financial income	$150,000	$0	$0	$0	
Temporary differences:					
Gross profit on installment sales	(40,000)				
Taxable amount—reversals		13,000	15,000	12,000	
Taxable income	$110,000	$13,000	$15,000	$12,000	
Enacted tax rate	40%	35%	32%	30%	**Total**
Income taxes payable	$ 44,000				$44,000 a
Deferred tax liability:					
Current		$ 4,550			$4,550 b
Noncurrent			$ 4,800	$ 3,600	$8,400 c

1991 Journal Entries — Dr. / Cr.

	Dr.	Cr.
Income Tax Expense—Current	44,000	
Income Taxes Payable		44,000 a
Income Tax Expense—Deferred	12,950	
Deferred Tax Liability—Current		4,550 b
Deferred Tax Liability—Noncurrent		8,400 c

1991 Income Statement Presentation

Income from continuing operations before income taxes		$140,000
Less income taxes:		
Current provision	$44,000	
Deferred provision	12,950	56,950
Income from continuing operations		$83,050

in 1992 creates a $4,550 current deferred tax liability, and the additional reversals in 1993 and 1994 create an $8,400 noncurrent deferred tax liability. The total amount reported as 1991 income tax expense is $56,950—a current provision of $44,000 and a deferred provision of $12,950.

Similar schedules will be required for each future year, and adjustments to the deferred tax accounts will be made based on the schedules. In reality, companies usually have several temporary differences arising and reversing each year. This complicates the scheduling and computation of the balance sheet amounts. Before discussing these complexities, the computation of deferred tax assets will be illustrated.

Example 2 **Temporary Differences Creating Future Year Deductible Amounts (Deferred Tax Assets)**

If a company's taxable income is more than taxable financial income because of temporary differences, the reversal in future years will create **deductible amounts** that must be analyzed to determine if a deferred tax asset is to be recognized. While deferred tax liabilities are created for any future year in which there is a net taxable amount shown on the schedule of temporary difference reversals, only in some cases do net deductible amounts result in deferred tax assets.

To illustrate the computation of deferred tax assets, assume that instead of the installment sale temporary difference, Delvado Inc. issues warranties with its product sales that obligate the company to provide maintenance service for four future years. For financial income purposes, the estimated warranty costs are fully deducted in the year of sale; however, for income tax purposes, warranty costs are deductible only when they are actually incurred. Assume that the future estimated warranty costs on 1991 sales are $35,000. Exhibit 20-3 shows the scheduling of reversals with the same declining income tax rates as used in Exhibit 20-2, the calculation of deductible amounts, and the carryback of the scheduled losses for the years 1992-1994.

Under FASB Statement No. 96, deductible amounts are viewed as net operating losses, and the carryback and carryforward provisions discussed earlier are applied to these scheduled future "losses." The tax rate used to compute the deferred tax asset is the rate enacted for the year to which the loss can be carried back or forward. In this example, losses for three years can be carried back to the current year, a year in which the enacted tax rate is 40%. The tax on the loss carryback from 1992 is classified as a current asset while the tax on the 1993 and 1994 losses is classified as a noncurrent asset. The $4,000 net deductible amount in 1995 cannot be carried back to 1991 because it exceeds the three-year carryback limitation. It cannot be carried forward because there are no taxable amounts in other future years against which the carryforward can be charged. Thus, for 1991, no tax effect for the $4,000 is reflected in the financial statements because no income is assumed in 1995. FASB Statement No. 96 does not allow the recognition of an asset that is based on anticipated future income. The entry to record the increase in deferred tax assets results in a deferred tax benefit and a reduction from the current provision to compute the net tax expense.

Exhibit 20-3   Deferred Tax Asset, Future Deductible Amounts

| | 1991 | Reversal years | | | |
		1992	1993	1994	1995
Pretax financial income (loss)	$140,000				
Nondeductible expense	10,000				
Taxable financial income (loss)	$150,000	$0	$0	$0	$0
Temporary differences:					
Estimated warranty payments in future years	35,000				
Deductible amount—warranty pmts.		(8,000)	(18,000)	(5,000)	(4,000)
Taxable income (loss)	$185,000	$(8,000)	$(18,000)	$(5,000)	$(4,000)
Loss carryback:					
1992 carryback to 1991	(8,000)	8,000			
1993 carryback to 1991	(18,000)		18,000		
1994 carryback to 1991	(5,000)			5,000	
Net taxable (deductible) amount	$154,000	$0	$0	$0	$(4,000)
Enacted tax rate	40%	35%	32%	30%	30%
Income taxes payable (40% × $185,000)	$ 74,000 a				
Deferred tax asset:					
Current (40% × $8,000)	$ 3,200 b				
Noncurrent (40% × $23,000)	$ 9,200 c				

1991 Journal Entries	**Dr.**	**Cr.**
Income Tax Expense—Current	74,000	
Income Taxes Payable		74,000a
Deferred Tax Asset—Current	3,200 b	
Deferred Tax Asset—Noncurrent	9,200 b	
Income Tax Benefit—Deferred		12,400

1991 Income Statement Presentation

Income from continuing operations before income taxes		$140,000
Less income taxes:		
Current provision	$74,000	
Deferred benefit	(12,400)	61,600
Income from continuing operations		$78,400

Example 3   Combination of Taxable and Deductible Amounts

Usually the scheduling of future reversals of temporary differences will result in a combination of deductible and taxable amounts. Exhibit 20-4 illustrates the reversal schedule for Delvado Inc., assuming that the taxable and deductible temporary differences illustrated in Exhibits 20-2 and 20-3 both occur. The $3,000 estimated deductible amount in 1993 can be carried back two years and used to reduce the current year's taxable income. This creates a noncurrent deferred tax asset of $1,200. The $4,000 estimated deductible amount in 1995 can be used to reduce the 1992 taxable amount from $5,000 to $1,000 (three-year carryback).

With one exception, the deferred asset or liability amount can be computed for a particular reversal year by applying the enacted rates for that year to the net taxable (deductible) amount. That is, for a given year, deductible amounts can be netted against taxable amounts, and only one asset or liability (either current or noncurrent) computed. The one exception to this netting process arises because it is not appropriate to net current amounts against noncurrent amounts, or vice versa. Thus, the exception applies only when the year in question is the next year following the current one and that next year has a taxable amount (a current liability) and is affected by the carryback of a deductible amount (a noncurrent asset). This occurs in Exhibit 20-4 for 1992, which has a $5,000 taxable amount and a $4,000 carryback of a projected 1995 deductible amount. In this situation, netting to compute the deferred tax asset and liability amount is inappropriate. Thus, instead of applying the 35% tax rate to a net taxable amount of $1,000, the rate is applied separately to the current taxable amount ($5,000) and the noncurrent deductible amount ($4,000). This results in a *current* deferred tax liability of $1,750 ($5,000 × 35%) and a *noncurrent* deferred tax asset of $1,400 ($4,000 × 35%).

Exhibit 20-4   Deferred Tax Assets and Liabilities

| | 1991 | Reversal years | | | |
		1992	1993	1994	1995
Pretax financial income (loss)	$140,000				
Nondeductible expense	10,000				
Taxable financial income (loss)	$150,000	$0	$0	$0	$0
Temporary differences:					
Gross profit on installment sales	(40,000)				
Taxable amount—collections		13,000	15,000	12,000	
Estimated warranty payments in					
future years	35,000				
Deductible amount—warranty					
pmts.		(8,000)	(18,000)	(5,000)	(4,000)
Taxable income (loss)	$145,000	$5,000	($3,000)	$7,000	($4,000)
Loss carryback:					
1993 loss carryback to 1991	(3,000)		3,000		
1995 loss carryback to 1992		(4,000)			4,000
Net taxable (deductible) amount	$142,000	$1,000	$0	$7,000	$0
Enacted tax rate	40%	35%	32%	30%	30%

	1991	1992		1994		Total
Income taxes payable						
(40% × $145,000)	$58,000 a					$58,000 a
Deferred tax asset:						
Noncurrent (40% × $3,000;						
35% × $4,000)	$1,200	$1,400				$2,600 b
Deferred tax liability:						
Current (35% × $5,000)		$1,750				$1,750 c
Noncurrent (30% × $7,000)				$2,100		$2,100 d

1991 Journal Entries	Dr.	Cr.
Income Tax Expense—Current	58,000	
Income Taxes Payable		58,000 a
Deferred Tax Asset—Noncurrent	2,600 b	
Income Tax Expense—Deferred	1,250	
Deferred Tax Liability—Current		1,750 c
Deferred Tax Liability—Noncurrent		2,100 d

1991 Income Statement Presentation

Income from continuing operations before income taxes		$140,000
Less income taxes:		
Current provision......................	$58,000	
Deferred provision.....................	1,250	59,250
Income from continuing operations		$80,750

Applying the netting rules to Exhibit 20-4, the total deferred tax asset—noncurrent is $2,600, the deferred tax liability—current is $1,750, and the deferred tax liability—noncurrent is $2,100. No separate computation of deferred tax assets or liabilities is necessary for 1993 and 1994 because of the netting of taxable and deductible amounts that are all noncurrent.

Example 4   Depreciation Temporary Differences

The illustrations so far have involved temporary differences whose reversals create either taxable or deductible amounts. Depreciation temporary differences are unique in that most often they involve both several years of deductible amounts and several years of taxable amounts. This occurs because most tax depreciation methods result in a higher tax depreciation charge on acquired assets for several years before accounting depreciation begins to exceed tax depreciation. As discussed in Chapter 12, all depreciation methods ultimately charge the same amount of depreciation, but in varying patterns.

Exhibit 20-5 illustrates the depreciation pattern for an asset acquired in 1991 by Allred, Inc. For this example, assume that the enacted tax rate for the current and future years is 40%. For three years, tax depreciation exceeds financial depreciation by a total of $40,000. For the next two years, financial depreciation exceeds tax depreciation by the same $40,000 amount. All of the 1992 deductible amount and $7,000 of the 1993 deductible amount can be carried back against the 1991 taxable income. The remaining $10,000 deductible amount for 1993 is carried forward to be offset against the $20,000 taxable amount. As shown in the exhibit, this creates a current asset of $7,200 and a noncurrent asset of $2,800. Net taxable amounts are shown for 1994 and 1995, and thus noncurrent liabilities of $12,000 are created. The net differences in the deferred accounts create a $2,000 deferred tax provision to accompany the $10,000 current tax provision, or total income tax expense of $12,000.

All of the illustrations thus far have assumed that the company is in its first year of operations and thus has no beginning balances in the deferred tax asset or liability accounts. In subsequent years, the adjustment to the deferred accounts is computed by determining the required ending balances from the schedule of future reversals, comparing these balances with the beginning balances, and determining the entries necessary to adjust the beginning balance to the ending balance. No transaction entries are made to the deferred tax accounts during a reporting period. Adjustments are made only when financial statements are prepared.

Exhibit 20-5   Depreciation Temporary Difference—Year 1

	1991	1992	1993	1994	1995
			Reversal years		
Taxable financial income (loss)	$30,000				
Temporary difference between tax and book depreciation	(5,000)	($18,000)	($17,000)	$20,000	$20,000
Taxable income (loss)	$25,000	($18,000)	($17,000)	$20,000	$20,000
Loss carrybacks:					
1992 carryback to 1991	(18,000)	18,000			
1993 carryback to 1991	(7,000)		7,000		
1993 carryforward to 1994			10,000	(10,000)	
Net taxable (deductible) amount	$0	$0	$0	$10,000	$20,000
Enacted tax rate	40%	40%	40%	40%	40%

		Total
Income taxes payable		
(40% × $25,000)	$10,000	$10,000 a
Deferred tax asset:		
Current (40% × $18,000)	$ 7,200	$7,200 b
Noncurrent (40% × $7,000)	$ 2,800	$2,800 c
Deferred tax liability:		
Noncurrent (40% × $10,000; 40% × $20,000)	$4,000 $8,000	$12,000 d

1991 Journal Entries	Dr.	Cr.
Income Tax Expense—Current	10,000	
Income Taxes Payable		10,000 a
Deferred Tax Asset—Current	7,200 b	
Deferred Tax Asset—Noncurrent	2,800 c	
Income Tax Expense—Deferred	2,000	
Deferred Tax Liability—Noncurrent		12,000 d

1991 Income Statement Presentation

Income from continuing operations before income taxes		$30,000
Less income taxes:		
Current provision	$10,000	
Deferred provision	2,000	12,000
Income from continuing operations		$18,000

Exhibit 20-6 illustrates the computation of deferred tax assets and liabilities for 1992, or year 2 of Allred, Inc.'s operations. It is assumed that taxable financial income is $30,000 for both 1991 and 1992. The $17,000 projected deductible amount for 1993 is carried back to 1991 and netted against the prior year's income. This creates a current tax asset of $6,800. Because the deductible amount from 1993 can now be fully used as a carryback to 1991 and the 1992 deductible amount can be offset against actual 1992 financial income, the 1994 and 1995 taxable amounts result in a $16,000 noncurrent deferred tax liability. Comparison of the ending balances in the deferred accounts with the beginning balances results in a reduction in both current and noncurrent deferred tax assets and an increase in the deferred tax liability.

Exhibit 20-6   Depreciation Temporary Difference—Year 2

	Prior Yr. 1991	Current Yr. 1992	Reversal years 1993	1994	1995
Taxable financial income (loss)	$30,000	$30,000	$0	$0	$0
Temporary difference between tax and book depreciation	(5,000)	(18,000)	(17,000)	20,000	20,000
Taxable income (loss)	$25,000	$12,000	($17,000)	$20,000	$20,000
Loss carrybacks:					
1993 carryback	(17,000)		17,000		
Net taxable (deductible) amount	$ 8,000	$12,000	$ 0	$20,000	$20,000
Enacted tax rate	40%	40%	40%	40%	40%
Income taxes payable (40% × $12,000)		$4,800a			

				Totals		
				Ending Balance	Beginning Balance (Exhibit 20-5)	1992 Adjustment
Deferred tax asset:						
Current (40% × $17,000)	$6,800					
Noncurrent				$ 6,800	$ 7,200	$(400) b
Deferred tax liability:				$0	$ 2,800	$(2,800) c
Noncurrent			$ 8,000	$ 8,000	$16,000	$12,000	$ 4,000 d

1992 Journal Entries

	Dr.	Cr.
Income Tax Expense—Current	4,800	
Income Taxes Payable		4,800 a
Income Tax Expense—Deferred	7,200	
Deferred Tax Asset—Current		400 b
Deferred Tax Asset—Noncurrent		2,800 d
Deferred Tax Liability—Noncurrent		4,000 d

1992 Income Statement Presentation

Income from continuing operations before income taxes		$30,000
Less income taxes:		
Current provision	$4,800	
Deferred provision	7,200	12,000
Income from continuing operations		$18,000

Example 5   Changing Tax Rates

When the enacted tax rates change, the existing deferred tax accounts must be adjusted to reflect the new rates. FASB Statement No. 96 requires that the effect of the change in rates be reported as a separate component of income tax expense in the year of the change. The computation of the adjustment for new rates can be made by rescheduling the temporary difference reversals for the most recent year using the newly enacted rates.

To illustrate the entry needed when tax rates change, assume that in 1992, legislation is enacted which changes tax rates for 1992 and subsequent years as follows:

Year	Original rate Exhibits 20-5 and 20-6	Revised Rates
1992	40%	35%
1993	40%	32%
1994	40%	30%
1995	40%	30%

Exhibit 20-7 is a revision of Exhibit 20-5 using the new rates. Since 1991 rates did not change, no adjustment is required to the deferred tax asset accounts that are created by carrying the 1992 and 1993 deductible amounts back to 1991. However, the deferred tax liabilities for 1994 and 1995 are affected by the decreased rates. Rather than $12,000, the revised balance is $9,000. Thus, an adjusting entry of $3,000 is required.

Exhibit 20-7   Depreciation Temporary Difference—Rate Change

		Reversal years							
	1991	1992	1993	1994	1995				
Taxable financial income (loss)	$30,000	$0	$0	$0	$0				
Temporary difference between tax and book depreciation	(5,000)	(18,000)	(17,000)	20,000	20,000				
Taxable income (loss)	$25,000	($18,000)	($17,000)	$20,000	$20,000				
Loss carrybacks:									
1992 carryback to 1991	(18,000)	18,000							
1993 carryback to 1991	(7,000)		7,000						
1993 carryforward to 1994			10,000	(10,000)					
Net taxable amount	$0	$0	$0	$10,000	$20,000				
Enacted tax rate	40%	35%	32%	30%	30%				
Income taxes payable (40% × $25,000)	$10,000					Revised Ending Balance	Original Ending Balance (Exhibit 20-5)	1992 Tax Rate Adjustment	
Deferred tax asset:									
Current (40% × $18,000)	$ 7,200					$7,200	$ 7,200	$0	
Noncurrent (40% × $7,000)	$ 2,800					$2,800	$ 2,800	$0	
Deferred tax liability: Noncurrent				$ 3,000	$ 6,000	$9,000	$12,000	$3,000 a	

1992 Rate Adjustment Entry	Dr.	Cr.
Deferred Tax Liability— Noncurrent	3,000	
Income Tax Benefit—Tax Rate Change		3,000 a

Exhibit 20-8 illustrates the computation of deferred tax balances at the end of Year 2 for Allred, Inc., assuming the rate change has occurred. The benefit arising from the tax rate change is reported as a separate part of the income tax expense computation as shown in the 1992 income statement.

Exhibit 20-8   Depreciation Temporary Difference—After Rate Change—Year 2

	Pior Yr. 1991	Current Yr. 1992	Reversal years 1993	1994	1995
Taxable financial income (loss)	$30,000	$30,000	$0	$0	$0
Temporary difference between tax and book depreciation	(5,000)	(18,000)	(17,000)	20,000	20,000
Taxable income (loss)	$25,000	$12,000	($17,000)	$20,000	$20,000
Loss carrybacks: 1993 carryback	(17,000)		17,000		
Net taxable (deductible) amount	$ 8,000	$12,000	$0	$20,000	$20,000
Enacted tax rate	40%	35%	32%	30%	30%
Income taxes payable (35% × $12,000)		$4,200a			

			Ending Balance	Revised Beginning Balance (Exhibit 20-7)	1992 Adjustment- Increase (Decrease)
Deferred tax asset: Current (40% × $17,000)	$ 6,800		$ 6,800	$7,200	$ (400) a
Noncurrent			$0	$2,800	$(2,800) c
Deferred tax liability: Noncurrent		$ 6,000 $ 6,000	$12,000	$9,000	$ 3,000 d

1992 Journal Entries	Dr.	Cr.
Income Tax Expense—Current	4,200	
Income Taxes Payable		4,200 a
Income Tax Expense—Deferred	6,200	
Deferred Tax Asset—Current		400 b
Deferred Tax Asset—Noncurrent		2,800 c
Deferred Tax Liability—Noncurrent		3,000 d

1992 Income Statement Presentation

Income from continuing operations before income taxes		$30,000
Less income taxes:		
Current provision	$4,200	
Deferred provision	6,200	
Tax rate change benefit—(Exhibit 20-7)	(3,000)	7,400
Income from continuing operations		$22,600

Example 6   Net Operating Loss Carryforwards

As indicated earlier, net operating loss carryforwards are not reported as assets because future income cannot be known in advance. However, to the extent a company has deferred tax liabilities, they may be reduced by application of the carryforward against future taxable amounts. The benefit arising from the application of the carryforward must be reported separately as an element of income tax expense for the current period, either in the income statement or in notes to the statement.

To determine the benefit available, the carryforward must be included on the schedule of future temporary difference reversals. These actual operating losses are used *before* any future deductible amounts are carried back or carried forward. If a company has only temporary differences that create deferred tax liabilities, the unused operating loss can be used to directly reduce the liabilities. For example, assume Royden Corp. has an unused operating loss carryforward of $30,000 and a future taxable amount of $20,000 arising from a temporary difference reversal. Assuming a 40% enacted tax rate for the reversal year, the $8,000 (40% × $20,000) deferred tax liability can be completely written off thus increasing the net assets of the company by $8,000. The income tax expense would reflect the $8,000 as a benefit from the NOL carryforward.

Exhibit 20-9 further illustrates the scheduling necessary in most applications of net operating loss carryforward offsets against deferred tax liabilities. Assume that Allred, Inc. had a financial loss in 1992 of $15,000 rather than an income of $30,000 as shown in Exhibit 20-6. The temporary depreciation difference in 1992 results in a taxable loss of $33,000. The carryback provision completely eliminates the $25,000 taxable income amount for 1991 and permits the filing of an amended return and a refund of $10,000 (40% × $25,000). This leaves an $8,000 operating loss carryforward. The schedule of temporary difference reversals in Exhibit 20-9 includes $20,000 taxable amounts in both 1994 and 1995. This permits the carryforward of $8,000 to 1994. The $17,000 deductible amount from 1993 can no longer be carried back to 1991 as was true in Exhibit 20-6 because the 1992 operating loss carryback was applied first. As shown in Exhibit 20-9, the $17,000 can be carried forward against taxable amounts in 1994 and 1995. After applying the carryback and carryforward rules, only 1995 has a balance remaining; a $15,000 taxable amount. The deferred tax liability on this amount is $6,000 (40% × $15,000). No deferred tax assets are indicated for 1992. The journal entry recognizes the tax benefit from the net operating loss as a separate credit. As was true in the other examples, the charge to Income Tax Expense-Deferred Provision is the amount necessary to balance the entry after adjusting all deferred tax accounts to their correct ending balances.

Exhibit 20-9   NOL Carryback and Carryforward

	Pior Yr. 1991	Current Yr. 1992	Reversal years		
			1993	1994	1995
Taxable financial income (loss)	$30,000	($15,000)	$0	$0	$0
Temporary difference between tax and book depreciation	(5,000)	(18,000)	(17,000)	20,000	20,000
Taxable income (loss)	$25,000	($33,000)	($17,000)	$20,000	$20,000
1992 net operating loss carryback to 1991	(25,000)	25,000			
1992 net operating loss carryforward to 1994		8,000		(8,000)	
Net taxable income (loss)	$0	$0	($17,000)	$12,000	$20,000
Loss carryforwards: 1993 carryforward to 1994			12,000	(12,000)	
1993 carryforward to 1995			5,000		(5,000)
Net taxable (deductible) amount	$0	$0	$0	$0	$15,000
Enacted tax rate	40%	40%	40%	40%	40%
Tax Refund Receivable ($25,000 × 40%)	$10,000 a				

Benefit from NOL Carryforward ($8,000 × 40%)		$3,200b			

			Totals		
			Ending Balance	Beginning Balance (Exhbt 20-6)	1992 Adjustment
Deferred tax asset:					
Current			$0	$ 7,200	$(7,200) c
Noncurrent			$0	$ 2,800	$(2,800) d
Deferred tax liability:					
Noncurrent			$ 6,000	$ 6,000	$12,000	$(6,000) e

1992 Journal Entries

	Dr.	Cr.
Income Tax Refund Receivable	10,000	
Refund of Income Tax from Net Operating Loss Carryback.		10,000a
Income Tax Expense—Deferred	7,200	
Deferred Tax Liability—Noncurrent	6,000 e	
Deferred Tax Asset—Current		7,200 c
Deferred Tax Asset—Noncurrent		2,800 d
Income Tax Benefit from NOL Carryforward		3,200 b

1992 Income Statement Presentation

Loss from operations before income taxes	($15,000)
Refund of income tax from NOL carryback	10,000
Less income taxes:	
Deferred provision	(7,200)
Benefit from NOL carryforward	3,200
Loss from operations	($ 9,000)

Other Changes in Estimates and Strategies

Although the illustrations in this section may seem complex, they have purposely been kept simple to illustrate the application of the asset and liability method. When new schedules of temporary difference reversals are prepared each financial reporting period, new estimates of amounts and timing of reversals must be made. FASB Statement No. 96 allows companies to consider reasonable tax strategies in making these estimates.

For example, if the scheduling results in certain deductible amounts that cannot be netted against scheduled taxable amounts, scheduled reversals can be accelerated or delayed based on possible early disposition of assets or refinancing of liabilities that were affected by temporary differences. Companies do not have to actually implement the tax strategy, but it must be a prudent and feasible strategy over which the organization has discretion and control and also has the ability and intent to implement. It must also meet the cost benefit constraint of FASB Concepts Statement No. 2.

The introduction of tax strategies makes the computation of deferred tax assets and liabilities very subjective. Depending on the strategy developed, the total income tax expense can be changed dramatically. Because the total income tax expense figure is determined based on the changes in the deferred balance sheet accounts, unusual variations in tax expense can be anticipated. Tax planning will undoubtedly take on a new level of importance as a result of FASB Statement No. 96. All earnings per share and income totals will be affected by the strategies assumed and by the estimates made.

Summary of Application of the Asset and Liability Method

The preceding pages have illustrated the application of the asset and liability method. In summary, the following steps that are enumerated in FASB Statement No. 96 must be taken each period to determine the deferred tax asset and liability balances.[5]

1. Schedule temporary differences for future years. Estimate the particular future years in which temporary differences will result in taxable or deductible amounts.

2. Determine the net taxable or deductible amount in each future year.

3. Consider operating loss carryforwards. Deduct operating loss carryforwards for tax purposes (as permitted or required by tax law) from net taxable amounts that are scheduled to occur in the future years included in the loss carryforward period.

4. Apply carryback and carryforward principle to deductible amounts. Carry back or carry forward (as permitted or required by law) net deductible amounts occurring in particular years to offset net taxable amounts that are scheduled to occur in prior or subsequent years.

5. Compute deferred tax asset balances. Recognize a deferred tax asset for

---

[5]Adapted from paragraph 17 of FASB Statement No. 96.

the tax benefit of net deductible amounts that could be realized by loss carryback from future years (1) to reduce a current deferred tax liability and (2) to reduce taxes paid in the current or prior year. (No asset is recognized for any additional net deductible amounts in future years.)

6. Compute preliminary deferred tax liability balances. Calculate the amount of tax for the remaining net taxable amounts that are scheduled to occur in each future year by applying presently enacted tax rates and laws for each of those years to the type and amount of net taxable amounts scheduled for those years.

7. Apply tax credit carryforwards to reduce deferred tax liability balances. Deduct tax credit carryforwards for tax purposes (as permitted or required by law) from the amount of tax (calculated above) for future years that are included in the carryforward periods. (No asset is recognized for any additional amount of tax credit carryforward).

8. Compute deferred tax liability balances. Recognize a deferred tax liability for the remaining amount of taxes payable for each future year.

9. Compute current and deferred income tax expense. Recognize as current income tax expense the current year tax liability. Recognize as deferred income tax expense the amount required to adjust all deferred tax asset and liability accounts to their computed ending balances.

Transition From Deferred To Asset and Liability Method

Companies adopting the asset and liability method for the first time must make transition adjustments to the deferred accounts recorded under the deferred method. Statement No. 96 is effective for fiscal years beginning after December 15, 1989. While earlier application was encouraged, the complexity of this new statement and the uncertainty of future tax rates did not result in many early adoptions. Because of the rate reductions included in the 1986 Tax Reform Act, many companies with deferred tax liabilities were able to show a significant reduction in their tax liabilities and increased net income when they adopted the new method. Many companies with deferred asset balances no longer can report them because of the limited deferred tax asset recognition under the new standard. This is especially true for those companies with extended reversal periods for their deferred tax assets.

The Financial Accounting Standards Board provided for two distinct methods for reporting these transition catch-up adjustments:

1. *Retroactively restating financial statements for prior years.* A company selecting this option may restate as many years as it chooses. Thus, if the year that includes October 22, 1986, the date of the 1986 Tax Reform Act, is restated, the full effects of that act would be reported in income of that year. If the financial statements do not include the earliest year

restated, the beginning balance of Retained Earnings should be adjusted for the effects of the restatement.[6]

2. *Reporting the catchup adjustment in the current year's income statement after income from continuing operations but before net income.* This method recognizes the adjustment as a cumulative change in accounting principle.

Financial Statement Presentation and Disclosure

In classified balance sheets, deferred tax assets and liabilities must be reported as either current or noncurrent depending on their expected reversal dates. FASB Statement No. 96 provides for some offsetting of deferred assets and liabilities. In order for offsetting to be acceptable, the asset and liability must both be current or both be noncurrent. A current asset cannot be offset against a noncurrent liability. Exhibit 20-4 (page 888) provides an example of a case in which offsetting would be permitted on the balance sheet. As indicated by the journal entries in the exhibit, there is a noncurrent deferred tax asset of $2,600 and a noncurrent deferred tax liability of $2,100. These amounts could be reported separately or offset to report a net noncurrent asset of $500. If offsetting is applied, the following income tax related amounts would be reported in the December 31, 1991 balance sheet.

Noncurrent assets		Current liabilities	
Deferred tax asset	$500	Income taxes payable	$58,000
		Deferred tax liability	1,750

Most companies are subject to state and municipal income taxes as well as Federal income taxes. If a business enterprise pays income taxes in more than one tax jurisdiction, no offsetting is permitted across jurisdictions.

The income statement must show, either in the body of the statement or in a note, the following selected components of income taxes related to continuing operations:[7]

1. Current tax expense or benefit
2. Deferred tax expense or benefit, except for 6 below
3. Investment tax credits
4. Government grants recognized as tax reduction
5. The benefits of operating loss carryforwards
6. Adjustments of a deferred tax liability or asset for enacted changes in tax laws or rates or a change in the tax status of an enterprise. All such changes are allocated to tax from continuing operations even if they relate to irregular or extraordinary items.

In addition to the above, the reported amount of income tax expense related to continuing operations must be reconciled with the amount of in-

---

[6]Statement of Financial Accounting Standards No. 96, par. 33.
[7]*Ibid*, par. 27.

come tax expense that would result from applying federal tax rates to pretax financial income from continuing operations. This reconciliation provides information to readers of the financial statements regarding how the entity has been affected by special provisions of the tax code such as permanent differences, tax credits, and operating loss carrybacks and carryforwards.

Concluding Comments

Accounting for income taxes has been, and will continue to be, a complex financial accounting issue. This chapter has introduced the major concepts and applications of this topic. FASB Statement No. 96 covers many areas besides those presented in this chapter. A significant part of the statement deals with the treatment of deferred taxes when businesses combine or merge. In addition, the effect of foreign income tax credits, the Alternative Minimum Tax, and varying tax planning strategies are all discussed in the statement.

The application of this new standard will be very difficult for most companies. It is not obvious that the benefits of the asset and liability method will outweigh the considerable costs to be incurred in its application by both large and small business entities. In an attempt to clarify the provisions of FASB Statement No. 96, the FASB issued an implementation special report in March 1989 that answered questions concerning the standard.[12] Many of the answers proposed methods to simplify the accounting required to implement FASB Statement No. 96. The implementation date of FASB Statement No. 96 was delayed until December 15, 1989 to give companies more time to study its provisions.

Most of the advantages of the asset and liability method relate to its conceptual superiority to the previously accepted deferred method. However, as discussed in the chapter, there are many implementation disadvantages. The following is a summary of the advantages and disadvantages attributed to this balance-sheet-oriented method.

The major advantages of the asset and liability method are as follows:

1. Because the assets and liabilities created under this method are in agreement with the FASB definitions of financial statement elements, the method is conceptually superior to the deferred method.

2. The asset and liability method is a flexible method that recognizes changes in circumstances and adjusts the reported amounts accordingly. This flexibility may make the predictive value of the statements superior to that of the deferred method.

The major disadvantages of the asset and liability method are as follows:

1. The scheduling of all future reversals of temporary differences each reporting period is time consuming and costly.

---

[12]*Special Report on Income Tax Accounting*, (Norwalk: Financial Accounting Standards Board, 1989).

2. Unrealistic assumptions about the effect of future reversals on net income must be made, i.e., it is assumed that the future financial income is always zero.

3. Computing income tax expense as a residual amount can result in a distorted net income figure in the financial statements.

4. The amount reported as a liability or asset is affected by changes in the tax laws. When laws change frequently, the reported tax accounts lose their predictability and stability.

5. By making deferred tax accounting dependent on income tax laws, which are complex, the accounting for deferred income taxes becomes potentially very complicated, and less understandable to statement users.

6. Because the asset and liability method prescribed by Statement No. 96 does not permit discounting, income tax assets and liabilities are not reported consistently with other items such as leases, pensions, and bonds that use discounted (present) values.

There is a need for research and analysis of the effects of this standard on the published financial statements and their usefulness to readers. There undoubtedly will be many interpretations and adjustments to accounting for income taxes in future years by the FASB.

Appendix A

Intraperiod Income Tax Allocation

As discussed in Chapter 4, when a company reports irregular or extraordinary items on its income statement, or when a prior period adjustment affects retained earnings, intraperiod tax allocation is appropriate. Under this approach, the income tax effect of each of these special items is reported with the individual item rather than being included with the income tax expense related to current operations. It was assumed in Chapter 4 that a single rate applied to each category of income, and that no special tax limitations were present for any of the income categories. With this assumption, intraperiod income tax allocation is not difficult.

When this simplifying assumption is not realistic and different levels of income are taxed at varying rates, decision rules must be developed to make the allocation among the various categories of income. Prior to adoption of FASB Statement No. 96, these allocation rules were broad and vague. However, paragraphs 74 and 75 of Statement No. 96 establish a definite priority for intraperiod tax allocation.

In summary, a with and without approach is applied as follows:[8]

1. Income taxes are computed for current operations *without* any of the irregular or extraordinary items.

2. Income taxes are computed *with* all income items considered. The difference between (1) and (2) is the total tax allocation to irregular and extraordinary items.

3. Income taxes are computed on total income *without* irregular and extraordinary *losses* considered to determine the tax effect of all losses. If there are several losses, the incremental tax effect of each loss category is considered, and the total tax impact of all loss categories is allocated among the separate losses in the ratio of their separate incremental impacts.

4. The difference between the income tax benefit allocated to all losses and the total irregular and extraordinary allocation (2) is attributed to irregular and extraordinary gains. If there are several gains, the incre-

---

[8]To simplify the discussion of intraperiod income tax allocation, it is assumed that financial and taxable income are equal, thus there are no deferred taxes. In many actual situations, deferred taxes may apply both to current operations and to irregular categories of income such as discontinued operations. The interplay of deferred taxes with intraperiod tax allocation adds another dimension of complexity not considered in this introductory presentation of accounting for income taxes.

mental tax effect of all gain categories is considered, and further allocation to gain items is made in the same manner as losses.

An example will illustrate the application of these decision rules. Assume Marble Corp. reports the following pretax income components on its income statement:

Income from continuing operations	$75,600
Loss on disposal of business segment	(19,000)
Extraordinary gain on early extinguishment of debt	30,000
Extraordinary loss on litigation claim	(16,000)
Cumulative effect of change in depreciation method	15,000
Total income before considering income taxes	$85,600

Assume the tax department has applied the current tax regulations and rates to Marble's various income categories, and computed the following tax information using the with and without concepts required for intraperiod tax allocation:

Tax on total income ($85,600)	$30,200
Tax on income from continuing operations ($75,600)	26,750
Tax on total income before considering all irregular and extraordinary losses ($85,600 + 19,000 + 16,000 = $120,600)	42,500

Based on this assumed tax information, the net income for the year is $55,400 ($85,600 − $30,200). The total intraperiod tax allocation is $3,450 tax expense ($30,200 − $26,750). The total tax benefit allocated to the two loss categories is $12,300 ($42,500 − $30,200) and the total tax expense allocated to the two gain categories is $15,750 ($12,300 + $3,450). This allocation can be shown graphically as follows:

Tax on income from continuing operations_____ $26,750
$15,750 (Tax on all gains)

Tax on total income before
considering all irregular and
extraordinary losses_____ $42,500
($12,300) (Tax benefit from all losses)

Tax on total income_____ $30,200
$3,450 (Net tax allocated to irregular and extraordinary items)

The loss and gain tax effects are further allocated to the specific gain and loss categories using the following assumed information also provided by the tax department. The incremental tax benefit or expense is determined by considering each component separately.

Incremental tax benefit—disposal loss	$ 9,000
Incremental tax benefit—extraordinary loss	6,000
Total tax benefits from losses	$15,000

Incremental tax expense—extraordinary gain	$10,200
Incremental tax expense—cumulative change	3,800
Total tax expense on gains	$14,000

Allocation of the $12,300 tax benefit to loss categories would be as follows:

Disposal loss ($9,000/$15,000) × $12,300	$ 7,380
Extraordinary loss ($6,000/$15,000) × $12,300	4,920
Total tax benefit	$12,300

Allocation of the $15,750 tax expense to gain categories would be as follows:

Extraordinary gain [($10,200/$14,000) × $15,750]	$11,475
Cumulative change [($3,800/$14,000) × $15,750]	4,275
Total tax expense	$15,750

The bottom portion of Marble Corp.'s income statement would be reported as follows:

Income from continuing operations before income taxes..........	$75,600
Income taxes	26,750
Income from continuing operations	$48,850
Loss on disposal of business segment (net of income tax benefit of $7,380)	(11,620)
Extraordinary gain from early extinguishment of debt (net of income taxes of $11,475)...................................	18,525
Extraordinary loss on litigation claim (net of income tax benefit of $4,920)	(11,080)
Cumulative effect of change in depreciation method (net of income taxes of $4,275)..	10,725
Net income	$55,400

If there are taxable direct entries to owners' equity accounts, the incremental approach is used to allocate tax benefits or tax expense to the equity accounts. For example, prior period adjustments usually are affected by income taxes and must be shown in the statement of retained earnings net of the tax effect.

Appendix B

The Investment Tax Credit

Tax credits are direct reductions in the amount of taxes due. They represent another way legislative bodies can stimulate economic growth. Unlike temporary differences that affect the amount of taxable income used to compute the taxes payable, tax credits are applied directly to the computed income tax liability. They represent the last adjustment made in computing income taxes payable.

One of the more common tax credits of the past thirty years has been the investment tax credit (ITC). In order to encourage investment in productive assets, the Revenue Act of 1962 permitted taxpayers to reduce their federal income tax by a credit equal to a specified percentage of the cost of certain depreciable assets acquired after December 31, 1961. Since this provision was first included in the tax code, there have been many modifications of the investment tax credit, including its temporary suspension. Whenever the economy has needed a stimulus, however, Congress has returned to the ITC as a way of encouraging business to invest in new productive assets and thus increase the gross national product. As part of the Tax Reform Act of 1986, Congress repealed the investment tax credit for property placed in service after December 31, 1985.

Although the investment tax credit was suspended by the 1986 Act, history suggests that it could be reinstated at any future time. With this in mind, a brief discussion of the accounting implications of the credit is warranted.

Accounting for the Investment Tax Credit

There are two methods that can be used to record the tax reduction resulting from the ITC: (1) the credit can be used to reduce the income tax expense for the year in which it is received, commonly referred to as the flow-through method of investment tax credit, or (2) the credit can be deferred and reflected as a reduction of tax expense over the period during which the asset is depreciated, commonly referred to as the deferred method of investment tax credit.

Flow-Through Method

Using the flow-through method, the investment tax credit is treated as a reduction of income tax expense in the year the credit is allowed. To illustrate, assume that a business acquired machinery in 1991 for $100,000, and the applicable investment tax credit rate is 10%. The federal income tax for 1991 is $75,000 reduced by an investment tax credit of $10,000 (10% of $100,000). The entry to record the federal income tax for 1991 would be:

Income Tax Expense	65,000	
Income Taxes Payable		65,000
Recognition of income tax of $75,000 less investment tax credit of $10,000.		

Deferred Method   Under the deferred method of accounting for the investment tax credit, the credit is viewed as a reduction of income tax expense over the life of the asset rather than in the year the credit is applied to the tax liability. Using the information in the previous example, the entry to record income tax in 1991 under the deferred method would be:

Income Tax Expense	75,000	
Deferred Investment Tax Credit		10,000
Income Taxes Payable		65,000

The following entry would be made each year to amortize the investment tax credit over the 5-year life of the asset.

Deferred Investment Tax Credit	2,000	
Income Tax Expense		2,000

Evaluation of Accounting Treatment of Investment Tax Credit   The Accounting Principles Board favored the deferred method and approved it in Opinion No. 2. Lack of support for this view among many prominent accountants led to the issuance in 1964 of Opinion No. 4 in which the Board accepted both methods, although still stating a preference for the deferred method. In 1968, a further attempt was made by the Accounting Principles Board to restore the deferred method as a single uniform method. Again, differences of opinion resulted in failure to adopt the original conclusions. In 1971, the Board once again made a serious effort to restore the deferred method. However, they had to postpone their work as a result of congressional action permitting the taxpayer to choose the method to be used in recognizing the benefit arising from the credit.

Good theoretical arguments can be presented for either method. Those who advocate using the deferred method argue that the cost of the asset is effectively reduced by the investment credit, and the tax benefit should be spread over the acquired asset's useful life. Those who advocate using the flow-through method argue that the tax credit is in reality a tax reduction in the current period. They argue that tax regulations establish the tax liability each year, and that amount is the proper expense to match against current revenues. This latter treatment affects current income more and is favored by political leaders when the investment tax credit is being used to stimulate a sluggish economy.

It is unfortunate that this issue has become such a political item. It is an example of an area where there seems to be no justification for having two methods. It is difficult to see how different economic circumstances among companies would justify dual treatment. If the investment tax credit is reinstated by Congress, the authors believe that a uniform accounting method for its treatment should be adopted by the accounting profession.

Key Terms

Asset and liability method of
   interperiod tax allocation 880
Current tax provision 883
Deductible amount 882
Deferred method of interperiod tax
   allocation 880
Deferred method of investment tax
   credit 904
Deferred tax assets 882
Deferred tax liability 882
Deferred tax provision 883
Financial income 874
Flow-through method of investment
   tax credit 904

Interperiod tax allocation 876
Intraperiod tax allocation 901
Investment tax credit 904
Net operating loss carryback 877
Net operating loss carryforward 878
Permanent differences 876
Pretax financial income 884
Taxable amount 882
Taxable financial income 884
Taxable income 874
Temporary differences 874
Timing differences 874

Questions

1. Accounting methods used by a company to determine income for financial reporting purposes frequently differ from those used to determine taxable income. What is the justification for these differences?
2. Distinguish between a nondeductible expense and a temporary difference that results in a larger current year taxable income.
3. Why is the ability to pay concept applied to income tax legislation?
4. In applying the net operating loss carryback and carryforward provisions, what order of application may be followed for federal tax purposes?
5. Under what circumstances, if any, may an operating loss carryforward be reported as an asset on an entity's balance sheet?
6. Why was the asset and liability method of income tax allocation adopted by the FASB?
7. Under FASB Statement No. 96, a liability or asset shall be recognized for the deferred tax consequences of all temporary differences. What financial statement elements are affected by these temporary differences?
8. Under what conditions may a company recognize a deferred tax asset under FASB Statement No. 96?
9. Tax consequences of earning income or incurring losses or expenses in future years or the future enactment of a change in tax laws or rates are not recognized under the asset and liability method. Why?
10. How is income tax expense computed under the asset and liability method?
11. Under what conditions will an entity report a current deferred tax asset or liability in its balance sheet?
12. How is the scheduling of depreciation reversals in the future different from scheduling other temporary differences such as bad debts?
13. Accounting for changing tax rates is different under the asset and liability method than under the deferred method. Describe the currently accepted accounting procedures when tax rates change.
14. Under what conditions may operating loss carryforwards be used to reduce deferred tax liabilities?
15. Tax strategies have an important role in accounting for income taxes. Describe briefly how a change in tax strategy could affect the amount reported as deferred taxes.

16. What transition alternatives have been provided for companies adopting FASB Statement No. 96?
17. How is income tax expense subdivided to provide additional information to statement readers?
18. What are the principal arguments against the use of the asset and liability method of interperiod tax allocation?
*19. Describe the with and without method of intraperiod tax allocation.
*20. What is the proper sequence for computing intraperiod tax allocation?
**21. Two methods of accounting for investment tax credits are acceptable. Identify and briefly describe both methods.

*Relates to Appendix A
**Relates to Appendix B

Discussion Cases   **Case 20-1   (What are deferred income taxes?)**

Hurst Inc. is a new corporation that has just completed a highly successful first year of operation. Hurst is a privately held corporation, but its president, Byron Hurst, has indicated that if the company continues to do as well for the next 4 or 5 years, it will go public. By all indications, the company should continue to be highly profitable on both a short-term and long-term basis.

The controller of the new company, Lori James, plans on using the MACRS method of depreciating Hurst's assets and using the installment sales method of recognizing income for tax purposes. For financial statement presentation, straight-line depreciation will be used and all sales will be fully recognized in the year of sale. There are no other differences between book and taxable income.

Hurst has hired your firm to prepare its financial statements. You are now preparing the income statement. The controller wants to show, as "income tax expense," the amount of the tax liability actually due. "After all," James reasons, "that's the amount we'll actually pay, and in light of our plans for continued expansion, it's highly unlikely that the temporary differences will ever reverse."

Draft a memo to the controller outlining your reaction to the plan. Give reasons in support of your decision.

*Case 20-2   (Should health of the economy govern GAAP?)

Perhaps no issue has created more controversy and discussion in the accounting profession, business, and government than the investment tax credit. The government's involvement has been an intriguing one. The purpose of the investment tax credit has been to stimulate investment in new business property and thus promote a steady growth in the Gross National Product and avoid severe recession or depression. In order to have the most significant impact possible on a company's income, legislative officials who enacted the investment tax credit legislation indicated a preference for the flow-through method of accounting. Many people in the business community agree with this approach because of its favorable impact on reported income. Accounting theorists, on the other hand, argue that the deferred method of accounting for the credit is preferable because it reflects more clearly the economic reality of the credit. Evaluate these two positions. What role, if any, should public policy and the impact of accounting principles on the economy have upon the establishment of GAAP?

*Relates to Appendix B

Case 20-3   (How do deferred taxes work?)

The Primrose Company appropriately uses the asset and liability method for interperiod income tax allocation.

Primrose reports depreciation expense for certain machinery purchased this year using the modified accelerated cost recovery system (MACRS) for income tax purposes and the straight-line basis for accounting purposes. The tax deduction is the larger amount this year.

Primrose received rent revenues in advance this year. These revenues are included in this year's taxable income. However, for accounting purposes, these revenues are reported as unearned revenues, a current liability.

(1) What is the theoretical basis for deferred income taxes under the asset and liability concept?
(2) How would Primrose determine and account for the income tax effect for depreciation and rent? Why?
(3) How should Primrose classify the income tax effect of the depreciation and rent on its balance sheet and income statement? Why?

Exercises   ### Exercise 20-1   (Net operating loss carryback)
The following historical financial data are available for the Bradshaw Manufacturing Company.

Year	Income	Tax Rate	Tax Paid
1988	$175,000	40%	$ 70,000
1989	230,000	42%	96,600
1990	310,000	35%	108,500

In 1991, the Bradshaw Company suffered a $750,000 net operating loss due to an economic recession. The company elects to use the carryback provision in the tax law.

(1) Using the information given, calculate the refund due arising from the loss carryback and the amount of the loss available to carryforward to future periods. Assume a 1991 tax rate of 34%. Also, assume that no adjustments need to be made to prior years' net income for purposes of the loss carryback and that there is no guarantee that future periods will be profitable.
(2) Give the entry necessary to record the refund due and the loss reduction.
(3) Using the answer from (1), prepare the bottom portion of the income statement reflecting the effect of the loss carryback on the 1991 statement.

Exercise 20-2   (Identification of temporary differences)
Indicate which of the following items are temporary differences and which are

nontaxable or nondeductible. For each temporary difference, indicate whether it affects the deferred tax asset or liability account.

(a) Tax depreciation in excess of book depreciation, $150,000.
(b) Excess of income on installment sales over income reportable for tax purposes, $130,000.
(c) Premium payment for insurance policy on life of president, $35,000.
(d) Earnings of foreign subsidiary received and taxed in the current year but recorded on the books in a previous year, $150,000.
(e) Amortization of goodwill, $60,000.
(f) Rent collected in advance of period earned, $75,000.
(g) Warranty provision accrued in advance of period paid, $40,000.
(h) Interest revenue received on municipal bonds, $30,000.

Exercise 20-3   (Temporary difference calculation—deductible amounts)

Pro-Tech-Tronics Company computed a pretax financial income of $35,000 for the first year of its operations ended December 31, 1991. Analysis of the tax and book basis of its liabilities disclosed $55,000 in unearned rental revenue on the books that had been recognized as taxable income in 1991 when the cash was received.

The unearned rent is expected to be recognized on the books in the following pattern.

1992	$15,000
1993	20,000
1994	12,000
1995	8,000
	$55,000

The enacted tax rates for this year and the next four years are as follows:

1991	38%	1993	30%	1995	32%
1992	34%	1994	30%		

Prepare a schedule showing the reversal of the temporary difference and the computation of income taxes payable and deferred tax assets or liabilities as of December 31, 1991.

Exercise 20-4   (Temporary differences calculation—deductible and taxable amounts)

Fibertek, Inc. computed a pretax financial income of $40,000 for the first year of its operations ended December 31, 1991. Included in financial income was $25,000 of nondeductible expenses, $22,000 gross profit on installment sales that was deferred for tax purposes until the installments were collected, and $18,000 in doubtful accounts expense that had been accrued on the books in 1991.

The temporary differences are expected to reverse in the following patterns.

Year	Gross Profit on Collections	Bad Debt Write-Offs
1992	$ 5,000	$ 6,000
1993	7,000	12,000
1994	4,000	
1995	6,000	
	$22,000	$18,000

The enacted tax rates for this year and the next four years are as follows:

1991	40%	1993	32%	1995	32%
1992	35%	1994	30%		

Prepare a schedule showing the reversal of the temporary differences and the computation of income taxes payable and deferred tax assets or liabilities as of December 31, 1991.

Exercise 20-5   (Computation of deferred asset and liability balances)

Nashua Engineering's schedule of temporary difference reversals reported the following taxable income (loss) amounts as of December 31, 1991, the end of its first fiscal year.

Year	Taxable Income (Loss)	Enacted Tax Rate
1991	$10,000	40%
1992	7,000	35%
1993	(12,000)	32%
1994	(8,000)	30%
1995	20,000	32%

Compute the net taxable (deductible) amounts after considering loss carrybacks and carryforwards and the deferred tax assets and liabilities that would be reported on Nashua's balance sheet as of December 31, 1991.

Exercise 20-6   (Computation of deferred asset and liability balances—current year operating loss)

Wasatch Computer, Inc.'s schedule of temporary difference reversals reported the following taxable income (loss) amounts as of December 31, 1991, the end of its first fiscal year.

Year	Taxable Income (Loss)	Enacted Tax Rate
1991	($5,000)	40%
1992	7,000	35%
1993	(5,000)	32%
1994	4,000	30%
1995	6,000	32%

Compute the net taxable (deductible) amounts after considering all carrybacks and carryforwards and the deferred tax assets and liabilities that would be reported on Wasatch Computer's balance sheet as of December 31, 1991.

Exercise 20-7   (Computation of deferred asset and liability balances)

Dixon Type and Supply Company's schedule of temporary difference reversals reported the following taxable income (loss) amounts as of December 31, 1991, the end of its first fiscal year.

Year	Taxable Income (Loss)	Enacted Tax Rate
1991	$ 8,000	40%
1992	(10,000)	35%
1993	(11,000)	32%
1994	6,000	30%
1995	4,000	32%

Compute the net taxable (deductible) amounts after considering any carrybacks and carryforwards and the deferred tax assets and liabilities that would be reported on Dixon Type and Supply Company's balance sheet as of December 31, 1991.

Exercise 20-8   (Computation of deferred asset and liability balances with subsequent tax rate change)

Quistguard Company's schedule of temporary difference reversals reported the following taxable income (loss) amounts as of December 31, 1991, the end of its first fiscal year. The enacted tax rate for 1991 and all future years was 40%.

Year	Taxable Income Loss
1991	$15,000
1992	12,000
1993	(4,000)
1994	5,000
1995	3,000
1996	(23,000)

In 1992, new tax legislation was passed with the following rates enacted for 1992 and future years:

1992	38%
1993	36%
1994 and beyond	34%

(1) Compute the net taxable (deductible) amounts after considering loss carrybacks and carryforwards, income taxes payable, and the deferred tax assets and liabilities that would be reported on Quistguard's balance sheet as of December 31, 1991.

(2) Compute the adjustment to be made in 1992 to reflect the change in enacted tax rates.

*Exercise 20-9   (Intraperiod income tax allocation)

The Hughes Enterprise Company paid $360,000 in income taxes for the year ended December 31, 1991. $20,000 of these taxes related to an extraordinary gain that was taxed at 25%. Hughes discontinued one of its segments during 1991, and had a tax savings of $50,000 resulting from the loss on disposition of the segment. The loss was treated for tax purposes as an ordinary loss, and was deducted from ordinary income that was taxed at 40%. Included in the $360,000 tax payment was $10,000 resulting from a gain on the sale of equipment. The tax rate on the gain was 25%. All other income items were from normal operations and were taxed at 40%. Hughes had 40,000 shares of common stock outstanding.

Prepare the income statement for Hughes Enterprise beginning with "Income from continuing operations before income taxes." Include intraperiod tax allocation procedures as may be appropriate.

*Relates to Appendix A

**Exercise 20-10   (Investment tax credit)

Brossard Electric Company purchased a new machine on January 1, 1991, for $350,000. The machine had a 10-year life and was depreciated by the straight-line method. Assuming a 10% investment tax credit, give the entries to record the recognition of income taxes for the first 2 years under (a) the flow-through method and (b) the deferred method. (Income tax before the credit in 1991 and 1992 was $217,500 and $312,000 respectively.)

**Relates to Appendix B

**Exercise 20-11   (Investment tax credit)

The Ferre Corporation purchased a stamping press for $1,360,000 on January 1, 1991. The press had an estimated useful life of 12 years and no salvage value. The corporation uses the straight-line method of depreciation. Assuming an income tax liability for the current year of $476,000 before an eligible investment tax credit of 6%, give the entries to record income tax for 1991 using (a) the flow-through method and (b) the deferred method.

**Relates to Appendix B

Problems   **Problem 20-1   (Operating loss carryback and carryforward)**

The following information is taken from the financial statements of Columbia Enterprises:

Year	Taxable and Pretax Financial Income	Income Tax Rate	Income Tax Paid
1987	$24,000	40%	$ 9,600
1988	27,400	40%	10,960
1989	31,500	34%	10,710
1990	21,240	34%	7,222
1991	(86,000)	36%	0

The company elects to use the carryback provisions of the tax law.

Instructions:

(1) Given the information from the financial statements, compute the amount of income tax refund due as a result of the operating loss.
(2) What is the amount, if any, of the operating loss carryforward?
(3) (a) Assume the foregoing information except that the loss in 1991 was $61,000. Calculate the refund due and prepare the journal entry to record the claim for income tax refund.
(b) Assume that in addition to (a), there was a loss in 1992 of $24,000. How much could be carried back and how much could be carried forward?

Problem 20-2   (Net operating loss carryback and carryforward)

The following financial history shows the income and losses for Steele and Associates for the 10-year period 1982-1991:

Year	Taxable and Pretax Financial Income (Before NOL)	Income Tax Rate	Income Tax Paid
1982	$ 8,800	50%	$ 4,400
1983	12,300	50%	6,150
1984	14,800	44%	6,512
1985	(29,250)	44%	0
1986	7,200	44%	3,168
1987	(21,750)	46%	0
1988	16,600	46%	?
1989	32,000	40%	12,800
1990	(58,700)	40%	0
1991	65,000	40%	?

Assume that no adjustments to taxable income are necessary for purposes of the net operating loss carryback and the company elects to use the carryback provisions of the tax code. (Assume the income tax provisions described in the text are in effect for all years.)

Instructions:

(1) Given the foregoing information, compute the amount of income tax refund for each year as a result of each loss carryback and the amount of the carryforward (if any).
(2) Calculate the amount of income tax paid, showing the benefit of the loss carryforward, for the years 1988 and 1991.
(3) For 1991, give the entry to record the income tax liability.

Problem 20-3   (Temporary difference calculation—taxable amounts)

Timpany Motors, Inc. computed a pretax financial income of $75,000 for its first year of operations ended December 31, 1991. In preparing the income tax return for the year, the tax accountant determined the following differences between 1991 financial income and taxable income:

1. Nondeductible expenses	$30,000
2. Nontaxable revenues	12,500
3. Temporary difference—Installment sales reported in financial income but not in taxable income	28,000

The temporary difference is expected to reverse in the following pattern.

1992	$ 6,000
1993	13,500
1994	8,500
	$28,000

The enacted tax rates for this year and the next three years are as follows:

1991	40%	1993	34%
1992	36%	1994	30%

Instructions:

(1) Prepare a schedule showing the reversal of the temporary differences and the computation of income taxes payable and deferred tax assets or liabilities as of December 31, 1991.

(2) Prepare journal entries to record income taxes payable and deferred income taxes.

(3) Prepare the income statement for Timpany Motors beginning with "Income from continuing operations before income taxes" for the year ended December 31, 1991.

Problem 20-4   (Temporary differences calculation—deductible amounts)

Davidson Gasket Inc. computed a pretax financial loss of $15,000 for the first year of its operations, ended December 31, 1991. Analysis of the tax and the book basis of its liabilities disclosed $55,000 in unearned rental revenue on the books that had been recognized as taxable income in 1991 when the cash was received and $20,000 in warranties payable that had been recognized as expense on the books in 1991 when product sales were made, but that are not deductible on the tax return until paid.

These temporary differences are expected to reverse in the following pattern.

Year	Rent Earned on Books	Warranty Payments
1992	$13,000	$ 5,000
1993	25,000	8,000
1994	12,000	7,000
1995	5,000	
	$55,000	$20,000

The enacted tax rates for this year and the next four years are as follows:

1991	38%	1993	32%	1995	30%
1992	36%	1994	30%		

Instructions:

(1) Prepare a schedule showing the reversal of the temporary differences and the computation of income taxes payable and deferred tax assets or liabilities as of December 31, 1991.

(2) Prepare journal entries to record income taxes payable and deferred income taxes.
(3) Prepare the income statement for Davidson Gasket Inc., beginning with "Income from continuing operations before income taxes" for the year ended December 31, 1991.

▌▌▌ Problem 20-5   (Temporary differences calculation—deductible and taxable amounts)

Stratco computed a pretax financial income of $40,000 for the first year of its operations ended December 31, 1991. Included in financial income was $50,000 of nontaxable revenue, $20,000 gross profit on installment sales that was deferred for tax purposes until the installments were collected, and $50,000 in warranties payable that had been recognized as expense on the books in 1991 when product sales were made.
The temporary differences are expected to reverse in the following patterns.

Year	Gross Profit on Collections	Warranty Payments
1992	$5,000	$9,000
1993	7,000	16,500
1994	2,000	20,500
1995	6,000	4,000
	$20,000	$50,000

The enacted tax rates for this year and the next four years are as follows:

1991	40%	1993	32%	1995	30%
1992	35%	1994	30%		

Instructions:

(1) Prepare a schedule showing the reversal of the temporary differences and the computation of income taxes payable and deferred tax assets or liabilities as of December 31, 1991.
(2) Prepare journal entries to record income taxes payable and deferred income taxes.
(3) Prepare the income statement for Stratco beginning with "Income from continuing operations before income taxes" for the year ended December 31, 1991.

Problem 20-6   (Temporary difference calculation—depreciation)

JGS Associates computed a pretax financial income of $48,000 for the first year of its operations ended December 31, 1991. JGS uses the modified accelerated cost recovery method on its tax return, and straight line depreciation on its books.
The differences between the tax and book deduction for depreciation over the five year life of the assets acquired in 1991 are as follows:

1991	$(12,000)
1992	(24,000)
1993	(6,000)
1994	18,000
1995	24,000
	0

The enacted tax rates for this year and the next four years are as follows:

1991	40%	1993	38%	1995	37%
1992	38%	1994	35%		

Instructions:

(1) Prepare a schedule showing the pattern of depreciation differences and the computation of income taxes payable and deferred tax assets or liabilities as of December 31, 1991.
(2) Prepare journal entries to record income taxes payable and deferred income taxes.
(3) Prepare the income statement for JGS Associates beginning with "Income from continuing operations before income taxes" for the year ended December 31, 1991.

Problem 20-7 (Temporary differences and net operating loss)

Topspin Company began operations at the beginning of 1991. At the end of the first year, it computed the following deferred tax asset and liability balances on its depreciation temporary difference:

Deferred tax asset—current	$5,200
Deferred tax liability—noncurrent	6,600

Topspin reported a pretax financial income of $20,000 in 1991 and $25,000 in 1992. Topspin uses the modified accelerated cost recovery method on its tax return, and straight line depreciation on its books.
The differences between the tax and book deduction for depreciation over the five year life of the assets acquired in 1991 are as follows:

1991	$(7,000)
1992	(15,000)
1993	(9,500)
1994	11,500
1995	20,000
	0

During 1992, Topspin recorded $21,000 gross profit on installment sales that will not be taxable until the cash is collected in subsequent years. This temporary difference is expected to reverse in the following pattern:

1993	$ 5,000
1994	13,000
1995	3,000
	$21,000

The enacted tax rates for the five year period 1991-1995 are as follows:

1991	40%	1993	35%	1995	33%
1992	38%	1994	35%		

Instructions:

(1) Prepare a schedule showing the pattern of depreciation differences and installment sale collections, the computation of income taxes payable or refunds receivable, and deferred tax assets or liabilities as of December 31, 1992. Include 1991 information in the schedule.

(2) Prepare journal entries to record income taxes payable (receivable) and deferred income taxes, taking into consideration the beginning balances in the deferred accounts.

(3) Prepare the income statement for Topspin Company beginning with "Income from continuing operations before income taxes" for the year ended December 31, 1992.

▐▐▐ Problem 20-8   (Adjustment for changing tax rates)

Moritz Company analyzed its temporary differences as of December 31, 1991. The enacted tax rate was 40% for 1991 and all future tax years. The computation of taxes payable for 1991 and deferred tax liabilities as of the end of 1991 were as follows:

Year	Taxable Amount	Taxes Payable	Deferred Tax Liability Current	Deferred Tax Liability Noncurrent
1991	$20,000	$8,000		
1992	45,000		$18,000	
1993	34,000			$13,600
1994	36,000			14,400
1995	12,000			4,800
		$8,000	$18,000	$32,800

Instructions:

(1) Assume in early 1992 the taxing authority changed the rates for 1992 and beyond as follows:

1992	38%
1993	36%
1994 and beyond	34%

Prepare the 1992 journal entry to record the tax decrease.

(2) Assume that the rates were increased rather than decreased in early 1992 as follows:

1992	42%
1993	42%
1994	43%
1995 and beyond	45%

Prepare the 1992 journal entry to record the tax increase.

*Problem 20-9 (Intraperiod tax allocation)

Assume Energy Corp. has the following income components on its income statement. Amounts are before tax.

Income from continuing operations	$37,500
Gain on disposal of business segment	19,000
Extraordinary gain on early extinguishment of debt	23,000
Extraordinary loss on property loss	(32,000)
Cumulative effect of change in depreciation method	(13,000)
Total income before considering income taxes	$34,500

Assume the tax department has applied the current tax regulations and rates to Energy's various income categories, and computed the following tax information using the with and without concepts required for intraperiod tax allocation:

Tax on total income ($34,500)	$13,100
Tax on income from continuing operations ($37,500)	$15,200
Tax on total income before considering all irregular and extraordinary losses	$27,030

Instructions:

(1) Compute the total tax to be allocated to all income components after income from continuing operations, the total tax benefit allocated to the two loss categories, and the total tax expense allocated to the two gain categories.

(2) Assume the tax department has computed the following incremental tax benefits and expenses on each individual gain or loss component:

Incremental tax expense—gain components	
Gain on disposal	$5,700
Extraordinary gain	6,500
Incremental tax benefit—loss components	
Extraordinary loss	9,600
Cumulative effect	5,000

Allocate the total tax benefit and tax expense from (1) to the separate gain and loss components.

*Relates to Appendix A

*Problem 20-10 (Intraperiod tax allocation cases)

Assume the following intraperiod tax allocation information for Cases A, B, and C:

	Case A	Case B	Case C
Tax on income from continuing operations	$23,000	$57,000	$7,000
Tax on total income before considering all irregular and extraordinary losses	$36,900	$61,000	$9,500
Tax on total income	$32,000	$46,000	$7,000
Incremental tax expense—Gains			
Gain on disposal	$4,300	$1,700	$800
Extraordinary gain—A	$6,500	$3,200	$3,000
Extraordinary gain—B	$3,900		
Incremental tax benefit—Losses			
Extraordinary loss	($2,500)	($12,500)	($1,600)
Cumulative effect of accounting changes	($3,000)	($6,000)	($900)

Instructions: Compute the tax expense and benefits in Cases A through C for all irregular and extraordinary items.
*Relates to Appendix A

**Problem 20-11   (Investment tax credit)

Granite Sand and Gravel purchased a gravel sifting machine from Steelco Fabrications in 1991. Granite also purchased from Steelco the patent on the machine. In conjunction with the acquisition, Granite hired an independent appraiser to assess the fair market values of the machine and the patent at the purchase date. Company records revealed the following information:

Machine and patent purchase price	$ 530,000
Fair market value of the machine	425,000
Fair market value of the patent	125,000
Useful life of the machine	10 years
Useful life of the patent	15 years
Precredit tax liability: 1991	650,800
1992	1,180,200

Assume that an investment tax credit of 10% is allowable in 1991.

Instructions: Give the journal entries to record the acquisition of the machine and the patent, the recognition of income taxes in 1991 and 1992, and any amortization of deferred investment tax credits under both (1) the flow-through method and (2) the deferred method (assume that the company records depreciation for a full year in the year of acquisition).
**Relates to Appendix B

Chapter 21

Accounting for Leases

A lease is a contract specifying the terms under which the owner of property, the lessor, transfers the right to use the property to a lessee. Leasing is widely used in our economy as a method of obtaining various kinds of assets. Individuals may lease houses, apartments, automobiles, televisions, appliances, furniture, and almost any other consumer good on the market. Business enterprises lease land, buildings, and almost any type of equipment. For example, the Black & Decker Corporation in its 1987 financial statements reported leased assets including "service centers, administrative headquarters, warehouses and equipment." Indeed, almost any asset that can be acquired through purchase can be obtained through leasing. Of the 600 companies surveyed in the annual AICPA publication, *Accounting Trends and Techniques*, 534 companies, or approximately 90%, reported some form of lease arrangement.[1]

Some leases are simple rental agreements, while others closely resemble a debt-financed purchase of property. A major issue for the accounting profession has been whether this latter type of lease should be accounted for as a rental agreement in accordance with its legal form, or as a purchase of property which reflects the economic substance of the transaction. To illustrate the issue, assume that Monroe Co. decides to acquire equipment costing $10,000. The equipment has a useful life of 5 years, with no expected residual value. Monroe Co. can purchase the equipment by issuing a 5-year, 10%, $10,000 note with principal and interest to be paid in 5 equal installments of $2,368. Alternatively, Monroe Co. can lease the asset for 5 years, making 5 annual "rental" payments of $2,368. In substance, the lease is equivalent to purchasing the asset, the only difference being the legal form of the transaction. However, if the lease is accounted for as a simple rental agreement, Monroe Co. will not report the equipment as an asset nor the obligation to the lessor as a liability. Under conditions such as these, recording the transaction as a rental agreement does not reflect the underlying economic substance of acquiring and using the equipment.

---

[1]*Accounting Trends and Techniques, 1988* (New York: American Institute of Certified Public Accountants, 1988), p. 175.

As illustrated by this simple example, leasing can be used to avoid reporting a liability on the balance sheet. As discussed in Chapter 15, "off-balance-sheet financing" continues to be a perplexing problem for the accounting profession, and leasing is probably the oldest and most widely used means of keeping debt off the balance sheet. The FASB has attempted to eliminate this practice by requiring leases which meet certain criteria to be treated as assets, or capital leases—in effect, purchases of property.

Economic Advantages of Leasing

It would be unfair and incorrect to imply that the only reason companies lease property is to avoid reporting the lease obligation in the financial statements. While the accounting issue is one factor, other financial and tax considerations also play an important role in the leasing decision. While every situation is different, there are two primary advantages to the lessee of leasing over purchasing:

(1) **No down payment.** Most debt-financed purchases of property require a portion of the purchase price to be paid immediately by the borrower. This provides added protection to the lender in the event of default and repossession. Lease agreements, in contrast, are frequently structured so that 100% of the value of the property is financed through the lease. This aspect of leasing makes it an attractive alternative to a company that does not have sufficient cash for a down payment or wishes to use available capital for other operating or investing purposes.

(2) **Avoids risks of ownership.** There are many risks accompanying the ownership of property. They include casualty loss, obsolescence, changing economic conditions, and physical deterioration. The lessee may terminate a lease, although usually with a certain penalty, and thus avoid assuming the risk of these events. This flexibility is especially important in businesses where innovation and technological change make the future usefulness of particular equipment or facilities highly uncertain. A prime example of this condition in recent years has been the electronics industry with its rapid change in areas such as computer technology, robotics, and telecommunication.

The lessor also may find benefits to leasing its property rather than selling it. Advantages of the lease to the lessor include the following:

(1) **Increased sales.** By offering potential customers the option of leasing its products, a manufacturer or dealer may significantly increase its sales volume. For the reasons suggested in the preceding paragraphs, customers may be unwilling or unable to purchase property.

(2) **Ongoing business relationship with lessee.** When property is sold, the purchaser frequently has no more dealings with the seller of the prop-

erty. In leasing situations, however, the lessor and lessee maintain contact over a period of time, and long-term business relationships can often be established through leasing.

(3) **Residual value retained.** In many lease arrangements, title to the leased property never passes to the lessee. The lessor benefits from economic conditions that may result in a significant residual value at the end of the lease term. The lessor may lease the asset to another lessee or sell the property and realize an immediate gain. Many lessors have realized significant profits from unexpected increases in residual values.

Historical Development of Lease Accounting

The earliest accounting recognition of the importance of leasing as a financing device occurred in 1949 when the Committee on Accounting Procedures issued Accounting Research Bulletin No. 38, "Disclosure of Long-Term Leases in Financial Statements of Lessees." When the Accounting Principles Board was formed in 1959, the topic of leases was one of the initial ones to be considered. The Board issued four opinions on the subject of leasing during its fourteen-year history. Two of the opinions dealt with accounting by lessees, the other two with accounting by lessors. But the profession was not satisfied with the results of these opinions. Inconsistencies developed between accounting by lessees and lessors, and much of the opinions dealt with note disclosure rather than the accounting procedures themselves. Criteria for capitalization of leases were vague, and few lessees actually reported leases as assets with the accompanying liabilities.

Leasing was one of the topics on the original agenda of the FASB, and in 1976 the Board issued Statement No. 13, "Accounting for Leases." The objective of the FASB in issuing Statement No. 13 was to reflect the economic reality of leasing by requiring that the majority of long-term leases be accounted for as capital acquisitions by the lessee and as sales by the lessor. However, comparatively few leases have been capitalized as a result of the statement because of the liberal interpretations applied to the criteria used to define a capital lease.[2] An example of the broad interpretation of Statement No. 13 can be observed in the financial statements of General Mills, Inc. reproduced in Appendix A. Note fourteen refers to the company's existing leases, all of which are apparently reported as rental agreements rather than capitalized, even though they are labeled non-cancellable, and require future rental payments totaling $252 million.

The failure of Statement No. 13 to achieve the desired objective forced the FASB to issue additional pronouncements in the area of leasing. By 1980, several Interpretations of Statement No. 13 and seven new statements had been issued in an attempt to achieve the original goal of in-

---

[2]For an interesting analysis of these problems, see Richard Dieter, "Is Lessee Accounting Working?" *CPA Journal* (August 1979), pp. 13-19.

creased lease capitalization. In May 1980, the FASB issued an integrated revision of Statement No. 13 and its amendments and interpretations.[3] Since that time, additional standards (FASB Statement Nos. 91 and 98) and Technical Bulletins have been issued to further clarify accounting and reporting for leases.

Nature of Leases

Leases vary widely in their contractual provisions. Variables include cancellation provisions and penalties, lease term, bargain renewal and purchase options, economic life of assets, residual asset values, minimum lease payments, interest rates implicit in the lease agreement, and the degree of risk assumed by the lessee, including payments of certain costs such as maintenance, insurance, and taxes. These and other relevant facts must be considered in determining the appropriate accounting treatment of a lease.

The many variables affecting lease capitalization have been given precise definitions which must be understood in order to account for the various types of leases found in practice. Each of these variables is defined and briefly discussed below.

Cancellation Provisions

Some leases may be termed as **noncancellable**, meaning that these lease contracts are cancellable only upon the outcome of some remote contingency or that the cancellation provisions and penalties of these leases are so costly to the lessee that, in all likelihood, cancellation will not occur. Only noncancellable leases are subject to capitalization.

Lease Term

An important variable in lease agreements is the lease term; that is, the time period from the beginning to the end of the lease. The **inception of the lease** is defined as the date of the lease agreement, or date of an earlier written commitment if all the principal provisions have been negotiated. The **beginning of the lease term** occurs when the lease agreement takes effect, i.e., when the leased property is transferred to the lessee.

The date of the beginning of the lease term may coincide with the date of the inception of the lease. In many cases, however, a considerable amount of time may elapse between the inception date and the beginning of the lease term. For example, property may be constructed by the lessor to the lessee's specifications following the execution of a written agreement specifying all the major provisions for leasing the property to the lessee when the construction is complete. The inception of the lease is the date of the agreement to construct the property, but the beginning of the lease

---

[3]*Statement of Financial Accounting Standards No. 13*, "Accounting for Leases" (Stamford: Financial Accounting Standards Board, 1976), as amended and interpreted through May 1980.

term is after the construction is completed and the property is turned over to the lessee.

The **end of the lease term** is the end of the fixed noncancellable period of the lease plus all periods, if any, covered by bargain renewal options, or other provisions that, at the inception of the lease strongly indicate that the lease will be renewed.[4] If a bargain purchase option, as defined in the next section, is included in the lease contract, the lease term includes any renewal periods preceding the date of the bargain purchase option. In no case does the lease term extend beyond the date of a bargain purchase option.

Bargain Purchase Option

Leases often include a provision giving the lessee the right to purchase leased property at some future date. A definite purchase or option price may be specified, although in some cases the price is expressed as the fair market value at the date the option is exercised. If the specified option price is expected to be considerably less than the fair market value at the date the purchase option may be exercised, a bargain purchase option is indicated.

Residual Value

The market value of the leased property at the end of the lease term is referred to as its residual value. In some leases, the lease term extends over the entire **economic life of the asset**, or the period in which the asset continues to be productive, and there is little if any residual value. In other leases, the lease term is shorter, and a residual value does exist. If the lessee can purchase the asset at the end of the lease term at a materially reduced price from its residual value, a bargain purchase option is present and it can be assumed that the lessee would exercise the option and purchase the asset.

Some lease contracts require the lessee, or a designated third party, to guarantee a minimum residual value. If the market value at the end of the lease term falls below the guaranteed residual value, the lessee or third party must pay the difference. This provision protects the lessor from loss due to unexpected declines in the market value of the asset. For example, assume a piece of equipment is expected to have a $25,000 residual value at the end of the lease term, and the lessee guarantees that amount. However, at the end of the lease term, the residual value is only $15,000. The lessee is obligated to pay the $10,000 differential to the lessor so that the lessor is in effect guaranteed the full amount of the residual value that was

---

[4]In some lease situations, such as sale-leasebacks, the lessee lends the lessor money to finance the lease or acts as a guarantor for third-party financing. As long as these financial arrangements are in place, the lease-term extends through ordinary renewal option periods. Thus, the lease term for a 10-year lease, with a 10-year ordinary renewal and a 20 year loan on the leased property from the lessee to the lessor, would be 20 years. *Statement of Financial Accounting Standards No. 98*, "Accounting for Leases: . . . Definition of Lease Term" (Norwalk: Financial Accounting Standards Board, 1988), par. 22a.

estimated at the beginning of the lease. The lessee or the third party may buy the property for the $25,000 guaranteed amount, but the terms do not require the purchase. As will be demonstrated later in the chapter, a guarantee of residual value by a third party requires lessees to account for leases differently than would be true if the lessee were making the guarantee.

If there is no bargain purchase option or guarantee of the residual value, the lessor reacquires the property and may offer to renew the lease, lease the asset to another lessee, or sell the property. The actual amount of the residual value is unknown until the end of the lease term; however, it must be estimated at the inception of the lease. The residual value under these circumstances is referred to as the unguaranteed residual value.

Minimum Lease Payments

The rental payments required over the lease term plus any amount to be paid for the residual value either through a bargain purchase option or a guarantee of the residual value are referred to as the minimum lease payments. If these payments are all made by the lessee, the minimum lease payments are the same for the lessee and the lessor. However, if a third party guarantees the residual value, the lessee would not include the guarantee as part of the minimum lease payments, but the lessor would.

Rental payments sometimes include charges for such items as insurance, maintenance, and taxes incurred for the leased property. These are referred to as executory costs, and are not included as part of the minimum lease payments. If the lessor includes a charge for profit on these costs, the profit is also considered an executory cost.

To illustrate the computation of minimum lease payments, assume that Dorney Leasing Co. leases road equipment for 3 years at $3,000 per month. Included in the rental payment is $500 per month for executory costs to insure and maintain the equipment. At the end of the 3-year period, Dorney is guaranteed a residual value of $10,000 by the lessee.

Minimum lease payments:
Rental payments exclusive of executory costs ($2,500 × 36)	$ 90,000
Guaranteed residual value	10,000
Total minimum lease payments	$100,000

Because the minimum lease payments are to be made in future periods, the present value of these payments is needed to account for capitalized leases. Two different discount rates must be considered in computing the present value of minimum lease payments: the lessee's incremental borrowing rate and the implicit interest rate. The incremental borrowing rate is the rate at which the lessee could borrow the amount of money necessary to purchase the leased asset, taking into consideration the lessee's financial situation and the current conditions in the marketplace. The implicit interest rate is that rate which would discount the minimum lease payments to the fair market value of the asset at the inception of the lease. The lessor uses the implicit interest rate in determining the present value of the minimum lease payments. The lessee, however, uses either the implicit rate or the incremental borrowing rate, whichever is lower. If the lessee does not know the implicit rate, the incremental borrowing rate is used.

To illustrate using the Dorney Leasing Co. example, assume that the $3,000 rental payments to Dorney are made at the beginning of each month, the implicit interest rate in the lease contract is 12% per year, and the lessee's incremental borrowing rate is 14%. Assuming the lessee knows the implicit rate, both the lessor and lessee would discount the minimum lease payments using the 12% rate. The present value of the $100,000 minimum lease payments would be:

Present value of 36 payments of $2,500 ($3,000 less executory costs of $500) at 1% interest (12% annual interest divided by 12 months per year):

$$PV_n = R(PVAF_{\overline{n-1}|i} + 1)$$
$$PV_n = \$2,500\ (29.4086^* + 1) \qquad\qquad \$76,022$$

Present value of $10,000 guaranteed residual value at the end of 3 years at 12% annual interest:

$$PV = A(PVF_{\overline{n}|i})$$
$$PV = \$10,000\ (.7118^{**}) \qquad\qquad\qquad \underline{7,118}$$

Present value of minimum lease payments $\qquad\qquad \underline{\underline{\$83,140}}$

*From Table IV
**From Table II

The present value of $83,140 would be the selling price or fair market value of the asset at the inception of the lease. The use of present value formulas and tables in discounting minimum lease payments is illustrated later in the chapter.

Lease Classification Criteria

As indicated earlier, FASB Statement No. 13 identified criteria to determine whether a lease is merely a rental contract, an operating lease, or is in substance a purchase of property, a capital lease. In considering this issue, the FASB was concerned with the fact that, under the APB pronouncements, leases were often reported differently by the lessee and the lessor. The Board felt that in most cases, there should be consistent treatment between the two parties; i.e., if the lessee treated the agreement as a purchase of property, the lessor should treat it as a sale of property. For this reason, the Board specified four criteria that apply to both the lessee and the lessor, any one of which would identify the lease agreement as a purchase and sale of property, or in other words, a capital lease. Two additional criteria were specified for lessors, both of which must be met before the lease can be treated as a sale by the lessor. The lease classification criteria and their applicability to lessees and lessors are summarized in Exhibit 21-1.

Exhibit 21-1   Lease Classification Criteria

> **General criteria applicable to both the lessee and the lessor:**
> 1. The lease transfers ownership of the property to the lessee by the end of the lease term.
> 2. The lease contains a bargain purchase option.
> 3. The lease term is equal to 75% or more of the estimated economic life of the leased property.
> 4. The present value of the minimum lease payments, excluding that portion representing executory costs, equals or exceeds 90% of the fair market value of the property.
>
> **Additional criteria applicable to lessors:**
> 5. Collectibility of the minimum lease payments is reasonably predictable.
> 6. No important uncertainties surround the amount of unreimbursable costs yet to be incurred by the lessor.
>
> **Lessee:** Capital lease if any one of criteria 1, 2, 3, or 4 is met.
>
> **Lessor:** Capital lease if any one of criteria 1, 2, 3, or 4 is met *and* both 5 and 6 are met.

Classification Criteria—Lessee and Lessor

The four general criteria that apply to all leases for both the lessee and lessor relate to transfer of ownership, bargain purchase options, economic life, and fair market value. The **transfer of ownership** criterion is met if the lease agreement includes a clause that transfers full ownership of the property to the lessee by the end of the lease term. Of all the classification criteria, transfer of ownership is the most objective and, therefore, the easiest to apply.

The second general criterion is met if the lease contains a **bargain purchase option** that makes it reasonably assured that the property will be purchased by the lessee at some future date. This criterion is more difficult to apply than the first criterion because the future fair market value of the leased property must be estimated at the inception of the lease and compared with the purchase option price to determine if a bargain purchase is indeed indicated.

The third criterion relates to the **economic life** of the asset. This criterion is met if the lease term is equal to 75% or more of the estimated economic life of the leased property. As defined earlier, the lease term includes renewal periods if renewal seems assured. This criterion is difficult to apply objectively because of the uncertainty of an asset's economic life. It can also be easily manipulated to achieve whatever result is desired. An exception to the economic life criterion was made for certain used property. The FASB recognized that used property may be leased near the end of the property's economic life, and this criterion would result in classifying all such leases as capital leases. The Board provided that this criterion would not be applicable to leases occurring in the last 25% of the leased property's economic life. It should also be recognized that this criterion cannot apply to land leases, since land has an unlimited life.

The fourth general criterion focuses on the **fair market value** of the property in relation to the provisions of the lease. This criterion is met if, at the beginning of the lease term, the present value of the minimum lease payments equals or exceeds 90% of the fair market value of the leased asset. This criterion was intended to be the key factor in determining the existence of a capital lease. If the lessee is obligated to pay, in present value terms, almost all of the fair market value of the leased property, the lease is in substance a purchase of the property. But the application of this criterion has also been difficult and subject to manipulation by lessees and lessors. The key variable in this criterion is the discounted minimum lease payments.

Since larger minimum lease payments cause the fair market value criteria to be met, the use of third parties to guarantee residual values has led to a lack of consistency between lessees and lessors in many lease arrangements. Many lessors want to report the lease as a sale and thus recognize income at the inception of the lease. However, lessees generally want to report the lease as a rental contract and gain the advantage of off-balance-sheet financing. Since third-party guarantees are considered minimum lease payments to the lessor but not to the lessee, a careful structuring of the lease terms can allow both parties to achieve their goals.

This variable, more than any other, has been used in lease arrangements to avoid the intent of the FASB to achieve increased consistency in reporting. In fact, a new industry of third-party financing has arisen to take advantage of this difference in defining minimum lease payments between the lessee and the lessor. This phenomenon will be illustrated later in the chapter.

The rate used to discount the future minimum lease payments is critical in determining whether the fair market value criterion is met. The lower the discount rate used, the higher the present value of the minimum lease payments and the greater the likelihood that the fair market value criterion of 90% will be met. As explained earlier in the chapter, the FASB specified that the lessor should use the implicit interest rate of the lease agreement, including consideration of residual values. The lessee also uses the lessor's implicit interest rate if it is known and if it is lower than the lessee's incremental borrowing rate. If the lessee cannot determine the lessor's implicit interest rate, the lessee must use its incremental borrowing rate.

Because incremental borrowing rates are often higher than the implicit interest rates, and because lessees do not generally want to capitalize leases, many lessees use the borrowing rate and do not attempt to estimate the implicit rate. If there is no residual value, the lessee can usually determine the implicit rate because the market value of the leased asset is usually known. If a residual value exists, however, the lessee must obtain knowledge of these values from the lessor.

The use of different discount rates between lessees and lessors is another cause of inconsistent accounting treatment between lessees and lessors.

Additional Classification Criteria—Lessor

In addition to meeting one of the four general criteria, a lease must meet two additional criteria in order to be classified by the lessor as a capital lease.[5] As indicated in Exhibit 21-1, the first of the two lessor-specific criteria relates to **collectibility**. Collection of the minimum lease payments, either from the lessee or a third party guarantor, must be reasonably predictable.

The second additional criterion requires **substantial completion** of performance by the lessor. This means that any unreimbursable costs yet to be incurred by the lessor under the terms of the lease are known or can be reasonably estimated. This criterion is to be applied at the inception of the lease or at the date the leased asset is acquired by the lessor, if acquisition occurs after the inception date. If the leased asset is constructed by the lessor, the criterion is applied at the later of the inception date or the date construction is completed.

Application of General Lease Classification Criteria

To illustrate the application of the classification criteria specified in FASB Statement No. 13, four different leasing situations are presented in Exhibit 21-2. A summary analysis of each lease is also presented in the exhibit. Following is a brief explanation of the analysis for each of the four leases.

Lease #1 will be treated as an operating lease by the lessee but as a capital lease by the lessor. Since the lessee does not know the implicit rate of the lessor, the incremental borrowing rate is used to test for criteria 4. The incremental borrowing rate is higher than the implicit rate, and the present value of the minimum lease payments is less than 90% of the fair market value of the property; thus criteria 4 is not met for the lessee. The lessor will use the implicit rate, and criteria 4 is met.

Lease #2 will be treated as a capital lease by both the lessee and the lessor, because title passes to the lessee at the end of the lease term. Because there is a third-party guaranteed residual value, the minimum lease payments are higher for the lessor than the lessee, and criteria 4 is met by the lessor but not by the lessee. Thus, if title had not passed, Lease #2 would be treated as an operating lease by the lessee but a capital lease by the lessor. Since title passes to the lessee, the economic life of the lease will be used as the amortization period.

Lease #3 will be treated as a capital lease by the lessee, but as an operating lease by the lessor. The difference is caused by the lease failing to meet the lessor criteria. The bargain purchase option meets criteria 2 and, since the lessee knows the implicit rate, both the lessee and lessor computations meet criteria 4. Because of the bargain purchase option, the economic life of the lease will be used as the amortization period.

Lease #4 will be treated as an operating lease by both the lessee and the lessor. The lease is a cancellable lease, and even though title passes to the lessee at the end of the lease, it would be classified as a rental agreement.

---

[5]*Statement of Financial Accounting Standards No. 13*, par. 8. If the lease involves real estate, these criteria are replaced by a criterion that requires a transfer of title at the end of the lease term. *Statement of Financial Accounting Standards No. 98*, par. 22c.

Exhibit 21-2 Application of FASB Statement No. 13 Criteria to Lease Situations

Lease provisions	Lease #1	Lease #2	Lease #3	Lease #4
Cancellable	No	No	No	Yes
Title passes to lessee	No	Yes	No	Yes
Bargain purchase option	No	No	Yes	No
Lease term	10 years	10 years	8 years	10 years
Economic life of asset	14 years	15 years	13 years	12 years
Present value of minimum lease payments as a percentage of fair market value—incremental borrowing rate	80%	79%	95%	76%
Present value of minimum lease payments as a percentage of fair market value—implicit rate	92%	91%	92%	82%
Lessee knows implicit rate	No	No	Yes	Yes
Unguaranteed residual value	Yes	No	No	No
Residual value guaranteed by third party	No	Yes	No	No
Present value of minimum lease payments exclusive of third-party guaranteed residual value as a percentage of fair market value—implicit rate	92%	80%	92%	82%
Rental payments collectible and lessor costs certain	Yes	Yes	No	Yes
Analysis of Leases:				
Lessee				
Treat as capital lease	No	Yes	Yes	No
Criteria met	None	1	2 and 4	must be non-
Use incremental borrowing rate	NA	Yes	No	cancellable
Amortization period	NA	15 years	13 years	
Lessor				
Treat as capital lease	Yes	Yes	No	No
First four criteria met	4	1 and 4	2 and 4	must be non-
Lessor criteria met	Yes	Yes	No	cancellable

Accounting For Leases—Lessee

All leases as viewed by the lessee may be divided into two types: operating leases and capital leases. If a lease meets any one of the four classification criteria discussed previously, it is treated as a capital lease. Otherwise, it is accounted for as an operating lease.

Accounting for operating leases involves the recognition of rent expense over the term of the lease. The leased property is not reported as an asset on the lessee's balance sheet nor is a liability recognized for the obligation to make future payments for use of the property. Information concerning the lease is limited to disclosure in notes to the financial statements. Accounting for a capital lease essentially requires the lessee to report on the balance sheet the present value of the future lease payments, both as an asset and a liability. The asset is depreciated as though it had been purchased by the lessee. The liability is accounted for in the same manner as would be a mortgage on the property. The difference in the impact of these two methods on the financial statements is frequently significant.

Accounting for Operating Leases—Lessee

Operating leases are considered to be simple rental agreements with debits being made to an expense account as the payments are made. For example, assume the lease terms for manufacturing equipment were $40,000 a year on a year-to-year basis. The entry to record the payment for a year's rent would be as follows:

Rent Expense	40,000	
Cash		40,000

Rent payments are frequently made in advance. In this event, if the lease period does not coincide with the lessee's fiscal year, or if the lessee prepares interim reports, a prepaid rent account would be required to record the unexpired portion of rent at the end of the accounting period involved. The prepaid rent account should be adjusted at the end of each period.

Operating Leases with Varying Rental Payments

Some operating leases specify rental terms that provide for varying rental payments over the lease term. Most commonly, these types of agreements call for lower initial payments and scheduled rent increases later in the life of the lease. They may even provide an inducement to prospective lessees in the form of a "rent holiday" (free rent). In some cases, however, the lease may provide for higher initial rentals. FASB Statement No. 13 requires that when rental payments vary over the lease term, rental expense be recognized on a straight-line basis "unless another systematic and rational basis is more representative of the time pattern in which use benefit is derived from the leased property, in which case that basis shall be used."[6]

When recording rent expense under these agreements, differences between the actual payments and the debit to expense would be reported as Rent Payable or Prepaid Rent, depending on whether the payments were accelerating or declining. For example, assume the terms of the lease for an aircraft by International Airlines provide for payments of $150,000 a year for the first 2 years of the lease and $250,000 for the next 3 years. The total lease payments for the 5 years would be $1,050,000, or $210,000 a year on a straight-line basis. The required entries in the first 2 years would be as follows:

Rent Expense	210,000	
Cash		150,000
Rent Payable		60,000

The entries for each of the last 3 years would be as follows:

Rent Expense	210,000	
Rent Payable	40,000	
Cash		250,000

The portion of Rent Payable due in the subsequent year would be classified as a current liability.

---

[6]*Ibid.*, par. 15.

<table>
<tr><td>

**Accounting for
Capital Leases—
Lessee**

</td><td>

Capital leases are considered to be more like a purchase of property than a rental. Consequently, accounting for capital leases by lessees requires entries similar to those required for the purchase of an asset with long-term credit terms. The amount to be recorded as an asset and as a liability is the present value of the future minimum lease payments as previously defined. The discount rates used by lessees to record capital leases are the same as those used to apply the classification criteria previously discussed, i.e., the lower of the implicit interest rate (if known) and the incremental borrowing rate. The minimum lease payments consist of the total rental payments, bargain purchase options, and lessee-guaranteed residual values.

</td></tr>
</table>

An important exception to the use of the present value of future minimum lease payments as a basis for recording a capital lease was included by the FASB in Statement No. 13 as follows:

> However, if the amount so determined exceeds the fair value of the leased property at the inception of the lease, the amount recorded as the asset and obligation shall be the fair value.[7]

This means that if the leased asset has a determinable sales price, the present value of the future minimum lease payments should be compared with that price. If the sales price is lower, it should be used as the capitalized value of the lease, and an implicit interest rate would have to be computed using the sales price as the capitalized value of the asset.

Illustrative Entries for Capital Leases

Assume that Marshall Corporation leases equipment from Universal Leasing Company with the following terms:

Lease period: 5 years, beginning January 1, 1992. Noncancellable.
Rental amount: $65,000 per year payable annually in advance;
                 includes $5,000 to cover executory costs.
Estimated economic life of equipment: 5 years.
Expected residual value of equipment at end of lease period: None.

Because the rental payments are payable in advance, the formula to find the present value of the lease is the annuity-due formula described in Chapter 6. Assuming the Marshall Corporation's incremental borrowing rate and the implicit interest rate on the lease are both 10%, the present value for the lease would be $250,194 computed as follows:[8]

$$PV_n = R(PVAF_{\overline{n-1}|i} + 1)$$
$$PV_n = \$60,000 \ (\text{Table IV}_{\overline{4}|10\%} + 1)$$
$$PV_n = \$60,000 \ (3.1699 + 1)$$
$$PV_n = \$250,194$$

[7]*Ibid.*, par. 10.

[8]All computations of present value in this chapter will be rounded to the nearest dollar. This will require some adjustment at times to the final figures in the tables to balance the amounts.

The journal entries to record the lease at the beginning of the lease term would be as follows:

```
1992
Jan. 1  Leased Equipment . . . . . . . . . . . . . . . . . . . . . . . . .    250,194
           Obligations Under Capital Leases . . . . . . . . . . .              250,194⁹
           To record the lease.

        Lease Expense . . . . . . . . . . . . . . . . . . . . . . . . . . .      5,000
        Obligations Under Capital Leases . . . . . . . . . . . .     60,000
           Cash . . . . . . . . . . . . . . . . . . . . . . . . . . . . . . . . . . .            65,000
           To record the first lease payment.
```

The asset value is amortized in accordance with the lessee's normal method of depreciation. The amortization period to be used depends on which of the criteria was used to qualify the lease as a capital lease. If the lease qualified under either of the first two criteria, ownership transfer or bargain purchase option, the economic life of the asset should be used. If the lease qualified under either of the last two criteria, economic life or investment recovery, and the lease term is shorter than the estimated life of the asset, the lease term should be used for amortization purposes. In the preceding example, the lease qualifies under the third criterion and presumably the fourth since the lessor would not lease the asset over its entire economic life if the present value of the lease payments were less than the fair market value of the asset at the inception of the lease. The liability should be reduced each period so as to produce a constant rate of interest expense on the remaining balance of the obligation. The lessee's incremental borrowing rate, or the lessor's implicit rate if lower, is the constant interest rate for the lessee under the provisions of FASB Statement No. 13. Table 1 shows how the $60,000 payments (excluding executory costs) would be allocated between payment on the obligation and interest expense. To simplify the schedule, it is assumed that all lease payments after the first payment are made on December 31 of each year. If the payments were made in January, an accrual of interest at December 31 would be required.

Table 1   **Schedule of Lease Payments [Five-Year Lease, $60,000 Annual Payments (Net of Executory Costs) 10% Interest]**

		Lease Payment			
Date	Description	Amount	Interest Expense*	Principal	Lease Obligation
1- 1-92	Initial balance				$250,194
1- 1-92	Payment	$ 60,000		$60,000	190,194
12-31-92	Payment	60,000	$19,019	40,981	149,213
12-31-93	Payment	60,000	14,921	45,079	104,134
12-31-94	Payment	60,000	10,413	49,587	54,547
12-31-95	Payment	60,000	5,453	54,547	0
		$300,000	$49,806	$250,194	

*Preceding lease obligation × 10%.

⁹It is also possible to record the liability at the gross amount of the payments ($300,000) and offset it with a discount account—Discount on Lease Contract. The net method is more common in accounting for leases by the lessee and will be used in this chapter.

If the normal company depreciation policy for this type of equipment is straight-line, the required entry at December 31, 1992, for amortization of the asset would be as follows:

```
1992
Dec. 31  Amortization Expense on Leased Equipment .....   50,039
             Accumulated Amortization on Leased
                Equipment..............................              50,039
         Computation:
         $250,194 ÷ 5 = $50,039
```

Similar entries would be made for each of the remaining 4 years. Although the credit could be made directly to the asset account, the use of a contra asset account provides the necessary disclosure information about the original lease value and accumulated amortization to date.

Another entry is required at December 31, 1992, to record the second lease payment, including a prepayment of next year's executory costs. As indicated in Table 1, the interest expense for 1992 would be computed by multiplying the incremental borrowing rate of 10% by the initial present value of the obligation less the immediate $60,000 first payment, or ($250,194 − $60,000) × .10 = $19,019.

```
1992
Dec. 31  Prepaid Executory Costs ....................    5,000
         Obligations Under Capital Leases ............   40,981
         Interest Expense ...........................   19,019
            Cash.......................................            65,000
```

Because of the assumption that all lease payments after the first payment are made on December 31, the portion of each payment that represents executory costs must be recorded as a prepayment and charged to lease expense in the following year.

The December 31, 1992, balance sheet of Marshall Corporation would include information concerning the leased equipment and related obligation as illustrated below:

Marshall Corporation
Balance Sheet (Partial)
December 31, 1992

Assets		Liabilities	
Current assets:		Current liabilities:	
Prepaid executory costs— leased equipment..................	$ 5,000	Obligations under capital leases, current portion	$ 45,079
Land, buildings, and equipment:		Noncurrent liabilities:	
Leased equipment	$250,194	Obligations under capital leases, exclusive of	
Less accumulated amortization	50,039	$45,079 included in current liabilities...................	$104,134
Net value	$200,155		

Note that the principal portion of the December 31, 1993, payment is reported as a current liability.[10]

The income statement would include the amortization on leased property of $50,039, interest expense of $19,019, and executory costs of $5,000 as expenses for the period. The total expense of $74,058 exceeds the $65,000 rental payment made in the first year. As the amount of interest expense declines each period, the total expense will be reduced and, for the last 2 years, will be less than the $65,000 payments (Table 2). The total amount debited to expense over the life of the lease will, of course, be the same regardless of whether the lease is accounted for as an operating lease or as a capital lease. If a declining-balance method of amortization is used, the difference in the early years between the expense and the payment would be even larger. In addition to this statement disclosure, a note to the financial statements would be necessary to explain the terms of the lease and future rental payments in more detail.

Table 2   Schedule of Expenses Recognized—Capital and Operating Leases Compared

	Expenses Recognized—Capital Lease				Expenses Recognized—Operating Lease	Difference
Year	Interest	Executory Costs	Amorti-zation	Total		
1992	$19,019	$ 5,000	$ 50,039	$ 74,058	$ 65,000	$9,058
1993	14,921	5,000	50,039	69,960	65,000	4,960
1994	10,413	5,000	50,039	65,452	65,000	452
1995	5,453	5,000	50,039	60,492	65,000	(4,508)
1996	—	5,000	50,038	55,038	65,000	(9,962)
	$49,806	$25,000	$250,194	$325,000	$325,000	$ 0

If in this example, the fair market value of the leased asset had been less than $250,194, the exception discussed previously would be applied, and the lower fair market value would be used for the capitalized value of the lease. For example, assume the fair market value, or sales price, of the leased asset is $242,250. By using the present value tables and the method illustrated in Chapter 6, the implicit interest rate of the lease can be computed as being approximately 12%. A table similar to Table 1 could then be constructed using $242,250 as the initial balance and 12% as the interest rate. For complex lease situations involving something other than equal annual lease payments, computation of the implicit rate of interest must be

---

[10]There have been some theoretical arguments advanced against this method of allocating lease obligations between current and noncurrent liabilities. See Robert J. Swierenga, "When Current is Noncurrent and Vice Versa," *Accounting Review* (January 1984), pp. 123-130. Professor Swierenga identifies two methods of making the allocation: the "change in present value" (CPV) approach that is used in the example, and the "present value of the next year's payment" (PVNYP) approach that allocates a larger portion of the liability to the current category. A later study shows that the CPV method is almost universally followed in practice. A. W. Richardson, "The Measurement of the Current Portion of Long-Term Lease Obligations—Some Evidence from Practice," *Accounting Review* (October 1985), pp. 744-752. While there is theoretical support for both positions, this text uses CPV in chapter examples and problem materials.

done from the present value formulas themselves. This computation is facilitated by use of a computer.

Accounting for Lease with Bargain Purchase Option

Frequently, the lessee is given the option of purchasing the property at some future date at a bargain price. As discussed previously, the present value of the bargain purchase option should be included in the capitalized value of the lease. Assume in the preceding example that there was a bargain purchase option of $75,000 exercisable after 5 years, and the economic life of the equipment was expected to be 10 years. The other lease terms remain the same. The present value of the minimum lease payments would be increased by the present value of the bargain purchase amount of $75,000 or $46,568 computed as follows:

$$PV = A(PVF_{\overline{n}|i})$$
$$PV = \$75,000(\text{Table II}_{\overline{5}|10\%})$$
$$PV = \$75,000 \ (.6209)$$
$$PV = \$46,568$$

The total present value of the lease is $296,762 ($250,194 + $46,568). This amount will be used to record the initial asset and liability. The asset balance of $296,762 will be amortized over the asset life of 10 years because of the existence of the bargain purchase option, which makes the transaction in reality a sale. The liability balance will be reduced as shown in Table 3 at the top of page 940.

At the date of exercising the option, the net balance in the asset account, Leased Equipment, and its related accumulated amortization account would be transferred to the regular equipment account. The entries at the exercise of the option would be as follows:

Obligations Under Capital Leases	68,183	
Interest Expense	6,817	
Cash		75,000
To record exercise of bargain purchase option.		

Equipment	148,381	
Accumulated Amortization on Leased Equipment	148,381	
Leased Equipment		296,762
To transfer remaining balance in leased asset account		
to equipment account.		

Computation:
Accumulated amortization:
  One-half amortized after 5 years of a 10-year life: $296,762 ÷ 2 = $148,381

Table 3   Schedule of Lease Payments
[Five-Year Lease with Bargain Purchase Option of $75,000 after Five Years,
$60,000 Annual Payments (Net of Executory Costs) 10% Interest]

		Lease Payment			
Date	Description	Amount	Interest Expense	Principal	Lease Obligation
1- 1-92	Initial balance				$296,762
1- 1-92	Payment	$60,000		$60,000	236,762
12-31-92	Payment	60,000	$23,676	36,324	200,438
12-31-93	Payment	60,000	20,044	39,956	160,482
12-31-94	Payment	60,000	16,048	43,952	116,530
12-31-95	Payment	60,000	11,653	48,347	68,183
12-31-96	Payment	75,000	6,817	68,183	0
		$375,000	$78,238	$296,762	

If the equipment is not purchased and the lease is permitted to lapse, a loss in the amount of the net remaining balance in the asset account, less any remaining liabilities, would have to be recognized by the following entry:

Loss from Failure to Exercise Bargain Purchase Option	73,381	
Obligations Under Capital Leases	68,183	
Interest Expense	6,817	
Accumulated Amortization on Leased Equipment	148,381	
Leased Equipment		296,762

Accounting for Lease with Lessee Guaranteed Residual Value

If the lease terms require the lessee to guarantee a residual value, the lessee treats the guarantee as a bargain purchase option and includes the present value of the guaranty as part of the capitalized value of the lease. At the expiration of the lease term, the amount of the guaranty will be reported as a liability under the lease. If the lessee is required to pay the guaranteed amount, the liability will be reduced accordingly. If only part of the guaranteed amount is paid, the difference can be reflected as an adjustment to the current lease expense.

Accounting for Purchase of Asset During Lease Term

When a lease does not provide for a transfer of ownership or a purchase option, it is still possible that a lessee may purchase leased property during the term of the lease. Usually the purchase price will differ from the recorded lease obligation at the purchase date. The FASB issued Interpretation No. 26 to cover this situation. The Board decided that no gain or loss should be recorded on the purchase, but the difference between the purchase price and the obligation still on the books should be charged or credited to the acquired asset's carrying value.[11]

[11]FASB Interpretation No. 26, "Accounting for Purchase of a Leased Asset by the Lessee during the Term of the Lease" (Stamford: Financial Accounting Standards Board, 1978), par. 5.

To illustrate, assume that on December 31, 1994, rather than making the lease payment due on that date the lessee purchased the leased property described on page 936 for $120,000. At that date, the remaining liability recorded on the lessee's books is $114,547 ($104,134 + $10,413), and the net book value of the recorded leased asset is $100,077, the original capitalized value of $250,194 less $150,117 amortization ($50,039 × 3). The entry to record the purchase on the lessee's books would be as follows:

Interest Expense	10,413	
Obligations Under Capital Leases	104,134	
Equipment	105,530	
Accumulated Amortization on Leased Equipment	150,117	
Leased Equipment		250,194
Cash		120,000

The purchased equipment is capitalized at $105,530, which is the book value of the leased asset, $100,077, plus $5,453, the excess of the purchase price over the carrying value of the lease obligation ($120,000 − $114,547).

Accounting For Leases—Lessor

The lessor in a lease transaction gives up the physical possession of the property to the lessee. If the transfer of the property is considered temporary in nature, the lessor will continue to carry the leased asset as an owned asset on the balance sheet, and the revenue from the lease will be reported as it is earned. Depreciation of the leased asset will be matched against the revenue. This type of lease is described as an **operating lease** and is similar to the operating lease described for the lessee. However, if a lease has terms that make the transaction similar in substance to a sale or a permanent transfer of the asset to the lessee, the lessor should no longer report the asset as though it were owned, but should reflect the transfer to the lessee.

As indicated on page 930, if a lease meets one of the four criteria that apply to both lessees and lessors, plus both of the lessor conditions, collectibility and substantial completion, it is classified by the lessor as a capital lease and recorded as either a direct financing lease or a sales-type lease. Direct financing leases involve a lessor who is primarily engaged in financial activities, such as a bank or finance company. The lessor views the lease as an investment. The revenue generated by this type of lease is interest revenue. Sales-type leases, on the other hand, involve manufacturers or dealers who use leases as a means of facilitating the marketing of their products. Thus, there are really two different types of revenue generated by this type of lease: (1) an immediate profit or loss which is the difference between the cost of the property being leased and its sales price, or fair value, at the inception of the lease, and (2) interest revenue to compensate for the deferred payment provisions.

For either an operating, direct financing, or sales type lease, a lessor may incur certain costs, referred to as initial direct costs, in connection with obtaining the lease. These costs include:[12]

1. Costs to originate a lease that result directly from and are essential to acquire that lease and would not have been incurred if that leasing transaction had not occurred.

2. Certain costs directly related to the following specified activities performed by the lessor for that lease: evaluating the prospective lessee's financial condition; evaluating and recording guarantees, collateral, and other security arrangements; negotiating lease terms; preparing and processing lease documents; and closing the transaction.

Initial direct costs are accounted for differently depending on which of the three types of leases is involved. Exhibit 21-3 summarizes the accounting treatment of initial direct costs. These costs will be discussed further as each type of lease is presented.

Exhibit 21-3	**Accounting for Initial Direct Costs**

Type of Lease	Accounting Treatment of Costs
Operating	Recorded as asset and amortized over lease term.
Direct financing	Recorded as asset and amortized over lease term with unearned income so as to produce a constant rate of return on the net investment in the lease.
Sales-type	Immediately recognized as reduction in manufacturer's or dealer's profit.

Accounting for Operating Leases— Lessor

Accounting for operating leases for the lessor is very similar to that described for the lessee. The lessor recognizes revenue as the payments are received. If there are significant variations in the payment terms, entries will be necessary to reflect a straight-line pattern of revenue recognition. Initial direct costs incurred in connection with an operating lease are deferred and amortized on a straight-line basis over the term of the lease, thus matching them against rent revenue.

To illustrate accounting for an operating lease on the lessor's books, assume that the equipment leased for 5 years by Marshall for $65,000 a year including executory costs of $5,000 per year had a cost of $400,000 to the lessor. Initial direct costs of $15,000 were incurred to obtain the lease. The equipment has an estimated life of 10 years, with no residual value. Assuming no purchase or renewal options or guarantees by the lessee, the lease does not meet any of the four general classification criteria and would be treated as an operating lease. The entries to record the payment of the initial direct costs and the receipt of rent would be as follows:

[12]*Statement of Financial Accounting Standards No. 91*, "Accounting for Non-refundable Fees and Costs Associated with Originating or Acquiring Loans and Initial Direct Costs of Leases" (Stamford: Financial Accounting Standards Board, 1986), par. 24.

```
1992
Jan. 1  Deferred Initial Direct Costs ...................    15,000
            Cash ........................................              15,000
      1  Cash .........................................    65,000
            Rent Revenue .............................              65,000
```

Assuming the lessor depreciates the equipment on a straight-line basis over its expected life of 10 years and amortizes the initial direct costs on a straight-line basis over the 5-year lease term, the depreciation and amortization entries at the end of the first year would be:

```
1992
Dec. 31  Amortization of Initial Direct Costs .............     3,000
             Deferred Initial Direct Costs .................              3,000
     31  Depreciation Expense on Leased Equipment.....    40,000
             Accumulated Depreciation on Leased
             Equipment.................................              40,000
```

Executory costs would be recognized as expense when paid or accrued. If the rental period and the lessor's fiscal year do not coincide, or if the lessor prepares interim reports, an adjustment would be required to record the unearned rent revenue at the end of the accounting period. Amortization of the initial direct costs would be adjusted to reflect a partial year.

Accounting for Direct Financing Leases

Accounting for direct financing leases for lessors is very similar to that used for capital leases by lessees, but with the entries reversed to provide for interest revenue rather than interest expense and reduction of an asset rather than a liability. In practice, the receivable is usually recorded by the lessor at the gross amount of the lease payments with an offsetting valuation account for the unearned interest revenue, rather than at a net figure as is true for lessee accounting. Unearned interest revenue is computed as the difference between the gross investment (total lease payments) and the fair market value, or cost, of the leased asset. The difference between the gross investment and the unearned interest revenue is the net lease investment.

Illustrative Entries for Direct Financing Leases

Referring to the lessee example on page 935, assume that the cost of the equipment to the Universal Leasing Company was the same as its fair market value, $250,194, and the purchase by the lessor had been entered into the account Equipment Purchased for Lease. The entry to record the initial lease would be as follows:

```
Lease Payments Receivable ........................    300,000
    Equipment Purchased for Lease...................              250,194
    Unearned Interest Revenue ......................               49,806
```

The first payment would be recorded as follows:

Cash	65,000	
Lease Payment Receivable		60,000
Executory Costs Payable		5,000

The lessor is paying the executory costs, but charging them to the lessee. The lessor can record the receipt of the executory costs by debiting cash and crediting Executory Costs Payable. As the lessor pays the costs, the liability account is decreased. The lessor is serving as a conduit for these costs to the lessee, and will have an expense only if the lessee fails to make the payments.

Interest revenue will be recognized over the lease term as shown in Table 4.

Table 4   **Schedule of Lease Receipts and Interest Revenue**
[Five-Year Lease, $60,000 Annual Payments (Exclusive of Executory Costs) 10% Interest]

Date	Description	Interest Revenue*	Lease Receipt	Lease Payments Receivable	Unearned Interest Revenue
1-1-92	Initial balance			$300,000	$49,806
1-1-92	Receipt		$60,000	240,000	49,806
12-31-92	Receipt	$19,019	60,000	180,000	30,787
12-31-93	Receipt	14,921	60,000	120,000	15,866
12-31-94	Receipt	10,413	60,000	60,000	5,453
12-31-95	Receipt	5,453	60,000	0	0
		$49,806	$300,000		

*Preceding lease payment receivable less unearned interest revenue × 10%.

At the end of the first year, the following entries would be made to record receipt of the second lease payment and to recognize interest revenue for 1992.

1992			
Dec. 31	Cash..	65,000	
	Minimum Lease Payments Receivable.........		60,000
	Executory Costs Payable		5,000
31	Unearned Interest Revenue	19,019	
	Interest Revenue		19,019

The balance sheet of the lessor at December 31, 1992, will report the lease receivable less the unearned interest revenue as follows:

Universal Leasing Company
Balance Sheet (Partial)
December 31, 1992

Assets		
Current assets:		
Lease payments receivable.....................	$ 60,000	
Less unearned interest revenue	14,921	$45,079
Noncurrent assets:		
Lease payments receivable (exclusive of $60,000		
included in current assets)	$120,000	
Less unearned interest revenue	15,866	104,134

If a direct financing lease contains a bargain purchase option, the amount of the option is added to the receivable and the interest included in the option amount is added to the unearned interest revenue account. The periodic entries and computations are made as though the bargain purchase amount was an additional rental payment.

Lessor Accounting for Direct Financing Lease with Residual Value

If leased property is expected to have residual value, the gross amount of the expected residual value is added to the receivable account. It does not matter whether the residual value is guaranteed or unguaranteed. If guaranteed, it is treated in the accounts exactly like a bargain purchase option. If unguaranteed, the lessor is expected to have an asset equal in value to the residual amount at the end of the lease term. The estimated residual value is added to the asset account and the interest attributable to the unguaranteed residual value is added to the unearned interest revenue account.

To illustrate the recording of residual values, assume the same facts for the Universal Leasing Company as the example on pages 939-940 except that the asset has a residual value at the end of the 5-year lease term of $75,000 (either guaranteed or unguaranteed) rather than a bargain purchase option. Assume the cost of the equipment to the Universal Leasing Company was again the same as its fair market value, $296,762.

The entries to record this lease and the first payment would be as follows:

Lease Payments Receivable	375,000	
Equipment Purchased for Lease....................		296,762
Unearned Interest Revenue		78,238
Cash	65,000	
Lease Payments Receivable		60,000
Executory Costs Payable		5,000

The difference between the Lease Payments Receivable of $375,000 and the cost of the equipment leased of $296,762 is the Unearned Interest Revenue of $78,238. The amortization of the unearned interest revenue would be identical to the interest expense computation illustrated in Table 3 for the lessee.

At the end of the first year the lessor would make the following entries:

Cash	65,000	
Lease Payments Receivable		60,000
Executory Costs Payable		5,000
Unearned Interest Revenue	23,676	
Interest Revenue		23,676

At the end of the lease term, the lessor would make the following entry to record the recovery of the leased asset assuming the residual value was the same as originally estimated:

Equipment	75,000	
Unearned Interest Revenue	6,817	
Lease Payments Receivable		75,000
Interest Revenue		6,817

The unguaranteed residual value should be reviewed at least annually by the lessor and adjusted for any decline that is considered other than temporary. Such adjustment is accounted for as a change in estimate.

Initial Direct Costs Related to Direct Financing Lease

If the lessor incurs any initial direct costs in conjunction with a direct financing lease, those costs are recorded as a separate asset and amortized, along with unearned interest revenue, so as to produce a constant rate of return on the net lease investment.[13] Because the net lease investment is increased by the initial direct costs, a lower implicit interest rate will be used to compute the amortization. In effect, this treatment spreads the initial costs over the lease term and reduces the amount of interest revenue that would otherwise be recognized.

To illustrate, assume that the lessor in the preceding example incurred initial direct costs of $15,000. The entry relating to these costs would be as follows:

Deferred Initial Direct Costs	15,000	
Cash		15,000
To record payment of initial direct costs.		

Accounting for Sales-Type Leases

Accounting for sales-type leases adds one more dimension to the lessor's revenue, an immediate profit or loss arising from the difference between the sales price of the leased property and the lessor's cost to manufacture or purchase the asset. If there is no difference between the sales price and the lessor's cost, the lease is not a sales-type lease. The lessor also will recognize interest revenue over the lease term for the difference between the sales price and the gross amount of the minimum lease payments. The three values that must be identified to determine these income elements, therefore, can be summarized as follows:

1. The minimum lease payments as defined previously for the lessee, i.e., rental payments over the lease term net of any executory costs included therein plus the amount to be paid under a bargain purchase option or guarantee of the residual value.
2. The fair market value of the asset.

[13]*Statement of Financial Accounting Standards No. 98*, "Accounting for Leases—Initial Direct Costs of Direct Financing Leases" (Norwalk: Financial Accounting Standards Board, 1988) par. 22i.

3. The cost or carrying value of the asset to the lessor increased by any initial direct costs to lease the asset.

The manufacturer's or dealer's profit is the difference between the fair market value of the asset [(2) above] and the cost or carrying value of the asset to the lessor [(3) above]. If cost exceeds the fair market value, a loss will be reported. The difference between the gross rentals [(1) above] and the fair market value of the asset [(2) above] is interest revenue and arises because of the time delay in paying for the asset as described by the lease terms. The relationship between these three values can be demonstrated as follows:

(1) Minimum lease payments _____

                                                Financial Revenue
                                                   (Interest)

(2) Fair market value of leased asset _____

                                                Manufacturer's or
                                                Dealer's Profit (Loss)

(3) Cost or carrying value of leased asset to lessor _____

To illustrate this type of lease, assume the lessor for the equipment described on page 935 is American Manufacturing Company rather than Universal Leasing. The fair market value of the equipment is equal to its present value (the future lease payments discounted at 10%), or $250,194. Assume the equipment cost American $160,000 and initial direct costs of $15,000 were incurred. The three values and their related revenue amounts would be as follows:

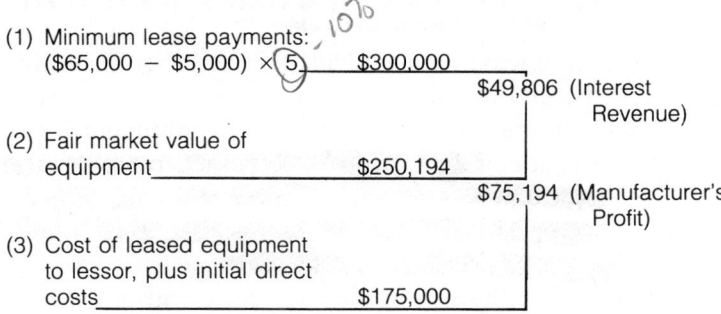

(1) Minimum lease payments:
    ($65,000 − $5,000) × 5 $300,000
                                          $49,806 (Interest
                                                   Revenue)

(2) Fair market value of
    equipment $250,194
                                          $75,194 (Manufacturer's
                                                    Profit)

(3) Cost of leased equipment
    to lessor, plus initial direct
    costs $175,000

Illustrative Entries for Sales-Type Leases

The interest revenue ($49,806) is the same as that illustrated for a direct financing lease on page 943, and it is recognized over the lease term by the same entries and according to Table 4. The manufacturer's profit is recognized as revenue immediately in the current period by including the fair market value of the asset as a sale and debiting the cost of the equipment carried in the finished goods inventory to Cost of Goods Sold. The initial direct costs previously deferred are recognized as an expense immediately by increasing Cost of Goods Sold by the amount expended for these costs.

This reduces the amount of immediate profit to be recognized. The reimbursement of executory costs is treated in the same way as illustrated for direct financing leases.

The entries to record this information on American Manufacturing Company's books at the beginning of the lease term would be as follows:

```
1992
Jan. 1  Lease Payments Receivable..................    300,000
        Cost of Goods Sold ........................    175,000
            Finished Goods Inventory ...................            160,000
            Unearned Interest Revenue ................             49,806
            Sales .....................................            250,194
            Deferred Initial Direct Costs ................            15,000
1992
Jan. 1  Cash ......................................     65,000
            Lease Payments Receivable.................             60,000
            Executory Costs Payable...................              5,000
```

The 1992 income statement would include the sales and cost of sales amounts yielding the manufacturer's profit of $75,194, and interest revenue of $19,019. A note to the statements would describe in more detail the nature of the lease and its terms.

In the preceding example, it was implied that the fair market value of the leased equipment was determined by discounting the minimum lease payments at a rate of 10%. Normally, however, the fair market value is known, and the minimum lease payments are set at an amount that will yield the desired rate of return to the lessor.

Accounting for Sales-Type Lease with Bargain Purchase Option or Guarantee of Residual Value

If the lease terms provide for the lessor to receive a lump-sum payment at the end of the lease term in the form of a bargain purchase option or a guarantee of residual value, the minimum lease payments include these amounts. The receivable is thus increased by the gross amount of the future payment, the unearned interest revenue account is increased by the interest on the end-of-lease payment, and sales are increased by the present value of the additional amount.

To illustrate a sales-type lease with a bargain purchase option, assume American Manufacturing was the lessor on the lease described on page 939 and Table 3. The initial entries when either a bargain purchase option or a guarantee of residual value of $75,000 is payable at the end of the 5-year lease term would be as follows:

```
1992
Jan. 1  Lease Payments Receivable..................    375,000
        Cost of Goods Sold ........................    175,000
            Finished Goods Inventory ...................            160,000
            Unearned Interest Revenue ................             78,238
            Sales .....................................            296,762
            Deferred Initial Direct Costs ................            15,000
```

```
1992
Jan. 1  Cash .......................................      65,000
            Lease Payments Receivable................               60,000
            Executory Costs Payable...................                5,000
```

Because the lease now includes a bargain purchase option, Sales increases by $46,568 (present value of the bargain purchase amount) over the amount recorded on page 948. The manufacturer's profit is also increased by this amount, and the difference between the $75,000 gross payment and the $46,568 increase in sales is recorded as a $28,432 increase in Unearned Interest Revenue.

Accounting for Sales-Type Leases with Unguaranteed Residual Value

When a sales-type lease does not contain a bargain purchase option or a guaranteed residual value, but the economic life of the leased asset exceeds the lease term, the residual value of the property will remain with the lessor. As indicated earlier, this is called an unguaranteed residual value. The only difference between accounting for an unguaranteed residual value and a guaranteed residual value or bargain purchase option is that rather than increasing Sales by the present value of the residual value as was illustrated above, the present value is *deducted* from the cost of the leased equipment. The entry to record the initial lease described above with an unguaranteed residual value, therefore, would be as follows:

```
1992
Jan. 1  Lease Payments Receivable..................     375,000
        Cost of Goods Sold .........................     128,432
            Finished Goods Inventory ...................             160,000
            Unearned Interest Revenue ................              78,238
            Sales .....................................             250,194
            Deferred Initial Direct Costs ...............              15,000
```

Note that the gross profit on the transaction is the same regardless of whether the residual value is guaranteed or unguaranteed as demonstrated below:

	Guaranteed Residual Value	Unguaranteed Residual Value
Sales	$296,762	$250,194
Cost of goods sold	175,000	128,432
Gross Profit	$121,762	$121,762

Sale of Asset During Lease Term   If the lessor sells an asset to the lessee during the lease term, a gain or loss is recognized on the difference between the receivable balance, after deducting any unearned finance charges, and the selling price of the asset. Thus, if the leased asset described in Table 4, page 944, is sold on December 31, 1994, for $140,000 before the $60,000 rental payment is made, a gain of $25,453 would be reported. ($140,000 − $120,000 + $15,866 − $10,413). The following journal entry would be made to record the sale.

Unearned Interest Revenue	15,866	
Cash	140,000	
Interest Revenue		10,413
Lease Payments Receivable		120,000
Gain on Sale of Leased Asset		25,453

It should be remembered that although the lessor does recognize a gain or loss on the sale, the lessee defers any gain or loss in the value placed on the purchased asset.

Disclosure Requirements For Leases

The Financial Accounting Standards Board has established specific disclosure requirements for all leases, regardless of whether they are classified as operating or capital leases. The required information supplements the disclosures required in the financial statements, and is usually included in a single note to the financial statements. For example, General Mills, Inc. reports information concerning its operating leases in Note Fourteen (see Appendix A at the end of the text).

The following information is required for all leases that have initial or remaining noncancellable lease terms in excess of one year:

Lessee

1. Gross amount of assets recorded as capital leases and related accumulated depreciation as of the date of each balance sheet presented by major classes according to the nature of the function.

2. Future minimum rental payments required as of the date of the latest balance sheet presented in the aggregate and for each of the five succeeding fiscal years. These payments should be separated between operating and capital leases. For capital leases, executory costs should be excluded.

3. Rental expense for each period for which an income statement is presented. Additional information concerning minimum rentals, contingent rentals, and sublease rentals is required for the same periods.

4. A general description of the lease contract including information about restrictions on such items as dividends, additional debt, and further leasing.

5. For capital leases the amount of imputed interest necessary to reduce the lease payments to present value.

A note accompanying the 1988 financial statements of Vulcan Materials Company reproduced on the next page, illustrates the required lessee disclosures for both operating and capital leases.

Lessor

1. The following components of the net investment in sales-type and direct financing leases as of the date of each balance sheet presented:

    (a) future minimum lease payments receivable with separate deductions for amounts representing executory costs and the accumulated allowance for uncollectible minimum lease payments receivable.

    (b) unguaranteed residual values accruing to the benefit of the lessor.

    (c) unearned revenue.

    (d) for direct financing leases only, initial direct costs.

2. Future minimum lease payments to be received for each of the five succeeding fiscal years as of the date of the latest balance sheet presented, including information on contingent rentals.

3. The amount of unearned revenue included in income to offset initial direct costs for each year for which an income statement is prepared.

4. For operating leases, the cost of assets leased to others and the accumulated depreciation related to these assets.

5. A general description of the lessor's leasing arrangements.

An example of lessor disclosure of sales-type direct financing and leveraged leases for Sun Company, Inc. is shown on page 952.

Exhibit 21-4   Vulcan Materials Company

---

6. Leases

Total rental expense of nonmineral leases, exclusive of rental payments made under leases of one month or less, is summarized as follows (in thousands of dollars):

	1988	1987	1986
Minimum rentals	$4,202	$4,399	$2,310
Contingent rentals (based principally on usage)	4,764	1,643	1,571
Total	$8,966	$6,042	$3,881

Future minimum lease payments under all leases with initial or remaining noncancellable lease terms in excess of one year, exclusive of mineral leases, at December 31, 1988 are as follows (in thousands of dollars):

Year Ending December 31	Capital Leases	Operating Leases
1989	$ 929	$ 6,008
1990	930	4,903
1991	924	4,436
1992	2,219	3,831
1993	838	3,408
Remaining years	2,473	12,689
Total minimum lease payments	8,313	$35,275
Less: Amount representing interest	2,500	
Present value of net minimum lease payments (including long-term obligations of $5,418)	$5,813	

Lease agreements frequently include renewal options and require that the company pay for utilities, taxes, insurance and maintenance expense. Options to purchase are also included in some lease agreements, particularly capital leases.

Loan agreements with insurance companies include covenants with regard to annual rentals on leases with a remaining term of more than five years, excluding capitalized leases and leases of mineral properties, office space and data processing equipment. For the company and its subsidiaries which are restricted under the loan agreements, those annual rentals may not exceed 3% of consolidated net worth, determined as of the end of the preceding year.

Exhibit 21-5   Sun Company, Inc.

---

8) Long-Term Receivables and Investments

	December 31	
	1987	1986
	(Millions of Dollars)	
Investment in:		
Leveraged leases	**$ 85**	$ 79
Direct financing and sales-type leases	**276***	271
	361	350
Accounts and notes receivable	**114**	68
Investments in and advances to affiliated companies	**27**	34
Other investments, at cost	**19**	12
	$521	$ 464

*Includes $129 million used with $26 million of other assets as collateral for $87 million recourse long-term debt—leasing notes associated with sales-type leases (Note 12).

Sun, as lessor, has entered into leveraged, direct financing and sales-type leases of a wide variety of equipment including ocean-going vessels, aircraft, mining equipment, railroad rolling stock and various other transportation and manufacturing equipment. The components of Sun's investment in these leases at December 31, 1987 and 1986 are set forth below (in millions of dollars):

December 31	Leveraged Leases		Direct Financing and Sales-Type Leases	
	1987	1986	**1987**	1986
Minimum rentals receivable	**$ 63***	$ 50*	**$ 401**	$ 417
Estimated unguaranteed residual value of leased assets	**61**	61	**60**	55
Unearned and deferred income	**(39)**	(32)	**(185)**	(201)
Investment in leases	**85**	79	**$ 276**	$ 271
Deferred taxes arising from leveraged leases	**(60)**	(54)		
Net investment in leveraged leases	**$ 25**	$ 25		

*Net of principal of and interest on related nonrecourse financing aggregating $234 and $247 million in 1987 and 1986, respectively.

The following is a schedule of minimum rentals receivable by years at December 31, 1987 (in millions of dollars):

Year ending December 31:	Leveraged Leases	Direct Financing and Sales-Type Leases
1988	$ 4	$ 51
1989	5	49
1990	5	48
1991	4	46
1992	6	37
Later years	39	170
	$63	$ 401

Dividends received from affiliated companies amounted to $15, $9 and $10 million in 1987, 1986 and 1985, respectively. Earnings employed in the business at December 31, 1987 include $12 million of undistributed earnings of affiliated companies.

Accounting For Sale-Leaseback Transactions

A common type of lease arrangement is referred to as a sale-leaseback transaction. Typical of this type of lease is an arrangement whereby one party sells the property to a second party, and then the first party leases the property back. Thus, the seller becomes a seller-lessee and the purchaser a purchaser-lessor. The accounting problem raised by this transaction is whether the seller-lessee should recognize the profit from the original sale immediately, or defer it over the lease term. The Financial Accounting Standards Board has recommended that if the initial sale produces a profit, it should be deferred and amortized in proportion to the amortization of the leased asset if it is a capital lease or in proportion to the rental payments if it is an operating lease. If the transaction produces a loss because the fair market value of the asset is less than the undepreciated cost, an immediate loss should be recognized.[14]

To illustrate the accounting treatment for a sale at a gain, assume that on January 1, 1992, Hopkins Inc. sells a warehouse having a carrying value of $7,500,000 on its books to Ashcroft Co. for $9,500,000 and immediately leases the warehouse back. The following conditions are established to govern the transaction.

1. The land value is less than 25% of the total fair market value.

2. The term of the lease is 10 years, noncancellable. A down payment of $2,000,000 is required plus equal rental payments of $1,071,082 at the beginning of each year.

3. The warehouse has a fair value of $9,500,000 on January 1, 1992, and an estimated economic life of 20 years. Straight-line depreciation is used on all owned assets.

4. The lessee has an option to renew the lease for $100,000 per year for 10 years, the rest of its economic life. Title passes at the end of the lease term.

5. The terms of the lease meet the requirements of FASB Statement No. 66 for sales of real estate.

Analysis of this lease shows that it qualifies as a capital lease under both the third and fourth criteria. Since the land value is less than 25% of the total fair value, the lease is treated as a single depreciable unit. It meets the third "75% of economic life" criterion because of the bargain renewal option which makes both the lease term and the economic life of the warehouse 20 years. It meets the fourth "90% of fair market value" criterion, because the present value of the rental payments is equal to the fair market value of the warehouse ($9,500,000).[15] The entries for recording the sale and the leaseback on both the seller-lessee's books and the purchaser-lessor's books for the first year of the lease are as shown on page 954.

---

[14]*Ibid.*, par. 32-33.

[15]*Computation of present value of lease:*
(a) Present value of 10 years' rentals:
   $R(PVAF_{\overline{10-1}|10\%} + 1) = \$1,071,082 \times 6.7590 = \$7,239,443$.
(b) Present value of second 10 years' rentals:
   $R(PVAF_{\overline{10-1}|10\%} + 1) = \$100,000 \times 6.7590 = \$675,900$, present value at beginning of second 10 years' lease period.
   Present value at beginning of lease, 10 years earlier:
   $A(PVF_{\overline{10}|10\%}) = \$675,900 \times .3855 = \$260,559$.
(c) Total present value, $7,239,443 + $260,559 + 2,000,000 down payment = $9,500,000 (rounded).

Hopkins Inc. (Seller-Lessee)

1992
Jan. 1 Cash 9,500,000
        Warehouse   7,500,000
        Unearned Profit on Sale-Leaseback   2,000,000
        Original sale of warehouse.

    1 Leased Warehouse 9,500,000
        Obligations Under Capital Lease   6,428,918
        Cash   3,071,082
        Lease of warehouse, including first payment.

Dec. 31 Amortization Expense on Leased Warehouse ...   475,000
        Accumulated Amortization on Leased
        Warehouse   475,000
        Amortization of warehouse over 20 year
        period ($9,500,000 ÷ 20).

   31 Interest Expense   642,892
     Obligations Under Capital Lease   428,190
        Cash   1,071,082
        Second lease payment. Interest expense:
        $6,428,918 × 10% = $642,892.

   31 Unearned Profit on Sale-Leaseback   100,000
     Revenue Earned on Sale-Leaseback   100,000
        Recognition of revenue over 20-year life in
        proportion to the amortization of
        the leased asset.

Ashcroft Co. (Purchaser-Lessor)

1992
Jan. 1 Warehouse 9,500,000
     Cash   9,500,000
        Purchase of warehouse.

    1 Cash 3,071,082
     Lease Payments Receivable 10,639,738
        Warehouse   9,500,000
        Unearned Interest Revenue   4,210,820
        Direct financing leaseback to Hopkins Inc.
        Total receivable = (10 × $1,071,082) +
        (10 × $100,000) = $11,710,820;
        $11,710,820 − $1,071,082 =
        $10,639,738.

Dec. 31 Cash 1,071,082
     Unearned Interest Revenue..................   642,892
        Lease Payments Receivable   1,071,082
        Interest Revenue   642,892
        Receipt of second lease payment. See
        computations under Hopkins Inc.

The amortization entries and recognition of the deferred gain on the sale for Hopkins Inc. would be the same each year for the 20-year lease term. The interest expense and interest revenue amounts would decline each year using the interest method of computation.

If the lease had not met the criteria, it would have been recorded as an operating lease. The gain on the sale would have been deferred and recognized in proportion to the lease payments. If the initial sale had been at a loss, an immediate recognition of the loss would have been recorded.

**Concluding
Comment**

This chapter has discussed the basics of accounting for leases. Special considerations applicable to real estate leases and leveraged leases are discussed in Appendix A and B, respectively, at the end of the chapter. Leveraged leases are often very complex arrangements involving third parties who assist in financing lease transactions.

As indicated at the beginning of this chapter, the Board is convinced that more leases should be reported as capital items. Until such time as companies respond, more statements and interpretations from the Board on leases can be expected. In the meantime, full disclosure of lease arrangements seems to be a minimum requirement to meet the spirit of Statement No. 13.

Appendix A

Criteria For Classifying
Real Estate Leases

A significant percentage of leases involve real estate. If the real estate includes both nondepreciable land and depreciable buildings and equipment, special problems arise in determining how the lease should be treated. Some of the criteria used to evaluate a lease do not apply to leases of land. The FASB treated leases of real estate separately in Statement No. 13. This treatment is summarized in the flowchart on page 957 and in subsequent sections.

Leases Involving Land Only or Buildings Only

Leases of land should be classified as capital leases only if title to the land is certain to be transferred in the future or if transfer is reasonably assured based on the existence of a bargain purchase option. Thus, only the first two general criteria listed on page 930 apply to the leasing of land. The third criterion cannot apply because land has an unlimited life. The fourth criterion was not felt to be applicable, because under this criterion no actual ownership transfer is contemplated. Ownership transfer is an important consideration, because the residual value of the land to the lessor would be material since there is no depreciation on land. Leases of land that meet either of the first two general criteria are capitalized on the lessee's books and treated as sales-type or direct financing leases on the lessor's books if both of the lessor's supplementary criteria are also met. Other leases of land are treated as operating leases.

No special problems arise when a lease involves only the building. The four general criteria for lessees and lessors and the two additional criteria for the lessor can be applied as discussed previously.

Leases Involving Land and Buildings

If a lease involves both land and buildings, the accounting treatment depends on which criteria the lease meets. If it meets either of the first two criteria, both the land and the buildings should be classified as capital leases using the fair market values of the properties to allocate the capital value between them. The building lease portion will be amortized by the lessee and the land will be left at originally allocated cost. The lessor treats the lease as a sale of a single unit and accounts for it as a sales-type or direct financing lease depending on the circumstances.

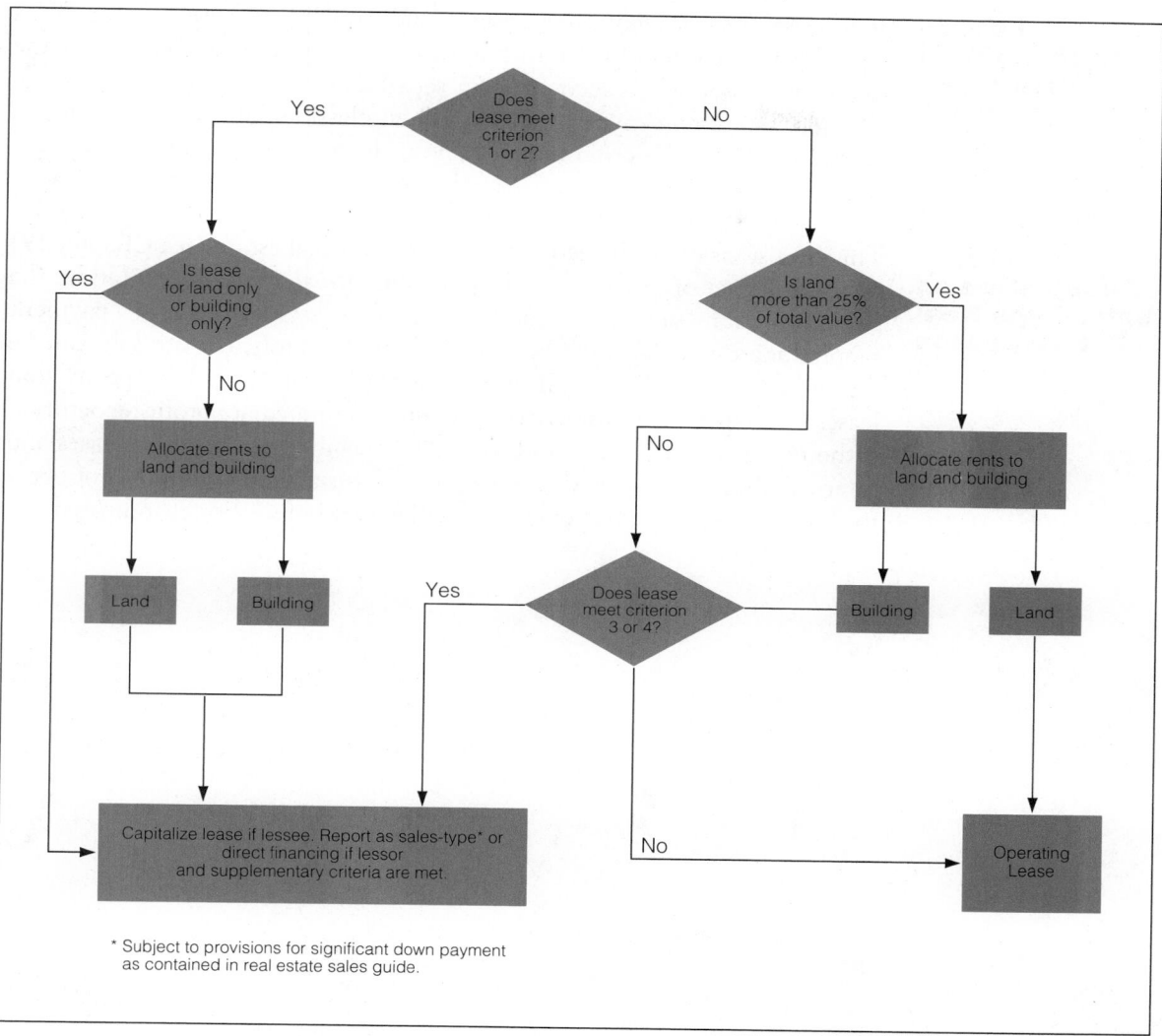

* Subject to provisions for significant down payment
as contained in real estate sales guide.

If the lease does not meet either of the first two criteria, then additional tests are prescribed by the FASB to determine if any portion should be capitalized. If the land fair market value is less than 25% of the total fair value, the lease is treated as a single unit and the third and fourth criteria are applied to the single unit to determine if it should be treated as an operating or a capital lease. The estimated economic life of the building is used in applying the third classification criterion. If the fair market value of the land exceeds 25% of the total fair value, the land portion is treated as an operating lease and the third and fourth criteria are applied to the building as a separate unit. If the test is met for the building, the building portion is classified as a capital lease; otherwise it is treated as an operating lease.

Leases Involving Real Estate and Equipment

If a lease includes both real estate and equipment, the equipment is considered separately in determining the appropriate classification by the lessee and lessor and is accounted for separately over the term of the lease. The real estate portion of the lease is then classified and accounted for in accordance with the criteria applicable to leases of real estate.

Profit Recognition on Sales-Type Real Estate Leases

The provisions of profit recognition on sales of real estate (see Chapter 19) have an impact on the lessor's classification of real estate leases. Under the guidelines for sales of real estate, a substantial down payment (approximately 25%) must be made before the profit on the sale can be recognized in full. The FASB amended Statement No. 13 to specify that leases that fail to meet the criteria for full and immediate profit recognition if the real estate had been sold should be classified as operating leases and no immediate profit should be recognized. This amendment does not apply to direct financing leases or sales-type leases where a loss is indicated.

Appendix B

Leveraged Leases

As indicated in the chapter, there are several potential economic advantages to a lessor in leasing property to others. A lessor who wishes to maximize its ability to lease often has to obtain outside financing for the investment in leased assets. A popular type of lease that has developed over the past twenty-five years to accommodate this type of situation is the **leveraged lease.** There are generally three parties in a leveraged lease: the **lessee**; the **owner-lessor**, or equity participant; and the **third-party long-term creditor**, or debt participant. Only direct financing leases are treated as leveraged leases.

A leveraged lease generally requires a down payment by the owner-lessor equivalent to 20-30% of the purchase price. The rest of the financing is provided by the debt participant as a nonrecourse loan on the general credit of the lessor. The interest rate charged on the loan is dependent on the credit rating of the owner-lessor. The owner-lessor enters into the lease arrangement with the lessee, receives rental payments, makes required principal and interest payments on the debt, and recognizes the difference as income. No special accounting is required by the lessee. The lessor records the investment in the leveraged lease net of the nonrecourse debt. The interaction of deferred income taxes, rental payments, and debt-related costs can result in complex accounting entries for the lessor. These complexities are not treated in this text.[16]

---

[16]For additional discussion and illustrations concerning leveraged leases, see *Statement of Financial Accounting Standards No. 13,* Appendix E, par. 123.

Key Terms

Bargain renewal options 927
Bargain purchase option 927
Capital leases 924
Direct financing leases 941
Executory costs 928
Guaranteed residual value 927
Implicit interest rate 928
Incremental borrowing rate 928
Initial direct costs 942
Lease 923
Lease term 926

Lessee 923
Lessor 923
Leveraged lease 955
Minimum lease payments 928
Net lease investment 943
Operating leases 933
Residual value 927
Sale-leaseback 952
Sales-type leases 941
Unguaranteed residual value 928

Questions

1. What are the principal advantages to a lessee in leasing rather than purchasing property?
2. What are the principal advantages to a lessor in leasing rather than selling property?
3. Why is the concept of residual value an important one in capital leases?
4. How is the lease term measured?
5. What criteria must be met before a lease can be properly accounted for as a capital lease on the books of the lessee?
6. The third and fourth criteria for classifying a lease as a capital transaction are not as restrictive as originally intended. Explain how each of these criteria can be circumvented.
7. In determining the classification of a lease, a lessor uses the criteria of the lessee plus two additional criteria. What are these additional criteria and why are they included in the classification of leases by lessors?
8. Under what circumstances are the minimum lease payments for the lessee different from that of the lessor?
9. (a) What discount rate is used to determine the present value of a lease by the lessee? (b) by the lessor?
10. What is the basic difference between an operating lease and a capital lease from the viewpoint of the lessee?
11. If an operating lease requires the payment of uneven rental amounts over its life, how should the lessee recognize rental expense?
12. What amount should be recorded as an asset and a liability for capital leases on the books of the lessee?
13. The FASB has identified a situation in which the present value of future minimum payments would not be used as the amount for the initial recording of an asset and liability for lessees under capital leases. Describe this situation and how an interest rate would be calculated for determining interest expense.
14. Why do asset and liability balances for capital leases usually differ after the first year?
15. A capitalized lease should be amortized in accordance with the lessee's normal depreciation policy. What life should be used for lease amortization?
16. The use of the capital lease method for a given lease will always result in a lower net income than the operating lease method. Do you agree? Explain fully.

17. If a lease contains a bargain purchase option, what entries are required on the books of the lessee under each of the following conditions?
    (a) The bargain purchase option is exercised.
    (b) The bargain purchase option is not exercised and no renewal of the lease is made.
    (c) The bargain purchase option is not exercised, but a renewal of the lease is obtained.
18. Distinguish a sales-type lease from a direct financing lease.
19. Under what circumstances would a lessor recognize as interest revenue over the lease term an amount greater than the difference between the gross amount of lease receivables and the cost of the asset to the lessor?
20. Terms of leases may provide for guaranteed residual values by third parties. Why have such agreements been popular in many leasing situations?
21. Unguaranteed residual values may accrue to the lessor at the expiration of the lease. How are these values treated in a sales-type lease?
22. Describe the specific lease disclosure requirements for lessees.
23. What disclosure is required by the FASB for lessors under sales-type and direct financing leases?
24. When should the profit or loss be recognized by the seller-lessee in a sale-leaseback arrangement?
*25. Real estate leases can include land and/or buildings. Explain how the four criteria for determining lease capitalization are applied to the following:
    (a) Leases involving land only.
    (b) Leases involving land and buildings.
    (c) Leases involving buidings only.
**26. What characteristics are unique to a leveraged lease?

*Relates to Appendix A
**Relates to Appendix B

Discussion Cases   **Case 21-1   (How should the lease be recorded?)**

Louise Corporation entered into a lease arrangement with Wilder Leasing Corporation for a certain machine. Wilder's primary business is leasing and it is not a manufacturer or dealer. Louise will lease the machine for a period of 3 years, which is 50% of the machine's economic life. Louise will take possession of the machine at the end of the initial 3-year lease and lease it to another smaller company that does not need the most current version of the machine. Louise does not guarantee any residual value for the machine and will not purchase the machine at the end of the lease term.

Louise's incremental borrowing rate is 10% and the implicit rate in the lease is 8½%. Louise has no way of knowing the implicit rate used by Wilder. Using either rate, the present value of the minimum lease payments is between 90% and 100% of the fair value of the machine at the date of the lease agreement.

Louise has agreed to pay all executory costs directly and no allowance for these costs is included in the lease payments.

Wilder is reasonably certain that Louise will pay all lease payments, and, because Louise has agreed to pay all executory costs, there are no important uncertainties regarding costs to be incurred by Wilder.

(1) With respect to Louise (the lessee) answer the following:
   (a) What type of lease has been entered into? Explain the reason for your answer.
   (b) How should Louise compute the appropriate amount to be recorded for the lease or asset acquired?
   (c) What accounts will be created or affected by this transaction and how will the lease or asset and other costs related to the transaction be matched with earnings?
   (d) What disclosures must Louise make regarding this lease or asset?
(2) With respect to Wilder (the lessor) answer the following:
   (a) What type of leasing arrangement has been entered into? Explain the reason for your answer.
   (b) How should this lease be recorded by Wilder and how are the appropriate amounts determined?
   (c) How should Wilder determine the appropriate amount of earnings to be recognized from each lease payment?
   (d) What disclosures must Wilder make regarding this lease?

(AICPA adapted)

Case 21-2 (Should we buy or lease?)

The Meeker Machine and Die Company has learned that a sophisticated piece of computer-operated machinery is available to either buy or rent. The machinery will result in 3 employees being replaced, and quality of the output has been tested to be superior in every demonstration. There is no doubt that this machinery represents the latest in technology; however, new inventions and research make it difficult to estimate when the machinery will be made obsolete by new technology. The physical life expectancy of the machine is 10 years; however, the estimated economic life is between 2 and 5 years.

Meeker has a debt-to-equity ratio of .75. If the machine is purchased, and the minimum down payment is made, the debt-to-equity ratio will increase to 1.1. The monthly payments if the machine is purchased are 20% lower than the rental payments if it is leased. The incremental borrowing rate for Meeker is 11%. The rate implicit in the lease is 12%. What factors should Meeker consider in deciding how to finance the acquisition of the machine?

Case 21-3 (How should the leases be classified and accounted for?)

On January 1, Toronto Company, a lessee, entered into three noncancellable leases for new equipment, Lease J, Lease K, and Lease L. None of the three leases transfers ownership of the equipment to Toronto at the end of the lease term. For each of the three leases, the present value at the beginning of the lease term of the minimum lease payments, excluding that portion of the payments representing executory costs such as insurance, maintenance, and taxes to be paid by the lessor, including any profit thereon, is 75% of the fair value of the equipment to the lessor at the inception of the lease.

The following information is peculiar to each lease:

(a) Lease J does not contain a bargain purchase option; the lease term is equal to 80% of the estimated economic life of the equipment.

(b) Lease K contains a bargain purchase option; the lease term is equal to 50% of the estimated economic life of the equipment.

(c) Lease L does not contain a bargain purchase option; the lease term is equal to 50% of the estimated economic life of the equipment.

(1) How should Toronto Company classify each of the 3 leases and why? Discuss the rationale for your answer.

(2) What amount, if any, should Toronto record as a liability at the inception of the lease for each of the 3 leases?

(3) Assuming that the minimum lease payments are made on a straight-line basis, how should Toronto record each minimum lease payment for each of the 3 leases?   (AICPA adapted)

Case 21-4 (More leases mean lower profits.)

Ultrasound, Inc. has introduced a new line of equipment that may revolutionize the medical profession. Because of the new technology involved, potential users of the equipment are reluctant to purchase the equipment, but they are willing to enter into a lease arrangement as long as they can classify the lease as an operating lease. The new equipment will replace equipment that Ultrasound has been selling in the past. It is estimated that a 25% loss of actual equipment sales will occur as a result of the leasing policy for the new equipment.

Management must decide how to structure the leases so that the lessees can treat them as operating leases. Some members of management want to structure the leases so that Ultrasound, as lessor, can classify the lease as a sales-type lease and thus avoid a further reduction of income. Others feel they should treat the leases as operating leases and minimize the income tax liability in the short term. They are uncertain, however, as to how the financial statements would be affected under these two different approaches. They also are uncertain as to how leases could be structured to permit the lessee to treat the lease as an operating lease and the lessor to treat it as a sales-type lease. You are asked to respond to their questions.

Exercises   Exercise 21-1 (Criteria for capitalizing leases)

Atwater Manufacturing Co. leases its equipment from Westside Leasing Company. In each of the following cases, assuming none of the other criteria for capitalizing leases is met, determine whether the lease would be a capital lease or an operating lease under FASB Statement No. 13 on leases. Your decision is to be based only on the terms presented, considering each case independently of the others.

(a) At the end of the lease term, the market value of the equipment is expected to be $20,000. Atwater has the option of purchasing it for $5,000.

(b) The fair market value of the equipment is $75,000. The present value of the lease payments is $71,000 (excluding any executory costs).

(c) Ownership of the property automatically passes to Atwater at the end of the lease term.

(d) The economic life of the equipment is 12 years. The lease term is for 9 years.

(e) The lease requires payments of $9,000 per year in advance, plus executory costs of $500 per year. The lease period is for 3 years, and Atwater's incremental borrowing rate is 12%. The fair market value of the equipment is $28,000.

(f) The lease requires payments of $6,000 per year in advance which includes executory costs of $500 per year. The lease period is for 3 years, and Atwater's incremental borrowing rate is 10%. The fair market value of the equipment is $16,650.

Exercise 21-2　(Entries for lease—lessor and lessee)

The Doxey Company purchased a machine on January 1, 1991, for $1,250,000 for the express purpose of leasing it. The machine was expected to have a 7-year life from January 1, 1991, no salvage value, and be depreciated on a straight-line basis. On March 1, 1991, Doxey leased the machine to Mondale Company for $300,000 a year for a 4-year period ending February 28, 1995. Doxey paid a total of $15,000 for maintenance, insurance, and property taxes on the machine for the year ended December 31, 1991. Mondale paid $300,000 to Doxey on March 1, 1991. Doxey retains title to the property and plans to lease it to someone else after the 4-year lease period. Give all the 1991 entries relating to the lease on (a) Doxey Company's books, (b) Mondale Company's books. Assume both sets of books are maintained on the calandar-year basis.　　　　　　　　　　　　　　　　　　　　(AICPA adapted)

Exercise 21-3　(Entries for operating lease—lessee)

Jonas Inc. leases equipment on a 5-year lease. The lease payments are to be made in advance as shown below.

January 1, 1991	$100,000
January 1, 1992	100,000
January 1, 1993	140,000
January 1, 1994	170,000
January 1, 1995	210,000
Total	$720,000

The equipment is to be used evenly over the 5-year period. For each of the 5 years, give the entry that should be made at the time the lease payment is made to allocate the proper share of rent expense to each period. The lease is classified as an operating lease by Jonas Inc.

Exercise 21-4　(Entries for lessee)

Bingham Smelting Company entered into a 15-year noncancellable lease beginning January 1, 1992, for equipment to use in its smelting operations. The term of the lease is the same as the expected economic life of the equipment. Bingham uses straight-line depreciation for all plant assets. The provisions of the lease call for annual payments of $290,000 in advance plus $20,000 per year to cover executory costs, such as taxes and insurance, for the 15-year period of the lease. At the end of the 15 years, the equipment is expected to be scrapped. The incremental borrowing rate of Bingham is 10%. The lessor's computed implicit interest rate is unknown to Bingham.

Record the lease on the books of Bingham and give all the entries necessary to record the lease for its first year plus the entry to record the second lease payment on December 31, 1992. (Round to the nearest dollar.)

Exercise 21-5   (Entries for lease—lessee)

On January 2, 1991, the Jaques Company entered into a noncancellable lease for a new warehouse. The warehouse was built to the Jaques Company's specifications and is in an area where rental to another lessee would be difficult. Rental payments are $300,000 a year for 10 years, payable in advance. The warehouse has an estimated economic life of 20 years. The taxes, maintenance, and insurance are to be paid directly by the Jaques Company, and the title to the warehouse is to be transferred to Jaques at the end of the lease term. Assume the cost of borrowing funds for this type of an asset by Jaques Company is 12%.

(1) Give the entry on Jaques' books that should be made at the inception of the lease.
(2) Give the entries for 1991 and 1992 assuming the second payment and subsequent payments are made on December 31 and assuming double-declining-balance amortization.

▌▌▌ Exercise 21-6   (Schedule of lease payments)

Carter Construction Co. is leasing equipment from Vasquez Inc. The lease calls for payments of $50,000 a year plus $4,000 a year executory costs for 5 years. The first payment is due on January 1, 1992, when the lease is signed, with the other 4 payments due on December 31 of each year. Carter has also been given the option of purchasing the equipment at the end of the lease at a bargain price of $100,000. Carter has an incremental borrowing rate of 10%, the same as the implicit interest rate of Vasquez. Carter has hired you as an accountant and asks for a schedule of its obligations under the lease contract. Prepare a schedule that shows all of the lessee's obligations.

Exercise 21-7   (Entry for purchase by lessee)

The Cordon Enterprise Company leases many of its assets and capitalizes most of the leased assets. At December 31, the company had the following balances on its books in relation to a piece of specialized equipment.

Leased Equipment	$70,000
Accumulated Amortization—Leased Equipment	49,300
Obligation Under Capital Leases	26,000

Amortization has been recorded up to the end of the year, and no accrued interest is involved. At December 31, Cordon decided to purchase the equipment for $32,000, and paid cash to complete the purchase. Give the entry required on Cordon's books to record the purchase.

Exercise 21-8   (Computation of implicit interest rate)

Tueller Leasing leases equipment to Tsoi Manufacturing. The fair market value of the equipment is $473,130. Lease payments, excluding executory costs, are $70,000 per year, payable in advance, for 10 years. What is the implicit rate of interest Tueller Leasing should use to record this capital lease on its books?

Exercise 21-9   (Direct financing lease—lessor)

The Deseret Finance Company purchased a printing press to lease to the Quality Printing Company. The lease was structured so that at the end of the lease period of 15 years Quality would own the printing press. Lease payments required in this lease were $190,000 (excluding executory costs) per year, payable in advance. The cost of the press to Deseret was $1,589,673, which is also its fair market value at the time of the lease.

(1) Why is this a direct financing lease?   *Purchase to lease*
(2) Give the entry to record the lease transaction on the books of Deseret Finance Company.
(3) Give the entry at the end of the first year on Deseret Finance Company's books to recognize interest revenue.

Exercise 21-10   (Direct financing lease with residual value)

The Massachusetts Casualty Insurance Company decides to enter the leasing business. It acquires a specialized packaging machine for $300,000 cash and leases it for a period of 6 years after which the machine is returned to the insurance company for disposition. The expected unguaranteed residual value of the machine is $20,000. The lease terms are arranged so that a return of 12% is earned by the insurance company.

(1) Calculate the annual rent, payable in advance, required to yield the desired return.
(2) Prepare entries for the lessor for the first year of the lease assuming the machine is acquired and the lease is recorded on January 1, 1991. The first lease payment is made on January 1, 1991, and subsequent payments are made each December 31.
(3) Assuming the packaging machine is sold by Massachusetts at the end of the 6 years for $32,000, give the required entry to record the sale.

Exercise 21-11   (Table for direct financing lease—lessor)

The Pioche Savings and Loan Company acquires a piece of specialized hospital equipment for $1,500,000 that it leases on January 1, 1991, to a local hospital for $391,006 per year, payable in advance. Because of rapid technological developments, the equipment is expected to be replaced after 4 years. It is expected that the machine will have a residual value of $200,000 to Pioche Savings at the end of the lease term. The implicit rate of interest in the lease is 10%.

(1) Prepare a 4-year table for Pioche Savings and Loan similar to Table 4 on page 944.
(2) How would the table differ, if the local hospital guaranteed the residual value to Pioche?

Exercise 21-12 (Direct financing lease with residual value)

The Mario Automobile Company leases automobiles under the following terms: A 3-year lease agreement is signed in which the lessor receives annual rental of $4,000 (in advance). At the end of the 3 years, the lessee agrees to make up any deficiency in residual value below $3,500. The cash price of the automobile is $13,251. The implicit interest rate is 12%, which is known to the lessee, and the lessee's incremental borrowing rate is 14%. The lessee estimates the residual value at the end of 3 years to be $4,200 and depreciates its automobiles on a straight-line basis.

(1) Give the entries on the lessee's books required in the first year of the lease including the second payment on April 30, 1992. Assume the lease begins May 1, 1991, the beginning of the lessee's fiscal year.
(2) What balances relative to the lease would appear on the lessee's balance sheet at the end of year 3?
(3) Assume the automobile is sold by the lessee for $3,100. Prepare the entries to record the sale and settlement with the lessor.

Exercise 21-13 (Sales-type lease—lessor)

Salcedo Co. leased equipment to Erickson Inc. on April 1, 1991. The lease is appropriately recorded as a sale by Salcedo. The lease is for an 8-year period ending March 31, 1999. The first of 8 equal annual payments of $175,000 (excluding executory costs) was made on April 1, 1991. The cost of the equipment to Salcedo is $940,000. The equipment has an estimated useful life of 8 years with no residual value expected. Salcedo uses straight-line depreciation and takes a full year's depreciation in the year of purchase. The cash selling price of the equipment is $1,026,900.

(1) Give the entry required to record the lease on Salcedo's books.
(2) How much interest revenue will Salcedo recognize in 1991?

Exercise 21-14 (Sales-type lease—lessor)

The Jacinto Leasing and Manufacturing Company uses leases as a means of financing sales of its equipment. Jacinto leased a machine to Hudson Construction for $22,000 per year, payable in advance, for a 10-year period. The cost of the machine to Jacinto was $108,000. The fair market value at the date of the lease was $120,000. Assume a residual value of zero at the end of the lease.

(1) Give the entry required to record the lease on Jacinto's books.
(2) How much profit will Jacinto recognize initially on the lease, excluding any interest revenue?
(3) How much interest revenue would be recognized in the first year?

Exercise 21-15 (Effect of lease on reported income—lessee and lessor)

On February 20, 1991, Topham, Inc. purchased a machine for $1,200,000 for the purpose of leasing it. The machine is expected to have a 10-year life, no residual value, and is depreciated on the straight-line basis to the nearest month. The machine was leased to Lutts Company on March 1, 1991, for a 4-year period at a monthly rental of $18,000. There is no provision for the renewal of the lease or purchase of the machine by the lessee at the expiration of the lease term. Topham paid $60,000 of commissions associated with negotiating the lease in February 1991.

(1) What expense should Lutts record as a result of the lease transaction for the year ended December 31, 1991? Show supporting computations in good form.
(2) What income or loss before income taxes should Topham record as a result of the lease transaction for the year ended December 31, 1991? Show supporting computations in good form.   (AICPA adapted)

Exercise 21-16   (Lease disclosures—lessee)

The following lease information was obtained by a staff auditor for a client, Kroller, Inc. at December 31, 1992. Indicate how this information should be presented in Kroeller's 2-year comparative financial statements. Include any notes to the statements required to meet generally accepted accounting principles. Lease payments are made on December 31 of each year.

Leased building; minimum lease payments per year; 10 years remaining life	$45,000
Executory costs per year	2,000
Capitalized lease value, 12% interest	343,269
Accumulated amortization of leased building at December 31, 1992	114,423
Amortization expense for 1992	22,885
Obligations under capital leases; balance at December 31, 1992	239,770
Obligations under capital leases; balance at December 31, 1991.	254,259

Exercise 21-17   (Sale-leaseback accounting)

On July 1, 1991, Baker Corporation sold equipment it had recently purchased to an unaffiliated company for $570,000. The equipment had a book value on Baker's books of $450,000 and a remaining life of 6 years. On that same day, Baker leased back the equipment at $135,000 per year, payable in advance, for a 5-year period. Baker's incremental borrowing rate is 10%, and it does not know the lessor's implicit interest rate. What entries are required for Baker to record the transactions involving the equipment during the first full year assuming the second lease payment is made on June 30, 1992? Ignore consideration of the lessee's fiscal year. The lessee uses the double-declining balance method of depreciation for similar assets it owns outright.

*Exercise 21-18   (Entries for real estate lease with residual value—lessee)

Atlantus Corporation leases its land and building from an investment company. The terms of the lease are as follows:

(a) Lease term is 20 years, after which title to the property can be acquired for 25% of the market value at that date. The estimated remaining life of the building is 30 years.
(b) Annual lease payments payable in advance are $250,000 (excluding executory costs). Expected residual value of the property in 20 years is $800,000.
(c) Assume the current market value of the combined land and buildings is

$2,370,945, of which the market value of the land is $350,000. The implicit interest rate of the lease is 10%.

What entries would be required on Atlantus Corporation's books for the first year of the lease? Assume the second lease payment is made on the last day of the first year.

*Relates to Appendix A

*Exercise 21-19 (Lease of real estate—lessee)

Maycomb Industries leases its land and buildings on a 10-year lease from E. L. Kimball. The property includes 10 acres of land that is used for parking and an amusement area. The market value of the leased land is $500,000, and the market value of the leased buildings is $1,200,000. The annual rent for the property payable in advance is $251,516. There is no provision in the lease for Maycomb to purchase the property at the conclusion of the lease. The buildings are estimated to have a 12-year remaining life, and are depreciated on a straight-line basis.

(1) Does the lease of Maycomb Industries qualify as a capital lease? If yes, what criteria apply?
(2) Record the lease on Maycomb's books and give the entries for the first full year of the lease assuming the first payment is made on January 1, 1991, and the second payment is made on December 31, 1991.

*Relates to Appendix A

Problems   ### Problem 21-1 (Entries for capital lease—lessee; lease criteria)

The Miner Company leased a machine on July 1, 1991, under a 10-year lease. The economic life of the machine is estimated to be 15 years. Title to the machine passes to Miner Company at the expiration of the lease and thus the lease is a capital lease. The lease payments are $83,000 per year, including executory costs of $3,000 per year, all payable in advance annually. The incremental borrowing rate of the company is 10% and the lessor's implicit interest rate is unknown. The Miner Company uses the straight-line method of depreciation and uses the calendar year as its fiscal year.

Instructions:

(1) Give all entries on the books of the lessee relating to the lease for 1991.
(2) Assume the lessor retains title to the machine at the expiration of the lease, there is no bargain renewal or purchase option, and that the fair market value of the equipment is $575,000 as of the lease date. Using the criteria for distinguishing between operating and capital leases according to FASB Statement No. 13, what would be the amortization or depreciation expense for 1991?

Problem 21-2 (Operating lease—lessee and lessor)

Calderwood Industries leases a large specialized machine to the Youngstown Company at a total rental of $1,800,000, payable in 5 annual installments in the following declining pattern: 25% for first 2 years, 22% in the third year, and 14% in each of the last 2 years. The lease begins January 1, 1992, with annual renewal for $150,000 available after that time. In addition to the rent, Youngstown is required to pay annual executory costs of $15,000 to cover unusual repairs and insurance. The lease does not qualify as a capital lease for reporting purposes. Calderwood incurred initial direct costs of $15,000 in obtaining the lease. The machine cost Calderwood $2,100,000 to construct and has an estimated life of 10 years with an estimated residual value of $100,000. Calderwood uses the straight-line depreciation method on its equipment. Both companies' fiscal year is the calendar year.

Instructions:

(1) Prepare the journal entries on Calderwood's books for 1992 and 1996 related to the lease.
(2) Prepare the journal entries on Youngtown's books for 1992 and 1996 related to the lease.

Problem 21-3   (Entries for capital lease—lessee)

Aldridge Enterprises has a long standing policy of acquiring company equipment by leasing. Early in 1991, the company entered into a lease for a new milling machine. The lease stipulates that annual payments will be made for 5 years. The payments are to be made in advance on December 31 of each year. At the end of the 5-year period, Aldridge may purchase the machine. Company financial records show the incremental borrowing rate to be less than the implicit interest rate. The estimated economic life of the equipment is 12 years. Aldridge has a calendar year for reporting purposes and uses straight-line depreciation for other equipment. In addition, the following information about the lease is also available.

Original cost of machine	$318,000
Annual lease payments	$55,000
Purchase option price	$25,000
Estimated fair market value of machine after 5 years	$75,000
Incremental borrowing rate	10%
Date of first lease payment	January 1, 1991

Instructions:

(1) Compute the amount to be capitalized as an asset for the lease of the milling machine.
(2) Prepare a table similar to Table 3, page 940, that shows the computation of the interest expense for each period.
(3) Give the journal entries that would be made on Aldridge's books for the first 2 years of the lease.
(4) Assume that the purchase option is exercised at the end of the lease. Give the Aldridge journal entry necessary to record the exercise of the option.

Problem 21-4   (Entries for capital lease—lessee, guaranteed residual value)

For some time, Balster, Inc. has maintained a policy of acquiring company equipment by leasing. On January 1, 1992, Balster entered into a lease with Edgemont Fabricators for a new concrete truck that had a selling price of $265,000. The lease stipulates that annual payments of $52,500 will be made for 6 years. The first lease payment is made on January 1, 1992, and subsequent payments are made on December 31 of each year. At the end of the 6-year period, Balster guarantees a residual value of $45,890. Balster has an incremental borrowing rate of 13%, and the implicit interest rate to Edgemont is 12% after considering the guaranteed residual value. The economic life of the truck is 9 years. Balster uses the calendar year for reporting purposes, and uses straight-line depreciation to depreciate other equipment.

Instructions:

(1) Compute the amount to be capitalized as an asset on the lessee's books for the concrete truck.
(2) Prepare a table showing the reduction of the liability by the annual payments after considering the interest charges. (See Table 1 as an example.)
(3) Give the journal entries that would be made on Balster's books for the first 2 years of the lease.
(4) Assume that the lessor sells the truck for $35,000 at the end of the 6-year period to a third party. Give the Balster journal entries necessary to record the payment to satisfy the residual guaranty and to write off the leased equipment accounts. Write off any remaining liability to lease expense—adjustment.

Problem 21-5   (Accounting for direct financing lease—lessee and lessor)

The Trost Leasing Company buys equipment for leasing to various manufacturing companies. On October 1, 1990, Trost leases a press to the Shumway Shoe Company. The cost of the machine to Trost, which approximated its fair market value on the lease date, was $196,110. The lease payments stipulated in the lease are $33,000 per year in advance for the 10-year period of the lease. The payments include executory costs of $3,000 per year. The expected economic life of the equipment is also 10 years. The title to the equipment remains in the hands of Trost Leasing Company at the end of the lease term, although only nominal residual value is expected at that time. Shumway's incremental borrowing rate is 10% and it uses the straight-line method of depreciation on all owned equipment. Both Shumway and Trost have fiscal years which end September 30, and lease payments are made on September 30.

Instructions:

(1) Prepare the entries to record the lease and the first lease payment on the books of the lessor and lessee assuming the lease meets the criteria of a direct-financing lease for the lessor and a capital lease for the lessee.
(2) Compute the implicit rate of interest of the lessor.
(3) Give all entries required to account for the lease on both the lessee's and lessor's books for the fiscal years 1991, 1992, and 1993 [exclusive of the initial entries required in (1)].

Problem 21-6   (Lease computations—lessee and lessor)

Computer Controls Corporation is in the business of leasing new sophisticated computer systems. As a lessor of computers, Computer Controls purchased a new system on December 31, 1991. The system was delivered the same day (by prior arrangement) to Edwards Investment Company, the lessee. The company accountant revealed the following information relating to the lease transaction:

Cost of system to Computer Controls	$550,000
Estimated useful life and lease term	8 years
Expected residual value (unguaranteed)	$40,000
Computer Controls implicit rate of interest	12%
Edwards' incremental borrowing rate	14%
Date of first lease payment	December 31, 1991

Additional information follows:

(a) At the end of the lease, the system will revert to Computer Controls.
(b) Edwards is aware of Computer Controls rate of implicit interest.
(c) The lease rental consists of equal annual payments.
(d) Computer Controls accounts for leases using the direct financing method. Edwards intends to record the lease as a capital lease. Both the lessee and the lessor are calendar-year corporations and elect to depreciate all assets on the straight-line bases.

Instructions:

(1) Compute the annual rental under the lease. (Round to the nearest dollar.)
(2) Compute the amounts of the lease payments receivable and the unearned interest revenue that Computer Controls should disclose at the inception of the lease.
(3) What total lease expense should Edwards record for the year ended December 31, 1992.

III Problem 21-7   (Sales type lease—lessor)

Aquatran Incorporated uses leases as a method of selling its products. In early 1991, the company completed construction of a passenger ferry for use on the Upper New York Bay between Manhattan and Staten Island. On April 1, 1991, the ferry was leased to the Manhattan Ferry Line on a contract specifying that ownership of the ferry will revert to the lessee at the end of the lease period. Annual lease payments do not include executory costs. Other terms of the agreement are as follows:

Original cost of the ferry	$1,500,000
Fair market value of ferry at lease date	$2,107,102
Lease payments (paid in advance)	$225,000
Estimated residual value	$78,000
Incremental borrowing rate—lessor	10%
Date of first lease payment	April 1, 1991
Lease period	20 years

Instructions:

(1) Compute the amount of financial revenue that will be earned over the

lease term and the manufacturer's profit that will be earned immediately by Aquatran.

(2) Give the entries to record the lease on Aquatran's books. Compute the implicit rate of interest on the lease.

(3) Give the journal entries necessary on Aquatran's books to record the operating of the lease for the first 3 years exclusive of the initial entry. Aquatran's accounting period is the calendar year.

(4) Indicate the balance of each of the following accounts at December 31, 1993:

Unearned Interest Revenue

Lease Payments Receivable

Problem 21-8 (Sales-type lease—Lessor)

Universal Enterprises adopted the policy of leasing as the primary method of selling its products. The company's main product is a small jet airplane that is very popular among corporate executives. Universal constructed such a jet for Executive Transport Services (ETS) at a cost of $8,329,784. Financing of the construction was acccomplished through borrowings at a 13% rate. The terms of the lease provided for annual advance payments of $1,331,225 to be paid over 20 years with the ownership of the airplane transferring to ETS at the end of the lease period. It is estimated that the plane will have a residual value of $800,000 at that date. The lease payments began on October 1, 1992. Universal incurred initial direct costs of $150,000 in finalizing the lease agreement with ETS. The sales price of similar airplanes is $11,136,734.

Instructions:

(1) Compute the amount of manufacturer's profit that will be earned immediately by Universal.

(2) Prepare the journal entries to record the lease on Universal's books at October 1, 1992.

(3) Prepare the journal entries to record the lease for the years 1992-1996 exclusive of the initial entry. Universal's accounting period is the calendar year.

(4) How much revenue did Universal earn from this lease for each of the first 3 years of the lease?

Problem 21-9 (Entries for capital lease—lessee and lessor)

The Alta Corporation entered into an agreement with Snowfire Company to lease equipment for use in its ski manufacturing facility. The lease is appropriately recorded as a purchase by Alta and as a sale by Snowfire. The agreement specifies that lease payments will be made on an annual basis. The cost of the machine is reported as inventory on Snowfire's accounting records. Because of extensive changes in ski manufacturing technology, the machine is not expected to have residual value. Alta uses straight-line depreciation and computes depreciation to the nearest month. After 3 years, Alta purchased the machine from Snowfire.

Annual lease payments will not include executory costs. Other terms of the agreement are as follows:

Machine cost recorded in inventory	$4,700,000
Price at purchase option date	$3,250,000
Lease payments (paid in advance)	$710,000
Contract interest rate	10%
Contract date/first lease payment	October 1, 1991
Date of Alta purchase	October 1, 1994
Lease period	8 years

Instructions: Prepare journal entries on the books of both the lessee and the lessor as follows:

(1) Entries in 1991 to record the first lease payment, and make adjustments necessary at December 31, the end of each company's fiscal year.
(2) All entries required in 1992. The companies do not make reversing entries.
(3) Entry in 1994 to record the sale and purchase assuming no previous entries have been made during the year in connection with the lease.

Problem 21-10   (Accounting for capital lease—lessee and lessor)

The Crosby Equipment Company both leases and sells its equipment to its customers. The most popular line of equipment includes a machine that costs $340,000 to manufacture. The standard lease terms provide for 5 annual payments of $130,000 each (excluding executory costs), with the first payment due when the lease is signed and subsequent payments due on December 31 of each year. The implicit rate of interest in the contract is 10% per year. Dannell Tool Co. leases one of these machines on January 2, 1992. Initial direct cost of $17,000 are incurred by Crosby on January 2, 1992, to obtain the lease. Dannell's incremental borrowing rate is determined to be 12%. The equipment is very specialized, and it is assumed it will have no salvage value after 5 years. Assume the lease qualifies as a capital lease and a sales-type lease for lessee and lessor respectively. Also assume that both the lessee and the lessor are on a calendar-year basis and that the lessee is aware of the lessor's implicit interest rate.

Instructions:

(1) Give all entries required on the books of Dannell Tool Co. to record the lease of equipment from Crosby Equipment Company for the year 1992. The depreciation on owned equipment is computed once a year on the straight-line basis.
(2) Give entries required on the books of Crosby Equipment Company to record the lease of equipment to Dannell Tool Co. for the year 1992.
(3) Prepare the balance sheet section involving lease balances for both the lessee's and lessor's financial statements at December 31, 1992.
(4) Determine the amount of expense Dannell Tool Co. will report relative to the lease for 1992 and the amount of revenue Crosby Equipment Company will report for the same period.

Problem 21-11   (Accounting for lease—lessee and lessor)

Astle Manufacturing Company manufactures and leases a variety of items. On

January 2, 1992, Astle leased a piece of equipment to Haws Industries Co. The lease is for 6 years with an annual amount of $32,000 payable in advance. The equipment has an estimated useful life of 9 years, and was manufactured by Astle at a cost of $120,000. The lease payment includes executory costs of $1,500 per year. It is estimated that the equipment will have a residual value of $60,000 at the end of the 6-year lease term. There is no guarantee by the lessee of this amount, nor is there any provision for purchase or renewal by Haws at the end of the lease term. The equipment has a fair market value at the lease inception of $187,176. The implicit rate of interest in the contract is 10%, the same rate at which Haws Industries Co. can borrow money at its bank. Haws depreciates assets on a double-declining balance basis. All lease payments after the first one are made on December 31 of each year.

Instructions:

(1) Give the entries required on the books of the lessor and lessee to record the incurrence of the lease and its operation for the first year.
(2) Show how the lease would appear on the balance sheet of Astle Manufacturing Company and Haws Industries Co. (if applicable) as of December 31, 1992.
(3) Assume Astle Manufacturing Company sold the equipment at the end of the 6-year lease for $70,000. Give the entry to record the sale assuming all lease entries have been properly made.
(4) Assume that a third party has guaranteed the residual value of $60,000. Give the entry required on the books of the lessor for the first year.

Problem 21-12   (Disclosure requirements—operating leases)

Jaquar Mining and Manufacturing Company leases from Emory Leasing Company three machines under the following terms:

Machine #1   Lease Period—10 years, beginning April 1, 1986.
             Lease Payment—$18,000 per year, payable in advance.
Machine #2   Lease Period—10 years, beginning July 1, 1990.
             Lease Payment—$30,000 per year, payable in advance.
Machine #3   Lease Period—15 years, beginning January 1, 1991.
             Lease Payment—$12,500 per year, payable in advance.

All of the leases are classified as operating leases.

Instructions: Prepare the note to the 1992 financial statements that would be required to disclose the lease commitments of Jaquar Mining and Manufacturing Company. Jaquar uses the calendar year as its accounting period.

Chapter 22

Accounting for Pensions and Other Postemployment Benefits

A widely recognized phenomenon of the 20th Century has been the increasing life expectancy of people in almost all countries of the world. For example, in 1900, the average life expectancy of people in the United States was 49 years; by 1985 it had increased to 74.7 years.[1] As people live longer, they must deal with the problem of financing their extended retirement years. The magnitude of the problem in the United States will increase in the next 15 to 20 years as the "baby-boomer" population of the 1940's and 50's moves into retirement. It is estimated that by the year 2020, 18 percent of America's population will be over 65 years of age.[2]

Financing retirement years is accomplished by establishing some type of **pension plan** that sets aside funds during an employee's working years so that at retirement the funds and earnings from investment of the funds may be returned to the employee in lieu of earned wages. In the United States, three major categories of pension plans have emerged:

1. Government plans, primarily social security
2. Individual plans, such as individual retirement accounts (IRAs)
3. Employer plans

The third category, employer pension plans, involves several difficult and controversial accounting and reporting issues. In 1985, the FASB issued two new pension accounting standards, Statement No. 87, "Employers' Accounting for Pensions," and Statement No. 88, "Employers' Accounting for Settlements and Curtailments of Defined Benefit Pension Plans and for Termination Benefits." These standards, particularly Statement No. 87, changed significantly the way in which pension costs are determined and reported by employers.

A related issue, and one that is currently generating a high level of interest and concern, is the employer's accounting for **postemployment benefits** other than pensions. These benefits that extend beyond the active years of employment include such items as health care, life insurance, legal

[1]*Information Please Almanac*, 1989, (Boston: Houghton Mifflin Company, 1989), p. 795.
[2]Carol J. Loomis, "The Killer Cost Stalking Business," *Fortune*, Feb. 27, 1989, pp. 58-68.

services, special discounts on items produced or sold by the employer, and tuition assistance. The costs of many of these benefits, especially health care, have escalated dramatically over the past several years. As explained in this chapter, pension costs have for many years been recognized on an accrual basis during the employees' working years rather than when the benefits are actually paid following retirement. In addition, employers set aside funds each period to cover, at least partially, the cost of future pension benefits. Unlike pension plans, the majority of other postemployment benefits have been accounted for on a "pay-as-you-go" basis. Few employers have accrued the cost of these benefits or set aside funds in advance of the actual payment, even though employees earn the right to the benefits while they are actively employed. This has led to a large, unrecorded liability for postemployment benefits, primarily health care. It is estimated that the liability for postretirement health care costs of America's corporations at the end of 1988 exceeded $168 billion.

In February 1989, the FASB issued an exposure draft entitled "Employers' Accounting for Postretirement Benefits Other Than Pensions." This proposed standard would require employers to accrue estimated costs of these benefits rather than charging them to expense when paid. Many of the recommendations of the exposure draft are extensions of those in the pension standards. This chapter focuses on employers' accounting for pension plans. The FASB's proposed requirements for other postemployment benefits are summarized in an appendix to the chapter.

Regulation of Pension Plans— ERISA

The United States Government introduced the social security system in the 1930s to help deal with the problems of the aged. This was accompanied by increased union demands on employers to initiate company pension plans to supplement the social security benefits. A majority of companies responded to these demands, and various types of private employer pension plans arose.

The tremendous growth in pension plan assets and a lack of pension regulation led to many abuses by both employers and unions. Many pension plans did not have adequate funds to make the required pension payments, and the rights of employees who were terminated prior to retirement were often almost nonexistent. Employees counting on pension benefits when they retired often found assets lacking, or provisions changed.

As a result of pension plan irregularities and abuses, Congress enacted a massive piece of legislation in 1974 officially known as the Employee Retirement Income Security Act of 1974 (ERISA). The act introduced a wide spectrum of reforms and regulations covering all types of pensions. The act included provisions requiring minimum funding of plans, minimum rights to employees upon termination of their employment, and minimum disclosure and audit requirements for trustees of pension plans. In addition to these provisions, the Act created a federal agency, the **Pension Benefit Guaranty Corporation (PBGC)**, to help protect employee benefits when pension plans are terminated as a result of employer bankruptcy or other causes. When a plan is terminted, ERISA requires the employer to contribute up to 30% of its net assets to provide benefits for the employees covered by the plan. To enforce this provision, the PBGC is given the right to impose a lien on the employer's assets that gives it priority over most creditor claims. In effect, PBGC actually becomes the trustee for pension plans that terminate. The PBGC also administers a fund supported by premiums charged to participating companies. The fund is used to pay retirement benefits if the employer is unable to do so.

A key element in all pension plans is the **vested benefits** provision. Vesting occurs when an employee has met certain specified requirements and is eligible to receive pension benefits at retirement regardless of whether the employee continues working for the employer. In early pension plans, vesting did not occur for many years. In extreme cases, vesting occurred only when an employee reached retirement. A major outcome of the ERISA was much earlier vesting privileges for employees. This change had a significant impact on accounting for pension costs.

Nature and Characteristics of Employer Pension Plans

The subject of employers' accounting for pensions is very complex, partly because of the many variations in plans that have been developed. Most pension plans are specifically designed for one employer and are known as **single-employer pension plans**. If several companies contribute to the same plan, it is called a multiemployer pension plan. This chapter, like the accounting standards, focuses on accounting for single-employer plans.

Funding of Employer Pension Plans

The basic purpose of all employer pension plans is the same—to provide retirement benefits to employees. A principal issue concerning pension plans is how to provide sufficient funds to meet the needs of retirees. The social security system of the Federal Government has frequently been criticized because it is not a "funded" plan. FICA taxes (contributions) paid by employers and employees in the current year are used to pay benefits to individuals who are currently retired. This means that the current employees must have faith that a future generation will do the same for them. Such a system creates much doubt and uncertainty.

Private plans are not permitted to operate in this way. Federal law requires companies to **fund** their pension plans in an orderly manner so that the employee is protected at retirement. Some pension plans are funded entirely by the employer and are referred to as **noncontributory pension plans**. In other cases, the employee also contributes to the cost of the pension plan, referred to as a **contributory pension plan**.[3] The amounts and

---

[3]Employee contributions are not considered in subsequent discussions and examples, since the chapter is concerned with employers' accounting for pensions.

timing of contributions depend on the particular circumstances and plan provisions. While the provisions of pension plans vary widely and in many cases are very complex, there are two basic classifications of pension plans: (1) defined contribution plans and (2) defined benefit plans.

Defined Contribution Pension Plans

Defined contribution pension plans are relatively simple in their construction and raise very few accounting issues for employers. Under these plans, a periodic contribution amount is paid by the employer into a separate trust fund, which is administered by an independent third-party trustee. The contribution may be defined as a fixed amount each period, a percentage of the employer's income, a percentage of employee earnings, or a combination of these or other factors. As contributions to the fund are made, they are invested by the fund administrator. When an employee retires, the accumulated value in the fund is used to determine the pension payout to the employee. The employee's retirement income therefore depends on how the fund has been managed. If investments have been made wisely, the employee will fare better than if the investments were managed poorly. In effect, the investment risk is borne by the employee. The employer's obligation extends only to making the specified periodic contribution.

Defined Benefit Pension Plans

Defined benefit pension plans are much more complex than defined contribution plans. Under defined benefit plans, the employee is guaranteed a specified retirement income often related to his or her average salary over a certain number of years. The periodic amount of contribution is based on the expected future benefits to be paid to employees and is affected by a number of variables. Because the benefits are defined, the contributions (funding) must vary as conditions change. Exhibit 22-1 illustrates the basic nature of a defined benefit plan. A defined contribution plan could be illustrated in the same manner except that the contributions (rather than the benefits) would be defined. This difference, however, is significant and accounts for the complexity of defined benefit plans.

Under defined benefit plans, the investment risk is, in substance, borne by the employer. While a separate trust fund is usually maintained for contributions and investment earnings, the employer is ultimately responsible to assure that employees receive the defined benefits provided by the plan. Pension plan assets may be viewed essentially as funds set aside to meet the employer's future pension obligation just as funds may be set aside for other purposes, e.g., to retire bonds at maturity. One major difference, however, is that a future obligation to retire bonds is a definite amount, while the employer's future obligation for retirement benefits is based on many estimates and assumptions.

Defined Benefits

Defined benefit pension plans provide for an increase in future retirement benefits as additional services are rendered by an employee. In effect, the employee's total compensation for a period consists of current wages or salaries plus the right to receive a defined amount of future benefits. The amount of future benefits earned by employees for a particular period is determined by actuaries, not accountants. However, an understanding of the basic concepts used in measuring future retirement benefits is necessary for understanding the accounting issues relating to pensions.

Exhibit 22-1   Defined Benefit Pension Plans

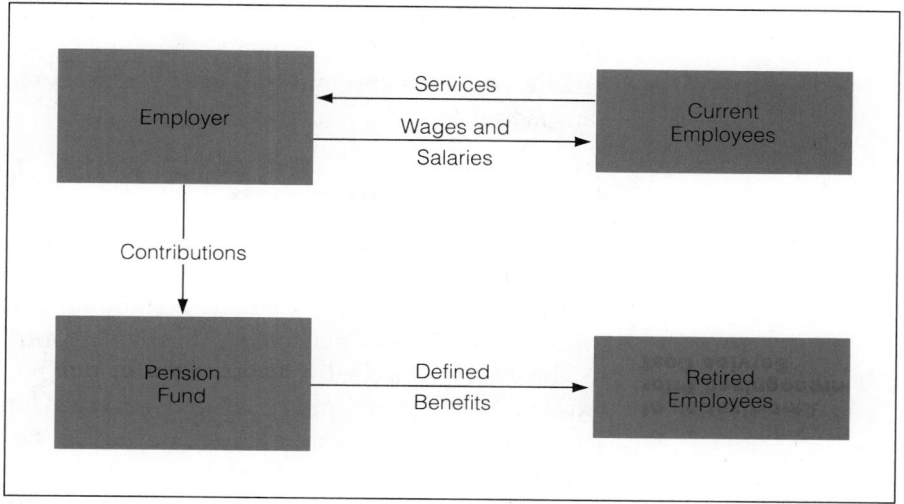

The amount of future benefits earned for a period is based on the plan's **benefit formula**, which specifies how benefits are **attributed** (assigned) to years of employee service. Some plans attribute equal benefits to each year of service rendered, e.g., a pension benefit of $20 per month for each year of employee service rendered. Thus an employee who retires after 30 years of service would be entitled to a monthly benefit of $600 ($20 per month × 30 years of service). The benefit attributed to each year of service would be $20 multiplied by the number of months of life expectancy after retirement. Some plans attribute different benefits to different years of service, e.g., a pension benefit of $20 per month for each year of service up to 20 years and $25 per month for each additional year of service. Many plans include a benefit formula based on current or future employee earnings. For example, a plan might provide monthly benefits of 2% of an employee's average annual earnings for the 5 years preceding retirement. This type of benefit formula requires an estimate of future earnings in determining the additional benefits earned in the current period.

Two different approaches are used to determine the amount of future benefits earned by employees under a defined benefit plan: (1) the accumulated benefit approach and (2) the projected benefit approach. The **accumulated benefit approach** is used when benefits are non-pay related (e.g., a fixed monthly benefit for each year of service) or based on current salary levels. When benefits are defined in terms of future salaries, the **projected benefit approach** is used.

Regardless of the approach used, the measurement of future benefits is highly subjective. The amount of benefits earned by employees for a period is based on many variables including the average age of employees, length of service, expected turnover, vesting provisions, and life expectancy. Thus, the actuaries must estimate how many of the current employees will retire and when they will retire, the number of employees who will leave the company prior to retirement, the number who will leave with vested benefits, the life expectancy of employees after retirement, and other relevant factors.

Funding of Defined Benefit Plans

The periodic amounts to be contributed to a defined benefit plan by the employer are directly related to the future benefits expected to be paid to current employees. The methods of funding pension plans vary widely. Most defined benefit plans require periodic contributions that accumulate to the balance needed to pay the promised retirement benefits to employees. Some plans specify an even amount for each year of employee service. Others require a lower amount in the early years of employee service, with an accelerating schedule over the years. Still other plans provide for a higher amount at first, then a declining pattern of funding. The contribution amounts are determined by actuarial formulas and must be adjusted as estimates and assumptions are revised to reflect changing conditions.

All funding methods are based on present values. The additional future benefits earned by employees each year must be discounted to their present value, referred to as the **actuarial present value**, using an assumed rate of return on pension fund investments. In many cases, employers contribute an amount equal to the present value of future benefits attributed to current services. As noted above, however, funding patterns vary and the amount contributed for a particular period may be less than or greater than the present value of the additional benefits earned for the period. Assume, for example, that the present value of future benefits earned in the current period is determined to be $30,000 using a discount rate of 10%. If the funding method requires a contribution of only $25,000 for the period, the employer has an **unfunded** obligation of $5,000. At the end of the following year, this obligation will have increased to $5,500 to reflect the interest cost of 10%. When contributions exceed the present value of the future benefits, lower contributions will be required in subsequent periods as a result of earnings on the "overfunded" amount.

Thus far the discussion has focused on the additional future benefits earned by employees for **current services**. When a pension plan is first adopted, provision must be made to give credit to current employees for prior services rendered. Some of the current employees may be near retirement with few years of future service remaining, but they will still receive full retirement benefits. Actuaries analyze the extent of the additional benefits attributable to **prior services**, and negotiate with the employer as to how these benefits will be funded. The entire amount could be funded immediately by one contribution equal to the present value of the additional future benefits. In many cases, the amount is relatively large, and the employer is permitted to fund the benefits over several years.

To illustrate, assume that a pension plan is adopted on January 1, 1992. The current employees are granted benefits "retroactively" for services rendered prior to the plan adoption and the present value of those benefits, as measured by actuaries, is $1,625,000. This amount is to be funded by the employer over a 12-year period, with an equal amount being contributed at the end of each year. If the interest rate is 10%, the annual contribution amount can be determined using the formula for the present value of an ordinary annuity and Table IV from Chapter 6.

$$PV_n = R(PVAF_{\overline{n}|i})$$

$$R = \frac{PV_n}{PVAF_{\overline{n}|i}}$$

$$R = \frac{\$1,625,000}{\text{Table IV}_{\overline{12}|10\%}}$$

$$R = \frac{\$1,625,000}{6.8137}$$

$$R = \$238,490 \text{ (rounded)}$$

As the computations indicate, 12 annual payments of $238,490 will liquidate the employer's prior service obligation by the end of 2003.

The problem of providing additional funds to cover prior services also arises whenever a plan amendment is adopted to provide for increased benefits. Inflation makes it necessary for many employers to amend their pension plans in order to provide an adequate retirement income for their employees. The additional benefits granted for services prior to the plan amendment must be measured and funded in some equitable manner as discussed previously in the context of plan adoption.

Scope of Pension Accounting Standards

Employer pension plans may be either defined contribution or defined benefit plans. Because accounting for defined contribution plans merely involves charging the employer's periodic contribution to pension expense, the FASB focused its work, and Statement No. 87, on defined benefit plans. This chapter follows the same emphasis.

Issues in Accounting for Defined Benefit Plans

Although the provisions of defined benefit pension plans can be extremely complex, and the application of accounting standards to a specific plan can be highly technical, the accounting issues themselves are more easily identified. Following is a list of these issues, all of which relate to accounting and reporting by employers:

1. The amount of net periodic pension cost to be recognized as expense
2. The amount of pension liability to be reported on the balance sheet
3. The amount of pension fund assets to be reported on the balance sheet
4. Accounting for pension settlements, curtailments, and terminations
5. Disclosures needed to supplement the amounts reported in the financial statements

The issue of funding pension plans is purposely omitted from the list. Funding decisions are affected by tax laws, governmental regulations, actuarial computations, and contractual terms, not by accounting standards. They should not directly affect the amount that is reported as net periodic pension cost (expense) under the accrual concept. However, differences between the amount funded and the amount expensed do have an impact on the balance sheet, as explained in a subsequent section of the chapter.

The five issues identified are not new. They are the same ones addressed by the Committee on Accounting Procedures in Accounting Research Bulletin No. 47, issued in 1956, and by the Accounting Principles Board in Opinion No. 8, issued in 1967. Dissatisfied with the wide diversity in accounting for pension costs permitted by APB Opinion No. 8, the FASB added the topic of pensions to its agenda in 1975. As indicated in Chapter 1 (see page 13), the project that resulted in the 1985 FASB standards lasted for more than ten years. During that time, there were many conflicting viewpoints, and the final pension standards differed in significant ways from the preliminary views and exposure drafts. In many instances, the final standards are not consistent with the FASB definitions of elements of financial statements as contained in the concepts statements. Three of the seven FASB members dissented from FASB Statement No. 87 and two dissented from FASB Statement No. 88. The dissenting members have documented the reasons for their dissent in Statements No. 87 and 88.

The next section of the chapter discusses accounting for pensions in the context of the five issues identified. Terms will be defined as they arise, and examples of how these issues have been resolved by the FASB will be presented.

Accounting for Pensions

The basic accounting entries for pensions are very straightforward. An entry is made to accrue the pension cost computed according to the applicable accounting standards, and another entry is made to record the contribution to the pension fund. If the accrual and the contribution are equal in amount, as they have often been in the past, there is no effect on the balance sheet. However, if the amounts differ, as they frequently will under FASB Statement No. 87, the difference is reported on the balance sheet as either a **prepaid pension cost** or an **accrued pension cost**. A single account, often labelled Prepaid/Accrued Pension Cost, is used to reflect either a debit or credit balance.

To illustrate, assume the Robertson Robotics Company computed pension cost for 1992 of $230,000 and made a contribution to the pension fund of $190,000. The journal entries would be as follows:

Pension Cost	230,000	
Prepaid/Accrued Pension Cost		230,000
To record 1992 pension cost.		
Prepaid/Accrued Pension Cost	190,000	
Cash		190,000
To record 1992 contribution to pension plan.		

As a result of these entries, pension cost of $230,000 would be reported as an expense on the income statement. Assuming there was a zero balance in the Prepaid/Accrued Pension Cost account at the beginning of the year, the balance sheet would report the accrued pension cost of $40,000 as a liability. If the contribution had exceeded the accrual, prepaid pension cost would be reported as an asset.

While the entries themselves are very simple, the determination of pension cost can be very complex. Likewise, there are many complexities that enter into the determination of amounts to be reported as liabilities or assets. These problems are discussed and illustrated in the following sections.

Determining Net Periodic Pension Cost

Net periodic pension cost is the annual expense recognized by the employer as a result of its pension plan.[4] For a given period, a company may recognize as many as six different components of net periodic pension cost (alternatively referred to, for simplicity, as pension cost). The six components are:

1. Service cost
2. Interest cost
3. Actual return on pension plan assets (if any)
4. Amortization of unrecognized prior service cost (if any)
5. Deferral of current period gain or loss and amortization of unrecognized net gain or loss
6. Effects (if any) of transition to Statement No. 87

---

[4]The FASB pension standards use the term "pension cost" rather than "pension expense" to recognize that cost may be expensed immediately or capitalized as part of an asset such as inventory. Cost and expense may be used interchangeably. We have chosen to follow the FASB and refer to the periodic charge as pension cost.

Before discussing these components of pension cost in depth, it is necessary to define and discuss two key measurements in pension accounting, the **projected benefit obligation (PBO)** and the **fair value of pension plan assets**. The **projected benefit obligation** is a present value measure of the future benefits expected to be paid to employees based on their employment to date but taking into consideration, if applicable, expected increases in wages that would affect their retirement benefits. The measurement is based on actuarial estimation of such factors as life expectancy, employee turnover, and interest rates. The projected benefit obligation increases each year as additional benefits are earned by employees through another year of service (service cost) and by the passage of time that brings employees one year closer to receiving their benefits (interest cost). The projected benefit obligation decreases each year by the pension payments to retired employees. In addition, the obligation may increase or decrease by changes in any of the actuarial assumptions enumerated above. These changes may be summarized as follows:

Projected benefit obligation, beginning of year	+	Service cost and interest cost	−	Retirement benefits paid	±	Change in actuarial assumptions	=	Projected benefit obligation, end of year

The **fair value of pension plan assets** is based on the market value of pension plan assets at a given measurement date. The fair value of pension plan assets increases each year by employer contributions to the fund and decreases by the retirement benefits paid. The fair value also changes by the amount of earnings on the pension plan assets, including changes in the market value of the assets. These changes may be summarized as follows:

Fair value of pension plan assets, beginning of year	+	Employer contributions	−	Retirement benefits paid	±	Actual return on pension plan assets	=	Fair value of pension plan assets, end of year

These two valuations are used extensively in the components of pension cost explained and illustrated in the following sections of this chapter.

Throughout the discussion of the components of pension cost, an illustration for a specific company, Thornton Electronics, Inc., will be used to compute the 1992 pension cost. The following data will be used in the examples:

Exhibit 22-2   1992 Pension Plan Information for Thornton Electronics, Inc.

Balances at January 1, 1992:	
Projected benefit obligation	$1,495,000
Fair value of pension plan assets	$1,385,000
Market-related value of pension plan assets (5 yr. weighted average)	$1,200,000
Unrecognized prior service costs	$495,000
Unrecognized net gain from prior years	$200,000
Unamortized transition gain	$200,000
Accrued pension liability	$15,000
1992 pension activity:	
Service cost as reported by actuaries	$75,000
Contributions to pension plan	$115,000
Benefits paid to retirees	$136,975
Actuarial change increasing projected benefit obligation	$10,000
Fair value of pension plan assets at December 31, 1992	$1,513,025
Settlement interest rate	10.5%
Long-term expected rate of return on pension plan assets	10.0%
Average remaining service life of employees	5.5 years

This data will be used as needed in computing the elements of pension cost and in determining the information to be disclosed.

Service Cost   Defined benefit plans provide for an increase in future retirement benefits as additional services are rendered by an employee. That is, each year employees earn the right to receive additional retirement benefits as part of their total compensation. The cost to the employer of the additional benefits earned during a period is called service cost. Because the retirement benefits will be paid in the future, the amount of service cost is the present value of the additional benefits. As explained earlier, the amount of future benefits is determined by actuaries based on the plan's benefit formula. Thornton Electronics' actuaries reported 1992 service cost of $75,000.

Interest Cost   The interest component of net periodic pension cost represents the fact that the estimated future retirement benefits are now one period closer than they were at the beginning of the year. Thus the present value of the future obligation is increased by the interest on the beginning projected benefit obligation. The settlement interest rate is used to discount the projected benefit obligation. This is the interest rate at which pension benefits could be effectively settled, that is, the rate implicit in the current prices of annuity contracts that could be purchased to settle the benefits owed to employees.

To illustrate the computation of the interest cost component, note that Thornton Electronics, Inc. had a projected benefit obligation as of January 1, 1992 of $1,495,000. The settlement interest rate for Thornton was 10.5%, thus the interest cost for 1992 would be $1,495,000 × 10.5%, or $156,975.

Actual Return on Pension Plan Assets

The assets created by employer contributions to a pension plan usually earn a return that reduces the reported amount of annual pension cost. The return is composed of such elements as interest revenue, dividends, rentals, and changes in the market value of the assets. If a decline in the market value of the pension plan assets exceeds the earnings on the assets, the actual return will be a negative figure that would increase the pension cost rather than decrease it. We will assume in our chapter illustrations that the net return is positive, and therefore represents a reduction in the employer's pension cost. The actual return can be computed by comparing the fair value of the pension plan assets at the beginning and end of the year. After adjusting for current-year contributions and benefits paid to retirees, any change is the actual return on pension plan assets. To illustrate using the data on page 987, the actual return on pension plan assets for Thornton Electronics in 1992 would be $150,000, computed as follows:

Fair value of pension plan assets December 31, 1992	$1,513,025
Fair value of pension plan assets January 1, 1992	1,385,000
Increase in fair value	$ 128,025
Add benefits paid	136,975
Deduct contributions made	(115,000)
Actual return on pension plan assets	$ 150,000

The actual return on pension plan assets is always computed in determining net periodic pension cost. However, as explained in a later section on the treatment of pension gains and losses under FASB Statement No. 87, the actual return may be adjusted to the expected return when there is a difference between the two amounts.

Amortization of Unrecognized Prior Service Cost

In some cases, an employer's net periodic pension cost will include a component referred to as amortization of unrecognized prior service cost. As explained earlier in the chapter, when a pension plan is initially adopted or amended to provide increased benefits, employees are granted additional benefits for services performed in years prior to the plan adoption or amendment. The cost of these additional benefits to the employer is called prior service cost. The amount of prior service cost is determined by actuaries and represents the increase in the projected benefit obligation arising from the adoption or amendment of the plan. The settlement interest rate is used to discount the prior service cost to its present value.

Although prior service costs arises from services rendered in prior periods, there has been general agreement in the accounting profession that the cost should not be recognized at the plan adoption or amendment date, but rather should be **amortized over future periods**. This is based on the assumption that the employer will receive future economic benefits accruing from the plan adoption or amendment in the form of improved employee morale, loyalty, and productivity. FASB Statement No. 87 states that unrecognized prior service cost should be amortized by "assigning an equal amount to each future period of service of each employee active at the date of the amendment who is expected to receive benefits under the plan."[5] This is referred to as the expected service period. Because employees will have varying years of remaining service, this amortization method will result in a declining amortization charge. For example, assume a company has 4 employees at the time of a plan amendment. The prior service cost is $30,000. Assume further that the employees had the following expected remaining years of service life.

Employee 1	1 year
Employee 2	2 years
Employee 3	4 years
Employee 4	5 years

The amortization fractions would be computed as follows:

Employee Number	Future Service Years	Year 1	Year 2	Year 3	Year 4	Year 5
1	1	1				
2	2	1	1			
3	4	1	1	1	1	
4	5	1	1	1	1	1
	12	4	3	2	2	1
Amortization fraction		$\frac{4}{12}$	$\frac{3}{12}$	$\frac{2}{12}$	$\frac{2}{12}$	$\frac{1}{12}$
Amortization amount (fraction × $30,000)		$10,000	$7,500	$5,000	$5,000	$2,500

When a company has many employees retiring or terminating in a systematic pattern, a method similar to the sum-of-the-years-digits depreciation method can be used. The FASB included an illustration of how this computation would be made in Statement No. 87, Appendix B.[6] A simplified version of the Board's illustration is included in Exhibit 22-3. Assume that Thornton Electronics, Inc. has 150 employees who are expected to receive benefits for prior services under a plan amendment adopted at the end of 1991. Ten percent of the employees (15 employees) are expected to leave (either retire or quit with vesting privileges) in each of the next 10 years. Employees hired after the plan amendment date do not affect the amortization. Note that under these assumptions, 825 service years will be rendered by the affected employees. The fraction used to determine the amortization has a numerator that declines by 15 employees each year and a denominator that is the sum of the service years, or 825. If the increase

[5]*Statement of Financial Accounting Standards No. 87*, "Employers' Accounting for Pensions" (Stamford: Financial Accounting Standards Board, 1985), par. 25.
[6]*Ibid.*, pp. 84-86.

in the projected benefit obligation, or prior service cost, arising from the plan amendment at the end of 1991 was $495,000, the amortization for 1992 would be 150/825 × $495,000, or $90,000. The annual amortization for the 10 years is shown in Exhibit 22-4.

Exhibit 22-3   Determination of Amortization Fraction Based on Service Years Rendered in Each Year

Employees	Future Service Yrs.	Year									
		1	2	3	4	5	6	7	8	9	10
A1-A15	15	15									
B1-B15	30	15	15								
C1-C15	45	15	15	15							
D1-D15	60	15	15	15	15						
E1-E15	75	15	15	15	15	15					
F1-F15	90	15	15	15	15	15	15				
G1-G15	105	15	15	15	15	15	15	15			
H1-H15	120	15	15	15	15	15	15	15	15		
I1-I15	135	15	15	15	15	15	15	15	15	15	
J1-J15	150	15	15	15	15	15	15	15	15	15	15
	825	150	135	120	105	90	75	60	45	30	15
Amortization fraction		150/825	135/825	120/825	105/825	90/825	75/825	60/825	45/825	30/825	15/825

Exhibit 22-4   Declining Amortization of Unrecognized Prior Service Cost

Year	Beginning-of-Year Balance	Amortization Rate	Amortization	End-of-Year Balance
1992	$495,000	150/825	$90,000	$405,000
1993	$405,000	135/825	$81,000	$324,000
1994	$324,000	120/825	$72,000	$252,000
1995	$252,000	105/825	$63,000	$189,000
1996	$189,000	90/825	$54,000	$135,000
1997	$135,000	75/825	$45,000	$90,000
1998	$90,000	60/825	$36,000	$54,000
1999	$54,000	45/825	$27,000	$27,000
2000	$27,000	30/825	$18,000	$9,000
2001	$9,000	15/825	$9,000	$0

It is not necessary to construct a future years of service table (Exhibit 22-3) each time an amortization schedule is desired. The formula for the sum-of-the-years-digits method illustrated in Chapter 12 can be used with a slight modification to reflect the decreased number of employees each period. Thus, the total service years for Thornton Electronics, Inc. could be computed with the following formula:

$$\frac{N(N + 1)}{2} \times D = \text{Total future years of service}$$

where
N = number of remaining years of service
D = decrease in number of employees working each year.

or,

$$\frac{10(11)}{2} \times 15 = 825$$

The numerator would begin with the total employees at the time of the plan amendment, and decline by D each period.

Although the FASB indicated a preference for this method, it also indicated that consistent use of an alternative amortization approach that more rapidly reduces the unrecognized prior service cost is acceptable.[7] As an example of such an alternative, a straight-line amortization of prior service cost over the average remaining service period of employees was presented in Statement No. 87, Appendix B.[8] To illustrate the straight-line approach using the Thornton Electronics example, the average remaining service life would be 5.5 years (825/150 employees), and the amortization schedule would be as shown in Exhibit 22-5.[9]

Exhibit 22-5	**Straight-Line Amortization of Unrecognized Prior Service Cost**		
Year	Beginning-of-Year Balance	Amortization	End-of-Year Balance
1992	$495,000	$90,000	$405,000
1993	$405,000	$90,000	$315,000
1994	$315,000	$90,000	$225,000
1995	$225,000	$90,000	$135,000
1996	$135,000	$90,000	$45,000
1997	$45,000	$45,000	$0

A separate amortization schedule is necessary for each plan amendment. There is no need to alter the schedule for new employees, as they would not receive benefits from prior services. If the planned termination or retirement pattern does not occur, adjustments may be necessary later to completely amortize the prior service cost.

Deferral and Amortization of Gains and Losses

Because pension costs include many assumptions and estimates, frequent adjustments must be made for variations between the actual results and the estimates or projections that were used in determining net periodic pension cost for previous periods. For example, the market value of pension plan assets may increase at a much higher or lower rate than anticipated, the employee turnover rate may differ from that projected in earlier periods, or changes in the interest rate may differ significantly from expectations. Such differences between expected results and actual experience give rise to a pension gain or loss.

[7]*Ibid.*, par. 26.

[8]*Ibid.*, p. 88.

[9]The straight-line amortization rate can be obtained more directly by using the simplified version of the formula on page 990. Since the number of employees is equal to DN in the formula, simplification results in
Average life = (N + 1) ÷ 2.
Thus, for Thornton it would be 11 ÷ 2 = 5.5 years. If N were 15, the average life would be 16 ÷ 2 or 8 years.

Recognition of these pension gains and losses was a subject of controversy during the FASB's study of pensions. Immediate recognition was opposed by many accountants who were concerned about the volatility of pension expense. Like its predecessors, the FASB decided to minimize the volatility of net periodic pension cost by allowing deferral of some gains and losses and amortization over future periods rather than requiring recognition of gains and losses in the period they arise.[10] The FASB's position, as reflected in FASB Statement No. 87, represented a compromise and created some unusual and complex accounting practices.

Although actuarial estimates may change for several reasons, only two will be considered in this illustration: (1) the current year difference between the actual and expected return on pension plan assets and (2) actuarial changes in determining the projected benefit obligation.

Deferral of Current Year Difference Between Actual and Expected Return on Pension Plan Assets

In estimating the return on pension plan assets, FASB Statement No. 87 indicates that the expected *long-term* rate of return on assets should be used rather than a more volatile short-run rate. Thus, in the short-run, the **actual return on pension plan assets** will usually differ from the expected return. By deferring the difference between the expected return and the actual return, pension cost will tend to be reduced by the expected long-term rate of return rather than by the more volatile short-term return rates. If the actual return on pension plan assets exceeds the expected return, the difference is a deferred gain; if the expected return exceeds the actual return, the difference is a deferred loss.

The **expected return on pension plan assets** is computed by multiplying the market-related value of pension plan assets by the expected long-term rate of return. The FASB defines **market-related value of pension plan assets** as either (1) the fair market value of pension plan assets at the beginning of the current year or (2) a weighted average value based on market values of pension plan assets over a period not to exceed five years.[11] If asset values have been increasing, the weighted average value will be lower than the beginning fair market value, resulting in a lower expected return and thus a larger deferred gain.

When the actual return on pension plan assets exceeds the expected return, the difference, a deferred gain, is added to the pension cost as part of the gain or loss component. When the actual return is less than the expected return, the difference, a deferred loss, is deducted from pension cost. Because the actual return on pension plan assets is deducted in com-

---

[10]Alternately, a company may elect to recognize all gains or losses immediately. If this election is made, the company must (1) apply the immediate recognition method consistently, (2) recognize all gains or losses immediately, and (3) disclose the fact that immediate recognition is being followed. *Special Report*, "A Guide to Implementation of Statement 87 on Employers' Accounting for Pensions—Questions and Answers," (Stamford: Financial Accounting Standards Board, 1986), p. 23. For purposes of this chapter, all illustrations and end-of-chapter material will assume the deferred recognition method is used.

[11]Different methods of calculating market-related value may be used for different classes of assets. However, a company must apply the methods consistently from year to year.

puting pension cost, the net effect of the deferred pension gain or loss adjustment is that the expected return, rather than the actual return, is used to reduce pension cost, thus achieving a smoothing of pension costs over time.

To illustrate the computation of the pension gain or loss arising from differences between actual and expected return, assume Thornton Electronics computes the expected return on pension plan assets using the five-year weighted average value. Based on the data on page 987, the expected return on pension plan assets for 1992 is $120,000 ($1,200,000 × 10%). Since the actual return for the year as computed on page 988 is $150,000, the $30,000 difference is treated as a deferred pension gain and is added to pension cost. Note that if Thornton had chosen to use the fair value of the pension plan assets at January 1, 1992 as its market-related value to compute the expected return, a gain of only $11,500 would have been deferred ($150,000 − $138,500).

Differences in Actuarial Estimates of Projected Benefit Obligation

As indicated earlier, the actuarial computation of the projected benefit obligation involves many estimates, including future interest rates, life expectancy rates, and future salary rates. The effects of changing these estimates are deferred and accumulated for possible amortization to pension cost over future periods. As indicated on page 987, Thornton's actuaries computed an increase in the projected benefit obligation of $10,000 as a result of changes in estimates. This increase is identified as a loss. No adjustment is made to pension cost in the current period for this deferral as was necessary for the deferral of the difference in the return on pension plan assets. The deferred loss arising from the adjustment to the projected benefit obligation becomes part of the **unrecognized net pension gain or loss** for future amortization. The ending projected benefit obligation for Thornton can be computed from the data on page 987 as follows:

Projected benefit obligation, January 1, 1992	$1,495,000
Plus:	
Service cost	75,000
Interest cost	156,975
Deferred loss—actuarial changes	10,000
Minus:	
Retirement benefits paid	(136,975)
Projected benefit obligation, December 31, 1992	$1,600,000

Amortization of Unrecognized Net Pension Gain or Loss from Prior Years

Under certain conditions, an employer's net periodic pension cost will include the **amortization of unrecognized net pension gain or loss**. The unrecognized pension gain or loss from prior years is amortized over future years if it accumulates to more than an amount defined by the FASB as a **corridor amount**. Amortization is required only for an unrecognized net gain or loss that exceeds 10% of the greater of the projected benefit obligation or the market-related value of the plan assets as of the beginning of the year. The Board indicated that any systematic method of amortization that equalled or exceeded the straight-line amortization over the remaining expected service years of the employees would be acceptable as long as the procedure is applied consistently to both gains and losses. The amortization of a deferred gain reduces the net periodic pension cost while the amortization of a deferred loss increases the net periodic pension cost.

To illustrate the computation of the corridor amount, Thornton would apply the 10% to the projected benefit obligation at the beginning of the year of $1,495,000 since that exceeded market-related value of pension plan assets. Thus, the corridor amount would be $149,500 ($1,495,000 × 10%). Because the unrecognized deferred gain at January 1, 1992 was $200,000, only the excess of $50,500 would be subject to amortization ($200,000 − $149,500). If the average remaining service life of 5.5 years were used to compute the amortization of this deferred gain, the 1992 amortization would be $9,182 ($50,500 ÷ 5.5). This amount represents amortization of a gain that is a deduction from the other components in computing pension cost.

Summary of Pension Gains and Losses

The deferral of the current-year net pension gain or loss and the amortization of prior years' pension gain or loss are added together to compute the gain or loss component of pension cost. For Thornton, the deferral of the $30,000 current-year gain is reduced by the amortization of prior year gains of $9,182, leaving a net addition to the pension cost for 1992 of $20,818.

As is true for unrecognized prior service costs, the unrecognized net pension gain or loss balance is not included in the formal accounting records, but must be kept in separate memorandum records in order to compute the amortization.[12] The unrecognized net pension gain for Thornton Electronics at the end of 1992 would be computed as follows:

Unrecognized net pension gain—January 1, 1992	$200,000
Deferral of gain arising from excess of actual return over expected return on pension plan assets	30,000
Deferral of loss arising from increase in projected benefit obligation caused by a change in actuarial assumptions	(10,000)
Amortization of prior period unrecognized net pension gain	(9,182)
Unrecognized net pension gain—December 31, 1992	$210,818

Amortization of Transition Gain or Loss

The last component of pension cost arises as a result of the transition between accounting for pensions under previous standards and those required under FASB Statement No. 87. The transition gain or loss is

---

[12]For an informative illustration of the interaction of recorded and memorandum entries in pension accounting, see Paul B. W. Miller, "The New Pension Accounting (part 2), *Journal of Accountancy*, February 1987, p. 84-94.

defined as the difference between the projected benefit obligation and the fair value of the pension plan assets at the time FASB Statement No. 87 was adopted by a company. For most companies, this occurred in their 1987 fiscal year. If the projected benefit obligation was the larger of these two values at the transition date, the difference was a loss. If the fair value of the pension plan assets was the larger value, the difference was a gain. The computed transition gain or loss was further adjusted by any balance sheet pension liability or asset amount at the balance sheet date. The resulting transition gain or loss is not recorded on the books, but is recognized by amortization on a straight-line basis over the average remaining service life of the participating employees. (See the straight-line amortization method illustrated for prior service costs on page 991). Alternatively, if the average service life is less than 15 years, the employer is permitted to use a 15-year amortization period. Amortized losses are increases in net periodic pension cost, while amortized gains are decreases in net periodic pension costs.

The use of a transition gain or loss provided employers' pension plans with a fresh start. Any previously unrecognized prior service cost or actuarial gains or losses were included in this one adjustment amount. To complete the illustration for Thornton Electronics, Inc., assume that Thornton made its transition to FASB Statement No. 87 on January 1, 1987, and that its transition gain at that date was $300,000. Assume further that Thornton elected to amortize this gain over 15 years, or $20,000 a year. Thus, the unrecognized transition gain at January 1, 1992 was $200,000 [($300,000 − 5($20,000)] and the deduction from pension cost for the amortization in 1992 is $20,000.

Summary of Pension Cost

The net periodic pension cost for a company is determined by combining the various components. The pension cost for Thornton Electronics, Inc. as illustrated in the preceding pages is computed as follows:

Service cost		$ 75,000
Interest cost		156,975
Actual return on plan assets		(150,000)
Amortization of prior service cost		90,000
Gain or Loss		
Deferral of excess of actual return over		
expected return on plan assets	$30,000	
Amortization of prior years' unrecognized net		
pension (gain) or loss.	(9,182)	20,818
Amortization of transition (gain) or loss		(20,000)
Net periodic pension cost		$172,793

The journal entry on Thornton's books to record the pension cost for 1992 would be as follows:

Pension Cost................................   172,793
   Prepaid/Accrued Pension Cost   172,793
      To record accrual of net pension cost for
      1992.

The funding for 1992 would be determined by the plan provisions, and would not necessarily be related to the determination of the pension cost. As indicated in the data on page 987, the contributions to the plan for 1992 are $115,000. The following journal entry would be made to record payment.

Prepaid/Accrued Pension Cost   115,000
   Cash.....................................   115,000
      To record 1992 contribution to the pension
      plan.

Since the beginning accrued pension liability was $15,000, the balance in the accrued pension liability account at December 31, 1992 after posting these two entries would be $72,793 ($15,000 + $172,793 − $115,000) and the income statement would report net pension cost of $172,793. If the accumulated contributions exceed the accrual of pension cost, the difference would be reported as a prepaid pension cost. In most cases, these accounts would be reported in the noncurrent section of the balance sheet unless the facts indicated that the amounts would be settled within the next fiscal year.

Determining Pension Liability

As described earlier, an employer under a defined benefit plan assumes the responsibility for making pension payments to retired employees based on the benefit formula in the plan. The exact amount of these future payments is not known until they occur. Most plans provide for pension payments that are related to the salary levels in the years preceding retirement. For example, in the authors' pension plan at their University, the formula is based on an average salary computed on the highest five consecutive salary years before retirement. The exact amount of the payments also depends on how long the retiree lives after retirement, and what option for payment is selected.

The greatest controversy in employers' accounting for pensions concerns how the employer's obligation for these highly uncertain future payments should be reported—more specifically, how the employer should report the obligation for future benefits that have been earned by employees but not yet funded by the employer. There are two conditions giving rise to these unfunded benefits: (1) when the annual net periodic pension cost exceeds the amount of the annual pension fund contribution, and (2) when the present value of the future benefits for services already rendered exceeds the amount of pension fund assets.

The liability for accrued pension cost arising from the first condition has been recognized in financial statements for many years. This situation was illustrated in the previous example on page 996. However, the existence of the second condition has seldom been recognized as a liability. The principal causes of the second condition are unrecognized prior service cost and unrecognized losses. Because these costs are amortized over future periods, there was seldom any recorded liability for these unfunded costs under accounting standards prior to FASB Statement No. 87. The failure to record a liability to reflect unfunded prior service cost has disturbed an increasing number of accountants and users of financial statements over the years. For example, in an article entitled "Pension Accounting: The Liability Question," the authors concluded that:

> Based on our work to date, we are not convinced by the arguments against recording a liability when a pension plan is established or amended. We believe that an accounting liability does exist and that including it with other liabilities in the balance sheet will significantly improve the usefulness of financial statements.[13]

As the Board members considered the issues involved, they were influenced by the conceptual framework they had established, especially its definitions of the elements and the qualitative characteristics. They were convinced that an improvement in reporting financial position was required. Some proponents of maintaining the existing standards argued that increased benefits provided by plan amendments are granted by the employer in exchange for future services and that a liability should be recognized only as the future services are rendered. They cited the FASB definition of liabilities which stresses that the obligation has to arise as a result of *past* transactions and events. The Board agreed that a plan amendment "is undertaken by the employer with the expectation of future economic benefits . . ." and "to the extent that an amendment increases benefits that will be attributable to future services . . .," no recognition of a liability is necessary.[14]

However, the Board members felt that prior service costs are more directly related to past services than to future periods. They recognized that for matching purposes, the prior service cost is assigned to future periods through the amortization process. They also recognized, however, that the historical policy of allocating prior service costs to future periods rather than past periods is at least partially done to avoid the continual changing of previously issued financial statements.

This analysis led the Board to accept the view that some recognition of a liability for unfunded prior service cost was warranted. FASB Statement No. 87 identified the concept of a **minimum pension liability** to reflect existing unfunded pension costs and established rules for an employer to apply in determining if an entry to record a minimum pension liability is

---

[13]Thomas S. Lucas and Betsy Ann Hollowell, "Pension Accounting: The Liability Question," *Journal of Accountancy* (October 1981), p. 66.

[14]*Statement of Financial Accounting Standards No. 87*, par. 145.

required. Because the pension benefit payments are future amounts, any reporting of a liability for future payments must be discounted to its present value using the settlement rate. In determining the minimum liability, the Board continued the practice of previous standards by allowing the rule of **offset** to be applied. This means that the discounted future benefits payable can be offset by the fair value of plan assets in determining the liability to be reported.

The major question remaining was how to measure both the liabilities and the assets. The Board had already decided to use the projected benefit obligation to determine the periodic service cost. This amount includes all the variables affecting the future payment of benefits, including estimates of future salary levels. Several respondents to the exposure draft of the pension standard argued that these values were unknown and highly subjective. The Board acknowledged this, but several Board members felt that a liability using these amounts would be more representationally faithful than one that used only historical salary levels. This issue became the most controversial one in the entire study, and was finally resolved by identifying a new obligation referred to as the **accumulated benefit obligation (ABO)**. The ABO is similar to the projected benefit obligation (PBO) except that current, rather than future, salary levels are used in computing the ABO. In most cases, the result is an amount lower than the projected benefit obligation.[15] The accumulated benefit obligation was identified as the amount to be used in computing the minimum pension liability to be reported on the employer's financial statements.

FASB Statement No. 87 requires the employer to report a minimum pension liability that is at least equal to the **unfunded accumulated benefit obligation (ABO)**, which is determined as follows:

$$\text{Unfunded ABO (minimum pension liability)} = \text{ABO} - \text{Fair value of pension plan assets}$$

If the employer already has an accrued pension liability resulting from accrued pension costs in excess of the amount funded, no **additional pension liability** is recognized if the accrued pension cost is equal to or greater than the minimum pension liability (unfunded ABO). If accrued pension costs are less than the minimum liability, then an additional liability is recognized for the difference. In this situation, the additional pension liability equals the minimum pension liability minus the accrued pension cost.

If a prepaid pension cost balance exists because funding has exceeded the accrual, the *total* amount of the liability to be reported is the minimum pension liability (unfunded ABO) plus the prepaid balance reported as an asset. Thus, the *net* pension liability reported is the minimum pension liability. To illustrate, assume that the unfunded ABO at December 31 is determined to be $250,000 and the accounts reflect prepaid pension cost of

---

[15]Under plans where benefits are not defined in terms of future salaries, the accumulated benefit obligation is the same as the projected benefit obligation.

$60,000. The prepaid cost of $60,000 would be reported with the assets on the balance sheet, and a separate liability of $310,000 would be reported. The result is a net pension liability equal to the minimum pension liability of $250,000 required by Statement No. 87.

Exhibit 22-6 illustrates the computation of the pension liability under four different conditions. The entries to record the liability are discussed and illustrated in the next section.

Exhibit 22-6   Pension Liability Computation

Case	(1) Accumulated Benefit Obligation	(2) Fair Value of Pension Plan Assets	(3) Minimum Pension Liability	(4) Prepaid Pension Costs	(5) Accrued Pension Costs	(6) Additional Pension Liability	(7) Total Pension Liability
1	2,564,500	1,685,600	878,900		125,000	753,900	878,900
2	2,564,500	2,480,000	84,500		125,000	0	125,000
3	2,150,000	2,480,000	0		125,000	0	125,000
4	2,564,500	2,480,000	84,500	32,000		116,500	84,500

(1) Present value of future benefits attributable to services already rendered by employees. The measurement of future benefits is based on current, rather than future, salary levels.
(2) Fair market value of pension plan assets.
(3) The minimum amount of net pension liability to be reported on the balance sheet (ABO − Fair value of pension plan assets).
(4) Excess of pension contributions over accrued pension costs reported as an asset.
(5) Excess of accrued pension costs over pension contributions reported as a liability.
(6) Additional pension liability, if any, necessary to reflect the minimum liability required by FASB Statement No. 87.
(7) Total amount of pension liability to be reported on the balance sheet.

Determining Pension Assets

There are two distinct types of assets related to defined benefit pension plans: (1) pension plan assets arising from employer contributions and earnings from investment of the contributions and (2) prepaid or deferred amounts arising from the recognition of pension costs or liabilities.

Pension Plan Assets

When the value of the pension plan assets is less than the present value of the pension obligation, the pension plan is said to be **underfunded**. In this situation, the rule of offset is applied and a net pension liability is reported. As indicated in the previous section, if the accumulated benefit obligation exceeds the fair value of the pension plan assets, a minimum liability equal to the unfunded obligation must be reported on the employer's balance sheet.

When the value of the pension plan assets is greater than the present value of the pension obligation, the pension plan is said to be **overfunded**. In this situation, however, **no recognition of the net asset position on the balance sheet is permitted**. The FASB's decision to exclude the reporting of net pension plan assets under these circumstances is another reflection of inconsistency in the interest of conservatism, and reflects the intense pressure that was exerted on the Board by various groups. In Appendix A of Statement No. 87, the Board stated that it "believes that . . . an employer with . . . an overfunded pension obligation has an asset."[16] The Board concluded, however, that recognition of all changes in plan asset values and in the present value of the obligation would not be practical at the present time and would be too drastic a change from previous reporting practices.

Prepaid Net Pension Cost

As has been discussed previously, if the amount funded for a pension plan exceeds the amount accrued, a prepaid net pension cost arises. Each year the total cumulative amount funded is compared to the cumulative amount accrued, and either an accrued liability or a prepaid cost is reported. As discussed previously, to simplify the accounting for these differences, a single account entitled **Prepaid/Accrued Pension Cost** can be used. If this account has a credit balance, it is reported as a liability; if it has a debit balance, it is reported as an asset.

Deferred Pension Cost

If an employer is required to record an additional pension liability as a result of applying the minimum liability provisions, the Board indicated that the offsetting charge should be to a **deferred pension cost** account (intangible asset) to the extent of any unrecognized prior service cost or any unamortized transition loss. If the additional liability exceeds these unrecognized amounts, the Board indicated the excess should be recorded as a separate **contra-equity adjustment**. The deferred account represents that portion of the additional liability that can be related to prior periods because of either the adoption of a plan or a plan amendment, or because of the transition to the new standards. These unrecognized costs will be recognized in future periods through the amortization procedures discussed earlier, and thus the deferred account is not directly amortized. It is adjusted each period to reflect the increases or decreases in the recorded minimum liability.

The contra-equity adjustment account represents that portion of the additional liability that reflects either changes in the value of pension plan assets or changes in the benefit obligation that are not related to unrecognized prior service costs or to the transition adjustment. These unrecognized losses are recognized through the gains and losses component of pension cost. The contra-equity account is also adjusted each period when the minimum liability is recorded.

To illustrate accounting for the minimum liability and its offsetting asset or equity adjustment, assume the Clapton Corporation computes the following balances as of December 31, 1992:

Accumulated benefit obligation	$1,250,000
Fair value of pension plan assets	$1,140,000
Accrued pension cost	$ 16,000
Unrecognized prior service cost	$ 80,000

[16]*Statement of Financial Accounting Standards No. 87*, par. 98.

The minimum pension liability is $110,000 ($1,250,000 − $1,140,000), and the recorded liability for accrued pension cost is only $16,000. An **additional pension liability** of $94,000 ($110,000 − $16,000) would be recorded as follows:

Deferred Pension Cost	80,000	
Excess of Additional Pension Liability over Unrecognized Prior Service Cost	14,000	
Additional Pension Liability		94,000
To recognize additional pension liability.		

For reporting purposes, the $16,000 accrued pension cost and the $94,000 additional pension liability may be combined into one pension liability of $110,000 on the balance sheet.

The minimum liability is accounted for in subsequent periods in a similar manner. For example, assume that the computed minimum liability at December 31, 1993, is $104,000 and accrued pension cost at that date is $18,000. The balance in the additional pension liability account would be adjusted to $86,000 ($104,000 − $18,000). If the unrecognized prior service cost at December 31, 1993 has declined to $70,000, the deferred pension cost would be adjusted to $70,000. The excess of additional pension liability over unrecognized prior service cost would be adjusted to $16,000 ($86,000 − $70,000). The following journal entry would be made to adjust the accounts at the end of 1993:

Additional Pension Liability	8,000[1]	
Excess of Additional Pension Liability over Unrecognized Prior Service Cost	2,000[2]	
Deferred Pension Cost		10,000[3]
To adjust additional pension liability and related asset and contra-equity accounts.		

Computations:

	Beginning Balance	Ending Balance	Adjustment
1	$94,000 cr	$86,000 cr	$ 8,000 dr
2	14,000 dr	16,000 dr	2,000 dr
3	80,000 dr	70,000 dr	10,000 cr

The deferred pension cost balance of $70,000 (the amount of unrecognized prior service cost) would be reported on the balance sheet as an intangible asset. The contra-equity account balance of $16,000 would be deducted in the stockholders' equity section. A combined pension liability of $104,000 ($18,000 accrued pension cost + $86,000 additional pension liability) would be reported as a liability, usually under the noncurrent liabilities section.

If Clapton Corporation had an unamortized transition loss, that amount would be treated the same as unrecognized prior service cost in recording the minimum pension liability. The combined amount of any unrecognized prior service cost and unamortized transition loss determine the maximum amount of deferred pension cost. If there is an unamoritized transition gain, the amount would be deducted from prior service cost in determining deferred pension cost. If the gain is greater than prior service cost, no deferred pension cost is recognized, and an amount equal to the additional pension liability would be reported in the contra-equity account.

One of the more difficult aspects of the pension standards is identifying which obligation and asset values are used for the different pension amounts. It is important to note that the *accumulated benefit obligation* is used only in determining the minimum pension liability. In all other determinations involving future benefits discussed in this chapter, the *projected benefit obligation* is used.

Pension Settlements and Curtailments and Termination Benefits

If a pension plan is settled or the benefits are curtailed, a question arises as to how a resulting gain or loss should be treated by the employer. Settlement of a pension plan occurs when an employer takes an irrevocable action that relieves the employer of primary responsibility for all or part of the obligation. Examples of a settlement transaction include the purchase by the employer of an annuity from an insurance company that would cover vested benefits, or a lump-sum cash payment to the employees in exchange for their rights to receive specified pension benefits. A curtailment of a pension plan arises from an event that significantly reduces the benefits that will be provided for present employees' future services. Curtailments include: (1) the termination of employees' services earlier than expected, for example, as a result of closing a plant or discontinuing a segment of the business and (2) the termination or suspension of a pension plan so that employees do not earn additional benefits for future services.[17]

As discussed throughout this chapter, FASB Statement No. 87 provides for delayed recognition of pension gains and losses arising from the ordinary operations of the pension plan. In addition, the statement provides for delayed recognition of prior service costs and transition adjustments. Thus, at any given time there are usually amounts of gains, losses, and prior service costs unrecognized in an employer's financial statements.

The FASB felt it was clear that if a pension plan is completely terminated and all pension obligations are settled and plan assets are disbursed, then previously unrecognized pension amounts should be recognized. What wasn't clear, however, is what happens when partial settlements or curtailments take place. The FASB considered this issue and presented their recommendations in FASB Statement No. 88. The statement also addresses the issue of termination benefits, i.e., benefits provided to employees in connection with the termination of their employment.

---

[17]*Statement of Financial Accounting Standards No. 88,* "Employers' Accounting for Settlements and Curtailments of Defined Benefit Pension Plans and for Termination Benefits" (Stamford: Financial Accounting Standards Board, 1985), par. 6.

Settlements

In recent years, many pension plans have become overfunded because of the rising stock market. To take advantage of this situation, many companies have **settled** their pension plans by purchasing annuity contracts from insurance companies for less than the amount in the pension fund. Subject to regulations such as ERISA, the excess funds can then be used for other corporate purposes.

The accounting issue surrounding settlements centers on whether the gain should be recognized immediately or deferred and recognized in future periods. Prior to Statement No. 88, settlement gains that were accompanied by asset withdrawals from the pension fund, referred to as "asset reversion transactions," were deferred and offset against future pension costs. The Board, however, decided that if the settlement was (1) an irrevocable action, (2) relieved the employer of primary responsibility for the pension benefit obligation, and (3) eliminated significant risks related to the obligation and the assets used to effect the settlement, the previously unrecognized net gain or loss should be recognized in the current period. If only part of the projected benefit obligation is settled, a pro rata portion of the gain should be recognized currently.[18]

The note accompanying the Manufacturers Hanover Corporation statement describing the effect of applying FASB Statement No. 88 to a settlement is reproduced below:

Exhibit 22-7   Manufacturers Hanover Corporation

Manufacturers Hanover Corporation

During 1985, the Corporation also adopted Statement of Financial Accounting Standards No. 88 (SFAS No. 88) which deals with the accounting for "settlements." In accordance with SFAS No. 88, the Retirement Plan purchased annuity contracts for approximately 4,100 members of the pension plan guaranteeing the payment of their future pension benefits. In connection with this transaction, no Retirement Plan assets were reverted and no cash was received. A gain was recognized in other revenue of approximately $53.5 million, which was equal to a pro-rata portion of the excess of the Retirement Plan's assets over the projected benefit obligation at January 1, 1985.

Curtailments

As indicated previously, a pension plan curtailment is an event that significantly reduces the expected years of future service of present employees or eliminates for a significant number of employees the accrual of defined benefits for their future services. Examples include termination of employees' services earlier than expected, such as occurs when a segment of

---

[18]*Ibid.*, par. 9.

the business is discontinued, or termination or suspension of a plan so that no further benefits are earned for future services.

Any unrecognized prior service cost or transition adjustment associated with years of service no longer expected to be rendered as a result of the curtailment is recognized as a loss. In addition, the projected benefit obligation of the pension plan may be changed as a result of the curtailment, giving rise to an additional gain or loss. The Board provided for offsetting previously unrecognized pension gains and losses against the gain or loss from changes in the projected benefit obligation and called the difference curtailment gains or losses. If the sum of all gains and losses attributed to the curtailment, including the write-off of unrecognized prior service cost, is a loss, it is recognized in the period when it is probable that the curtailment will occur and the effects are estimable. If the sum of all gains and losses attributed to the curtailment is a gain, it is recognized when the related employees terminate or when the plan suspension or amendment is adopted.[19]

These rules were adopted by the Board to allow consistency between this standard and other standards related to disposal of a business segment and accounting for contingencies, both of which affect the concept of accounting for pension curtailments. They do, however, result in a conflict with the delayed recognition of gains and losses and prior service costs adopted in Statement No. 87. This latter inconsistency led to a strong dissent by one of the Board members.[20]

Termination Benefits

Termination benefits to employees may be either **special-termination benefits** arising from a plan amendment that covers only a short period of time, or **contractual termination benefits** provided in the original pension contract only if a certain event, such as a plant closing, occurs. In the case of special benefits, a loss and liability are recognized by the employer when the employees accept the offer of the special benefits. The loss and liability relating to contractual benefits should be recognized when it is both probable that the employees will be entitled to termination benefits because of the occurrence of the triggering event and the amount can be reasonably estimated. If the termination benefits are payable immediately, the entire amount is recognized as a loss. If they are to be paid in the future, the present value of the termination benefits is recognized.[21]

The rules relating to these changes in pension plans are complex and are often in conflict with one or more parts of the conceptual framework. A careful reading of Statements No. 87 and No. 88, including the dissents and the appendices, reveals the continual trade-offs that were required in arriving at the final pension standards.

---

[19]*Statement of Financial Accounting Standards No. 88*, par. 12-14.
[20]*Ibid.*, p. 8.
[21]*Ibid.*, par. 15.

Disclosure of Pension Plans

The FASB recognized that all of the useful information concerning an employer's pension plans cannot be provided in the body of the financial statements. The Board identified as a major objective:

> To provide disclosures that will allow users to understand better the extent and effect of an employer's undertaking to provide employee pensions and related financial arrangements.[22]

Statement No. 87 therefore requires extensive disclosure in the notes accompanying the general purpose financial statements. Following is a list of the required disclosures for defined benefit plans.[23]

1. A description of the plan including employee groups covered, type of benefit formula, funding policy, types of assets held and significant non-benefit liabilities, if any, and the nature and effect of significant matters affecting comparability of information for all periods presented

2. The amount of the net periodic pension cost for the period showing separately the service cost component, the interest cost component, the actual return on assets for the period, and the net total of the other components

3. A schedule reconciling the funded status of the plan with amounts shown in the employer's statement of financial position, showing separately,
    (a) The fair value of pension plan assets
    (b) The projected benefit obligation, the accumulated benefit obligation, and the vested benefit obligation
    (c) The amount of unrecognized prior service cost
    (d) The amount of unrecognized net pension gain or loss
    (e) The amount of any remaining unrecognized transition adjustment
    (f) The amount of any additional liability arising from application of the minimum liability provision
    (g) The net result of the preceding items recognized in the statement of financial position

4. The assumed discount rate (settlement interest rate), the rate of compensation increase used to measure the projected benefit obligation, and the expected long-term rate of return on pension plan assets

5. The amounts and types of securities included in plan assets and approximate amount of annual benefits to employees covered by annuity contracts.

As indicated in item (3), the required disclosures include a reconciliation of the funded status of the plan with amounts reported in the employer's statement of financial position. Illustrations of the required reconciliation are included in Appendix B of FASB Statement No. 87.

---

[22]*Statement of Financial Accounting Standards No. 87*, par. 6c.
[23]*Ibid.*, par. 54.

Essentially, the reconciliation is prepared in two parts: (1) Compute the funded status of the pension plan as the difference between the projected benefit obligation and the fair value of pension plan assets. (2) Identify the unrecognized items that have not yet been included on the employer's balance sheet, such as unrecognized prior service cost, unrecognized transition adjustments, and unrecognized pension gains and losses. The difference between the funding status and the unrecognized items should reconcile with the pension assets and liabilities reported on the balance sheet.

To illustrate the reconciliation, Exhibit 22-8 summarizes the pension information for Thornton Electronics, Inc. for 1992 as presented in this chapter. This information would be presented in the notes to Thornton's financial statements in the following reconciliation format:

Projected benefit obligation, December 31, 1992	$(1,600,000)
Fair value of pension plan assets, December 31, 1992	1,513,025
Excess of obligation over assets (underfunding)	$ (86,975)
Unamortized transition gain, December 31, 1992	(180,000)
Unrecognized net pension gain, December 31, 1992	(210,818)
Unrecognized prior service costs, December 31, 1992	405,000
Accrued pension liability, December 31, 1992	$ (72,793)

Of the above account balances, only the accrued pension liability is a recorded balance sheet account. The unrecognized and unamortized balances are computed outside the traditional recording system as illustrated in Exhibit 22-8. Each year adjustments are made to these balances as illustrated in the following example for Thornton Electronics, Inc.[24]

Disclosure of pension plans is much more complete as a result of the FASB standards. The two required schedules disclosing (1) the components of net pension cost and (2) the reconciliation of the pension funding status to the balance sheet are usually part of the note disclosure. In 1987, Westinghouse Electric Corporation reported an underfunded plan (Exhibit 22-10, page 1009) and Phillip Morris Companies, Inc. reported an overfunded plan (Exhibit 22-9, page 1008). Note the interplay of the various components of pension cost in the following schedules for these two corporations.

[24]For an interesting graphical presentation of this reconciliation, see Dennis M. Bline and Ted D. Skekel, "Effective Classroom Presentation of FAS 87 Footnote Reconciliation," *Issues in Accounting Education*, Fall 1988, pp. 215-227.

Exhibit 22-8   Thornton Electronics Inc.
Summary of 1992 Pension Information

	Recorded in Accounts		Memorandum Records				
	Pension Cost/ Expense	Prepaid/ (Accrued) Pension Cost	Projected Benefit Obligation	Fair Value of Pension Plan Assets	Unamortized Transition (Gain) Loss	Unrecognized Net Pension (Gains) Losses	Unrecognized Prior Service Cost
Balance, January 1, 1992		($15,000)	($1,495,000)	$1,385,000	($200,000)	($200,000)	$495,000
Recognition of components of net pension cost:							
Service cost	$ 75,000	(75,000)	(75,000)				
Interest cost	156,975	(156,975)	(156,975)				
Actual return on pension plan assets	(150,000)	150,000		150,000			
Amortization of prior service cost	90,000	(90,000)					(90,000)
Deferral of gain on pension plan assets	30,000	(30,000)				(30,000)	
Amortization of unrecognized pension (gain) loss	(9,182)	9,182				9,182	
Amortization of transition (gain) loss	(20,000)	20,000			20,000		
Contributions to fund		115,000		115,000			
Retirement benefits paid			136,975	(136,975)			
Change in PBO assumptions			(10,000)			10,000	
Balance December 31, 1992	$172,793	($72,793)	($1,600,000)	$1,513,025	($180,000)	($210,818)	$405,000

Exhibit 22-9   Philip Morris Companies Inc.

NOTES CONTINUED

Pension Plans:

Effective January 1, 1986, the company adopted Statement of Financial Accounting Standards No. 87, "Employers' Accounting for Pensions" ("SFAS 87"), for its U.S. pension plans. Pension cost and related disclo-sures for non-U.S. plans in 1987 and 1986 and for all plans in 1985 were determined under the provisions of the previous accounting principles.

U.S. Plans

The company and its subsidiaries sponsor noncontribu-tory defined benefit pension plans covering substantially all employees. The plans generally provide retirement benefits for salaried employees based on years of service and compensation during the last years of employment.

Retirement benefits for hourly employees generally are a flat dollar amount for each year of service. The company funds these plans in amounts consistent with the funding requirements of federal law and regulations. Net pension cost included the following components:

(in millions)	1987	1986
Service cost—benefits earned during the year	$ 93	$ 88
Interest cost on projected benefit obligation	190	172
Return on assets—actual	(148)	(436)
—deferred gain (loss)	(94)	211
Amortization of net gain upon adoption of SFAS 87	(28)	(28)
Net pension cost	$ 13	$ 7

The adoption of SFAS 87 decreased 1986 pension cost by approximately $76 million. Pension cost for 1985 was $74 million.

The funded status of the plans at December 31 was as follows:

(in millions)	1987	1986
Actuarial present value of accumulated benefit obligation—vested	$1,756	$1,758
—nonvested	104	94
	1,860	1,852
Benefits attributable to projected salaries	561	551
	2,421	2,403
Plan assets at fair value	2,936	2,917
Excess of assets over projected benefit obligation	515	514
Unamortized net gain upon adoption of SFAS 87	(373)	(401)
Unrecognized net loss from experience differences and assumption changes	42	77
Prepaid pension cost	$ 184	$ 190

The projected benefit obligation at December 31, 1987 and 1986 was determined using assumed discount rates of 8½% and 7¾% and assumed compensation increases of 7½% and 6¾%, respectively. The assumed long-term rate of return on plan assets was 9% at both dates. Plan assets consist principally of common stocks and fixed income securities.

The company sponsors a deferred profit-sharing plan covering certain salaried, nonunion and union employees. Contributions and cost are determined as a percentage of consolidated pre-tax earnings, as defined by the plan. Subsidiaries of the company also maintain other defined contribution plans. Amounts charged to expense for defined contribution plans totaled $118 million, $99 mil-lion and $77 million in 1987, 1986 and 1985, respectively.

Exhibit 22-10   Westinghouse Electric Corporation

Note 2: Pensions and Other Postretirement Benefits

The parent and its domestic subsidiaries have defined benefit pension plans covering substantially all employees. Plan benefits are based on either years of service and compensation levels at the time of retirement or a formula based on career earnings. These pension benefits are paid from trusts, which are funded by contributions from employees and the Corporation. The Corporation's funding policy is consistent with the funding requirements of federal law and regulations.

Effective January 1, 1987, the Corporation adopted the provisions of Statement of Financial Accounting Standards No. 87 (SFAS No. 87), "Employers' Accounting for Pensions," which supersedes all previous standards for pension accounting.

In contrast to prior years when pension expense and benefit obligations were determined using the unit credit actuarial method, SFAS No. 87 requires that the projected unit credit actuarial method be used to determine pension cost and the projected benefit obligation. This latter method utilizes both the employee's future service and projected future compensation in the determination of projected benefits. The new standard further requires the calculation of a "transition obligation" at January 1, 1987, to reflect the excess of the plan's projected benefit obligation over the fair market value of plan assets. The transition obligation is being amortized over a period of 15 years. Plan amendments which increase benefits for service to date are amortized over the average remaining service lives of employees. Additionally, SFAS No. 87 requires that pension expense reported in prior years not be restated to reflect the retroactive application of the new standard.

The projected benefit obligation is the actuarial present value of that portion of the projected benefits that is attributable to employee service rendered to date. Service cost is the actuarial present value of that portion of the projected benefits that is attributable to employee service rendered for the year.

Net periodic pension cost for domestic plans was $112 million in 1987, $113 million in 1986, and $117 million in 1985. The 1987 amount included a reduction resulting from the adoption of SFAS No. 87, which was offset by an increase for plan benefit improvements for service rendered in prior years.

Net periodic pension cost for 1987 included the following components, in millions:

Service cost — benefits earned during the period		$ 66.2
Interest cost on projected benefit obligation		393.7
Actual return on plan assets	$ 18.1	
Amount deferred	(424.4)	
Recognized return on plan assets		(406.3)
Amortization of unrecognized net obligation		47.3
Amortization of unrecognized prior service cost		10.8
Net periodic pension cost		$111.7

The following table sets forth the domestic plans' funded status and amounts recognized in the Corporation's Consolidated Balance Sheet at December 31, 1987, in millions:

Actuarial present value of benefit obligation:	
Vested	$(3,832.1)
Nonvested	(399.9)
Accumulated benefit obligation	(4,232.0)
Effect of projected future compensation levels	(445.3)
Projected benefit obligation for service rendered to date	(4,677.3)
Plan assets at fair value, primarily listed stocks, fixed income and real estate investments	3,629.5
Projected benefit obligation in excess of plan assets	(1,047.8)
Unrecognized net loss	429.4
Prior service cost not yet recognized in net periodic pension cost	124.6
Unrecognized net obligation at January 1, 1987, net of amortization	663.0
Prefunded pension contribution	$ 169.2

For the principal United States pension plans, the discount rate and rate of increase in future compensation levels used in determining the actuarial present value of the projected benefit obligation were 9.0 percent and 6.0 percent, respectively. The expected long-term rate of return on assets was 11.0 percent. For 1986 and 1985, the earnings assumption used to determine pension expense and the discount rate used to determine the actuarial present value of accumulated benefits were 12.25 percent for plan participants who were retired or inactive-vested at December 31, 1982, and 8.25 percent for all other plan participants.

Conclusion   It is too early to evaluate the overall impact of FASB Statement No. 87 and 88 on financial statements and on their usefulness to decision makers. The failure to recognize completely market changes as they occur will conceivably lead to management actions to recognize gains earlier and defer losses longer. Unless carefully monitored, this could lead to abuses of pension plans and leave employees with less protection than they had expected. The Board had to compromise its final pension standards, modifying exposure drafts which had recommended earlier and more complete recognition of the impact of economic change on pension plans.

This led to a more complicated standard, and one that leaves considerable doubt as to its ultimate effects.

The Board included the following conclusion in Appendix A of Statement No. 87.

> After considering the range of comments . . ., the Board concluded that the changes required by this Statement represent a worthwhile improvement in financial reporting. Opinion 8 noted in 1966 that "accounting for pension cost is in a transitional stage" (paragraph 17). The Board believes that is still true in 1985. FASB Concepts Statement No. 5, *Recognition and Measurement ins Financial Statements of Business Enterprises*, paragraph 2, indicates that "the Board intends future change [in practice] to occur in the gradual, evolutionary way that has characterized past change." The Board realizes that the evolutionary change in some areas may have to be slower than in others. The Board believes that it would be conceptually appropriate and preferable to recognize a net pension liability or asset measured as the difference between the projected benefit obligation and plan assets, either with no delay in recognition of gains and losses, or perhaps with gains and losses reported currently in comprehensive income but not in earnings. However, it concluded that those approaches would be too great a change from past practice to be adopted at the present time. In light of the differences in respondents' views and the practical considerations noted, the Board concluded that the provisions of this Statement as a whole represent an improvement in financial reporting.[25]

The postretirement benefits exposure draft discussed earlier in the chapter is receiving much attention by all segments of the business world. The major provisions of the proposed standard are summarized in the following appendix.

---

[25]*Statement of Financial Standards No. 87*, par. 107.

Appendix

Postemployment Benefits Other Than Pensions

In 1979, the FASB added a project on postemployment benefits other than pensions to its agenda and made it part of its project on pensions. In 1984, the other postemployment benefits project (OPEB) was identified as a separate project so that the pension project could be expedited. As soon as FASB Statements No. 87 and 88 were issued, the Board turned significant attention to the OPEB project.

Postemployment benefits include any benefits that are paid to employees after their service employment has ended, whether retired or not. Because health care costs paid after retirement have become such a large dollar outlay, the Board focused its attention on this area, and in February, 1989, issued an exposure draft, "Employers' Accounting for Postretirement Benefits Other than Pensions." Although technically the exposure draft includes any postretirement benefits, the health care benefits were the primary focus. Other postemployment benefits that are not necessarily related to retirement are still under study and could become a subject for later pronouncements by the FASB.

Nature of Postretirement Health Care Plans

Before discussing the principal recommendations of the exposure draft, it is important to understand more clearly what these postretirement benefits really are. After World War II, many companies not only initiated pension plans, but they began programs to provide health care benefits for their employees. In many arrangements, these benefits were extended not only to currently employed individuals, but also to retired former employees. Often these plans were not formalized into an agreement, but their existence became an accepted fact. Because the costs of health care were not onerous at first, most employers were not concerned about funding for these costs. As claims arose, they were paid and the payments were charged to expense. In some instances, a separate insurance carrier, such as Blue Cross, was used to cover the risk. But in many cases, especially for larger companies, a form of self-insurance developed.

Over the years, factors such as longer life expectancy, improved medical treatment facilities, and early retirements have combined to cause health care costs for retired employees to increase dramatically. In 1965, health care costs in the United States amounted to an estimated $38 billion. Employers paid 18% of those costs. In 1988, just 23 years later, health care costs had risen to an estimated $532 billion annually, with employers paying 28% of the bill.[26] Because most employer health care plans provide specific types of benefits rather than specific dollar amounts, as is true for most pension plans, these increased health costs have a direct impact on a company's cash outflow.

Most retirement health care plans are non-pay related. In other words, an employee receives specific health care benefits upon retirement regardless of the level of pay earned. The benefits are paid as health care is needed. Usually the plan provides for a minimum level of service before an employee becomes eligible to receive the benefits, but after a certain period of time, known as the full eligibility date, full benefits are paid.

As has been mentioned earlier, a majority of pension plans are pay related, with benefits increasing as the employee earns a higher salary and works additional years. Income tax laws have been favorable to early deduction of pension accruals, but similar favorable treatment has not been granted to other postretirement benefits. This decreases the incentive to fund these costs that cannot be deducted from taxable revenue until they are actually paid.

FASB Recommendations on Accounting for Postretirement Benefits

After studying postretirement benefits, especially, postretirement health care costs, the FASB concluded that they were, in reality, very similar to pension costs. Benefits are earned while employees provide service to the company, at least up to the eligibility date; thus, they are a form of deferred compensation. Because of this similarity, the Board recommended that these costs be accrued and that the unfunded liability be reported on the balance sheet. Because these costs have not been recorded in the past, the magnitude of their impact on U.S. corporations is unknown. Estimates have ranged from $168 billion made by the Employees Benefit Research Institute[27] to $2 trillion mentioned in a 1988 Wall Street Journal article.[28] It is also estimated that the implementation of this exposure draft would, on the average, result in additional expense amounting to 15-20% of the annual income reported by U.S. corporations.[29]

Realizing this impact, the FASB recommended a 15-year transition period to accrue fully all accumulated earned postretirement benefits, rather than requiring immediate recognition of these liabilities. In discussing the accrual and reporting of these costs, the Board has recognized four different categories of employees and their benefits as follows:

---

[26]Carol J. Loomis, "The Killer Cost Stalking Business', op. cit., p. 61.

[27]As reported by Dennis Salisbury, President of the Employee Benefit Research Institute in the FASB video "Other Postemployment Benefits Project," February 1989.

[28]Lee Berton, "FASB Plan Would Make Firms Deduct Billions for Potential Retiree Benefits", The Wall Street Journal, August 17, 1988, p. 3.

[29]Dennis Salisbury, loc. cit.

1. Retired employees.
2. Employees not retired, but who are eligible to receive full postretirement benefits.
3. Active employees who have not reached their full eligibility date.
   a. Portion of benefits earned through service before full eligibility date.
   b. Portion of benefits not yet earned, but expected to be earned in the future as employee reaches the full eligibility date.

The FASB recommends in the exposure draft that costs for categories 1, 2, and 3a should be accrued. The Board recommends that these costs be attributed to the period of service from the date of hire to the full eligibility date rather than to the retirement date that is used for most pension plans. It also recommends that postretirement benefit costs generally contain the same components as defined for pension costs under FASB Statement No. 87.[30] Because of differences between pension costs and postretirement benefits, however, some of the components are computed differently.

The exposure draft also provides for the computation of a minimum liability similar to that required for pension plans in FASB Statement No. 87. The proposal, however, provides for computing the minimum liability only for categories 1 and 2 above, or in other words, only for employees who have reached the full eligibility date. It is proposed that implementation of this provision be delayed until 1997. It is expected that the accrual provision that would begin in 1992 will result in most companies reaching the minimum liability level by 1997.

A disclosure policy similar to that for pensions is proposed. In addition, information on the assumed health care cost trend rate and a sensitivity analysis of how health care costs would be affected by a 1% change in these assumptions must also be disclosed.

While the exposure draft stresses health care costs, other postretirement benefits such as the cost of life insurance contracts, legal assistance benefits, and tuition assistance must also be reported on an accrual basis. For some companies, these costs may also be material and have a significant impact on the company's income.

There is a high level of interest in this proposed standard. Companies are focusing on these costs with greater interest, and some have considered reducing or changing postretirement plans and benefits to avoid the significant consequences of recording these costs in the short run and paying for them in the long run. However, trying to change benefits for those employees who have earned them has proven difficult, and many lawsuits have resulted when reductions in benefits have been proposed by companies. The accounting profession has not created the problems arising from the escalating costs of postretirement benefits, but it has focused national attention on them as it applies the conceptual framework to this important area.

---

[30]Exposure draft, *Proposed Statement of Financial Accounting Standards*, "Employers' Accounting for Postretirement Benefits Other Than Pensions", (Norwalk: Financial Accounting Standards Board, 1989), par. 39

Key Terms

Accrued pension cost 985

Accumulated benefit obligation (ABO) 998

Actual return on pension plan assets 988

Actuarial present value 982

Additional pension liability 998

Amortization of unrecognized net pension gain or loss 993

Amortization of unrecognized prior service cost 988

Contributory pension plan 979

Corridor amount 993

Curtailment of a pension plan 1002

Deferred pension cost 1000

Defined benefit pension plans 980

Defined contribution pension plans 980

Employee Retirement Income Security Act of 1974 (ERISA) 978

Expected return on pension plan assets 992

Expected service period 989

Fair value of pension plan assets 986

Full eligibility date 1012

Market-related value of pension plan assets 992

Minimum pension liability 997

Net periodic pension cost 985

Noncontributory pension plans 979

Pension gain or loss 991

Pension plan 977

Pension plan assets 980

Pension Benefit Guaranty Corportion (PBGC) 979

Postemployment benefits 977

Postretirement benefits 1011

Prepaid pension cost 985

Prior service cost 988

Projected benefit obligation (PBO) 986

Service cost 987

Settlement of a pension plan 1002

Settlement interest rate 987

Single-employer pension plans 979

Termination benefits 1002

Transition gain or loss 994

Unrecognized net pension gain or loss 993

Unrecognized prior service cost 989

Vested benefits 979

Questions

1. What conditions led to a growth in private pension plans in America?

2. (a) What conditions led to the enactment in 1974 of the Employee Retirement Income Security Act (ERISA)? (b) What provisions in ERISA affected the safety of pension benefits for employees?

3. What is meant by the term *vesting*?

4. Distinguish between: (a) a defined benefit plan and a defined contribution plan, (b) a contributory plan and a noncontributory plan, (c) a single-employer and a multiemployer plan.

5. Distinguish between the accumulated benefit approach and the projected benefit approach in determining the amount of future benefits earned by employees under a defined benefit pension plan.

6. What factors must be considered by actuaries in determining the amount of future benefits under a defined benefit plan?

7. Explain how prior period pension costs arise (a) at the inception of a pension plan, and (b) at the time of a plan amendment.

8. What five accounting issues were addressed by the FASB in relation to defined benefit plans?

9. List and briefly describe the six basic components of net periodic pension cost.

10. How is the service cost portion of net periodic pension cost to be measured according to FASB Statement No. 87?

11. Since prior service costs are related to years of service already rendered, why are they considered to be a future pension cost?

12. How does the FASB recommend that prior service cost be amortized?

13. Does pension cost include the actual return on plan assets or the expected return? Explain.

14. The FASB identified 2 parts to the gain or loss component of pension cost. Identify the parts and explain how they are computed and used.

15. Why is a corridor amount identified in recognizing gain or loss from pension plans?

16. (a) How is the transition gain or loss arising from adoption of FASB Statements No. 87 and 88 computed. (b) How is the unrecognized transition gain or loss amortized?

17. What two types of liabilities can be identified as arising from pension plans?

18. (a) What conditions give rise to recognizing a minimum pension liability according to FASB Statement No. 87? (b) What conditions give rise to recognizing assets in a pension plan on the employer's books according to FASB Statement No. 87?

19. The FASB permits the use of an average market value of plan assets for some pension computations. In other cases, the fair market value at a specific measurement date must be used. Under what circumstances is the average market value permissible?

20. (a) Under what conditions does FASB Statement No. 87 provide for recording a contra-equity account? (b) How is it adjusted from period to period?

21. Distinguish between a pension settlement and a pension curtailment.

22. How are gains and losses arising from pension settlements recognized according to FASB Statement No. 88?

23. What is the function of the pension disclosure requirement included in the pension standards?

*24. What is meant by postretirement benefits, and what is the primary issue in accounting for their costs?

*25. What is the full eligibility date, and why is it an important date in accounting for postretirement benefits?

*Relates to Appendix

Discussion Cases   **Case 22-1   (I don't understand the note!)**

The following excerpts from a note were included with the 1985 financial statements for Dupont (E.I.) de Nemours at December 31, 1985, and presented to stockholders at the annual stockholders' meeting in early 1986. Dupont elected to apply FASB Statements No. 87 and 88 to their financial statements effective January 1, 1985. The amounts presented in the note are in millions of dollars.

The Company has noncontributory defined benefit plans covering most U.S. employees. The benefits for these plans are based primarily on years of service and employees' pay near retirement. The company's funding policy is consistent with the funding requirements of Federal law and regulations. Plan assets consist principally of common stocks and U.S. governmental obligations.

1985 Pension costs include the following components:		
Service cost—benefits earned during the period		$ 111
Interest cost on projected benefit obligation		587
Return on assets—actual	$(2,214)	
—deferred gain	1,525	(689)
Amortization of net gain at January 1, 1985		(167)
Net pension cost		$(158)

The funded status of U.S. plans at December 31, 1985, was as follows:

Actuarial present value of vested benefit obligation	$(5,165)	
Accumulated benefit obligation	$(5,502)	
Projected benefit obligation		$(5,763)
Plan assets at fair value		9,401
Excess of assets over projected benefit obligation		$3,638
Unrecognized net gain at January 1, 1985		(2,720)
Unrecognized 1985 gain		(840)
Prepaid pension cost at December 31, 1985		$ 78

The projected benefit obligation was determined using an assumed discount rate of 11% (12.25% at January 1, 1985), and an assumed long-term rate of compensation increase of 5%. The assumed long-term rate of return on plan assets is 9%.

As the external auditor, you were present at the meeting and were asked the following questions. How would you respond to the queries?

(1) Since the plan assets' value exceeds the vested benefit obligation, why isn't there an asset on the balance sheet for the excess?
(2) What does the note mean by "net gain?"
(3) Explain the two components of return on assets, actual and deferred gain.
(4) How does the return on assets of $(689) relate to the amortization of net gain of $(167)?
(5) How is the interest cost on projected benefit obligation computed?
(6) What is the difference between the accumulated benefit obligation and the projected benefit obligation?
(7) Does the DuPont note disclosure meet the requirements of FASB Statement No. 87?

Case 22-2   (Why fix something that isn't broken?)

The FASB's study of pension accounting for employers generated considerable interest among business executives. During the extended discussion period, pressure was brought to bear against the FASB by several individuals and the companies they represented to leave pension accounting alone. These business executives felt that the existing standards (APB Opinion No. 8) were adequate, and that further tinkering with the pension provisions was unnecessary.

What are some of the factors that caused the FASB to "hold on" to the pension issue until a standard was released?

Case 22-3 (What theoretical support is there for the pension standards?)

The topic of pensions was considered at length in an accounting theory class. The discussion centered around the following terms:

(a) Representational faithfulness
(b) Substance over form
(c) Verifiability
(d) Usefulness
(e) Present value
(f) Conservatism
(g) Adequate disclosure

How would these terms be helpful in resolving the issue of how to account for pension plans on the employer's books? Based on your understanding of these terms, assess the treatment of pension plans by the FASB in Statements No. 87 and 88.

*Case 22-4 (Are those postretirement benefits really accruable?)

George Logan, controller of Dyatine, Inc. has just finished reading a *Wall Street Journal* article about accounting for postretirement health costs. Dyatine has informally agreed to pay the medical costs of its retirees and their spouses for as long as they lived. Because the company has a young work force, very little has been paid under this program. Last year, an analysis of the potential liability indicated that there would not be significant risk of payment for at least ten years. No liability for future benefits has been accrued on Dyatine's books. But, according to the *Journal* article, this could change if the FASB's proposed standard becomes final. George has always felt that Dyatine was being generous with its employees, and that, if economic circumstances changed, the plan could be easily altered or terminated. George calls his CPA, Debra Adams, to ask her about the exposure draft and to see how she feels about the FASB proposal. He is surprised to learn that Debra is very supportive of the exposure draft. He asks for reasons and Debra, in turn, asks George to support his position.

Prepare a summary of the pros and cons surrounding the implementation of this exposure draft.

*Relates to Appendix

Exercises

Exercise 22-1 (Computation of pension service cost)

Pension plan information for Springfield Metro Company is as follows:

January 1, 1992	Projected benefit obligation	$3,620,000
	Accumulated benefit obligation	$2,850,000
1992 transactions	Pension benefits paid to retired employees	$136,000
December 31, 1992	Projected benefit obligation	$4,150,000
	Accumulated benefit obligation	$3,125,000
Discount (settlement) rate		12%

Assuming no change in actuarial assumptions, what is the pension service cost for 1992?

Exercise 22-2   (Amortization of prior service cost—plan amendment)
Queensland Company has 5 employees belonging to its pension plan. Expected years of future service for these employees are as follows:

Employee	Future Service Years
1	3
2	6
3	7
4	9
5	10

On January 1, 1992, Queensland initiated an amendment to its pension plan that increased the projected benefit obligation for the plan by $390,000. If Queensland amortizes the prior service cost of the pension plan by assigning an equal amount to each future period of service of each employee who is active at the date of the amendment and expected to receive benefits under the plan, determine the amortization for the years 1992, 1994, 1998, and 2001.

Exercise 22-3   (Amount of funding and amortization of prior service cost)
Stratosphere, Inc. has a work force of 200 employees. A new pension plan is negotiated on January 1, 1992, with the labor union. Based on the provisions of the pension agreement, prior service cost related to the new plan amounts to $3,726,000. The cost is to be funded evenly with annual contributions over a 10-year period, with the first payment due at the end of 1992. The cost is to be amortized over the average remaining service life of the covered employees. The interest rate for funding purposes is 10%. It is anticipated that, on the average, 10 employees will retire each year over the next 20 years.

(1) Compute the annual amount Stratosphere will pay to fund its prior service cost.
(2) Compute the amount of amortization of prior service cost for 1992, 1994, and 1999.

Exercise 22-4   (Amortization of prior service cost; straight-line method)
Osvaldo Awning Co. has unrecognized prior service cost of $1,262,000 arising from a pension plan amendment. The board of directors decided to amortize this cost over the average remaining service period for its 45 employees on a straight-line basis. It is assumed that employees will retire at the rate of 3 employees each year over a 15-year period. (1) Compute the average remaining service life and the annual amortization of prior service cost for Osvaldo. (2) Assuming that pension cost other than amortization of prior service cost was $370,000 for the year, and $450,000 was contributed by the employer to the pension fund, prepare the journal entries relating to the pension plan for the current year.

Exercise 22-5   (Computation of actual return on plan assets)

The Longlee Electrical Company maintains a fund to cover its pension plan. The following data relate to the fund for 1992:

January 1	Fair value of pension plan assets	$875,000
	Market-related value of plan assets (5 year weighted average)	$715,000
During year	Pension benfits paid	$62,000
	Contributions made to the fund	$50,000
December 31	Fair value of pension plan assets	$980,000
	Market-related value of plan assets (5 year weighted average)	$730,000

Compute the 1992 actual return on plan assets for Longlee Electrical.

Exercise 22-6   (Return on plan assets—expected and actual)

Tingey Originals has a pension plan covering its 75 employees. Tingey anticipates a 12% return on its pension plan assets. The fund trustee furnishes Tingey with the following information relating to the pension fund for 1992:

January 1	Fair value of pension plan assets	$1,350,000
	Market-related value of pension plan assets (5 year weighted average)	$1,220,000
During year	Actual return on pension plan assets	$155,000
December 31	Fair value of pension plan assets	$1,470,000
	Market-related value of pension plan assets (5 year weighted average)	$1,210,000

Compute the difference between the actual and expected return on plan assets. How should the difference be treated in determining pension cost for 1992, assuming Tingey bases expected return on the market-related value of the plan assets?

Exercise 22-7   (Amortization of unrecognized gain on plan assets)

Melba Enterprises has an unrecognized gain of $425,000 relating to its pension plan as of January 1, 1992. Management has chosen to amortize this deferral on a straight-line basis over the 10-year average remaining service life of its employees, subject to the limitation of the corridor amount. Additional facts about the pension plan as of January 1, 1992 are as follows:

Projected benefit obligation	$1,950,000
Accumulated benefit obligation	$1,850,000
Fair value of pension plan assets	$1,500,000
Market-related value of pension plan assets (5 year weighted average)	$1,350,000

Compute the minimum amortization of unrecognized gain to be recognized by Melba in 1992.

Exercise 22-8   (Computation of gain or loss component)

The gain or loss component of pension cost consists of (a) a deferral of the difference between actual and expected return on pension plan assets and (b) amortization of unrecognized pension gains and losses. Determine the proper addition (deduction) to pension cost related to the gain or loss component under each of the following independent conditions.

	a	b	c	d
(1) Actual return on pension plan assets	$200,000	$200,000	$500,000	$500,000
(2) Expected return on pension plan assets	$180,000	$230,000	$400,000	$550,000
(3) Unrecognized (gain) loss at beginning of year	$200,000	$275,000	$(100,000)	$(75,000)
(4) Average service life of employees used for amortization	10 years	5 years	8 years	12 years
(5) Corridor amount	$100,000	$150,000	$50,000	$175,000

Exercise 22-9   (Computation of pension cost and journal entries)

The accountants for Bern Financial Services provide you with the following detailed information at December 31, 1992. Based on these data, prepare the journal entries related to the accrual and funding of pension cost for 1992.

Service cost	$45,000
Actual return on pension plan assets	$75,000
Interest cost	$52,000
Excess of expected return over actual return on pension plan assets	$20,000
Amortization of deferred pension loss from prior years	$15,000
Amortization of transition loss	$8,000
Amortization of prior service cost	$30,000
Contribution to pension fund	$72,000

Exercise 22-10   (Pension cost computation)

Fredco's defined benefit pension plan had a projected benefit obligation of $10,000,000 at the beginning of the year. This was based on a 10% discount rate (settlement interest rate). The fair value of pension plan assets at the beginning of the year was $10,400,000. These assets were expected to earn a long-term rate of return on the fair value of 8%. During the year, service cost was $800,000. At the date of transition to FASB Statement No. 87, a net pension asset of $400,000 existed. This was equal to the amount by which the plan was overfunded at that date. At the transition date, the average service life of the employees expected to receive the benefits was 20 years. There was no unrecognized prior service cost or unrecognized net pension gain (loss) at the beginning of the year. The actual return on pension plan assets for the year was $900,000. The accumulated benefit obligation was $9,500,000 at the beginning of the year. Compute Fredco's net periodic pension cost for the year.

Exercise 22-11   (Computing and recording minimum pension liability)

Tacoma Energy Corp. has had a retirement program for its employees for several years. It adopted the new FASB pension standards beginning January 1, 1988. The following information relates to the plan for 1992:

Balances at December 31, 1992:	
Projected benefit obligation	$967,500
Accumulated benefit obligation	$825,000
Fair value of pension plan assets	$640,000
Market-related value of pension plan assets (5 year weighted average)	$610,000
Prepaid pension cost	$21,000
Unamortized transition loss	$76,000
Unrecognized prior service cost	$80,000

In prior years, no additional liability was required. Compute the minimum pension liability, if any for 1992, and prepare any necessary journal entries to record the liability.

Exercise 22-12 (Computing minimum pension liability)

Chateau Furniture and Cabinet Mfg. Co. computes the following balances for its defined benefit pension plan as of the end of its fiscal year (000's omitted).

Projected benefit obligation	$1,625
Accumulated benefit obligation	$1,380
Fair value of pension plan assets	$1,460
Market-related value of pension plan assets (5-year weighted average)	$1,336
Accrued pension cost	$61
Unamortized transition loss	$115
Unrecognized prior service cost	$180

(1) According to FASB Statement No. 87, what is the amount of additional liability, if any, required to reflect the minimum pension liability?

(2) Some FASB members felt that the minimum pension liability should consider expected future salary levels rather than the current levels. If this approach had been adopted in the standard, what additional liability adjustment, if any, would have been required?

Exercise 22-13 (Reconciliation of funding status)

From the following information for each of three independent cases, prepare the reconciliation that would be included in the pension note according to FASB Statement No. 87.

	Case 1	Case 2	Case 3
Projected benefit obligation	$12,500	$6,290	$890
Accumulated benefit obligation	9,700	5,400	700
Fair value of pension plan assets	15,300	4,200	650
Market-related value of pension plan assets	12,800	5,000	560
Unamortized transition (gain) or loss	(400)	1,200	(75)
Unrecognized net (gain) or loss from prior years	(200)	(500)	100
Unrecognized prior service cost	1,200	1,100	200
Recorded additional liability	-0-	-0-	100
Prepaid/(accrued) pension cost	3,400	(290)	85

Problems

Problem 22-1 (Entries to record accrual and funding of pension costs)

The Allied Rental Company reported the following information related to its pension plan for the years 1992-1995. The fund is administered by a separate outside trustee.

Year	Pension Cost Accrual	Contribution	Benefit Payments to Retirees	Actual Return on Pension Plan Assets
1992	$560,700	$625,000	$300,000	$350,000
1993	725,000	670,000	300,000	400,000
1994	685,000	620,000	275,000	450,000
1995	726,500	625,000	400,000	525,000

Instructions:

(1) Prepare the required summary journal entries for each year to record applicable pension items.

(2) Assuming Allied had an accrued pension liability of $25,000 at January 1, 1992, compute the prepaid/accrued pension account balance at December 31, 1995.

(3) Assuming that the fair value of the pension plan assets at January 1, 1992, was $2,600,000, compute the fair value of the pension plan assets at December 31, 1995.

Problem 22-2   (Computation of prior service cost funding and amortization)

The Staybrite Electronics Co. amended its pension plan effective January 1, 1992. The increase in the pension benefit obligation occurring as a result of the plan amendment is $6,290,000. Staybrite arranged to fund the prior service cost by equal annual contributions over the next 15 years at 10% interest. The first payment will be made December 31, 1992. The company decides to amortize the prior service cost on a straight-line basis over the average remaining service life of its employees. The company has 225 employees at January 1, 1992, who are entitled to the benefits of the amendment. It is estimated that, on the average, 15 employees will retire each year.

Instructions:

(1) Compute the amount Staybrite will pay each year to fund the prior service cost arising from the plan amendment.

(2) Compute Staybrite's annual prior service cost amortization.

Problem 22-3   (Computation of gain or loss component)

The Birnberg Equipment Co. has a defined benefit pension plan. As of January 1, 1992, the following balances were computed for the pension plan:

Unrecognized pension gain	$500,000
Fair value of pension plan assets	$3,100,000
Market-related value of plan assets (5 year weighted average)	$2,600,000
Projected benefit obligation	$3,600,000
Accumulated benefit obligation	$3,300,000

It was anticipated that the pension plan assets would earn 11% in 1992. The actual return on pension plan assets was $275,000. The company has elected to amortize the unrecognized pension gains and losses over 10 years.

Instructions:

(1) Compute the amount of gain or loss deferral for 1992.

(2) Compute the amount of amortization of unrecognized pension gain or loss for 1992.

(3) If net periodic pension cost, exclusive of the gain or loss component, is $626,000, what is the net periodic pension cost after including the gain or loss component.

(4) What is the unrecognized pension gain or loss that Birnberg will carry forward to 1993 as a result of changes in the return on pension plan assets?

▌▌▌ Problem 22-4   (Computation, recording, and funding of pension cost)

Averon Industrial, Inc. computed the following components of pension cost for the years 1992-1994.

Components of Pension Cost	(000's omitted)		
	1992	1993	1994
Service cost	$330	$415	$580
Interest cost	150	170	220
Actual return on pension plan assets	35	50	40
Expected return on pension plan assets	30	45	50
Amortization of unrecognized pension (gain) or loss—above corridor amount	(20)	(10)	18
Amortization of unrecognized prior service cost	90	105	105
Amortization of transition (gain) or loss	(20)	(15)	(15)
Amount contributed to fund	520	580	750

Instruction:

(1) Compute the net periodic pension cost for the years 1992-1994.
(2) Prepare the journal entries to record the computed pension cost in (1) and the funding of the pension plan.
(3) If the prepaid pension cost balance at January 1, 1992, was $75, compute the balance of the prepaid/(accrued) pension cost account at December 31, 1994.

Problem 22-5   (Computation of transition amortization and minimum liability)

Atlas Wholesale Company adopted FASB Statement No. 87 as of January 1, 1987, for its defined benefit pension plan and computed a transition loss of $6,300 at that date. The following information was provided relative to the plan for the years 1991-1993:

	January 1, 1991	December 31, 1991	December 31, 1992	December 31, 1993
Accrued pension cost	$ 625			
Projected benefit obligation	27,525	$29,700	$32,600	$34,300
Accumulated benefit obligation	22,900	23,800	29,300	37,000
Fair value of pension plan assets	20,600	24,200	27,900	31,500
Market-related value of pension plan assets (5 year weighted average)	17,900	18,600	21,300	26,950
Net pension cost exclusive of transition amortization		1,920	2,410	2,860
Contributions made to pension fund		1,970	3,510	2,410

Assume the average remaining service life of employees in the pension plan at the transition date was 15 years.

Instructions:

(1) Compute the amount of net periodic pension cost for each of the 3 years.
(2) Prepare the journal entries for recording the net pension cost and the pension funding for the 3 years.
(3) Compute any additional liability to be recorded for each of the 3 years under the minimum liability requirements of FASB Statement No. 87.
(4) Identify the pension balance sheet accounts and their amounts as of December 31, 1992. There is no unrecognized prior service cost at this date.

Problem 26-6   (Computing and recording additional pension liability)

The following balances relate to the defined benefit pension plan of Cameron Industries:

	12/31/91	12/31/92
Fair value of pension plan assets	$149,000	$160,000
Market-related value of pension plan assets (5 year weighted average)	145,000	152,000
Projected benefit obligation	173,200	191,600
Accumulated benefit obligation	159,100	172,900
Prepaid/(accrued) pension cost	4,200	(1,950)
Unrecognized prior service cost	8,200	6,300

Instructions:

(1) Determine the additional pension liability, if any, at December 31, 1991 and December 31, 1992.
(2) Prepare journal entries for the additional pension liability adjustment, if any, at December 31, 1991 and December 31, 1992. Assume that the company had not previously recognized additional pension liability under FASB Statement No. 87.

Problem 22-7   (Adjusting additional pension liability)

The Adamson Corporation adopted FASB Statement No. 87 as of January 1, 1987. A transition loss of $2,500,000 was calculated at the transition date. At the end of 1989, an additional pension liability of $1,200,000 was recorded for the first time, the offset being charged to Deferred Pension Cost. Minimum pension liability computations for 1990-1993 indicated the following additional pension liability amounts:

December 31, 1990	$1,300,000
December 31, 1991	$1,600,000
December 31, 1992	$900,000
December 31, 1993	$1,100,000

The transition loss is being amortized over a 10-year period, and no plan amendments occurred during these years.

Instructions: For each of the 4 years, prepare the journal entry to adjust the minimum pension liability account to the balance indicated above.

Problem 22-8 (Journal entries and minimum pension liability)

Rienstern Transportation Co. adopted the provisions of FASB Statements No. 87 and 88 effective January 1, 1987. At that time, a transition gain of $330,000 was computed. A 15-year amortization period is used for this gain. The following balances relate to the pension plan at December 31, 1991 and 1992.

	(000's omitted)	
	December 31, 1991	December 31, 1992
Projected benefit obligation	$3,075	$3,160
Accumulated benefit obligation	2,650	2,775
Fair value of pension plan assets	2,600	2,400
Market-related value of pension plan assets	2,550	2,750
Unrecognized prior service cost	240	215
Prepaid/(accrued) pension cost	15	(30)

Instructions:

(1) Determine if a minimum pension liability adjustment is required at December 31, 1991 and 1992.
(2) Prepare journal entries at December 31, 1991 and 1992, to record any additional liability.

Problem 22-9 (Disclosure of pension plan information)

The following information relates to the pension plan of Circle Manufacturing Company at December 31, 1992. Assume that Circle adopted FASB Statement No. 87 effective January 1, 1987.

Balances at December 31, 1992:	(000's omitted)
Projected benefit obligation	$11,750
Fair value of pension plan assets	$10,800
Accumulated benefit obligation	$9,900
Vested benefit obligation	$7,400
Unrecognized transition loss	$850
Unrecognized net loss (arose in 1992)	$60
Accrued pension cost	$40
1992 activity:	
Service cost	$875
Interest cost	$1,100
Actual return on pension plan assets	$1,250
Expected return on pension plan assets	$1,310
Amortization of transition loss	$75

Instructions: Prepare the pension note at December 31, 1992 that discloses the component parts of pension cost and the reconciliation of the funded status of the plan.

▌▌Problem 22-10 (Comprehensive computation of pension cost components)

The actuaries for Viewmont Cable Company provided Viewmont's accountants with the following information related to the company's pension plan.

	(000's omitted)
December 31, 1992:	
Increase in PBO arising from plan amendment	$732
January 1, 1992:	
Projected benefit obligation	$3,800
Accumulated benefit obligation	$3,420
Fair value of pension plan assets	$2,530
Market-related value of pension plan assets—5 year weighted average	$2,100
Accrued pension cost	$ 488
Unamortized transition loss from Jan. 1, 1987	$110
Settlement discount rate	12%
Average service life for amortization of transition gain or loss	10 years
Average service life for amortization of gain and prior service costs	12 years
Unamoritized pension gain—prior year	$60
Expected rate of return	10%
For year 1992:	
Benefit payments to retirees	$185
Contributions to pension plan	$300
December 31, 1992:	
Projected benefit obligation	$4,161
Fair value of pension plan assets	$2,865

Instructions: Based on the data provided, prepare a schedule similar to that of Exhibit 22-8 for Viewmont Cable Company for 1992.

Chapter 23

Accounting Changes and Error Corrections

The financial statements of companies sometimes report significantly different results from year to year. This may be due to changes in economic circumstances as reflected in the statements. But it may also be due to changes in accounting methods or to corrections of errors in recording past transactions. As an example, during 1987 General Electric Company changed its method of accounting for income taxes and its method of accounting for inventory manufacturing costs. These changes increased 1987 net income by $858 millon, an increase of almost 17 percent. Without these changes, G.E. would have reported a 15 percent decrease in earnings for 1987. As another example, during 1987 Amerada Hess corporation adopted Financial Accounting Statement No. 96, "Accounting for Income Taxes." This accounting change resulted in a decrease in retained earnings prior to 1985 of $201.8 millon and a restatement of 1985 and 1986 earnings with increases of $38.3 and $36.3 million respectively. In addition, Amerada Hess reported an increase of $47.4 million in net income in 1987 because of this change.

As these examples show, changing the accounting methods used can have a dramatic impact on the financial statements of a company. Because of this impact, one can argue that accounting changes detract from the informational characteristics of *comparability* and *consistency* discussed in Chapter 2. So why are these accounting changes made? The main reasons for such changes may be summarized as follows:

1. A company, as a result of experience or new information, may change its estimates of revenues or expenses, for example, the estimate of uncollectible accounts receivable, or the estimated service lives of depreciable assets.

2. Due to changes in economic conditions, companies may need to change methods of accounting to more clearly reflect the current economic situation.

3. Accounting standard-setting bodies may require the use of a new ac-

counting method or principle, such as the new income tax requirements as noted in the Amerada Hess example.

4. The acquisition or divestiture of companies, which has been particularly prevalent in the 1980's, may cause a change in the reporting entity.

Whatever the reason, accountants must keep the primary qualitative characteristic of *usefulness* in mind. They must determine if the reasons for accounting changes are appropriate, and then how best to report the changes to facilitate understanding of the financial statements.

The detection of errors in accounting for past transactions presents a similar problem. The errors must be corrected and appropriate disclosures made so that the readers of the financial statements will clearly understand what has happened. The purpose of this chapter is to discuss the different types of accounting changes and error corrections, and the appropriate accounting procedures that should be used.

Treatment of Accounting Changes and Error Corrections

The accounting profession has identified three main categories of accounting changes:[1]

1. Change in accounting estimate
2. Change in accounting principle
3. Change in reporting entity

In addition, while not an accounting change, past **accounting errors** resulting from mathematical mistakes, improper application of accounting principles, or omissions of material facts must be corrected.

As pointed out in Chapter 1, a major objective of published financial statements is to provide users with information to help them predict, compare, and evaluate future earning power and cash flows of the reporting entity. When a reporting entity adjusts its past estimates of revenues earned or costs incurred, changes its accounting principles from one method to another, changes its nature as a reporting entity, or corrects past errors, it becomes more difficult for a user to predict the future from past historical statements. The basic accounting issue is whether these changes and error corrections should be reported as adjustments of the prior periods' statements, and thus increase their comparability with the current and future statements, or whether the changes and error corrections should affect only the current and future years.

Several alternatives have been suggested for reporting accounting changes and correction of errors.

1. Restate the financial statements presented for prior periods to reflect the effect of the change or correction. Adjust the beginning Retained

---

[1] *Opinions of the Accounting Principles Board, No. 20, "Accounting Changes"* (New York: American Institute of Certified Public Accountants, 1971).

Earnings balance for the current period for the cumulative effect of the change or correction.

2. Make no adjustment to statements presented for prior periods. Report the cumulative effect of the change or correction in the current year as a direct entry to Retained Earnings.

3. Same as (2) except report the cumulative effect of the change or correction as a special item in the income statement instead of directly to Retained Earnings.

4. Report the cumulative effect in the current year as in (3), but also present limited pro forma information for all prior periods included in the financial statements reporting "what might have been" if the change or correction had been made in the prior years.

5. Make the change effective only for current and future periods with no catch-up adjustment. Correct errors only if they still affect the statements.

Each of these methods for reporting an accounting change or correcting an error has been used by companies in the past, and arguments can be made for each of the various approaches. For example, some accountants argue that accounting principles should be applied consistently for all reported periods. Therefore, if a new accounting principle is used in the current period, the financial statements presented for prior periods should be restated so that the results shown for all reported periods are based on the same accounting principles. Other accountants contend that restating financial statements may dilute public confidence in those statements. Principles applied in earlier periods were presumably appropriate at that time and should be considered final. The only exceptions would be for changes in a reporting entity or for corrections of errors. In addition, restating financial statements is costly, requires considerable effort, and is sometimes impossible due to lack of data.

Because of the diversity of practice and the resulting difficulty in user understandability of the financial statements, the Accounting Principles Board issued Opinion No. 20. The Board's objective was to bring increased uniformity to reporting practice. Evidence of compromise exists in the final opinion, as the Board attempted to reflect both its desire to increase comparability of financial statements and to improve user confidence in published financial statements. Depending on the type of accounting change or error correction, different accounting treatment is required, as explained in the following sections.

Change in Accounting Estimate

Contrary to what many people believe, accounting information cannot always be measured and reported precisely. Also, to be reported on a timely basis for decision making, accounting data often must be based on estimates of future events. The financial statements incorporate these estimates, which are based on the best professional judgment given the information available at that time. At a later date, however, additional experience or new facts sometimes make it clear that the estimates need to be revised to more accurately reflect the existing business circumstances. When this happens, a **change in accounting estimate** occurs.

Examples of areas where changes in accounting estimates often are needed include:

1. Uncollectible receivables
2. Useful lives of depreciable or intangible assets
3. Residual vaues for depreciable assets
4. Warranty obligations
5. Quantities of mineral reserves to be depleted
6. Actuarial assumptions for pensions or other post-employment benefits
7. Number of periods benefited by deferred costs

Accounting for a change in estimate has already been discussed in Chapter 4 and throughout the text in areas where changes in estimates are common. By way of review, all changes in estimates should be reflected either in the current period or in current and future periods. No retroactive adjustments or pro forma statements are to be prepared for a change in accounting estimate. Changes in estimates are considered to be part of the normal accounting process and not corrections or changes of past periods.

However, disclosures such as the following, made by Crown Central Petroleum Corporation, are useful in helping readers of financial statements understand the impact of changes in estimates.

Exhibit 23-1   Crown Central Petroleum Corporation

Note N — Change in Accounting Estimate

In the second quarter of 1987, the Company increased the estimated remaining useful lives of its refinery units based upon available technology and anticipated severity of service. Remaining asset lives which averaged 9 years were increased to an average of 20 years. The effects of this change in accounting estimate were to decrease 1987 depreciation expense by approximately $3,224,000 and increase 1987 net income by approximately $1,799,000, or $.25 per primary share, ($.18 per fully diluted share).

Change in Accounting Principle

A **change in accounting principle** involves a change from one generally accepted principle or method to another.[2] A change in principle, as defined in APB Opinion No. 20, does not include the initial adoption of an accounting principle as a result of transactions or events that had not occured (or were immaterial) in previous periods. Also, a change from a principle that is not generally accepted to one that is generally accepted is

---

[2]The classification "change in accounting principle" includes changes in methods used to account for transactions. No attempt was made by the Accounting Principles Board in Opinion No. 20 to distinguish between a principle and a method.

considered to be an error correction rather than a change in accounting principle.

If an asset is affected by both a change in principle and a change in estimate during the same period, APB Opinion No. 20 requires that the change be treated as a change in estimate rather than a change in principle.[3] For example, if a company changes its depreciation method at the same time it recognizes a change in estimated asset life, this would involve both a change in method and a change in estimate. According to APB Opinion No. 20, such circumstances would be treated as a change in estimate.

As indicated in previous chapters, companies may select among alternative accounting principles to account for business transactions. For example, for financial reporting purposes a company may depreciate its buildings and equipment using the straight-line depreciation method, the double-declining-balance method, the sum-of-the-years-digits method, or any other consistent and rational allocation procedure. Long-term construction contracts may be accounted for by the percentage-of-completion or the completed-contract method. Inventory may be accounted for using FIFO, LIFO, or other acceptable methods. These alternative methods are often equally available to a given company, but in most instances criteria for selection among the methods are inadequate. As a result, companies have found it rather easy to justify changing from one accounting principle or method to another.

Current Recognition of Cumulative Effect of Change in Principle.

The APB concluded that, in general, companies should not change their accounting principles from one period to the next. "Consistent use of accounting principles from one period to another enhances the utility of financial statements to users by facilitating analysis and understanding of comparative accounting data."[4] A company may change its accounting principles, however, if it can justify a change because of a new pronouncement by the authoritative accounting standard-setting body or because of a change in its economic circumstances. Just what constitutes an acceptable change in economic circumstances is not clear. It presumably could include a change in the competitive structure of an industry, a significant change in the rate of inflation in the economy, a change resulting from government restrictions due to economic or political crisis, and so forth.

In general, the effect of a change from one accepted accounting principle to another is reflected by **reporting the cumulative effect of the change in the income statement** in the period of the change. This cumulative adjustment is shown as a separate item on the income statement after extraordinary items and before net income. When a change in accounting

[3]*Opinions of the Accounting Principles Board, No. 20*, par. 32.
[4]*Ibid.* par. 15.

principle occurs, the financial statements for all prior periods reported for comparative purposes with the current year financial statements are presented as previously reported. To enhance trend analysis, however, pro forma information also is required to reflect the income before extraordinary items and net income that would have been reported if the new accounting principle had been in effect for the respective prior years. Pro forma earnings per share figures also should be reported.

To illustrate the general treatment of a change in accounting principle, assume Telstar Company, a high-powered telescope sales and manufacturing firm, elected in 1991 to change from the double-declining-balance (DDB) method of depreciation to the straight-line method to make its financial reporting more consistent with the majority of its competitors. For tax purposes, assume Telstar has elected to use the straight-line method and will continue to do so. Assume further that Telstar presents comparative income statements for three years, and that the past difference in book and tax depreciation is the only difference in accounting treatment impacting Telstar's financial and taxable income.

These and other assumptions are necessary because, in most instances, a change in accounting principle involves temporary differences between book and tax income, creating the need for **interperiod tax allocation**. As noted in Chapter 20, the exact amounts of any deferred income tax liabilities or potential deferred income tax assets are dependent on several factors, such as current tax laws, current and future tax rates, and future reversal schedules. Therefore, in this chapter, including the end-of-chapter material, the impact of income tax either is ignored or the assumed amounts are provided to simplify the illustrations and focus on the effects of accounting changes and error corrections.

For Telstar, the change to straight-line depreciation for reporting purposes means that tax and book depreciation will be the same in future years. It is assumed, however, that the greater depreciation charged on the books in prior years, as compared to the tax depreciation taken, resulted in a previously recorded deferred tax asset. This and other relevant information for Telstar are presented below:

Years	Double-Declining-Balance Depreciation	Straight-Line Depreciation	Depreciation Difference	Assumed Tax Effects	Effects on Income (Net of taxes)
Prior to 1989	$163,000	$ 90,000	$ 73,000	$21,900	$51,100
1989	60,000	32,000	28,000	8,400	19,600
1990	65,000	35,000	30,000	9,000	21,000
	$288,000	$157,000	$131,300	$39,000	$91,700

The data indicate that depreciation expense for the years prior to 1991 would have been $131,000 less if the straight-line method had been used. Thus, income would have been $131,000 higher, less the applicable assumed income taxes of $39,300. Based on these data, the journal entry to record the cumulative effect adjustment and to eliminate the previously recorded deferred tax asset is as follows:

Accumulated Depreciation.........................	131,000	
Deferred Tax Asset		39,300
Cumulative Effect of Change in Accounting Principle. ..		91,700

The $131,000 debit to Accumulated Depreciation represents the excess depreciation charged to the books in prior years. The $39,300 credit would eliminate the previously established deferred tax asset amount. The $91,700 after-tax cumulative effect would be reported in the income statement for 1991, the year of the change.

Continuing the Telstar example, assume that net income for the two preceding years as originally reported was $450,000 in 1989 and $500,000 in 1990, and that all net income in both years was from continuing operations. Using the new depreciation method, in 1991 Telstar reported $560,000 income from continuing operations and an extraordinary gain of $70,000 net of income taxes of $30,000. Following is a partial income statement for 1991 with comparative information for 1990 and 1989.

Telstar Company
Partial Comparative Income Statement
For Years Ended December 31

	1991	1990	1989
Income from continuing operations	$560,000	$500,000	$450,000
Extraordinary gain (net of income taxes of $30,000)	70,000		
Cumulative effect on prior years of change in accounting principle—change to the straight-line method of depreciation from double-declining-balance method (net of income taxes of $39,300)	91,700		
Net income...............................	$721,700	$500,000	$450,000

Note that in 1991 the cumulative effect is shown net of tax and as a separate item after the extraordinary item. As explained in Chapter 4, all below-the-line items, such as extraordinary gains or losses and the cumulative effect of a change in accounting principle, are to be reported net of related income taxes. This is referred to as **intraperiod tax allocation**. With this disclosure technique, the appropriate amount of income taxes is associated with income from continuing operations and with the individual below-the-line items reported separately. Also note that the amounts of income from continuing operations for the two prior years are presented as originally reported. In addition, the disclosure of pro forma (as if) income for the prior years is required and would be shown on the face of the income statement (using assumed data) as follows:

Pro Forma Income Data

	1990	1989
Net income from continuing operations as previously reported	$500,000	$450,000
Extraordinary gain (net of tax)		
Effect of change in accounting principle (net of tax)	21,000	19,600
Pro forma income (restated)	$521,000	$469,600

Pro forma earnings per share amounts reflecting the revised income figures also would be presented.

Reporting and disclosure requirements for a change in accounting principle are further illustrated on page 1037. The income statement and the related note disclosures were presented in the 1988 annual report of AIM Telephones, Inc.

In a few cases, past records are inadequate to prepare pro forma statements for individual years. This fact should be disclosed when applicable. For example, a change to the LIFO method of inventory valuation is usually made effective with the beginning inventory in the year of change rather than with some prior year because of the difficulty in identifying prior year layers or dollar-value pools. Thus, the beginning inventory in the year of change becomes the same as the previous inventory valued using another costing method, and this becomes the base LIFO layer. No cumulative effect adjustment is required.

Restatement of Prior Periods for Change in Principle

If a change in accounting principle is caused by a new pronouncement of an authoritative accounting body, the cumulative effect may be reported retroactively or currently, depending on the instructions contained in the pronouncement. The APB generally favored the reporting procedures described in the previous section, i.e., current recognition of the cumulative effect. However, the Board identified four specific changes as being of such a nature that the "advantages of retroactive treatment in prior period reports outweigh the disadvantages."[5] These exceptions are:

1. Change from LIFO method of inventory pricing to another method.
2. Change in the method of accounting for long-term construction contracts.
3. Change to or from the "full cost" method of accounting used in the extractive industries.
4. Changes made at the time of an initial distribution of company stock.[6]

---

[5]*Ibid.*, par. 27.

[6]This exception is available only once for a company, and may be used for (a) obtaining additional equity capital from investors, (b) effecting business combinations, or (c) registering securities, whenever a company first issues financial statements, *Ibid.*, par. 29.

Exhibit 23-2   Aim Telephones, Inc.

Consolidated Statements of Income

Year Ended	February 29, 1988	February 28 1987	February 28 1986
Revenues:			
Installation contracts	$16,948,000	$17,014,000	$ 8,643,000
Customer additions, service and maintenance	13,119,000	8,392,000	3,989,000
	30,067,000	25,406,000	12,632,000
Costs and Expenses:			
Cost of revenues	18,116,000	16,155,000	8,382,000
Selling, general and administrative	9,254,000	6,763,000	3,487,000
Interest expense	1,177,000	372,000	166,000
	28,547,000	23,290,000	12,035,000
Income Before Income Taxes	1,520,000	2,116,000	597,000
Income Taxes (Note *)	723,000	1,105,000	256,000
Income Before Extraordinary Item and Cumulative Effect on Prior Years of a			
Change in Accounting Principle	797,000	1,011,000	341,000
Extraordinary Item—Tax benefit of net operating loss carryforward	—	141,000	233,000
Cumulative Effect on Prior Years of a Change in Accounting Principle—Change in Allocation of Overhead Costs to Inventories, Net of Income Taxes of $170,000	221,000	—	—
Net Income	$ 1,018,000	$ 1,152,000	$ 574,000
Per Common Share and Equivalents:			
Income before extraordinary item and cumulative effect of accounting change	$ .19	$ .27	$ .12
Extraordinary item	—	.04	.08
Cumulative effect on prior years of a change in accounting principle	.05	—	—
Net income	$ .24	$ .31	$ .20
Pro Forma Amounts Assuming the Change in Allocating Overhead Costs is Applied Retroactively:			
Income before extraordinary item		$ 1,131,000	$ 377,000
Earnings per share		$ .31	$ .13
Net income		$ 1,272,000	$ 610,000
Earnings per share		$ .34	$ .21
Weighted Average Number of Shares of Common Stock and Equivalents Outstanding	4,276,000	3,695,000	2,906,000

Accounting Change—

Effective March 1, 1987, the Company adopted the Inventory Costing Rules under the Tax Reform Act of 1986 for financial and tax reporting purposes. Such rules require including certain costs in inventories which had previously been expensed. This change is considered preferable because costs are expected to be better matched with related revenue. The effect of the change for the year ended February 29, 1988 was to increase income before extraordinary item by approximately $244,000 ($.06 per share). The adjustment of $221,000 to apply retroactively the new method is included in income of 1988. The pro forma amounts shown on the income statement have been adjusted for the effects of retroactive application on cost of revenues and related income taxes.

In addition to these exceptions, several FASB statements also require retroactive restatement.

In those cases where retroactive restatement is required, the cumulative effect of the change is recorded directly as an adjustment to the beginning retained earnings balance for the earliest year presented. Income statement data reported for comparative purposes also must be adjusted to reflect the new principle.

To illustrate the procedures required for restatement, assume that in 1991 the Forester Company changed from the LIFO inventory costing method to the FIFO method for both financial reporting and income tax purposes. There are no deferred tax consequences because both the old and new methods apply to both financial and tax reporting. However, additional taxes will be payable for prior years as a result of changing the inventory method used for tax purposes. The following data are applicable, and a tax rate of 30% is assumed for all years.

Years	Pretax Income FIFO	Pretax Income LIFO	Pretax Income Difference	Income Tax Effect (30%)	Effect on Income (Net of Tax)
Prior to 1989	$190,000	$160,000	$ 30,000	$ 9,000	$21,000
1989	110,000	75,000	35,000	10,500	24,500
1990	120,000	100,000	20,000	6,000	14,000
Totals—beginning of 1991	$420,000	$335,000	$ 85,000	$25,500	$59,500
1991 Results	$125,000	$100,000	$ 25,000	$ 7,500	$17,500

The entry in 1991 to record the prior period effects of the change in accounting principle would be

Inventory	85,000	
Income Taxes Payable		25,500
Retained Earnings		59,500

The $85,000 debit to Inventory adjusts the beginning 1991 inventory to its FIFO cost. The $59,500 reflects the after-tax effect on cost of goods sold in years prior to 1991. Cost of goods sold would have been lower using FIFO and pretax income would have been higher, resulting in additional taxes of $25,500. Assumed comparative income statement data, restated for 1990 and 1989, would be presented as follows:

Forester Company
Partial Income Statement
For Years Ended December 31

	1991	1990	1989
Income before income taxes.................	$125,000	$120,000	$110,000
Income taxes (30%)	37,500	36,000	33,000
Net income.................................	$ 87,500	$ 84,000	$ 77,000
Earnings per share (10,000 shares outstanding)	$8.75	$8.40	$7.70

The adjustment for the cumulative effect of the change in principle would be reported in Forester Company's statement of retained earnings.

Assuming a beginning retained earnings balance in 1989 of $351,000 and no dividends, a comparative retained earnings statement would appear as follows:

Forester Company
Statement of Retained Earnings
For Years Ended December 31

	1991	1990	1989
Retained earnings at beginning of year, as previously reported	$473,500	$403,500	$351,000
Add adjustment for cumulative effect on prior years of applying retroactively the FIFO method of inventory costing (See Note A) . . .	59,500	45,500	21,000
Adjusted retained earnings, beginning of year	$533,000	$449,000	$372,000
Net income	87,500	84,000	77,000
Retained earnings, end of year	$620,500	$533,000	$449,000

Note A Change in Accounting Principle
Forester Company has changed its inventory costing method from last-in, first out (LIFO) to first-in, first-out (FIFO), effective January 1, 1991. The new inventory method was adopted to better reflect company earnings and inventory values. The financial statements have been restated to apply the new method retroactively. Because income tax laws permit the use of LIFO for tax purposes only if it is also used for financial reporting, the FIFO method has also been adopted for income tax reporting. As a result, an additional tax liability of $25,500 was incurred for years prior to 1991. The effect of the accounting change on income in 1991 (net of taxes of $7,500) was an increase of $17,500, or $1.75 per share. The net of tax effect in 1990 was an increase of $14,000, and in 1989, an increase of $24,500. The retained earnings balance for 1991, 1990, and 1989 have been adjusted to reflect the cumulative effect of applying retroactively the new method of inventory costing, net of applicable taxes.

Note that no pro forma information is required with the retroactive approach because the statements for prior years are restated directly. If prior-year income statements cannot be presented because of inadequate data, that fact should be disclosed. Under those circumstances, the cumulative effect would be reported only in the retained earnings statement.

Change in Reporting Entity

Companies sometimes change their structures or report their operations in such a way that the financial statements are in effect those of a different reporting entity. Specifically, a change in reporting entity includes: (a) presenting consolidated or combined statements in place of statements of individual companies; (b) changing specific subsidiaries comprising the group of companies for which consolidated statements are presented; (c) changing the companies included in combined financial statements; and (d) a business combination accounted for as a pooling of interest.[7]

Because of the basic objective of comparability, the APB required that financial statements be adjusted retroactively to disclose what the statements would have looked like if the current entity had been in existence in the prior years.

Thus, previous years' financial statements presented for comparison with the current year (the year of change) must be restated to reflect results of operations, financial condition, and cash flows as if the current reporting entity had been in existence in those years. Also, in the period of the

[7]*Ibid.*, par. 12.

change, the financial statements should disclose the nature of, and reasons for the change, as illustrated in the following note included in Alcoa's 1987 annual report.

Exhibit 23-3	**Aluminum Co. of America (ALCOA)**

B. Accounting Changes

Effective December 31, 1987, Alcoa revised its consolidation accounting policy to conform to the Financial Accounting Standard Board's (FASB) newly issued Statement No. 94–Consolidation of All Majority-owned Subsidiaries. Prior to the change Alcoa had consolidated only wholly-owned subsidiaries (except Alcoa Properties, Inc.). All prior year data included in this report has been restated to conform to the change. See Note T for additional information regarding the subsidiaries that are now being consolidated.

The statements also should disclose the effect of the change on income from continuing operations, net income, and the related earnings per share amounts for all periods presented. Subsequent years' statements do not need to repeat the disclosures.[8] Changes in reporting entities are covered in more depth in advanced accounting texts.

Error Corrections   As noted earlier, error corrections are not considered accounting changes, but their treatment is specified in APB Opinion No. 20 and reaffirmed in FASB Statement No. 16.[9] In effect, **accounting errors** made in prior years that have not already been "counterbalanced" or reversed are reported as prior period adjustments and recorded directly to Retained Earnings.

Kinds of Errors

There are a number of different kinds of errors. Some errors are discovered in the period in which they are made, and these are easily corrected. Others may not be discovered currently and are reflected on the financial statements until discovered. Some errors are never discovered; however, the effects of these errors may be counterbalanced in subsequent periods and after this takes place, account balances are again accurately stated. Errors may be classified as follows.

1. **Errors discovered currently in the course of normal accounting procedures.** Examples of this type of error are clerical errors, such as an addition error, posting to the wrong account, or misstating or omitting an account from the trial balance. These types of errors usually are detected during the regular summarizing process of the accounting cycle and are readily corrected.

---

[8]*Ibid.*, par. 35.
[9]*Statement of Financial Accounting Standards No. 16*, "Prior Period Adjustments" (Stamford: Financial Accounting Standards Board, 1977), p. 5.

2. **Errors limited to balance sheet accounts.** Examples include debiting Marketable Securities instead of Notes Receivable, crediting Interest Payable instead of Notes Payable, or crediting Interest Payable instead of Salaries Payable. Another example is not recording the exchange of convertible bonds for stock. Such errors are frequently discovered and corrected in the period in which they are made. When such errors are not found until a subsequent period, corrections must be made at that time and balance sheet data subsequently restated for comparative reporting purposes.

3. **Errors limited to income statement accounts.** The examples and correcting procedures for this type of error are similar to those in (2). For example, Office Salaries may be debited instead of Sales Salaries. This type of error should be corrected as soon as it is discovered. Even though the error would not affect net income, the misstated accounts should be restated for analysis purposes and comparative reporting.

4. **Errors affecting both income statement accounts and balance sheet accounts.** Certain errors, when not discovered currently, result in the misstatement of net income and thus affect both the income statement accounts and the balance sheet accounts. The balance sheet accounts are carried into the succeeding period; hence, an error made currently and not detected will affect earnings of the future. Such errors may be classified into two groups:

   (a) **Errors in net income that, when not detected, are automatically counterbalanced in the following fiscal period.** Net income amounts on the income statements for two successive periods are inaccurately stated; certain account balances on the balance sheet at the end of the first period are inaccurately stated, but the account balances in the balance sheet at the end of the succeeding period are accurately stated. In this class are errors such as the misstatement of inventories and the omission of adjustments for prepaid and accrued items at the end of the period.

   (b) **Errors in net income that, when not detected, are not automatically counterbalanced in the following fiscal period.** Account balances on successive balance sheets are inaccurately stated until such time as entries are made compensating for or correcting the errors. In this class are errors such as the recognition of capital expenditures as revenue expenditures and the omission of charges for depreciation and amortization.

When errors affecting income are discovered, careful analysis is necessary to determine the required action to correct the account balances. As indicated, most errors will be caught and corrected prior to closing the books. The few material errors not detected until subsequent periods and those that have not already been counterbalanced must be treated as prior period adjustments.

The following sections describe and illustrate the procedures to be applied when error corrections require prior period adjustments. It is assumed that each of the errors is material. When errors are discovered, they usually affect the income tax liability for a prior period. Amended tax returns are usually prepared either to claim a refund or to pay any additional tax assessment. For simplicity, the examples on the following pages and the exercises and problems ignore the income tax effect of errors.

Illustrative Example of Error Correction

Assume the Hiedleberg Co. began operations at the beginning of 1989. An auditing firm is engaged for the first time in 1991. Before the accounts are adjusted and closed for 1991, the auditor reviews the books and accounts and discovers the errors summarized on pages 1044 and 1045. Effects of these errors on the financial statements, before any correcting entries, are indicated as follows: a plus sign $(+)$ indicates an overstatement; a minus sign $(-)$ indicates an understatement. Each error correction is discussed in the following paragraphs.

(1) Understatement of merchandise inventory It is discovered that the merchandise inventory as of December 31, 1989, was understated by $1,000. The effects of the misstatement were as follows:

	Income Statement	Balance Sheet
For 1989:	Cost of goods sold overstated (ending inventory too low)	Assets understated (inventory too low)
	Net income understated	Retained earnings understated
For 1990:	Cost of goods sold understated (beginning inventory too low)	Balance sheet items not affected, retained earnings understatement for 1989 being corrected
	Net income overstated	by net income overstatement for 1990

Since this type of error counterbalances after two years, no correcting entry is required in 1991.

If the error had been discovered in 1990 instead of 1991, an entry should have been made to correct the account balances so that operations for 1990 would be reported accurately. The beginning inventory for 1990 would have been increased by $1,000, the asset understatement, and Retained Earnings would have been credited for this amount representing the income understatement in 1989. The correcting entry in 1990 would have been:

Merchandise Inventory 1,000
    Retained Earnings   1,000

(2) Failure to record merchandise purchases It is discovered that purchase invoices as of December 28, 1989, for $850 were not recorded until 1990.

The goods were included in the inventory at the end of 1989. The effects of failure to record the purchases were as follows:

	Income Statement	Balance Sheet
For 1989:	Cost of goods sold understated (purchases too low)	Liabilities understated (accounts payable too low)
	Net income overstated	Retained earnings overstated
For 1990:	Cost of goods sold overstated (purchases too high)	Balance sheet items not affected, retained earnings overstatement for 1989 being corrected by net income understatement for 1990
	Net income understated	

Since this is a counterbalancing error, no correcting entry is required in 1991.

If the error had been discovered in 1990 instead of 1991, a correcting entry would have been necessary. In 1990, Purchases was debited and Accounts Payable credited for $850 for merchandise acquired in 1989 and included in the ending inventory of 1989. Retained Earnings would have to be debited for $850, representing the net income overstatement for 1989, and Purchases would have to be credited for the same amount to reduce the Purchases balance in 1990. The correcting entry in 1990 would have been:

Retained Earnings	850	
Purchases		850

(3) Failure to record merchandise sales It is discovered that sales on account for the last week of December, 1990, for $1,800 were not recorded until 1991. The goods sold were not included in the inventory at the end of 1990. The effects of the failure to report the revenue in 1990 were:

	Income Statement	Balance Sheet
For 1990:	Revenue understated (sales too low)	Assets understated (accounts receivable too low)
	Net income understated	Retained earnings understated

When the error is discovered in 1991, Sales is debited for $1,800 and Retained Earnings is credited for this amount representing the net income understatement for 1990. The following entry is made:

Sales	1,800	
Retained Earnings		1,800

Analysis Sheet to Show Effects

| | At End of 1989 | | | |
| | Income Statement | | Balance Sheet | |
	Section	Net Income	Section	Retained Earnings
(1) Understatement of merchandise inventory of $1,000 on December 31, 1989	Cost of Goods Sold +	−	Current Assets −	−
(2) Failure to record merchandise purchases on account of $850 in 1989, purchases were recorded in 1990.	Cost of Goods Sold −	+	Current Liabilities −	+
(3) Failure to record merchandise sales on account of $1,800 in 1990. (It is assumed that the sales for 1990 were recognized as revenue in 1991.)				
(4) Failure to record accrued sales salaries; expense was recognized when payment was made. On December 31, 1989, $450	Selling Expense −	+	Current Liabilities −	+
On December 31, 1990, $300.				
(5) Failure to record prepaid taxes of $275 on December 31, 1989; amount was included as miscellaneous general expense.	General Expense +	−	Current Assets −	−
(6) Failure to record accrued interest on notes receivable of $150 on December 31, 1989; revenue was recognized when collected in 1990.	Other Revenue −	−	Current Assets −	−
(7) Failure to record unearned service fees; amounts received were included in Miscellaneous Revenue. On December 31, 1989, $175	Other Revenue +	+	Current Liabilities −	+
On December 31, 1990, $225.				
(8) Failure to record depreciation of delivery equipment. On December 31, 1989, $1,200.	Selling Expense −	+	Noncurrent Assets +	+
On December 31, 1990, $1,200.				

(4) Failure to record accrued expense Accrued sales salaries of $450 as of December 31, 1989, and $300 as of December 31, 1990, were overlooked in adjusting the accounts on each of these dates. Sales Salaries is debited for salary payments. The effects of the failure to record the accrued expense of $450 as of December 31, 1989, were as follows:

of Errors on Financial Statements

At End of 1990				At End of 1991			
Income Statement		Balance Sheet		Income Statement		Balance Sheet	
Section	Net Income	Section	Retained Earnings	Section	Net Income	Section	Retained Earnings
Cost of Goods Sold −	+						
Cost of Goods Sold +	−						
Sales −	−	Accounts Receivable −	−	Sales +	+		
Selling Expense +	−						
Selling Expense −	+	Current Liabilities −	+	Selling Expense +	−		
General Expense −	+						
Other Revenue +	+						
Other Revenue −	−						
Other Revenue +	+	Current Liabilities −	+	Other Revenue −	−		
		Noncurrent Assets +	+			Noncurrent Assets +	+
Selling Expense −	+	Noncurrent Assets +	+			Noncurrent Assets +	+

	Income Statement	**Balance Sheet**
For 1989:	Expenses understated (sales salaries too low)	Liabilities understated (accrued sales salaries not reported)
	Net income overstated	Retained earnings overstated
For 1990:	Expenses overstated (sales salaries too high)	Balance sheet items not affected, retained earnings overstatement for 1989 being corrected by net income understatement for 1990
	Net income understated	

The effects of failure to recognize the accrued expense of $300 on December 31, 1990, were as follows:

Income Statement	Balance Sheet
For 1990: Expenses understated (sales salaries too low)	Liabilities understated (accrued sales salaries not reported)
Net income overstated	Retained earnings overstated

No entry is required in 1991 to correct the accounts for the failure to record the accrued expense at the end of 1989, the misstatement in 1989 having been counterbalanced by the misstatement in 1990. An entry is required, however, to correct the accounts for the failure to record the accrued expense at the end of 1990 if the net income for 1991 is not to be misstated. If accrued expenses were properly recorded at the end of 1991, Retained Earnings would be debited for $300, representing the net income overstatement for 1990, and Sales Salaries would be credited for a similar amount, representing the amount to be subtracted from salary payments in 1991. The correcting entry is:

Retained Earnings	300	
Sales Salaries		300

If the failure to adjust the accounts for the accrued expense of 1989 had been recognized in 1990, an entry similar to the preceding one would have been required in 1990 to correct the account balances. The entry in 1990 would have been:

Retained Earnings	450	
Sales Salaries		450

The accrued salaries of $300 as of the end of 1990 would be recorded at the end of that year by an appropriate adjustment.

(5) Failure to record prepaid expense It is discovered that Miscellaneous General Expense for 1989 included taxes of $275 that should have been deferred in adjusting the accounts on December 31, 1989. The effects of the failure to record the prepaid expense were as follows:

Income Statement	Balance Sheet
For 1989: Expenses overstated (miscellaneous general expense too high)	Assets understated (prepaid taxes not reported)
Net income understated	Retained earnings understated
For 1990: Expenses understated (miscellaneous general expense too low)	Balance sheet items not affected, retained earnings understatement for 1989 being corrected
Net income overstated	by net income overstatement for 1990

Since this is a counterbalancing error, no entry to correct the accounts is required in 1991.

If the error had been discovered in 1990 instead of 1991, a correcting entry would have been necessary. If prepaid taxes were properly recorded at the end of 1990, Miscellaneous General Expense would have to be debited for $275, the expense relating to operations of 1990 and Retained Earnings would have to be credited for the same amount representing the net income understatement for 1989. The correcting entry in 1990 would have been:

Miscellaneous General Expense	275	
Retained Earnings		275

(6) Failure to record accrued revenue Accrued interest on notes receivable of $150 was overlooked in adjusting the accounts on December 31, 1989. The revenue was recognized when the interest was collected in 1990. The effects of the failure to record the accrued revenue were:

	Income Statement	**Balance Sheet**
For 1989:	Revenue understated (interest revenue too low)	Assets understated (interest receivable not reported)
	Net income understated	Retained earnings understated
For 1990:	Revenue overstated (interest revenue too high)	Balance sheet items not affected, retained earnings understatement for 1989 being corrected by net income overstatement for 1990
	Net income overstated	

Since the balance sheet items at the end of 1990 were correctly stated, no entry to correct the accounts is required in 1991.

If the error had been discovered in 1990 instead of 1991, an entry would have been necessary to correct the account balances. If accrued interest on notes receivable had been properly recorded at the end of 1990, Interest Revenue would have to be debited for $150, the amount to be subtracted from receipts of 1990, and Retained Earnings would have to be credited for the same amount representing the net income understatement for 1989. The correcting entry in 1990 would have been:

Interest Revenue	150	
Retained Earnings		150

(7) Failure to record unearned revenue Fees received in advance for miscellaneous services of $175 as of December 31, 1989, and $225 as of December 31, 1990, were overlooked in adjusting the accounts on each of these dates. Miscellaneous Revenue had been credited when fees were received. The effects of the failure to recognize the unearned revenue of $175 at the end of 1989 were as shown on page 1048:

Income Statement	**Balance Sheet**
For 1989: Revenue overstated (miscellaneous revenue too high)	Liablitities understated (unearned service fees not reported)
Net income overstated	Retained earnings overstated
For 1990: Revenue understated (miscellaneous revenue too low)	Balance sheet items not affected, retained earnings overstatement for 1989 being corrected by net income understatement for 1990
Net income understated	

The effects of the failure to recognize the unearned revenue of $225 at the end of 1990 were as follows:

Income Statement	**Balance Sheet**
For 1990: Revenue overstated (miscellaneous revenue too high)	Liabilities understated (unearned service fees not reported)
Net income overstated	Retained earnings overstated

No entry is required in 1991 to correct the accounts for the failure to record the unearned revenue at the end of 1989, the misstatement in 1989, having been counterbalanced by the misstatement in 1990. An entry is required, however, to correct the accounts for the failure to record the unearned revenue at the end of 1990 if the net income for 1991 is not to be misstated. If the unearned revenue were properly recorded at the end of 1991, Retained Earnings would be debited for $225, representing the net income overstatement for 1990, and Miscellaneous Revenue would be credited for the same amount, representing the revenue that is to be identified with 1991. The correcting entry is:

```
Retained Earnings ....................................    225
    Miscellaneous Revenue ...........................          225
```

If the failure to adjust the accounts for the unearned revenue of 1989 had been recognized in 1990, instead of 1991, an entry similar to the preceding one would have been required in 1990 to correct the account balances. The entry at that time would have been:

```
Retained Earnings ....................................    175
    Miscellaneous Revenue ...........................          175
```

The unearned service fees of $225 as of the end of 1990 would be recorded at the end of that year by an appropriate adjustment.

(8) Failure to record depreciation Delivery equipment was acquired at the beginning of 1989 at a cost of $6,000. The equipment has an estimated 5-year life, and depreciation of $1,200 was overlooked at the end of 1989 and 1990. The effects of the failure to record depreciation for 1989 were as follows:

	Income Statement	**Balance Sheet**
For 1989:	Expenses understated (depreciation of delivery equipment too low) Net income overstated	Assets overstated (accumulated depreciation of delivery equipment too low) Retained earnings overstated
For 1990:	Expenses not affected Net income not affected	Assets overstated (accumulated depreciation of delivery equipment too low) Retained earnings overstated

It should be observed that the misstatements arising from the failure to record depreciation are not counterbalanced in the succeeding year.

Failure to record depreciation for 1990 affected the statements as shown below:

	Income Statement	**Balance Sheet**
For 1990:	Expenses understated (depreciation of delivery equipment too low) Net income overstated	Assets overstated (accumulated depreciation of delivery equipment too low) Retained earnings overstated

When the omission is recognized, Retained Earnings must be decreased by the net income overstatements of prior years and accumulated depreciation must be increased by the depreciation that should have been recorded. The correcting entry in 1991 for depreciation that should have been recognized for 1989 and 1990 is as follows:

Retained Earnings	2,400	
Accumulated Depreciation—Delivery Equipment		2,400

Working Papers to Summarize Corrections

It is assumed in this section that the errors previously discussed are discovered in 1991 before the accounts for 1991 are adjusted and closed. Accounts are corrected so that revenue and expense accounts report the balances identified with the current period and asset, liability, and retained earnings accounts are accurately stated. Instead of preparing a separate entry for each correction, a single compound entry may be made for all of the errors discovered. The entry to correct earnings of prior years as well as to correct current earnings may be developed by the preparation of working papers. Assume the following retained earnings account for the Hiedleberg Co.:

Account   Retained Earnings

Date		Item	Debit	Credit	Balance Debit	Balance Credit
1989 Dec.	31	Balance.........................				12,000
1990 Dec.	20	Dividends declared	5,000			7,000
	31	Net income....................		15,000		22,000

Hiedleberg Co.
Working Papers for Correction of Account Balances
December 31, 1991

Explanation	Retained Earnings Dec. 31, 1989		Net Income Year Ended Dec. 31, 1990		Accounts Requiring Correction in 1991		
	Debit	Credit	Debit	Credit	Debit	Credit	Account
Reported retained earnings balance, Dec. 31, 1989		12,000					
Reported net income for year ended Dec. 31, 1990				15,000			
Corrections.*							
(1) Understatement of merchandise inventory on Dec. 31, 1989, $1,000 . . .		1,000	1,000				
(2) Failure to record merchandise purchases in 1989, $850	850			850			
(3) Failure to record merchandise sales in 1990, $1,800				1,800	1,800		Sales
(4) Failure to record accrued sales salaries: (a) On Dec. 31, 1989, $450 . . . . (b) On Dec. 31, 1990, $300	450		300	450		300	Sales Salaries
(5) Failure to record prepaid taxes on Dec. 31, 1989, $275		275	275				
(6) Failure to record accrued interest on notes receivable on Dec. 31, 1989, $150		150	150				
(7) Failure to record unearned service fees: (a) On Dec. 31, 1989, $175 . . . . (b) On Dec. 31, 1990, $225	175		225	175		225	Misc. Revenue
(8) Failure to record depreciation of delivery equipment: (a) On Dec. 31, 1989, $1,200 . . . . . . (b) On Dec. 31, 1990, $1,200	1,200		1,200			1,200 1,200	Accumulated Depr.—Delivery Equipment
Corrected retained earnings balance, Dec. 31, 1989	10,750 13,425	13,425					
Corrected net income for 1990			15,125 18,275	18,275			
Net correction to retained earnings as of Jan. 1, 1991					1,125 2,925	2,925	Retained Earnings

*For a more detailed description of the individual errors and their correction, refer to pages 1042-1049.

The working papers to determine the corrected retained earnings balance on December 31, 1989, and the corrected net income for 1990 are shown on page 1050. As indicated earlier, no adjustment is made for income tax effects in this example.

The working papers indicate that Retained Earnings is to be decreased by $1,125 as of January 1, 1991, as shown below.

Retained earnings overstatement as of December 31, 1989:		
Retained earnings as originally reported	$12,000	
Retained earnings as corrected	10,750	$1,250
Retained earnings understatement in 1990:		
Net income as corrected	$15,125	
Net income as orignially reported	15,000	125
Retained earnings overstatement as of January 1, 1991		$1,125

The following entry is prepared from the working papers to correct the account balances in 1991:

Retained Earnings	1,125	
Sales	1,800	
Sales Salaries		300
Miscellaneous Revenue		225
Accumulated Depreciation—Delivery Equipment		2,400

The retained earnings account after correction will appear with a balance of $20,875, as follows:

Account   Retained Earnings

Date		Item	Debit	Credit	Balance Debit	Balance Credit
1991						
Jan.	1	Balance				22,000
Dec.	31	Corrections in net incomes of prior periods discovered during the course of the audit	1,125			20,875

Summary of Accounting Changes and Correction of Errors

The following summary presents the appropriate accounting procedures applicable to each of the four main categories covered in APB Opinion No. 20. Naturally, accountants must apply these guidelines with judgment and should seek to provide the most relevant and reliable information possible.

**Summary of Procedures for Reporting Accounting Changes
and Corrections of Errors**

Category	Accounting Procedures
I. Change in estimate	1. Adjust only current period results or current and future periods. 2. No separate, cumulative adjustment or restated financial statements. 3. No pro forma disclosure needed.
II. Change in accounting principle a. Current recognition of cumulative effect	1. Adjust for cumulative effect, i.e., a "catch-up" adjustment in current period as special item in income statement. 2. No restated financial statements. 3. Pro forma data required showing income and EPS information for all periods presented.
b. Restatement of prior periods	1. Direct cumulative adjustment to beginning Retained Earnings balance. 2. Restate financial statements to reflect new principle for comparative purposes. 3. No pro forma information required because prior period statements are changed directly.
III. Change in reported entity	1. Restate financial statements as though new entity had been in existence for all periods presented.
IV. Error correction	1. If detected in period error occurred, correct accounts through normal accounting cycle adjustments. 2. If detected in a subsequent period, adjust for effect of material errors by prior period adjustments directly to Retained Earnings.

Key Terms   Accounting changes 1030   Change in accounting principle 1032
Accounting errors 1030   Change in reporting entity 1039
Change in accounting estimate 1032

Questions   1. How do accounting changes detract from the informational characteristics of
comparability and consistency as described in FASB Concepts Statement No.
2?

2. List the three categories of accounting changes and explain briefly why such
changes are made.

3. What alternative procedures have been suggested as solutions for reporting
accounting changes and corrections of errors?

4. (a) List several examples of areas where changes in accounting estimates are
often made. (b) Explain briefly the proper accounting treatment for a change
in estimate. (c) Why is this procedure considered proper for recording changes
in accounting estimates?

5. (a) List several examples of changes in accounting principle that a company
may make. (b) Explain briefly the proper accounting treatment for
recognizing currently a change in accounting principle.

6. What information should pro forma statements include?

7. Why does a change in accounting principle require justification?

8. (a) When should the effects of a change in accounting principle be reported as
a restatement of prior periods? (b) Although no justification was given by the
APB for selecting certain items for special treatment, what might be a possible
reason?

9. The Stice Company purchased a delivery van in 1988. At the time of
purchase, the van's service life was estimated to be 7 years with a salvage value
of $500. The company has been using the straight-line method of
depreciation. In 1991, the company determined that because of extensive use,
the van's service life would be only 5 years with no salvage value. Also, the
company has decided to change the depreciation method used from straight-
line to the sum-of-the-years digits method. How would these changes be
treated?

10. (a) List the 4 types of changes in reporting entities that might occur. (b) How
are these changes treated? (c) What assumption does the treatment of a
change in reporting entity make?

11. Describe the effect on current net income, beginning retained earnings,
individual asset accounts, and contra-asset accounts when:

    (a) Depreciation is changed from the straight-line method to an accelerated
    method.

    (b) Depreciation is changed from an accelerated method to the straight-line
    method.

    (c) Income on construction contracts that had been reported on a completed-
    contract basis is now reported on the percentage-of-completion basis.

    (d) The valuation of inventories is changed from a FIFO to a LIFO basis.

    (e) It is determined that warranty expenses in prior years should have been
    5% of sales instead of 4%.

    (f) The valuation of inventories is changed from a LIFO to a FIFO basis.

    (g) Your accounts receivable clerk has learned that a major customer has
    declared bankruptcy.

(h) Your patent lawyer informs you that your rival has perfected and patented a new invention making your product obsolete.

12. (a) How are accounting errors to be treated? (b) What are counterbalancing errors?

13. The Foreign Manufacturing Co. failed to record accrued interest for 1988, $800; 1989, $700; and 1990, $950. What is the amount of overstatement or understatement of retained earnings at December 31, 1991?

14. Goods purchased F.O.B. shipping point were shipped to Merkley & Co. on December 31, 1991. The purchase was recorded in 1991, but the goods were not included in ending inventory. (a) What effect would this error have had on reporting income for 1991 had it not been discovered? (b) What entry should be made on the books to correct this error assuming the books have not yet been closed for 1991?

Discussion Cases   **Case 23-1   (Accounting changes)**

Situation 1

Stewart Company has determined that the depreciable lives of several operating machines are too long and therefore do not fairly match the cost of the assets with the revenues produced. Stewart therefore decides to reduce the depreciable lives of these machines by 3 years.

Situation 2

Scott Company decides that at the beginning of the year it will adopt the straight-line method of depreciation for plant equipment. The straight-line method will be used for new acquisitions as well as for the previously acquired plant equipment, which had been accounted for using an accelerated depreciation method.

What types of accounting changes were involved in the two situations? Describe the method of reporting the changes under current GAAP. Where applicable, explain how the reported amounts are computed.   (AICPA adapted)

Case 23-2   (Change in principle or change in estimate?)

Jill Stanton, President of Central Company, is confused about why your accounting firm has recommended that she report certain events as changes in principle instead of changes in estimate, which is what Jill thought they should be. She has asked you for an explanation. Describe a change in an accounting principle and a change in accounting estimate. Explain how each would be reported in the income statement of the period of change.

Exercises   **Exercise 23-1   (Change in estimate and in accounting principle)**

Motor Manufacturing purchased a machine on January 1, 1987, for $50,000. At the time, it was determined that the machine had an estimated useful life of 10 years and an estimated residual value of $2,000. The company used the double-declining-balance method of depreciation. On January 1, 1991, the company decided to change its depreciation method from double-declining-balance to straight-line. The machine's remaining useful life was estimated to be 5 years with a residual value of $1,000.

(1) Give the entry required to record the company's depreciation expense for 1991.
(2) Give the entry, if any, to record the effect of the change in depreciation methods.

Exercise 23-2 (Change in estimate)

The Curtis Company purchased a machine on January 1, 1988, for $1,500,000. At the date of acquisition, the machine had an estimated useful life of 6 years with no residual value. The machine is being depreciated on a straight-line basis. On January 1, 1991, Curtis determined, as a result of additional information, that the machine had an estimated useful life of 8 years from the date of acquisition with no residual value.

(1) Give the journal entry, if any, to record the cumulative effect on prior years of changing the estimated useful life of the machine.
(2) What is the amount of depreciation expense on the machine that should be charged to Curtis Company's income statement for the year ended December 31, 1991?

Exercise 23-3 (Change in accounting principle)

High Quality Construction Company has used the completed-contract method of accounting since it began operations in 1984. In 1991, for justifiable reasons, management decided to adopt the percentage-of-completion method.

The following schedule, reporting income for the past 3 years, has been prepared by the company.

	1988	1989	1990
Total revenues from completed contracts	$500,000	$1,200,000	$1,000,000
Less cost of completed contracts	350,000	925,000	760,000
Income from operations	$150,000	$ 275,000	$ 240,000
Extraordinary loss			45,000
Income	$150,000	$ 275,000	$ 195,000

Analysis of the accounting records disclosed the following income by projects, earned in the years 1988-1990 using the percentage-of-completion method.

	1988	1989	1990
Project A	$150,000		
Project B	100,000	$175,000	
Project C	70,000	200,000	$ 10,000
Project D		10,000	60,000
Project E			(40,000)

Give the journal entry required in 1991 to reflect the change in accounting principle. Ignore income taxes.

Exercise 23-4   (Change in accounting principle)

Diversified Manufacturing Company decides to change from an accelerated depreciation method it has used for both reporting and tax purposes to the straight-line method for reporting purposes. From the following information, prepare the income statement for 1991.

Year	Net Income As Reported	Excess of Accelerated Depreciation Over Straight-Line Depreciation	Income Effect (Net of Tax)
Prior to 1988		$12,500	$ 7,500
1988	$62,500	6,250	3,750
1989	54,500	7,500	4,500
1990	78,000	11,250	6,750
		$37,500	$22,500

In 1991, net sales were $190,000; cost of goods sold, $92,500; selling expenses, $47,500, and general and administrative expenses, $14,000. The income tax on operating income was $14,400. In addition, Diversified had a tax deductible extraordinary loss of $12,000 net of $8,000 income tax savings. Assume the fiscal year ends on December 31.

Exercise 23-5   (Change in accounting principle involving LIFO)

Assume the change in net income as shown in Exercise 23-4 is the result of a change from the LIFO method of inventory pricing to another method. During 1991, dividends of $17,500 were paid. Based on this information, prepare the retained earnings statement for 1991. The December 31, 1990 retained earnings balance as reported was $260,000.

Exercise 23-6   (Changes in estimates and accounting principles)

Due to changing economic conditions and to make its financial statements more comparable to those of other companies in its industry, the management of Kelsea Inc. decided in 1991 to review its accounting practices.

On January 1, management decided to change its allowance for uncollectible accounts from 2% to 3½% of its outstanding receivables balance.

On July 1, Kelsea decided to begin using the straight-line method of depreciation on its main frame computer instead of the sum-of-the-years-digits method. Based on further information, it also was decided that the computer has 10 more years of useful life. Kelsea bought the computer on January 1, 1981, at a cost of $550,000. At that time, Kelsea estimated it would have a 15 year useful life. The computer has no expected salvage value. Prior years' depreciation is as follows:

1981	$68,750	1986	$45,833
1982	64,167	1987	41,250
1983	59,583	1988	36,667
1984	55,000	1989	32,083
1985	50,417	1990	27,500

On October 1, Kelsea determined that starting with the current year it would depreciate the company's printing press using hours of use as the depreciation base. The press, which had been purchased on January 1, 1978, at a cost of

$930,000, was being depreciated for 25 years using the straight-line method. No salvage value was anticipated. It is estimated that this type of press provides 200,000 total hours of use and, as of January 1, 1991, it had been used 76,000 hours. At the end of 1991, the plant manager determined the press had been run 6,250 hours during the year. Ignore income taxes relating to this change.

(1) Evaluate each of the foregoing changes and determine whether it is a change in estimate or a change in accounting principle.
(2) Give the journal entries required at December 31, 1991, to account for the above changes. Kelsea's receivable balance at December 31, 1991, was $345,000. The allowance for doubtful accounts carried a $1,000 debit balance before adjustment.

Exercise 23-7 (Accounting errors)

The following errors in the accounting records of the Reed & Kinsey Partnership were discovered on January 10, 1991.

Year of Error	Ending Inventories Overstated	Depreciation Understated	Accrued Rent Revenue Not Recorded	Accrued Interest Expense Not Recorded
1988	$20,000		$ 6,000	
1989		$5,000	22,000	
1990	24,000			$2,000

The partners share net income and losses as follows: 40%, Reed; 60%, Kinsey.

(1) Prepare a correcting journal entry on January 10, 1991, assuming that the books were closed for 1990.
(2) Prepare a correcting journal entry on January 10, 1991, assuming that the books are still open for 1990 and that the partnership uses the perpetual inventory system.

Exercise 23-8 (Analysis of errors)

State the effect of each of the following errors made in 1990 on the balance sheets and the income statements prepared in 1990 and 1991:

(a) The ending inventory is understated as a result of an error in the count of goods on hand.
(b) The ending inventory is overstated as a result of the inclusion of goods acquired and held on a consignment basis. No purchase was recorded on the books.
(c) A purchase of merchandise at the end of 1990 is not recorded until payment is made for the goods in 1991; the good purchased were included in the inventory at the end of 1990.
(d) A sale of merchandise at the end of 1990 is not recorded until cash is received for the goods in 1991; the goods sold were excluded from the inventory at the end of 1990.
(e) Goods shipped to consignees in 1990 were reported as sales; goods in the hands of consignees at the end of 1990 were not recognized for inventory purposes; sale of such goods in 1991 and collections on such sales were recorded as credits to the receivables established with consignees in 1990.

(f) One week's sales total during 1990 was credited to Gain on Sales—Machinery.

(g) No depreciation is taken in 1990 for machinery sold in April, 1990. The company is on a calender year and computes depreciation to the nearest month.

(h) No depreciation is taken in 1990 for machinery purchased in October, 1990. The company is on a calender year and computes depreciation to the nearest month.

(i) Customers' notes receivable are debited to Accounts Receivable.

Exercise 23-9   (Correction of errors—working papers)

The Hickory Co. reports net incomes for a 3-year period as follows: 1988, $36,000; 1989, $21,000; 1990, $25,000.

In reviewing the accounts in 1991, after the books for the prior year have been closed, you find that the following errors have been made in summarizing activities:

	1988	1989	1990
Overstatement of ending inventories as a result of errors in count	$1,600	$2,800	$1,800
Understatement of advertising expense payable	300	600	450
Overstatement of interest receivable	250	—	200
Omission of depreciation on property items still in use	900	800	750

(1) Prepare working papers summarizing corrections and reporting corrected net incomes for 1988, 1989, and 1990.

(2) Give the entry to bring the books of the company up to date in 1991.

Exercise 23-10   (Journal entries to correct accounts)

The first audit of the books for the Balm Corporation was made for the year ended December 31, 1991. In reviewing the books, the auditor discovered that certain adjustments had been overlooked at the end of 1990 and 1991, and also that other items had been improperly recorded. Omissions and other failures for each year are summarized below:

	December 31	
	1990	1991
Sales salaries payable	$1,300	1,100
Interest receivable	325	215
Prepaid insurance	450	300
Advances from customers	1,750	2,500
(Collections from customers had been included in sales but should have been recognized as advances from customers since goods were not shipped until the following year.)		
Equipment	1,400	1,200
(Expenditures had been recognized as repairs but should have been recognized as cost of equipment; the depreciation rate on such equipment is 10% per year, but depreciation in the year of the expenditure is to be recognized at 5%.)		

Prepare journal entries to correct revenue and expense accounts for 1991 and record assets and liabilities that require recognition on the balance sheet as of December 31, 1991. Assume the nominal accounts for 1991 have not yet been closed into the income summary account.

Problems   **Problem 23-1   (Change in accounting principle)**

Yuki, Inc. acquired the following assets on January 3, 1988:

Equipment, estimated service life 5 years; residual value $13,000	$513,000
Building, estimated service life 40 years; no residual value	900,000

The equipment has been depreciated using the sum-of-the-years-digits method for the first 3 years. In 1991, the company decided to change the method of depreciation to straight-line. No change was made in the estimated service life or residual value. The company also decided to change the total estimated service life of the building from 40 to 45 years with no change in the estimated residual value. The building is depreciated on the straight-line method.

The company has 200,000 shares of capital stock outstanding. Partial results of operations for 1991 and 1990 are as follows:

	1991	1990
Income before cumulative effect of change in computing depreciation for 1991; depreciation for 1991 was computed on a straight-line basis for equipment and building.*	$890,000	$856,000
Earnings per share before cumulative effect of change in computing depreciation for 1991	$4.45	$4.28

*The computations for depreciation expense for 1991 and 1990 for the building were based on the original estimate of service life of 40 years.

Instructions:

(1) Compute the cumulative effect of the change in accounting principle to be reported in the income statement for 1991, and prepare the journal entry to record the change (ignore tax effects.)

(2) Present comparative data for the years 1990 and 1991, starting with income before cumulative effect of accounting change. Prepare pro forma data. (Ignore income tax effects.)

III Problem 23-2   (Accounting changes)

Barney Corporation has released the following condensed financial statements for 1989 and 1990 and has prepared the following proposed statements for 1991.

Barney Corporation
Comparative Balance Sheet
December 31

Assets	1991	1990	1989
Current assets	$249,000	$219,000	$165,000
Land	60,000	45,000	30,000
Equipment	150,000	150,000	150,000
Accumulated depreciation—equipment	(45,000)	(30,000)	(15,000)
Total assets	$414,000	$384,000	$330,000
Liabilities and Stockholders' Equity			
Current liabilities	$177,000	$177,000	$147,000
Common stock	60,000	60,000	60,000
Retained earnings	177,000	147,000	123,000
Total liabilities and stockholders' equity	$414,000	$384,000	$330,000

Barney Corporation
Comparative Income Statement
For Years Ended December 31

	1991	1990	1989
Sales	$315,000	$300,000	$255,000
Cost of goods sold.........................	$240,000	$225,000	$189,000
Other expenses except depreciation...........	30,000	36,000	33,000
Depreciation expense—equipment	15,000	15,000	15,000
Total costs..................................	$285,000	$276,000	$237,000
Net income	$ 30,000	$ 24,000	$ 18,000

Barney Corporation acquired the equipment for $150,000 on January 1, 1989, and began depreciating the equipment over a 10-year estimated useful life with no salvage value, using the straight-line method of depreciation. The double-declining-balance method of depreciation, under the same assumptions, would have required the following depreciation expense:

$$1989 \quad 20\% \times \$150,000 = \$30,000$$
$$1990 \quad 20\% \times \$120,000 = \$24,000$$
$$1991 \quad 20\% \times \$\ 96,000 = \$19,200$$

Instructions: In comparative format, prepare a balance sheet and a combined statement of income and retained earnings for 1991, giving effect to the following changes. Ignore any income tax effect. Barney Corporation has 10,000 shares of common stock outstanding. The following situations are independent of each other.

(1) For justifiable reasons, Barney Corporation changed to the double-declining-balance method of depreciation in 1991. The effect of the change should be included in the net income of the period in which the change was made.
(2) During 1991, Barney Corporation found the equipment was fast becoming obsolete and decided to change the estimated useful life from 10 years to 5 years. The books for 1991 had not yet been closed.
(3) During 1991, Barney Corporation found additional equipment, also acquired on January 1, 1989, costing $24,000, had been recorded in the land account and had not been depreciated. This error should be corrected using straight-line depreciation over a 10-year period.

Problem 23-3 (Change in accounting estimate and principle)
The following information relates to depreciable assets of Brillantez Electronics:

(a) Machine A was purchased for $30,000 on January 1, 1986. The entire cost was expensed in the year of purchase. The machine had a 15-year useful life and no residual value.
(b) Machine B cost $105,000 and was purchased January 1, 1987. The straight-line method of depreciation was used. At the time of purchase the expected useful life was 12 years with no residual value. In 1991, it was estimated that the total useful life of the asset would be only 8 years and that there would be a $5,000 residual value.
(c) Building A was purchased January 1, 1988, for $600,000. The straight-line

method of depreciation was originally chosen. The building was expected to be useful for 20 years and to have zero residual value. In 1991, a change was made from the straight-line depreciation method to the sum-of-the-years-digits method. Estimates relating to the useful life and residual value remained the same.

Income before depreciation expense was $520,000 for 1991. Depreciation on assets other than those described totaled $50,000. Net income for 1990 was $415,000.

Instructions: (Ignore all income tax effects)

(1) Prepare all entries for 1991 relating to depreciable assets.
(2) Prepare partial income statements for 1990 and 1991. Begin with income before the cumulative effects of any accounting changes. Show all computations.

Problem 23-4   (Reporting accounting changes)

Listed below are three independent, unrelated sets of facts concerning accounting changes.

Case 1 The Davis Company determined that the amortization rate on its patents is unacceptably low due to current advances in technology. The company decided at the beginning of 1991, the current year, to increase the amortization rate on all existing patents from 10% to 20%. Patents purchased on January 1, 1986, for $2,400,000 had a book value of $1,200,000 on January 1, 1991.

Case 2 Landon Enterprises decided on January 1, 1991, to change its depreciation method on manufacturing equipment from an accelerated method to the straight-line method. The straight-line method is to be used for new acquisitions as well as for previously acquired equipment. It has been determined that the excess of accelerated depreciation over straight-line depreciation for the years 1988 through 1990 totals $634,000.

Case 3 On December 31, 1990, Bradley Inc. owned 27% of the Clubb Company, at which time Bradley reported its investment using the equity method. During 1991, Bradley has increased its ownership in Clubb by 24%. Accordingly, Bradley is planning to prepare consolidated financial statements for Bradley and Clubb for the year ended December 31, 1991.

Instructions: For each of the situtations described:

(1) Identify the type of accounting change.
(2) Explain how the accounting change should be reported under current generally accepted accounting principles, and provide, where applicable, the journal entries to effect the accounting change. (Ignore the effect of income taxes.)
(3) Explain the effect of the change on the statement of financial position and income statement.   (AICPA adapted)

Problem 23-5   (Change in accounting principle)

During 1991, All Seasons Company changed its method of depreciating equipment from an accelerated depreciation method to the straight-line method. The following information shows the effect of this change.

Years	Net Income as Reported	Excess of Accelerated Depreciation Over Straight-Line Depreciation	Assumed Tax Effects
Prior to 1989		$68,000	$27,200
1989	$190,000	14,000	5,600
1990	210,000	17,000	6,800

Instructions:

(1) Compute the effect of the change in accounting principle on income (net of tax).
(2) Prepare a partial income statement for 1991 if income before extraordinary items was $225,000 and an extraordinary loss of $21,600 (net of $14,400 income tax reduction) was incurred. Assume 100,000 shares of common stock are outstanding.
(3) Present pro forma income data for the years 1989-1991. Assume 100,000 shares of common stock were outstanding in all years.

Problem 23-6   (Change in accounting principle—LIFO to FIFO)

On January 1, 1991, Overland Inc. decided to change from the LIFO method of inventory pricing to the FIFO method. The reported income for the 4 years Overland had been in business was as follows:

1987	$250,000	1989	$310,000
1988	260,000	1990	330,000

Analysis of the inventory records disclosed that the following inventories were on hand at the end of each year as valued under both the LIFO and FIFO methods.

	LIFO Method	FIFO Method
January 1, 1987	0	0
December 31, 1987	$228,000	$256,000
December 31, 1988	240,000	238,000
December 31, 1989	270,000	302,000
December 31, 1990	288,000	352,000

The income tax effect is assumed to be as follows:

1987	$11,200
1988	(12,000)
1989	13,600
1990	12,800

Instructions:

(1) Compute the restated net income for the years 1987-1990.
(2) Prepare the retained earnings statement for Overland Inc. for 1991 if the 1990 ending balance had been previously reported at $600,000, 1991 net income using the FIFO method is $360,000, and dividends of $200,000 were paid during 1991.

Problem 23-7 (Correction of errors)

Twain Textile Corporation is planning an expansion of its current plant facilities. Twain is in the process of obtaining a loan at City Bank. The bank has requested audited financial statements. Twain has never been audited before. It has prepared the following comparative financial statements for the years ended December 31, 1991, and 1990.

Twain Textile Corporation
Balance Sheet
December 31, 1991 and 1990

Assets	1991	1990
Current assets:		
Cash.	$ 407,500	$ 205,000
Accounts receivable.	980,000	740,000
Allowance for doubtful accounts	(92,500)	(45,000)
Marketable securities (at cost)	195,000	195,000
Inventory	517,500	505,000
Total current assets	$2,007,500	$1,600,000
Plant assets:		
Property, plant and equipment	$ 417,500	$ 423,750
Accumulated depreciation	(304,000)	(266,000)
Total plant assets	113,500	157,750
Total assets	$2,121,000	$1,757,750
Liabilities and Stockholder's Equity		
Liabilities:		
Accounts payable.	$ 303,500	$ 490,250
Stockholder's equity:		
Common stock, par value $25; authorized, 30,000 shares; issued and outstanding, 26,000 shares.	$ 650,000	$ 650,000
Retained earnings	1,167,500	617,500
Total stockholders' equity	$1,817,500	$1,267,500
Total liabilities and stockholders' equity	$2,121,000	$1,757,750

Twain Textile Corporation
Income Statement
For Years Ended December 31, 1991 and 1990

	1991	1990
Sales	$2,500,000	$2,250,000
Cost of good sold	1,075,000	987,500
Gross margin	$1,425,000	$1,262,500
Operating expenses.	$ 575,000	$ 512,500
General and administrative expense	300,000	262,500
	$ 875,000	$ 775,000
Net income	$ 550,000	$ 487,500

The following facts were disclosed during the audit.

(a) On January 20, 1990, Twain had charged a 5-year fire insurance premium to expense. The total premium amounted to $15,500.

(b) All marketable securities were purchased in 1990. The entire portfolio was properly classified as current and includes only equity securities. The market valuation at the end of each year was as follows:

1990	$202,500
1991	$178,250

(c) Over the last two years, the amount of loss due to bad debts has steadily decreased. Twain has decided to reduce the amount of bad debt expense from 2% to 1½% of sales, beginning with 1991. (A charge of 2% has already been made for 1991.)

(d) The inventory account (maintained on a periodic basic) has been in error the last 2 years. The errors were as follows:

1990:   Ending inventory overstated $37,750
1991:   Ending inventory overstated $49,500

(e) A machine costing $75,000, purchased on January 4, 1990, was incorrectly charged to operating expense. The machine had a useful life of 10 years and a residual value of $12,500. The straight-line depreciation method is used by Twain.

Instructions:

(1) Prepare the journal entries to correct the books at December 31, 1991. The books for 1991 have not been closed. Ignore income taxes.

(2) Prepare a schedule showing the computation of corrected net income for the years ended December 31, 1990 and 1991, assuming that any adjustments are to be reported on the comparative statements for the two years. Begin your schedule with the net income for each year. Ignore income taxes.

(AICPA adapted)

Problem 23-8   (Correction of errors—working papers)

The auditors for the Wharton Co. in inspecting accounts on December 31, 1991, the end of the fiscal year, find that certain prepaid and accrued items had been overlooked in prior years and in the current year as follows:

	End of			
	1988	1989	1990	1991
Prepaid expenses	$700	$600	$750	$1,900
Expenses payable	500	800	950	1,000
Unearned revenues	140			420
Revenues receivable		150	125	200

Retained earnings on December 31, 1988, had been reported at $25,600; and net income for 1989 and for 1990 were reported at $9,500 and $12,250 respectively. Revenue and expense balances for 1991 were transferred to the income summary account and the latter shows a credit balance of $12,500 prior to correction by the auditors. No dividends had been declared in the 3-year period.

Instructions:

(1) Prepare working papers to develop a corrected retained earnings balance as of December 31, 1988, and corrected income for 1989, 1990, and 1991. Disregard effects of corrections on income tax.
(2) Prepare a corrected statement of retained earnings for the 3-year period ending December 31, 1991.
(3) Give the entry or entries required as of December 31, 1991, to correct the income summary account and retained earnings account and to establish the appropriate balance sheet accounts as of this date.

Problem 23-9   (Analysis and correction of errors)

A CPA is engaged by the Alpine Corp. in 1991 to examine the books and records and to make whatever corrections are necessary.

An examination of the accounts discloses the following:

(a) Dividends had been declared on December 15 in 1988 and 1989 but had not been entered in the books until paid.
(b) Improvements in buildings and equipment of $4,800 had been debited to expense at the end of April, 1987. Improvements are estimated to have an 8-year life. The company uses the straight-line method in recording depreciation and computes depreciation to the nearest month.
(c) The physical inventory of merchandise had been understated by $1,500 at the end of 1988 and by $2,150 at the end of 1990.
(d) The merchandise inventories at the end of 1989 and 1990 did not include merchandise that was then in transit and to which the company had title. These shipments of $1,900 and $2,750 were recorded as purchases in January of 1990 and 1991 respectively.
(e) The company had failed to record sales commissions payable of $1,050 and $850 at the end of 1989 and 1990 respectively.
(f) The company had failed to recognize supplies on hand of $600 and $1,250 at the end of 1989 and 1990 respectively.

The retained earnings account appeared as follows on the date the CPA began the examination.

Account   **Retained Earnings**

Date		Item	Debt	Credit	Balance Debit	Balance Credit
1988						
Jan. . .	1	Balance				40,500
Dec.	31	Net income for year		9,000		49,500
1989						
Jan. . .	10	Dividends paid	7,500			42,000
Mar. . .	6	Stock sold—excess over par		16,000		58,000
Dec.	31	Net loss for year	5,600			52,400
1990						
Jan. . .	10	Dividends paid	7,500			44,900
Dec.	31	Net loss for year	6,200			38,700

Instructions:

(1) Prepare working papers for the correction of account balances using the following columns (disregard effects of corrections on income tax):

Explanation	Retained Earnings Jan. 1, 1988		Net Income Year Ended Dec. 31, 1988		Net Income Year Ended Dec. 31, 1989		Net Income Year Ended Dec. 31, 1990		Accounts Requiring Correction in 1991		
	Debit	Credit	Debit	Credit	Debit	Credit	Debit	Credit	Debit	Credit	Account

(2) Journalize the necessary corrections.
(3) Prepare a statement of retained earnings covering the 3-year period beginning January 1, 1988. The statement should report the corrected retained earnings balance on Janaury 1, 1988, the annual changes in the account, and the corrected retained earnings balances as of December 31, 1988, 1989 and 1990.
(4) Set up an account for retained earnings before correction, and post correcting data to this account for part (2). Balance the account, showing the corrected retained earnings as of January 1, 1991.

Problem 23-10   (Accounting changes and correction of errors)

Stevens Company is in the process of adjusting its books at the end of 1991. Stevens' records reveal the following information.

(a) Stevens failed to accrue sales commissions at the end of 1989 and 1990 as follows:
     1989 $27,000
     1990 $15,333
The sales commissions were paid in January of the following year.

(b) On December 31, 1991, Stevens changed its depreciation method for machinery from double-declining-balance to the straight-line method. Stevens has already recorded the 1991 depreciation using the double-declining-balance method. The following information also was provided:

	Double-Declining-Balance Depreciation	Straight-Line Depreciation	Depreciation Difference
Before 1991	$233,333	$133,333	$100,000
1991	40,000	33,333	6,667

(c) Errors in ending inventories for the last 3 years were discovered to be as follows:

     1989 $43,333 understated
     1990   56,667 understated
     1991   10,000 overstated

The incorrect amount has already been recorded for 1991.

(d) Early in 1991, Stevens changed from the percentage-of-completion method of accounting for long-term construction contracts to the completed contract method. The income for 1991 was recorded using the completed contract method. The following information also was available:

	Pre-Tax Income	
	Percentage of Completion	Completed Contract
Before 1991	$583,333	$166,667
1991	200,000	66,667

Instructions:

(1) Prepare the necessary journal entries at December 31, 1991, to record the above information. Assume the books are still open for 1991. Ignore all income tax effects.

(2) Assuming income from continuing operations before taxes of $500,000, taxes of $150,000 on operating income, and no applicable taxes on the cumulative effect of changing depreciation methods, prepare a partial income statement (beginning with income from continuing operations before taxes) for Stevens Company for 1991. (Ignore earnings per share.)

(3) Assuming Retained Earnings at the beginning of 1991 was $1,985,000 and that dividends of $125,000 were declared during 1991, prepare a statement of retained earnings for Stevens Company, reflecting appropriate adjustments from (1). Assume no applicable taxes on the cumulative effect of changing to the completed-contract method.

PART FIVE

Financial Reporting

Chapter 24

Statement of Cash Flows

Assessing the amounts, timing, and uncertainty of future cash flows is one of the primary objectives of financial reporting.[1] The statement that provides information needed to meet this objective is a **statement of cash flows.** Chapter 5 provided an overview of reporting cash flows; this chapter details the techniques for preparing and analyzing a cash flow statement.

Historical Perspective

As discussed in Chapters 4 and 5, the primary financial statements for a business enterprise include the balance sheet, the income statement, and the statement of cash flows. The balance sheet reports the financial position of a business at a given time. The income statement reports the operating results for the period and may be accompanied by a statement summarizing the changes in retained earnings or stockholders' equity in successive periods. The statement of cash flows provides information about the cash receipts and cash payments of an entity during a period of time. It has replaced the previously required **statement of changes in financial position** or **funds statement.**

The funds statement went through several years of development in becoming one of the primary financial statements. In 1961, Accounting Research Study No. 2, sponsored by the AICPA, recommended that a funds statement be prepared and included with the income statement and balance sheet in annual reports to shareholders.[2] Two years later APB Opinion No. 3 was issued to provide guidelines for the preparation of the funds statement.[3] Even though Opinion No. 3 did not require a funds statement, most businesses recognized the value of the funds statement and included it in their annual reports. Thus, it was somewhat anticlimactic when, in 1971, the APB issued Opinion No. 19 officially requiring that a funds

---

[1]*Statement of Financial Accounting Concepts No. 1*, "Objectives of Financial Reporting by Business Enterprises" (Stamford: Financial Accounting Standards Board, 1978), par 37.

[2]Perry Mason, *Accounting Research Study No. 2*, " 'Cash Flow' Analysis and the Funds Statement" (New York: American Institute of Certified Public Accountants, 1961).

[3]*Opinions of the Accounting Principles Board, No. 3*, "The Statement of Source and Application of Funds" (New York: American Institute of Certified Public Accountants, 1963).

statement be included as one of the three primary financial statements in annual reports to shareholders and that it be covered by the auditor's report.[4]

Opinion No. 19 did not specify a single definition or concept of funds to be used in preparing the funds statement or a required format for the statement. Thus, companies were allowed considerable flexibility in the reporting of funds flow information. In late 1987, the FASB issued Statement No. 95, which supersedes APB Opinion No. 19. Instead of allowing various definitions of funds, such as cash or working capital, and a variety of formats, the FASB called for a statement of cash flows to replace the more general statement of changes in financial position. In addition, the FASB specified a format that highlights cash flows from operating, investing, and financing activities.[5] A major reason for the FASB's actions was the desire to help investors and creditors better predict future cash flows, which is considered an important financial reporting objective.

Nature and Purpose of a Statement of Cash Flows

As previously noted, the major purpose of a statement of cash flows is to provide relevant information about the cash receipts and cash payments of an entity during a period of time. This information should help investors and creditors assess an entity's ability to generate positive future net cash flows and to meet its current and long-term obligations, including possible future dividend payments. In addition, the statement of cash flows should help users assess the reasons for the differences between net income and the related cash receipts and payments. Finally, the statement of cash flows should help to determine the effects of both cash and noncash investing and financing transactions on an entity's financial position.[6]

To achieve these objectives, the FASB concluded that a statement of cash flows should report the cash effects of an entity's operations, its investing transactions, and its financing transactions. Additional disclosures should be made of any significant investing or financing transactions that affect an enterprise's financial position but do not directly affect cash flows during the period. Finally, a reconciliation of accrual net income and net cash flow from operating activities also should be provided.

Cash and Cash Equivalents

A statement of cash flows explains the change during the period in cash and cash equivalents—short-term, highly liquid investments that can be converted easily into cash. To qualify as a cash equivalent an item must be:[7]

---

[4]Opinions of the Accounting Principles Board, No. 19, "Reporting Changes in Financial Position" (New York: American Institute of Certified Public Accountants, 1971).

[5]Statement of Financial Accounting Standards No. 95, "Statement of Cash Flows" (Stamford: Financial Accounting Standards Board, November 1987).

[6]Ibid, par. 5.

[7]Ibid, par. 8.

1. Readily convertible to cash, and
2. So near its maturity that there is insignificant risk of changes in value due to changes in interest rates.

Generally, only investments with original maturities of three months or less qualify as cash equivalents. **Original maturity** in this case is determined from the date an investment was acquired by the reporting entity, which may not coincide with the date of issuance of the security. For example, both a three-month U.S. Treasury bill and a three-year Treasury note purchased three months prior to maturity qualify as cash equivalents. However, if the Treasury note were purchased three years ago, it would not qualify as a cash equivalent during the last three months prior to its maturity.[8] In addition to U.S. Treasury obligations, cash equivalents can include such items as money market funds and commercial paper. Investments in marketable *equity* securities (common and preferred stock) normally would not be classified as cash equivalents because such securities have no definite maturity date and are subject to fluctuations in value.

Not all investments qualifying as cash equivalents need be reported as such. Management is required to establish a policy concerning which short-term, highly liquid investments are to be treated as cash equivalents. Once a policy is established, management should disclose which items are being treated as cash equivalents in presenting its cash flow statement. Any change in the established policy would be considered a change in accounting principle.

Major Classifications of Cash Flows

The traditional funds statement classified the flow of resources simply as sources and uses of funds. The statement of cash flows, as mentioned previously, should classify cash receipts and payments according to three main categories: operating activities, investing activities, and financing activities. Exhibit 24-1 summarizes the major types of cash receipts and cash payments included in each category. Note that these are general classifications. Specific items might be classified differently for certain types of businesses. For example, activities normally classified as investing might be classified as operating activities for a bank or other financial institution.[9]

Operating Activities

Operating activities include those transactions and events that normally

---

[8]*Ibid.*

[9]With the issuance of Statement No. 102, the FASB has specifically modified Statement No. 95 with respect to the classification of certain securities or debt instruments held in a trading portfolio. Thus, the cash receipts or cash payments from acquisitions or sales of securities or other assets that are acquired specifically for resale and that are carried at market values in trading accounts should be classified as operating cash flows instead of investing cash flows. A similar reclassification should be made for loans that are acquired specifically for resale and that are carried at market or lower of cost or market values. See *Statement of Financial Accounting Standards No. 102*, "Statement of Cash Flows—Exemption of Certain Enterprises and Classification of Cash Flows from Certain Securities Acquired for Resale," (Norwalk: Financial Accounting Standards Board, February 1989), p. 3.

Exhibit 24–1   Major Classifications of Cash Flows

Operating Activities
Cash receipts from:
  Sale of goods or services
  Interest revenue
  Dividend revenue
Cash payments to:
  Suppliers for inventory purchases
  Employees for services
  Governments for taxes
  Lenders for interest expense
  Others for other expenses (e.g., utilities, rent)
Investing Activities
Cash receipts from:
  Sale of plant assets
  Sale of a business segment
  Sale of investments in equity securities of other entities or debt securities (other than
    cash equivalents)
  Collection of principal on loans made to other entities
Cash payments to:
  Purchase plant assets
  Purchase equity securities of other entities or debt securities (other than cash
    equivalents)
  Make loans to other entities
Financing Activities
Cash receipts from:
  Issuance of own stock
  Borrowing (e.g., bonds, notes, mortgages)
Cash payments to:
  Stockholders as dividends
  Repay principal amounts borrowed
  Repurchase an entity's own stock (treasury stock)

enter into the determination of operating income. Cash receipts from selling goods or from providing services would be the major cash inflow for most businesses. Other cash receipts might come from interest, dividends, and similar items. Major cash outflows would include payments to purchase inventory and to pay wages, taxes, interest, utilities, rent, and similar expenses. The net amount of cash provided or used by operating activities is a key figure that should be highlighted on a statement of cash flows.

While cash inflows from interest or dividends logically might be classified as investing or financing activities, the FASB decided to classify them as operating activities, which conforms to their presentation on the income statement. Note, too, that investments in short-term, highly liquid securities that are considered cash equivalents are included as part of the cash balance.

Investing Activities

Transactions and events involving the purchase and sale of securities (excluding cash equivalents), land, buildings, equipment, and other assets not generally held for resale, and the making and collecting of loans are classified as **investing activities**. These activities occur regularly and result in cash receipts and payments. They are not classified as operating activities since they relate only indirectly to the central, ongoing operation of an entity, which is usually the sale of goods or services.

Financing Activities

Financing activities include transactions and events whereby cash is obtained from or repaid to owners (equity financing) and creditors (debt financing). For example, the cash proceeds from issuing capital stock or bonds would be classified under financing activities. Similarly, the payments to reacquire stock (treasury stock) or to retire the principal amounts owed, and the payment of dividends are considered financing activities. This classification scheme is not totally consistent since the receipt of dividends and the receipt and payment of interest, as noted earlier, are classified under operating activities. The classifications, however, are consistent with the presentation in an income statement.

Noncash Investing and Financing Activities

Some investing and financing activities affect an entity's financial position but not the entity's cash flows during the period. For example, equipment may be purchased with a note payable or land may be acquired by issuing stock. Such noncash investing and financing activities were previously reported in a traditional funds statement under the "all-financial-resources concept," as both a source and a use of funds. Now, according to FASB Statement No. 95, significant noncash investing and financing activities should be disclosed separately, either in the notes to the financial statements or in an accompanying schedule, not in the statement itself.[10] The statement of cash flows reports only operating, investing, and financing activities involving cash.

Reporting Alternatives   Exhibit 24-2 illustrates the general format, with details and amounts omitted, for a statement of cash flows. The statement should report the net cash provided (used) by operating, investing, and financing activities, and the net effect of total cash flows on cash and cash equivalents during the period. While the exact format of the statement is not specified by the FASB, the information is to be presented in a manner that reconciles beginning and ending cash and cash equivalent amounts.[11]

---

[10]*FASB Statement No. 95*, par. 32.

[11]Additional disclosures are required in reconciling the change in cash and cash equivalents for a company that has foreign currency transactions or foreign operations. Such entities must report the equivalent of foreign currency cash flows and should show the effect of any exchange rate fluctuations on the cash balances as a separate item in the cash flow statement. The complexities involved in reporting these foreign currency cash flows are considered beyond the scope of this text.

Exhibit 24–2	**General Format for a Statement of Cash Flows**

Cash provided (used) by:
Operating activities . . . . $XXX
Investing activities   XXX
Financing activities   XXX
Net increase (decrease) in cash and cash equivalents . . . . $XXX
Cash and cash equivalents at beginning of year   XXX
Cash and cash equivalents at end of year . . . . $XXX

There are two methods that may be used in calculating and reporting the amount of net cash flow from operating activities: the direct method and the indirect method. The direct method shows the major operating cash receipts (such as cash collected from customers and receipts of interest and dividends) and cash payments (for example, to suppliers for inventory, to employees for wages, to creditors for interest, and to government agencies for taxes). The difference between these operating cash receipts and payments is the net cash flow provided (used) by operating activities.

The indirect method involves a reconciliation of net income, as reported on the income statement, and net cash flow provided (used) by operating activities, as shown on the statement of cash flows. In effect, this requires adjusting accrual net income for any items that do not affect cash, such as depreciation or amortization, and also converting the accrual-based amounts reflected on the income statement to a cash basis.

Both methods produce identical results, i.e., the same amount of net cash flow provided (used) by operations. The direct method is favored by many statement readers because it is straightforward and is not likely to be misunderstood. The indirect method is favored and used by most accountants because it is easy to apply and because it helps explain the reasons for the difference between net income and net cash flow from operations. Furthermore, some accountants are concerned that use of the direct method might imply that cash-basis income is a better measure of company performance than accrual-basis income, which is contrary to generally accepted accounting principles.

The Direct Method   A statement of cash flows prepared using the **direct method** essentially requires analysis of the cash account, resulting in the cash receipts and payments being classified according to their impact on operating, financing, and investing activities. With this approach, each cash transaction could be analyzed separately to derive total cash receipts and payments for the period. Usually, however, summarized data provided in the financial statements is analyzed to convert accrual-basis revenues and expenses to cash receipts and payments.

To illustrate the analytical process that is used in preparing a cash flow statement with the direct method, consider sales revenue as an example. The amount of sales reported on the income statement must be adjusted for changes in accounts receivable balances to determine the cash collected during the period. The beginning receivables balance represents sales from the previous period. These receivables are assumed to have been collected in cash during the current period. The ending receivables represent sales of the current period that will be collected in a future period. Thus, to determine the cash collected from customers during the current period, the beginning receivables must be added to, and the ending receivables subtracted from, the accrual sales figure. If we assume reported sales of $500,000 and beginning and ending accounts receivable balances of $125,000 and $110,000, respectively, the computation would be:

	Sales (reported on income statement)	$500,000
+	Beginning Accounts Receivable	125,000
−	Ending Accounts Receivable	(110,000)
=	Cash Receipts from Customers	$515,000

The above example makes two important assumptions. First, it is assumed that all the accounts receivable were trade receivables and therefore related totally to cash collected from customers, an operating activity. If part of the receivables were nontrade receivables, the cash collected on those receivables would be classified as an investing activity. In this chapter, unless otherwise noted, it will be assumed that all accounts receivable amounts (as well as accounts payable amounts) are related to operations.

The second assumption is that no accounts were written off as uncollectible. The adjustments for accounts receivable balances were made at "gross" amounts, i.e., without deducting any allowance for doubtful accounts. When this procedure is used, any write-offs for uncollectible accounts also must be deducted from accrual sales to derive the cash collected from customers. Using the above example and assuming a $1,000 account was written-off during the period, the cash collected would be $514,000 ($500,000 + $125,000 − $110,000 − $1,000). The write-off reduced the ending accounts receivable balance but did not produce cash.

If in the above example the receivable balances were "net" of appropriate allowances for doubtful accounts, a write-off of an uncollectible account would be ignored. The write-off would reduce the allowance account as well as the receivable account and leave the net balance unchanged. However, the amount of cash collected from customers would have to be reduced by the amount of the bad debt expense provision for the period since part of the change in the net receivable balance did not come from cash flows, but rather from an adjusting entry, debiting the bad debt expense account and crediting the allowance for doubtful accounts.

The adjustment process applicable to sales also is required for other revenues and their related receivable balances. Revenues collected in advance are an exception to the above rule. For example, when rent revenue is collected in advance, the cash is received before it is earned. For these types of revenue items, the ending unearned rent liability is added and the beginning unearned rent is subtracted from the reported rent revenue amount to compute the cash received for rent during the period.

A similar process and rationale are applicable for converting expenses reported on an accrual basis to the amount of cash paid during the period. To illustrate, if $150,000 of wages expense is reported on the income statement and the beginning and ending wages payable amounts are $40,000 and $45,000, respectively, the amount of cash paid for wages would be as follows:

	Wages Expense (reported on income statement)	$150,000
+	Beginning Wages Payable	40,000
−	Ending Wages Payable	(45,000)
=	Cash Paid for Wages During the Period	$145,000

The conversion process would be the same for all expenses that are incurred prior to being paid, e.g., utilities, interest, property taxes, and income taxes. Prepaid expenses, however, are generally paid and recorded as assets prior to becoming an expense. An example would be prepaid insurance. For these types of expenses, an opposite calculation is required. Assume that insurance expense reported for the current period is $4,000 and the beginning and ending balances in Prepaid Insurance are $1,000 and $500, respectively. The amount of cash paid for insurance would be calculated as follows:

	Insurance Expense (reported on the income statement)	$4,000
+	Ending Prepaid Insurance	500
−	Beginning Prepaid Insurance	(1,000)
=	Cash Paid for Insurance	$3,500

The amount of cash paid for inventory also must be calculated. If a company is using a periodic inventory system, the amount of purchases can be determined directly from the purchases accounts. That amount would then be adjusted by adding the beginning accounts payable balance and subtracting the ending accounts payable balance to determine the cash paid for inventory. If a perpetual inventory system is used, the cost of goods sold is known, but the amount of purchases would have to be calculated by adding the ending inventory and subtracting the beginning inventory amounts. Then purchases would be adjusted to a cash basis by considering the beginning and ending accounts payable balances. The following calculations, with assumed numbers, illustrate this point.

	Cost of Goods Sold (from perpetual inventory records)	$240,000
+	Ending Inventory	43,000
−	Beginning Inventory	(38,000)
=	Purchases	$245,000
+	Beginning Accounts Payable	27,000
−	Ending Accounts Payable	(30,000)
=	Cash Paid for Inventory	$242,000

Exhibit 24-3 summarizes the adusting procedures used to convert accrual amounts to the cash basis. The exhibit includes an example of each basic type of revenue and expense adjustment. If a company earns dividend revenue or incurs interest expense, FASB Statement No. 95 requires that those items be reported under operating activities. Dividend revenue is adjusted in the same manner as interest revenue. Interest expense is converted using the approach illustrated for wages expense.

Exhibit 24—3   Cash Flows from Operating Activities—Direct Method

Accrual Basis	± Adjustments Required	= Cash Basis
Net credit sales	+ Beginning accounts receivable − Ending accounts receivable	= Cash receipts from customers
Other revenues (e.g., rent and interest):		
Rent revenue	+ Ending unearned rent − Beginning unearned rent	= Cash received for rent
Interest revenue	+ Beginning interest receivable − Ending interest receivable	= Cash received for interest
Cost of goods sold	+ Ending inventory − Beginning inventory + Beginning accounts payable − Ending accounts payable	= Cash paid for inventory
Operating expenses (excluding depreciation and other noncash items; e.g., insurance and wages):		
Insurance expense	+ Ending prepaid insurance − Beginning prepaid insurance	= Cash paid for insurance
Wages expense	+ Beginning wages payable − Ending wages payable	= Cash paid for wages
Income tax expense	+ Beginning income taxes payable − Ending income taxes payable	= Cash paid for income taxes
		Net cash flow provided (used) by operating activities

The Indirect Method   The **indirect method**, like the direct method, reports the net cash flow provided or used by operating activities by converting accrual revenues and expenses to cash receipts and payments. The conversion process, however, is somewhat different. The indirect method begins with reported net income, adjusts that amount for any items not affecting cash, and converts the accrual numbers to a cash basis by adding or subtracting changes in the operating accounts that affect net income. This reconciliation of net income to cash flow from operations generally is reported directly on the cash flow statement.

Adjustments for Noncash Items

Some items reported in the income statement do not affect cash. Examples of noncash items include depreciation on buildings and equipment, amortization of intangible assets such as goodwill, amortization of bond premium or discount, estimates of bad debt expense and warranty obligations, lower of cost or market adjustments, and other items that are reported as revenues or expenses in the income statement but that do not result in cash receipts or payments during the period.

Under the direct method, only cash transactions are analyzed and reported; therefore, no adjustments for noncash items are needed. (An exception, as noted earlier, would be for bad debt expense when adjusting sales for accounts receivable balances on a net basis.) Under the indirect method, however, the computation of cash flows from operating activities begins with net income, which already includes the effects of noncash items. For example, depreciation has been deducted as an operating expense to derive net income. Because the entry to record depreciation does not involve cash, the amount of depreciation expense must be added back to the reported net income in computing cash flows from operating activities. Similarly, any noncash item that has increased net income (such as the amortization of a bond premium) would be subtracted on a cash flow statement prepared using the indirect method.

Adjustments for Gains and Losses

The net income amount used as a starting point with the indirect method also may include gains or losses on the sale of assets. These gains and losses are the result of activities that are incidental or peripheral to the central operations of a business. Generally, sales of assets result in cash inflows and should be reported in the statement of cash flows, but under investing activities, not operating activities.

Under the indirect method, the gain (loss) reported in the income statement is subtracted from (added to) net income in computing operating cash flow. To illustrate, assume that Halifax Corporation sold for $75,000 land that cost $50,000. This land had been held for possible expansion, but was no longer needed. The entry for the sale would be:

Cash	75,000	
Land		50,000
Gain on Sale of Land		25,000

Since the $25,000 gain was included in net income, that amount would be subtracted in deriving net cash flows from operating activities using the indirect method. Note that no adjustment for gains and losses is required under the direct method, because that method reports *directly* the operating cash receipts and payments.

The cash effect of the transaction is reported on the statement of cash flows under investing activities. Regardless of which method (direct or indirect) is used to report operating cash flows, the $75,000 would be reported as cash received from investing activities.

Adjustments for Changes in Current Operating Accounts

In addition to noncash items and gains and losses, the net income amount must be adjusted for changes in current asset and liability account balances that affect net cash flow from operations. These adjustments are necessary to convert accrual-basis revenues and expenses reflected in net income to the cash basis. This conversion process is based on the same rationale as that discussed and illustrated for the direct method.

Changes in Current Asset Accounts Increases in accounts receivable are subtracted from net income in deriving cash flows from operations. Decreases in accounts receivable are added to net income. For example, assume the ending balance in Accounts Receivable was $20,000 more than the beginning balance, receivables being reported net of applicable allowances for doubtful accounts. This indicates that the amount of cash collected during the period was $20,000 less than the sales revenue reported in the income statement on an accrual basis. Thus, the $20,000 increase would be subtracted from net income to reflect the cash received for the period on the cash flow statement. If a receivable balance decreases, the opposite would be true; the decrease would be added to net income because more cash was collected than is reflected in the revenue reported in the income statement.

It should be noted that under the indirect method when net income is adjusted for the change in receivable balances reported *net* of the allowance for doubtful accounts, any write-offs of uncollectible accounts and the provision for bad debt expense can be ignored. Both the write-off and the estimated bad debt expense have already been netted against the receivable balances. However, if only *gross* change in receivables is added or subtracted to net income, then net income must be adjusted further for the bad debt expense for the period.

To illustrate, assume the following data:

	Beginning Balances	Ending Balances
Accounts Receivable	$20,000	$25,000
Allowance for Doubtful Accounts	4,000	5,000
Net Accounts Receivable	$16,000	$20,000
Net income for the year	$100,000	
Bad Debt Expense for the year	$ 2,000	
Write-Off of Uncollectible Accounts for the year	$ 1,000	

Using the net versus the gross approach, the cash collected would be computed as follows:

	Net Approach	Gross Approach
Net income	$100,000	$100,000
Increase in Accounts Receivable	(4,000)	(6,000)*
Bad Debt Expense		2,000
Cash collected	$96,000	$96,000

*$25,000 Ending Balance − $20,000 Beginning Balance + $1,000 Write-Off

As with receivables, an increase in inventory is subtracted from net income because more cash was used for purchases than is reflected in cost of goods sold on the income statement. A decrease in inventory is added to net income because less cash was used to acquire goods than is reflected in the income statement.

Adjustments also must be made for changes in prepaid asset accounts. An increase in a prepaid asset, such as Prepaid Insurance, is subtracted from net income to reflect the amount of cash paid for insurance. A decrease in a prepaid account is added to net income.

The changes in most current asset accounts affect operating income and require adjustment as described above. Changes in temporary investments, on the other hand, generally do not affect operating activities but are considered investing activities. An exception to this general statement is when short-term marketable securities are written down to the lower of cost or market (or when there is a recovery of a write-down) and the loss (or gain) is included in operating income. Such a write-down (or recovery) does not involve cash, and, under the indirect method, net income would have to be adjusted in the same manner as it is for other noncash items.

Those short-term investments that qualify as cash equivalents would be included with cash. The changes in other temporary investments would be included under the category of investing activities. For brokerage firms and financial institutions, as mentioned earlier, purchases and sales of trading account securities would be considered operating activities. Nontrading account securities, even for these firms, would be classified as investing activities.

Changes in Current Liability Accounts Changes in accounts payable balances have the opposite effect of changes in accounts receivable balances. For example, an increase in accounts payable means less cash was used than the amount of purchases or cost of goods sold recorded on an accrual basis. Thus, an increase in accounts payable is added to net income in deriving cash flow from operations. A decrease in accounts payable is deducted from net income because more cash was paid than is reflected in accrual net income.

Similar adjustments for other current payables that affect income would be required. For example, the amount of wages expense, interest expense, and taxes expense reported on the income statement would have to be adjusted for increases and decreases in applicable payable balances to report the net cash flow provided (used) by operating activities. Adjustments for increases or decreases in other current payables that do not affect income (e.g., dividends payable) would also have to be made. These adjustments would be reflected in the investing or financing activities section of the cash flow statement rather than in the operating section.

Adjustments also must be made for changes in unearned revenue accounts such as Advances from Customers or Unearned Rent Revenue. An increase in an unearned revenue account is added to net income, while a decrease is subtracted to adjust the revenue reported in the income statement to a cash basis.

Exhibit 24-4 summarizes the procedures for determining net cash flow from operating activities using the indirect method. A comparison of Exhibits 24-3 and 24-4 reveals the differences between the two approaches. The direct method, as the name implies, reports directly the operating cash receipts and payments, while the indirect method starts with net income and adjusts that figure to a cash basis.

Exhibit 24—4   Cash Flows from Operating Activities—Indirect Method

---

Net income reported on the income statement
Adjustments for noncash items:

- \+ Depreciation
- \+ Amortization of intangible assets
- \+ Amortization of bond discount
- − Amortization of bond premium
- \+ Bad debt expense*
- \+ Recognized decline in value of current marketable equity securities
- − Recovery of recognized decline in value of current marketable equity securities
- ± Other noncash items included in net income

Adjustments for gains and losses:

- − Gains on sales of assets
- \+ Losses on sales of assets

Adjustments for changes in current operating accounts:

- − Increases in current asset accounts (except cash and cash equivalents)
- \+ Decreases in current asset accounts (except cash and cash equivalents)
- \+ Increases in current liability accounts
- − Decreases in current liability accounts

Net cash flow provided (used) by operating activities
*When adjusting for gross receivables

FASB Statement No. 95 encourages use of the direct method for preparing a statement of cash flows, with a separate schedule to reconcile net income and net cash flow from operating activities. A company may choose, however, to use the indirect method, which already includes the required reconciliation. If the indirect method is used, the company should disclose separately, in the notes or related disclosures, the amounts of interest and income taxes paid during the period, since these items are considered particularly significant by the FASB.

Regardless of which method is used, the amount reported as net cash flow provided (used) by operating activities will be the same. As will be illustrated, only the format and extent of detail on the statement of cash flows will differ for the two methods. Since most accounting systems are set up to report revenues and expenses on an accrual basis for the income statement, it is likely that most companies will start with net income, make the necessary adjustments, and report net cash flows from operations using the indirect method.

Four steps are generally required in preparing a statement of cash flows:

1. *Determine the change in cash* (including cash equivalents). This is simply the difference between beginning and ending cash balances for the period being analyzed. The change in cash is the "target figure"—the amount that will be explained by the statement of cash flows.

2. *Determine the net cash flow provided (used) by operating activities*, using either the direct or the indirect method. This step requires analysis of comparative balance sheet amounts, income statement data, and specific transactions that relate to company operations.

3. *Determine the net cash flow provided (used) by investing and financing activities*. This step requires analysis of the cash flow impact of all accounts and transactions relating to investing and financing activities.

4. *Prepare a formal statement of cash flows*, classified according to operating, investing, and financing activities. Note that the amount determined in Step 1 should equal the total net increase (decrease) in cash reported on the statement of cash flows and will, therefore, reconcile the beginning and ending cash balances for the period. Any significant noncash investing or financing transactions should be reported separately, not on the statement of cash flows.

To illustrate the process of analyzing accounts and preparing a statement of cash flows, a simple example will be considered. The balance sheets, income statement, and additional information for the Taylor Company provide the necessary data for the illustrations. Use of the indirect method for computing and reporting operating cash flows is illustrated first, followed by the direct method. To emphasize the nature of the account analysis required in preparing a statement of cash flows, it is assumed that no other information is available. In practice, however, the data for preparing a cash flow statement can be taken directly from the accounting records.

Taylor Company
Comparative Balance Sheets
December 31, 1991 and 1990

Assets	1991	1990
Cash and cash equivalents..........................	$ 82,000	$ 40,000
Accounts receivable (net)	180,000	150,000
Inventory..	170,000	200,000
Equipment	200,000	140,000
Accumulated depreciation..........................	(72,000)	(60,000)
	$560,000	$470,000

Liabilities and Stockholders' Equity		
Accounts payable..................................	$100,000	$ 80,000
Long-term notes payable...........................	100,000	50,000
Common stock	250,000	250,000
Retained earnings.................................	110,000	90,000
	$560,000	$470,000

Taylor Company
Income Statement
For the Year Ended December 31, 1991

Revenues		$345,000
Less: Cost of goods sold...........................	$120,000	
Operating expenses (excluding depreciation, bad debts, and interest).....................................	53,000	
Depreciation.....................................	40,000	
Bad debt expense	5,000	
Interest expense	2,000	220,000
Operating income		$125,000
Gain from sale of equipment		5,000
Income before income taxes........................		$130,000
Less income tax expense		30,000
Net income......................................		$100,000

Additional information:
1. Equipment costing $30,000, with a book value of $2,000, was sold for $7,000 during the year.
2. Retained Earnings was affected only by net income and cash dividends paid during the year.

Illustration—Indirect Method   Determining the change in cash and cash equivalents[12] is the first step in preparing a statement of cash flows. For Taylor Company, the cash balance has increased $42,000.

Since the primary purpose of the statement is to identify the cash receipts and payments for the period, and thus explain the change in the

---

[12]Throughout the remainder of the chapter, the term *cash* includes cash equivalents where appropriate.

cash balance, the statement can be prepared by analyzing all noncash balance sheet accounts to determine what operating, investing, and financing transactions took place and what effect they had on cash flow.

To assist in the analysis of accounts, it is often helpful to use T-accounts, especially for certain accounts such as Retained Earnings where the net change in the balance does not clearly show the total picture of the inflows and outflows of cash. To illustrate, the balance sheet shows that the December 31, 1990, balance in Retained Earnings for the Taylor Company was $90,000. It has increased $20,000 during 1991 to $110,000. Since the reported net income was $100,000 for 1991, there must have been reductions in Retained Earnings totaling $80,000. An analysis of the retained earnings account indicates a reduction of $80,000 for dividends. The following T-account illustrates:

Retained Earnings			
Dividends	80,000	Beginning balance	90,000
		Net income	100,000
		Ending balance	110,000

Based on this analysis, the $100,000 of net income, prior to any adjustments, would be shown as an operating source of cash and the $80,000 of dividends as a use of cash for financing activities. These items would appear on a partially completed cash flow statement as shown below:

Cash flows from operating activities:	
Net income	$100,000
Cash flows from financing activities:	
Payment of dividends	$ (80,000)

Continuing the example, Taylor Company's net income of $100,000 must be adjusted for any noncash items and for any gains or losses. The entry to record depreciation has no effect on cash. Depreciation is a valid expense, however, and is deducted from revenues in arriving at net income. Therefore, depreciation and similar noncash items such as amortization of intangible assets must be added to net income to arrive at cash provided (used) by operations. As mentioned previously, some noncash items increase the amount of net income reported in the income statement. Examples include amortization of bond premium and a recognized recovery in the value of marketable equity securities. These noncash items would be subtracted from net income in determining cash flows from operations.

The amount of depreciation expense for the period for Taylor Company can be determined from the income statement. If limited information were available (e.g., if depreciation were included with other operating expenses in the income statement), an analysis of Accumulated Depreciation and the related equipment account would be necessary. The following T-accounts facilitate the analysis.

Equipment

Beginning balance	140,000	Sale of equipment	30,000
Purchase of equipment	90,000		
Ending balance	200,000		

Accumulated Depreciation

Sale of equipment	28,000	Beginning balance	60,000
		Depreciation expense	40,000
		Ending balance	72,000

As illustrated, the net change in the equipment account is $60,000. Since $30,000 of equipment was sold, $90,000 of equipment must have been purchased, and this should be reflected on the cash flow statement as an investing activity. Similarly, the net change in Accumulated Depreciation is $12,000. The account was decreased by $28,000 due to the sale of equipment. The $40,000 of depreciation expense, a noncash item, should be added to net income as an adjustment to derive cash flow from operations.

Note that no adjustment is required for the noncash item, bad debt expense. This is because accounts receivable are reported "net." As explained previously, with the indirect method and the "net" approach, there is no need to adjust for either write-offs or bad debt expense.

In addition to adjustments for noncash items, net income must also be adjusted for gains and losses reported in the income statement. For Taylor Company, the $5,000 gain from the sale of equipment (selling price of $7,000 less book value of $2,000) must be subtracted from net income because it does not reflect the amount of cash received in the transaction. The proceeds from the sale of equipment, $7,000 in this illustration, provide the cash, and this amount should be included in the cash flow statement as part of cash flows from *investing* activities. Because the $5,000 gain on the sale is included in net income, it must be subtracted from net income to avoid counting the gain twice.

If a loss had been recognized on the sale (i.e., if the selling price were less than the book value), net income would be adjusted by adding the amount of loss reported, and the proceeds would be reported as a cash flow from investing activities.

The approach described and illustrated in this section highlights the amount of cash generated by normal, recurring operations. It also recognizes cash provided from other activities such as the sale of assets, which may not occur with regularity. A similar approach would be followed in reporting any gains or losses from the disposal of a business segement or from an extraordinary item.

The adjustments for Taylor Company for depreciation, to eliminate the gain on sale of equipment, and to record the increase and decrease in cash from the sale and purchase of equipment are illustrated in the developing statement of cash flows as follows:

Cash flows from operating activities:	
Net income	$100,000
Adjustments:	
Depreciation expense	40,000
Gain on sale of equipment	(5,000)
Cash flows from investing activities:	
Sale of equipment	$ 7,000
Purchase of equipment	(90,000)
Cash flows from financing activities:	
Payment of dividends	$(80,000)

In the Taylor Company example, the amount of net income adjusted for items not requiring cash is $135,000 ($100,000 net income + $40,000 depreciation − $5,000 gain). When preparing a cash flow statement, this amount must be further adjusted to reflect net income measured on a cash basis. As discussed previously in the chapter, with the indirect method changes in current operating accounts are recognized as adjustments to accrual net income in deriving net cash flow from operations.

T-accounts for the noncash current asset accounts and the current liability account of Taylor Company are presented below:

Receivables (net)

Beginning balance	150,000		
Net increase	30,000		
Ending balance	180,000		

Inventory

Beginning balance	200,000	Net decrease	30,000
Ending balance	170,000		

Accounts Payable

		Beginning balance	80,000
		Net increase	20,000
		Ending balance	100,000

The $30,000 increase in net receivables is deducted from net income, since cash receipts for goods and services sold were less than the revenue recognized in arriving at accrual net income. The $30,000 decrease in inventory is added to net income since purchases were less than the charge made against revenue for cost of sales in arriving at net income. The $20,000 increase in accounts payable requires an addition to net income since the cash disbursements for goods and services purchased were less than the charges made for these items in arriving at net income. These adjustments would result in the following presentation of the net cash flow provided (used) by operations for Taylor Company.

Cash flows from operating activities:
Net income $100,000
Adjustments:
Depreciation expense 40,000
Gain on sale of equipment .... (5,000)
Increase in receivables .... (30,000)
Decrease in inventories 30,000
Increase in accounts payable 20,000
Net cash flow provided (used) by operations $155,000

At this point all noncash accounts have been analyzed except Long-Term Notes Payable and Common Stock. In the Taylor Company example, there is no change in the common stock account, but there is an increase of $50,000 in the long-term notes payable account, due to additional borrowing. Thus, the complete statement of cash flows, using the indirect method, would appear as in the following illustration:

Taylor Company
Statement of Cash Flows (Indirect Method)
For the Year Ended December 31, 1991

Cash flows from operating activities:
Net income $100,000
Adjustments:
Depreciation expense 40,000
Gain on sale of equipment .... (5,000)
Increase in receivables .... (30,000)
Decrease in inventories 30,000
Increase in accounts payable 20,000
Net cash flow provided (used) by operations* $155,000

Cash flows from investing activities:
Sale of equipment $7,000
Purchase of equipment .... (90,000)
Net cash flow provided (used) by investing activities ..... (83,000)

Cash flows from financing activities:
Payment of dividends .... $(80,000)
Increase in long-term notes payable 50,000
Net cash flow provided (used) by financing activities ..... (30,000)
Net increase (decrease) in cash and cash equivalents .... $ 42,000
Cash and cash equivalents at beginning of year 40,000
Cash and cash equivalents at end of year .... $ 82,000

*The amounts of interest and taxes paid during the period were $2,000 and $30,000, respectively.

The completed statement highlights the major categories of inflows and outflows of cash. Taylor Company generated $155,000 from its operations. It used $83,000 for investments and another $30,000 for financing activities. The remaining $42,000 represents an increase in the cash balance, and is the amount needed to reconcile the beginning-of-year and end-of-year cash and cash equivalent balances. The amounts paid for interest and taxes are disclosed separately, as required by FASB Statement No. 95.

A statement of cash flows prepared using the direct method shows the major cash receipts (e.g., from customers) and payments (e.g., for wages) on the statement itself and does not reconcile to net income like the indirect method. The reported amounts can be determined by analyzing specific cash transactions or by adjusting accrual-based amounts from the financial statements to a cash basis. Since only summary data are available for Taylor Company, the latter approach is used here.

To determine the amount of cash collected from customers for Taylor Company, the $345,000 of revenues must be converted to a cash basis. Following the approach described earlier, the computation is as follows:

	Revenues	$345,000
+	Beginning receivables (net)	150,000
−	Ending receivables (net)	(180,000)
−	Bad debt expense	(5,000)
	Cash receipts from customers	$310,000

Note that the accrual revenue amount of $345,000 must be adjusted for the change in receivables, which are reported net, as well as for the bad debt expense. The net receivable balance was reduced when Bad Debt Expense was debited and Allowance for Doubtful Accounts was credited, but that reduction did not come from collecting cash, and therefore the $5,000 must be subtracted, as shown in the example.

Similar adjustments must be made to determine the cash paid for inventory purchases.

	Cost of goods sold	$120,000
+	Ending inventory	170,000
	Total goods available	$290,000
−	Beginning inventory	(200,000)
	Goods purchased during year	$ 90,000
+	Beginning accounts payable	80,000
−	Ending accounts payable	(100,000)
	Cash paid for inventory purchases	$ 70,000

For Taylor Company, the $53,000 of operating expenses (excluding depreciation, bad debts, and interest) do not require adjustment since no related current asset or current liabilty balances changed during this period. The same is true for Taylor Company's interest expense and income tax expense. Thus, the cash paid for operating expenses was $53,000; for interest, $2,000; for income taxes, $30,000. Note also that no adjustments are needed for noncash items, such as the $40,000 depreciation expense and the $5,000 gain, when using the direct method.

Based on the above analysis, the statement of cash flows for Taylor Company, using the direct approach, would be as follows:

Taylor Company
Statement of Cash Flows (Direct Method)
For the Year Ended December 31, 1991

Cash flows from operating activities:

Cash receipts from customers		$310,000
Cash payments for:		
Inventory	$ 70,000	
Operating expenses	53,000	
Interest	2,000	
Income taxes	30,000	155,000
Net cash flow provided (used) by operations		$155,000

Cash flows from investing activities:

Sale of equipment....................................	$ 7,000	
Purchase of equipment	(90,000)	
Net cash flow provided (used) by investing activities		(83,000)

Cash flows from financing activities:

Payment of dividends.............................	$(80,000)	
Increase in long term notes payable	50,000	
Net cash flow provided (used) by financing activities		(30,000)

Net increase (decrease) in cash and cash

equivalents		$ 42,000
Cash and cash equivalents at beginning of year		40,000
Cash and cash equivalents at end of year		$ 82,000

Note that the only differences in the two formal cash flow statements prepared for Taylor Company (page 1089 and above) are in the details provided and the approach used to compute net cash flow from operations. The amount of cash provided from operations, $155,000, is the same and the investing and financing sections of the statements are identical. If the direct approach is used, the FASB requires that a schedule be included that reconciles net income to net cash flow provided (used) by operations. A schedule to accompany Taylor Company's cash flow statement prepared using the direct method is provided below. If the indirect approach is used, this reconciliation is already part of the statement, as illustrated.

Taylor Company
Schedule Reconciling Net Income to Net Cash Flow
Provided by Operating Activities
For the Year Ended December 31, 1991

Net income...		$100,000
Adjustments to reconcile net income to net cash flow		
provided by operations:		
Depreciation expense	$40,000	
Gain on sale of equipment	(5,000)	
Increase in receivables (net)........................	(30,000)	
Decrease in inventories	30,000	
Increase in accounts payable.......................	20,000	55,000
Net cash flow provided by operations		$155,000

Comprehensive Illustration of Cash Flow Statement

Examples in the preceding sections were relatively simple. Ordinarily, however, more complex circumstances are encountered and some type of work sheet generally is used in preparing a statement of cash flows. In the pages that follow, a work sheet approach for use with the indirect method is described first. A modified work sheet for use with the direct method is then discussed. The appendix to this chapter describes and illustrates a T-account approach to preparing a statement of cash flows.

Indirect Method— Work Sheet Approach to Preparing a Statement of Cash Flows

Using a work sheet, such as the one illustrated on page 1095, facilitates the analysis of account changes when using the indirect method. The format of the work sheet is straightforward. The first column contains the beginning balances, then there are two columns for analysis of transactions to arrive at the ending balances in the fourth column.

In preparing a work sheet, accumulated depreciation balances, instead of being reported as credit balances in the debit (asset) section, may be more conveniently listed with liability and owners' equity balances in the credit section. Similarly, contra liability accounts and contra owners' equity balances may be separately recognized and more conveniently listed with assets in the debit section.

The lower portion of the work sheet shows the major categories of cash flow: operating, investing, and financing. A debit in the lower section means an increase in cash, while a credit reflects a decrease in cash. It is from the lower section of the work sheet that the formal statement of cash flows is prepared.

The illustrations and analysis that follow are based on the comparative balance sheet data for Western Resources, Inc., as shown on page 1094, and the following information.

- The statement of retained earnings summarizes activities during 1991 as follows:

Balance, December 31, 1990		$234,300
Add net income		44,000
		$278,300
Deduct:		
Cash dividends	$25,100	
40% stock dividend on common stock	100,000	
Prior period adjustment resulting from understatement of depreciation on equipment	3,500	128,600
Balance, December 31, 1991		$149,700

- The income statement for 1991 summarizes operations as follows:

Income from continuing operations	$36,000
Extraordinary gain on involuntary conversion of building (net of income taxes)	8,000
Net income	$44,000

- Marketable securities that do not qualify as cash equivalents were purchased at a cost of $2,000.
- An extraordinary gain was recorded to reflect the total destruction by a tornado of a building costing $40,000 with a book value of $2,000. The insurance company paid $10,000 cash; a new building was then constructed at a cost of $105,000.
- Long-term investments, cost $96,000, were sold for $102,500. The cost method was used to account for the investment.
- Land was acquired for $108,500, the seller accepting in payment $40,000 of common stock and cash of $68,500.
- New machinery was purchased for $12,000 cash. Additional machinery and equipment were overhauled, extending the useful life at a cost of $26,000, the cost being debited to the accumulated depreciation account.
- The amortization of patent cost and depreciation expense on buildings and equipment were recorded as follows:

Buildings—depreciation	$ 5,600
Machinery and equipment—depreciation	15,300
Patents—amortization	5,000
Total depreciation and amortization	$25,900

- Ten-year bonds of $60,000 were issued at a discount of $3,000 at the beginning of the year; discount amortization for the year was $300.
- Western Resources had certain temporary differences between taxable and financial income, which created a need for interperiod tax allocation. Based on expected reversals of these temporary differences for future years, Western's noncurrent deferred income tax liability increased by $6,000 during 1991.

In preparing a cash flow statement for Western Resources, Inc., we begin by determining the change in cash balance, in this case a $7,700 decrease. All noncash accounts may now be analyzed using the work sheet illustrated on page 1095. The cash flow statement is prepared directly from the work sheet and is illustrated on page 1100.

Generally, the most efficient approach to developing a work sheet for a statement of cash flows is to begin with an analysis of the change in Retained Earnings (see items (a) through (d) on the work sheet). In the process, the income from continuing operations and other income components should be reported separately (item (a)). After the change in Retained Earnings has been accounted for, the remaining noncash accounts should be reviewed in conjunction with the income statement and supplementary information to determine what additional adjustments are required. Operating income should be adjusted to determine the actual amount of cash provided or used by operations (items (a), (g), (l), and (n)-(u)). Analysis must also be made to determine all other cash flows from investing and financing activities (items (a), (b), (e), (f), (g), (h), (j), (k), (m), and (v)), and to reflect significant investing and financing activities that have no effect on cash (item (i)).

Western Resources, Inc.
Comparative Balance Sheets
December 31, 1991 and 1990

	1991		1990	
Assets				
Current assets:				
Cash and cash equivalents	$ 47,300		$ 55,000	
Marketable securities	12,000		10,000	
Accounts receivable (net)	60,000		70,500	
Inventories	75,000		76,500	
Prepaid operating expenses ...	16,500	$210,800	12,000	$224,000
Investments (at cost)		10,000		106,000
Land, buildings, and equipment:				
Land	$183,500		$ 75,000	
Buildings..................	290,000		225,000	
Less accumulated depreciation	(122,600)		(155,000)	
Machinery and equipment.....	132,000		120,000	
Less accumulated depreciation	(36,300)	446,600	(43,500)	221,500
Patents		35,000		40,000
Total assets		$702,400		$591,500
Liabilities				
Current liabilities:				
Accounts payable	$ 65,000		$ 81,200	
Income taxes payable	10,000		9,500	
Salaries payable	5,000		1,500	
Dividends payable	4,400	$ 84,400	—	$ 92,200
Bonds payable	$ 60,000			
Less discount on bonds payable	(2,700)	57,300		
Deferred income tax liability ...		21,000		15,000
Total liabilities		$162,700		$107,200
Stockholders' Equity				
Common stock	$390,000		$250,000	
Retained earnings............	149,700	539,700	234,300	484,300
Total liabilities and stockholders' equity		$702,400		$591,500

Explanations for individual adjustments recorded on the work sheet for Western Resources, Inc. follow. The letter preceding each explanation corresponds with that used on the work sheet.

(a) Net income included in the ending retained earnings balance is composed of income from continuing operations and an extraordinary gain. Net income, then, is recorded on the work sheet as follows:

Cash Provided by Income from Continuing Operations	36,000	
Cash Provided by Involuntary Conversion of Building	8,000	
Retained Earnings		44,000

Western Resources, Inc.
Work Sheet for Statement of Cash Flows—Indirect Method
For the Year Ended December 31, 1991

Accounts	Balance Dec. 31, 1990	Adjustments DR		Adjustments CR		Balance Dec. 31, 1991
Debits						
Cash and Cash Equivalents..............	55,000			(w)	7,700	47,300
Marketable Securities	10,000	(v)	2,000			12,000
Accounts Receivable (net)...............	70,500			(p)	10,500	60,000
Inventories........................	76,500			(q)	1,500	75,000
Prepaid Operating Expenses............	12,000	(r)	4,500			16,500
Investments...........................	106,000			(g)	96,000	10,000
Land.......................	75,000	(h)	68,500			183,500
		(i)	40,000			
Buildings	225,000	(f)	105,000	(e)	40,000	290,000
Machinery and Equipment	120,000	(j)	12,000			132,000
Patents...........................	40,000			(l)	5,000	35,000
Discount on Bonds Payable.............		(m)	3,000	(n)	300	2,700
Total	790,000					864,000
Credits						
Accum. Depr.—Buildings	155,000	(e)	38,000	(l)	5,600	122,600
Accum. Depr.—Mach. and Equip.	43,500	(k)	26,000	(d)	3,500	36,300
				(l)	15,300	
Accounts Payable	81,200	(t)	16,200			65,000
Income Taxes Payable	9,500			(s)	500	10,000
Salaries Payable	1,500			(u)	3,500	5,000
Dividends Payable....................				(b)	4,400	4,400
Bonds Payable........................				(m)	60,000	60,000
Deferred Income Tax Liability	15,000			(o)	6,000	21,000
Common Stock.......................	250,000			(c)	100,000	390,000
				(i)	40,000	
Retained Earnings	234,300	(b)	25,100	(a)	44,000	149,700
		(c)	100,000			
		(d)	3,500			
	790,000		443,800		443,800	864,000
Cash flows from operating activities:						
Income from continuing operations		(a)	36,000			
Adjustments:						
Amortization of patents		(l)	5,000			
Depreciation expense		(l)	20,900			
Amortization of bond discount		(n)	300			
Increase in deferred income tax liability		(o)	6,000			
Gain on sale of investments...........				(g)	6,500	
Decrease in accounts receivable (net)		(p)	10,500			
Decrease in inventories		(q)	1,500			
Increase in prepaid operating expenses				(r)	4,500	
Increase in income taxes payable		(s)	500			
Increase in salaries payable		(u)	3,500			
Decrease in accounts payable				(t)	16,200	
Cash flows from investing activities:						
Involuntary conversion of building		(a)	8,000			
		(e)	2,000			
Construction of building				(f)	105,000	
Sale of long-term investments		(g)	102,500			
Purchase of land				(h)	68,500	
Purchase of machinery and equipment ...				(j)	12,000	
Overhaul of machinery and equipment ...				(k)	26,000	
Purchase of marketable securities				(v)	2,000	
Cash flows from financing activities:						
Issuance of bonds at discount		(m)	57,000			
Payment of cash dividends				(b)	20,700	
			253,700		261,400	
Net decrease in cash		(w)	7,700			
			261,400		261,400	

The operating income must be adjusted to arrive at the total cash provided by operations; the extraordinary item requires separate recognition and must also be adjusted to reflect the amount of cash provided. Since a number of adjustments are usually required in arriving at the actual amount of net cash flow from operating activities, adequate space should be allowed below this line on the work sheet.

(b) The cash dividends declared and deducted from retained earnings are adjusted for the change in the dividends payable balance in arriving at the amount of dividends actually paid during the year. The work sheet adjustment would be as follows:

Retained Earnings	25,100	
Dividends Payable		4,400
Cash Used for Payment of Dividends		20,700

(c) The transfer of retained earnings to common stock as a result of a stock dividend has no effect on cash, and the changes in the account balances are reconciled by the following adjustment:

Retained Earnings	100,000	
Common Stock		100,000

(d) The recognition that depreciation had been understated on equipment in prior periods is recorded by a debit to Retained Earnings and a credit to Accumulated Depreciation—Machinery and Equipment. The correction of earnings of prior periods has no effect on cash, and the changes in the account balances may be reconciled as follows:

Retained Earnings	3,500	
Accumulated Depreciation—Machinery and Equipment		3,500

(e) The destruction of the building and the subsequent insurance reimbursement produced an extraordinary gain of $8,000. This gain was recorded as "Cash Provided by Involuntary Conversion of Building," in entry (a), as the result of the earlier recognition of the individual component of net income. Since the effect of the destruction was to provide cash of $10,000, the proceeds from the insurance company, the cash of $8,000 recognized in entry (a) must be adjusted to show the full amount of cash received:

Accumulated Depreciation—Buildings	38,000	
Cash Provided by Involuntary Conversion of Building . . .	2,000	
Buildings		40,000

(f) The buildings account was increased by the cost of constructing a new building, $105,000. The cost of the new building is reported separately as an investment of cash by the following entry:

Buildings	105,000	
Cash Used for Construction of Building		105,000

(g) The sale of long-term investments was recorded by a credit to the asset account at cost $96,000, and a credit to a gain on sale of investment account. At the end of the period, the gain account was closed to retained earnings as part of income from continuing operations. Since the effect of the sale was to provide cash of $102,500, this amount is reported as cash provided by investing activities. The investments account balance is reduced, and cash provided by operations is decreased by the amount of the gain. The following adjustment is made on the work sheet:

Cash Provided by Sale of Long-Term Investments	102,500	
Long-Term Investments		96,000
Income from Continuing Operations—Gain on Sale of		
Investments		6,500

(h) and (i) Land was acquired at a price of $108,500; payment was made in common stock valued at $40,000 and cash of $68,500. Two separate entries are made to segregate the cash and noncash components of this transaction:

Land	68,500	
Cash used to Purchase Land		68,500
Land	40,000	
Common Stock		40,000

The issuance of common stock for land has no effect on cash, but it is a significant transaction that should be disclosed separately. The cash flow statement reports only transactions affecting cash, in accordance with FASB Statement No. 95.

(j) and (k) Machinery costing $12,000 was acquired during the year. Payment was made in cash and is reported as cash used for investing purposes. The cost of overhauling other machinery and equipment also represents a use of cash for investing purposes. The cost of overhauling, $26,000, was debited to the accumulated depreciation account. The work sheet adjustments for the acquisition (j) and overhauling (k) of machinery and equipment are:

Machinery and Equipment	12,000	
Cash Used to Purchase Machinery and Equipment		12,000
Accumulated Depreciation—Machinery and Equipment	26,000	
Cash Used to Overhaul Machinery and Equipment		26,000

(l) The changes in the patents account and in the accumulated depreciation accounts result from the recognition of amortization of the patents and depreciation on the plant assets. Cash provided by operations is increased by the charges against earnings not involving current cash outflows by the following adjustment:

Income from Continuing Operations—Amortization of Patents......	5,000	
Income from Continuing Operations—Depreciation Expense......	20,900	
Patents......		5,000
Accumulated Depreciation—Buildings......		5,600
Accumulated Depreciation—Machinery and Equipment......		15,300

(m) and (n) During the year, bonds were issued at a discount. The result of this transaction was to credit Bonds Payable for $60,000 and debit Discount on Bonds Payable for $3,000. The net cash provided by financing through the bond issuance of $57,000 is recognized by entry (m). Subsequently, the bond discount was amortized by reducing the bond discount account. This decrease in the discount account is explained by increasing cash provided by operations by the amount of the charge against earnings not involving the use of cash—entry (n). The entries are as follows:

Discount on Bonds Payable	3,000	
Cash Provided by Issuance of Bonds	57,000	
Bonds Payable......		60,000
Income from Continuing Operations—Amortization of Bond Discount	300	
Discount on Bonds Payable......		300

(o) The impact of the temporary differences between taxable and financial income was recognized as a debit to Income Tax Expense— Deferred and a credit to Deferred Income Tax Liability (Noncurrent). For 1991, the deferred tax liability increased $6,000. This is shown on the work sheet as an increase in the deferred income tax liability account and an increase in cash provided by operations. The $6,000 is added back to income from operations because it represents income taxes recognized as an expense of the current period for which no cash was paid. Since there was no outflow of cash, the following entry is made:

Income from Continuing Operations—Increase in Deferred Taxes	6,000	
Deferred Income Tax Liability		6,000

(p)-(u) In preparing a cash flow statement, operating income must be adjusted from an accrual basis to a cash basis, as explained earlier in the chapter. The entries (p) through (u) reflect that analysis for

Western Resources, Inc. A compound entry to reflect these adjustments might be made as follows:

Prepaid Operating Expenses (r)	4,500	
Accounts Payable (t)	16,200	
Income from Continuing Operations—net adjustment to Cash Basis		4,700
Accounts Receivable (p)		10,500
Inventories (q)		1,500
Income Taxes Payable (s)		500
Salaries Payable (u)		3,500

The net credit (reduction in cash) of $4,700 does not appear in the lower portion of the work sheet, because the individual account changes are reported in the statement of cash flows. Separate entries could be made for each current operating account rather than one compound entry as shown above. For example, the separate entry for the change in receivables would be:

Income from Continuing Operations—Decrease in Accounts Receivable	10,500	
Accounts Receivable		10,500

(v) As noted earlier in the chapter, marketable securities are treated differently from other current assets in preparing a cash flow statement, since marketable securities transactions usually are investing rather than operating activities. The adjustment to reflect the purchase of $2,000 of marketable securities would be:

Marketable Securities	2,000	
Cash Used to Purchase Marketable Securities		2,000

(w) After all changes in account balances have been reconciled and the effects of the changes on cash flow have been recorded in the work sheet, the total debits and credits in the lower portion of the Adjustments columns are $253,700 and $261,400, respectively. The excess of credits (decreases in cash) over debits (increases in cash) is equal to the net change in the cash balance for the period of $7,700. The following entry is made to reflect the net decrease in cash and balance the work sheet.

Net Decrease in Cash	7,700	
Cash		7,700

The work sheet is now complete, and a statement of cash flows for Western Resources, Inc. can be prepared in an appropriate format, such as the one presented here:

Western Resources, Inc.
Statement of Cash Flows
For the Year Ended December 31, 1991

Cash flows from operating activities:

Income from continuing operations	$ 36,000	
Adjustments:		
Amortization of patents	5,000	
Depreciation expense	20,900	
Amortization of bond discount	300	
Increase in deferred income tax liability	6,000	
Gain on sale of investments	(6,500)	
Decrease in accounts receivable (net)	10,500	
Decrease in inventories	1,500	
Increase in prepaid operating expenses	(4,500)	
Increase in income taxes payable	500	
Increase in salaries payable	3,500	
Decrease in accounts payable	(16,200)	
Net cash flow provided (used) by operations		$ 57,000

Cash flows from investing activities:

Involuntary conversion of building	$ 10,000	
Construction of building	(105,000)	
Sale of long-term investments	102,500	
Purchase of land	(68,500)	
Purchase of machinery and equipment	(12,000)	
Overhaul of machinery and equipment	(26,000)	
Purchase of marketable securities	(2,000)	
Net cash flow provided (used) by investing activities		(101,000)

Cash flows from financing activities:

Issuance of bonds at discount	$ 57,000	
Payment of cash dividends	(20,700)	
Net cash flow provided (used) by financing activities		36,300
Net increase (decrease) in cash		$ (7,700)
Cash and cash equivalents at beginning of year		55,000
Cash and cash equivalents at end of year		$ 47,300

A reader analyzing the cash flow statement for Western Resources, Inc. can readily see that $57,000 cash was provided internally from operating activities. This amount was not sufficient to satisfy the investment needs of the company, and so additional cash was generated from external financing activities involving the issuance of bonds. The company would also disclose in a separate schedule or note to the financial statements that land valued at $40,000 was acquired by issuing common stock, a significant noncash financing transaction. The cash generated from operations clearly met the need for payment of cash dividends, but when other cash needs are considered, the total cash outflow exceeded the total inflow of cash for the period, causing the cash balance to decrease by $7,700, or 14%.

In addition to the formal statement of cash flows, when using the indirect method, Western Resources should disclose the amount of cash paid during the period for interest and taxes. A schedule similar to the following might be prepared to accompany Western's cash flow statement.

Western Resources, Inc.
Schedule of Cash Paid for Interest and Income Taxes
For the Year Ended December 31, 1991

Interest

Interest Expense	$ 3,900 *	
Deduct bond discount amortization	(300)	
Adjust for change in interest payable account during the period	0	
Amount of cash paid for interest		$3,600

Income Taxes

Income Tax Expense	$24,000 *	
Deduct: Increase in noncurrent deferred income tax liability	(6,000)	
Increase in income taxes payable	(500)	
Amount of cash paid for income taxes		$17,500

*These amounts would be taken from the income statement or other records of Western Resources, Inc.

**Direct Method—
Modified Work Sheet
Approach to
Preparing a
Statement of Cash
Flows**

When using the direct method with a work sheet approach, adjustments are made to individual revenue and expense items rather than in total to income from operations. Thus, the operating activities section of the work sheet must be expanded to develop the detail needed, as illustrated below.

The first column of the illustrated work sheet shows the revenue and expense detail as would be provided on the income statement for Western Resources, Inc. Note that these amounts are reported on an accrual basis. The adjustments columns are used to eliminate items and to convert accrual based amounts to a cash basis. The formal statement of cash flows may be prepared from the last column of the work sheet. Only the detail provided in the operating activities section will differ from that shown when using the indirect method. The rest of the statement of cash flows will be exactly the same.

Western Resources, Inc.
Partial Work Sheet for Statement of Cash Flows—Direct Method
For the Year Ended December 31, 1991

Item	Accrual Basis	Adjustments Debits	Adjustments Credits	Cash Basis
Cash flows from operating activities:				
Sales	753,800		(1) 10,500	764,300
Deduct:				
Cost of goods sold (Except depreciation and amortization)	524,100	(3) 16,200	(2) 1,500	538,800
Depreciation and amortization	25,900		(4) 25,900	-0-
Selling and general expenses	146,400	(5) 4,500	(6) 3,500	147,400
Operating income	57,400			78,100
Add gain on sale of long-term investment	6,500	(7) 6,500		-0-
Deduct interest expense	3,900		(8) 300	3,600
Income before taxes	60,000			74,500
Deduct income taxes	24,000		(9) 6,000 } 500	17,500
Income from continuing operations	36,000			57,000
Add extraordinary gain on involuntary conversion of building	8,000	(10) 8,000		-0-
Net income	44,000	**Net cash flow provided (used) by operations**		57,000

Key to adjustments
(1) Decrease in accounts receivable (previous sales collected this period).
(2) Decrease in inventories (inventory sold this period but purchased last period).
(3) Decrease in accounts payable (purchases made last period but paid for this period).
(4) Depreciation and amortization are noncash items (ignored with direct method).
(5) Increase in prepaid operating expenses (additional prepaid expenses paid for this period).
(6) Increase in salaries payable (salaries expense incurred this period but not yet paid).
(7) Elimination of gain on sale of long-term investments (proceeds to be reported as investing activity).
(8) Bond discount amortization a noncash item.
(9) Increase in deferred income tax liability and increase in income taxes payable (income taxes of this period not yet paid).
(10) Elimination of extraordinary gain (to be reported as investing activity).

Cash flows from operations, as summarized above, may be presented on the statement of cash flows using the direct method as follows:

Western Resources, Inc.
Statement of Cash Flows
For the Year Ended December 31, 1991

Cash flows from operating activities:		
Cash receipts from customers		$764,300
Cash payments for:		
Inventory	$538,800	
Selling and general expenses.....................	147,400	
Interest expense	3,600	
Income taxes	17,500	707,300
Net cash flow provided (used) by operations		$ 57,000
Cash flows from investing activities:		
Involuntary conversion of building	$ 10,000	
Construction of building	(105,000)	
Sale of long-term investments.......................	102,500	
Purchase of land	(68,500)	
Purchase of machinery and equipment	(12,000)	
Overhaul of machinery and equipment	(26,000)	
Purchase of marketable securities	(2,000)	
Net cash flow provided (used) by investing activities		(101,000)
Cash flows from financing activities:		
Issuance of bonds at discount	$ 57,000	
Payment of cash dividends	(20,700)	
Net cash flow provided (used) by financing activities		36,300
Net increase (decrease) in cash..................		$ (7,700)
Cash and cash equivalents at beginning of year		55,000
Cash and cash equivalents at end of year........		$ 47,300

A reconciliation of net income to net cash flow from operations, similar to that illustrated for Taylor Company on page 1091, would be presented along with the cash flow statement prepared using the direct method.

Summary The FASB's conceptual framework suggests that a statement of cash flows is essential in meeting the informational needs of investors and creditors. Statement No. 95 now requires that such a statement be presented as one of the three primary financial statements prepared for external users. The cash flows for the period are to be classified according to three main categories: operating activities, investing activities, and financing activities. A "sources and uses" format is no longer acceptable. The statement is to focus on cash receipts and payments and must explain the changes in cash and cash equivalents. Significant financing and investing transactions not involving cash are to be reported in notes to the financial statements or in separate schedules, not in the statement of cash flows.

Companies may choose to use the direct or the indirect method in presenting the net cash flows from operations. If the direct method is used, a schedule reconciling net cash flow from operations to net income is required. If the indirect method is used, specific disclosures of cash paid for interest and income taxes are required. As a result of these specific reporting guidelines from Statement No. 95, external users can expect greater uniformity and comparability in the presentation of the statement of cash flows.

IBM Corporation's 1988 statement of cash flows, presented on page 1104, illustrates how this company is complying with Statement No. 95. IBM chose to include a summary of cash inflows and outflows in graphic form.

Exhibit 24–5   IBM Corporation and Subsidiary Companies

Consolidated Statement of Cash Flows
for the year ended December 31:

International Business Machines Corporation
and subsidary Companies

(Dollars in millions)	1988		1987		1986	
Cash Flow from Operating Activities:						
Net earnings	$ 5,806		$ 5,258		$ 4,789	
Adjustments to reconcile net income to cash						
provided from operating activities:						
Depreciation	3,871		3,534		3,331	
Amortization of software	893		863		672	
(Gain) on disposition of investment assets	(133)		(128)		(68)	
(Increase) in accounts receivable	(2,322)		(2,542)		(275)	
(Increase) decrease in inventory	(1,232)		129		1,120	
(Increase) in other assets	(1,587)		(808)		(1,626)	
Increase (decrease) in accounts payable	265		300		(394)	
Increase in other liabilities	519		134		1,690	
Net cash provided from operating activities		$ 6,080		$ 6,740		$ 9,239
Cash Flow from Investing Activities:						
Payments for plant, rental machines and other property	(5,390)		(4,195)		(4,639)	
Proceeds from disposition of plant, rental machines						
and other property	409		353		672	
Investment in software	(1,318)		(1,048)		(907)	
Purchases of marketable securities and other investments	(2,555)		(4,815)		(7,239)	
Proceeds from marketable securities and other investments	4,734		5,900		5,362	
Net cash used in investing activities		(4,120)		(3,805)		(6,751)
Cash Flow from Financing Activities:						
Proceeds from new debt	4,540		2,963		3,069	
Payments to settle debt	(3,7007)		(1,980)		(2,340)	
Short-term borrowings less than 90 days—net	1,028		(399)		150	
Proceeds from employee stock plans—net	(11)		105		23	
Payments to purchase and retire capital stock	(992)		(1,425)		(1,488)	
Cash dividends paid	(2,609)		(2,654)		(2,698)	
Net cash used in financing activities		(1,051)		(3,390)		(3,284)
Effect of Exchange Rate Changes						
on Cash and cash Equivalents		(201)		330		234
Net Change in Cash and Cash Equivalents		708		(125)		(562)
Cash and Cash Equivalents at January 1		3,467		3,592		4,154
Cash and Cash Equivalents at December 31		$ 4,175		$ 3,467		$ 3,592

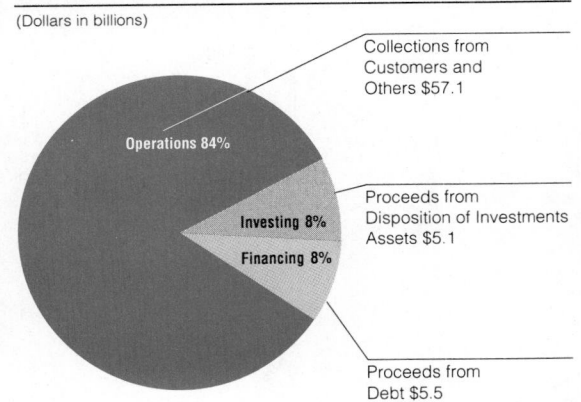

Summary of Cash Inflows
(Dollars in billions)

Collections from Customers and Others $57.1

Operations 84%

Investing 8%

Financing 8%

Proceeds from Disposition of Investments Assets $5.1

Proceeds from Debt $5.5

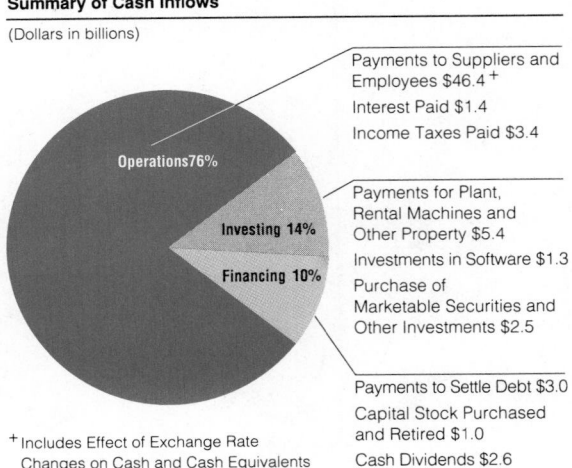

Summary of Cash Inflows
(Dollars in billions)

Payments to Suppliers and Employees $46.4 [+]

Interest Paid $1.4

Income Taxes Paid $3.4

Operations 76%

Investing 14%

Financing 10%

Payments for Plant, Rental Machines and Other Property $5.4

Investments in Software $1.3

Purchase of Marketable Securities and Other Investments $2.5

Payments to Settle Debt $3.0

Capital Stock Purchased and Retired $1.0

Cash Dividends $2.6

[+] Includes Effect of Exchange Rate Changes on Cash and Cash Equivalents

Appendix

T-Account Approach to Preparing a Cash Flow Statement

This appendix illustrates a T-account approach to preparing a cash flow statement. As shown, this approach produces the same results as the columnar work sheet illustrated in the chapter; only the format is different. To highlight the similarities in the two approaches, the information and account analysis used in the work sheet illustration for Western Resources, Inc. will also be used for the T-account illustration.

With the T-account approach, special "cash flows" T-accounts may be established. These accounts are used to summarize cash flows from operations and from significant investing and financing activities during the period and provide the basis for preparing the formal cash flow statement. Individual T-accounts are also established for Cash and all other balance sheet accounts.

During the process of analysis, the change in each account is explained as providing or using cash. In following the illustration, it may be helpful to refer to the detailed explanations for individual adjustments described on pages 1094–1099 of the chapter. Once the changes in all accounts have been reconciled and the Cash Flows T-accounts balanced, the formal cash flow statement can be prepared as illustrated on page 1100.

Cash Flows—Operating

(a)	36,000		
		(g)	6,500
(l)	5,000		
(l)	20,900		
(n)	300		
(o)	6,000		
(p)	10,500		
(q)	1,500	(r)	4,500
(s)	500	(t)	16,200
(u)	3,500		
Net cash provided by operations	57,000		

Cash Flows—Investing

(a)	8,000	(f)	105,000
(e)	2,000	(h)	68,500
(g)	102,500	(j)	12,000
		(k)	26,000
		(v)	2,000
			101,000

Net cash used by investing activities

Cash Flows—Financing

(m)	57,000	(b)	20,700
	36,300		

Net cash provided by financing activities

Cash Flows—Summary

Net cash provided by operations	57,000	
Net cash used by investing		101,000
Net cash provided by financing	36,300	
Net decrease in cash	(w) 7,700	
	101,000	101,000

Cash
Beginning bal.	55,000	(w)	7,700
Ending bal.	47,300		

Marketable Securities
Beginning bal.	10,000		
(v)	2,000		
Ending bal.	12,000		

Accounts Receivable (net)
Beginning bal.	70,500	(p)	10,500
Ending bal.	60,000		

Inventories
Beginning bal.	76,500	(q)	1,500
Ending bal.	75,000		

Prepaid Operating Expenses
Beginning bal.	12,000		
(r)	4,500		
Ending bal.	16,500		

Investments
Beginning bal.	106,000	(g)	96,000
Ending bal.	10,000		

Land
Beginning bal.	75,000	
(h)	68,500	
(i)	40,000	
Ending bal.	183,500	

Buildings
Beginning bal.	225,000	(e)	40,000
(f)	105,000		
Ending bal.	290,000		

Accumulated Depreciation—Buildings
(e)	38,000	Beginning bal.	155,000
		(l)	5,600
		Ending bal.	122,600

Machinery and Equipment
Beginning bal.	120,000	
(j)	12,000	
Ending bal.	132,000	

Accumulated Depreciation— Machinery and Equipment
(k)	26,000	Beginning bal.	43,500
		(d)	3,500
		(l)	15,300
		Ending bal.	36,300

Patents

Beginning bal.	40,000	(l)	5,000
Ending bal.	35,000		

Accounts Payable

		Beginning bal.	81,200
(t)	16,200		
		Ending bal.	65,000

Income Taxes Payable

		Beginning bal.	9,500
		(s)	500
		Ending bal.	10,000

Salaries Payable

		Beginning bal.	1,500
		(u)	3,500
		Ending bal.	5,000

Dividends Payable

		Beginning bal.	0
		(b)	4,400
		Ending bal.	4,400

Bonds Payable

		Beginning bal.	0
		(m)	60,000
		Ending bal.	60,000

Discount on Bonds Payable

Beginning bal.	0		
(m)	3,000	(n)	300
Ending bal.	2,700		

Deferred Income Tax Liability

		Beginning bal.	15,000
		(o)	6,000
		Ending bal.	21,000

Common Stock

		Beginning bal.	250,000
		(c)	100,000
		(i)	40,000
		Ending bal.	390,000

Retained Earnings

(b)	25,100	Beginning bal.	234,300
(c)	100,000	(a)	44,000
(d)	3,500		
		Ending bal.	149,700

Key Terms

Cash equivalents 1072
Direct method 1076
Financing activities 1073
Indirect method 1076
Investing activities 1073

Noncash items 1080
Noncash investing and financing
  activities 1075
Operating activities 1073
Statement of cash flows 1071

Questions

1. (a) Why is the statement of cash flows one of three primary financial statements required to be presented to financial reporting users? (b) What are the major purposes of a cash flow statement?
2. What information does the cash flow statement provide that is not provided by an income statement or by comparative balance sheets?
3. Why has the statement of cash flows replaced the traditional funds statement previously required by generally accepted accounting principles?
4. What uses might each of the following find for a cash flow statement?
   (a) Manager of a small laundry.
   (b) Stockholder interested in regular dividends.
   (c) Bank granting short-term loans.
   (d) Officer of a labor union.
5. What criteria must be met for an item to be considered a cash equivalent in preparing a statement of cash flows?
6. Why does the FASB in Statement No. 95 treat dividend payments as a financing activity but treat the receipt of dividends as an operating activity?
7. Either the direct method or the indirect method may be used to determine the net cash flow from operations. What is the difference in approach for the two methods?
8. Why do users seem to prefer the direct method? Why do preparers seem to prefer the indirect method?
9. What additional disclosures are required by FASB Statement No. 95 if a company elects to use the direct method in preparing its statement of cash flows? What disclosures are required if the indirect method is used?
10. (a) Why is it important to disclose separately the amount of net cash flow provided from operations?
    (b) To compute net cash flow from operations, what adjustments are applied to net income on a cash flow statement when using the indirect method?
11. How are significant noncash investing and financing transactions to be reported in connection with a statement of cash flows?
12. What alternatives exist to using work sheets in developing a statement of cash flows?

Discussion Cases   **Case 24–1   (Is depreciation a source of cash?)**

Brad Berrett and Jim Wong are roommates in college. Berrett is an accounting major while Wong is a finance major. Both have recently studied the statement of cash flows in their classes. Wong's finance professor stated that depreciation is a major source of cash for some companies. Berrett's accounting professor indicated in class that depreciation cannot be a source of cash because cash is not affected by the recording of depreciation.

Berrett and Wong wonder which professor is correct. Explain the positions taken by both professors and indicate which viewpoint you support and why?

Case 24-2   (Where does all the money go?)

Price Brothers Auto Parts has hired you as a consultant to analyze the company's financial position. One of the owners, David Price, is in charge of the financial affairs of the company. He makes all the deposits and pays the bills, but has an accountant prepare a balance sheet and an income statement once a year. The business has been quite profitable over the years. In fact, 2 years ago Price Brothers opened a second store and is considering a third outlet. However, the economy has slowed and the cash position has become very tight. The company is having an increasingly difficult time paying its bills. David has not been able to satisfactorily explain to his brothers what is happening. What factors should you consider and what recommendations might you make to Price Brothers?

Case 24-3   (Why do we have more cash?)

Hot Lunch Delivery Service has always had a policy to pay stockholders annual dividends in an amount exactly equal to net income for the year. Joe Alberg, the company's president, is confused because the cash balance has been consistently increasing ever since Hot Lunch began operations 5 years ago, in spite of their faithful adherence to the dividend policy. Assuming no errors have been made in the bookkeeping process, explain why this situation might occur.

Case 24-4   (Which method should we use: the direct or the indirect method?)

Do-It-Right Company has prepared a working capital funds statement each year for several years. The company must now prepare a statement of cash flows. As the assistant controller of Do-It-Right, you have been given the assignment to study FASB Statement No. 95 and make recommendations on how the company should prepare its statement of cash flows. Specifically, you are to indicate which method should be used in determining net cash flow from operations: the direct method or the indirect method. Which method do you recommend and why?

Exercises   **Exercise 24-1   (Classification of cash flows)**

Indicate whether each of the following items would be classified as (1) an operating, investing, or financing activity, or (2) as a noncash transaction or noncash item.

(a) Cash collected from customers
(b) Cash paid to suppliers for inventory
(c) Cash received for interest on a nontrade note receivable
(d) Cash received from issuance of stock
(e) Cash paid for dividends
(f) Cash received from bank on a loan
(g) Cash paid for interest on a loan

(h) Cash paid to retire bonds
(i) Cash paid to purchase stock of another company as a long-term investment
(j) Cash received from the sale of a business segment
(k) Cash paid for property taxes
(l) Cash received for dividend revenue
(m) Cash paid for wages
(n) Cash paid for insurance
(o) Preferred stock retired by issuing common stock
(p) Depreciation expense for the year
(q) Cash paid to purchase machinery
(r) Cash received from the sale of land

Exercise 24–2   (Cash flow analysis)

State how each of the following items would be reflected on a statement of cash flows.

(a) Marketable securities (not cash equivalents) were purchased for $5,000.
(b) At the beginning of the year, equipment with a book value of $2,000 was traded for dissimilar equipment costing $3,500; a trade-in value of $700 was allowed on the old equipment; the balance of the purchase price is to be paid in 12 monthly installments.
(c) Buildings were acquired for $187,500, the company paying $50,000 cash and signing a 12% mortgage note payable in 5 years for the balance.
(d) Uncollectible accounts of $225 were written off against the allowance for doubtful accounts.
(e) Cash of $62,500 was paid to purchase business assets consisting of: merchandise, $22,500; furniture and fixtures, $7,500; land and buildings, $23,750; and goodwill, $8,750.
(f) A cash dividend of $1,250 was declared in the current period, payable at the beginning of the next period.
(g) Accounts payable shows a decrease for the period of $3,750.

Exercise 24–3   (Cash receipts and cash payments)

The accountant for Alpine Hobby Stores prepared the following selected information for the year ended December 31, 1991.

	December 31, 1991	December 31, 1990
a. Equipment	$25,000	$30,000
b. Accumulated depreciation	11,000	9,500
c. Long-term debt	11,000	20,000
d. Common stock	20,000	15,000

Equipment with a book value of $20,000 was sold for $17,000. The original cost of the equipment was $25,000.
What is the amount of cash received or paid for each item listed?

Exercise 24–4   (Cash computations)

Comparative balance sheets and income statement data for the Xavier Metals Company are presented on the next page.

	December 31,	
	1991	1990
Assets		
Current assets:		
Cash..	$ 119,000	$ 98,000
Marketable securities (not cash equivalents)	59,000	
Accounts receivable (net)	312,000	254,000
Inventory	278,000	239,000
Prepaid expenses....................................	35,000	21,000
Total current assets	$ 803,000	$ 612,000
Property, plant, and equipment	$ 536,000	$ 409,000
Less accumulated depreciation	76,000	53,000
	$ 460,000	$ 356,000
Total assets	$1,263,000	$ 968,000
Liabilities and Equity		
Current liabilities:		
Accounts payable.....................................	$ 212,000	$ 198,000
Accrued expenses	98,000	76,000
Dividends payable	40,000	
Total current liabilities	$ 350,000	$ 274,000
Notes payable—due 1994	125,000	—
Total liabilities	$ 475,000	$ 274,000
Stockholders' equity:		
Common stock	$ 600,000	$ 550,000
Retained earnings	188,000	144,000
Total stockholders' equity	$ 788,000	$ 694,000
Total liabilities and equity	$1,263,000	$ 968,000

	Year Ended December 31,	
	1991	1990
Net sales	$3,561,000	$3,254,000
Cost of goods sold....................................	2,789,000	2,568,000
Gross profit	$ 772,000	$ 686,000
Expenses...	521,000	486,000
Net income	$ 251,000	$ 200,000

Additional information for Xavier:

(a) All accounts receivable and accounts payable relate to trade merchandise.
(b) The proceeds from the notes payable were used to finance plant expansion.
(c) Capital stock was sold to provide additional working capital.

Compute the following for 1991:

(1) Cash collected from accounts receivable, assuming all sales are on account.
(2) Cash payments made on accounts payable to suppliers, assuming that all purchases of inventory are on account.
(3) Cash dividend payment.
(4) Cash receipts that were not provided by operations.
(5) Cash payments for assets that were not reflected in operations.

Exercise 24–5   (Net cash flow provided (used) by operations—indirect method)

The following data were taken from the books of Tapwater Company. Compute the amount of net cash flow provided by operations during 1991 using the indirect method.

	December 31, 1991	December 31, 1990
Accounts receivable	$18,900	$16,750
Accounts payable	11,500	14,000
Accumulated depreciation (no plant assets were retired during the year)	26,000	22,000
Inventories	26,500	22,000
Other current liabilities	5,000	3,000
Short-term prepayment	1,200	2,000
Net income	35,500	

Exercise 24–6 (Net cash flow provided (used) by operations—direct method)

A summary of revenues and expenses for Stanton Company for 1991 follows:

Sales	$6,000,000
Cost of goods manufactured and sold	2,800,000
Gross profit	$3,200,000
Selling, general, and administrative expenses	2,000,000
Income before income tax	$1,200,000
Income tax	520,000
Net income	$ 680,000

Net changes in working capital items for 1991 were as follows:

	Debit	Credit
Cash	$104,000	
Trade accounts receivable (net)	400,000	
Inventories		$ 60,000
Prepaid expenses (selling and general)	10,000	
Accrued expenses (75% of increase related to manufacturing activities and 25% to general operating activities)		32,000
Income taxes payable		48,000
Trade accounts payable		140,000

Depreciation on plant and equipment for the year totaled $600,000; 70% was related to manufacturing activities and 30% to general and administrative activities.

Prepare a schedule of net cash flow provided by operations for the year using the direct method.

Exercise 24–7 (Cash provided by operations—direct method)

The following information was taken from the comparative financial statements of Buttercup Corporation.

Net income for year	$ 90,000
Sales revenue	500,000
Cost of goods sold (except depreciation)	300,000
Depreciation expense for year	60,000
Amortization of goodwill for year	10,000
Interest expense on short-term debt for year	3,500
Dividends declared and paid during year	65,000

<u>Selected Account Balances</u>

	Beginning of year	End of year
Accounts Receivable (net)	$43,000	$30,000
Inventory	42,000	50,000
Accounts Payable	59,400	56,000
Interest Payable	1,000	0

Using the direct method, compute the net amount of cash provided (used) by operating activities for the year.

Exercise 24–8   (Cash provided by operations—indirect method)

Based on the information given in exercise 24-7 and using the indirect method, compute the net amount of cash provided (used) by operating activities for the year.

Exercise 24–9   (Statement of cash flows)

Below is information for Boswell Manufacturing Company:

	December 31, 1990	December 31, 1991
Current assets:		
Cash and cash equivalents	$ 80,000	$108,100
Inventory	162,000	192,000
Accounts receivable (net)	200,000	213,000
Marketable securities (LCM)*	60,000	39,000
Current liabilities:		
Accounts payable	85,800	51,000
Dividends payable	18,000	27,000
Interest payable	3,000	11,100
Wages payable	12,000	84,000

*Noncash equivalents

(a) Long-term debt of $450,000 was retired at face value.
(b) New machinery was purchased for $48,000.
(c) Common stock with a par value of $120,000 was sold for $150,000.
(d) Dividends of $18,000 declared in 1990 were paid in January, 1991, and dividends of $27,000 were declared in December, 1991, to be paid in 1992.
(e) Included in net income for 1991 was an unrealized loss on the short-term marketable equity securities portfolio in the amount of $21,000.
(f) Income of $19,200 was recognized from an investment accounted for by the equity method even though no cash dividends were received during the year.
(g) Net income was $300,000. Included in the computation were depreciation expense of $60,000 and goodwill amortization of $30,000.

Prepare a statement of cash flows for the year ended December 31, 1991, using the indirect method.

Exercise 24–10   (Statement of cash flows)

The Sunnyvale Corporation prepared for 1991 and 1990 the following balance sheet data:

| | December 31 | |
	1991	1990
Cash and cash equivalents	$ 349,500	$ 255,000
Marketable securities	69,000	420,000
Accounts receivable (net)	360,000	345,000
Merchandise inventory	750,000	654,000
Prepaid insurance	4,500	6,000
Buildings and equipment	5,515,500	4,350,000
Accumulated depreciation—buildings and equipment	(2,235,000)	(1,995,000)
Total	$ 4,813,500	$ 4,035,000
Accounts payable	$ 613,500	$ 945,000
Salaries payable	75,000	105,000
Notes payable—bank (current)	150,000	600,000
Mortgage payable	1,500,000	0
Capital stock, $5 par	2,400,000	2,400,000
Retained earnings (deficit)	75,000	(15,000)
Total	$ 4,813,500	$ 4,035,000

Cash needed to purchase new equipment and to improve the company's
working capital position was raised by selling marketable securities costing
$351,000 for $360,000 and by issuing a mortgage. Equipment costing $75,000
with a book value of $15,000 was sold for $18,000; the gain on sale was
included in net income. The company paid cash dividends of $90,000 during
the year and reported earnings of $180,000 for 1991. There were no entries in
the retained earnings account other than to record the dividend and the net
income for the year. Marketable securities are carried at cost which is lower
than market; these securities do not qualify as cash equivalents.

Prepare a statement of cash flows using the indirect method.

Problems   **Problem 24–1   (Statement of cash flows—indirect method)**
Comparative balance sheet data for the Amber Company are presented below.

	1991	1990
Cash	$ 2,000	$ 10,000
Marketable securities	9,000	18,000
Accounts receivable	94,000	86,000
Inventory	110,000	100,000
Property, plant and equipment	550,000	500,000
Accumulated depreciation on property, plant and equipment	(277,500)	(250,000)
Total	$ 487,500	$ 464,000
Short-term notes payable		$ 20,000
Accounts payable	$105,000	80,000
Long-term notes payable	100,000	75,000
Bonds payable	50,000	100,000
Common stock, $5 par	100,000	100,000
Additional paid-in capital	75,000	75,000
Retained earnings	57,500	14,000
Total	$ 487,500	$ 464,000

The marketable securities qualify as cash equivalents. New equipment was
purchased for $50,000, consisting of $25,000 cash and a long-term note for

$25,000. Proceeds from the short-term notes payable were used for operating purposes. Cash dividends of $10,000 were paid in 1991; all other changes to retained earnings were caused by the net income for 1991, which amounted to $53,500.

Instructions: Prepare a statement of cash flows for the year ended December 31, 1991, using the indirect method.

Problem 24–2   (Statement of cash flows—direct method)

Based on an analysis of the cash and other accounts the following information was provided by the controller of Lumbercamp, Inc., a manufacturer of wood burning stoves, for the year 1991.

(a) Cash sales for the year were $150,000; sales on account totaled $180,000.
(b) Cost of goods sold was 50 percent of total sales.
(c) All inventory is purchased on account.
(d) Depreciation on equipment was $93,000 for the year.
(e) Amortization of goodwill was $6,000.
(f) Collection of accounts receivable was $114,000.
(g) Payments on accounts payable for inventory equaled $117,000.
(h) Rent expense paid in cash was $33,000.
(i) 60,000 shares of $10 par stock were issued for $720,000.
(j) Land was acquired by issuance of a $300,000 bond that sold for $318,000.
(k) Equipment was purchased for cash at a cost of $252,000.
(l) Dividends of $138,000 were declared.
(m) $45,000 of dividends that had been declared the previous year were paid.
(n) A machine used on the assembly line was sold for $36,000. The machine had a book value of $21,000.
(o) Another machine with a book value of $1,500 was scrapped and was reported as an ordinary loss. No cash was received on this transaction.
(p) The Cash account increased $573,000 during the year.

Instructions: Use the direct method to prepare a statement of cash flows for Lumbercamp, Inc., for the year ending December 31, 1991.

▐▌▌ Problem 24–3   (Cash flow statement—indirect method)

Comparative balance sheet data for the firm of Young and Jones are as follows:

	December 31,	
	1991	1990
Cash.	$ 14,000	$ 10,500
Accounts receivable	22,000	25,500
Inventory	112,500	85,000
Prepaid expenses	3,500	4,250
Furniture and fixtures	64,500	42,000
Accumulated depreciation	(33,875)	(25,425)
Total	$182,625	$141,825
Accrued expenses	$ 7,000	$ 5,200
Accounts payable	19,425	28,875
Long-term note	17,700	-0-
Donna Young, capital	51,375	50,875
Diane Jones, capital	87,125	56,875
Total	$182,625	$141,825

Income from operations for the year was $43,000 and this was transferred in equal amounts to the partners' capital accounts. Further changes in the capital accounts arose from additional investments and withdrawals by the partners. The change in the furniture and fixtures account arose from a purchase of additional furniture; part of the purchase price was paid in cash and a long-term note was issued for the balance.

Instructions: Using the indirect method, prepare a statement of cash flows for 1991 (work sheets are not required).

Problem 24—4 (Statement of cash flows—conversion from working capital funds statement)

Presented below are the funds statement on a working capital basis for the Perk Building Company for the year ended December 31, 1991, and a schedule of changes in working capital.

The balance sheet for December 31, 1990, appears on page 1117.

Perk Building Company
Statement of Changes in Financial Position—Working Capital Basis
For the Year Ended December 31, 1991

Working capital was provided by:		
Net income	$188,500	
Adjustments:		
Depreciation	37,500	
Amortization of patent	3,750	
Gain on sale of investments	(21,750)	
Working capital provided by operations		$208,000
Proceeds from sale of investments		78,000
Proceeds from sale of common stock		108,300
Long-term borrowing		79,200
Total working capital provided		$473,500
Working capital was applied to:		
Purchase of land	$ 57,250	
Dividends declared	37,500	
Reclassification of portion of long-term debt as current	7,500	
Purchase of machinery	225,000	
Total working capital applied		$327,250
Net increase in working capital		$146,250

Schedule of Changes in
Working Capital Components
Perk Building Company
For the Year Ended December 31, 1991

	Working Capital Changes
Cash	$ 33,750
Accounts receivable	(7,500)
Inventory	60,000
Prepaid insurance	15,000
Accounts payable	22,500
Dividends payable	18,750
Current portion of long-term debt	3,750
	$146,250

Perk Building Company
Balance Sheet
December 31, 1990

Assets

Cash..		$ 22,500
Accounts receivable		33,750
Inventory		15,000
Prepaid insurance		7,500
Land...		6,500
Machinery	$150,000	
Accumulated depreciation	(37,500)	112,500
Patents...		30,000
Investments (at cost)		75,000
Total assets		$302,750

Liabilities and Stockholders' Equity

Accounts payable	$ 60,000
Dividends payable	56,250
Current portion of long-term debt	11,250
Long-term debt...	37,500
Common stock	112,500
Retained earnings	25,250
Total liabilities and stockholders' equity	$302,750

Instructions:

(1) Convert the funds statement on a working capital basis to a statement of cash flows.

(2) Prepare a classified balance sheet for Perk Building Company as of December 31, 1991.

Problem 24—5 (Cash flow statement)

Berclay Tile Co. reported net income of $6,160 for 1991 but has been showing an overdraft in its bank account in recent months. The manager has contacted you as the auditor for an explanation. The information below was given to you for examination.

Berclay Tile Co.
Comparative Balance Sheet
Decmber 31, 1991 and 1990

	1991		1990	
Assets				
Current assets:				
Cash		$ (960)		$ 4,780
Accounts receivable		4,000		1,000
Inventory		2,350		750
Prepaid insurance		70		195
Total current assets		$ 5,460		$ 6,725
Land, buildings, and equipment:				
Land		$12,500		$12,500
Buildings.....................................	$25,000		$25,000	
Less accumulated depreciation...............	15,000	10,000	14,000	11,000
Equipment	$37,250		$30,850	
Less accumulated depreciation...............	22,500	14,750	18,400	12,450
Total land, buildings, and equipment		37,250		35,950
Total assets		$42,710		$42,675

Liabilities and Stockholders' Equity

Current liabilities:		
Accounts payable	$ 4,250	$ 3,500
Taxes payable	1,400	2,350
Wages payable	750	1,675
Notes payable—current portion	1,500	3,500
Total current liabilities	$ 7,900	$11,025
Long-term liabilities:		
Notes payable	10,500	11,500
Capital stock	$17,500	$15,000
Retained earnings	6,810	5,150
Total stockholders' equity.......................	24,310	20,150
Total liabilities and stockholders' equity	$42,710	$42,675

You also determine the following:

(a) Equipment was sold for $1,500, its cost was $2,500 and its book value was $500. The gain was reported as Other Revenue.

(b) Cash dividends of $4,500 were paid.

Instructions: Prepare a statement of cash flows using the indirect method (work sheets are not required).

Problem 24–6 (Statement of cash flows—direct method)

The following data show the account balances of Novations, Inc., at the beginning and end of the company's accounting period.

Debits	Dec. 31, 1991	Jan. 1, 1991
Cash and Cash Equivalents	$176,400	$ 58,000
Accounts Receivable	34,000	29,000
Inventory	21,000	25,400
Prepaid Insurance	5,600	4,000
Long-Term Investments (at cost)	6,000	16,800
Equipment	80,000	66,000
Treasury Stock (at cost)	10,000	20,000
Cost of Goods Sold	368,000	
Operating Expenses	187,000	
Income Tax Expense	37,600	
Loss on Sale of Equipment	1,000	
Total debits	$926,600	$219,200

Credits		
Allowance for Doubtful Accounts	$ 4,000	$ 2,400
Accumulated Depreciation—Equipment	19,000	18,000
Accounts Payable	7,000	11,200
Interest Payable	1,000	2,000
Income Taxes Payable	12,000	8,000
Notes Payable—Long Term	16,000	24,000
Common Stock	110,000	100,000
Paid-In Capital in Excess of Par	32,000	30,000
Retained Earnings	19,600*	23,600
Sales	704,000	
Gain on Sale of Long-Term Investments	2,000	
Total credits	$926,600	$219,200

*Pre-closing balance

The following information was also available:

(a) All purchases and sales were on account.

(b) Equipment costing $10,000 was sold for $3,000; a loss of $1,000 was recognized on the sale.

(c) Among other items, the operating expenses included depreciation expense of $7,000; doubtful accounts expense of $2,000; interest expense of $2,800; and insurance expense of $2,400.

(d) Equipment was purchased during the year by issuing common stock and by paying the balance ($12,000) in cash.

(e) Treasury stock was sold for $4,000 less than it cost; the decrease in owners' equity was recorded by reducing retained earnings.

(f) No dividends were paid during the year.

Instructions:

1. Prepare a statement of cash flows for the year ended December 31, 1991, using the direct method of reporting net cash flow from operations.

2. Comment on the lack of dividend payment. Does a "no dividend" policy seem appropriate under the current circumstances for Novations, Inc.?

Problem 24-7 (Statement of cash flows—indirect method)

Refer to the data in problem 24-6 for Novations, Inc.

Instructions:

1. Prepare an income statement for Novations, Inc., for the year ended December 31, 1991.

2. Prepare a statement of cash flows for the year ended December 31, 1991, using the indirect method.

Problem 24-8 (Cash flow from operations—direct method work sheet)

The following combined income and retained earnings statement, along with selected balance sheet data, are provided for the Timberdale Company.

Timberdale Company
Combined Income and Retained Earnings Statement
for the Year Ended December 31, 1991

Net sales revenue		$170,000
Other revenues		9,000*
Total revenues		$179,000
Expenses:		
Cost of goods sold	$102,000	
Selling and administrative expenses	29,400	
Depreciation expense	6,400	
Interest expense	2,800	
Total expenses		140,600
Income before taxes		$ 38,400
Income taxes		(11,520)
Net income		$ 26,880
Retained earnings, January 1, 1991		67,000
		$ 93,880
Dividends declared and paid		(5,000)
Retained earnings, December 31, 1991		$ 88,880

*Gain on sale of equipment (cost $19,000; book value, $12,000; sales price $21,000).

Balance Sheet Amounts

	Beginning of Year	End of Year
Accounts receivable (net)	$21,000	$22,000
Inventory	38,600	36,000
Prepaid expenses	1,900	1,400
Accounts payable	14,400	16,000
Interest payable	3,000	2,000
Income taxes payable	1,000	5,000

Instructions:

1. Using a work sheet and the direct method, compute the amount of net cash flow from operations for Timberdale Company for 1991.
2. What is the impact of dividends paid on net cash flow from operations? Explain.

Problem 24–9   (Cash flow statement with work sheet)

The following data are provided for the Dallas Department Store.

	Dr. (Cr.)	
	December 31, 1990 Post-Closing Trial Balance	December 31, 1991 Trial Balance
Cash and Equivalents	12,000	28,800
Accounts Receivable (net)	36,000	24,000
Inventory	96,000	144,000
Prepaid Expenses	6,000	7,200
Plant Assets	480,000	624,000
Accumulated Depreciation—Plant Assets	(48,000)	(122,400)
Accounts Payable	(24,000)	(30,000)
Accrued Liabilities	(9,600)	(12,000)
Mortgage Payable	(60,000)	(84,000)
Bonds Payable	(240,000)	(240,000)
Common Stock	(180,000)	(210,000)
Capital in Excess of Par	(30,000)	(36,000)
Retained Earnings	(38,400)	(26,400)
Sales	—	(840,000)
Cost of Goods Sold	—	480,000
Operating Expenses	—	252,000
Gain on Sale of Plant Assets	—	(12,000)
Income Tax Expense	—	52,800
Total	0	0

The following additional information was obtained from Dallas Department Store's accounting records:

(a) All accounts receivable were from sales to customers.
(b) The inventory and accounts payable were for merchandise purchased for resale.
(c) The prepaid expenses and accrued liabilities were for operating expenses.
(d) During the year, plant assets were purchased by paying $180,000 cash and signing a $24,000 mortgage.

(e) Plant assets with a cost of $60,000 and accumulated depreciation of $24,000 were sold for $48,000 cash.

(f) Depreciation expense for the year was included in operating expenses.

(g) Common stock was sold for $36,000 cash.

(h) Cash dividends of $12,000 were paid during the year.

Instructions: Using a work sheet, prepare a cash flow statement for the year ended December 31, 1991.   (AICPA adapted)

Problem 24–10   (Work sheet for a statement of cash flows—direct method)

Financial statement data for Hometown Corporation are provided below. (All numbers are shown rounded to the nearest thousand dollars.)

Hometown Corporation
Income and Retained Earnings Statements
for the Year Ended December 31, 1991

Sales revenue	$2,466	
Cost of goods sold	2,036	
Gross margin		$430
Operating expenses:		
Depreciation expense	$ 112	
Administrative expenses	218	
Other expenses	84	
Total operating expenses		414
Income from operations		$ 16
Gain on sale of real estate		220
Income before taxes		$236
Income taxes		82
Net income		$154
Dividends paid		-0-
Increase in retained earnings		$154

Hometown Corporation
Balance Sheets
as of December 31, 1991 and 1990

Assets	1991	1990
Cash and cash equivalents	$ 298	$1,522
Accounts receivable	326	302
Inventory	2,442	1,424
Land	2,318	3,278
Equipment	2,562	510
Accumulated depreciation, equipment	(162)	(50)
Total assets	$7,784	$6,986
Liabilities and Stockholders' Equity		
Accounts payable	$ 742	$ 982
Long-term debt	2,378	2,804
Common stock ($1 par)	1,500	1,000
Paid-in capital in excess of par	1,680	870
Retained earnings	1,484	1,330
Total liabilities and stockholders' equity	$7,784	$6,986

Instructions:

1. Prepare a work sheet using the direct method to compute the net cash flow from operations.
2. Prepare a statement of cash flows for Hometown Corporation for the period ended December 31, 1991.
3. Comment on the impression an investor may have in comparing Hometown's income statement with its cash flow statement.

Problem 24–11 (Comprehensive cash flow statement)

The following schedule showing net changes in balance sheet accounts at December 31, 1990, compared to December 31, 1991, was prepared from the records of the Willard Company. The statement of cash flows for the year ended December 31, 1991 has not yet been prepared.

	Increase (Decrease)
Assets	
Cash and cash equivalents	$ 60,000
Accounts receivable (net)	66,000
Inventories	37,000
Prepaid expenses	2,000
Property, plant, and equipment (net)	63,000
Total assets	$228,000
Liabilities	
Accounts payable	$(46,000)
Short-term notes payable	(20,000)
Accrued liabilities	28,500
Bonds payable	(28,000)
Less amortized bond discount	1,200
Total liabilities	$(64,300)
Stockholders' Equity	
Common stock, $10 par	$500,000
Paid-in capital in excess of par	200,000
Retained earnings	(437,700)
Appropriation of retained earnings for possible future inventory price decline	30,000
Total stockholders' equity	$292,300

Additional information includes:

(a) The net income for the year ended December 31, 1991, was $172,300. There were no extraordinary items.

(b) During the year ended December 31, 1991, uncollectible accounts receivable of $26,400 were written off by a debit to Allowance for Doubtful Accounts.

(c) A comparison of Property, Plant, and Equipment, as of the end of each year follows:

	December 31		Increase
	1991	1990	(Decrease)
Property, plant, and equipment	$570,500	$510,000	$60,500
Less accumulated depreciation	225,500	228,000	(2,500)
Property, plant and equipment	$345,000	$282,000	$63,000

During 1991, machinery was purchased at a cost of $45,000. In addition, machinery that was acquired in 1984 at a cost of $48,000 was sold for $3,600. At the date of sale, the machinery has an undepreciated cost of $4,200. The remaining increase in property, plant and equipment resulted from the acquisition of a tract of land for a new plant site.

(d) The bonds payable mature at the rate of $28,000 every year.

(e) In January 1991, the company issued an additional 10,000 shares of its common stock at $14 per share upon the exercise of outstanding stock options held by key employees. In May, 1991, the company declared and issued a 5% stock dividend on its outstanding stock. During the year, a cash dividend was paid on the common stock. On December 31, 1991, there were 840,000 shares of common stock outstanding.

(f) The appropriation of retained earnings for possible future inventory price declines was provided by a debit to Retained Earnings in anticipation of an expected future drop in the market related to goods in inventory.

(g) The notes payable relate to operating activities.

Instructions: Based on the information presented, prepare a statement of cash flows for the year ended December 31, 1991.   (AICPA adapted)

Problem 24—12   (Analysis of cash flows)

The schedule on page 1124 shows the account balances of the Beneficio Corporation at the beginning and end of the fiscal year ended October 31, 1991.

The following information was also available:

(a) All purchases and sales were on account.

(b) The sinking fund will be used to retire the long-term bonds.

(c) Equipment with an original cost of $15,000 was sold for $7,000.

(d) Selling and general expenses include the following expenses:

Building depreciation	$ 3,750
Equipment depreciation	19,250
Doubtful accounts expense	4,000
Interest expense	18,000

(e) A 6-month note payable for $50,000 was issued toward the purchase of new equipment.

(f) The long-term note payable requires the payment of $20,000 per year plus interest until paid.

(g) Treasury stock was sold for $1,000 more than its cost.

(h) All dividends were paid by cash.

Instructions:

(1) Prepare schedules computing: (a) collections of accounts receivable, (b) payments of accounts payable.

(2) Prepare a statement of cash flows using the direct approach. Supporting computations should be in good form.   (AICPA adapted)

Debits	October 31, 1991	November 1, 1990	Increase (Decrease)
Cash and Cash Equivalents	$ 226,000	$ 50,000	$176,000
Accounts Receivable	148,000	100,000	48,000
Inventories	291,000	300,000	(9,000)
Prepaid Insurance	2,500	2,000	500
Long-Term Investments (at cost)	10,000	40,000	(30,000)
Sinking Fund	90,000	80,000	10,000
Land and Building	195,000	195,000	
Equipment	215,000	90,000	125,000
Discount on Bonds Payable	8,500	9,000	(500)
Treasury Stock (at cost)	5,000	10,000	(5,000)
Cost of Goods Sold	539,000		
Selling and General Expenses	287,000		
Income Taxes	35,000		
Loss on Sale of Equipment	1,000		
Total debits	$2,053,000	$876,000	

Credits			
Allowance for Doubtful Accounts	$ 8,000	$ 5,000	$ 3,000
Accumulated Depreciation—Building	26,250	22,500	3,750
Accumulated Depreciation—Equipment	39,750	27,500	12,250
Accounts Payable	55,000	60,000	(5,000)
Notes Payable—current	70,000	20,000	50,000
Miscellaneous Expenses Payable	18,000	15,000	3,000
Taxes Payable	35,000	10,000	25,000
Unearned Revenue	1,000	9,000	(8,000)
Notes Payable—Long-Term	40,000	60,000	(20,000)
Bonds Payable—Long-Term	250,000	250,000	
Common Stock	300,000	200,000	100,000
Retained Earnings Appropriated for Sinking Fund	90,000	80,000	10,000
Unappropriated Retained Earnings	94,000	112,000	(18,000)
Paid-In Capital in Excess of Par Value	116,000	5,000	111,000
Sales	898,000		
Gain on Sale of Investments	12,000		
Total credits	$2,053,000	$876,000	

Chapter 25

Reporting the Impact of Changing Prices

A troublesome problem for individuals and businesses alike is how to deal with changing prices. Most consumers are well aware that the prices of goods and services have risen significantly over the past fifty years. This increase in the general price level is called **inflation**. The following schedule shows the general price level in the U.S. for selected years since 1920, as measured by the consumer price index. The schedule illustrates the long-term inflationary trend that has characterized the U.S. economy in the post-depression years. In some parts of the world, for example in South America, the rate of inflation has been much higher, at times over 1,000% a year.

Consumer Price Index for All Urban Consumers (CPI-U) (1967 = 100)

Selected Years	Average for Year
1920	60.0
1930	50.0
1940	42.0
1950	72.1
1960	88.7
1967*	100.0
1970	116.3
1980	246.8
1984	311.1
1985	322.2
1986	328.4
1987	340.4
1988	354.4

*The base year.
Source: U.S. Department of Labor, Bureau of Labor Statistics

Financial statements of business enterprises have traditionally reflected transactions in terms of the number of dollars exchanged. These statements are often referred to as **historical cost/nominal dollar** or simply **historical cost** statements, meaning statements reporting unadjusted original dollar amounts. The justification for reporting original dollar amounts is objectivity. Historical costs generally are based on arm's-length transactions that are considered to measure appropriate exchange values at a transaction date.

The problem is that historical cost statements do not reflect the impact of price changes subsequent to the transaction date. To some, this is a serious limitation of traditional accounting, especially in periods of high inflation or rapidly increasing replacement costs for certain assets. When the inflation rate is low, the concern over accounting for changing prices tends to diminish.

Regardless of existing economic conditions, and the related level of interest in accounting for changing prices, there are some basic concepts that should be understood. This chapter explains these concepts and provides simple examples to illustrate the procedures involved in accounting for changing prices.

Reporting the Effects of Changing Prices

Two kinds of price changes have been identified. The first deals with changes in the general price level for all commodities and services. The second kind of price change relates to changes in prices of specific items. Prices for individual items may fluctuate up or down and by differing magnitudes; the average of all specific price changes determines the change in the general price level. With respect to terminology, accounting for the first kind of price change is referred to as **constant dollar accounting** or general price-level adjusted accounting. Accounting for the second kind of price change is referred to as **current cost accounting** or current value accounting. This distinction is important in order to understand the reporting alternatives identified in the next section.

Reporting Alternatives

The major financial reporting alternatives, including the currently used historical cost/nominal dollar basis, may be classified as follows:

	Historical Cost Valuation	Current Cost Valuation
Nominal Dollar Measurement	HC/ND Historical Cost/ Nominal Dollar	CC/ND Current Cost/ Nominal Dollar
Constant Dollar Measurement	HC/CD Historical Cost/ Constant Dollar	CC/CD Current Cost/ Constant Dollar

The two distinct aspects of changing prices are highlighted by the matrix: the change in the unit of measurement (nominal and constant dollars) and the change in basis of valuation (historical and current costs). These distinctions are important since the accounting for and the effects on the financial statements are significantly different.

The first cell reflects financial statements that are currently reported in terms of nominal dollars using historical cost valuation. The dollar measurement is not adjusted for changes in the general price level, and the valuation basis represents the historical exchange prices of transactions, not the current costs of the items reported. This is contrasted to the cell labeled HC/CD. Reporting on this basis maintains historical cost valuation but measures the items in terms of constant dollars. This means that the original or nominal dollars are adjusted to constant dollars—dollars of equivalent purchasing power. Sometimes constant dollars are referred to as **general purchasing power dollars** because they represent quantities of goods or services that can be purchased given a general price level. This concept is explained in greater detail later in this chapter.

The cell identified as CC/ND does not adjust the dollar measurement; it reports nominal dollars. However, it changes the valuation basis from historical costs to current costs. This basis of reporting reflects changes in specific prices but does not account for changes in the general price level. The term **current cost** is used throughout this chapter in a general sense to mean the current value of an asset. Measures of current cost include: replacement cost, reproduction cost, sales value, net realizable value, and net present value of expected cash flows. The terms current cost and current value are used interchangeably.

The cell identified as CC/CD combines current cost valuation with constant dollar measurement. Reporting on this basis reflects both specific price changes and general purchasing power changes.

In summary, reporting on the traditional basis (represented by HC/ND) does not reflect the impact of general price changes or specific price changes until assets are sold or otherwise disposed of. Reporting on the HC/CD basis considers general purchasing power changes but not specific price changes. The CC/ND basis is just the opposite. It reports the impact of specific price changes because of its current cost valuation but does not reflect changes in the general purchasing power of the dollar. Only by reporting on a CC/CD basis are both types of price changes accounted for.

The extent and manner of reporting the impact of changing prices is also an issue. One possibility is to choose one of the three nontraditional cells and require preparation of primary financial statements on the basis selected. Another alternative is to continue reporting the primary financial statements on the historical cost/nominal dollar basis, but to provide supplemental information adjusted to constant dollars and/or reflecting current costs. If the latter alternative were chosen, a remaining question would be whether to restate all items or only selected items.

Historical Perspective   The issues involved and the proposed alternatives for reporting the effects of changing prices are not new. In the 1920s and 1930s Henry Sweeney and others advocated constant dollar accounting under the names of "stabilized" or price-level accounting.[1]

In 1963, the AICPA published Accounting Research Study No. 6, "Reporting the Financial Effects of Price-Level Changes." This study recommended that supplementary data be presented showing comprehensive restatement of all elements of financial statements using a general price index.[2] Later, in 1969, the APB issued Statement No. 3, which again recognized the potential benefits of general price-level adjusted information and suggested supplemental disclosure of such data.[3]

At the end of 1974, the FASB issued an exposure draft entitled "Financial Reporting in Units of General Purchasing Power." This proposed statement would have required constant dollar accounting, although still as supplemental information.[4] However, before the FASB adopted a final statement, the SEC issued ASR No. 190, which required many companies to disclose current replacement costs of selected assets.[5] Because this conflicted with the FASB's constant dollar exposure draft, the Board withdrew its proposal.

In 1979, after careful evaluation, the FASB decided to experiment with alternative ways of reporting the impact of changing prices by issuing Statement No. 33, "Financial Reporting and Changing Prices.[6] This statement required certain companies to disclose supplemental information for selected items on *both* a constant dollar and a current cost basis. Subsequently, the SEC modified its requirements, as established in ASR No. 190, to comply with the more comprehensive FASB Statement No. 33.

In December 1986, after careful review of the Statement No. 33 experiment, the FASB issued Statement No. 89, superseding Statement No. 33 and various related amendments to that statement. Thus, the FASB has made voluntary the supplementary disclosure of current cost/constant dollar information after concluding that such disclosure should be encouraged, but not required.[7]

Since some companies will continue to report changing price data and since this topic will no doubt continue to be debated, accounting students should be familiar with the underlying concepts of constant dollar accounting and current cost accounting.

[1]See, for example, Henry W. Sweeney, *Stabilized Accounting*, (New York: Harper & Brothers, 1936).

[2]*Accounting Research Study No. 6*, "Reporting the Financial Effects of Price-Level Changes" (New York: American Institute of Certified Public Accountants, 1963).

[3]*Statement of the Accounting Principles Board, No. 3*, "Financial Statements Restated for General Price-Level Change" (New York, American Institute of Certified Public Accountants, 1969).

[4]*FASB Exposure Draft*, "Financial Reporting in Units of General Purchasing Power" (Stamford: Financial Accounting Standards Board, 1974).

[5]Securities and Exchange Commission, *Accounting Series Release No. 190*, "Disclosure of Certain Replacement Cost Data," (Washington: U.S. Government Printing Office, 1976).

[6]*Statement of Financial Accounting Standards No. 33*, "Financial Reporting and Changing Prices" (Stamford: Financial Accounting Standards Board, 1979); Also see, Robert W. Berliner and Dale L. Gerboth, "FASB Statement No. 33 'The Great Experiment,' *Journal of Accountancy* (May 1980), pp. 48–54.

[7]*Statement of Financial Accounting Standards No. 89*, "Financial Reporting and Changing Prices" (Stamford: Financial Accounting Standards Board, 1986).

Constant Dollar Accounting

Recording transactions in terms of the number of nominal dollars exchanged ignores the fact that the dollar is *not* a stable monetary unit. As a unit of measurement, the dollar has significance only in reference to a particular price level. Thus, nominal dollar measurements represent diverse amounts of purchasing power. Unless statements are adjusted, readers are likely to regard dollars in terms of current general purchasing power rather than the general purchasing power at the time the dollars were exchanged. The objective of constant dollar accounting is to convert all dollar measurements into **equivalent purchasing power units** so that a company's position and progress may be viewed in proper perspective.

To illustrate, it would not seem proper to add 100 U.S. dollars to 100 British pounds. It would seem necessary to first convert one of the figures to its exchange equivalent before adding, subtracting, or comparing amounts. Similarly, the number of dollars spent years ago for land or buildings should be converted into current equivalent purchasing power units to arrive at meaningful asset totals. This conversion of nominal dollar amounts to equivalent purchasing power units is the essence of constant dollar accounting. Historical costs, the original exchange values, are maintained as the valuation basis, but are adjusted for changes in the general price level. The basis of measurement changes from nominal dollar amounts to constant dollar amounts or equivalent purchasing power units. The conversion is accomplished using a general price index.

Price Indexes

The value or purchasing power of a monetary unit is inversely related to the price of goods or services for which it can be exchanged. Over a period of time, the prices of specific goods or services will move up or down depending on the relative scarcity and desirability of the goods or services. It would be possible to adjust for specific items, but those price changes may be different than changes in the general price level.

The general price level cannot be measured in absolute terms, but relative changes from period to period and the direction of change can be determined. To measure changes in the general price level, a sample of commodities and services is selected and the current prices of these items are compared with their prices during a base period. The prices during the base period are assigned a value of 100, and the prices of all other periods are expressed as percentages of this amount. The resulting series of numbers is called a **price index**.

Price indexes are valuable aids in measuring inflation or deflation. However, these measurements do have limitations. In the first place, all price indexes are based on samples. Since all prices do not fluctuate in the same degree or direction, the selection of commodities to be included in the sample affects the computed amounts. In addition, improvements in products affect the general level of prices, but such qualitative changes are difficult to measure.

Although there is no perfect way to measure the changing value of the dollar, indexes have been developed that provide reasonable estimates of changes in the dollar's general purchasing power. Among these are the Consumer Price Index and the Wholesale Price Index, both provided by the Bureau of Labor Statistics, and the GNP (Gross National Product) Implicit Price Deflator provided by the Department of Commerce.

Each of these indexes exhibits a similar pattern of price-level change, but reports different values. This is because each index is based on a different sample. The index recommended by the FASB is the Consumer Price Index for all Urban Consumers (CPI-U), which is published monthly.

Mechanics of Constant Dollar Restatement

Constant dollar accounting requires that nominal dollar amounts be restated to equivalent purchasing power units, i.e., constant dollars, usually for the current period. The general formula for restatement is:

$$\text{Nominal dollar amount} \times \frac{\text{Price index converting \textbf{to}}}{\text{Price index converting \textbf{from}}} = \text{Constant dollar amount}$$

To illustrate the conversion process, assume that a company issued capital stock worth $50,000 in exchange for inventory valued at $50,000. Further assume that the current end-of-year price index is 105 and that the exchange took place when the general price index was 100. The company holds inventory during the year without engaging in any other activities. A conventional balance sheet prepared at the end of the year will show both inventory and invested capital at their nominal amounts, $50,000. In preparing a constant dollar balance sheet at the end of the year, however, inventory and capital stock will be reported as follows:

1. Inventory needs to be restated for the change in the general price level since its acquisition. Inventory, with a nominal acquisition cost of $50,000, is expressed in constant dollars as $52,500:

$$\$50,000 \times \frac{\text{Index converting to (105)}}{\text{Index converting from (100)}} = \$52,500$$

2. Capital stock also requires restatement so that it expresses the stockholders' investment in terms of the current general price level. The capital stock balance is expressed in constant dollars as $52,500:

$$\$50,000 \times \frac{\text{Index converting to (105)}}{\text{Index converting from (100)}} = \$52,500$$

Conversion ratios may be used that express the relationship of one index to another. Thus, in the example cited, 105/100 may be stated as a conversion ratio of 1.05.

In the example presented, the price index converted "to" was the end-of-year index. Alternatively, an average index for the current year could have been used. If such an approach were taken, the conversion factor would have been 102.5/100 rather than 105/100. Another approach would be to restate all amounts in terms of the price level of an earlier period, e.g., the year of purchase of an item or a base year. Then events occuring during the current year would be restated in terms of constant dollars of the earlier period selected. Nominal dollars can be restated to constant dollars of any period by modifying the indexes used for the conversion factor.

If current-year constant dollars are used to prepare comparative summaries, all past year data, including monetary assets and liabilities (defined in the next section), must be "rolled forward" to the current year. In this manner, data presented for several years will all be stated in terms of the same purchasing power units. To illustrate, assume that land was purchased in 1985 for $100,000. Assume further that the general price level was 150 when the land was purchased, 200 at the end of 1990, and 215 at the end of 1991. In reporting the land on the balance sheet at the end of 1990, the land would be reported in current end-of-year constant dollars as follows:

$$\text{Land}\left(\$100,000 \times \frac{200}{150}\right) = \$133,333$$

However, in reporting comparative amounts at the end of 1991 in current end-of-year constant dollars, the 1990 amount would have to be rolled forward as follows:

$$\text{Land}\left(\$133,333 \times \frac{215}{200}\right) = \$143,333$$

Alternatively, the 1991 amount could be computed directly as follows:

$$\$100,000 \times \frac{215}{150} = \$143,333$$

Thus, the comparative balance sheet at December 31, 1991, would show the following:

	1990	1991
Land	$143,333	$143,333

This correctly shows no increase in the land account during 1990 and 1991 when amounts are all stated in terms of the same constant dollars. For comparative balance sheet purposes at the end of 1992, the $143,333 would again have to be rolled forward to reflect 1992 dollars.

As indicated earlier, all terms may be reported in terms of constant dollars of an earlier base year. This would eliminate the need for a roll-forward adjustment because all items would be stated in terms of a base year's constant dollars. Even though restating amounts to current-year constant dollars requires a roll-forward procedure, it provides information that relates to the current general price level as opposed to some earlier price level. Current price levels are usually more understandable and relevant for decision-making purposes.

To illustrate the application of constant dollar accounting to the balance sheet, consider a simple example—Campus Supply. All amounts are restated to current end-of-year constant dollars. Assume that the beginning-of-year index was 220; the end-of-year index was 260. The entire ending inventory was all purchased when the index was 225; the land was bought when the index was 125; all capital stock was issued when the index was 110.

Campus Supply
Balance Sheet
December 31, 1991
(Constant Dollar Basis)

Assets	HC/ND Amounts	Conversion Factor	HC/CD Amounts
Cash	$22,000		$22,000
Accounts receivable	14,000		14,000
Inventory	9,000	260/225	10,400
Land	20,000	260/125	41,600
Total assets	$65,000		$88,000
Liabilities and Stockholder's Equity			
Accounts payable	$ 4,000		$ 4,000
Mortgage payable	15,000		15,000
Capital stock	22,000	260/110	52,000
Retained earnings	24,000		17,000*
Total liabilities and stockholders' equity	$65,000		$88,000

*$88,000 − ($4,000 + $15,000 + $52,000)

Note that conversion is not made for cash, receivables, and payables. As explained in the next section, these "monetary items" are fixed in amount regardless of changes in the price level, except when rolling forward past year data for comparative statements. It also should be observed that Retained Earnings cannot be converted directly, since it represents a composite of many different price levels.

Purchasing Power Gains and Losses

In preparing an income statement on the historical cost/constant dollar basis, revenues and expenses are restated by applying the appropriate indexes in the same manner as illustrated in the preceding section. In addition, reported income is adjusted for any **purchasing power gain or loss** that results from holding monetary items. Monetary items are assets, liabilities, and equities whose balances are fixed in terms of numbers of dollars regardless of changes in the general price level. All items not representing a right to receive or an obligation to pay a fixed sum are nonmonetary items.

Monetary assets include cash and items such as accounts and notes receivable, loans to employees, cash surrender value of life insurance, and certain marketable securities, such as bonds, that are expected to be held to maturity and redeemed at a fixed number of dollars. Regardless of changes in the general price level, these balances are fixed and provide for the recovery of neither more nor less than the stated amounts. Monetary liabilities include such items as accounts and notes payable, cash dividends payable, and fixed payments for accruals under pension plans. Regardless of changes in the price level, these balances are fixed and call for the payment of neither more nor less than the stated amounts. Nonconvertible preferred stock is a monetary equity item while common stock is a non-monetary item. (For a more extensive classification of monetary and non-monetary items, see Appendix D of FASB Statement No. 33.)

To illustrate the concept of purchasing power gain or loss, assume that a person placed $1,000 cash under the mattress for "safekeeping" when the price index was 100. If the price index were to rise to 110 a year later, the individual would have suffered a purchasing-power loss because it would require $1,100 to purchase the same amount of goods that $1,000 would have bought a year ago. On the other hand, a debt of $1,000 payable a year later, again assuming an increase in the price index to 110 from 100, would result in a purchasing power gain. The equivalent purchasing power would be $1,100 yet the debt can be settled for the fixed amount of $1,000.

Nonmonetary assets include such items as inventories and supplies; land, buildings, and equipment; and intangible assets. These items are nonmonetary because with changes in the general price level, the nominal dollar amounts at which they are reported on the conventional financial statements will differ from the resources they actually represent. On the other hand, nonmonetary liabilities generally include such items as obligations to furnish goods or services, advances on sales contracts, and warranties on goods sold. These items are nonmonetary because with changes in the general price level, the dollar demands they actually make will differ from the dollar amounts reported on conventional financial statements.

The difference between a company's monetary assets and its monetary liabilities and equities is referred to as its **net monetary position**. With the number of dollars relating to monetary items remaining fixed, and reflecting current dollars regardless of the change in the price level, purchasing power gains and losses arise as prices change. In any given period, the gain or loss from holding monetary assets is offset by the loss or gain from maintaining monetary liabilities and equities. The net gain or loss for a period, then, depends on whether a company's position in net monetary items is positive—monetary assets exceeding monetary liabilities and equities—or negative—monetary liabilities and equities exceeding monetary assets. Gains and losses are associated with a company's net monetary position as follows:

	Rising Prices	Declining Prices
Positive Net Monetary Position	Loss	Gain
Negative Net Monetary Position	Gain	Loss

Constant dollar accounting requires that purchasing power gains and losses be determined. The steps to be followed in determining these gains and losses are explained and illustrated using the financial information for Campus Supply on page 1134 and the following additional information.

Sales for the year were $90,000, purchases were $60,000, and other expenses were $24,000. These revenues and expenses were incurred evenly throughout the year.

The net monetary positions as of January 1, 1991, and December 31, 1991, are as follows:

	January 1, 1991	December 31, 1991
Cash	$19,000	$22,000
Accounts receivable	11,000	14,000
Accounts payable	(3,000)	(4,000)
Mortgage payable	(16,000)	(15,000)
Net monetary position	$11,000	$17,000

The purchasing power gain or loss is calculated as follows assuming conversion to end-of-year constant dollars:

1. The company's net monetary position at the beginning of the period is restated to end-of-year constant dollars. Campus Supply's net monetary position as of January 1, 1991, is $11,000. This amount can be restated to end-of-year dollars by multiplying it by the ratio of the year-end price index to the index at the beginning of the year: $11,000 \times 260/220 = $13,000.

2. Transactions involving monetary items during the year are expressed in terms of year-end constant dollars and are added to or subtracted from the beginning net monetary position. For Campus Supply, monetary items were increased by sales and decreased by purchases and other expenses. Because these items were incurred evenly during the year, the ratio of the year-end price index to the average index for 1991 can be used to restate them to end-of-year dollars.

	HC/ND	Conversion Factor	HC/CD
Sales	$90,000	260/240	$97,500
Purchases	(60,000)	260/240	(65,000)
Other expenses	(24,000)	260/240	(26,000)
Increase in net monetary position	$ 6,000	260/240	$ 6,500

If no gain or loss in purchasing power had occurred during the year, the ending net monetary position would be $19,500 computed as follows:

	HC/CD
Net monetary position, January 1, 1991	$13,000
Increase in net monetary position	6,500
Net monetary position, December 31, 1991	$19,500

3. The actual net monetary position at the end of the year is compared with the results from Step 2. If the actual net monetary position is less than the amount computed in Step 2, the company has sustained a loss

in purchasing power. If it is greater, the company has experienced a gain. Campus Supply's actual net monetary position at the end of 1991 is $17,000. Since this amount is less than the $19,500 computed above, the company has sustained a $2,500 purchasing power loss. The foregoing calculations can be summarized in the following schedule:

Campus Supply
Schedule of Purchasing Power Loss
For the Year Ended December 31, 1991

	HC/ND	Conversion Factor	HC/CD*
Net monetary position, January 1, 1991	$11,000	260/220	$13,000
Increase in net monetary position	6,000	260/240	6,500
			$19,500
Net monetary position, December 31, 1991	$17,000		17,000
Purchasing power loss.....................			$ 2,500

*End of year dollars

This schedule shows several things. First, the beginning net monetary position plus the net increase (or less the net decrease) will always equal the ending net monetary position, all stated in nominal dollars. This amount can be computed directly from the balance sheet data. Second, the $19,500 represents the amount that the ending monetary position should be in terms of current end-of-year purchasing power units (constant dollars) if no gain or loss had occurred. However, the actual net monetary position is $17,000 because monetary items are fixed in amount. The result is a purchasing power loss of $2,500, the difference between what the monetary position would be if purchasing power had been maintained and the actual amount. On a constant dollar income statement, the purchasing power gain or loss is added to or subtracted from the constant dollar operating income and becomes a part of the ending retained earnings balance.

As indicated earlier, the objective of constant dollar accounting is to convert all nominal dollar amounts to dollars of equivalent purchasing power. Thus, nominal dollars may be converted to constant dollars of a prior period or to average dollars for the current year. The latter approach is frequently encountered in practice and is illustrated in the following schedule for Campus Supply.

Campus Supply
Schedule of Purchasing Power Loss
For the Year Ended December 31, 1991

	HC/ND	Conversion Factor	HC/CD*
Net monetary position, January 1, 1991	$11,000	240/220	$12,000
Increase in net monetary position	6,000		6,000
			$18,000
Net monetary position, December 31, 1991	$17,000	240/260	15,692
Purchasing power loss.....................			$ 2,308

*Average dollars

When average-for-the-year constant dollars are used to determine purchasing power gain or loss, both beginning and ending amounts must be restated in terms of the average price index. No restatement was required for the ending balance in the previous example since this amount reflected end-of-year dollars. When using an average current-year index, the net increase or decrease in monetary position is not converted since revenues and expenses are assumed to occur evenly throughout the period; therefore, these amounts already reflect average price levels for the year. The purchasing power loss of $2,308 differs from the $2,500 loss in the previous example because it reflects a different price level. The $2,308 can be restated to end-of-year dollars as follows: $2,308 × 260/240 = $2,500.

Arguments For and Against Constant Dollar Accounting

Proponents of constant dollar accounting maintain that meaningful comparisons of accounting data are not possible unless the measuring units are comparable. They argue that the purchasing power of the dollar is not stable, fluctuating with changes in the general price level. Constant dollar accounting corrects this deficiency by measuring transactions in terms of equivalent purchasing power units, thus giving proper recognition to changes in the general price level. Those in favor of constant dollar accounting also point out that recognition of purchasing power gains and losses highlights the impact of inflation with respect to monetary assets, liabilities, and equities. They conclude that constant dollar information is relevant to decision makers and can be provided on a reliable basis without undue cost.

Those opposed to constant dollar accounting note that changes in specific prices of goods are not considered. Constant dollar accounting reflects only changes in the general price level. It ignores many underlying reasons for specific price changes—for example, those due to improvements in quality and specialized industry circumstances. In addition, the general price index used may not be relevant to particular industries. Constant dollar opponents also point out that price indexes are based on statistical averages and have many weaknesses. They question the reliability of the data, especially if used indiscriminately. Many accountants also question whether the benefits exceed the costs of providing constant dollar data. They fear companies will incur substantial costs, only to have users of the data be confused by or uninterested in the information.

Current Cost Accounting

The objective of current cost accounting is different from constant dollar accounting. Constant dollar accounting seeks to use comparable measuring units to reflect equivalent purchasing power for a specified general price level. Current cost accounting attempts to measure the current values of assets, liabilities, and equities. The current values may be measured in nominal dollars or in constant dollars, but they are intended to represent the current exchange prices of goods or services, not historical costs.

Current cost accounting measures changes in specific prices rather than changes in the general price level. While the general price level may have increased an average 12% during the past year, the current values of land may be up 22%, inventories may be up only 8%, and certain types of equipment, perhaps due to technological advancements, may have even decreased in value.

Concept of Well-Offness

From an income measurement perspective, current cost accounting is based on a concept of *well-offness*. This concept is attributed to an economist, J. R. Hicks, and maintains that operating gross profit, often called economic income, is the amount a firm can spend during a period and be as well-off at the end of the period as at the beginning. Operationalized, economic income (loss) is the difference between the sales price of an item and the cost to replace that item. Alternatively, it may be viewed as the change in net assets during a period measured on a current value basis. For example, if an entity's net assets, in terms of current costs, equaled $250,000 at the beginning of a period, and $300,000 at the end of the period, given no additional investments or withdrawals and holding the general price level constant, economic income would be $50,000.

Current cost may be defined in several ways. Among the most common are: (1) input prices, i.e., replacement or reproduction costs; (2) exit prices, i.e., sales values; (3) net realizable values, i.e., expected sales prices less costs to complete and sell; and (4) economic values, i.e., present values of future cash flows. These distinctions are technical refinements in implementing the general approach of reflecting current values in financial statements.

Different circumstances may require different approaches to presenting current cost information. For example, the current cost of inventory or plant assets is generally thought of as the cost to replace or reproduce those assets at the balance sheet date. However, assets such as timber can be replaced only over a long period of time; minerals and oil and gas reserves may not be renewable at all. In these circumstances, economic values probably offer better representations of current costs than do replacement costs. This again points out the need for accountants to use judgment, within the guidelines established by the profession, in applying accounting principles.

Holding Gains or Losses

Current cost accounting not only emphasizes economic income but also makes it possible to isolate any gains or losses resulting from holding nonmonetary assets. Traditionally, accountants have recognized income at the point of sale, measuring the difference between the sales price and the historical cost of the item sold. Under current cost accounting, changes in asset values during a period would be recognized whether the assets were sold or not. The recognition of **holding gains or losses** is therefore an essential ingredient of current cost accounting.

Two types of gains and losses from holding assets need to be accounted for. **Realized holding gains and losses** indicate the differences between the current costs and the historical costs of assets sold or used during a period. **Unrealized holding gains and losses** are increases (or decreases) in the current values of assets held during a period but not sold or used. For example, in the earlier illustration assume that the land of Campus Supply had a current value of $60,000 at the end of 1991. On a December 31, 1991, current cost balance sheet, the land would be reported at its current value of $60,000 rather than its historical cost of $20,000 or its end-of-year constant dollar value of $41,600, thus disclosing a $40,000 unrealized holding gain.

To further illustrate the concept of holding gains or losses, assume that Current Value Company made a sale of $100,000. The cost of goods sold was $65,000, and the cost to replace the inventory sold was $80,000. The total gross profit recognized under historical cost accounting is $35,000 (sales price minus historical cost of inventory sold). However, the $35,000 includes an operating gross profit of $20,000 (sales price minus current cost of inventory sold) and an inventory holding gain of $15,000. The realized holding gain of $15,000 represents the difference between the historical cost and the replacement cost of the inventory sold. This may be illustrated as follows:

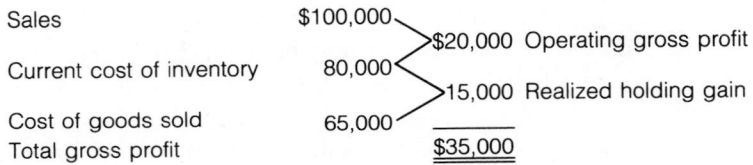

Sales	$100,000
	$20,000 Operating gross profit
Current cost of inventory	80,000
	15,000 Realized holding gain
Cost of goods sold	65,000
Total gross profit	$35,000

If, in the example, Current Value Company had additional inventory that was not sold but that had a change in value, it would have an unrealized holding gain or loss. Assume inventory that was not sold cost $50,000 and had a replacement cost of $75,000. There would be a $25,000 unrealized holding gain on the inventory.

To show how these concepts would be applied over time, assume $10,000 of inventory was purchased by a company at the beginning of Year 1. At the end of Year 1 no inventory had been sold but its current cost was $12,000. At the end of Year 2, the inventory was sold for $18,000 and was replaced at a cost of $15,000. A comparison of the historical cost and current cost approaches over time is shown in the following illustration. For simplicity, assume that the only expense is cost of goods sold.

	Historical Cost			Current Cost		
	Year 1	Year 2	Total	Year 1	Year 2	Total
Sales revenue	-0-	$18,000	$18,000	-0-	$18,000	$18,000
Cost of goods sold	-0-	10,000	10,000	-0-	15,000	15,000
Operating income	-0-	$ 8,000	$ 8,000	-0-	$ 3,000	$ 3,000
Holding gain (loss)	-0-	-0-	-0-	$2,000	3,000	5,000
Net income	-0-	$ 8,000	$ 8,000	$2,000	$ 6,000	$ 8,000

Note that total income recognized is the same under either method. Under current cost accounting, however, changes in the prices of inventory are recognized as they occur. The $2,000 increase in the value of the inventory during Year 1 was an unrealized holding gain, since the inventory had not been sold.

In Year 2, the difference between the current cost of the inventory and its historical cost, $5,000, is a realized holding gain. Note that this realized holding gain includes the $2,000 unrealized holding gain recognized in Year 1 as well as $3,000 realized in Year 2. There is no unrealized holding gain on the inventory in Year 2, since the ending inventory was acquired at the end of Year 2 resulting in the historical cost and the current value being the same.

Current cost net income in this example consists of operating income and holding gains, both realized and unrealized. The total net income would be reflected in retained earnings and would offset changes in net asset values shown on the balance sheet. Some accountants argue, however, that holding gains and losses should be reported as a special account in the owners' equity section of the balance sheet and should not be included in the determination of net income. Another position is that only realized holding gains and losses should be reported as income, and unrealized gains or losses should be reported in an owners' equity account.

Mechanics of Current Cost Accounting

The major problem in current cost accounting is determining appropriate current values. There are two recommended approaches: (1) **indexing** through internally or externally developed specific price indexes for the class of goods or services being measured, and (2) **direct pricing** from current invoice prices, vendors' price lists, or standard manufacturing costs that reflect current costs. If indexing is used, restatement is mechanically the same as for constant dollar accounting. The difference is that specific price indexes are used rather than a general price index. The direct pricing approach assigns current values, determined by analysis and estimate, to particular assets.

Arguments for and Against Current Cost Accounting

Many accountants were not in favor of the replacement cost reporting requirements of ASR 190. Some were opposed to FASB Statement No. 33, being especially critical of its complexity and the confusion it might cause. However, proponents of current cost accounting argue that historical cost financial statements, even if adjusted for general price-level changes, do not adequately reflect the economic circumstances of a business. The balance sheet is deficient because only historical costs are presented, and these measurements do not reflect the current financial picture of an enterprise. The income statement is deficient because charges against revenues are based on historical costs that may differ from current costs. Also, increases in net asset values are not recognized at the time of a change in asset value but must await realization at time of sale. Under current cost accounting, assets are reported at their current values, thus more closely reflecting the actual financial position of a business. Expenses are based on the expiration of current costs of assets utilized, thus providing a more meaningful income measure, and changes in values of assets held are recognized as they occur.

Opponents of current cost accounting argue that determining current values is too subjective. For example, the current cost of a particular item may not be readily available and may have to be determined by appraisal or estimation. It may be difficult or impossible to even find an identical replacement item to consider its replacement cost. If an identical asset is not used, a subjective adjustment for differences in the quality of a similar but not identical item would have to be made.

Another disadvantage is the increased subjectivity of the income measurement if changes in current values are recognized as income prior to transactions that confirm arm's-length exchange values.

Additional arguments against current cost accounting include the lack of understanding of current cost financial statements; the question of whether the benefits are worth the extra costs involved; and the uncertainty of whether financial statement users will be better served by current cost accounting.

Current Cost/ Constant Dollar Accounting

A number of accountants argue against both constant dollar and current cost accounting, pointing out that each approach solves only one of the problems of accounting for changing prices. Constant dollar accounting adjusts for general price changes; current cost accounting recognizes the impact of specific price changes. Current cost/constant dollar accounting combines both approaches and reflects current cost valuation on a constant dollar basis. Such an approach recognizes that adjustments for specific and general price changes are neither mutually exclusive nor competing alternatives. Conceptually, this is the best reporting alternative if the objective is to give full effect to the impact of changing prices on business enterprises. Its primary disadvantage, in addition to the shortcomings ascribed to the other approaches considered separately, is its complexity.

Again referring to the Campus Supply example, on a December 31, 1991, current cost/constant dollar balance sheet, the land would be reported at its current cost stated in end-of-year constant dollars of $60,000. Note that this is the same amount as reported under the current cost/nominal dollar approach. For the $60,000 to be a current cost it would have to be a year-end amount. Conversion would be required, however, if average-year or base-year dollars were used.

In the example, the $60,000 current cost/constant dollar land amount is $40,000 higher than the $20,000 reported under the historical cost/nominal dollar approach. As explained earlier, this is an unrealized holding gain. However, only part of the $40,000 total unrealized holding gain is real; a portion of it is an inflationary component or fictitious holding gain due to changes in the general purchasing power of the dollar. This concept can be illustrated by the following diagram:

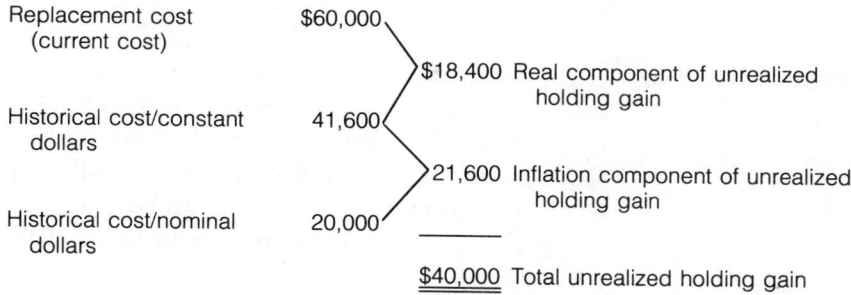

Replacement cost (current cost)	$60,000	
		$18,400 Real component of unrealized holding gain
Historical cost/constant dollars	41,600	
		21,600 Inflation component of unrealized holding gain
Historical cost/nominal dollars	20,000	
		$40,000 Total unrealized holding gain

However, it should be noted that in presenting financial statements on a current cost/constant dollar basis, the inflationary component is not reported separately. The constant dollar adjustment is made for all non-monetary items, and only the real component of unrealized holding gains is shown as a separate item. In the Campus Supply example, only the $18,400 holding gain on the land would be disclosed.

This example shows the impact of both general and specific price changes on only one item. It is indeed a complex problem to determine and report such information for all items on a balance sheet as well as to trace the impact of real and inflationary and realized and unrealized holding gains and losses through the income and retained earnings statements.

The FASB Experiment

FASB Statement No. 33 was published in September 1979 as an experiment in requiring supplementary information concerning the effects of changing prices on business enterprises. The statement initially required large, public companies to disclose both constant dollar and current cost information for the current year as well as summary data for the most recent five-year period. Subsequently, requirements for the disclosure of certain constant dollar data were eliminated, and other disclosure requirements were modified.

When Statement No. 33 was issued, the FASB indicated that it would review the results of the reporting requirements after five years. The Board has now completed that review and has concluded that further supplementary disclosures should be encouraged, but are not required. The primary basis for this decision seems to be a lack of public interest in and use of the supplemental data and a feeling that whatever benefits may be derived from the disclosures are not equal to the costs of providing the information.

The decision of the FASB to, in effect, rescind Statement No. 33 was not unanimous. Some members of the Board, and no doubt others, believe that inflation and specific price changes cause historical cost statements to show illusory profits and to hide the erosion of capital. These accountants view supplemental disclosures of changing prices as being relevant information necessary to prevent users from making incorrect economic decisions.

Prospects For The Future

It is possible that some companies will continue to disclose supplemental information concerning changing prices. Other companies, however, will discontinue the supplementary disclosures since there is no reporting requirement and little public interest. If inflation rates increase to higher levels, however, this topic may again become controversial, with increased pressure to consider additional reporting on a basis other than historical cost/nominal dollar.

Key Terms   Constant dollar accounting 1128
Current cost accounting 1128
Current cost 1139
Historical cost/nominal dollar 1127
Inflation 1127
Monetary items 1134
Net monetary position 1135

Nonmonetary items 1134
Price index 1131
Realized holding gains and losses
 1139
Unrealized holding gains and losses
 1140

Questions   1. (a) Why have accountants traditionally preferred to report historical costs rather than current costs in conventional statements? (b) What are some of the limitations of historical cost statements?

2. What are the 3 alternatives to reporting historical cost/nominal dollar financial statements and how do they differ from conventional reporting practice.

3. (a) What are general purchasing power dollars? (b) How are they different from equivalent purchasing power units?

4. Historically, what has caused an increased interest in reporting financial statements adjusted for price changes?

5. (a) How does constant dollar reporting differ from current cost reporting? (b) What is the objective of constant dollar reporting and how is this objective accomplished?

6. (a) How are general price indexes computed? (b) What are some of their limitations? (c) Which index is recommended by the FASB?

7. If equipment was purchased for $85,000 at the beginning of the year when the CPI-U was 160, how would the equipment be recorded on a constant dollar end-of-year balance sheet if the year-end CPI-U was 180?

8. (a) Distinguish between monetary assets and nonmonetary assets. (b) Which of the following are monetary assets?
    (1) Cash
    (2) Investment in common stock
    (3) Investment in bonds
    (4) Merchandise on hand
    (5) Prepaid expenses
    (6) Buildings
    (7) Patents
    (8) Sinking fund—uninvested cash
    (9) Sinking fund—investments in real estate
   (10) Deferred development costs

9. Assume a company holds property or maintains the obligations listed below during a year in which there is an increase in the general price level. State in each case whether the real position of the company at the end of the year is better, worse, or unchanged.
    (a) Cash
    (b) Cash surrender value of life insurance
    (c) Land
    (d) Unearned subscription revenue
    (e) Accounts receivable
    (f) Notes payable
    (g) Inventory
    (h) Long-term warranties on sales

10. Indicate whether a company sustains a gain or loss in purchasing power under each of the following conditions.
    (a) A company maintains an excess of monetary assets over monetary liabilities during a period of general price-level increase.
    (b) A company maintains an excess of monetary liabilities over monetary assets during a period of general price-level increase.
    (c) A company maintains an excess of monetary assets over monetary liabilities during a period of general price-level decrease.
    (d) A company maintains an excess of monetary liabilities over monetary assets during a period of general price-level decrease.
11. (a) What is the objective of current cost accounting? (b) Give examples of definitions of current costs?
12. Define the concept of well-offness.
13. (a) Distinguish between realized and unrealized holding gains and losses. (b) Distinguish between the real and inflationary components of total holding gains and losses.
14. What are the two recommended approaches used to determine appropriate current values?
15. Briefly explain the advantages and disadvantages of current cost accounting as compared to constant dollar and historical cost accounting.
16. Distinguish between the current cost/constant dollar approach and the current cost/nominal dollar approach to financial reporting.

Discussion Cases

Case 25–1   (Which reporting alternative is best?)

At a recent executive committee meeting, the officers of Celebrar Corporation entered into a lively discussion concerning changing prices in the economy and financial reporting. Kyle Jones, the controller, argued that the FASB was smart to experiment with reporting alternatives in Statement No. 33 since something must be done to reflect price changes. The economic analyst, Marie Colton, argued strongly for a current cost approach. Colton had little good to say about "irrelevant" historical costs, even if adjusted to constant dollars. Ted Starley, the marketing V.P., on the other hand, felt comfortable with historical cost data. Starley understands that approach and has confidence in the objectivity of the numbers reported. As president of the company, what position do you take?

Case 25–2   (Constant dollar theory)

Published financial statements of United States companies are currently prepared on a "stable-dollar" assumption even though the general purchasing power of the dollar has declined considerably because of inflation over the past several years. To account for this changing value of the dollar, many accountants suggest that financial statements should be adjusted for general price-level changes. Two independent statements regarding constant dollar financial statements follow. Each statement contains some fallacious reasoning.

Statement 1

The accounting profession has not seriously considered constant dollar financial statements before because the rate of inflation usually has been so small from year-to-year that the adjustments would have been immaterial in amount. Constant dollar financial statements represent a departure from the historical-cost basis of accounting. Financial statements should be prepared from facts, not estimates.

Statement 2

If financial statements were adjusted for general price-level changes, depreciation charges in the earnings statement would permit the recovery of dollars of current purchasing power and, thereby, equal the cost of new assets to replace the old ones. Constant dollar adjusted data would yield balance sheet amounts closely approximating current values. Furthermore, management can make better decisions if constant dollar financial statements are published.

Evaluate each of the independent statements and identify the areas of fallacious reasoning in each and explain why the reasoning is incorrect.

(AICPA adapted)

Case 25–3 (Current valuation of assets)

The financial statements of a business entity could be prepared by using historical cost or current value as a measurement basis. In addition, the basis could be stated in terms of unadjusted dollars or dollars restated for changes in purchasing power. The various combinations of these two separate and distinct areas are shown in the following matrix:

	Unadjusted dollars	Dollars restated for changes in purchasing power
Historical cost	1	2
Current value	3	4

Block number 1 of the matrix represents the traditional method of accounting for transactions, wherein the absolute (unadjusted) amount of dollars given up or received is recorded for the asset or liability obtained (relationship between resources). Amounts recorded in the method described in block 1 reflect the original cost of the asset or liability and do not take into account any change in value of the unit of measure (standard of comparison). This method assumes the validity of the accounting concepts of going concern and stable monetary unit. Any gain or loss (including holding and purchasing power gains or losses) resulting from the sale or satisfaction of amounts recorded under this method is deferred in its entirety until sale or satisfaction.

For each of the remaining matrix blocks respond to the following questions. Limit your discussion to nonmonetary assets only.

(1) How will this method of recording assets affect the relationship between resources and the standard of comparison?

(2) What is the theoretic justification for using each method?

(AICPA adapted)

Exercises   **Exercise 25–1   (Classification of monetary and nonmonetary items)**

Classify the following accounts as either monetary or nonmonetary.

<table>
<tr><td align="center">Assets</td><td align="center">Liabilities and Stockholders' Equity</td></tr>
<tr><td valign="top">

Current assets:
  Cash
  Marketable securities (stocks)
  Receivables (net of allowance)
  Inventories
  Prepaid rent
  Discount on notes payable
  Deferred tax asset
Long-term investments:
  Affiliated companies, at cost
  Cash surrender value of life insurance
  Bond sinking fund
  Investment in bonds
Land, buildings, and equipment:
  Land
  Buildings
  Equipment
Intangible assets:
  Patents
  Goodwill
Advances paid on purchase contracts

</td><td valign="top">

Current liabilities:
  Accounts and notes payable
  Dividends payable
  Refundable deposits on returnable
    containers
  Advances on sales contracts
Long-term liabilities:
  Bonds payable
  Premium on bonds payable
Stockholders' equity:
  Preferred stock (at fixed liquidation price)
  Common stock
  Retained earnings

</td></tr>
</table>

Exercise 25–2   (Computing purchasing power gains or losses)

On January 1, 1991, Camden Corporation had monetary assets of $5,000,000 and monetary liabilities of $2,000,000. During 1991, Camden's monetary inflows and outflows were relatively constant and equal so that it ended the year with net monetary assets of $3,000,000.

(1) Assume that the CPI-U was 200 on January 1, 1991, and 220 on December 31, 1991. In end-of-year constant dollars, what is Camden's purchasing power gain or loss for 1991?

(2) Assume that the CPI-U was 200 on January 1, 1991, and 180 on December 31, 1991. In average-year constant dollars, what is Camden's purchasing power gain or loss for 1991?   (AICPA adapted)

Exercise 25–3   (Adjusting expenses to constant dollars)

Assuming prices rise evenly by 6% during the year, compute the amount of expenses stated in terms of year-end constant dollars in each of the following independent cases:

(a) Expenses of $1,000,000 were paid at the beginning of the year for services received during the first half of the year.

(b) Expenses of $250,000 were paid at the end of each quarter for services received during the quarter.

(c) Expenses of $250,000 were paid at the beginning of each quarter for services received during the quarter.

(d) Expenses of $1,000,000 were paid evenly throughout the year for services received during the year.

Exercise 25–4 (Constant dollar depreciation)

The financial statements for Superior Corp. showed the original cost of depreciable assets purchased over the years as $3,500,000 at December 31, 1990, and $4,200,000 at December 31, 1991. These assets are being depreciated on a straight-line basis over a 10-year period with no residual value. Acquisitions of $700,000 were made on January 1, 1991. A full year's depreciation was taken in the year of acquisition.

Superior presents constant dollar financial statements as supplemental information to its historical cost financial statements. The December 31, 1991, depreciable asset balance (before accumulated depreciation) restated to reflect 1991 average purchasing power was $4,060,000.

Compute the amount of depreciation expense that should be shown in the constant dollar income statement for 1991 if the general price-level index was 110 at December 31, 1990, and 130 at December 31, 1991. Assume that the constant dollar financial statements are to be expressed in average 1991 dollars.

Exercise 25–5 (Constant dollar restatement of income and retained earnings statement)

A comparative income statement for the Linquist Company for the first 2 years of operations appears below.

	Results of Operations			
	First Year		Second Year	
Sales		$750,000		$900,000
Cost of goods sold:				
Beginning inventory		—	$300,000	
Purchases	$750,000		500,000	
Goods available for sale	$750,000		$800,000	
Ending inventory	300,000	450,000	400,000	400,000
Gross profit on sales		$300,000		$500,000
Operating expenses:				
Depreciation	$ 30,000		$ 30,000	
Other	240,000	270,000	350,000	380,000
Net income		$ 30,000		$120,000
Dividends		15,000		30,000
Increase in retained earnings		$ 15,000		$ 90,000

Prepare a comparative income and retained earnings statement expressing items in constant dollars at the end of the second year, considering the following data:

(a) Prices rose evenly and index numbers expressing the general price-level changes were:

Beginning of first year	100
End of first year	110
End of second year	140

(b) Sales and purchases were made and expenses were incurred evenly each year.

(c) Inventories were reported at cost using first-in, first-out pricing; average indexes for the year are applicable in restating inventories.

(d) Depreciation relates to equipment acquired at the beginning of the first year.

(e) Dividends were paid at the middle of each year.

(f) Assume no purchasing power gain or loss in either year.

Exercise 25–6   (Constant dollar restatement of balance sheet)

Comparative balance sheet data for Fletch Inc., since its formation appear below. The general price level during the 2-year period went up steadily; index numbers expressing the general price-level changes are listed following the balance sheet. Restate the comparative balance sheet data in terms of constant dollars at the end of the second year.

	End of First Year	End of Second Year
Cash	$ 90,000	$ 75,000
Receivables	60,000	84,000
*Land, buildings, and equipment (net)	156,000	138,000
	$306,000	$297,000
Payables	$ 81,000	$ 54,000
Capital stock	192,000	192,000
Retained earnings	33,000	51,000
	$306,000	$297,000

*Acquired at the beginning of the first year.

General Price Index	
At the beginning of the first year	106
At the end of the first year	120
At the end of the second year	130

Exercise 25–7   (Adjustment to average-year constant dollars)

The historical cost/constant dollar income statement of the Dunn Corporation shows a puchasing power loss of $3,000 based on end-of-year constant dollars. Price indexes were as follows:

Beginning of year	120
Average	145
End of year	170

Calculate the purchasing power loss in average-year dollars.

Exercise 25–8   (Current cost income)

On January 1, 1991, Outerspace Corp. purchased 1,000 robots at $25 per robot. As of December 31, 1991, Outerspace had sold three-fourths of the robots at $32 per robot, and the robot manufacturer (supplier) was selling to retailers (Outerspace) at $28 per robot.

Compute the operating gross profit for 1991 on a current-cost basis. Also identify the amount of realized holding gain and unrealized holding gain. Ignore income taxes.

Exercise 25–9 (Current cost depreciation)

Detmer Company began operating on December 31, 1988, at which time it purchased operating machinery for $3,000,000. These assets were expected to have a 15-year life with no residual value and are to be depreciated using the straight-line method:

The following information is available:

(a) Current value of assets (as if new)
December 31, 1990	$5,000,000
December 31, 1991	5,500,000

(b) General price-level index values:
December 31, 1988	120
December 31, 1990	140
December 31, 1991	155
1991 average (rounded)	148

Compute the following:

(1) Current value depreciation expense for 1991 in terms of average dollars from 1991.

(2) Realized holding gains from the use (and depreciation) of the asset during 1991 measured in terms of average dollars from 1991.

Exercise 25–10 (Current cost/constant dollar balance sheet)

The current cost/nominal dollar balance sheet for the Josh Corporation at December 31, 1991, is shown below. The equipment and land were purchased at year end. The inventory is valued at year-end current prices. The capital stock was issued when the consumer price index was 240. The consumer price index at December 31, 1991 was 270. Prepare a current cost/constant dollar balance sheet for the Josh Corporation at December 31, 1991, stated in end-of-year constant dollars.

Josh Corporation
Balance Sheet
December 31, 1991
(Current Cost/Nominal Dollar Basis)

Assets		Liabilities and Stockholders' Equity	
Cash	$ 10,000	Accounts payable	$ 20,000
Accounts receivable	15,000	Interest payable	10,000
Inventory	30,000	Total liabilities	$ 30,000
Equipment (net)	50,000	Captial stock	$ 80,000
Land	45,000	Retained earnings	40,000
		Total stockholders' equity	$120,000
		Total liabilities and	
Total assets	$150,000	stockholders' equity	$150,000

Exercise 25–11 (Reporting alternatives)

Gifford Company purchased land for $150,000 in 1990 when the price index was 150. At the end of 1991 when the price index was 175, the land had a fair market value of $180,000. How would the land be reported on the balance sheet under each of the following approaches?

(a) Historical cost/nominal dollar
(b) Historical cost/constant dollar
(c) Current cost/nominal dollar
(d) Current cost/constant dollar (year-end dollars)

Problems   **Problem 25–1   (Constant dollar adjustments and replacement costs)**

Valuation to reflect constant dollar adjustments would yield differing amounts on a firm's financial statements as opposed to replacement costs.

Transactions regarding one asset of a company whose calendar year is from January 1 to December 31 are as follows:

> 1989 Purchased land for $48,000 cash on December 31. Replacement cost at year-end was $48,000.
> 1990 Held land all year. Replacement cost at year-end was $62,400.
> 1991 December 31—sold land for $81,600.

General price-level index at:	
December 31, 1989	120
December 31, 1990	132
December 31, 1991	144

Instructions: Duplicate the following schedule and complete the information required based on the foregoing transactions. Express all constant dollar amounts in year-end dollars. Do not distinguish between realized and unrealized holding gains.

	Historical Cost		Replacement Costs	
	Nominal Dollar	Constant Dollar	Unadjusted for Inflation	Adjusted for Inflation
Valuation of land:				
December 31, 1989				
December 31, 1990				
Gain on income statement:				
1989				
1990				
1991				
Total				

(AICPA adapted)

▌ Problem 25–2   (Constant dollar adjustment for cost of goods sold and depreciation)

The following information was taken from the books of the Top Value Company during its first 2 years of operations:

	Useful Life	1990	1991
Beginning inventory		$150,000	$200,000
Purchases		550,000	500,000
Ending inventory.......................		200,000	160,000
Building (acquired 1/1/90).............	25 years	400,000	—
Office equipment (acquired 7/1/90).....	12 years	30,000	—
Machinery (acquired 10/1/90)...........	8 years	16,000	—
Price index (1/1).......................		190	202
Price index (12/31)*....................		202	214

*Assume prices rose evenly throughout the year.

Instructions:

(1) Calculate the cost of goods sold for 1990 and 1991 in terms of respective year-end dollars assuming a LIFO inventory cost flow with average costs used for any increments. Assume the 1990 beginning inventory was purchased on January 1, 1990. Round to the nearest dollar amount.

(2) Restate depreciable assets and accumulated depreciation (straight-line, ignore salvage values) reporting the depreciation for 1990 and 1991 in terms of 1990 and 1991 year-end dollars respectively.

Problem 25—3   (Converting nominal dollar financial data to constant dollars)

Midwest Inc., a retailer, was organized during 1988. Midwest's management has decided to supplement its December 31, 1991, historical dollar financial statements with constant dollar financial statements. The following general ledger trial balance (historical dollar) and additional information have been furnished.

Midwest, Inc.
Trial Balance
December 31, 1991

	Debits	Credits
Cash and Receivables (net)	432,000	
Marketable Securities (common stock)	320,000	
Inventory	352,000	
Equipment	520,000	
Equipment—Accumulated Depreciation		131,200
Accounts Payable		240,000
6% First-Mortgage Bonds, Due 1996		400,000
Common Stock, $8 par		800,000
Retained Earnings, December 31, 1990 (Deficit)......	36,800	
Sales		1,520,000
Cost of Sales.......................................	1,206,400	
Depreciation	52,000	
Other Operating Expenses and Interest	172,000	
Total	3,091,200	3,091,200

(a) Monetary assets (cash and receivables) exceeded monetary liabilities (accounts payable and bonds payable) by $356,000 at December 31, 1990.

(b) Purchases ($1,152,000 in 1991) and sales are made evenly throughout the year.

(c) Depreciation is computed on a straight-line basis, with a full year's depreciation being taken in the year of acquisition and none in the year of retirement. The depreciation rate is 10%, and no residual value is anticipated. Acquisitions and retirements have been made evenly over each year, and the retirements in 1991 consisted of assets purchased during 1989 that were scrapped. No cash was received.

An analysis of the equipment account reveals the following:

Year	Beginning Balance	Additions	Retirements	Ending Balance
1989		440,000		440,000
1990	440,000	8,000		448,000
1991	448,000	120,000	48,000	520,000

(d) The bonds were issued in 1989, and the marketable securities were purchased evenly over 1991. Other operating expenses and interest were incurred evenly throughout the year and paid with cash.

(e) Assume that the relevant price-index values were as follows:

Annual Average		Quarterly Average	
1989	110	1990	
1990	122	Fourth	123
1991	128	1991	
		First	124
		Second	128
		Third	127
		Fourth	130

Instructions: In completing the following requirements, use constant dollars from the fourth quarter of 1991.

(1) Prepare a schedule to convert the equipment account balance at December 31, 1991, from nominal to constant dollars.

(2) Prepare (in nominal dollars) an analysis of the Accumulated Depreciation—Equipment account for the years 1989 through 1991.

(3) Prepare a schedule to express the Accumulated Depreciation—Equipment account balance as of December 31, 1991, in terms of constant dollars.

(4) Prepare a schedule to compute Midwest's purchasing power gain or loss on its net holdings or monetary assets for 1991.   (AICPA adapted)

Problem 25-4   (Analysis of EPS & ROI in terms of constant dollars)

To obtain a more realistic appraisal of her investment, Sheri West, your client, has asked you to adjust certain financial data of the International Company for general price-level changes. On January 1, 1989, West invested $50,000 in the International Company in return for 10,000 shares of common stock. Immediately after her investment, the trial balance data appeared as follows:

Cash and Receivables	65,200	
Merchandise Inventory	4,000	
Building	50,000	
Accumulated Depreciation—Building		8,000
Equipment	36,000	
Accumulated Depreciation—Equipment		7,200
Land	10,000	
Current Liabilities		50,000
Capital Stock, $5 par		100,000
	165,200	165,200

Balances in certain selected accounts as of December 31, 1989-1991, were as follows:

	1989	1990	1991
Sales	$39,650	$39,000	$42,350
Inventory	4,500	5,600	5,347
Purchases	14,475	16,350	18,150
Operating expenses (excluding depreciation)	10,050	9,050	9,075

Assume the 1989 price level as the base year and all changes in the price level take place at the beginning of each year. Further assume the 1990 price level is 10% above the 1989 price level and the 1991 price level is 10% above the 1990 level.

The building was constructed in 1985 at a cost of $50,000 with an estimated life of 25 years. The price level at that time was 80% of the 1989 price level.

The equipment was purchased in 1987 at a cost of $36,000 with an estimated life of 10 years. The price level at that time was 90% of the 1989 price level.

The LIFO method of inventory valuation is used. The original inventory was acquired in the same year the building was constructed and was maintained at a constant $4,000 until 1989. In 1989 a gradual buildup of the inventory was begun in anticipation of an increase in the volume of business.

West considers the return on her investment as the dividend she actually receives. In 1989 and also in 1991 the International Company paid cash dividends in the amount of $4,000.

Instructions:

(1) Compute the 1991 earnings per share of common stock in terms of 1989 dollars.
(2) Compute the percentage return on the investment for 1989 and 1991 in terms of 1989 dollars.

(AICPA adapted)

Problem 25–5   (Restatement of balance sheet to constant dollars)

The Layton Co. began operations in 1960. At the end of 1991 it was decided to furnish stockholders with a balance sheet restated in terms of constant 1991 dollars as a supplement to the conventional financial statements. This is the first time such a statement was prepared. The balance sheet prepared in conventional form at the end of 1991 follows.

Layton Co.
Balance Sheet
December 31, 1991

Cash.....................	$ 187,600	Accounts payable	$ 379,900
Accounts receivable	342,400	Mortgage note payable	450,000
Inventory	742,300	Bonds payable	1,250,000
Land......................	1,720,000	Capital stock	1,000,000
Building	2,115,000	Additonal paid-in captial	200,000
Less accumulated depreciation	(705,000)	Retained earnings	1,122,400
		Total liabilities and	
Total assets.................	$4,402,300	stockholders' equity	$4,402,300

All the stock was issued in 1960. Land was purchased subject to a mortgage note of $1,000,000 at the time the company was formed. The present building is being depreciated on a straight-line basis with a 30-year life and no salvage value. The bonds were issued in 1970. The company uses the first-in, first-out method in pricing inventories.

Instructions: Prepare a balance sheet for the Layton Co. restated in terms of 1991 constant dollars. Use the following indexes in making adjustments; assume the index for each year is regarded as repesentative of the price level for the entire year.

Year	Price Index	Year	Price Index
1960	54.9	1988	160.1
1970	70.7	1989	168.0
1980	93.0	1990	178.6
1982	100.0	1991	185.2
1987	146.5		

Problem 25—6   (Restatement of income statement to constant dollars)

The income statement prepared at the end of the year for Novasano Corporation follows:

Novasano Corporation
Income Statement
For Year Ended December 31, 1991

Sales		$350,000
Less sales discount		15,000
Net sales		$335,000
Cost of goods sold:		
Inventory, January 1................................	$125,000	
Purchases	180,000	
Goods available for sale	$305,000	
Inventory, December 31	120,000	
Cost of goods sold................................		185,000
Gross profit on sales		$150,000
Operaing expenses:		
Depreciation	$ 21,250	
Other operating expenses.........................	50,000	
Total operating expenses		71,250
Income before income tax		$ 78,750
Income tax		31,300
Net income		$ 47,450

The following additional data are available:

(a) The price index rose evenly throughout the year from 120 on January 1 to 130 on December 31.

(b) Sales were made evenly throughout the year; expenses were incurred evenly throughout the year.

(c) The inventory was valued at cost using first-in, first-out pricing; average indexes for the year are used in restating inventories. The beginning inventory was acquired in the preceding period when the average index was 122.

(d) The depreciation charge related to the following items:

	Asset Cost	Index at Date of Acquisition	Deprecation Rate
Building	$75,000	95	3 %
Equipment	80,000	95	12½%
Equipment	20,000	98	12½%
Equipment*	39,000	120	16⅔%

*Acquired at the beginning of the current year.

(e) Semiannual dividends of $7,500 were declared and paid at the end of June and at the end of December.

(f) The balance sheet position for the company changed during the year as follows:

	January 1	December 31
Current assets	$180,000	$174,700
Building and equipment (net)	120,000	137,750
	$300,000	$312,450
Current liabilities	$ 55,000	$ 35,000
Captial stock	200,000	200,000
Retained earnings	45,000	77,450
	$300,000	$312,450

Instructions: Prepare an income statement in which items are stated in end-of-year dollars accompanied by a schedule summarizing the purchasing power gain or loss for 1991.

III Problem 25–7   (Restatement of financial statements to constant dollars)

Financial statements are prepared for the Missouri Company at the end of each year in nominal dollars and are also measured in constant dollars. Balance sheet data summarized in nominal dollars and in constant dollars at the end of 1990 are given on the following page:

	Nominal Dollars	Constant Dollars (Reporting Purchasing Power at End of Year)
Assets:		
Cash.............................	$ 23,000	$ 23,000
Accounts receivable...............	70,000	70,000
Inventory	105,000	106,500
Buildings and equipment........... $120,000		$153,600
Less accumulated depreciation ... 48,000	72,000	61,440 92,160
Land................................	50,000	64,000
Total assets......................	$320,000	$355,660
Liabilities:		
Accounts payable.................	$ 48,000	$ 48,000
Long-term liabilities	40,000	40,000
Total liabilities	$ 88,000	$ 88,000
Stockholders' equity:		
Capital stock	$150,000	$192,000
Retained earnings	82,000	75,660
Total stockholders' equity	$232,000	$267,660
Total liabilities and stockholders' equity	$320,000	$355,660

Data from statements measured in nominal dollars at the end of 1991 are given below:

Balance Sheet		Income and Retained Earnings Statement	
Assets		Sales	$1,100,000
Cash......................	$ 83,840	Cost of goods sold	600,000
Accounts receivable	72,500	Gross profit on sales	$ 500,000
Inventory	125,000	Operating expenses	308,000
Buildings and equipment	120,000	Income before income tax	$ 192,000
Accumulated depreciation ...	(56,000)	Income tax	85,660
Land.......................	50,000	Net income	$ 106,340
	$395,340	Dividends	20,000
Liabilites and Stockholders' Equity		Increase in retained earnings	$ 86,340
Accounts payable	$ 37,000		
Long-term liabilities	40,000		
Capital stock	150,000		
Retained earnings	168,340		
	$395,340		

The following additional data are available at the end of 1991:

(a) Price indexes were as follows for the year:

January 1	150
December 31	153

(b) Sales and purchases were made evenly, and expenses were incurred evenly, throughout the year.

(c) The first-in, first-out method was used to compute inventory cost; average indexes for the year are used in restating inventories.

(d) All the land, buildings, and equipment were acquired when the compnay was formed.

(e) Dividends were declared and paid at the end of the year.

Instructions: Prepare in terms of end-of-year constant dollars: (1) an income and retained earnings statement accompanied by a schedule summarizing the purchasing power gain or loss for 1991, (2) a balance sheet as of December 31, 1991.

Problem 25–8 (Reporting constant dollar information)

The historical cost income statement for the Colorado Company is presented below.

Colorado Company
Income Statement
For the Year Ended December 31, 1991

Sales		$180,000
Cost of goods sold:		
Beginning inventory	$ 20,000	
Purchases	140,000	
Goods available for sale	$160,000	
Ending inventory	50,000	
Cost of goods sold		110,000
Gross profit		$ 70,000
Operating expenses:		
Depreciation expense	$ 10,000	
Other expenses	20,000	30,000
Net income		$ 40,000

The following additional information is provided:

(a) Sales, purchases, and other expenses were incurred evenly over the year.
(b) The beginning inventory was purchased when the price index was 180. Assume the ending inventory was acquired when the price index was 220.
(c) Price indexes were as follows:

Beginning of year	200
Average for year	220
End of year	240

(d) The equipment on which the depreciation expense is computed was purchased when the price index was 110.

Instructions: Prepare a statement showing income from continuing operations in average-year constant dollars.

Problem 25–9 (Current cost accounting)

Hastings Inc. adopted a current cost system in its first year of operations. At the start of the first year, 1991, the company purchased $168,000 of inventory, and at the end of the year had an inventory of $100,800 on a historical cost basis and $164,500 on a current cost basis. At the time the inventory was sold, the current cost of the inventory was $107,800. Sales for the year were $182,000. Ignore all tax effects and assume that CPI-U did not change over this period. Other expenses were $8,400 on both historical cost and current cost basis.

Instructions:

(1) Prepare a current cost income statement.
(2) What is the increase in the specific price of inventory during the year?

Chapter 26

Financial Statement Analysis

Accounting provides information to assist various individuals in making economic decisions. A significant amount of information relevant to this purpose is presented in the primary financial statements of companies. Additional useful information is provided by financial data reported by means other than the financial statements. However, as explained in Chapter 2, financial data are only part of the total information needed by decision makers. Nonfinancial information may also be relevant. Thus, the total information spectrum is broader than just financial reporting. It encompasses financial statements, financial reporting by means other than the financial statements, and additional nonfinancial information.

The Financial Accounting Standards Board has restricted its focus to general-purpose external financial reporting by business enterprises. This chapter concentrates on analysis of information in the primary financial statements. Notes are an integral part of financial statements, and significant accounting policies and other information included in notes should be considered carefully in performing an analysis and in evaluating results. Supplementary information should also be considered in interpreting financial statement data.

Objectives of Financial Statement Analysis

Financial analysis is necessary for intelligent decision making. Nearly all businesses prepare financial statements of some type; the form and complexity of the statements vary according to the decisions to be made by those who use them. The owner of a small business might simply list the firm's cash receipts and disbursements and use this to prepare an income tax return. On the other hand, a large corporation's accounting staff spends considerable time in preparing the company's complex financial statements that can be used for many types of decisions.

Whatever their form, financial statements provide information about a business and its operation to interested users. For example, questions concerning matters such as a company's sales, net income, and trends for these items; the amount of working capital and changes in working capital; the relationship of income to sales, and of income to investments may be raised by creditors making a lending decision. Identifying these relationships requires analysis of data reported on the income statement, the balance sheet, and the statement of cash flows. Internal management is also concerned with analyzing the general-purpose financial statements, but requires additional special information in setting policies and making decisions. Questions may arise on matters such as the performance of various company divisions, the income from sales of individual products, and whether to make or buy product parts and equipment. Decisions on these matters can be made by establishing internal information systems to provide the necessary data. Thus, in analyzing financial data, the nature of analysis and the information needed depend on the decision needs of users and the issues involved.

The analyses of financial data described in this chapter are directed primarily to the information needs of external users who must generally rely on the financial reports prepared by a company. Many groups are interested in the data found in financial statements, including:

1. Owners—sole proprietor, partners, or stockholders.
2. Management, including board of directors.
3. Creditors.
4. Government—local, state, and federal (including regulatory, taxing, and statistical units).
5. Prospective owners and prospective creditors.
6. Stock exchanges, investment bankers, and stockbrokers.
7. Trade associations.
8. Employees of a business and their labor unions.
9. The general public.

Questions raised by these groups can generally be answered by analyses that develop comparisons and measure relationships between components of financial statements. The analyses will form a basis for decisions made by the user.

Analysis is generally directed toward evaluating four aspects of a business: (1) liquidity, (2) stability, (3) profitability, and (4) growth potential.

Liquidity relates to the ability of an enterprise to pay its liabilities as they mature. Financial statements are analyzed to determine whether a business is currently liquid and whether it could retain its liquidity in a period of adversity. The analysis includes studies of the relationship of current assets to current liabilities, the size and nature of creditor and ownership interests, the protection afforded creditors and owners through sound asset values, and the amounts and trends of net income. Creditors are especially concerned with the liquidity of their debtors.

Stability is measured by the ability of a business to make interest and principal payments on outstanding debt and to pay regular dividends to its stockholders. In judging stability, data concerning operations and financial position are studied. For example, there must be a regular demand for the goods or services sold, and the gross profit on sales must be sufficient to cover operating expenses, interest, and dividends. There should be a satisfactory turnover of assets, and all business resources should be productively employed.

Profitability is measured by the ability of a business to increase its ownership equity from its operations. The nature and amount of income, as well as its regularity and trend, are significant factors affecting profitability.

The **growth potential** of a company is also of primary importance to stockholders. This element, along with profitability, directly affects future cash flows derived from increased income and/or appreciation in stock values. Growth potential is measured by the expansion and growth into new markets, the rate of growth in existing markets, the rate of growth in earnings per share, and the amount of expenditures for research and development.

An analysis must serve the needs of those for whom it is made. For example, owners are interested in a company's ability to obtain additional capital for current needs and possible expansion. Creditors are interested not only in the position of a business as a going concern but also in its position should it be forced to liquidate.

Analytical Procedures

Analytical procedures fall into two main categories: (1) comparisons and measurements based on financial data for two or more periods, and (2) comparisons and measurements based on financial data of only the current fiscal period. The first category includes comparative statements, ratios and trends for data on successive statements, and analyses of changes in the balance sheet, income statement, and statement of cash flows. The second category includes determining current balance sheet and income statement relationships and analyzing earnings and earning power. A review of financial data usually requires both types of analysis.

The analytical procedures commonly employed may be identified as: comparative statements, index-number trend series, common-size statements, and analysis of financial statement components. These techniques are described and illustrated in the following sections. It should be emphasized that the analyses illustrated herein are simply guides to the evaluation of financial data. Sound conclusions can be reached only through intelligent use and interpretation of such data. The AC&W Corporation is used as an example throughout the chapter.

Comparative Statements

Financial data become more meaningful when compared with similar data for preceding periods. Statements reflecting financial data for two or more periods are called **comparative statements**. Annual data can be compared with similar data for prior years. Monthly or quarterly data can be compared with similar data for previous months or quarters or with similar data for the same months or quarters of previous years.

Comparative data allow statement users to analyze trends in a company, thus enhancing the usefulness of information for decision making. The Accounting Principles Board stated that comparisons between financial statements are most informative and useful under the following conditions:

1. The presentations are in good form; that is, the arrangement within the statements is identical.
2. The content of the statements is identical; that is, the same items from the underlying accounting records are classified under the same captions.
3. Accounting principles are not changed or, if they are changed, the financial effects of the changes are disclosed.
4. Changes in circumstances or in the nature of the underlying transactions are disclosed.[1]

To the extent that the foregoing criteria are not met, comparisons may be misleading. Consistent practices and procedures and reporting periods of equal and regular lengths are also important, especially when comparisons are made for a single enterprise.

Comparative financial statements may be even more useful to investors and others when the reporting format highlights absolute changes in dollar amounts as well as relative percentage changes. Statement users will benefit by considering both amounts as they make their analyses. For example, an investor may decide that any change in a financial statement amount of 10% or more should be investigated further. A 10% change in an amount of $1,000, however, is not as significant as a 5% change in an amount of $100,000. When absolute or relative amounts appear out of line, conclusions, favorable or unfavorable, are not justified until investigation has disclosed reasons for the changes.

The development of data measuring changes taking place over a number of periods is known as horizontal analysis. Using the AC&W Corporation's income statement as an example, and a reporting format that discloses dollar and percentage changes, horizontal analysis is illustrated on the following page.

Index-Number Trend Series

When comparative financial statements present information for more than two or three years, they become cumbersome and potentially confusing. A technique used to overcome this problem is referred to as an **index-number trend series**.

To compute index numbers, the statement preparer must first choose a base year. This may be the earliest year presented or some other year considered particularly appropriate. Next, the base year amounts are all expressed as 100%. The amounts for all other years are then stated as a percentage of the base year amounts. Index numbers can only be computed when amounts are positive. The set of percentages for several years may

[1]*Statements of the Accounting Principles Board, No. 4,* "Basic Concepts and Accounting Principles Underlying Financial Statements of Business Enterprises" (New York: American Institute of Certified Public Accountants, 1970), par. 95–99.

AC&W Corporation
Comparative Income Statement
For Years Ended December 31

	1992	1991	1990	Increase (Decrease)			
				1991-1992		1990-1991	
				Amount	Percent	Amount	Percent
Gross sales	$1,500,000	$1,750,000	$1,000,000	$(250,000)	(14%)	$750,000	75%
Sales returns	75,000	100,000	50,000	(25,000)	(25%)	50,000	100%
Net sales	$1,425,000	$1,650,000	$ 950,000	$(225,000)	(14%)	$700,000	74%
Cost of goods sold..	1,000,000	1,200,000	630,000	(200,000)	(17%)	570,000	90%
Gross profit on sales	$ 425,000	$ 450,000	$ 320,000	$ (25,000)	(6%)	$130,000	41%
Selling expense.....	$ 280,000	$ 300,000	$ 240,000	$ (20,000)	(7%)	$ 60,000	25%
General expense ...	100,000	110,000	100,000	(10,000)	(9%)	10,000	10%
Total operating expenses	$ 380,000	$ 410,000	$ 340,000	$ (30,000)	(7%)	$ 70,000	21%
Operating income (loss)	$ 45,000	$ 40,000	$ (20,000)	$ 5,000	13%	$ 60,000	—
Other revenue items	85,000	75,000	50,000	10,000	13%	25,000	50%
	$ 130,000	$ 115,000	$ 30,000	$ 15,000	13%	$ 85,000	283%
Other expense items	30,000	30,000	10,000	—	—	20,000	200%
Income before income tax	$ 100,000	$ 85,000	$ 20,000	$ 15,000	18%	$ 65,000	325%
Income tax.........	30,000	25,000	5,000	5,000	20%	20,000	400%
Net income	$ 70,000	$ 60,000	$ 15,000	$ 10,000	17%	$ 45,000	300%

thus be interpreted as trend values or as a series of index numbers relating to a particular item. For example, AC&W Corporation had gross sales of $1,000,000 in 1990, $1,750,000 in 1991, and $1,500,000 in 1992. These amounts, expressed in an index-number trend series with 1990 as the base year, would be 100, 175, and 150, respectively.

The index-number trend series technique is a type of horizontal analysis. It can give statement users a long-range view of a firm's financial position, earnings, and cash flow. The user needs to recognize, however, that long-range trend series are particularly sensitive to changing price levels.

Data expressed in terms of a base year are frequently useful for comparisons with similar data provided by business or industry sources or government agencies. When information used for making comparisons does not employ the same base period, it will have to be restated. Restatement of a base year calls for the expressing of each value as a percentage of the value for the base-year period.

To illustrate, assume the gross sales data for the AC&W Corporation for 1990-1992 are to be compard with a sales index for its particular industry. The industry sales indexes are as follows:

	1992	**1991**	**1990**
(1986 = 100)	146	157	124

Recognizing 1990 as the base year, industry sales are restated as follows:

1990		100
1991 (157 ÷ 124)		127
1992 (146 ÷ 124)		118

Industry sales and net sales for the AC&W Corporation can now be expressed in comparative form as follows:

	1992	1991	1990
Industry sales index	118	127	100
AC&W Corporation sales index*	150	175	100

*From comparative income statement on page 1165.

Common-Size Financial Statements

Horizontal analysis measures changes over a number of accounting periods. Statement users also need data that express relationships within a single period, which is known as **vertical analysis**. Preparation of **common-size financial statements** is a widely used vertical analysis technique. The common-size relationships may be stated in terms of percentages or in terms of ratios. Common-size statements may be prepared for the same business as of different dates or periods, or for two or more business units as of the same date or for the same period.

Common-size financial statements are useful in analyzing the internal structure of a financial statement. For example, a common-size balance sheet expresses each amount as a percentage of total assets usually expressed as a decimal fraction. A common-size income statement usually shows each revenue or expense item as a percentage of net sales. As an illustration, a comparative balance sheet for AC&W Corporation with each item expressed in both dollar amounts and percentages is shown below. Other types of common-size financial statements, e.g., a common-size retained earnings statement or statement of cash flows, may be prepared. When a supporting schedule shows the detail for a group total, individual items may be expressed as percentages of either the base figure or the group total.

Common-size analysis can also be used when comparing a company with other companies or with an entire industry. Differences in sizes of numbers in the financial statement are neutralized by reducing them to common-size ratios. Industry statistics are frequently published in common-size form, which facilitates making these types of comparisons. When comparing a company with other companies or with industry figures, it is important that the financial data for each company reflect comparable price levels. Furthermore, the financial data should be developed using comparable accounting methods, classification procedures, and valuation bases. Comparisons should be limited to companies engaged in similar activities. When the financial policies of two companies are different, these differences should be recognized in evaluating comparative reports. For example, one company may lease its properties while the other may purchase such items; one company may finance its operations using long-term borrowing while the other may rely primarily on funds supplied by stockhold-

AC&W Corporation
Comparative Balance Sheet
December 31

	1992		1991		1990	
	Amount	Common Size Ratio	Amount	Common Size Ratio	Amount	Common Size Ratio
Assets						
Current assets	$ 855,000	.38	$ 955,500	.40	$ 673,500	.38
Land, buildings, and equipment (net)	1,275,000	.56	1,275,000	.54	925,000	.52
Intangible assets	100,000	.04	100,000	.04	100,000	.06
Other assets	48,000	.02	60,500	.02	61,500	.04
Total assets	$2,278,000	1.00	$2,391,000	1.00	$1,760,000	1.00
Liabilities						
Current liabilities	$ 410,000	.18	$ 546,000	.23	$ 130,000	.07
Long-term liabilities—10% bonds	400,000	.18	400,000	.17	300,000	.17
Total liabilities	$ 810,000	.36	$ 946,000	.40	$ 430,000	.24
Stockholders' Equity						
Preferred 6% stock	$ 350,000	.15	$ 350,000	.15	$ 250,000	.14
Common stock	750,000	.33	750,000	.31	750,000	.43
Additional paid-in capital	100,000	.04	100,000	.04	100,000	.06
Retained earnings	268,000	.12	245,000	.10	230,000	.13
Total stockholders' equity	$1,468,000	.64	$1,445,000	.60	$1,330,000	.76
Total liabilities and stockholders' equity	$2,278,000	1.00	$2,391,000	1.00	$1,760,000	1.00

ers and by earnings. Financial statements for two companies under these circumstances cannot be wholly comparable.

All this suggests that comparisons between different companies should be evaluated with care, and should be made with a full understanding of the inherent limitations. Reference was made earlier to the criteria that the Accounting Principles Board identified if comparisons are to be meaningful. Comparability between enterprises is more difficult to obtain than comparability within a single enterprise. Ideally, differences in companies' financial reports should arise from basic differences in the companies themselves or from the nature of their transactions and not from differences in accounting practices and procedures.

Other Analytical Procedures

In addition to the financial statement analysis procedures described in the preceding sections, various measures may be developed with respect to specific components of financial statements. Some measurements are of general interest, while others have special significance to particular groups. Creditors, for example, are concerned with the ability of a company to pay its current obligations and seek information about the relationship of current assets to current liabilities. Stockholders are concerned with dividends and seek information relating to earnings that will form the basis for dividends. Managements are concerned with the activity of the merchandise stock and seek information relating to the number of times goods have turned over during the period. All users are vitally interested in profitability and wish to be informed about the relationship of income to both liabilities and owners' equity.

The computation of percentages, ratios, turnovers, and other measures of financial position and operating results for a period is a form of vertical analysis. Comparison with the same measures for other periods is a form of horizontal analysis. These comparisons can be made within a company's financial statements or with other companies, individually or in industry groups. The measures described and illustrated in the following sections should not be considered all-inclusive; other measures may be useful to various groups, depending on their particular needs. It should be emphasized again that sound conclusions cannot be reached from an individual measurement. But this information, together with adequate investigation and study, may lead to a satisfactory evaluation of financial data.

Liquidity Analysis   Generally, the first concern of a financial analyst is a firm's liquidity. Will the firm be able to meet its current obligations? If a firm cannot meet its obligations in the short run, it may not have a chance to be profitable or to experience growth in the long run. The two most commonly used measures of liquidity are the current ratio and the acid-test ratio.

Current Ratio

The comparison of current assets with current liabilities is regarded as a fundamental measurement of a company's liquidity. Known as the **current ratio** or **working capital ratio**, this measurement is computed by dividing total current assets by total current liabilities.

The current ratio is a measure of the ability to meet current obligations. Since it measures liquidity, care must be taken to determine that proper items have been included in the current asset and current liability categories. A ratio of current assets to current liabilities of less than 2 to 1 for a trading or manufacturing unit has frequently been considered unsatisfactory. However, because liquidity needs are different for different industries and companies, any such arbitrary measure should not be viewed as meaningful or appropriate in all cases. A comfortable margin of current assets over current liabilities suggests that a company will be able to meet maturing obligations even in the event of unfavorable business conditions or losses on such assets as marketable securities, receivables, and inventories.

For the AC&W Corporation, current ratios for 1992 and 1991 are developed as follows[2]:

	1992	1991
Current assets	$855,000	$955,500
Current liabilities	$410,000	$546,000
Current ratio	2.1:1	1.8:1

[2]Comparative data for more than two years are generally required in evaluating financial trends. Analyses for only two years are given in the examples in this chapter, since these are sufficient to illustrate the analytical procedures involved.

A current ratio of 2.1 to 1 means that AC&W could liquidate its total current liabilities 2.1 times using only its current assets.

The AC&W Corporation increased the current ratio in 1992 from 1.8:1 to 2.1:1. If no other information is available, this change may indicate some improvement in AC&W's liquidity position with improved ability to meet its current obligations. This conclusion may be in error, however, since the ratios do not disclose anything about the composition of the current assets. For example, past due receivables and slow moving inventories are generally classified as current assets, but they would not represent liquid assets. There is also the possibility, given the business risk in the organization and industry, that these ratios are too high. Assets may be kept unnecessarily liquid and thus not earn the higher returns associated with longer-term investments. Nevertheless, the current ratio is useful in analyzing the liquidity position of the organization. Added meaning is obtained when it is compared with the company's past data and industry standards.

Acid-Test Ratio

A test of a company's immediate liquidity is made by comparing the sum of cash, marketable securities, notes receivable, and accounts receivable, commonly referred to as quick assets, with current liabilities. The total quick assets divided by current liabilities gives the acid-test ratio or quick ratio. Considerable time may be required to convert raw materials, goods in process, and finished goods into receivables and then into cash. A company with a satisfactory current ratio may be in a relatively poor liquidity position when inventories comprise most of the total current assets. This is revealed by the acid-test ratio. In developing the ratio, the receivables and securities included in the total quick assets should be examined closely. In some cases these items may actually be less liquid than inventories.

Usually, a ratio of quick assets to current liabilities of at least 1 to 1 is considered desirable. Again, however, special conditions of the particular business must be evaluated. Questions such as the following should be considered: What is the composition of the quick assets? What special requirements are made by current activities upon these assets? How soon are current payables due?

Acid-test ratios for AC&W Corporation are computed as follows:

	1992	1991
Quick assets:		
Cash:	$ 60,000	$100,500
Marketable securities	150,000	150,000
Receivables (net)	420,000	375,000
Total quick assets	$630,000	$625,500
Total current liabilities	$410,000	$546,000
Acid-test ratio	1.5:1	1.1:1

Other Measures of Liquidity

Other ratios may help to analyze a company's liquidity. For example, it may be useful to show the relationship of total current assets to total assets and the relationship of individual current assets, such as receivables and inventories, to total current assets. In the case of liabilities, it may be useful to show the relationship of total current liabilities to total liabilities and the relationship of individual current liabilities to total current liabilities. Such comparisons may provide information concerning the relative liquidity of total assets and the maturity of total obligations as well as the structure of working capital and shifts within the working capital group.

Activity Analysis   There are special tests that may be applied to measure how efficiently a firm is utilizing its assets. Several of these measures also relate to liquidity because they involve significant working capital elements, such as receivables, inventories, and accounts payable.

Accounts Receivable Turnover

The amount of receivables usually bears a close relationship to the volume of credit sales. The receivable position and approximate collection time may be evaluated by computing the accounts receivable turnover. This rate is determined by dividing net credit sales (or total net sales if credit sales are unknown) by the average trade notes and accounts receivable outstanding. In developing an average receivables amount, monthly balances should be used if available.

Assume in the case of AC&W Corporation that all sales are made on credit, that receivables arise only from sales, and that receivable totals for only the beginning and the end of the year are available. Receivable turnover rates are computed as follows:

	1992	1991
Net credit sales	$1,425,000	$1,650,000
Net receivables:		
Beginning of year	$ 375,000	$ 333,500
End of year	$ 420,000	$ 375,000
Average receivables	$ 397,500	$ 354,250
Receivables turnover for year	3.6	4.7

Number of Days' Sales in Receivables

Average receivables are sometimes expressed in terms of the **number of days' sales in receivables,** which shows the average time required to collect receivables. Average receivables divided by average daily sales then gives the number of days' sales in average receivables. This procedure for AC&W Corporation is illustrated below.

	1992	1991
Average receivables	$ 397,500	$ 354,250
Net credit sales	$1,425,000	$1,650,000
Average daily credit sales (net credit sales ÷ 365)	$ 3,904	$ 4,521
Number of days' sales in average receivables (average receivable ÷ average daily credit sales)	102	78

This same measurement can be obtained by dividing the number of days in the year by the receivable turnover.

In some cases, instead of developing the number of days' sales in average receivables, it may be more useful to report the number of days' credit sales in receivables at the end of the period. This information would be significant in evaluating current position, and particularly the receivable position as of a given date. This information for AC&W Corporation is presented below:

	1992	1991
Receivables at end of year	$420,000	$375,000
Average daily credit sales	$ 3,904	$ 4,521
Number of days' sales in receivables at end of year	108	83

What constitutes a reasonable number of days in receivables varies with individual businesses. For example, if merchandise is sold on terms of net 60 days, 40 days' sales in receivables would be reasonable; but if terms are net 30 days, a receivable balance equal to 40 days' sales would indicate slow collections.

Sales activity just before the close of a period should be considered when interpreting accounts receivable measurements. If sales are unusually light or heavy just before the end of the fiscal period, this affects total receivables as well as the related measurements. When such unevenness prevails, it may be better to analyze accounts receivable according to their due dates, as was illustrated in Chapter 8.

The problem of minimizing accounts receivable without losing desirable business is important. Receivables often do not earn interest revenue, and the cost of carrying them must be covered by the profit margin. The longer accounts are carried, the smaller will be the percentage return realized on invested capital. In addition, heavier bookkeeping and collection charges and increased bad debts must be considered.

To attract business, credit is frequently granted for relatively long periods. The cost of granting long-term credit should be considered. Assume that a business has average daily credit sales of $5,000 and average accounts receivable of $250,000, which represents 50 days' credit sales. If collections and the credit period can be improved so that accounts receivable represent only 30 days' sales, then accounts receivable will be reduced to $150,000. Assuming a total cost of 10% to carry and service the accounts, the $100,000 decrease would yield annual savings of $10,000.

Inventory Turnover

The amount of inventory carried frequently relates closely to sales volume. The inventory position and the appropriateness of its size may be evaluated by computing the **inventory turnover**. The inventory turnover is computed by dividing cost of goods sold by average inventory. Whenever possible, monthly figures should be used to develop the average inventory balance.

Assume that for AC&W Corporation the inventory balances for only the beginning and the end of the year are available. Inventory turnover rates are computed as follows:

	1992	1991
Cost of goods sold	$1,000,000	$1,200,000
Inventory:		
Beginning of year	$ 330,000	$ 125,000
End of year	$ 225,000	$ 330,000
Average inventory	$ 277,500	$ 227,500
Inventory turnover for year	3.6	5.3

Number of Days' Sales in Inventories

Average inventories are sometimes expressed as the **number of days' sales in inventories**. Information is thus afforded concerning the average time it takes to turn over the inventory. The number of days' sales in inventories is calculated by dividing average inventory by average daily cost of goods sold. The number of days' sales can also be obtained by dividing the number of days in the year by the inventory turnover rate. The latter procedure for AC&W Corporation is illustrated below:

	1992	1991
Inventory turnover for year	3.6	5.3
Number of days' sales in average inventory (assuming a year of 365 days)	101	69

As was the case with receivables, instead of developing the number of days' sales in average inventories, it may be more useful to report the number of days' sales in ending inventories. The latter measurement is determined by dividing ending inventory by average daily cost of goods sold. This information is helpful in evaluating the current asset position and particularly the inventory position as of a given date.

A company with departmental classifications for inventories will find it desirable to support the company's inventory measurements with individual department measurements, since there may be considerable variation among departments. A manufacturing company may compute separate turnover rates for finished goods, goods in process, and raw materials. The finished goods turnover is computed by dividing cost of goods sold by average finished goods inventory. Goods in process turnover is computed by dividing cost of goods manufactured by average goods in process inventory. Raw materials turnover is computed by dividing the cost of raw materials used by average raw materials inventory.

The same valuation methods must be employed for inventories in successive periods if the inventory measurements are to be comparable. Maximum accuracy is possible if information relating to inventories and amount of goods sold is available in terms of physical units rather than dollar costs.

The effect of seasonal factors on the size of year-end inventories should be considered in inventory analyses. Inventories may be abnormally high or low at the end of a period. Many companies adopt a fiscal year ending when operations are at their lowest point. This is called a **natural business year**. Inventories will normally be lowest at the end of such a period, so that the organization can take inventory and complete year-end closing most conveniently. Under these circumstances, monthly inventory balances should be used to arrive at a representative average inventory figure. When a periodic inventory system is employed, monthly inventories may be estimated using the gross profit method as explained in Chapter 10.

With an increased inventory turnover, the investment necessary for a given volume of business is smaller, and consequently the return on invested capital is higher. This conclusion assumes an enterprise can acquire goods in smaller quantities sufficiently often at no price disadvantage. If merchandise must be bought in very large quantities in order to get favorable prices, then the savings on quantity purchases must be weighed against the additional investment, increased costs of storage, and other carrying charges.

The financial advantage of an increased turnover rate may be illustrated as follows. Assuming cost of goods sold of $1,000,000 and average inventory at cost of $250,000, inventory turnover is 4 times. Assume further that, through careful buying, the same business volume can be maintained with turnover of 5 times, or an average inventory of only $200,000. If interest on money invested in inventory is 10%, the savings on the $50,000 will be $5,000 annually. Other advantages include decreased inventory spoilage and obsolescence, savings in storage cost, taxes, and insurance, and reduction in risk of losses from price declines.

Inventory investments and turnover rates vary among businesses, and each business must be judged in terms of its financial structure and operations. Management must establish an inventory policy that will avoid the extremes of a dangerously low stock, which may impair sales, and an overstocking of goods involving a heavy capital investment and risks of spoilage and obsolescence, price declines, and difficulties in meeting purchase obligations.

Total Asset Turnover

A measure of the overall efficiency of asset utilization is the ratio of net sales to total assets called the **total asset turnover**. This ratio is calculated by dividing net sales by total assets. The resulting figure indicates the contribution made by total assets to sales. With comparative data, judgments can be made concerning the relative effectiveness of asset utilization. A ratio increase may suggest more efficient asset utilization, although a point may be reached where there is a strain on assets and a company is unable to achieve its full sales potential. An increase in total assets accompanied by a ratio decrease may suggest overinvestment in assets or inefficient utilization.

In developing the asset turnover rate, long-term investments should be excluded from total assets when they make no contribution to sales. On the other hand, a valuation for leased property should be added to total assets to permit comparability between companies owning their properties and those that lease them. If monthly figures for assets are available, they may be used in developing a representative average for total assets employed. Often the year-end asset total is used for the computation. When sales can be expressed in terms of units sold, ratios of sales units to total assets offer more reliable interpretations than sales dollars, since unit sales are not affected by price changes.

Assume that for AC&W Corporation only asset totals for the beginning and end of the year are available, and that sales cannot be expressed in terms of units. Ratios of net sales to total assets are computed as follows:

	1992	1991
Net sales	$1,425,000	$1,650,000
Total assets (excluding long-term investments):		
Beginning of year	$2,391,000	$1,760,000
End of year	$2,278,000	$2,391,000
Average total assets	$2,334,500	$2,075,500
Ratio of net sales to average total assets	0.6:1	0.8:1

Other Measures of Activity

Turnover analysis, as illustrated for receivables, inventories, and total assets, can also be applied to other assets or groups of assets. For example, current asset turnover is calculated by dividing net sales by average current assets. This figure may be viewed as the number of times current assets are replenished, or as the number of sales dollars generated per dollar of current assets. Similarly, if net sales are divided by plant assets, a plant asset turnover can be computed. This figure measures the efficiency of plant asset management and indicates the volume of sales generated by the operating assets of a company. Increases in turnover rates generally indicate more efficient utilization of assets.

Similar procedures may also be used to analyze specific liabilities. An accounts payable turnover, for example, may be computed by dividing purchases by average payables; the number of days' purchases in accounts payable may be computed by dividing accounts payable by average daily purchases.

Analysis of liabilities in terms of due dates may assist management in cash planning. Useful relationships may also be obtained by comparing specific assets or liabilities with other assets or liabilities, or with asset or liability totals. For example, data concerning the relationship of cash to accounts payable or of cash to total liabilities may be useful.

Profitability Analysis   Profitability analysis provides evidence concerning the earnings potential of a company and how effectively a firm is being managed. Since the reason most firms exist is to earn profits, the profitability ratios are among the most significant financial ratios. The adequacy of earnings may be measured in terms of (1) the rate earned on sales, (2) the rate earned on total assets, (3) the rate earned on stockholders' equity, and (4) the availability of earnings to common stockholders. Thus, the most popular profitability measurements are profit margin on sales, return on investment ratios, and earnings per share.

Profit Margin on Sales

The ratio of net income to sales determines the net profit margin on sales. This measurement represents the net income percentage per dollar of sales. The percentage is computed by dividing net income by net sales for a period. For AC&W Corporation, the net profit margin on sales is:

	1992	1991
Net income	$ 70,000	$ 60,000
Net sales	$1,425,000	$1,650,000
Net profit margin rate	4.9%	3.6%

This means that for 1992, AC&W generated almost five cents of profit per dollar of sales revenue. Because net income is used in the computation, any extraordinary or irregular items may distort the profit margin rate with respect to normal operating activities. Adjustments may be needed in the analysis to account for such items.

For merchandising and manufacturing companies, gross profit margin on sales is often a significant ratio for evaluating the profitability of a company. In these companies, cost of goods sold is the most significant expense, and careful inventory control is necessary to assure profitable operations. For AC&W, the gross profit margin on sales is:

	1992	1991
Gross profit on sales	$ 425,000	$ 450,000
Net sales	$1,425,000	$1,650,000
Gross profit margin rate	29.8%	27.2%

Rate Earned on Total Assets

Overall asset productivity may be expressed as the rate earned on total assets, also referred to as the return on investment (ROI) or the asset productivity rate. The rate is computed by dividing net income by the total assets used to produce net income. This rate measures the efficiency in using resources to generate net income. If total assets by months are available, they should be used to develop an average for the year. Frequently, however, the assets at the beginning of the year or the assets at the end of the year are used. In some cases it may be desirable to use net income from operations by excluding revenue from investments, such as interest, dividends, and rents, or from gains or losses resulting from nonoperating transactions. When this is the case, total assets should be reduced by the investments or other assets. Sometimes comparisons are developed for the rate of operating income to total assets or the rate of pretax income to total assets, so that results are not affected by financial management items or by changes in income tax rates.

Rates earned on total assets for AC&W Corporation are determined as follows:

	1992	1991
Net income	$ 70,000	$ 60,000
Total assets:		
Beginning of year	$2,391,000	$1,760,000
End of year	$2,278,000	$2,391,000
Average total assets	$2,334,500	$2,075,500
Rate earned on average total assets	3.0%	2.9%

An analysis, referred to as the DuPont Method, illustrates the factors that affect this ratio. The DuPont method explicitly recognizes that return on total assets equals the profit margin on sales multiplied by the total asset turnover. The formulas for these ratios show clearly why this relationship exists.

$$\text{Profit margin} \times \text{Total asset turnover} = \text{Return on total assets}$$

$$\frac{\text{Net income}}{\text{Sales}} \times \frac{\text{Sales}}{\text{Total assets}} = \frac{\text{Net income}}{\text{Total assets}}$$

Sales cancels out of the formula leaving the return on assets ratio. Ratios previously computed for the AC&W Corporation in 1992 further illustrate this analysis.

Profit Margin on Sales (p. 1175)	X	Total Asset Turnover (p. 1174)	=	Rate Earned on Total Assets (p. 1176)
4.9	X	.6	=	3% (rounded)

This analytical tool helps explain how discount organizations compete with full service companies. Generally, the discount store operates on a relatively small margin and plans for a high turnover of assets, whereas the full service organization has a higher margin but lower turnover.

For example, assume that Company A is a full service organization and Company B is a discount store. Company A has a margin of 22.6% on sales and a total asset turnover of 1.1. Company B has a margin of 4.5% and a turnover of 5.2. Company A's percentage return on assets equals 24.9% (22.6% x 1.1), and Company B's return is 23.4% (4.5% x 5.2). Thus, the return on total assets for Company A is very close to that of Company B, although their asset turnover and profitability ratios are quite different.

Rate Earned on Stockholders' Equity

Net income may be expressed as the **rate earned on stockholders' equity** (or return on stockholders' equity) by dividing net income by stockholders' equity. In developing this rate, it is preferable to calculate the average stockholders' equity for a year from monthly data, particularly when significant changes have occurred during the year, such as the sale of additional stock, retirement of stock, and accumulation of earnings. Sometimes the beginning or the ending stockholders' equity is used.

For AC&W Corporation, rates earned on stockholders' equity are as follows:

	1992	1991
Net income	$ 70,000	$ 60,000
Stockholders' equity:		
Beginning of year	$1,445,000	$1,330,000
End of year	$1,468,000	$1,445,000
Average stockholders' equity	$1,456,500	$1,387,500
Rate returned on average stockholders' equity	4.8%	4.3%

As a company's liabilities increase in relationship to stockholders' equity, the spread between the rate earned on stockholders' equity and the rate earned on total assets rises. This difference measures the way a company is using leverage in its business financing. The rate earned on stockholders' equity is important to investors who must reconcile the risk of debt financing with the potentially greater profitability.

Rate Earned on Common Stockholders' Equity

As a refinement to the rate earned on total stockholders' equity, earnings may be measured in terms of the residual common stockholders' equity. The **rate earned on common stockholders' equity** is computed by dividing net income after preferred dividend requirements by common stockholders' equity. The average equity for common stockholders should be determined, although the rate is frequently based on beginning or ending common equity.

In the case of AC&W Corporation, preferred dividend requirements are 6%. The rate earned on common stockholders' equity, then, is calculated as follows:

	1992	1991
Net income	$ 70,000	$ 60,000
Less dividend requirements on preferred stock	21,000	21,000
Net income related to common stockholders' equity	$ 49,000	$ 39,000
Common stockholders' equity:		
Beginning of year	$1,095,000	$1,080,000
End of year	$1,118,000	$1,095,000
Average common stockholders' equity	$1,106,500	$1,087,500
Rate earned on average common stockholders' equity	4.4%	3.6%

Earnings per Share

Earnings per share calculations were described in detail in Chapter 18. Recall that the Accounting Principles Board in Opinion No. 15 indicated that earnings per share data were of such importance to investors and others that such data should be presented prominently on the income statement. In computing earnings per share on common stock, earnings are first reduced by the prior dividend rights of preferred stock. Computations are made in terms of the weighted average number of common shares outstanding for each period presented. Adjustments are required when a corporation's capital structure includes potentially dilutive securities. If the total potential dilution is material, both primary earnings per share and fully diluted earnings per share must be disclosed. When net income includes below-the-line items, earnings per share should be reported for each major component of income as well as for net income.

For AC&W Corporation, there are no potentially dilutive securities. Earnings per share on common stock is calculated as follows.

	1992	1991
Net income	$70,000	$60,000
Less dividend requirements on preferred stock	21,000	21,000
Income related to common stockholders' equity	$49,000	$39,000
Number of shares of common stock outstanding	75,000	75,000
Earnings per share on common stock	$.65	$.52

Dividends per Share

In addition to earnings per share, many companies report dividends per share in the financial statements. This amount is computed simply by dividing cash dividends for the year by the number of shares of common stock outstanding. When a significant number of common shares have been issued or retired during a period, an average should be computed; otherwise, the number of common shares outstanding at the end of the period is normally used. For AC&W Corporation, the number of shares of common stock outstanding has remained constant for the past 3 years. Therefore, the dividends per share are $.35 for 1992 and $.32 for 1991. Another way of analyzing dividends is to compute the **dividend payout rate,** or the percentage of net income paid out in dividends. This may be computed by dividing the dividends per share by the earnings per share, or by dividing dividends paid by net income. The dividend payout rates for AC&W are 54% in 1992 and 62% in 1991.

Yield on Common Stock

Dividends per share may be used to compute a rate of return on the market value of common stock. Such a rate, referred to as the **yield on common stock**, is found by dividing the annual dividends per common share by the latest market price per common share. For AC&W Corporation the yield on the common stock is computed as follows:

	1992	1991
Dividends for year per common share	$ .35	$ .32
Market value per common share at end of year	$10.00	$6.50
Yield on common stock	3.5%	4.9%

Price-Earnings Ratio

The market price of common stock may be expressed as a multiple of earnings to evaluate the attractiveness of common stock as an investment. This measurement is referred to as the **price-earnings ratio** and is computed by dividing the market price per share of stock by the annual earnings per share. Instead of using the average market value of shares for the period covered by earnings, the latest market value is normally used. The lower the price-earnings ratio, the more attractive the investment. Assuming market values per common share of AC&W Corporation stock at the end of 1992 of $10 and at the end of 1991 of $6.50, price-earnings ratios would be computed as follows:

	1992	1991
Market value per common share at end of year	$10.00	$6.50
Earnings per share (calculated on page 1178)	$ .65	$ .52
Price-earnings ratio	15.4	12.5

As an alternative to the price-earnings ratio, earnings per share can be presented as a percentage of the market price of the stock.

Capital Structure Analysis The composition of a company's capital structure has significant implications for stockholders, creditors, potential investors and potential creditors. Creditors look to the stockholders' equity as a margin of safety. As stockholders' equity increases in relation to total liabilities, the margin of protection to creditors also increases. Should a company have financial difficulty and have to terminate its operations through bankruptcy, the higher the margin of safety the more probable that creditors will recover their investment in the company.

However, from the perspective of the common stockholders, it is often advantageous to use borrowed capital or preferred stock to expand operations rather than issuing additional common stock. If a company can earn a return on the funds obtained through borrowing or from preferred stock that is greater than the cost of the funds, the excess earnings will benefit the common stockholders through an increase in the return on common stockholders' equity. This result is commonly referred to as **trading on the equity** or applying **financial leverage**. On the other hand, if the company earns a return that is less than the cost of the funds, the common stockholders must bear the excess cost. There is a legal obligation to pay interest, and preferred stock dividends are usually cumulative thus they must be paid before any distribution to the common stockholders.

To illustrate the impact trading on the equity has on common stockholders, assume that a company with 10,000 shares of stock outstanding reports assets of $500,000 and has no liabilities. The company estimates that its income before income taxes will be $80,000 without any borrowed capital. Income taxes are estimated to be 30% of income, therefore net income is estimated to be $56,000 ($80,000-$24,000). This would result in a return on common stockholders' equity of 11.2% ($56,000 ÷ $500,000).

Exhibit 26-1 illustrates the effects of borrowing an extra million dollars at 12% interest under (1) the assumption the extra funds earn 15% before interest and taxes, or more than the cost of the borrowed funds, and (2) the assumption the extra funds earn 5% before interest and taxes, or less than the cost of the borrowed funds. Using financial leverage favorably under the first assumption results in an increase in the return on common stockholders' equity from 11.2% to 15.4%. The market would probably react to this increase favorably and the market price of the stock would rise. Additional dividends could also be paid with the increase of $21,000 in net income. On the other hand, the unfavorable result of trading on the equity can be seen under the second assumption as the return on common stockholders' equity decreases from 11.2% to 1.4%. The $49,000 decrease in net income will probably result in an unfavorable impact on both the stock's market price and the dividend payments.

The illustration used borrowed funds that had a tax deductible interest cost attached to them. If the funds had been acquired with preferred stock, the computations would have differed because of the nondeductibility of preferred dividends for income tax purposes. However, the same advantages and disadvantages to the common stockholder apply depending on the relationship between the cost of the funds and the amount that can be earned from the funds.

Stockholders, creditors, and other interested parties often make use of capital structure measurements including the equity to debt ratio, number of times interest is earned, fixed charge coverage, and book value per share. These methods are illustrated in the following sections.

Exhibit 26–1   Trading on the Equity

	Assumption 1 Borrowed Capital Earns 15%	Assumption 2 Borrowed Capital Earns 5%
Income before interest and taxes:		
Without borrowed funds	$ 80,000	$ 80,000
On $1,000,000 borrowed	150,000	50,000
	$230,000	$130,000
Interest (12% × $1,000,000)	120,000	120,000
Income before taxes	$110,000	$ 10,000
Income taxes (30%)	33,000	3,000
Net income	$ 77,000	$ 7,000
Common stockholders' equity	$500,000	$500,000
Return on common stockholders' equity	15.4%	1.4%

Ratio of Stockholders' Equity to Total Liabilities

Stockholders' and creditors' equities may be expressed in terms of total assets or in terms of each other. For example, stockholders may have a 60% interest in total assets and creditors a 40% interest. This can be expressed as an equity to debt ratio of 1.5 to 1.

For AC&W Corporation, the relationships of stockholders' equity to total liabilities are calculated as follows:

	1992	1991
Stockholders' equity	$1,468,000	$1,445,000
Total liabilities	$ 810,000	$ 946,000
Ratio of stockholders' equity to total liabilities	1.8:1	1.5:1

In analyzing the relationship of stockholders' equity to total liabilities, particular note should be made of lease arrangements. Both property rights provided under the leases and the accompanying liabilities should be considered in evaluating the equities and changes in equities from period to period.

Often the reciprocal of the equity to debt ratio is used. The debt to equity ratio is computed by dividing total liabilities by total stockholders' equity. This shows the reciprocal relationship to that just described. It is still a measure of the amount of leverage used by a company. Investors generally prefer a higher debt to equity ratio to obtain the advantages of financial leverage while creditors favor a lower ratio to increase the safety of their debt.

Number of Times Interest Earned

A measure of the debt position of a company in relation to its earnings ability is the number of times interest is earned. The calculation is made by dividing income before any charges for interest or income tax by the interest requirements for the period. The resulting figure reflects the company's ability to meet interest payments and the degree of safety afforded the creditors. The number of times interest was earned by AC&W Corporation follows:

	1992	1991
Income before income tax	$100,000	$ 85,000
Add bond interest (10% of $400,000)	40,000	40,000
Amount available in meeting bond interest requirements	$140,000	$125,000
Number of times bond interest requirements were earned	3.5	3.1

Pretax income was used in the computation since income tax applies only after interest is deducted, and it is pretax income that protects creditors.

A computation similar to times interest earned, but more inclusive, is the **fixed charge coverage**. Fixed charges include such obligations as interest on bonds and notes, lease obligations, and any other recurring financial commitments. The number of times fixed charges are covered is calculated by adding the fixed charges to pretax income and then dividing the total by the fixed charges.

Book Value Per Share

Stockholders' equity can be measured by calculating the **book value per share**, which is the dollar equity in corporate capital of each share of stock. This amount is frequently used by investors in conjunction with the market value per share to evaluate the attractiveness of the stock for investment purposes.

When there is only one class of stock outstanding, the calculation of book value is relatively simple; the total stockholders' equity is divided by the number of shares of stock outstanding at the close of the reporting period. When a company is holding treasury stock, its cost is deducted from stockholders' equity and the treasury shares are deducted from the shares issued. When more than one class of stock is outstanding, a portion of the stockholders' equity must be allocated to the other classes of stock before the book value of the common stock is computed. Usually the par or liquidation value of the other classes of stock is used to make this allocation.

In the case of AC&W Corporation, the par value of the preferred stock is equal to the liquidation value, and there are no preferred dividends in arrears. The book value per share is computed as follows:

	1992	1991
Common stockholders' equity	$1,118,000	$1,095,000
Number of shares of common stock outstanding	75,000	75,000
Book value per share on common stock	$14.91	$14.60

Since the market value of the stock is lower than the book value, many investors would consider AC&W an attractive investment. However, the nature and limitations of the per share book value measurements must be considered in using these data. Carrying values of assets may vary significantly from their present fair values or immediate realizable values. This would directly affect the per share amount that could be realized in the event of a company liquidation.

Summary of Analytical Measures

Financial ratios, percentages, and other measures are useful tools for analyzing financial statements. They enable statement users to make meaningful judgments about an enterprise's financial condition and operating results. These measures, like financial statements, are more meaningful when compared with similar data for more than one period and with industry averages or other available data. A summary of the major analytical measures discussed in this chapter is presented below and on the following page.

Summary of Major Analytical Measures

Liquidity Analysis

(1) Current ratio	$\dfrac{\text{Current assets}}{\text{Current liabilities}}$	Measures ability to pay short-term debts.
(2) Acid-test ratio	$\dfrac{\text{Quick assets}}{\text{Current liabilities}}$	Measures immediate ability to pay short-term debts.

Activity Analysis

(3) Accounts receivable turnover	$\dfrac{\text{Net credit sales}}{\text{Average accounts receivable}}$	Measures receivable position and approximate average collection time.
(4) Number of days' sales in receivables	$\dfrac{\text{Average accounts receivable}}{\text{Average daily credit sales}}$	Measures receivable position and approximate average collection time.
(5) Inventory turnover	$\dfrac{\text{Cost of goods sold}}{\text{Average inventory}}$	Measures appropriateness of inventory levels in terms of time required to sell or "turn over" goods.
(6) Number of days' sales in inventories	$\dfrac{\text{Average inventory}}{\text{Average daily cost of goods sold}}$	Measures appropriateness of inventory levels in terms of time required to sell or "turn over" goods.
(7) Total asset turn over	$\dfrac{\text{Net sales}}{\text{Average total assets}}$	Measures effectiveness of asset utilization.

Profitability Analysis

(8) Net profit margin on sales	$\dfrac{\text{Net income}}{\text{Net sales}}$	Measures profit percentage per dollar of sales.
(9) Gross profit margin on sales	$\dfrac{\text{Gross profit}}{\text{Net sales}}$	Measures gross profit percentage per dollar of sales.

Profitability Analysis (continued)

(10) Rate earned on total assets	$$\frac{\text{Net income}}{\text{Average total assets}}$$	Measures overall asset productivity.
(11) Rate earned on stockholders' equity	$$\frac{\text{Net income}}{\text{Average stockholders' equity}}$$	Measures rate of return on average stockholders' equity.
(12) Rate earned on common stockholders' equity.	$$\frac{\text{Net income—preferred dividend requirements}}{\text{Average common stockholders' equity}}$$	Measures rate of return on average common stockholders' equity.
(13) Earnings per share	$$\frac{\text{Net income—preferred dividend requirements}}{\text{Weighted average number of shares of common stock outstanding}}$$	Measures net income per share of common stock.
(14) Dividends per share	$$\frac{\text{Dividends on common stock}}{\text{Average number of shares of common stock outstanding}}$$	Measures dividends per share of common stock.
(15) Yield on common stock	$$\frac{\text{Dividends per share of common stock}}{\text{Market value per share of common stock}}$$	Measures rate of cash return to stockholders.
(16) Price-earnings ratio	$$\frac{\text{Market price per share of common stock}}{\text{Earnings per share of common stock}}$$	Measures attractiveness of stock as an investment.

Capital Structure Analysis

(17) Equity-to-debt ratio	$$\frac{\text{Stockholders' equity}}{\text{Total liabilities}}$$	Measures use of debt to finance operations.
(18) Number of times interest is earned	$$\frac{\text{Income before taxes and interest expense}}{\text{Interest expense}}$$	Measures ability to meet interest payments.
(19) Book value per share	$$\frac{\text{Common stockholders' equity}}{\text{Number of shares of common stock outstanding}}$$	Measures equity per share of common stock.

Use of Industry Data For Comparative Analysis

As indicated earlier in the chapter, comparisons of common-size information or other measurements may be made over time within a company or with similar companies individually or in industry groups. There are many general and industry sources that can be used to obtain comparative information. The major difficulty in using comparative data is the selection of specific companies or an industry that is similar to the company being examined. The government has established a standard for classifying industries known as the **Standard Industrial Code (SIC)**. Over 800 industries are identified, and general survey information is compiled according to these codes.

If the company being analyzed operates only in one general business area, it usually isn't difficult to find a category for comparison. However, many businesses today are large, complex organizations engaged in a variety of activities that bear little relationship to each other. For example, a company might manufacture airplane engines, operate a real estate business, and manage a professional hockey team. Such companies, referred to as **diversified companies** or **conglomerates**, operate in multiple industries and do not fit any one specific industry category. Thus, comparative analysis for a highly diversified company requires either an assumption that the company operates primarily in one area or separate data for each subindustry or segment. Generally, comparisons are more meaningful when separate data for segments are analyzed, and many companies are required to include such data with their financial statements.

Segment Reporting   When a company is diversified, the different statements of the company often operate in distinct and separate markets, involve different management teams, and experience different growth patterns, profit potentials, and degrees of risk. In effect, the segments of the company behave almost like, and in some cases are, separate companies within an overall corporate structure. Yet, if only total company information is presented for a highly diversified company, the different degrees of risk, profitability, and growth potential for major segments of the company cannot be analyzed and compared.

Recognizing this problem, the FASB issued Statement No. 14, which requires disclosure of selected information for segments of diversified companies.[3] Information to be reported includes revenues, operating profit, and identifiable assets for each significant industry segment of a company. Essentially, a **segment** is considered significant if its sales, profits, or assets are 10% or more of the respective total company amounts. A practical limit of 10 segments is suggested, and at least 75% of total company sales must be accounted for. The segment data may be reported in the audited financial statements, or in a separate schedule considered an integral part of the statements. Other provisions of Statement No. 14 require disclosure of revenues from major customers and information about foreign operations and export sales.

Reporting by lines of business presents several problems. For example, how does one determine which business segments should be reported on? Certainly not all companies are organized in the same manner, even if they are engaged in similar business activities. Reporting on a particular division or profit-center in one company may not be comparable to another company. Another problem relates to transfer pricing. Not all companies use the same method of pricing goods or services that are "sold" among the different divisions or units of a company. This could lead to distorted segment profit data. Another related problem is the allocation of common costs among segments of a company. Certain costs, such as general and administrative expenses, are very difficult to assign to particular segments

---

[3]*Statement of Financial Accounting Standards No. 14*, "Financial Reporting for Segments of a Business Enterprise" (Stamford: Financial Accounting Standards Board, 1976).

of a company on anything other than an arbitrary basis. This, again, could result in misleading information.

In spite of these difficulties, the accounting profession has concluded that segment reporting is necessary to assist readers of financial statements in analyzing and understanding an enterprise's past performance and future prospects and making comparisons with other companies. An example of segment reporting, from the 1987 annual report of Capital Cities/ABC, is presented on page 1187. The disclosures made by General Mills in Note Fifteen in Appendix A provide another illustration of segment reporting by a diversified company.

Interim Reporting

Statements showing financial position and operating results for intervals of less than a year are referred to as interim financial statements. Interim reports are considered essential in providing investors and others with more timely information as to the position and progress of an enterprise. This information is most useful in comparative form because of the relationship it shows to data for similar reporting intervals and to data in the annual report.

Notwithstanding the need for interim reports, there are significant difficulties associated with them. One problem is caused by the seasonal factors of certain businesses. For example, in some companies, revenues fluctuate widely among interim periods; in other businesses, significant fixed costs are incurred during a single period but are to benefit several periods. Not only must costs be allocated to appropriate periods of benefit, but they must be matched against the realized revenues for the interim period to determine a reasonable income measurement.

In preparing interim reports, adjustments for accrued items, generally required only at year end, have to be considered at the end of each interim period. Because of the additional time and extra costs involved to develop complete information, many estimates of expenses are made for interim reports. The increased number of estimates adds an element of subjectivity to these reports.

Another problem is that extraordinary items or the disposal of a business segment will have a greater impact on an interim period's earnings than on the results of operations for an entire year. In analyzing interim financial statements, special attention should be given to these and similar considerations.

Partially because of some of the above problems and partially because of differing views as to the objective of interim reports, there has been a variety of practices in presenting interim financial information. Two prominent viewpoints exist. One viewpoint is that each reporting interval is to be recognized as a separate accounting period. Thus, the results of operations for each interim period are determined in essentially the same manner as for the annual accounting period. Under this approach, the same judgments, estimations, accruals, and deferrals are recognized at the end of each interim period as for the annual period.

The other viewpoint, and the one accepted by the APB in Opinion No. 28, is

Exhibit 26–2   **Capital Cities/ABC**

Notes to Consolidated Financial Statements—(Continued)

8. Segment Data

The Company operates the ABC Television Network and eight affiliated television stations, six radio networks and 21 radio stations, and provides programming for cable television. The Company publishes newspapers, shopping guides, various specialized business and consumer periodicals and books; and also distributes information from data bases. Operations are classified into two business segments: Broadcasting and Publishing. There are no product transfers between segments of the Company, and virtually all of the Company's business is conducted within the United States. Prior to 1986, the Company owned and operated cable television systems. They were classified as a separate business segment and are included below in the Broadcasting segment. Cable television net revenues and income from operations for 1985 were $84,580,000 and $5,206,000, respectively. The segment data follows (000's omitted):

	1987	1986	1985	1984	1983
Broadcasting					
Net revenues	$ 3,433,749	$ 3,153,619	$ 378,297	$ 348,106	$ 302,785
Direct operating costs	2,680,582	2,554,932	192,249	172,867	151,608
Depreciation	73,730	78,952	26,711	23,257	18,889
Total operating costs	2,754,312	2,633,884	218,960	196,124	170,492
Income before amortization of intangible assets	679,437	519,735	159,337	151,982	132,293
Amortization of intangible assets	46,527	45,200	8,367	7,800	7,597
Income from operations	$ 632,910	$ 474,535	$ 150,970	$ 144,182	$ 124,696
Assets at year-end	$ 4,018,775	$ 4,186,650	$ 537,797	$ 507,433	$ 455,341
Capital expenditures	102,425	104,278	26,327	26,370	36,782
Publishing					
Net revenues	$ 1,006,597	$ 970,755	$ 642,583	$ 591,616	$ 459,510
Direct operating costs	822,123	778,201	482,333	438,414	342,253
Depreciation	18,878	15,353	10,395	10,190	8,646
Total operating costs	841,001	793,554	492,728	448,604	350,899
Income before amortization of intangible assets	165,596	177,201	149,855	143,012	108,611
Amortization of intangible assets	18,879	18,202	11,343	9,833	4,577
Income from operations	$ 146,717	$ 158,999	$ 138,512	$ 133,179	$ 104,034
Assets at year-end	$ 908,193	$ 920,896	$ 455,274	$ 430,997	$ 287,523
Capital expenditures	13,114	48,589	45,869	26,700	10,666
Consolidated					
Net revenues	$ 4,440,346	$ 4,124,374	$ 1,020,880	$ 939,722	$ 762,295
Income from operations	$ 779,627	$ 633,534	$ 289,482	$ 277,361	$ 228,730
General corporate expense	(33,637)	(30,856)	(11,981)	(9,849)	(8,366)
Operating income	745,990	602,678	277,501	267,512	220,364
Interest expense	(190,806)	(185,511)	(22,738)	(27,161)	(14,633)
Interest and other income	8,794	5,576	22,059	28,442	18,773
Income before income taxes	$ 563,978	$ 422,743	$ 276,822	$ 268,793	$ 224,504
Assets employed by segments	$ 4,926,968	$ 5,107,546	$ 993,071	$ 938,430	$ 742,864
Investments and corporate assets	451,404	83,870	891,860	269,742	310,048
Total assets at year-end	$ 5,378,372	$ 5,191,416	$ 1,884,931	$ 1,208,172	$ 1,052,912

that the interim period is an integral part of the annual period.[4] Essentially, the revenues and expenses for the total period are allocated among interim periods on some reasonable basis, e.g., time, sales volume, or productive activity.

Under the **integral part of annual period concept,** the same general accounting principles and reporting practices employed for annual reports are to be utilized for interim statements, except modifications may be required so the interim results will better relate to the total results of operations for the annual period. As an example of the type of modification that may be required, assume a company uses the LIFO method of inventory valuation and encounters a situation where liquidation of the base period inventory occurs at an interim date but the inventory is expected to be replaced by the end of the annual period. Under these circumstances, the inventory reported at the interim date should not reflect the LIFO liquidation, and the cost of goods sold for the interim period should include the expected cost of replacing the liquidated LIFO base.[5]

Another example of a required modification deals with a change in accounting principle during an interim period. In general, these changes should follow the provisions of APB Opinion No. 20.[6] However, the FASB has concluded in Statement No. 3 that for any cumulative effect-type change, other than a change to LIFO, if the change is made "in other than the first interim period of an enterprise's fiscal year, the cumulative effect of the change on retained earnings at the beginning of that year shall be included in the determination of net income of the first interim period of the year of change."[7]

Applying generally accepted accounting practices to interim financial statements can become complex. This is an area that is developing to meet the perceived needs of users. For example, the SEC has adopted rules requiring increased disclosure of interim financial information. Interpretations of old standards and the development of new standards will assist in presenting interim financial data that should help investors and others in analyzing and interpreting the financial picture and operating results of a company.

Sources of Industry Data

Whether a company operates in one industry or in several different industries, financial analysis is enhanced if company data can be compared with industry statistics. Ratio information concerning various industries is available from different sources. These sources can be divided into two categories: (1) general sources and (2) specific industry sources. The following two general sources are kept reasonably current and are quite comprehensive:

1. Dun and Bradstreet, Inc., "Key Business Ratios"
2. Robert Morris and Associates, "Annual Statement Studies"

---

[4]*Opinions of the Accounting Principles Board, No. 28,* "Interim Financial Reporting" (New York: American Institute of Certified Public Accountants, 1973), par 9.

[5]*Ibid.,* par. 14.

[6]*Opinions of the Accounting Principles Board, No. 20,* "Accounting Changes" (New York American Institute of Certified Public Accountants, 1971).

[7]*Statement of Financial Accounting Standards No. 3,* "Reporting Accounting Changes in Interim Financial Statements" (Stamford: Financial Accounting Standards Board, 1974), par. 4.

"Key Business Ratios" features 14 financial ratios for over 800 retailing, wholesaling, and manufacturing lines of business. The computations are made using data for over 400,000 companies. In addition, common-size statement information is provided for each line of business. "Key Business Ratios" is published annually, but data are collected continuously throughout the year. A sampling of data for 118 companies is contained in *Dun's Review* each November.

The second general source is Robert Morris Associates "Annual Statement Studies." Ratios for about 300 lines of business are prepared based on data furnished by member banks of Robert Morris Associates from customer-submitted financial reports. The ratios are presented for 5 years, and additional trend data are also provided. In contrast, the Dun and Bradstreet ratios and common-size data are presented for a single year. Because the submission of data for the Robert Morris publication is on a voluntary basis, the number of companies included in "Annual Statement Studies" is much lower than the number included in Dun and Bradstreet's "Key Business Ratios."

Other general sources of information include limited ratio information published occasionally in business periodicals such as *Forbes, Business Week,* and *Fortune.* This information is usually classified by industry and often includes rankings of factors such as growth and profitability. The annual "Fortune 500" listing and analysis of the 500 largest American companies is perhaps the best known of these sources.

Specific industry sources for comparative data include a large number of industry associations that collect, summarize, and disseminate information about their members. Often this information is of greater use in financial analysis than information from general sources because of its greater detail and more current data.

Interpretation of Analyses

The analyses discussed in this chapter are designed to help an analyst arrive at certain conclusions with regard to a business. As previously stated, these are merely guides to intelligent interpretation of financial data.

Only those ratios and measurements that will actually assist in arriving at informed conclusions with respect to questions raised need be used. The measurements developed need to be interpreted in terms of the circumstances of a particular enterprise, the conditions of the particular industry in which the enterprise operates, and the general business and economic environment. If measurements are to be of maximum value, they must be compared with similar data developed for the particular enterprise for past periods, with standard measurements for the industry as a whole, and with pertinent data relating to general business conditions and price fluctuations affecting the individual enterprise. Only through intelligent use and integration of the foregoing sources of data can financial weaknesses and strengths be identified and reliable opinions be developed concerning business structure, operations, and growth.

Key Terms

Accounts receivable turnover 1170	Natural business year 1173
Acid-test ratio 1169	Net profit margin on sales 1175
Book value per share 1182	Number of time interest is earned 1181
Common-size financial statements 1166	Price-earnings ratio 1179
Comparative statements 1163	Profitability 1163
Conglomerates 1185	Quick assets 1169
Current ratio 1168	Quick ratio 1169
Debt to equity ratio 1181	Rate earned on common stockholders' equity 1177
Diversified companies 1185	Rate earned on stockholders' equity 1177
Dividends per share 1178	
Earnings per share 1178	Rate earned on total assets 1175
Equity to debt ratio 1181	Return on investment (ROI) 1175
Financial leverage 1180	Segment 1185
Fixed charge coverage 1182	Stability 1162
Gross profit margin on sales 1175	Total asset turnover 1173
Horizontal analysis 1164	Trading on the equity 1180
Integral part of annual period concept 1188	Vertical analysis 1166
Interim financial statements 1186	Working capital ratio 1168
Inventory turnover 1172	Yield on common stock 1179
Liquidity 1162	

Questions

1. What groups may be interested in a company's financial statements?
2. What types of questions requiring financial statement analysis might be raised by external users, such as investors and creditors, as contrasted to internal management?
3. What are the factors that one would look for in judging a company's (a) liquidity, (b) stability, (c) profitability, (d) growth potential?
4. Why are comparative financial statements considered more meaningful than statements prepared for a single period? What conditions increase the usefulness of comparative statements?
5. Distinguish between horizontal and vertical analysis. What special purpose does each serve?
6. What information is provided by analysis of comparative statements of cash flows that is not available from analysis of comparative balance sheets and income statements?
7. What is meant by a *common-size* statement? What are its advantages?
8. Mention some factors that may limit the comparability of financial statements of two companies in the same industry.
9. What factors may be responsible for a change in a company's net income from one year to the next?
10. The Black Co. develops the following measurements for 1992 as compared with the year 1991. What additional information would you require before arriving at favorable or unfavorable conclusions for each item?
    (a) Net income has increased $70,000.
    (b) Sales returns and allowances have increased by $25,000.
    (c) The gross profit rate has increased by 5%.
    (d) Purchase discounts have increased by $5,000.

(e) Working capital has increased by $85,000.

(f) Accounts receivable have increased by $150,000.

(g) Inventories have decreased by $110,000.

(h) Retained earnings have decreased by $300,000.

11. Define working capital and appraise its significance.

12. Distinguish between the current ratio and the acid-test ratio.

13. Balance sheets for the Rich Corporation and the Poor Corporation each show a working capital total of $500,000. Does this indicate that the short-term liquidity of the two corporations is approximately the same? Explain.

14. (a) How is the accounts receivable turnover computed? (b) How is the number of days' purchases in accounts payable computed?

15. (a) How is the merchandise inventory turnover computed? (b) What precautions are necessary in arriving at the basis for the turnover calculation? (c) How would you interpret a rising inventory turnover rate?

16. The ratio of stockholders' equity to total liabilities offers information about the long-term stability of a business. Explain.

17. Indicate how each of the following measurements is calculated and appraise its significance:

(a) The number of times bond interest requirements were earned.

(b) The number of times preferred dividend requirements were earned.

(c) The rate of earnings on the common stockholders' equity.

(d) The earnings per share on common stock.

(e) The price-earnings ratio on common stock.

(f) The dividends per share on common stock.

(g) The yield on common stock.

18. Briefly explain how the sources of assets, liabilities, and owners' equity affect the rate of return to the residual owners of the organization.

19. Explain how the turnover of assets may affect return on assets.

20. Identify the major financial relationships that reflect the components of the rate of return to the residual owners.

21. Explain under what conditions the rate of return on total assets equals the rate of return to the common shareholder.

22. Under what circumstances is the use of industry ratios beneficial in analyzing a company's activity?

23. (a) What are the principal sources of industry data for use in comparative analysis? (b) What are the advantages and disadvantages of each source?

24. In what ways can segment information assist in the analysis of a company's financial statements?

25. Distinguish between the two primary viewpoints concerning the preparation of interim financial statements.

26. Why must investors be careful in interpreting interim reports?

Discussion Cases   **Case 26–1   (How should we finance our expansion?)**

The Detweiler Co. is considering expanding its operations. The company's balance sheet at December 31, 1991 is presented on the following page.

Detweiler Co.
Balance Sheet
December 31, 1991

Assets		Liabilities		
Cash	$ 325,000	Accounts payable	$ 300,000	
Accounts receivable	525,000	Bonds payable	1,100,000	
Inventory	1,150,000	Total liabilities		$1,400,000
Land	1,200,000	Stockholders' Equity		
Buildings and equipment (net)	2,500,000	Preferred stock, 8% cumulative, par		
		$100	$ 300,000	
		Common stock, par $25	1,000,000	
		Retained earnings	3,000,000	
		Total stockholders' equity		4,300,000
Total assets	$5,700,000	Total liabilities and stockholders' equity		$5,700,000

Each $1,000 bond is convertible at the option of the bondholder to 15 shares of common stock. The bonds carry an interest rate of 12%, and are callable at 100. The company's 1991 income before taxes was $2,200,000 and was $1,520,000 after taxes. The preferred stock is callable at par. The common stock has a market price of $60 per share.

The company's management has identified several alternatives to raise $1,000,000.

(a) Issue additional bonds.
(b) Call in the convertible bonds to force conversion and then issue additional bonds.
(c) Issue additional 8% cumulative preferred stock.
(d) Issue additional common stock.

Evaluate the company's leverage position and discuss the advantages and disadvantages of each alternative.

Case 26–2   (Analyzing earnings)

Royer Donahoe owns two businesses: a drug store and a retail department store. The investment in land, buildings, and equipment is approximately the same in either business.

Drug Store		Department Store	
Net sales	$1,050,000	Net sales	$670,000
Cost of goods sold	1,000,000	Cost of goods sold	600,000
Average inventory	50,000	Average inventory	200,000
Operating expenses	39,500	Operating expenses	36,500

Which business earns more income? Which business earns a higher return on its investment in inventory? Which business would you consider more profitable?

Case 26–3   (Evaluating alternative investments)

Judy Snow is considering investing $10,000 and wishes to know which of two companies offers the better alternative.

The Hoffman Company earned net income of $63,000 last year on average total assets of $280,000, and average stockholders' equity of $210,000. The company's shares are selling on the market at $100 per share; 6,300 shares of common stock are outstanding.

The McMahon Company earned $24,375 last year on average total assets (net of interest and taxes) of $125,000 and average stockholders' equity of $100,000. The company's common shares are selling on the market at $78 per share; 2,500 shares are outstanding.

Which stock should Snow buy?

Case 26–4   (Should the FASB set standards for financial ratios?)

Financial ratios can be computed using many different formulas. In an article in the CPA Journal, the author recommends that the FASB become involved in identifying common formulas and ratios that would be included in all financial statements. What are the advantages in pursuing such a recommendation? What are the difficulties?

Exercises   ### Exercise 26–1   (Index numbers)

Sales for the Montrek Company for a 5-year period and an industry sales index for this period are listed below. Convert both series into indexes employing 1988 as the base year.

	1992	1991	1990	1989	1988
Sales of Montrek Company (in thousands of dollars)	$8,400	$9,205	$8,710	$8,850	$8,530
Industry sales index (1978-1982 = 100)	192	212	200	170	158

Exercise 26–2   (Comparative cost of goods sold schedule)

Cost of goods sold data for P. Lohner Corporation are presented below. The company's fiscal year ends June 30.

	1991-1992	1990-1991
Inventory, July 1	$ 75,000	$ 60,000
Purchases	410,000	320,000
Goods available for sale	$485,000	$380,000
Less inventory, June 30	55,000	75,000
Cost of goods sold	$430,000	$305,000

Prepare a comparative schedule of cost of goods sold showing dollar and percentage changes. Round to nearest whole percentage.

Exercise 26–3   (Vertical analysis)

The financial position of the Islandic Co. at the end of 1992 and 1991 is as follows:

	1992	1991
Assets		
Current assets	$ 70,000	$ 60,000
Long-term investments	15,000	14,000
Land, buildings, and equipment (net)	100,000	75,000
Intangible assets	10,000	10,000
Other assets	5,000	6,000
Total assets	$200,000	$165,000
Liabilities		
Current liabilities..	$ 30,000	$ 35,000
Long-term liabilities	88,000	62,000
Total liabilities	$118,000	$ 97,000
Stockholders' Equity		
Preferred 8% stock	$ 10,000	$ 9,000
Common stock	54,000	42,000
Additional paid-in capital..................................	5,000	5,000
Retained earnings	13,000	12,000
Total stockholders' equity	$ 82,000	$ 68,000
Total liabilities and stockholders' equity	$200,000	$165,000

Prepare a comparative balance sheet including a percentage analysis of component items in terms of total assets and total liabilities and stockholders' equity for each year (Common-size statement). Round to nearest whole percentage.

Exercise 26—4   (Liquidity ratios)

The following data are taken from the comparative balance sheet prepared for the McCabe Resources Company:

	1992	1991
Cash	$ 25,000	$ 10,000
Marketable securities (net)	9,000	45,000
Trade receivables (net)	43,000	30,000
Inventories	65,000	40,000
Prepaid expenses	3,000	2,000
Land, buildings, and equipment (net)	79,000	75,000
Intangible assets	10,000	15,000
Other assets	2,000	8,000
Total assets	$236,000	$225,000
Current liabilities	$ 80,000	$ 65,000

(1) From the data given, compute for 1992 and 1991: (a) the working capital, (b) the current ratio, (c) the acid-test ratio, (d) the ratio of current assets to total assets, (e) the ratio of cash to current liabilities.
(2) Evaluate each of the changes.

Exercise 26—5   (Analysis of inventory position)

Income statements for the Eldermon Sales Co. show the following:

	1992	1991	1990
Sales	$125,000	$100,000	$75,000
Cost of goods sold:			
Beginning inventory	$ 30,000	$ 25,000	$ 5,000
Purchases	105,000	80,000	85,000
	$135,000	$105,000	$90,000
Ending inventory	45,000	30,000	25,000
	$ 90,000	$ 75,000	$65,000
Gross profit on sales	$ 35,000	$ 25,000	$10,000

Give whatever measurements may be developed in analyzing the inventory position at the end of each year. What conclusions would you make concerning the inventory trend?

Exercise 26—6 (Analysis of accounts payable)

The total purchases of goods by The Gerald Company during 1991 were $720,000. All purchases were on a 2/10, n/30 basis. The average balance in the vouchers payable account was $76,000. Was the company prompt, slow, or average in paying for goods? How many days' average purchases were there in accounts payable, assuming a 365 day year?

Exercise 26—7 (Inventory turnover)

The following data are taken from the Clayburgh Corporation records for the years ending December 31, 1992, 1991, and 1990.

	1992	1991	1990
Finished goods inventory	$ 60,000	$ 40,000	$ 30,000
Goods in process inventory	60,000	65,000	60,000
Raw materials inventory	60,000	40,000	35,000
Sales	400,000	340,000	300,000
Cost of goods sold	225,000	230,000	210,000
Cost of good manufactured	260,000	250,000	200,000
Raw materials used in production	150,000	130,000	120,000

(1) Compute turnover rates for 1992 and for 1991 for (a) finished goods, (b) goods in process, and (c) raw materials.
(2) Analyze the turnover results as to reasonableness, and the message they provide to a statement reader.

Exercise 26—8 (Analysis of capital structure)

The Vijay Corporation estimates that pretax earnings for the year ended December 31, 1991, will be $200,000 if it operates without borrowed capital. Income tax is 30% of earnings. Owners' equity is $750,000 for the entire year. Assuming that the company is able to borrow $1,200,000 at 12% interest, indicate the effects on net income and return on owners' equity if borrowed capital earns (1) 20%, and (2) 10%. Explain the cause of the variations.

Exercise 26—9 (Profitability analysis)

The balance sheets for the Fargo Paint Corp. showed long-term liabilities and stockholders' equity balances at the end of each year as follows:

	1992	1991	1990
10% Bonds payable	$ 600,000	$600,000	$600,000
Preferred 8% stock, $100 par	600,000	400,000	400,000
Common stock, $25 par	1,200,000	900,000	900,000
Additional paid-in capital	150,000	100,000	100,000
Retained earnings	300,000	100,000	50,000

Net income after income tax was: 1992, $280,000; 1991, $130,000. Using the foregoing data, compute for each year:

(a) The rate of earnings on average total stockholders' equity.
(b) The number of times bond interest requirements were earned (income after tax).
(c) The number of times preferred dividend requirements were earned.
(d) The rate earned on average common stockholders' equity.
(e) The earnings per share on common stock.

Exercise 26–10   (Inventory turnover)

The controller of the Montoya Manufacturing Co. wishes to analyze the activity of the finished goods, goods in process, and raw materials inventories. The following information is produced for the analysis.

Finished goods inventory, 12/31/91	$112,500
Finished goods inventory, 12/31/92	215,000
Goods in process inventory, 12/31/91	211,000
Goods in process inventory, 12/31/92	239,000
Raw materials inventory, 12/31/91	140,000
Raw materials inventory, 12/31/92	175,000
Cost of goods sold, 1992	245,000
Cost of goods manufactured, 1992	306,000
Cost of materials used, 1992	250,000

(1) Compute the inventory turnovers.
(2) Based upon the foregoing data and the turnover computations, evaluate the company's control over inventories.

Exercise 26–11   (Return on stockholders' equity)

Fay Cutler wishes to know which of two companies will yield the greater rate of return on an investment in common stock. Financial information for 1991 for the Joslyn Company and the Troy Company is presented below:

	Joslyn Co.	Troy Co.
Net income	$ 150,000	$ 293,000
Preferred stock (7%)	600,000	970,000
Common stockholders' equity:		
January 1, 1991	1,450,000	2,465,000
December 31, 1991	1,350,000	2,670,000

Determine which company earned the greater return on common stockholders' equity in 1991.

Exercise 26–12   (Profitability analysis for two companies)

The following information is obtained from the primary financial statements of two retail companies. One company markets its merchandise in a resort area, the other company is a discount household goods store. Neither company has any interest-bearing debt. By analyzing these data, indicate which company is more likely to be the gift shop and which is the discount household goods store. Support your answer.

	Company A	Company B
Revenue	$6,000,000	$6,000,000
Average total assets	$1,200,000	$6,000,000
Net income	$125,000	$600,000

Exercise 26–13   (Analysis of financial data)

For each of the following numbered items, you are to give the lettered financial statement effects for that item. If there is no appropriate response among the effects listed, leave the item blank. If more than one effect is applicable to a particular item, be sure to list *all* applicable letters. (Assume the state statutes do not permit declaration of nonliquidating dividends except from earnings.)

Item	Effect
(1) Declaration of a cash dividend due in one month on preferred stock.	A. Reduces working capital.
(2) Declaration and payment of an ordinary stock dividend.	B. Increases working capital.
	C. Reduces current ratio.
(3) Receipt of a cash dividend, not previously recorded, on stock of another corporation.	D. Increases current ratio.
	E. Reduces the dollar amount of total capital stock.
(4) Passing of a dividend on preferred stock.	F. Increases the dollar amount of total capital stock.
(5) Receipt of preferred shares as a dividend on stock held as a temporary investment. This was not a regularly recurring dividend.	G. Reduces total retained earnings.
	H. Increases total retained earnings.
	I. Reduces equity per share of common stock.
(6) Payment of dividend mentioned in (1).	J. Reduces equity of each common stockholder.
(7) Issue of new common shares in a 5-for-1 stock split.	

(AICPA adapted)

Exercise 26–14   (Analysis of financial data)

The December 31, 1991 balance sheet of Copepper's Inc. is presented below. These are the only accounts in Copepper's balance sheet. Amounts indicated by a question mark (?) can be calculated from the additional information given.

Assets		Liabilities and Stockholders' Equity	
Cash......................	$ 25,000	Accounts payable (trade)	$?
Accounts receivable (net)	?	Income taxes payable (current)	25,000
Inventory	?	Long-term debt.............	?
Property, plant, and equipment		Common stock	300,000
(net)	294,000	Retained earnings	?
	$432,000		$?

Additional information:

Current ratio (at year end)	1.5 to 1
Total liabilities divided by total stockholders' equity	.8
Inventory turnover based on sales and ending inventory	15 times
Inventory turnover based on cost of goods sold and ending inventory	10.5 times
Gross margin for 1991	$315,000

(1) What was Copepper's December 31, 1991 balance in trade accounts payable?
(2) What was Copepper's December 31, 1991 balance in retained earnings?
(3) What was Copepper's December 31, 1991 balance in the inventory account?　　　　　　　　　　　　　　　　　(AICPA adapted)

Exercise 26–15   (Reporting segment information)

Lutz Industries operates in five different industries. From the information given below, determine which segments should be classified as reportable segments according to FASB Statement No. 14. Provide justification for your answer.

Lutz Industries
Information About Company Operations in Different Industries
For Year Ended December 31, 1991
(In Millions of Dollars)

	Industry 1	Industry 2	Industry 3	Industry 4	Industry 5	Total
Revenues	$ 577	$ 84	$ 93	$117	$ 96	$ 967
Operating profit	66	11	9	10	10	106
Identifiable assets	2,124	298	328	314	353	3,417

Exercise 26–16   (Interim income statements)

The income statement for the year ended December 31, 1991, of Essex Technology Inc. appears below. Using the yearly income statement and the supplemental information, reconstruct the third-quarter interim statement for Essex.

Essex Technology Inc.
Income Statement
For Year Ended December 31, 1991

Sales	$900,000
Cost of goods sold	560,000
Gross profit on sales	$340,000
Operating expenses	96,000
Operating income	$244,000
Gain on sale of equipment	28,000
Income from continuing operations before income taxes	$272,000
Income taxes	108,800
Income from continuing operations	$163,200
Extraordinary loss (less applicable income tax reduction of $40,000)	(60,000)
Net income	$103,200

Supplemental information:

(a) Assume a 30% tax rate.

(b) Third-quarter sales were 20% of total sales.

(c) For interim reporting purposes, a gross profit rate of 38% can be justified.

(d) Variable operating expenses are allocated in the same proportion as sales. Fixed operating expenses are allocated based on the expiration of time. Of the total operating expenses, $60,000 relate to variable expenses.

(e) The equipment was sold June 1, 1991.

(f) The extraordinary loss occurred September 1, 1991.

Problems

Problem 26–1   (Comparative statements)

Operations for the Gordo Company for 1992 and 1991 are summarized below:

	1992	1991
Sales	$500,000	$450,000
Sales returns	20,000	10,000
Net sales	$480,000	$440,000
Cost of goods sold	350,000	240,000
Gross profit on sales	$130,000	$200,000
Selling and general expenses	100,000	120,000
Operating income	$ 30,000	$ 80,000
Other expenses	35,000	30,000
Income (loss) before income tax	$ (5,000)	$ 50,000
Income tax (refund)	(2,000)	20,000
Net income (loss)	$ (3,000)	$ 30,000

Instructions:

(1) Prepare a comparative income statement showing dollar changes and percentage changes for 1992 as compared with 1991.

(2) Prepare a comparative income statement offering a percentage analysis of component revenue and expense items of net sales for each year.

(3) Based on the above percentages, prepare an analysis of Gordo's operations for 1992 and 1991.

Problem 26–2   (Common-size statements)

Balance sheet data for the Stay-Trim Company and the Tone-Up Company are as follows:

	Stay-Trim Company	Tone-Up Company
Assets		
Current assets	$ 51,000	$ 240,000
Long-term investments	5,000	280,000
Land, buildings, and equipment (net)	48,000	520,000
Intangible assets	6,000	100,000
Other assets	5,000	60,000
Total assets	$115,000	$1,200,000

	Liabilities		
Current liabilities		$ 15,000	$ 180,000
Long-term liabilities		25,000	300,000
Deferred revenues		5,000	70,000
Total liabilities		$ 45,000	$ 550,000
	Stockholders' Equity		
Preferred stock		$ 5,000	$ 100,000
Common stock		30,000	200,000
Additional paid-in capital		25,000	185,000
Retained earnings		10,000	165,000
Total stockholders' equity		$ 70,000	$ 650,000
Total liabilities and stockholders' equity		$115,000	$1,200,000

Instructions:

(1) Prepare a common-size statement comparing balance sheet data for the year.

(2) What analytical conclusions can be drawn from this comparative common-size statement?

Problem 26–3   (Index numbers)

Sales for Leong Mfg. Co. and its chief competitor, La Ultima Company, and the sales index for the industry, are as follows:

	1992	1991	1990	1989	1988
Sales of Leong Mfg. Co. (in thousands of dollars)	$ 7,000	$7,280	$7,735	$8,450	$8,385
Sales of La Ultima Company (in thousands of dollars)	$10,100	$9,690	$9,975	$9,785	$9,880
Industry sales index (1983 = 100)	140	152	161	144	133

Instructions:

(1) Convert the three series to index numbers using 1988 as the base year.

(2) Prepare a short report for the management of Leong Mfg. Co. summarizing your findings.

Problem 26–4   (Computation of various ratios)

The balance sheet data for the Fielding Supply Corp. on December 31, 1991, are as follows:

Assets		Liabilities and Stockholders' Equity	
Cash	$ 120,000	Notes and accounts payable	$ 150,000
Marketable securities	25,000	Income tax payable	40,000
Notes and accounts receivable (net)	175,000	Wages and interest payable	10,000
Inventories	590,000	Dividends payable	25,000
Prepaid expenses	15,000	Bonds payable	380,000
Bond redemption fund (securities of		Deferred revenues	20,000
other companies)	400,000	Common stock $20 par	1,200,000
Land, buildings, and equipment (net)	730,000	Preferred 6% stock, $20 par (noncumu-	
Intangible assets	420,000	lative, liquidating value at par)	200,000
		Retained earnings appropriated for plant	
		expansion	200,000
		Retained earnings	250,000
	$2,475,000		$2,475,000

Instructions: From the balance sheet data, compute the following:

(1) The amount of working capital.
(2) The current ratio.
(3) The acid-test ratio.
(4) The ratio of current assets to total assets.
(5) The ratio of stockholders' equity to total liabilities.
(6) The ratio of land, buildings, and equipment to bonds payable.
(7) The book value per share of common stock.

▌▌▌ Problem 26–5   (Liquidity analysis)

The following are comparative data for Sunshine State Equipment, Inc. for the 3-year period 1990-1992.

Income Statement Data

	1992	1991	1990
Net sales	$1,200,000	$900,000	$1,020,000
Cost of goods sold......................	760,000	600,000	610,000
Gross profit on sales	$ 440,000	$ 300,000	$ 410,000
Selling, general, and other expenses	340,000	280,000	250,000
Operating income.......................	$ 100,000	$ 20,000	$ 160,000
Income tax	40,000	9,000	72,000
Net income	$ 60,000	$ 11,000	$ 88,000
Dividends paid	35,000	30,000	30,000
Net increase (decrease) in retained earnings	$ 25,000	$ (19,000)	$ 58,000

Balance Sheet Data

	1992	1991	1990
Assets			
Cash..................................	$ 50,000	$ 40,000	$ 75,000
Trade notes and accounts receivable (net) ..	300,000	320,000	250,000
Inventory (at cost)	380,000	420,000	350,000
Prepaid expenses	30,000	10,000	40,000
Land, buildings, and equipment (net)	760,000	600,000	690,000
Intangible assets	110,000	100,000	125,000
Other assets	70,000	10,000	20,000
	$1,700,000	$1,500,000	$1,550,000
Liabilities and Stockholders' Equity			
Trade notes and accounts payable	$ 120,000	$ 185,000	$ 220,000
Wages, interest, dividends payable.........	25,000	25,000	25,000
Income tax payable	29,000	5,000	30,000
Miscellaneous current liabilities	10,000	4,000	10,000
8% bonds payable......................	300,000	300,000	250,000
Deferred revenues	10,000	10,000	25,000
Preferred 6% stock, cumulative, $100 par and liquidating value	200,000	200,000	200,000
No-par common stock, $10 stated value	500,000	400,000	400,000
Additional paid-in capital.................	310,000	200,000	200,000
Retained earnings—appropriated	90,500	60,000	60,000
Retained earnings—unappropriated	105,500	111,000	130,000
	$1,700,000	$1,500,000	$1,550,000

Instructions:

(1) From the foregoing data, calculate comparative measurements for 3 years,

1990-1992 as follows: (for ratios using averages, assume 1989 figures are the same as 1990).

   (a) The amount of working capital.
   (b) The current ratio.
   (c) The acid-test ratio.
   (d) The average days' sales in trade receivables at the end of the year (assume a 365-day year and all sales on a credit basis).
   (e) The trade payables turnover rate for the year.
   (f) The inventory turnover rate.
   (g) The number of days' sales in the inventory at the end of the year.
   (h) The ratio of stockholders' equity to total liabilities.
   (i) The ratio of land, buildings, and equipment to bonds payable.
   (j) The ratio of stockholders' equity to land, buildings, and equipment.
   (k) The book value per share of common stock.
(2) Based on the measurements made in (1), evaluate the liquidity position of Sunshine State Equipment, Inc. at the end 1992 as compared with the end of 1991.

▌ Problem 26–6   (Profitability analysis)

Use the comparative data for Sunshine State Equipment, Inc. as given in Problem 26-5.

Instructions:

(1) Compute comparative measurements for the 3 years 1990-1992 as follows:
   (a) The ratio of net sales to average total assets.
   (b) The ratio of net sales to average land, buildings, and equipment.
   (c) The rate earned on net sales.
   (d) The gross profit rate on net sales.
   (e) The rate earned on average total assets.
   (f) The rate earned on average stockholders' equity.
   (g) The number of times bond interest requirements were earned (before income tax).
   (h) The number of times preferred dividend requirements were earned.
   (i) The rate earned on average common stockholders' equity.
   (j) The earnings per share on common stock.
(2) Based on the measurements made in (1), evaluate the profitability of Sunshine State Equipment, Inc. for 1992 as compared with 1991 and 1990.

Problem 26–7   (Analysis of inventory, receivables, and payables)

Inventory and receivable balances and also gross profit data for Balboa Arrow Co. appear below:

	1992	1991	1990
Balance sheet data:			
Inventory, December 31	$100,000	$ 90,000	$ 80,000
Accounts receivable, December 31	55,000	50,000	20,000
Accounts payable, December 31	70,000	50,000	45,000
Net purchases	140,000	110,000	80,000
Income statement data:			
Net sales	$320,000	$260,000	$250,000
Cost of goods sold	215,000	200,000	180,000
Gross profit on sales	105,000	$ 60,000	$ 70,000

Instructions: Assuming a 300-day business year and all sales on a credit basis, compute the following measurements for 1992 and 1991.

(1) The receivables turnover rate.

(2) The average days' sales in receivables at the end of the year.

(3) The inventory turnover rate.

(4) The number of days' sales in inventory at the end of the year.

(5) The accounts payable turnover rate.

Problem 26—8 (Profitability analysis of three companies)

Financial information relating to three different companies appears below.

Item	Company A	Company B	Company C
Revenues	$60,000,000	$28,000,000	$21,000,000
Net income	$9,600,000	$1,850,000	$360,000
Net income to common stockholders*	$6,100,000	$1,140,000	$300,000
Average year-end balances:			
Total assets	$155,400,000	$21,500,000	$3,200,000
Common stockholders' equity	$61,000,000	$11,300,000	$1,690,000

*Net income less preferred stock dividends

Instructions:

(1) Compute the following ratios:
   (a) Net profit margin on sales.
   (b) Total asset turnover.
   (c) Rate earned on total assets.
   (d) Rate earned on stockholders' equity.

(2) Assume the three companies are (a) a large department store, (b) a large grocery store, and (c) a large utility. Based on the above information, identify each company. Explain your answer.

Problem 26—9 (Reporting segment data)

Abcom Industries operates in several different industries, some of which are appropriately regarded as reportable segments. Total sales for Abcom are $12,000,000 and total common costs are $6,000,000 for 1991. Abcom allocates common costs based on the ratio of a segment's sales to total sales, which is considered an appropriate method of allocation. Additional information regarding the different segments is contained in the following schedule:

	Segment 1	Segment 2	Segment 3	Segment 4	Other Segments
Contribution to total sales	23%	8%	31%	28%	10%
Identifiable assets as percent of total company assets	36%	9%	32%	8%	15%
Traceable costs	$800,000	$350,000	$1,200,000	$1,000,000	$650,000

Instructions: Prepare a schedule from which operating profit is derived for Abcom Industries which conforms to the reporting criteria set forth in FASB Statement No. 14.

Problem 26–10   (Comprehensive analysis of financial data)

The partially condensed balance sheet and income statement for Maxfield Company are shown below.

Maxfield Company
Balance Sheet
December 31, 1991

Assets

Cash.	$ 63,000
Trade receivables, less estimated uncollectibles of $12,000	238,000
Inventories.	170,000
Prepaid expenses	7,000
Land, buildings, and equipment, cost less $182,000 charged to operations . .	390,000
Other assets	13,000
	$881,000

Liabilities and Stockholders' Equity

Accounts and notes payable—trade	$ 98,000
Accrued liabilities payable	17,000
Income tax payable	18,000
First-mortgage, 7% bonds, due in 1998	150,000
$7 Preferred stock—no par value (entitled to $110 per share in liquidation); authorized 1,000 shares; in treasury 400 shares; outstanding 600 shares . . .	108,000
Common stock—no par; authorized 100,000 shares, issued and outstanding 10,000 shares stated at a nominal value of $10 per share	100,000
Paid-in capital from sale of common stock at more than stated value	242,000
Retained earnings appropriated for plant expansion	50,000
Retained earnings appropriated for cost of treasury stock.	47,000
Retained earnings	98,000
Cost of 400 shares of treasury stock.	(47,000)
	$881,000

Notes: (1) Working capital—December 31, 1990, was $205,000. (2) Trade receivables—December 31, 1990, were $220,000 gross, $206,000 net. (3) Dividends for 1991 have been declared and paid. (4) There has been no change in amount of bonds outstanding during 1991.

Maxfield Company
Income Statement
For the Year Ended December 31, 1991

	Cash	Credit	Total
Gross sales.	$116,000	$876,000	$992,000
Less: Sales discount	$ 3,000	$ 12,000	$ 15,000
Sales returns and allowances	1,000	6,000	7,000
	$ 4,000	$ 18,000	$ 22,000
Net sales	$112,000	$858,000	$970,000
Cost of goods sold:			
Inventory of finished goods, January 1		$ 92,000	
Cost of goods manufactured		680,000	
Inventory of finished goods, December 31		(100,000)	672,000
Gross profit on sales			$298,000
Selling expenses		$173,000	
General expenses		70,000	243,000
Income from operations.			$ 55,000
Other additions and deductions (net)			3,000
Income before income tax			$ 58,000
Income tax (estimated)			18,000
Net income			$ 40,000

Instructions: Compute the following:

(1) Acid-test ratio.
(2) Number of days sales in receivables.
(3) Average finished goods turnover.
(4) Number of times bond interest was earned (before tax).
(5) Number of times preferred dividend was earned.
(6) Earnings per share of common stock.
(7) Book value per share of common stock.
(8) Current ratio.

(AICPA adapted)

Appendix A

Illustrative Financial Statements

REPORT OF MANAGEMENT RESPONSIBILITIES

The management of General Mills, Inc. includes corporate executives, operating managers, controllers and other personnel working full time on company business. These managers are responsible for the fairness and accuracy of our financial statements. The Audit Committee of the Board of Directors meets periodically to satisfy itself that management, internal auditors and independent auditors are properly discharging their duties regarding internal control and financial reporting.

The statements have been prepared in accordance with generally accepted accounting principles, using management's best estimates and judgments where appropriate. The financial information throughout this report is consistent with our financial statements.

Management has established a system of internal controls which we believe provides reasonable assurance that, in all material respects, assets are maintained and accounted for in accordance with management's authorization, and transactions are recorded accurately on our books. Our internal controls provide for appropriate separation of duties and responsibilities, and there are documented policies regarding utilization of company assets and proper financial reporting. These formally stated and regularly communicated policies demand high ethical conduct from all employees.

We maintain a strong internal audit program that independently evaluates the adequacy and effectiveness of internal controls. The independent auditors, internal auditors and the Controller have full and free access to the Audit Committee at any time.

Peat Marwick Main & Co., independent certified public accountants, are retained to examine the consolidated financial statements. Their opinion follows.

H. B. Atwater, Jr.

H. B. Atwater, Jr.
Chairman of the Board and Chief Executive Officer

F. C. Blodgett

F. C. Blodgett
Vice Chairman of the Board,
Chief Financial and Administrative Officer

Mark H. Willes

M. H. Willes
President

REPORT OF THE AUDIT COMMITTEE

The Audit Committee of the Board of Directors is composed of six outside directors. Its primary function is to oversee the Company's system of internal controls, financial reporting practices and audits to ensure their quality, integrity and objectivity are sufficient to protect stockholder resources.

The Audit Committee met twice during fiscal 1988 to review the overall audit scope, plans and results of the internal auditor and independent auditor, the Company's internal controls, emerging accounting issues, officer and director expenses, audit fees, goodwill and other intangible values, and pension plans. Audit Committee meeting results were reported to the full Board of Directors. The Committee also met, without management present, with the independent auditor to discuss the results of their examination. Acting with the other Board members, the Com-

pany's annual financial statements were also reviewed and approved before issuance. The Audit Committee recommended to the Board of Directors that Peat Marwick Main & Co. be reappointed for fiscal 1989, subject to the approval of the stockholders at the annual meeting.

The Audit Committee is satisfied with the adequacy of the internal control system and that the stockholders of General Mills are protected by appropriate accounting and auditing procedures.

William F. Pounds

W. F. Pounds
Chairman, Audit Committee

INDEPENDENT AUDITORS' REPORT

The Stockholders and the Board of Directors of
General Mills, Inc.:

We have audited the accompanying consolidated balance sheets of General Mills, Inc. and subsidiaries as of May 29, 1988 and May 31, 1987, and the related consolidated statements of earnings, retained earnings and changes in financial position for each of the fiscal years in the three-year period ended May 29, 1988. These consolidated financial statements are the responsibility of the Company's management. Our responsibility is to express an opinion on these consolidated financial statements based on our audits.

We conducted our audits in accordance with generally accepted auditing standards. Those standards require that we plan and perform the audit to obtain reasonable assurance about whether the financial statements are free of material misstatement. An audit includes examining, on a test basis, evidence supporting the amounts and disclosures in the financial statements. An audit also includes assessing the accounting principles

used and significant estimates made by management, as well as evaluating the overall financial statement presentation. We believe that our audits provide a reasonable basis for our opinion.

In our opinion, the consolidated financial statements referred to above present fairly, in all material respects, the financial position of General Mills, Inc. and subsidiaries at May 29, 1988 and May 31, 1987, and the results of their operations and their changes in financial position for each of the fiscal years in the three-year period ended May 29, 1988 in conformity with generally accepted accounting principles.

As described in note 11 to the consolidated financial statements, the Company changed its method of accounting for pension costs in fiscal 1988.

Peat Marwick Main & Co.

Minneapolis, Minnesota
June 30, 1988

CONSOLIDATED STATEMENTS OF EARNINGS

Amounts in Millions, Except Per Share Data	Fiscal Year Ended		
	May 29, 1988	May 31, 1987	May 25, 1986
Continuing Operations:			
Sales	$5,178.8	$4,699.0	$4,112.3
Costs and Expenses:			
Cost of sales, exclusive of items below	2,847.8	2,576.7	2,289.1
Selling, general and administrative expenses	1,710.5	1,564.0	1,376.9
Depreciation and amortization expenses	140.0	122.8	104.5
Interest expense, net	37.7	29.7	31.6
Total Costs and Expenses	4,736.0	4,293.2	3,802.1
Earnings from Continuing Operations before Taxes	442.8	405.8	310.2
Income Taxes	177.4	197.5	135.1
Earnings from Continuing Operations	265.4	208.3	175.1
Earnings per Share – Continuing Operations	$ 3.05	$ 2.35	$ 1.96
Discontinued Operations after Taxes	17.7	13.7	8.4
Net Earnings	$ 283.1	$ 222.0	$ 183.5
Net Earnings per Share	$ 3.25	$ 2.50	$ 2.06
Average Number of Common Shares	87.0	88.7	89.2

CONSOLIDATED STATEMENTS OF RETAINED EARNINGS

Amounts in Millions, Except Per Share Data	Fiscal Year Ended		
	May 29, 1988	May 31, 1987	May 25, 1986
Retained Earnings at Beginning of Year	$ 924.1	$ 812.9	$1,201.7
Net Earnings	283.1	222.0	183.5
Deduct dividends of $1.60 per share in 1988, $1.25 per share in 1987 and $1.13 per share in 1986	(139.3)	(110.8)	(100.9)
Distribution of equity to stockholders from spin-offs of Toy and Fashion operations	—	—	(471.4)
Retained Earnings at End of Year	$1,067.9	$ 924.1	$ 812.9

See accompanying notes to consolidated financial statements.

CONSOLIDATED BALANCE SHEETS

In Millions	May 29, 1988	May 31, 1987
ASSETS		
Current Assets:		
Cash	$ 11.4	$ 48.7
Short-term investments	3.2	131.0
Receivables, less allowance for doubtful accounts of $6.1 in 1988 and $5.9 in 1987	230.0	236.7
Inventories	423.5	388.6
Prepaid expenses and other current assets	60.8	60.9
Deferred income taxes	80.6	75.0
Net assets of discontinued operations	176.4	—
Total Current Assets	985.9	940.9
Land, Buildings and Equipment, at cost:		
Land	129.2	115.8
Buildings	691.3	652.4
Equipment	1,124.0	1,028.2
Construction in progress	194.5	142.7
Total Land, Buildings and Equipment	2,139.0	1,939.1
Less accumulated depreciation	(762.6)	(689.6)
Net Land, Buildings and Equipment	1,376.4	1,249.5
Other Assets:		
Intangible assets, principally goodwill	72.9	56.4
Investments and miscellaneous assets	236.7	108.6
Total Other Assets	309.6	165.0
Total Assets	$2,671.9	$2,355.4
LIABILITIES AND STOCKHOLDERS' EQUITY		
Current Liabilities:		
Accounts payable	$ 460.8	$ 434.0
Current portion of long-term debt	1.5	94.4
Notes payable	370.1	2.2
Accrued taxes	75.3	116.4
Accrued payroll	110.1	105.1
Other current liabilities	173.6	170.9
Total Current Liabilities	1,191.4	923.0
Long-Term Debt	361.5	285.5
Deferred Income Taxes	176.5	140.7
Deferred Income Taxes — Tax Leases	230.6	216.9
Other Liabilities and Deferred Credits	63.4	58.9
Total Liabilities	2,023.4	1,625.0
Stockholders' Equity:		
Common stock	223.3	220.9
Retained earnings	1,067.9	924.1
Less common stock in treasury, at cost	(608.2)	(379.4)
Cumulative foreign currency adjustment	(34.5)	(35.2)
Total Stockholders' Equity	648.5	730.4
Total Liabilities and Stockholders' Equity	$2,671.9	$2,355.4

See accompanying notes to consolidated financial statements.

CONSOLIDATED STATEMENTS OF CHANGES IN FINANCIAL POSITION

	Fiscal Year Ended		
In Millions	May 29, 1988	May 31, 1987	May 25, 1986
Funds Provided (Used) by Operations:			
Earnings from continuing operations	$ 265.4	$ 208.3	$ 175.1
Depreciation and amortization	140.0	122.8	104.5
Deferred income taxes	28.1	9.4	22.8
Other, net	(27.8)	22.8	7.3
Funds provided by continuing operations	405.7	363.3	309.7
(Increase) decrease in working capital used by continuing operations	(75.8)	66.3	119.7
Cash provided by continuing operations	329.9	429.6	429.4
Cash provided (used) by discontinued operations	16.0	(15.4)	(78.1)
Cash Provided by Operations	345.9	414.2	351.3
Funds Provided (Used) by Investments:			
Purchase of land, buildings and equipment	(410.7)	(329.1)	(244.9)
Investments in businesses, intangibles and affiliates	(36.2)	(10.5)	—
Proceeds from disposal of land, buildings and equipment	13.0	17.7	19.0
Proceeds from dispositions	23.1	94.7	385.2
Other, net	(14.4)	9.7	(11.3)
Cash Provided (Used) by Investments	(425.2)	(217.5)	148.0
Funds Used for Dividends	(139.3)	(110.8)	(100.9)
Funds Provided (Used) by Financing:			
Increase (decrease) in notes payable	367.2	(3.5)	(376.0)
Issuance of long-term debt	87.1	50.9	99.1
Reduction of long-term debt	(108.2)	(176.5)	(144.5)
(Increase) decrease in long-term security investments	(68.3)	38.5	11.2
Cash flows from tax leases	2.1	54.4	113.3
Purchase of common stock for treasury	(246.6)	(80.7)	—
Common stock issued	20.2	20.4	22.0
Cash Provided (Used) by Financing	53.5	(96.5)	(274.9)
Increase (Decrease) in Cash and Short-Term Investments	$ (165.1)	$ (10.6)	$ 123.5
(Increase) Decrease in Working Capital Used by Continuing Operations:			
Receivables	$ (14.4)	$ (14.5)	$ 80.7
Inventories	(101.2)	(52.2)	28.6
Prepaid expenses and other current assets	(10.1)	(3.4)	20.2
Accrued taxes	(21.5)	96.5	3.1
Accounts payable and other current liabilities	71.4	39.9	(12.9)
(Increase) Decrease in Working Capital Used by Continuing Operations	$ (75.8)	$ 66.3	$ 119.7

See accompanying notes to consolidated financial statements.

NOTES TO CONSOLIDATED FINANCIAL STATEMENTS

NOTE ONE: SUMMARY OF SIGNIFICANT ACCOUNTING POLICIES

A. Principles of Consolidation

The consolidated financial statements include the following domestic and foreign operations: parent company and 100% owned subsidiaries other than General Mills Finance, Inc.; and General Mills' investment in and share of net earnings or losses of 20-50% owned companies. General Mills Finance, Inc. is accounted for by the equity method because of the different nature of its operations.

Our fiscal year ends on the last Sunday of May. Fiscal years 1988 and 1986 each consisted of 52 weeks and fiscal year 1987 consisted of 53 weeks. The fiscal years of foreign operations (other than Canada) generally end in April.

Certain 1987 and 1986 amounts have been reclassified to conform to the 1988 presentation.

B. Land, Buildings, Equipment and Depreciation

Buildings and equipment are depreciated over estimated useful lives ranging from 3-50 years, primarily using the straight-line method. Accelerated depreciation methods are generally used for income tax purposes.

When an item is sold or retired, the accounts are relieved of cost and the related accumulated depreciation; the resulting gains and losses, if any, are recognized.

C. Inventories

Inventories are valued at the lower of cost or market. Certain domestic inventories are valued using the LIFO method, while other inventories are generally valued using the FIFO method.

D. Amortization of Intangibles

Goodwill represents the difference between purchase prices of acquired companies and the related fair values of net assets acquired and accounted for by the purchase method of accounting. Any goodwill acquired after October 1970 is amortized on a straight-line basis over 40 years or less.

The costs of patents, copyrights and other intangible assets are amortized evenly over their estimated useful lives. Most of these costs were incurred through purchases of businesses.

The Audit Committee of the Board of Directors annually reviews goodwill and other intangibles. At its meeting on April 25, 1988, the Board of Directors affirmed that the remaining amounts of these assets have continuing value.

E. Research and Development

All expenditures for research and development are charged against earnings in the year incurred. The charges for fiscal 1988, 1987 and 1986 were $40.7 million, $38.0 million and $41.4 million, respectively.

F. Income Taxes

Income taxes include deferred income taxes that result from timing differences between earnings for financial reporting and tax purposes. Investment tax credits are reflected as reductions of income taxes in the year eligible assets are placed in service.

G. Earnings Per Share

Earnings per share has been determined by dividing net earnings by the weighted average number of common shares outstanding during the year. Common share equivalents were not material.

H. Foreign Currency Translation

For most foreign operations, local currencies are considered the functional currency. Assets and liabilities are translated using the exchange rates in effect at the balance sheet date. Results of operations are translated using the average exchange rates prevailing throughout the period. Translation effects are accumulated as part of the foreign currency adjustment in stockholders' equity.

Gains and losses from foreign currency transactions are generally included in net earnings for the period.

NOTE TWO: DISCONTINUED OPERATIONS

In the fourth quarter of fiscal 1988, the Board of Directors authorized disposition of the Specialty Retailing segment of our business. The sales of Talbots and Eddie Bauer were closed subsequent to year end and will result in a net gain in the first quarter of fiscal 1989.

Operating income for the Specialty Retailing segment for fiscal 1988, net of income tax expense of $11.8 million, was $17.7 million ($.20 per share). This includes $6.4 million of interest expense allocated to the segment based on their capital using an appropriate debt-to-capital ratio.

The net assets of the discontinued operations included on the Consolidated Balance Sheet as of May 29, 1988, amounted to $176.4 million and consisted primarily of receivables, inventories, fixed assets, certain intangibles and miscellaneous liabilities. The prior year's Consolidated Balance Sheet has not been restated.

In fiscal 1987, we sold The Furniture Group America, Inc., consisting of our Pennsylvania House and Kittinger furniture operations. The discontinuation of this line of business, including the gain on the transaction and operating losses, resulted in a net after-tax gain of $12.3 million ($.14 per share).

Also during fiscal 1987, we recorded additional after-tax charges related to our previously discontinued businesses of $12.3 million ($.14 per share). These adjustments were primarily due to additional estimated tax costs, as well as the estimated effects of the Tax Reform Act of 1986 and other minor adjustments to established reserves. No adjustments to these reserves were recorded in fiscal 1986.

Sales for the discontinued operations were $598.9 million, $509.2 million and $474.3 million for fiscal 1988, 1987 and 1986, respectively.

The Consolidated Statements of Earnings have been restated to show continuing operations for the periods presented with discontinued operations shown separately. The Notes to Consolidated Financial Statements relate to continuing operations only.

NOTE THREE: UNUSUAL ITEMS

During fiscal 1988, we disposed of our Pioneer Products and Leeann Chin's operations and recorded a charge for closing of poorly performing York's units, resulting in a decrease in net earnings of $3.1 million ($.04 per share). In fiscal 1987, unusual items included insurance settlements, a land condemnation and the sale of a grain terminal elevator, which resulted in an increase in net earnings of $8.6 million ($.10 per share).

NOTE FOUR: FOREIGN CURRENCY TRANSLATION

The following is an analysis of the changes in the cumulative foreign currency adjustment equity account:

	Fiscal Year	
In Millions	1988	1987
Balance, beginning of year	$35.2	$32.2
Adjustments during the year, including applicable income taxes of $5.8 in 1988 and $5.1 in 1987	(0.7)	3.0
Balance, end of year	$34.5	$35.2

NOTE FIVE: INVENTORIES

The components of year-end inventories are as follows:

In Millions	May 29, 1988	May 31, 1987
Raw materials, work in process and supplies	$206.2	$156.4
Finished goods	209.1	259.0
Grain	61.2	24.7
Reserve for LIFO valuation method	(53.0)	(51.5)
Total inventories	$423.5	$388.6

At May 29, 1988, and May 31, 1987, respectively, $185.2 million and $151.5 million were valued at LIFO. If the FIFO method of inventory accounting had been used in place of LIFO, reported earnings per share would have been higher by $.01 in fiscal 1988, $.03 in fiscal 1987, and lower by $.01 in fiscal 1986.

NOTE SIX: SHORT-TERM BORROWINGS

The components of year-end notes payable are as follows:

In Millions	May 29, 1988	May 31, 1987
U.S. commercial paper	$285.1	$ —
Banks	85.0	2.2
Total notes payable	$370.1	$ 2.2

To ensure availability of funds, we maintain domestic bank credit lines sufficient to cover our outstanding commercial paper. As of May 29, 1988, we had $160.0 million fee-paid lines and $150.0 million uncommitted, no-fee lines available. Foreign subsidiaries had $18.3 million of unused credit lines.

Subsequent to year end, our fee-paid bank credit lines expired and we entered into a revolving credit agreement. This agreement provides for a $150.0 million fee-paid credit line for three years, extendable to five years at our option.

NOTE SEVEN: LONG-TERM DEBT

In Millions	May 29, 1988	May 31, 1987
Zero coupon notes, yield 11.14%, $566.6		
due August 15, 2013	$ 37.6	$ 34.6
9¾% sinking fund debentures due March 1, 2009	113.3	113.3
Zero coupon notes, yield 11.73%, $92.7		
due August 15, 2004	14.7	13.8
12% notes due December 19, 1991	69.3	71.6
Zero coupon notes, yield 14⅝%, $49.2		
due June 30, 1991	31.9	27.7
14% Australian dollar notes due July 27, 1990	70.2	—
Zero coupon notes, yield 13.3%, $100.0		
due January 4, 1988	—	92.7
Other, no individual item greater than $3.2	26.0	26.2
	363.0	379.9
Less amounts due within one year	(1.5)	(94.4)
Total long-term debt	$361.5	$285.5

In fiscal 1988, we issued from our shelf registration statements 100 million Australian dollar notes (approximately $70 million), due July 27, 1990, at 14%. In a related transaction we entered into an agreement to convert the Australian dollar principal and interest obligations into U.S. dollars. This agreement also converts the fixed interest rate to a variable interest rate (6.7% at May 29, 1988).

In fiscal 1988, we filed an additional shelf registration statement with the Securities and Exchange Commission. Our shelf registrations now permit the issuance of up to $229.6 million net proceeds in unsecured debt securities to reduce short-term debt and for other general corporate purposes.

In fiscal 1987, we purchased $53.3 million face amount of the zero coupon notes, 14 ⅝% yield, which decreased net earnings by $4.4 million ($.05 per share).

In fiscal 1987, certain debt warrants that expire on December 19, 1989, were exercised, resulting in the issuance of $25.2 million principal amount of the 12% Series B notes. We called $33.8 million of the 12% Series A notes. We also purchased $29.9 million principal amount of 12% Series B notes which decreased net earnings by $2.5 million ($.03 per share).

In fiscal 1987 and 1986, we purchased $343.9 million and $75.9 million face amount of the zero coupon notes, 11.14% yield, and $79.5 million and $73.4 million face amount of the zero coupon notes, 11.73% yield, respectively. These transactions decreased fiscal 1987 and 1986 net earnings by $9.9 million ($.11 per share) and $2.9 million ($.03 per share), respectively. In related transactions, we sold U.S. Treasury securities (which we purchased with the original debt proceeds) and increased fiscal 1987 and 1986 net earnings by $13.7 million ($.15 per share) and $5.0 million ($.06 per share), respectively.

We have an agreement that converts the fixed interest rate on our 12% notes to a variable rate (7.2% at May 29, 1988).

The sinking fund and principal payments due on long-term debt are (in millions) $1.5, $1.1, $71.3, $108.2 ($125.5 face amount) and $8.0 in fiscal years ending 1989, 1990, 1991, 1992, and 1993, respectively.

Certain debt issues have been removed from our Consolidated Balance Sheets through the creation of irrevocable trusts. The principal and interest of the funds deposited with the trustee will be sufficient to fund the scheduled principal and interest payments of these debt issues. At May 29, 1988, there was $98.1 million of this debt outstanding.

NOTE EIGHT: CHANGES IN CAPITAL STOCK

	$.75 Par Value Common Stock (250.0 Million Shares Authorized)			
	Issued		In Treasury	
Dollars in Millions	Shares	Amount	Shares	Amount
Balance at May 26, 1985	102,076,666	$213.7	13,195,018	$333.9
Stock option, profit sharing and employee stock ownership plans	—	2.2	(786,038)	(19.8)
Balance at May 25, 1986	102,076,666	215.9	12,408,980	314.1
Stock option, profit sharing and employee stock ownership plans	—	5.0	(587,154)	(15.4)
Shares repurchased on open market	—	—	2,022,600	80.7
Balance at May 31, 1987	102,076,666	220.9	13,844,426	379.4
Stock option, profit sharing and employee stock ownership plans	—	2.4	(626,768)	(17.8)
Shares repurchased on open market	—	—	5,204,200	246.6
Balance at May 29, 1988	102,076,666	$223.3	18,421,858	$608.2

Cumulative preference stock of 5.0 million shares, without par value, is authorized but unissued.

During fiscal 1986, the Board of Directors declared a distribution of one right for each outstanding share of common stock. As a result of the stock split in November 1986, one-half right is now associated with each such share. Each right entitles the holder to purchase one one-hundredth of a share of cumulative preference stock (or, in certain circumstances, common stock or other securities), exercisable upon the occurrence of certain events. The rights are not exercisable or transferable apart from the common stock until a person or group has acquired 20 percent or more, or makes a tender offer for 30 percent or more, of the common stock. If the Company is acquired in a merger or other business combination transaction, each right will entitle the holder (other than the acquiring company) to receive, upon exercise, common stock of either the Company or the acquiring company having a value equal to two times the exercise price of the right. The rights are redeemable by the Board in certain circumstances and expire on March 7, 1996. At May 29, 1988, there were 41.8 million rights issued and outstanding.

The Board of Directors has authorized the repurchase, from time to time, of common stock for our treasury, provided that the number of shares in the treasury shall not exceed 25.0 million.

NOTE NINE: STOCK OPTIONS

The following table contains information on stock options:

	Shares	Average Option Price Per Share
Granted:		
1988	778,872	$51.76
1987	869,400	44.11
1986	447,900	29.73
Exercised:		
1988	715,392	$19.47
1987	526,420	19.48
1986	707,598	17.83
Expired:		
1988	155,234	$27.40
1987	59,929	26.42
1986	145,888	21.73
Outstanding at year-end:		
1988	3,618,953	$32.77
1987	3,710,707	25.99
1986	3,427,656	20.40
Exercisable at year-end:		
1988	2,340,327	$24.84
1987	2,283,259	19.33
1986	2,331,756	18.29

Options for a total of 1,557,220 shares are available for grant to officers and key employees under our 1984 stock option plan, under which grants may be made until September 30, 1988. The options may be granted subject to approval of the Compensation Committee of the Board of Directors at a price not less than 100% of the fair market value on the date the option is granted. Options now outstanding include some granted under the 1975 and 1980 option plans, under which no further options may be granted. All options expire within 10 years plus one month after the date of grant. The plans provide for full vesting of benefits, except in limited circumstances, in the event there is a change of control.

The 1980 and 1984 plans permit the granting of performance units corresponding to stock options granted. The value of performance units will be determined by return on equity and growth in earnings per share measured against preset goals over three-year performance periods. For seven years after a performance period, holders may elect to receive the value of performance units (with interest) as an alternative to exercising corresponding stock options. On May 29, 1988, there were 1,923,068 outstanding options with corresponding performance units or performance unit accounts.

The 1984 plan provides for granting of incentive stock options as well as non-qualified options. No incentive stock options have yet been granted.

NOTE TEN: INTEREST EXPENSE

The components of net interest expense are as follows:

	Fiscal Year		
In Millions	1988	1987	1986
Interest expense	$56.2	$46.3	$56.9
Capitalized interest	(5.1)	(3.0)	(4.1)
Interest income	(13.4)	(13.6)	(21.2)
Interest expense, net	$37.7	$29.7	$31.6

The Tax Reform Act of 1986 reduced the income tax rate from 46% to 34% effective July 1, 1987. This change in the rate affected the assumptions made in accounting for our tax benefit leases and resulted in an after-tax decrease in net interest expense of $7.7 million ($.09 per share) in fiscal 1987.

NOTE ELEVEN: EMPLOYEES' RETIREMENT PLANS

We have defined benefit plans covering most employees. Benefits for salaried employees are based on length of service and final average compensation. The hourly plans include various monthly amounts for each year of credited service. Our funding policy is consistent with the funding requirements of federal law and regulations. Our principal plan covering salaried employees has a provision that any excess pension assets would be vested in plan participants if the plan is terminated within five years of a change in control. Plan assets consist principally of listed equity securities and corporate obligations, insurance contracts and U.S. government bonds.

In fiscal 1988, we adopted Statement of Financial Accounting Standards No. 87, "Employers' Accounting for Pensions." The effect of the change was to reduce pension expense in fiscal 1988 by $41.9 million. Components of the net pension credit for fiscal 1988 are as follows:

In Millions

Service cost—benefits earned	$ 10.4
Interest cost on projected benefit obligation	41.0
Actual return on plan assets	1.2
Net amortization and deferral	(86.6)
Net pension credit	$ (34.0)

The weighted-average discount rate and rate of increase in future compensation levels used in determining the actuarial present value of the benefit obligations were 10.67% and 6%, respectively. The expected long-term rate of return on assets was 11.35%.

The funded status of the plans and the amount recognized on the year-end Consolidated Balance Sheet (as determined on May 31, 1988) are as follows:

In Millions

Actuarial present value of benefit obligations:	
Vested benefits	$320.8
Nonvested benefits	35.7
Accumulated benefit obligation	356.5
Projected benefit obligation	412.4
Plan assets at fair value	595.2
Plan assets in excess of the projected benefit obligation	182.8
Unrecognized net loss	74.5
Unrecognized transition asset	(214.4)
Prepaid pension asset	$ 42.9

The new Statement was adopted on a prospective basis as required; therefore, the fiscal 1987 and 1986 pension expense has not been restated. Defined benefit plan pension expense for fiscal 1987 and 1986 was $7.8 million and $19.2 million, respectively. The decrease in fiscal 1987 pension expense resulted from changes to the investment return assumption and actuarial cost method. The actuarial present value of accumulated plan benefits at January 1, 1987, was $470 million (of which $55 million was nonvested), compared with net assets available for benefits of $558 million. Actuarial present values of accumulated benefits were determined using discount rates established by the Pension Benefit Guaranty Corporation (PBGC) for valuing plan benefits. The PBGC rates ranged from 4% to 7.5% for 1987, with the latter of the range being the principal rate.

We have a few defined contribution plans that provide for benefits based on accumulated contributions and investment income. Our contributions to the plans expensed in fiscal 1988, 1987 and 1986 were $11.0 million, $12.0 million and $10.6 million, respectively.

We sponsor a variety of plans that provide health care benefits to the majority of our retirees. Some of these plans require contributions from the retirees. We recognized total costs of $4.9 million, $4.7 million and $4.3 million in fiscal 1988, 1987 and 1986, respectively, for these benefits on a pay-as-you-go basis.

NOTE TWELVE: PROFIT-SHARING PLANS

We have profit-sharing plans to provide incentives to key individuals who have the greatest potential to contribute to current earnings and successful future operations. These plans were approved by the Board of Directors upon recommendation of the Compensation Committee. The awards under these plans depend on profit performance in relation to pre-established goals. The plans are administered by the Compensation Committee, which consists of directors who are not members of our management. Profit-sharing expense, including performance unit accruals, was $8.8 million in fiscal 1988, $10.7 million in fiscal 1987 and $9.4 million in fiscal 1986.

NOTE THIRTEEN: INCOME TAXES

The components of earnings before income taxes and the income taxes thereon are as follows:

	Fiscal Year		
In Millions	1988	1987	1986
Earnings before income taxes:			
U.S.	$414.7	$381.0	$293.2
Outside U.S.	28.1	24.8	17.0
Total earnings before income taxes	$442.8	$405.8	$310.2
Income taxes:			
Current:			
Federal taxes	$114.1	$158.3	$101.4
U.S. investment tax credit	(0.1)	(6.2)	(10.3)
State and local taxes	28.2	27.4	15.0
Foreign taxes	7.1	8.6	6.2
Total current income taxes	149.3	188.1	112.3
Deferred income taxes (principally U.S.)	28.1	9.4	22.8
Total income taxes	$177.4	$197.5	$135.1

In prior years we purchased certain income tax items from other companies through tax lease transactions. Total current income taxes charged to earnings in fiscal 1988, 1987 and 1986 reflect the amounts attributable to operations and have not been materially affected by tax leases. Actual current taxes payable on fiscal 1988 operations were increased by approximately $2 million and fiscal 1987 and 1986 operations were reduced by approximately $55 million and $112 million, respectively, due to the effect of tax leases. These tax benefits are temporary in nature and do not affect taxes for statement of earnings purposes since the amount of benefits (net of the consideration paid to the sellers) will be repaid to the government in future years over the terms of the leases. The repayment liability is classified as "Deferred Income Taxes—Tax Leases."

Deferred income taxes result from timing differences in the recognition of revenue and expense for tax and financial statement purposes. The tax effects of these differences follow:

	Fiscal Year		
In Millions	1988	1987	1986
Depreciation	$13.2	$22.1	$17.1
Prepaid pension asset	16.6	—	—
Utilization of contribution carryover	9.1	—	—
Interest	0.7	(11.2)	(3.9)
Provision for losses on dispositions	(1.1)	5.6	22.1
Accrued expenses	(10.8)	(0.1)	(8.0)
Other	0.4	(7.0)	(4.5)
Total deferred income taxes	$28.1	$ 9.4	$22.8

The following table reconciles the U.S. statutory income tax rate with the effective income tax rate:

	Fiscal Year		
	1988	1987	1986
U.S. statutory rate	35.0%	46.0%	46.0%
U.S. investment tax credit	—	(1.5)	(3.3)
State and local income taxes, net of federal tax benefits	5.0	3.7	3.8
Other, net	0.1	0.5	(2.9)
Effective income tax rate	40.1%	48.7%	43.6%

Provision has been made for foreign and U.S. taxes that would be payable on foreign operations' earnings that are not considered permanently reinvested. Additional income taxes have not been provided on unremitted earnings of foreign operations amounting to $76.2 million that are expected by management to be permanently reinvested. If a portion were to be remitted, income tax credits would substantially offset any resulting tax liability.

NOTE FOURTEEN: LEASES

An analysis of rent expense by property leased follows:

	Fiscal Year		
In Millions	1988	1987	1986
Restaurant space	$16.1	$13.6	$11.4
Warehouse space	7.2	6.5	5.9
Office space	4.0	3.7	3.7
Transportation	3.1	2.8	2.7
All other	3.2	3.1	3.1
Total rent expense	$33.6	$29.7	$26.8

Some leases require payment of property taxes, insurance and maintenance costs in addition to the rent payments. Contingent and escalation rent in excess of minimum rent payments totaled approximately $2.1 million in fiscal 1988, $1.7 million in fiscal 1987 and $1.4 million in fiscal 1986. Sublease income netted in rent expense was insignificant.

Noncancelable future lease commitments are (in millions) $26.3 in 1989, $22.9 in 1990, $19.7 in 1991, $17.6 in 1992, $15.7 in 1993 and $149.9 after 1993, or a cumulative total of $252.1.

NOTE FIFTEEN: SEGMENT INFORMATION

In Millions	Consumer Foods	Restaurants	Unallocated Corporate Items (a)	Consolidated Total
Sales				
1988	**$3,752.6**	**$1,426.2**		**$5,178.8**
1987	3,449.9	1,249.1		4,699.0
1986	3,061.3	1,051.0		4,112.3
Operating Profits				
1988(b)	**411.3**	**88.9**	**$ (57.4)**	**442.8**
1987	369.5	92.5	(56.2)	405.8
1986	284.2	84.8	(58.8)	310.2
Identifiable Assets (c)				
1988	**1,441.7**	**772.0**	**458.2**	**2,671.9**
1987	1,211.7	594.0	549.7	2,355.4
1986	1,091.8	467.8	612.7	2,172.3
Capital Expenditures				
1988	**191.2**	**163.8**	**55.7**	**410.7**
1987	151.5	145.3	32.3	329.1
1986	153.6	74.0	17.3	244.9
Depreciation Expense				
1988	**88.0**	**47.9**	**1.4**	**137.3**
1987	78.9	39.4	1.6	119.9
1986	69.2	32.7	1.0	102.9

(a) Corporate expenses reported here include net interest expense and general corporate expenses. Corporate capital expenditures include capital expenditures of discontinued Speciality Retailing operations through the date disposition was authorized.

(b) The effect of the change in method of accounting for pension costs on operating profits was an increase for Consumer Foods of $38.7 million and Restaurants of $2.1 million in fiscal 1988.

(c) Identifiable assets for our segments consist of receivables, inventories, prepaid expenses, net land, buildings and equipment, intangible assets and investments and miscellaneous assets. Corporate identifiable assets consist mainly of cash, short-term investments, deferred income taxes, other miscellaneous investments and net assets of discontinued Specialty Retailing operations.

NOTE SIXTEEN:QUARTERLY DATA (UNAUDITED)

Summarized quarterly data for fiscal 1988 and 1987 follows:

In Millions, Except Per Share and Market Price Amounts	First Quarter		Second Quarter		Third Quarter		Fourth Quarter		Total Year	
	1988	1987	**1988**	1987	**1988**	1987	**1988**	1987	**1988**	1987
Sales	**$1,273.8**	$1,109.0	**$1,334.7**	$1,196.9	**$1,263.9**	$1,163.1	**$1,306.4**	$1,230.0	**$5,178.8**	$4,699.0
Gross profit *	**577.7**	505.7	**606.7**	559.1	**571.2**	539.9	**575.4**	517.6	**2,331.0**	2,122.3
Earnings after taxes –										
Continuing operations	**79.7**	61.0	**72.7**	54.3	**65.2**	51.9	**47.8**	41.1	**265.4**	208.3
Earnings per share –										
Continuing operations	**.90**	.68	**.82**	.61	**.76**	.59	**.57**	.47	**3.05**	2.35
Discontinued operations after taxes	**(2.5)**	(1.9)	**6.9**	15.6	**6.2**	5.0	**7.1**	(5.0)	**17.7**	13.7
Net earnings	**77.2**	59.1	**79.6**	69.9	**71.4**	56.9	**54.9**	36.1	**283.1**	222.0
Net earnings per share	**.87**	.66	**.90**	.79	**.83**	.64	**.65**	.41	**3.25**	2.50
Dividends per share	**.40**	.29	**.40**	.32	**.40**	.32	**.40**	.32	**1.60**	1.25
Market price of common stock:										
High	**62⅛**	45⅝	**59¼**	47⅜	**52¾**	51⅞	**51⅜**	56	**62⅛**	56
Low	**52¼**	37	**40¾**	37⅜	**41½**	41¼	**43⅛**	43	**40¾**	37

* Before charges for depreciation.

ELEVEN YEAR FINANCIAL SUMMARY AS REPORTED

Amounts in Millions, Except Per Share Data	May 29, 1988	May 31, 1987	May 25, 1986
FINANCIAL RESULTS			
Earnings (loss) per share (a)	$ 3.25	$ 2.50	$ 2.06
Return on average equity	41.1%	31.4%	21.5%
Dividends per share (a)	$ 1.60	1.25	1.13
Sales (b)	$5,178.8	5,189.3	4,586.6
Costs and expenses:			
Cost of sales, exclusive of items below (b)	$2,847.8	2,834.0	2,563.9
Selling, general and administrative (b)	$1,710.5	1,757.5	1,547.2
Depreciation and amortization (b)	$ 140.0	131.7	113.1
Interest (b)(c)	$ 37.7	32.9	38.8
Earnings before income taxes (b)	$ 442.8	433.2	323.6
Net earnings (loss)	$ 283.1	222.0	183.5
Net earnings (loss) as a percent of sales	5.5%	4.3%	4.0%
Weighted average number of common shares(a)(g)	87.0	88.7	89.2
Taxes (income, payroll, property, etc.) per share (a)(b)	$ 3.32	3.60	2.67
FINANCIAL POSITION			
Total assets	$2,671.9	2,280.4	2,086.2
Land, buildings and equipment, net (b)	$1,376.4	1,249.5	1,084.9
Working capital at year-end	$ (205.5)	(57.1)	41.6
Long-term debt, excluding current portion	$ 361.5	285.5	458.3
Stockholders' equity	$ 648.5	730.4	682.5
Stockholders' equity per share (a)	$ 7.75	8.28	7.61
OTHER STATISTICS			
Funds provided by operations (b)	$ 405.7	388.5	333.2
Total dividends	$ 139.3	110.8	100.9
Gross capital expenditures (h)	$ 410.7	329.1	244.9
Research and development (b)	$ 40.7	38.3	41.7
Advertising media expenditures (b)	$ 345.9	330.0	317.0
Wages, salaries and employee benefits (b)	$ 911.3	958.6	895.8
Number of employees (b)	74,453	65,619	62,056
Accumulated LIFO reserve (b)	$ 53.0	51.5	45.8
Common stock price range (a)	$ 62⅛–	56–	40⅛–
	40¾	37	26

(a) Years prior to fiscal 1987 have been adjusted for the two-for-one stock split in November 1986.

(b) Includes continuing operations only; years prior to fiscal 1988 include the discontinued Specialty Retailing apparel operations, years prior to fiscal 1987 include the discontinued furniture operations, and years prior to fiscal 1985 include the discontinued Toy, Fashion and Specialty Retailing non-apparel operations.

(c) Interest expense is net of interest income; amounts for years prior to fiscal 1986 are interest expense only with interest income included in selling, general and administrative expenses.

FINANCIAL DATA FOR CONTINUING OPERATIONS (years prior to fiscal 1988 restated)

Amounts in Millions, Except Per Share Data	Fiscal Year Ended					
	May 29, 1988	May 31, 1987	May 25, 1986	May 26, 1985	May 27, 1984	May 29, 1983
Sales	$5,178.8	$4,699.0	$4,112.3	$3,911.9	$3,793.5	$3,777.5
Earnings after taxes	$ 265.4	208.3	175.1	135.8	208.8	158.5
Earnings per share	$ 3.05	2.35	1.96	1.52	2.23	1.58

May 26, 1985	May 27, 1984	May 29, 1983	May 30, 1982	May 31, 1981	May 25, 1980	May 27, 1979	May 28, 1978
$ (.81)	$ 2.49	$ 2.45	$ 2.23	$ 1.95	$ 1.68	$ 1.46	$ 1.36
(6.5)%	19.0%	19.9%	19.1%	18.2%	17.6%	17.0%	17.6%
1.12	1.02	.92	.82	.72	.64	.56	.48½
4,285.2	5,600.8	5,550.8	5,312.1	4,852.4	4,170.3	3,745.0	3,243.0
2,474.8	3,165.9	3,123.3	3,081.6	2,936.9	2,578.5	2,347.7	2,026.1
1,443.9	1,841.7	1,831.6	1,635.5	1,384.0	1,145.5	1,021.3	883.8
110.4	133.1	127.5	113.2	99.5	81.1	73.3	58.6
60.2	61.4	58.7	75.1	57.6	48.6	38.8	29.3
195.9(d)	398.7	409.7	406.7	374.4	316.6	263.9	245.2(e)
(72.9)(f)	233.4	245.1	225.5	196.6	170.0	147.0	135.8
(1.7)%	4.2%	4.4%	4.2%	4.1%	4.1%	3.9%	4.2%
89.5	93.7	100.2	101.2	100.8	100.9	100.7	99.9
2.01	3.11	2.85	2.94	2.79	2.33	1.99	1.85
2,662.6	2,858.1	2,943.9	2,701.7	2,301.3	2,012.4	1,835.2	1,612.7
956.0	1,229.4	1,197.5	1,054.1	920.6	747.5	643.7	587.0
229.4	244.5	235.6	210.7	337.3	416.3	441.6	285.1
449.5	362.6	464.0	331.9	348.6	377.5	384.8	259.9
1,023.3	1,224.6	1,227.4	1,232.2	1,145.4	1,020.7	916.2	815.1
11.51	13.53	12.84	12.25	11.37	10.16	9.12	8.19
241.3	348.3	401.6	353.6	317.8	262.7	237.5	197.9
100.4	96.0	92.7	82.3	72.3	64.4	56.1	48.2
209.7	282.4	308.0	287.3	246.6	196.5	154.1	140.5
38.7	63.5	60.6	53.8	45.4	44.4	37.3	30.5
274.3	349.6	336.2	284.9	222.0	213.1	188.9	170.5
860.2	1,121.6	1,115.2	1,028.4	907.0	781.2	717.1	622.0
63,162	80,297	81,186	75,893	71,225	66,032	64,229	66,574
47.5	79.7	79.7	75.5	73.7	60.3	46.5	29.3
30¼–	28½–	28⅞–	21–	17⅞–	14⅛–	17–	15¾–
23⅞	20¾	19¼	16¼	11⅝	9½	12	13⅛

(d) Includes pretax redeployment charge of $75.8 million.

(e) Before discontinued Chemical operations.

(f) Includes after-tax discontinued operations charge of $188.3 million.

(g) Years prior to fiscal 1983 include common share equivalents.

(h) Includes capital expenditures of continuing operations and capital expenditures of discontinued operations through the date disposition was authorized.

Appendix B

Glossary

A

Accelerated Cost Recovery System (ACRS). An alternative to traditional depreciation methods introduced for tax purposes in 1981 and subsequently modified. *See* Modified Accelerated Cost Recovery System (MACRS).

Account form of balance sheet. A balance sheet that presents assets on the left-hand side and liabilities and owners' equity on the right-hand side.

Account. A record used to classify and summarize the effects of transactions; a separate account is maintained for each asset, liability, owners' equity, revenue, and expense item, showing increases, decreases, and the account balance.

Accounting and Audit Guides. Publications by special committees of the AICPA that deal with specific industries. These guides not only contain information concerning the auditing of these entities, but also discuss alternative accounting methods that could be used.

Accounting and Auditing Enforcement Releases (AAERs). SEC reports of substandard or fraudulent reporting in SEC filings and actions taken against the parties involved.

Accounting changes. A general term used to describe the use of different estimates or accounting principles or reporting entities from those used in a prior year.

Accounting cycle. *See* Accounting process.

Accounting errors. Incorrect accounting treatment resulting from mathematical mistakes, improper application of accounting principles, or omissions of material facts.

Accounting periods. The time intervals used for financial reporting; due to the need for timely information, the life of a business or other entity is divided into specific accounting periods for external reporting purposes. One year has been established as the normal reporting period, although some entities also provide interim (e.g., quarterly) statements.

Accounting Principles Board (APB). A board of the AICPA that issued opinions establishing accounting standards during the period 1959-1973.

Accounting process. The procedures used for analyzing, recording, classifying, and summarizing the information to be presented in accounting reports; also referred to as the accounting cycle.

Accounting Research Bulletins (ARBs). The publications of the Committee on Accounting Procedure that established accounting standards during the years 1939-1959.

Accounting system. The procedures and methods used, including use of data processing equipment, to collect and report accounting data.

Accounting. A service activity whose "function is to provide quantitative information, primarily financial in nature, about economic entities that is intended to be useful in making economic decisions—in making reasoned choices among alternative courses of action" (APBO Statement No. 4., par. 40).

Accounts receivable turnover. An analytical measurement of how rapidly customers' accounts are being collected. The net accounts receivable formula is net credit sales divided by average accounts receivable for a period.

Accounts receivable. Trade receivables that are not evidenced by a formal agreement or "note"; accounts receivable are usually unsecured "open accounts" and represent an extension of short-term credit to customers.

Accrual accounting. A basic assumption that revenues are recognized when earned and expenses are recognized when incurred, without regard to when cash is received or paid.

Accrued pension cost. The cumulative excess of annual pension costs over annual pension contributions. It is reported as a liability on a company's balance sheet.

Accumulated benefit obligation (ABO). The actuarial present value of pension benefits based on the plan formula for employee service earned to date using the existing salary structure. It is used to compute the minimum liability.

Acid-test ratio. An analytical measurement of the short-term liquidity of an entity. The acid-test ratio formula is quick assets divided by the current liabilities at a specified time.

Actual return on pension plan assets. A component of net periodic pension costs measured by the difference between the fair value of pension plan assets at the end of the period and the fair value at the beginning of the period, adjusted for contributions and payments of benefits during the period.

Actuarial present value. The present value of pension obligations determined by using stated actuarial assumptions and estimates.

Additional markups. Increases that raise prices above original retail.

Additional paid-in capital. The investment by stockholders in excess of the amounts assignable to capital stock as par or stated value as well as invested capital from other sources, such as donations of property or sale of treasury stock.

Additional pension liability. An additional liability reported for underfunded pension plans. It is computed as the difference between the minimum pension liability and accrued pension cost or as the sum of the minimum pension liability and the prepaid pension cost.

Additions. Expenditures that add to asset usefulness by either extending life or increasing future cash flows. No replacement of components is involved. Additions add to the cost of the asset.

Adjunct account. An account used to record additions to a related account. An example is Freight-In, which is added to the purchases account.

Adjusting entries. Entries required at the end of each accounting period to update the accounts as necessary and to fully recognize, on an accrual basis, revenues and expenses for the period.

Aging receivables. The most commonly used method for establishing an Allowance for Doubtful Accounts based on outstanding receivables. This method involves analyzing individual accounts to determine those not yet due and those past due. Past due accounts are classified in terms of length of the period past due.

Allowance method. A method of recognizing the estimated losses from uncollectible accounts as expenses during the period in which the sales occur; this method is required by GAAP.

American Accounting Association (AAA). An organization for accounting academicians. Its role in establishing accounting standards includes research projects to help the FASB and a forum for representing different points of view on various issues.

American Institute of Certified Public Accountants (AICPA). A professional organization for CPAs. Membership in the AICPA is voluntary. It publishes a monthly journal, the *Journal of Accountancy.*

Amortization of unrecognized net pension gain or loss. The systematic recognition as a component of net pension cost over several periods of previously unrecognized net pension gain or loss. Amortization of unrecognized prior service cost. The systematic recognition as a component of net pension cost over several periods of previously unrecognized prior service cost.

Amortization. Periodic cost allocation process for intangible assets.

Annuity due. An annuity that consists of payments (receipts) at the beginning of each period; also known as an annuity in advance.

Annuity. A series of equal payments (receipts) over a specified number of equal time periods.

Antidilution of earnings. Assumed conversion of convertible securities or exercise of stock options that results in an increase in earnings per share or a decrease in loss per share.

Antidilutive securities. Securities whose assumed conversion or exercise results in an antidilution of earnings per share.

Appropriated retained earnings. The restricted portion of retained earnings.

Arm's-length transactions. Exchanges between parties who are independent of each other; a traditional assumption in accounting is that recorded transactions and events are executed between independent parties, each of whom is acting in its own best interests.

Asset and liability method of interperiod tax allocation. A method of income tax allocation that determines deferred tax assets or tax liabilities based on scheduling future expected temporary difference reversals. If tax rates change, the asset or liability balances are adjusted to reflect the tax rates legislated to be in effect in the year when reversal is expected to occur.

Asset turnover rate. *See* Total asset turnover.

Assets. The resources of an entity: technically defined by the FASB in Concepts Statement No. 6 as "probable future economic benefits obtained or controlled by a particular entity as a result of past transactions or events."

Assignment of receivables. The borrowing of money with receivables pledged as security on the loan.

Average amount of accumulated expenditures. A weighted average of the expenditures incurred in the self-construction of an operating asset. Expenditures mean cash disbursements, not accruals. The expenditures are weighted by the portion of the year left after payment is made.

Average cost method. An inventory costing method that assigns the same average cost to each unit sold and each item in the inventory. Under a periodic inventory system, the unit cost is a *weighted average* for the entire period. Under a perpetual inventory system, the unit cost is computed as a *moving average* which changes with each new purchase of goods.

Average cost retail inventory method. A method of estimating inventory that approximates an average cost valuation.

B

Balance sheet. A statement that reports as of a given point in time the resources (assets) of a business, its obligations (liabilities), and the residual ownership claims against its resources (owners' equity); an alternative title for the statement is the *statement of financial position.*

Bank discounting. The process of transferring negotiable notes to a bank or other financial institution in return for cash.

Bank reconciliation statement. A report that identifies differences between the cash balance on the depositor's books and the balance reported on the bank statement. The reconciliation provides information needed to adjust the book balance to a corrected cash amount.

Bank service charge. Monthly fee usually charged by a bank to service the depositor's account.

Bargain purchase option. A lease provision that allows for the purchase of a leased asset by the lessee at a price significantly lower than the expected fair market value of the leased asset at the date the bargain purchase option can be exercised.

Bargain renewal option. A lease provision that allows for renewal of the lease by the lessee at significantly reduced lease payments from the original lease. The bargain terms strongly imply that the lease will be renewed, and the lease term is assumed to extend through the bargain renewal period.

Bearer or coupon bonds. Bonds for which owners receive periodic interest by clipping a coupon from the bond and sending it to the issuer as evidence of ownership.

Betterments. *See* Additions.

Bond certificates. Certificates of indebtedness issued by a company or government agency guaranteeing payment of a principal amount at a specified future date plus periodic interest; usually issued in denominations of $1,000.

Bond discount. The difference between the face value and the sales price when bonds are sold below their face value.

Bond indenture. The contract between the issuing entity and the bondholders specifying the terms, rights, and obligations of the contracting parties.

Bond issuance costs. Costs incurred by the issuer for legal services, printing and engraving, taxes, and underwriting in connection with the sale of a bond.

Bond premium. The difference between the face value and the sales price when bonds are sold above their face value.

Book value per share. A measure of an entity's value per share of common stock outstanding. The book value per share formula is common stockholders' equity divided by the number of common shares outstanding.

Business combination. The combining of two ongoing business entities, usually by the exchange of capital stock for the net assets acquired.

Business documents. Business records used as the basis for analyzing and recording transactions; examples include invoices, check stubs, receipts, and similar business papers. They are also referred to as Source documents.

C

Callable bonds. Bonds for which the issuer reserves the right to pay the obligation prior to the maturity date.

Callable obligation. A debt instrument that is (1) payable on demand or (2) has a specified due date but is payable on demand if the debtor defaults on the provisions of the loan agreement.

Capital lease. A lease that is, in substance, a contract to purchase an asset.

Capital stock. The portion of the contribution by stockholders assignable to the shares of stock as par or stated value.

Capitalized interest. The amount of interest expenditures included as part of the cost of a self-constructed asset.

Cash basis accounting. A system of accounting in which revenues and expenses are recorded as they are received and paid.

Cash dividend. The payment (receipt) of a dividend in the form of cash.

Cash equivalents. Short-term, highly liquid investments that can be converted easily to cash. Generally, only investments with original maturities of three months or less qualify as cash equivalents; U.S. Treasury bills, money market funds, and commercial paper are examples of instruments that are commonly classified as cash equivalents.

Cash or sales discount. A reduction in the selling price, allowed if payment is received within a specified period, usually offered to customers to encourage prompt payment.

Cash overdraft. A credit balance in the cash account; results from checks being written for more than the cash amount on deposit; should be reported as a current liability.

Cash surrender value. The investment portion of a life insurance policy that is available to the policyholder upon cancellation of the policy.

Cash. Coin, currency, and other items that are acceptable for deposit at face value; serves as a medium of exchange and provides a basis of measurement for accounting.

Ceiling limitation. The net realizable value used as an upper limit in defining market when valuing inventory at the lower of cost or market.

Change in accounting estimate. A specific type of accounting change that modifies predictions of future events, e.g., the useful life of a depreciable asset; changes in estimates are to be reflected in current and future periods.

Change in accounting principle. A specific type of accounting change that uses a different accounting principle or method from that used previously, e.g., using straight-line depreciation instead of the declining-balance method; generally, changes in principle require the reporting of a cumulative effect of the change in the current year's income statement, as well as "pro forma" information.

Change in reporting entity. A specific type of accounting change that reflects financial statements for a different unit of accountability, e.g., after a business merger; a change in reporting entity requires restatement of the financial results of prior periods so as to provide comparative data.

Change orders. Modifications to the original terms of a contract.

Chart of accounts. A systematic listing of all accounts used by a particular business entity.

Closing entries. Entries that reduce all nominal, or temporary, accounts to a zero balance at the end of each accounting period, transferring the pre-closing balances to real, or permanent, accounts.

Coinsurance clause. A clause written into a fire insurance policy by insurance companies to offset the tendency by the buyer to purchase only minimum insurance. The insured shares in the risk of loss if less than the minimum coverage is carried.

Committee on Accounting Procedures (CAP). A committee of the AICPA that issued Accounting Research Bulletins during the period 1939-1959.

Commodity-backed bonds or asset-linked bonds. Bonds that may be redeemed in terms of commodities, such as oil or precious metals.

Common stock equivalent. A security which, because of its terms or the circumstances

under which it was issued, is in substance equivalent to common stock.

Common stock. The class of stock issued by corporations that represents the basic residual ownership interest; allows shareholders the right to vote and to receive dividends if declared, although the right to dividends is generally secondary to that of preferred stock.

Common-size financial statements. Financial statements that reflect the components of the financial statement as a percentage of a total, e.g., percentage of total liabilities or total revenues.

Comparability. A secondary quality of useful accounting information, based on the premise that information is more useful when it can be related to a benchmark or standard, such as data for other firms within the same industry.

Comparative statements. Financial statements reflecting data for two or more periods.

Compensated absences. Payments by employers for vacation, holiday, illness, or other personal activities.

Compensating balances. The portion of a demand deposit that must be maintained as support for existing borrowing arrangements.

Compensatory plans. Stock option plans that are offered to a select group of employees and that provide a form of compensation.

Completed-contract method. An accounting method that recognizes revenues and expenses on long-term construction contracts only when completed.

Complex capital structure. A corporate structure that includes convertible securities and/or stock options, warrants, or rights that could result in the issuance of additional common stock through exercise or conversion.

Composite depreciation. A method of computing depreciation in which dissimilar assets are aggregated and depreciation is computed for the aggregation based on a weighted average life expectancy.

Compound interest. Interest that is computed on the principal amount plus previously accumulated interest.

Comprehensive income. A concept of income measurement and reporting that includes all changes in owners' equity except investments by and distributions to owners. Comprehensive income is specifically defined in FASB Concepts Statement No. 5 and is not currently reported in general-purpose financial statements.

Conceptual framework. A theoretical foundation underlying accounting standards and practice. Today's framework encompasses the objectives, fundamental concepts, and implementation guidelines described in FASB Concepts Statement Nos. 1-6, as well as traditional assumptions. (See Exhibit 2-1, page 33, and Exhibit 2-6, page 51.)

Conglomerates. *See* Diversified companies.

Conservatism. A constraint underlying the reporting of accounting information based on the notion that when doubt exists concerning two or more reporting alternatives, users of information are best served by selecting the alternative with the least favorable impact on owners' equity.

Consigned goods. Inventory that is physically located at a dealer (consignee), however the title (ownership) is retained by another entity (consignor) until the consignee sells the inventory.

Consignment. A transfer of property without a transfer of title and risk of ownership. The recipient of the property (consignee) acts as a selling agent on behalf of the owner (consignor).

Consistency. A secondary quality of useful accounting information requiring that accounting methods be followed consistently from one period to the next unless conditions indicate that changing to another method would provide more useful information.

Consolidation method. An accounting method that combines the financial statement balances of the parent and subsidiary companies as if they were one total economic unit; this method is appropriate where the parent company has control (more than 50 percent of the voting stock) over the subsidiary company.

Constant dollar accounting. A method of reporting whereby original costs are adjusted to reflect the changes in the general price level of the economy; with this approach, historical costs are converted to measuring units of equal purchasing power.

Contingent liability. A potential obligation, the existence of which is uncertain because it is dependent on the outcome of a future event, such as a pending lawsuit. The amount of the potential obligation may or may not be determinable.

Contra account. An account used to record subtractions from a related account; sometimes referred to as an "offset account." Examples include Allowance for Doubtful Accounts, which is subtracted from Accounts Receivable, and Accumulated Depreciation, which is subtracted from a plant asset account.

Contributed capital. The portion of corporate capital that represents investments by the owners, or stockholders. Also referred to as paid-in capital.

Contribution clause. A clause normally included in a casualty insurance policy specifying that if other policies are carried on the same property, recovery of a loss is limited to the ratio which the face amount of the policy bears to the total insurance carried on the property.

Contributory pension plan. A pension plan in which employees make contributions to the plan and thus bear part of the cost.

Control account. A general ledger account that summarizes the detailed information in a subsidiary ledger. For example, Accounts Receivable is the control account for the individual customer accounts in the subsidiary accounts receivable ledger.

Conventional retail inventory method. A method of estimating inventory that approximates a lower of average cost or market valuation.

Convertible bonds. Bonds that provide for conversion into some other security at the option of the stockholder.

Convertible securities. Securities, such as bonds and preferred stock, whose terms permit the holder to convert the investment into common stock of the issuing companies.

Corporation. A business entity that is a separate, legal entity owned by its shareholders, who are given stock certificates as evidence of ownership; the owners' equity is divided between contributed capital (Capital Stock and paid-in capital accounts) and earned capital (Retained Earnings account).

Corridor amount. An amount established as a minimum before amortization of pension gains and losses is required. Only amortization of unrecognized pension gains and losses that exceed 10% of the greater of the projected benefit obligation or the market-related asset value as of the beginning of the period is included in the net periodic pension cost. Any systematic method of amortization that exceeds the minimum may be used as long as it is consistently applied to both gains and losses and it is disclosed in the statements.

Cost effectiveness. A pervasive constraint underlying the reporting of accounting information; to be cost effective, information must provide benefits in excess of its cost. Analysis of the cost-benefit relationship is an important consideration in selecting or requiring reporting alternatives.

Cost method. The method of accounting for long-term investments in the stock of another company where significant influence does not exist (generally less than 20 percent ownership); the initial investment is recorded and maintained at cost with dividends being recognized as revenue when received and no adjustment made for a proportionate share of investee earnings.

Cost percentage (retail inventory method). Cost of goods available for sale valued at cost divided by the goods available for sale at retail.

Cost recovery method. A revenue recognition method which requires recovery of the total cost (investment) prior to the recognition of revenue.

Cost recovery period. A period of time defined by tax legislation over which the cost of noncurrent operating assets may be written-off (deducted) for tax purposes. Currently, there are six recovery periods for personal property and two for real estate.

Cost-to-cost method. A method for determining the percentage of completion for long-term construction contracts using a ratio of the actual cost incurred to date to the estimated total costs.

Credit. An entry on the right side of an account.

Cumulative preferred stock. Preferred stock that has a right to receive current dividends as well as any dividends in arrears before common stockholders receive any dividends.

Current assets. Cash and resources that are reasonably expected to be converted into cash during the normal operating cycle of a business or within one year, whichever period is longer.

Current cost. The current value of an asset (i.e., the current exchange price) as measured by its replacement cost, reproduction cost, sales value, net realizable value, or net present value of future cash flows.

Current cost accounting. A method of reporting whereby original costs are adjusted to reflect the changes in the specific prices of individual items; with this approach, historical costs are converted to measurements reflecting the current values of individual items.

Current liabilities. Obligations that are reasonably expected to be paid using current assets or by creating other current liabilities within one year. For operating liabilities, such as accounts payable and accrued liabilities, the time period is extended to cover the operating cycle of a business if the cycle is longer than one year.

Current market value. The cash equivalent price that could be obtained currently by selling an asset in an orderly liquidation.

Current ratio. An analytical measurement of the short-term liquidity of an entity. The current ratio formula is current assets divided by current liabilities. Sometimes referred to as the working capital ratio.

Current replacement cost. The cash equivalent price that would be paid currently to purchase or replace goods or services.

Current tax provision. The amount of income tax expense for a given year that is equal to the tax payable for the year based on tax regulations. The current tax provision is identified as a separate component of income tax expense on the income statement.

Curtailment of a pension plan. An event that significantly reduces the expected years of future services of present employees or eliminates for a significant number of employees the accrual of defined benefits for their future services.

D

Debit. An entry on the left side of an account.

Debt securities. Instruments, such as bonds and notes, issued by corporations and other entities to obtain funds from creditors.

Debt to equity ratio. A ratio that measures the relationship between the debt and equity of an entity. The debt to equity formula is total debt divided by total stockholders' equity.

Decision usefulness. The overriding quality or characteristic of accounting information.

Declining-balance depreciation. A depreciation method providing decreasing periodic charges for depreciation by applying a constant percentage to a declining asset book value.

Decreasing-charge deprecation methods. Any method of computing depreciation that provides a decreasing charge against revenue over time. Most common of the decreasing-charge methods are sum-of-the-years-digits depreciation and declining-balance depreciation.

Deductible amount. The net amount of tax deductions for a given year arising from scheduling the expected reversals of temporary differences. This amount may be carried back to reduce income already reported to a taxing authority or forward to net against future taxable amounts.

Deferred method of interperiod tax allocation. A method of interperiod tax allocation that defers the effect of timing differences between financial income and taxable income and allocates the deferred tax expense to the years

when the reversal occurs. No adjustment is made when tax rates change. The deferral is based on the rates in effect when the timing difference originates.

Deferred method of investment tax credit. A method of reporting investment tax credits that defers the credit and recognizes its effect over the life of the asset that gave rise to the credit.

Deferred pension cost. A noncurrent asset resulting from recognition of an additional pension liability for underfunded pension plans. The balance in this account should not exceed the sum of any unrecognized transition (gain) or loss plus prior service cost.

Deferred tax asset. The amount of income tax recognized as an asset through scheduling of the reversals of temporary differences. It may be classified as a current or noncurrent asset depending on the timing of the expected tax benefit.

Deferred tax liability. The amount of income tax recognized as a liability through scheduling of the reversals of temporary differences. It may be classified as a current or noncurrent liability depending on the timing of the expected tax payment.

Deferred tax provision. The net amount of income tax expense for a given year arising from adjusting deferred tax assets and liabilities at the end of a fiscal year to the amount determined from scheduling the reversals of temporary differences. Identified as a separate component of income tax expense on the income statement.

Deficit. An excess of dividend payments and losses over net income resulting in a negative (debit) balance in retained earnings.

Defined benefit pension plans. Pension plans that define the benefits that employees will receive at retirement. In these plans, it is necessary to determine what the contribution s should be to meet the future benefit requirements. FASB Statement No. 87 deals primarily with this type of pension plan.

Defined contribution pension plans. Pension plans that specify the employer's contributions based on a formula that includes such factors as age, length of service, employer's profits, and compensation levels. FASB Statement No. 87 does not deal with these types of plans except for disclosure requirements. The pension expense is the amount funded each year.

Demand deposits. Funds deposited in a bank that can be withdrawn upon demand.

Depletion. The periodic allocation of the cost of natural resources; depletion expense represents a charge for the using up of the resources and is computed in a manner similar to the productive-output method of depreciation, i.e., cost is divided by estimated total resources available to determine the depletion charge per unit removed or extracted.

Deposit in transit. A deposit made near the end of the month and recorded on the depositor's books but that is not received by the bank in time to be reflected on the bank statement.

Deposit method. An accounting method which recognizes the receipt of cash and the unearned revenue prior to the completion of a contract.

Depreciation. Periodic allocation of the cost of tangible noncurrent operating assets over the periods benefited by use of the asset.

Development activities. Application of research findings to develop a plan or design for new or improved products and processes.

Dilution of earnings. A reduction in earnings per share (or increase in loss per share) resulting from the assumption that convertible securities have been converted or that options and warrants have been exercised or other shares have been issued upon the fulfillment of certain conditions.

Dilutive securities. Securities whose assumed exercise or conversion results in a reduction in earnings per share or an increase in loss per share.

Direct financing lease. A lease in which the lessor is primarily engaged in financial activities and views the lease activity as an investment.

Direct method. An approach to calculating and reporting the net cash flow from operating activities that shows the major operating cash receipts and cash payments. The difference between cash receipts and cash payments is the net cash flow provided (used) by operations.

Direct write-off method. A method of recognizing the actual losses from uncollectible accounts as expenses during the period in which the receivables are determined to be uncollectible; this method is not in accordance with GAAP.

Discontinued operations. The disposal of a major segment of a business either through sale or abandonment. The segment may be a product line, a division, or a subsidiary company. The assets and related activities of the segment must be clearly distinguishable from other activities of the company, both physically and operationally.

Discussion Memorandum. A document issued by the FASB that identifies the principal issues involved with financial accounting and reporting topics. It includes a discussion of the various points of view as to the resolution of issues, but does not reach a specific conclusion.

Diversified companies. Business entities that have a wide variety of product and service lines of business. Sometimes referred to as conglomerates.

Dividend payout percentage (payout rate). Dividend per share divided by earnings per share. Dividends in arrears. Dividends on cumulative preferred stock for prior years that were not paid and that still are an obligation that must be satisfied before dividends can be declared and paid on common stock.

Dividends per share. A measure of the distribution to stockholders by an entity. The dividends per share formula is the dividends paid to the common shareholders divided by the number of common shares issued and outstanding. Dividends are not paid on treasury stock.

Dividends. Periodic distributions of earnings in the form of cash, stock, or other property to the stockholders (owners) of a corporation.

Dollar-Value LIFO inventory method. An adaptation of the LIFO inventory concept that measures inventory by total dollar amount rather than by individual units. LIFO incremental layers are determined based on total dollar changes.

Dollar-value LIFO retail method. An inventory valuation method in which retail inventory values are classified by total dollar amounts. The retail values are then converted to cost by use of index numbers and LIFO incremental layers are determined based on incremental dollar changes.

Double extension index. An internal LIFO index computed by double-extending a sample of inventory items at base-year prices and end-of-year prices. The derived index is then used to compute the dollar-value LIFO balance for all inventory items.

Double extension. A method of determining the valuation of inventory using the dollar-value LIFO method by extending all inventory quantities twice: once at a base-year cost and once at current-year cost.

Double-declining-balance depreciation. A decreasing charge depreciation method that uses twice the straight-line depreciation rate as the constant percentage to be applied to the decreasing book value.

Double-entry accounting. A system of recording transactions in a way that maintains the equality of the accounting equation: Assets = Liabilities + Owners' Equity.

E

Early extinguishment of debt. The retirement of debt prior to the maturity date of the obligation; any gain or loss arising from early extinguishment of debt must be classified as an extraordinary item on the income statement.

Earnings per share (EPS). Income for the period reported on a per share of common stock basis. The presentation of earnings per share on the income statement is required by generally accepted accounting principles. Seperate EPS amounts are required for income from continuing operations and for each irregular or extraordinary component of reported income.

Earnings. A new term found in the FASB's concepts statements that is the equivalent of net income without including the effects of changes in accounting principles.

Economic entity. A specific reporting unit; a traditional assumption in accounting is that the business enterprise or other reporting unit is viewed as separate and distinct from its owners or other entities.

Effective rate of interest. The rate of interest used in compound interest problems; also known as the yield or true rate of interest.

Effective-interest method. An amortization method which provides for recognition of an equal rate of amortization of bond premium or discount each period; uses a constant interest rate times a changing investment balance.

Efforts-expended methods. Methods for determining the percentage of completion for long-term construction contracts using an estimate of work or service performed. The estimates may be based on labor hours, labor dollars, or estimates of experts.

Emerging Issues Task Force (EITF). A task force of representatives from the accounting profession and industry created by the FASB to deal with taking timely action on emerging issues of financial reporting. The task force identifies significant emerging issues and develops consensus positions when possible.

Employee Retirement Income Security Act of 1974 (ERISA). A legislative act passed by Congress in 1974 that made significant changes in requirements for employer pension plans.

Entry cost. The acquisition cost of an asset.

Equity method. The method of accounting for long-term investments in the stock of another company where significant influence exists (generally 20-50 percent to ownership); the initial investment is recorded at cost but is increased by a proportionate share of investor's income and decreased by dividends and a proportionate share of losses to reflect the underlying claim by the investor on the net assets of the investee company.

Equity security. An instrument representing ownership shares, e.g., common stock, or the right to acquire ownership shares (e.g., options).

Equity to debt ratio. A ratio that measures the relationship between the equity and debt of an entity. The equity to debt ratio formula is total stockholders' equity divided by total assets. (See debt to equity ratio.)

Executory costs. Costs to maintain property such as repairs, insurance and taxes. These costs may be paid by the lessee or the lessor. If paid by the lessor, part of each lease payment should be related to the executory costs.

Exit value. The value received for an asset when sold.

Expected return on pension plan assets. An amount calculated as a basis for determining the extent of delayed recognition of the effects of changes in the fair value of pension plan assets. The expected return on pension plan assets is determined based on the expected long-term rate of return on pension plan assets and the market-related value of pension plan assets.

Expected service period. Estimated number of years an employee will work before receiving pension benefits. Can be estimated as the average computed life based on the total expected future years of service divided by the number of employees. The expected future years of service may be computed by the formula $[N(N + 1) \div 2] \times D$, where N equals the number of years over which service is to be performed and D is the decrease in number of employees through retirement or termination of services per year.

Expense recognition. The process of determining the period in which expenses are to be recorded. Expense recognition is divided into three categories: (1) direct matching, (2) immediate recognition, and (3) systematic and rational allocation.

Expenses. Outflows or other using up of assets or incurrences of liabilities (or a combination of both) from delivering or producing goods, rendering services, or carrying out other activities that constitute the entity's ongoing major or central operations.

Exposure Draft. A preliminary statement of a standard that includes specific recommendations made by the FASB.

Reaction to the Exposure Draft is requested from the accounting and business community, and the comments received are carefully considered before a Statement of Financial Accounting Standards is issued.

External audit. The independent examination of the financial statements to be furnished to external users and issuance of an opinion as to the fairness of the presentation in accordance with generally accepted accounting principles.

Extraordinary items. Gains or losses resulting from events and transactions that are both unusual in nature and infrequent in occurrence or otherwise defined as an extraordinary item per APB Opinion No. 30.

F

Face amount, par value, maturity value. The amount that will be paid on a bond at the maturity date.

Factory overhead. All manufacturing costs other than direct materials and direct labor; alternatively referred to as *manufacturing overhead*.

Factory receivables. The sale of receivables without recourse for cash to a third party, usually a bank or other financial institution.

Fair value of pension plan assets. The amount that could be received from the sale of plan assets in a current sale between a willing buyer and seller. Fair value is used to determine the minimum liability and the transition amount.

Feedback value. A key ingredient of relevant accounting information; helps to confirm or change a decision maker's expectations.

Financial Accounting Foundation (FAF). An organization responsible for selecting members of the FASB, GASB, and their Advisory Councils; also responsible for funding the standard-setting bodies.

Financial Accounting Standards Advisory Council. A council that consults with the FASB concerning major policy questions, selects major project task forces to work on specific projects, and conducts such other activities as may be requested by the FASB.

Financial Accounting Standards Board (FASB). An

independent private organization consisting of seven full-time members with the responsibility of studying accounting issues and establishing accounting standards to govern financial reporting to external users.

Financial accounting. The activity associated with the development and communication of financial information for external users, primarily in the form of general purpose financial statements.

Financial Analysts Federation. An organization of financial analysts who advise the investing public on the meaning of financial reports.

Financial capital maintenance. A concept under which income is defined as the excess of net assets at the end of an accounting period over the net assets at the beginning of the period, excluding effects of transactions with owners.

Financial Executives Institute (FEI). A national organization composed of financial executives employed by large corporations. The FEI membership includes treasurers, controllers, and financial vice-presidents.

Financial income. Income reported on the financial statements as opposed to taxable income that is reported to taxing authorities in accordance with tax regulations.

Financial leverage. A measure of an entity's ability to increase profitability to residual shareholders by using borrowed funds whose cost is less than the profit that can be earned with the borrowed funds.

Financial Reporting Releases (FRRs). SEC statements dealing with reporting and disclosure requirements in documents filed with the SEC.

Financing activities. One of three major categories included in a statement of cash flows; includes transactions and events whereby cash is obtained from or paid to owners and creditors; examples include cash receipts from issuing stocks and bonds and the payment of cash dividends.

Finished goods. Manufactured products for which the manufacturing process is complete.

First-In, First-Out (FIFO) method. An inventory costing method that assigns historical unit costs to expense (cost of goods sold) in the order in which the costs are incurred.

Fixed charge coverage. A measure of the number of times earnings covers the fixed charges of an entity for a period. Fixed charges include interest, lease payments, and specified periodic principal statements.

Floor limitation. The net realizable value less a normal profit used as a lower limit in defining market when valuing inventory at the lower of cost or market.

Flow-through method of investment tax credit. A method of reporting investment tax credits that recognizes the full credit from income tax expense in the year it is taken as a deduction from income taxes payable.

FOB (free on board) destination. Terms of sale under which title of goods passes to the purchaser at the point of destination.

FOB (free on board) shipping point. Terms of sale under which title of goods passes to the purchaser at the point of shipment.

Freight in. Cost of transporting goods from the supplier to the purchaser; part of the cost of inventory.

Full cost approach. An amortization approach in the oil and gas industry that defers all exploratory costs and writes them off against revenues as depletion expense.

Full disclosure principle. A basic accounting concept which requires that all relevant information be presented in an unbiased, understandable, and timely manner.

Full eligibility date. The date at which an employee attains full eligibility for the benefits that employee is expected to earn under the terms of a postretirement benefit plan.

Fully diluted earning per share. The amount of current earnings per share reflecting the maximum dilution that would have resulted from conversions, exercises and other contingent issuances of stock that individually would have decreased earnings per share and in the aggregate would have had a dilutive effect.

Funds. Cash and other assets set apart for certain designated purposes.

Future value. The amount of cash that will be accumulated in the future if an investment is made today at a certain interest rate.

G

Gains. Increases in equity (net assets) from peripheral or incidental transactions of an entity and from all other transactions and other events and circumstances affecting the entity except those that result from revenues or investments by owners.

General journal. An accounting record used to record all business activities for which special journals are not maintained.

General ledger. A record of all accounts used by a business. Some accounts in the general ledger, e.g., accounts receivable, are supported by detail contained in subsidiary ledgers. (*See* Control account and Subsidiary ledger.)

General purpose financial statements. A balance sheet, income statement, statement of cash flows, and usually a statement of changes in retained earnings or in owners' equity.

Generally accepted accounting principles (GAAP). Accounting standards recognized by the profession as required in the preparation of financial statements for external users. Currently, the Financial Accounting Standards Board is the principal issuer of generally accepted accounting principles.

Going concern. An entity that is expected to continue in existence for the foreseeable future; a traditional assumption in accounting is that an entity is viewed as a going concern in the absence of evidence to the contrary.

Goods in process. Inventory of a manufacturer that is partly processed and requires further work before it can be sold. Alternatively referred to as *work in process.*

Goodwill. The ability of an organization to earn above-normal income. Above-normal income means a rate of return greater than that normally required to attract investors into a particular type of business. Recorded goodwill is the excess amount paid for a company in a business combination over the fair market value of the company's identifiable assets.

Governmental Accounting Standards Board (GASB). An independent private organization responsible for establishing standards in the governmental area. Appointed by the Financial Accounting Foundation.

Gross method. A method of inventory accounting that records inventory cost before considering purchase discounts.

Gross profit margin on sales. A measure of the profitability of sales in relation to the cost of the goods sold. The gross profit margin on sales formula is the gross profit for a financial period divided by sales for the same period.

Gross profit method. An inventory estimation technique based on the relationship between gross profit and revenue (sales). The gross profit, as a percentage of sales, is applied to sales to determine cost of goods sold which, in turn, is used to determine the value of the inventory not yet sold.

Gross profit. Revenue (sales) less cost of goods sold.

Group depreciation. A method of computing depreciation in which like assets are grouped together and depreciation is computed for the group rather than for individual assets.

Guaranteed residual value. A guarantee by lessee or a third party of a minimum value for the residual value of a leased asset. If the residual value is less than the guarantee, the guarantor must pay the difference to the lessor.

H

Historical cost. The cash equivalent price of goods or services at the date of acquisition.

Historical cost/nominal dollar. A method of reporting in terms of the numbers of dollars exchanged at the original transaction date; with this approach historical costs are not adjusted for any price changes.

Horizontal analysis. Analysis of a company's statements over a number of reporting periods.

I

If-converted method. A method used to adjust the earnings per share computation to consider the impact of the possible conversion of convertible securities. Under this method, the earnings per share computation is made as if the convertible securities were converted at the beginning of the year or the date the convertible security was issued, whichever is later.

Impairment. Unexpected reduction in the value of an asset that significantly reduces its current value below its reported value.

Implicit interest rate. The interest rate that would discount the minimum lease payments to the fair market value of the asset at the inception of the lease.

Implicit or effective interest. The actual interest rate earned or paid on a note, bond, or similar instrument.

Imprest petty cash system. A petty cash fund in which all expenditures are documented by vouchers or vendor receipts or invoices.

Imputed interest rate. A rate of interest assigned to a note when there is no current market price for either the property, goods or services or the note. The assigned rate of interest is used to discount future receipts or payments to the present in computing the present value of the note.

In-substance defeasance. A process involving the transfer of assets (generally cash and securities) to a trust and the use of the assets and earnings therefrom to satisfy long-term obligations as they come due; a gain or loss is recognized as an extraordinary item and the debt is removed from the balance sheet.

Income Summary. A temporary clearing account used at the end of a period to accumulate amounts from closing entries to revenues and expenses. For a corporation, the income summary account is closed to Retained Earnings; for a proprietorship or partnership, it is closed to the appropriate capital accounts.

Incremental borrowing rate. The interest rate at which the lessee could borrow the amount of money necessary to purchase the leased asset, taking into consideration the lessee's financial situation and the current conditions in the marketplace.

Incremental shares. The number of shares issued upon exercise of options or warrants less the assumed number of shares reacquired after applying the treasury stock method of stock reacquisition.

Indirect method. An approach to calculating and reporting the net cash flow from operating activities that reconciles net income, as reported on the income statement, with net cash flow provided (used) by operations, as shown on the statement of cash flows; net income is adjusted for noncash items, for any gains or losses, and is adjusted from an accrual amount to a cash amount.

Inflation. An increase in the general price level of goods and services.

Initial direct costs. Costs such as commissions, legal fees, and preparation of documents that are incurred by the lessor in negotiating and completing a lease transaction.

Initial markup. The difference between the initial retail price of merchandise and the original historical cost.

Input measures. Measures of the earning process in percentage-of-completion accounting based on cost or efforts devoted to a contract.

Installment sales method. A revenue recognition method which recognizes revenue and related expenses as cash is received.

Intangible noncurrent operating assets. Economic resources with future benefit that are used in the normal operating activity of the organization that cannot be physically observed e.g., copyrights, patents, trade names, and goodwill.

Integral part of annual period concept. A concept of preparing interim financial statements that utilizes the same accounting principles and practices for the interim statements that would be used for the annual statement, except that modifications are permitted to allow the interim results to relate better to the annual statements. An alternate concept would require the interim period to be treated the same way as an annual statement with no flexibility for interim modifications.

Interest-bearing note. A note written in a form in which the maker promises to pay the face amount plus interest at a specified rate; in this form, the face amount is usually equal to the present value upon issuance of the note.

Interest. The payment (cost) for the use of money; it is the excess cash paid or received over the amount of cash borrowed or loaned.

Interim financial statements. Financial statements for a period of time less than one year. Typically, corporations issue quarterly statements that are subject to limited auditor's review.

Interperiod tax allocation. An accounting method that recognizes the tax effect of temporary differences between financial and taxable income in the financial statement rather than reporting as tax expense the actual tax liability in each year. The allocation may be made either by the (1) deferred method or (2) the asset and liability method. The latter method is currently required by GAAP.

Interpolation. A method of finding future or present value table factors when the exact factor does not appear in the table; this method assumes linear relationships.

Interpretation of a Statement of Financial Accounting Standards. A supplemental pronouncement that expands the discussion of an existing Statement of Financial Accounting Standards. These are issued by the FASB, and are considered equal in authority to the Statements issued by the FASB.

Intraperiod tax allocation. A method of income statement presentation of irregular or extraordinary items in which the tax effect of each of these special items is reported with the individual item rather than in the income tax expense related to current operations.

Inventory turnover. An analytical measurement of how rapidly inventories are being used and/or sold during a year. If a company has one inventory, the formula is the cost of goods sold divided by the average inventory. If there are different types of inventory, such as raw materials and work in process, the numerator would be related to the type of inventory. Thus, the numerator for the raw materials inventory would be raw material purchases

and the numerator for work in process inventory would be cost of goods completed.

Inventory. Assets held for sale in the normal course of business.

Investing activities. One of three major categories included in a statement of cash flows; includes transactions and events that occur regularly but that relate only indirectly to the central, ongoing operations of an entity; examples include the purchase or sale of securities or other assets not generally held for resale and the making or collecting of loans to other entities.

Investment tax credit. A tax provision that permits taxpayers to deduct a percentage of the cost of new investment in qualifying assets from the income tax liability for a given year.

Involuntary conversions. Retirement of assets caused by uncontrollable events such as fire, earthquake, flood, or condemnation.

J

Journals. Accounting records in which transactions are first entered, providing a chronological record of business activity. (*See* General journal and Special journal.)

Junk bonds. High-risk, high-yield bonds issued by companies in a weak financial condition.

L

Last-In, First-Out (LIFO) method. An inventory costing method that assigns the most recent historical unit costs to expense (cost of goods sold) and the oldest unit cost to the asset inventory).

Lease term. The noncancellable period of lease designated in the lease contract, plus the period of any bargain renewal periods or other provisions that, at the inception of the lease, strongly indicate that the lease will be renewed.

Lease. A contract specifying the terms under which the owner of the property, the lessor, transfers the right to use the property to a lessee.

Ledgers. Records used for summarizing the effects of transactions upon individual accounts. A ledger may be in the form of a book of accounts or a computer printout. (*See* General ledger and Subsidiary ledgers.)

Lessee. The entity that receives a right to use property under the terms of a lease.

Lessee. The party using property that is owned by another party (lessor).

Lessor. The owner of leased property who transfers the right to use the property to a second party, the lessee.

Lessor. The party who owns property that is used by another party.

Leveraged buy-out (LBO). An acquisition of a company where a substantial amount of the purchase price, often 90 percent or more, is debt financed.

Leveraged lease. A lease contract usually involving three parties; the lessee, the owner-lessor, and the third-party, a long-term creditor. Only direct financing leases are treated as leveraged leases.

Liabilities. The claims of creditors against an entity's resources: technically defined by the FASB as "probable future sacrifices of economic benefits arising from present obligations of a particular entity to transfer assets or provide services to other entities in the future as a result of past transactions or events."

LIFO allowance. A valuation account that adjusts a nonLIFO inventory cost to a LIFO cost.

LIFO conformity rule. A federal tax regulation that requires the use of LIFO for financial reporting purposes if LIFO is used for income tax purposes.

LIFO inventory pools. Classification of inventory into groups of items having common characteristics and then assuming the LIFO cost method for each classification or grouping.

Link-chain index. An internal LIFO index computed by double-extending a sample of inventory items at beginning-of-year prices and at end-of-year prices. The derived index is then used to compute the dollar-value LIFO balance for all inventory items.

Liquidating dividend. A distribution to stockholders representing a return of a portion of contributed capital.

Liquidity. The ability of a company to meet its obligations as they come due.

Loan value. The amount that an insurance company will lend on a life insurance policy.

Long-term (noncurrent) investments. Investments that are either not readily marketable or not expected to be converted to cash within a year; these investments are usually reported on the balance sheet under a separate noncurrent heading.

Long-term debt. Obligations that are not expected to be paid in cash or other current assets within one year or the normal operating cycle.

Losses. Decreases in equity (net assets) from peripheral or incidental transactions of an entity and from all other transactions and other events and circumstances affecting the entity except those that result from expenses or distributions to owners.

Lower of cost or market (LCM). Generally accepted method for valuation of certain assets including inventories and marketable equity securities; this method can be applied on an aggregate or individual item basis for inventories but must be applied on an aggregate basis for marketable securities.

M

Maintenance. The normal cost of keeping property in operating condition. Maintenance is charged to expense in the period in which it is incurred.

Management accounting. The activity associated with financial reporting for internal users. Information needed for internal decisions may relate to such items as specific product lines, specific financing alternatives, detailed expense classifications, and differences between actual and budgeted revenues and costs.

Markdown cancellations. Decreases in the markdowns that do not raise the sales prices above original retail.

Markdowns. Decreases that reduce sales prices below original retail.

Market (lower of cost or market). The replacement cost adjusted for an upper and/or lower limit that reflects the estimated realizable value.

Market, yield, or effective interest rate. The actual rate of interest earned or paid on a bond. Market-related value of pension plan assets. A balance used to calculate the expected return on pension plan assets and the corridor amount. Market-related value can be either fair market value or a calculated value that recognizes changes in fair value in a systematic and rational manner over not more than five years.

Marketable securities. Securities that have a day-to-day market and that can be sold on short notice.

Markup cancellations. Decreases in additional markups that do not reduce sales prices below original retail.

Matching principle. A basic accounting concept that is applied to determine when expenses are recognized (recorded). Under this principle, expenses for a period are determined by associating or "matching" them with specific revenues or a particular time period.

Material dilution. Decrease of 3 percent or more in simple earnings per share when computing primary or fully diluted earnings per share.

Materiality. An important constraint underlying the reporting of accounting information; it determines the threshold for recognition of an item in the financial statements. Materiality decisions focus on the size of a judgment item in a given set of circumstances.

Minimum lease payments. The rental payments required over the lease term plus any amount to be paid for the residual value either through a bargain purchase option or a guarantee of residual value.

Minimum pension liability. The net amount of pension liability that must be reported when a plan is underfunded. The minimum liability is measured as the difference between the accumulated benefit obligation and the fair value of the pension plan assets.

Modified Accelerated Cost Recovery System (MACRS). The accelerated cost recovery system as revised by the Tax Reform Act of 1986. It is applicable for assets acquired after December 31, 1986.

Monetary items. Assets, liabilities, and equities whose balances are fixed in terms of number of dollars regardless of changes in the general price level.

N

National Association of Accountants (NAA). An organization of management accountants that is concerned with the development and use of accounting data within the business organization.

Natural business year. A year that ends when a company's operations are at its lowest point. This type of a fiscal year relates primarily to those business that have seasonal sales.

Natural resources. Assets produced by nature as opposed to those produced by man. They include such wasting assets as oil, gas, timber, and ore deposits.

Negative goodwill. The excess of fair market values of a company's net assets over the purchase price for the company in a business combination.

Negotiable note. A note that is legally transferable by endorsement and delivery.

Net Assets. *See* Owners' equity.

Net lease investment. The carrying value of a lease on the lessor's books; equals the difference between total lease payments receivable (gross investment) and unearned interest revenue.

Net markdowns. Markdowns less markdown cancellations.

Net markups. Additional markups less markup cancellations.

Net method. A method of inventory accounting that records inventory net of any purchase discount.

Net monetary position. The difference between a

company's monetary assets and its monetary liabilities.

Net operating loss carryback. The amount of operating loss that can be carried back and offset against the income of earlier profitable years to obtain a refund of previously paid income taxes.

Net operating loss carryforward. The amount of operating loss that can be carried forward and offset against income of future profitable years to reduce the tax liability for those years.

Net periodic pension cost. The amount recognized in an employer's financial statements as a cost of a pension plan for a period. Components of net periodic pension cost are service cost, interest cost, actual return on plan assets, pension gain or loss, amortization of unrecognized prior service cost, and amortization of unrecognized transition gain or loss.

Net profit margin on sales. A measure of the profitability of a company that relates net income to the sales of the company. The formula is net income divided by net sales.

Net realizable value. The amount of cash expected to be received from the conversion of assets in the normal course of business; net realizable value equals selling price less normal selling costs for inventory and equals gross receivables less the allowance for doubtful accounts for accounts receivable.

Neutrality. A key ingredient of reliable accounting information requiring that information be presented in an unbiased manner; relates to the concept of fairness to users.

Nominal accounts. Accounts that are closed to a zero balance at the end of an accounting period; they include all income statement accounts (revenues, expenses, gains, and losses) and the dividends account. They are also referred to as Temporary accounts.

Non-interest-bearing note. A note written in a form in which the face amount includes an interest charge; in this form, the difference between the face amount and the present value of the note is the implicit or effective interest.

Noncash investing and financing activities. Investing and financing transactions that affect an entity's financial position but not the entity's cash flows during the period; an example would be the purchase of land by issuing stock. Significant noncash financing and investing activities should be disclosed separately, not reported in the statement of cash flows.

Noncash items. Certain items that are reported on the income statement but that do not affect cash; examples include depreciation on buildings and equipment and amortization of intangibles and bond discount or premium.

Noncompensatory plans. Stock option plans that are offered to all employees equally and that are not considered to provide additional compensation.

Noncontributory pension plans. Plans in which the employer bears the total cost of the plan.

Noncumulative preferred stock. Preferred stock that has no claim on any prior year dividends that may have been "passed."

Nonmonetary items. All items that do not represent rights or obligations to receive or pay a fixed sum regardless of changes in the general price level.

Nonreciprocal transfer of a nonmonetary asset. A transfer of a nonmonetary asset with no sacrifice (cost) incurred by the organization receiving the asset e.g., donated assets, discovered assets.

Nontrade notes payable. A note issued to nontrade creditors for purposes other than to purchase goods or services.

Nontrade receivables. Any receivables arising from transactions that are not directly associated with the normal operating activities of a business.

Normal operating cycle. The time required for cash to be converted to inventories, inventories into receivables, and receivables ultimately into cash.

Not-sufficient-funds (NSF) check. A check that is not honored by a bank because of insufficient cash in the maker's account.

Notes receivable. Receivables that are evidenced

by a formal written promise to pay a certain sum of money at a specified date.

Number of times interest is earned. A measure of the safety for creditors that relates the interest expense to the income before interest. The formula is income before taxes and interest expense divided by interest expense.

O

Objective acceleration clause. A clause in a debt instrument that identifies specific conditions that will cause the debt to be callable immediately.

Off-balance-sheet financing. Procedures used by companies to avoid disclosing all their debt on the balance sheet in order to make their financial position look stronger.

Operating activities. One of three major categories included in a statement of cash flows; includes transactions and events that normally enter into the determination of operating income; examples include selling goods or services and purchasing inventory.

Operating leases. Simple rental agreements, usually for a relatively short period of time, for one entity (lessee) to use property that is owned by another entity (lessor).

Opinions. Statements of accounting standards issued by the Accounting Principles Board during the period 1959-1973.

Ordinary annuity. An annuity that consists of payments (receipts) at the end of each period; also known as an annuity in arrears.

Original retail. The initial sales price, including the original increase over cost referred to as the initial markup.

Output measures. Measures of the earnings process in percentage-of-completion accounting based on units produced, contract milestones reached, and values added.

Outstanding checks. Checks written near the end of the month that have reduced the depositor's cash balance but have not yet cleared the bank as of the bank statement date.

Owners' equity. The residual interest in the assets of an entity that remains after deducting its liabilities: sometimes referred to as net assets.

P

Paid-in capital. *See* Contributed capital.

Par value. A value that may be assigned to stock by the terms of a corporation's charter; the par value is printed on the stock certificate.

Parent company. A company that exercises control over another company, known as a subsidiary through majority ownership (more than 50 percent) of the subsidiary's voting stock.

Partnership. A business entity owned by two or more people; the owner's equity is recorded in individual partner capital accounts.

Pension Benefit Guaranty Corporation (PBGC). A federal agency established to protect employees when pension plans are terminated.

Pension gain or loss. A component of net periodic pension costs that is the sum of (a) the difference between the actual return on plan assets and the expected return on plan assets and (b) the amortization of the unrecognized net gain or loss arising in a prior period from a change in the value of either the projected benefit obligation or the plan assets because of an experience different from that assumed or from a change in an actuarial assumption.

Pension plan assets. Assets arising from contributions to the pension plan. Generally comprised of cash and investments that have been segregated and designated for use of the pension plan only.

Pension plan. An agreement, usually written, that provides for benefits to employees upon retirement from active employment. The plan usually includes provisions as to how the benefits are to be funded, who receives benefits, the amount of benefits to be paid, and restrictions on investments of pension plan assets.

Percentage-of-completion accounting. An accounting method for long-term construction contracts which recognizes revenue and related expenses prior to delivery of the goods. Recognition is based on either an input or output measure of the earning process.

Period costs. Costs that are recognized as expenses during the period in which cash is spent or liabilities are incurred for goods and services that are used up either simultaneously with acquisition or soon after.

Periodic inventory system. A method of accounting for inventory in which cost of goods sold is determined and inventory is adjusted to the proper balance at the end of the accounting period, not when inventoriable merchandise is bought or sold. Throughout the period, all purchases of inventoriable merchandise are recorded in the purchases account, and ending inventory is determined by a physical count of merchandise on hand.

Permanent accounts. *See* Real accounts.

Permanent differences. Nondeductible expenses or nontaxable revenues that are recognized for financial reporting purposes but that are never part of taxable income.

Perpetual inventory system. A method of accounting for inventory in which detailed records of each inventory purchase and sale are maintained. This system provides a current record of inventory on hand and cost of goods sold to date.

Petty cash fund. A small amount of cash kept on hand for the purpose of making miscellaneous payments.

Physical capital maintenance. A concept under which income is defined as the excess of physica l productive capacity at the end of an accounting period over the physical productive capacity at the beginning of the period, excluding the effects of transactions with owners.

Pooling of interest. A method of accounting for a business combination whereby all the asset, liability, and owners' equity values are combined; under this approach, the retained earnings amounts are added together to become the total retained earnings for the combined entity.

Post-balance sheet events. *See* Subsequent events.

Post-closing trial balance. A list of all real accounts and their balances after the closing process has been completed.

Postemployment benefits. A term used to describe all benefits granted to employees after termination of employment. Includes benefits granted after retirement as well as those benefits granted for any period between the termination of employment and retirement.

Posting. The process of summarizing transactions by transferring amounts from the journal to the ledger accounts.

Postretirement benefits. Benefits other than pensions provided by an employer to former employees. Includes health insurance, life insurance, and disability payments. Some companies charge these costs to accounts on a pay-as-you-go basis. Others accrue them. The FASB still has recommended in an exposure draft that these costs be accrued.

Predictive value. A key ingredient of relevant accounting information; helps a decision maker predict future consequences based on information about past transactions and events.

Preferred stock. A class of stock that usually confers dividend and liquidation rights that take precedence over those of common stock; preferred stock is often nonvoting stock.

Prepaid pension cost. The cumulative excess of annual pension contributions over annual pension costs. It is reported as an asset on a company's balance sheet.

Present (or discounted) value. The amount of net future cash inflows or outflows discounted to their present value at an appropriate rate of interest

Pretax financial income. The difference between all revenues and expenses, except income taxes, reported in the income statement.

Price index. A series of numbers that compares a sample of commodity prices during a base period with equivalent prices at other periods of time; the base period is assigned a value of 100, and the prices of all other periods are expressed as percentages of this amount.

Price-earnings ratio. A measure of the relationship between the market price of a company's stock and its profitability. The formula is the market price per share of common stock divided by the earnings per share of common stock.

Price-earnings ratio. Market price of stock divided by earnings per share.

Primary earnings per share. The amount of earnings attributable to each share of commo n stock outstanding, including common stock equivalents.

Principal or face amount. The amount, excluding interest, that the maker of a note or the issuer of a bond agrees to pay at the maturity date; this amount is printed on the note or bond contract.

Prior period adjustment. An adjustment made directly to the Retained Earnings account to correct errors made in prior accounting periods.

Prior service cost. The present value of the increased benefits granted by a pension plan amendment (or initial adoption of a plan). Recognized as a component of net periodic pension cost through amortization over the future service life of the covered employees.

Private Companies Practice Section (PCPS). A section of the AICPA for firms that do not have clients regulated by the SEC. Membership in the section is voluntary. Periodic peer review is required of all firms with membership in the PCPS.

Productive-output depreciation. A use-factor method based on the theory that an asset is acquired for the service it can provide in the form of production output. Depreciable cost is divided by the total estimated output to determine the depreciation rate per unit of output.

Profitability. The ability of a company to earn a satisfactory return on its assets.

Projected benefit obligation (PBO). The actuarial present value of benefits using the benefits/ years of service approach that requires assumptions about future compensation levels. Increases over time by interest, amendments to plan, additional service years, and changes in actuarial assumptions.

Promissory note. A formal written promise to pay a certain amount of money at a specified future date.

Property dividend. The payment (receipt) of a dividend in the form of some asset other than cash.

Proportional performance method. An accounting method for recording service revenue and related expenses prior to completion of a service contract.

Proprietorship. A business entity owned by one person; the owner's equity is recorded in a single (proprietor) capital account.

Purchase. A method of accounting for a business combination whereby the value of the stock in excess of the net assets acquired is recorded as Goodwill; under this approach, the retained earnings of the acquired company do not become part of the combined retained earnings.

Q

Quasi-reorganization. A procedure, when permitted by state law, whereby a company eliminates a deficit in retained earnings by restating its invested capital balance; provides a "fresh start" for a company, changing retained earnings from a negative to a zero balance.

Quick assets. Assets that are very liquid. They include cash, cash equivalents, marketable securities, and usually accounts receivable. Inventories and prepaid expenses to do not qualify as quick assets.

Quick ratio. *See* Acid-test ratio.

R

Rate earned on common stockholders' equity. An analytical measurement of profitability for the residual owners of a company. The formula is net income divided by the average stockholders' equity.

Rate earned on stockholders' equity. An analytical measurement of profitability for all stockholders, residual and preferred. The formula is net income divided by the average stockholders' equity.

Rate earned on total assets. An analytical

measurement of profitability for a company as an entity regardless of the source of funds.

Raw materials. Inventory acquired by a manufacturer for use in the production process. Also referred to as *direct materials*.

Real accounts. Accounts that are not closed to a zero balance at the end of each accounting period; also referred to as Permanent accounts. They include all balance sheet accounts (assets, liabilities, and owners' equity).

Realized holding gains and losses. The differences between the current costs and the historical costs of assets that are sold or used during a period.

Receivables. Claims against others for money, goods, or services; usually, receivable claims are settled by the receipt of cash.

Recognition. The process of formally recording an item in the accounting records and eventually reporting it in the financial statements; includes both the initial recording of an item and any subsequent changes related to that item.

Redeemable preferred stock. Preferred stock that may be redeemed at the option of the holder, or at a fixed price on a specific date, or upon other conditions not solely within the control of the issuer; redemption requirements for this type of stock must be disclosed.

Refundable deposits. An obligation of a company to refund amounts previously collected from customers as deposits.

Registered bonds. Bonds for which the bondholders' names and addresses are kept on file by the issuing company.

Relevance. One of two primary qualities inherent in useful accounting information; essentially information is relevant if it will affect a decision. The key ingredients of relevance are feedback value, predictive value, and timeliness.

Reliability. One of two primary qualities inherent in useful accounting information; to be reliable, information must contain the key ingredients of verifiability, neutrality, and representational faithfulness.

Renewals. Unplanned replacements of a component of an asset which may or may not extend the asset's useful life or increase future cash flows. If the asset's life is extended or if future cash flows will increase, then a renewal is properly recorded as an asset. If the life of the asset will not increase and no future cash flows are expected as a result of the renewal, then the renewal is charged to expense in the period in which it is incurred.

Replacement cost. The cost that would be required to replace an existing asset.

Replacements. *See* Renewals.

Report form of balance sheet. A balance sheet that presents assets, liabilities, and owners' equity sections in a vertical arrangement.

Representational faithfulness. A key ingredient of reliable accounting information requiring that the amounts and descriptions reported in the financial statements reflect the actual results of economic transactions and events.

Research activities. Activities undertaken to discover new knowledge that may be used in developing new products, services, or processes or that may result in significant improvements of existing products or processes.

Research and development (R&D). A functional activity engaged in by a company to discover an d develop new products, designs, methods etc.

Reserve Recognition Accounting (RRA). A method of accounting that recognizes the value of oil and gas reserves rather than their historical cost. RRA was proposed as a method by the SEC, but later withdrawn from active consideration.

Residual value. Estimated amount that can be realized upon the retirement of a depreciable asset; sometimes referred to as salvage value.

Residual value (leased property). The value of leased property at the end of the lease term. This value may be retained by the lessor, purchased by the lessee, or sold to a third person.

Retail inventory method. A procedure that converts the retail value of inventory to an estimation of cost by using a cost percentage that reflects the relationship of inventory available for sale valued at retail and cost

Retained earnings. The portion of owners' equity that represents the net accumulated earnings of a corporation; generally, equal to total owners' equity less contributed capital.

Return on investment (ROI). A general term for various analytical measurements of profitability related to input of resources. See "rate earned on common stockholders' equity', "rate earned on assets."

Revenue recognition principle. A basic accounting concept that is applied to determine when revenue should be recognized (recorded). Generally, under this principle, revenues are recognized when two criteria are met: the earnings process is substantially complete and the revenues are realized or realizable.

Revenue recognition. The process of determining the period in which revenue is recorded. Revenue is generally recognized when it has been realized or is realizable and when it has been earned through substantial completion of the activities involved in the earnings process.

Revenues. Inflows or other enhancements of assets of an entity or settlements of its liabilities (or a combination of both) from delivering or producing goods, rendering services, or other activities that constitute the entity's ongoing major or central operations.

Reversing entries. Entries made at the beginning of a period that exactly reverse certain adjusting entries made at the end of the previous period. Reversing entries are optional, and their purpose is to facilitate subsequent recording of transactions.

S

Sale-leaseback. A contractual arrangement in which one party, the seller, sells a leased asset to a second party, and in the same agreement, the seller leases back the property. The seller becomes the seller-lessee and the purchaser the purchaser-lessor. Any profit made on the sale must be deferred and recognized over the lease term. Losses are recognized immediately.

Sales-type lease. A lease in which the lessor is a manufacturer or dealer utilizing the lease to facilitate the sale of goods.

Salvage value. *See* Residual value

SEC Practice Section (SECPS). A section of the AICPA for firms that have clients that are subject to government regulations through the Securities and Exchange Commission. Membership in the section is voluntary. Periodic peer review is required of all firms with membership in SECPS. Member firms are subject to more regulation than is true for the member firms belonging to the Private Companies Practice Section.

Secured bonds. Bonds for which assets are pledged to guarantee repayment.

Securities and Exchange Commission (SEC). A governmental body created to regulate the issuance and trading of securities by corporations to the general public. As part of this function, the SEC is vitally interested in financial accounting and reporting standards. While this body has the authority to establish accounting standards, it has historically relied heavily on the private sector to perform this function.

Securities Industry Associates. An organization of investment bankers who manage the portfolios of large institutional investors.

Segment. A subdivision of a company that can be identified in relationship to its cash flows, profitability, assets and debt.

Serial bonds. Bonds that mature in a series of installments at future dates.

Service cost. A component of net periodic pension cost representing the actuarial present value of benefits accruing to employees for services rendered during that period.

Service-hours depreciation. A use-factor depreciation method based on the theory that the purchase of an asset represents the purchase of a number of hours of direct service. Depreciable cost is divided by total service hours during the useful life of the asset to determine the depreciation rate per hour.

Settlement interest rate. The interest rate used to compute the interest component of net periodic pension cost and the interest rate used to discount projected and accumulated benefit obligations to their present values. It is the rate at which pension plan obligations could be effectively settled; that is, the rate implicit in the current prices of annuity contracts that could be purchased to settle the benefits owed to employees.

Settlement of a pension plan. An irrevocable action taken by an employer that relieves the employer of primary responsibility for all or part of the pension obligation. Examples include purchasing from an insurance company an annuity that would cover employees' vested benefits, or a lump-sum payment to employees in exchange for their rights to receive specified pension benefits.

Similar assets. Assets that are similar in nature and can be exchanged under certain conditions without recognition of a gain on the transfer.

Simple capital structure. A corporate structure that includes only common and nonconvertible preferred stock and has no convertible securities, stock options, warrants or other rights outstanding.

Simple earnings per share. An earnings per share computation that considers only common stock issued and outstanding. It is computed as the net income less preferred dividends divided by the weighted-average common shares outstanding for the year.

Simple interest. Interest that is computed on the principal amount only.

Single-employer pension plans. Pension plans established for a single employer. FASB Statement No. 87 primarily refers to this type of plan.

Solvency. The ability of an entity to pay all current and long-term debts as they come due.

Source documents. *See* Business documents.

Special journal. An accounting record used to record a particular type of frequently recurring transaction.

Specific Identification method. An inventory costing method that assigns the actual cost of the asset to the inventory (unsold) or cost of goods sold (when sold). The cost flow matches the physical flow of the asset.

Stability. The ability of a company to make interest and principal payments on outstanding debt and to pay regular dividends to its stockholders.

Stable monetary unit. An accounting assumption that the measuring unit maintains constant purchasing power; based on this assumption, U.S. financial statements have traditionally reported items in nominal dollars without adjustment for changes in purchasing power.

Stated or contract rate. The rate of interest printed on the bond.

Stated value. A value that may be assigned to no-par stock by the board of directors of a corporation; similar in concept to par value.

Statement of cash flows. One of three primary financial statements required to be included in the full set of general-purpose statements presented to external users. The statement provides information about the cash receipts (inflows) and cash payments (outflows) of an entity during a period of time. The statement is separated into cash flows from operating, investing, and financing activities.

Statement of changes in stockholders' equity. A report that shows the total changes in all stockholders' equity accounts during a period of time; provides a reconciliation of the beginning and ending stockholders' equity amounts.

Statement of financial position. *See* Balance sheet.

Statements of Financial Accounting Concepts. A set of guidelines established by the FASB to provide a conceptual framework for establishing and administering accounting standards.

Statements of Financial Accounting Standards (SFAS). The official statements of the Financial Accounting Standards Board that govern external financial reporting. These statements are prepared after extensive review and discussion by the FASB with the various groups involved in preparing and using general purpose financial statements.

Statements of Position. Statements issued by the Accounting Standards Executive Committee of the AICPA that deal with emerging issues that have not yet been placed on the FASB agenda.

Stock dividend. The payment (receipt) of a dividend in the form of additional shares of a company's own stock.

Stock options. Rights granted to officers or employees, sometimes as part of compensation plan; term also may be used interchangeably with stock rights and stock warrants.

Stock rights. Rights issued to existing shareholders to permit maintenance of a proportionate ownership interest; term also may be used interchangeably with stock warrants and stock options.

Stock split. A reduction in the par or stated value of stock accompanied by a proportionate increase in number of shares outstanding.

Stock warrants. Rights sold separately for cash, generally in conjunction with another security; term also may be used interchangeably with stock rights and stock options.

Straight-line depreciation. A time-factor method of depreciation that recognizes equal periodic depreciation charges for each year of an asset's useful life.

Straight-line method. An amortization method which provides for recognition of an equal amount of bond premium or discount amortization each period.

Subjective acceleration clause. A clause in a debt instrument that identified general conditions that can cause the debt to be callable immediately but violation of the conditions cannot be determined objectively.

Subsequent events. Events occurring between the balance sheet date and the date financial statements are issued and made available to external users.

Subsidiary company. A company that is owned or controlled by another company, known as the parent company.

Subsidiary ledger. A grouping of individual accounts that in total equal the balance of a control account in the general ledger; provides additional detail in support of general ledger balances.

Substantial performance. A criterion for recognizing revenue from a franchising agreement which requires that all provisions of the contract agreement be substantially complete before revenue and related expenses may be recognized.

Successful efforts approach. An amortization method employed in the gas and oil industry that expenses the cost of unsuccessful projects and records as assets only the exploratory costs for successful oil and gas projects.

Sum-of-the-years-digits depreciation. A depreciation method providing decreasing periodic depreciation charges by applying a series of fractions to the asset cost, where the denominator is the sum of the digits l through n, and n equals the asset life in years.

T

Tangible noncurrent operating assets. Economic resources with future benefit that are used in the normal operating activity of the organization that can be physically observed, e.g., land, buildings, and equipment.

Taxable amount. The net amount of taxable income for a given year arising from the scheduling of expected reversals of temporary differences. It becomes the basis for determining the deferred tax liability based on the enacted rates for the reversal year.

Taxable financial income. The amount of financial income subject to income taxes; determined by adjusting pretax financial income for any nontaxable revenues and nondeductible expenses.

Taxable income. Income as defined by income tax regulations as the basis for determining the income tax liability for a given entity.

Technical Bulletins. Publications issued by the staff of the FASB that give guidance for specific problems that arise in practice. They are advisory in nature and do not have as much authority as the FASB Statements or Interpretations.

Technological feasibility. The attainment of a detailed program design and working model for computer software.

Temporary accounts. *See* Nominal accounts.

Temporary differences. Differences between the tax and book basis of assets and liabilities that will reverse over time.

Temporary investments. Investments in securities that: (1) have a ready market, and (2) management intends to sell if the need for cash arises.

Term bonds. Bonds that mature in one lump sum at a specified future date.

Termination benefits. Benefits that arise either from a special amendment to the pension plan that covers only a short period of time, or from the original pension contract that provides special benefits if a certain event, such as a plant closing, occurs.

Time deposits. Funds deposited in a bank that legally require prior notification before they can be withdrawn.

Time-factor depreciation methods. Methods of depreciation in which the factor that measures the declining usefulness of an asset is related to time more than to use. The most widely used depreciation methods, such as straight-line, declining-balance, and ACRS, rely on this factor.

Timeliness. A key ingredient of relevant accounting information; to be relevant and therefore useful for decision making, information must be provided on a timely basis.

Timing differences. Differences between taxable and financial income in a given year that will reverse over time. These differences are a significant part of temporary differences.

Total asset turnover. An analytical measurement of the relationship between asset cost and sales generated by those assets. If a company can generate more sales with the same assets, it will increase its level of profitability. The formula is net sales divided by average total assets.

Trade discount. A reduction in the "list" sales price of an item to the "net" sales price actually charged the customer; trade discounts are generally dependent on the volume of business or size of order from the customer.

Trade notes payable. A note issued to trade creditors for the purchase of goods or services.

Trade receivables. Receivables associated with the normal operating activities of a business e.g., credit sales of goods or services to customers.

Trading on the equity. *See* Financial leverage.

Transaction approach. A method of determining income by defining the financial statement effects of certain events classified as revenues, gains, expenses, and losses. Also known as the *matching concept,* this is the traditional accounting approach to measuring and defining income.

Transaction. An exchange of goods or services between entities or some other event having an economic impact on a business enterprise.

Transfer of receivables with recourse. A hybrid form of receivables financing; depending on the specific circumstances, these may be treated for accounting purposes as a sale (factoring) transaction or as a borrowing (assignment) transaction.

Transition gain or loss. The difference between the projected benefit obligation and the fair value of pension fund assets existing at the time FASB Statement No. 87 is adopted, adjusted by an accrued pension cost or prepaid pension cost at the time of transition. This gain or loss is amortized over the average remaining service life of employees. If average service life is less than 15 years, the employer may use 15 years of amortization purposes.

Treasury stock. Stock issued by a corporation but subsequently reacquired by the corporation and held for possible future reissuance or retirement.

Treasury stock method. A method of recognizing the use of proceeds that would be obtained upon exercise of options and warrants in computing earnings per share. It assumes that any proceeds would be used to purchase common stock at current market prices.

Trial balance. A list of all accounts and their balances; provides a means of testing whether total debits equal total credits for all accounts.

Troubled debt restructuring. A situation involving a concession by creditors to allow debtors to eliminate or significantly modify debt obligations due to the debtor's financial difficulties.

Trust indenture. A legal agreement specifying how a fund should be administered by its trustee(s).

U

Unappropriated (free) retained earnings. The unrestricted portion of retained earnings.

Understandability. An essential, use-specific quality of accounting information.

Unearned revenues. Liabilities resulting from amounts that are received before they have been earned; e.g., advances from customers or unearned rent.

Unguaranteed residual value. A residual value of leased property that remains with the lessor at the end of the lease term. Since there is no guarantee of the residual value, market factors and asset condition determine the value of the leased asset at the end of the lease.

Unit depreciation. Depreciation computed on an individual asset as opposed to computation on groups of assets.

Unrealized holding gains and losses. Increases (decreases) in the current value of assets held during a period but not sold or used.

Unrecognized net pension gain or loss. The cumulative net pension gain or loss that has not been recognized as a part of net periodic pension cost.

Unrecognized prior service cost. That portion of prior service cost that has not been recognized as a part of net periodic pension cost.

Unsecured bonds (debentures). Bonds for which no specific collateral has been pledged.

Use-factor depreciation methods. Methods of depreciation in which the factor that measures the declining usefulness of an asset is related to use more than to time. The units-of-production method is the most common depreciation method that emphasizes the use factor.

Useful life. An estimated measure of time or of production capacity a noncurrent operating asset will yield. All noncurrent operating assets, other than land, have a limited useful life. Physical factors such as wear and tear, deterioration, damage or destruction limit the useful life of an asset. Functional factors such as inadequacy or obsolescence may also limit the useful life of an asset.

V

Verifiability. A key ingredient of reliable accounting information; reported information should be based on objectively determined facts that can be verified by other accountants using the same measurement methods.

Vertical analysis. Analysis of a company's single year financial statements by comparing elements within the statements with each other and with statement totals.

Vested benefits. The amount of pension benefits an employee will retain if employment with the employer is terminated.

W

Warranties. Obligations of a company to provide free service on units failing to perform satisfactorily or to replace defective goods.

Weighted-average interest rate. An interest rate determined by relating interest expenditures for a period with the amount of weighted borrowings during the same period.

Work in process. *See* Goods in process.

Work sheet. A columnar schedule used to summarize accounting data; often used to facilitate the preparation of adjusting entries and financial statements.

Working capital ratio. *See* Current ratio.

Working capital. Current assets less current liabilities: a measure of liquidity.

Y

Yield on common stock. A measure of the cash return to common stockholders. The formula is dividends per share of common stock divided by market value per share of common stock.

Z

Zero-interest bonds or deep-discount bonds. Bonds that do not bear interest but instead are sold at significant discounts, providing the investor with a total interest payoff at maturity.

Appendix C

Index of References to APB and FASB Pronouncements

The following list of pronouncements by the Accounting Principles Board and the Financial Accounting Standards Board (as of June 1, 1989) is provided to give students an overview of the standards issued since 1962 and to reference these standards to the relevant chapters in this book. Earlier pronouncements by the Committee on Accounting Procedure of the AICPA have been largely superseded or amended. In those cases where no change has been made by subsequent standard-setting bodies, the earlier pronouncements and still accepted as official.

Accounting Principles Board Opinions

Date Issued	Opinion Number	Title	Chapter References
Nov. 1962	1	New Depreciation Guidelines and Rules	12
Dec. 1962	2	Accounting for the "Investment Credit"; addendum to Opinion No. 2—Accounting Principles for Regulated Industries	N/A
Oct. 1963	3	The Statement of Source and Application of Funds	24
Mar. 1964	4	Accounting for the "Investment Credit"	20
Sep. 1964	5	Reporting of Leases in Financial Statements of Lessee	21
Oct. 1965	6	Status of Accounting in Research Bulletins	16
May 1966	7	Accounting for Leases in Financial Statements of Lessors	21
Nov. 1966	8	Accounting for the Cost of Pension Plans	22
Dec. 1966	9	Reporting the Results of Operations	4
Dec. 1966	10	Omnibus Opinion—1966	20
Dec. 1967	11	Accounting for Income Taxes	20
Dec. 1967	12	Omnibus Opinion—1967	12

APB Opinions (concluded)

Date Issued	Opinion Number	Title	Chapter References
Mar. 1969	13	Amending Pargraph 6 of ABP Opinion No. 9, Application to Commerical Banks	N/A
Mar. 1969	14	Accounting for Convertible Debt and Debt Issued with Stock Purchase Warrants	15, 16
May 1969	15	Earnings per Share	18
Aug. 1970	16	Business Combinations	N/A
Aug. 1970	17	Intangible Assets	11, 12
Mar. 1971	18	The Equity Method of Accounting for Investments in Common Stock	13
Mar. 1971	19	Reporting Changes in Financial Position	24
Jul. 1971	20	Accounting Changes	23
Aug. 1971	21	Interest on Receivables and Payables	8, 14
Apr. 1972	22	Disclosures of Accounting Policies	5
Apr. 1972	23	Accounting for Income Taxes—Special Areas	20
Apr. 1972	24	Accounting for Income Taxes—Investments in Common Stock Accounted for by the Equity Method (Other than Subsidiaries and Corporate Joint Ventures)	20
Oct. 1972	25	Accounting for Stock Issued to Employees	16, 18
Oct. 1972	26	Early Extinguishment of Debt	15
Nov. 1972	27	Accounting for Lease Transactions by Manufacturer or Dealer Lessors	21
May 1973	28	Interim Financial Reporting	N/A
May 1973	29	Accounting for Nonmonetary Transactions	11, 13, 15
Jun. 1973	30	Reporting the Results of Operations	4, 23
Jun. 1973	31	Disclosures of Lease Commitments by Lessees	21

Accounting Principles Board Statements

Date Issued	Statement Number	Title	Chapter References
Apr. 1962	1	Statement by the Accounting Principles Board (on Accounting Research Studies Nos. 1 and 3)	2
Sep. 1967	2	Disclosure of Supplemental Financial Information by Diversified Companies	26
Jun. 1969	3	Financial Statements Restated for General Price-Level Changes	25
Oct. 1970	4	Basic Concepts and Accounting Principles Underlying Financial Statements of Business Enterprises	2

Financial Accounting Standards Board Statements of Financial Accounting Standards

Date Issued	Statement Number	Title	Chapter References
Dec. 1973	1	Disclosure of Foreign Currency Translation Information	N/A
Oct. 1974	2	Accounting for Research and Development Costs	11
Dec. 1974	3	Reporting Accounting Changes in Interim Financial Statements	N/A
Mar. 1975	4	Reporting Gains and Losses from Extinquishment of Debt	4, 15
Mar. 1975	5	Accounting for Contingencies	14
May 1975	6	Classification of Short-Term Obligations Expected to be Refinanced	5, 14
Jun. 1975	7	Accounting and Reporting by Development Stage Enterprises	11

FASB Statements (continued)

Date Issued	Statement Number	Title	Chapter References
Oct. 1975	8	Accounting for the Translation of Foreign Currency Transactions and Foreign Currency Financial Statements	N/A
Oct. 1975	9	Accounting for Income Taxes—Oil and Gas Producing Companies	N/A
Oct. 1975	10	Extension of "Grandfather" Provisions for Business Combinations	N/A
Dec. 1975	11	Accounting for Contingencies—Transition Method	14
Dec. 1975	12	Accounting for Certain Marketable Securities	7, 13
Nov. 1976	13	Accounting for Leases	21
Dec. 1976	14	Financial Reporting for Segments of a Business Enterprise	26
Jun. 1977	15	Accounting by Debtors and Creditors for Troubled Debt Restructurings	15
Jun. 1977	16	Prior Period Adjustments	17, 23
Nov. 1977	17	Accounting for Leases—Initial Direct Costs	21
Nov. 1977	18	Financial Reporting for Segments of a Business Enterprise—Interim Financial Statements	N/A
Dec. 1977	19	Financial Accounting and Reporting by Oil and Gas Producing Companies	12
Dec. 1977	20	Accounting for Forward Exchange Contracts	N/A
Apr. 1978	21	Suspension of the Reporting of Earnings per Share and Segment Information by Nonpublic Enterprises	18, 26
Jun. 1978	22	Changes in the Provisions of Lease Agreements Resulting from Refundings of Tax-Exempt Debt	N/A
Aug. 1978	23	Inception of the Lease	21
Dec. 1978	24	Reporting Segment Information in Financial Statements That Are Presented in Another Enterprise's Financial Report	N/A
Feb. 1979	25	Suspension of Certain Accounting Requirements for Oil and Gas Producing Companies	12
Apr. 1979	26	Profit Recognition on Sales-Type Leases of Real Estate	21
May 1979	27	Classification of Renewals or Extensions of Existing Sales-Type or Direct Financing Leases	21
May 1979	28	Accounting for Sales with Leasebacks	21
Jun. 1979	29	Determining Contingent Rentals	21
Aug. 1979	30	Disclosures of Information About Major Customers	26
Sep. 1979	31	Accounting for Tax Benefits Related to U.K. Tax Legislaton Concerning Stock Relief	N/A
Sep. 1979	32	Specialized Accounting and Reporting Principles and Practices in AICPA Statements of Position and Guides on Accounting and Auditing Matters	19
Sep. 1979	33	Financial Reporting and Changing Prices	25
Oct. 1979	34	Capitalization of Interest Cost	11
Mar. 1980	35	Accounting and Reporting by Defined Benefit Pension Plans	22
May 1980	36	Disclosure of Pension Information	22
Jul. 1980	37	Balance Sheet Classification of Deferred Income Taxes	20
Sep. 1980	38	Accounting for Preacquisition Contingencies of Purchased Enterprises	N/A
Oct. 1980	39	Financial Reporting and Changing Prices: Specialized Assets—Mining and Oil and Gas	N/A
Nov. 1980	40	Financial Reporting and Changing Prices: Specialized Assets—Timberlands and Growing Timber	N/A
Nov. 1980	41	Financial Reporting and Changing Prices: Specialized Assets—Income-Producing Real Estate	N/A
Nov. 1980	42	Determining Materiality for Capitalization of Interest Cost	11
Nov. 1980	43	Accounting for Compensated Absences	14
Dec. 1980	44	Accounting for Intangible Assets of Motor Carriers	N/A
Mar. 1981	45	Accounting for Franchise Fee Revenue	19
Mar. 1981	46	Financial Reporting and Changing Prices: Motion Picture Films	N/A
Mar. 1981	47	Disclosure of Long-Term Obligations	15
Jun. 1981	48	Revenue Recognition When Right of Return Exists	19
Jun. 1981	49	Accounting for Product Financing Arrangements	N/A

FASB Statements (continued)

Date Issued	Statement Number	Title	Chapter References
Nov. 1981	50	Financial Reporting in the Record and Music Industry	N/A
Nov. 1981	51	Financial Reporting by Cable Television Companies	N/A
Dec. 1981	52	Foreign Currency Translation	N/A
Dec. 1981	53	Financial Reporting by Producers and Distributors of Motion Picture Films	N/A
Jan. 1982	54	Financial Reporting and Changing Prices: Investment Companies	N/A
Feb. 1982	55	Determining Whether a Convertible Security Is a Common Stock Equivalent	18
Feb. 1982	56	Designation of AICPA Guide and Statement of Position (SOP) 81-1 on Contractor Accounting and SOP 81-2 Concerning Hospital-Related Organizations as Preferable for Purposes of Applying APB Opinion 20	19
Mar. 1982	57	Related Party Disclosures	N/A
Apr. 1982	58	Capitalization of Interest Cost in Financial Statements that Include Investments Accounted for by the Equity Method	N/A
Apr. 1982	59	Deferral of the Effective Date of Certain Accounting Requirements for Pension Plans of State and Local Governmental Units	N/A
Jun. 1982	60	Accounting and Reporting by Insurance Enterprises	N/A
Jun. 1982	61	Accounting for Title Plant	N/A
Jun. 1982	62	Capitalization of Interest Cost in Situations Involving Certain Tax-Exempt Borrowings and Certain Gifts and Grants	N/A
Jun. 1982	63	Financial Reporting by Broadcasters	N/A
Sep. 1982	64	Extinguishments of Debt Made to Satisfy Sinking-Fund Requirements	15
Sep. 1982	65	Accounting for Certain Mortgage Banking Activities	N/A
Oct. 1982	66	Accounting for Sales of Real Estate	19
Oct. 1982	67	Accounting for Costs and Initial Rental Operations of Real Estate Projects	N/A
Oct. 1982	68	Research and Development Arrangements	15
Nov. 1982	69	Disclosures About Oil and Gas Producing Activities	N/A
Dec. 1982	70	Financial Reporting and Changing Prices: Foreign Currency Translation	N/A
Dec. 1982	71	Accounting for the Effects of Certain Types of Regulation	N/A
Feb. 1983	72	Accounting for Certain Acquisitions of Banking or Thrift Institutions	N/A
Aug. 1983	73	Reporting a Change in Accounting for Railroad Track Structures	N/A
Aug. 1983	74	Accounting for Special Termination Benefits Paid to Employees	22
Nov. 1983	75	Deferral of the Effective Date of Certain Acccounting Requirements for Pension Plans of State and Local Governmental Units	N/A
Nov. 1983	76	Extinguishment of Debt	15
Dec. 1983	77	Reporting by Transferors for Transfers of Receivables with Recourse	8
Dec. 1983	78	Classification of Obligations That Are Callable by the Creditor	5, 15
Feb. 1984	79	Elimination of Certain Disclosures for Business Combinations by Nonpublic Enterprises	N/A
Aug. 1984	80	Accounting for Futures Contracts	N/A
Nov. 1984	81	Disclosure of Postretirement Health Care and Life Insurance Benefits	22
Nov. 1984	82	Financial Reporting and Changing Prices: Elimination of Certain Disclosures	25
Mar. 1985	83	Designation of AICPA Guides and Statement of Position on Accounting by Brokers and Dealers in Securities, by Employee Benefit Plans, and by Banks as Preferable for Purposes of Applying APB Opinion 20	N/A
Mar. 1985	84	Induced Conversion of Covertible Debt	15
Mar. 1985	85	Yield Test for Determining Whether a Convertible Security Is a Common Stock Equivalent	18
Aug. 1985	86	Accounting for the Costs of Computer Software to Be Sold, Leased, or Otherwise Marketed	11
Dec. 1985	87	Employers' Accounting for Pensions	22
Dec. 1985	88	Employers' Accounting for Settlements and Curtailments of Defined Benefit Pension Plans and for Termination Benefits	22
Dec. 1986	89	Financial Reporting and Changing Prices	25

FASB Statements (continued)

Date Issued	Statement Number	Title	Chapter References
Dec. 1986	90	Regulated Enterprises—Accounting for Abandonments and Disallowances of Plant Costs	N/A
Dec. 1986	91	Accounting for Nonrefundable Fees and Costs Associated with Originating or Acquiring Loans and Initial Direct Costs of Leases	21
Aug. 1987	92	Regulated Enterprises—Accounting for Phase-In Plans	N/A
Aug. 1987	93	Recognition of Depreciation by Not-for-Profit Organizations	N/A
Oct. 1987	94	Consolidation of all Majority-Owned Subsidiaries	N/A
Nov. 1987	95	Statement of Cash Flows	24
Dec. 1987	96	Accounting for Income Taxes	20
Dec. 1987	97	Accounting and Reporting by Insurance Enterprises for Certain Insurance Enterprises for Certain Long-Duration Contracts and for Realized Gains and Losses from the Sale of Investments	N/A
May 1988	98	Accounting for Leases: · Sale-Leaseback Transactions Involving Real Estate · Sales-Type Leases of Real Estate · Definition of the Lease Term · Initial Direct Costs of Direct Financial Leases	21
Sep. 1988	99	Deferral of the Effective Date of Recognition of Depreciation by Not-for-Profit Organizations	N/A
Dec. 1988	100	Accounting for Income Taxes—Deferral of the Effective Date FASB Statement No. 96	20
Dec. 1988	101	Regulated Enterprises—Accounting for the Discontinuation of Application of FASB Statement No. 71	N/A
Feb. 1989	102	Statement of Cash Flows—Exemption of Certain Enterprises and Classification of Cash Flows from Certain Securities Aquired for Resale	24

Financial Accounting Standards Board Statements of Financial Accounting Concepts

Date Issued	Statement Number	Title	Chapter References
Nov. 1978	1	Objectives of Financial Reporting by Business Enterprises	2
May 1980	2	Qualitative Characteristics of Accounting Information	2
Dec. 1980	3	Elements of Financial Statements of Business Enterprises	2
Dec. 1980	4	Objectives of Financial Reporting by Nonbusiness Organizations	N/A
Dec. 1984	5	Recognition and Measurement in Financial Statements of Business Enterprises	2
Dec. 1985	6	Elements of Financial Statements	2

Selected FASB Exposure Draft

Date Issued	Title	Chapter References
Feb. 1989	Employer's Accounting for Postretirement Benefits Other than Pensions	22

Index